ANALOG ELECTRONICS

ANALOG ELECTRONICS

A. K. MAINI
VARSHA AGRAWAL

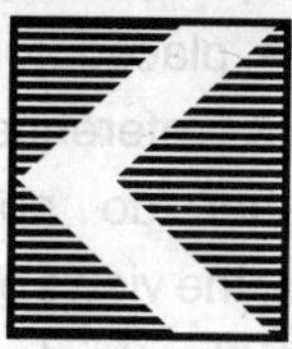

KHANNA BOOK PUBLISHING CO. (P) LTD.

Publisher of Engineering and Computer Books

4C/4344, Ansari Road, Darya Ganj, New Delhi-110002
Phone : 011-23244447-48 **Mobile:** +91-9910909320
E-mail : contact@khannabooks.com
Website : www.khannabooks.com

Dear Readers,

To prevent the piracy, this book is secured with HIGH SECURITY HOLOGRAM on the front title cover. In case you don't find the hologram on the front cover title, please write us to at contact@khannabooks.com or whatsapp us at +91-99109 09320 and avail special gift voucher for yourself.

Specimen of Hologram on front Cover title:

Moreover, there is a SPECIAL DISCOUNT COUPON for you with EVERY HOLOGRAM.

How to avail this SPECIAL DISCOUNT:

Step 1: Scratch the hologram
Step 2: Under the scratch area, your "coupon code" is available
Step 3: Logon to www.khannabooks.com
Step 4: Use your "coupon code" in the shopping cart and get your copy at a special discount
Step 5: Enjoy your reading!

ISBN: 978-93-86173-58-4

Analog Electronics
by A.K. Maini & Varsha Agrawal

First Edition: 2018
Reprint Edition: 2022, 2025, **2026**

To view complete list of books, Please scan the QR Code:

Published by:
Khanna Book Publishing Co. (P) Ltd.
CIN: U22110DL1998PTC095547

Visit us at: **www.khannabooks.com**
Write us at: **contact@khannabooks.com**

Printed in Bharat.

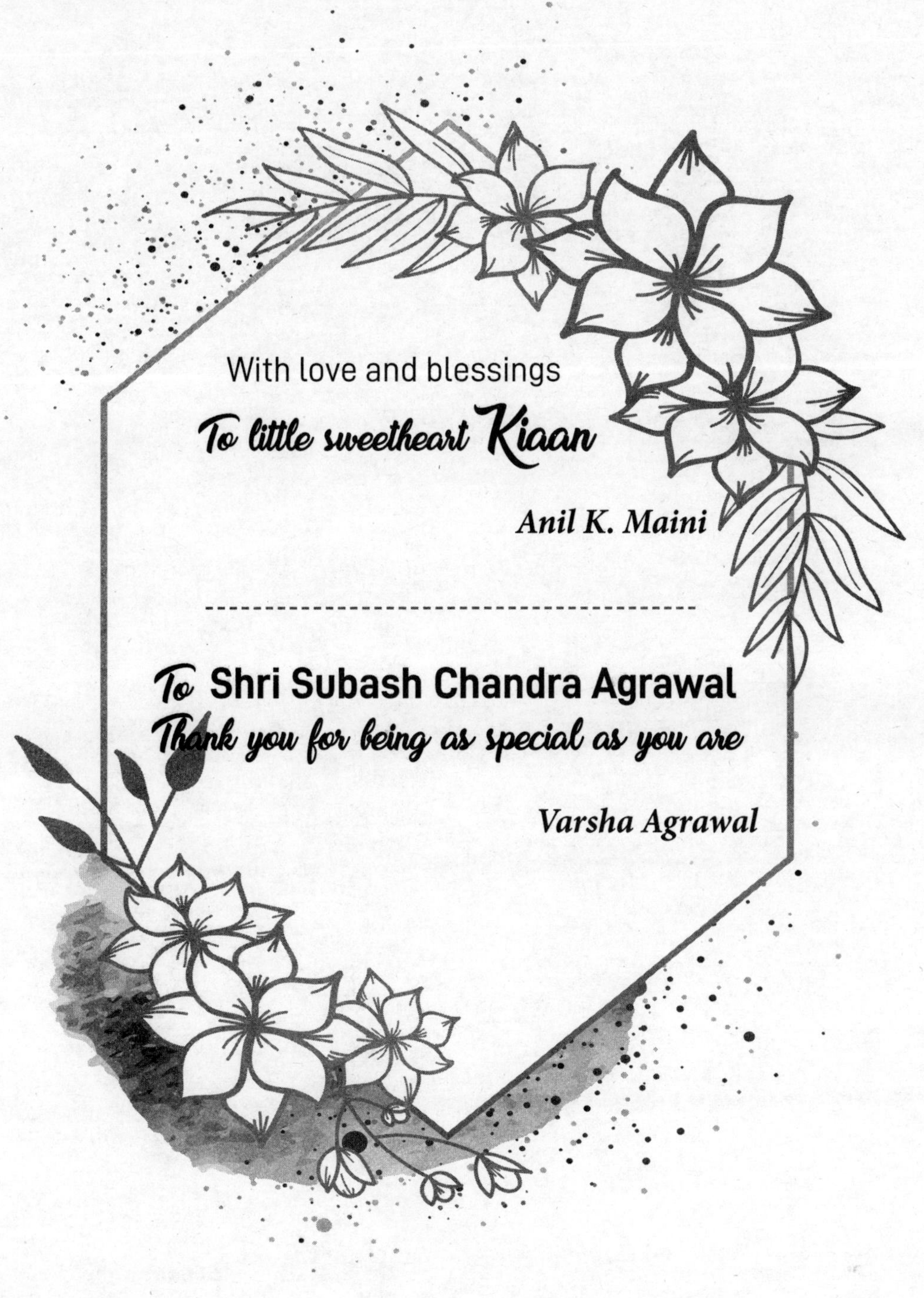

With love and blessings

To little sweetheart Kiaan

Anil K. Maini

To Shri Subash Chandra Agrawal

Thank you for being as special as you are

Varsha Agrawal

PREFACE

Analog Electronics with its focus on both passive and active discrete electronic devices and the application circuits configured around them is invariably an essential subject in the curriculum of **Electronics and Communication Engineering, Electrical Engineering, Computer Science and Information Technology Engineering and Instrumentation Engineering.** It is so because it is essential to understanding the operational basics and design of linear integrated circuits, digital electronics devices and electronic circuits and to some extent instrumentation also. It is therefore essential for students and engineers to understand **Analog Electronics**, which includes fundamentals of discrete electronics devices and integrated circuits and also circuits built around them. The book is intended to be a comprehensive textbook covering all topics of **Analog Electronics** as recommended by the AICTE curriculum for Indian institutes of engineering and technology. Analog Electronics is a complete book that provides comprehensive coverage of different topics of analog electronics related to electronics devices including discrete devices as well as integrated circuits and electronic circuits. Choice of topics is strictly based on the curriculum recommended by AICTE for Electronics and Electrical engineering disciplines for undergraduate level. Each chapter in the book, whether it is related to operational fundamentals or applications, is amply illustrated with diagrams and design examples. Each chapter includes a set of review questions, numerical problems and a comprehensive self-evaluation exercise comprising multiple-choice questions and other types of objective-type questions. Solutions to problems and multiple choice questions are provided towards the end of each chapter. Unlike most of the books in print on the subject that are either too brief, lacking in illustrated examples and examination-oriented study material, or too voluminous, containing lot of redundant material, the book has been written keeping in mind the topics taught in the subject at undergraduate and graduate levels. The book should also be of interest to practicing engineers and scientists who wish to update their knowledge on the subject.

The book is divided into 12 chapters, which includes **semiconductor device fundamentals (Chapters 1 to 3)** including Semiconductor Diodes in chapter-1, Bipolar Junction Transistors in chapter-2 and Field Effect Transistors in chapter-3. Small Signal Amplifiers and their low and high frequency responses are covered in chapter-4.This is followed by a detailed discussion on **analysis of various amplifier configurations** built around bipolar junction transistors and field effect transistors. Large Signal Amplifiers in chapter-5. Multistage amplifiers are discussed in chapter-6. **Negative Feedback Amplifiers and Oscillators** are covered next respectively in chapters 7 and 8. Chapters 9 and 10 are devoted to **operational amplifiers**. Chapter-9 exhaustively covers operational amplifier fundamentals followed a comprehensive treatment of a large number of application circuits configured around opamps in chapter-10. Chapter-11 focuses on **Digital-to-Analog and Analog-to-Digital circuits**. The concluding chapter i.e. chapter-12 introduces another very important analog building block of **Switched Capacitors** and **Switched Capacitor Circuits**.

The first three chapters cover the fundamentals of the semiconductor devices. These include semiconductor diodes, bipolar junction transistors (BJT), field effect transistors (FET) and Metal Oxide Semiconductor Field Effect Transistors (MOSFETs).Each device is first introduced by explaining its internal behaviour which is then followed up by a discussion on its characteristics, important performance parameters and equivalent circuit. Application circuits are also discussed at length in these chapters. Analysis of amplifiers including **small signal analysis** using h-parameter and hybrid-p models, low and high frequency response, **large signal analysis and cascaded arrangement of amplifiers** are covered in chapters 4 to 6. **Concept of negative feedback** and its associated advantages, different types of feedback topologies and their circuit implementations are exhaustively covered in chapter-7. Chapter-8 discusses both **sinusoidal and non-sinusoidal oscillators.** R-C, L-C and crystal oscillators are discussed in detail. The chapter covers concept behind initiation of oscillations, Bark hausen criterion and different types of R-C, L-C and crystal oscillators. The chapter on oscillators also covers different types of non-sinusoidal oscillators including multi vibrators and blocking oscillator.

Chapter-9 covers **operational amplifier fundamentals**. Beginning with internal architecture of an opamp, it goes on to discuss important performance parameters and different types of opamps. Chapter-10 covers a large number of **application circuits using opamps**. These include inverting and non-inverting amplifiers, voltage follower, averager, absolute value circuit, integrators and differentiators, adders and subtractors, non-linear amplifiers, active filters, instrumentation amplifiers, phase shifters, rectifiers, clipping and clamping circuits.

Chapter-11 is devoted to **D/A and A/D converters**. Major topics discussed in this chapter include device fundamentals, performance parameters and types of D/A and A/D converters. Chapter-12 discusses fundamentals of **switched capacitor circuits** including switched capacitor resistors, switched capacitor amplifiers, switched capacitor integrators and switched capacitor filters.

The purpose and motivation to write this book and the selection of topics to be covered were driven mainly by the revised curriculum of the Electronics, Communication and Electrical Engineering streams as recommended by AICTE and the absence of a textbook which covers all the topics contained therein. As the authors, we have made an honest attempt to cover the subject in entirety by including comprehensive treatment of all topics on the subject of Analog Electronics including devices and circuits. The book has been written to facilitate its use as self-study material. Particular attention has been paid to the requirements of undergraduate students from the viewpoint of examination by including comprehensive self-evaluation exercises at the end of each chapter. We, the authors, do hope that the book will be well received by the targeted readers. Constructive suggestions, if any, will be welcome as this would facilitate us to orient the book more towards the needs of the readers in future editions of the book.

Anil K. Maini
Varsha Agrawal

CONTENTS

1 Semiconductor Diodes Fundamentals, Types and Circuits

Learning Objectives

After completing this chapter, you will learn the following topics.

— Intrinsic and extrinsic semiconductors and their properties
— N-type semiconductors and p-type semiconductors
— Law of mass action
— Drift and diffusion carriers
— PN junction diode (structure, forward biased diode, reverse biased diode, ideal and practical diodes)
— I-V characteristics of a diode and their dependence on temperature
— Diode's resistances and capacitance
— Diode's equivalent circuit
— Electrical specifications of a diode
— Load line analysis of a diode circuit (DC load line analysis and AC load line analysis)
— Zener and avalanche diodes
— Varactor diodes
— Schottky diodes
— Tunnel diodes
— Review of half wave and full-wave rectifiers
— Clipping circuits
— Clamping circuits

Introduction

The topics covered in this module include P-N junction diode, I-V characteristics of a diode, half-wave and full-wave rectifiers, Zener diodes, clamping and clipping circuits. In addition, basic topics like intrinsic and extrinsic semiconductors, law of mass action and carrier charge densities in a semiconductor are covered to facilitate a better understanding of a P-N junction diode. P-N junction diode's resistances and capacitances, its equivalent circuit and specifications are also discussed in brief. The DC and AC load line analysis is discussed next to understand how to use a diode in DC and AC circuits respectively. Different types of diodes including Zener, avalanche, varactor, Schottky, tunnel and point contact diodes are also discussed. Important formulae and keywords are listed at the end of the chapter. Different topics discussed in the chapter are amply illustrated with solved examples. In addition, there are a number of problems given towards the end of the chapter along with brief solutions. A self-evaluation exercise containing multiple-choice questions along with answers concludes the chapter.

1.1 INTRINSIC AND EXTRINSIC SEMICONDUCTORS

Intrinsic and extrinsic semiconductors are respectively pure semiconductors and semiconductors with some percentage of specified impurities added to them. Extrinsic semiconductors are further N-type and P-type semiconductors. Intrinsic and extrinsic semiconductors are discussed in the following paragraphs.

1.1.1 Intrinsic Semiconductors

Intrinsic semiconductors are semiconductors with very low level of impurity concentration. They are essentially as pure as can be available through modern technology wherein the purity levels are of the order of 1 part in 10 billion. Conduction in intrinsic semiconductors is either due to thermal excitation or due to crystal defects. Silicon, Germanium, Gallium Arsenide and Indium Antimonide are some of the examples of common semiconductors.

We shall illustrate the behaviour of intrinsic semiconductors by briefly considering the cases of Silicon and Germanium. Silicon has 14 orbiting electrons. The innermost shell has two electrons, the middle shell eight electrons and the outermost shell four electrons. Hence, it has four valence electrons and is referred to as a tetravalent atom. These four electrons are shared by four neighbouring atoms in the crystal. It is the sharing of these four electrons of an atom with their respective neighboring atoms that constitutes a total of eight electrons in its valence shell. This bonding of atoms due to sharing of electrons is called covalent bonding. Fig. 1.1 (a) shows the crystal structure of Silicon at absolute zero temperature (0°K). Owing to the covalent bonding, the valence electrons are tightly bound to the nucleus and hence the crystal has poor conductivity at low temperature. At room temperature, the thermal energy is sufficient to break some of the covalent bonds as shown in Fig. 1.1 (b). The electrons are raised to the conduction band and are referred to as free electrons that are available for conduction. The absence of electron in the covalent bond means that the atom now has a positive charge referred to as a hole [represented by a small circle in Fig. 1.1 (b)]. Holes serve as a carrier of electricity in a manner similar to free electrons. In fact, the motion of hole in one direction is equivalent to the motion of negative charge in the opposite direction.

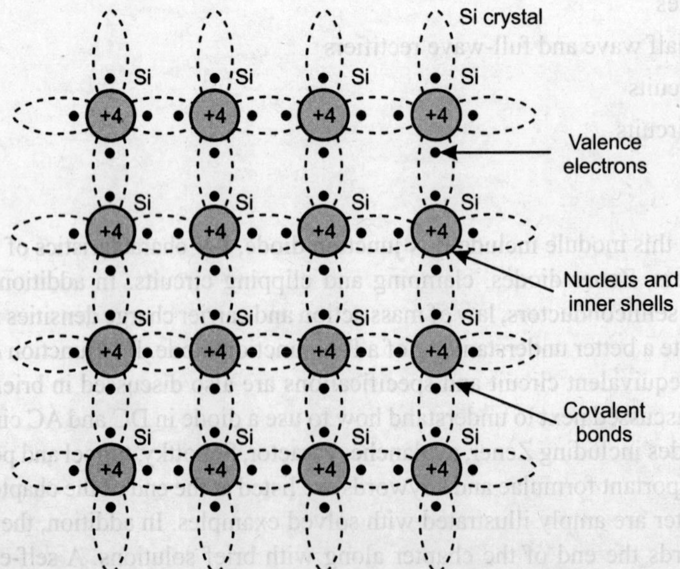

Fig. 1.1: Crystal structure of Silicon at (a) absolute zero temperature

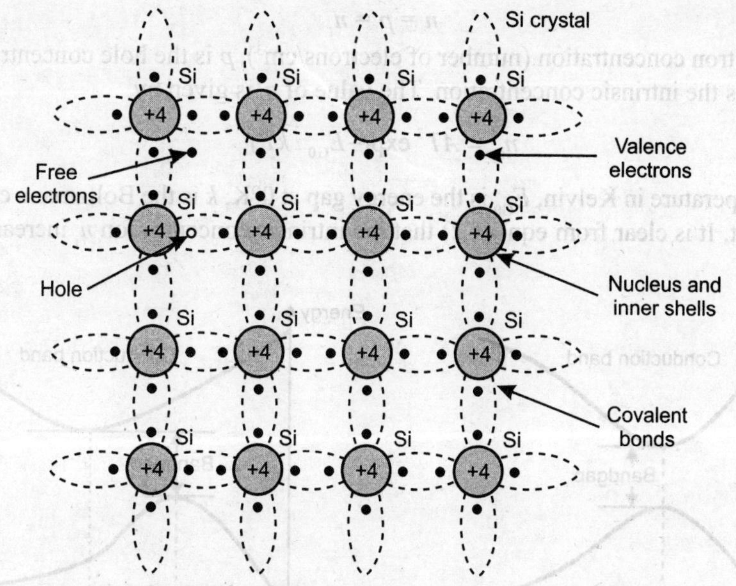

Fig. 1.1: Crystal structure of Silicon at (b) room temperature

Germanium also has four electrons in the valence shell. Intrinsic semiconductors are also formed by combination of atoms having three valence electrons with those having five valence electrons. Examples include Gallium Arsenide (GaAS) and Indium Antimonide (InSb). In Gallium Arsenide, Gallium atom has three valence electrons and Arsenic atom has five valence electrons. Other combinations are also possible, for example Mercury, Cadmium and Tellurium bond to form Mercury Cadmium Telluride (HgCdTe). To summarize, at low temperatures of the order of 0°K, the intrinsic semiconductor behaves as an insulator as no free carriers of electricity are available.

1.1.1.1 Types

Intrinsic semiconductors can be further classified as *direct band gap semiconductors* and *indirect band gap semiconductors*. In a *direct band gap semiconductor*, the maximum energy of the valence band occurs at the same momentum value as the minimum energy of the conduction band [Fig. 1.2 (a)]. Thus, in a direct band gap semiconductor, electrons present at the minimum of conduction band combine with holes present at the maximum of valence band while conserving momentum. The energy released due to recombination is emitted in the form of photon of light. Therefore, these semiconductors are used in making light-emitting diodes (LED) and laser diodes. Examples of direct band gap semiconductors include Gallium Arsenide and Mercury Cadmium Telluride. In an *indirect band gap semiconductor*, the maximum energy of the valence band occurs at a different momentum value than the minimum energy of the conduction band [Fig. 1.2 (b)]. Hence, a direct transition across the band gap does not conserve momentum and does not emit photons of light. Instead, the energy in this case is released in the form of heat. Silicon and Germanium are examples of indirect band gap semiconductors.

1.1.1.2 Charge Concentration

In an intrinsic semiconductor, the number of holes is equal to the number of electrons. Hole and electron pairs are generated by thermal agitation and disappear due to recombination. Therefore, in an intrinsic semiconductor,

$$n = p = n_i \tag{1.1}$$

where n is the electron concentration (number of electrons/cm^3), p is the hole concentration (number of holes/cm^3) and n_i is the intrinsic concentration. The value of n_i is given by

$$n_i^2 = AT^3 \exp(-E_{G0} / kT) \tag{1.2}$$

where T is the temperature in Kelvin, E_{G0} is the energy gap at 0°K, k is the Boltzmann constant in eV/°K and A is a constant. It is clear from eqn. (1.2) that the intrinsic concentration n_i increases with increase in temperature.

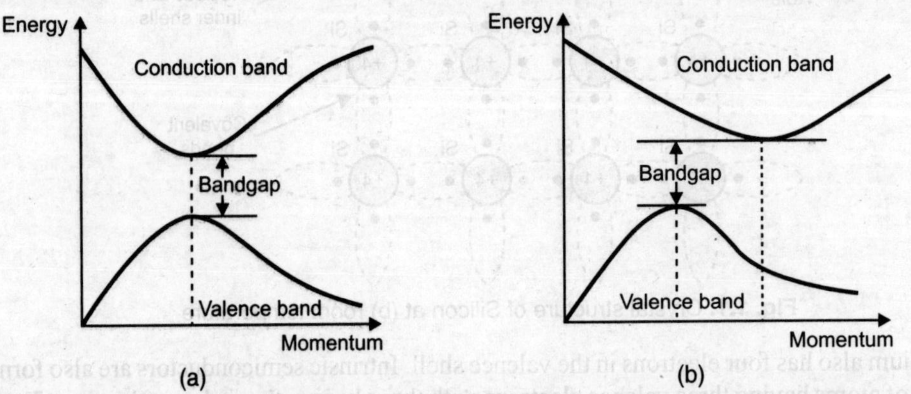

Fig. 1.2: (a) Direct band gap intrinsic semiconductor (b) indirect band gap intrinsic semiconductor

1.1.1.3 Electrical Properties

A semiconductor is a bipolar device; that is, both electrons and holes contribute to the flow of current. It may be mentioned here that metals are unipolar devices; that is, only electrons act as current carriers. In a semiconductor, there are two different mechanisms of current flow, namely, the 'electron flow in the conduction band' and the 'hole flow in the valence band'. When an external potential is applied, the free electron may either contribute to the current by drifting through the crystal or combine with a hole in the valence band. The first component constitutes the electron flow in the conduction band. When an electron combines with a hole, it leaves a hole in its initial position. This hole may now be filled by an electron from another covalent bond creating a hole in its position and the process continues. This results in the motion of holes in the direction opposite to the direction of motion of electrons. The mathematical expression for the current density in any material is given by eqn. 1.3.

$$J = (n\mu_n + p\mu_p)q\varepsilon \tag{1.3}$$

where J is the current density in Amp/cm^2, n is the electron concentration (number of electrons/cm^3), p is the hole concentration (number of holes/cm^3), μ_n is the mobility of an electron in the material in cm^2/Vs, μ_p is the mobility of a hole in the material in cm^2/Vs, q is the charge of an electron (1.6×10^{-19} C) and ε is the applied electric field in V/cm.

This current is due to the potential gradient created by the applied electric field and is referred to as drift current density. The expression for conductivity is given by eqn. (1.4) and is denoted by σ:

$$\sigma = (n\mu_n + p\mu_p)q \tag{1.4}$$

Since in an intrinsic semiconductor, $n = p = n_i$, therefore from eqns. (1.3) and (1.4), respectively, we obtain eqns. 1.5 and 1.6 respectively for current density and conductivity.

$$J = (\mu_n + \mu_p)n_i q\varepsilon \tag{1.5}$$

$$\sigma = (\mu_n + \mu_p)n_i q \tag{1.6}$$

1.1.1.4 Energy Band Gap

The forbidden energy band gap (also called energy band gap) of a semiconductor depends on its temperature and decreases with increase in temperature. For Silicon, the energy band gap [$E_G(T)$] at temperature T (°K) is given by:

$$E_G(T) = 1.21 - 3.60 \times 10^{-4}\, T \tag{1.7}$$

and for Germanium, it is given by:

$$E_G(T) = 0.785 - 2.23 \times 10^{-4}\, T \tag{1.8}$$

where T is the temperature in Kelvin. At room temperature (taken as 300°K), the band gap for Silicon and Germanium are 1.1 and 0.72 eV, respectively.

1.1.1.5 Fermi Level

The probability that an energy level in a semiconductor is occupied by an electron is given by

$$f(E) = \frac{1}{1 + \exp[(E - E_F)/kT]} \tag{1.9}$$

Where, $f(E)$ is the Fermi–Dirac probability function (i.e., probability of finding an electron in the energy state E), k is the Boltzmann constant (8.642×10^{-5} eV/°K), T is the temperature in Kelvin and E_F is the Fermi level in eV.

Fermi level represents the energy state with 50% probability of being filled by an electron if no forbidden energy band gap exists. In an intrinsic semiconductor at absolute zero temperature, the probability of finding an electron in the valence band is 100% and the probability of finding the electron in the conduction band is 0%. The Fermi level in an intrinsic semiconductor at absolute zero temperature lies at the center of the forbidden band gap as shown in Fig. 1.3 (a). As the temperature increases, some of the electrons are excited to higher energy levels. They leave the valence band and jump to the conduction band. Thus, the probability of finding an electron in the valence band decreases and the probability of finding an electron in the conduction band increases [Fig. 1.3 (b). The Fermi level remains at the center of the forbidden band gap.

1.1.2 N-type Semiconductors

Intrinsic semiconductors have very limited applications as they conduct a very small amount of current. However, the electrical characteristics of an intrinsic semiconductor are changed significantly by adding impurity atoms to the pure semiconductor material. The impurities added are of the order of 1 part in 10^5 parts to 1 part in 10^8 parts. However, this small alteration results in a large change in the semiconductor material properties. For example, the conductivity is increased about 1000 times. This process of adding impurities is called doping and the resultant semiconductor is called an extrinsic semiconductor. If the added impurity is a pentavalent atom, then the resultant semiconductor is called an N-type semiconductor; and if the impurity added is trivalent in nature, then it is called a P-type semiconductor. N-type semiconductors are discussed in this sub-section, while the P-type semiconductors are covered in the next sub-section.

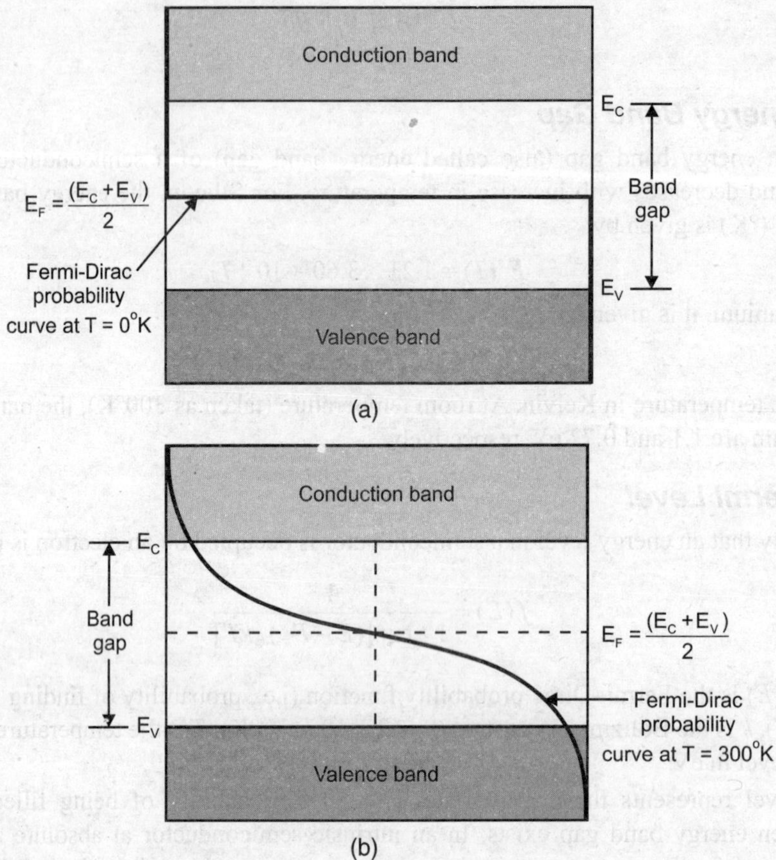

Fig. 1.3: Fermi–Dirac probability function of an intrinsic semiconductor at (a) absolute zero temperature (b) 300°K.

An N-type semiconductor material is created by adding approximately 1 part in 10^8 parts of pentavalent impurities to the intrinsic semiconductor material. Pentavalent atoms are those atoms that have five valence electrons. Some examples of pentavalent atoms are Phosphorus, Antimony, Arsenic, etc. Pentavalent impurity atoms are called the donor atoms. Fig. 1.4 shows the crystal structure of an N-type semiconductor material where four of the five electrons of the pentavalent impurity atom (Antimony) form covalent bonds with four intrinsic semiconductor atoms; the fifth electron is loosely bound to the pentavalent atom, is relatively free to move within the crystal and is referred to as the free electron. The energy required to detach this fifth electron from the atom is very small, of the order of 0.01 eV for Germanium and 0.05 eV for Silicon.

The effect of doping creates a discrete energy level called donor energy level in the forbidden band gap with energy level (E_D) slightly less than the conduction band (Fig. 1.5). The difference between the energy levels of the conduction band and the donor energy level is the energy required to free the electron (0.01 eV for Germanium and 0.05 eV for Silicon). At room temperature, almost all the "fifth" electrons from the donor materials are raised to the conduction band and hence the number of electrons in the conduction band increases significantly.

In an N-type semiconductor, the number of electrons increases and the number of holes decreases compared to those available in an intrinsic semiconductor. The decrease in the number of holes is attributed to the increase in the rate of recombination of electrons with holes. The current in the N-type semiconductor is dominated by electrons, which are referred to as majority carriers. Holes are the minority carriers in the N-type semiconductor. Fig. 1.6 shows flow of current in an N-type semiconductor. Here I is total conventional current flow, I_e the current flow due to electrons and I_h the current flow due to holes.

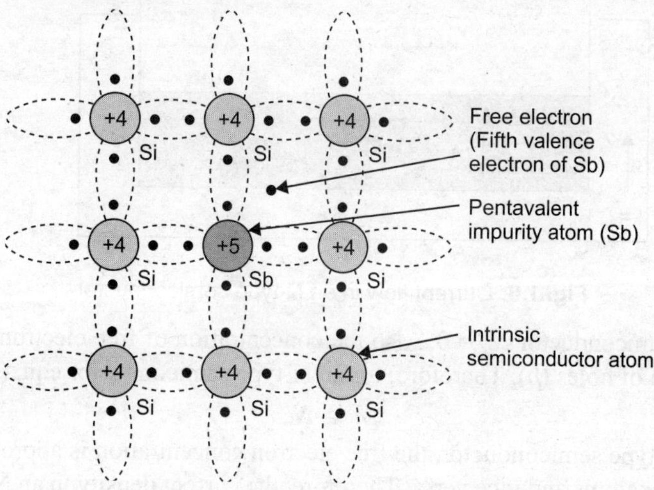

Fig. 1.4: Crystal structure of an N-type semiconductor

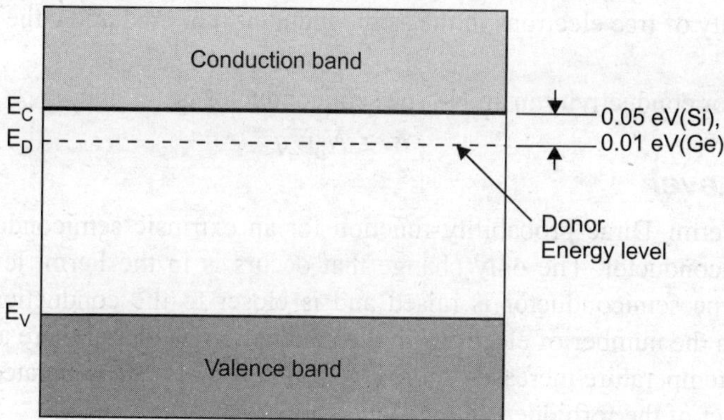

Fig. 1.5: Energy band diagram of an N-type semiconductor

1.1.2.1 Electrical Properties

Let us consider a semiconductor that has N_D donor atoms per cubic centimeter and N_A acceptor atoms per cubic centimeter, that is, the concentrations of donor and acceptor atoms are N_D and N_A, respectively. Therefore, N_D positively charged ions per cubic centimeter are contributed by the donor atoms and N_A negatively charged ions per cubic centimeter are contributed by the acceptor atoms. Let us assume that the concentration of free electrons and holes in the semiconductor are n and p, respectively.

Therefore according to the law of electrical neutrality,

$$N_D + p = N_A + n \tag{1.10}$$

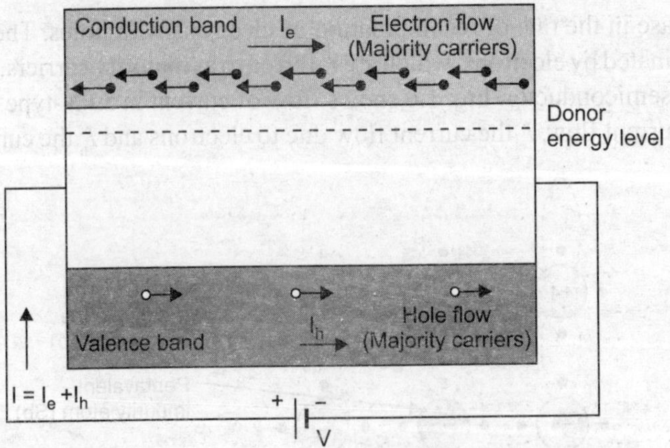

Fig. 1.6: Current flow in an N-type semiconductor

For an N-type semiconductor $N_A = 0$. Also the concentration of free electrons (n) is much greater than the concentration of holes (p). Therefore, for an N-type semiconductor eqn. (1.10) reduces to

$$n \cong N_D \tag{1.11}$$

Hence, for an N-type semiconductor, the free electron concentration is approximately equal to the concentration of donor atoms and vice versa. Therefore, the current density in an N-type semiconductor is given by

$$J \cong N_D \mu_n q \varepsilon \tag{1.12}$$

where μ_n is the mobility of free electrons in the semiconductor (cm²/Vs) and e the applied electric field (V/cm).

The expression for conductivity in an N-type semiconductor is

$$\sigma \cong N_D \mu_n q \tag{1.13}$$

1.1.2.2 Fermi Level

The expression for Fermi–Dirac probability function for an extrinsic semiconductor is same as that for the intrinsic semiconductor. The only change that occurs is in the Fermi level. The Fermi level (Fig. 1.7) in an N-type semiconductor is raised and is closer to the conduction band as there is a significant increase in the number of electrons in the conduction band and there are fewer holes in the valence band. As the temperature increases, more electron–hole pairs are generated and the Fermi level shifts toward the center of the forbidden energy band gap.

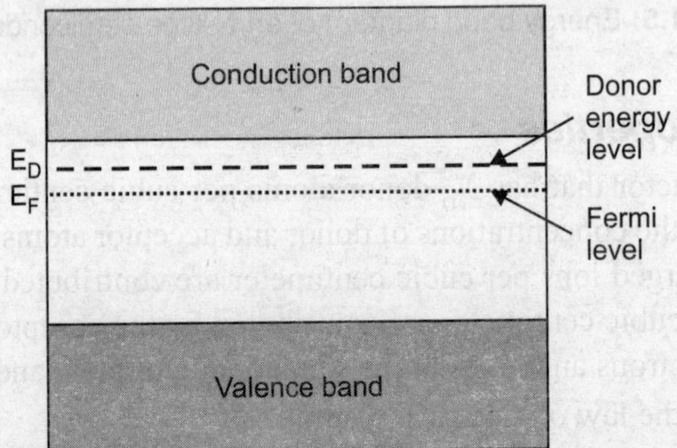

Fig. 1.7: Fermi level in an N-type semiconductor

The Fermi level is given by

$$E_F = E_C - kT \ln\left(\frac{N_C}{N_D}\right) \tag{1.14}$$

where E_C is the energy at the bottom of the conduction band, k the Boltzmann constant in eV/°K (8.642 × 10^{-5} eV/°K), T the temperature in Kelvin, N_C the density of states in the conduction band, which is constant for a material at a given temperature, and N_D the donor atom concentration (number of atoms/ cm^3).

The value of N_C is given by

$$N_C = 2\left(\frac{2\pi m_n kTq}{h^2}\right)^{3/2}$$

where m_n is the effective mass of an electron, T the temperature in Kelvin, h the Planck's constant and q the electronic charge (1.6 × 10^{-19} C).

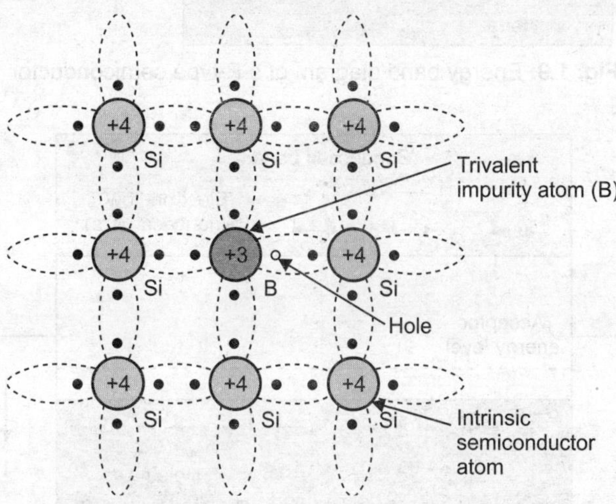

Fig. 1.8: Crystal structure of a P-type semiconductor

1.1.3 P-type semiconductors

A P-type semiconductor is created by adding approximately 1 part in 10^5 parts of trivalent impurity to the intrinsic semiconductor. Trivalent atoms have three electrons in their valence shell and are called acceptor atoms in the context of semiconductor devices. Examples of trivalent impurities include Boron (B), Indium (In) and Gallium (Ga). As there are three electrons in the valence shell of these trivalent impurity atoms, only three covalent bonds can be formed with the neighboring intrinsic semiconductor atoms and a vacancy exists in the fourth bond as shown in Fig. 1.8. This vacancy is referred to as the hole and is represented by a small circle. The hole is ready to accept an electron from the neighboring atom, thereby creating a hole in the neighboring atom. This hole in turn is ready to accept an electron, thereby creating another hole. In this way, the hole moves through the crystal.

The effect of doping creates a discrete energy level called acceptor level in the forbidden energy band gap with energy level (E_A) just above the valence band (Fig. 1.9). The difference between the energy levels of the acceptor band (E_A) and the valence band (E_V) is the energy required by an electron to leave the valence band and occupy the acceptor band, thereby leaving a hole in the valence band. This difference ($E_A - E_V$) is of the order of 0.08 eV for Silicon and 0.01 eV for Germanium. Since very small energy is required for the electron to leave the valence band and occupy the acceptor energy level, large number of electrons jump to the acceptor energy level resulting in a large number of holes in the valence band.

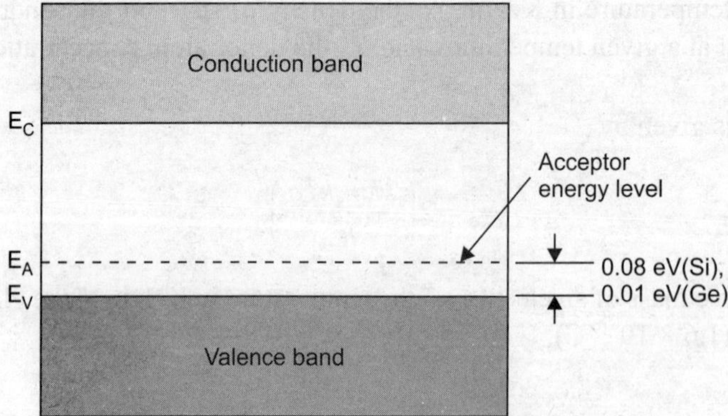

Fig. 1.9: Energy band diagram of a P-type semiconductor

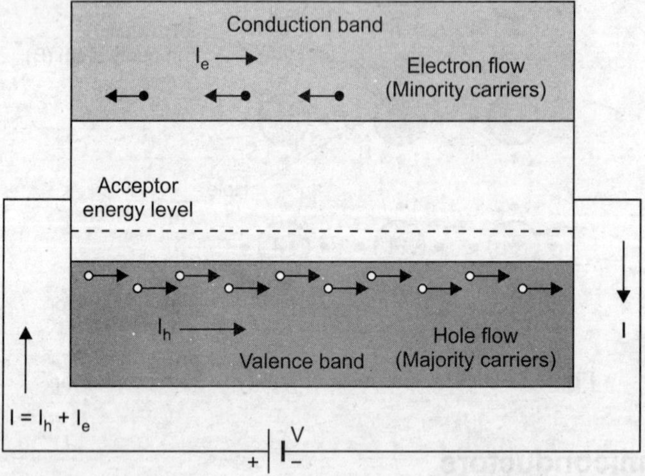

Fig. 1.10: Current flow in a P-type semiconductor

In a P-type semiconductor, the number of electrons decreases, and the number of holes increases compared to those available in an intrinsic semiconductor. The decrease in the number of electrons is attributed to the increase in the rate of recombination of electrons with holes. The current in the P-type semiconductor is dominated by holes, which are referred to as majority carriers. Electrons are the minority carriers in a P-type semiconductor material. Fig. 1.10 shows current flow in P-type semiconductor. Here I is total conventional current flow, I_e the current flow due to electrons and I_h the current flow due to holes. Please remember that the conductivity of an N-type semiconductor is higher than that of a P-type semiconductor as the mobility of electrons is greater than that of holes. For the same level of doping in the N-type and the P-type semiconductors, the conductivity of an N-type semiconductor is around twice that of a P-type semiconductor. Also, in practical semiconductors that the concentration of dopants is greater in P-type semiconductors (approximately 1 part in 10^5 parts) than in N-type semiconductors (approximately 1 part in 10^8 parts).

1.1.3.1 Electrical Properties

For a P-type semiconductor, $N_D = 0$. Also the concentration of free electrons (n) is much less than the concentration of holes (p). Therefore, for a P-type semiconductor, the hole concentration is approximately equal to the acceptor atom concentration, that is,

$$p \cong N_A \tag{1.15}$$

Alternatively, the number of holes in a P-type semiconductor is approximately equal to the number of acceptor atoms. Therefore, the current density in a P-type semiconductor is given by

$$J \cong N_A \mu_p q \varepsilon \tag{1.16}$$

where μ_p is the mobility of holes in the semiconductor (cm²/Vs) and e the applied electric field (V/cm).

The expression for conductivity is

$$\sigma \cong N_A \mu_p q \tag{1.17}$$

1.1.3.2 Fermi Level

As mentioned before, the Fermi–Dirac probability function for an extrinsic semiconductor is the same as that for an intrinsic semiconductor. The only change that occurs is the change in the Fermi level. The Fermi level in a P-type semiconductor (Fig. 1.11) is lower than that of an intrinsic semiconductor and is closer to the valence band; this is because there is a significant increase in the number of holes in the valence band and decrease in the number of electrons in the conduction band. As the temperature increases, more electron–hole pairs are generated and the Fermi level shifts toward the center of the energy gap.

The Fermi level can be derived using the expression

$$E_F = E_V + kT \ln\left(\frac{N_V}{N_A}\right) \tag{1.18}$$

where E_V is the energy at the top of the valence band, N_V the density of states in the valence band, which is constant for a material at a given temperature, and T the temperature in Kelvin.

The value of N_V is calculated using eqn. 1.19.

$$N_V = 2\left(\frac{2\pi m_p kTq}{h^2}\right)^{3/2} \tag{1.19}$$

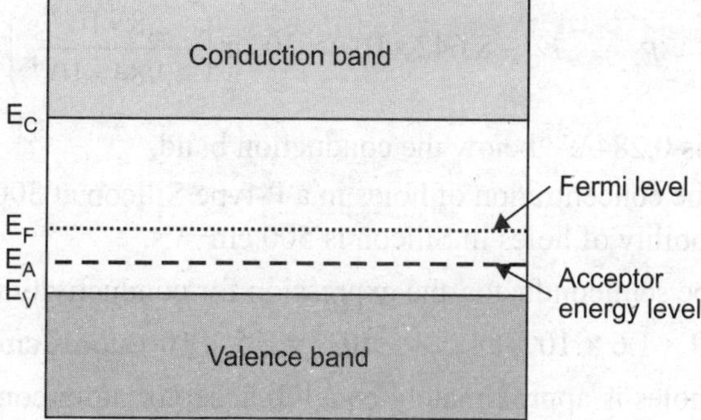

Fig. 1.11: Fermi level in a P-type semiconductor

where m_p is the effective mass of a hole, h the Planck's constant, T the temperature in Kelvin, q the electronic charge (1.6×10^{-19} C), k the Boltzmann constant in eV/°K (= 8.642×10^{-5} eV/°K) and N_A the donor atom concentration (number of atoms/cm³).

Example-1.1: A pentavalent impurity is added to an intrinsic Silicon semiconductor with 1 part in 10^8 parts. Find the concentration of donor atoms and the resistivity of the semiconductor. Also find the Fermi level of the semiconductor. It is given that atomic weight of Silicon is 28.1, density is 2.33 g/cm³, Avogadro's number is 6.023×10^{23}, effective mass of an electron is 1.08 × mass of an electron, mass of the electron is 9.11×10^{-31} kg, mobility of electron is 1300 cm²/V s, Boltzmann constant is 8.642×10^{-5} eV/°K, Planck's constant is 6.626×10^{-34} Js and temperature is 300°K.

Solution: Concentration of donor atoms refers to the number of donor atoms per cubic centimeter of the semiconductor material.

As we know, there are 6.023×10^{23} atoms in one mole of an element.

Atomic weight of Silicon is 28.1. Therefore, in 1 g of Silicon the number of atoms is $6.023 \times 10^{23}/28.1 = 2.14 \times 10^{22}$

Density of Silicon is 2.33 g/cm³. Therefore, the number of atoms of Silicon in 1 cm³ is $2.33 \times 2.14 \times 10^{22} = 4.986 \times 10^{22}$

It is given that there is one dopant atom per 10^8 Silicon atoms. Therefore, the dopant concentration is $4.986 \times 10^{22}/1 \times 10^8 = 4.986 \times 10^{14}$ atoms/cm³

The conductivity of an N-type semiconductor is given by $\sigma \cong N_D \mu_n q$. That is conductivity is $4.986 \times 10^{14} \times 1300 \times 1.6 \times 10^{-19} = 0.103$ (Ω-cm)$^{-1}$

Therefore, resistivity is (1/conductivity), that is (1/0.103) = 9.642 Ω-cm.

The expression for Fermi level in an N-type semiconductor is given by

$$E_F = E_C - kT \ln\left(\frac{N_C}{N_D}\right)$$

$$N_C = 2\left(\frac{2\pi m_n kTq}{h^2}\right)^{3/2}$$

where

$$= 2\left(\frac{2\times 3.14\times 1.08\times 9.11\times 10^{-31}\times 8.642\times 10^{-5}\times 300\times 1.6\times 10^{-19}}{(6.626\times 10^{-34})^2}\right)^{3/2}$$

$$= 2.8 \times 10^{25} \text{ atoms/m}^3 = 2.8 \times 10^{19} \text{ atoms/cm}^3$$

Therefore,

$$E_F = E_C - 8.642\times 10^{-5}\times 300 \ln\left(\frac{2.8\times 10^{19}}{4.984\times 10^{14}}\right) = E_C - 0.284 \text{ eV}$$

Thus, the Fermi level is 0.284 eV below the conduction band.

Example-1.2: Find the concentration of holes in a P-type Silicon at 300°K if its conductivity is 2 (Ω-cm)$^{-1}$, given that the mobility of holes in Silicon is 500 cm²/Vs.

Solution: For a P-type semiconductor, the expression for conductivity is $\sigma = N_A \mu_p q$.

Therefore, $N_A = 2/(500 \times 1.6 \times 10^{-19}) = 2/8 \times 10^{-17} = 2.5 \times 10^{16}$ atoms/cm³

The concentration of holes is approximately equal to acceptor atom concentration. Therefore, the concentration of holes is 2.5×10^{16}.

Example-1.3: A sample of Germanium is doped with both donor and acceptor impurities with donor concentration of 10^{14} donor atoms/cm^3 and acceptor concentration of 10^{15} acceptor atoms/cm^3. Find the resistivity of the semiconductor material. Also find the conduction current density for an applied electric field of 4.5 V/cm. It is given that the mobility of holes and electrons in Germanium is 1800 cm^2/Vs and 3800 cm^2/Vs, respectively.

Solution: The given semiconductor is doped with both donor and acceptor impurities. The concentration of free electrons is approximately equal to the donor impurity concentration and the concentration of holes is approximately equal to the acceptor impurity concentration.

Therefore, the concentration of free electrons (n) = 10^{14} and the concentration of holes (p) = 10^{15}. The conductivity is

$$\sigma = (n\mu_n + p\mu_p) \times q$$

$$= (10^{14} \times 3800 + 10^{15} \times 1800) \times 1.6 \times 10^{-19} = 0.3488\ (\Omega\ \text{cm})^{-1}$$

Now resistivity is given by

$$\text{Resistivity} = \frac{1}{\text{Conductivity}} = \frac{1}{0.3488\ (\Omega\ \text{cm})^{-1}} = 2.867\ \Omega\ \text{cm}$$

Current density in a semiconductor is given by

$$J = \sigma\varepsilon$$

where e is the applied electric field. Substituting the values in this equation we get

$$J = 0.3488 \times 4.5\ \text{A/cm}^2 = 1.5696\ \text{A/cm}^2$$

1.2 LAW OF MASS ACTION

The concentration of holes and electrons in a semiconductor is governed by the law of mass action. According to the law of mass action, the product of free electron concentration and hole concentration in any semiconductor is constant and is given by $np = n_i^2$ where n is the free electron concentration (negatively charged carriers), p the hole concentration (positively charged carriers) and n_i is the intrinsic concentration.

Therefore, the product of concentration of negative and positive charge carriers in a semiconductor is independent of the type and amount of doping and is equal to the square of the intrinsic concentration. Hence, in an N-type semiconductor as the number of electrons increases, the number of holes decreases and in a P-type semiconductor as the number of holes increases the number of electrons decreases.

For an N-type semiconductor, $n \cong N_D$

Therefore,

$$p \cong \frac{n_i^2}{N_D} \tag{1.20}$$

For a P-type semiconductor, $p \cong N_A$

Therefore,

$$n \cong \frac{n_i^2}{N_A} \tag{1.21}$$

Example-1.4: If the concentration of concentration of holes is 1.5×10^{15} atoms/cm^3, find the concentration of electrons. Also, determine the ratio of holes to the free electrons. It is given that the intrinsic concentration of Silicon is 1.5×10^{10}.

Solution: Using the mass action law, the concentration of free electrons is given by

$$n = \frac{n_i^2}{p} = \frac{(1.5\times10^{10})^2}{1.5\times10^{15}} = 150000$$

The concentration of free electrons is 150000 electrons/cm^3, which is much less than the concentration of holes.

$$\frac{\text{Number of holes}}{\text{Number of free electrons}} = \frac{1.5\times10^{15}}{150000}$$

$$= 1\times10^{10}$$

1.3 DRIFT AND DIFFUSION CARRIERS

The current in a semiconductor is the sum of the drift current and the diffusion current as opposed to a conductor where the current flow is only due to the drift phenomenon. Drift current is due to the potential gradient in the semiconductor and is given by the eqn. 1.22.

$$J = (n\mu_n + p\mu_p)q\varepsilon \tag{1.22}$$

where J is the current density in A/cm^2, n the free electron concentration in the material (number of free electrons/cm^3), p the hole concentration in the material (number of holes/cm^3), μ_n the mobility of an electron in the material (cm^2/Vs), μ_p the mobility of a hole in the material (cm^2/Vs), q the charge of an electron (1.6×10^{-19} C) and e the applied electric field (V/cm).

The drift current density due to holes is given by eqn. 1.23.

$$J_p = p\mu_p q\varepsilon \tag{1.23}$$

The drift current density due to electrons is given by eqn. 1.24

$$J_n = n\mu_n q\varepsilon \tag{1.24}$$

Diffusion current is caused by the concentration gradient in the semiconductor, that is, when there is non-uniform concentration of charge particles in a semiconductor.

The hole diffusion current density is given by the eqn. 1.25.

$$J_p = -qD_p\frac{dp}{dx} \tag{1.25}$$

where D_p is the diffusion constant of holes in cm^2/s and dp/dx the variation in hole concentration with distance x (it is positive when the hole concentration increases with distance and is negative if the hole concentration decreases with distance).

Similarly, the electron diffusion current density is given by eqn. 1.26.

$$J_n = qD_n\frac{dn}{dx} \tag{1.26}$$

where D_n is the diffusion constant of electrons in cm^2/s and dn/dx is the variation of electron concentration with distance x (it is positive when the concentration of electrons increases with distance and is negative if the concentration of electrons decreases with distance).

The diffusion constant of a carrier is related to its mobility and is given by eqn. 1.27.

$$\frac{D_p}{\mu_p} = \frac{D_n}{\mu_n} = V_T \tag{1.27}$$

where V_T is the volt equivalent of temperature and is equal to kT (k is the Boltzmann constant in eV/°K and T is the temperature in Kelvin). Therefore, the total current is the sum of the diffusion and drift currents. The total hole current density is given by eqn. 1.28.

$$J_p = p\mu_p q\varepsilon - qD_p \frac{dp}{dx} \quad (1.28)$$

The total electron current density is given by the eqn. 1.29.

$$J_n = n\mu_n q\varepsilon + qD_n \frac{dn}{dx} \quad (1.29)$$

Example-1.5: The silicon sample with unit cross-sectional area shown in Fig. 1.12 is in thermal equilibrium. The following information is given: T = 300 K, electronic charge = 1.6×10^{-19} C, thermal voltage = 26mV and electron mobility = 1350 cm^2/Vs.

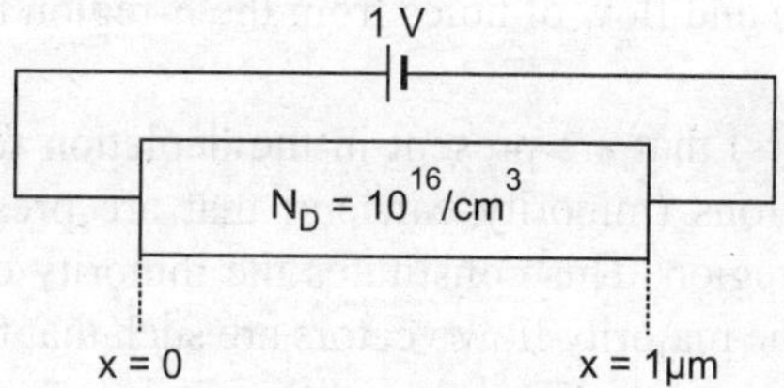

Fig. 1.12: Example-1.5

Find the magnitude of the electric field and electron drift current density at $x = 0.5$ μm?

Solution: Given that the sample is in thermal equilibrium, therefore

$$\varepsilon = \frac{v}{d} = \frac{1}{1\times10^{-6}} = 10^6 \ V/\text{m} = 10kV/\text{cm}$$

We have $J = N_D q\mu_n \varepsilon$

Substituting different given values in the above equation, we get

$$J = 10^{16} \times (1.6 \times 10^{-19}) \times (1350) \times (10 \times 10^3) = 2.16 \times 10^4 \ A/\text{cm}^2$$

1.4 P-N JUNCTION DIODES

A semiconductor diode is a polarity-sensitive two-terminal device comprising a P-N junction formed between a P-type semiconductor material and an N-type semiconductor material [Fig. 1.13 (a)]. The P-N junction is formed by introducing the donor impurities on one side and acceptor impurities on the other side of a single crystal of a semiconductor. Fig. 1.13 (b) shows the circuit symbol of a P-N junction diode. The arrow is associated with the P-region and the vertical line with the N-region. The

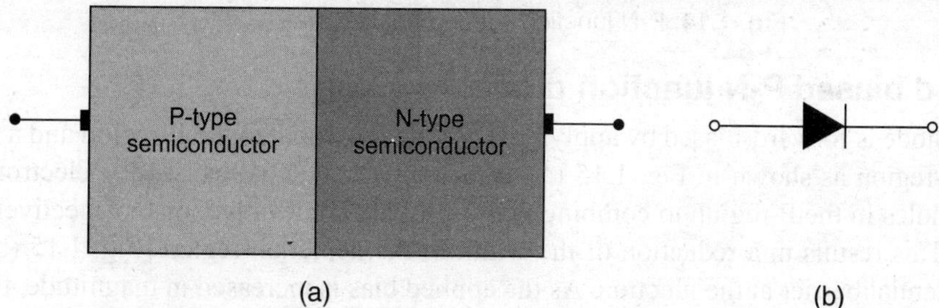

Fig. 1.13: (a) P-N junction; (b) symbol of a P-N junction diode

P- and N-regions are referred to as the anode and the cathode, respectively. Silicon and Germanium are the most commonly used materials for fabricating semiconductor diodes. The electrons in the N-region and the holes in the P-region combine near the junction, resulting in a region near the junction that is devoid of free electrons and holes. This region of uncovered positive and negative ions is called the *depletion region* because of the depletion of free carriers in this region. The thickness of this region is of the order of 0.5 μm.

Electrons (majority carriers) in the N-region and negatively charged ions in the P-region repel each other near the junction. Similarly, holes in the P-region (majority carriers) and positively charged ions in the N-region also repel each other near the junction. An effective potential of the order of few tenths of a volt, referred to as the *contact potential* or the *barrier potential*, is developed across the depletion region. However, some of these holes and electrons have sufficient kinetic energy to overcome the contact potential and be able to pass through the depletion region. This results in a flow of electrons from the N-region to the P-region and flow of holes from the P-region to the N-region. This constitutes the majority carrier flow vector.

Also, holes (minority carriers) that are present in the depletion region of the N-region will pass to the P-region. Similarly, electrons (minority carriers) that are present in the depletion region of the P-region will pass to the N-region. This constitutes the minority carrier flow vector. The relative magnitudes of the minority and the majority flow vectors are such that the net flow in either direction is zero. This is referred to as the open-circuit condition of the semiconductor diode where no bias voltage is applied to the diode. In other words, in the absence of an applied bias voltage, the net flow of current in a semiconductor diode is zero. Fig. 1.14 shows the P-N junction with no applied bias.

In the subsequent paragraphs, we will discuss the response of the semiconductor diode under forward-bias and reverse-bias conditions.

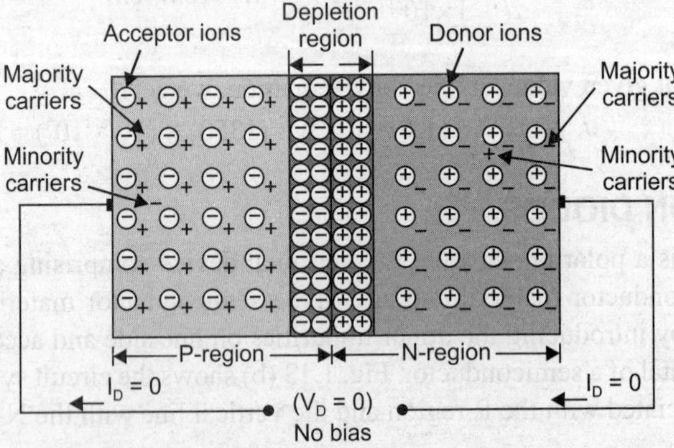

Fig. 1.14: P-N junction with no applied bias

1.4.1 Forward biased P-N junction diode

A semiconductor diode is forward-biased by applying a positive potential to the P-region and a negative potential to the N-region as shown in Fig. 1.15 (a). This applied potential causes the electrons in the N-region and the holes in the P-region to combine with positive and negative ions, respectively, in the depletion region. This results in a reduction of the width of the depletion region [Fig. 1.15 (b)] and a decrease in the potential barrier at the junction. As the applied bias is increased in magnitude, the width of the depletion region decreases until a point is reached where there is a sharp rise in the number of majority carriers crossing the junction. In other words, a large number of holes cross the junction from the P-region to the N-region and a large number of electrons cross the junction in the reverse direction, that is, from the N-region to the P-region. It may be mentioned here that holes traveling from left to right constitute a current in the same direction as the electrons traveling from right to left. This results in exponential rise in the current due to the majority carriers. The current due to the majority carriers is referred to as the *forward current* and is in the range of few tens of milliamperes (except for power diodes where the current is of the order of few amperes). Typically, the voltage across the forward-biased diode is less than 1 V and depends upon the diode material. As an example, the forward voltage for Silicon and Germanium diodes is typically 0.7 V and 0.3 V, respectively.

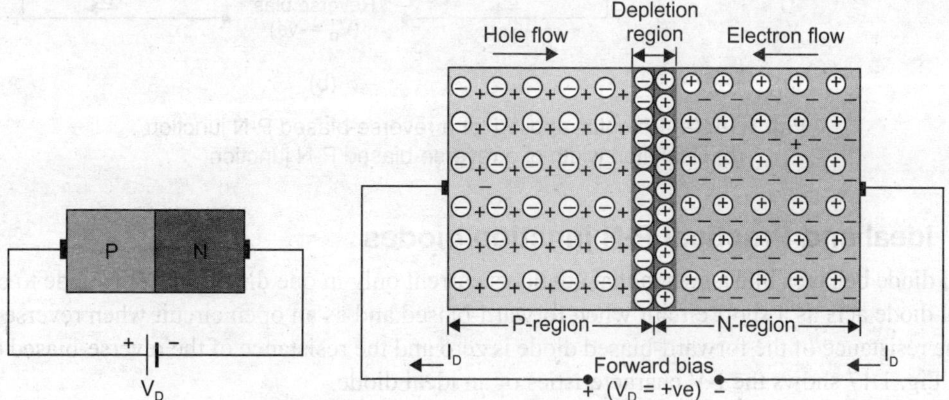

Fig. 1.15: Potential applied for (a) forward-biased P-N junction (b) Depletion width of a forward biased P-N junction

The flow of the minority carriers remains the same as in the case of diode with no applied bias. The current contributed by the minority carriers is referred to as the *reverse saturation current* or *reverse leakage current* and is of the order of a few nanoamperes to a few microamperes. The reverse saturation current is in the opposite direction to the forward current. However, its magnitude is negligible as compared to the forward current. V-I characteristics of the diode are discussed in detail in section below.

1.4.2 Reverse biased P-N junction diode

A diode is said to be reverse-biased when an external potential applied across it is such that the positive terminal is connected to the N-region and the negative terminal is connected to the P-region [Fig. 1.16 (a)]. This results in widening of the depletion region as electrons and holes are drawn away from the junction due to the polarity of the applied voltage [Fig. 1.16 (b)]. Widening of the depletion region reduces the flow of majority carriers to approximately zero.

The minority carrier flow remains the same as in case of diode with no applied bias. As mentioned before, this current is referred to as the reverse saturation current and is of the order of a few nanoamperes to a few microamperes. The reverse saturation current does not significantly change with change in the reverse-bias potential. However, it is a strong function of the diode temperature and increases with increase in diode temperature. When the applied reverse-bias is increased beyond the breakdown voltage of the diode, there is a sharp increase in the reverse current.

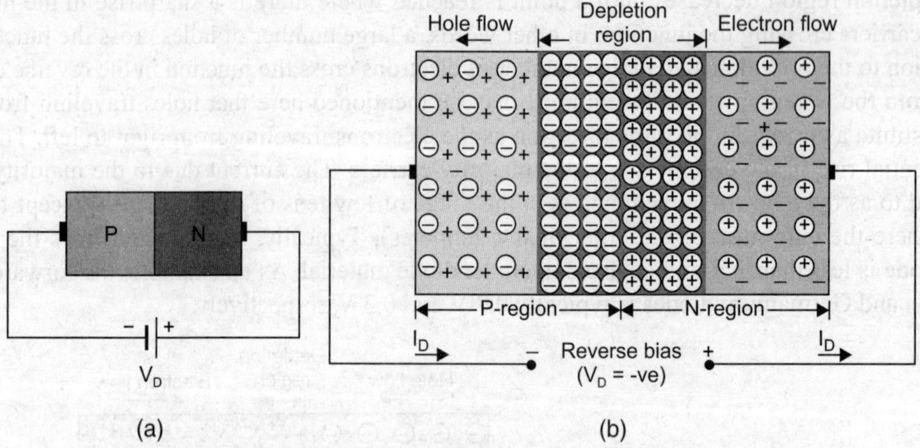

Fig. 1.16: (a) Potential applied for a reverse-biased P-N junction
(b) Depletion width of a reverse-biased P-N junction

1.4.3 Ideal and Practical P-N junction diodes

An ideal diode behaves like a switch that conducts current only in one direction from anode to cathode. An ideal diode acts as a short circuit when forward-biased and as an open circuit when reverse-biased. Thus, the resistance of the forward-biased diode is zero and the resistance of the reverse-biased diode is infinite. Fig. 1.17 shows the I-V characteristics of an ideal diode.

A practical or actual P-N junction diode differs from the ideal diode. In the forward-bias condition, the ideal diode acts as a closed switch with zero ON-resistance that allows the current to flow in one direction from anode to cathode. However, practical diodes do not conduct until a certain value of forward voltage is applied to them. This voltage, referred to as the *cut-in voltage* or the *knee voltage* or the *threshold voltage*, is of the order of less than 1 V for semiconductor diodes. Also, the ON-resistance of the practical diode is not zero and varies from few ohms to few hundreds of ohms. In the reverse-bias state, the practical diode differs from the ideal diode that behaves like an open switch. In the case of a practical diode in reverse-bias condition, a small amount of current, referred to as the reverse saturation current, flows through the diode. Also, there is a sharp increase in the reverse current when the applied reverse-bias voltage exceeds the reverse breakdown voltage.

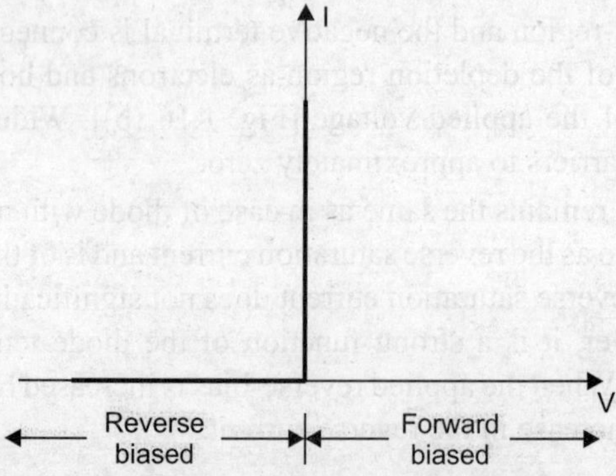

Fig. 1.17: I-V characteristics of an ideal diode

1.5 I-V CHARACTERISTICS OF A DIODE

The I-V characteristics of a semiconductor diode both in the forward-bias and reverse-bias conditions are expressed by the universal diode equation also known as *Shockley's diode equation* expressed by eqn. 1.30.

$$I_D = I_0(e^{V_D/\eta V_T} - 1), \qquad (1.30)$$

where V_D is the voltage across the diode (in V); I_D the diode current (in mA); I_0 the reverse saturation current (in mA); $\eta = 1$ for Germanium and Silicon (for relatively higher values of diode current) and $\eta = 2$ for Silicon at relatively low levels of diode current, that is below the cut-in-voltage or the knee-point of the diode characteristics; V_T the volt equivalent of temperature (in V).

It may be mentioned here that, the value of $V_T = kT/q$, where k is the Boltzmann constant (8.642 × 10^{-5} eV/K); q the electron charge (1.6 × 10^{-19} C); T the temperature (in °K); V_T the volt equivalent of temperature (in V). Also, diode voltage (V_D) and diode current (I_D) are positive when the diode is forward-biased and negative when the diode is reverse-biased. The I-V characteristics of a Silicon P-N junction diode are shown in Fig. 1.18 (a) and that of a Germanium P-N junction diode in Fig. 1.18 (b). As is evident from the curves shown in the two figures; when the diode is forward-biased, there is a minimum voltage that must be exceeded before there is sufficient conduction of current through the diode. In other words, current flows through the diode when it is forward-biased, with the applied voltage greater than the cut-in voltage (V_γ) of the diode. The cut-in voltage is 0.7 V in the case of Silicon diodes and 0.3 V in the case of Germanium diodes.

When the applied forward voltage exceeds the cut-in voltage, there is a sharp rise in the current through the diode. In other words, a very small increment in the forward voltage (V_D) results in a very large increase in the forward current (I_D). For positive values of V_D, we can see from Eqn. (1.30) that the first term of the equation will grow exponentially and overpower the effect of the second term. The first term corresponds to the forward current through the diode and the second term corresponds to the reverse saturation current. Thus, the current through the diode varies exponentially with the applied voltage, provided that the applied voltage is greater than the cut-in voltage. The forward current is measured in milliamperes and is generally in the range of few tens of milliamperes.

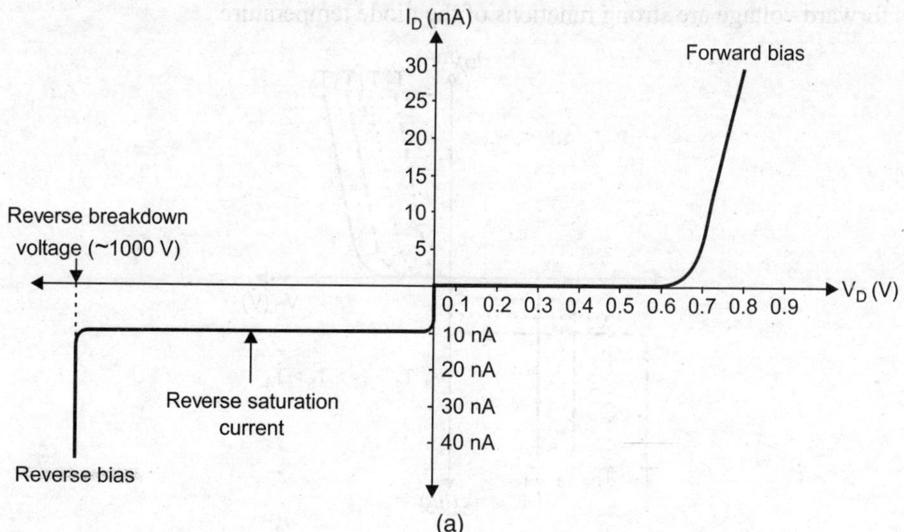

(a)

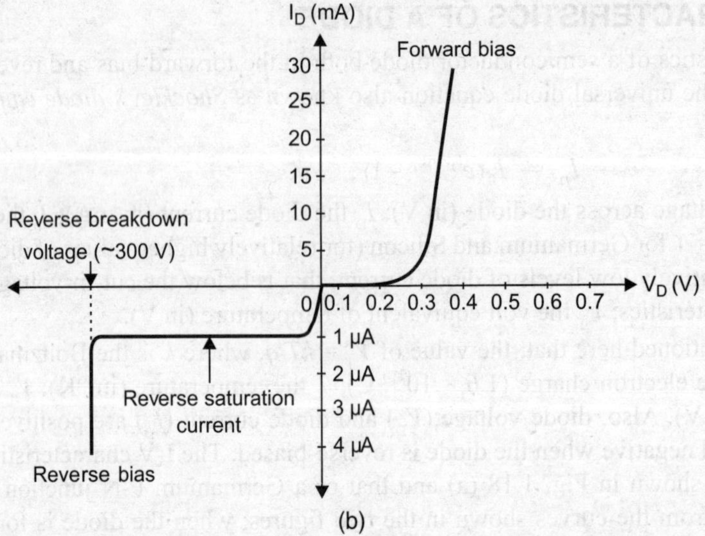

Fig. 1.18: I-V characteristics of (a) Silicon diode and (b) Germanium diode

In the reverse-bias mode, the small current that flows through the diode is the reverse saturation current. It is of the order of few nanoamperes for Silicon diodes and typically 1 μA for Germanium diodes. This current is independent of the applied reverse voltage until the semiconductor junction breaks down at a voltage known as the *reverse breakdown voltage* or the *peak inverse voltage.* The breakdown of the junction results in a sudden rise of current that ends up in damaging the diode. Hence, when the diodes are operated in the reverse-bias mode; their operating voltage should be less than the breakdown voltage. Some diodes known as breakdown diodes are designed to operate in the breakdown region.

1.5.1 Temperature Dependence of the I-V Characteristics

Fig. 1.19 shows the variation in the diode's I-V characteristic curves with change in temperature. As is evident from the figure, the reverse saturation current, reverse breakdown voltage, cut-in voltage and the diode's forward voltage are strong functions of the diode temperature.

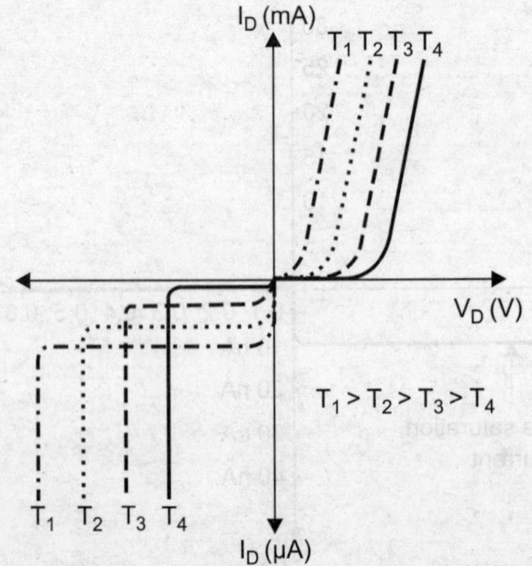

Fig. 1.19: Temperature dependence of the diode I-V characteristics

As an approximation it can be said that reverse saturation current doubles itself for every 10°C rise in diode temperature. As an example, the reverse saturation current of the Germanium diode is of the order of 1 μA at 25°C and increases to around 100 μA at 100°C. The variation of the reverse saturation current with temperature is given by eqn. 1.31.

$$I_0(T) = I_0(T_1)\times 2^{(T-T_1)/10} \qquad (1.31)$$

where $I_0(T)$ is the reverse saturation current at temperature T and $I_0(T_1)$ the reverse saturation current at temperature T_1. The reverse breakdown voltage of the diode increases with increase in temperature. Also, the cut-in-voltage (V_γ) and the forward voltage across the diode for a given current decrease with increase in temperature. The variation of cut-in voltage and the forward voltage with temperature is given by eqn. 1.32.

$$\frac{dV}{dT} = 2.5 \text{ mV/°C} \qquad (1.32)$$

Example-1.6: A semiconductor junction diode has a reverse saturation current of 1 μA at an ambient temperature of 30°C. What should be the approximate value of reverse saturation current at 80°C?

Solution: The reverse saturation current approximately doubles for every 10°C rise in temperature. The temperature increases by 50°C in the present case. Thus, the reverse saturation current increases by a factor of (2^5) = 32. The reverse saturation current at 80°C is therefore 32 × 1μA = 32μA.

Example-1.7: Calculate the reverse current of a silicon diode at a temperature of 27°C if a forward voltage of 0.5V causes a current of 1A.

Solution: We know that diode current,

$$I_D = I_0(e^{V_D/\eta V_T}-1),$$

where V_D is the voltage across the diode (in V); I_0 the reverse saturation current (in μA); η = 2 for Silicon; $V_T = kT/q$, where k is the Boltzmann constant (1.38 × 10^{-23} J/K); q the electron charge (1.6 × 10^{-19} C); T is the temperature in Kelvin.

Substituting the values of K and q in the equation, we get

$$I = I_o\left[e^{\frac{5800V}{T}}-1\right], T = 27°C = 300K$$

$$I = 1A,\ V = 0.5V$$

Substituting the values of T, I and V, we get

$$I_o\left[e^{\frac{5800\times0.5}{300}}-1\right] = 1$$

$$I_0\,[e^{9.67}-1] = 1$$

$$I_0\,[15835-1] = 1$$

This gives I_0 = 63μA

Example-1.8: A silicon diode operating at a temperature of 25°C and a forward biased-voltage of 0.6V has a forward current of 0.8A flowing through it. If the current is held constant, what would be the voltage across the diode at an operating temperature of 75°C?

Solution: From the previous example, we have seen that for a silicon diode,

$$I_D = I_0\left[e^{\frac{5800V}{T}}-1\right]$$

Substituting the values of I, V and T, we get (for 25°C)

$$I_0\left[e^{\frac{5800\times0.6}{298}}-1\right] = 0.8 \quad = 0.8$$

$$I_0\,[117008-1] = 0.8$$

This gives $I_0 = 6.837\mu A$

When the operating temperature becomes 75°C (348K); the new voltage across the diode can be computed from:

$$I_D = I_0'\left[e^{\frac{5800V}{T}}-1\right]$$

Where, $T = 348K$, I is held constant at 0.8A and I_0' is the new value of reverse saturation current. We know that I_0 doubles for every 10°C rise in temperature. Therefore,

$$I_0 = (2^5)\,I_0 = 32I_0 = 32 \times 6.837\mu A = 218.8\mu A$$

Therefore,

$$0.8 = 218.8\times10^{-6}\left[e^{\frac{5800V}{348}}-1\right]$$

Solving the above equation, we get $V = 0.492V$

The required value of voltage across the diode, therefore, is 0.492V

1.6 DIODE'S RESISTANCES AND CAPACITANCES

1.6.1 Diode Resistances

As the I-V characteristics of a diode are non-linear; the diode resistance varies with change in the applied voltage. Two terms very commonly used to define the resistance of the diode are the *static resistance* and the *dynamic resistance*.

1.6.1.1 Static Resistance

Static resistance or the DC resistance (R) of the diode is the resistance offered by the diode when a steady DC voltage is applied across it. This results in the flow of a steady DC current through the diode. Let us consider that application of voltage (V_{D1}) results in current (I_{D1}) through the diode as shown in Fig. 1.20 (a). Then the static resistance of the diode is given by eqn. 1.33.

$$R = \frac{V_{D1}}{I_{D1}} \tag{1.33}$$

The static resistance of the diode when forward-biased will be higher near the knee region or below it as compared to the vertical region of the I-V characteristics. In the reverse-biased state, the value of the static resistance will be very high. Typical values of static resistance for Silicon diodes varied from few tens to hundreds of ohms in the forward-biased region and from few mega-ohms to few hundreds of mega-ohms in the reverse-biased region.

1.6.1.2 Dynamic Resistance

Dynamic resistance or the AC resistance of a diode is defined as the resistance offered by the diode to a time-varying input signal. The dynamic resistance of the diode having the I-V characteristics as shown in Fig. 1.20 (b) is given by Eqn. (1.34). In other words, the dynamic resistance at a particular point in the operating region of the diode is defined by the slope of the tangent drawn at that point.

$$r = \frac{\Delta V_d}{\Delta I_d} \tag{1.34}$$

By taking the derivative of universal diode equation given in eqn. (1.30) with respect to applied forward voltage and reversing the result we get the expression for the dynamic resistance of the diode. The derivation is as follows.

Universal diode equation is $I_D = I_0(e^{V_D/\eta V_T} - 1)$. Substituting $V_T = kT/q$ in the above equation and taking derivative of the equation with respect to the forward voltage (V_D) we get,

$$\frac{dI_D}{dV_D} = \frac{qI_0 e^{qV/\eta kT}}{\eta kT}$$

Substituting $I_0 e^{qV/\eta kT} = I_D + I_0$ in the above equation we get,

$$\frac{dI_D}{dV_D} = \frac{q(I_D + I_0)}{\eta kT}$$

For $I_D >> I_0$,

$$\frac{dI_D}{dV_D} \cong \frac{qI_D}{\eta kT}$$

Taking the reciprocal of the above equation, we obtain

$$\frac{dV_D}{dI_D} \cong \frac{\eta kT}{qI_D}$$

Substituting the value of $k = 8.642 \times 10^{-5}$ eV/°K and $T = 300$°K we get,

$$\frac{dV_D}{dI_D} = r \cong \frac{26\eta}{I_D}$$

Dynamic resistance (r) of a diode in the forward-biased region is given by eqn. 1.35.

$$r \cong \frac{26\eta}{I_D} \tag{1.35}$$

Where $\eta = 1$ for Germanium and Silicon (for relatively higher values of diode current); $\eta = 2$ for Silicon at relatively low levels of diode current, that is below the cut-in-voltage or the knee-point of the diode characteristics; I_D is the forward diode current. In the reverse-biased region, the value of the dynamic resistance of the diode is given by eqn. 1.36.

$$\text{Dynamic resistance of the diode in the reverse-biased region} \cong \frac{26\eta}{I_0} \tag{1.36}$$

where I_0 is the reverse saturation current. However, the change in the value of reverse saturation current (I_0) is very small with change in the reverse-bias voltage from 0 V to the reverse breakdown voltage resulting in very high value of dynamic resistance. Hence, for all practical purposes the diode can be assumed to be an open circuit in the reverse-bias region. The typical value of dynamic resistance of Silicon diodes is of the order of few ohms in the forward-biased region and around few hundreds of mega-ohms in the reverse-biased region.

1.6.1.3 Average AC Resistance

Another term sometimes used to define the resistance of a diode is the *average AC resistance*. When a sufficiently large input signal is applied to the diode to produce a broad swing as shown in Fig. 1.20 (c); the resistance associated with the diode is called the average AC resistance. It is determined by the slope of the straight line formed by joining the two points on the I-V characteristics of the diode corresponding to the maximum and minimum input voltages. It is expressed by eqn. 1.37.

$$\text{Average AC resistance} = \frac{(V_{D2} - V_{D1})}{(I_{D2} - I_{D1})} \tag{1.37}$$

The static, dynamic and average AC resistances discussed thus far are all contributed by the P-N junction. Other than the junction resistance, the resistance of the semiconductor material (called the body resistance) and the resistance introduced by the connection between the semiconductor material and the external metallic conductor (called the contact resistance) are also present. These resistances together can range from 0.1 Ω to around 2 Ω and in most cases can be ignored.

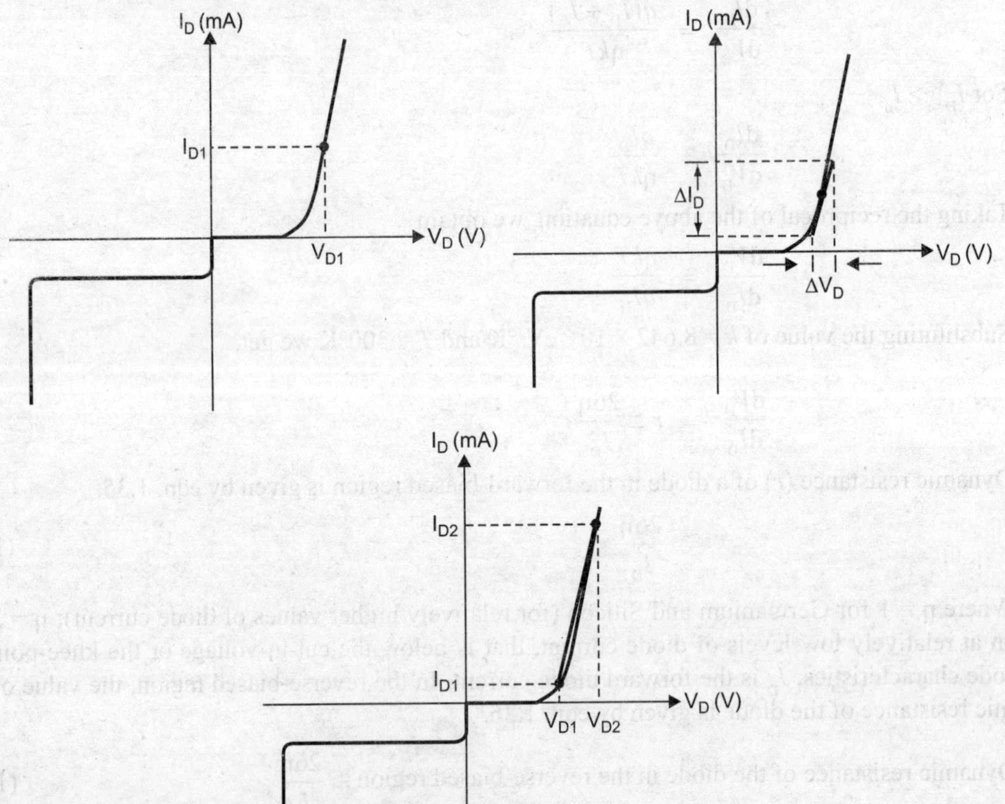

Fig. 1.20: (a) Static resistance of a diode; (b) dynamic resistance of a diode; (c) average AC resistance of a diode

1.6.3 Diode Junction Capacitances

There are two types of capacitances associated with a junction diode, namely, the *transition capacitance* (C_T) and the *diffusion capacitance* (C_D). These capacitances in effect come in parallel with the ideal diode as shown in Fig. 1.21 (a). For low- and mid-frequency low-power applications, the effect of these capacitances on the diode performance is negligible and hence can be ignored. However, in high-frequency and high-power applications, the effects of these capacitances have to be taken into consideration. The two types of diode capacitances are briefly discussed in the following paragraphs.

1.6.3.1 Transition Capacitance

The P-N junction acts as a parallel plate capacitor with the P- and the N-regions as the parallel plates and the depletion region as the insulator or the dielectric. As we can recall, the capacitance of a parallel plate capacitor is given by the formula $C_P = (\varepsilon A/d)$, where ε is the permittivity of the dielectric used, A is the area of the plates and d is the separation between the plates. With no applied bias, the width of the depletion region is around 0.5 μm and the associated capacitance is of the order of 20 pF. In the forward-biased state, the width of the depletion region decreases and hence the capacitance increases. In the reverse-biased condition, the depletion region widens with the applied reverse voltage so the corresponding capacitance reduces with increase in applied reverse bias. This capacitance is referred to as the transition capacitance or the space charge capacitance. Fig. 1.21 (b) shows the variation of the transition capacitance with the applied reverse voltage. The dependence of the diode capacitance on the applied reverse bias is made use of in a number of electronic devices and systems, for example in variable voltage capacitors known as the varactors. The effect of transition capacitance in the forward-biased state is overshadowed by the presence of diffusion capacitance.

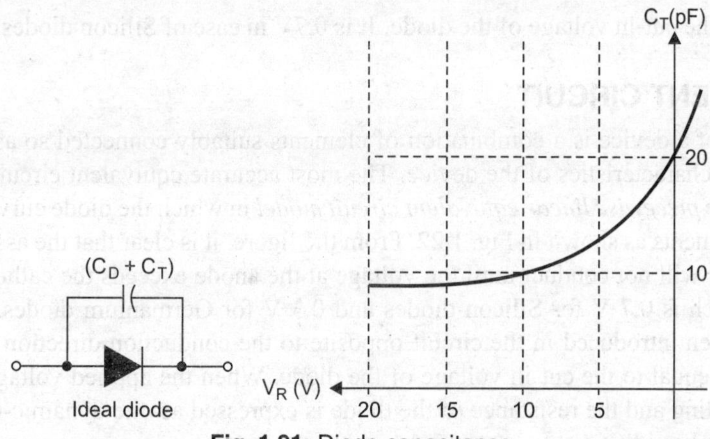

Fig. 1.21: Diode capacitance

1.6.3.2 Diffusion Capacitance

In the forward-biased state, the capacitance that is predominant is the diffusion capacitance or the storage capacitance. It is defined by the equation $C_D = dq/dv$, where dq represents the change in the number of minority carriers stored outside the depletion region when a change in voltage (dv) is applied across the diode. In other words, it is dependent on the rate at which the charge is inducted into the P- and the N-regions just outside the depletion region. Its value in the forward-biased region is in the range of 10 μF to 20 μF. In the reverse-bias region, its value is much smaller than the transition capacitance and hence the transition capacitance predominates in this region. Diffusion capacitance affects the switching time of the diode. The switching time constant of the diode is equal to $r_d \times C_D$, where r_d is the dynamic forward resistance of the diode. The value of switching time constant is very small due to the extremely small value of r_d. Hence, the switching time of the diode is not taken into consideration for normal diode applications and it assumes importance only when the diode is used as a switching device in very high speed applications.

Example-1.9: A 12-Volt Zener diode operating at a current of 12mA has an observed dynamic resistance value of 10 ohms. What would be the change in Zener voltage produced if the operating current changes by 10μA?

Solution: The dynamic resistance is given by

$$Z = \frac{\Delta V_z}{\Delta I_z}$$

Where,

ΔV_z is the change in the Zener voltage

DI_z is the change in the operating current

$$DV_z = Z \times \Delta I_z = 12 \times 10 \times 10^{-6} = 0.12mV$$

Example-1.10: A Silicon P-N junction diode has a forward voltage drop of 1V for a forward DC current of 100 mA. It has a reverse current of 2μA for a reverse voltage of 5V. Find the bulk resistance of the diode in ohms.

Solution: Bulk resistance of a diode is given by:

$$\left(\frac{V_F - V_B}{I_F}\right) = \left(\frac{1-0.7}{100\times 10^{-3}}\right) = 3\Omega$$

Where, VB is the cut-in voltage of the diode. It is 0.7V in case of Silicon diodes.

1.7 EQUIVALENT CIRCUIT

Equivalent circuit of a device is a combination of elements suitably connected so as to best represent the actual terminal characteristics of the device. The most accurate equivalent circuit model for a P-N junction diode is the *piecewise linear equivalent circuit model* in which the diode curves are represented by straight-line segments as shown in Fig. 1.22. From the figure, it is clear that the assumption has been made that the diode will not conduct until the voltage at the anode exceeds the cathode voltage by the cut-in voltage, which is 0.7 V for Silicon diodes and 0.3 V for Germanium diodes. Hence, a battery voltage (V_B) has been introduced in the circuit opposite to the conduction direction of the diode. The magnitude of V_B is equal to the cut-in voltage of the diode. When the applied voltage exceeds V_B; the diode starts conducting and the resistance of the diode is expressed as the dynamic-ON resistance (r_d) in the forward-biased condition.

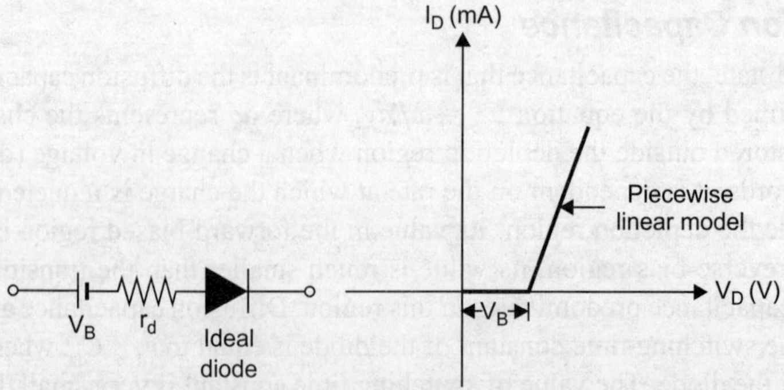

Fig. 1.22: Piecewise linear equivalent model of a diode

A line is drawn on the equivalent model curve with a slope equal to the inverse of the value of the dynamic resistance ($1/r_d$). The ideal diode shown in the circuit is an ideal switch that conducts only in one direction. The piecewise linear equivalent circuit model is the most accurate equivalent model of a diode. Also, the model is equally valid for both DC as well as AC applications. However, it does not result in the actual duplication of the diode characteristics, especially in the knee region.

When the network resistance is much larger than the value of the diode resistance (r_d); then the above model can be simplified as shown in Fig. 1.23. Here the diode resistance is assumed to be zero. The model makes an assumption that the diode will not conduct until the cut-in voltage is reached and after that it acts as an ideal closed switch that conducts only in one direction.

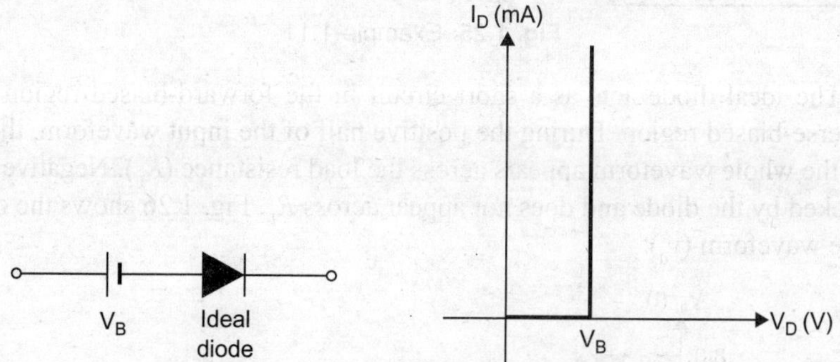

Fig. 1.23: Simplified equivalent diode model

Another possible simplification model is shown is shown in Fig. 1.24. Here, the curve has been approximated by a straight line through the origin and the slope of the straight line is given by the inverse of the static diode resistance at the point of intersection of the line with the diode I-V characteristics.

Ideal diode is the simplest equivalent diode model. This model is applicable when the applied voltage levels are much larger than the diode's cut-in voltage and the network resistance is of a much larger value than the diode's dynamic-ON resistance. The I-V characteristics of an ideal diode were shown earlier in Fig. 1.17.

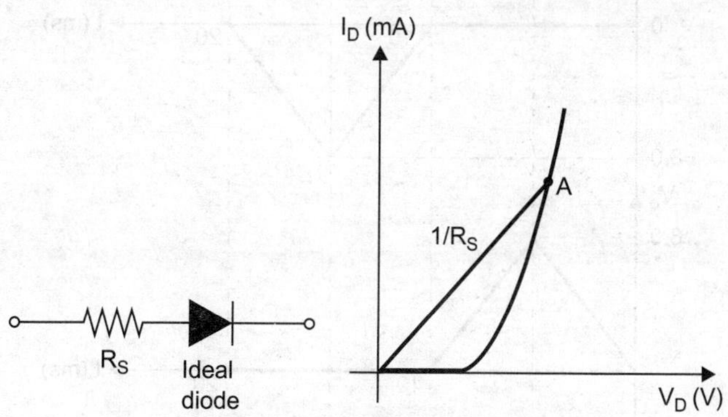

Fig. 1.24: Another simplified diode model

Example-1.11: Fig. 1.25 (a) shows a simple diode circuit. The input waveform applied to the circuit is shown in Fig. 1.25 (b). Draw the waveforms for the output voltage (v_o) and voltage across the diode (v_d) assuming the diode to be ideal.

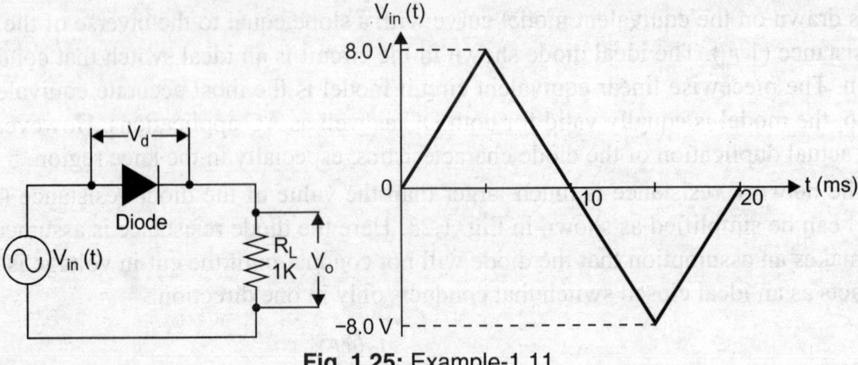

Fig. 1.25: Example-1.11

Solution: The ideal diode acts as a short circuit in the forward-biased region and as an open circuit in the reverse-biased region. During the positive half of the input waveform, the diode acts as a short circuit and the whole waveform appears across the load resistance (R_L). Negative half of the input waveform is blocked by the diode and does not appear across R_L. Fig. 1.26 shows the output waveform (v_o) and the diode waveform (v_d).

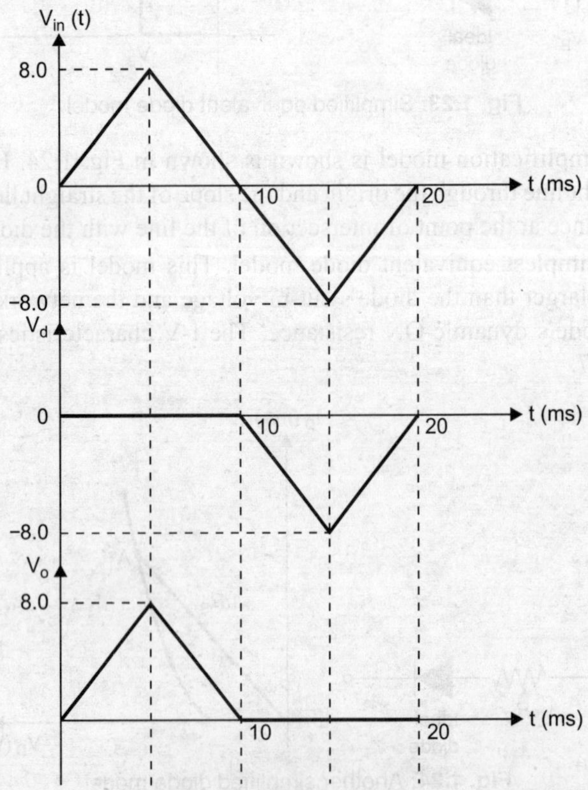

Fig. 1.26: Solution to Example-1.11

Example-1.12: Draw the piecewise linear equivalent circuit model for the diode shown in Fig. 1.27.

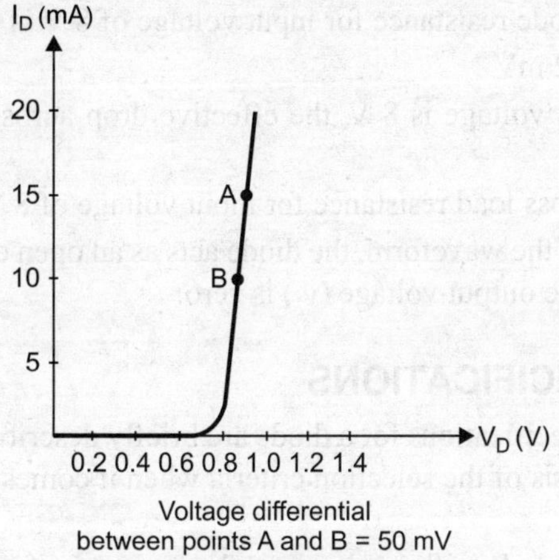

Fig. 1.27: Example-1.12

Solution: Refer to Fig. 1.28(a). From Fig. 1.28 (a), we can see that the cut-in voltage is approximately 0.8 V.

The slope of the curve is given by taking two points A and B in the linear region as shown in Fig. 1. 28 (a).

Slope = $(V_A - V_B) / (I_A - I_B)$ = 50 mV/5 mA = 10 Ω

The piecewise equivalent model is shown in Fig. 1.28 (b). It comprises a battery voltage of 0.8 V, a resistance of 10 Ω and an ideal diode. The I-V characteristic curve for the equivalent model is also shown in the figure.

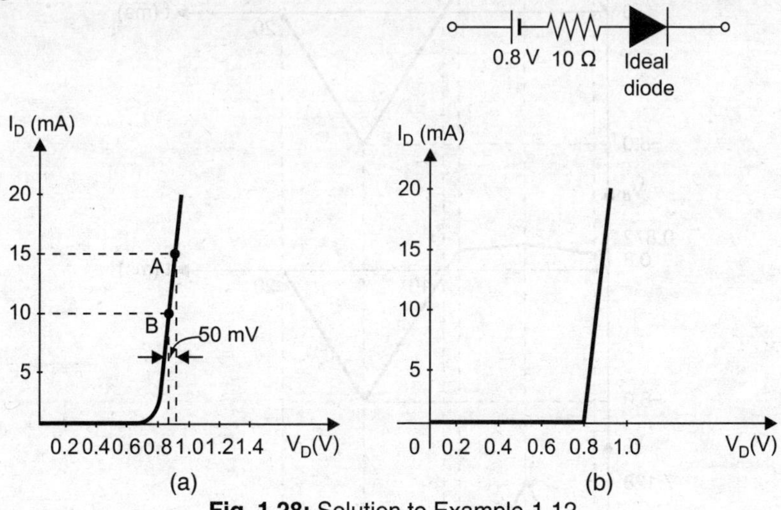

Fig. 1.28: Solution to Example-1.12

Example-1.13: Using the equivalent model of the diode in Example-1.12, draw the output voltage (v_o) and the diode voltage (v_d) waveforms for the circuit and the input waveform of Example-1.11.

Solution: The output voltage (v_o) and diode voltage (v_d) waveforms are shown in Fig. 1.29.

The diode acts as an open circuit until the input voltage reaches 0.8 V. After that it acts as a resistance with a value of 10 Ω

Voltage drop across the diode resistance for input voltage of 8 V is given by:

[(8 – 0.8) × 10)/ 1000 = 72 mV

Therefore, when the input voltage is 8 V, the effective drop across the diode = 0.8 + 0.072 V = 0.872V

Therefore, the voltage across load resistance for input voltage of 8 V = 8 – 0.872 V = 7.128 V

For the negative portion of the waveform, the diode acts as an open circuit. The whole input voltage appears across the diode and the output voltage (v_o) is zero.

1.8 ELECTRICAL SPECIFICATIONS

Some of the major electrical specifications for a diode are briefly described in the following paragraphs. These specifications are the basis of the selection criteria when it comes to choosing the right diode for a given application.

1. ***Forward Voltage (V_F):*** It is the voltage applied across a forward-biased diode. It is not a specification in itself. It is given along with the corresponding forward current value at which it has been measured. It indicates the diode's static resistance. For example, general purpose diode 1N3611 is specified as 1.1 V@1000 mA, which also indicates that its static resistance is 1.1 Ω.

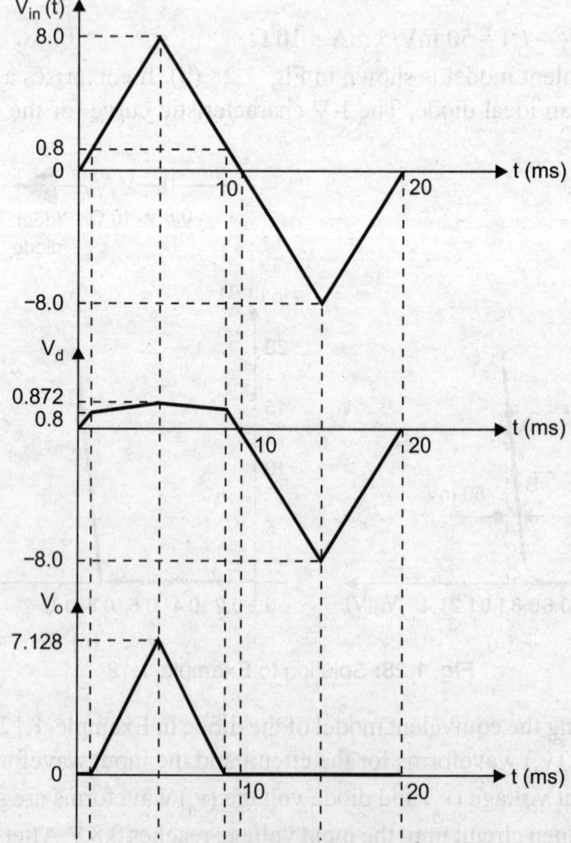

Fig. 1.29: Example-1.13

2. ***Forward Current (I_F):*** It is the direct current flowing through the diode when it is forward-biased.
3. ***Reverse Voltage (V_R):*** It is the voltage across a reverse-biased diode. It is specified along with corresponding reverse current value at which it has been measured. It also indicates the diode's reverse-biased resistance.
4. ***Reverse Current (I_R):*** It is the direct current flowing through a reverse-biased diode.
5. ***Reverse Breakdown Voltage or the Peak Inverse Voltage (V_{BR}, PIV):*** It is the maximum reverse voltage that a diode can withstand without breaking down. There are usually two different PIV ratings specified in case of diodes. One is the *repetitive peak inverse voltage* (V_R or V_{RRM}) and the other is the *non-repetitive peak inverse voltage* (V_{RSM}). The non-repetitive rating is obviously greater than the repetitive rating. The one that needs to be considered depends upon the intended application of the diode. As an example, in a rectifier application, it is the repetitive peak inverse voltage rating that is to be considered.
6. ***Power Dissipation (P_D):*** The power dissipated in a diode for a given value of diode voltage (V_D) and current (I_D) is given by

$$P_D = V_D \times I_D \tag{1.38}$$

7. ***Maximum Power Dissipation Rating [$P_{D(max)}$]:*** The maximum power that can be safely dissipated in a diode is referred to as the *maximum power dissipation rating* [$P_{D(max)}$]. The value of maximum power dissipation is specified at 25°C. At higher operating temperature, its value should be derated as per the power–temperature derating curve of the diode. The maximum power rating decreases linearly with the increase in temperature. Fig. 1.30 shows the typical power derating curve for a diode.

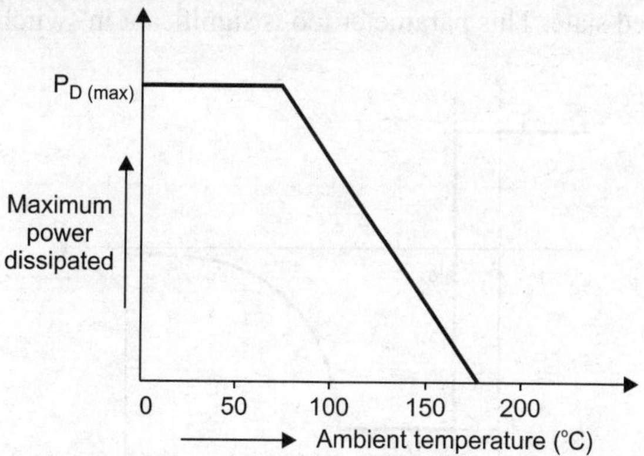

Fig. 1.30: Typical power derating curve of a diode

8. ***Maximum Junction Temperature (T_j):*** It is the maximum allowable junction temperature of the diode. It is significant in the case of power diodes and helps in finding the size of the heat sink to be used for a given diode current.
9. ***Maximum Average Rectified Current ($I_{F(av)}$):*** It is the maximum average forward rectified output current that can be allowed to pass through the diode.
10. ***Peak Repetitive Forward Current:*** This is the maximum instantaneous value of the repetitive forward current.

11. ***Peak Forward Surge Current:*** During turn-on, malfunction, switching, etc., high values of current may flow through the diode for brief time intervals. Surge current ratings define the maximum value and time duration of such surges in the current level. For instance, a surge rating of 10 A for 10 ms implies that the diode can handle a maximum of 10 A of forward current for time duration not exceeding 10 ms. The surge current rating is significantly higher than the peak forward current rating.
12. ***Ampere Square Seconds (I^2t):*** It indicates the sub-cycle current capability of diode when used as a rectifier. It is usually specified for one complete cycle of a 50 Hz operation.
13. ***Reverse Recovery Time (t_{rr}):*** When the diode is switched from the forward-biased condition to the reverse-biased condition abruptly, it is the time required by the reverse current or voltage to reach a specified value. Fig. 1.31 shows the current versus time waveform of a diode when the voltage across the diode is abruptly changed to reverse-bias the diode from its forward-bias condition. On application of the reverse voltage, the diode current reverses its direction as shown in the figure and stays at this level for time t_s (storage time). It is the time required for the carriers in the N-region to move to the P-region and the carriers in the P-region to move to the N-region. After this, the current reduces and eventually reaches the reverse saturation value after a certain time called the transition time (t_t). The reverse recovery time is the sum of the storage time and the transition time. The reverse recovery time is a very significant parameter in fast recovery rectifier diodes used in switched mode power supplies and in diodes used for high-frequency switching applications. The reverse recovery time varies from a few nanoseconds (for ultrafast diodes) to about 500 ns (for a typical fast recovery rectifier).
14. ***Forward Recovery Time (t_{ff}):*** It is the time required for the forward current or voltage to reach a specified value after the diode has been abruptly switched from the reverse-biased state to the forward-biased state. This parameter too is significant in switching applications.

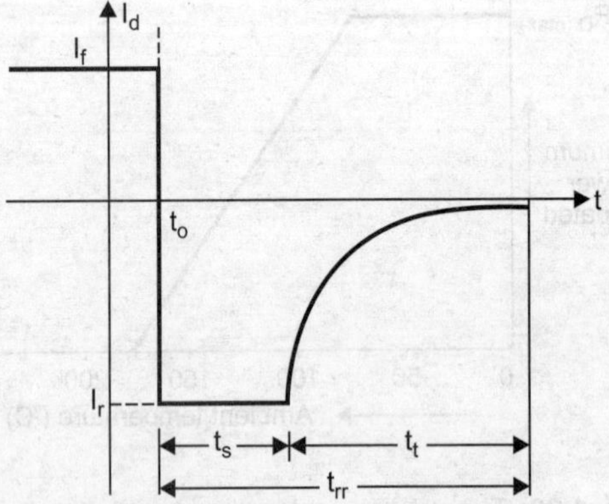

Fig. 1.31: Reverse recovery time

15. ***Diode Resistance:*** The diode offers resistance both in the forward- and the reverse-biased conditions. The diode resistance in the forward-biased region varies from few ohms to few hundreds of ohms, while in the reverse-biased region it is in the range of few to few hundreds of MW.
16. ***Diode Capacitance:*** It is the inherent capacitance of the diode junction. There are two types of capacitances present, namely, the *transition capacitance* and the *diffusion capacitance*. In the reverse-bias condition, the transition or the depletion capacitance (C_T) is of importance

whereas in the forward-bias region diffusion or storage capacitance (C_D) dominates. Diode capacitance plays a very significant role in the functioning of switching diodes. Smaller value of diode capacitance results in faster switching times.

1.9 LOAD LINE ANALYSIS

Load-line analysis is a graphical method of analyzing a circuit. In this method, a load line is drawn on the actual characteristic curve or on the equivalent model curve of the active device used in the circuit. It provides a very accurate method of analyzing the circuit when the actual characteristic curve of the active device is used for analysis. The load resistance decides the slope of the load line, which in turn has an impact on the point or region of operation of the device. The active device of concern in this section is the semiconductor diode.

1.9.1 DC load line analysis

Fig. 1.32 (a) shows the basic diode circuit where a DC input voltage source (V_I) is applied to a series connection of a diode (D) and load resistance (R_L). Applying Kirchhoff's voltage law to the circuit of Fig. 1.32(a) we get

$$V_I = V_D + I_D R_L \tag{1.39}$$

where V_D is the diode voltage and I_D the diode current.

The straight line represented by eqn. (1.39) is called the *load line*. This single equation is not sufficient to determine the two unknown variables: diode voltage (V_D) and diode current (I_D). However, these two variables are the same as the diode's I-V characteristics axis variables [Fig. 1. 32 (b)]. Therefore, a second relationship between the two variables is given by the I-V characteristic curve of the diode. The intersection of the load line with the I-V characteristic curve of the diode determines the *operating point* of the circuit also called the *quiescent point* or the *Q-point*.

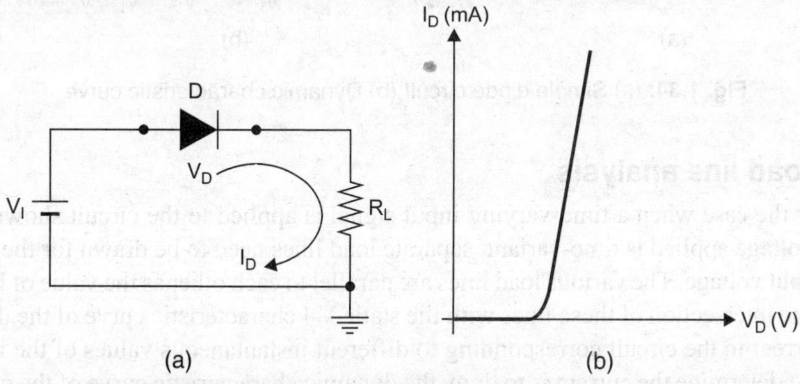

Fig. 1.32: Simple diode circuit; (b) V-I characteristics of a diode

The load line can be drawn by determining its intercepts on the voltage and the current axes. For $V_D = 0$, $I_D = V_I/R$ and for $I_D = 0$, $V_D = V_I$. The straight line joining these two points is the load line. The slope of the line is dependent on the value of load resistance (R_L) and is given by $-1/R_L$. Thus, for a given input voltage (V_I), lower the value of the load resistance, steeper is the load line resulting in a higher value of the current at the Q-point. The process of drawing the load line and determining the Q-point is better illustrated in Fig. 1.33. The operating point for the circuit is (V_{DQ}, I_{DQ}), where $V_{DQ} = V_{DD} - I_{DQ}$ ' R_L.

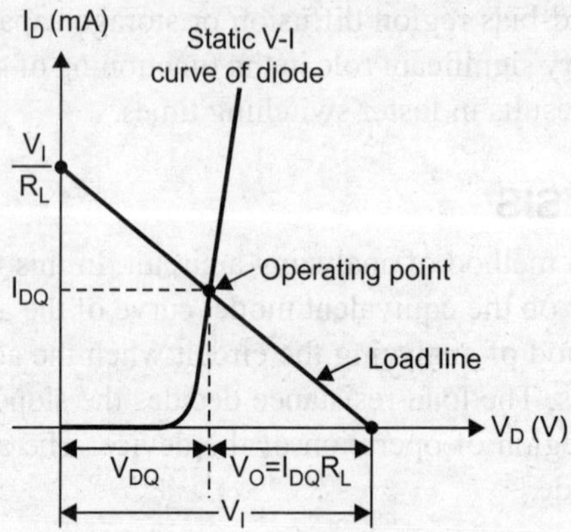

Fig. 1.33: Load-line analysis of a diode circuit for DC input voltage

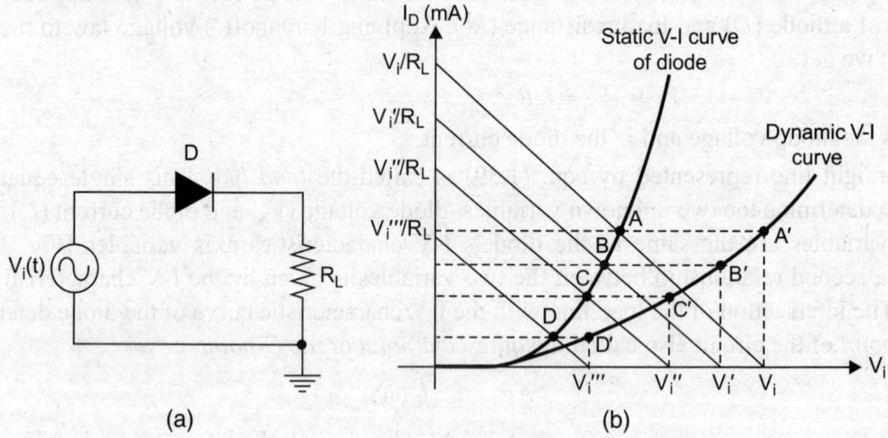

Fig. 1.34: (a) Simple diode circuit (b) Dynamic characteristic curve

1.9.2 AC load line analysis

Let us consider the case when a time-varying input signal is applied to the circuit shown in Fig. 1. 34 (a). Since the voltage applied is time-variant, separate load lines need to be drawn for the instantaneous values of the input voltage. The various load lines are parallel to each other as the value of load resistance (R_L) is fixed. The intersection of these lines with the static V-I characteristic curve of the diode gives the value of the current in the circuit corresponding to different instantaneous values of the input signal. A better method to determine the current is to draw the dynamic characteristic curve of the circuit which is a plot between the diode current and the input voltage. Fig. 1.34 (b) shows the procedure for drawing the dynamic characteristic curve. The load line for the maximum value of the input signal is drawn. From the Q-point a horizontal line is drawn. The point where this line intersects with the vertical line drawn from the X-axis corresponding to that input voltage gives a point on the dynamic curve. The process is repeated for a few other values of input voltage to yield sufficient points to construct the dynamic curve.

As an illustration, let us construct the output waveform for the diode circuit of Fig. 1.34 (a) for an input waveform of Fig. 1.35 (a) applied to the circuit input. The dynamic curve can be used to draw the output current waveform as shown in Fig. 1.35 (b). The figure is self-explanatory. It may be mentioned here that the dynamic curve applies only to the circuit containing the same value of load resistance for which it is drawn. Also, in the discussion we have assumed the diode to be an open circuit in the reverse-bias region. However, the dynamic curve for the diode in the reverse-bias region can be drawn on similar lines as drawn for the forward-bias region.

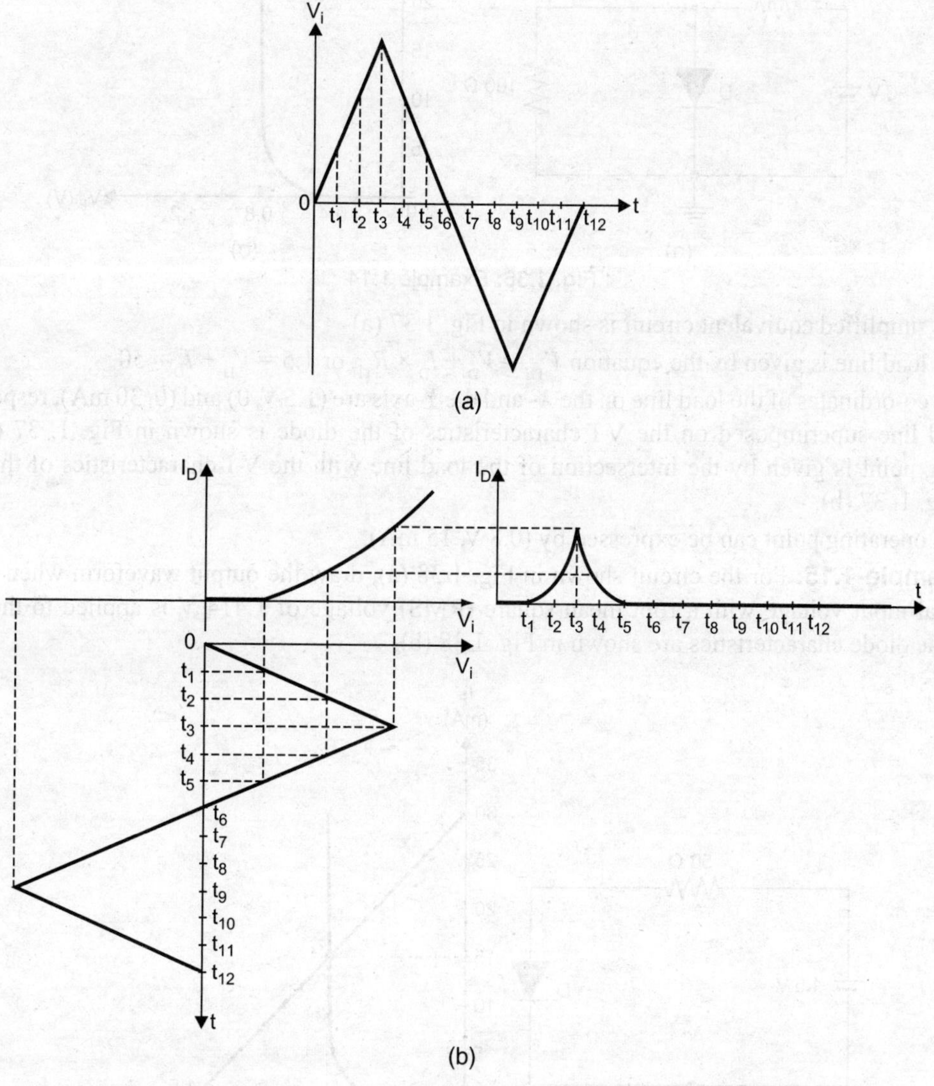

Fig. 1.35: (a) Input waveform; (b) construction of output waveform

Example-1.14: Draw the load line for the diode circuit of Fig. 1.36(a). The forward characteristics of the diode are shown in Fig. 1.36(b). Also determine the operating point.

Solution: The circuit of Fig. 1.36(a) can be simplified using the Thevenin's theorem. Thevenin's equivalent voltage $V_{TH} = (3 \times 100/200) = 1.5$ V.

Thevenin's equivalent resistance $R_{TH} = (100 \times 100/200) = 50\ \Omega$.

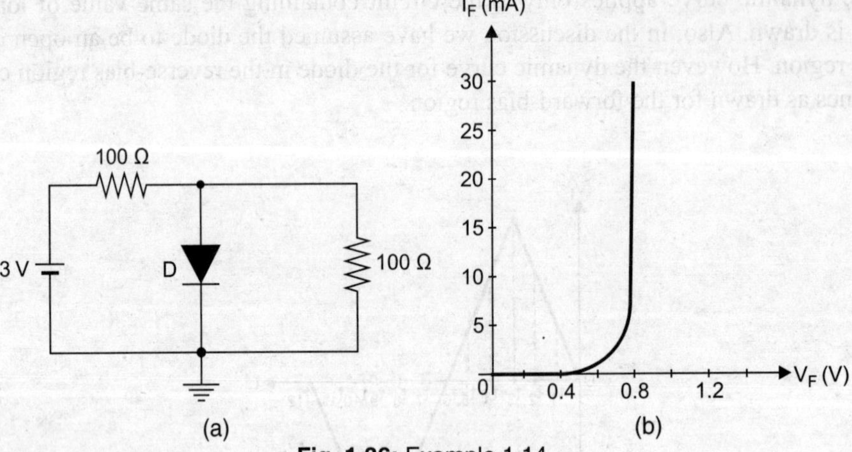

Fig. 1.36: Example 1.14

The simplified equivalent circuit is shown in Fig. 1.37 (a)

The load line is given by the equation $V_{TH} = V_D + I_D \times R_{TH}$ or $1.5 = V_D + I_D \times 50$

The co-ordinates of the load line on the *X*- and the *Y*-axis are (1.5 V, 0) and (0, 30 mA), respectively. The load line superimposed on the V-I characteristics of the diode is shown in Fig. 1. 37 (b). The operating point is given by the intersection of the load line with the V-I characteristics of the diode. From Fig. 1. 37 (b),

The operating point can be expressed by (0.8 V, 15 mA).

Example-1.15: For the circuit shown in Fig. 1.38 (a), draw the output waveform when a 50 Hz sinusoidal input voltage with a root mean square (RMS) voltage of 1.414 V is applied to the circuit input. The diode characteristics are shown in Fig. 1.38 (b).

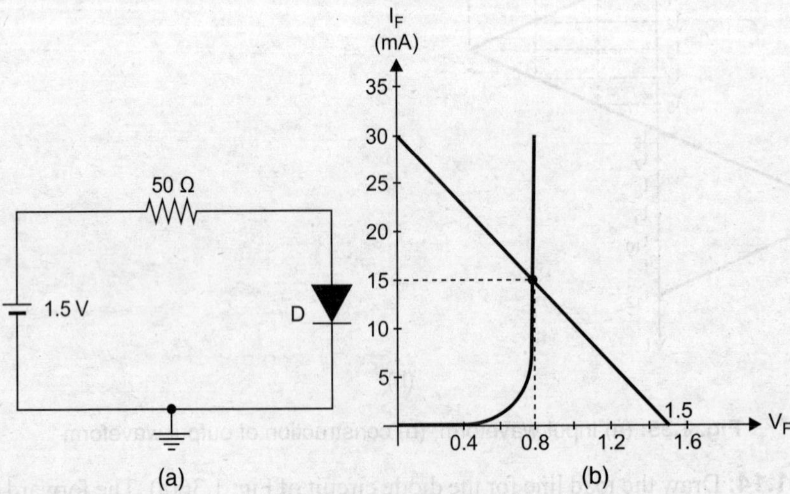

Fig. 1.37: Example-1.15

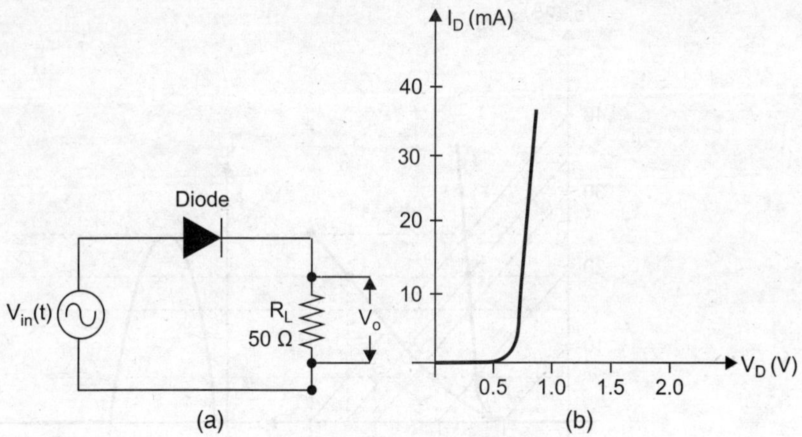

Fig. 1.38: Example 1.15

Solution: For RMS voltage = 1.414 V, Peak value of voltage = 2 V

For frequency = 50 Hz, time period = 20 ms

Load line is drawn for the peak value of the input waveform.

The load-line equation in this case is given by $2 = v_D + i_D \times 50$. The coordinates of the line on the voltage and the current axes are (2 V, 0) and (0, 40 mA), respectively.

The procedure is repeated for other values of the input waveform and the dynamic curve is drawn. The relevant waveforms are shown in Fig. 1.39. From the figure, we see that the maximum output current is 24 mA. The peak output voltage across the load resistor is 1.2 V.

1.10 ZENER AND AVALANCHE DIODES

Zener and *avalanche* diodes are P-N junction diodes designed with sufficient power dissipation capabilities to operate in the breakdown region. They are generally employed as constant-voltage devices or as voltage references. Depending upon the mechanism which leads to breakdown they can be further classified as *Zener diodes* and *avalanche diodes*. Figures-1.40 (a) and (b) respectively show the circuit symbol and the I-V characteristics of breakdown diodes. As is clear from Fig. 1.40 (b), for reverse voltages less than the breakdown voltage (V_Z), the diode acts as an open circuit, and for voltages greater than the breakdown voltage, the voltage across the diode remains constant irrespective of the current flowing through it. It may be mentioned here that the shape of the I-V characteristics is the same for both the Zener and avalanche diodes. The parameters of interest for the breakdown diodes are the breakdown voltage, the dynamic impedance and the power dissipation capability.

1.10.1 Avalanche Diodes

In the case of avalanche diodes, on the application of reverse-bias voltage the thermally generated carriers have sufficient energies to disrupt covalent bonds, thereby resulting in free electrons. These free electrons knock out more electrons from the adjacent bonds. The process is regenerative and is referred to as *avalanche multiplication*. Avalanche breakdown mechanism is predominant in lightly doped diodes with broad depletion region and low field intensity. Generally, the avalanche diodes have breakdown voltages greater than 6 V and their breakdown voltage increases with increase in temperature, that is, they have positive temperature coefficient of breakdown voltage. As the temperature increases, the

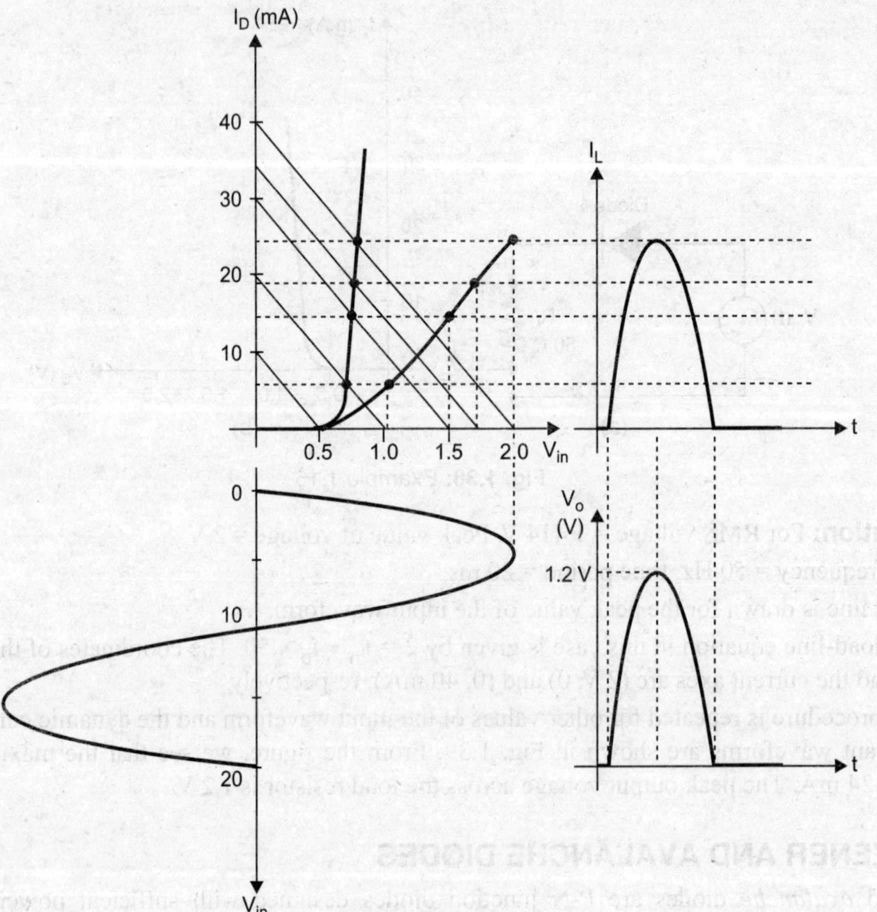

Fig. 1.39: Solution to Example-1.15

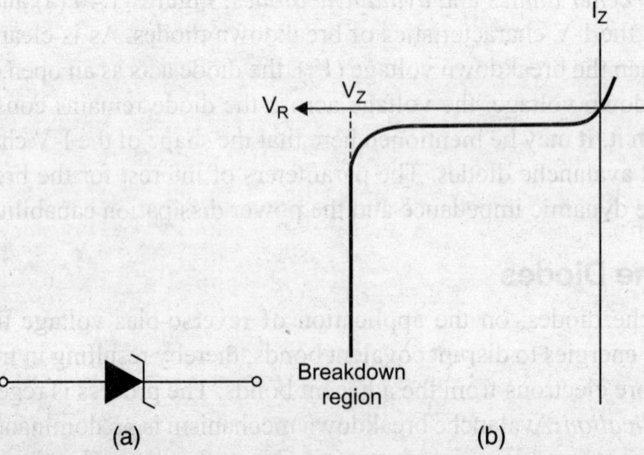

Fig. 1.40: (a) Circuit symbol of breakdown diodes and (b) V-I characteristic of breakdown diodes

vibrational displacement of atoms in the crystal grows which increases the probability of collision of carriers with the lattice atoms as they cross the depletion region. Hence, they do not have sufficient energy to start the avalanche process resulting in an increase in the breakdown voltage. Silicon diodes with avalanche breakdown phenomenon are available with breakdown voltages ranging from several volts to several hundreds of volts and with power ratings up to 50 W.

1.10.2 Zener Diodes

The breakdown phenomenon in the case of a Zener diode is the result of electrons breaking their covalent bonds due to the existence of a strong electric field at the junction. The new hole–electron pair created increases the reverse current. It does not involve collisions of carriers with the lattice atoms. A Zener breakdown phenomenon occurs for heavily doped diodes having a narrow depletion-region width and high-field intensity. They have breakdown voltages below 6 V. With increase in temperature, the energy of the valence electrons increases, making it easier for these electrons to break the covalent bonds and hence the breakdown voltage decreases. Hence, these diodes have a negative temperature coefficient of breakdown voltage. Diodes with breakdown voltages between 5 V and 6 V have almost zero temperature coefficient of breakdown voltage. It may be mentioned here that the term Zener diode is generally used for breakdown diodes even with avalanche breakdown phenomenon.

Both Zener and avalanche diodes are used in voltage regulators to regulate the load voltage against variations in load current and input voltage. They are used in these applications because in the breakdown region large change in the diode current produces only a small change in the diode voltage. Fig. 1.41 shows a simple voltage regulator circuit employing a Zener diode. The voltage across the load resistor is the same as the Zener breakdown voltage.

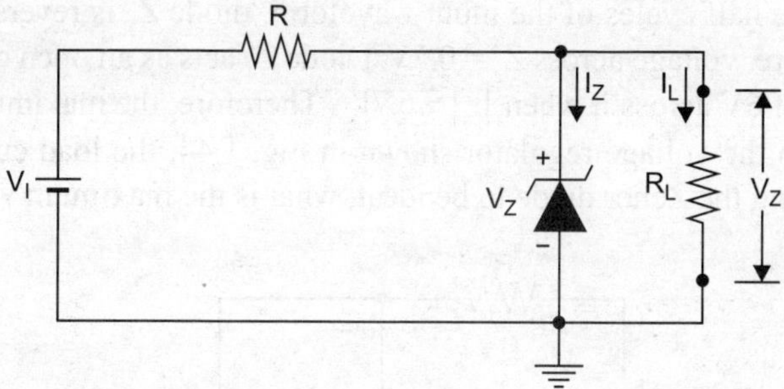

Fig. 1.41: Simple voltage regulator circuit using Zener diode

Example-1.16: A Zener diode regulator in the Fig. 1.42 is to be designed to meet the following specifications: $I_L = 10\text{mA}$, $V_o = 10\text{V}$ and V_i varied from 30V to 50V. The Zener diode has $V_Z = 10\text{V}$ and I_{ZK} (knee current) equal to 1mA. Determine the value of R for satisfactory operation.

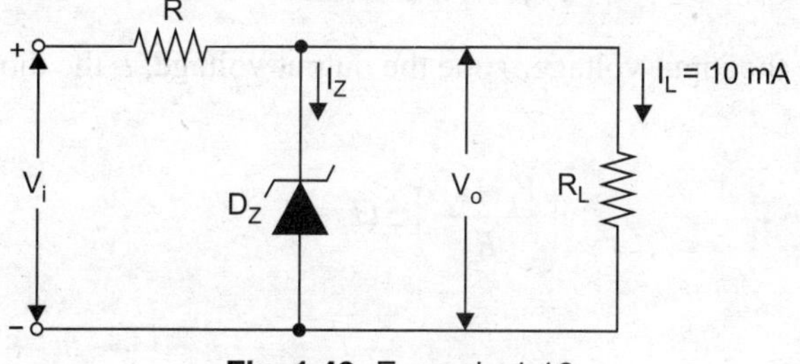

Fig. 1.42: Example-1.16

Solution: $\left(\frac{V_i - V_o}{R}\right) \geq (I_Z + I_L)$

Therefore, for $V_i = 30V$, we get $R \leq 1818$ W and for $V_i = 50V$, we get $R \leq 3636\ \Omega$

Therefore, $R < 1818\ \Omega$

Example-1.17: For the circuit shown in Fig. 1.43, find the maximum value of output voltage? (Given that the breakdown voltage and cut-in voltage of both the Zener diodes is 6V and 0.7V respectively. The input v_i is a sine wave signal with peak amplitude of 10V.

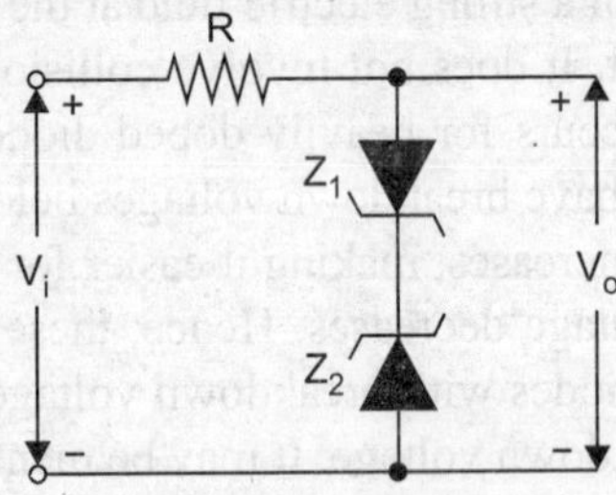

Fig. 1.43: Example-1.17

Solution: During both positive and negative half cycles, the maximum value of $|v_o|$ is the same.

During the positive half cycles of the input waveform, diode Z_1 is forward biased and diode Z_2 is reverse biased. Therefore, voltage across $Z_1 = 0.7V$. Diode Z_2 acts as an open circuit till $|v_i| < 6.7V$ and has a constant voltage of 6V across it when $|v_i| > 6V$. Therefore, the maximum value of $|v_o|$ is 6.7V.

During the negative half cycles of the input waveform, diode Z_1 is reverse biased and diode Z_2 is forward biased. Therefore, voltage across $Z_2 = 0.7V$. Diode Z_1 acts as an open circuit till $|v_i| < 6.7V$ and has a constant voltage of 6V across it when $|v_i| > 6.7V$. Therefore, the maximum value of $|v_o|$ is 6.7V.

Example-1.18: In the voltage regulator shown in Fig. 1.44, the load current can vary from 100 mA to 500 mA. Assuming the Zener diode to be ideal, what is the maximum value of R?

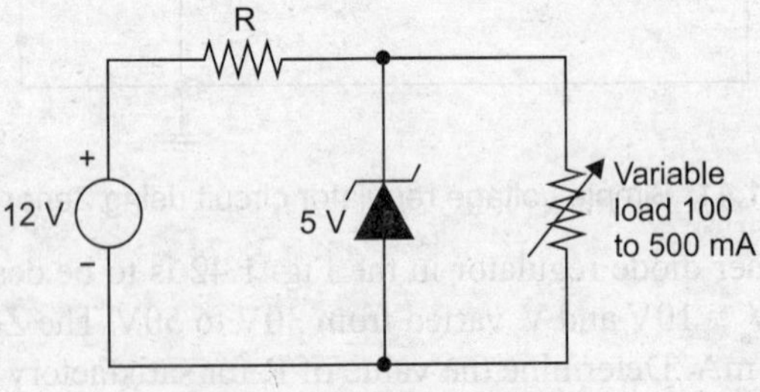

Fig. 1.44: Example-1.18

Solution: Let V_i be the input voltage, V_o be the output voltage, I_z the diode current and I_L the load current.

$$\left(\frac{V_i - V_o}{R}\right) \geq (I_z + I_L)$$

For $I_L = 100$mA

$$\left(\frac{12-5}{R}\right) \geq (0+100\times10^{-3})$$

Solving the above equation we get

$R \leq 70\Omega$

For I_L = 500mA, $R \leq 14\Omega$

Hence, the maximum value of R is 14 ohms.

1.11 VARACTOR DIODES

Varactor diodes are used as variable voltage capacitors. They are also referred to as *varicaps* or *variable voltage capacitance diodes* or *tunable diodes*. Their mode of operation depends on the transition capacitance that exists across a reverse-biased P-N junction diode. Fig. 1.45 shows the characteristics of a typical commercially available varactor diode. As shown in the figure, there is a sharp decrease in the transition capacitance initially with increase in reverse-bias voltage. As the reverse-bias voltage increases further, the rate of change of capacitance with voltage decreases. Varactor diodes are normally operated with reverse voltages in 20–30 V range. The relationship between the transition capacitance and the applied reverse bias is expressed by eqn. (1.40).

$$C_T = \frac{K}{(V_\gamma + V_R)^n} \tag{1.40}$$

where K is a constant (depends on the semiconductor material and the diode construction technique); V_g the knee potential of the diode; V_R the magnitude of the applied reverse bias; n = 1/2 for alloy junction and 1/3 for diffused junction.

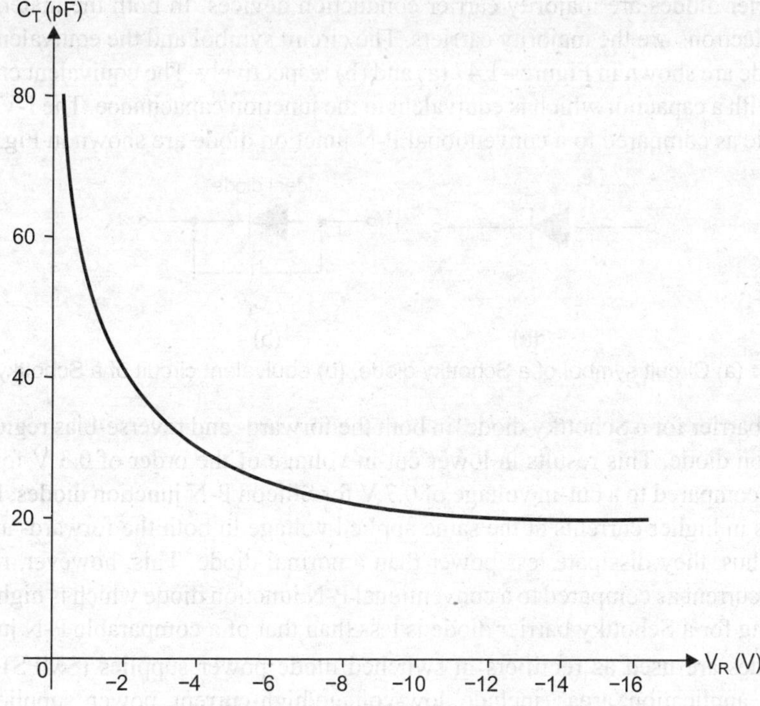

Fig. 1.45: Characteristics of a varactor diode

Fig. 1.46: (a) Circuit symbol of a varactor diode; (b) equivalent circuit of a varactor diode

The circuit symbol and the equivalent circuit of varactor diodes are shown in Figures-1.46 (a) and (b), respectively. R_R is the resistance of the diode in the reverse-bias region and is of the order of greater than equal to 1 MΩ; R_S is the geometric resistance of the diode and is of the order of few ohms. The magnitude of C_T varies from few picofarads to around hundred picofarads. In different varactor diode types, the values of minimum and maximum capacitances may vary; however, the ratio of maximum to minimum capacitance is typically 2.5 to 3. Typical application areas of varactor diodes include FM modulators, automatic frequency control devices, adjustable bandpass filters and parametric amplifiers.

1.12 SCHOTTKY DIODES

Schottky diodes, also known as *hot-carrier diodes*, have a metal–semiconductor junction instead of a semiconductor–semiconductor junction (P-N junction) of a conventional P-N junction diode. Normally N-type Silicon is used as the semiconductor material while the metal used can be Aluminium, Platinum, Tungsten or Molybdenum. This different construction technique renders these diodes some special characteristics such as lower cut-in voltage, increased frequency of operation, etc. as compared to P-N junction diodes.

Schottky barrier diodes are majority carrier conduction devices. In both the materials (metal and semiconductor), electrons are the majority carriers. The circuit symbol and the equivalent circuit model for a Schottky diode are shown in Figures-1.47 (a) and (b) respectively. The equivalent circuit is an ideal diode in parallel with a capacitor which is equivalent to the junction capacitance. The I-V characteristics of a Schottky diode as compared to a conventional P-N junction diode are shown in Fig. 1.48.

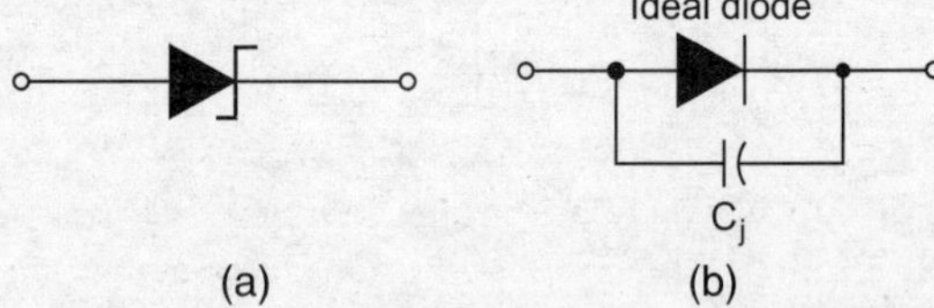

Fig. 1.47: (a) Circuit symbol of a Schottky diode; (b) equivalent circuit of a Schottky diode

The junction barrier for a Schottky diode, in both the forward- and reverse-bias regions, is less than that of P-N junction diode. This results in lower cut-in voltage of the order of 0.3 V for Silicon-metal Schottky diode as compared to a cut-in voltage of 0.7 V for Silicon P-N junction diodes. Lower junction barrier also results in higher currents at the same applied voltage in both the forward- and the reverse-bias conditions. Thus, they dissipate less power than a normal diode. This, however, results in larger reverse saturation current as compared to a conventional P-N junction diode which is highly undesirable. Also, the PIV rating for a Schottky barrier diode is less than that of a comparable P-N junction diode.

Schottky diodes are used as rectifiers in switched mode power supplies (SMPS) and switching regulators. Other application areas include low-voltage/high-current power supplies, AC to DC converters, mixers and detectors in communication systems. The absence of minority carriers in Schottky diodes results in significantly lower value of reverse recovery time (as low as 20 ns). Thus, they are effective at operating frequencies extending up to several Gigahertz.

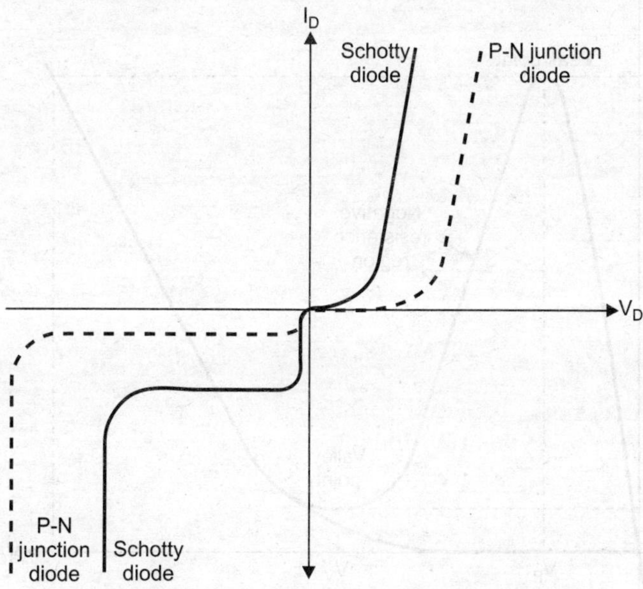

Fig. 1.48: I-V characteristics of a Schottky diode

1.13 TUNNEL DIODES

Tunnel diodes have heavily doped P- and N-regions with about 100–1000 times dopant concentration than that of a typical semiconductor diode. Heavy doping results in narrowing of the depletion region. The width of the depletion region of a tunnel diode is about 100–1000 times less than that of a typical semiconductor diode. Owing to this narrow depletion region, the charge carriers instead of climbing up the potential barrier may pierce through the potential barrier resulting in "tunnelling" of carriers both in the forward-bias and the reverse-bias regions, hence rendering the diode bi-directional conduction property. In the forward direction, the current reaches the maximum value I_P (called the peak current) at a voltage V_P (peak voltage). At this point, referred to as *peak point*, slope of the V-I curve is zero, that is, $di/dv = 0$. Beyond the peak point, the current starts to decrease with increase in voltage as there are no more carriers available for tunnelling. The current approaches zero for a forward voltage of 0.4 V to 0.5 V but then the normal P-N junction effect starts. The forward current of P-N junction diode adds to the current due to the tunnelling effect. The current decreases beyond the peak point until a point, referred to as the *valley point*. The region between the peak point and the valley point has negative resistance characteristics as the voltage decreases with increase in current. At the valley point also, the slope of the I-V curve is zero ($di/dv = 0$). Beyond the valley point, the current starts increasing again with increase in voltage and the current reaches the peak value I_P again at a voltage V_F. This is further illustrated in Fig. 1.49, showing the I-V characteristics of the tunnel diode. These characteristics may be considered to be composed of two characteristics, one due to the P-N junction and other due to the tunnelling phenomenon. The value of voltage swing ($V_F - V_P$) is of the order of 1 V for Gallium Arsenide tunnel diodes and 0.45 V for Germanium tunnel diodes.

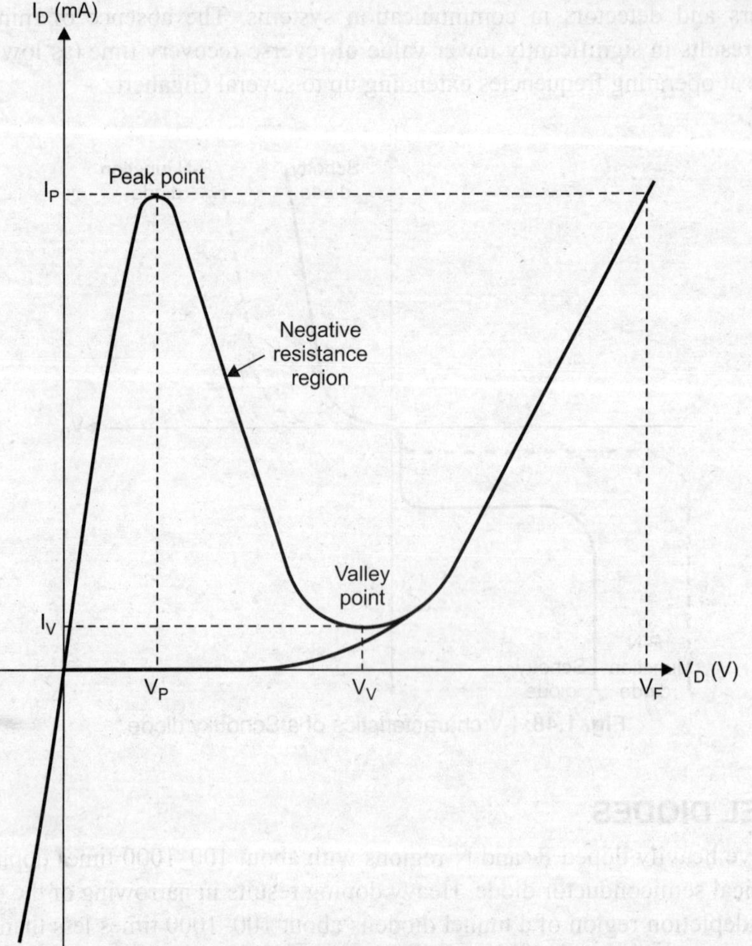

Fig. 1.49: I-V characteristics of a tunnel diode

The symbol of the tunnel diode and its equivalent circuit in the negative resistance region are shown in Figures-1.50 (a) and (b), respectively. The semiconductor material used in construction of tunnel diodes is either Germanium or Gallium Arsenide. Silicon is not used for constructing tunnel diodes. This is because the ratio of the peak current to the valley current (I_P/I_V) in Gallium Arsenide and Germanium is quite high, approximately 15 for Gallium Arsenide and 8 for Germanium. The value in the case of Silicon is very small (approx. 3).

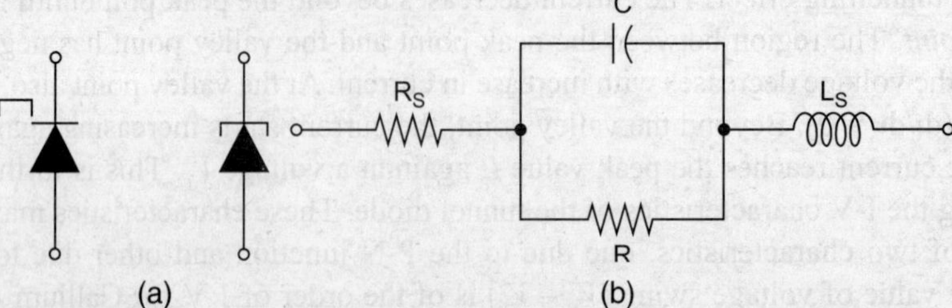

Fig. 1.50: (a) Circuit symbol of a tunnel diode; (b) equivalent circuit of the tunnel diode in the negative resistance region

Tunnel diodes are used in high-speed applications such as in computers with switching times of the order of few nanoseconds to several picoseconds. Owing to their negative resistance characteristics these diodes were earlier used as microwave oscillators. However, now they have been replaced by other devices that have surpassed them in performance.

1.14 POINT CONTACT DIODES

These diodes are intended primarily for radio frequency (RF) applications owing to their extremely small internal capacitance, considerably less than that of a conventional junction diode. They basically have a metal–semiconductor junction and have been replaced by Schottky barrier diodes because of their lower forward resistance, wide dynamic range and better noise performance as compared to point-contact diodes.

1.15 RECTIFIER CIRCUITS

A rectifier circuit converts the AC voltage into a unidirectional voltage. There are three basic rectifier circuit configurations. These include (a) half-wave rectifier, (b) conventional two-diode full-wave rectifier that requires a center-tapped secondary winding and (c) bridge rectifier. Rectifier circuits are characterized by several parameters, which include *ripple frequency*, *ripple factor*, *ratio of rectification*, *transformer utilization factor* and the required *peak inverse voltage* of the rectifier diodes in the circuit. These parameters are briefly discussed in the following paragraphs. Different types of rectifier circuits are discussed next.

1.15.1 Characteristic Parameters

Performance of a rectifier circuit is often judged on the basis of the parameters outlined in the previous paragraph. These parameters are briefly covered in the following paragraphs.

1.15.1.1 Ripple Frequency

Ripple frequency is the frequency of the unidirectional periodic voltage waveform present at the output of the rectifier circuit. In the case of half-wave rectifier, it is f, where f is the frequency of AC signal present at the input of rectifier circuit. In the case of full-wave rectifiers, conventional and bridge, it is $2f$. Higher ripple frequency means lower ripple factor and less stringent filtering requirement.

1.15.1.2 Ripple Factor

Ripple factor is ratio of root mean square (RMS) amplitude of AC component to the DC component in the rectified waveform. Ripple factor tells how close the rectified waveform is to the true DC. It can be computed as ratio of RMS value of the AC component of the rectified voltage signal to the DC value of the rectified voltage signal. It can also be computed from the ratio of the RMS value of the AC component of rectified current signal to the DC value of the rectified current signal.

That is, ripple factor (r) is given by

$$r = \frac{V_r(\text{RMS})}{V_{DC}} = \frac{I_r(\text{RMS})}{I_{DC}}$$

where V_r (RMS) is the RMS value of ripple voltage; V_{DC} the DC value of rectified voltage; I_r (RMS) the RMS value of ripple current; I_{DC} the RMS value of rectified current.

Also, $V_r(\text{RMS}) = \sqrt{(V_{RMS}^2 - V_{DC}^2)}$, where V_{RMS} is the RMS value of the rectified voltage. And

$I_r(\text{RMS}) = \sqrt{(I_{\text{RMS}}{}^2 - I_{\text{DC}}{}^2)}$, where I_{RMS} is the RMS value of the rectified current. This gives ripple factor as:

$$r = \sqrt{\frac{(V_{\text{RMS}}{}^2 - V_{\text{DC}}{}^2)}{V_{\text{DC}}{}^2}} = \sqrt{\frac{(I_{\text{RMS}}{}^2 - I_{\text{DC}}{}^2)}{I_{\text{DC}}{}^2}} \tag{1.41}$$

$$r = \sqrt{\left(\frac{V_{\text{RMS}}}{V_{\text{DC}}}\right)^2 - 1} = \sqrt{\left(\frac{I_{\text{RMS}}}{I_{\text{DC}}}\right)^2 - 1}.$$

1.15.1.3 Ratio of Rectification

Ratio of rectification is the ratio of DC power delivered to the load to the AC power input from transformer secondary. Like ripple factor, it also determines the effectiveness of a rectifier circuit in converting AC into DC.

DC power delivered to the load resistance (R_L) = $I_{\text{DC}}{}^2 \times R_L$.

AC power input from transformer secondary = $I_{\text{RMS}}{}^2 \times (R_f + R_L)$. Here R_f is the resistance offered by forward-biased rectifier diode. Since R_f is much smaller than R_L,

AC power available from transformer secondary $\cong I_{\text{RMS}}{}^2 \times R_L$.

This gives,

$$\text{Ratio of rectification} = \frac{I_{\text{DC}}{}^2}{I_{\text{RMS}}{}^2} = \left(\frac{I_{\text{DC}}}{I_{\text{RMS}}}\right)^2. \tag{1.42}$$

From eqns. (1.41) and (1.42) we can see that ratio of rectification and ripple factor are interrelated. One can be expressed in the form of the other and vice versa.

1.15.1.4 Transformer Utilization Factor

Transformer utilization factor (TUF) is defined as the ratio of DC power delivered to the load to the AC power rating of the transformer secondary.

$$\text{TUF} = \frac{\text{DC power delivered to the load}}{\text{AC power rating of transformer secondary}}.$$

It may be mentioned here that rating of the transformer in a power supply is governed by the intended DC power to be delivered to the load and the type of rectifier circuit. TUF parameter should not be confused with the ratio of rectification. Rating of transformer secondary is different from the actual AC power delivered by it. AC power rating of transformer secondary is the product of V_{RMS} across secondary and RMS value of current flowing through secondary. The transformer utilization factor tells us about the maximum DC power that can be delivered to the load for a given transformer rating. A lower TUF implies lower DC power delivered to load for a given power rating of the transformer. We will see in the following paragraphs that TUF values for half-wave and full-wave rectifiers, respectively, are 0.287 and 0.574. This implies that a 1 kVA transformer can at the most deliver a DC power of 287 W to a resistive load when used with a half-wave rectifier. The same for a full-wave rectifier is 574 W.

1.15.1.5 *Peak Inverse Voltage*

Peak inverse voltage (PIV) is the maximum reverse voltage appearing across the diodes used in the rectifier circuit. It is important as it decides the PIV rating of the diode to be used in the rectifier circuit. It is yet another parameter that can be used to compare merits/demerits of different rectifier circuits. It is V_m, $2V_m$ and V_m in the case of half-wave, conventional two-diode full-wave rectifier and bridge rectifier circuits, respectively.

1.15.2 Half-wave rectifier circuits

Fig. 1.51 shows the half-wave rectifier circuit for positive output voltage along with input and output waveforms. Fi3g. 1.52 shows the same for negative output voltage. In the case of positive output rectifier circuit of Fig. 1.51, diode D_1 is forward-biased during positive half cycles and reverse-biased during negative half cycles of the input. In the case of negative output rectifier circuit of Fig. 1.52, diode D_1 is forward-biased during negative half cycles and reverse-biased during positive half cycles of the input. This explains the output waveforms in the two cases.

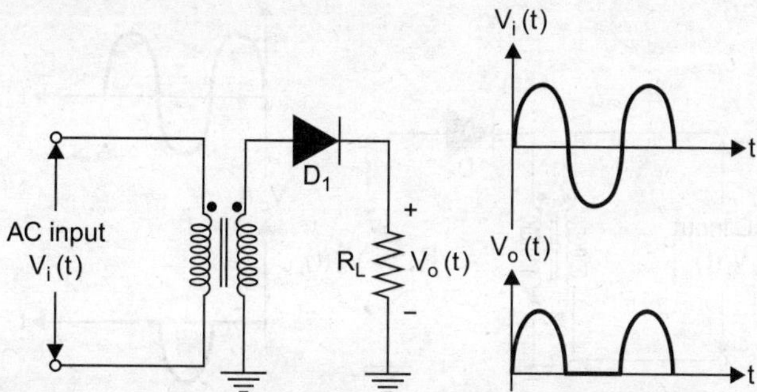

Fig. 1.51: Half-wave rectifier circuit for positive output voltage

Ripple factor in the case of half-wave rectifier circuit can be computed from eqn. (1.41).

$$r = \sqrt{\left(\frac{I_{RMS}}{I_{DC}}\right)^2 - 1}.$$

In the case of a half-wave rectified waveform,

$$I_{RMS} = \frac{I_m}{2} \text{ and } I_{DC} = \frac{I_m}{\pi}.$$

where I_m is the peak value of the current waveform. This gives:

$$r = \sqrt{\left(\frac{(I_m/2)}{(I_m/\pi)}\right)^2} - 1 = \sqrt{(\pi^2/4) - 1} = 1.21.$$

Ratio of rectification can be computed as:

$$\text{Ratio of rectification} = \left(\frac{I_{DC}}{I_{RMS}}\right)^2 = \left(\frac{(I_m/\pi)}{(I_m/2)}\right)^2 = \frac{4}{\pi^2} = 0.406.$$

Transformer utilization factor can be computed as follows:

$$\text{DC power delivered to load} = \left(\frac{I_m}{\pi}\right)^2 \times R_L.$$

$$\text{AC power rating of transformer secondary} = \frac{V_m}{\sqrt{2}} \times \frac{I_m}{2} = \frac{V_m \times I_m}{2\sqrt{2}}.$$

Also, ignoring the forward-biased diode's resistance, $V_m = I_m' R_L$. This gives

$$\text{AC power rating or transformer secondary} = \frac{V_m \times I_m}{2\sqrt{2}} = \frac{I_m^2 \times R_L}{2\sqrt{2}}.$$

Therefore,

$$\text{Transformer utilization factor} = \frac{[(I_m/\pi)^2 \times R_L]}{[(I_m^2 \times R_L)/2\sqrt{2}]} = \frac{2\sqrt{2}}{\pi^2} = 0.287.$$

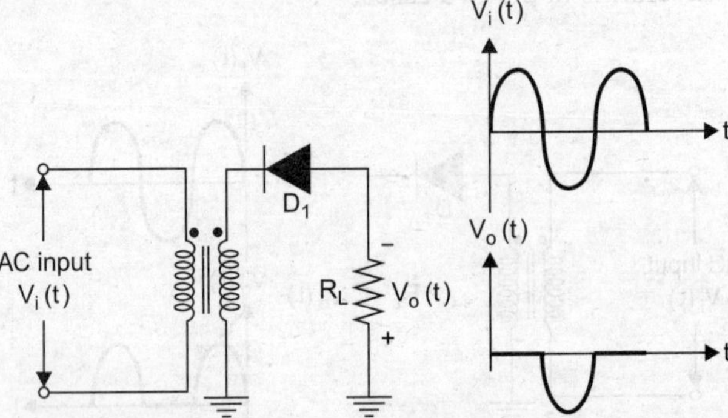

Fig. 1.52: Half-wave rectifier for negative output voltage.

1.15.3 Full-wave rectifier circuits

Fig. 1.53 shows the full-wave rectifier circuit for positive output voltage along with input and output waveforms. Fig. 1.54 shows the same for negative output voltage. In the case of positive output rectifier circuit of Fig. 1.53, diode D_1 is forward-biased and diode D_2 is reverse-biased during positive half cycles of the input. During negative half cycles, diode D_2 is forward-biased and diode D_1 is reverse-biased. In both half cycles, current through load resistance R_L flows in the same direction as shown. In the case of negative output rectifier circuit of Fig. 1.54, diode D_2 is forward-biased and diode D_1 is reverse-biased during positive half cycles of the input. During negative half cycles, diode D_1 is forward-biased and diode D_2 is reverse-biased. In both half cycles, current through load resistance R_L flows in the same direction, which is opposite to the direction of flow of current in the case of positive output circuit. This explains the output waveforms in the two cases.

Ripple factor in the case of full-wave rectifier circuit can be computed from:

$$r = \sqrt{\left(\frac{I_{RMS}}{I_{DC}}\right)^2 - 1}$$

In the case of a full-wave rectified waveform,

$$I_{RMS} = \frac{I_m}{\sqrt{2}} \quad \text{and} \quad I_{DC} = \frac{2I_m}{\pi}$$

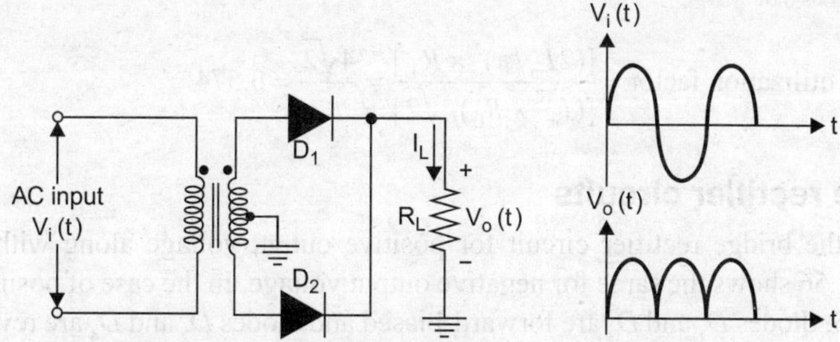

Fig. 1.53: Full-wave rectifier circuit for positive output voltage

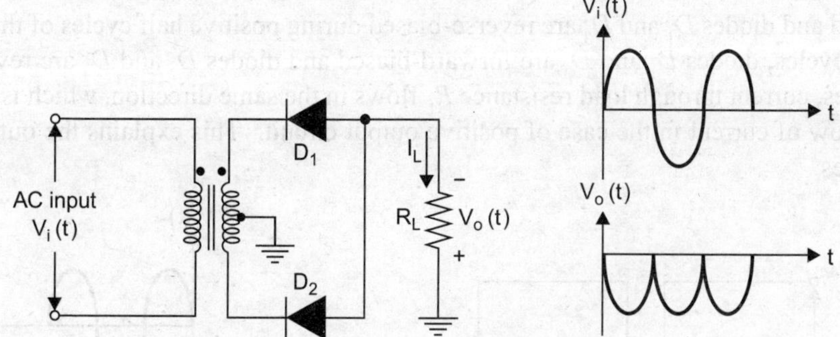

Fig. 1.54: Full-wave rectifier for negative output voltage

where I_m is the peak value of the current waveform.

$$r = \sqrt{\left(\frac{(I_m/\sqrt{2})}{(2I_m/\pi)}\right)^2 - 1} = \sqrt{(\pi^2/8) - 1} = 0.482$$

Ratio of rectification can be computed as

$$\text{Ratio of rectification} = \left(\frac{I_{DC}}{I_{RMS}}\right)^2 = \left(\frac{(2I_m/\pi)}{(I_m/\sqrt{2})}\right)^2 = \frac{8}{\pi^2} = 0.812$$

Transformer utilization factor can be computed as follows:

$$\text{DC power delivered to load} = \left(\frac{2I_m}{\pi}\right)^2 \times R_L$$

Transformer utilization factor can be computed as follows:

$$\text{DC power delivered to load} = \left(\frac{2I_m}{\pi}\right)^2 \times R_L$$

$$\text{AC power rating of transformer secondary} = 2 \times \left(\frac{V_m}{\sqrt{2}} \times \frac{I_m}{2}\right) = \frac{V_m \times I_m}{\sqrt{2}}$$

Also, ignoring the forward-biased diode's resistance, we get $V_m = I_m \times R_L$. This gives

$$\text{AC power rating of transformer secondary} = \frac{V_m \times I_m}{\sqrt{2}} = \frac{I_m{}^2 \times R_L}{\sqrt{2}}$$

Therefore,

$$\text{Transformer utilization factor} = \frac{[(2I_m/\pi)^2 \times R_L]}{[(I_m{}^2 \times R_L)/\sqrt{2}]} = \frac{4\sqrt{2}}{\pi^2} = 0.574$$

1.15.4 Bridge rectifier circuits

Fig. 1.55 shows the bridge rectifier circuit for positive output voltage along with input and output waveforms. Fig. 1.56 shows the same for negative output voltage. In the case of positive output rectifier circuit of Fig. 1.55, diodes D_1 and D_3 are forward-biased and diodes D_2 and D_4 are reverse-biased during positive half cycles of the input. During negative half cycles, diode D_2 and D_4 are forward-biased and diodes D_1 and D_3 are reverse-biased. In both half cycles, current through load resistance R_L flows in the same direction as shown. In the case of negative output rectifier circuit of Fig. 1.56, diodes D_2 and D_4 are forward-biased and diodes D_1 and D_3 are reverse-biased during positive half cycles of the input. During negative half cycles, diodes D_1 and D_3 are forward-biased and diodes D_2 and D_4 are reverse-biased. In both half cycles, current through load resistance R_L flows in the same direction, which is opposite to the direction of flow of current in the case of positive output circuit. This explains the output waveforms in the two cases.

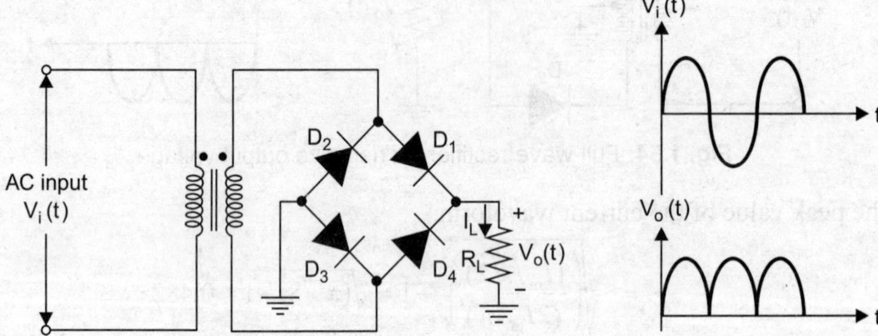

Fig. 1.55: Bridge rectifier for positive output voltage

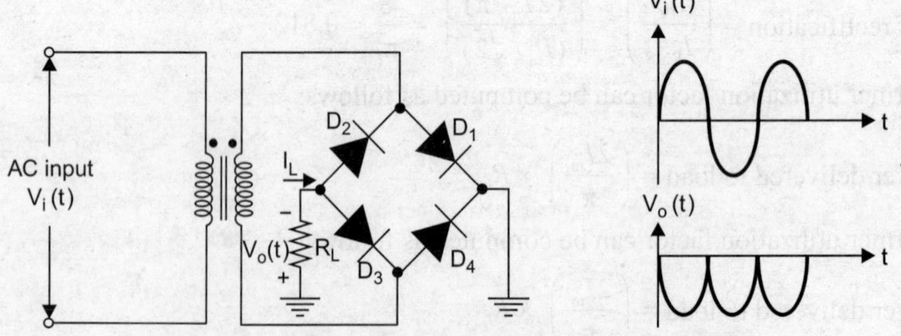

Fig. 1.56: Bridge rectifier for negative output voltage

Ripple factor and ratio of rectification parameters in the case of bridge rectifier are the same as those computed in the case of two-diode full-wave rectifier. That is, ripple factor = 0.482 and ratio of rectification = 0.812.

Transformer utilization factor can be computed as follows:

DC power delivered to load $= \left(\frac{2I_m}{\pi}\right)^2 \times R_L$

AC power rating of transformer secondary $= \frac{V_m}{\sqrt{2}} \times \frac{I_m}{\sqrt{2}} = \frac{V_m \times I_m}{2}$

Also, ignoring the forward biased diode's resistance, we get $V_m = I_m \times R_L$. This gives

AC power rating of transformer secondary $= \frac{V_m \times I_m}{2} = \frac{I_m^2 \times R_L}{2}$

Therefore,

Transformer utilization factor $= \frac{[(2I_m/\pi)^2 \times R_L]}{[(I_m^2 \times R_L)/2]} = \frac{8}{\pi^2} = 0.812$

Table-1.1 gives a comparison of different rectifier circuits.

Example-1.19: Ripple factor and ratio of rectification are related to each other. Derive an expression to show how ratio of rectification can be expressed in terms of ripple factor.

Solution: Ripple factor, r, is given by:

$$r = \sqrt{\left(\frac{I_{RMS}}{I_{DC}}\right)^2 - 1}$$

This gives $\left(\frac{I_{RMS}}{I_{DC}}\right)^2 = 1 + r^2$ or $\left(\frac{I_{DC}}{I_{RMS}}\right)^2 = \frac{1}{1+r^2}$

Ratio of rectification is given by:

Ratio of rectification $= \left(\frac{I_{DC}}{I_{RMS}}\right)^2 = \frac{1}{1+r^2}$

Example-1.20: Determine the transformer rating if it were to deliver a DC power of 500 W to a resistive load using (a) half-wave rectifier, (b) conventional two-diode full-wave rectifier and (c) bridge rectifier.

Solution: (a) In the case of half-wave rectifier,

Transformer utilization factor = 0.287 = DC power delivered to load/transformer rating

Therefore, transformer rating = DC power delivered to load/0.287 = 500/0.287 = 1742 W.

(b) In the case of conventional two-diode full-wave rectifier,

Transformer utilization factor = 0.574 = DC power delivered to load/transformer rating

Therefore, transformer rating = DC power delivered to load/0.693= 500/0.574 = 871 W.

(c) In the case of bridge rectifier,

Transformer utilization factor = 0.812 = DC power delivered to load/transformer rating

Therefore, transformer rating = DC power delivered to load/0.812 = 500/0.812 = 616 W.

Example-1.21: A 220 V, 50 Hz AC is applied to the primary of 5:1 step-up transformer with a tapped secondary winding. The transformer along with a two-diode full-wave rectifier feeds a resistive load of 1000 Ω. Determine (a) DC power delivered to the load, (b) power rating of the transformer secondary, (c) PIV across each diode and (d) ripple frequency and ripple factor.

Solution: (a) Peak value of primary voltage = 220 × √2 = 311 V.

Peak value of secondary voltage = 311 × 5 = 1555 V.

Peak value of secondary current = 1555/1000 = 1.555 A.

DC power delivered to the load = $(2 \times 1.555/\pi)^2 \times 1000$ = 981 W.

(b) In the case of two-diode full-wave rectifier, transformer utilization factor = 0.574. Therefore, power rating of transformer secondary = 981/0.574 = 1709 W.

(c) PIV across each diode = 2 × 1555 = 3.11 kV.

(d) Ripple frequency = 2 × f = 2 × 50 = 100 Hz.

Ripple factor = $\sqrt{[(I_{RMS}/I_{DC})^2 - 1]}$.

I_{RMS} = 1.555/√2 = 1.1 A.

I_{DC} = (2 × 1.555/π) = 0.99 A.

Therefore, ripple factor = $\sqrt{[(1.1/0.99)^2 - 1]}$ = 0.484

Table-1.1: Comparison of rectifier circuits

Parameter	Half Wave	Full Wave	Bridge
Secondary voltage Line-to-line (RMS)	$\frac{V_m}{\sqrt{2}}$	$\sqrt{2} \times V_m$	$\sqrt{2} \times V_m$
Number of diodes	1	2	4
Peak inverse voltage	V_m	$\sqrt{2} \times V_m$	V_m
No load DC output	$\frac{V_m}{\pi}$	$\frac{V_m}{\pi}$	$\frac{2V_m}{\pi}$
Ripple frequency	f	$2f$	$2f$
Ripple factor	1.21	0.482	0.482
Ratio of rectification	0.406	0.812	0.812
TUF	0.287	0.574	0.812

1.16 CLIPPER CIRCUITS

Diode-based clipper circuits can be used for clipping or removing whole or part of positive or negative portion of bidirectional waveforms. This class of wave-shaping circuits is also called non-linear wave-shaping circuits as one or more than one element has non-linear current-to-voltage characteristics. Four basic diode-based clipper circuits are shown in Figures-1.57 (a) to (d). The non-linear element in the circuits of Fig. 1.57 is the diode. In the following paragraphs, we will study the response of each of these circuits to a sinusoidal input. Diodes are assumed to be ideal. That is, the cut-in voltage of the diodes is zero.

The input and output waveforms for the clipping circuit of Fig. 1.57 (a) are shown in Fig. 1.58 (a). The figure is self-explanatory. The circuit configuration is similar to that of a half-wave rectifier circuit. During the positive and negative half cycles of the input waveform, the diode is respectively forward- and reverse-biased. The positive half cycles therefore appear across the output.

Similarly, the output waveform for the circuit of Fig. 1.57 (b) is shown in Fig. 1.58 (b). The circuit is again a half-wave rectifier circuit that allows negative half cycles to appear across the output. The diode in this case is forward-biased during negative half cycles of the input waveform.

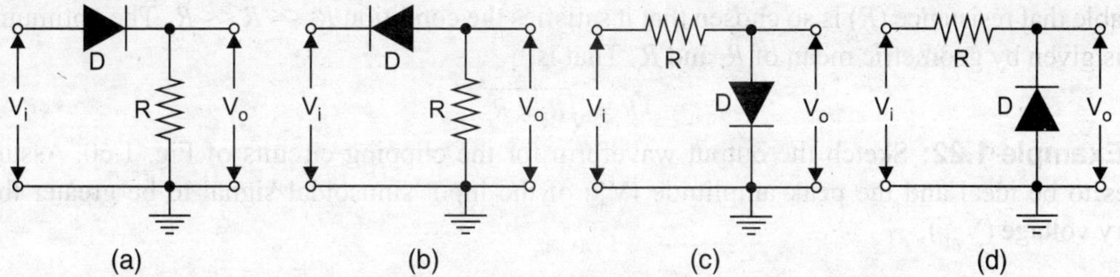

Fig. 1.57: Basic clipper circuits

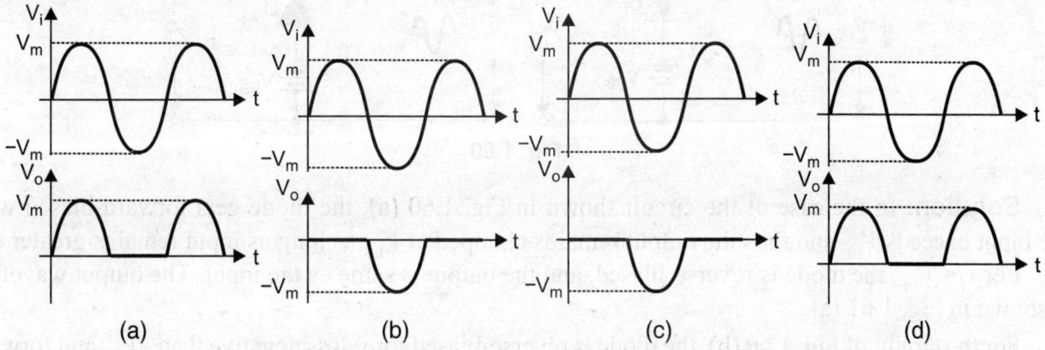

Fig. 1.58: Input and output waveforms for the clipper circuits of Fig. 1.57 for ideal diodes

For the clipping circuit of Fig. 1.57(c), the diode is forward-biased during positive half cycles and reverse-biased during negative half cycles. The output is therefore clipped to zero during positive half cycles and the negative half cycles are allowed to appear across the output as the diode is then reverse-biased. For the circuit of Fig. 1.57 (d), the negative half cycles would be clipped to zero.

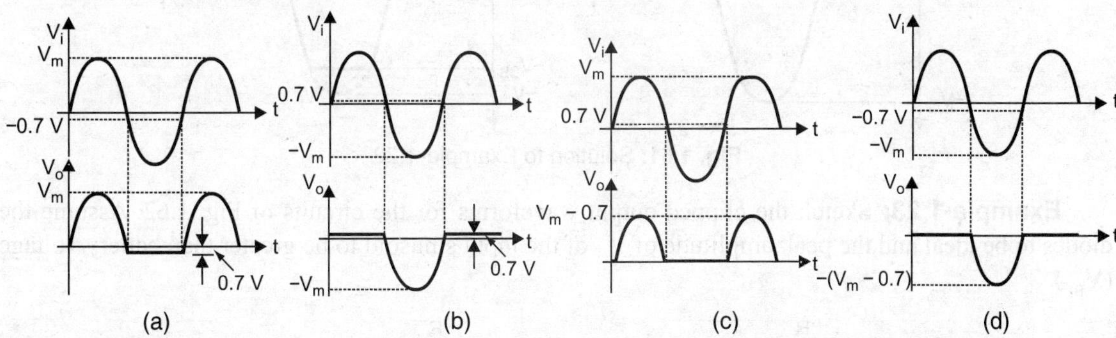

Fig. 1.59: Output waveforms for clipper circuits of Fig. 1.57 when the diodes are non-ideal

In case the diodes used in the circuits of Figures-1.57 were non-ideal, the output waveforms would be similar to those shown in Fig. 1.58 except that the diode would have a cut-in voltage of 0.7 V for silicon diodes and 0.3 V for germanium diodes instead of zero as assumed in the case of ideal diodes. The waveforms for clipping circuits with silicon diodes of Fig. 1.57 are shown in Fig. 1.59. The other important issue is that of choice of resistance (R). In the case of non-ideal diodes, the forward-biased resistance is not zero and also the reverse-biased resistance is not infinite. In such a situation, it is desirable that resistance (R) is so chosen that it satisfies the condition $R_f << R << R_r$. The optimum value of R is given by geometric mean of R_f and R_r. That is,

$$R = \sqrt{R_f \times R_r} \tag{1.43}$$

Example-1.22: Sketch the output waveform for the clipping circuits of Fig. 1.60. Assume the diodes to be ideal and the peak amplitude (V_m) of the input sinusoidal signal to be greater than the battery voltage (V_{BB}).

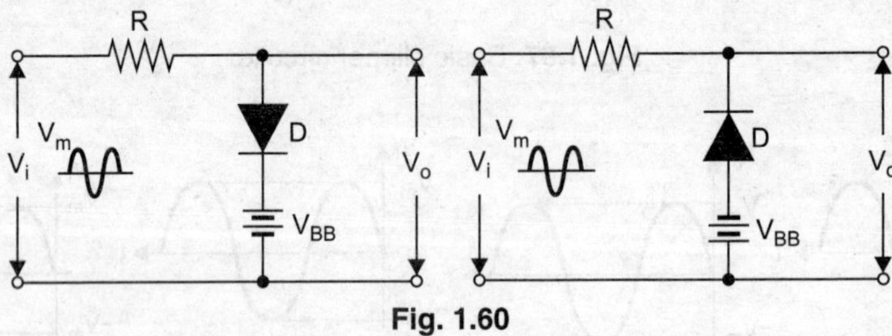

Fig. 1.60

Solution: In the case of the circuit shown in Fig. 1.60 (a), the diode gets forward-biased when the input exceeds V_{BB} and thus the output remains clamped at V_{BB} as long as input remains greater than V_{BB}. For $v_i < V_{BB}$, the diode is reverse-biased, and the output is same as the input. The output waveform is shown in Fig. 1.61 (a).

For the circuit of Fig. 1.60 (b), the diode is reverse-biased for v_i less negative than $-V_{BB}$ and forward-biased for v_i more negative than $-V_{BB}$. The output waveform is shown in Fig. 1.61 (b).

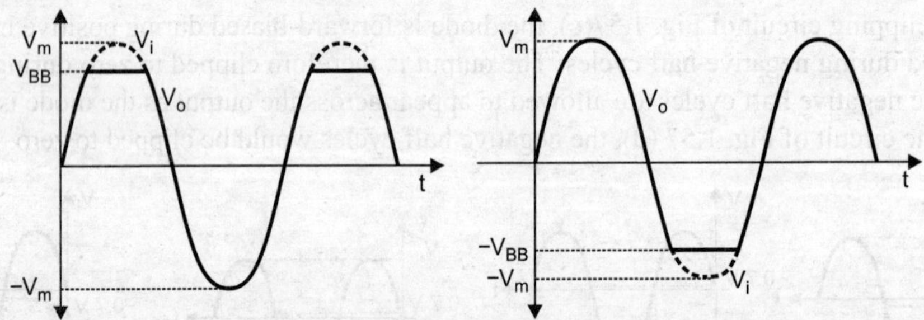

Fig. 1.61: Solution to Example-1.22

Example-1.23: Sketch the clipped output waveforms for the circuits of Fig. 1.62. Assume the diodes to be ideal and the peak amplitude of V_m of the input sinusoid to be greater than battery voltage (V_{BB}).

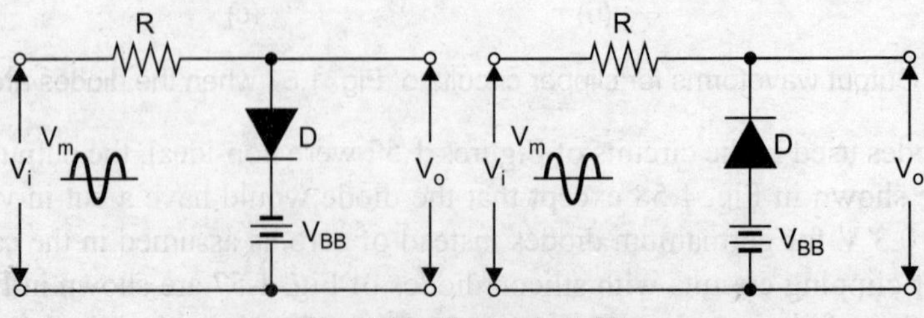

Fig. 1.62: Example-1.23

Solution: For the circuit shown in Fig. 1.62 (a), the diode is forward-biased for all input voltages except for the period when v_i is more negative than the battery voltage ($-V_{BB}$) where it is reverse-biased. Fig. 1.63 (a) shows the output waveform. For the circuit shown in Fig. 1.62(b), the diode is forward-biased for v_i less than equal to battery voltage (V_{BB}) and reverse-biased for v_i greater than V_{BB}. Fig. 1.63 (b) shows the output waveform.

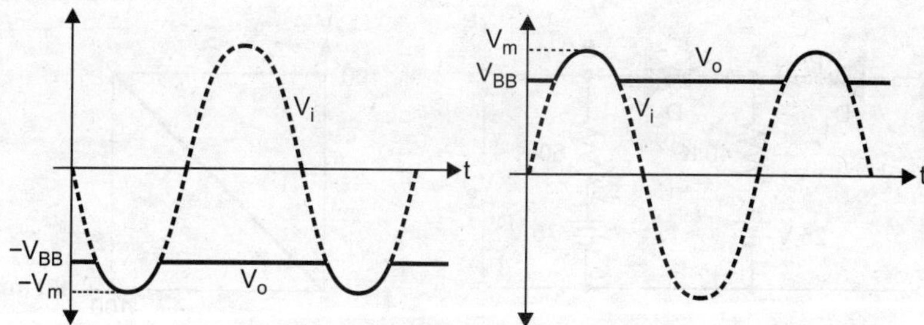

Fig. 1.63: Solution to Example-1.23

Example-1.24: Sketch the clipped output waveforms for the double-diode circuits of Figures-1.64 (a) and (b). Assume diodes D_1 and D_2 to be ideal and the forward-biased voltage drops of the Zener diodes to be zero.

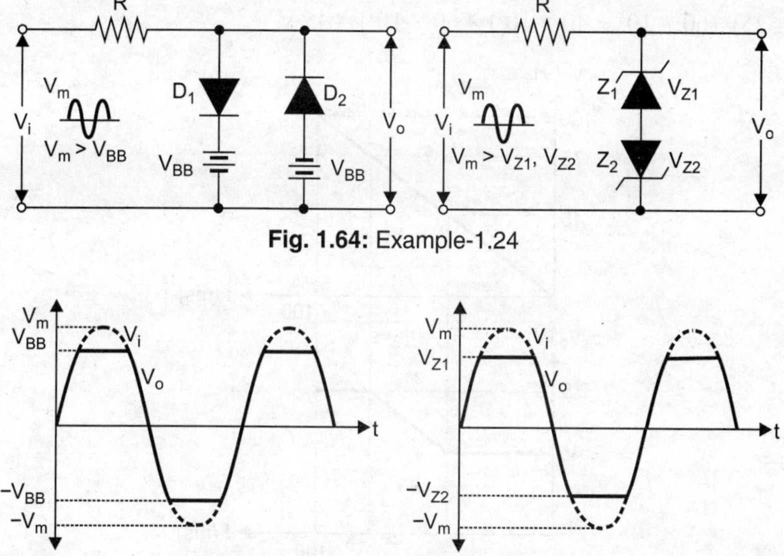

Fig. 1.65: Solution to Example-1.24

Solution: For the circuit shown in Fig. 1.64 (a), during the whole of positive half-cycle, diode D_2 remains reverse-biased and the diode D_1 gets forward-biased for v_i greater than V_{BB}.

During the negative half cycle, diode D_1 remains reverse-biased and diode D_2 is forward-biased only for the period where v_i is more negative than $-V_{BB}$.

The output waveform is shown in Fig. 1.65 (a).

For the clipper circuit shown in Fig. 1.64 (b), Zener diode Z_2 is forward-biased during positive half cycle and Zener diode Z_1 breaks down for v_i greater than V_{z1}.

During the negative half cycle, Zener diode Z_1 is forward-biased and Zener diode Z_2 breaks down for v_i more negative than $-V_{z2}$.

The output waveform is shown in Fig. 1.65 (b).

Example-1.25: Refer to the two diode clipper circuit of Fig. 1.66. The input to this circuit is a linear ramp varying from 0 to 100 V. Plot the output waveform. The diodes can be assumed to be ideal.

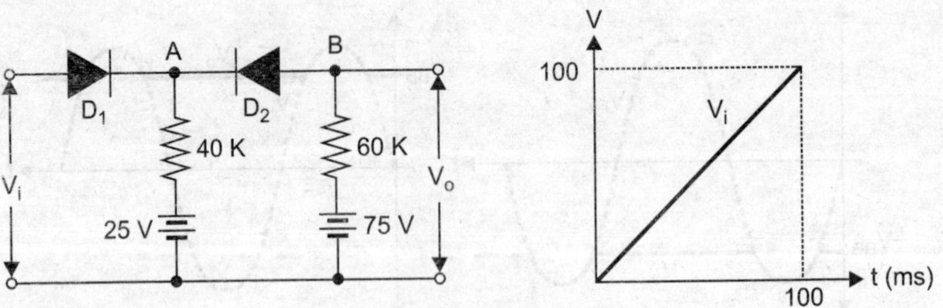

Fig. 1.66: Example-1.25

Solution: When the input voltage (v_i) is less than the potential at node A, the diode D_1 is reverse-biased.

When diode D_1 is reverse-biased and the diode D_2 is forward-biased, potential at node A is equal to potential at node B. The potential at nodes A and B is equal to:

$[75 - (75 - 25)/ (60 \times 10^3 + 40 \times 10^3) \times 60 \times 10^3] = 45$ V

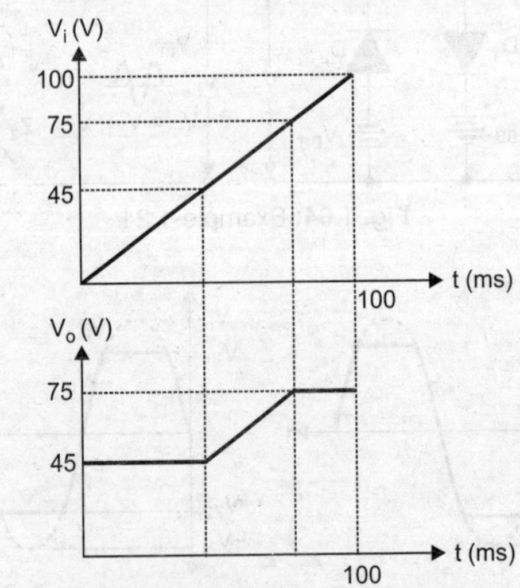

Fig. 1.67: Solution to Example-1.25

Therefore, for v_i less than 45 V, diode D_1 is reverse-biased and diode D_2 is forward-biased with nodes A and B at a potential of 45 V.

As v_i exceeds 45 V, D_1 gets forward-biased and from then onwards, potential at A is same as v_i. Diode D_2 remains forward-biased as long as v_i does not exceed 75 V. Thus, for v_i greater than 45 V and less than 75 V, v_o is same as v_i.

As v_i exceeds 75 V, D_2 is also reverse-biased. From then onwards, the output is constant at 75 V.

The input and output waveforms are shown in Fig. 1.67.

Example-1.26: Draw the transfer characteristics (*i.e.*, v_o versus v_i) for the two diode clipper circuit of Fig. 1.68. Assume the diodes to be ideal.

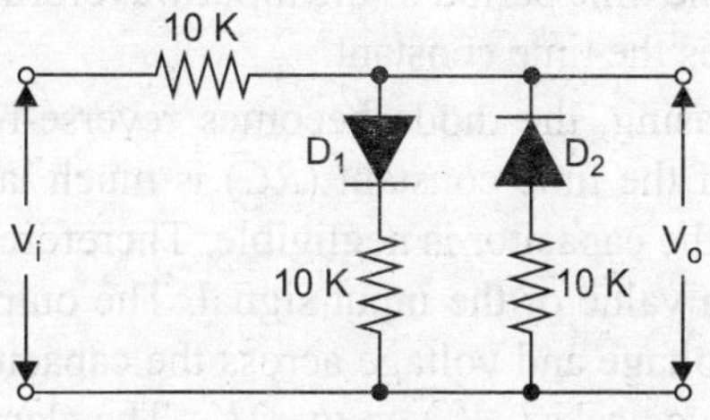

Fig. 1.68: Example-1.26

Solution: As v_i increases in the positive direction, D_1 is forward-biased and D_2 is reverse-biased. v_o in this case is always equal to $v_i/2$.

For negative values of v_i, diode D_2 is forward-biased and diode D_1 is reverse-biased. Again, the output is $-v_i/2$.

The transfer characteristics are shown in Fig. 1.69.

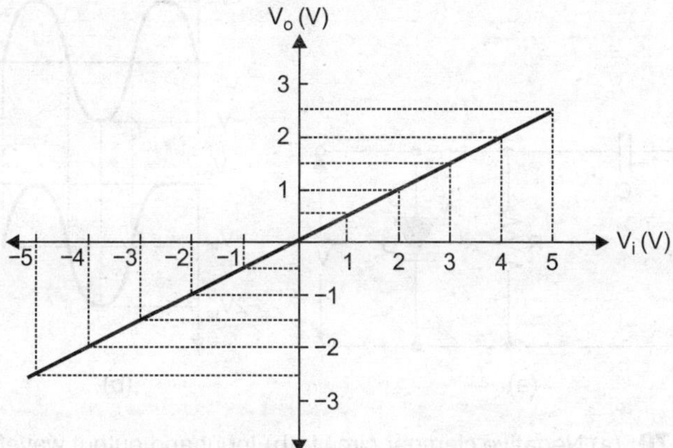

Fig. 1.69: Solution to Example-1.26

1.17 CLAMPER CIRCUITS

Clamper circuits are used to clamp either positive or negative extremities of an AC signal to zero or a specified DC voltage. These are also called as DC restorer circuits for obvious reasons. Both positive and negative clamper circuits are briefly described in the following paragraphs.

1.17.1 Negative Clamper

A negative clamper circuit clamps the positive peaks of the input AC signal to zero or a specified DC voltage. Fig. 1.70 (a) shows the negative clamper circuit, which clamps the positive peaks of the AC signal to zero. Fig. 1.70 (b) shows the clamped output waveform for a given sinusoidal input. The circuit functions as follows. As the input v_i rises towards the positive peak V_m from zero in the first quarter of the cycle, capacitor (C) charges to V_m through the forward-biased diode. The overall charging resistance is sum of source resistance (R_s), not shown in the figure, and the parallel combination of R and diode's forward resistance (R_f). If R is much larger than R_f then the capacitor C charges with a time constant of [($R_s + R_f$) ′ C]. Now for given R_s and R_f, C should be such that it charges to V_m in a time which in no case is greater than one-fourth of the time period of the input waveform. The total charging time may be considered to be equal to five times the time constant.

When the input starts decreasing, the diode becomes reverse-biased. The capacitor now tends to discharge through resistor R. If the time constant (RC) is much larger than the time period of the input waveform, the discharge of the capacitor is negligible. Therefore, the voltage across the capacitor remains constant at the maximum value of the input signal. The output at any instant of time is then equal to algebraic sum of input voltage and voltage across the capacitor. Thus, all positive peaks (V_m) are clamped to zero and all negative peaks ($-V_m$) go to $-2V_m$. The clamping circuit as can be seen from the clamped output waveform, does not alter the wave shape, it only changes the DC level.

If the peak amplitude of the input changes, the capacitor must charge or discharge to the new value depending upon whether input amplitude has increased or decreased. When the peak value of the input signal increases, the capacitor charges through the forward-biased diode again to the new larger value and when the peak value of the input signal decreases, it discharges through R to the new lower value.

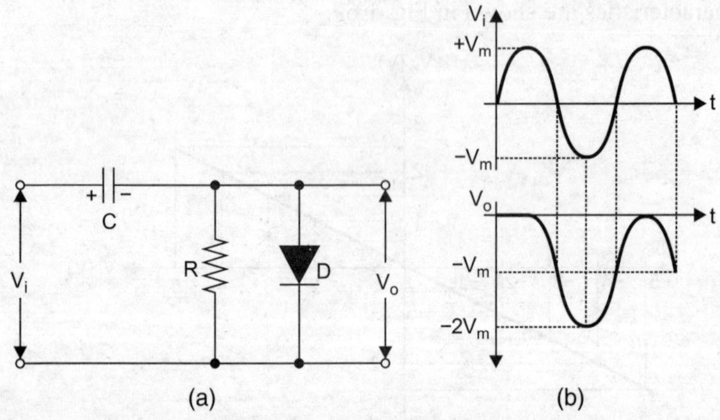

Fig. 1.70: (a) Negative clamper circuit; (b) Input and output waveforms

If there were no resistance R connected across the diode; the capacitor will be forced to discharge through the reverse-biased diode resistance (R_r), which may be as large as 100 MW. Therefore, it may even be seconds before the capacitor discharges to new lower value, in case the peak amplitude of the input waveform decreases and the output again clamped to the desired voltage. As R is chosen to be much smaller than R_r, this problem is not encountered, and the clamping is usually restored within a few cycles of the input waveform at the most even after the input undergoes a step change in peak amplitude. The optimum value of R is given by geometric mean of R_f and R_r. That is,

$$R = \sqrt{R_f \times R_r} \tag{1.44}$$

It may be mentioned here that the clamping circuit will function even in the absence of R provided that the peak input amplitude remains constant. In the event of peak input amplitude decreasing, one has to wait for a sufficiently long time depending upon (R_r × C) time constant before normal clamping operation is restored. After having calculated the value of R for a given diode, C should be so chosen that it does not discharge appreciably during the time the diode remains reverse-biased. The time constant when the diode is reverse-biased is given by eqn. 1.45.

$$R_s + \frac{R_r \times R}{R_r + R} \times C \tag{1.45}$$

The time constant of the discharge circuit should at least be 100 times the reverse-biased time period. It is more appropriate to choose C to meet extremely slow discharge requirement rather than fast charging requirement through R_f. R_f is usually so small that C chosen by the discharge criterion almost always satisfies the charge criterion.

1.17.2 Positive Clamper

A positive clamper circuit clamps the negative peaks of input AC signal to zero or specified DC voltage. Fig. 1.71 (a) shows the positive clamper circuit. The input and output waveforms are shown in Fig. 1.71 (b). The circuit functions in the same way as the negative clamper circuit except that the capacitor would charge to $-V_m$ during the first negative half cycle when the diode gets forward-biased. Negative peaks are clamped to zero as for all negative peaks of the input waveform, the output (v_o) given by algebraic sum of v_i and v_c will be zero. R is determined by eqn. 1.44, which is reproduced here for convenience.

$$R = \sqrt{R_f \times R_r}$$

and C is given by eqn. 1.46.

$$\left(R_s + \frac{R_r \times R}{R_r + R} \right) \times C \geq 100T \tag{1.46}$$

where T is the time period of the input waveform.

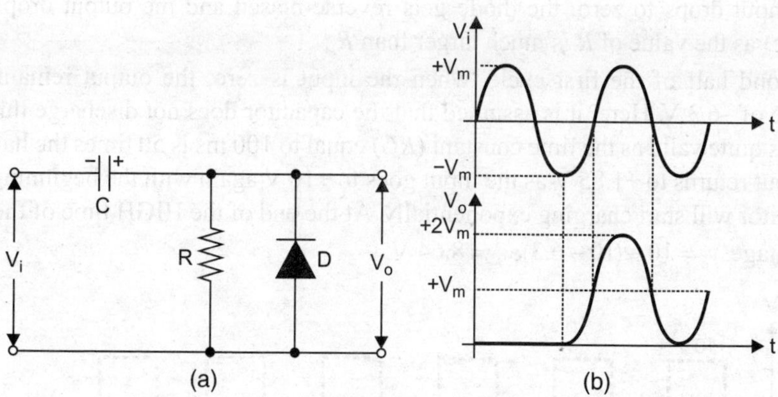

Fig. 1.71: (a) Positive clamper circuit; (b) Input and output waveforms

Example-1.27: For the clamping circuit of Fig. 1.72(a) and the input waveform of Fig. 1.72(b), plot the output waveform for the first five cycles. Comment on the results obtained. (Assume the diodes to be ideal.)

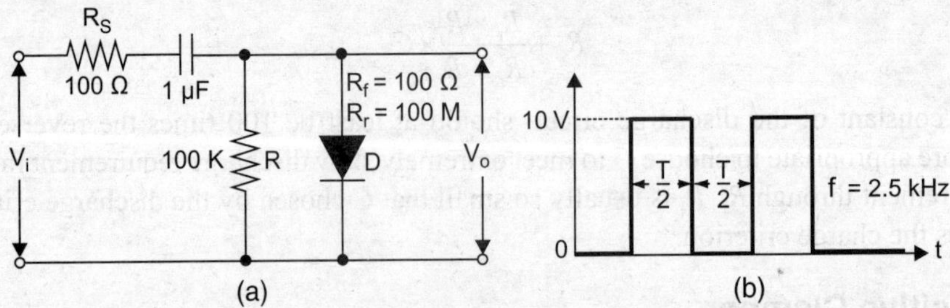

Fig. 1.72: Example-1.27

Solution: As the input goes from 0 to +10 V, the diode gets forward-biased. Since the voltage across the capacitor cannot change instantaneously, the output voltage (v_o) abruptly rises to only +5 V due to the potential divider arrangement of R_s (= 100 Ω) and R_f (= 100 Ω). The capacitor then starts charging towards +10 V with a time constant $(R_f + R_s) \times C$.

Now, the capacitor charges with a time constant = (100 + 100) × 10^{-6} = 200 μs.

Also, for f = 2.5 kHz, the time period of input waveform = (1000/2.5) μs = 400 μs

Therefore, during the first cycle, when the diode is forward-biased; the capacitor would exponentially charge as per the following equation.

$$v_c = 10(1 - e^{-t/200 \times 10^{-6}})$$

For, t = 200 μs, $v_c = 10(1 - e^{-1}) = 6.3$ V . This gives, v_o = (10 – 6.3)/2 = 1.85 V

When the input drops to zero, the diode gets reverse-biased and the output drops to –6.3 V (= capacitor voltage) as the value of R is much larger than R_s.

For the second half of the first cycle, when the input is zero, the output remains equal to the capacitor voltage of –6.3 V. Here, it is assumed that the capacitor does not discharge through R during this time which is quite valid as the time constant (RC) equal to 100 ms is 50 times the half cycle time of 200 μs. The output returns to +1.85 V as the input goes to +10 V again with the beginning of the second cycle. The capacitor will start charging exponentially. At the end of the HIGH time of the second cycle, the capacitor voltage $v_c = 10 - (10 - 6.3)e^{-1} = 8.64$ V

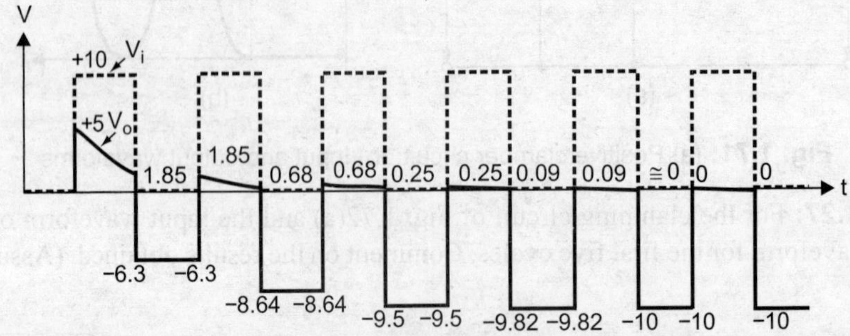

Fig. 1.73: Solution to Example-1.27

This gives, v_o = (10 – 8.64)/2 = 0.68 V

When the input drops to zero, the output drops to –8.64 V. The output waveform progresses in the same fashion for the subsequent cycles. Refer to Fig. 1.73. As shown in the figure, the output is nearly clamped in the fifth cycle. From then onwards, the output has the positive extremities of the input waveform clamped to zero.

Example-1.28: Sketch the steady-state clamped output waveforms for the circuits shown in Figures-1.74(a) to (c). Assume a zero forward-biased voltage drop for diode.

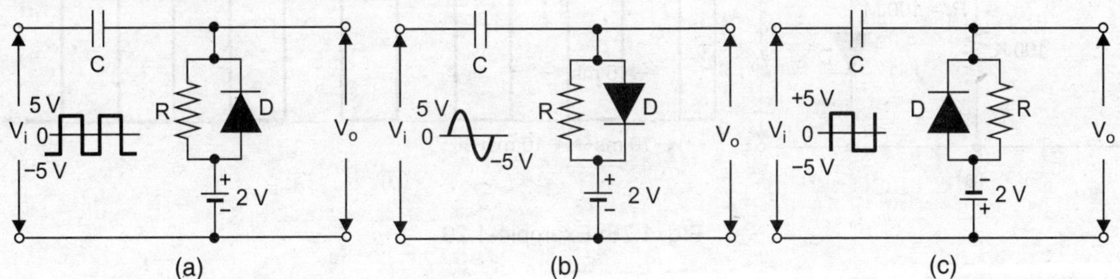

Fig. 1.74: Example-1.28

Solution: Fig. 1.74 (a): In the absence of the 2-Volt battery, the negative extremities of the input waveform would be clamped to zero. In the presence of the battery, the waveform will be clamped to –2 V. Fig. 1.75 (a) shows the clamped waveform.

Fig. 1.74 (b): In this case, the positive peaks instead of being clamped to zero are clamped to +2 V. Fig. 1.75 (b) shows the clamped waveform.

Fig. 1.74 (c): The circuit is similar to the one shown in Fig. 1.74 (a) except that the polarity of battery has been reversed. As a result, the negative peak is clamped to +2 V. Fig. 1.75 (c) shows the waveform.

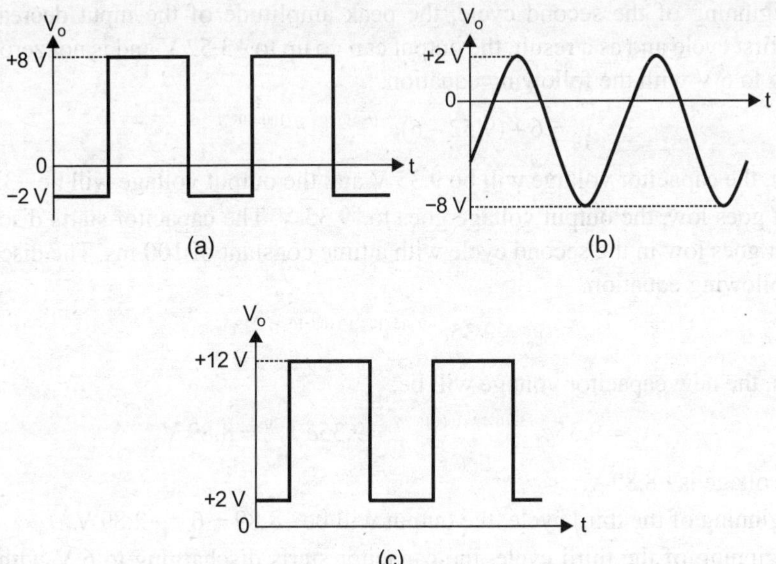

Fig. 1.75: Solution to Example-1.28

Example-1.29: Refer to the clamping circuit of Fig. 1.76 (a). The input waveform to this circuit is shown in Fig. 1. 76 (b) for the first six cycles. Sketch the clamped output waveform for the first six cycles.

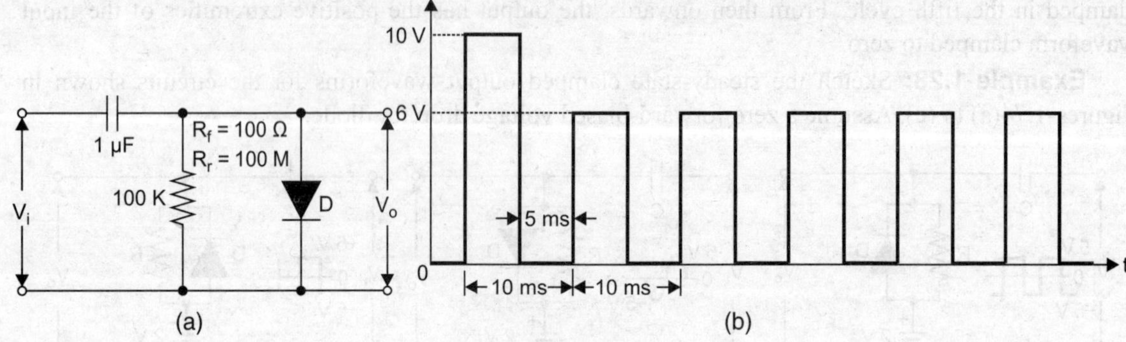

Fig. 1.76: Example-1.29

Solution: With $C = 1$ μF and $R_f = 100\ \Omega$, the time constant = 100 μs. The capacitor (C) would therefore charge to 10 V in about half a millisecond during the 5 ms high time of the first cycle.

As the input drops to zero, the output too drops by 10 V and the output is at –10 V. The capacitor starts discharging the moment input goes low in the second cycle through the resistor R with a time constant of 100 ms. The discharge equation is given by:

$$v_c = 10e^{-(t-5\times10^{-3})/(100\times10^{-3})}$$

At $t = 10$ ms, the new capacitor voltage can be computed as follows.

$$v_c = 10e^{-(5\times10^{-3})/(100\times10^{-3})} = 10e^{-1/20} = 9.52\text{ V}$$

Therefore, the output voltage at $t = 10$ ms = –9.52 V.

With the beginning of the second cycle, the peak amplitude of the input decreases by 4 V as compared to the first cycle and as a result, the output can go up to –3.52 V and is not zero. The capacitor starts discharging to 6 V with the following equation.

$$v_c = 6 + (9.52 - 6)e^{-(t-10\times10^{-3})/(100\times10^{-3})}$$

At $t = 15$ ms, the capacitor voltage will be 9.35 V and the output voltage will be –3.35 V.

As the input goes low, the output voltage goes to -9.35 V. The capacitor starts discharging to 0 V the moment input goes low in the second cycle with a time constant of 100 ms. The discharge equation is given by the following equation.

$$v_c = 9.35e^{-(t-15\times10^{-3})/(100\times10^{-3})}$$

At $t = 20$ ms, the new capacitor voltage will be:

$$v_c = 9.35e^{-(5\times10^{-3})/(100\times10^{-3})} = 9.35e^{-1/20} = 8.89\text{ V}$$

The output voltage is –8.89 V.

With the beginning of the third cycle, the output will be –8.89 + 6 = –2.89 V.

With the beginning of the third cycle, the capacitor starts discharging to 6 V with the following equation.

$$v_c = 6 + (8.89 - 6)e^{-(t-20\times10^{-3})/(100\times10^{-3})}$$

At $t = 25$ ms, the capacitor voltage will be 8.75 V and the output voltage will be –2.75 V.

As the input goes low, the output goes to -8.75V. The capacitor starts discharging to 0 V the moment input goes low in the third cycle with a time constant of 100 ms. The discharge equation is given by the following equation.

$$v_c = 8.75e^{-(t-25\times10^{-3})/(100\times10^{-3})}$$

At $t = 30$ ms, the new capacitor voltage can be computed from the following equation.

$$v_c = 8.75e^{-(5\times10^{-3})/(100\times10^{-3})} = 8.75e^{-1/20} = 8.32 \text{ V}$$

The output voltage is –8.32 V. Similar calculations can be done for the fourth, fifth and sixth cycles. The output waveform is plotted in Fig. 1.77.

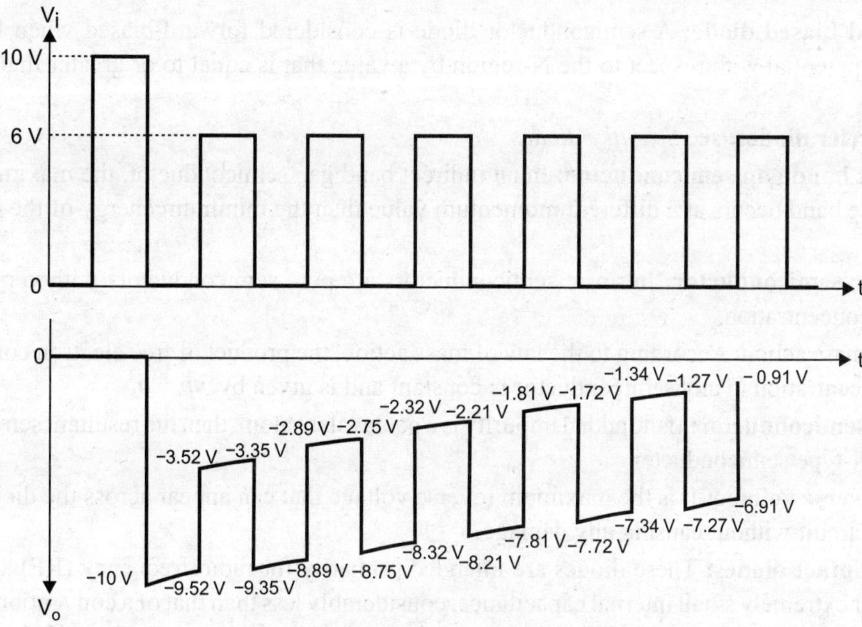

Fig. 1.77: Solution to Example-1.29

GLOSSARY

AC resistance of a diode: see *dynamic resistance of a diode*

Avalanche diode: In the case of an avalanche diode, on the application of reverse-bias voltage the thermally generated carriers have sufficient energies to disrupt covalent bonds, thereby resulting in free electrons. These free electrons knock out more electrons from the adjacent bonds. The process is regenerative and is referred to as avalanche multiplication.

Avalanche multiplication: see *avalanche diode*

Clamper circuit: Clamper circuits are used to clamp either positive or negative extremities of an AC signal to zero or a specified DC voltage. These are also called as DC restorer circuits.

Clipper circuit: Clipper circuits are used for clipping or removing whole or part of positive or negative portion of bidirectional waveforms.

DC resistance of a diode: see *static resistance of a diode*

Diode: A semiconductor diode is a polarity-sensitive two-terminal device comprising a P-N junction formed between a P-type semiconductor material and an N-type semiconductor material.

Direct band gap semiconductor: In a direct band gap semiconductor, the maximum energy of the valence band occurs at the same momentum value as the minimum energy of the conduction band.

Doping: The process of adding impurities to a semiconductor material is called doping and the resultant semiconductor is called an extrinsic semiconductor.

Dynamic resistance of a diode: Dynamic resistance or the AC resistance of a diode is defined as the resistance offered by the diode to a time-varying input signal.

Extrinsic semiconductor: The semiconductor formed after adding impurities is called extrinsic semiconductor.

Forward biased diode: A semiconductor diode is considered forward-biased when P-region is at a positive potential with respect to the N-region by a value that is equal to or greater than the cut-in voltage.

Hot-carrier diodes: see *Schottky diodes*

Indirect band gap semiconductor: In an indirect band gap semiconductor, the maximum energy of the valence band occurs at a different momentum value than the minimum energy of the conduction band

Intrinsic semiconductor: Intrinsic semiconductors are pure semiconductors with very low level of impurity concentration.

Law of mass action: According to the law of mass action, the product of free electron concentration and hole concentration in any semiconductor is constant and is given by $np = n_i^2$

N-type semiconductor: If the added impurity is a pentavalent atom, then the resultant semiconductor is called an N-type semiconductor

Peak inverse voltage: It is the maximum reverse voltage that can appear across the diodes used in the rectifier circuit without causing any damage.

Point contact diodes: These diodes are intended primarily for radio frequency (RF) applications owing to their extremely small internal capacitance, considerably less than that of a conventional junction diode. They basically have a metal–semiconductor junction and have been replaced by Schottky barrier diodes.

P-type semiconductor: If the impurity added is trivalent in nature, then it is called a P-type semiconductor.

Ratio of rectification: It is the ratio of DC power delivered to the load to the AC power input from transformer secondary. Like ripple factor, it also determines the effectiveness of a rectifier circuit in converting AC into DC.

Rectifier circuit: The job of a rectifier circuit is to convert the AC voltage appearing across the transformer secondary into a unidirectional voltage. There are three basic rectifier circuit configurations. These include (a) half-wave rectifier, (b) conventional two-diode full-wave rectifier that requires a center-tapped secondary winding and (c) bridge rectifier.

Reverse biased diode: A diode is said to be reverse-biased when an external potential applied across it is such that the P-region is negative with respect to N-region.

Ripple factor: It is ratio of root mean square (RMS) amplitude of AC component to the DC component in the rectified waveform.

Ripple frequency: It is the frequency of the unidirectional periodic voltage waveform present at the output of the rectifier circuit.

Schottky diode: A Schottky diode has a metal - semiconductor junction instead of a semiconductor -semiconductor junction of a conventional P-N junction diode. Normally N-type Silicon is used as the semiconductor material while the metal used can be Aluminium, Platinum, Tungsten or Molybdenum.

Shockley's diode equation: The I-V characteristics of a semiconductor diode both in the forward-bias and reverse-bias conditions are expressed by the universal diode equation, referred to as the Shockley's diode equation given by $I_D = I_0(e^{V_D/\eta V_T} - 1)$.

Static resistance of a diode: The static resistance or the DC resistance of the diode is the resistance offered by the diode when a steady DC voltage is applied to the diode.

Transformer utilization factor (TUF): It is defined as the ratio of DC power delivered to the load to the AC power rating of the transformer secondary

Tunnel diode: A tunnel diode has heavily doped P- and N-regions with a dopant concentration that is about 100–1000 times higher than that of a typical semiconductor diode.

Varactor diode: A varactor diode is a voltage variable capacitor. The capacitance is provided by transition capacitance that exists at the P-N junction when the diode is reverse-biased. The capacitance is varied by varying the reverse-bias voltage.

Zener diodes: The breakdown phenomenon in the case of a Zener diode is the result of electrons breaking their covalent bonds due to the existence of a strong electric field at the junction. The new hole - electron pair created increases the reverse current.

SUMMARY OF IMPORTANT FORMULAE

1. For an intrinsic semiconductor,

$$n = p = n_i$$

$$n_i^2 = AT^3 \exp(-E_{G0}/kT)$$

$$J = (\mu_n + \mu_p)n_i q\varepsilon$$

$$\sigma = (\mu_n + \mu_p)n_i q$$

The terms have their usual meaning.

2. For Silicon, the energy band gap [$E_G(T)$] at temperature T (°K) is $E_G(T) = 1.21 - 3.60 \times 10^{-4} T$
3. For Germanium, the energy band gap [$E_G(T)$] at temperature T (°K) is $E_G(T) = 0.785 - 2.23 \times 10^{-4} T$
4. The probability that an energy level in a semiconductor is occupied by an electron is given by:

$$f(E) = \frac{1}{1 + \exp[(E - E_F)/kT]}$$

5. For a N-type semiconductor, $n \cong N_D$, $p \cong \dfrac{n_i^2}{N_D}$
6. The Fermi level for an N-type semiconductor is $E_F = E_C - kT \ln\left(\dfrac{N_C}{N_D}\right)$

7. The value of N_C is given by $N_C = 2\left(\frac{2\pi m_n kTq}{h^2}\right)^{3/2}$

8. For a P-type semiconductor, $p \cong N_A$, $n \cong \frac{n_i^2}{N_A}$

9. Current density in a P-type semiconductor is $J \cong N_A \mu_p q \varepsilon$

10. Conductivity in a P-type semiconductor is $\sigma \cong N_A \mu_p q$

11. The Fermi level for a P-type semiconductor is $E_F = E_V + kT \ln\left(\frac{N_V}{N_A}\right)$

12. The value of N_V is $N_V = 2\left(\frac{2\pi m_p kTq}{h^2}\right)^{3/2}$

13. Law of mass action $np = n_i^2$

14. $\frac{D_p}{\mu_p} = \frac{D_n}{\mu_n} = V_T$

15. Shockley's diode equation $I_D = I_0(e^{V_D/\eta V_T} - 1)$

16. Variation of diode current with temperature is $I_0(T) = I_0(T_1) \times 2^{(T-T_1)/10}$

17. The variation of cut-in voltage and the forward voltage with temperature is $\frac{dV}{dT} = -2.5$ mV/°C

18. Static resistance of the diode is $R = \frac{V_{D1}}{I_{D1}}$

19. Dynamic resistance of the diode in the reverse-biased region $\cong \frac{26\eta}{I_0}$

20. Dynamic resistance (r) of a diode in the forward-biased region is $r \cong \frac{26\eta}{I_D}$

21. For a Varactor Diode, relation between capacitance and the applied reverse bias is $C_T = \frac{K}{(V_\gamma + V_R)^n}$

22. Ripple factor (r) is $r = \frac{V_r(\text{RMS})}{V_{DC}} = \frac{I_r(\text{RMS})}{I_{DC}}$

23. $r = \sqrt{\frac{(V_{RMS}^2 - V_{DC}^2)}{V_{DC}^2}} = \sqrt{\frac{(I_{RMS}^2 - I_{DC}^2)}{I_{DC}^2}}$

$$r = \sqrt{\left(\frac{V_{RMS}}{V_{DC}}\right)^2 - 1} = \sqrt{\left(\frac{I_{RMS}}{I_{DC}}\right)^2 - 1}.$$

24. Ratio of rectification $= \frac{I_{DC}^2}{I_{RMS}^2} = \left(\frac{I_{DC}}{I_{RMS}}\right)^2$.

25. $\text{TUF} = \frac{\text{DC power delivered to the load}}{\text{AC power rating of transformer secondary}}$.

REVIEW QUESTIONS

1. What is the difference between intrinsic and extrinsic semiconductors?
2. What are N-type and P-type semiconductors?
3. Explain the formulation of PN junction with no applied bias? What is barrier potential?
4. What is Zener diode? Draw its circuit symbol and its characteristics?
5. Show how a Zener diode can be used to regulate the voltage?
6. Draw the I-V characteristics of a diode and explain its dependence on temperature?
7. What is a tunnel diode? How does it differ from an ordinary diode?
8. Draw the circuit of a positive and a negative clipper and explain the difference between them?
9. Draw the circuit of a bridge rectifier and compare its performance with that of a half wave rectifier?
10. Can two diodes connected, back to back form a transistor?
11. Explain in detail
    (a) The effect of temperature on Zener diode.
    (b) The depletion region and the N- and the P-regions of a P-N junction diode form a parasitic capacitance. What is the effect of the applied reverse-bias voltage on this capacitance?
    (c) How is it possible to determine the polarity of a rectifying diode (which terminal is the anode and which terminal is the cathode) from its physical appearance?
    (d) What do you understand by the term "derating"? What is its significance for semiconductor evices?
    (e) The effect of temperature on the reverse saturation current of the diode.
12. "Tunnel diode is a voltage controllable device." Comment.
13. What are Schottky diodes? How are they different from conventional P-N junction diodes? What are their major applications?
14. For a Silicon diode, calculate the amount by which the diode voltage would have to be increased to double the diode current.
15. Mention two instruments which can be used to check the health of a diode. Also explain the checking procedure.
16. Briefly describe the following terms:
    (a) Static resistance (b) Dynamic resistance
    (c) Junction capacitance (d) Tunnelling effect
17. Show the basic diode action diagrammatically when it is
    (a) Unbiased (b) Reverse-biased
    (c) Forward-biased
18. With the help of relevant circuit diagrams, briefly describe the operation of clipping circuits that can be used to:
    (a) Clip portion of positive half cycles of a sinusoidal input with amplitude greater than a certain specified DC voltage V_{BB} assuming that the peak amplitude of sinusoidal input is greater than V_{BB}.

(b) Clip portion of negative half cycles of a sinusoidal input with amplitude more negative than a certain specified DC voltage $-V_{BB}$ assuming that the peak amplitude of sinusoidal input is greater than V_{BB}.

19. With the help of circuit diagram, briefly describe the operation of a positive clamper circuit. What is role of resistor (R) in the clamping circuit? How does one choose an optimum value of the resistance?

20. With the help of circuit diagram, briefly describe the operation of a negative clamper circuit. What is role of resistor (R) in the clamping circuit? How does one choose an optimum value of the resistance?

PROBLEMS

1. An N-type silicon bar 0.1 cm long and 100μm² in cross-sectional area has a majority carrier concentration of 5×10^{20} /m³ and the carrier mobility is 0.13 m²/Vs at 300K. If the charge of an electron is 1.6×10^{-19} coulomb, find the value of resistance of the bar?

2. A heavily doped N-type semiconductor has the following data: Hole-electron mobility ratio = 0.4, doping concentration 4.2×10^{8} atoms/m³, intrinsic concentration = 1.5×10^{4} atoms/m³. Find the ratio of conductance of the N-type semiconductor to that of the intrinsic semiconductor of the same material and at the same temperature?

3. Fig. 1.78 shows a circuit along with an input waveform. Draw the output waveform.

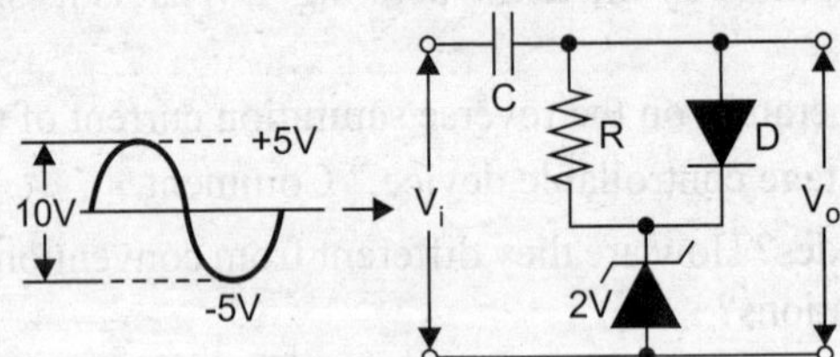

Fig. 1.78: Problem-3

4. In the circuit shown in Fig. 1.79, the diode is ideal. Find the value of voltage V?

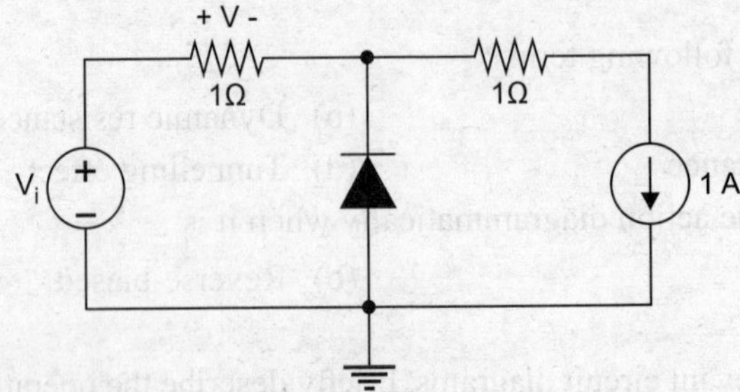

Fig. 1.79: Problem-4

5. Find the output voltage V_o in volts of the circuit shown in Fig. 1.80?

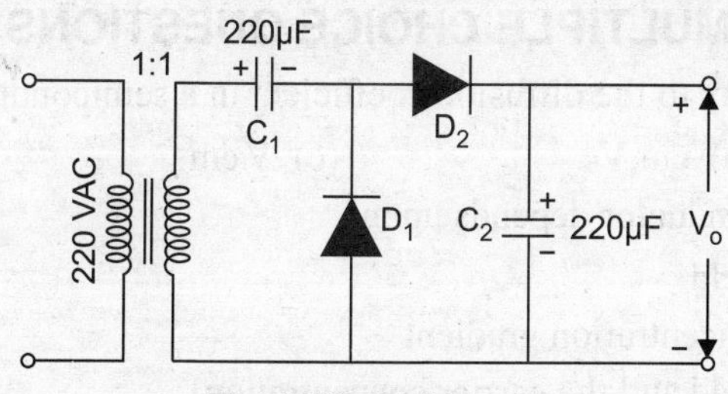

Fig. 1.80: Problem-5

6. In the basic clamper circuit, positive or negative, a resistance R is always connected across the diode. If the forward-biased and reverse-biased resistances of the diode were 10 ohms and 10 Mega-ohms respectively, find the most optimum value of R in Kilo-ohms.

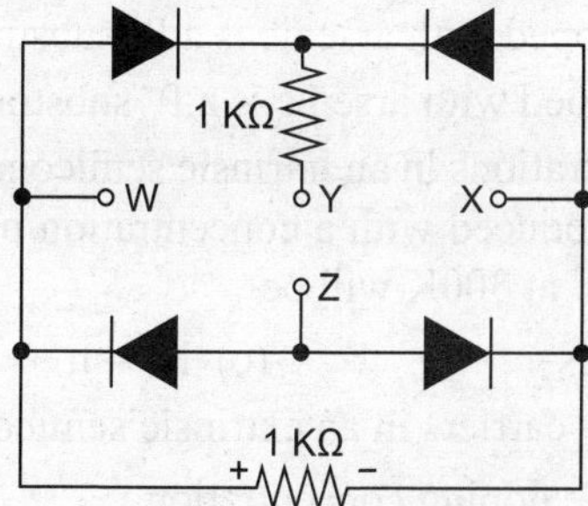

Fig. 1.81: Problem-7

7. Refer to Fig. 1.81. A voltage 1000 sin ωt (in volts) is applied across Y – Z. Assuming ideal diodes, the voltage measured across W – X (in volts) is:
8. Refer to Fig. 1.82. A triangular waveform as shown in the figure is applied to the input of the circuit. Draw the v_O, v_{O1} and v_{O2} waveforms assuming the diode to be ideal.

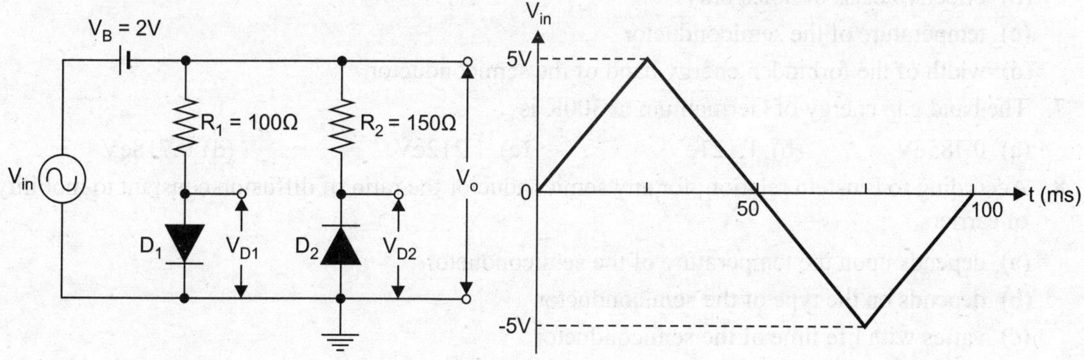

Fig. 1.82: Problem-8

9. Given that the ripple factor in the case of a full wave rectifier is 0.482. Determine the ratio of rectification of the same.
10. If ripple factor and ratio of rectification are denoted by r and R respectively, prove that $r = \sqrt{\dfrac{1-R}{R}}$

MULTIPLE CHOICE QUESTIONS

1. The ratio of the mobility to the diffusion coefficient in a semiconductor has the unit
   (a) V^{-1} (b) $cm.V^{-1}$ (c) $V.cm^{-1}$ (d) V.s
2. Drift current in semiconductor depends upon
   (a) only the electric field
   (b) only the carrier concentration gradient
   (c) both the electric field and the carrier concentration
   (d) both the electric field and carrier concentration gradient
3. Which of the following is true?
   (a) A silicon wafer heavily doped with boron is a P^+ substrate
   (b) A silicon wafer lightly doped with boron is a P^+ substrate
   (c) A silicon wafer heavily doped with arsenic is a P^+ substrate
   (d) A silicon wafer lightly doped with arsenic is a P^+ substrate
4. The electron and hole concentrations in an intrinsic semiconductor are n_i per cm^3 at 300K. Now, if acceptor impurities are introduced with a concentration of N_A per cm^3 (where $N_A >> n_i$), the electron concentration per cm^3 at 300K will be
   (a) n_i (b) $n_i + N_A$ (c) $N_A - n_i$ (d) n_i^2/N_A
5. The concentration of minority carriers in an extrinsic semiconductor under equilibrium is
   (a) directly proportional to the doping concentration
   (b) inversely proportional to the doping concentration
   (c) directly proportional to the intrinsic concentration
   (d) inversely proportional to the intrinsic concentration
6. In an intrinsic semiconductor, the free-electron concentration depends on
   (a) effective mass of electrons only
   (b) effective mass of holes only
   (c) temperature of the semiconductor
   (d) width of the forbidden energy band of the semiconductor
7. The band gap energy of Germanium at 300K is
   (a) 0.785eV (b) 1.121eV (c) 1.212eV (d) 0.718eV
8. According to Einstein relation, for any semiconductor the ratio of diffusion constant to mobility of carriers
   (a) depends upon the temperature of the semiconductor
   (b) depends on the type of the semiconductor
   (c) varies with life time of the semiconductor
   (d) is a universal constant
9. A varactor diode may be advantageous at microwave frequencies (indicate false answer)
   (a) for electronic tuning (b) as an oscillator
   (c) as a parametric amplifier (d) for frequency multiplication
10. There are two semiconductor diodes A and B. One of them is Zener whereas other is avalanche. Their ratings are 5.6 V and 24 V, respectively, then

(a) A is Zener, B is avalanche (b) A is avalanche, B is Zener
(c) Both of them are Zener diodes (d) Both of them are avalanche diodes

11. A forward potential of 20V is applied to a Si diode. A resistance of 1kΩ is in series with the diode. The current flowing through the diode is
(a) 19.3mA (b) 9.3mA (c) 20mA (d) 10mA

12. For two energy levels E_1 and E_2 E eV above and below the Fermi level respectively, let P_1 and P_2 be the probability of E_1 being occupied by an electron and E_2 being empty. Then which of the following statements is true
(a) $P_1 > P_2$
(b) $P_1 = P_2$
(c) $P_1 < P_2$
(d) P_1 and P_2 depend on the number of free electrons

13. A general purpose diode is more likely to suffer avalanche breakdown rather than Zener breakdown as
(a) Its leakage current is small (b) It has weak covalent bonds
(c) It is lightly doped (d) It has low reverse resistance

14. In a half wave and full wave rectifier, if the input frequency is 50Hz, then the output frequency will be
(a) 50Hz, 50Hz (b) 100Hz, 50Hz (c) 50Hz, 100Hz (d) 100Hz, 50Hz

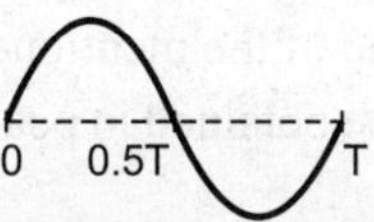

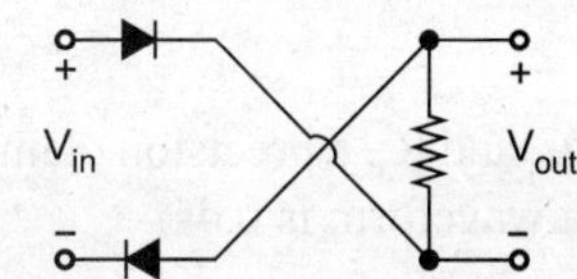

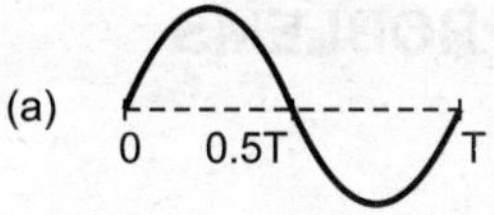

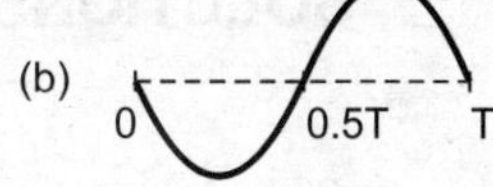

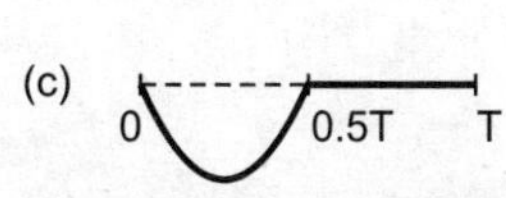

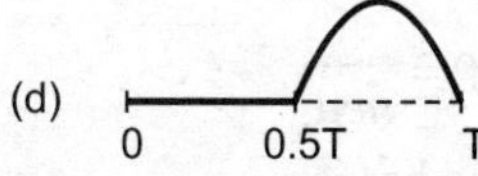

Fig. 1.83: Q-15

15. For the circuit with ideal diodes shown in the Fig. 1.83, the shape of the output (V_{out}) for the given sine wave input (V_{in}) will be
(a) V_{in} for +ve half cycle and 0 for –ve half cycle
(b) 0 for +ve half cycle and V_{in} for –ve half cycle
(c) $-V_{in}$ for +ve half cycle and 0 for –ve half cycle
(d) 0 for +ve half cycle and $-V_{in}$ for –ve half cycle

16. If the circuit shown in Fig. 1.84 has to function as a clamping circuit, then which one of the following conditions should be satisfied for the sinusoidal signal of period T?
(a) RC << T (b) RC = 0.35T (c) RC = T (d) RC >> T

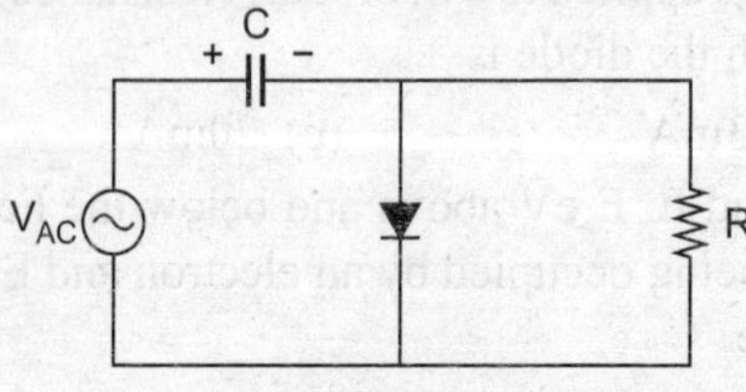

Fig. 1.84: Q-16

17. When a reverse bias is applied to a diode, it will
(a) Raise the potential barrier
(b) Lower the potential barrier
(c) Increases the majority-carrier a current greatly
(d) None of these

18. The depletion region of a semiconductor diode is due to
(a) absence of the current carriers (b) Reverse Biasing
(c) Forward Biasing (d) Crystal doping

19. In a positive clipper, the diode conducts when
(a) $V_{in} < V_{ref}$ (b) $V_{in} = V_{ref}$
(c) $V_{in} > V_{ref}$ (d) None of the mentioned

20. At what values of C_i and R_d, a precision clamping can be obtained in peak clamper when the time period of the input waveform is 0.4s?
(a) C_i=0.1μF and R_d=10kΩ (b) C_i=0.47μF and R_d=10MΩ
(c) C_i=33μF and R_d=10MΩ (d) C_i=2.5F and R_d=10kΩ

SOLUTIONS TO PROBLEMS

Problem-1:

Conductivity $\sigma = ne\mu_n + pe\mu_p$

As, silicon-bar is N-type, conductivity is given by $\sigma \cong ne\mu_n$

Hence, resistivity, $\rho \cong \dfrac{1}{ne\mu_n}$

The resistance of the bar is

$$R = \frac{\rho l}{A} = \frac{l}{ne\mu_n A} = \frac{10^{-3}}{5\times10^{20}\times1.6\times10^{-19}\times0.13\times100\times10^{-12}} \cong 1M\Omega$$

Problem-2:

For N-type semiconductor, $\sigma_n \cong nq\mu_n$

For an intrinsic semiconductor, $\sigma_i = n_i q(\mu_n + \mu_p)$

$$\frac{\sigma_n}{\sigma_i} = \frac{nq\mu_n}{n_i q(\mu_n + \mu_p)} = \frac{n\mu_n}{n_i(\mu_n + \mu_p)} = \frac{4.2\times10^8 \times \mu_n}{1.5\times10^4 \times \mu_n\left[1+(\mu_p/\mu_n)\right]} = 20000$$

Problem-3:

The circuit acts as a basic negative clamper, in the absence of the Zener diode. With the Zener diode connected, the output gets clamped to a maximum voltage of 2V. Fig. 1.85 shows the output waveform.

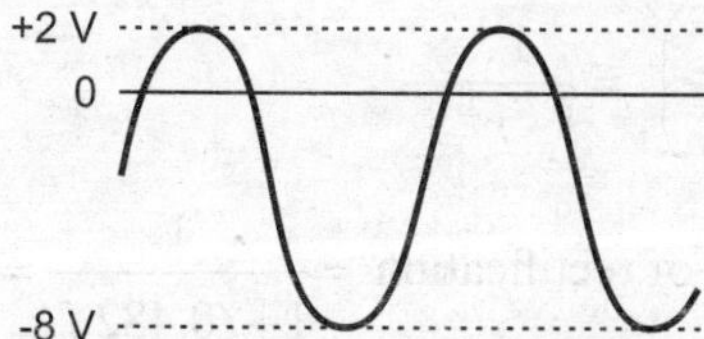

Fig. 1.85: Solution to Problem-3

Problem-4:

Due to the current source of 1A, the diode is reverse biased by 1V. When the input voltage V_i is less than -1V, the diode gets forward biased and the voltage V is equal to V_i. When the input voltage V_i is greater than -1V, the diode is reverse biased, and the voltage V is equal to 1V. Therefore, the voltage V is min(V_i, 1)

Problem-5:

It is a half-wave voltage doubler circuit. The peak value of the input waveform is $(220\times\sqrt{2})V = 310V$

Therefore, the output voltage is 2 × 310V = 620V

Problem-6:

$$R = \sqrt{R_f \times R_r} = \sqrt{10\times10\times10^6} = 10^4\Omega = 10k\Omega$$

Problem-7:

When VYZ is positive, then all the four diodes are reverse biased. Therefore, $V_W - V_X = 0$ or $V_{WX} = 0V$

When VYZ is negative, then all the four diodes are forward biased. Since all the diodes are given to be ideal, they will act as short circuit. Therefore, $V_W = V_X$. Hence, $V_{WX} = 0V$.

Therefore, for all conditions $V_{WX} = 0V$.

Problem-8:

The waveform V_o is the addition of the input waveform and 2V. Therefore, it has a positive peak of 7V and negative peak of -3V.

Diode D_1 conducts for V_o greater than 0V and acts as an open circuit for V_o less than 0V. Therefore, V_{o1} is 0V when V_o is positive and follows V_o when it is negative.

Diode D_2 conducts for V_o less than 0V and acts as an open circuit for positive value of V_o. Therefore, V_{o2} is zero when V_o is negative and follows V_o when it is positive.

Fig. 1.86 shows the waveforms.

Problem-9:

$$\text{Ripple factor } r = \sqrt{\left(\frac{I_{RMS}}{I_{DC}}\right)^2 - 1}$$

$$\text{Ratio of rectification} = \left(\frac{I_{DC}}{I_{RMS}}\right)^2 = \frac{1}{1+r^2}$$

As $r = 0.482$, therefore, ratio of rectification $= \dfrac{1}{1+(0.482)^2} = 0.812$

Problem-10:

$$\text{Ripple factor } r = \sqrt{\left(\frac{I_{RMS}}{I_{DC}}\right)^2 - 1}$$

$$\text{Ratio of rectification} = \left(\frac{I_{DC}}{I_{RMS}}\right)^2$$

Substituting the value of R in the expression of r, we get $r = \sqrt{\dfrac{1}{R} - 1} = \sqrt{\dfrac{(1-R)}{R}}$

SOLUTIONS TO MULTIPLE CHOICE QUESTIONS

1. (a) As we know, $\dfrac{D}{\mu} = V_T$

   Hence, $\dfrac{\mu}{D} = \dfrac{1}{V_T}$

   $\dfrac{\mu}{D}$ = Mobility

   Therefore, mobility has units of V^{-1}.

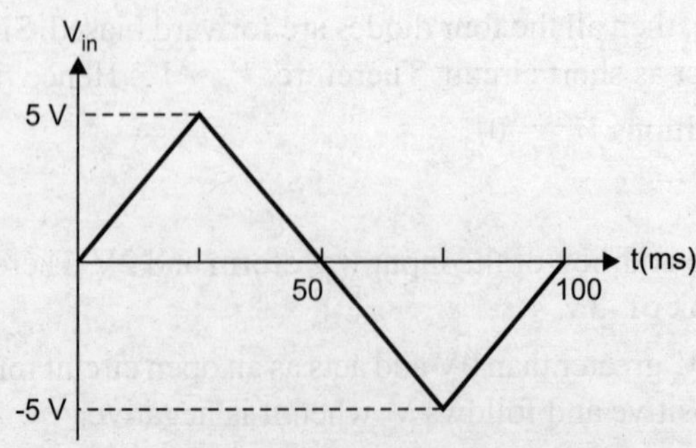

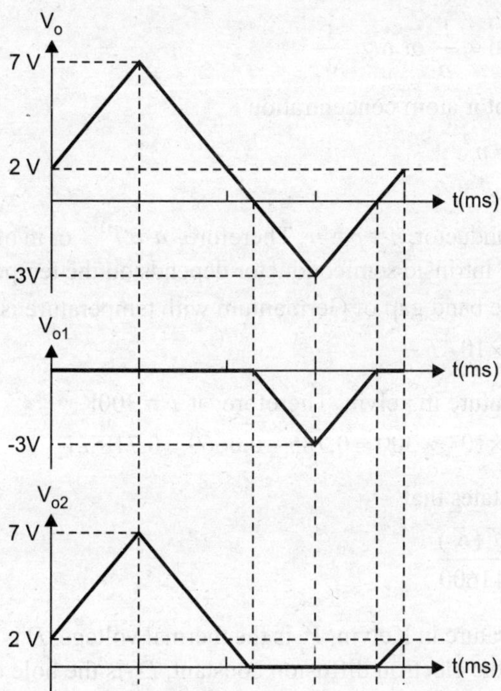

Fig. 1.86: Solution to Problem-8

2. (c) Drift current density $J = ne\mu\varepsilon$
   Therefore, drift current $I = ne\mu\varepsilon A$
   Where, A is the cross-sectional area of the semi-conductor
   Hence, I depends upon both the carrier concentration and the electric field
3. (a) Boron is an acceptor impurity. Hence, silicon wafer doped with high concentration of boron is a P+ substrate.
4. (d) By the law of electrical neutrality, $p + N_D = n + N_A$
   As $N_D = 0$, and $N_A >> n_i$ in this problem. Therefore, $p = N_A$
   Using the law of mass action,
   $np = n_i^2$
   $n = \frac{n_i^2}{p} = \frac{n_i^2}{N_A}$
5. (b) We know that $np = n_i^2$
   For a N-type semiconductor, p is the minority carrier concentration.
   Therefore, $p = \frac{n_i^2}{n}$ or $p \propto \frac{1}{n}$ or $p \propto \frac{1}{N_D}$
   Where, N_D is the donor atom concentration
   For a P-type semiconductor, n is the minority carrier concentration.

Therefore, $n = \frac{n_i^2}{p}$ or $n \propto \frac{1}{p}$ or $n \propto \frac{1}{N_A}$

Where, N_A is the acceptor atom concentration

6. (c) We know that $np = n_i^2$

Also, $n_i \propto T^{3/2}$

For an intrinsic semiconductor, $n = p = n_i$. Therefore, $n \propto T^{3/2}$ or in other words, the free electron concentration in an intrinsic semiconductor depends on the temperature.

7. (d) The variation of the band gap of Germanium with temperature is given by

$E_g(T) = 0.785 - 2.23 \times 10^{-4} T$

Where T is the temperature in kelvin. Therefore, at $T = 300$K,

$E_g(T) = 0.785 - 2.23 \times 10^{-4} \times 300 = 0.785 - 0.0669 = 0.7181 eV$

8. (a) Einstein equation states that

$$\frac{D}{\mu} = \frac{D_n}{\mu_n} = \frac{D_p}{\mu_p} = V_T = \frac{T(K)}{11600}$$

Where, T is the temperature in Kelvin, V_T is the thermal voltage, D is the diffusion constant, m is the mobility, D_n is the electron diffusion constant, D_p is the hole diffusion constant, μ_n is the electron mobility and μ_p is the hole mobility. From the equation, we see that the ratio of the diffusion constant to the mobility of carriers depends on the temperature of the semiconductor.

9. (b)
10. (a)
11. (a) Forward voltage across the diode = 0.7V

Voltage across the resistance = 19.3V.

Current flowing through the resistor = 19.3/ 1 × 10^3 A = 19.3mA

Current flowing the diode is the same as that flowing through the resistor. Therefore, current flowing through the diode is 19.3mA

12. (c) Given that the Fermi level probability $P_1 = E_1$ and Fermi level probability $P_2 = E_2$

We know that

$$f(E) = \frac{1}{1 + e^{(E-E_F)/KT}}$$

Where f(E) is the Fermi-Dirac probability function and E_F is the Fermi level. Therefore, $P_1 < P_2$.

13. (c)
14. (c) In a half-wave rectifier, the output frequency is the same as the input frequency

In a full-wave rectifier, the output frequency is double that of the input frequency

15. (c). Refer to Fig. 1.87.

For positive half cycle of the input, diodes D_1 and D_2 are ON and the output voltage $V_{out} = -V_{in}$

For negative half cycle of the input, diodes D_1 and D_2 are OFF and the output voltage $V_{out} = 0V$

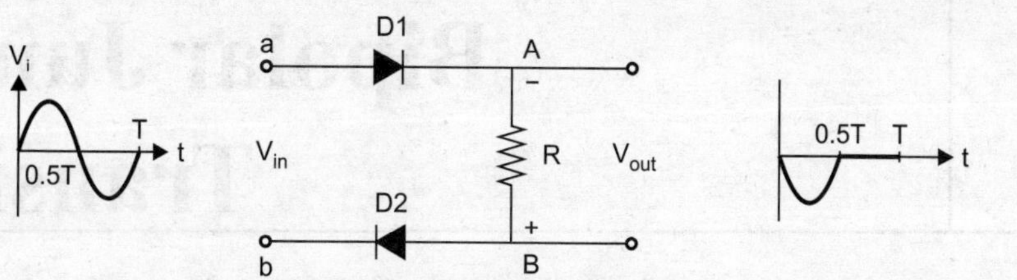

Fig. 1.87: Solution to MCQ-15

16. (d) The given circuit is that of a negative clamper which has a load resistor connected in shunt. When the diode is OFF, the capacitor discharges through the resistor R. The output falls exponentially with time constant RC to avoid the discharge of the capacitor significantly. Therefore, RC >> T, where T is the period of the sinusoidal waveform applied to the given circuit.
17. (a)
18. (a)
19. (b) In a positive clipper, the diode conducts until $V_{in} = V_{ref}$ (during the positive half cycle of the input), because when $V_{in} < V_{ref}$, the voltage (V_{ref}) at the negative input is higher than that at the positive input.
20. (a) For precision clamping, $(C_i \times R_d) << T/2$. So, $(0.1\mu F \times 10\ k\Omega) << (0.4/2)$ or $1 \times 10^{-3} << 0.2$. Therefore, $C_i = 0.1\mu F$ and $R_d = 10k\Omega$.

2 Bipolar Junction Transistors

Learning Objectives

After completing this chapter, you will learn the following.

- — Structure of a bipolar junction transistor (NPN and PNP)
- — BJT amplifier configurations (common emitter, common collector and common base configurations)
- — I-V characteristics of a BJT
- — BJT specifications and absolute maximum ratings
- — BJT as a switch
- — BJT as an amplifier (BJT biasing circuits) - common-emitter configuration (fixed bias configuration, voltage divider bias configuration, collector-to-base bias configuration), common-base configuration, common-collector configuration
- — Bias stabilization, Stability factor
- — Bias compensation
- — Thermal runaway

INTRODUCTION

In this chapter, the structure of bipolar junction transistors including NPN and PNP transistors and their I-V characteristics are discussed.The BJT amplifier configurations (common emitter, common collector and common base) and biasing circuits and BJT as a switch are covered in detail. Bias stabilization, bias compensation techniques and thermal runaway are discussed at the end of the chapter. Important formulae and keywords are listed at the end of the chapter. The chapter is amply illustrated with a large number of solved examples and unsolved problems with solutions provided at the end of the chapter. Theory type questions are also given in the section on review questions.

2.1 BIPOLAR JUNCTION TRANSISTOR

A *Bipolar Junction Transistor* (BJT) is a three-layer, three-terminal semiconductor device having two PN junctions. BJT are so named as both holes and electrons contribute to the flow of current.It comprises three differently doped semiconductor regions; namely the emitter region, the base region and the collector region. The base region is physically sandwiched between the emitter and the collector regions. The width of the base region is much smaller than the width of the emitter and the collector regions. Typically, ratio of the total width of the transistor to the width of the base region is of the order of few hundreds. The emitter region is the most heavily doped, the collector region moderately doped and the base region very lightly doped. The doping of the base region is around 10 times less than that of the emitter region. This results in reduced conductivity of the base region. Bipolar transistors are classified as NPN and PNP transistors depending upon the type of doping of the three regions

2.1.1 NPN and PNP Transistors

Figure-2.1(a) shows the structure of an *NPN transistor*. The collector and the emitter regions are N-type semiconductors and the base region is a P-type semiconductor. The collector, emitter and base terminals are designated as C, E and B, respectively. Figure-2.1(b) shows the circuit symbol of an NPN transistor. The arrow on the emitter lead specifies the direction of the conventional current flow when the emitter-base junction is forward biased. In an NPN transistor, most of the current flow is due to flow of electrons.

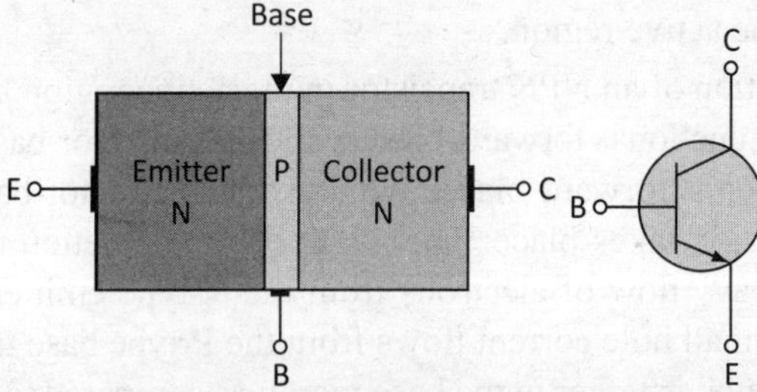

Fig. 2.1: NPN transistor (a) structure and (b) circuit symbol of an NPN transistor

Figure-2.2(a) and (b) respectively show the structure and circuit symbol of a PNP transistor. The collector and the emitter regions are P-type semiconductors and the base region is an N-type semiconductor. The arrow on the emitter lead specifies the direction of the conventional current flow when the emitter–base junction is forward-biased. In a PNP transistor, holes majorly contribute to the flow of current.

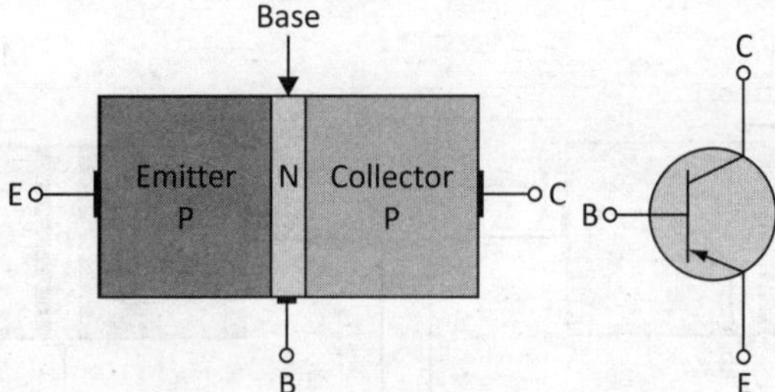

Fig. 2.2: PNP transistor (a) structure and (b) circuit symbol of a PNP transistor

2.1.2 Operation of NPN and PNP Transistors

NPN transistors are more commonly used as compared to PNP transistors as they offer higher current density and faster switching times. This is so because the electron mobility is higher than the hole mobility. The basic operation of an NPN transistor is described in this section. The operation of a PNP transistor is same as that of an NPN transistor except that the roles of electrons and holes are interchanged and the polarities of the voltages and the direction of current reversed. Transistors may be looked upon as two PN junction diodes connected back to back. The two junctions are the emitter-base and the collector-base junctions. We know that when the PN junction diode is an open circuit, no current flows through it and the diode voltage is equal to the diode's contact potential. Similarly, when no external voltage is applied to the transistor, the currents flowing through the transistor are zero and the potential at the two junctions is equal to their respective contact potentials.

Transistors operate in four regions, namely the active region, the reverse-active region, the saturation region and the cut-off region depending upon the polarity of voltages applied to the emitter-base and the collector-base junctions. In the *active region,* the emitter–base junction is forward-biased, and the collector-base junction is reverse-biased. Transistors when operating in the active region function as amplifiers. In the *reverse-active region*, the biasing condition is reversed, that is, the emitter-base junction is reverse-biased, and the collector-base region is forward-biased. Transistors are seldom operated in the reverse-active region. In the *saturation region*, both the emitter-base and the collector-base junctions are forward-biased and in the *cut-off region*, both the junctions are reverse-biased. When the transistor is used as a switching device it operates either in the saturation or the cut-off region. It acts as a closed switch in the saturation region and as an open switch in the cut-off region. When used as an amplifier, the transistor is operated in the active region.

Let us consider the operation of an NPN transistor in the active region. As mentioned before, in the active region the emitter-base junction is forward-biased, and the collector-base junction is reverse-biased. When the emitter–base junction is forward-biased with an open collector-base junction [Figure-2.3(a)], normal PN junction diode action takes place. The width of the depletion region decreases due to the applied bias and there is a heavy flow of electrons from the N-type emitter to the P-type base. As the base is lightly doped, a very small hole current flows from the P-type base to the N-type emitter region. The width of the depletion region is larger in the base region as compared to that in the emitter region as the base is lightly doped compared to the emitter region. If the collector-base junction is reverse-biased with the emitter-base junction open [Figure-2.3(b)], it behaves like a normal reverse-biased junction diode. There is a small current flow due to the minority carriers; that is, the flow of electrons from the base region to the collector region and flow of holes from the collector to the base region. The depletion width increases with the increase in the reverse-bias voltage and is larger in the base region than that in the collector region.

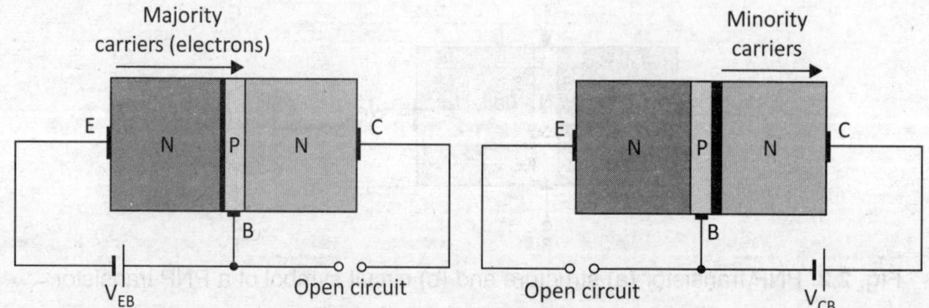

Fig. 2.3: NPN transistor (a) forward-biased emitter-base junction and (b) reverse-biased collector-base junction

Figure-2.4 shows the flow of current in an NPN transistor in the active region; that is, both the forward and the reverse voltages are applied simultaneously to the emitter-base and the collector-base junctions, respectively. The emitter current (I_E) comprises electron current (due to flow of electrons from emitter to base) and hole current (due to the flow of holes from base to emitter). As the base is very lightly doped as compared to the emitter; the emitter current consists mainly of electrons. Not all the electrons crossing the emitter-base junction reach the base-collector junction as some of them remain in the base region and constitute the base current (I_B). As the base region is very thin and has low level of conductivity due to light doping, only a very few electrons remain in the base region. The rest of the electrons diffuse across the reverse-biased collector-base junction to reach the N-type collector and constitute the collector current (I_C). The magnitude of the base current is of the order of few microamperes as compared to several milliamperes for the collector and the emitter current. Applying Kirchhoff's current law to the transistor, considering it as a node, we get

$$I_E = I_C + I_B \tag{2.1}$$

where I_E is the emitter current, I_C the collector current and I_B the base current.

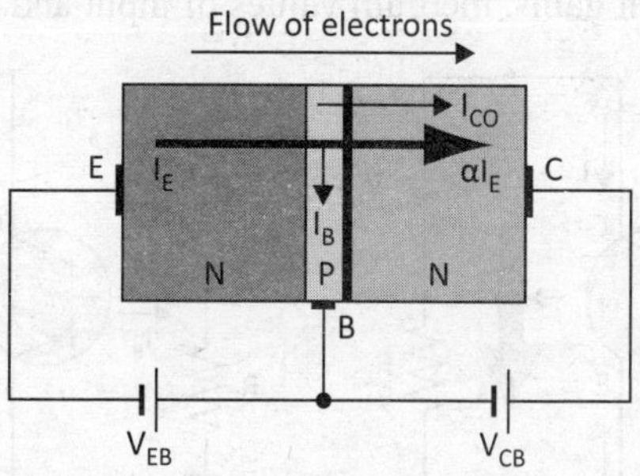

Fig. 2.4: Flow of current in an NPN transistor in the active region

From eqn.2.1, we can infer that the emitter current is the sum of the collector current and the base current. The collector current comprises two components: the majority-carrier component and the leakage-current component. The majority-carrier component is due to the electrons that have travelled from the emitter region across the base to the collector region. This component is equal to aI_E, where a is the fraction of emitter electrons that reach the collector region. The leakage current (I_{CO}) is the minority current of the reverse-biased base-collector junction with an open-circuit emitter-base junction. I_{CO} is in the range of few hundreds of nanoamperes to few microamperes. The expression for collector current is given by eqn. 2.2.

$$I_C = \alpha I_E + I_{CO} \tag{2.2}$$

The above equation is only valid in the active region of the transistor. The generalized expression for the collector current in a transistor is given by eqn. 2.3.

$$I_C = \alpha I_E + I_{CO}\left[1 - \exp\left(-\frac{V_{CB}}{V_T}\right)\right] \tag{2.3}$$

Where, V_{CB} is the voltage across the collector–base junction and V_T the volt equivalent of temperature. When the collector-base junction is sufficiently reverse-biased; the term $\exp(-V_{CB}/V_T)$ tends to zero and eqn. 2.3 reduces to eqn. 2.2. Operation of a PNP bipolar junction transistor can be explained on similar lines.

2.2 BASIC TRANSISTOR AMPLIFIER CONFIGURATIONS

Transistors are connected in any of the following three configurations.

1. Common-emitter (CE) configuration
2. Common-base (CB) configuration
3. Common-collector (CC) configuration

The configurations discussed below are the basic ones and only show the mode of operation of the transistor. The associated circuitry to be used in these configurations for providing required biasing to the two junctions will be discussed in detail in a later part of the chapter.

2.2.1 Common-Emitter Configuration

The *common-emitter (CE) configuration* has emitter terminal common to both the input and the output sections, as shown in Figures 2.5(a) and (b), for the NPN and the PNP transistors, respectively. The input signal is applied to the base-emitter section and the output is taken from the collector-emitter section. It is the most commonly used transistor configuration. Salient features of CE transistor configuration are high values of voltage and current gains, medium values of input and output impedances.

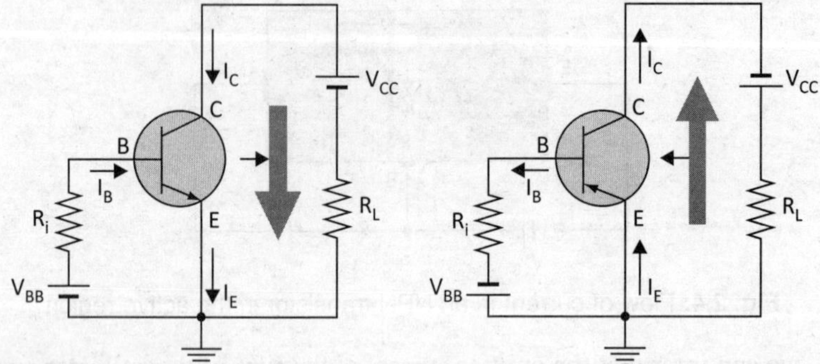

Fig. 2.5: Common-emitter configuration for (a) NPN transistor and (b) PNP transistor

2.2.2 Common-Base Configuration

In the *common-base (CB) configuration*, the base terminal is common to both the input and the output sections. Figures-2.6(a) and (b) show the basic circuit of the transistor in the CB configuration for the NPN and the PNP transistors, respectively. The directions of currents shown are used for conventional current flow. Also, the current flowing into the transistor is taken as positive and the current leaving the transistor is taken as negative.

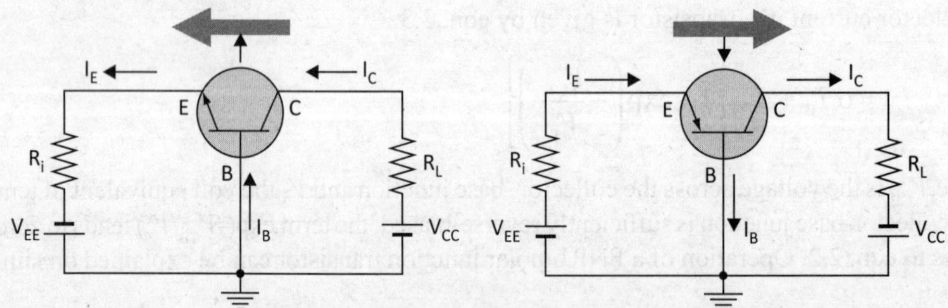

Fig. 2.6: Common-base configuration (a) NPN transistor (b) PNP transistor

2.2.3 Common-Collector Configuration or Emitter Follower Configuration

In the *common-collector (CC) configuration*, also known as the *emitter-follower configuration*, the collector terminal is common to both the input and the output sections. Figures-2.7(a) and (b) show the NPN and PNP transistors connected in the CC configuration. The configuration is similar to the common-emitter configuration with the output taken from the emitter terminal rather than the collector terminal.

CC configuration offers high input impedance and low output impedance and hence it is used for impedance matching applications, that is, for driving low-impedance load from a high-impedance source. The voltage gain offered by CC configuration is less than unity and the value of current gain is high. Table-2.1 gives the salient features of the three basic transistor configurations.

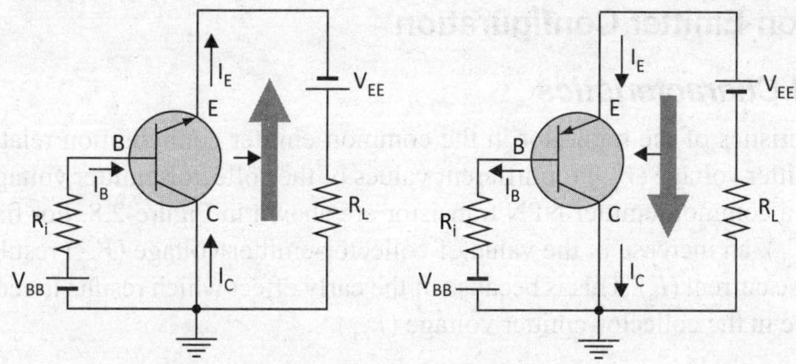

Fig. 2.7: Common-collector configuration for (a) NPN transistor and (b) PNP transistor

Table 2.1: Salient features of the three transistor configurations

Configuration	Current gain	Voltage gain	Input impedance	Output impedance
Common emitter (CE)	High (≈50–100)	Very high (≈500)	Medium (≈800 Ω)	Medium (≈50 kΩ)
Common collector (CC)	High (≈80–100)	Approximately unity	High (≈800 kΩ)	Very low (≈50 Ω)
Common base (CB)	Approximately unity	High (≈150)	Low (≈100 Ω)	Very high (≈500 kΩ)

2.2.4 Alpha (a) and Beta(b) of Bipolar Junction Transistor

Alpha (a) and beta (b) of a bipolar transistor are defined as the forward DC current gains of the transistor when connected as common-base and common-emitter configurations respectively. That is, b = I_C/I_B and a = I_C/I_E. Also, since $I_E = I_C + I_B$, (a) and (b) are related by eqn. 2.4.

$$\beta = \alpha/(1-\alpha) \tag{2.4}$$

As is evident from eqn. (2.4), a very small change in the value of *a* is reflected as a very large change in the value of *b*.

Relationship between collector and emitter currents is also given by eqn. 2.5.

$$I_C = I_{CO} + \alpha I_E \tag{2.5}$$

Combining eqns. (2.4) and (2.5) we get,

$$I_C = \frac{\alpha}{(1-\alpha)} I_B + \frac{1}{(1-\alpha)} I_{CO} \tag{2.6}$$

If we substitute, then eqn. (2.6) becomes,

$$I_C = \beta I_B + (\beta + 1) I_{CO} \tag{2.7}$$

2.3 I-V CHARACTERISTICS

There are two important types of I-V characteristics related to the three basic bipolar transistor amplifier configurations. These are the *Input Characteristics* and the *Output Characteristics*. The input and output characteristics in the case of the three basic amplifier configurations are briefly described in the following sub-sections.

2.3.1 Common-Emitter Configuration

2.3.1.1 *Input Characteristics*

The input characteristics of the transistor in the common-emitter configuration relate the base current (I_B) to the base-emitter voltage (V_{BE}) for different values of the collector-emitter voltage (V_{CE}). The input characteristics for a common-emitter NPN transistor are shown in Figure-2.8. For fixed value of base-emitter voltage (V_{BE}), an increase in the value of collector-emitter voltage (V_{CE}) results in a decrease in the value of the base current (I_B). This is because of the early effect which results in reduction of the base width with increase in the collector-emitter voltage (V_{CE}).

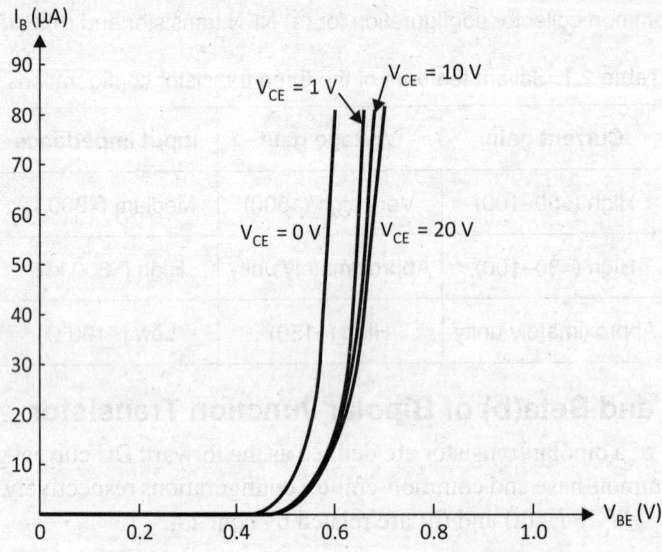

Fig. 2.8: Input characteristics of CE transistor

2.3.1.2 *Output Characteristics*

Output characteristics of the transistor in common emitter configuration relate the collector current (I_C) to the collector-emitter voltage (V_{CE}) for different values of base current (I_B). The output characteristics are shown in Figure-2.9. The output curves for CE configuration are not as horizontal as that for CB configuration, indicating that the collector-emitter voltage has an influence on the value of collector current.

The CE characteristics of the transistors of the same type number differ significantly from one device to another. The value of β varies considerably with changes in both the operating temperature and collector current as shown in Figure-2.10.

The output characteristics can be divided into three distinct regions namely the active region, the saturation region and the cut-off region. The *active region* in the output characteristics corresponds to the portion of the graph to the right of the line at $V_{CE(sat)}$ and above the curve for $I_B = 0$. As can be seen from the figure, the curves of collector current (I_C) for different values of base current (I_B) are not as horizontal and parallel as the curves for the CB configuration which are shown latter in Figure-2.14. Transistors in the CE configuration operating in the active mode are used as voltage, current and power amplifiers. In the active region . As mentioned before *b* is the DC forward current transfer ratio or the DC current gain of the transistor. It is also denoted as h_{FE}. Typical value of *b* is in the range of 50–100. Hence, the

CE configuration provides a high current gain. It also provides a large value of voltage and power gain. For AC applications ac beta (β_{ac}) is defined as:

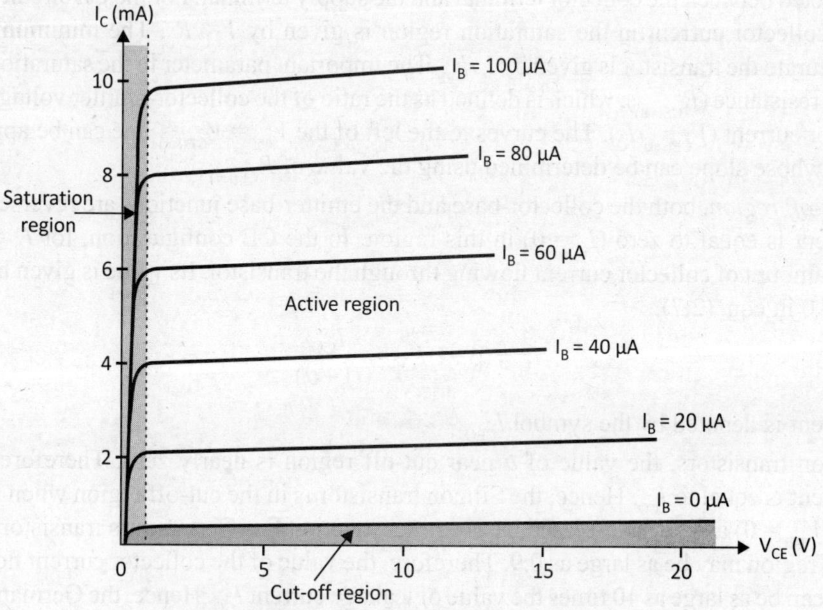

Fig. 2.9: Output characteristics of CE transistor

$$\beta_{ac} = \left(\frac{\Delta I_C}{\Delta I_B}\right)_{V_E = \text{constant}}$$

β_{ac} is referred to as the CE forward-current amplification factor and is also denoted by h_{fe}.

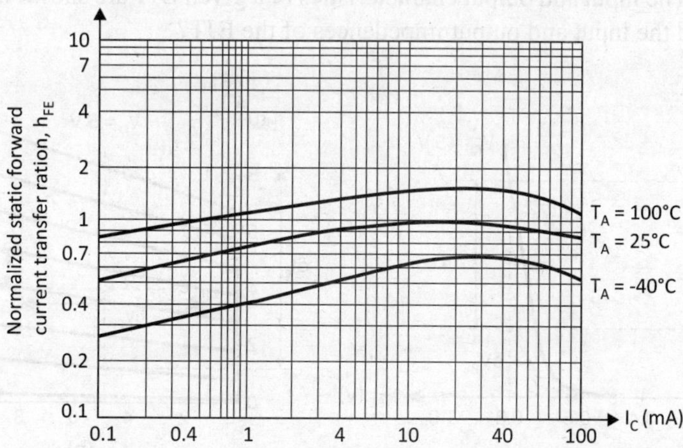

Fig. 2.10 : Variation of β with change in temperature and collector current

In the *saturation region*, both the collector-base and the emitter-base junctions are forward-biased. In thesaturation regionof the output characteristics, magnitudes of collector-base voltage (V_{CB}) and emitter-base voltage (V_{EB}) are equal to the cut-in voltages of the base-collector and the base-emitter junctions, respectively. Therefore, the value of V_{CE} (= V_{CB}-V_{BE}) is few tenths of volts in the saturation region. The region to the left of $V_{CE} = V_{CE(sat)}$ line in the output characteristics is the saturation region. In the saturation region, the value of the collector current is independent of the base current and depends on the value of resistor connected between the collector terminal and the supply terminal. For the CE circuit of Figure-2.5, the value of collector current in the saturation region is given by V_{CC}/R_L. The minimum base current required to saturate the transistor is given by I_C/h_{FE}. The important parameter in the saturation region is the CE saturation resistance ($R_{CE(sat)}$), which is defined as the ratio of the collector-emitter voltage at saturation to the collector current ($V_{CE(sat)}/I_C$). The curves to the left of the $V_{CE} = V_{CE(sat)}$ line can be approximated as straight lines whose slope can be determined using the value of $R_{CE(sat)}$.

In the *cut-off region*, both the collector-base and the emitter-base junctions are reverse-biased. Also, the base current is equal to zero ($I_B = 0$) in this region. In the CE configuration, for $I_B = 0$, there is a considerable amount of collector current flowing through the transistor. Its value is given by substituting the value $I_B = 0$ in eqn. (2.7).

$$I_C = (\beta + 1) I_{CO} = \frac{I_{CO}}{(1-\alpha)} \tag{2.8}$$

This current is denoted by the symbol I_{CEO}.

For Silicon transistors, the value of á near cut-off region is nearly zero. Therefore, the value of collector current is equal to I_{CO}. Hence, the Silicon transistor is in the cut-off region when $I_B = 0$ both for short circuit ($V_{BE} = 0$) and reverse-biased base-emitter junction.For Germanium transistors, the value of á near cut-off region may be as large as 0.9. Therefore, the value of the collector current flowing through the transistor can be as large as 10 times the value of leakage current I_{CO}. Hence, the Germanium transistor is not in the cut-off region for $I_B = 0$. A reverse bias needs to be applied to the base-emitter junction to bring the transistor to cut-off. The bias voltage applied should bring the value of collector current (I_C) less than or equal to reverse saturation current (I_{CO}). Reverse-bias voltage of 0.1 V is sufficient to reduce the collector current to this value. Therefore, the Germanium transistor is in cut-off region when $I_B = 0$ for reverse-biased base-emitter junction with V_{BE} greater than 0.1 V.

Example-2.1: The input and output characteristics of a given BJT are shown in Figure-2.11(a) and (b) respectively. Find the input and output impedances of the BJT?

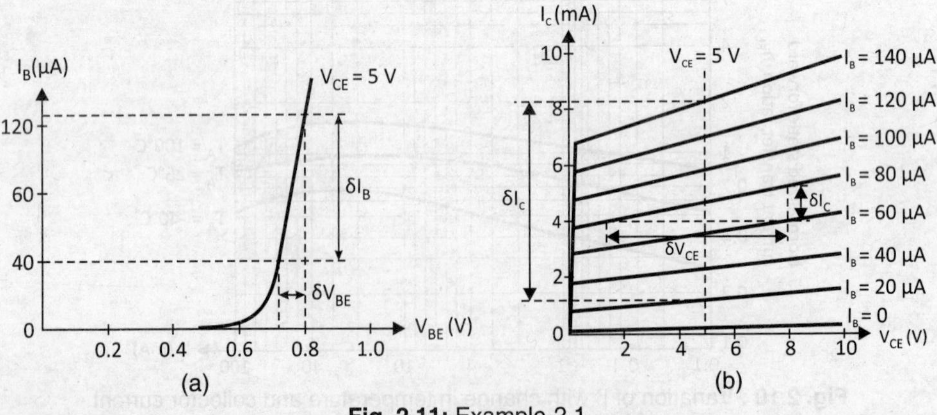

Fig. 2.11: Example-2.1

Solution: Using the linear portion of the input characteristics, for a change in V_{BE} of 85mV, the corresponding change of I_B is 88μA. Therefore,

$$R_{in} = \frac{\delta V_{BE}}{\delta I_B} = \frac{85\times10^{-3}}{88\times10^{-6}} = 966\Omega$$

From the output characteristics for $I_B = 80\mu A$, a change of V_{CE} from 8 to 1.4V results in a corresponding change in I_C from 5.2 to 4mA.

$$\delta V_{CE} = -6.6V \qquad \delta I_C = -1.2mA$$

$$R_{out} = \frac{\delta V_{CE}}{\delta I_C} = \frac{-6.6}{-1.2\times10^{-3}} = 5.5k\Omega$$

Example-2.2: (a) The DC current gain (β) of a BJT is 50. Determine (α).
(b) If for a BJT, $\alpha = 0.99$, what would be the value of β?

Solution: (a) Given that $\beta = 50$

Now, $\beta = \alpha / (1 - \alpha)$

Therefore, $\alpha = \dfrac{\beta}{\beta+1} = \dfrac{50}{51} = 0.98$

(b) $\beta = \alpha / (1 - \alpha) = 0.99/(1–0.99) = 99$

2.3.2 Common-Base Configuration

2.3.2.1 Input Characteristics

The *input characteristics* of common base configuration relate the emitter current (I_E) to the emitter-base voltage (V_{EB}) for various levels of the collector-base voltage (V_{CB}). Figure-2.12 shows the input characteristics of an NPN Silicon transistor connected in common-base configuration. The current I_E is considered negative as the current flows out of the emitter terminal. The input characteristics of PNP transistors are same with the reversal of polarity of the voltages and currents.

From the Figure 2.12, we can infer that there is a cut-in or threshold voltage below which the value of emitter current is very small. The typical values of cut-in voltage for Silicon and Germanium transistors are approximately 0.5 and 0.1 V, respectively. The curve for open condition is the same as that for a forward-biased PN junction diode. Another feature of the input characteristics is that for a fixed value of collector-base voltage (V_{CB}), the emitter-base voltage (V_{EB}) increases with increase in the emitter current (I_E). This behavior is the same as that of a PN junction diode in the forward-biased state. Since a small change in the emitter-base voltage causes a very large change in the emitter current, the input resistance (r_i) of the common-base configuration is very small. The value of r_i in the linear portion of the input characteristics is of the order of hundred ohms. Also, it can be interpreted from the curves shown in Figure-2.12 that for fixed value of emitter-base voltage (V_{EB}), the emitter current (I_E) increases with increase in the collector-base voltage (V_{CB}). This is because of the early effect phenomenon in transistors. This is explained in the following paragraph.

Early effect or the *base width modulation* phenomenon refers to the change in the width of the base region with the change in the collector-base voltage. As the emitter-base junction is forward-biased, the width of the depletion region is negligible. For the reverse-biased collector-base junction, the width of the depletion region is substantial. The width of the depletion region increases with increase in the reverse voltage at the collector-base junction. As the base region is lightly doped, the penetration of the depletion region is much larger in the base region than in the collector region. As a result of this the effective width of the base region decreases. This phenomenon of change in the effective width of the base region with change in the collector-base voltage is referred to as the early effect.

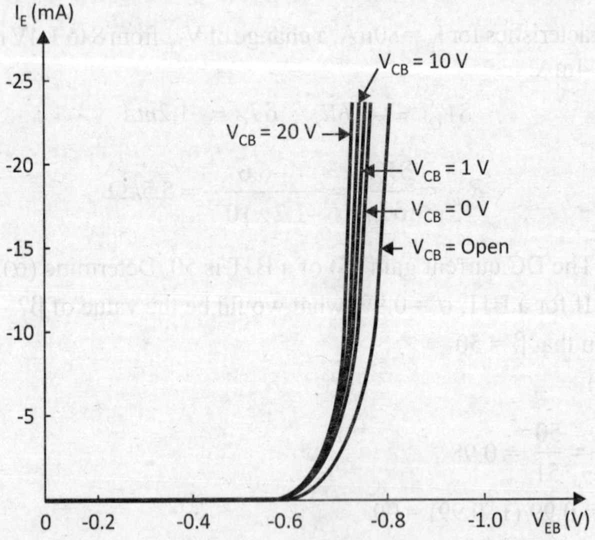

Fig. 2.12: Input characteristics of CB transistor

Due to the early effect, at increased reverse potential, the rate of recombination of the electrons and holes decreases. This results in increase in the value of . Also, the concentration of the minority carriers becomes zero at effective base width ($W_B{}^{¢}$) instead of W_B (Figure-2.13). Hence, the concentration gradient of minority carriers (P_n) is increased within the base region. As the emitter current is proportional to the gradient of minority carriers at the emitter junction (J_E), the value of emitter current also increases.

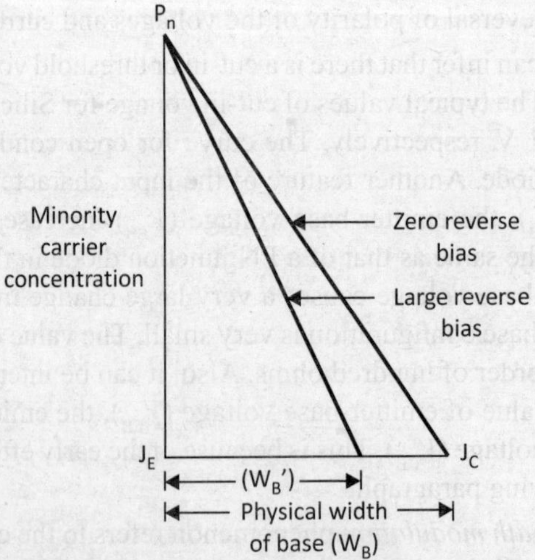

Fig. 2.13: Early effect

2.3.2.2 Output Characteristics

The *output characteristics*of commonbase configuration (Figure-2.14) relate the collector current (I_C) to the collector–base voltage (V_{CB}) for various levels of the emitter current (I_E). For a fixed value of emitter current, the collector current almost remains constant with changes in the value of the collector-base voltage. However, near the origin the collector current drops rapidly with the decrease in the value of the collector-base voltage. The output characteristics can be divided into three regions, namely the active region, the cut-off region and the saturation region.

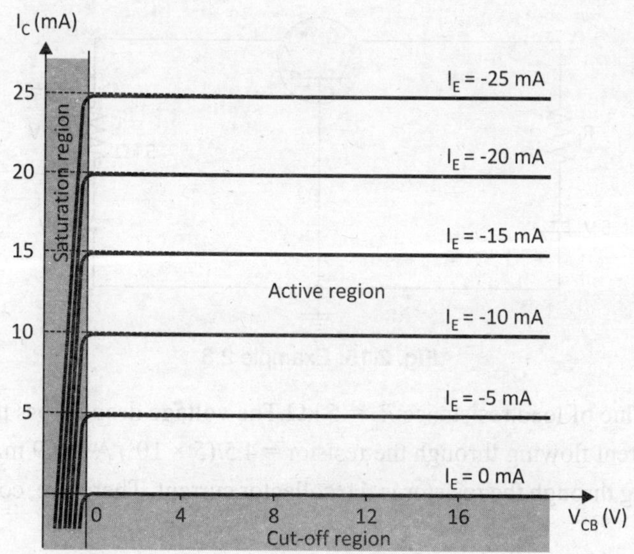

Fig. 2.14: Output characteristics of the common-base transistor

In the *active region*, the collector-base junction is reverse-biased while the emitter-base junction is forward-biased. The unshaded portion of Figure-2.14 corresponds to the active region. The collector current (I_C) is almost independent of the collector-base voltage (V_{CB}) and depends only on the value of the emitter current (I_E). Therefore, the output characteristics curves are straight parallel lines. As we can see from the figure, the collector current increases slowly with the collector-base voltage (around 0.5%). This is because of the early effect phenomenon. But for most applications, this increase can be ignored, and the collector current can be considered to be constant for a fixed value of emitter current. The output resistance (r_o) offered by the CB-configuration is very high as a very large change in the collector-base voltage produces a very small change in the collector current. When the emitter-base junction is open-circuited; the emitter current is zero. The collector current that flows in this condition is the reverse saturation current (I_{CO}). This condition corresponds to the lowest curve in the output characteristics. The current I_{CO} is of the order of few microamperes for Germanium transistors and several nanoamperes for Silicon transistors.

In the *cut-off region*, both the collector-base and the emitter-base junctions of the transistor are reverse-biased. The region below the $I_E = 0$ curve corresponds to the cut-off region. In this region, the transistor acts as an open circuit and does not conduct any current. As mentioned before, the value of collector current at $I_E = 0$ is equal to the reverse saturation current (I_{CO}). I_{CO} increases rapidly with increase in temperature. I_{CO} is also referred to as I_{CBO}, the collector current with base open-circuited. I_{CBO} can be ignored in most transistor applications except for power transistors and transistors operating at high temperatures.

In the *saturation region*, both the collector-base and the emitter-base junctions are forward-biased. The region to the left of $V_{CB} = 0$ line corresponds to the saturation region. As is clear from the figure, the collector-base voltage (V_{CB}) is slightly negative in the saturation region. This is because the collector-base junction is also forward-biased. There is an exponential increase in the collector current with a small increase in the collector-base voltage.

Example-2.3: For the common-base configuration shown in Figure-2.15, determine the values of base current (I_B), emitter current (I_E) and collector current (I_C).It is given that the value of a is 0.9

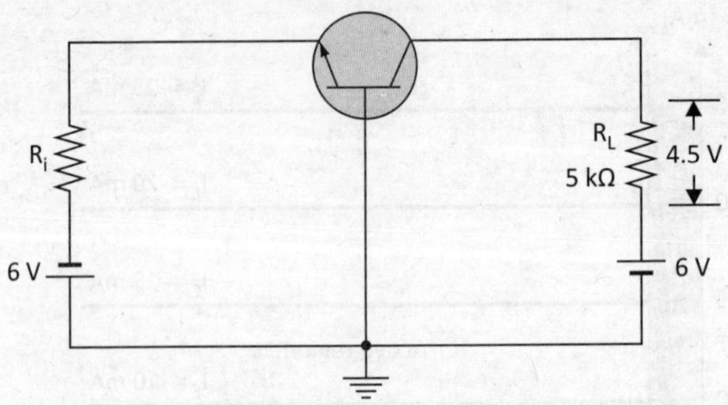

Fig. 2.15: Example 2.3

Solution: The value of load resistance R_L = 5 kΩ.The voltage drop across the resistor is 4.5 V.

Therefore, the current flowing through the resistor = $4.5/(5 \times 10^3)$ A = 0.9 mA.

The current flowing through the resistor is the collector current. Therefore, collector current is equal to 0.9 mA.

The emitter current is $I_C/a = 0.9 \times 10^{-3}/0.9$ A = 1 mA.

The base current is $I_E – I_C = (1\times 10^{-3} – 0.9 \times 10^{-3})$ = 100 μA.

2.3.3 Common-Collector Configuration

2.3.3.1 Input Characteristics

The *input characteristics* of common collector configuration relate the base current (I_B) to the base-collector voltage (V_{BC}) for different values of the emitter-collector voltage (V_{EC}). The input characteristics for an NPN transistor connected in CC-configuration are shown in Figure-2.16.

2.3.3.2 Output Characteristics

Output characteristics of the common collector configuration relate the emitter current (I_E) to the emitter–collector voltage (V_{EC}) for different values of base current (I_B). Figure-2.17 shows the output characteristics for an NPN transistor connected in the CC-configuration. The characteristics are similar to that for the CE configuration.

Current gain in case of common collector configuration is denoted by Gamma (g). For any transistor configuration, the emitter, collector and base currents are related to each other by eqn. 2.9.

$$I_E = I_C + I_B \tag{2.9}$$

Relationship between collector and emitter currents is given by eqn. 2.10.

$$I_C = I_{CO} + \alpha I_E \tag{2.10}$$

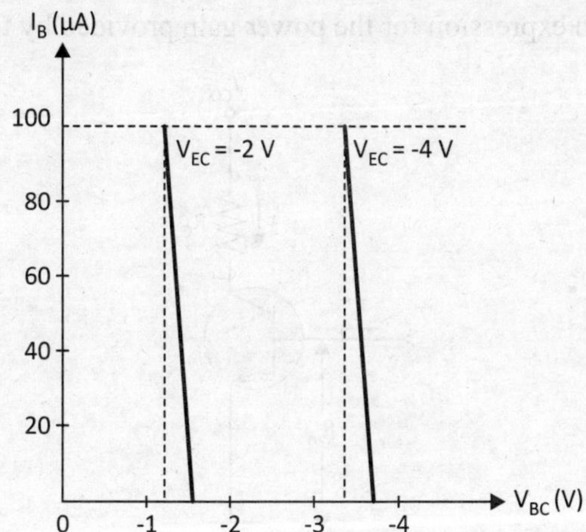

Fig. 2.16: Input characteristics of the CC configuration

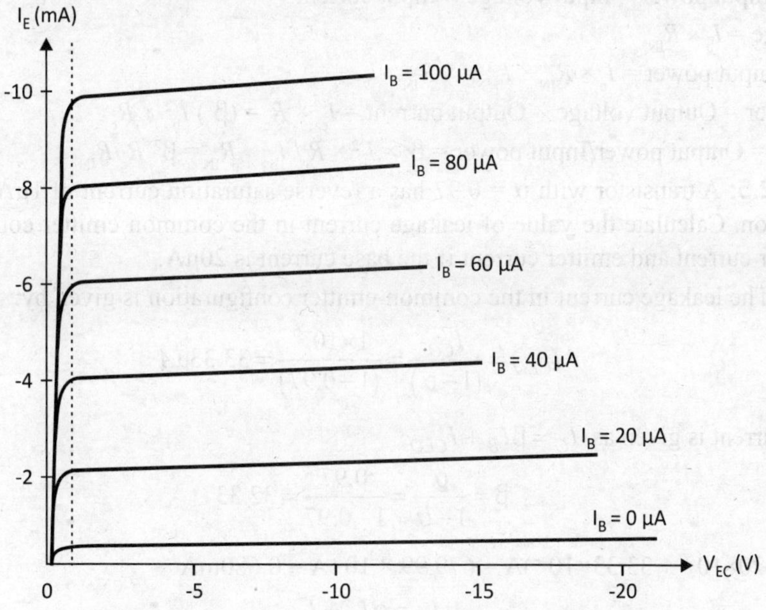

Fig. 2.17: Output characteristics of the CC configuration

Combining eqns. (2.9) and (2.10) we get,

$$I_E = \frac{I_B}{(1-\alpha)} + \frac{I_{CO}}{(1-\alpha)} \tag{2.11}$$

Now, $\gamma = \beta + 1$. If we substitutein $\gamma = (\beta+1) = 1/(1-\alpha)$ in eqn. 2.11, then eqn. (2.11) becomes

$$I_C = \gamma I_B + \gamma I_{CO} \tag{2.12}$$

Example-2.4: Derive an expression for the power gain provided by the transistor in Figure-2.18.

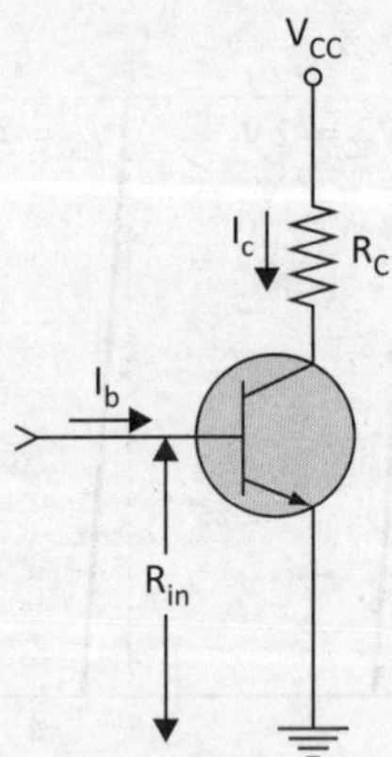

Fig. 2.18: Example-2.4

Solution: Input power = Input voltage × Input current.

Input voltage = $I_b \times R_{IN}$.

Therefore, Input power = $I_b \times R_{IN} \times I_b^2 = \times R_{IN}$.

Output power = Output voltage × Output current = $I_c^2 \times R_c = (\beta^2)\, I_b^2 \times R_c$

Power gain = Output power/Input power = $\beta^2 \times I_b^2 \times R_c / I_b^2 \times R_{IN} = \beta^{2\prime} R_c / R_{IN}$

Example-2.5: A transistor with $\alpha = 0.97$ has a reverse saturation current of 1μA in the common base configuration. Calculate the value of leakage current in the common emitter configuration. Also find the collector current and emitter current if the base current is 20μA.

Solution: The leakage current in the common-emitter configuration is given by:

$$I_{CEO} = \frac{I_{CO}}{(1-\alpha)} = \frac{1\times10^{-6}}{(1-0.97)} = 33.33\mu A$$

Collector current is given as $I_C = \beta I_B + I_{CEO}$

$$\beta = \frac{\alpha}{1-\alpha} = \frac{0.97}{1-0.97} = 32.33$$

$I_c = (32.33\times20\times10^{-6} + 33.33\times10^{-6})A = 679.99\times10^{-6}A = 0.680mA$

$$I_C = \alpha I_E + I_{CO}$$

$$I_E = \frac{I_C - I_{CO}}{\alpha} = \left(\frac{0.680\times10^{-3} - 1\times10^{-6}}{0.97}\right)A = 0.7mA$$

2.4 EBERS–MOLL MODEL OF TRANSISTORS

Ebers–Moll transistor model was developed by Ebers and Moll in the year 1954. It is also known as the coupled diode model. Ebers-Moll model is a simple and elegant way of representing the transistor as a circuit modeland is applicable for all four regions of transistor operation. The model involves two ideal diodes and two ideal current sources. Figures-2.19(a) and (b) show the Ebers-Moll model for the NPN and the PNP transistor, respectively.

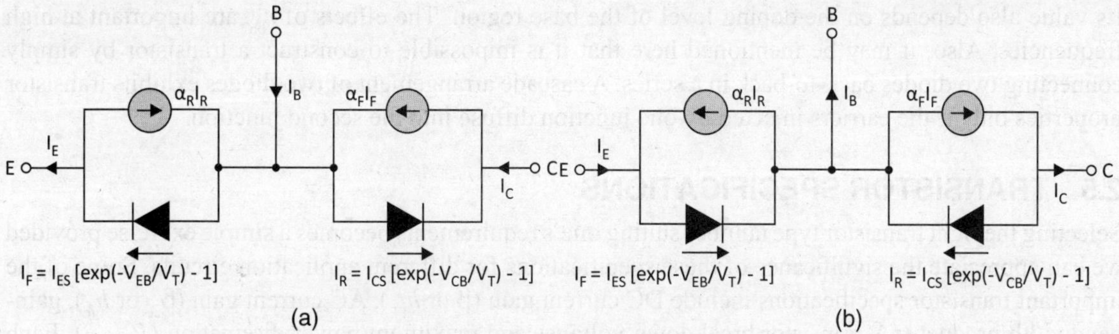

Fig. 2.19: Ebers–Moll model for (a) NPN transistor and (b) PNP transistor

To understand the model, let us consider the generalized current equation of a transistor given by eqn. 2.13.

$$I_C = I_{CO}\left[1 - \exp\left(-\frac{V_{CB}}{V_T}\right)\right] + \alpha I_E \tag{2.13}$$

Eqn. (2.13) can be rewritten for the active region as eqn. 2.14.

$$I_C = I_{CS}\left[1 - \exp\left(-\frac{V_{CB}}{V_T}\right)\right] + \alpha_F I_E \tag{2.14}$$

where a_F is the CB current gain in the normal operating mode (base-emitter junction is forward-biased and base-collector junction is reverse-biased) and I_{CS} the saturation current of the base-collector diode. For the reverse-active region the Eq. (2.13) can be rewritten as eqn. 2.15.

$$I_E = I_{ES}\left[1 - \exp\left(-\frac{V_{EB}}{V_T}\right)\right] + \alpha_R I_C \tag{2.15}$$

where a_R is the CB current gain in the inverting operating mode (base–emitter junction is reverse-biased and the base–collector junction is forward-biased) and I_{ES} the saturation current of the base–emitter diode. The two diodes shown in Figure-2.19 represent the base-emitter and the base-collector diodes and are connected back-to-back. The reverse saturation currents through the base-emitter and the base–collector diodes are I_{ES} and I_{CS}, respectively. Two current sources are in shunt with the diodes and their values depend upon the current flowing through the diodes. They quantify the transport of minority carriers through the base region, that is, they account for the minority-carrier transport across the base.

From Figure-2.19, the equations for the collector, emitter and base currents in the Ebers–Moll model are given by eqns. 2.16, 2.17 and 2.18.

$$I_C = -I_R + \alpha_F I_F \tag{2.16}$$

$$I_E = I_F - \alpha_R I_R \tag{2.17}$$

$$I_B = (1 - \alpha_R)I_R + (1 - \alpha_F)I_F \tag{2.18}$$

$$I_{ES}\alpha_F = I_{CS}\alpha_R$$

The expression above is referred to as the *reciprocity relation*.

In the above discussion, we have not considered the effect of base-spreading resistance ($r_{bb'}$) of a transistor. It is the resistance offered by the base region to the flow of current through it. Typical value of $r_{bb'}$ is of the order of 100 Ω and it increases with the increase in the reverse-bias collector-base voltage.

Its value also depends on the doping level of the base region. The effects of $r_{bb'}$ are important at high frequencies. Also, it may be mentioned here that it is impossible to construct a transistor by simply connecting two diodes back-to-back in a series. A cascade arrangement of two diodes exhibits transistor properties only if the carriers injected by one junction diffuse into the second junction.

2.5 TRANSISTOR SPECIFICATIONS

Selecting the right transistor type number suiting one's requirements becomes a simple exercise provided we can appreciate the significance of these specifications for different application circuits. Some of the important transistor specifications include DC current gain (β or h_{FE}), AC current gain (β_{ac} or h_{fe}), gain-bandwidth product (f_T), transistor breakdown voltages and maximum power dissipation ($P_{D(max)}$). Each of these is briefly described in the following paragraphs.

2.5.1 DC Current Gain (β or h_{FE})

The parameter β (also denoted as h_{FE}) is called the *DC current gain*, that is, the ratio of the collector current to the base current of the transistor in common-emitter configuration. It specifies the base current required to keep the transistor conducting for a given collector current. It is an important parameter for switching transistors as it tells about the minimum base current required to drive the transistor to the saturation region for a certain collector current. A transistor with smaller h_{FE} needs a harder base drive for a given collector current.

2.5.2 AC Current Gain (β_{ac} or h_{FE})

AC current gain is defined as the ratio of the change in the collector current to a small change in the base current for a constant collector-emitter voltage. It is expressed by eqn. 2.19.

$$h_{fe} = \left(\frac{\Delta I_C}{\Delta I_B}\right)_{V_{CE}=\text{constant}} \tag{2.19}$$

2.5.3 Gain-Bandwidth Product (f_T)

The gain-bandwidth product (f_T) tells us about the high frequency response of the transistor. It is the frequency for which gain on the high-frequency side falls to unity or 0 dB. It is an important parameter that needs to be considered when the transistor is to be used for IF/RFapplications.

2.5.4 Transistor Breakdown Voltages

There are two types of breakdown phenomena possible in a transistor, namely the avalanche breakdown and reach-through phenomenon. The breakdown voltages associated with the avalanche multiplication are V_{CEO} and V_{CBO}. V_{CEO} is the maximum voltage that can be applied across the collector-emitter junction with the base open in the CE configuration. It is the worst case of collector-emitter breakdown voltage and is a very important specification particularly in switching transistors used in switched-mode power supplies. This parameter is often specified in different ways. Quite often, V_{CER} (collector-emitter breakdown voltage with a specified resistance typically of the value of 100–200 Ω connected between the base and emitter) and V_{CES} (collector-emitter breakdown voltage with base shorted to the emitter) ratings are also given in addition to the V_{CEO} rating of the switching transistors. It may be mentioned that V_{CEO} is the lowest of all and if the design is such that the V_{CEO} rating is not exceeded, the possibility of collector-emitter junction breakdown gets eliminated. V_{CBO} is the reverse output breakdown voltage when the transistor is connected in the CB configuration with the emitter terminal open.

The second mechanism that leads to transistor breakdown is the reach-through or the punch-through effect. It results from the increase in the width of the collector-base junction depletion region with increase in the reverse voltage. As the base region is very thin, even at moderate values of reverse voltages, the depletion region spreads completely across the base and reaches the emitter junction. This results in large flow of emitter current leading to transistor breakdown. The collector-base breakdown voltage due to the punch-through effect is independent of the transistor configuration. The lower of the breakdown voltages either due to avalanche or reach-through breakdown is considered as the maximum voltage limit.

2.5.5 Peak Collector Current [$I_{C(max)}$]

It is the peak collector current rating of the transistor. It is specified for continuous or pulsed mode of operation of a transistor.

2.5.6 Power Dissipation [$P_{D(max)}$]

It is the maximum power dissipation capability of a transistor. The curve for maximum power dissipation can be plotted using eqn. 2.20.

$$P_{D(max)} = V_{CE} \times I_C \tag{2.20}$$

The maximum collector current, collector-emitter voltage and the power ratings limit the active region of operation of a transistor as shown in Figure-2.20. $V_{CE(sat)}$ specifies the minimum collector-emitter voltage required to drive the transistor in the active region. The area enclosed by dotted lines represents the safe operating area of the transistor.

$P_{D(max)}$ is usually specified at a given ambient temperature and it should be derated at higher temperatures as per the derating curve supplied by the manufacturer. The use of heat sink results in increased power dissipation capability of the transistor. The actual dissipation capability can be determined from known values of maximum operating junction temperature, ambient temperature and the associated thermal resistances. There are two types of thermal resistances associated with a transistor: the junction-to-case thermal resistance and the case-to-ambient thermal resistance. The former tells about how effectively heat is conducted away from the junction to the case, and the latter tells about how effectively the heat is conducted away from the case to ambient.

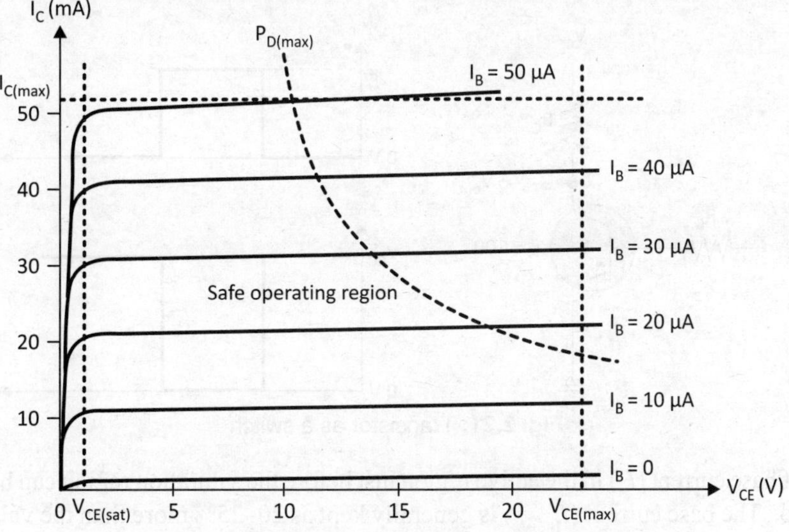

Fig. 2.20: Maximum ratings of a transistor

The case-to-ambient thermal resistance depends upon the transistor's package size. It is, for instance 300°C/W for TO-18 package, 150°C/W for TO-5 and TO-39 packages, 60°C/W for TO-66 package and only 30°C/W for TO-3 package. The effective case-to-ambient thermal resistance can be reduced by using an appropriate heat sink that basically increases the effective radiating area.

All of the above mentioned specifications are not equally important for all application requirements. Table-2.2 lists some typical applications and the corresponding transistor parameters that would significantly affect the choice criteria.

Table 2.2: Typical transistor applications and important specifications

S. No.	Application requirements	Important specifications
1.	General purpose, low-level amplifier and switching transistors	h_{FE}, $I_{C(max)}$, f_T, V_{CEO}
2.	Power-switching Applications	V_{CEO}, V_{CBO}, h_{FE}, $I_{C(max)}$, $f_{o(max)}$
3.	Low-level IF/RF amplification	$I_{C(max)}$, f_T, V_{CEO}
4.	Audio amplification	h_{FE}, $I_{C(max)}$, $P_{D(max)}$, V_{CEO}
5.	High-voltage transistors	V_{CEO}, V_{CBO}, h_{FE}, $I_{C(max)}$, f_T

2.6 BJT AS A SWITCH

Other than their use in amplifier circuits, another major application of transistors is their use as switching devices in computers and other control applications. Figure-2.21 shows the use of a transistor as an inverting switch; that is, the transistor output is at logic-HIGH level for a logic-LOW input applied at its base terminal and the output is at logic-LOW level for a logic-HIGH input. When a logic-LOW input is applied, the transistor is in the cut-off region and acts as an open switch. It is in the saturation region for a logic-HIGH input and acts as a closed switch.

While designing the transistor-based switch, the designer should ensure that the transistor is heavily saturated for a logic-HIGH input signal. The saturation collector current ($I_{C(sat)}$) is given by the eqn. 2.21.

$$I_{C(sat)} = \frac{V_{CC}}{R_C} \tag{2.21}$$

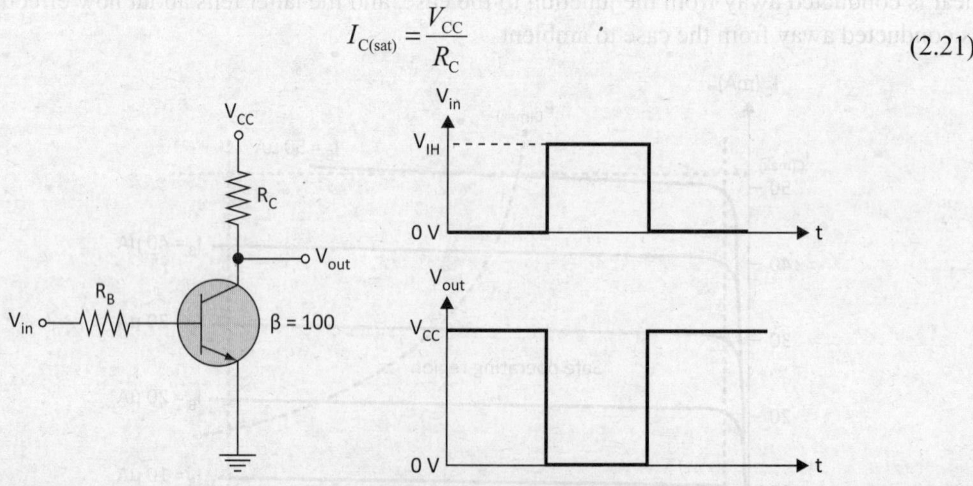

Fig. 2.21: Transistor as a switch

The level of base current (I_B) in the active region just before the saturation region can be approximated by $I_{B\,(sat)} = I_{C(sat)}/\beta$. The base current ($I_{B(max)}$) is generally kept as 20–25% more than the value of $I_{B(sat)}$ so as to ensure that the transistor is in deep saturation. Therefore, the ratio of the collector current to the base current when the logic-HIGH input is applied is less than the transistor current gain (β). The minimum value of input voltage (V_{IH}) required to drive the transistor into deep saturation so that it acts as a closed switch is given by eqn. 2.22.

$$V_{IH} = I_{B(max)} R_B + V_{BE} \tag{2.22}$$

The resistance between the emitter and the collector terminals when the transistor is in saturation is given by eqn. 2.23.

$$R_{sat} = \frac{V_{CE(sat)}}{I_{C(sat)}} \tag{2.23}$$

The resistance offered by the transistor switch when in saturation is equal to R_{sat}. The value of R_{sat} is in the range of few ohms to few tens of ohms. For input voltage equal to zero, the collector current (I_C) is equal to the leakage current (I_{CO}), which is negligible. Therefore, the collector voltage is at the logic-HIGH level and the collector-emitter resistance is very high in the range of several hundreds of kilo-ohms to few mega-ohms. The circuit thus acts as an open circuit.

2.6.1 Transistor Switching Delays

Figure-2.22 shows the response of a transistor switch when an input pulse is applied to it. When the input voltage is 0 V, the transistor is in the cut-off region. It is in the saturation region when the input voltage is at the voltage level V_{IH}. When the input voltage changes from 0 V to V_{IH}, the transistor does not immediately respond to the input signal and there is a time delay before the collector current reaches the saturation value. The time delay between the time the input pulse is applied to the time the collector current rises to 10% of the final value is called the *delay time* (t_d).

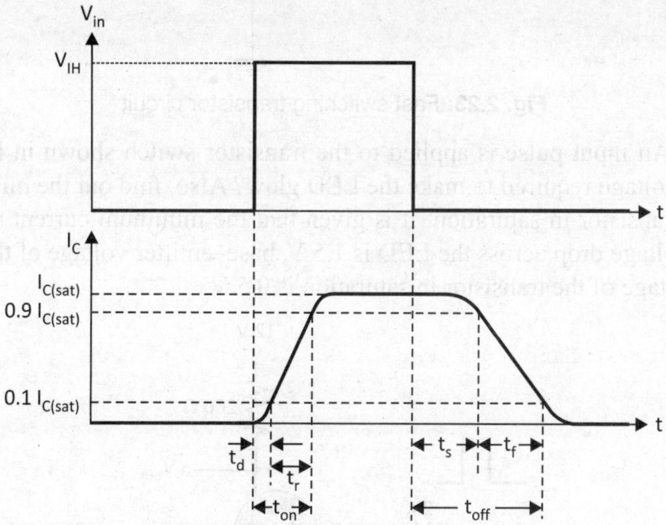

Fig. 2.22: Transistor switching times

The time required for the collector current to rise from 10% to 90% of the final value is called the *rise time* (t_r). The total time ($t_d + t_r$) is known as the *turn-on time* (t_{on}) of the transistor. Delay time (t_d) is contributed by three factors: First, the time required to charge the emitter-junction capacitance so that the transistor is brought from the cut-off to the active region; second, the time required to move the carriers from the base junction to the collector junction; third, the time required by the collector current to rise to 10% of its final value. Rise time (t_r) is due to the time taken by the collector current to traverse the active region.

When the input signal returns to 0 V, again there is a delay between the transition of the input waveform and the time when the collector current reduces to zero. The time interval between the input pulse transition to the time when the collector current drops to 90% of its value at saturation is called the *storage time* (t_s). Storage time delay is because the transistor in saturation has a saturation charge of excess minority carriers stored in the base region and the transistor cannot respond until this excess charge has been removed. *Fall time* (t_f) is the time required by the collector current to fall from 90% to 10% of the saturation level. Fall time is caused due to the time required by the collector current to traverse the active region. *Turn-off time* (t_{off}) is defined as the sum of the storage time (t_s) and the fall time (t_f).

When the transistor is used in fast switching applications; a capacitor (C) is added across the base resistor (R_B) to reduce the storage time (Figure-2.23). The capacitor will act as a short circuit when switching occurs and an impulse current will flow out of the base at the negative transition of the input pulse facilitating rapid removal of stored minority carrier charge.

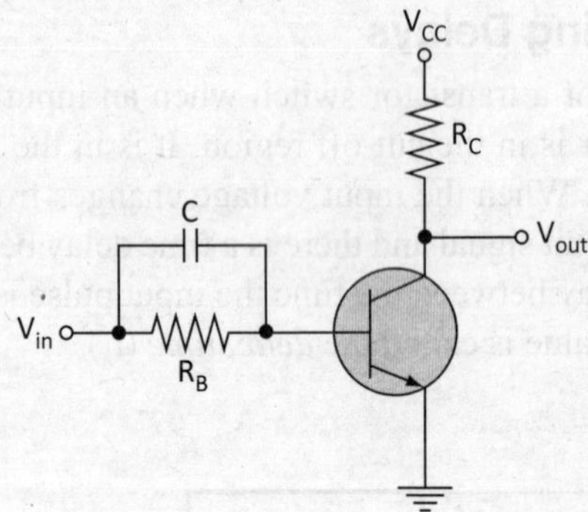

Fig. 2.23: Fast switching transistor circuit

Example-2.6: An input pulse is applied to the transistor switch shown in Figure-2.24. What is the minimum input voltage required to make the LED glow? Also, find out the minimum input voltage required to put the transistor in saturation. It is given that the minimum current required by the LED to glow is 10 mA, voltage drop across the LED is 1.5 V, base–emitter voltage of the transistor is 0.7 V, collector–emitter voltage of the transistor in saturation is 0.5 V.

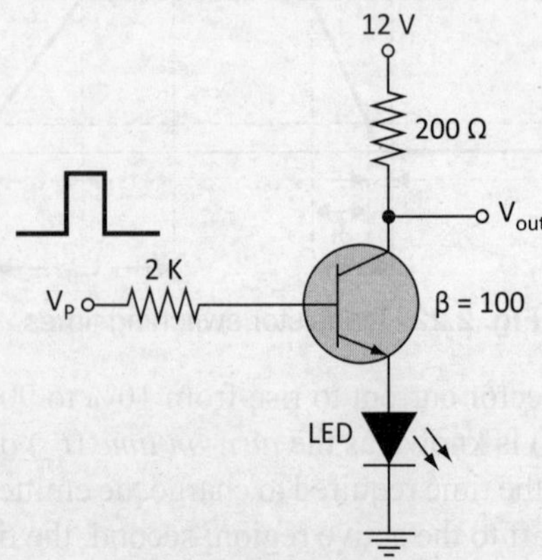

Fig. 2.24: Example-2.6

Solution: The minimum current required to make the LED glow is 10 mA and the voltage drop across the LED is 1.5 V. Therefore, the collector current required to make the LED glow is 10 mA. As β of the transistor is 100, therefore the base current (I_B) required is given by:

$10/(100 \times 10^{-3})$A = 100 µA

Applying Kirchhoff's voltage law to the base-emitter loop, we get:

$V_P - 2 \times 10^3 \times 100 \times 10^{-6} - 0.7 - 1.5 = 0$

Therefore, $V_P = 2.4$ V

Therefore, the minimum voltage required to make the LED glow is 2.4 V

When the transistor is in saturation, $V_{CE(sat)} = 0.5$ V. Therefore, applying Kirchhoff's voltage law to the collector-emitter loop, we get:

$12 - 200 \times I_{C(sat)} - 0.5 - 1.5 = 0$ or $I_{C(sat)} = 50$ mA

The value of $I_{B(sat)}$ corresponding to this value of $I_{C(sat)}$ is therefore given by:

$50/(100 \times 10^{-3})$ A = 500 µA.

The value of $I_{B(max)}$ is kept 1.25 times this value of $I_{B(sat)}$ to ensure that the transistor is in saturation. Therefore, $I_{B(max)} = 625$ µA

Applying Kirchhoff's voltage law to the base-emitter loop and solving for V_P, we get:

$V_P = 0.7 + 1.5 + 2 \times 10^3 \times 625 \times 10^{-6} = 3.45$ V

The input voltage required to put the transistor into saturation is 3.45 V

Example-2.7: Figure-2.25(a) shows a simple logic circuit. The input voltages V_3 and V_4 applied to the circuit are plotted in Figure-2.25(b). Draw the output waveform across resistor R_5. Assume $V_{CE(sat)} = 0$.

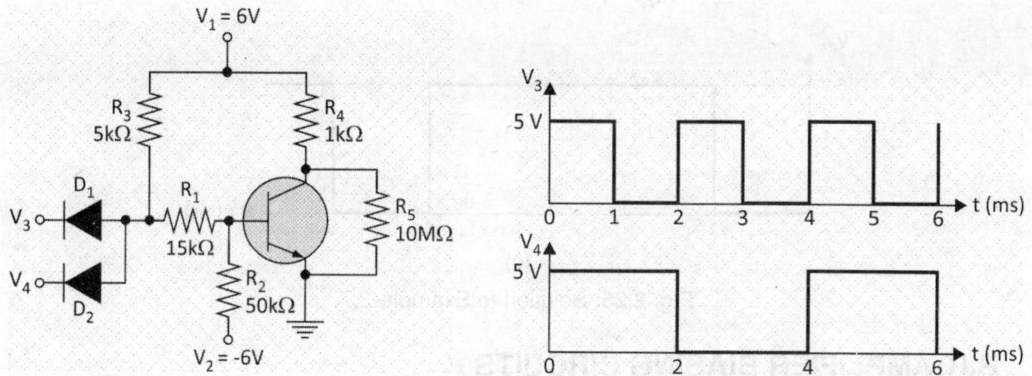

Fig. 2.25 (a): (a) Logic circuit for example 2.7; (b) Input waveforms applied to the circuit in

Solution: The waveform across R_5 is same as the collector-emitter voltage. shows the output waveform. This is explained as follows. When either or both of the inputs are low; then one or both of the diodes D_1 and D_2 are conducting. Therefore, the voltage at the R_1–R_3 node is 0.7 V. The transistor is not-conducting and the collector-emitter voltage is 6V. This explains the 6V output across R_5 from 1 to 4 ms and from 5 ms onwards.

When both inputs are high; then diodes D_1 and D_2 are not conducting and the base voltage is determined by voltages V_1 and V_2 and resistors R_1, R_2 and R_3. The base voltage can be determined using superposition theorem.

Assuming $V_1 = 0$ [Figure-2.26(a)], the voltage due to V_2 at base terminal is given by:

$$V_{B2}=-(5+15)\times\frac{6}{5+15+50}=-20\times\frac{6}{70}=-1.7\text{ V}$$

Assuming $V_2 = 0$ [Figure-2.26(b)], the voltage due to V_1 at base terminal is given by:

$$V_{B1}=50\times\frac{6}{5+15+50}=50\times\frac{6}{70}=4.3\text{ V}$$

Base voltage = 4.3 V – 1.7 V = 2.6 V

This base voltage drives the transistor into saturation. Since the collector-emitter voltage when the transistor is in saturation is given to be zero;the waveform across R_5, which is same as that of the collector-emitter voltage of the transistor, is also zero [Figure-2.26(c)].

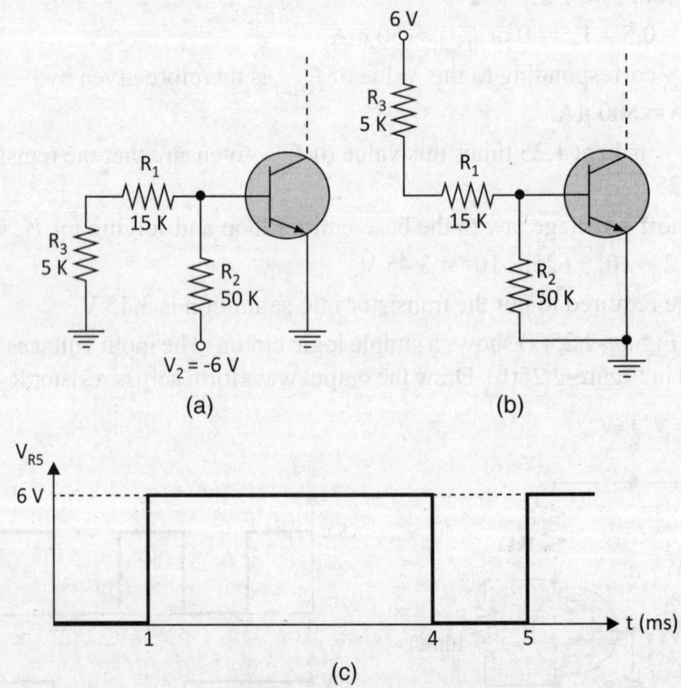

Fig. 2.26: Solution to Example-2.7

2.7 BJT AMPLIFIER BIASING CIRCUITS

In a BJT-based amplifier circuit,the BJT is operated in the active region. This is done using a transistor-biasing circuit. This section focuses on the importance of transistor biasing and the various transistor-basing configurations including fixed bias, emitter bias, collector-to-base bias and voltage-divider bias with emitter bias. The stability offered by each of the configurations against variations in temperature and other parameters and the phenomenon of thermal runaway are covered in subsequent sections of the chapter.

2.7.1 Operating Point

The first step in designing a transistor amplifier is to design a circuit so as to enable the transistor to operate in its linear active region. This is done by using external components such as resistors and capacitors and applying DC voltages to the transistor so as to establish proper collector current (I_C) and collector-emitter voltage (V_{CE}) across the transistor. This process is referred to as *transistor biasing* and the circuit used for transistor biasing is called a *biasing circuit*. Transistor biasing is done so that the transistor amplifies the input signal linearly and without distortion. There are four conditions that should be met for a transistor to act as a faithful amplifier.

1. The emitter-base junction should be forward-biased, and the collector-base junction should be reverse-biased for all levels of input signal. For the emitter-base junction to be forward-biased, the base–emitter voltage (V_{BE}) should not fall below 0.3 V for Germanium transistors and below 0.7 V for Silicon transistors for all values of input signal.
2. The collector-emitter voltage (V_{CE}) should not fall below the knee voltage ($V_{CE(sat)}$) for any part of the input signal. For V_{CE} less than the $V_{CE(sat)}$ (0.5 V for Germanium transistor and 1.0 V for Silicon transistor), the collector-base junction is not properly reverse-biased.
3. The value of collector current (I_C) when no signal is applied should at least be equal to the maximum collector current due to signal alone.
4. The maximum ratings of the transistor ($I_{C(max)}$, $V_{CE(max)}$ and $P_{D(max)}$) should not be exceeded at any value of the input signal.

The DC collector current (I_C) and the collector-emitter voltage (V_{CE}) when no input signal is applied is referred to as the *operating point*. Since the operating point is a fixed point on the output characteristics of the transistor; it is also referred to as the *quiescent point* (Q-point). Judicious selection of the operating point is important for faithful amplification of the input signal. Figure-2.27 shows the output characteristics of a common-emitter amplifier with four different operating points. The functioning of the transistor amplifier for each of these operating points is discussed in the following paragraphs. This will help in understanding the importance of selecting the correct operating point.

Operating point A represents a condition when no bias is applied to the transistor. The transistor is in the cut-off region and there is no collector current through the transistor. Also, the base-emitter voltage is zero. It does not satisfy any of the conditions necessary for faithful amplification and hence A is not a suitable operating point.

Point B would allow some positive and negative variations of the output signal, but the peak-to-peak output voltage is limited due to the proximity of the operating point to the knee point ($V_{CE(sat)}$). Also, non-linearities will be introduced in the amplification as the spacing between the I_B curves is not linear near the knee region.

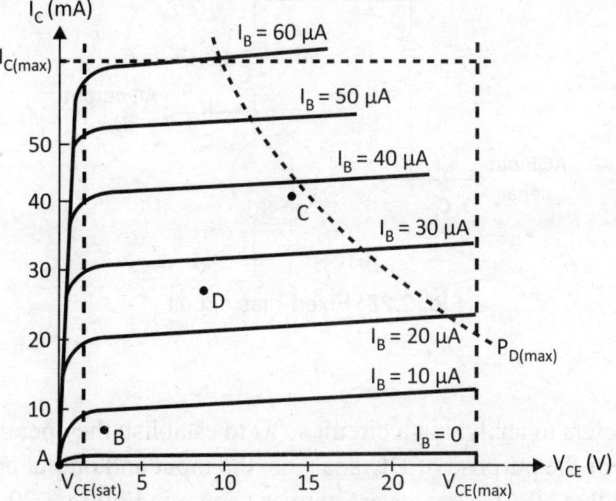

Fig. 2.27: Selecting a suitable operating point

Point C is too close to the $P_{D(max)}$ curve of the transistor. Therefore, the output voltage swing in the positive direction is limited.

Point D is located in the middle of the active region of the transistor characteristics. It will allow both the positive and the negative excursions in the output signal. It also provides linear gain and largest possible output voltage and current swing. Therefore, the operating point for a transistor amplifier is selected to be in the middle of the active region.

It may be mentioned here that after having selected the operating point, the effect of temperature should also be taken into account. A rise in the temperature results in increase in the value of transistor gain (*b*) and the leakage current (I_{CO}). This results in a shift in the operating point. The biasing network should also provide temperature stability so that there is minimum variation in the operating point with change in temperature.

2.7.2 Common-Emitter configuration

In this section, we shall discuss different biasing circuits for common-emitter configuration as it is the most popular of the three transistor amplifier configurations because of its capability to provide considerable current gain as well as voltage gain. There are several common-emitter biasing circuits, namely the fixed bias, emitter bias, voltage-divider bias with emitter bias and collector-to-base bias circuits. Different biasing circuits are discussed in detail in this section in terms of DC analysis, load-line analysis and merits and demerits of each of the configurations.

2.7.2.1 Fixed bias

Consider the circuit shown in Figure-2.28. It is referred to as the *fixed-bias circuit* and is one of the simplest possible transistor-biasing circuits. The biasing components include two resistors, base resistor (R_B) and collector resistor (R_C), and a supply voltage (V_{CC}). The base-emitter junction gets forward-biased through V_{CC} and R_B. The supply voltage also reverse-biases the collector-base junction through resistor R_C. Resistor R_B is of the order of few hundreds of kilo-ohms whereas typical value of R_C is of few kilo-ohms. Capacitors C_i and C_o are referred to as the input and the output coupling capacitors, respectively.

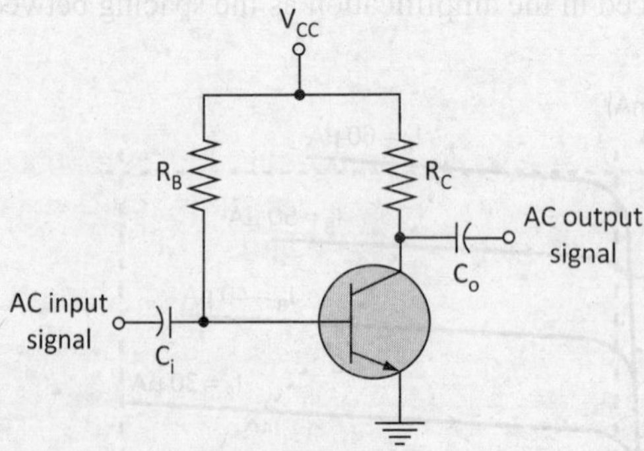

Fig. 2.28: Fixed-bias circuit

DC Analysis

DC analysis of a circuit refers to analyzing a circuit so as to establish the operating point in the absence of any input AC signal. For the purpose of DC analysis, the input and output capacitors are considered as open and it is assumed that all AC sources are zero as shown in Figure-2.29.

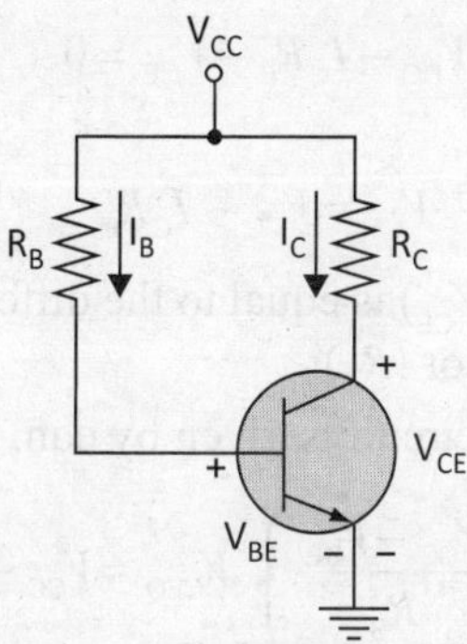

Fig. 2.29: DC equivalent of fixed-bias circuit

The base-emitter section of the fixed-bias circuit comprises the supply voltage (V_{CC}), the base resistor (R_B) and the transistor base-emitter junction. Base current (I_B) can be determined by applying Kirchhoff'svoltage law to the base-emitter section and is given by eqn. (2.24).

$$V_{CC} - I_B R_B - V_{BE} = 0 \tag{2.24}$$

Rearranging the terms in eqn. (2.24), we get the value of base current (I_B) as:

$$I_B = \frac{V_{CC} - V_{BE}}{R_B} \tag{2.25}$$

From eqn. (2.25) it is clear that the base current (I_B) is given by ratio of the voltage drop across the base resistor (R_B) to the value of R_B. The value of base-emitter voltage (V_{BE}) is small as compared to the supply voltage (V_{CC}) and hence can be neglected without causing much error. Therefore, eqn. (2.25) can be approximated as

$$I_B \cong \frac{V_{CC}}{R_B}$$

The collector current (I_C) of the transistor is directly related to the base current (I_B) and is expressed as:

$$I_C = \beta I_B$$

That is,

$$I_C = \beta\left(\frac{V_{CC} - V_{BE}}{R_B}\right) \cong \frac{\beta V_{CC}}{R_B} \tag{2.26}$$

Where *b*is the transistor current gain.

We can infer from eqn. (2.34) that the collector current (I_C) is dependent on the supply voltage (V_{CC}) and the base resistor (R_B) and is independent of the value of collector resistor (R_C). Any change in the value of R_C will not have any effect on the base current or the collector current as long as the transistor is operating in the active region. However, the transistor collector-emitter voltage (V_{CE}) depends on the value of R_C.

The collector-emitter section comprises the supply voltage (V_{CC}),collector resistor (R_C) and the transistor collector-emitter junction. Applying Kirchhoff's voltage law to the collector-emitter section we get:

$$V_{CC} - I_C R_C - V_{CE} = 0 \tag{2.27}$$

Rearranging the terms, we get:

$$V_{CE} = V_{CC} - I_C R_C \tag{2.28}$$

Thus, the collector-emitter voltage (V_{CE}) is equal to the difference between the supply voltage (V_{CC}) and the voltage across the collector resistor (R_C).

The quiescent point for a fixed-bias circuit is given by eqn. (2.29).

$$I_{CQ} = \beta\left(\frac{V_{CC} - V_{BE}}{R_B}\right),\ V_{CEQ} = V_{CC} - I_{CQ} R_C \tag{2.29}$$

Load-Line Analysis

Eqn. (2.28) relates to two variables; namely, the collector current (I_C) and the collector-emitter voltage (V_{CE}). The transistor output characteristics curve also relates these two variables. If we superimpose the straight line defined by eqn. (2.28) on the transistor output characteristics, we can determine the operating point of the circuit and also the way the operating point changes with change in the value of circuit parameters. This is referred to as load-line analysis. Figure-2.30 shows the load line as superimposed on the output characteristics.

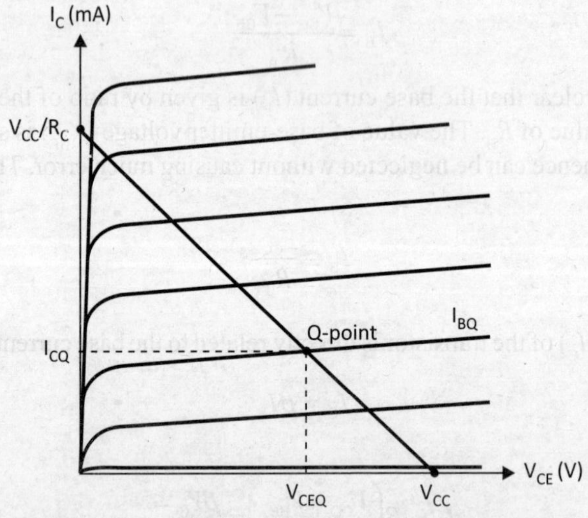

Fig. 2.30: Load-line analysis of the fixed-bias circuit

To draw the load line, substitute $I_C = 0$ in eqn. (2.28). We get

$$V_{CE} = V_{CC}\big|_{I_C=0}$$

This point appears on the horizontal axis (0, V_{CC}) of the output characteristics. I_C can be evaluated by substituting $V_{CE} = 0$ in eqn. (2.28) as

$$I_C = \frac{V_{CC}}{R_C}\bigg|_{V_{CE}=0}$$

This point appears on the vertical axis (V_{CC}/R_C, 0) of the output characteristics.

The load line is obtained by joining these two points as shown in Figure-2.30. The operating point is established on the load line by determining the level of base current (I_B) using eqn. (2.25). The point of intersection of the load line with the curve corresponding to the calculated value of I_B gives the operating point as shown in the figure. The operating point shifts with the change in the value of circuit parameters.

The operating point moves up the load line if the value of I_B increases and moves down the load line when the value of I_B decreases (Figure-2.31). The value of I_B can be changed by changing the value of resistor R_B. If the supply voltage (V_{CC}) is held constant and the value of the collector resistor (R_C) is changed, then the load line shifts as shown in Figure-2.32. Therefore, the operating point also shifts for the same value of base current (I_B) as shown in the figure. The variation of the load line and the operating point due to change in the supply voltage (V_{CC}) is illustrated in Figure-2.33.

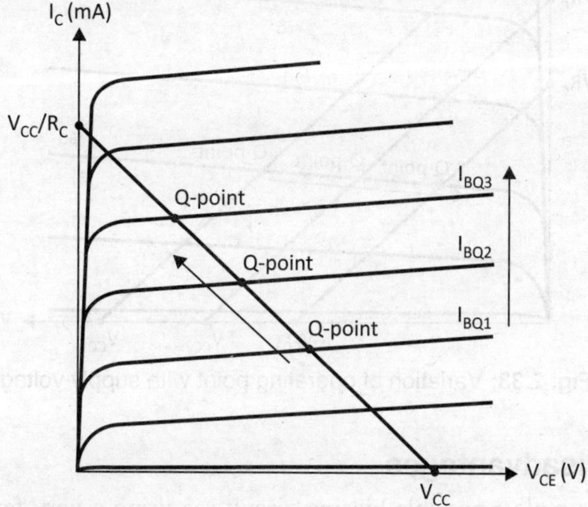

Fig. 2.31: Variation of operating point with base current

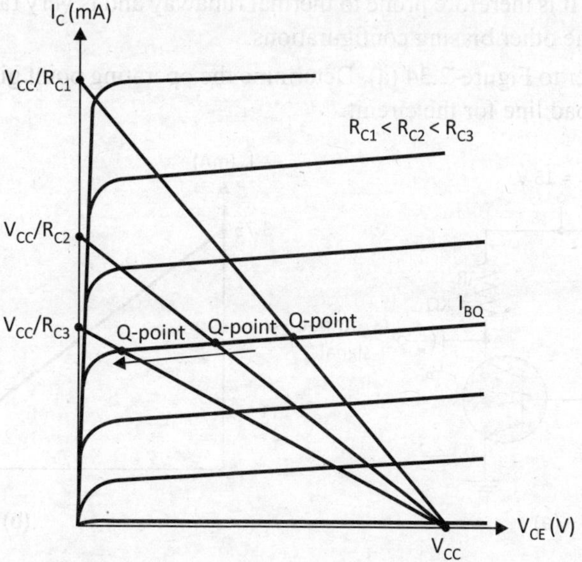

Fig. 2.32: Variation of operating point with collector resistor

The circuit shown employs NPN transistor and the network equations have been derived for NPN transistors. Same analysis applies to PNP transistors with the direction of currents and the polarities of the voltages reversed.

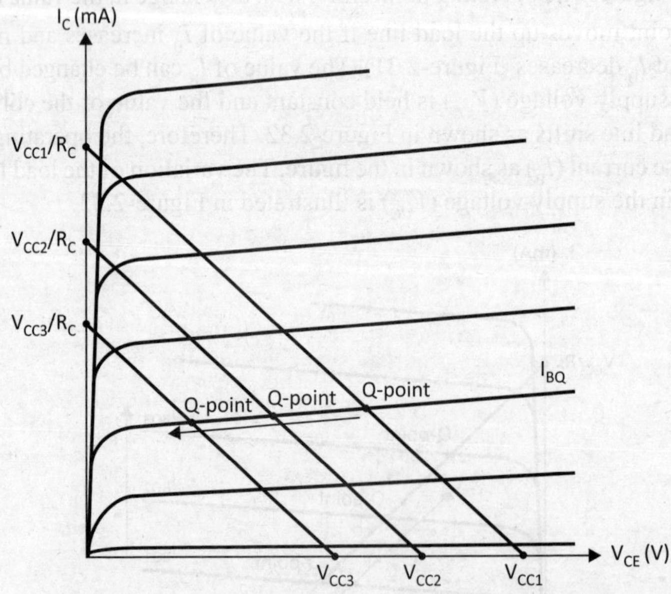

Fig. 2.33: Variation of operating point with supply voltage

Advantages and Disadvantages

Fixed-bias circuit is the simplest possible biasing circuit requiring a very few components. However, the circuit offers worst stability against variations in temperature or transistor gain (*â*) as compared to the other configurations. It is therefore prone to thermal runaway and is very rarely used. Things will get clearer when we study the other biasing configurations.

Example-2.8: Refer to Figure-2.34 (a). Determine the operating point given that $\beta = 100$ and $V_{BE} = 0.7$ V. Also draw the load line for the circuit.

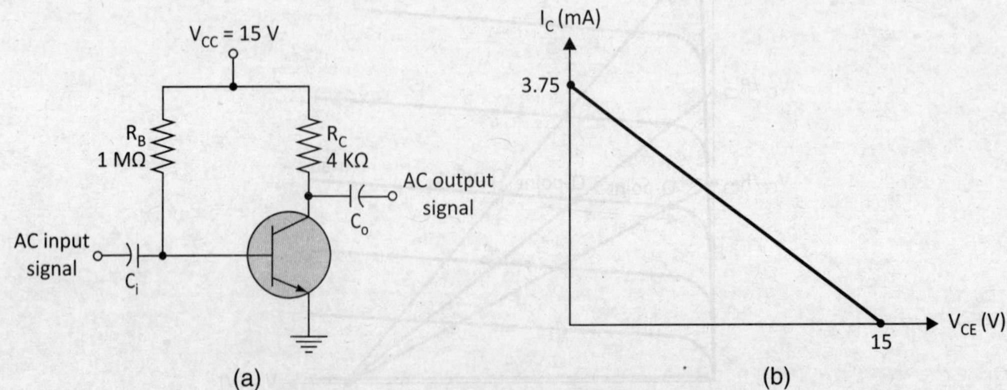

Fig. 2.34: Example-2.8 (a) circuit (b) solution

Solution: The value of collector current (I_{CQ}) is given by:

$$I_{CQ} = \beta\left(\frac{V_{CC} - V_{BE}}{R_B}\right)$$

Substituting the values of different parameters, we get,

$$I_{CQ} = 100 \times (15 - 0.7)/1 \times 10^6 = 1.43 \text{ mA}$$

The value of the collector-emitter voltage (V_{CEQ}) is given by $V_{CEQ} = V_{CC} - I_{CQ}R_C$

That is $V_{CEQ} = 15 - 1.43 \times 10^{-3} \times 4 \times 10^3 = 15 - 5.72 = 9.28$ V

The load-line equation for a fixed-bias circuit is given by $V_{CE} = V_{CC} - I_C R_C$

Substituting $I_C = 0$, $V_{CE} = V_{CC} = 15$ V, the coordinates of the load line on the *X*-axis are obtained as (0 mA, 15 V).

For $V_{CE} = 0$, $I_C = V_{CC}/R_C = 15/4 \times 10^3 = 3.75$ mA

The coordinates of the load line on the *Y*-axis are obtained as (3.75 mA, 0 V).

The load line is obtained by joining the two points as shown in Figure-2.34 (b).

2.7.2.2 Emitter or self-bias

Emitter-bias configuration, also referred to as *self-bias circuit*, has an additional emitter resistor (R_E) between the transistor's emitter terminal and ground as compared to the fixed-bias circuit (Figure-2.35). Resistor R_E introduces negative feedback thereby providing improved stabilization.It is a current-series feedback as a voltage proportional to the output current is fed-back into the input.

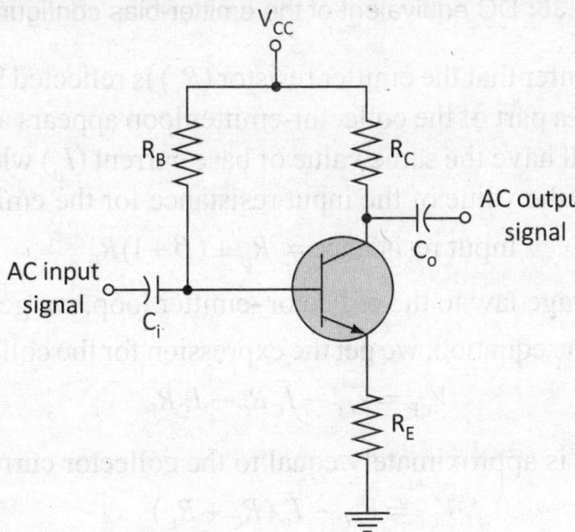

Fig. 2.35: Emitter-bias or self-bias

DC Analysis

The DC equivalent of the emitter-bias circuit of Figure-2.35 is shown in Figure-2.36. The DC analysis is done on similar lines as that done for the fixed-bias circuit. Applying Kirchhoff's voltage law to the base-emitter loop we get,

$$V_{CC} - I_B R_B - V_{BE} - I_E R_E = 0$$

Substituting the value of emitter current (I_E) as $I_E = (\beta + 1)I_B$ in the above equation and rearranging the terms, the expression for I_B can be written as eqn. (2.30).

$$I_B = \frac{V_{CC} - V_{BE}}{R_B + (\beta + 1)R_E} \tag{2.30}$$

Voltage V_{BE} is small as compared to V_{CC} and can therefore be neglected. The expression for base current (I_B) is then given by eqn. (2.31).

$$I_B = \frac{V_{CC}}{R_B + (\beta + 1)R_E} \tag{2.31}$$

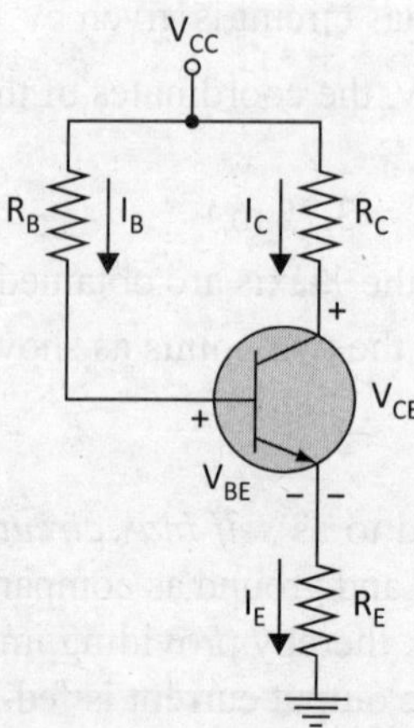

Fig. 2.36: DC equivalent of the emitter-bias configuration

From eqn. (2.30), we can infer that the emitter resistor (R_E) is reflected into the input circuit as (β + 1) R_E. In other words, R_E which is a part of the collector-emitter loop appears as (b+ 1)R_E in the base-emitter loop. The fixed-bias circuit will have the same value of base current (I_B) when it has a base resistor equal to [R_B + (β + 1)R_E]. Therefore, the value of the input resistance for the emitter-bias circuit is given by

$$\text{Input resistance} = R_B + (\beta + 1)R_E \tag{2.32}$$

Applying Kirchhoff's voltage law to the collector–emitter loop, we get $V_{CC} - I_C R_C - V_{CE} - I_E R_E = 0$

Rearranging the terms of the equation, we get the expression for the collector-emitter voltage (V_{CE}) as:

$$V_{CE} = V_{CC} - I_C R_C - I_E R_E$$

As the emitter current (I_E) is approximately equal to the collector current (I_C), therefore

$$V_{CE} = V_{CC} - I_C (R_C + R_E) \tag{2.33}$$

The voltage of the emitter terminal of the transistor (V_E) is given by eqn. (2.34).

$$V_E = I_E R_E \cong I_C R_E \tag{2.34}$$

The Q-point for the emitter-bias circuit is given by eqn. (2.35).

$$I_{CQ} = \beta\left(\frac{V_{CC} - V_{BE}}{R_B + (\beta + 1)R_E}\right), \; V_{CEQ} = V_{CC} - I_{CQ}(R_C + R_E) \tag{2.35}$$

The emitter-bias circuit offers stability against variations in collector current due to change in temperature or change in the transistor gain (β). When the collector current increases, the emitter voltage increases. This results in a decrease in the base-emitter potential, which further leads to a decrease in the value of base current. Therefore, the collector current also decreases, thereby compensating for the initial increase in its value.

Load-line Analysis

The load-line analysis of the emitter-bias network differs slightly from that of the fixed-bias configuration. The load line in this configuration is given by eqn. (2.36).

$$V_{CE} = V_{CC} - I_C(R_C + R_E) \tag{2.36}$$

To draw the load line, substitute $I_C = 0$ in eqn. (2.36) following which we get,

$$V_{CE} = V_{CC}\Big|_{I_C=0}$$

This point appears on the horizontal axis (0, V_{CC}) of the output characteristics. Substituting $V_{CE} = 0$ in eqn. (2.36), we obtain I_C as:

$$I_C = \frac{V_{CC}}{(R_C + R_E)}\Bigg|_{V_{CE}=0}$$

This point appears on the vertical axis [($V_{CC}/(R_C + R_E)$, 0] of the output characteristics. The load line is obtained by joining these two points as shown in Figure-2.37. The operating point is established on the load line by determining the level of I_B using eqn. (2.30) or eqn. (2.31).

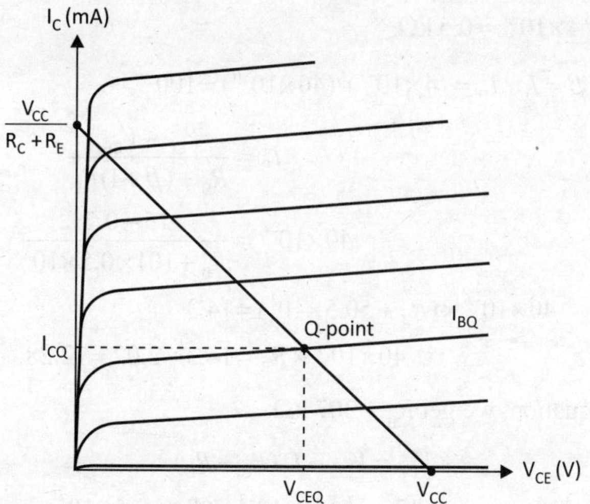

Fig. 2.37: Load-line analysis of the emitter-bias circuit

Advantages and Disadvantages

The emitter-bias circuit offers better stability than the fixed-bias circuit. However, maximum stability is offered by the circuit when theratio of the base resistor (R_B) to the emitter resistor (R_E), that is R_B/R_E, is as small as possible. Thus, R_E should have a large value or R_B should be small. For large values of resistor R_E, larger collector supply voltage (V_{CC}) is needed. Also increase in R_E increases the negative feedback and reduces the gain of the circuit. For small values of resistor R_B, a separate base supply voltage is needed which adds to circuit complexity and is often not feasible. The disadvantages of the emitter-bias circuit are removed in the voltage-divider bias with emitter-bias circuit.

Example-2.9: Refer to Figure-2.38. Find the values of resistors R_B, R_C and R_E and the transistor gain b, given that $I_B = 40\ \mu A$, $I_C = 4$ mA, $V_E = 2$ V, $V_{CE} = 12$ V and supply voltage $V_{CC} = 15$ V. Assume that the transistor used in the circuit is a Silicon transistor.

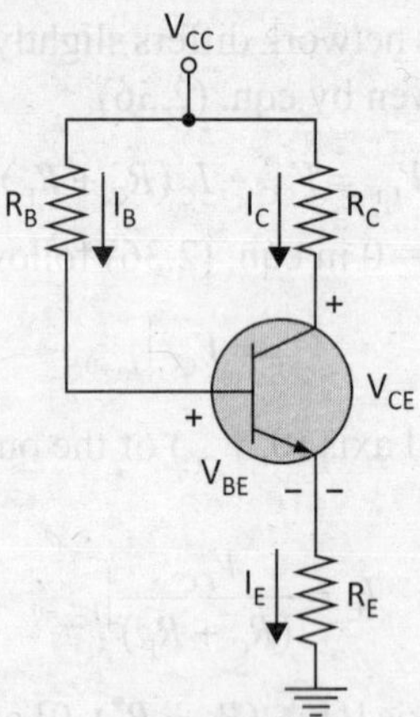

Fig. 2.38: Example-2.9

Solution: $V_E = I_E R_E \cong I_C R_E$

$$R_E = V_E / I_C = 2/4\times10^{-3} = 0.5\ \text{k}\Omega.$$

$I_C = \beta I_B$. Therefore, $\beta = I_C / I_B = (4\times10^{-3})/(40\times10^{-6}) = 100$

$$I_B = \frac{V_{CC} - V_{BE}}{R_B + (\beta+1)R_E}$$

$$40\times10^{-6} = \frac{15-0.7}{R_B + 101\times0.5\times10^3}$$

$$40\times10^{-6}\times(R_B + 50.5\times10^3) = 14.3$$

$$40\times10^{-6}\times R_B = 14.3 - 2.02 = 12.28$$

Solving the above equation, we get $R_B = 307$ kΩ.

$$V_{CE} = V_{CC} - I_C(R_C + R_E)$$

$$12 = 15 - 4\times10^{-3}\times(R_C + 0.5\times10^3)$$

$$4\times10^{-3}\times R_C = 15 - 12 - 2 = 1$$

Therefore, $R_C = 0.25$ kΩ.

Example-2.10: For the circuit shown in Figure-2.39, $V_{CC} = 15$ V, $V_{EE} = -10$ V, $R_C = 2$ kΩ, $R_E = 5$ kΩ, $R_B = 400$ kΩ and $\beta = 60$. Find the value of collector current (I_C) and the collector-to-emitter voltage (V_{CE}).

Solution: Applying Kirchhoff's voltage law to the base-emitter loop of the circuit in Figure-2.39, we get

$$V_{CC} - I_B R_B - V_{BE} - I_E R_E - V_{EE} = 0$$

Substituting $I_E = (b + 1)I_B$ in the above equation, we obtain the expression for I_B as

$$I_B = \frac{V_{CC} - V_{EE} - V_{BE}}{R_B + (\beta + 1)R_E}$$

$$I_B = \frac{15 + 10 - 0.7}{400\times10^3 + 61\times5\times10^3}$$

$$= 24.3/(705\times10^3) = 34.46\ \text{A}$$

$I_C = \beta I_B$. Therefore, $I_C = 60 \times 34.46 \times 10^{-6}$ A = 2.07 mA.

Applying Kirchhoff's law to the collector-emitter loop of the circuit in Figure-2.39, we get

$$V_{CC} - I_C R_C - V_{CE} - I_E R_E - V_{EE} = 0$$

As $I_C \cong I_E$,, therefore $V_{CE} = V_{CC} - V_{EE} - I_C(R_C + R_E)$.

$V_{CE} = 15 + 10 - 2.07 \times 10^{-3} \times (2\ 10^3 + 5 \times 10^3) = 25 - 14.49 = 10.51$ V.

Therefore, $I_C = 2.07$ mA, $V_{CE} = 10.51$ V.

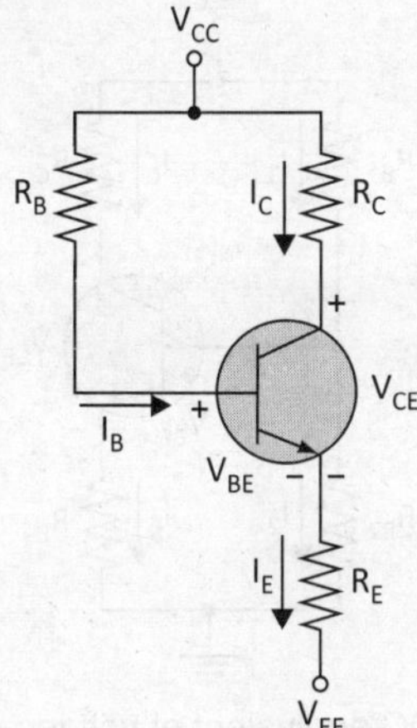

Fig. 2.39: Example 2.10

2.7.2.3 *Voltage divider bias*

The stability of the emitter-bias configuration is further improved if its input side is modified as shown in Figure-2.40. The circuit configuration is referred to as voltage-divider bias with emitter-bias or simply the voltage-divider bias configuration. It is the most commonly used transistor-biasing configuration. The name voltage-divider comes from the fact that the input section comprises a voltage divider of resistors R_{B1} and R_{B2} across the supply voltage V_{CC}. The circuit offers improved stability against variations in the temperature and the transistor gain.

DC Analysis

The DC equivalent of the voltage-divider bias circuit of Figure-2.40 is shown in Figure-2.41. The circuit can be analyzed using two methods, namely, the accurate method and the approximate method. The accurate method is applicable to all circuits whereas the approximate method can be applied if certain conditions are met. We will discuss both the methods in subsequent paragraphs.

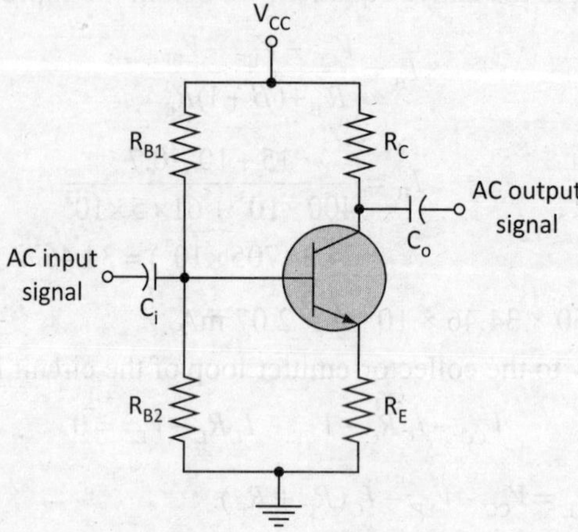

Fig. 2.40: Voltage-divider bias with emitter-bias

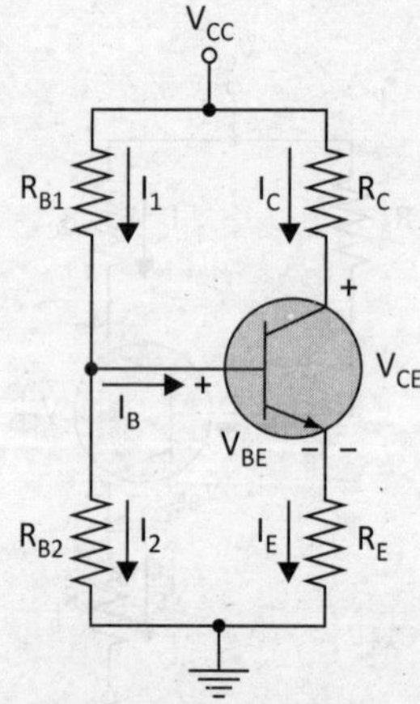

Fig. 2.41: DC equivalent of voltage-divider bias

Accurate Method: Accurate method makes use of Thevenin's equivalent model of the input section. The input section of the circuit can be redrawn as shown in Figure-2.42 (a) and can be simplified using Thevenin's equivalent theorem. Figure-2.42 (b) shows the Thevenin's equivalent model. R_{TH} is the Thevenin's equivalent resistance and is found by replacing the voltage source by a short circuit and calculating the resultant resistance of the circuit. R_{TH} is equal to the parallel combination of resistors R_{B1} and R_{B2} and is given by eqn. (2.37).

$$R_{TH} = R_{B1} \| R_{B2} = \frac{R_{B1}R_{B2}}{R_{B1} + R_{B2}} \tag{2.37}$$

V_{TH} is the open-circuit Thevenin's voltage and is given by eqn. (2.38).

$$V_{TH} = \frac{R_{B2}V_{CC}}{R_{B1} + R_{B2}} \tag{2.38}$$

Figure-2.43 shows the complete circuit using Thevenin's equivalent model.

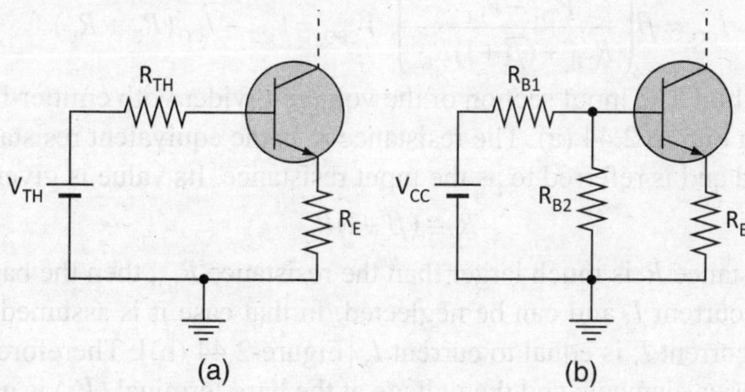

Fig. 2.42: (a) Input section of the voltage-divider bias configuration (b) Thevenin's equivalent of the input section

Applying Kirchhoff's voltage law to the base–emitter loop of the circuit in Figure-2.43, we get,

$$V_{TH} - I_B R_{TH} - V_{BE} - I_E R_E = 0 \tag{2.39}$$

Substituting $I_E = (\beta + 1)I_B$, we get the expression for I_B as eqn. (2.40)

$$I_B = \frac{V_{TH} - V_{BE}}{R_{TH} + (\beta + 1)R_E} \tag{2.40}$$

The expression is similar to the one derived for emitter-bias with the term R_B being replaced by R_{TH}. If the base-emitter voltage (V_{BE}) is small as compared to the Thevenin's voltage (V_{TH}), then eqn. (2.40) can be simplified to

$$I_B = \frac{V_{TH}}{R_{TH} + (\beta + 1)R_E} \tag{2.41}$$

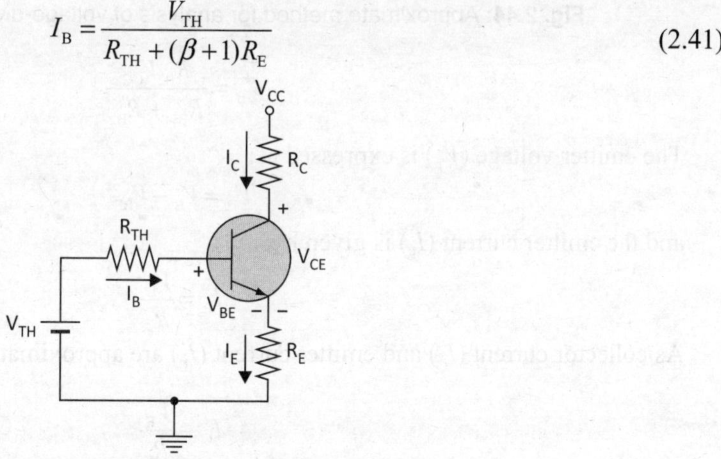

Fig. 2.43: Thevenin's equivalent of voltage-divider bias configuration

After determining the base current (I_B), the collector–emitter voltage (V_{CE}) can be determined by applying Kirchhoff's voltage law to the collector–emitter loop,

$$V_{CC} - I_C R_C - V_{CE} - I_E R_E = 0$$

As $I_C @ I_E$, the value of collector–emitter voltage (V_{CE}) is given by eqn. (2.42).

$$V_{CE} = V_{CC} - I_C(R_C + R_E) \tag{2.42}$$

The operating point is given by eqn. (2.43).

$$I_{CQ} = \beta\left(\frac{V_{TH} - V_{BE}}{R_{TH} + (\beta+1)R_E}\right),\ V_{CEQ} = V_{CC} - I_{CQ}(R_C + R_E) \tag{2.43}$$

Approximate Method The input section of the voltage-divider with emitter-bias configuration can be redrawn as shown in Figure-2.44 (a). The resistance R_i is the equivalent resistance between the base terminal and the ground and is referred to as the input resistance. Its value is given by

$$R_i \cong (\beta+1)R_E \tag{2.44}$$

If the value of resistance R_i is much larger than the resistance R_{B2}, then the base current (I_B) will be much smaller than the current I_2 and can be neglected. In that case it is assumed that the base current I_B is equal to zero and current I_1 is equal to current I_2 [Figure-2.44 (b)]. Therefore, resistors R_{B1} and R_{B2} can be considered as series elements and the voltage at the base terminal (V_B) is given by eqn. (2.44).

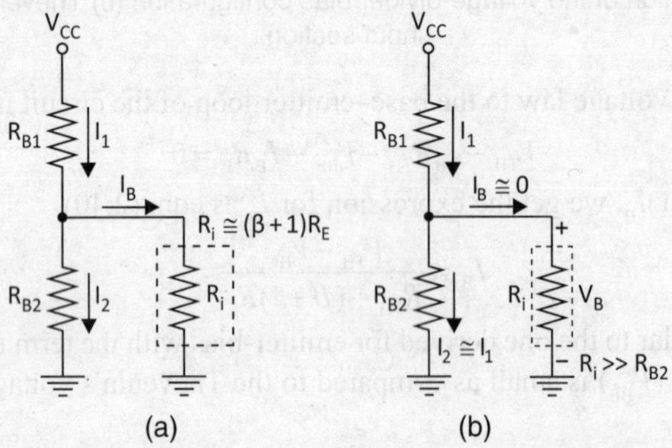

Fig. 2.44: Approximate method for analysis of voltage-divider bias configuration

$$V_B = \frac{R_{B2}V_{CC}}{R_{B1} + R_{B2}} \tag{2.44}$$

The emitter voltage (V_E) is expressed as:

$$V_E = V_B - V_{BE} \tag{2.45}$$

and the emitter current (I_E) is given by:

$$I_E = \frac{V_E}{R_E} \tag{2.46}$$

As collector current (I_C) and emitter current (I_E) are approximately equal, the value of I_C is

$$I_C \cong \frac{V_E}{R_E} \tag{2.47}$$

The collector–emitter voltage (V_{CE}) is given by

$$V_{CE} = V_{CC} - I_C(R_C + R_E) \tag{2.48}$$

It may be mentioned here that the approximate method can be applied if the value of the input resistance R_i is equal to greater than 10 times the resistance R_{B2}. That is,

$$(\beta+1)R_E \geq 10R_{B2} \tag{2.49}$$

Load-line Analysis

The output circuit of the voltage-divider bias configuration is the same as that of the emitter-bias configuration. This results in the same load line for the two configurations. The level of base current (I_B) is however determined by a different equation in this case.

Advantages and Disadvantages

Voltage-divider bias configuration is the most commonly used configuration as it provides excellent stabilization against variations in temperature and transistor gain (b). This is because, the emitter resistor introduces negative feedback in the circuit. But negative feedback results in reduction of AC gain of the circuit. This problem can be solved by using a capacitor C_E in parallel with resistor R_E (Figure-2.45). The capacitor does not affect the DC analysis as it acts as an open circuit for DC voltages. For AC inputs, it acts as a short circuit, making the voltage across the emitter resistor (R_E) equal to zero and thus removing the problem of AC negative feedback.

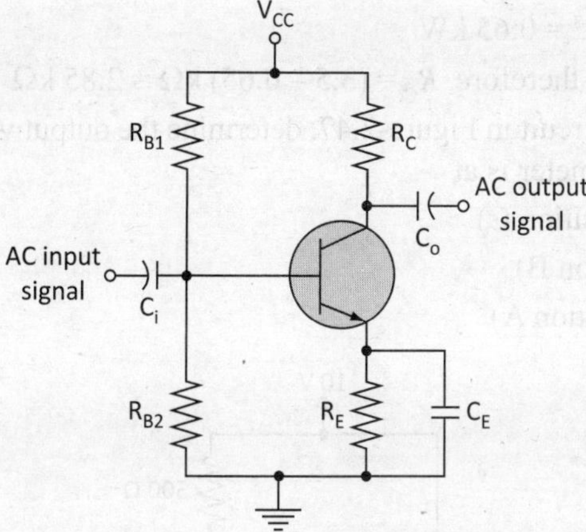

Fig. 2.45: Voltage-divider bias configuration with emitter bypass capacitor

Example-2.11: Determine the values of the resistors R_C and R_E for the circuit in Figure-2.46. Given that $R_1 = 5k\Omega$, $R_2 = 1\ k\Omega$, $\beta = 200$, $V_{BE} = 0.7$ V, $I_1 >> I_B$, $V_{CEQ} = 5$ V and $I_C = 2$ mA.

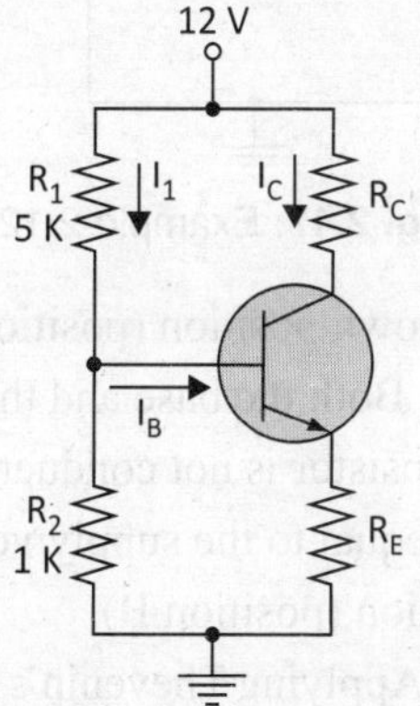

Fig. 2.46: Example-2.11

Solution: Applying Kirchhoff's voltage loop to the collector–emitter loop of the circuit, we get

$$V_{CC} - I_C R_C - V_{CE} - I_E R_E = 0$$

Assuming that $I_C \cong I_E$ and substituting the values in the above equation, we get

$$12 - 2\times10^{-3} \times R_C - 5 - 2\times10^{-3} \times R_E = 0$$

Therefore, $R_C + R_E = 3.5$ kΩ

It is given that current I_1 is much greater that the base current I_B. Therefore, the approximate method can be used to analyze the circuit. The base voltage (V_B) is given by:

$V_B = 12 \times R_2/(R_1 + R_2) = 12 \times 110^3/(5 \times 10^3 + 1 \times 10^3) = 2$ V

The emitter voltage (V_E) is given by:

$V_E = V_B - V_{BE}$. As $V_{BE} = 0.7$ V, therefore $V_E = (2 - 0.7)$ V = 1.3 V

$V_E = I_E R_E$.

Therefore, $R_E = 1.3/2 \times 10^{-3} = 0.65$ kW

Also, as $R_C + R_E = 3.5$ kΩ, therefore, $R_C = (3.5 - 0.65)$ kΩ = 2.85 kΩ

Example-2.12: For the circuit in Figure-2.47, determine the output voltage of the circuit when the adjust terminal of the potentiometer is at

(a) full-down position (position C)

(b) middle position (position B)

(c) top-most position (position A)

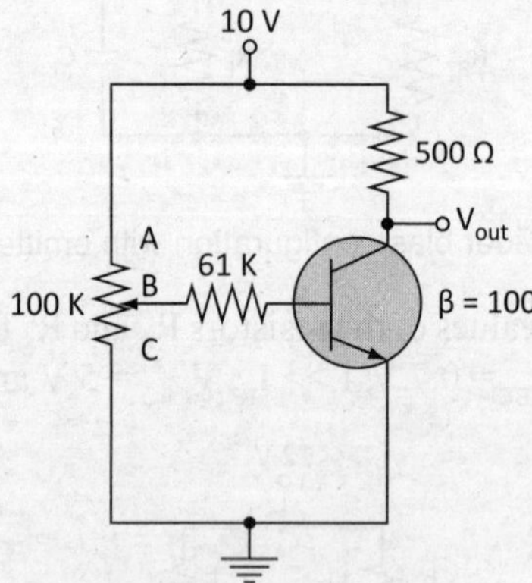

Fig. 2.47: Example-2.12

Solution: (a) Potentiometer in full-down position (position C)

Figure-2.48 (a) shows the circuit. Both the base and the emitter voltages are zero. Therefore $V_{BE} = 0$. Hence, the transistor is not conducting.

As a result, the output voltage is equal to the supply voltage, that is 10 V.

(b) Potentiometer in the middle position (position B)

Figure-2.48 (b) shows the circuit. Applying Thevenin's theorem to the input section of the circuit in Figure-2.48 (b), Thevenin's equivalent resistance (R_{TH}) is given by:

$R_{TH} = (50 \times 10^3 \times 50 \times 10^3)/(50 \times 10^3 + 50 \times 10^3) = 25$ kΩ

The open-circuit Thevenin's equivalent voltage (V_{TH}) is given by:

$V_{TH} = (10 \times 50 \times 10^3)/(50 \times 10^3 + 50 \times 10^3) = 5$ V

The simplified circuit is shown in Figure-2.48 (c).

Applying Kirchhoff's voltage law to the input circuit, we get $5 - 25 \times 10^3 I_B - 61 \times 10^3 I_B - 0.7 = 0$

Therefore, $I_B = (4.3/86) \times 10^{-3}$ A = 50 μA. $I_C = \beta \times I_B$. Therefore, $I_C = 100 \times 50 \times 10^{-6} = 5$ mA.

Applying Kirchhoff's voltage law to the output section of the circuit and solving for output voltage (V_{out}) we get $V_{out} = 10 - 0.5 \times 10^3 \times 5 \times 10^{-3} = 7.5$ V

(c) Potentiometer in top-most position (position A)

Figure-2.48 (d) shows the circuit when the adjust terminal of the potentiometer is at position A.

Applying Kirchhoff's voltage law to the input section we get:

$10 - 61 \times 10^3 \times I_B - 0.7 = 0$

$I_B = (9.3/61) \times 10^3$ A = 152 μA

$I_C = I_C = \beta \times I_B = 100 \times 152 \times 10^{-6}$A = 15.2 mA

Applying Kirchhoff's voltage law to the output section and solving for the output voltage (V_{out}) we get,

$V_{out} = 10 - 0.5 \times 10^3 \times 15.2 \times 10^{-3} = 10 - 7.6 = 2.4$ V

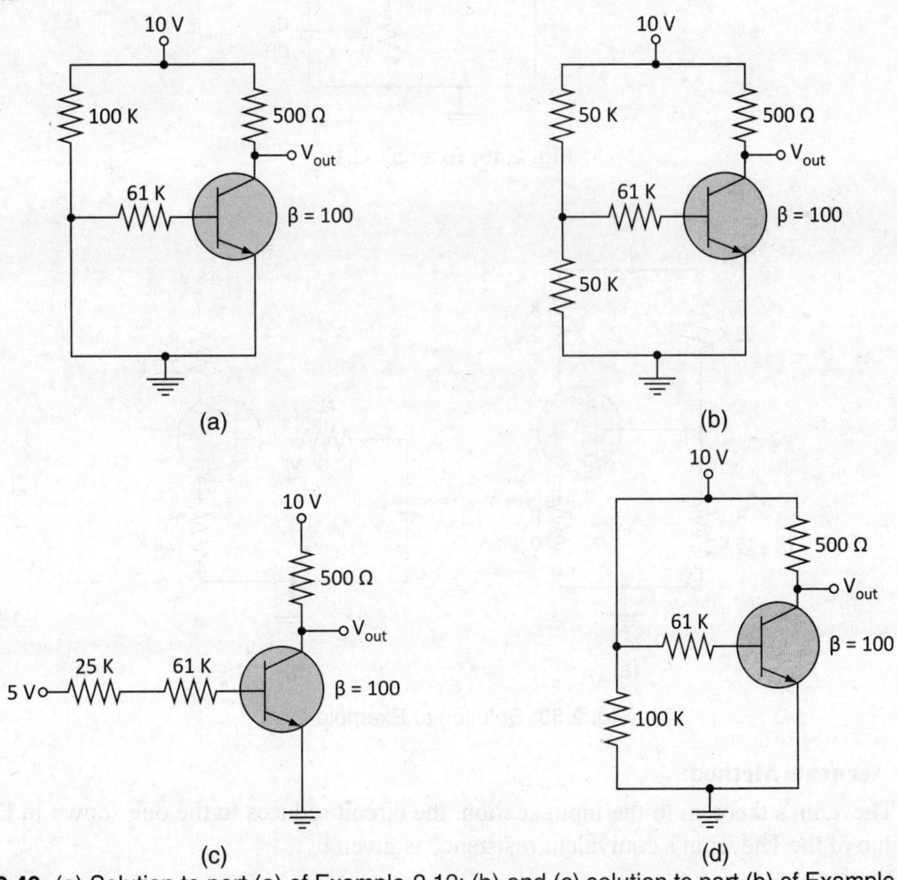

Fig. 2.48: (a) Solution to part (a) of Example-2.12; (b) and (c) solution to part (b) of Example-2.12; (d) solution to part (c) of Example-2.12.

Example-2.13: Draw the DC equivalent of the circuit shown in Figure-2.49. Calculate the quiescent value of emitter current (I_{EQ}) using both the approximate and the accurate method. What is the percentage error introduced using the approximate method, given that transistor gain β is 165?

Solution: The DC equivalent circuit is shown in Figure-2.50 (a). The DC equivalent circuit is drawn by making all capacitors open and considering all the AC sources to be zero. Resistor R_E is equal to the sum of the resistors R_{E1} and R_{E2}.

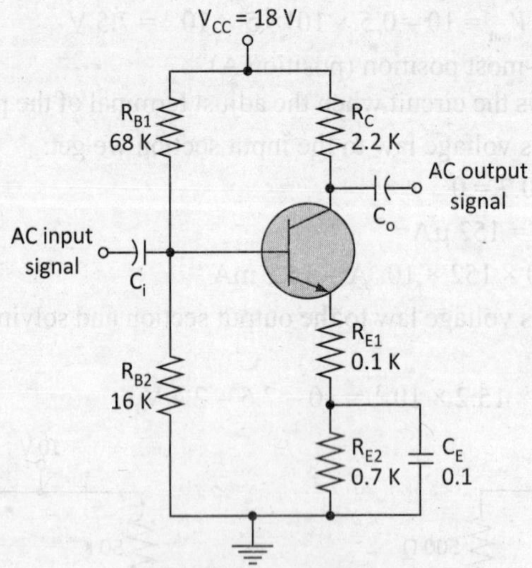

Fig. 2.49: Example-2.13

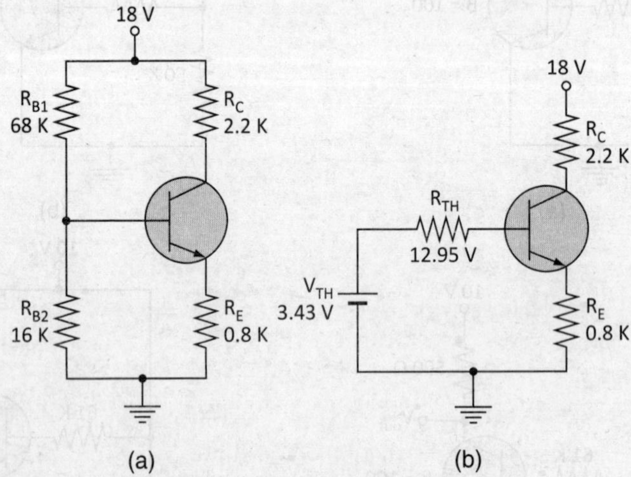

Fig. 2.50: Solution to Example-2.13

Using the Accurate Method:

Applying Thevenin's theorem to the input section, the circuit reduces to the one shown in Figure-2.50 (b). The value of the Thevenin's equivalent resistance is given by:

$$R_{TH} = 68\ k\Omega \| 16\ k\Omega = 12.95\ k\Omega$$

The value of the Thevenin's equivalent voltage (V_{TH}) is given by:

$$V_{TH} = (18 \times R_{B2})/(R_{B1} + R_{B2})$$
$$= (18 \times 16 \times 10^3)/(68 \times 10^3 + 16 \times 10^3) = 3.43 \text{ V}$$

Applying Kirchhoff's voltage law to the emitter-base loop of the circuit in Figure-2.50 (b), we get

$3.43 - 12.95 \times 10^3 \times I_B - 0.7 - 0.8 ' 10^3 \times I_E = 0$

Substituting $I_E = (\beta + 1)I_B = 166 \times I_B$ in the above equation, we obtain

$$2.73 - 12.95 \times 10^3 \times I_B - 132.8 \times 10^3 \times I_B = 0$$

$I_B = 18.7\ \mu A$

$I_C = \beta I_B$. Therefore, $I_C = 165 \times 18.7 \times 10^{-6} = 3.08$ mA

Applying Kirchhoff's voltage law to the collector-emitter loop of the circuit in Figure-2.50 (b), we get

$18 - 2.2 \times 10^3 \times I_C - V_{CE} - 0.8 \times 10^3 \times I_E = 0$

Assuming, $I_C \cong I_E$ in the above equation, we get

$V_{CE} = 18 - 3 \times 10^3 \times I_C = 18 - 3 \times 10^3 \times 3.08 \times 10^{-3} = 18 - 9.24 = 8.76$ V

Therefore, $V_{CE} = 8.76$ V

The operating point as calculated using accurate method is ($I_C = 3.08$ mA, $V_{CE} = 8.76$ V)

Using the Approximate Method:

The voltage at the base terminal (V_B) is given by:

$V_B = 18 \times R_{B2}/(R_{B1} + R_{B2}) = 18 \times 16 \times 10^3/(68 \times 10^3 + 16 \times 10^3) = 3.43$ V

Therefore, the voltage at the emitter terminal (V_E) is given by:

$V_E = V_B - V_{BE} = (3.43 - 07)$ V $= 2.73$ V

$V_E = R_E \times I_E$, therefore the emitter current (I_E) is given by:

$I_E = 2.73/0.8 \times 10^3 = 3.41$ mA

Applying Kirchhoff's voltage law to the collector–emitter loop, we get

$18 - 2.2 \times 10^3 \times I_C - V_{CE} - 0.8 \times 10^3 \times I_E = 0$

Assuming, $I_C \cong I_E$, in the above equation, we get

$V_{CE} = 18 - 3 \times 10^3 \times 3.41 \times 10^{-3} = 7.77$ V

The operating point as calculated using the approximate method is ($I_C = 3.41$ mA, $V_{CE} = 7.77$ V)

The percentage error in the value of I_C using approximate method is given by:

$[(3.41 - 3.08)/3.08] \times 100\% = 10.71\%$

The percentage error in the value of V_{CE} using the approximate method is given by:

$[(7.77 - 8.76)/8.76] \times 100\% = -11.3\%$

2.7.2.4 Collector-to-Base Bias

In *collector-to-base bias* configuration, the base-bias voltage is obtained from the collector of the transistor instead of the collector supply voltage (V_{CC}) as shown in Figure-2.51. This configuration is also referred to as feedback-bias. The circuit offers better stability of the operating point against variations in temperature and transistor gain (β) due to negative feedback. The configuration has voltage-shunt feedback as the output voltage is fed-back in shunt to the input through base resistor (R_B).

DC Analysis

Figure-2.52 shows the DC equivalent of the collector-to-base bias circuit inFigure-2.51. The current in the resistor R_C through supply voltage V_{CC} is split into two parts at the collector junction;(I_C) flowing into the collector terminal and (I_B) flowing through the base resistor (R_B). The current in resistor R_B is equal to the base current (I_B). Therefore, the current through resistor R_C is the sum of the base current (I_B) and the collector current (I_C).

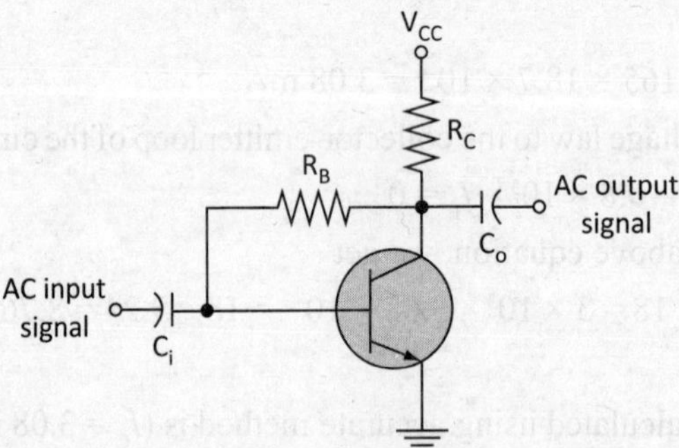

Fig. 2.51: Collector-to-base bias configuration

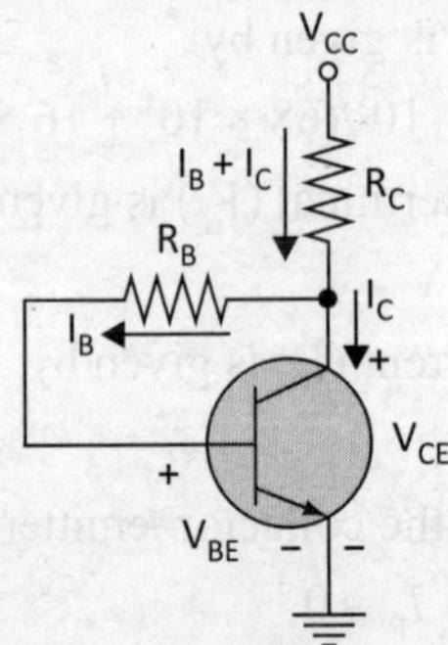

Fig. 2.52: DC equivalent of collector-to-base bias configuration

Applying Kirchhoff's voltage law to the base-emitter loop of the circuit in Figure-2.52, we obtain:

$$V_{CC} - (I_B + I_C)R_C - I_B R_B - V_{BE} = 0$$

Substituting $I_C = \beta I_B$ in the above equation and solving the equation for I_B we get:

$$I_B = \frac{V_{CC} - V_{BE}}{R_B + (\beta + 1)R_C} \tag{2.50}$$

This equation can be compared with that of emitter-bias configuration where the base current (I_B) was given by:

$$I_B = \frac{V_{CC} - V_{BE}}{R_B + (\beta + 1)R_E}$$

The term R_E in the expression for base current (I_B) for emitter-bias configuration has been replaced by the term R_C in the collector-to-base bias configuration.

The value of collector current (I_C) is given by $I_C = bI_B$. Therefore,

$$I_C = \beta\left(\frac{V_{CC} - V_{BE}}{R_B + (\beta+1)R_C}\right) \tag{2.51}$$

As the value of b is very large, (β + 1) can be approximated as β. Therefore, collector current (I_C) is given by:

$$I_C = \beta\left(\frac{V_{CC} - V_{BE}}{R_B + \beta R_C}\right)$$

If the value of βR_C is much greater than R_B, then the term $R_B + \beta R_C$ can be approximated as βR_C and in this case the value of collector current I_C is given by:

$$I_C \cong \beta\left(\frac{V_{CC} - V_{BE}}{\beta R_C}\right) = \frac{V_{CC} - V_{BE}}{R_C}$$

Therefore, the collector current becomes independent of the value of transistor gain (β). In other words, the stability offered by the collector-to-base configuration improves as the value of the collector resistor (R_C) increases.

Applying Kirchhoff's voltage law to the collector–emitter loop, we get:

$$V_{CC} - (I_B + I_C)R_C - V_{CE} = 0$$

Ignoring base current (I_B) because its value is negligible compared to the collector current (I_C), we get

$$V_{CE} = V_{CC} - I_C R_C \tag{2.52}$$

The value of the operating point for collector-to-base bias configuration is given by eqn. (2.53).

$$V_{CEQ} = V_{CC} - I_{CQ}R_C,\ I_{CQ} = \beta\left(\frac{V_{CC} - V_{BE}}{R_B + (\beta+1)R_C}\right) \tag{2.53}$$

Load-line Analysis

The load-line analysis for collector-to-base bias can be carried on similar lines to that done in the case of emitter-bias configuration. Another variation of the collector-to-base bias circuit is to place an emitter resistor (R_E) between the emitter terminal of the transistor and the ground as shown in Figure-2.53. In that case, the equations for the base current (I_B), collector current (I_C) and the collector-emitter voltage (V_{CE}) are given by eqns. (2.54), (2.55) and (2.56).

$$I_B = \frac{V_{CC} - V_{BE}}{R_B + (\beta+1)(R_C + R_E)} \tag{2.54}$$

$$I_C = \beta\left(\frac{V_{CC} - V_{BE}}{R_B + (\beta+1)(R_C + R_E)}\right) \tag{2.55}$$

$$V_{CE} = V_{CC} - I_C(R_C + R_E) \tag{2.56}$$

The collector-to-base bias configuration with emitter resistor offers better stability than emitter-bias and collector-to-base bias configuration without emitter resistor.

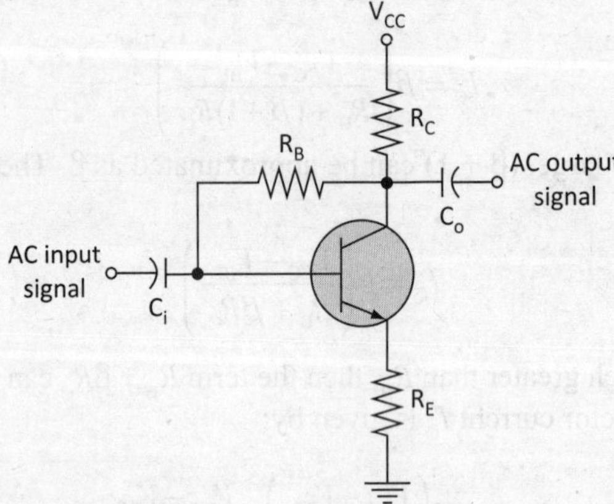

Fig. 2.53: Collector-to-base bias configuration with emitter resistor

Advantages and Disadvantages

The collector-to-base bias circuit provides stability to the operating point against variations in temperature and transistor gain (β). However, due to negative feedback, the AC voltage gain of the amplifier is reduced. This problem is partially solved by splitting the resistor R_B into two parts and by connecting a capacitor C_B as shown in Figure-2.54. For the AC signal, capacitor C_B acts as a short circuit and the effective base resistance R_B is reduced to half. This reduces the AC negative feedback and increases the AC voltage gain offered by the circuit.

Also, the base resistor (R_B) in collector-to-base bias has a smaller value than that used in fixed-bias or the emitter-bias circuit. Therefore, in this case the base current changes more with temperature. Hence, the advantage of better stability factor offered by collector-to-base bias circuit is offset by the larger variation in the base current.

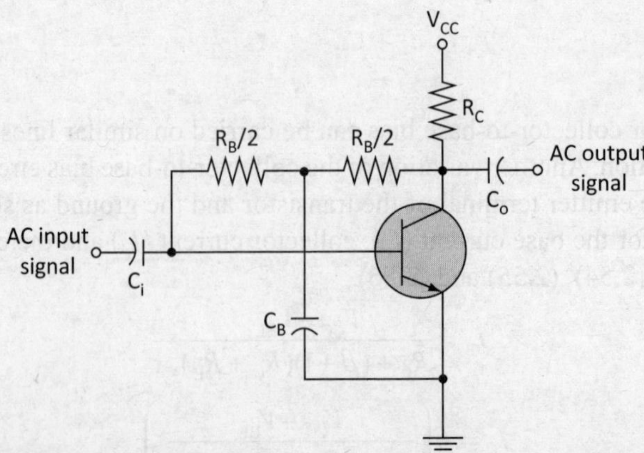

Fig. 2.54: Collector-to-base bias with capacitor to reduce AC negative feedback

Example-2.14: Determine the operating point of the collector-to-base bias circuit of Figure-2.55. The value of the transistor gain β is 100 and the base–emitter voltage (V_{BE}) of the transistor is 0.7 V. Also find the percentage change in the value of operating point when the value of b increases by 50%.

Solution: The value of base current is given by:

$$I_B = \frac{V_{CC} - V_{BE}}{R_B + (\beta + 1)(R_C + R_E)}$$

$$= \frac{15 - 0.7}{200 \times 10^3 + 101 \times (5 \times 10^3 + 1 \times 10^3)}$$

$$= \frac{14.3}{806 \times 10^3} = 17.74\ \mu A$$

Collector current $I_C = \beta I_B = 100 \times 17.74 \times 10^{-6} = 1.77$ mA

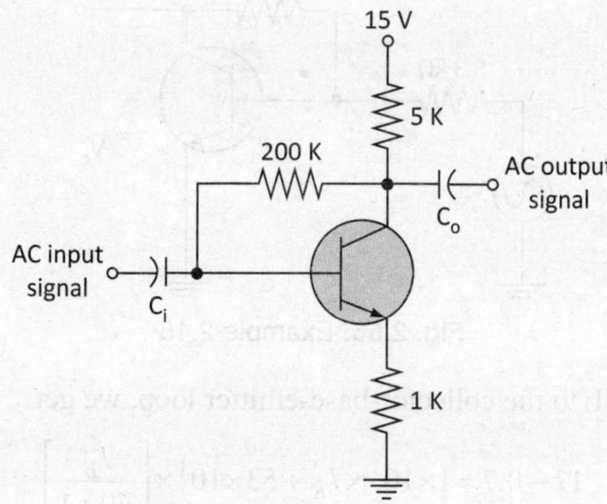

Figure-2.55: Example-2.14

The value of collector–emitter voltage is given by:

$$V_{CE} = V_{CC} - I_C(R_C + R_E)$$

$$= 15 - 1.77 \times 10^{-3} \times (5 \times 10^3 + 1 \times 10^3)$$

$$= 15 - 10.62 = 4.38\ V$$

The operating point for β = 100 is (1.77 mA, 4.38 V)

When the value of β increases by 50%, value of new β is equal to 150

The value of base current is given by:

$$I_B = \frac{V_{CC} - V_{BE}}{R_B + (\beta + 1)(R_C + R_E)}$$

$$= \frac{15 - 0.7}{200 \times 10^3 + 151 \times (5 \times 10^3 + 1 \times 10^3)} = \frac{14.3}{1106 \times 10^3} = 12.93\ \mu A$$

Collector current $I_C = \beta I_B = 150 \times 12.93 \times 10^{-6} = 1.94$ mA

The value of collector–emitter voltage is given by:

$$V_{CE} = V_{CC} - I_C(R_C + R_E)$$
$$= 15 - 1.94 \times 10^{-3} \times (5 \times 10^3 + 1 \times 10^3) = 15 - 11.64 = 3.36 \text{ V}$$

The operating point for $\beta = 150$ is (1.94 mA, 3.36 V)

Percentage change in collector current = [(1.94 – 1.77)/1.77] × 100% = 9.6%

Percentage change in collector-emitter voltage = [(3.36 – 4.38)/4.38] × 100% = –23.3%

Example-2.15: In the BJT amplifier circuit shown in the Figure-2.56, calculate the V_{CE} voltage under the DC conditions (given that $\beta_{DC} = 60$, $V_{BE} = 0.7V$, $h_{ie} \to \infty$, $h_{fe} \to \infty$, $CC \to \infty$).

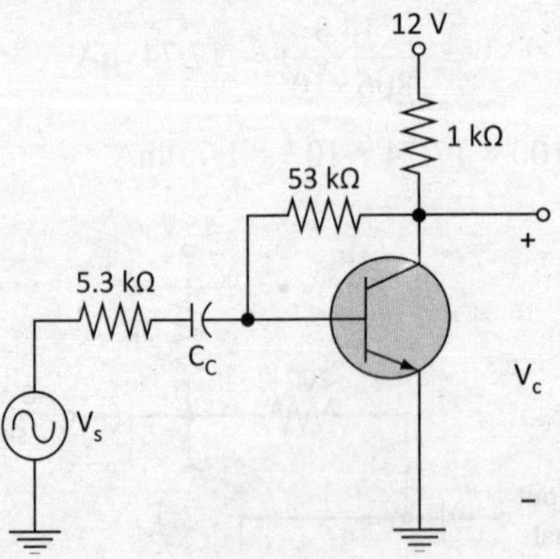

Fig. 2.56: Example-2.15

Solution: Applying KVL to the collector-base-emitter loop, we get

$$12 - 0.7 = 1 \times 10^3 \times I_E + 53 \times 10^3 \times \left[\frac{I_E}{60+1}\right]$$

Therefore, $I_E = 6mA$

Applying KVL to the collector-emitter loop, we get

$$V_{CE} = 12 - 6 \times 10^{-3} \times 1 \times 10^3 = 6V$$

Example-2.16: If in Example-2.15, β_{DC} is increased by 10%, determine change in V_{CE}?

Solution: New $\beta = 66$. From the equations in Example-2.15, the new values of $I_E = 6.31mA$ and $V_{CE} = 5.7V$. The percentage change in V_{CE} is $\left(\frac{6-5.7}{6}\right) \times 100\% = 5\%$.

Therefore, V_{CE} decreases by 5%.

2.7.3 Common-Base configuration

In the common-base circuit, the input is applied to the emitter terminal and the output is taken from the collector terminal. The base terminal is common to both the input and the output sections. Figure-2.57 (a) shows the circuit for common-base configuration. The DC equivalent of the circuit is shown in Figure-2.57 (b).

The analysis of the input section determines the emitter current (I_E). Applying Kirchhoff's voltage law to the input section (emitter–base loop), we get:

$$V_{EE} - I_E R_E - V_{BE} = 0$$

Therefore, the emitter current (I_E) is given by eqn. (2.57).

$$I_E = \frac{V_{EE} - V_{BE}}{R_E} \tag{2.57}$$

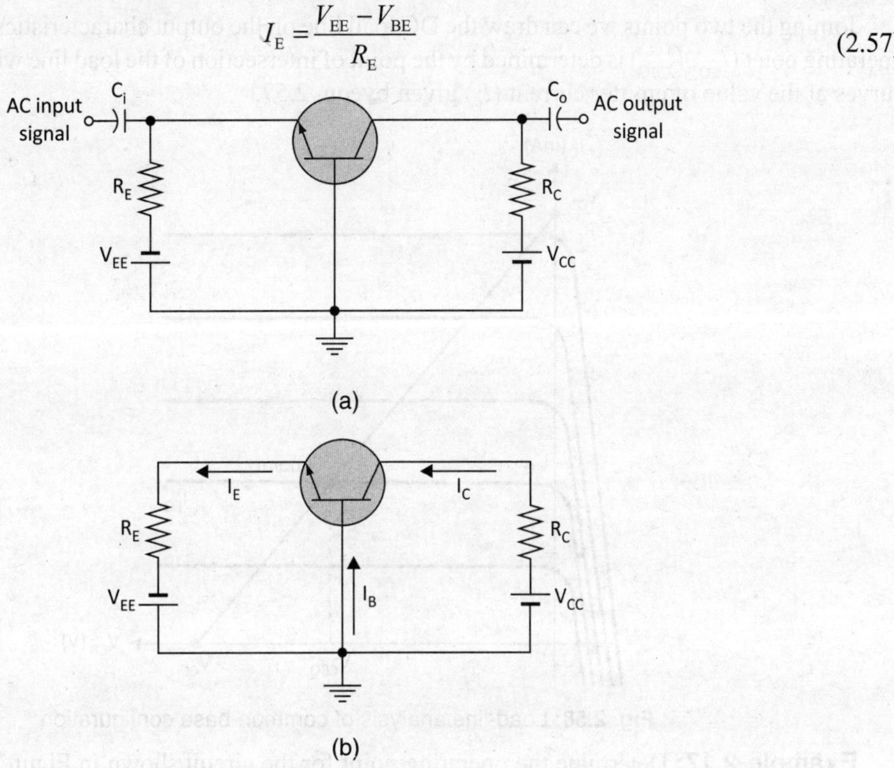

Fig. 2.57: Common-base configuration (a)Basiccircuit (b) DC equivalent of common-base circuit

As the collector current (I_C) ≅ emitter current (I_E), the value of collector current (I_C) is also given by eqn. (2.57). Applying Kirchhoff's voltage law to the output section (collector–emitter loop), we get

$$V_{CC} - V_{CB} - I_C R_C = 0$$

Therefore,

$$V_{CB} = V_{CC} - I_C R_C \tag{2.58}$$

The operating point for the common-base configuration is given by

$$I_C = \frac{V_{EE} - V_{BE}}{R_E}, \; V_{CB} = V_{CC} - I_C R_C \tag{2.59}$$

2.7.3.1 Load-line Analysis

The load line is drawn using the output equation given by eqn. 2.58.Substituting $I_C = 0$ in eqn. 2.58, we get,

$$V_{CB} = V_{CC}\big|_{I_C=0}$$

Substituting $V_{CB} = 0$ in eqn. 2.58, we get,

$$I_C = \frac{V_{CC}}{R_C}\bigg|_{V_{CB}=0}$$

Joining the two points we can draw the DC load line on the output characteristics (Figure-2.58). The operating point (I_{CQ}, V_{CBQ}) is determined by the point of intersection of the load line with the characteristic curves at the value of emitter current (I_E) given byeqn. 2.57.

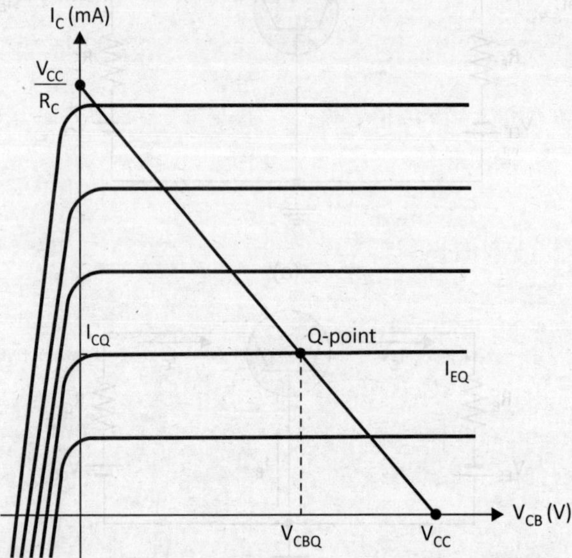

Fig. 2.58: Load-line analysis of common-base configuration

Example-2.17: Determine the operating point for the circuit shown in Figure-2.59 given that the transistor base–emitter voltage (V_{BE}) is 0.7 V.

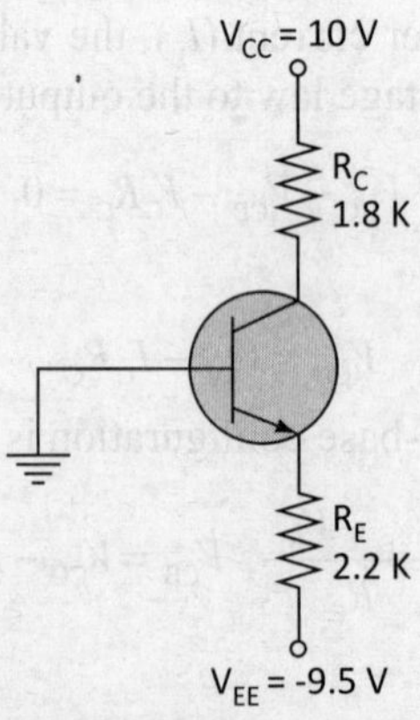

Fig. 2.59: Example-2.17

Solution: The value of the emitter current is given by:

$$I_E = \frac{V_{EE} - V_{BE}}{R_E}$$

$$I_E = (9.5 - 0.7)/2.2\times10^3 = 4 \text{ mA}$$

The value of collector current $I_C \cong I_E$. Therefore, $I_C = 4$ mA

The output voltage (V_{CB}) is given by:

$V_{CB} = 10 - 4\times10^{-3} \times 1.8 \times 10^3 = 10 - 7.2 = 2.8$

The operating point is $I_C = 4$ mA, $V_{CB} = 2.8$ V

2.7.4 Common-Collector configuration

In the *common-collector configuration*, also referred to as *emitter-follower configuration*, the input voltage is applied to the base terminal and the output is taken from the emitter leg. The collector terminal is common to both the input and the output sections. Common-collector configuration exhibits 100% voltage-series feedback as whole output voltage is fed-back in series with the input voltage.

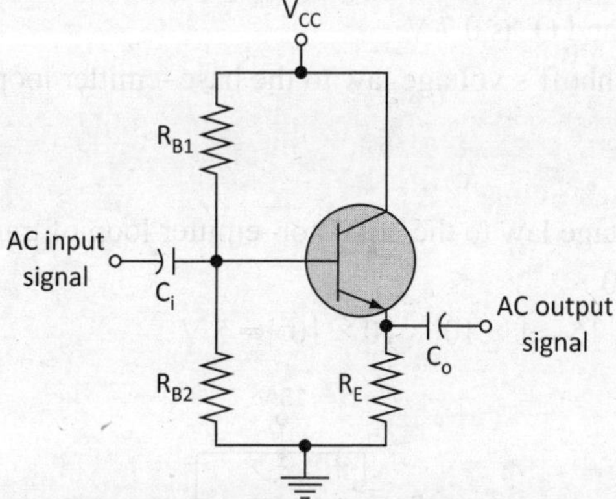

Fig. 2.60: Common-collector circuit

Figure-2.60 shows one of the possible circuits of common-collector configuration. The circuit is similar to that of voltage-divider bias with the difference that there is no collector resistor (R_C) and the output is taken from the emitter resistor (R_E) instead of the collector terminal. Figure-2.61 (a) shows another possible common-collector circuit. Figure-2.61 (b) shows the DC equivalent of the circuit in Figure-2.61(a). Applying Kirchhoff's voltage law to the base–emitter loop, we get,

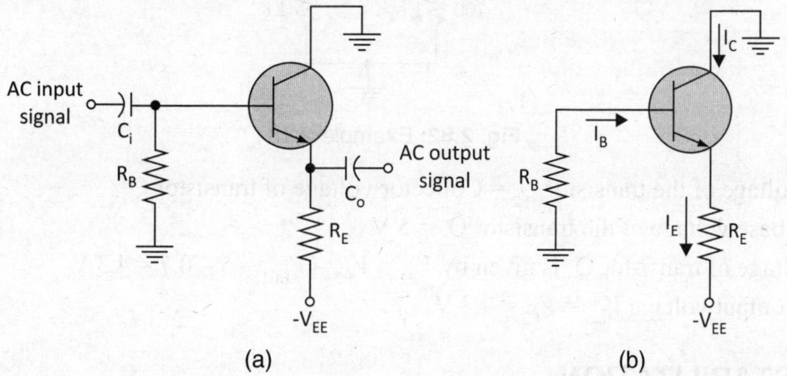

Fig. 2.61: (a) One possible common-collector configuration; (b) DC equivalent of the circuit in (a)

$$-I_B R_B - V_{BE} - I_E R_E + V_{EE} = 0$$

Substituting $I_E = (\beta + 1)I_B$ in the above equation and solving for base current (I_B), we get,

$$I_B = \frac{V_{EE} - V_{BE}}{R_B + (\beta + 1)R_E} \tag{2.60}$$

Applying Kirchhoff's voltage law to the emitter–collector loop, we get

$$-V_{EE} + I_E R_E + V_{CE} = 0 \tag{2.61}$$

$$V_{CE} = V_{EE} - I_E R_E$$

Load-line analysis can be done on similar lines as done earlier for the common-emitter configuration.

Example-2.18: Determine the output voltage (V_{out}) of the circuit shown in Figure-2.62, given that V_{BE} voltage for transistors Q_1 and Q_2 is 0.7 V.

Solution: Applying Kirchhoff's voltage law to the base–emitter loop of transistor Q_1, we get

$1.7 - 0.7 - 100 \times I_{E1} = 0$

$I_{E1} = 10$ mA

Applying Kirchhoff's voltage law to the collector–emitter loop of transistor Q_1, we get

$15 - 1 \times 10^3 \times I_{C1} - V_{C1} = 0$

As $I_{E1} \cong I_{C1}$, therefore $V_{C1} = 15 - 1 \times 10^3 \times 10 \times 10^{-3} = 5$ V

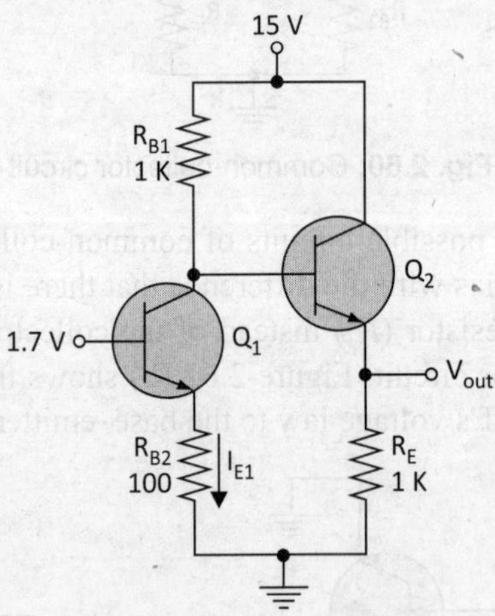

Fig. 2.62: Example-2.18

The base voltage of the transistor Q_2 = Collector voltage of transistor Q_1

Therefore, base voltage of the transistor $Q_2 = 5$ V

Emitter voltage of transistor Q_2 is given by $V_{E2} = V_{B2} - V_{BE2} = 5 - 0.7 = 4.3$ V

Therefore, output voltage $V_{out} = V_{E2} = 4.3$ V

2.8 BIAS STABILIZATION

Bias stabilization refers to the ability of a bias circuit to maintain a fixed operating point against variations in temperature and transistor gain (β). Bias stabilization is important as the transistor parameters are strongly dependent on temperature. The transistor gain (β) increases with increase in temperature, the base–emitter voltage (V_{BE}) of the transistor decreases with increase in temperature at a rate of 2.5 mV/°C for constant collector current and the leakage current (I_{CO}) doubles itself for every 10°C rise in temperature. As the base current (I_B) depends on V_{BE}; therefore it also varies with temperature. Collector current (I_C) is given by the expression $I_C = \beta I_B + (\beta + 1)I_{CO}$. Therefore, it varies with change in temperature as all the three parameters in its expression are temperature-dependent.

Figure-2.63 shows the typical output characteristics of a common–emitter transistor at two different temperatures. As it is evident from the figure, the CE output characteristics shift upwards with increase in temperature as the leakage current (I_{CO}) increases with increase in temperature. The spacing between the adjacent curves also increases as the gain (β) of the transistor increases. Thus for the same base current, the operating point shifts and it may be possible that the transistor biased in the active region at one temperature finds itself in the saturation region at an elevated temperature.

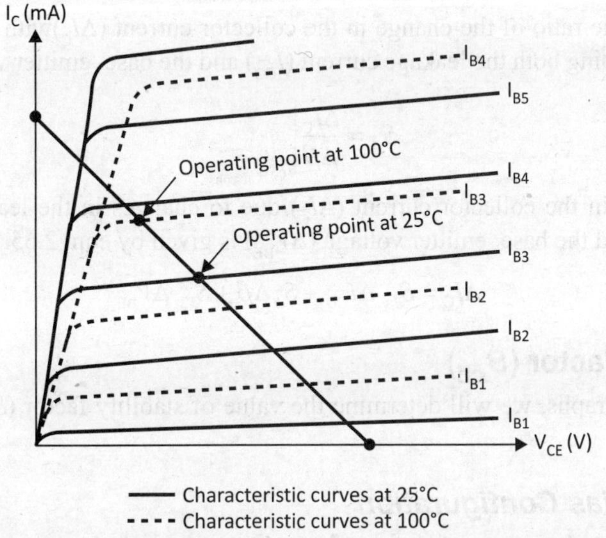

Fig. 2.63: Variation in the output characteristics of a transistor with change in temperature

Another important cause of variation in collector current (I_C) is the widespread variation in the value of transistor gain (β) of the order of three times for two transistors of the same type number. Thus for the same base current, the collector current varies with change in the transistor used in the circuit. Each of the biasing circuits described in preceding sections offers different amount of stability to the operating point. The amount of stability offered by the circuit is measured in terms of stability factor, which is described in the following section.

2.8.1 Stability Factor

Stability factor defines the extent to which the collector current (I_C) of a transistor is stable against variations in the transistor parameters, namely, the leakage current (I_{CO}), the transistor gain (β) and the base-emitter voltage (V_{BE}). The three types of stability factors are defined with respect to transistors, namely, SI_{CO}, Sâ and SV_{BE}. Small value of stability factor indicates good bias stability whereas large value of stability factor indicates poor bias stability. Ideal value of stability factor is zero.

There are three different stability factors namely SI_{CO}, SV_{BE} and $S\beta$ that describe change in collector current with respect to change in leakage current (I_{CO}), base-emitter voltage (V_{BE}) and transistor gain (β).SI_{CO} is defined as the ratio of the change in the collector current ($\ddot{A}I_C$)with respect to change in the leakage current (ΔI_{CO}) with the base-emitter voltage (V_{BE}) and the transistor gain (β) held constant. It can be expressed mathematically by eqn. 2.62.

$$S_{I_{CO}} = \left.\frac{\Delta I_C}{\Delta I_{CO}}\right|_{V_{BE},\beta\text{const.}} \tag{2.62}$$

SV_{BE} is defined as the ratio of change in the collector current (ΔI_C)with respect to change in the base-emitter voltage (ΔV_{BE}) with both the leakage current (I_{CO}) and the transistor gain (β) held constant:

$$S_{V_{BE}} = \left.\frac{\Delta I_C}{\Delta V_{BE}}\right|_{I_{CO},\beta\text{const.}} \tag{2.63}$$

$S\beta$ is defined as the ratio of the change in the collector current (ΔI_C)with respect to change in the transistor gain (β) keeping both the leakage current (I_{CO}) and the base–emitter voltage (V_{BE}) as constant:

$$S_\beta = \left.\frac{\Delta I_C}{\Delta \beta}\right|_{I_{CO},V_{BE}\text{const.}} \tag{2.64}$$

The total change in the collector current (ΔI_C) due to changes in the leakage current (ΔI_{CO}), the transistor gain (Δβ) and the base–emitter voltage (ΔV_{BE}) is given by eqn. 2.65.

$$\Delta I_C = S_{I_{CO}}\Delta I_{CO} + S_\beta \Delta\beta + S_{V_{BE}}\Delta V_{BE} \tag{2.65}$$

2.8.2 Stability Factor (S_{ICO})

In the following paragraphs, we will determine the value of stability factor (S_{ICO}) offered by different biasing circuits.

2.8.2.1 Fixed-Bias Configuration

The collector current (I_C) is expressed in terms of the base current (I_B) as:

$$I_C = \beta I_B + (\beta+1)I_{CO}$$

Differentiating collector current (I_C) with respect to the leakage current (I_{CO}) and keeping the transistor gain (β) and the base–emitter voltage (V_{BE}) as constant, we get,

$$\frac{dI_C}{dI_{CO}} = (\beta+1)$$

he stability factor S_{ICO} for a fixed-bias circuit is given by eqn. 2.66.

$$S_{I_{CO}} = \beta + 1 \tag{2.66}$$

If β = 100, then S_{ICO} = 101, which implies that the collector current increases by 101 times than the increase in the leakage current. Therefore, for fixed-bias circuit, the collector current (I_C) is strongly dependent on the change in the leakage current (I_{CO}) and hence on the temperature. In other words, fixed-bias circuit offers very poor stability against variations in the leakage current.

2.8.2.2 Emitter-Bias Configuration

As derived in the section on DC analysis, the voltage-current equation of the base-emitter loop of the emitter-bias configuration is given by eqn. 2.67.

$$V_{CC} - V_{BE} - I_E R_E - I_B R_B = 0 \tag{2.67}$$

Substituting $I_E = I_B + I_C$ in eqn. (2.67) and rearranging the terms, we get eqn. 2.68.

$$(R_B + R_E) I_B = V_{CC} - V_{BE} - I_C R_E$$

$$I_B = \frac{V_{CC} - V_{BE} - I_C R_E}{R_B + R_E} \tag{2.68}$$

As $V_{BE} << V_{CC}$, eqn. (2.68) can be rewritten as eqn. 2.69.

$$I_B = \frac{V_{CC} - I_C R_E}{R_B + R_E} \tag{2.69}$$

The collector current (I_C) is expressed by eqn. 2.70.

$$I_C = \beta I_B + (\beta + 1) I_{CO} \tag{2.70}$$

Substituting the value of I_B given by eqn. (2.69) in eqn. (2.70) we get,

$$I_C = \beta \frac{(V_{CC} - I_C R_E)}{R_B + R_E} + (\beta + 1) I_{CO} \tag{2.71}$$

Rearranging the terms of eqn. (2.71) we get eqn. 2.72.

$$\frac{(R_B + R_E + \beta R_E) I_C}{R_B + R_E} = \frac{\beta V_{CC}}{R_B + R_E} + (\beta + 1) I_{CO}$$

$$I_C = \frac{\beta V_{CC}}{R_B + (\beta + 1) R_E} + \frac{(\beta + 1)(R_B + R_E) I_{CO}}{R_B + (\beta + 1) R_E} \tag{2.72}$$

Differentiating I_C in eqn. (2.72) with respect to I_{CO} keeping b and V_{BE} constant we get,

$$\frac{dI_C}{dI_{CO}} = \frac{(\beta + 1)(R_B + R_E)}{R_B + (\beta + 1) R_E} = \frac{(\beta + 1)(1 + R_B/R_E)}{1 + \beta + R_B/R_E}$$

Therefore, the stability factor S_{ICO} for emitter-bias configuration is given by eqn. 2.73.

$$S_{I_{CO}} = \frac{(\beta + 1)(1 + R_B/R_E)}{1 + \beta + R_B/R_E} \tag{2.73}$$

For $(R_B/R_E) >> (\beta + 1)$, eqn. (2.73) becomes

$$S_{I_{CO}} \cong \beta + 1 \tag{2.74}$$

For the other extreme, when $(R_B/R_E) << 1$

$$S_{I_{CO}} \cong 1 \tag{2.75}$$

Thus, the stability factor (S_{ICO}) for an emitter-bias circuit varies from approximately 1 to (b + 1) as the ratio of base resistor (R_B) to emitter resistor (R_E) increases from a very small value to a very large value (Figure-2.64). As we know, the stability factor should be as small as possible, therefore, the ratio R_B/R_E should be as small as possible. Thus, resistor R_E should be sufficiently large. Increase in the value of R_E increases the negative feedback factor and reduces the gain of the circuit. Therefore, a trade-off needs to be applied that satisfies both the stability and circuit gain criteria.

To sum up, the emitter-bias configuration offers stability against variations in the leakage current $I_{CO.}$ However, the stability offered is not very high as the ratio of R_B/R_E cannot be reduced beyond a certain value. This problem is overcome in the voltage-divider bias with emitter-bias configuration.

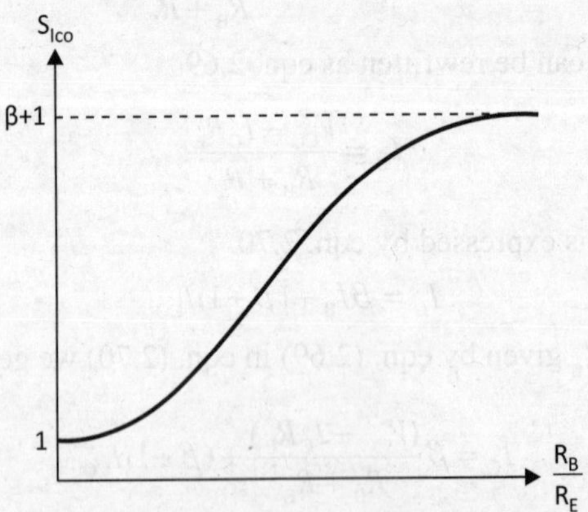

Fig. 2.64: Stability factor for emitter-bias circuit

The fact that the emitter-bias configuration offers stability can also be explained logically, without going deep into mathematical calculations, with the help of the expression of the base current (I_B) for the configuration given as

$$I_B = \frac{V_{CC} - V_{BE} - I_C R_E}{R_B + R_E} \tag{2.76}$$

When the collector current (I_C) increases due to increase in the leakage current (I_{CO}), the value of the base current (I_B) decreases, which in turn reduces the value of the collector current (I_C). This compensates for the initial increase in I_C. Thus, the circuit tries to maintain a constant collector current.

2.8.2.3 Voltage-Divider Bias with Emitter-Bias Configuration

In the case of voltage-divider bias configuration, the expression for S_{ICO} is similar to that of emitter-bias configuration, with the base resistor (R_B) being replaced by Thevenin'sequivalent resistance (R_{TH}):

$$S_{I_{CO}} = \frac{(\beta+1)(1+R_{TH}/R_E)}{1+\beta+R_{TH}/R_E} \tag{2.77}$$

The circuit offers highest stability when the value of emitter resistor (R_E) is much larger than the Thevenin's equivalent resistance (R_{TH}). It must be remembered that in voltage-divider configuration, Thevenin's equivalent resistance (R_{TH}) is much smaller than corresponding base resistor (R_B) of the emitter-bias configuration. Thus, the ratio R_E/R_{TH} is higher as compared to R_E/R_B in emitter-bias configuration. Hence, this configuration offers better stability as compared to the emitter-bias configuration.

2.8.2.4 Collector-to-Base Bias Configuration

The expression for S_{ICO} for collector-to-base bias configuration can be obtained in a manner similar to that for the emitter-bias configuration. The expression is given by eqn. 2.78.

$$S_{I_{CO}} = \frac{(\beta+1)(1+R_B/R_C)}{1+\beta+R_B/R_C} \tag{2.78}$$

Hence, the ratio R_B/R_C should be as small as possible for better stability.

2.8.3 Stability Factor (S_{VBE})

SV_{BE} is defined as the ratio of change in the collector current (ΔI_C) with respect to change in the base-emitter voltage (ΔV_{BE})with both the leakage current (I_{CO}) and the transistor gain (β) held constant. In the following sub-sections we derive the expression for S_{VBE} for different biasing circuits.

2.8.3.1 Fixed-Bias Circuit

The expression for collector current (I_C) is given by:

$$I_C = \beta I_B + (\beta+1)I_{CO}$$

In the case of fixed-bias circuit, the expression for base current (I_B) is given by

$$I_B = \frac{V_{CC} - V_{BE}}{R_B} \tag{2.79}$$

Substituting the value of base current (I_B) in the expression for collector current (I_C), we get,

$$I_C = \frac{\beta(V_{CC} - V_{BE})}{R_B} + (\beta+1)I_{CO} \tag{2.80}$$

Differentiating eqn. (2.80) with respect to V_{BE} with I_{CO} and $b$constant, we get,

$$\frac{dI_C}{dV_{BE}} = \frac{-\beta}{R_B}$$

Therefore, the stability factor S_{VBE} for a fixed-bias configuration is given by eqn. 2.81.

$$S_{V_{BE}} = \frac{-\beta}{R_B} \tag{2.81}$$

As is clear from this equation, the stability factor (S_{VBE}) of the fixed-bias circuit improves as the value of base resistor (R_B) increases.

2.8.3.2 Emitter-Bias Configuration

In the emitter-bias configuration the base current (I_B) is given by eqn. 2.82.

$$I_B = \frac{V_{CC} - V_{BE} - I_C R_E}{R_B + R_E} \tag{2.82}$$

Collector current (I_C) is given by eqn. 2.83.

$$I_C = \beta I_B + (\beta+1)I_{CO} \tag{2.83}$$

Substituting this value of base current (I_B) in eqn. (2.83), we get,

$$I_C = \frac{\beta(V_{CC} - V_{BE} - I_C R_E)}{R_B + R_E} + (\beta + 1)I_{CO} \tag{2.84}$$

Rearranging the terms in eqn.(2.84), we get,

$$I_C = \frac{\beta(V_{CC} - V_{BE}) + (\beta + 1)(R_B + R_E)I_{CO}}{R_B + (\beta + 1)R_E} \tag{2.85}$$

Differentiating I_C in eqn. (2.85) with respect to V_{BE} keeping β and I_{CO} constant, we get,

$$\frac{dI_C}{dV_{BE}} = \frac{-\beta}{R_B + (\beta + 1)R_E} = \frac{-\beta / R_E}{R_B / R_E + (\beta + 1)}$$

Thus, the stability factor S_{VBE} for the emitter-bias configuration is given by eqn. 2.86.

$$S_{V_{BE}} = \frac{-\beta / R_E}{R_B / R_E + (\beta + 1)} \tag{2.86}$$

When (β + 1) >> (R_B/R_E), the value of stability factor is given by eqn. 2.87.

$$S_{V_{BE}} = \frac{-\beta / R_E}{\beta + 1} \cong \frac{-1}{R_E} \tag{2.87}$$

As is evident from eqn. (2.87), the stability of the circuit against variations in base-emitter voltage (V_{BE}) improves with an increase in the value of emitter resistance (R_E).

2.8.3.3 Voltage-Divider Bias with Emitter-Bias Configuration

In the case of voltage-divider bias configuration, the expression for S_{VBE} is similar to that of emitter-bias configuration with the base resistor (R_B) replaced by Thevenin's equivalent resistance (R_{TH}).

$$S_{V_{BE}} = \frac{-\beta / R_E}{R_{TH} / R_E + (\beta + 1)} \tag{2.88}$$

2.8.3.4 Collector-to-Base Bias Configuration

In the case of collector-to-base bias, the expression for S_{VBE} is similar to that of emitter-bias configuration with the emitter resistor (R_E) being replaced by collector resistor (R_C).

$$S_{V_{BE}} = \frac{-\beta / R_C}{R_B / R_C + (\beta + 1)} \tag{2.89}$$

2.8.4 Stability Factor (S_β)

Sâ is defined as the ratio of the change in the collector current (ΔI_C) with respect to change in the transistor gain (β) keeping both I_{CO} and V_{BE} constant.

2.8.4.1 Fixed-Bias Configuration

The expression for collector current is given by:

$$I_C = \beta I_B + (\beta + 1)I_{CO}$$

As $I_{CO} << I_B$, therefore $I_C = \beta I_B$

For $\beta = \beta_1$,

$$I_{C1} = \beta_1 I_B \tag{2.90}$$

For $\beta = \beta_2$,

$$I_{C2} = \beta_2 I_B \tag{2.91}$$

Subtracting eqn. (2.90) from eqn. (2.91), we get,

$$I_{C2} - I_{C1} = (\beta_2 - \beta_1) I_B \tag{2.92}$$

Substituting $(I_{C2} - I_{C1})$ as ΔI_C and $(\beta_2 - \beta_1)$ as $\Delta\beta$ in eqn. (2.92), we get,

$$\Delta I_C = \Delta\beta I_B \tag{2.93}$$

Eqn. (2.93) can be rewritten as eqn. 2.94.

$$\frac{\Delta I_C}{\Delta\beta} = I_B = \frac{I_{C1}}{\beta_1} \tag{2.94}$$

Therefore, the value of stability factor S_β for the fixed-bias circuit is given by

$$S_\beta = \frac{I_{C1}}{\beta_1} \tag{2.95}$$

2.8.4.2 Emitter-Bias Configuration

In the emitter-bias configuration the base current (I_B) is given by eqn. 2.105.

$$I_B = \frac{V_{CC} - V_{BE} - I_C R_E}{R_B + R_E} \tag{2.96}$$

As we know, the expression for collector current (I_C) is given by eqn. 2.97.

$$I_C = \beta I_B + (\beta + 1) I_{CO} \tag{2.97}$$

Substituting this value of I_B given by eqn. (2.96) in Eq. (2.97), we get,

$$I_C = \frac{\beta(V_{CC} - V_{BE} - I_C R_E)}{R_B + R_E} + (\beta + 1) I_{CO} \tag{2.98}$$

Rearranging the terms in eqn. (2.98), we get,

$$I_C(R_B + R_E + \beta R_E) = \beta V_{CC} - \beta V_{BE} + (\beta + 1)(R_B + R_E) I_{CO}. \tag{2.99}$$

As $V_{BE} << V_{CC}$ and $I_{CO} << I_C$, eqn. (2.99) can be approximated as:

$$I_C(R_B + R_E + \beta R_E) = \beta V_{CC} \tag{2.100}$$

For $\beta = \beta_1$, eqn. (2.100) can be written as:

$$I_{C1}(R_B + R_E + \beta_1 R_E) = \beta_1 V_{CC} \tag{2.101}$$

For $\beta = \beta_2$, eqn. (2.101) can be written as:

$$I_{C2}(R_B + R_E + \beta_2 R_E) = \beta_2 V_{CC} \tag{2.102}$$

Subtracting eqn. (2.101) from eqn. (2.102), we get,

$$(I_{C2} - I_{C1})(R_B + R_E) + I_{C2}\beta_2 R_E - I_{C1}\beta_1 R_E = (\beta_2 - \beta_1)V_{CC} \tag{2.103}$$

Substituting $(I_{C2} - I_{C1})$ as ΔI_C and $(\beta_2 - \beta_1)$ as Δb in eqn. (2.103), we get,

$$\Delta I_C(R_B + R_E) + I_{C2}\beta_2 R_E - I_{C1}\beta_1 R_E = \Delta\beta V_{CC} \tag{2.104}$$

Adding and subtracting $I_{C1}\beta_2 R_E$ in eqn. (2.104) and then solving we get,

$$\Delta I_C(R_B + R_E) + \Delta I_C \beta_2 R_E + I_{C1}\Delta\beta R_E = \Delta\beta V_{CC} \tag{2.105}$$

Rearranging the terms in eqn. (2.105) we get,

$$\Delta I_C(R_B + R_E + \beta_2 R_E) = \Delta\beta(V_{CC} - I_{C1}R_E) \tag{2.106}$$

Rearranging the terms in eqn. (2.101) we get,

$$V_{CC} = \frac{I_{C1}(R_B + R_E + \beta_1 R_E)}{\beta_1} \tag{2.107}$$

Substituting this value of V_{CC} in eqn. (2.106), we get,

$$\Delta I_C(R_B + R_E + \beta_2 R_E) = \Delta\beta\left[\frac{I_{C1}(R_B + R_E + \beta_1 R_E)}{\beta_1} - I_{C1}R_E\right]$$

Therefore,

$$\frac{\Delta I_C}{\Delta\beta} = \frac{I_{C1}(R_B + R_E)}{\beta_1(R_B + R_E + \beta_2 R_E)}$$

$$\frac{\Delta I_C}{\Delta\beta} = \frac{I_{C1}(1 + R_B/R_E)}{\beta_1(1 + \beta_2 + R_B/R_E)}$$

The value of stability factor (S_β) for the emitter-bias configuration is given by eqn. 2.108.

$$S_\beta = \frac{I_{C1}(1 + R_B/R_E)}{\beta_1(1 + \beta_2 + R_B/R_E)} \tag{2.108}$$

2.8.4.3 Voltage-Divider Bias with Emitter-Bias Configuration

In the case of voltage-divider bias configuration, the expression for S_a is similar to that of emitter-bias configuration with the base resistor (R_B) being replaced by Thevenin's equivalent resistance (R_{TH}):

$$S_\beta = \frac{I_{C1}(1 + R_{TH}/R_E)}{\beta_1(1 + \beta_2 + R_{TH}/R_E)} \tag{2.109}$$

2.8.4.4 Collector-to-Base Bias Configuration

In the case of collector-to-base bias, the expression for S_β is similar to that of emitter-bias configuration with the resistance R_E being replaced by R_C. It is given by eqn. 2.110.

$$S_{\beta} = \frac{I_{C1}(1+R_B/R_C)}{\beta_1(1+\beta_2+R_B/R_C)} \tag{2.110}$$

Table-2.3 summarizes the values of collector current (I_C), collector-to-emitter voltage (V_{CE}) and stability factors S_{ICO}, S_{VBE} and S_{β} for the various transistor-biased circuits.

Table 2.3: Important parameters of different biasing configurations

	I_C	V_{CE}	S_{ICO}	S_{VBE}	S_b
Fixed bias	$\beta\left(\frac{V_{CC}-V_{BE}}{R_B}\right)$	$V_{CC}-I_{CQ}R_C$	$\beta+1$	$\frac{-\beta}{R_B}$	$\frac{I_{C1}}{\beta_1}$
Emitter bias	$\beta\left(\frac{V_{CC}-V_{BE}}{R_B+(\beta+1)R_E}\right)$	$V_{CC}-I_{CQ}(R_C+R_E)$	$\frac{(\beta+1)(1+R_B/R_E)}{1+\beta+R_B/R_E}$	$\frac{-\beta/R_E}{R_B/R_E+(\beta+1)}$	$\frac{I_{C1}(1+R_B/R_E)}{\beta_1(1+\beta_2+R_B/R_E)}$
Voltage-divider bias	$\beta\left(\frac{V_{TH}-V_{BE}}{R_{TH}+(\beta+1)R_E}\right)$	$V_{CC}-I_{CQ}(R_C+R_E)$	$\frac{(\beta+1)(1+R_{TH}/R_E)}{1+\beta+R_{TH}/R_E}$	$\frac{-\beta/R_E}{R_{TH}/R_E+(\beta+1)}$	$\frac{I_{C1}(1+R_{TH}/R_E)}{\beta_1(1+\beta_2+R_{TH}/R_E)}$
Collector-to-base bias	$\beta\left(\frac{V_{CC}-V_{BE}}{R_B+(\beta+1)R_C}\right)$	$V_{CC}-I_{CQ}R_C$	$\frac{(\beta+1)(1+R_B/R_C)}{1+\beta+R_B/R_C}$	$\frac{-\beta/R_C}{R_B/R_C+(\beta+1)}$	$\frac{I_{C1}(1+R_B/R_C)}{\beta_1(1+\beta_2+R_B/R_C)}$

Example-2.19: Determine the stability factors S_{ICO}, S_{VBE} and S_{β} for each of the following bias arrangements. Also, determine the total change in collector current when the temperature changes from +25°C to +175°C. The various transistor parameters at different temperatures are listed in Table 2.4.

(a) Fixed-bias circuit (R_B = 300 K, I_C = 2 mA, β = 50).

(b) Emitter-bias circuit (R_B = 300 K, R_E = 2 K, I_C = 2 mA, β = 50).

(c) Voltage-divider bias circuit (R_{B1} = 50 K, R_{B2} = 10 K, R_E = 2 K, I_C = 2 mA, β = 50).

Table-2.4: Example 2.19

T (°C)	I_{CO} (nA)	b	V_{BE} (V)
–65	2×10^{-4}	25	0.85
25	0.2	50	0.7
100	25	80	0.5
175	3×10^3	125	0.32

Solution: (a) Fixed-bias circuit

S_{ICO} = β + 1. Therefore, S_{ICO} = 51

$$S_{\beta} = \frac{I_{C1}}{\beta_1}$$

where I_{C1} and β_1 are the values of collector current and transistor gain at 25 °C, I_{C1} = 2 mA and β_1 = 50

Therefore, $S_{\beta} = 2 \times 10^{-3}/50 = 4 \times 10^{-5}$

$S_{VBE} = -\beta/R_B$. Therefore, $S_{VBE} = -50/(300 \times 10^3) = -16.6 \times 10^{-5}$

Total change in the collector current ΔI_C is $\Delta I_C = S_{I_{CO}}\Delta I_{CO} + S_{\beta}\Delta\beta + S_{V_{BE}}\Delta V_{BE}$.

$\Delta I_{CO} = (3 \times 10^3 - 0.2)$ nA $= 2.8 \times 10^3$ nA $= 2.8\mu$A

$\Delta b = 125 - 50 = 75.$

$\Delta V_{BE} = 0.32 - 0.7 = -0.38.$

$\Delta I_C = [51 \times 3 \times 10^{-6} + 4 \times 10^{-5} \times 75 + (-16.6 \times 10^{-5})(-0.38)]$ A $= (153 + 3000 + 63.08)$ μA $= 3.22$ mA

(b) Emitter-bias circuit

$$S_{I_{CO}} = \frac{(1+\beta)(1+R_B/R_E)}{1+\beta+R_B/R_E}$$

$$S_{I_{CO}} = (51)[1+\{(300\times10^3)/(2\times10^3)\}]/[1+50+\{(300\times10^3)/(2\times10^3)\}]$$

$$= 51\times151/201 = 38.31$$

$$S_\beta = \frac{I_{C1}(1+R_B/R_E)}{\beta_1(1+\beta_2+R_B/R_E)}$$

where I_{C1} and β_1 are the values of collector current and transistor gain at 25 °C. $I_{C1} = 2$ mA and $\beta_1 = 50$. β_2 is the transistor gain at 175 °C and is given by $\beta_2 = 125$

Therefore, $S = (2 \times 10^{-3})[1 + \{(300 \times 10^3)/(2 \times 10^3)\}]/[50(1 + 125 + \{(300 \times 10^3)/(2 \times 10^3)\}]$
$= (302 \times 10^{-3})/(50 \times 276) = 2.19 \times 10^{-5}$

$$S_{V_{BE}} = \frac{-\beta/R_E}{R_B/R_E + (\beta+1)}$$

$$S_{V_{BE}} = \{-50/(2\times10^3)\}/[\{(300\times10^3)/(2\times10^3)\}+51]$$

$$= -25\times10^{-3}/201 = 0.1243\times10^{-3} = -12.43\times10^{-5}$$

Total change in the collector current ΔI_C is $\Delta I_C = S_{I_{CO}}\Delta I_{CO} + S_\beta\Delta\beta + S_{V_{BE}}\Delta V_{BE}$.

$\Delta I_C = [38.31 \times 3 \times 10^{-6} + 2.19 \times 10^{-5} \times 75 + (-12.43 \times 10^{-5})(-0.38)]$ A $= 1.8$ mA

(c) Voltage-divider bias with emitter-bias circuit

$$R_{TH} = \frac{R_{B1}\times R_{B2}}{R_{B1}+R_{B2}}$$

$$R_{TH} = (50\times10^3\times10\times10^3)/(50\times10^3+10\times10^3) = 500/60 = 8.3\text{ K}$$

$$S_{I_{CO}} = \frac{(1+\beta)(1+R_{TH}/R_E)}{1+\beta+R_{TH}/R_E}$$

$$S_{I_{CO}} = [(51)\{1+(8.3\times10^3)/(2\times10^3)\}]/\{1+50+(8.3\times10^3)/(2\times10^3)\}$$

$$= 51\times5.15/55.15 = 4.76$$

$$S_\beta = \frac{I_{C1}(1+R_{TH}/R_E)}{\beta_1(1+\beta_2+R_{TH}/R_E)}$$

where I_{C1} and β_1 are the values of collector current and transistor gain at 25 °C. $I_{C1} = 2$ mA and $\beta_1 = 50$. β_2 is the transistor gain at 175 °C, that is $\beta_2 = 125$.

Therefore,

$$S_\beta = [(2\times10^{-3})\{1+(8.3\times10^3)/(2\times10^3)\}]/(50[1+125+\{(8.3\times10^3)/(2\times10^3)\}])$$

$$= 10.3\times10^{-3}/6507.5 \;=\; 1.58\times10^{-6}$$

$$S_{V_{\rm BE}} = \frac{-\beta/R_{\rm E}}{R_{\rm TH}/R_{\rm E}+(\beta+1)}$$

$$S_{V_{\rm BE}} = \{-50/(2\times10^3)\}/[\{(8.3\times10^3)/(2\times10^3)\}+50+1]$$

$$= -25\times10^{-3}/55.15 \;=\; 0.453\times10^{-3} = -45.3\times10^{-5}$$

Total change in the collector current ΔI_C is given by:

$$\Delta I_{\rm C} = S_{I_{\rm CO}}\Delta I_{\rm CO} + S_\beta \Delta\beta + S_{V_{\rm BE}}\Delta V_{\rm BE}$$

$$\Delta I_{\rm C} = [4.76\times3\times10^{-6} + 1.58\times10^{-6}\times75 + (-45.3\times10^{-5})(-0.38)]\ \text{A} \;=\; 0.305\ \text{mA}$$

Example-2.20: Design an emitter-bias circuit with the following specifications:

(a) change in collector current due to change in leakage current for a temperature range of 25ºC to 100ºC to be less than or equal to 1 µA;

(b) change in collector current due to change in transistor gain b for a temperature range of 25°C to 100°C to be less than or equal to 50 µA;

(c) change in collector current due to change in base-emitter voltage (V_{BE}) for a temperature range of 25°C to 100°C to be less than or equal to 400 µA;

(d) the quiescent collector-to-emitter voltage is 4 V.

Given that at 25 °C I_{CO} = 0.1 nA, β = 50, V_{BE} = 0.7; and at 100 °C I_{CO} = 25.1 nA, β = 70, V_{BE} = 0.4.

Solution: The desired value of the stability factor $S_{ICO} \le 1 \times 10^{-6}/(25.1 - 0.1) \times 10^{-9} \le 40$. Therefore, the maximum value of S_{ICO} is 40.

For an emitter-bias circuit,

$$S_{I_{\rm CO}} = \frac{(1+\beta)(1+R_{\rm B}/R_{\rm E})}{1+\beta+R_{\rm B}/R_{\rm E}}$$

Substituting β = 50 in the above expression we get

$40 = [51 \times (1 + R_B/R_E)]/(51 + R_B/R_E)$

Therefore, $40\ (51 + R_B/R_E) = [51 \times (1 + R_B/R_E)]$. Therefore, $R_B/R_E = 180.8$.

The desired value of the stability factor $S_{VBE} \le 50 \times 10^{-6}/(-0.3) \le -16.6 \times 10^{-5}$.

The maximum value of S_{VBE} is -16.6×10^{-5}.

For an emitter-bias circuit,

$$S_{V_{\rm BE}} = \frac{-\beta/R_{\rm E}}{R_{\rm B}/R_{\rm E}+(\beta+1)}$$

Substituing β = 50 in the above equation, we get

$-16.6 \times 10^{-5} = (-50/R_E)/(R_B/R_E + 51)$

Therefore, $-16.6 \times 10^{-5} (R_B/R_E + 51) = -50/R_E$. That is $R_B/R_E + 51 = 3 \times 10^5/R_E$.

Substituting $R_B/R_E = 180.8$ in the above equation, we get

$R_E = (3 \times 10^5)/231.8 = 1.294\ k\Omega$

The value of $R_B = 180.8 \times 1.294\ K = 234\ k\Omega$

The desired value of the stability factor $S_\beta \leq (400 \times 10^{-6})/(20) \leq 2 \times 10^{-5}$.

For an emitter-bias circuit,

$$S_\beta = \frac{I_{C1}(1 + R_B/R_E)}{\beta_1(1 + \beta_2 + R_B/R_E)}$$

Substituting the value of $\beta_1 = 50$ and $\beta_2 = 70$ in the above expression, we get,

$2 \times 10^{-5} = I_{C1} \times 181.8/50(71 + 180.8)$

$I_{C1} = 2 \times 10^{-5} \times 50 \times 251.8/181.8 = 1.38$ mA.

For the emitter-bias circuit the collector current (I_C) is given by:

$$I_C = \frac{\beta(V_{CC} - V_{BE})}{R_B + (\beta + 1)R_E}$$

Therefore,

$$1.38 \times 10^{-3} = 50(V_{CC} - 0.7)/(234 \times 10^3 + 51 \times 1.294 \times 10^3)$$
$$V_{CC} = 8.98\ V \cong 9\ V$$

Refer to the emitter-bias circuit of Figure-2.35 given earlier in the chapter. Applying Kirchhoff's voltage law to the collector-emitter loop, we get,

$9 - I_C R_C - V_{CE} - I_E R_E = 0$

$9 - 1.38 \times 10^{-3} \times R_C - 4 - 1.38 \times 10^{-3} \times 1.294 \times 10^3 = 0$ (Assuming $I_C \cong I_E$)

Therefore, $R_C = 2.3\ k\Omega$.

Figure-2.65 shows the design.

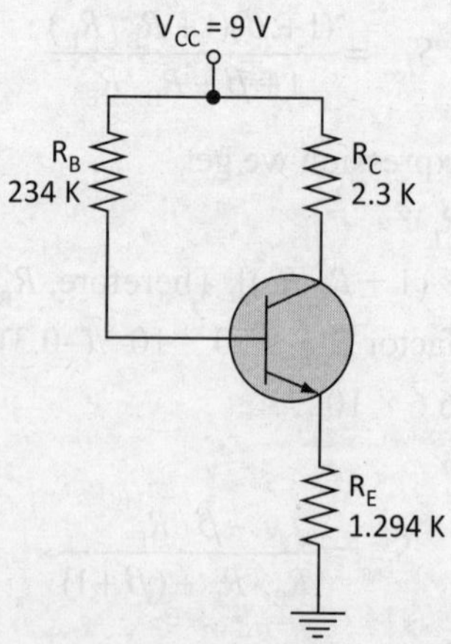

Fig. 2.65: Example 2.20

2.9 BIAS COMPENSATION

The biasing techniques discussed so far offer stability to the operating point (I_{CQ}, V_{CEQ}) by virtue of negative feedback. Although, negative feedback improves stability but it also reduces the gain of the circuit. In applications where the reduction in gain is intolerable; compensation techniques are used to reduce the drift in the operating point.

Compensation techniques make use of temperature-sensitive devices such as diodes, thermistors, transistors, sensitorsetc. to compensate for the changes in the operating point caused due to changes in temperature. In the following sub-sections, we will discuss some of the commonly used compensation circuits.

2.9.1 Diode Compensation for Base-Emitter Voltage

Figure-2.66 shows a circuit using diode for compensation against variations in base-emitter voltage (V_{BE}) due to change in temperature. The diode is made of the same material as the transistor with the result that there is same variation in the transistor's base-emitter voltage (V_{BE}) and diode's forward voltage (V_D) due to temperature. If we examine the circuit, we will see that the circuit is basically an emitter-bias circuit with additional diode circuitry in the emitter leg. The diode is kept in forward-bias mode through voltage (V_{DD}) and resistance (R_D).

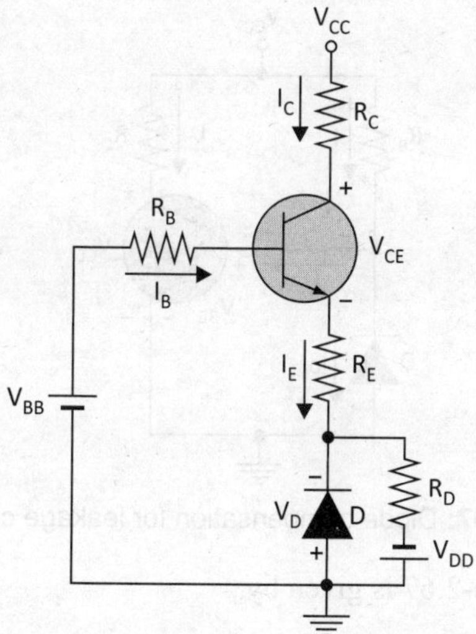

Fig. 2.66: Diode compensation for base-emitter voltage

Applying Kirchhoff's voltage law to the base-emitter loop, we get,

$$V_{BB} - I_B R_B - V_{BE} - I_E R_E + V_D = 0$$

Substituting $I_E = (\beta + 1)I_B$ in the above equation and solving for base current (I_B), we get,

$$I_B = \frac{V_{BB} - (V_{BE} - V_D)}{R_B + (\beta+1)R_E} \tag{2.111}$$

Collector current (I_C) is related to the base current by the following expression.

$$I_C = \beta I_B + (\beta+1)I_{CO}$$

Substituting the value of I_B in the expression for collector current, we get,

$$I_C = \frac{\beta[V_{BB} - (V_{BE} - V_D)]}{R_B + (\beta+1)R_E} + (\beta+1)I_{CO} \quad (2.112)$$

As is clear from eqn. (2.112), the change in the base-emitter voltage (V_{BE}) of the transistor due to the change in temperature will be nullified by a similar change in the forward voltage (V_D) of the diode. In other words, the diode forward voltage (V_D) tracks the changes in the base-emitter voltage (V_{BE}) of the transistor and compensates for its changes.

2.9.2 Diode Compensation for Leakage Current

To compensate for the variation in the leakage current (I_{CO}), the diode is placed across the base-emitter terminals of the transistor as shown in Figure-2.67. The diode is reverse-biased and hence the reverse saturation current (I_D) flows through it. The diode is chosen to be of the same material as the transistor, so that the reverse saturation current of the diode increases with temperature at the same rate as the leakage current of the transistor.

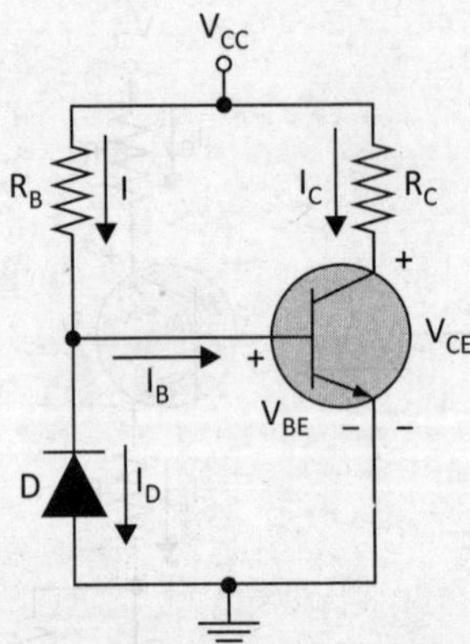

Fig. 2.67: Diode compensation for leakage current

The base current (I_B) in Figure-2.67 is given by:

$$I_B = I - I_D$$

Substituting this value of base current (I_B) in the expression for collector current (I_C), we get,

$$I_C = \beta(I - I_D) + (\beta+1)I_{CO}$$

As β and (β + 1) are nearly equal, the expression for I_C can be written as:

$$I_C = \beta I - \beta I_D + \beta I_{CO}$$

Rearranging the terms, we get,

$$I_C = \beta I - \beta(I_D - I_{CO}) \tag{2.113}$$

The diode reverse current (I_D) tracks the transistor leakage current (I_{CO}) over the desired temperature range.

2.9.3 Thermistor Compensation

Figure-2.68 shows a thermistor-based compensation circuit. The thermistor having negative temperature coefficient of resistance is placed in parallel with R_{B2}. Values of the resistances are so chosen as to establish the desired value of collector current (I_C) at the normal operating temperature. As the temperature increases, the value of the thermistor resistance decreases. This reduces the forward bias and hence the base and collector currents of the transistor. When the temperature decreases, the thermistor resistance increases resulting in an increase in the value of base-emitter voltage. This in turn increases the base and the collector currents. Therefore, the thermistor compensates for the increase in collector current due to increase in temperature.

2.10 THERMAL RUNAWAY

The power dissipation capability of a transistor depends upon its physical size, its construction and its mounting arrangement in the system. The maximum power rating is limited by the temperature that

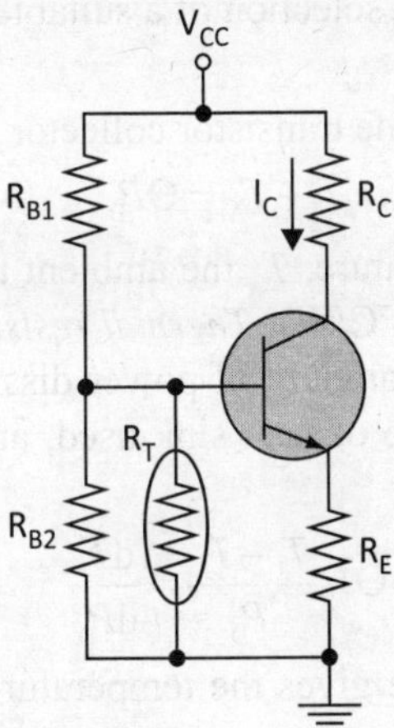

Fig. 2.68: Thermistor compensation

the collector-to-base junction can withstand and the ambient temperature. As the ambient temperature increases; the power rating of the transistor decreases. This is referred to as power derating. The power dissipation capability of transistor varies from few milliwatts to several hundreds of milliwatts in the case of small signal transistors to around 250 W in the case of power transistors. The maximum permissible temperature that the collector-to-base junction of a transistor can handle is in the range of 150°C to 225°C for silicon transistors and 60°C to 100°C for germanium transistors. Figure-2.69 shows the typical power derating curve of a silicon transistor with change in transistor case temperature. It may be mentioned here that in the case of small signal transistors, the case temperature is only slightly higher than the ambient temperature and the case and the ambient temperatures are generally considered to be equal. However, in the case of power transistors, case temperature may exceed the ambient temperature by a large amount.

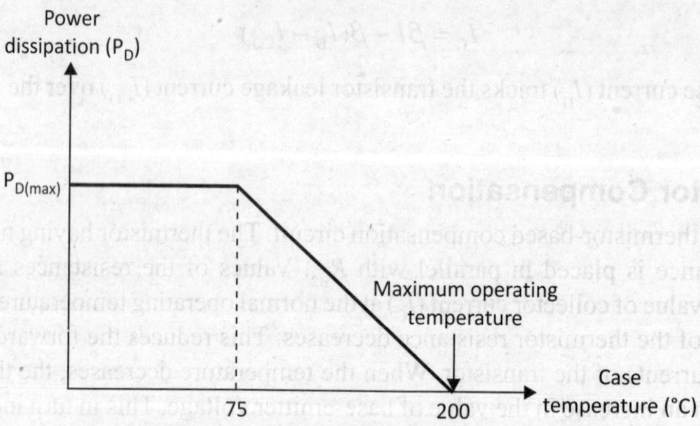

Fig. 2.69: Typical power derating curve of a transistor

If the transistor circuit is not designed properly; it may lead to the phenomenon of *thermal runway*. When the transistor is in operation, it dissipates power and its junction temperature rises, which in turn causes the collector current to increase. This may lead to more power dissipation and further increase in junction temperature and subsequently an increase in collector current. If this cycle continues, it may result in permanently damaging the transistor. This phenomenon is referred to as thermal runaway. Proper design of the transistor circuit and selection of a suitable operating point is necessary to prevent the phenomenon of thermal runaway.

The steady-state temperature rise at the transistor collector junction is given by eqn. (2.114).

$$T_J - T_A = \Theta P_D \tag{2.114}$$

where T_J is the transistor junction temperature; T_A the ambient temperature; P_D the power dissipated in the transistor; Θ the thermal resistance (°C/W). *Thermal resistance* is defined as the ratio of the rise in transistor junction temperature to the amount of power dissipated. The value of thermal resistance depends upon the transistor size, the size of heat sink used, and other cooling methods used such as forced-air cooling, etc.

$$\Theta = \frac{T_J - T_A}{P_D} = \frac{dT_J}{dP_D} \tag{2.115}$$

The inverse of the thermal resistance gives the temperature rate at which the power is dissipated under steady-state conditions.

$$\frac{dP_D}{dT_J} = \frac{1}{\Theta} \tag{2.116}$$

The condition for thermal stability is therefore the following: *The rate at which heat is generated at the collector junction should not exceed the rate at which it can be dissipated under steady-state conditions.*

2.10.1 Operating-Point Considerations in Thermal Runaway

The position of the operating point of the transistor amplifier determines whether the transistor is inherently stable against thermal runaway or not. Figure-2.70 shows the various power dissipation curves of a transistor and a typical DC load line for an emitter-bias configuration. Let us consider the operating point Q_1. The DC load line is tangent to the 200 mW power dissipation curve at the operating point. An increase in the collector current due to internal heating or increase in the ambient temperature causes the operating point to shift upwards on the DC load line. The operating point is now between the 100 mW and the 200 mW power dissipation curves. Therefore, with increase in temperature the power generated decreases. Hence, the circuit is inherently stable against variations in temperature.

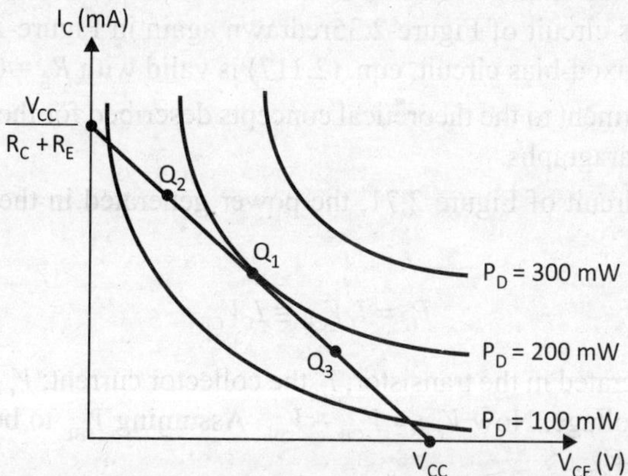

Fig. 2.70: Operating-point considerations against thermal runaway

For the operating point Q_2, the increase in collector current causes the operating point to shift upwards and move towards the 100 mW curve. This results in reduction in the power generated. Hence, the circuit is inherently thermally stable. However, if the operating point is at Q_3, increase in the collector current causes the operating point to shift upwards towards the 200 mW curve. This results in increase in the power generated. Hence, the circuit is not inherently thermally stable and may lead to thermal runaway. Such a circuit needs to be checked for thermal stability.

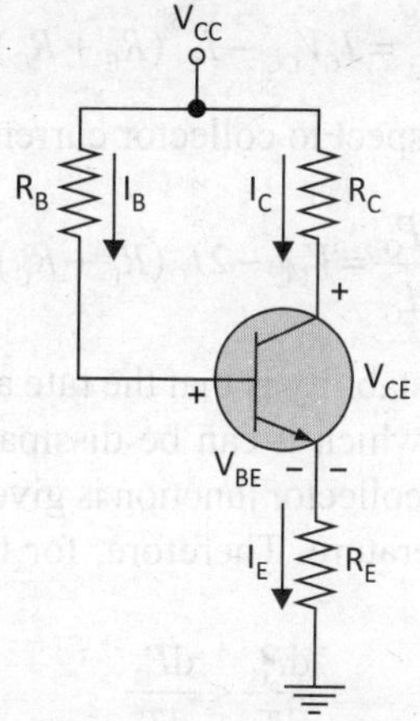

Fig. 2.71: Emitter-bias circuit

The thumb rule to decide whether the operating point is in the safe region of operation is as follows. For operating point with collector-to-emitter voltage (V_{CEQ}) less than $V_{CC}/2$, the circuit is thermally stable as increase in collector current results in reduced power generation. In the case of operating points having V_{CEQ} greater than $V_{CC}/2$, the circuit is not inherently thermally stable. In such cases, it is necessary to check the thermal characteristics of the transistor and the circuit design to ensure thermal stability.

For such circuits to be thermally stable they should satisfy the following condition.

$$[V_{CC} - 2I_C(R_E + R_C)](S_{I_{CO}})(0.07I_{CO}) < 1/\Theta \tag{2.117}$$

where V_{CC} is the supply voltage; I_C the collector current; R_E the emitter resistor; R_C the collector resistor; S_{ICO} the stability factor; I_{CO} the leakage current; Θ the thermal resistance of the transistor. This equation is valid for the emitter-bias circuit of Figure-2.35redrawn again in Figure-2.71 for the convenience of the readers. In the case of fixed-bias circuit, eqn. (2.117) is valid with $R_E = 0$.

The mathematical treatment to the theoretical concepts described for thermal runaway phenomenon is given in the following paragraphs.

For the emitter-bias circuit of Figure-2.71, the power generated in the transistor is given by eqn. (2.118).

$$P_G = I_C V_{CB} \cong I_C V_{CE} \tag{2.118}$$

where P_G is the power generated in the transistor; I_C the collector current; V_{CB} the collector-base voltage; V_{CE} the collector-emitter voltage. Now $V_{CE} = V_{CB} - V_{BE}$. Assuming V_{BE} to be negligible as compared to V_{CB} and V_{CE}, we have $V_{CE} \cong V_{CB}$.

The collector-emitter voltage (V_{CE}) in emitter-bias circuit is expressed by eqn. (2.119).

$$V_{CE} = V_{CC} - I_E R_E - I_C R_C \tag{2.119}$$

As $I_E \cong I_C$, eqn. (2.119) can be approximated as eqn. (2.120).

$$V_{CE} = V_{CC} - I_C(R_E + R_C) \tag{2.120}$$

Substituting the value of V_{CE} given in eqn. (2.120) in eqn. (2.119), we get,

$$P_G = I_C V_{CC} - I_C^2(R_E + R_C) \tag{2.121}$$

Differentiating eqn. (2.121) with respect to collector current (I_C), we get,

$$\frac{dP_G}{dI_C} = V_{CC} - 2I_C(R_E + R_C) \tag{2.122}$$

The required condition for thermal stability is that the rate at which heat is produced at the collector junction should not exceed the rate at which it can be dissipated by the transistor under steady-state conditions. Rate of heat generated at the collector junction is given by differentiating the power generated (P_G) with respect to the junction temperature. Therefore, for thermal stability the following equation should be satisfied.

$$\frac{dP_G}{dT_J} < \frac{dP_D}{dT_J} \tag{2.123}$$

We know that,

$$\frac{dP_D}{dT_J} = \frac{1}{\Theta}$$

Therefore, the requirement for thermal stability is given by eqn. (2.124).

$$\frac{dP_G}{dT_J} < \frac{1}{\Theta} \tag{2.124}$$

Multiplying and dividing the LHS of Eq. (2.124) by dI_C we get,

$$\frac{dP_G}{dT_J}\times\frac{dI_C}{dI_C}<\frac{1}{\Theta}$$

Rearranging the terms on the LHS of the equation we get,

$$\frac{dP_G}{dI_C}\times\frac{dI_C}{dT_J}<\frac{1}{\Theta} \tag{2.125}$$

where dI_C/dT_J is the rate at which the collector current changes with junction temperature. Since $1/\Theta$ and dI_C/dT_J are both positive, therefore the above equation is always true when dP_G/dI_C is negative. From eqn. (2.122) we know that

$$\frac{dP_G}{dI_C}=V_{CC}-2I_C(R_E+R_C)$$

Therefore, to ensure thermal stability, the following equation should be satisfied.

$$V_{CC}-2I_C(R_E+R_C)<0 \tag{2.126}$$

Rearranging the terms in eqn. (2.126), we get

$$I_C>\frac{V_{CC}}{2(R_E+R_C)} \tag{2.127}$$

We know that in emitter-bias configuration

$$V_{CE}=V_{CC}-I_C(R_E+R_C)$$

Substituting the value of I_C in the equation, we infer that when the collector-emitter voltage (V_{CE}) is less than half the supply voltage ($V_{CE}<V_{CC}/2$), then the circuit is thermally stable under all conditions. For $V_{CE}>V_{CC}/2$, the term dP_G/dI_C is positive and therefore the circuit design should be done such that eqn. (2.125) is satisfied.

The collector current (I_C) changes with temperature as the leakage current (I_{CO}), the base-emitter voltage (V_{BE}) and the transistor gain (β) change with temperature. The rate of change of collector current with junction temperature is given by:

$$\frac{dI_C}{dT_J}=S_{I_{CO}}\frac{dI_{CO}}{dT_J}+S_{V_{BE}}\frac{dV_{BE}}{dT_J}+S_\beta\frac{d\beta}{dT_J} \tag{2.128}$$

However, in most cases, the effect of leakage current (I_{CO}) is far more than that of transistor gain (β) and the base-emitter voltage (V_{BE}). Therefore,

$$\frac{dI_C}{dT_J}\cong S_{I_{CO}}\frac{dI_{CO}}{dT_J} \tag{2.129}$$

Substituting the value of dI_C/dT_J in eqn. (2.125), we get,

$$\left(\frac{dP_G}{dI_C}\right)(S_{I_{CO}})\left(\frac{dI_{CO}}{dT_J}\right)<\frac{1}{\Theta} \tag{2.130}$$

$dI_{CO}/dT_J = 0.07I_{CO}$ as the reverse saturation current increases at a rate of approximately 7%/°C. Substituting the value of dP_G/dI_C [eqn. (2.122)] and the value of dI_{CO}/dT_J in eqn. (2.130), we get,

$$[V_{CC} - 2I_C(R_C + R_E)](S_{I_{CO}})(0.07I_{CO}) < \frac{1}{\Theta} \quad (2.131)$$

From eqn. (2.131), we can infer that for small signal transistors, the problem of thermal runaway is not so critical as these transistors have small value of collector current (I_C) and small value of stability factor (S_{ICO}). However, power transistors have higher value of collector current (I_C) and stability factor and hence thermal management is a major problem in the case of power transistors. One of the thermal management techniques to increase the power handling capability of transistors is to make use of heat sinks.

Example-2.21: Figure-2.72 shows the circuit of a transformer-coupled power amplifier. Determine whether the circuit is thermally stable. If not, determine the junction to ambient thermal resistance (Θ_{J-A}) required so that the transistor operates safely at an ambient temperature of 25°C. It is given that the transistor gain β at 25 °C is 100, the leakage current I_{CO} at 25°C is 1 mA, the maximum junction operating temperature is 100°C, the base–emitter voltage of the transistor is 0.7 V.

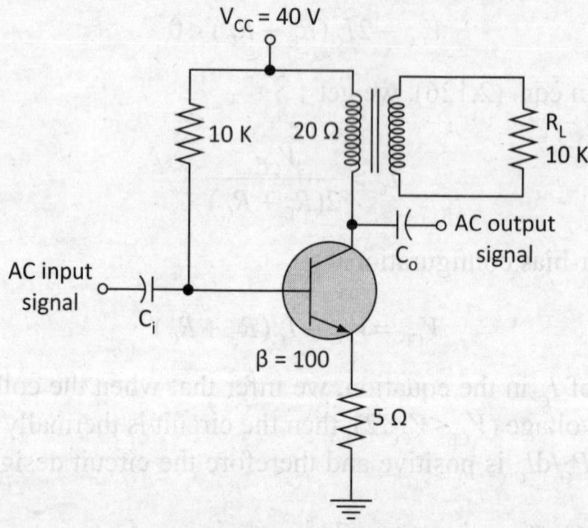

Fig. 2.72: Example-2.21

Solution:

$$I_C = \beta I_B + (\beta + 1)I_{CO}$$

$$= 100 \times I_B + 101 \times 1 \times 10^{-3}$$

$$= 100I_B + 0.101$$

Applying Kirchhoff's voltage law to the base emitter loop, we get,

$$40 - 10 \times 10^3 \times I_B - 0.7 - 5 \times I_E = 0$$

Subtituting $I_E = (\beta + 1)I_B = 101I_B$, we get $I_B = 3.74$ mA and $I_C = 374$ mA.

Applying Kirchhoff's voltage law to the collector–emitter loop, we get

$$40 - 20 \times I_C - V_{CE} - 5 \times I_E = 0$$

$$V_{CE} = 40 - 20 \times 374 \times 10^{-3} - 5 \times 374 \times 10^{-3} = 30.65$$

As $V_{CE} > V_{CC}/2$, therefore the circuit is not inherently thermally stable.

The quiescent power generated is given by:

$V_{CEQ} \times I_{CQ} = 30.65 \times 374 \times 10^{-3} = 11.46$ W

The power dissipation capability is given by $(T_J - T_A)/\Theta_{J\text{-}A}$.

For thermal stability $(100 - 25)/(\Theta_{J\text{-}A}) \geq 11.46$. Therefore, $(\Theta_{J\text{-}A}) \leq 6.54$ °C/W

Infact, transformer-coupled transistor amplifiers are very much susceptible to thermal runaway as they have very small DC resistance in the collector circuit (transformer primary and the emitter resistor).

Therefore, the circuit is not thermally stable. For the circuit to be thermally stable, the thermal resistance should be less than 6.54 °C/W.

GLOSSARY

AC Current Gain (β_{ac} or h_{FE}): AC current gain is defined as the ratio of the change in the collector current to a small change in the base current for a constant collector-emitter voltage.

Active region: In the active region, the emitter–base junction is forward-biased and the collector-base junction is reverse-biased. Transistors when operating in the active region function as amplifiers.

Alpha (α): Alpha (α) is the fraction of emitter current that contributes to the collector current.

Base width modulation: Refer to early effect.

Bias stabilization: Bias stabilization refers to the ability of a bias circuit to maintain a fixed operating point against variations in temperature and transistor gain (β). Bias stabilization is important as the transistor parameters are strongly dependent on temperature.

BJT:A BJT is a three-layer, three-terminal semiconductor device having two PN junctions. It comprises three differently doped semiconductor regions, namely the emitter region, the base region and the collector region.

Collector-to-Base Bias Configuration: In collector-to-base bias configuration, the base-bias voltage is obtained from the collector of the transistor instead of the collector supply voltage (V_{CC}). The circuit offers better stability of the operating point against variations in temperature and transistor gain (β) due to negative feedback. The configuration has voltage-shunt feedback as the output voltage is fed-back in shunt to the input through base resistor (R_B).

Common-Base (CB) Configuration: In the CB configuration, the base terminal is common to both the input and the output sections. The input signal is applied to the emitter-base section and the output is taken from the collector-base section.

Common-Collector (CC) Configuration: In CC configuration, the collector terminal is common to both the input and the output sections. The configuration is similar to the common-emitter configuration with the output taken from the emitter terminal rather than the collector terminal.

Common emitter (CE) configuration: The CE configuration has emitter terminal common to both the input and the output sections. The input signal is applied to the base-emitter section and the output is taken from the collector-emitter section.

Compensation techniques: Compensation techniques make use of temperature-sensitive devices such as diodes, thermistors, transistors, sensitors, etc. to compensate for the changes in the operating point caused due to changes in temperature.

Cut-off region: In the cut-off region both the junctions are reverse-biased. When the transistor is used as a switching device; it operates either in the saturation or the cut-off region. It acts as an open switch in the cut-off region.

DC Current Gain (β or h_{FE}): The variable β (also denoted as h_{FE}) is called the DC current gain, that is, the ratio of the collector current to the base current of the transistor in common-emitter configuration.

Early effect: It refers to the change in the width of the base region with the change in the collector-base voltage.

Ebers–Moll Model of Transistors: Ebers–Moll transistor model is an ideal model for a bipolar transistor and is applicable for all four regions of transistor operation. The model involves two ideal diodes and two ideal current sources.

Emitter follower configuration: Refer to common collector configuration.

Emitter or self-bias: Emitter-bias configuration, also referred to as self-bias circuit, has an additional emitter resistor (R_E) between the transistor's emitter terminal and ground as compared to the fixed-bias circuit. The addition of the resistor R_E provides improved stabilization as it introduces current-series feedback negative feedback into the circuit.

Fall time: Fall time (t_f) is the time required by the collector current to fall from 90% to 10% of the saturation level. Fall time is caused due to the time required by the collector current to traverse the active region.

Feedback-bias configuration: Refer to collector-to-base bias configuration.

Fixed bias circuit: It is one of the simplest possible transistor-biasing circuits. The biasing components include two resistors, base resistor (R_B) and collector resistor (R_C), and a supply voltage (V_{CC}). The base-emitter junction gets forward-biased through V_{CC} and R_B. The supply voltage also reverse-biases the collector-base junction through resistor R_C. Resistor R_B is of the order of few hundreds of kilo-ohms whereas typical value of R_C is of few kilo-ohms. Capacitors C_i and C_o are referred to as the input and the output coupling capacitors, respectively.

Gain-Bandwidth Product (f_T): The gain-bandwidth product (f_T) tells us about the high frequency response of the transistor. It is the frequency for which gain on the high-frequency side falls to unity or 0 dB. It is an important parameter that needs to be considered when the transistor is to be used for IF/RF applications.

$I_{C(max)}$: It is the peak collector current rating of the transistor. It is specified for continuous or pulsed mode of operation of a transistor.

Input Characteristics: The input characteristics of a transistor are a plot of the input current versus the input junction voltage for different values of output junction voltage.

NPN Transistor: Inan NPN transistor, the collector and the emitter regions are N-type semiconductors and the base region is a P-type semiconductor.

Operating point: The DC collector current (I_C) and the collector-emitter voltage (V_{CE}) when no input signal is applied is referred to as the operating point. Since the operating point is a fixed point on the output characteristics of the transistor; it is also referred to as the quiescent point (Q-point).

Output Characteristics: The output characteristics of a transistor are a plot of the output current and the output junction voltage for different values of input current.

PNP Transistor: Ina PNP transistor, the collector and the emitter regions are P-type semiconductors and the base region is an N-type semiconductor.

Power Dissipation ($P_{D(max)}$): It is the maximum power dissipation capability of a transistor. $P_{D(max)}$ is usually specified at a given ambient temperature and it should be derated at higher temperatures as per the derating curve supplied by the manufacturers.

Reverse region: In the reverse-active region, the emitter-base junction is reverse-biased and the collector-base region is forward-biased. Transistors are seldom operated in the reverse-active region.

Rise time: The time required for the collector current to rise from 10% to 90% of the final value is called the rise time (t_r).

Saturation region: In the saturation region, both the emitter-base and the collector-base junctions are forward-biased. When the transistor is used as a switching device; it operates either in the saturation or the cut-off region. It acts as a closed switch in the saturation region.

***SI*$_{CO}$: SI_{CO}** is defined as the ratio of the change in the collector current (ΔI_C)with respect to change in the leakage current (ΔI_{CO}) with the base-emitter voltage (V_{BE}) and the transistor gain (β) held constant.

Stability Factor: Stability factor defines the extent to which the collector current (I_C) of a transistor is stable against variations in the transistor parameters, namely, the leakage current (I_{CO}), the transistor gain (β) and the base-emitter voltage (V_{BE}). The three types of stability factors are defined with respect to transistors, namely, SI_{CO}, S_β and SV_{BE}. Small value of stability factor indicates good bias stability whereas large value of stability factor indicates poor bias stability. Ideal value of stability factor is zero.

***SV*$_{BE}$:** SV_{BE} is defined as the ratio of change in the collector current (ΔI_C)with respect to change in the base-emitter voltage (ΔV_{BE}) with both the leakage current (I_{CO}) and the transistor gain (*â*) held constant:

S$_\beta$: S_β is defined as the ratio of the change in the collector current (ΔI_C)with respect to change in the transistor gain (β) keeping both the leakage current (I_{CO}) and the base-emitter voltage (V_{BE}) as constant:

Transistor biasing: To design a transistor-based amplifier circuit, it is necessary to operate the transistor in the active region. This process is referred to as transistor biasing and the circuit used for transistor biasing is called a biasing circuit. Transistor biasing is done so that the transistor amplifies the input signal linearly and without distortion.

Turn-Off time: Turn-Off time (t_{off}) is defined as the sum of the storage time (t_s) and the fall time (t_f).

Turn-On time: The total time of the time delay and rise time ($t_d + t_r$) is known as the turn-on time (t_{on}) of the transistor.

SUMMARY OF IMPORTANT FORMULAE

1. $I_C = \alpha I_E + I_{CO}$

2. $I_C = \alpha I_E + I_{CO}\left[1-\exp\left(-\frac{V_{CB}}{V_T}\right)\right]$

3. $I_C = \beta I_B + (\beta+1)I_{CO}$

4. $\beta_{ac} = \left(\frac{\Delta I_C}{\Delta I_B}\right)_{V_E=\text{constant}}$

5. $\alpha_{ac} = \left(\frac{\Delta I_C}{\Delta I_E}\right)_{V_{CB}=\text{constant}}$

6. $I_C = \gamma I_B + \gamma I_{CO}$

7. $h_{fe} = \left(\frac{\Delta I_C}{\Delta I_B}\right)_{V_{CE}=\text{constant}}$

8. $P_{D(max)} = V_{CE} \times I_C$

9. $I_{B(sat)} = \frac{I_{C(sat)}}{\beta}$

10. The Q-point for a fixed-bias circuit is $I_{CQ} = \beta\left(\frac{V_{CC} - V_{BE}}{R_B}\right)$, $V_{CEQ} = V_{CC} - I_{CQ}R_C$

11. The Q-point for the emitter-bias circuit is $I_{CQ} = \beta\left(\frac{V_{CC} - V_{BE}}{R_B + (\beta+1)R_E}\right)$, $V_{CEQ} = V_{CC} - I_{CQ}(R_C + R_E)$

12. The Q-point for the Voltage divider bias is $I_{CQ} = \beta\left(\frac{V_{TH} - V_{BE}}{R_{TH} + (\beta+1)R_E}\right)$, $V_{CEQ} = V_{CC} - I_{CQ}(R_C + R_E)$

13. TheQ-pointforCollector-to-BaseBiasConfigurationis $V_{CEQ} = V_{CC} - I_{CQ}R_C$, $I_{CQ} = \beta\left(\frac{V_{CC} - V_{BE}}{R_B + (\beta+1)R_C}\right)$

14. The Q-point for the common-base configuration is $I_C = \frac{V_{EE} - V_{BE}}{R_E}$, $V_{CB} = V_{CC} - I_C R_C$

15. $S_{I_{CO}} = \left.\frac{\Delta I_C}{\Delta I_{CO}}\right|_{V_{BE},\beta\text{const.}}$

16. $S_{V_{BE}} = \left.\frac{\Delta I_C}{\Delta V_{BE}}\right|_{I_{CO},\beta\text{ const.}}$

17. $S_\beta = \left.\frac{\Delta I_C}{\Delta \beta}\right|_{I_{CO},V_{BE}\text{ const.}}$

18. $\Delta I_C = S_{I_{CO}}\Delta I_{CO} + S_\beta \Delta\beta + S_{V_{BE}}\Delta V_{BE}$

19. **Stability factor S_{ICO} for a fixed-bias circuit is** $S_{I_{CO}} = \beta + 1$

20. **Stability factor S_{ICO} for emitter-bias configuration is** $S_{I_{CO}} = \frac{(\beta+1)(1+R_B/R_E)}{1+\beta+R_B/R_E}$

21. **Stability factor S_{ICO} for Voltage-Divider Bias with Emitter-Bias Configuration is**

$$S_{I_{CO}} = \frac{(\beta+1)(1+R_{TH}/R_E)}{1+\beta+R_{TH}/R_E}$$

22. **Stability factor SI_{CO} for collector-to-base bias configuration is** $S_{I_{CO}} = \frac{(\beta+1)(1+R_B/R_C)}{1+\beta+R_B/R_C}$

23. Stability factor SV_{BE} for a fixed-bias configuration is $S_{V_{BE}} = \frac{-\beta}{R_B}$

24. Stability factor SV_{BE} for emitter-bias configuration is $S_{V_{BE}} = \frac{-\beta / R_E}{R_B / R_E + (\beta + 1)}$

25. For circuits to be thermally stable they should satisfy the conditions

$$[V_{CC} - 2I_C(R_E + R_C)](S_{I_{CO}})(0.07 I_{CO}) < 1/\Theta$$

or

$$[V_{CC} - 2I_C(R_C + R_E)](S_{I_{CO}})(0.07 I_{CO}) < \frac{1}{\Theta}$$

REVIEW QUESTIONS

1. Draw the structure of NPN and PNP transistors showing the direction of flow of currents through the transistor.
2. How do you distinguish between
   (a) β and α (b) h_{FE} and h_{fe} (c) I_{CBO} and I_{CEO}
3. The input impedance of a BJT affects the power gain provided by it. How is it then that the input impedance parameter does not figure in the transistor manuals?
4. Sketch the typical input and output characteristics of a bipolar transistor when connected in
   (a) Common-emitter configuration (b) Common-base configuration
5. Explain how a BJT in common-collector configuration can be used for impedance matching applications?
6. Define and interpret the following transistor ratings and specifications:
   (a) V_{CBO} (b) V_{CEO} (c) $P_{D(max)}$ (d) α
7. Explain in detail the early effect phenomenon. How does it affect the transistor characteristics?
8. How will you identify the terminals of a transistor using (a) an ohmmeter and (b) a multimeter?
9. List any four differences in the characteristic curves of Silicon and Germanium transistors.
10. Give reasons for the following:
    (a) Why is the collector current slightly less than the emitter current?
    (b) Why is a transistor referred to as a bipolar junction device?
    (c) The power rating of a transistor decreases with increase in the ambient temperature.
    (d) The concentration of minority carriers in the base region increases with increase in the reverse-bias voltage of the collector-base junction.
11. With the help of common emitter amplifier configuration, explain the criteria for selection of a suitable operating point and the factors affecting its stability.
12. Derive the mathematical expression to prove that the operating point in voltage-divider bias is independent of transistor gain β.
13. Explain the operation of a transistor switch. What are the steps to be followed to design a transistor switch?
14. What is the drawback of emitter-bias configuration? How is the drawback removed in the voltage-divider bias with emitter-bias configuration?

15. Draw the following circuits using PNP transistors and derive the expressions for the operating point for each of the cases:
    (a) fixed-bias configuration
    (b) voltage-divider bias configuration
    (c) collector-to-base bias configuration
16. What do you understand by thermal instability of the operating point? What are the consequences? Define the overall stability factor for an amplifier?
17. Give reasons for the following:
    (a) Why is bias compensation required?
    (b) Power transistors are more prone to thermal runaway as compared to small signal transistors?
    (c) Why is fixed-bias circuit not commonly used?
    (d) Why is the operating point chosen near the center of the active region of the transistor characteristics in a transistor amplifier?
18. Define the following terms
    (a) power derating
    (b) thermal resistance of a transistor
    (c) turn-on time of a transistor switch
    (d) bias-compensation
19. What is the significance of thermal resistance of a power transistor? How do you define (θ_{J-C}) and (θ_{C-A})
20. Is it theoretically possible to realize the maximum dissipation capability of a transistor? If so, under what conditions can we do so? What are the practical limitations?

PROBLEMS

1. For a transistor, the value of α is specified to be 0.98 at a particular collector–base voltage. The value of a increases by 0.5% when the collector–base voltage is increased. Find the percentage change in the value of β. Comment on the result.
2. Refer to Figure-2.73. Given that the emitter area of BJT Q_1 is half that of BJT Q_2. Find the value of the current I_o?

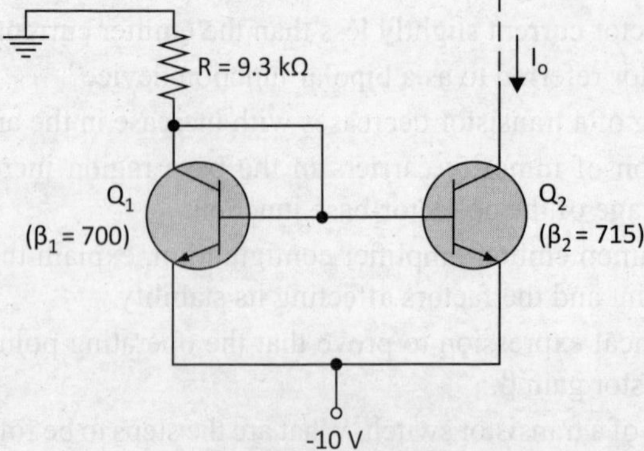

Fig. 2.73: Problem-2

3. For the circuit shown in Figure-2.74, find the values of emitter current (I_E), collector current (I_C) and base current (I_B). It is given that $\beta = 50$, $V_{BE} = 0.7$ V and $I_{CO} = 0\ \mu$A.

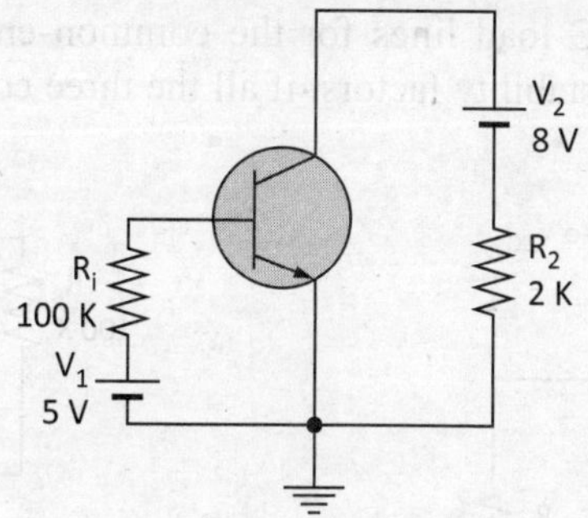

Fig. 2.74: Problem-3

4. Figure-2.75 shows the input characteristics of a common-emitter transistor. Find the input resistance for the linear portion of the curves for collector-emitter voltage of 1V and 20V.

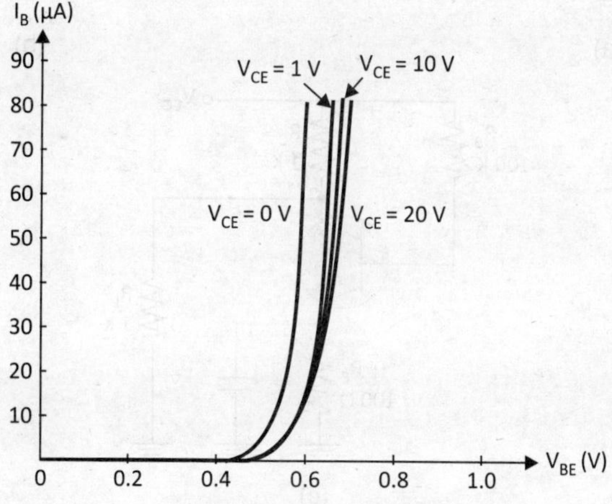

Fig. 2.75: Problem-4

5. If for a Silicon NPN transistor, the base-to-emitter voltage (V_{BE}) is 0.7V and the collector-to-base voltage (V_{CB}) is 0.2V, then the transistor is operating in which of the modes?
6. For the circuit shown in Figure-2.76, find the value of R_1? (Given that V_{BE} = 0.7V and I_{CO} = 0)

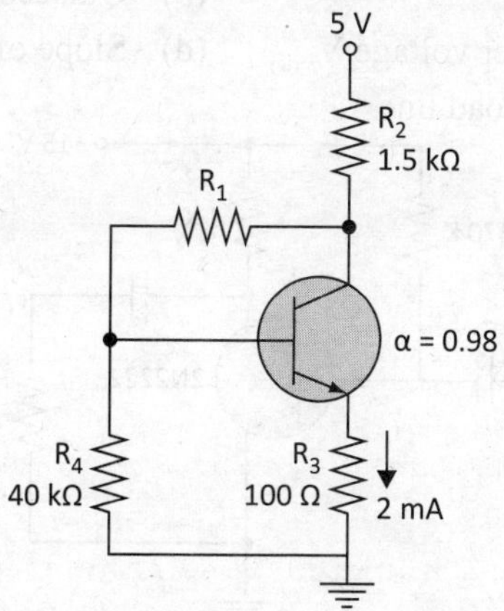

Fig. 2.76: Problem-6

7. Determine the slopes of DC load lines for the common-emitter amplifier configurations of Figure-2.77. Compare their stability factors, if all the three configurations have a β of 50 at the operating point.

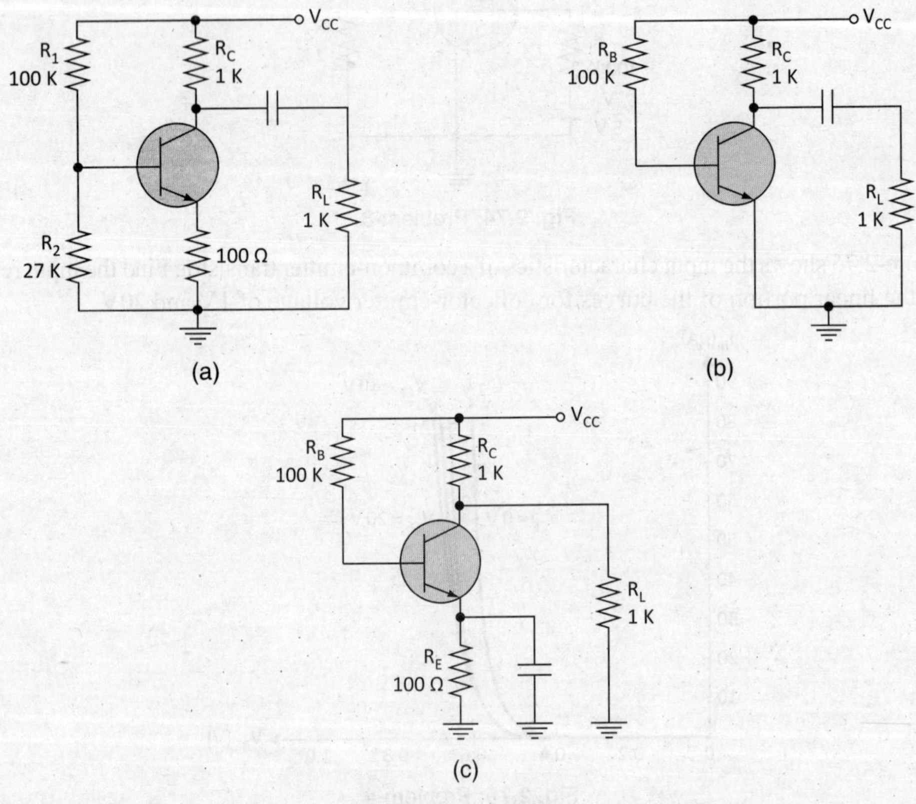

Fig. 2.77: Problem-7

8. For the common-emitter amplifier circuit of Figure-2.78 (a) and the output characteristics of transistor 2N2222 used in the circuit of Figure-2.78 (b), calculate the following.
   (a) Quiscent base current I_{BQ}
   (b) Quiscent collector current I_{CQ}
   (c) Quiscent collector-emitter voltage V_{CEQ}
   (d) Slope of the DC load line
   (e) Co-ordinates of the AC load line

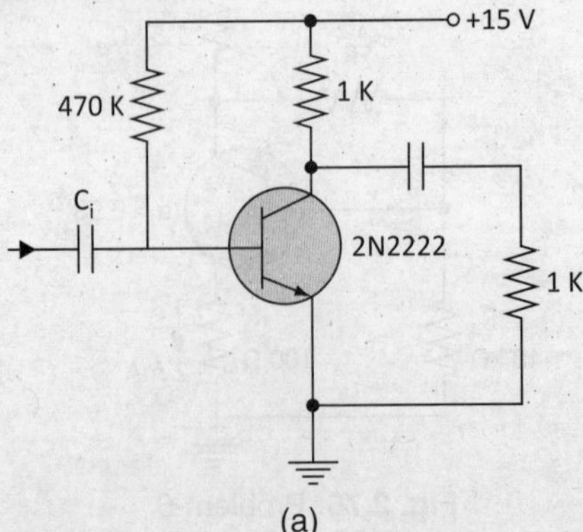

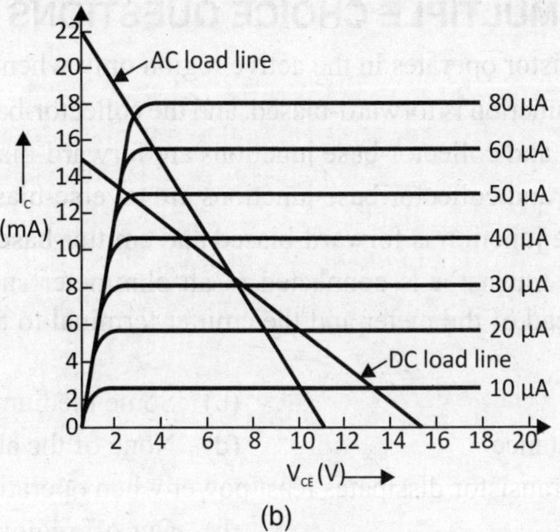

Fig. 2.78: Problem-8

9. For the circuit shown in Figure-2.79, find the voltage across the load resistor R_L? (Given that V_{BE} = 0.7V, α = 0.98 and I_{CO} = 0)

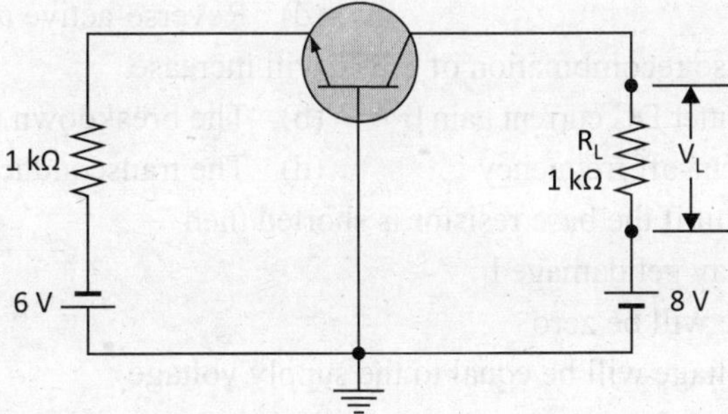

Fig. 2.79: Problem-9

10. Figure-2.80 shows a circuit using a PNP transistor. Assuming that the transistor is a Si transistor, find the value of voltage V_{out}?

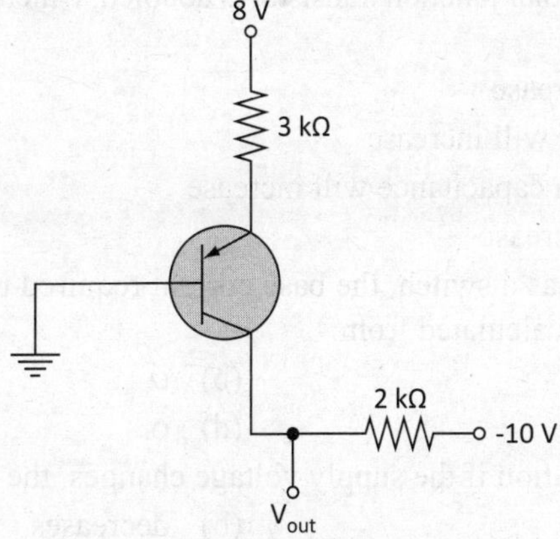

Fig. 2.80: Problem-10

MULTIPLE CHOICE QUESTIONS

1. A semiconductor transistor operates in the active region only when
   (a) The emitter-base junction is forward-biased, and the collector-base junction is reverse-biased.
   (b) Both emitter-base and collector-base junctions are forward-biased.
   (c) Both emitter-base and collector-base junctions are reverse-biased.
   (d) The collector-base junction is forward-biased and emitter-base junction is reverse-biased.
2. When a healthy NPN transistor is connected to an ohmmeter such that the base terminal is connected to the red lead of the meter and the emitter terminal to the black lead then the meter shows
   (a) An open circuit (b) Some medium resistance
   (c) A very small resistance (d) None of the above
3. A conducting bipolar transistor dissipates least power when operating in the
   (a) Saturation region (b) Cut-off region
   (c) Active region (d) Reverse-active region
4. A bipolar transistor in sinusoidal oscillator configuration is operating in the
   (a) Active region (b) Saturation region
   (c) Cut-off region (d) Reverse-active region
5. An increase in the base recombination of a BJT will increase
   (a) The common emitter DC current gain β (b) The breakdown voltage BV_{CEO}
   (c) The unity-gain-cut-off frequency f_T (d) The transconductance g_m
6. In the fixed-bias circuit if the base resistor is shorted then
   (a) The transistor may get damaged
   (b) The base voltage will be zero
   (c) The collector voltage will be equal to the supply voltage
   (d) The collector current is zero
7. The maximum reverse collector to emitter breakdown voltage with base open is referred to as
   (a) V_{CEO} (b) V_C
   (c) V_{CBO} (d) V_{EBO}
8. If the base width of in a bipolar junction transistor is doubled, which one of the following statements will be TRUE?
   (a) Current gain will increase
   (b) Unity gain frequency will increase
   (c) Emitter-base junction capacitance will increase
   (d) Early voltage will increase
9. When a transistor is used as a switch, the base current required to switch on the transistor for a given collector current is calculated from:
   (a) h_{FE} (b) α
   (c) γ (d) σ
10. In the fixed-bias configuration if the supply voltage changes, the slope of the load line
    (a) increases (b) decreases
    (c) remains the same (d) may increase or decrease

11. The biasing configuration that offers least stability is
    (a) fixed-bias configuration
    (b) collector-to-base bias configuration
    (c) voltage-divider bias configuration
    (d) none of the above
12. With increase in the collector–base reverse voltage
    (a) The base width increases
    (b) The base width decreases
    (c) The base width is not effected
    (d) The base width can increase or decrease
13. Which of the transistor configurations is capable of providing both voltage and current gains?
    (a) Common base
    (b) Common collector
    (c) Common emitter
    (d) Both common emitter and common base
14. Which of the following conditions ensures that the transistor does not undergo thermal runaway?
    (a) $V_{CE} = V_{CC}/2$
    (b) $V_{CE} < V_{CC}/2$
    (c) $V_{CE} < V_{CC}$
    (d) $V_{CE} > V_{CC}/2$
15. The delay time of the transistor switch is due to
    (a) time required to charge the emitter-junction capacitance so that the transistor is brought from the cut-off to the active region.
    (b) time required to move the carriers from the base to the collector junction.
    (c) time required by the collector current to rise to 10% of its final value.
    (d) All the above

SOLUTIONS TO PROBLEMS

Problem 1:

Original value of $\alpha = 0.98$.
Value of $\beta = \alpha/(1 - \alpha) = 0.98/(1 - 0.98) = 49$.
New value of $\alpha = 0.98 + 0.5 \times 0.98/100 = 0.985$.
Value of β for $\alpha = 0.985$ is $\beta = 0.985/(1 - 0.985) = 66$
Percentage change in $\beta = [(66 - 49)/49] \times 100\% = 34.69\%$.
From the above result it is clear that a small change in the value of $\alpha = 0.5\%$ results in a large change in the value of $\beta = 34.69\%$.

Problem-2:

The given circuit can be represented as shown in Figure-2.81.

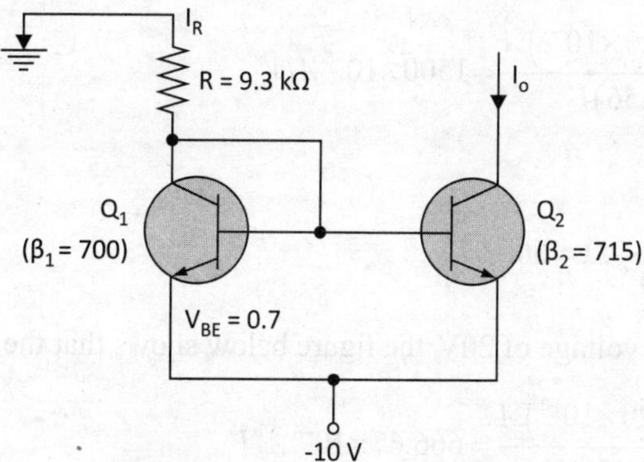

Fig. 2.81: Solution to Problem-2

Assuming that both the transistors are in the active region, the voltage at Q_1 base is

$V_{BQ1} = 0.7 - 10 = -9.3V$

The current through resistor R, $I_R = \frac{9.3}{9.3\times10^3} = 1mA = I_{C1}$

Given that the emitter area of transistor Q_1 is equal to half the emitter area of transistor Q_2.

Therefore, $(\beta_2)_{effective} = 2\beta_1 = 1430$

Since the effective value of â for transistor Q_2 is double that for transistor Q_1, so collector current of transistor Q_2, will also be nearly the double that of transistor Q_1 that is

$I_o = I_{C2} = 2I_{C1} = 2mA$

Problem-3:

The polarity of the voltage V_1 applied to the input section forward biases the emitter–base junction. Therefore the transistor is in active region or in the saturation region. Let us assume that the transistor is in the active region.

Applying Kirchhoff's voltage law to the input section: $5 - 100 \times 10^3 \times I_B - V_{BE} = 0$.

Substituting $V_{BE} = 0.7$ V, $I_B = (5 - 0.7)/(100 \times 10^3) = 43$ µA.

$I_C = \beta I_B$ (as $I_{CO} \cong 0$). Therefore, $I_C = 50 \times 43 \times 10^{-6}$ A $= 2.15$ mA.

Applying Kirchhoff's voltage law to the output section, we get

$$8 - 2\times10^3 \times 2.15\times10^{-3} - V_{CE} = 0$$

$$V_{CE} = 8 - 2\times10^3 \times 2.15\times10^{-3} = 8 - 4.3 = 3.7 \text{ V}$$

$V_{CE} = V_{CB} - V_{BE}$. Therefore, $V_{CB} = 3.7 - 0.7 = 3$ V.

For the NPN transistor, positive value of V_{CB} represents a reverse-biased collector–base junction and hence the assumption that the transistor is in the active region is correct.

$I_E = I_C + I_B$

$I_E = 2.15 \times 10^{-3} + 43 \times 10^{-6} = 2.193$ mA.

Problem-4:

For collector-emitter voltage of 1V, figure below shows that the slope of the input curve is

$$\frac{\Delta I_B}{\Delta V_{BE}} = \frac{(80\times10^{-6} - 20\times10^{-6})A}{(0.6-0.56)V} = 1500\times10^{-6}\ A/V$$

The input resistance

$$r_i = \frac{\Delta V_{BE}}{\Delta I_B} = \frac{1}{1500\times10^{-6}}\Omega = 666.67\Omega$$

For collector-emitter voltage of 20V, the figure below shows that the slope of the input curve is

$$\frac{\Delta I_B}{\Delta V_{BE}} = \frac{(80\times10^{-6} - 20\times10^{-6})A}{(0.71-0.62)V} = 666.67\times10^{-6}\ A/V$$

The input resistance

$$r_i = \frac{\Delta V_{BE}}{\Delta I_B} = \frac{1}{666.67 \times 10^{-6}} \Omega = 1500\Omega$$

Problem-5:

As the base-emitter voltage is 0.7V, the base-emitter junction is forward biased. As the collector-base voltage is 0.2V, the base-collector junction is reverse biased. Therefore, the given NPN transistor is operating in the normal active mode.

Problem-6:

Voltage across resistor $R_3 = 100 \times 2 \times 10^{-3}$ V $= 0.2$V

Base voltage $V_B = V_{BE} + V_E = 0.7V + 0.2V = 0.9V$

Current through resistor $R_4 = \left(\frac{V_B}{R_4}\right) = \left(\frac{0.9}{40 \times 10^3}\right) A = 22.5 \mu A$

$I_E = 2mA$, $I_C = \alpha I_E = 0.98 \times 2 \times 10^{-3}$ A $= 1.96$ mA

$I_B = I_E - I_C = (2 \times 10^{-3} - 1.96 \times 10^{-3})$ A $= 40\mu A$

Current through resistor $R_1 = 40 \times 10^{-6} A + 22.5 \times 10^{-6} A = 62.5 \mu A$

Voltage drop across $R_2 = (I_C + 62.5 \times 10^{-6}) \times 1.5 \times 10^3 V = (1.96 \times 10^{-3} + 62.5 \times 10^{-6}) \times 1.5 \times 10^3$ V $= 3.03$V

Voltage across $R_1 = (5 - 3.03)V - 0.9V = 1.07V$

Voltage across $R_1 = \left(\frac{1.07}{62.5 \times 10^{-6}}\right) = 17.12 k\Omega$

Problem-7:

Fig. 2.77 (a): Slope of DC load line = -1/1100 A/V

$$\text{Stability} = \left(\frac{\beta + 1}{1 + \left(\frac{\beta R_E}{R_E + R_B'}\right)}\right), \text{ where } R_B' = \frac{R_1 R_2}{R_1 + R_2}$$

$$\text{Therefore, stability} = \frac{50 + 1}{1 + \left(\frac{50 \times 100}{100 + 2126}\right)} = \frac{51}{\left(1 + \frac{5000}{2226}\right)} \cong 15$$

Fig. 2.77 (b): slope of DC load line = -1/1000

Stability factor = $\beta + 1 = 51$

Fig. 2.77 (c): Slope of DC load line = –1/1100 A/V

$$\text{Stability} = \left(\frac{\beta + 1}{1 + \left(\frac{\beta R_E}{R_E + R_B} \right)} \right)$$

$$\text{Therefore, stability} = \frac{50+1}{1+\left(\frac{50\times100}{100000}\right)} = \frac{51}{(21/20)} = \frac{1020}{21} \cong 48.5$$

Problem-8:

$$\text{Quiscent base current} = \frac{15-0.7}{470} mA = 30\mu A$$

Quiscent collector current (I_{CQ}) and quiescent collector-emitter voltage (V_{CEQ}) can be determined from the load line, as superimposed on the output characteristics I_{CQ} = 8mA

V_{CEQ} = 7V

Slope of the DC load line = – 1/1000

Slope of the AC load line = –1/500

The equation for the AC load line can now be written as $I_C - 8\times10^{-3} = -\frac{1}{500}(V_{CE} - 7)$

For I_C = 0, V_{CE} = 11V and for V_{CE} = 0V, I_C = 22mA

The co-ordinates of the AC load line are therefore (11,0) and (0,22)

Problem-9:

$$\text{Emitter current } I_E = \left(\frac{6-0.7}{1\times10^3}\right)A = 5.3mA$$

$$I_C = \alpha I_E = 0.98\times5.3\times10^{-3} = 5.2mA$$

Voltage across load resistance R_L = $\left(5.2\times10^{-3}\times1\times10^3\right) = 5.2V$

Problem-10:

Applying Kirchhoff's voltage law to the base-emitter loop we get $8 - I_E\times3\times10^3 - 0.7 = 0$

$$I_E = \left(\frac{7.3}{3\times10^3}\right)A = 2.43mA$$

Assuming $I_C \cong I_E$. Applying Kirchhoff's voltage law to the collector-base loop

$$-10 + 2\times10^3\times2.43\times10^{-3} - V_{out} = 0$$

Therefore, V_{out} = –5.14V

Answers to Multiple Choice Questions

1. (a)	2. (c)	3. (a)	4. (a)	5. (b)
6. (a)	7. (a)	8. (d)	9. (a)	10. (c)
11. (a)	12. (b)	13. (c)	14. (b)	15. (d)

3 Field-Effect Transistors

After completing this chapter, you will learn the following topics.

- Difference between FET and BJT
- Construction of p-channel and n-channel JFETs
- I-V characteristics of p-channel and n-channel JFETs
- Construction of p-channel and n-channel depletion MOSFETs
- I-V characteristics of p-channel and n-channel depletion MOSFETs
- Construction of p-channel and n-channel enhancement MOSFETs
- I-V characteristics of p-channel and n-channel enhancement MOSFETs
- Characteristic parameters and specifications of JFETS and MOSFETs
- Biasing circuits of JFETs
- Biasing circuits of depletion and enhancement MOSFETs
- Applications of FETs

Introduction

This chapter covers both types of field effect transistors (FETs) i.e. Junction Field Effect Transistors (JFETs) and Metal Oxide Field Effect Transistors (MOSFETs). The chapter begins with an outline on differences between FETs and Bipolar Junction Transistors (BJTs) and the construction and I-V characteristics of n-channel and p-channel JFETs and MOSFETs (both depletion and enhancement MOSFETs). This is followed by the discussion on the characteristic parameters and specifications of FETs and differences between FETs and MOSFETs. Operational aspects of FETs like operation of FET as a switch and as an amplifier are discussed next. Biasing circuits of both JFETs and MOSFETs including common-source configuration, common-drain configuration and common-gate configuration are discussed next. This is followed by discussion on FET applications. Important formulae and keywords are listed at the end of the chapter. Different topics discussed in the chapter are amply illustrated with solved examples. In addition, there are a number of problems given towards the end of the chapter along with brief solutions. A self-evaluation exercise containing multiple-choice questions along with answers concludes the chapter.

3.1 FIELD EFFECT TRANSISTORS VERSUS BIPOLAR JUNCTION TRANSISTORS

Both BJTs and FETs are semiconductor devices. The major differences between the two devices include the following.

1. BJTs are current-controlled devices whereas FETs are voltage-controlled devices. In a BJT, the collector current (I_C) is a direct function of the base current (I_B) whereas in an FET, the drain current (I_D) depends upon the gate-source voltage (V_{GS}). In other words, in a BJT, the output current is controlled by the input current whereas in an FET it is controlled by the input voltage.

2. BJTs are bipolar devices whereas FETs are unipolar devices. In other words, in a BJT both electrons and holes contribute to the flow of current whereas in an FET either holes or electrons contribute to the current. In an n-channel FET electrons are the current carriers whereas in a p-channel FET holes are the current carriers.
3. The input impedance of FET devices is much higher (of the order of several hundred mega-ohms) as compared to that of BJT transistor configurations (varying from hundred ohms to less than 1 MW). Input impedance is a very important characteristic parameter in the design of linear AC amplifiers.
4. FET devices, in general, are more temperature stable and smaller in construction as compared to BJTs. Owing to their smaller size, FETs are extensively used in the fabrication of integrated circuits.
5. Gain of an FET-based amplifier is smaller than that of a BJT amplifier.That is, FET amplifiers have poorer sensitivity to changes in the input signal.
6. FETs are more sensitive to handling than BJTs.

3.2 JUNCTION FIELD EFFECT TRANSISTORS – STRUCTURE AND I-V CHARACTERISTICS

Junction FET (JFET) is the simplest of the FETs. It is a three-terminal device where the voltage applied at one terminal controls the current through the other two terminals. JFETs comprise a semiconductor channel embedded into semiconductor layers of opposite polarity. Depending upon whether the semiconductor channel is an n-type semiconductor or a p-type semiconductor, JFETs are classified as n-channel or p-channel JFETs, respectively.

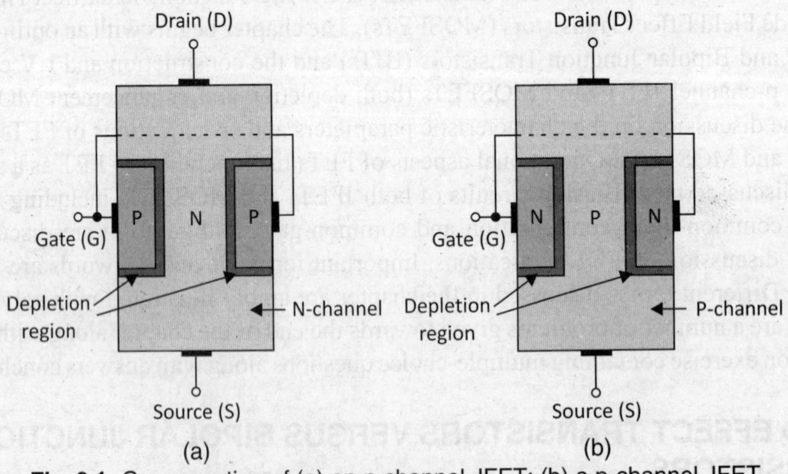

Fig. 3.1: Cross-section of (a) an n-channel JFET; (b) a p-channel JFET

3.2.1 Construction

Figures-3.1(a) and (b) show the cross-sectional view of n-channel and p-channel JFETs respectively. In an n-channel JFET, an n-type semiconductor material forms a channel between embedded layers of p-type material whereas in a p-channel JFET, a p-type semiconductor forms a channel between the embedded layers of n-type material. Therefore, two P-N junctions are formed between the semiconductor channel and the embedded semiconductor layers. Ohmic contacts are made at the top and bottom of the channel and are referred to as the *drain* (D) and the *source* (S) terminals, respectively. The channel behaves as a resistive element between its drain and source terminals. In an n-channel JFET, both the embedded p-type layers are connected together and form the *gate* (G) terminal. Similarly, in a p-channel JFET, the gate terminal is formed by connecting the two n-type embedded layers. Figures-3.2(a) and (b) show the circuit symbols for the n-channel and p-channel JFETs respectively.

In the absence of any externally applied potential, both the P-N junctions are open circuited, and a small depletion region is formed at each of the junctions as shown in Figure-3.1. The externally applied potential between gate and source terminals controls the flow of drain current for a given potential between the drain and source terminals. The operation of JFET devices is explained in the subsequent sections.

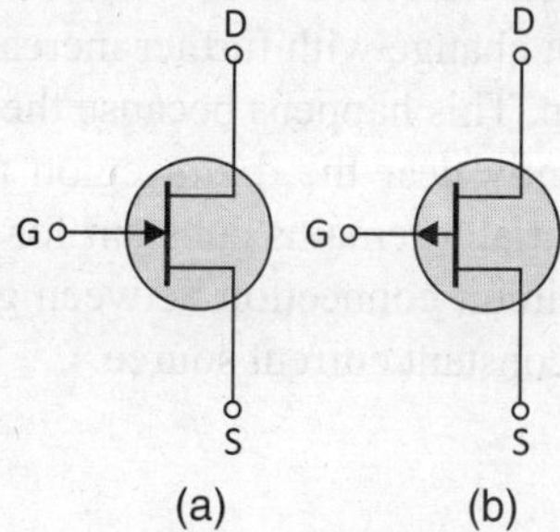

Fig. 3.2: Circuit symbol of (a) an n-channel JFET; (b) a p-channel JFET

3.2.2 I-V Characteristics

In this section, the principle of operation of an n-channel JFET is explained. The operation of a p-channel JFET is similar to that of an n-channel JFET with the polarities of voltages and direction of currents reversed. Let us consider the situation when a positive drain-source voltage (V_{DS}) is applied to the JFET with gate terminal shorted to the source terminal ($V_{GS} = 0$).

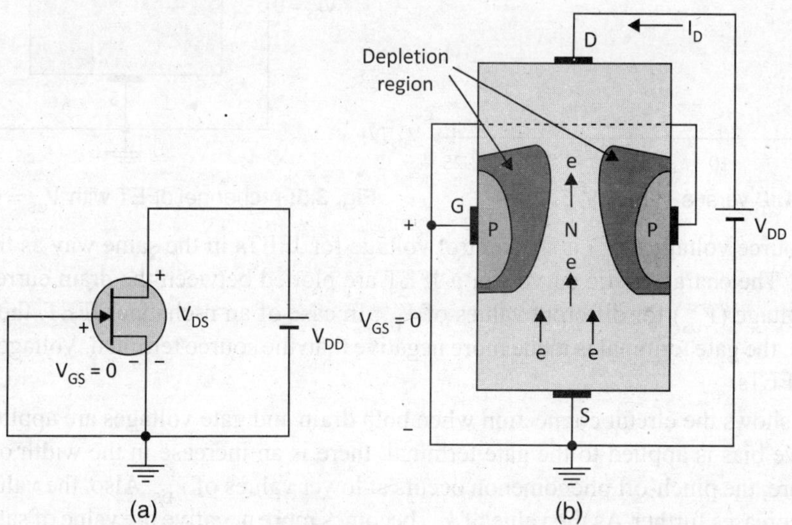

Fig. 3.3: n-channel JFET with $V_{GS} = 0$ and positive value of V_{DS}

Figure 3.3(a) shows the circuit connection. When the drain-source voltage is applied, the electrons in the n-channel are attracted to the drain-terminal establishing the flow of drain current (I_D) as shown in Figure-3.3(b). The value of I_D is determined by the value of the applied V_{DS} and the resistance of the n-channel between the drain and the source terminals. Owing to the flow of I_D, there is a uniform voltage drop across the channel resistance, which reverse-biases the two P-N junctions. This results in increase in the width of the depletion region. It may be mentioned here that the depletion region is wider near the drain-region than the source-region. This is because I_D and the channel resistance establish more reverse-bias voltage at the P-N junction near the D-region than near the source-region.

I_D increases linearly with increase in V_{DS} till the V_{DS} reaches a value where the saturation effect sets in. This is evident from Figure-3.4 which shows the relationship between I_D and V_{DS} for zero V_{GS} (V_{GS} = 0). The value of V_{DS} where the saturation effect sets in is referred to as the pinch-off voltage (V_P). When V_{DS} reaches V_P, the value of I_D does not change with further increase in the value of V_{DS}. This condition is referred to as the pinch-off condition. This happens because the width of the depletion regions of the P-N junctions has increased significantly near the drain-region resulting in reduction of the channel width (Figure-3.5). Therefore, I_D essentially remains constant for $V_{DS}>V_P$. This current is referred to as the drain-to-source current for short circuit connection between gate and source (I_{DSS}). In nutshell, for $V_{DS}>V_P$, JFET has characteristics of a constant current source.

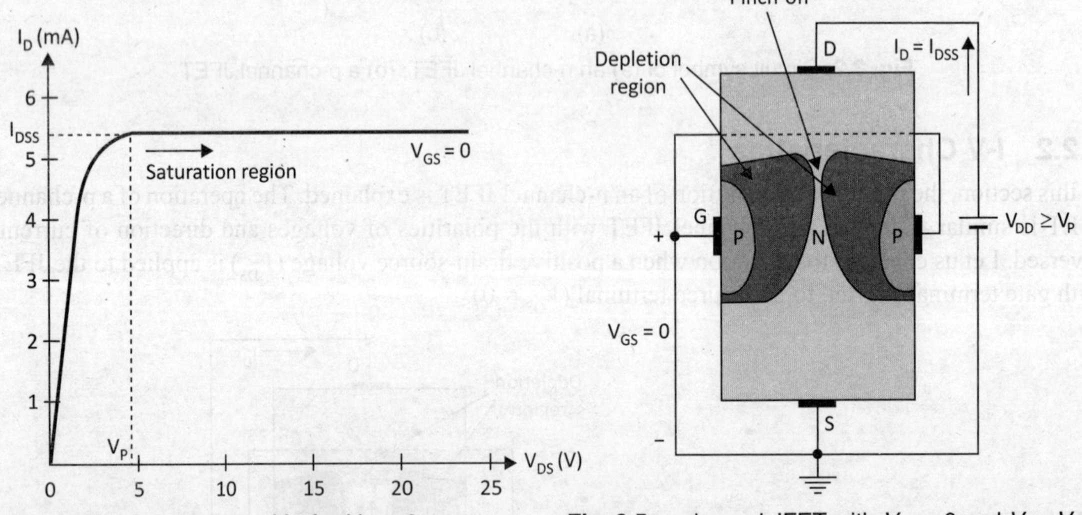

Fig. 3.4: I_D versus V_{DS} for V_{GS} = 0 **Fig. 3.5:** n-channel JFET with V_{GS} = 0 and $V_{DS}>V_P$

The gate-source voltage (V_{GS}) is the control voltage for JFETs in the same way as the base current (I_B) is for BJTs. The characteristic curves for a JFET are plotted between the drain current (I_D) and the drain-source voltage (V_{DS}) for different values of V_{GS}. In case of an n-channel JFET, the voltage V_{GS} is negative, that is, the gate terminal is made more negative than the source terminal. Voltage V_{GS} is positive for p-channel JFETs.

Figure-3.6 shows the circuit connection when both drain and gate voltages are applied to the JFET. When a negative bias is applied to the gate terminal, there is an increase in the width of the depletion region. Therefore, the pinch-off phenomenon occurs at lower values of V_{DS}. Also, the value of saturation drain current decreases further. As the value of V_{GS} becomes more negative the value of saturation current decreases. The drain current becomes zero for V_{GS} equal to $-V_P$. This voltage is referred to as the gate-source cut-off voltage or the gate-source pinch-off voltage ($V_{GS(off)}$).

In fact, the value of drain-source pinch-off voltage decreases in a parabolic manner with the V_{GS} becoming more negative. Figure-3.7 shows the output characteristic curves for the n-channel JFET. The region to the left of the locus of pinch-off voltages is the *ohmic region* or the *voltage-controlled resistance region*. Region to the right of the locus of the pinch-off voltages is the *saturation region* or the *constant-current region*. In the ohmic region, JFET acts as a variable resistor whose resistance is controlled by the applied gate-source voltage.

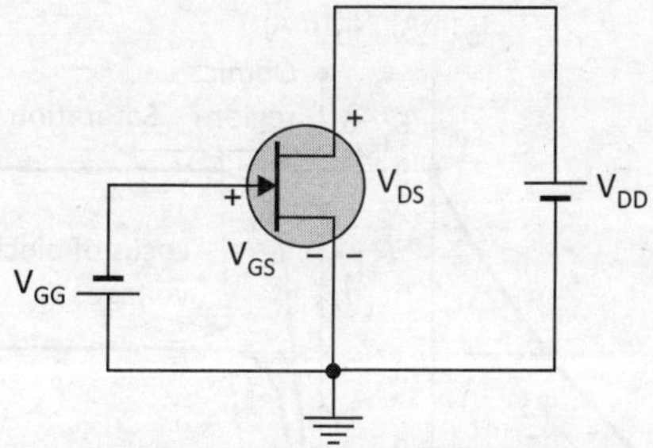

Fig. 3.6: n-channel JFET biasing circuit

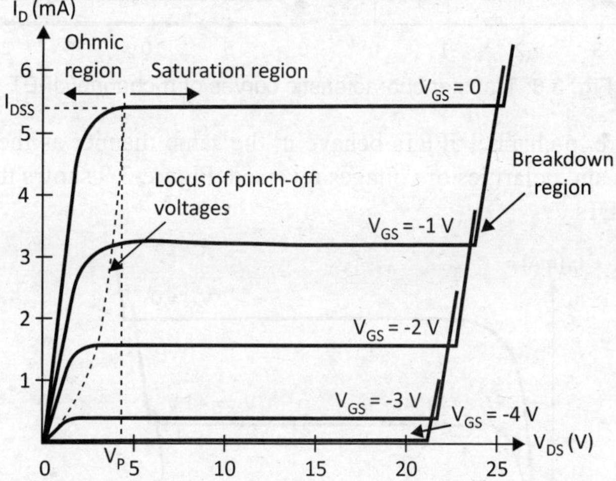

Fig. 3.7: Output characteristic curves of an n-channel JFET

The drain resistance (r_d) in the saturation region is given by eqn. (3.1)

$$r_d = \frac{r_o}{(1 - V_{GS}/V_P)^2} \tag{3.1}$$

Where, r_o is the resistance at $V_{GS} = 0$; r_d is the resistance at a particular value of V_{GS}; V_P is the pinch-off voltage.The relationship between the output current I_D in the saturation region for a given value of input V_{GS} is given by eqn. (3.2)

$$I_D = I_{DSS}\left(1 - \frac{V_{GS}}{V_P}\right)^2 \tag{3.2}$$

Where I_{DSS} is the drain current for short circuit connection between gate and source. This expression is referred to as the Shockley's equation. As is clear from the equation, there is a non-linear square law relationship between the output I_D and the input V_{GS} as opposed to a linear relation between the output collector current (I_C) and the input base current (I_B) in case of BJTs. Because of the square law characteristics, JFETs are very useful devices in radio tuners and TV receivers.

The transfer characteristics of a FET device is a plot between I_D and V_{GS} and can be plotted using Shockley's equation or using the output characteristic curves. Figure-3.8 shows how we can obtain the transfer characteristics curve using the output characteristics curve.

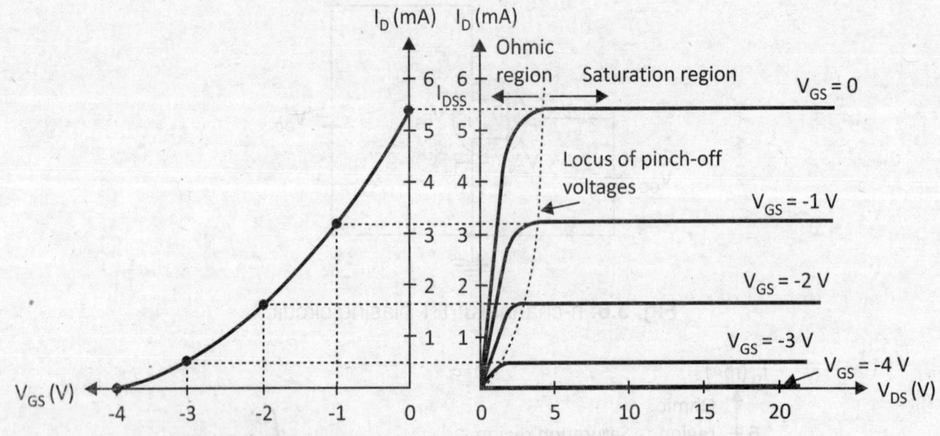

Fig. 3.8: Transfer characteristic curves of n-channel JFET

As mentioned before, p-channel JFETs behave in the same manner as the n-channel JFETs with the direction of currents and polarities of voltages reversed. Figure-3.9 shows the output ch aracteristic curves for p-channel JFETs.

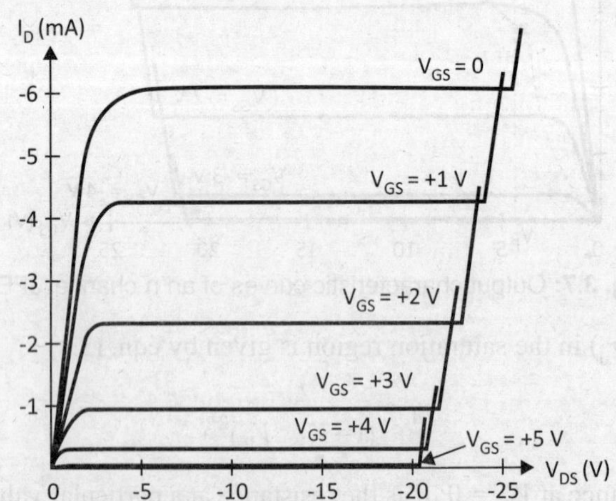

Fig. 3.9: Output characteristic curve of p-channel JFET

3.2.3 Effect of Temperature on JFET Parameters

JFETs offer better thermal stability as compared to BJTs. Increase in JFET temperature results in decrease in the depletion region width and decrease in the carrier mobility. Decrease in the depletion region results in increase in channel width, which in turn increases the value of I_D. This results in positive temperature coefficient for I_D. Increase in I_D with temperature results in increase in $V_{GS(off)}$ with temperature. $V_{GS(off)}$ also has a positive temperature coefficient of the order of 2.2 mV/°C.

Decrease in carrier mobility gives I_D a negative temperature coefficient. Since both the mechanisms occur simultaneously, the effect of one mechanism compensates for the other. Therefore, JFETs offer better temperature stability. It is even possible to bias the JFET so as to establish zero temperature coefficient.

3.3 MOSFET STRUCTURE AND I-V CHARACTERISTICS

Metal oxide field-effect transistors (MOSFETs) are another class of FETs. They are named so as the metal gate in a MOSFET is insulated from the semiconductor channel by a very thin oxide layer. MOSFETs are also referred to as insulated gate field-effect transistors (IGFETs). Like a JFET, a MOSFET is also a three-terminal device where the drain current is controlled by the applied gate voltage.

MOSFETs are further classified into two types depending upon their construction and mode of operation. These include the depletion MOSFET (or DE-MOSFET) and the enhancement MOSFET (or E-MOSFET). In this section, we discuss the construction, principle of operation and characteristic parameters of both the types of MOSFETs. Also discussed are the precautions to be taken while handling MOSFETs.

3.3.1 Depletion MOSFETs

In a DE-MOSFET, a channel is physically constructed between the drain and the source terminals. DE-MOSFETs are further of two types namely n-channel DE-MOSFETs and p-channel DE-MOSFETs depending on whether the channel material is an n-type semiconductor or a p-type semiconductor.

The cross-sectional view of an n-channel DE-MOSFET is shown in Figure-3.10. It comprises a substrate made of a p-type semiconductor material. Two n+ type regions linked by an n-channel are formed on the substrate. The source and the drain terminals are formed by connecting metal contacts to the two n+ regions as shown in Figure-3.10. The gate terminal is connected to the insulating silicon dioxide (SiO_2) layer on top of the n-channel. Therefore, there is no direct electrical connection between the gate terminal and the channel of a DE-MOSFET. It is the same In case of E-MOSFETs also and there is no direct electrical connection between the gate terminal and the channel.There is a capacitance that exists between the gate and the channel as the metal gate contact and the channel act as walls of a parallel plate capacitor and the SiO_2 layer forms the dielectric. Hence the input impedance of a DE-MOSFET is very high of the order of 10^{10}–10^{15}W.

The construction of a p-channel DE-MOSFET (Figure-3.11) is similar to that of an n-channel DE-MOSFET with the difference being that the substrate is an n-type semiconductor while the channel is a p-type material. Figures-3.12 (a) and (b) show the circuit symbols for n-type and p-type DE-MOSFETs, respectively.

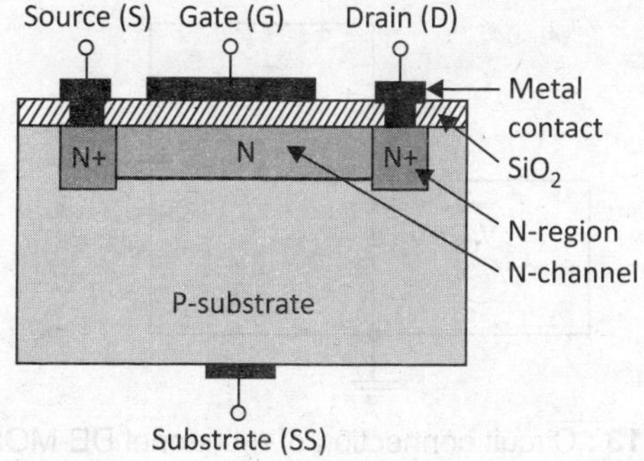

Fig. 3.10: Cross-section of an n-channel DE-MOSFET

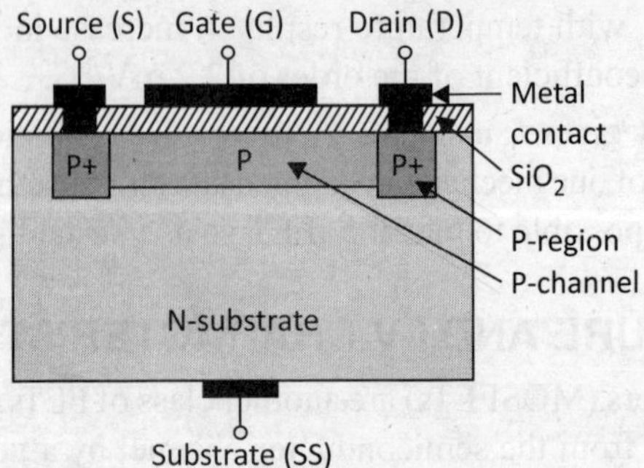

Fig. 3.11: Cross-section of a p-channel DE-MOSFET

An n-channel DE-MOSFET operates as follows. Refer to Figure-3.13. When the gate and the source terminals are shorted, that is, the voltage $V_{GS} = 0$ and a positive voltage is applied between the drain and the source terminals, that is, voltage V_{DS} is positive, there is a flow of current in the n-channel as the electrons are attracted by positive potential at the drain terminal. The current increases with increase in V_{DS} and after a certain value of V_{DS} it becomes constant. This current is represented as I_{DSS} and is similar to that established in a JFET with $V_{GS} = 0$. When the gate terminal is at a negative potential as compared to the source terminal, electrons in the n-channel are repelled by this negative potential towards the p-type substrate. Also, the holes in the p-type substrate are attracted towards the gate. This results in recombination of holes and electrons and there is reduction in the number of free electrons in the n-channel as shown in Figure-3.14. The higher the negative potential, more is the rate of recombination and less the number of free electrons in the channel. Therefore, the drain current decreases with increase in the value of the negative gate-source potential.

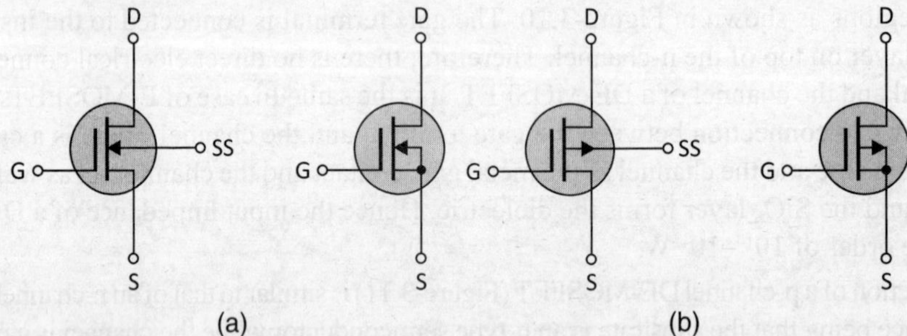

Fig. 3.12: Circuit symbol of DE-MOSFET (a) n-channel DE-MOSFET (b) p-channel DE-MOSFET

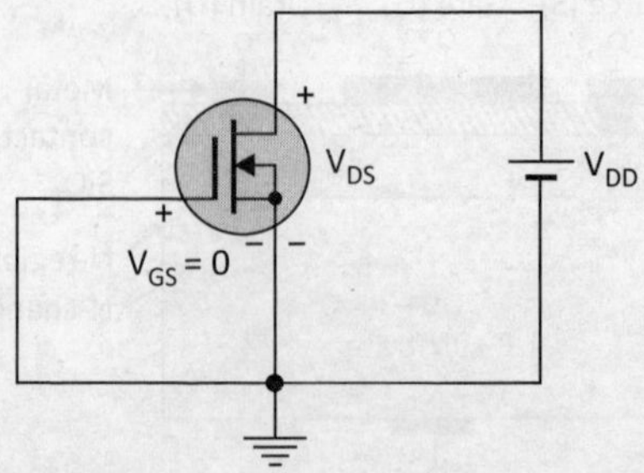

Fig. 3.13 : Circuit connection of n-channel DE-MOSFET

For positive values of gate-source voltage, electrons (minority carriers) in the p-type substrate are attracted into the channel and establish new carriers through the collisions between accelerating particles. Thus, the drain current increases rapidly with increase in the positive value of gate-source voltage. As the application of positive gate-source voltage increases the value of drain current, the region of positive gate-source voltages is referred to as the enhancement region. The region for zero and negative values of gate-source voltage is referred to as the depletion region. It may be mentioned here that Shockley's equation as defined for JFETs is applicable for the DE-MOSFET also in both the depletion and the enhancement regions. Figure-3.15 shows the output characteristic curves for an n-channel DE-MOSFET.

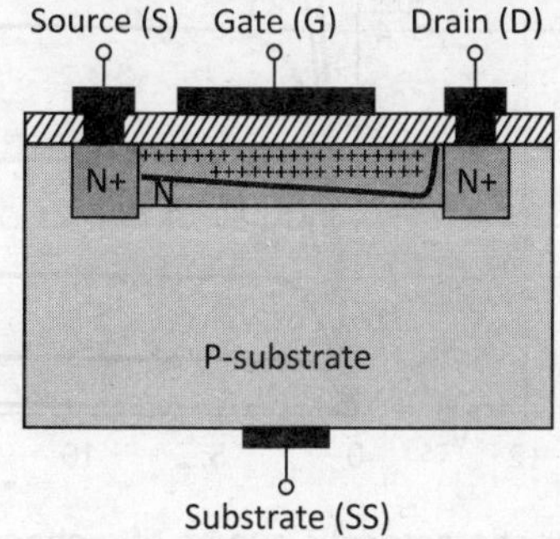

Fig. 3.14 : n-channel DE-MOSFET

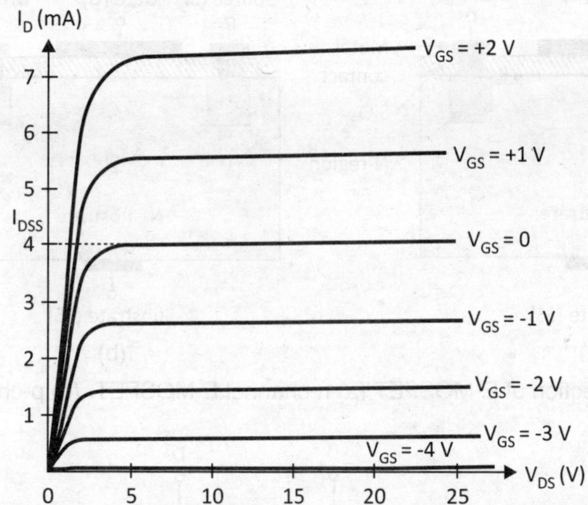

Fig. 3.15 : Output characteristic curves of n-channel DE-MOSFET

The transfer characteristics for DE-MOSFET can be plotted in a similar fashion like it was done in case of a JFET. Figure-3.16 shows the transfer characteristics for an n-channel DE-MOSFET.

3.3.2 Enhancement MOSFETs

The construction of an E-MOSFET is similar to that of a DE-MOSFET with the difference that there is no physical channel between the source and drain terminals in the E-MOSFET. The invention of E-MOSFETs has revolutionized the computer industry and they are extensively used in digital electronics and computers. Figures-3.17 (a) and (b) show the cross-section of n-channel and p-channel E-MOSFETs, respectively. Figures-3.18 (a) and (b) respectively, show the circuit symbols of the n-channel and p-channel MOSFETs. The broken line in the symbol indicates the absence of a channel.

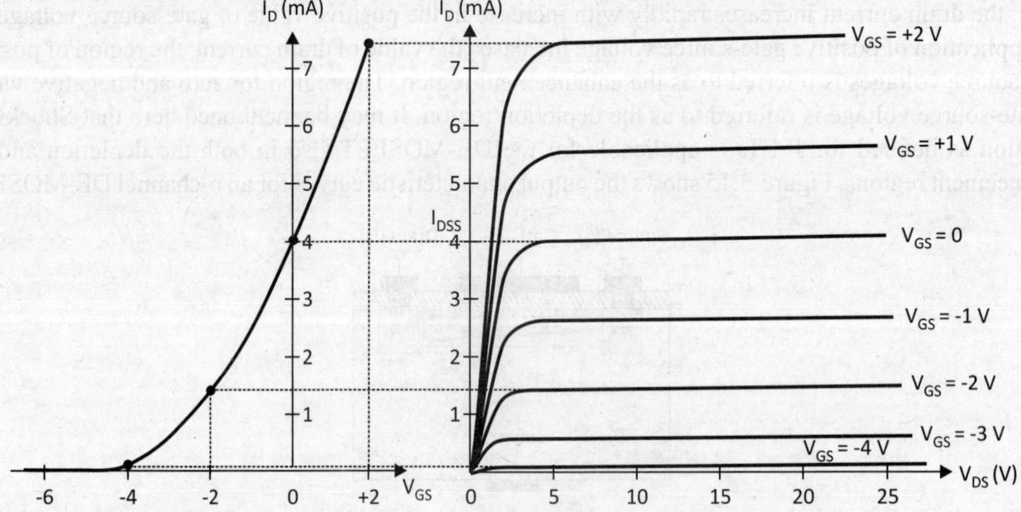

Fig. 3.16: Transfer characteristic curves of n-channel DE-MOSFET

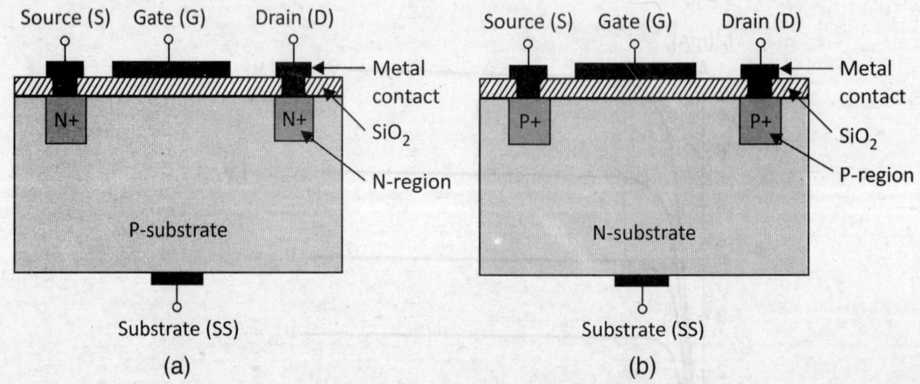

Fig. 3.17: Cross-section of E-MOSFET (a) n-channel E-MOSFET. (b) p-channel E-MOSFET

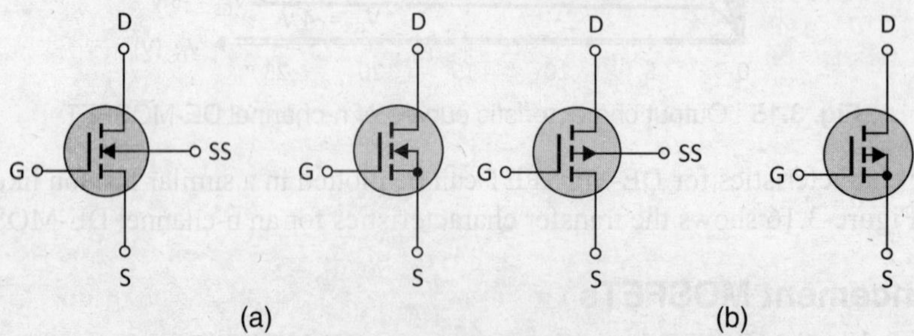

Fig. 3.18: Circuit symbol of E-MOSFET (a) n-channel E-MOSFET. (b) p-channel E-MOSFET

The n-channel E-MOSFET functions as follows. When the gate-source voltage is zero and some positive drain-source voltage is applied; there is no drain current as there is no channel available for flow of drain current. E-MOSFETs are also normally called off-MOSFETs as they do not conduct when $V_{GS} = 0$. The drain current flows only when a positive voltage is applied to the gate terminal with respect to the source terminal as this induces a channel by drawing the electrons (minority carriers) in the p-type substrate to accumulate near the surface of the SiO_2 layer. Also, holes in the p-substrate are forced to move away from the edge of the SiO_2 layer as shown in Figure-3.19. As the SiO_2 layer is insulating, it prevents the electrons from being absorbed at the gate terminal. These electrons lead to the flow of current between the drain and the source terminals. As the value of gate-source voltage is increased, more and more electrons accumulate leading to an enhanced flow of drain current. The level of gate-source voltage that leads to significant flow of drain current is referred to as threshold voltage and is denoted by V_T. For a fixed gate-source voltage and increasing the level of drain-source voltage leads to an initial increase in the drain current which eventually saturates due to the reduction in the gate-drain voltage (V_{GD}) with increase in the drain-source voltage (V_{DS}). Reduction in the gate-drain voltage reduces the attractive forces for the free carriers in the induced channel near the drain region, resulting in the reduction of effective channel width near the drain region. This effect is referred to as the pinching effect. Pinching effect refers to the reduction in the width of the channel near the drain region with increase in the drain-source voltage as shown in Figure-3.20. The value of the drain-source voltage at which the drain current saturates is given by $V_{DS(sat)}$.

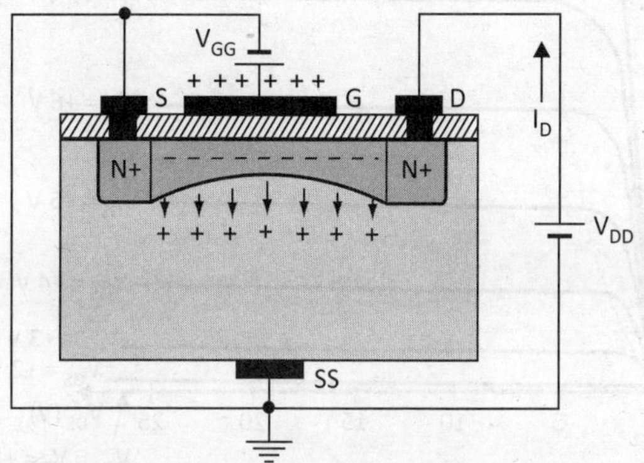

Fig. 3.19: Working of n-channel E-MOSFET

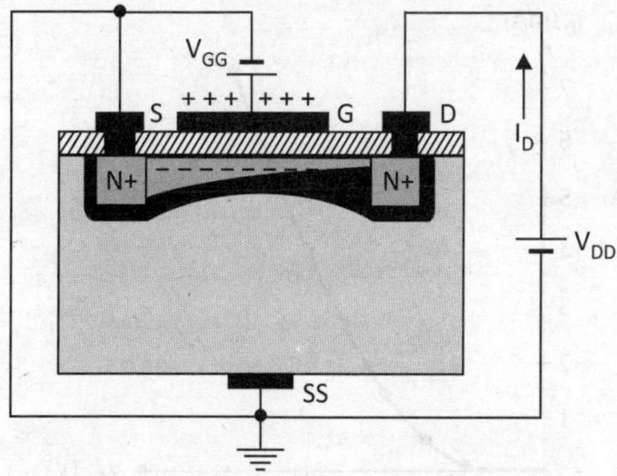

Fig. 3.20: Pinching phenomenon in E-MOSFET

Figure-3.21 shows the output characteristic curves for an n-channel E- MOSFET. It can be observed from the curve that the $V_{DS(sat)}$ voltage increases with the increase in the applied gate-source voltage. The relationship between $V_{DS(sat)}$ and V_{GS} is given by eqn. 3.3.

$$V_{DS(sat)} = V_{GS} - V_T \tag{3.3}$$

where V_T is the threshold gate-source voltage.

Also, the drain current is zero for gate-source voltage less than the threshold voltage V_T. For voltages greater than the threshold voltage the drain current is given by eqn. 3.4.

$$I_D = k(V_{GS} - V_T)^2 \tag{3.4}$$

As is clear from eqn. 3.4, the relationship between the drain current and the gate-source voltage is nonlinear, and the current is proportional to the square of the voltage. The relationship is shown in Figure-3.22. The characteristics of Figure-3.22 are referred to as the transfer characteristics.

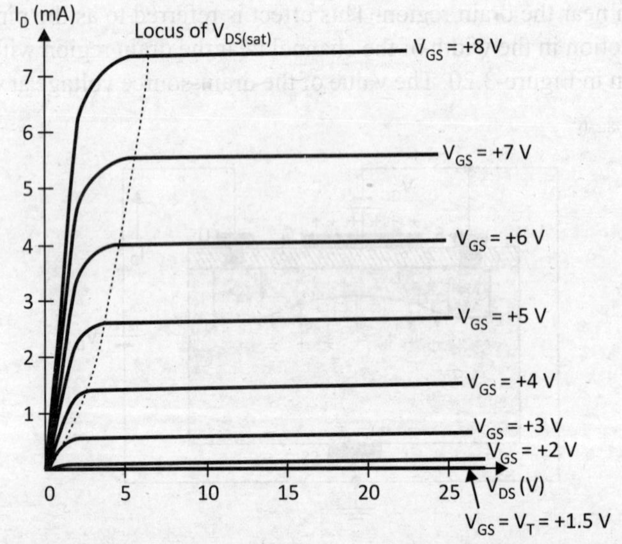

Fig. 3.21: Output characteristic curves for an n-channel E-MOSFET

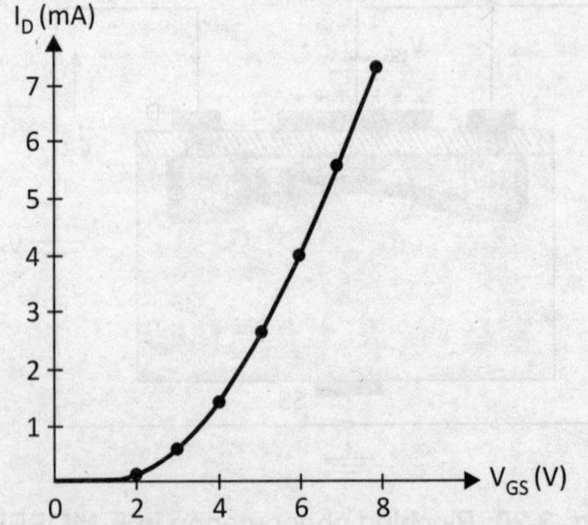

Fig. 3.22: Transfer characteristics of an n-channel E-MOSFET

Example-3.1: Figure-3.23 shows a certain MOSFET. Identify the MOSFET. If V_T is the threshold voltage of the MOSFET and I_{DSS} is the drain current of the MOSFET with gate-source voltage equal to twice the threshold voltage; draw its output characteristics. V_{GG} is the externally applied supply voltage between the gate and the drain terminals. Draw the curve between the drain current I_D and drain-source voltage V_{DS} for $V_{GG} = V_T/2$.

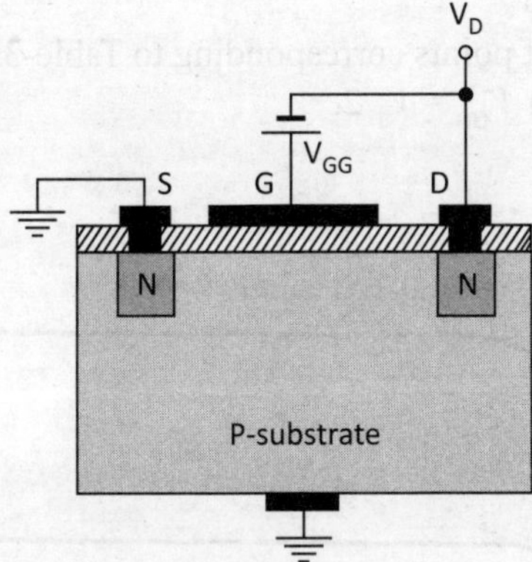

Fig. 3.23 : Example-3.1

Solution:

The MOSFET shown in Figure-3.23 is an n-channel enhancement MOSFET. An enhancement MOSFET conducts for V_{GS} greater than the threshold voltage (V_T). The current in an E-MOSFET is given by $I_D = k(V_{GS} - V_T)^2$. As I_{DS} is the current for $V_{GS} = 2V_T$, therefore $k = I_{DS}/V_T^2$.

The output characteristics can be plotted using the equations $I_D = \frac{I_{DS}}{V_T^2}(V_{GS} - V_T)^2$ and

$V_{DS(sat)} = V_{GS} - V_T$

By calculating the values of I_D for different values of V_{GS} we can plot the output characteristic curves for the given MOSFET. As an example, consider $V_{GS} = 3.5V_T$, $I_D = 6.25I_{DS}$ and $V_{DS(sat)} = 2.5V_T$. Figure-3.24 shows the output characteristics of an E-MOSFET.

Table 3.1: Solution to Example 3.1

V_D	V_{DS}	V_{GS}	I_D
0	0	$0.5V_T$	0
$0.5V_T$	$0.5V_T$	V_T	0
V_T	V_T	$1.5V_T$	$0.25I_{DS}$
$1.5V_T$	$1.5V_T$	$2V_T$	I_{DS}
$2V_T$	$2V_T$	$2.5V_T$	$2.25I_{DS}$
$2.5V_T$	$2.5V_T$	$3V_T$	$4I_{DS}$
$3V_T$	$3V_T$	$3.5V_T$	$6.25I_{DS}$

The voltage V_{GG} is applied between the gate and the drain terminals. The gate-source voltage (V_{GS}) is given by $V_{GS} = V_{GG} + V_{DS} = V_{GG} + V_D$(The voltage V_D is equal to the drain-source voltage V_{DS}).

As $V_{GG} = V_T/2$, the voltage V_{GS} will be less than the threshold voltage V_T until voltage V_{DS} is less than $V_T/2$. When $V_D = V_T/2$, $V_{GS} = V_T$ and the MOSFET starts conducting after that. Table-3.1 lists the values of V_{GS}, I_D for various values of V_D.

Figure-3.25 shows the plot of points corresponding to Table-3.1. The curve obtained by joining the points is the I_D versus V_{DS} plot for $V_{GG} = V_T/2$.

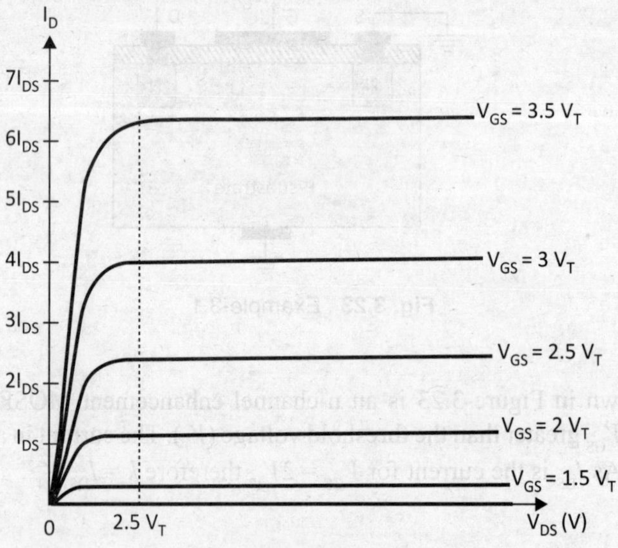

Fig. 3.24

Fig. 3.25

3.3.3 Dual-gate MOSFETs

In a dual-gate MOSFET, an additional second insulated gate is provided as compared to a conventional MOSFET. The flow of current through the MOSFET is controlled by voltages at both the gate terminals. Since the control is exerted by two gates, the dual-gate MOSFET may be considered to be the counterpart of a tetrode. Figure-3.26(a) shows the cross-section of an n-channel dual-gate DE-MOSFET and Figure-3.26(b) shows the circuit symbol. The device acts if two MOSFETs are connected in series. The n+ region in the middle acts as a drain for MOSFET-1 and a source for the MOSFET-2. The flow of current through the MOSFET is controlled by both gate voltages. For the dual-gate n-channel DE-MOSFET shown in the figure, the drain current decreases when the gate voltage at either of the two gate terminals is made negative. It may be mentioned here that the gate terminal-1 provides higher transconductance as compared to the gate terminal-2. Owing to simultaneous control of two gate voltages, the device is used in applications such as AGC amplifier, mixers and demodulators. When it is used in AGC amplifier, the signal to be amplified is connected to Gate-1 and the voltage to control the gain is applied to Gate-2.

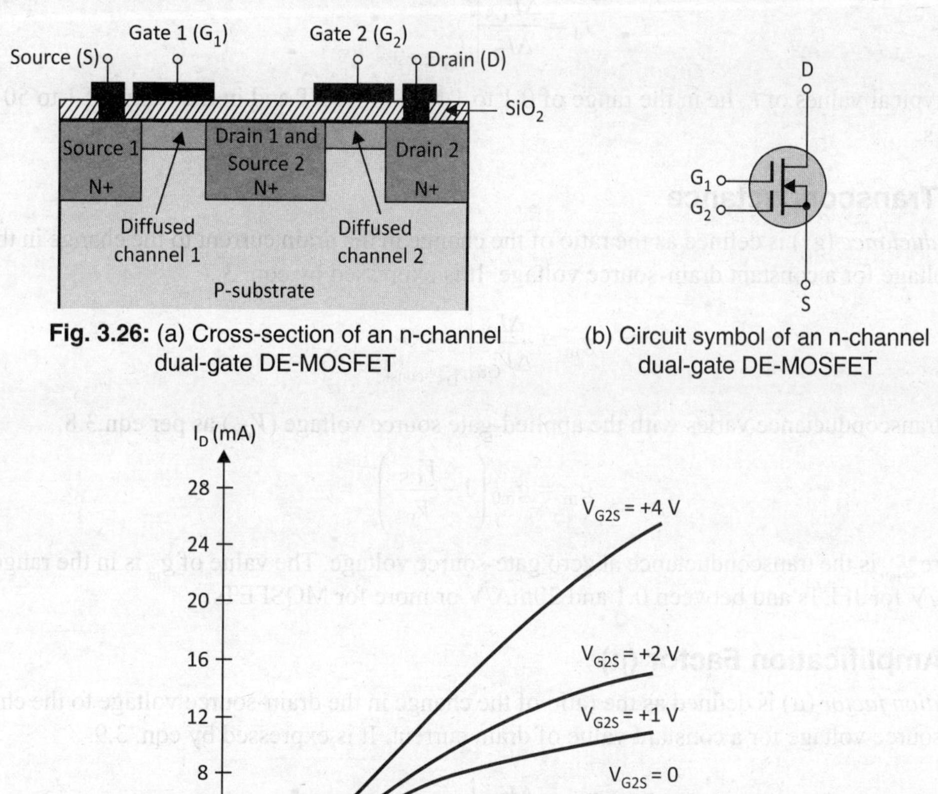

Fig. 3.26: (a) Cross-section of an n-channel dual-gate DE-MOSFET (b) Circuit symbol of an n-channel dual-gate DE-MOSFET

Fig. 3.27: Transfer characteristics of an n-channel dual-gate DE-MOSFET

Figure-3.27 shows the transfer characteristics of a popular n-channel dual-gate DE-MOSFET. The drain characteristics are similar to that of a conventional n-channel DE-MOSFET.

3.4 CHARACTERISTIC PARAMETERS

The four key parameters that define the performance of an FET device are static drain resistance, dynamic drain resistance, transconductance (g_m) and amplification factor (m).

3.4.1 Drain Resistance

Static drain resistance (R_D) is defined as the ratio of the drain-source voltage (V_{DS}) to the drain current (I_D). It is expressed by eqn. 3.5.

$$R_D = \frac{V_{DS}}{I_D} \tag{3.5}$$

Dynamic drain resistance (r_d) is defined as the ratio of change in the drain-source voltage to the change in the drain current at a constant gate-source voltage. It is expressed by eqn. 3.6.

$$r_d = \left.\frac{\Delta V_{DS}}{\Delta I_D}\right|_{V_{GS}=\text{const.}} \tag{3.6}$$

The typical values of r_d lie in the range of 0.1 to 1 MΩ for JFET and in the range of 1 to 50 kΩ for MOSFETs.

3.4.2 Transconductance

Transconductance (g_m) is defined as the ratio of the change in the drain current to the change in the gate-source voltage for a constant drain-source voltage. It is expressed by eqn. 3.7.

$$g_m = \left.\frac{\Delta I_D}{\Delta V_{GS}}\right|_{V_{DS}=\text{const.}} \tag{3.7}$$

The transconductance varies with the applied-gate source voltage (V_{GS}) as per eqn.3.8.

$$g_m = g_{m0}\left(1 - \frac{V_{GS}}{V_P}\right) \tag{3.8}$$

where g_{m0} is the transconductance at zero gate-source voltage. The value of g_m is in the range of 0.1 to 10 mA/V for JFETs and between 0.1 and 20mA/V or more for MOSFETs.

3.4.3 Amplification Factor (μ)

Amplification factor (μ) is defined as the ratio of the change in the drain-source voltage to the change in the gate-source voltage for a constant value of drain current. It is expressed by eqn. 3.9.

$$\mu = \left.\frac{\Delta V_{DS}}{\Delta V_{GS}}\right|_{I_D=\text{const.}} \tag{3.9}$$

Substituting the value of r_d given in eqn.(3.6) and the value of g_m given in eqn.(3.7) in eqn.(3.9), we get eqn. 3.10.

$$\mu = \frac{\Delta V_{DS}}{\Delta V_{GS}} = \frac{\Delta V_{DS}}{\Delta I_D} \times \frac{\Delta I_D}{\Delta V_{GS}} = r_d \times g_m \tag{3.10}$$

Therefore, the amplification factor is the product of the dynamic drain resistance and the transconductance of the JFET. Amplification factor in a JFET can be as high as 100.

Example-3.2: A certain JFET device has a drain current of 8 mA when a drain voltage of 5 V is applied to it with its gate-source terminals shorted. When the drain voltage is increased to 10 V,the drain current is observed to increase to 8.2 mA. When the gate-source voltage is made equal to –0.5 V, the drain current decreases to 7.2 mA. Determine the type of the JFET, its drain resistance, transconductance and amplification factor.

Solution: Since application of negative gate-source voltage results in decrease of the drain current, the JFET is an *n*-channel JFET. Drain resistance is given by:

$$r_d = \left.\frac{\Delta V_{DS}}{\Delta_D}\right|_{V_{GS}=\text{const.}} = (10-5)/(8.2\times10^{-3}-8.0\times10^{-3}) = 5/(0.2\times10^{-3}) = 25\text{ k}\Omega$$

$$\text{Transconductance } g_m = \left.\frac{\Delta I_D}{\Delta V_{GS}}\right|_{V_{DS}=\text{const.}}$$

$$g_m = (7.2\times10^{-3}-8.2\times10^{-3})/(-0.5-0) = -1\times10^{-3}/(-0.5) = 2\text{ mA/V}$$

$$\text{Amplification factor } \mu = r_d \times g_m = (25\times10^3)\times(2\times10^{-3}) = 50$$

Example-3.3: Derive the expression for the transconductance (g_m) of the JFET indicating how the gm would vary with V_{GS} from its initial value of g_{m0} for $V_{GS} = 0$.

Solution: Drain current (I_D) in a JFET is given by:

$$I_D = I_{DSS}\left(1-\frac{V_{GS}}{V_P}\right)^2$$

Differentiating both sides of the equation w.r.t. the gate-source voltage (V_{GS}) we get,

$$\frac{dI_D}{dV_{GS}} = 2I_{DSS}\times\left(1-\frac{V_{GS}}{V_P}\right)\times\left(\frac{-1}{V_P}\right)$$

As $g_m = dI_D/dV_{GS}$. Therefore,

$$g_m = 2I_{DSS}\times\left(1-\frac{V_{GS}}{V_P}\right)\times\left(\frac{-1}{V_P}\right)$$

Let g_{m0} be the transconductance for $V_{GS} = 0$. Therefore,

$$g_{m0} = 2I_{DSS}\times\left(\frac{-1}{V_P}\right)$$

Substituting the value of g_{m0} in the expression for g_m we get,

$$g_m = g_{m0}\times\left(1-\frac{V_{GS}}{V_P}\right)$$

3.5 FET SPECIFICATIONS

The common electrical specifications of JFET and MOSFET devices are as follows:

1. **Reverse Gate-Source Breakdown Voltage (BV_{GS}):** It is defined as the reverse gate-source voltage with either the drain open (BV_{GSO}) or drain shorted to the source (BV_{GSS}). It is typically few tens of volts.
2. **Power Dissipation (P_D):** Power dissipation rating of the JFET is the product of the drain-source voltage (V_{DS}) and the drain current (I_D). The power dissipation rating must be derated with increase in temperature. It is usually specified at an ambient temperature of 25 °C. JFETs are available in power ratings of hundreds of milliwatts while MOSFETs are available in a wide range of power ratings starting from a few milliwatts to more than hundred watts.
3. **Saturation Drain Current (I_{DSS}):** It is the maximum drain current when the gate terminal is shorted to the source terminal. It is usually specified at a given drain-source voltage somewhere in the channel pinch-off region.
4. **Pinch-Off Voltage (V_P or $V_{GS(off)}$):** It is the gate-source voltage for which the drain current reduces to zero. It is also specified for a given value of drain-source voltage. It is specified in case of JFETs and DE-MOSFETs only.
5. **Gate Leakage current (I_{GSS}):** It is the gate-to-source leakage current with the drain terminal shorted to the source terminal. It is given for a specific value of gate reverse bias voltage. Typical value of gate leakage current is few nanoamperes for JFETs and few pico-amperes for MOSFETs.
6. **Forward Transconductance (g_{fs}):** Itis usually given for specified values of gate-source voltage (V_{GS}) and drain-source voltage (V_{DS}). It is typically few thousand micro-mhos to few milli-mhos for both JFETs and MOSFETs.
7. **Output Conductance (g_{os}):** It is the reciprocal of the dynamic drain resistance (r_d). It is usually specified as an admittance parameter (y_{os}). y_{os} equals g_{os} at low frequencies. Admittance is in the range of few milli-mhos for both JFETs and MOSFETs.
8. **Input Capacitance (C_{iss}):** It is the input capacitance of the FET when connected in common source configuration. It is typically of the order of few pFs for both JFETs and MOSFET devices. The overall input capacitance (C_i) in a common source amplifier configuration using an FET is larger than C_{iss} due to the presence of Miller component of the gate-drain inter-electrode capacitance (C_{gd} or C_{rss}). It is also referred to as the reverse transfer capacitance. The overall input capacitance is given by:

$$C_i = C_{iss} + (1 - A_V)C_{rss} \tag{3.11}$$

   where A_V is the voltage gain.
9. **Reverse Transfer Capacitance (C_{rss}):** It is the reverse transfer capacitance for the common source configuration. It is of the order of few picofarads in JFETs but only a small fraction of a picofarad in some MOSFETs.
10. **Output Capacitance (C_{oss}):** It is the drain-source capacitance for the common source configuration. This too is typically few picofarads for both JFETs and MOSFET devices.
11. **Threshold Voltage ($V_{GS(th)}$):** It is the gate-source threshold voltage where the MOSFET begins to conduct. It is specified for E-MOSFETs only.

12. **Drain-Source ON Voltage ($V_{DS(on)}$):** It is the drain-source voltage for a particular level of gate-source voltage and drain current when the MOSFET is in the ON state. It is specified for E-MOSFETs only.

13. **ON-State Drain Current ($I_{D(on)}$):** It is a typical value of drain current for a particular value of gate-source voltage when the MOSFET is in the ON state. It is specified for E-MOSFETs only. As mentioned earlier, the drain current in an E-MOSFET is given by:

$$I_D = k(V_{GS} - V_T)^2$$

Therefore, the values of V_T, $V_{GS(on)}$ and $I_{D(on)}$ help in determining the value of *k*. The value of *k* is given by:

$$k = \frac{I_{D(on)}}{(V_{GS(on)} - V_T)^2} \tag{3.12}$$

3.6 JFETS VERSUS MOSFETS

JFETs and MOSFETs are similar devices in the sense that both are unipolar, and both are voltage controlled devices. There are however some differences between the two devices in terms of their principle of operation and the values of their characteristic parameters. These are as follows:

1. JFETs are operated in depletion mode only. DE-MOSFETs can be operated in both depletion and enhancement modes and E-MOSFETs are operated only in enhancement mode.
2. The input resistance offered by MOSFETs is much higher than that by JFETs. Input resistance for JFETs is greater than $10^9\Omega$ whereas it is around $10^{13}\Omega$ in case of MOSFETs.
3. JFETs have higher drain resistance than MOSFETs and hence their characteristic curve is flatter than that of MOSFETs. Drain resistance for JFETs is in the range of 100 kΩ to 1 MΩ while in case of MOSFETs, it is in the range of 1 to 50 kΩ.
4. The leakage gate current in MOSFETs is much smaller than that in JFETs. The gate current for MOSFETs is in the range of 100 nA to 10 pA whereas the same for JFETs is in the range of 100 mA to 10 nA.
5. MOSFETs are easier to construct and are used more widely than JFETs.

3.7 FET AS A SWITCH

FETs are used as analog switches. Both JFETs and MOSFETs can be operated as a switch by operating them in two regions, namely the cut-off and the saturation regions. When the voltage $V_{GS} = 0$, the FET operates in the saturation region and the maximum current flows through it. Therefore, it is like a fully ON switch. Similarly, when the applied gate-source voltage V_{GS} is more negative than the pinch-off voltage, the FET operates in the cut-off region and does not allow any current to flow through the device. Hence, the FET is in the fully OFF condition.

3.7.1 JFET as a switch

Figure-3.28 shows one possible switching configuration using an *n*-channel JFET. When no gate voltage (V_{GG}) is applied, the FET operates in the saturation region and acts as a closed switch. When a negative gate voltage (V_{GG}) is applied, the FET operates in the cut-off region. Therefore, it offers a very high resistance and acts as an open switch. This circuit is referred to as the parallel switch circuit.

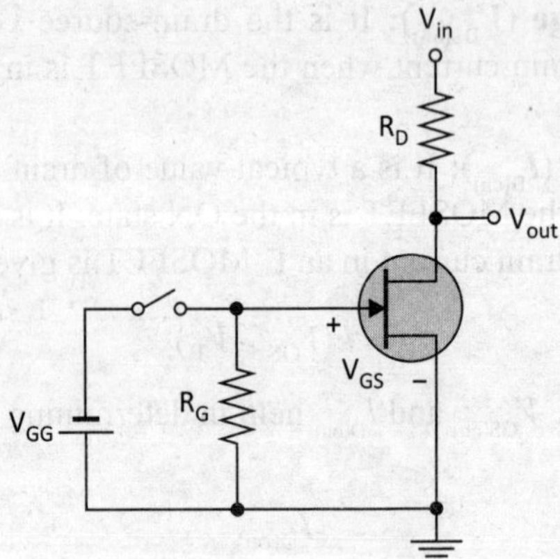

Fig. 3.28: JFET as a parallel switch

FET can also be used as a series switch. It acts as a closed switch if the control voltage is zero and as an open switch if the control voltage is negative. When the FET is ON, the input signal will appear at the output and when it is OFF, the output is zero. Figure-3.29 shows the series FET switch.

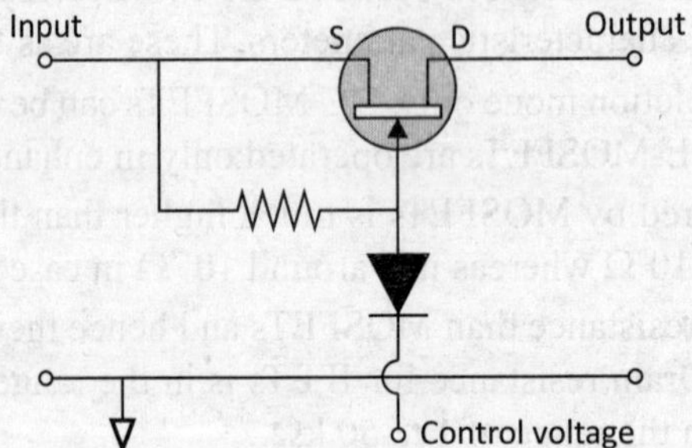

Fig. 3.29: JFET as a series switch

3.7.2 MOSFET as a switch

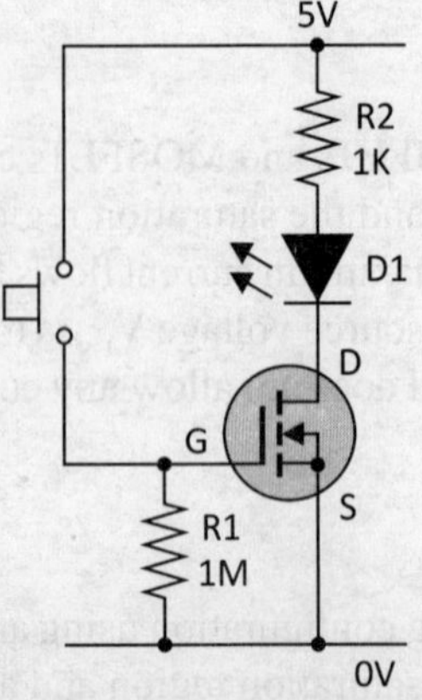

Fig. 3.30: MOSFET as a switch

MOSFET operates in the cut-off mode when V_{GS} is below the threshold level. There is no drain current flowing in this mode. Hence, it acts as an open switch. When the gate terminal of the MOSFET is connected to V_{DD}, the voltage applied at the gate terminal is maximum. This makes the channel resistance so small that the maximum drain current flows. In this mode, the MOSFET acts as a closed switch. Figure-3.30 shows the use of MOSFET as a switch. When the switch is pressed, 5V is applied at the gate terminal of the MOSFET and the MOSFET is turned ON. Otherwise the MOSFET remains in the cut-off condition.

3.8 FET AS AN AMPLIFIER

FET devices are commonly used as low-noise amplifiers and as buffer amplifiers. FETs are low-noise devices and hence they are used in the front-end of receivers and other electronic equipment and systems. JFETs in common-drain configuration (source follower) offer high input impedance and low output impedance and hence they are used as buffer amplifiers to isolate the preceding stage from the following stage. The biasing circuits commonly used for operating FETs as amplifiers are discussed in the following section.

3.9 BIASING CIRCUITS OF JFETS

DC biasing of an FET is done to produce the required gate-to-source voltage (V_{GS}) to get the desired value of drain current (I_D). There are large variations in the maximum and the minimum values of FET parameters even for a given type. The biasing circuits should maintain the drain current and the drain-source voltage within reasonable limits even for the maximum and minimum values of its parameters. It may be mentioned here that the phenomenon of thermal runaway does not occur in FETs. In this section, we discuss the common configurations used for biasing JFETs. The biasing configurations for DE-MOSFETs and E-MOSFETs are discussed in the next section. There are three biasing configurations used with JFETs, namely, the common source, common drain and common gate configurations. Each of these configurations is discussed in the subsequent paragraphs.

3.9.1 Common-Source configuration

Common-source configuration offers high input impedance, low output impedance, high voltage gain and the output voltage is 180° out-of-phase with the input voltage. The commonly used common-source biasing configurations include fixed-bias configuration, self-bias configuration and voltage-divider configurations.

3.9.1.1 Fixed-Bias Configuration

Fixed-bias configuration is the simplest of the three biasing configurations. Figure-3.31 (a) shows the fixed-bias circuit for *n*-channel JFET. The biasing components include drain resistor (R_D), gate resistor (R_G), input and output coupling capacitors (C_i and C_o), drain supply voltage (V_{DD}) and gate supply voltage (V_{GG}). The gate supply voltage ensures that the gate terminal is negative w.r.t. to the source. Resistor R_G is used so that the input AC signal develops across it. The DC equivalent of the circuit is shown in Figure-3.31 (b).

In a JFET, the gate current (I_G) is approximately equal to zero ($I_G \cong 0$). Therefore, the voltage drop across the resistor R_G, given by the product of the gate current and the value of resistor R_G, is approximately zero.

$$V_{RG} = I_G \times R_G \cong 0 \tag{3.13}$$

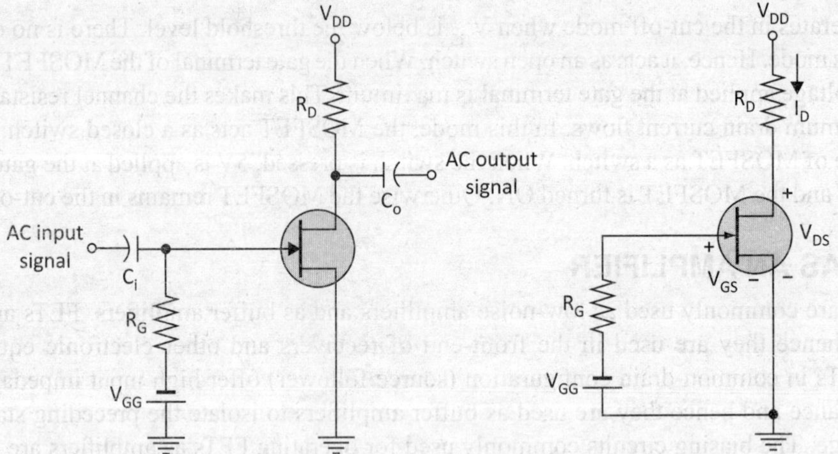

Fig. 3.31: (a) Fixed-bias circuit for *n*-channel JFET (b) DC equivalent of fixed-bias circuit

Applying Kirchhoff's voltage law to the input section we get,

$$-V_{GG} - V_{GS} = 0 \tag{3.14}$$

Therefore, the value of gate-source voltage is given by $V_{GS} = -V_{GG}$

The gate-source voltage (V_{GS}) is negative and equal in magnitude to the applied gate voltage (V_{GG}). As the voltage V_{GG} is fixed, V_{GS} is also fixed. Therefore, the configuration is named as fixed-bias configuration. This value of gate-source voltage is denoted as V_{GSQ}.

The drain current (I_D) in a JFET is given by Shockley's equation as eqn. 3.15.

$$I_D = I_{DSS}\left(1 - \frac{V_{GS}}{V_P}\right)^2 \tag{3.15}$$

Therefore, the value of quiescent drain current (I_{DQ}) is given by eqn. 3.16.

$$I_{DQ} = I_{DSS}\left(1 - \frac{V_{GSQ}}{V_P}\right)^2 \tag{3.16}$$

Since the value of gate-source voltage (V_{GS}) in a fixed-bias configuration is fixed, therefore the level of drain current (I_D) is also fixed.

Applying Kirchhoff's voltage law to the output section we get,

$$V_{DD} - I_D R_D - V_{DS} = 0 \tag{3.17}$$

$$V_{DSQ} = V_{DD} - I_{DQ} R_D \tag{3.18}$$

The operating point is defined as (I_{DQ}, V_{DSQ}). The operating point can also be obtained graphically, by superimposing the vertical line $V_{GS} = -V_{GG}$ on the transfer characteristics of the JFET (Figure-3.32).

The operating point can also be obtained by superimposing the load line on the output characteristic curves of the JFET. The load line is defined by eqn. (3.17).

Substituting $V_{DS} = 0$ in eqn. (3.17), we get $I_D = V_{DD}/R_D$
Substituting $I_D = 0$ in eqn. (3.17), we get $V_{DS} = V_{DD}$

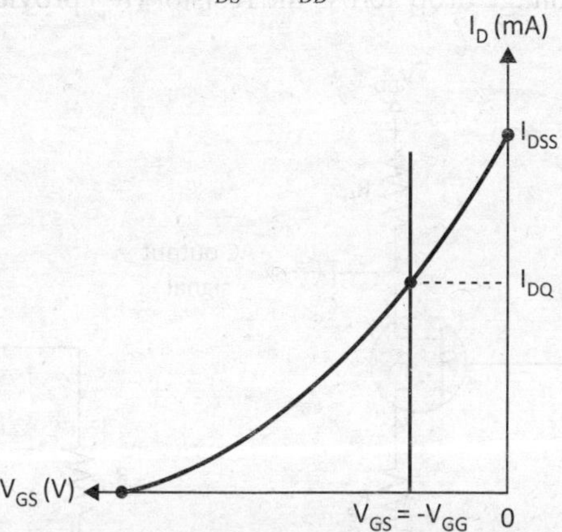

Fig. 3.32: Graphical analysis of the fixed-bias circuit

The line formed by joining the two points $(0, V_{DD})$ and $(V_{DD}/R_D, 0)$ is the DC load line. As we have studied in the chapter on BJT biasing, the operating point defines the DC conditions that exist when no input AC signal is applied. The bias point is selected so as to have the maximum possible drain-source voltage swing for the AC input signal. Figure-3.33 shows the load line analysis.

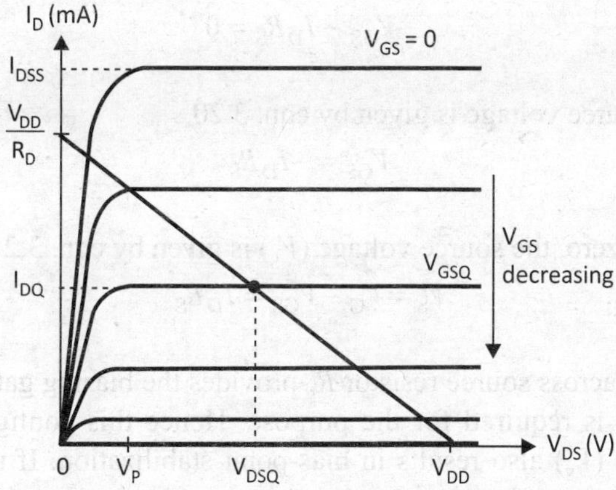

Fig. 3.33: Load line analysis for the fixed-bias circuit

The fixed-bias configuration is not used much as the wide differences in the minimum and maximum values of the JFET parameters make drain current levels unpredictable with simple fixed-bias circuits. Another disadvantage of the fixed-biasing circuit is that it needs an additional supply voltage for biasing the gate terminal. Self-bias and potential-divider biasing configurations require a single supply voltage and maintain the quiescent drain current and drain-source voltage within desirable limits.

3.9.1.2 Self-Bias Configuration

Self-bias configuration is the most commonly used biasing scheme for FETs. Self-bias configuration offers stabilization of the operating point against variations in FET parameters. Figure-3.34 (a) shows the self-bias circuit for an *n*-channel JFET. The difference between the fixed-bias and the self-bias configurations is the addition of source resistor (R_S) between the source and the ground terminals and the removal of the gate supply voltage. The voltage drop across the resistor (R_S) provides the controlling gate voltage.

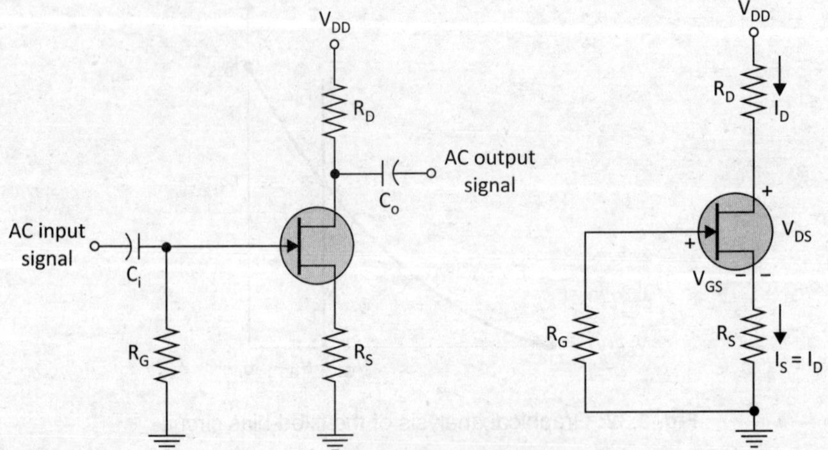

Fig. 3.34: (a) Self-bias configuration for *n*-channel JFET (b) DC equivalent of self-bias configuration

The analysis of the self-bias circuit can be done by drawing its DC equivalent circuit as shown in Figure-3.34 (b). As the gate current (I_G) is zero, there is no voltage drop across the resistor R_G. Therefore the gate voltage V_G is equal to zero. Applying Kirchhoff's voltage law to the input section we get,

$$-V_{GS} - I_D R_S = 0 \tag{3.19}$$

Therefore, the gate-source voltage is given by eqn. 3.20.

$$V_{GS} = -I_D R_S \tag{3.20}$$

As the gate voltage is zero, the source voltage (V_S) is given by eqn. 3.21.

$$V_S = V_G - V_{GS} = I_D R_S \tag{3.21}$$

The voltage drop (V_S) across source resistor R_S provides the biasing gate-source voltage and hence no external power supply is required for the purpose. Hence this configuration is named self-bias configuration. The voltage (V_S) also results in bias-point stabilization. If the transconductance of the JFET decreases, the drain current decreases resulting in decrease in the voltage across resistor R_S. Thus the voltage V_{GS} becomes less negative resulting in increase in drain current. This compensates for the initial decrease in the drain current. Now, drain current (I_D) in a JFT is given by:

$$I_D = I_{DSS}\left(1 - \frac{V_{GS}}{V_P}\right)^2$$

Substituting the value of V_{GS} in the expression for drain current (I_D) we get eqn. 3.22.

$$I_D = I_{DSS}\left(1 - \frac{-I_D R_S}{V_P}\right)^2 \tag{3.22}$$

Therefore, the drain current is given by eqn. 3.23.

$$I_D = I_{DSS}\left(1+\frac{I_D R_S}{V_P}\right)^2 \quad (3.23)$$

Applying Kirchhoff's voltage law to the output section we get eqn. 3.24.

$$V_{DD} - I_D R_D - V_{DS} - I_D R_S = 0 \quad (3.24)$$

Therefore, the drain-source voltage (V_{DS}) is given by eqn. 3.25.

$$V_{DS} = V_{DD} - I_D(R_D + R_S) \quad (3.25)$$

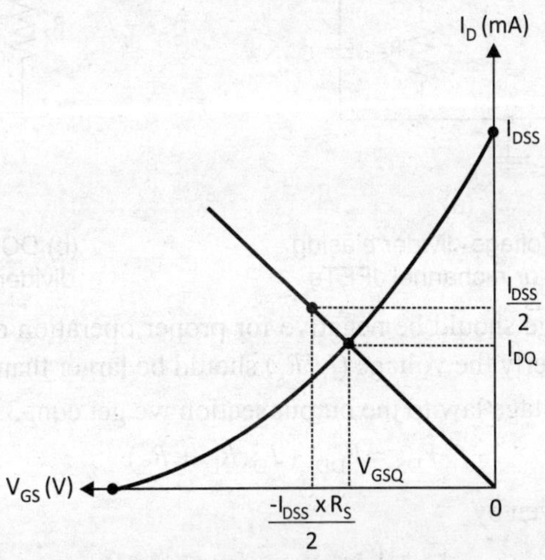

Fig. 3.35: Graphical analysis of self-bias configuration for *n*-channel JFETs

The graphical analysis can be done in a similar manner to that for fixed-bias configuration as shown in Figure-3.35. The operating point is determined by superimposing the straight line corresponding to the equation $V_{GS} = -I_D R_S$ on the transfer characteristic curve of the JFET. The load line analysis can also be done in the same manner as done for the fixed-bias circuit. The only difference is that the load line is now defined by eqn. (3.25).

3.9.1.3 Voltage-Divider Biasing

Voltage-divider biasing configuration used in the case of BJTs is also applicable to JFETs. The voltage-divider configuration offers improved bias stability. The voltage-divider biasing configuration for *n*-channel JFET is shown in Figure-3.36 (a). The resistors R_1 and R_2 form the potential divider. Voltage across resistor R_2 provides the necessary bias to the JFET. Figure-3.36 (b) shows the DC equivalent of the configuration.

As the gate current I_G@ 0, the gate voltage is given by eqn. 3.26.

$$V_G = \frac{R_2 \times V_{DD}}{R_1 + R_2} \quad (3.26)$$

The gate-source voltage (V_{GS}) is given by eqn. 3.27.

$$V_{GS} = V_G - V_S = V_G - I_D R_S \quad (3.27)$$

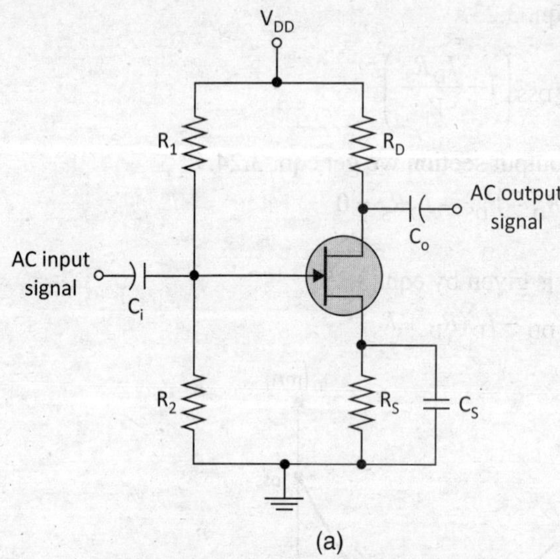

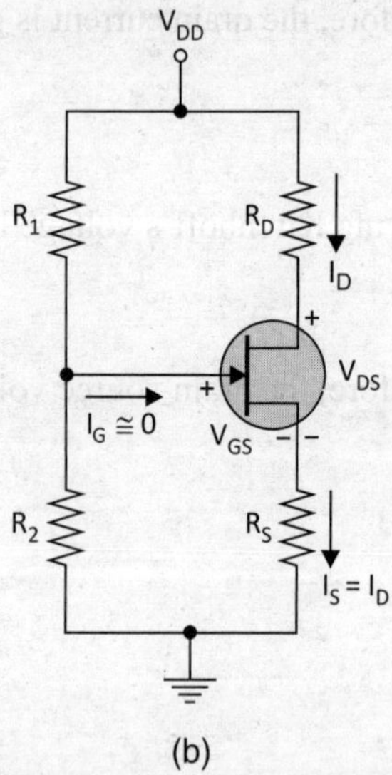

Fig. 3.36: (a) Voltage-divider biasing configuration or *n*-channel JFETs (b) DC equivalent of voltage-divider biasing configuration

As the gate-source voltage should be negative for proper operation of n-channel JFETs, therefore for the circuit to operate properly the voltage ($I_D{'}R_S$) should be larger than voltage V_G.

Applying Kirchhoff's voltage law to the output section we get eqn. 3.28.

$$V_{DS} = V_{DD} - I_D(R_D + R_S) \tag{3.28}$$

The operating point is given by:

$$I_{DQ} = \frac{V_G - V_{GS}}{R_S}, \; V_{DSQ} = V_{DD} - I_{DQ}(R_D + R_S)$$

Figure-3.37 shows the graphical method to determine the operating point. The figure is self-explanatory. Load line analysis can also be done to establish the operating point as explained in the case of fixed-bias circuit.

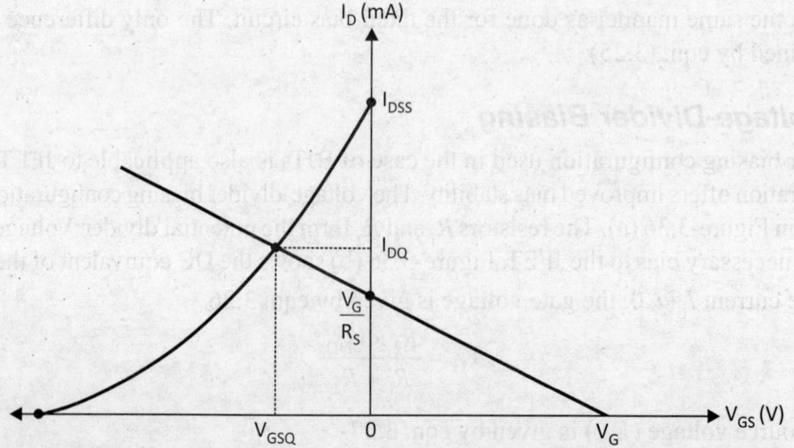

Fig. 3.37: Graphical analysis of voltage-divider bias configuration

Example-3.4: Refer to the self-bias circuit of Figure 3.38. Determine the value of drain current (I_D) and gate-source voltage (V_{GS}).

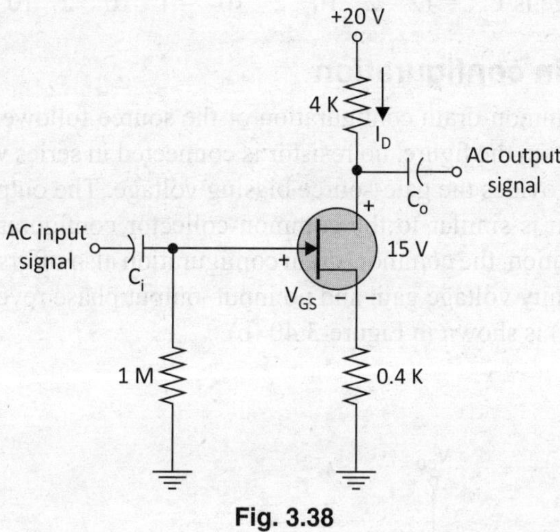

Fig. 3.38

Solution: The value of drain current is given by:

$$I_D = \frac{V_{DD} - V_{DS}}{R_D + R_S}$$

Therefore, $I_D = (20 - 15)/ (4 \times 10^3 + 0.4 \times 10^3) = 5/4.4 \times 10^3 = 1.14$ mA

The gate-source voltage is given by $V_{GS} = -I_D \times R_S = -1.14 \times 10^{-3}{'}\ 0.4 \times 10^3 = 0.456$ V

Example-3.5: For the circuit in Figure-3.39, determine the value of drain-source voltage (V_{DS}). (Given that the gate-source voltage is –0.8 V).

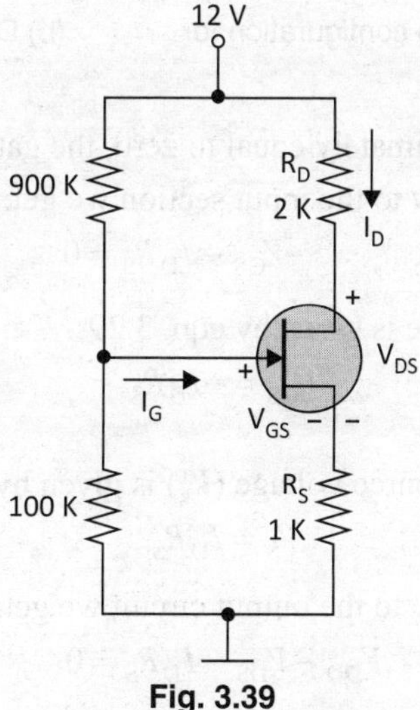

Fig. 3.39

Solution: The gate voltage is given by $V_G = 12\ '\ 100\ '\ 10^3/ (100\ '\ 10^3 +\ '\ 900\ '\ 10^3\ ) = 1.2$ V

The gate-source voltage is equal to $V_{GS} = V_G - V_S$

Therefore, –0.8 = 1.2 – V_S or V_S = 2.0 V
The drain current is equal to $I_D = V_S/R_S$ = 2/(1 ´ 10³) = 2 mA
The drain-source voltage is V_{DS} = 12 – 2 ´ 10³´ 2 ´ 10⁻³ – 1 ´ 10³ ´ 2 ´ 10⁻³ = 12 – 4 – 2 = 6 V

3.9.2 Common-Drain configuration

The basic circuit for the common-drain configuration or the source follower configuration is shown in Figure-3.40. As is evident from the figure, no resistor is connected in series with the drain terminal. The voltage across resistor R_S provides the gate-source biasing voltage. The output is taken from the source terminal. This configuration is similar to the common-collector configuration for the BJTs. Like the common-collector configuration, the common-drain configuration also offers high input impedance, low output impedance, nearly unity voltage gain and no input–output phase reversal. The DC equivalent of the circuit in Figure-3.40 (a) is shown in Figure-3.40 (b).

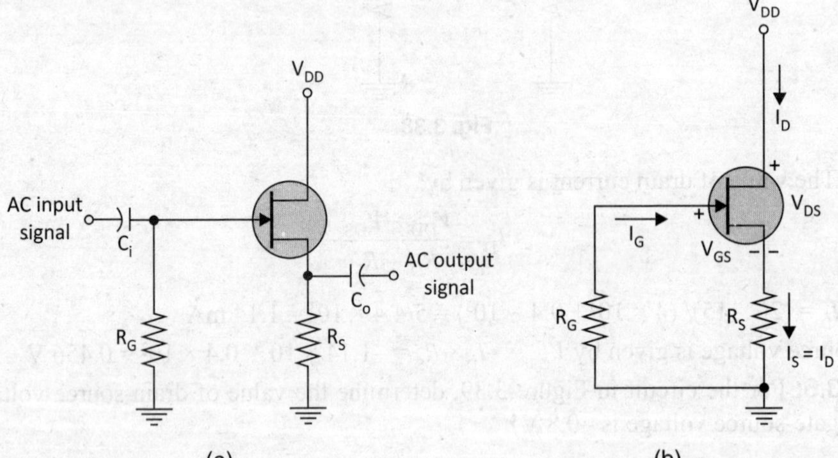

Fig. 3.40: (a) Common-drain configuration for *n*-channel (b) DC equivalent of the common-drain JFET configuration

As the gate current (I_G) is approximately equal to zero, the gate voltage V_G is also equal to zero. Applying Kirchhoff's voltage law to the input section we get:

$$-V_{GS} - I_D R_S = 0$$

Therefore, the gate-source voltage is given by eqn. 3.29.

$$V_{GS} = -I_D R_S \tag{3.29}$$

As the gate voltage is zero, the source voltage (V_S) is given by eqn. 3.30.

$$V_S = I_D R_S \tag{3.30}$$

Applying Kirchhoff's voltage law to the output circuit we get:

$$V_{DD} - V_{DS} - I_D R_S = 0$$

Therefore, the drain-source voltage is given by eqn. 3.31.

$$V_{DS} = V_{DD} - I_D R_S \tag{3.31}$$

Another possible common-drain configuration is shown in Figure 3.41(a). This configuration is based on the boot-strapped bias configuration and provides increased input resistance. Figure 3.41(b) shows the voltage-divider common-drain amplifier. The gate-bias voltage V_G is derived from V_{DD} by means of potential divider formed by resistors R_1 and R_2. In this case also, no resistor is connected in series with the drain terminal. The analysis for both the circuits can be done on similar lines as outlined earlier.

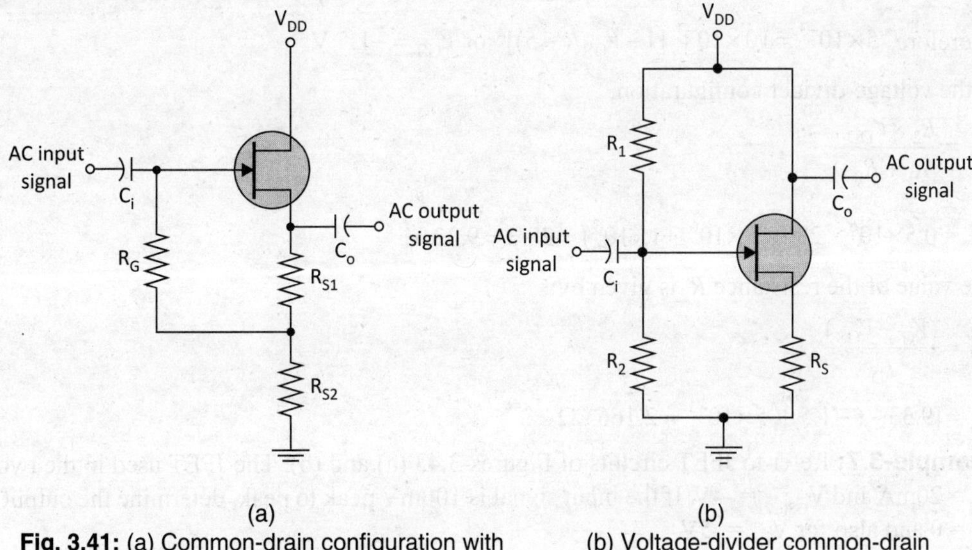

Fig. 3.41: (a) Common-drain configuration with boot-strapping for *n*-channel JFET (b) Voltage-divider common-drain configuration for *n*-channel JFET

3.9.3 Common Gate configuration

Figure-3.42 shows the common-gate configuration for an *n*-channel JFET. The input is applied between the source and the gate terminals and the output is taken between the drain and the gate terminals.

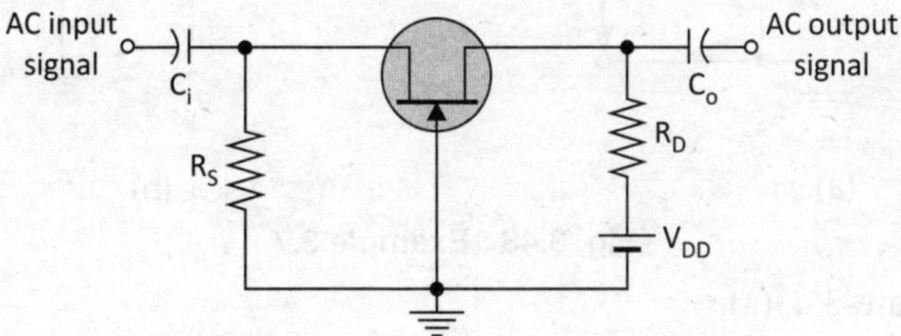

Fig. 3.42: Common-gate configuration

Common-gate configuration offers low input impedance, high output impedance, high voltage gain and the output voltage is in phase with the input voltage. The analysis for the circuit can be done on similar lines as that outlined earlier. The values of the gate-source and drain-source voltages are given by eqns. (3.32) and (3.33), respectively.

$$V_{GS} = -I_D R_S \tag{3.32}$$

$$V_{DS} = V_{DD} - I_D(R_S + R_D) \tag{3.33}$$

Example-3.6: In an n-channel JFET-based voltage-divider common-drain configuration, determine the value of resistor (R_S) so as to have the operating point as $I_{DQ} = 5$ mA, $V_{DSQ} = 10$ V.

Given that V_{DD} = 28 V, R_1 = 1 MW, R_2 = 0.5 MW, saturation drain current of the JFET = 10 mA and gate-source pinch-off voltage = –5 V

Solution: In a JFET, $I_D = I_{DSS}\left(1-\frac{V_{GS}}{V_P}\right)^2$

Therefore, $5\times10^{-3} = 10\times10^{-3}\ [1-V_{GS}/(-5)]^2$ or $V_{GS} = -1.5$ V

In the voltage-divider configuration,

$$V_G = \frac{R_2 \times V_{DD}}{R_1 + R_2}$$

$$V_G = 0.5\times10^6 \times 28/(0.5\times10^6 + 1\times10^6) = 28/3 = 9.33 \text{ V}$$

The value of the resistance R_s is given by:

$$R_S = \frac{(V_G - V_{GS})}{I_D}$$

$$R_S = [9.33-(-1.5)]/\ 5\times10^{-3} = 2.166 \text{ k}\Omega$$

Example-3.7: Refer to JFET circuits of Figures-3.43 (a) and (b). The JFET used in the two cases has I_{DSS} = 20mA and $V_{GS(off)}$ = -4V. If the input signal is 100mV peak to peak, determine the output signal for V_{GS} = 0 and also for V_{GS} = -5V.

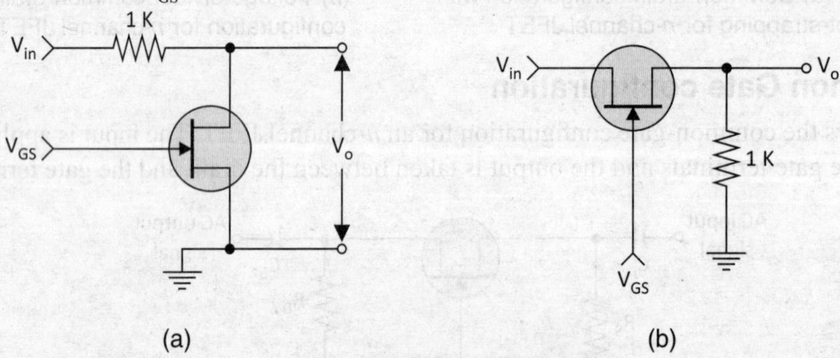

Fig. 3.43 : Example 3.7

Solution: For Figure-3.43(a),

Drain current for V_{GS} = 0 is I_{DSS}. The value of I_{DSS} = 20mA.

$V_{GS(off)} = -4V = -V_P$

Where, V_P is the pinch-off voltage

Therefore, V_P = 4V

$$R_{DS} = \frac{4}{20\times10^{-3}} = 200\Omega$$

For $V_{GS} = 0$, $v_o = \frac{v_{in}\times 200}{200+1000} = \frac{v_{in}}{6}$

Therefore, for V_{GS} = 0, v_o = 100/6 mV p-t-p = 16.67mV p-t-p

For V_{GS} = -5V, JFET is in cut-off.

Therefore, $v_o = v_{in}$ = 100mV p-t-p

For Figure-3.43 (b)

For V_{GS} = 0, $v_o = v_{in}$ = 100mV p-t-p

For V_{GS} = -5V, v_o = 0 as JFET is in cut-off

Example-3.8: Figure-3.44 shows the transfer characteristics of a junction FET. Determine the drain current for V_{GS} = -3V. Also determine the maximum value of transconductance.

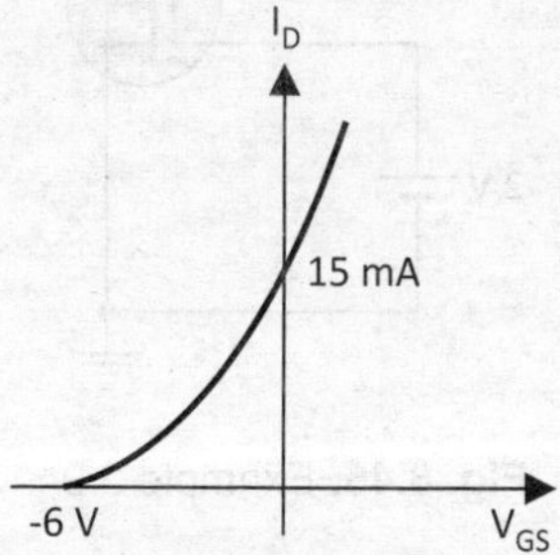

Fig. 3.44: Example 3.8

From the characteristics, I_{DSS} = 15mA and $V_{GS(off)}$ = -6V.

The transfer characteristics of Figure-3.44 can be expressed by:

$$I_D = I_{DSS}\left[1 - \frac{V_{GS}}{V_{GS(off)}}\right]^2$$

Therefore,

$$I_D = 15\times10^{-3}\left[1 + \frac{V_{GS}}{6}\right]^2$$

For V_{GS} = -3V, $I_D = 15 \times 10^{-3} (1 - 0.5)^2 = 15 \times 10^{-3} \times 0.25$ = 3.75mA

Maximum value of transconductance $g_{mo} = -\frac{2I_{DSS}}{V_{GS(off)}} = \frac{I_{DSS}}{3}$ = 5milli-mhos

3.10 BIASING CIRCUITS OF MOSFETS

In this section we will discuss the commonly used biasing configurations for the DE-MOSFETs and the E-MOSFETs.

3.10.1 Depletion MOSFETs

The biasing schemes for DE-MOSFETs are the same as that for JFETs because of the similarities in their characteristics. The only difference being that DE-MOSFETs also operate in enhancement mode, that is, with positive values of gate-source voltage (V_{GS}) in addition to the depletion mode. The operation of the DE-MOSFET in the enhancement mode is explained with the help of example-3.9.

Example-3.9: Figure-3.45 shows a biasing configuration using DE-MOSFET. Given that the saturation drain current is 8 mA and the pinch-off voltage is –2 V, determine the value of gate-source voltage, drain current and the drain-source voltage.

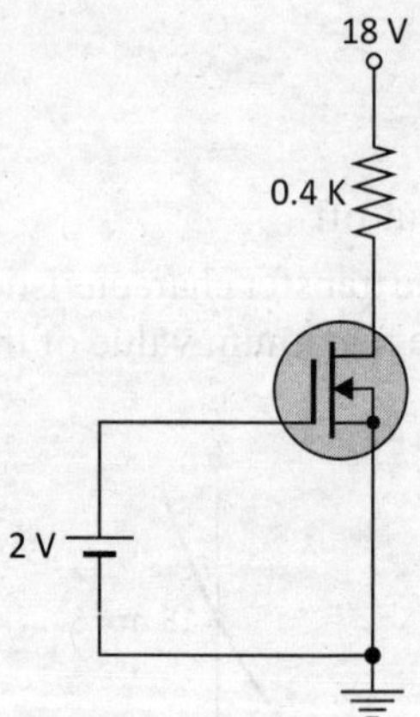

Fig. 3.45: Example 3.9

Solution: The gate-source voltage (V_{GS}) is equal to 2 V.

The polarity of the voltage applied between the gate and the source terminals is such that the MOSFET operates in the enhancement region of its output characteristics.

In a DE-MOSFET, $I_D = I_{DSS}\left(1 - \dfrac{V_{GS}}{V_P}\right)^2$

Now I_{DSS} = 8 mA, V_{GS} = 2 V, V_P = –2 V. Substituting in the above equation we get

$I_D = 8 \times 10^{-3} \times [1 - 2/(-2)]^2 = 32 \times 10^{-3}$ A = 32 mA

Applying Kirchhoff's voltage law to the output section we get $18 - 0.4 \times 10^3 \times 32 \times 10^{-3} - V_{DS} = 0$

Therefore, $V_{DS} = 18 - 6.4 = 18 - 12.8 = 5.2$ V

Example-3.10: Design a voltage-divider bias network using a DE-MOSFET with supply voltage V_{DD} = 16 V, I_{DSS} = 10 mA and V_P = –5V to have a quiescent drain current of 5 mA and gate voltage of 4V. (Assume the drain resistor R_D to be four times the source resistor R_S)

Solution: As the quiescent drain current is less than saturation drain current, the MOSFET is operated in the depletion mode.

The drain current (I_D) is given by $I_D = I_{DSS}\left(1 - \dfrac{V_{GS}}{V_P}\right)^2$

Therefore, $5\times10^{-3} = 10\times10^{-3}\times[1-\{V_{GS}/(-5)\}]^2$ or $V_{GS} = -1.5$ V

The gate-source voltage (V_{GS}) is given by $V_{GS} = V_G - V_S = V_G - I_D R_S$

Therefore, $I_D \times R_S = 4 + 1.5 = 5.5$ V

Substituting the value of I_D in the above equation, we get $R_S = 5.5/5 \times 10^{-3} = 1.1$ kΩ

$R_D = 4 \times R_S = 4 \times 1.1 \times 10^3 = 4.4$ kΩ

The gate voltage is $V_G = [R_2/(R_1 + R_2)] \times 16$

Let us assume R_2 = 1kΩ

Therefore, $4 = 16 \times 1 \times 10^3 / (R_1 + 1 \times 10^3)$

$(R_1 + 1 \times 10^3) = 4 \times 10^3$ or $R_1 = 3 \times 10^3 = 3\text{k}\Omega$

Figure-3.46 shows the circuit configuration.

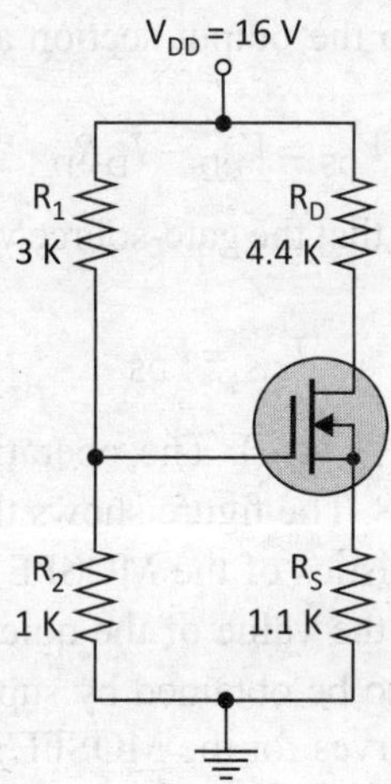

Fig. 3.46: Solution to Example-3.10

3.10.2 Enhancement MOSFETs

Two most popular biasing configurations for E-MOSFETs are the feedback biasing configuration and the voltage-divider configuration. These two biasing configurations are described in this section.

3.10.2.1 Feedback Biasing Configuration

Figure-3.47(a) shows the circuit for the feedback biasing configuration. The feedback connection to the gate terminal is taken from the drain terminal through resistor R_G. The resistor R_G brings bias voltage to the gate terminal to turn the MOSFET ON. Figure-3.47 (b) shows the DC equivalent circuit. Since the gate current (I_G) is approximately equal to zero, therefore the voltage drop across resistor R_G is also approximately equal to zero. Applying Kirchhoff's voltage law to the input section we get eqn. 3.34.

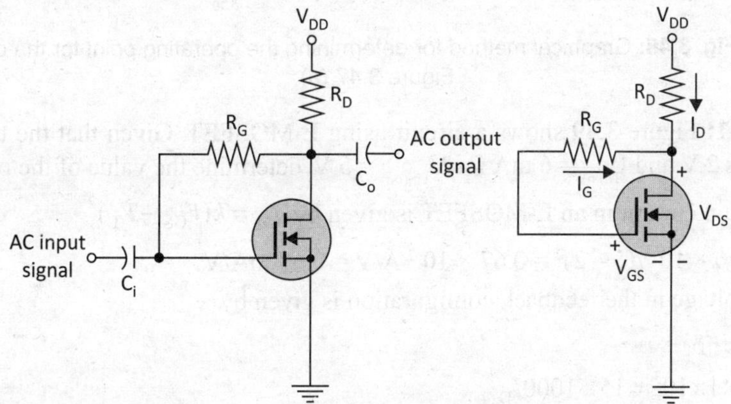

Figure 3.47: Feedback biasing configuration for E-MOSFET

$$V_{DD} - I_D R_D - V_{GS} = 0 \tag{3.34}$$

Therefore, gate-source voltage (V_{GS}) is given by eqn. 3.35.

$$V_{GS} = V_{DD} - I_D R_D \tag{3.35}$$

Applying Kirchhoff's voltage law to the output section and solving for the drain-source voltage (V_{DS}) we get eqn. 3.36.

$$V_{DS} = V_{DD} - I_D R_D \tag{3.36}$$

It is clear from eqns. (3.35) and (3.36) that the gate-source voltage (V_{GS}) and the drain-source voltage (V_{DS}) are equal, that is,

$$V_{GS} = V_{DS} \tag{3.37}$$

The operating point is given by (I_{DSQ}, V_{DSQ}). The operating point can also be established using graphical method as shown in Figure-3.48. The figure shows that the straight line given by eqn. (3.37) is superimposed on the transfer characteristics of the MOSFET. The point of intersection between the straight line and the transfer curve gives the value of the quiescent gate-source voltage and quiescent drain current. The operating point can also be obtained by superimposing the DC load line defined by eqn. (3.37) on the output characteristic curves for the MOSFET.

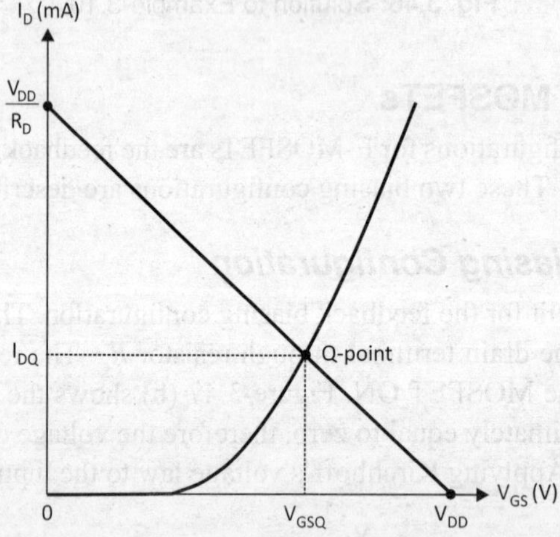

Fig. 3.48: Graphical method for determining the operating point for the circuit in Figure 3.47 (a)

Example-3.11: Figure-3.49 shows a circuit using E-MOSFET. Given that the threshold voltage for the MOSFET is 2 V and $I_{D(on)}$ = 6 mA for $V_{GS(on)}$ = 5 V, determine the value of the operating point.

Solution: Drain current in an E-MOSFET is given by $I_D = k(V_{GS} - V_T)^2$

Therefore, $k = 6 \times 10^{-3}/(5 - 2)^2 = 0.67 \times 10^{-3}$ A/V = 0.67 mA/V

Gate-source voltage in the feedback configuration is given by

$V_{GS} = V_{DD} - I_D R_D$

$V_{GS} = 15 - I_D \times 1 \times 10^3 = 15 - 1000 I_D$

Substituting this value of I_D in the expression $I_D = k(V_{GS} - V_T)^2$ we get

$I_D = 0.67 \times 10^{-3} (15 - 1000I_D - 2)^2$

$I_D = 0.67 \times 10^{-3} (13 - 1000I_D)^2$

Solving for I_D we get $I_D = 9.3 ' 10^{-3}$ A = 9.3 mA

The value of the drain-source voltage (V_{DS}) is given by:

$$V_{DS} = V_{DD} - I_D R_D$$

$$V_{DS} = 15 - 9.3 \times 10^{-3} \times 1 \times 10^3$$

$$= 15 - 9.3 = 5.7 \text{ V}$$

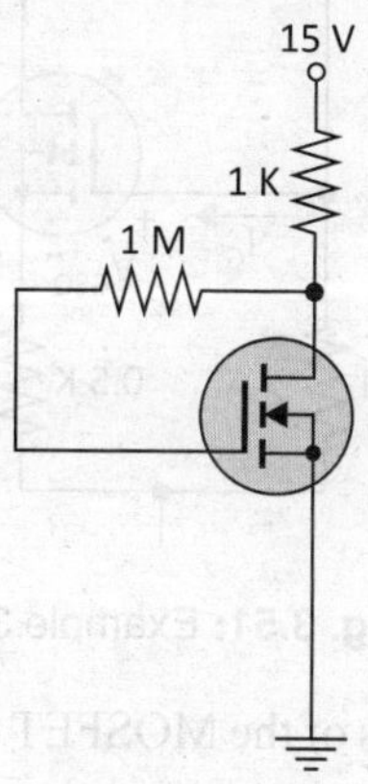

Fig. 3.49 : Example 3.11

3.10.2.2 Voltage-Divider Biasing Configuration

Voltage-divider biasing configuration is another popular biasing arrangement with E-MOSFETs. Figure-3.50(a) shows the biasing configuration. The arrangement is the same as that for BJTs and JFETs. The DC equivalent circuit is shown in Figure-3.50 (b). The analysis can be done in a manner similar to that done in the case of JFETs.

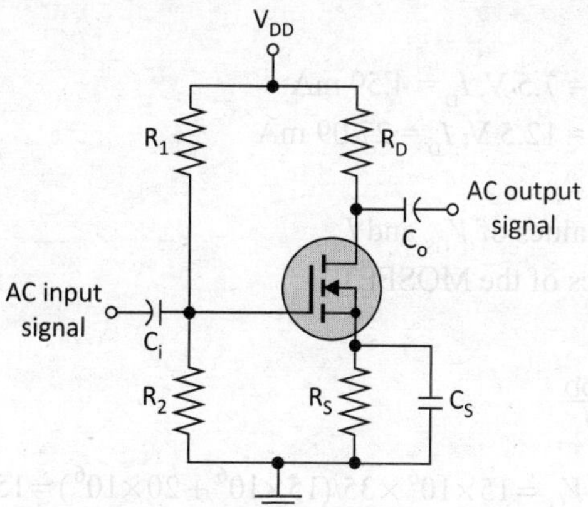

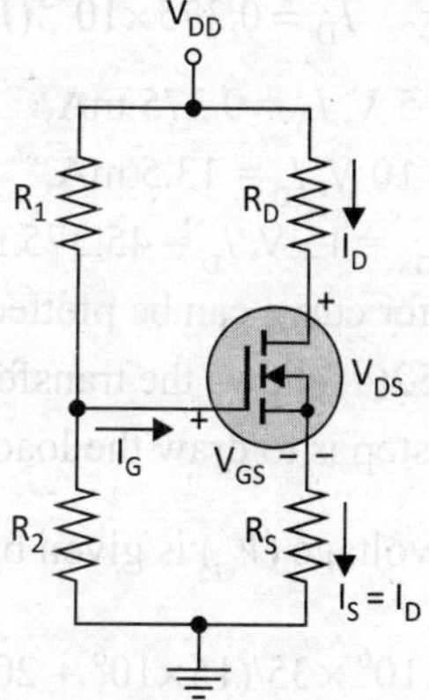

Fig. 3.50: (a) Voltage-divider biasing configuration for E-MOSFET (b) DC equivalent of the voltage-divider biasing configuration

Example-3.12: Figure-3.51 shows a voltage-divider configuration for the E-MOSFET. Given that the threshold voltage for the MOSFET is 4 V and the value of $I_{D(on)}$ = 6 mA for $V_{GS(on)}$ = 8 V, use graphical method to determine the value of the quiescent value of drain current, gate-source voltage and drain-source voltage.

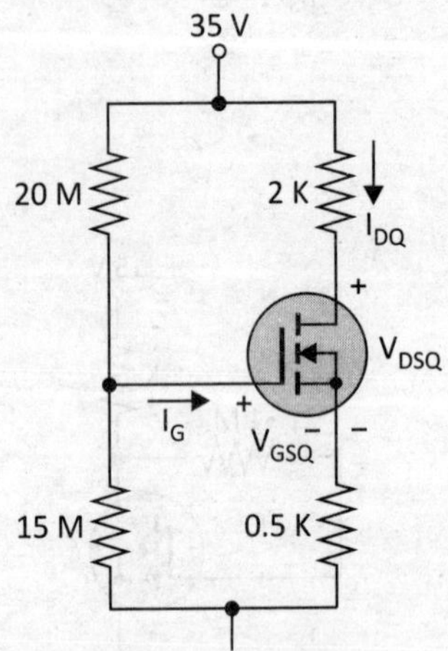

Fig. 3.51: Example 3.12

Solution: The transfer characteristics of the MOSFET can be plotted by finding the value of k using

$$k = \frac{I_{D(on)}}{(V_{GS(on)} - V_{GS(th)})^2}$$

Given that

$$I_{D(on)} = 6 \text{ mA}, V_{GS(on)} = 8 \text{ V and } V_{GS(th)} = 4\text{V}$$

Therefore,

$$k = 6 \times 10^{-3}/(8-4)^2 = 0.375 \times 10^{-3} \text{ A/V}^2$$

Therefore, the value of drain current is given by

$$I_D = 0.375 \times 10^{-3}(V_{GS} - V_{GS(th)})^2$$

For V_{GS} = 5 V, I_D = 0.375 mA, For V_{GS} = 7.5 V, I_D = 4.59 mA

For V_{GS} = 10 V, I_D = 13.5 mA, For V_{GS} = 12.5 V, I_D = 27.09 mA

and for V_{GS} = 15 V, I_D = 45.375 mA

The transfer curve can be plotted using these values of V_{GS} and I_D.

Figure 3.52(a) shows the transfer characteristics of the MOSFET.

The next step is to draw the load line.

The gate voltage (V_G) is given by $V_G = \dfrac{R_2 \times V_{DD}}{R_1 + R_2}$

$V_G = 15 \times 10^6 \times 35/(15 \times 10^6 + 20 \times 10^6) = 15$ V $V_G = 15 \times 10^6 \times 35/(15 \times 10^6 + 20 \times 10^6) = 15$ V

The gate-source voltage (V_{GS}) is given by:

$V_{GS} = V_G - V_S = V_G - I_D R_S$, For I_D = 0, V_{GS} = 15 V

For V_{GS} = 0, I_D = 15/0.5 × 10^3 = 30 mA

The next step is to draw the load line with coordinates (15 V, 0) and (0, 30 mA) on the transfer characteristics [Figure 3.52(b)].

From Figure 3.52 (b), the quiescent values of gate-source voltage and drain current are 9.4 V and 11 mA respectively.

The value of the drain-source voltage is given by:

$$V_{DS} = V_{DD} - I_D(R_D + R_S)$$

$$V_{DS} = 35 - 11 \times 10^{-3} (2 \times 10^3 + 0.5 \times 10^3) = 35 - 11 \times 2.5 = 7.5 \text{ V}$$

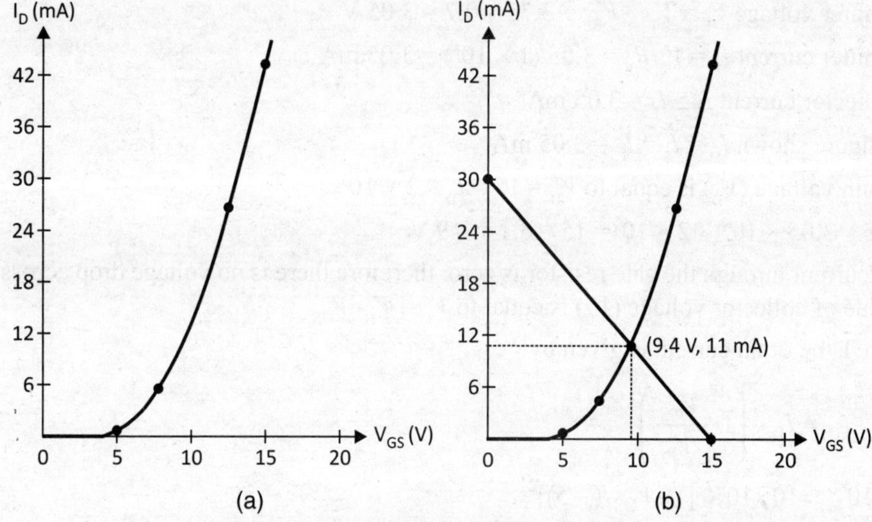

Fig. 3.52: Solution to Example-3.12

Example-3.13: Determine the values of voltages V_D and V_C for the circuit shown in Figure 3.53, given that the transistor b is 100, $V_{BE} = 0.7V$, saturation drain current of JFET is 10 mA and the pinch-off voltage is –5 V.

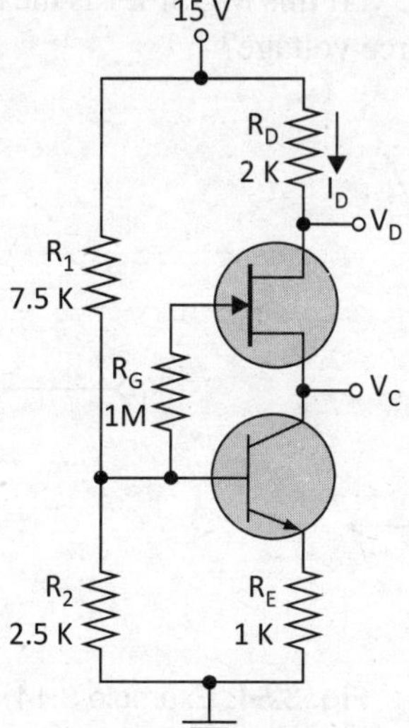

Fig. 3.53 : Example 3.13

Solution: The figure shows the voltage-divider transistor configuration with an additional JFET connected between the base and the collector terminals.

Value of $b \times R_E = 100 \times 1 \times 10^3 = 10^5$

Value of $10 \times R_2 = 10 \times 2.5 \times 10^3 = 2.5 \times 10^4$

As the value of $(b \times R_E)$ is much large than $(10 \times R_2)$, approximate analysis can be done to analyze the voltage-divider transistor configuration.

The base voltage $V_B = 15 \times 2.5 \times 10^3/(2.5 \times 10^3 + 7.5 \times 10^3) = 3.75$ V

The emitter voltage $V_E = V_B - V_{BE} = 3.75 - 0.7 = 3.05$ V

The emitter current $I_E = V_E/R_E = 3.05/(1 \times 10^3) = 3.05$ mA

The collector current $I_C \cong I_E = 3.05$ mA

In the figure shown $I_D = I_S = I_C = 3.05$ mA

The drain voltage (V_D) is equal to $V_D = 15 - I_D \times 2 \times 10^3$

$V_D = 15 - 3.05 \times 10^{-3} \times 2 \times 10^3 = 15 - 6.1 = 8.9$ V

As the current through the gate resistor is zero, therefore there is no voltage drop across the resistor R_G. The value of collector voltage (V_C) is equal to $V_C = V_B - V_{GS}$

In a JFET the drain current is given by:

$$I_D = I_{DSS}\left(1 - \frac{V_{GS}}{V_P}\right)^2$$

$$3.05 \times 10^{-3} = 10 \times 10^{-3}\ [1 - V_{GS}/(-5)]^2$$

$$V_{GS} = -2.24 \text{ V}$$

Therefore, $V_C = 3.75 - (-2.24) = -5.99$ V

Example-3.14: Figure-3.54(a) shows the transfer characteristics of an enhancement mode MOSFET. Determine the drain current for $V_{GS} = 5$V. If this MOSFET is the type chose for the circuit of Figure-3.54 (b), then what would be the drain-source voltage?

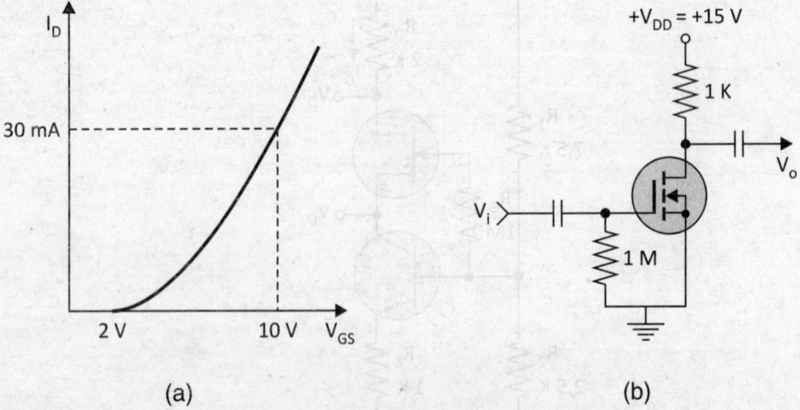

Fig. 3.54: Example 3.14

Solution: The transfer characteristics of an enhancement MOSFET are expressed by:

$I_D = KI_{D(on)}$

Where,

$$K = \left[\frac{V_{GS} - V_{GS(th)}}{V_{GS(on)} - V_{GS(th)}}\right]^2$$

Here, $V_{GS(th)} = 2V$, $V_{GS(on)} = 10V$, $I_{D(on)} = 30mA$

$$\text{Therefore, } K = \left[\frac{V_{GS} - 2}{10 - 2}\right]^2 = \left[\frac{V_{GS} - 2}{8}\right]^2$$

For $V_{GS} = 5V$, $K = (3/8)^2 = 9/64$

Therefore, I_D (for $V_{GS} = 5V$) $= (9/64) \times 30 \times 10^{-3}$ A $= 4.22$mA

In the circuit shown in Figure-3.54 (b), $V_{GS} = 0$ which means that the MOSFET is in cut-off. Therefore, the drain source voltage for $V_{GS} = 0V$ is +15V.

3.11 FET APPLICATIONS

The major shortcoming of BJTs is their low input impedance which leads to loading of the input source. As FETs offer very high input impedance as compared to BJTs, they are ideal for many applications where BJTs can be used. FETs are widely used as input amplifiers in oscilloscopes, electronic voltmeters and other test and measurement instruments, as low-noise amplifiers in front end of TV and radio receivers. FETs in the common-drain configuration are used as buffer amplifiers. E-MOSFETs are very commonly used in the fabrication of integrated circuits. Another common application of FETs is in switching applications and as voltage variable resistors (VVRs) in operational amplifiers. Some of the common applications of FETs are discussed in this section.

3.11.1 Amplifiers

FET devices are commonly used as low-noise amplifiers and as buffer amplifiers. FET amplifiers are discussed in sections 3.8, 3.9 and 3.10.

3.11.2 Analog Switch

FETs are used as analog switches. The use of FETs as switches has been described in detail in section 3.7.

3.11.3 Multiplexers

Field effect transistors are used in multiplexer circuits where each device acts as a single-pole single-throw switch. Figure-3.55 shows an *n*-channel JFET-based multiplexer. The input signals are applied to the drain terminals of the JFETs while the corresponding control inputs are applied to the gate terminals of the corresponding JFETs. When the control input corresponding to one of the input channels is made zero, that input is transmitted to the output. The control inputs for the other channels are made more negative than the $V_{GS(off)}$ voltage. Hence, all the other input signals are blocked.

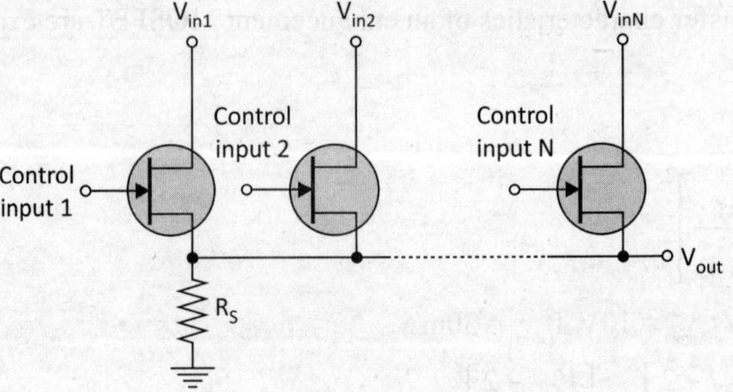

Fig. 3.55: FET as a multiplexer

3.11.4 Current Limiters

Field effect transistors can also be used in current-limiting applications as shown in Figure-3.56. During the normal operation of the circuit, the JFET operates in the ohmic region. When the load current increases substantially due to short circuit or any other reason, the JFET operates in the saturation region. Hence it acts as a constant current source and prevents excessive current through the load.

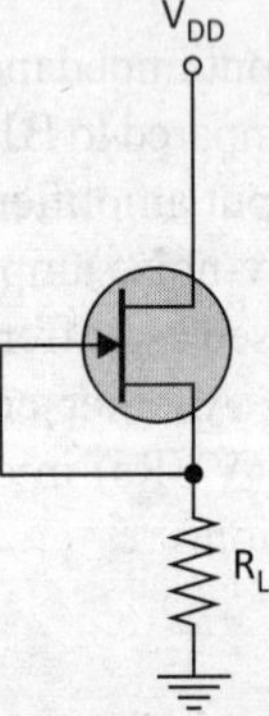

Fig. 3.56: FET for current limiting

3.11.5 Voltage Variable Resistor

FETs act as voltage variable resistors (VVR) when operated in the ohmic region (for small positive values of drain-to-source voltage V_{DS}) of their characteristics. In this region the drain resistance R_D can be controlled by the gate-to-source voltage (V_{GS}). For an *n*-channel JFET, the value of R_D increases with increase in the negative value of V_{GS} as shown in Figure-3.57. As we can see from the figure, the curve is symmetrical near the origin. That is, for small negative values of drain-source voltage, the curves are symmetrical to that of positive values of drain-source voltage. Thus, if an AC voltage (with small peak-to-peak voltage) is applied between the drain and the source terminals, then the FET acts as a linear resistor for a given gate-source voltage. FET-based VVRs are used in automatic gain control circuits.

3.11.6 Oscillators

FETs are also used in phase-shift oscillators (Figure-3.58) and pierce type of crystal-controlled oscillators (Figure-3.59). Oscillators are described in detail in chapter on sinusoidal oscillators.

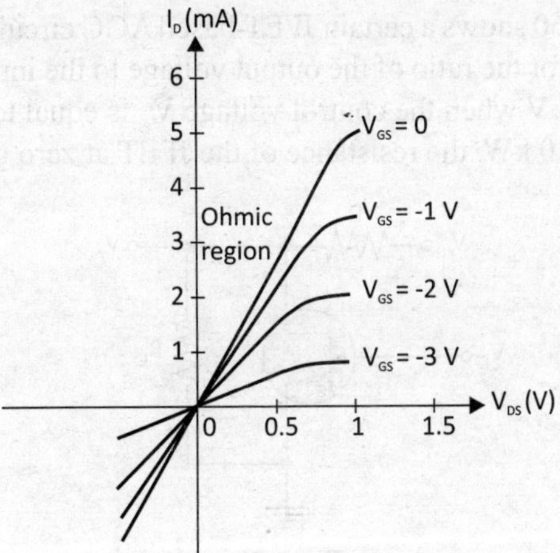

Fig. 3.57: Characteristics of an *n*-channel JFET in the ohmic region

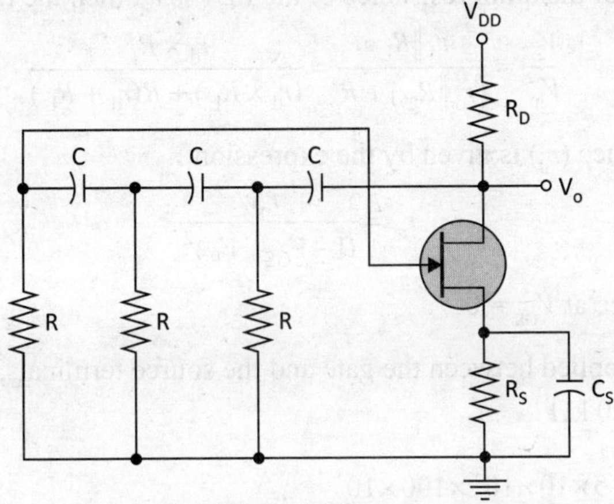

Fig. 3.58: FET-based phase-shift oscillator

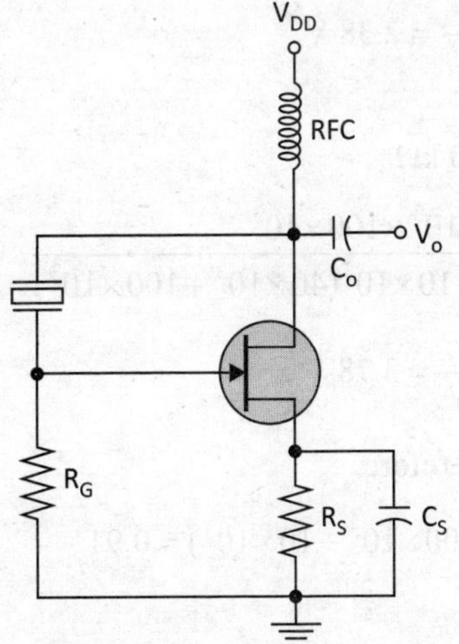

Fig. 3.59: FET-based pierce oscillator

Example-3.15: Figure-3.60 shows a certain JFET-based AGC circuit. The voltage V_C is the control voltage. Derive the expression for the ratio of the output voltage to the input voltage. Also find the value of the output voltage for V_{in} = 5 V when the control voltage V_C is equal to (a) 0 V (b) 0.5 V_P and (c) V_P. (Given that R_L = 100 kW, R = 10 kW, the resistance of the JFET at zero gate-source voltage is 10 kW.)

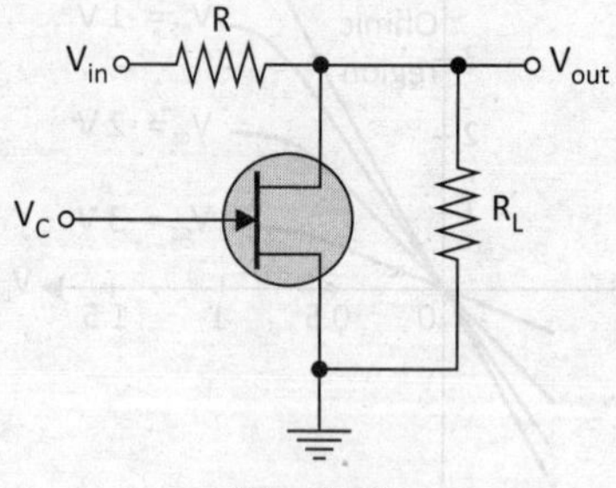

Fig. 3.60

Solution: If the value of the drain resistance of the FET is r_d, then the ratio V_o to V_{in} is given by:

$$\frac{V_o}{V_{in}} = \frac{r_d \| R_L}{(r_d \| R_L) + R} = \frac{r_d \times R_L}{(r_d \times R_L) + R(r_d + R_L)}$$

The value of the resistance (r_d) is given by the expression

$$r_d = \frac{r_o}{(1 - V_{GS}/V_P)^2}$$

where, r_o is the resistance at $V_{GS} = 0$.

The control voltage is applied between the gate and the source terminals, therefore $V_C = V_{GS}$

When $V_C = 0$, $r_d = r_o = 10$ kΩ

$$V_o = \frac{5 \times 10 \times 10^3 \times 100 \times 10^3}{(10 \times 10^3 \times 100 \times 10^3) + 10 \times 10^3 (10 \times 10^3 + 100 \times 10^3)}$$

$$= \frac{5 \times 1000 \times 10^6}{1000 \times 10^6 + 1100 \times 10^6} = 2.38 \text{ V}$$

When $V_C = 0.5\, V_P$, $r_d = 4 \times r_o = 40$ kΩ

$$V_o = \frac{5 \times 40 \times 10^3 \times 100 \times 10^3}{(40 \times 10^3 \times 100 \times 10^3) + 10 \times 10^3 (40 \times 10^3 + 100 \times 10^3)}$$

$$= \frac{5 \times 4000 \times 10^6}{4000 \times 10^6 + 1400 \times 10^6} = 3.78 \text{ V}$$

When $V_C = V_P$, r_d tends to ∞. Therefore,

$$\frac{V_o}{V_{in}} = \frac{R_L}{R_L + R} = 100 \times 10^3 / (100 \times 10^3 + 10 \times 10^3) = 0.91$$

$$V_o = 5 \times 0.91 = 4.55 \text{ V}$$

GLOSSARY

Amplification factor (m): It is defined as the ratio of the change in the drain-source voltage to the change in the gate-source voltage for a constant value of drain current.

Common Gate configuration: In this case, the input is applied between the source and the gate terminals and the output is taken between the drain and the gate terminals. Common-gate configuration offers low input impedance, high output impedance, high voltage gain and the output voltage is in phase with the input voltage.

Common-Drain configuration: In the common-drain configuration or the source follower configuration, the output is taken from the source terminal. This configuration is similar to the common-collector configuration for the BJTs. Like the common-collector configuration, the common-drain configuration also offers high input impedance, low output impedance, nearly unity voltage gain and no input–output phase reversal.

Common-Source configuration: In the common-source configuration, the source terminal is common to the input and the output sections. Common-source configuration offers high input impedance, low output impedance, high voltage gain and the output voltage is 180° out-of-phase with the input voltage. The commonly used common-source biasing configurations include fixed-bias configuration, self-bias configuration and voltage-divider configurations.

Depletion MOSFET (DE-MOSFET): In a DE-MOSFET, a channel is physically constructed between the drain and the source terminals. DE-MOSFETs are further classified as n-channel DE-MOSFETs and p-channel DE-MOSFETs depending on whether the channel material is an n-type semiconductor or a p-type semiconductor.

Dual-gate MOSFET: In a dual-gate MOSFET, an additional second insulated gate is provided as compared to a conventional MOSFET. The flow of current through the MOSFET is controlled by voltages at both the gate terminals. Since the control is exerted by two gates, the dual-gate MOSFET may be considered to be the counterpart of a tetrode.

Dynamic drain resistance (r_d): It is defined as the ratio of change in the drain-source voltage to the change in the drain current at a constant gate-source voltage.

Enhancement MOSFET (E-MOSFET): The construction of an E-MOSFET is similar to that of a DE-MOSFET with the difference that there is no physical channel between the source and drain terminals in the E-MOSFET.

Feedback Biasing Configuration: In this configuration, the feedback connection to the gate terminal is taken from the drain terminal through a resistor which brings bias voltage to the gate terminal to turn the MOSFET on.

Fixed-Bias Configuration: Fixed-bias configuration is the simplest of the biasing configurations. The biasing components include drain resistor (R_D), gate resistor (R_G), input and output coupling capacitors (C_i and C_o), drain supply voltage (V_{DD}) and gate supply voltage (V_{GG}). The gate supply voltage ensures that the gate terminal is negative w.r.t. to the source. Resistor R_G is used so that the input AC signal develops across it.

Forward Transconductance (g_{fs}): It is usually given for specified values of gate-source voltage (V_{GS}) and drain-source voltage (V_{DS}). It is typically few thousand micro-mhos to few milli-mhos for both JFETs and MOSFETs.

Gate Leakage current (I_{GSS}): It is the gate-to-source leakage current with the drain terminal shorted to the source terminal. It is given for a specific value of gate reverse bias voltage. Typical value of gate leakage current is few nanoamperes for JFETs and few pico-amperes for MOSFETs.

Input Capacitance (C_{iss}): It is the input capacitance of the FET when connected in common source configuration. It is typically of the order of few pF for both JFETand MOSFET devices. The overall input capacitance (C_i) in a common source amplifier configuration using an FET is larger than C_{iss} due to the presence of Miller component of the gate-drain inter-electrode capacitance (C_{gd} or C_{rss}). It is also referred to as the reverse transfer capacitance. The overall input capacitance is given by:

$$C_i = C_{iss} + (1 - A_V)C_{rss}$$

Junction FET (JFET): JFET is the simplest of the FETs. It is a unipolar, voltage controlled three-terminal device where the voltage applied at one terminal controls the current through the other two terminals. JFETs comprise a semiconductor channel embedded into semiconductor layers of opposite polarity.

Metal oxide field-effect transistors (MOSFETs): MOSFETs are another class of FETs. They are named so as the metal gate in a MOSFET is insulated from the semiconductor channel by a very thin oxide layer. MOSFETs are also referred to as insulated gate field-effect transistors (IGFETs). Like a JFET, a MOSFET is also a unipolar, voltage controlled three-terminal device where the drain current is controlled by the applied gate voltage.

Ohmic region: The region to the left of the locus of pinch-off voltages is the Ohmic region or the voltage-controlled resistance region. In the Ohmic region, JFET acts as a variable resistor whose resistance is controlled by the applied gate-source voltage.

Output Capacitance (C_{oss}): It is the drain-source capacitance for the common source configuration. This too is typically few pF for both JFETs and MOSFET devices.

Output Conductance (g_{os}): It is the reciprocal of the dynamic drain resistance (r_d). It is usually specified as an admittance parameter (y_{os}). y_{os} equals g_{os} at low frequencies. Admittance is in the range of few milli-mhos for both JFETs and MOSFETs.

Pinch-Off Voltage (V_P or $V_{GS(off)}$): It is the gate-source voltage for which the drain current reduces to zero. It is also specified for a given value of drain-source voltage. It is specified in case of JFETs and DE-MOSFETs only.

Power Dissipation (P_D): Power dissipation rating of the JFET is the product of the drain-source voltage (V_{DS}) and the drain current (I_D). The power dissipation rating must be derated with increase in temperature. It is usually specified at an ambient of 25 °C. JFETs are available in power ratings of hundreds of milliwatts while MOSFETs are available in a wide range of power ratings starting from a few milliwatts to more than hundred watts.

Reverse Gate-Source Breakdown Voltage (BV_{GS}): It is defined as the reverse gate-source voltage with either the drain open (BV_{GSO}) or drain shorted to the source (BV_{GSS}). It is typically few tens of volts.

Reverse Transfer Capacitance (C_{rss}): It is the reverse transfer capacitance for the common source configuration. It is of the order of few pF in JFETs but only a small fraction of a picofarad in some MOSFETs.

Saturation Drain Current (I_{DSS}): It is the maximum drain current when the gate terminal is shorted to the source terminal. It is usually specified at a given drain-source voltage somewhere in the channel pinch-off region.

Saturation region: Region to the right of the locus of the pinch-off voltages is the saturation region or the constant-current region.

Self-Bias Configuration: Self-bias configuration is the most commonly used biasing scheme for FETs. Self-bias configuration offers stabilization of the operating point against variations in FET parameters. Here a source resistor (R_S) is added between the source and the ground terminals and the gate supply voltage is removed. The voltage drop across the resistor (R_S) provides the controlling gate voltage.

Static drain resistance (R_D): It is defined as the ratio of the drain-source voltage (V_{DS}) to the drain current (I_D).

Threshold Voltage ($V_{GS(th)}$): It is the gate-source threshold voltage where the MOSFET begins to conduct. It is specified for E-MOSFETs only.

Transconductance (g_m): It is defined as the ratio of the change in the drain current to the change in the gate-source voltage for a constant drain-source voltage.

Voltage-divider biasing configuration: Voltage-divider biasing configuration used in the case of BJTs is also applicable to JFETs. The voltage-divider configuration offers improved bias stability.

REVIEW QUESTIONS

1. What is a Field Effect Transistor (FET) and how does it differ from a conventional transistor?
2. Write short notes on the following:
   (a) JFET as a voltage variable resistance
   (b) Handling MOSFETs
   (c) FETs as switches
   (d) Comparison between JFETs and MOSFETs
   (e) Comparison between enhancement MOSFET and depletion MOSFET
3. 'FET is a unipolar device'. Elaborate on the statement.Give one important reason why n-channel FETs are preferred over p-channel FETs?
4. Why do junction FETs have a very high input impedance?
5. What is an Insulated gate field effect transistor (IGFET)? How is it different from a MOSFET?
6. Explain the difference between the drain characteristics of depletion MOSFETs and enhancement MOSFETs?
7. Briefly describe different biasing circuits used for enhancement MOSFETs. Which of the biasing circuits used with MOSFETs offer the maximum stability?
8. Briefly describe application of JFET as:
   (a) Analog switch
   (b) Multiplexer
   (c) Current limiting device

PROBLEMS

1. An experimental set-up using a JFET gave the following readings:
   (i) With $V_{GS} = 0$ and $V_{DS} = 15V$, $I_D = 15mA$
   (ii) With $V_{GS} = 0$ and $V_{DS} = 10V$, $I_D = 14mA$
   (iii) With $V_{GS} = -1V$ and $V_{DS} = 15V$, $I_D = 13mA$
   Determine the values of
   (a) Drain resistance (b) Transconductance
   (c) Amplification factor (d) Type of FET
2. When the gate-to-source voltage (V_{GS}) of a MOSFET with threshold voltage of 400mV, working in saturation is 900mV the drain current is observed to be 1mA. Neglecting the channel width modulation effect and assuming that the MOSFET is operating at saturation, find the drain current for an applied V_{GS} of 1400mV?
3. Refer to the circuit shown in Figure-3.61. Given that the transistor â is 100, $V_{BE} = 0.7V$, saturation drain current of JFET is 10mA and the pinch-off voltage is -5V, determine the values of voltages V_D and V_E.

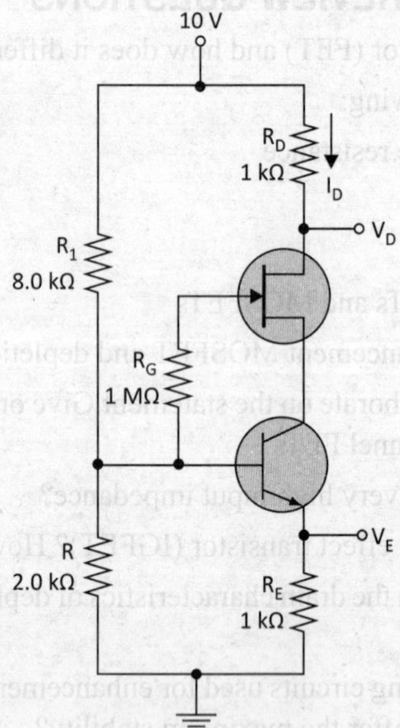

Fig. 3.61: Problem-3

4. Two identical NMOS transistors M_1 and M_2 are connected as shown in Figure-3.62. The circuit is used as an amplifier with the input connected between the G and S terminals and the output taken between D and S terminals. V_{bias} and V_D are so adjusted that both the transistors are in saturation. The transconductance of this combination is defined as $g_m = \dfrac{\partial i_D}{\partial v_{GS}}$ while the output resistance is $r_o = \dfrac{\partial v_{DS}}{\partial i_D}$, where i_D is the current flowing into the drain of M_2. Let g_{m1} and g_{m2} be

the transconductances and r_{o1} and r_{o2} be the output resistances of the transistors M_1 and M_2 respectively.

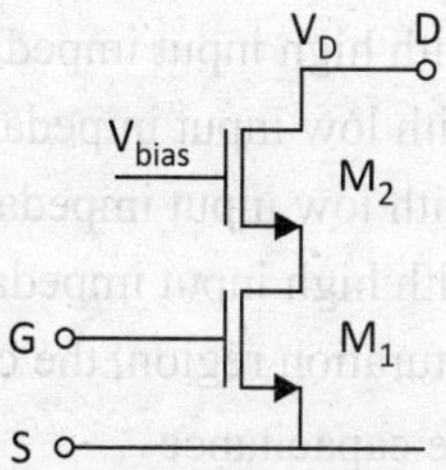

Fig. 3.62: Problem-4

Derive approximate expressions for g_m and r_o.

5. Identify the circuit shown in Figure-3.63. What is the value of current I_{OUT}?

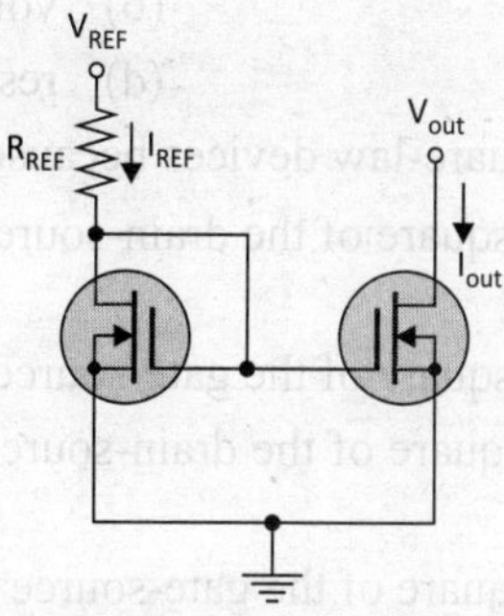

Fig. 3.63: Problem-5

6. For the AGC circuit shown in Figure-3.64, derive the expression for voltage gain. Given that r_o is the drain resistance at $V_{GS} = 0$ and assume $V_C^2 << V_P^2$

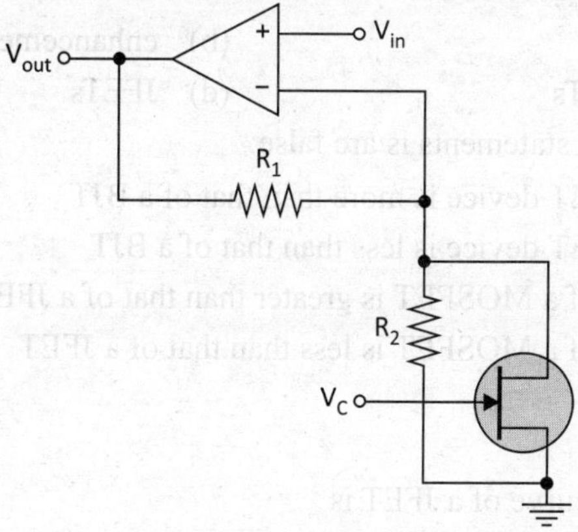

Fig. 3.64: Problem-6

MULTIPLE CHOICE QUESTIONS

1. FETs are
   (a) voltage controlled devices with high input impedance
   (b) current controlled devices with low input impedance
   (c) voltage controlled devices with low input impedance
   (d) current controlled devices with high input impedance
2. In a MOSFET operating in the saturation region, the channel length modulation effect causes
   (a) an increase in the gate-source capacitance
   (b) a decrease in the transconductance
   (c) a decrease in the unity-gain cut-off frequency
   (d) a decrease in the output resistance
3. For low values of drain-source voltages, the JFET acts as a
   (a) current source (b) voltage source
   (c) BJT (d) resistor
4. JFETs are also referred to as square-law devices because
   (a) the drain current varies as square of the drain-source voltage for fixed value of gate-source voltage
   (b) the drain current varies as square of the gate-source voltage for fixed drain-source voltage
   (c) the gate current varies as square of the drain-source voltage for fixed value of gate-source voltage
   (d) the gate current varies as square of the gate-source voltage for fixed drain-source voltage
5. For an N-channel enhancement-type MOSFET, if the source is connected at a higher potential then that of the bulk (i.e. $V_{SB} > 0$), the threshold voltage V_{TH} of the MOSFET will
   (a) remain unchanged (b) decrease
   (c) change polarity (d) increase
6. Which of the following devices has revolutionized the field of computers:
   (a) BJTs (b) enhancement MOSFETs
   (c) depletion MOSFETs (d) JFETs
7. Which of the following statements is/are false:
   (a) Noise level of a FET device is more than that of a BJT
   (b) Noise level of a FET device is less than that of a BJT
   (c) Input impedance of a MOSFET is greater than that of a JFET
   (d) Input impedance of a MOSFET is less than that of a JFET
   (e) (a) and (c)
   (f) (b) and (c)
8. The transconductance curve of a JFET is
   (a) parabolic (b) linear
   (c) hyperbolic (d) none of the above

9. Depletion MOSFETs can operate in
   (a) depletion mode only
   (b) enhancement mode only
   (c) both depletion and enhancement modes
   (d) none of the above
10. Dual-gate MOSFETs can be considered to be counterpart of
   (a) triodes (b) diodes
   (c) tetrodes (d) pentodes
11. The principle of operation of a VMOS device is similar to that of
   (a) enhancement MOSFET (b) depletion MOSFET
   (c) insulated gate bipolar transistor (d) junction FET

SOLUTIONS TO PROBLEMS

Problem-1:

(a) Drain resistance

$$r_d = \left.\frac{\Delta V_{DS}}{\Delta I_D}\right|_{V_{GS}=\text{constant}} = \frac{(10-15)}{\left(14\times10^{-3}-15\times10^{-3}\right)}\Omega = 5k\Omega$$

(b) Transconductance

$$g_m = \left.\frac{\Delta I_D}{\Delta V_{GS}}\right|_{V_{DS}=\text{constant}} = \frac{\left(13\times10^{-3}-15\times10^{-3}\right)}{(-1-0)} A/V = 2mA/V$$

(c) Amplification factor $\propto = r_d \times g_m = 5\times10^3\times2\times10^{-3} = 10$

(d) The FET used is an N-channel JFET as the value of drain current I_D decreases with increase in negative value of V_{GS}.

Problem-2:

For a MOSFET, the drain current (I_D), gate-source voltage (V_{GS}) and threshold voltage (V_{Th}) are related as:

$$I_D = K\left(V_{GS}-V_{Th}\right)^2$$

Hence, $1\times10^{-3} = K(0.9-0.4)^2$

Therefore,

$$K = \frac{1\times10^{-3}}{0.25} A/V^2 = \frac{1}{25\times10^4} mA/mV^2$$

When, $V_{GS} = 1400mV$ then,

$$I_D = \frac{1}{25\times10^4}\times(1400-400)^2 = 4mA$$

Problem-3:

The value of $\beta R_E = 100\times1\times10^3 = 100k\Omega$

Value of $10R_2 = 10\times2\times10^3 = 20k\Omega$

Value of $\beta R_E > 10R_2$, therefore approximate analysis can be done

Voltage at transistor base is given by

$$V_B = \left(\frac{R_2}{R_1+R_2}\right)\times10 = \left(\frac{2\times10^3}{2\times10^3+8\times10^3}\right)\times10V = 2V$$

The emitter voltage is given by $V_E = V_B - V_{BE} = 2-0.7 = 1.3V$

The emitter current $I_E = \frac{V_E}{R_E} = \frac{1.3}{1\times10^3}A = 1.3mA$

Now, the emitter current is the same as the drain current. Therefore,

$V_D = \left(10-1\times10^3\times1.3\times10^{-3}\right)V = (10-1.3)V = 8.7V$

The drain of an N-channel MOSFET is shorted to the gate so that $V_{GS} = V_{DS}$. The threshold voltage (V_{Th}) of MOSFET is 1V. If the drain current (I_D) is 1mA for $V_{GS} = 2V$, then for $V_{GS} = 3V$, the value of I_D is given by:

$$I_D = k\left(V_{GS}-V_{Th}\right)^2$$

Therefore, $1\times10^{-3} = k(2-1)^2$. Hence, K = 1mA/V²

For $V_{GS} = 3V$, drain current is given by $I_D = 1\times10^{-3}(3-1)^2 = 4mA$

Problem-4:

The small signal equivalent of the given circuit is shown in Figure-3.65 (a).

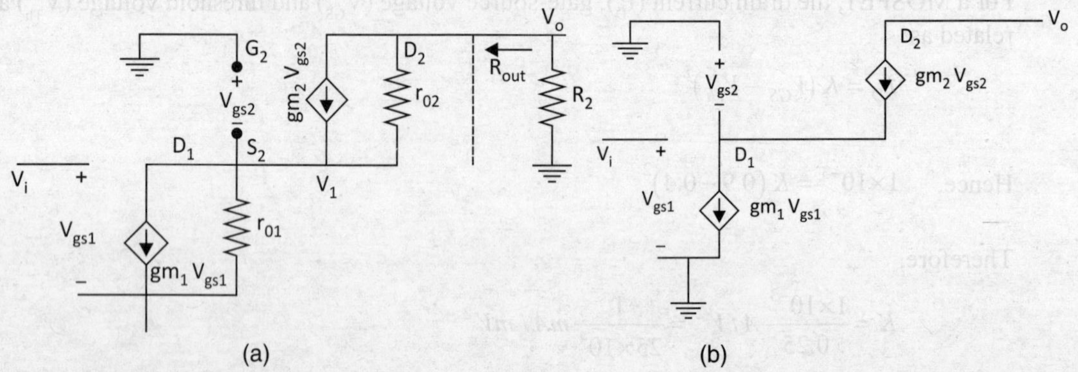

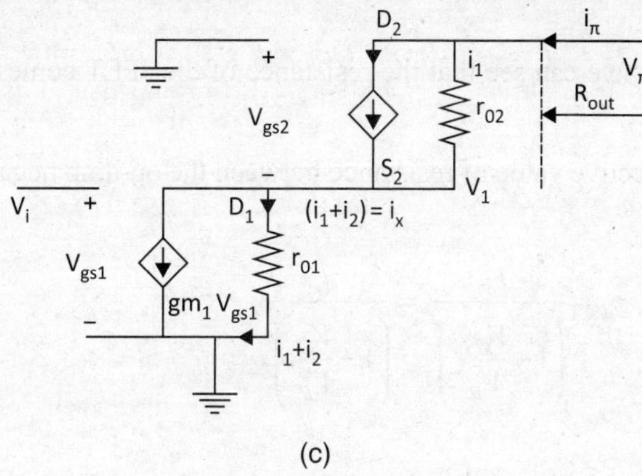

Fig. 3.65: Solution to Problem-4

r_{o1} and r_{o2} can be neglected to find the approximate value of g_{meq}. The approximate circuit is shown in Figure-3.65 (b).

Drain current $I_{D1} = I_{D2} = g_m V_{gs1} = g_m V_i$

Transconductance $g_{meq} = \dfrac{\partial I_d}{\partial V_i} = \dfrac{\partial (g_{m1} V_i)}{\partial V_i}$

$$g_{meq} = g_{m1}$$

For calculation of R_{out}, the circuit looks like as shown in Figure-3.65 (c).

As $V_{gs1} = 0$, therefore $g_m V_{gs1} = 0$

$V_{gs2} = -V_1$

$i_2 = g_{m2} V_{gs2} = -g_{m2} V_1 = -g_{m2} i_x r_{o1}$

Now, $i_x = i_1 + i_2$

Therefore, $\quad i_1 = i_x - i_2 = i_x + i_x g_{m2} r_{o1} = i_x \left(1 + g_{m2} r_{o1}\right)$

Using KVL we get, $V_x = i_1 r_{o2} + i_x r_{o1} = i_x \left(1 + g_{m2} r_{o1}\right) r_{o2} + i_x r_{o1}$

Therefore, $\dfrac{V_x}{i_x} = \left(1 + g_{m2} r_{o1}\right) r_{o2} + r_{o1} \approx g_{m2} r_{o1} r_{o2}$

Problem-5:

The current I_{OUT} is equal to the current I_{REF}. Therefore, the circuit is a current mirror circuit, where the output current is equal to the input current.

Problem-6:

From Figure-3.64, we can see that the resistance of the JFET comes in parallel with resistance R_2.

Therefore, the effective value of resistance between the op-amp negative terminal and ground is $R_2 \| r_d$.

For a JFET, $$r_d = \frac{r_o}{\left(1 - \frac{V_{GS}}{V_P}\right)^2} = \frac{r_o}{\left(1 - \frac{V_C}{V_P}\right)^2}$$

It is given that $V_C^2 << V_P^2$

Therefore, $$r_d = \frac{r_o}{\left(1 - 2\frac{V_C}{V_P}\right)}$$

The effective resistance between the negative terminal of op-amp and ground is given by:

$$R_2 \left\| \frac{r_o}{\left(1 - 2\frac{V_C}{V_P}\right)} \right. = \frac{R_2 \times \frac{r_o}{\left(1 - 2\frac{V_C}{V_P}\right)}}{R_2 + \frac{r_o}{\left(1 - 2\frac{V_C}{V_P}\right)}} = \frac{R_2 \times r_o}{R_2\left(1 - 2\frac{V_C}{V_P}\right) + r_o}$$

The gain of the circuit is given by:

$$1 + \frac{R_1}{\frac{R_2 \times r_o}{R_2\left(1 - 2\frac{V_C}{V_P}\right) + r_o}} = 1 + \frac{R_1 \times R_2\left(1 - 2\frac{V_C}{V_P}\right) + r_o \times R_1}{R_2 \times r_o}$$

$$= 1 + \frac{R_1}{r_o}\left(1 - 2\frac{V_C}{V_P}\right) + \frac{R_1}{R_2} \quad = 1 + \frac{R_1}{R_2} + \frac{R_1}{r_o}\left(1 - 2\frac{V_C}{V_P}\right)$$

SOLUTIONS TO MULTIPLE CHOICE QUESTIONS

1. (a) 2. (d) 3. (d) 4. (b)
5. (d)

Consider the Figure-3.66. As the MOSFET is an N-channel enhancement type MOSFET, the source being at higher potential than the substrate, implies that there is reverse bias potential between the source and the body ($V_{SB} > 0V$). The reverse-bias voltage will result in widening of the depletion region which in turn leads to reduction in channel depth as shown in the figure above. To return the channel to its former state, the gate-source voltage (V_{GS}) has to be increased. Hence, increase in V_{SB} results in increase in threshold voltage V_{TH}.

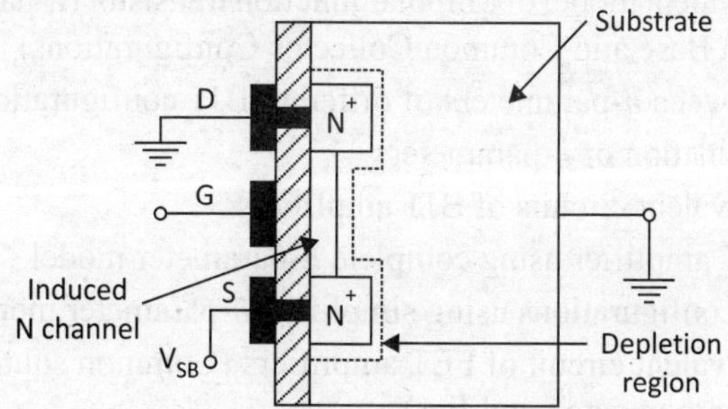

Fig. 3.66: Solution to MCQ-5

6. (b) 7. (f) 8. (a) 9. (c)
10. (c) 11. (a)

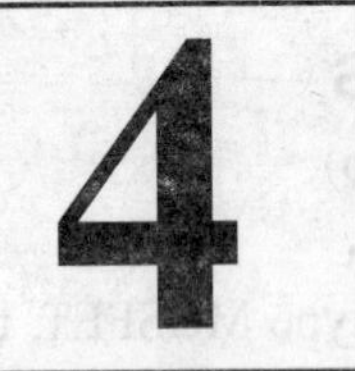

Small Signal Analysis of Amplifiers

Learning Objectives

After completing this chapter, you will learn the following topics.

- Hybrid parameters (*h*-parameters)
- Small signal equivalent model of a bipolar junction transistor (h-parameter model for Common-Emitter, Common Base and Common Collector Configurations)
- Relationships between *h*-parameters of different BJT configurations
- Graphical determination of *h*-parameters
- Small signal equivalent circuits of BJT amplifiers
- Analysis of a BJT amplifier using complete *h*-parameter model
- Analysis of BJT configurations using simplified *h*-parameter model
- Small signal equivalent circuit of FET amplifiers (Common source amplifier, Common drain amplifier and Common gate amplifier)
- Low frequency response and equivalent circuits of BJTand FET amplifiers
- High frequency response and equivalent circuits of BJT and FET amplifiers
- Miller's theorem

Introduction

In this chapter, the small signal analysis of BJT and FET amplifiers is discussed in detail along with their low and high frequency responses. The chapter begins with an introduction to h-parameter model for an amplifier. This is followed by discussion on the small signal equivalent model of a bipolar junction transistor (BJT) *i.e.* the *h*-parameter model for the common emitter, common base and common collector BJT configurations. This is followed by detailed discussion on small signal equivalent circuits of bipolar transistor amplifiers which covers analysis of a transistor amplifier using complete h-parameter model and analysis of different transistor configurations using simplified h-parameter models. Small signal equivalent circuit of FET amplifiers for different configurations are covered next. Low frequency and high frequency response of different BJT and FET amplifier configurations are covered in detail next. Miller's theorem is also discussed in the chapter. Important formulae and keywords are listed at the end of the chapter. Different topics discussed in the chapter are amply illustrated with solved examples. In addition, there are a number of problems given towards the end of the chapter along with brief solutions. A self-evaluation exercise containing multiple-choice questions along with answers concludes the chapter.

4.1 HYBRID PARAMETERS (H-PARAMETERS)

A two-port, four-terminal device such as an amplifier with two input and two output terminals,as shown in Figure-4.1, can be represented by an equivalent circuit model making use of two currents and two voltages provided that it meets the following two conditions. First, there is a common connection between the input and the output. Second, it should contain only linear elements. Two of the four variables including input and output currents and input and output voltages can be chosen as the independent variables and the remaining two variables can be expressed in terms of these independent variables. The choice of the independent variables depends upon the nature of the device.

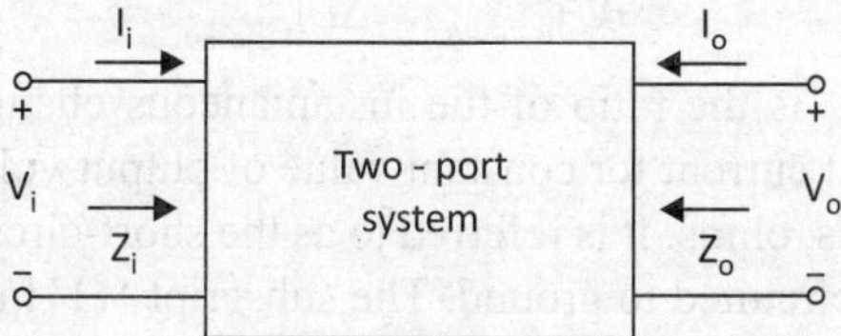

Fig. 4.1: Block diagram representation of a two-port, four-terminal device

Bipolar transistors are generally modeled using the hybrid parameter model or the h-parameter model. Their datasheets provide the values of these h-parameters. In the case of h-parameter model, input current (I_i) and output voltage (V_o) are taken as independent variables. The other two variables, namely, the input voltage (V_i) and the output current (I_o) are then related to these variables by eqns. 4.1 and 4.2.

$$V_i = h_{11}I_i + h_{12}V_o \tag{4.1}$$

$$I_o = h_{21}I_i + h_{22}V_o \tag{4.2}$$

The quantities h_{11}, h_{12}, h_{21} and h_{22} are referred to as the hybrid parameters or the h-parameters. The term *hybrid* has its origin in the fact that different h-parameters have different dimensions. Figure-4.2 shows the representation of the network in terms of the h-parameters. As we can see from the figure, the h-parameter model makes use of the Thevenin's voltage equivalent model at the input and the Norton's current equivalent model at the output. It may be mentioned here that V_i and I_i are the RMS voltage and current values, respectively, of the applied input signal. V_o and I_o are the RMS voltage and current values of the resulting output signal.

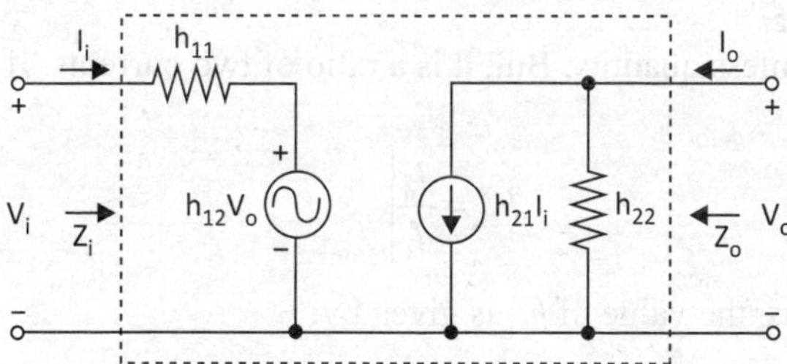

Fig. 4.2: *h*-parameter model of a two-port network

4.1.1 Determination of h-Parameters

In the following paragraphs, we shall determine generalized expressions for various hybrid parameters (*h*-parameters) outlined in the previous paragraphs.

4.1.1.1 *Parameter h_{11}*

h_{11} is an *impedance parameter* as would be evident from the following description. In eqn. (4.1), short circuiting the output terminals, *i.e.* substituting $V_o = 0$, we get,

$$h_{11} = \left.\frac{V_i}{I_i}\right|_{V_o=0} \tag{4.3}$$

where V_i and I_i are the RMS values of input voltage and current, respectively. Using partial calculus, the value of h_{11} can be calculated as

$$h_{11} = \left.\frac{\partial v_i}{\partial i_i}\right|_{V_o=\text{const.}} = \left.\frac{\Delta v_i}{\Delta i_i}\right|_{V_o=\text{const.}} \tag{4.4}$$

Therefore, the parameter h_{11} is the ratio of the instantaneous change in the input voltage to the instantaneous change in the input current for constant value of output voltage. Hence, the parameter h_{11} has the units of impedance, that is, ohms. It is referred to as the short-circuit input impedance parameter as it is defined for output short-circuited to ground. The subscript '11' indicates that it is dependent on the values of the input quantities. h_{11} is also represented as h_i.

4.1.1.2 Parameter h_{12}

h_{12} is a dimensionless quantity and is the ratio of two voltages. In eqn.(4.1), if the input terminals are open circuited, that is if we substitute $I_i = 0$, we get,

$$h_{12} = \left.\frac{V_i}{V_o}\right|_{I_i=0} \tag{4.5}$$

Using partial calculus, the value of h_{12} can be written as eqn. 4.6.

$$h_{12} = \left.\frac{\partial v_i}{\partial v_o}\right|_{I_i=\text{const.}} = \left.\frac{\Delta v_i}{\Delta v_o}\right|_{I_i=\text{const.}} \tag{4.6}$$

Here h_{12} is the ratio of the instantaneous change in the input voltage to the instantaneous change in the output voltage for constant value of input current and is therefore referred to as the *open-circuit reverse transfer voltage ratio* parameter. h_{12} is also represented as h_r.

4.1.1.3 Parameter h_{21}

h_{21} like h_{12} too is a dimensionless quantity. But, it is a ratio of two currents. If in eqn. 4.2, we substitute $V_o = 0$, then

$$h_{21} = \left.\frac{I_o}{I_i}\right|_{V_o=0} \tag{4.7}$$

Applying partial calculus, the value of h_{21} is given by:

$$h_{21} = \left.\frac{\partial i_o}{\partial i_i}\right|_{V_o=\text{const.}} = \left.\frac{\Delta i_o}{\Delta i_i}\right|_{V_o=\text{const.}} \tag{4.8}$$

Parameter h_{21} is the ratio of the change in the instantaneous value of output current to the change in the instantaneous value of the input current for constant value of output voltage. It is referred to as the *short-circuit forward transfer current ratio* parameter. h_{21} is also represented as h_f.

4.1.1.4 Parameter h_{22}

h_{22} is an admittance parameter. If the input terminals are open circuit, that is, $I_i = 0$, then eqn. (4.2) simplifies to eqn. 4.9.

$$h_{22} = \left.\frac{I_o}{V_o}\right|_{I_i=0} = \left.\frac{I_o}{V_o}\right|_{I_i=0} \tag{4.9}$$

Applying partial calculus, we get,

$$h_{22} = \left.\frac{\partial i_o}{\partial v_o}\right|_{I_i=\text{const.}} = \left.\frac{\Delta i_o}{\Delta v_o}\right|_{I_i=\text{const.}} \quad (4.10)$$

Parameter h_{22} is the ratio of the change in the instantaneous value of output current to the change in the instantaneous value of the output voltage for constant value of input current. It is referred to as the *open-circuit output admittance* parameter and is measured in Siemens. h_{22} is also represented as h_o.

Example 4.1: For the circuit shown in Figure-4.3, determine the h-parameters.

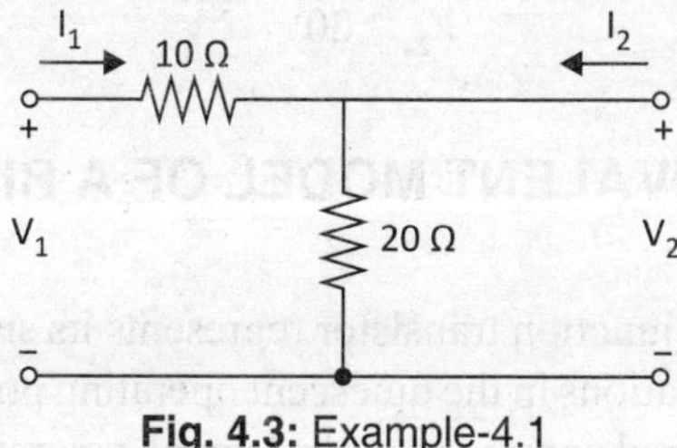

Fig. 4.3: Example-4.1

Solution: Parameters h_{11} and h_{21} are given by:

$$h_{11} = \left.\frac{V_1}{I_1}\right|_{V_2=0}$$

$$h_{21} = \left.\frac{I_2}{I_1}\right|_{V_2=0}$$

With $V_2 = 0$, the circuit can be redrawn as shown in Figure-4.4.

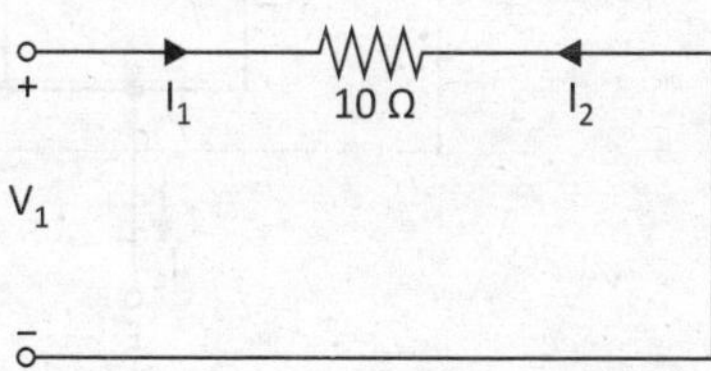

Fig. 4.4: Solution to Example-4.1

From Figure-4.4, $I_1 = -I_2$ and $V_1 = 10I_1$.

Therefore, $h_{21} = \frac{I_2}{I_1} = -1$ and

$$h_{11} = \frac{V_1}{I_1} = 10$$

Parameters, h_{12} and h_{22} are given by:

$$h_{12} = \left.\frac{V_1}{V_2}\right|_{I_1=0}$$

$$h_{22} = \left.\frac{I_2}{V_2}\right|_{I_1=0} = \left.\frac{I_2}{V_2}\right|_{I_1=0}$$

When $I_1 = 0$, then $V_1 = V_2$. Since there is no drop in the 10Ω resistance,
Therefore,

$$h_{12} = \frac{V_1}{V_2} = 1$$

Also, $V_2 = 20I_2$.
Therefore,

$$h_{22} = \frac{I_2}{V_2} = \frac{1}{20} = 0.05$$

4.2 SMALL SIGNAL EQUIVALENT MODEL OF A BIPOLAR JUNCTION TRANSISTOR

The *h*-parameter model of a bipolar junction transistor represents its small signal equivalent model. The basic assumption here is that the variations in the quiescent operating point (Q-point) are small, so that the transistor parameters can be considered constant over the signal excursion. It may be mentioned here that the *h*-parameter model is applicable to all the three BJT configurations. The values of h-parameters are more or less constant for a given transistor, although they vary slightly with change in collector current. However, they have different values for each of the three transistor configurations. In this section we shall discuss the *h*-parameter model for the three transistor configurations.

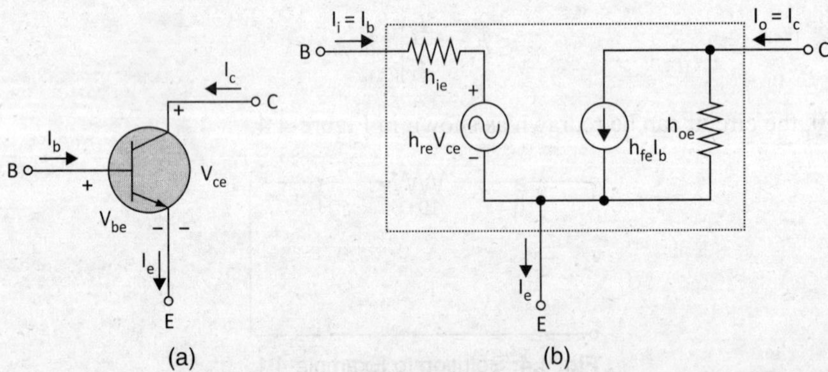

Fig. 4.5: (a) Circuit symbol of common-emitter transistor configuration (b) h-parameter equivalent model for the common-emitter transistor configuration

4.2.1 h-parameter model of Common-Emitter Configuration

Figures-4.5(a) and (b) show the circuit symbol and the h-parameter equivalent model for the common-emitter configuration, respectively. As we can see from the figure, a second subscript has been added to the nomenclature of the h-parameters. This is so done as to distinguish between the h-parameters of the three transistor configurations. In the case of common-emitter configuration, parameters h_{11}, h_{21}, h_{12} and h_{22} are respectively denoted as h_{ie} and referred to as the input impedance of the transistor; h_{fe} and called forward current transfer ratio; h_{re} and referred to as the reverse voltage transfer ratio and h_{oe} and called the output admittance. Note that in this case, current I_i is the base current I_b, current I_o is the collector current I_c, voltage V_i is the voltage V_{be} and voltage V_o is the voltage V_{ce}. The h-parameter equations for the common-emitter configuration are given by eqns. (4.11) and (4.12).

$$V_{be} = h_{ie} I_b + h_{re} V_{ce} \quad (4.11)$$

$$I_c = h_{fe} I_b + h_{oe} V_{ce} \quad (4.12)$$

The values of the parameters h_{ie}, h_{re}, h_{fe} and h_{oe} are given by the following set of equations, respectively.

$$h_{ie} = \left.\frac{\partial v_{be}}{\partial i_b}\right|_{V_{ce}=\text{const.}} = \left.\frac{\Delta v_{be}}{\Delta i_b}\right|_{V_{ce}=\text{const.}} \quad (4.13)$$

$$h_{re} = \left.\frac{\partial v_{be}}{\partial v_{ce}}\right|_{I_b=\text{const.}} = \left.\frac{\Delta v_{be}}{\Delta v_{ce}}\right|_{I_b=\text{const.}} \quad (4.14)$$

$$h_{fe} = \left.\frac{\partial i_c}{\partial i_b}\right|_{V_{ce}=\text{const.}} = \left.\frac{\Delta i_c}{\Delta i_b}\right|_{V_{ce}=\text{const.}} \quad (4.15)$$

$$h_{oe} = \left.\frac{\partial i_c}{\partial v_{ce}}\right|_{I_b=\text{const.}} = \left.\frac{\Delta i_c}{\Delta v_{ce}}\right|_{I_b=\text{const.}} \quad (4.16)$$

The symbol Δ refers to a small variation around the quiescent point of operation, that is, the *h*-parameters are determined in the region of operation for the applied signal. The effect of the parameter h_{re} is so small on the transistor amplifier that it can be neglected. Figure-4.6 shows the simplified equivalent model for the common-emitter transistor configuration. Here, h_{re} is assumed to be zero, therefore the magnitude of the voltage source $h_{re}V_{ce}$ is also equal to zero. In other words, it results in short-circuit equivalent for the feedback element. In cases where the value of $1/h_{oe}$ is very large as compared to the value of load resistance, it is assumed to be open in comparison with the load resistance connected across the output terminals.

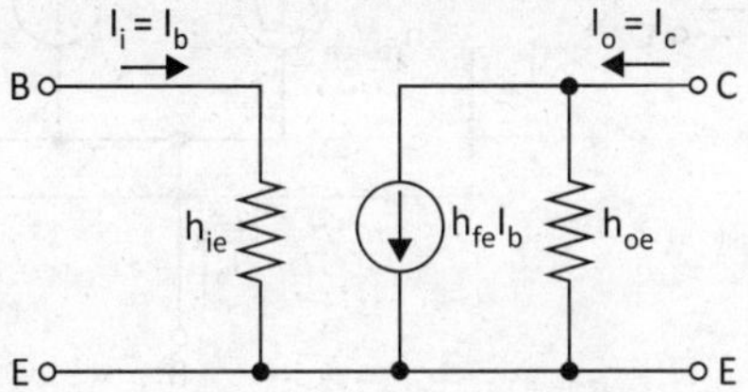

Fig. 4.6: Simplified equivalent h-parameter model for the common-emitter transistor

Example 4.2: For the transistor amplifier of Figure-4.7, find the small signal voltage gain of the amplifier given that $\beta_{DC} = 60$ and $V_{BE} = 0.7V$. Assume value of h_{ie} and h_{fe} to be equal to infinity.

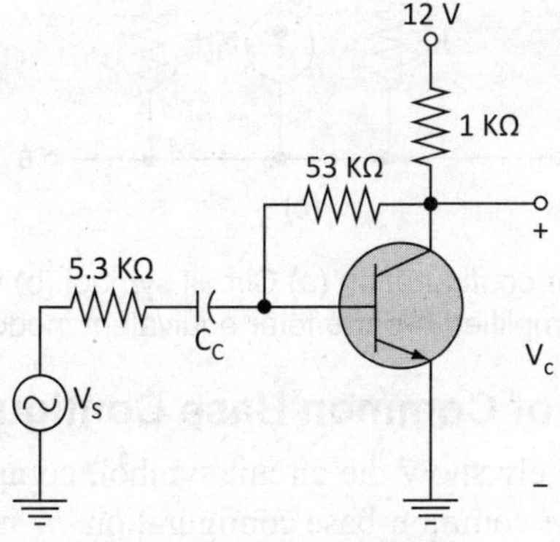

Fig. 4.7: Example-4.2

Solution: For small-signal gain calculations the capacitance C_C is assumed to be short circuit. As h_{ie} and h_{fe} are given to be infinity, the h-parameter equivalent circuit of the amplifier is shown in Figure-4.8.

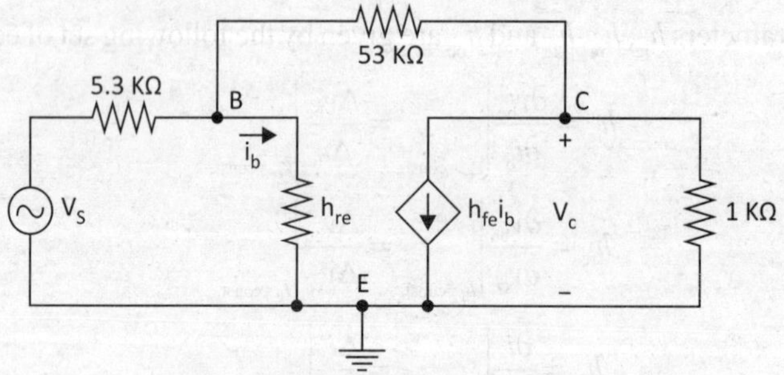

Fig. 4.8: Solution to Example 4.2

The circuit is same as an ideal opamp with input impedance and voltage gain as infinite.

Assuming virtual ground condition and applying KCL at node B, we get,

$$\frac{0-V_s}{5.3\times10^3}+\frac{0-V_c}{53\times10^3}=0$$

Therefore, $\frac{V_c}{V_s}=-10$

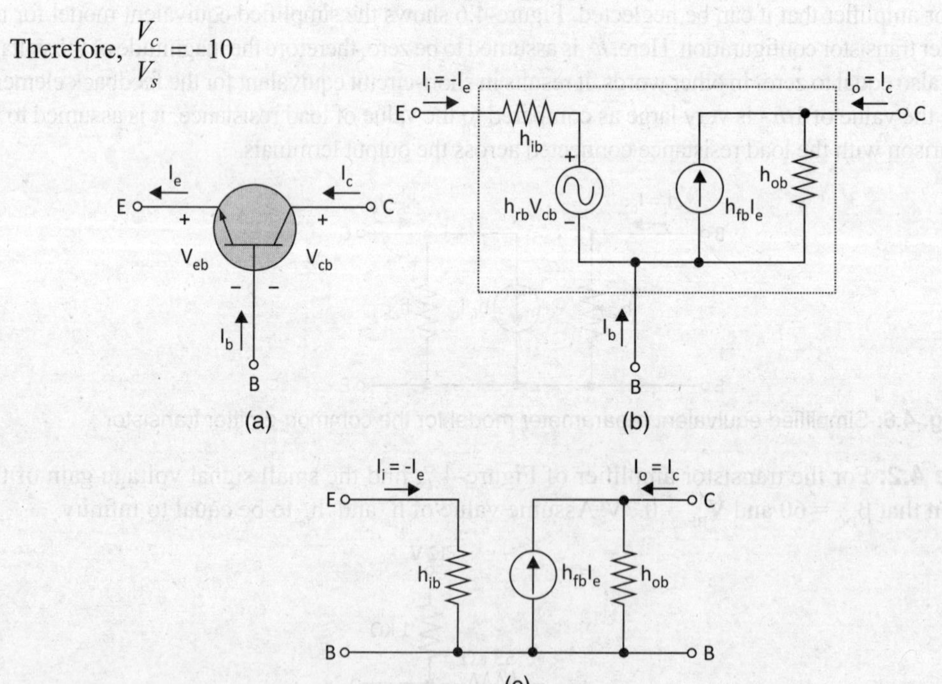

Fig. 4.9: Common-base transistor configuration (a) Circuit symbol (b) h-parameter equivalent model (c) simplified h-parameter equivalent model.

4.2.2 h-parameter model of Common Base Configuration

Figures-4.9(a), (b) and (c) respectively show the circuit symbol, complete h-parameter model and the simplified h-parameter model for the common-base configuration. h_{ib} is the input impedance parameter,

h_{fb} is the forward current transfer ratio, h_{rb} is the reverse voltage transfer ratio and h_{ob} is the output admittance parameter.

4.2.3 h-parameter model of Common Collector Configuration

Figures-4.10(a), (b) and (c) respectively show the circuit symbol, complete h-parameter model and simplified h-parameter model of the common-collector configuration. The parameter h_{ic} is referred to as the input impedance of the transistor in the common-collector configuration. Parameter h_{fc} stands for forward current transfer ratio and parameter h_{rc} is referred to as the reverse voltage transfer ratio. Parameter h_{oc} is the output admittance in the common-collector configuration. The h-parameters for the common-collector configuration can be determined in a similar fashion as that for the common-emitter configuration.

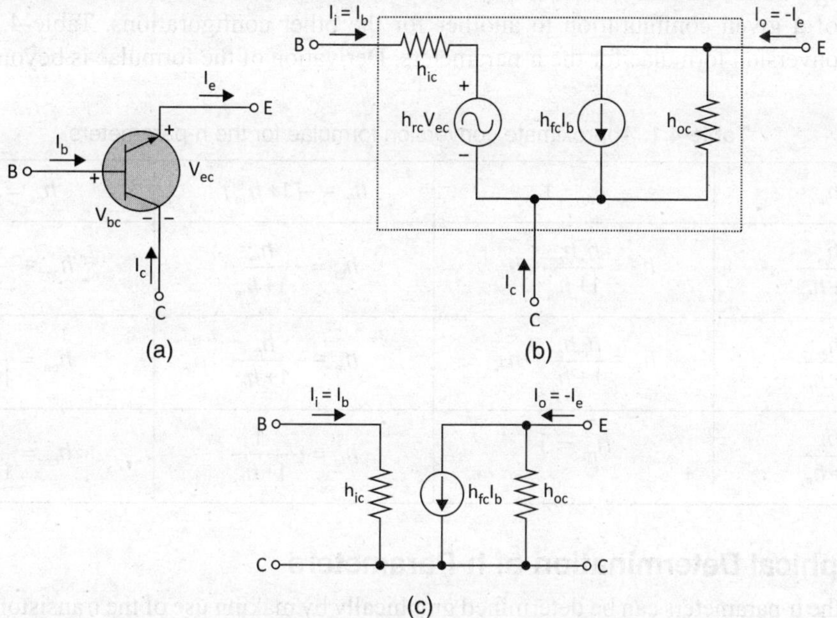

Fig. 4.10: Common-collector transistor configuration (a) Circuit symbol (b) h-parameter equivalent model (c) simplified h-parameter equivalent model

Example 4.3: Refer to the amplifier circuit of Figure-4.11. Find the expression for the voltage gain of the amplifier?

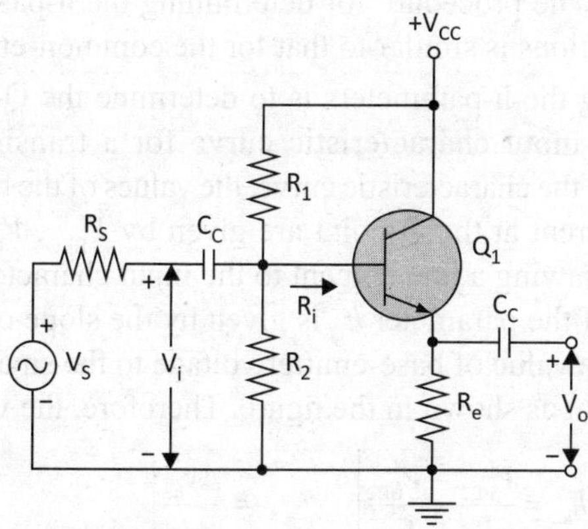

Fig. 4.11: Example 4.3

Solution: Assuming that $(1/h_{oe})$ is infinite, the output voltage is given by $V_o = h_{fe} \times I_b \times R_e$

Also, assuming that parallel combination of R_1, R_2 and h_{ie} is approximately equal to h_{ie},

$V_s/I_b = R_s + h_{ie}$

Therefore, the voltage gain is $A_V = \dfrac{V_o}{V_s} = \dfrac{h_{fe} \times I_b \times R_e}{V_s} \cong h_{fe} \times \dfrac{R_e}{R_s + h_{ie}}$

It may be mentioned here that the above assumptions are realistic.

4.2.4 Relationships between h-Parameters of Different Transistor Configurations

While designing a transistor-based amplifier, it may be necessary to convert from one set of transistor's h-parameters of a given configuration to another for the other configurations. Table-4.1 gives the approximate conversion formulae for the h-parameters. Derivation of the formulae is beyond the scope of the book.

Table-4.1: Approximate conversion formulae for the h-parameters

$h_{ic} = h_{ie}$	$h_{rc} = 1$	$h_{fc} = -(1 + h_{fe})$	$h_{oc} = h_{oe}$
$h_{ib} = \dfrac{h_{ie}}{1 + h_{fe}}$	$h_{rb} = \dfrac{h_{ie}h_{oe}}{1 + h_{fe}} - h_{re}$	$h_{fb} = -\dfrac{h_{fe}}{1 + h_{fe}}$	$h_{ob} = \dfrac{h_{oe}}{1 + h_{fe}}$
$h_{ie} = \dfrac{h_{ib}}{1 + h_{fb}}$	$h_{re} = \dfrac{h_{ib}h_{ob}}{1 + h_{fb}} - h_{rb}$	$h_{fe} = -\dfrac{h_{fb}}{1 + h_{fb}}$	$h_{oe} = \dfrac{h_{ob}}{1 + h_{fb}}$
$h_{ic} = \dfrac{h_{ib}}{1 + h_{fb}}$	$h_{rc} = 1$	$h_{fc} = -\dfrac{1}{1 + h_{fb}}$	$h_{oc} = \dfrac{h_{ob}}{1 + h_{fb}}$

4.2.5 Graphical Determination of h-Parameters

The values of the h-parameters can be determined graphically by making use of the transistor's input and output characteristics. The parameters h_i and h_r are determined from the input characteristic curves of the transistor whereas the parameters h_f and h_o are determined from the output characteristic curves. In this section we shall describe the procedure for determining the h-parameters graphically for common-emitter transistor configuration. The procedure for determining the h-parameters of the common-base and common-collector configurations is similar to that for the common-emitter configuration.

The first step in determining the h-parameters is to determine the Q-point or the operating point. Figure-4.12 shows the typical input characteristic curve for a transistor in the common-emitter configuration. As we can see from the characteristic curve, the values of the base-emitter voltage, collector-emitter voltage and the base current at the Q-point are given by V_{BEQ}, V_{CEQ} and I_{BQ}, respectively. The parameter h_{ie} is determined by drawing a line tangent to the input characteristic curve corresponding to V_{CEQ} at the Q-point. The value of the parameter h_{ie} is given by the slope of this line. In other words, h_{ie} is the ratio of small change in the value of base-emitter voltage to the small change in the value of base current around the operating point as shown in the figure. Therefore, the value of h_{ie} is given by

$$h_{ie} = \left.\frac{V_{BE2} - V_{BE1}}{I_{B2} - I_{B1}}\right|_{V_{CE} = V_{CEQ}} = \left.\frac{\Delta v_{be}}{\Delta i_b}\right|_{V_{CE} = V_{CEQ}} \tag{4.17}$$

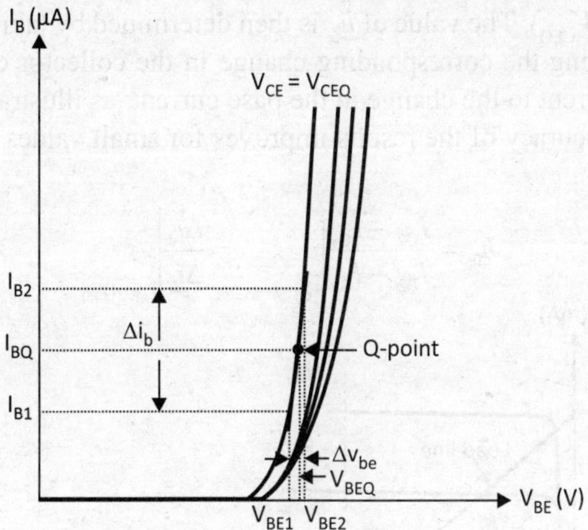

Fig. 4.12: Determination of h-parameter h_{ie}

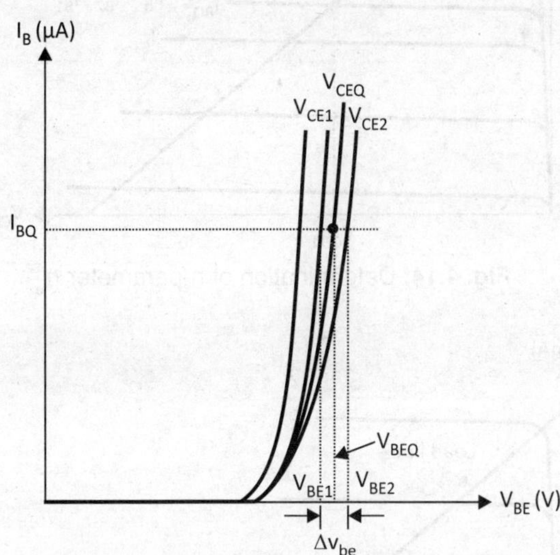

Fig. 4.13: Determination of h-parameter h_{re}

The parameter h_{re} is also determined using the input characteristic curve. Refer to Figure-4.13. A horizontal line is drawn at I_B equal to I_{BQ}, that is, for the value of the base current equal to the quiescent value of the base current. The change in base-emitter voltage is determined for a small change in the value of collector-emitter voltage around the operating point. The value of h_{re} is then determined by the ratio of the change in the value of base-emitter voltage to the change in the value of collector-emitter voltage for a constant value of base current. The value of h_{re} is given by eqn. 4.18.

$$h_{re} = \left.\frac{V_{BE2} - V_{BE1}}{V_{CE2} - V_{CE1}}\right|_{I_B = I_{BQ}} = \left.\frac{\Delta v_{be}}{\Delta v_{ce}}\right|_{I_B = I_{BQ}} \tag{4.18}$$

The other two parameters, that is, h_{fe} and h_{oe} are determined from the output characteristics. The value of parameter h_{fe} is determined by drawing a vertical line corresponding to the quiescent value of collector-emitter voltage (V_{CEQ}). The value of h_{fe} is then determined by taking a small change in the base current and then determining the corresponding change in the collector current. h_{fe} is the ratio of the change in the collector current to the change in the base current as illustrated in Figure 4.14. It may be mentioned here that the accuracy of the results improves for small values of the changes. The value of h_{fe} is given by eqn. 4.19.

$$h_{fe} = \left.\frac{I_{C2} - I_{C1}}{I_{B2} - I_{B1}}\right|_{V_{CE}=V_{CEQ}} = \left.\frac{\Delta i_c}{\Delta i_b}\right|_{V_{CE}=V_{CEQ}} \tag{4.19}$$

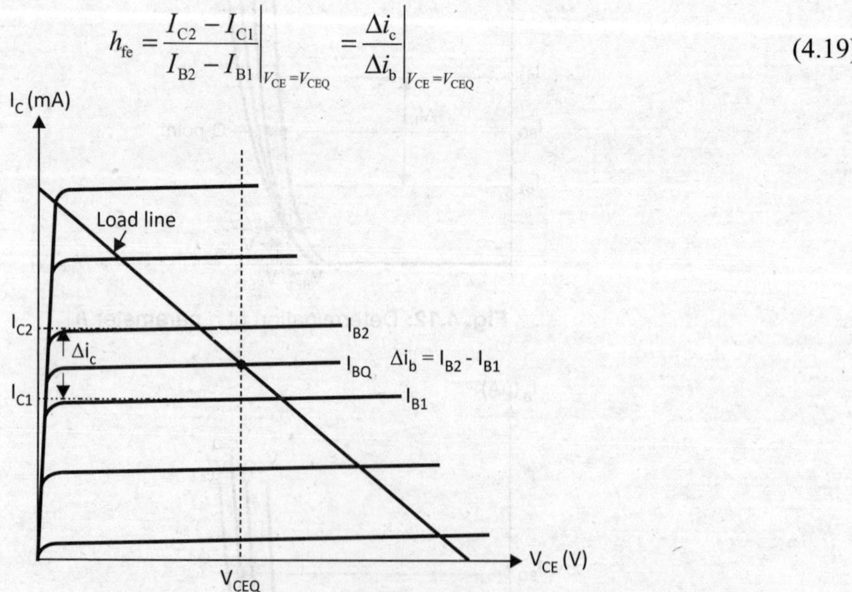

Fig. 4.14: Determination of h-parameter h_{fe}

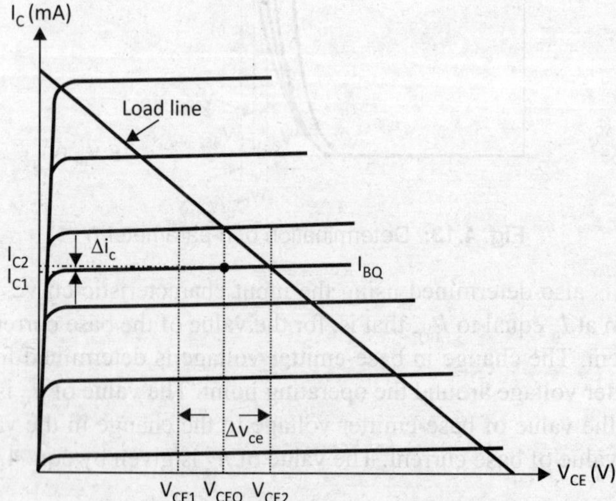

Fig. 4.15: Determination of h-parameter h_{oe}

The value of the parameter h_{oe} is determined by drawing a tangent to the output curve corresponding to base current equal to the quiescent base current. The value of the h_{oe} parameter is then determined by taking the ratio of the change in the collector current corresponding to a small change in the collector emitter voltage to the change in the collector emitter voltage as illustrated in Figure-4.15. The value of h_{oe} is given by eqn. 4.20.

$$h_{oe} = \frac{I_{C2} - I_{C1}}{V_{CE2} - V_{CE1}}\bigg|_{I_B = I_{BQ}} = \frac{\Delta i_c}{\Delta v_{ce}}\bigg|_{I_B = I_{BQ}} \tag{4.20}$$

Typical h-parameter values for the three BJT configurations for a silicon transistor are given in Table-4.2.

Table 4.2: Typical h-parameter values for silicon transistor

Parameter	Common emitter	Common collector	Common base
h_i	1 – 6.5 kΩ	1 – 6.5 kΩ	20 – 30 Ω
h_r	(1.5 Ω 10⁻⁴) – (2.5 Ω 10⁻⁴)	1	(0.1 × 10⁻⁴) – (3 × 10⁻⁴)
h_f	50 – 250	(–50) – (–250)	–1
h_o	5 – 25 μmhos	5–25 μmhos	0.02–0.5 μmhos

4.3 SMALL SIGNAL EQUIVALENT CIRCUITS OF BIPOLAR TRANSISTOR AMPLIFIERS

In the following sections, we shall present detailed analysis of bipolar transistor amplifiers in three configurations namely common-emitter, common-base and common-collector configurations using h-parameter models.

4.3.1 Analysis of a Transistor Amplifier using Complete h-Parameter Model

Figure-4.16 shows a generalized transistor-based amplifier where the transistor is replaced by its h-parameter model. As we can see from the figure, resistor R_L is the external load and V_S is the input signal source. The important parameters of any amplifier are the current gain, input impedance, voltage gain and the output impedance. The expressions for these parameters will be derived in this section.

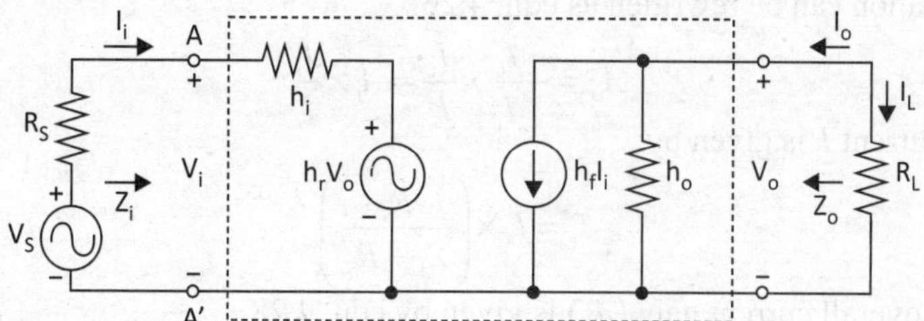

Fig. 4.16: Generalized h-parameter model of a transistor-based amplifier

4.3.1.1 *Current gain or the current amplification (A_i)*

Current gain is defined as the ratio of the current through the load resistance (I_L) to the input current (I_i). Eqn. 4.21 gives the expression for the current gain:

$$A_i = \frac{I_L}{I_i} \tag{4.21}$$

As the current $I_L = -I_o$,

Therefore,

$$A_i = -\frac{I_o}{I_i} \tag{4.22}$$

Applying Kirchhoff's current law to the output section of the circuit shown in Figure-4.16, the value of I_o is given by eqn. 4.23.

$$I_o = h_f I_i + h_o V_o \tag{4.23}$$

The value of the output voltage V_o is given by eqn. 4.24.

$$V_o = I_L R_L = -I_o R_L \tag{4.24}$$

Therefore, the current gain (A_i) is given by eqn. 4.25.

$$A_i = -\frac{h_f}{1 + h_o R_L} \tag{4.25}$$

This is the current gain without taking the source resistance (R_S) into account. The overall current gain taking source resistor into account can be determined by replacing the voltage source with its Norton's equivalent as shown in Figure-4.17.

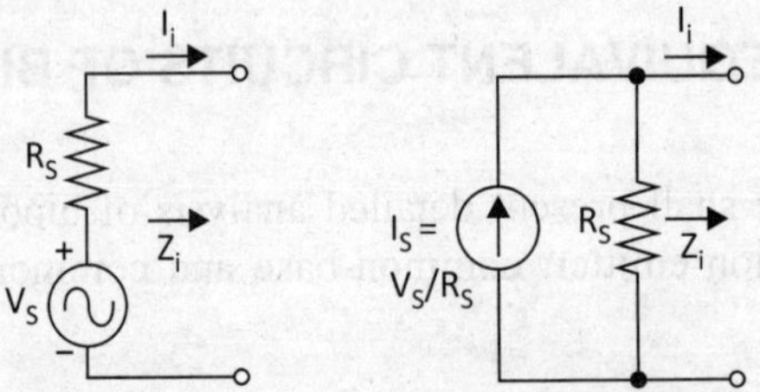

Fig. 4.17: Norton's equivalent of a voltage source

The overall current gain is determined using the following expression.

$$A_{is} = \frac{I_o}{I_s}$$

The above equation can be rewritten as eqn. 4.26.

$$A_{is} = -\frac{I_o}{I_i} \times \frac{I_i}{I_s} = A_i \times \frac{I_i}{I_s} \tag{4.26}$$

The value of current I_i is given by:

$$I_i = I_s \times \left(\frac{R_S}{Z_i + R_S}\right) \tag{4.27}$$

Therefore, the overall current gain (A_{is}) is given by eqn. 4.28.

$$A_{is} = A_i \times \left(\frac{R_S}{Z_i + R_S}\right) \tag{4.28}$$

From eqn. (4.28), it is clear that when $R_S \to \infty$, $A_{is} \to A_i$. Therefore, A_i is the current gain for an ideal current source.

4.3.1.2 Input impedance (Z_i)

The input impedance Z_i is defined as the impedance seen looking into the input terminals A–A' of the amplifier. It is given by eqn. 4.29.

$$Z_i = \frac{V_i}{I_i} \tag{4.29}$$

Applying Kirchhoff's voltage law to the input section of the amplifier we get,

$$V_i = h_i I_i + h_r V_o \tag{4.30}$$

Substituting the value of V_i given by eqn. (4.30) in eqn. (4.29), we get,

$$Z_i = \frac{h_i I_i + h_r V_o}{I_i} \tag{4.31}$$

The output voltage V_o is given by

$$V_o = -I_o R_L = A_i I_i R_L \tag{4.32}$$

Substituting the value of V_o in eqn. (4.31), we get,

$$Z_i = \frac{h_i I_i + h_r A_i I_i R_L}{I_i} = h_i + h_r A_i R_L$$

Substituting the value of A_i given in eqn. (4.25) in the above equation we get

$$Z_i = h_i - \frac{h_r h_f R_L}{1 + h_o R_L} \tag{4.33}$$

4.3.1.3 Voltage gain (A_v)

The voltage gain A_v is given by the ratio of the output voltage (V_o) to the input voltage (V_i).

$$A_v = \frac{V_o}{V_i}$$

Substituting the value of V_o given in eqn. (4.32) in the above equation, we get

$$A_v = \frac{A_i I_i R_L}{V_i} \tag{4.34}$$

Substituting $V_i/I_i = Z_i$, we get, $$A_v = \frac{A_i R_L}{Z_i}$$

The voltage gain taking source resistance R_S into account (A_{vs}) is given by eqn. 4.35.

$$A_{vs} = \frac{V_o}{V_S} = \frac{V_o}{V_i} \times \frac{V_i}{V_S} = A_v \times \frac{V_i}{V_S} \tag{4.35}$$

From the equivalent input circuit of the amplifier, the voltage (V_i) is expressed in terms of the signal voltage (V_S) by eqn. 4.36.

$$V_i = \frac{V_S Z_i}{Z_i + R_S} \tag{4.36}$$

Therefore, the expression for A_{vs} is given by eqn. 4.37.

$$A_{vs} = \frac{A_v Z_i}{Z_i + R_S} \tag{4.37}$$

When $R_S \to 0$ then $A_{vs} \to A_v$. In other words, A_v is the voltage gain for an ideal voltage source, that is, the one with zero internal resistance.

4.3.1.4 Output admittance (Y_o)

The output admittance (Y_o) is defined as the reciprocal of the output impedance (Z_o). The output impedance (Z_o) is determined by setting the voltage source (V_S) to zero and the load impedance R_L to infinity and by driving the output terminals from a voltage source (V_o). Z_o is then given by the ratio of the applied voltage (V_o) to output current (I_o).

$$Y_o = \left.\frac{I_o}{V_o}\right|_{V_s=0, R_L=\infty} \tag{4.38}$$

Substituting the value of I_o from eqn. (4.23) in eqn. (4.38), we get eqn. 4.39.

$$Y_o = h_f \frac{I_i}{V_o} + h_o \tag{4.39}$$

Applying Kirchhoff's voltage law to the input section of the circuit in Figure-4.16, we get,

$$V_s - R_s I_i - h_i I_i - h_r V_o = 0 \tag{4.40}$$

As $V_s = 0$, therefore

$$R_s I_i + h_i I_i + h_r V_o = 0 \tag{4.41}$$

Rearranging the terms in eqn. (4.41), we get,

$$\frac{I_i}{V_o} = -\frac{h_r}{h_i + R_s} \tag{4.42}$$

Substituting the value of I_i/V_o given by eqn. (4.42) in eqn. (4.39), we get

$$Y_o = h_o - \frac{h_f h_r}{h_i + R_s} \tag{4.43}$$

In this expression, it is assumed that the load R_L is external to the amplifier. If the effect of load resistor R_L is included, then the total impedance is given by the parallel combination of Z_o and R_L.

Example-4.4: Given a BJT with I_C = 3mA and h_{fe} = 150 at a room temperature with kT/q = 25mV. What is the value of h_{ie} in ohms?

Solution: $h_{ie} = h_{fe} \times \frac{kT}{q} \times \frac{1}{I_C} = \frac{150 \times 25 \times 10^{-3}}{3 \times 10^{-3}} = 1250\Omega$

Example-4.5: Refer to the amplifier shown in Figure-4.18. Determine the input impedance, overall voltage gain and current gain and output impedance. The values of the h-parameters of the transistor are h_{ie} = 1.5 kΩ, h_{fe} = 100, $h_{re} = 1 \times 10^{-4}$ and h_{oe} = 25 μA/V.

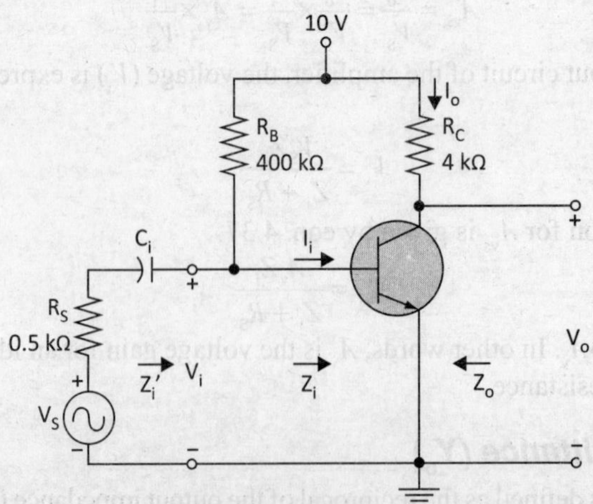

Fig. 4.18: Example-4.5

Solution: The complete hybrid equivalent model for the network is shown in Figure-4.19(a). Figure-4.19(b) shows the simplified circuit of the network shown in Figure-4.19(a) with the input section being replaced by the Thevenin's equivalent network. As the resistor $R_B >> R_S$, therefore the Thevenin's equivalent voltage V_{TH} is approximately equal to the source voltage V_S and the Thevenin's equivalent resistance R_{TH} is approximately equal to the resistor R_S.

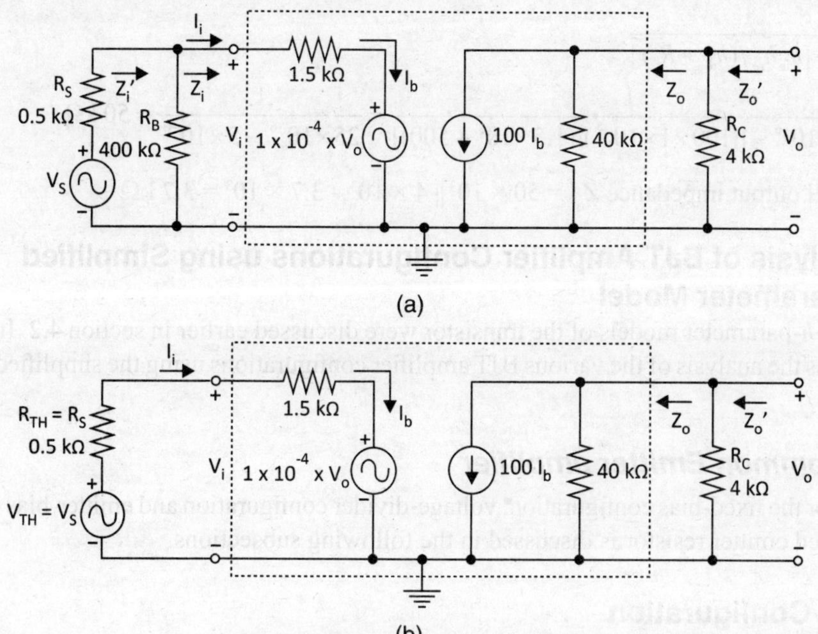

Fig. 4.19: Solution to Example-4.5

The input impedance Z_i is given by:

$$Z_i = h_{ie} - \frac{h_{fe} h_{re} R_C}{1 + h_{oe} R_C}$$

$$= 1.5 \times 10^3 - \frac{100 \times 1 \times 10^{-4} \times 4 \times 10^3}{1 + 25 \times 10^{-6} \times 4 \times 10^3} = 1.5 \times 10^3 - \frac{40}{1.1} = 1500 - 36.36 = 1.464 \text{ k}\Omega$$

The voltage gain A_v is given by:

$$A_v = \frac{V_o}{V_i} = \frac{-h_{fe} R_C}{h_{ie} + (h_{ie} h_{oe} - h_{fe} h_{re}) R_C}$$

$$= \frac{-100 \times 4 \times 10^3}{1.5 \times 10^3 + (1.5 \times 10^3 \times 25 \times 10^{-6} - 100 \times 1 \times 10^{-4}) \times 4 \times 10^3}$$

$$= \frac{-4 \times 10^5}{1.5 \times 10^3 + 0.0275 \times 4 \times 10^3} = \frac{-4 \times 10^5}{1.61 \times 10^3} = -248.45$$

The current gain A_i is equal to

$$A_i = \frac{h_{fe}}{1+h_{oe}R_C} = \frac{-100}{1+25\times10^{-6}\times4\times10^3} = -90.91$$

The output impedance Z_o' is parallel combination of Z_o and R_C. Z_o is given by:

$$Z_o = \frac{1}{h_{oe} - [h_{fe}h_{re}/(h_{ie}+R_s)]}$$

$$= \frac{1}{25\times10^{-6} - [(100\times1\times10^{-4})/(1.5\times10^3+500)]} = \frac{1}{25\times10^{-6} - 5\times10^{-6}} = 50\text{ k}\Omega$$

The overall output impedance $Z_o' = 50\times10^3 \,||\, 4\times10^3 = 3.7\times10^3 = 3.7\text{ k}\Omega$

4.3.2 Analysis of BJT Amplifier Configurations using Simplified *h*-Parameter Model

The simplified *h*-parameter models of the transistor were discussed earlier in section 4.2. In this section, we shall discuss the analysis of the various BJT amplifier configurations using the simplified h-parameter model.

4.3.2.1 Common Emitter amplifier

The analysis for the fixed-bias configuration, voltage-divider configuration and emitter-bias configuration with unbypassed emitter resistor is discussed in the following subsections.

Fixed-Bias Configuration

Figure-4.20(a) shows the circuit diagram of the fixed-bias configuration and Figure-4.20(b) shows the simplified h-parameter equivalent model.

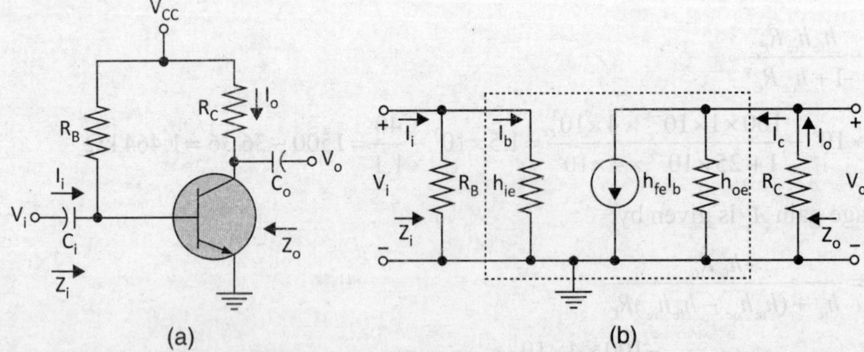

Fig. 4.20: (a) Circuit diagram of fixed-bias configuration (b) simplified *h*-parameter equivalent model.

The input impedance Z_i is given by a parallel combination of resistor R_B and transistor's h_{ie} parameter.

$$Z_i = R_B \| h_{ie} \tag{4.44}$$

The output impedance is given by the parallel combination of resistor R_C and the inverse of the output admittance h-parameter h_{oe}.

$$Z_o = R_C \| (1/h_{oe}) \tag{4.45}$$

The voltage gain A_v is given by:

$$A_v = \frac{V_o}{V_i} \quad (4.46)$$

The magnitude of the output voltage V_o is given by:

$$V_o = -I_o Z_o = -I_c Z_o \quad (4.47)$$

The collector current (I_c) is given by:

$$I_c = h_{fe} I_b \quad (4.48)$$

The base current (I_b) in turn is expressed in terms of the input voltage V_i as

$$I_b = \frac{V_i}{h_{ie}} \quad (4.49)$$

Substituting the value of I_C given by eqn. (4.48) and value of I_B given by eqn. (4.49) in eqn. (4.47), we get

$$V_o = -h_{fe} \times \frac{V_i}{h_{ie}} \times Z_o \quad (4.50)$$

Substituting this value of V_o in the eqn. (4.46), the voltage gain is given by:

$$A_v = \frac{-h_{fe} \times (V_i / h_{ie}) \times Z_o}{V_i} = \frac{-h_{fe} \times Z_o}{h_{ie}} = \frac{-h_{fe} \times [R_C \| (1/h_{oe})]}{h_{ie}} \quad (4.51)$$

The current gain A_i is given by:

$$A_i = \frac{I_o}{I_i} \quad (4.52)$$

The magnitude of I_o is given by:

$$I_o = I_c = h_{fe} I_b \quad (4.53)$$

Base current I_b is expressed in terms of the input current I_i as:

$$I_b = \frac{R_B}{R_B + h_{ie}} \times I_i \quad (4.54)$$

Therefore, the current gain A_i is given by:

$$A_i = \frac{h_{fe} I_b}{I_i} = \frac{h_{fe}}{I_i} \times \frac{R_B}{R_B + h_{ie}} \times I_i = \frac{h_{fe} \times R_B}{R_B + h_{ie}} \quad (4.55)$$

Assuming $R_B >> h_{ie}$

$$A_i \cong h_{fe}$$

Voltage-Divider Configuration

Figure-4.21(a) shows the voltage-divider configuration and Figure-4.21(b) shows its h-parameter equivalent circuit. As we can see from the Figure-, the equivalent circuit is the same as in the case of fixed-bias circuit with the difference that the resistor R_B is replaced by resistors R_{B1} and R_{B2}. The analysis for the voltage-divider configuration is done on similar lines as that for the fixed-bias configuration. Input impedance Z_i is given by:

$$Z_i = (R_{B1} \| R_{B2}) \| h_{ie} \quad (4.56)$$

The output impedance Z_o is given by the parallel combination of resistor R_C and the inverse of the output admittance h-parameter h_{oe}.

$$Z_o = R_C \| (1/h_{oe}) \tag{4.57}$$

The voltage gain A_v is given by:

$$A_v = \frac{-h_{fe} \times [R_C \| (1/h_{oe})]}{h_{ie}} \tag{4.58}$$

The current gain A_i is given by:

$$A_i = \frac{h_{fe} \times (R_{B1} \| R_{B2})}{(R_{B1} \| R_{B2}) + h_{ie}} \tag{4.59}$$

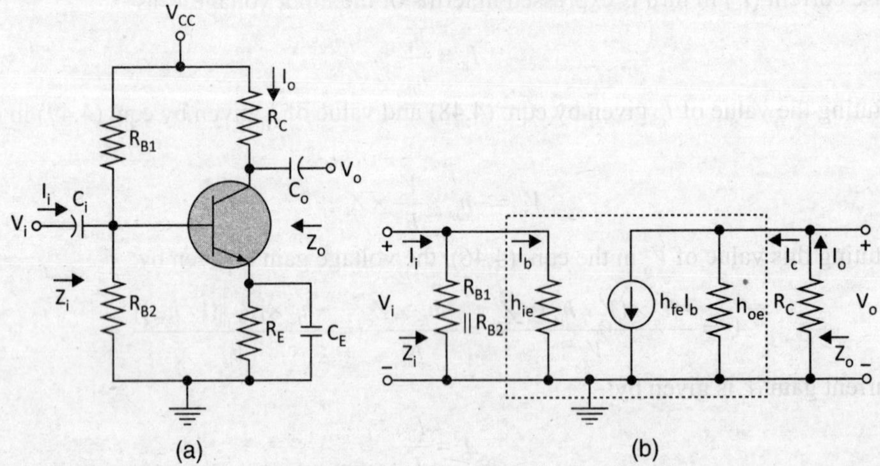

Fig. 4.21: (a) Circuit diagram of voltage-divider configuration (b) simplified h-parameter equivalent model

Emitter-Bias Configuration with Unbypassed Emitter Resistor

Figures-4.22(a) and (b) show the circuit diagram and the equivalent circuit of the emitter-bias configuration with unbypassed emitter resistor.

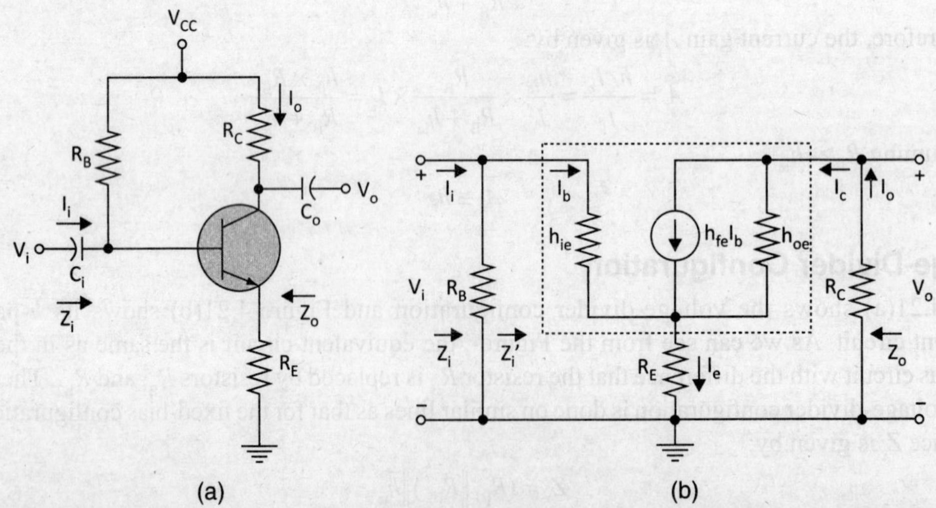

Fig. 4.22: (a) Circuit diagram of emitter-bias configuration with unbypassed emitter resistor; (b) simplified h-parameter equivalent model

Applying Kirchhoff's voltage law to the input section we get,

$$V_i = I_b h_{ie} + I_e R_E = I_b h_{ie} + (h_{fe}+1)I_b R_E = [h_{ie} + (h_{fe}+1)R_E]I_b$$

The input impedance looking into the network to the right of resistor R_B is given by eqn. 4.60.

$$Z_i' = \frac{V_i}{I_b} = h_{ie} + (h_{fe}+1)R_E \tag{4.60}$$

The overall input impedance Z_i is given by parallel combination of resistor R_B and impedance Z_i'.

$$Z_i = R_B \| Z_i' \tag{4.61}$$

The voltage gain A_v is given by:

$$A_v = \frac{V_o}{V_i} \tag{4.62}$$

The output voltage V_o is given by:

$$V_o = -I_o R_C = -I_c R_C = -h_{fe} I_b R_C \tag{4.63}$$

The base current I_b is given by:

$$I_b = \frac{V_i}{Z_i'} \tag{4.64}$$

Therefore, the magnitude of voltage gain A_v is given by:

$$A_v = -\frac{h_{fe} I_b R_C}{V_i} = -\frac{h_{fe} R_C}{Z_i'} = -\frac{h_{fe} R_C}{h_{ie} + (h_{fe}+1)R_E} \tag{4.65}$$

The magnitude of current gain A_i is given by:

$$A_i = \frac{I_o}{I_i} \tag{4.66}$$

The output current I_o is given by:

$$I_o = I_c = h_{fe} I_b \tag{4.67}$$

The base current I_b is expressed in terms of the input current I_i as eqn. 4.68.

$$I_b = \frac{R_B}{R_B + Z_i'} \times I_i \tag{4.68}$$

The value of the current gain A_i is then given by eqn. 4.69.

$$A_i = \frac{h_{fe} I_b}{I_i} = \frac{h_{fe} R_B}{R_B + Z_i'} = \frac{h_{fe} R_B}{R_B + h_{ie} + (h_{fe}+1)R_E} \tag{4.69}$$

4.3.2.2 Common Base amplifier

Figure-4.23(a) shows the circuit diagram of common-base configuration and Figure-4.23 (b) shows its simplified h-parameter equivalent model.

Input impedance Z_i is given by parallel combination of resistor R_E and parameter h_{ib}. That is,

$$Z_i = R_E \| h_{ib} = R_E \| [h_{ie} / (h_{fe}+1)] \tag{4.70}$$

The output impedance Z_o is equal to the parallel combination of collector resistor R_C and $1/h_{ob}$.

$$Z_o = R_C \| (1/h_{oe}) \cong R_C \tag{4.71}$$

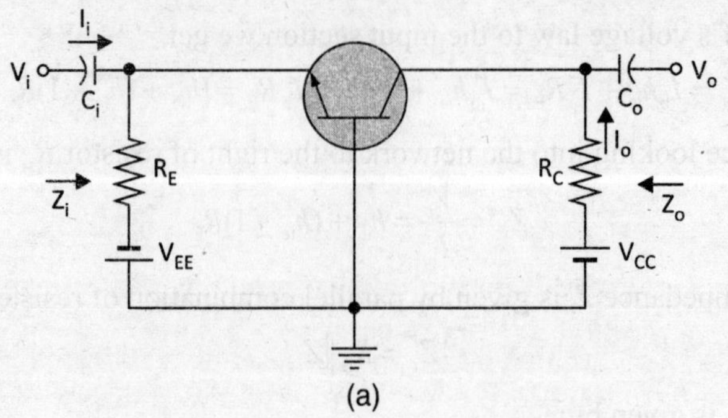

(a)

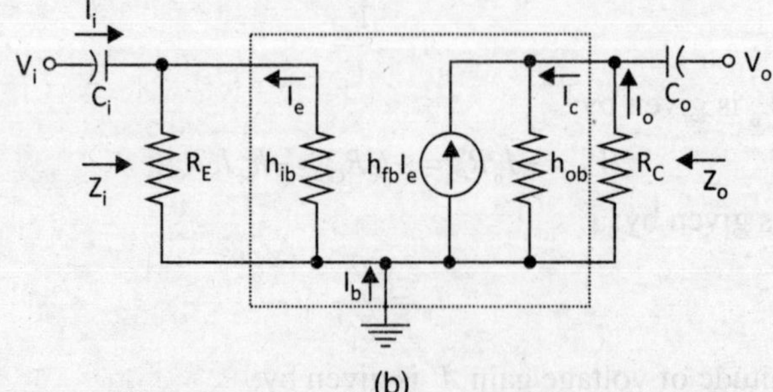

(b)

Fig. 4.23: (a) Circuit diagram of common-base configuration (b) simplified h-parameter equivalent model.

The output voltage V_o is given by:

$$V_o = -I_o R_C = h_{fb} I_e R_C \tag{4.72}$$

The emitter current I_e is expressed in terms of the input voltage V_i as eqn. 4.73.

$$I_e = -\frac{V_i}{h_{ib}} \tag{4.73}$$

Therefore, expression for voltage gain A_v can be written as:

$$A_v = \frac{V_o}{V_i} = \frac{+h_{fb} I_e R_C}{-h_{ib} I_e} = -\frac{h_{fb} R_C}{h_{ib}} = \frac{h_{fe} R_C}{h_{ie}} \tag{4.74}$$

The current gain A_i is given by:

$$A_i = \frac{I_o}{I_i} = \frac{-h_{fb} I_e}{I_i} \tag{4.75}$$

The emitter current I_e is expressed in terms of the input current I_i by:

$$I_e = \frac{-R_E}{R_E + h_{ib}} \times I_i \tag{4.76}$$

Therefore, current gain is given by:

$$A_i = \frac{h_{fb} R_E}{R_E + h_{ib}} = \frac{h_{fb} R_E}{R_E + h_{ie}/(1 + h_{fe})} \cong h_{fb} \tag{4.77}$$

Example-4.6: Refer to Figure-4.24. Determine the value of overall voltage gain V_o/V_s and current gain I_o/I_i.

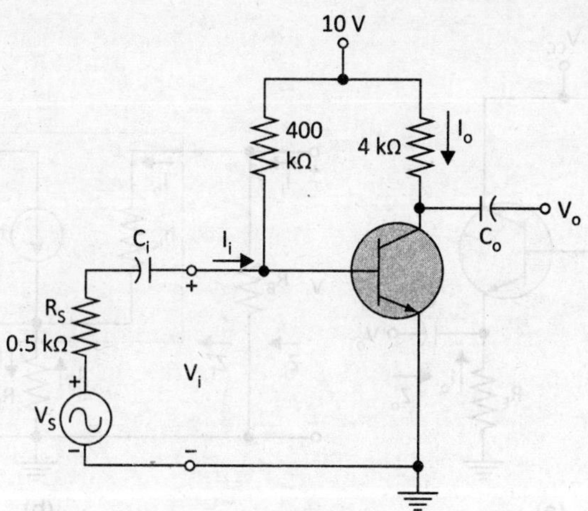

Fig. 4.24: Example-4.6

Voltage gain

$$A_V = \frac{V_o}{V_i} = -h_{fe} \times \frac{R_C \| 1/h_{oe}}{h_{ie}} = -h_{fe} \times \frac{R_C}{h_{ie}} = \frac{-100 \times 4 \times 10^3}{4 \times 10^3} = -400$$

$$A_{VS} = \frac{V_o}{V_s} = \frac{V_o}{V_i} \times \frac{V_i}{V_s} = -400 \times \frac{Z_i}{Z_i + R_s}$$

$$Z_i = R_B \| h_{ie} = 400 \times 10^3 \| 1 \times 10^3 = 0.997 k\Omega$$

$$A_{VS} = -400 \times \frac{997}{997 + 500} = -266.31$$

Current gain

$$A_i = \frac{I_o}{I_i} = \frac{h_{fe} \times R_B}{(R_B + h_{ie})} = \frac{100 \times 400 \times 10^3}{400 \times 10^3 + 1 \times 10^3} = 99.75$$

4.3.2.3 Common Collector amplifier

Figure-4.25(a) shows the emitter-follower configuration and Figure-4.25(b) shows its h-parameter equivalent model.

The input impedance is determined in a similar manner as that for the emitter-bias configuration with unbypassed emitter resistor. The input impedance looking into the network to the right of resistor R_B is given by eqn. 4.78.

$$Z_i' = \frac{V_i}{I_b} = h_{ic} - h_{fc} R_E = h_{ie} + (h_{fe} + 1) R_E \tag{4.78}$$

The overall input impedance Z_i is given by parallel combination of resistor R_B and impedance Z_i'.

$$Z_i = R_B \| Z_i' \tag{4.79}$$

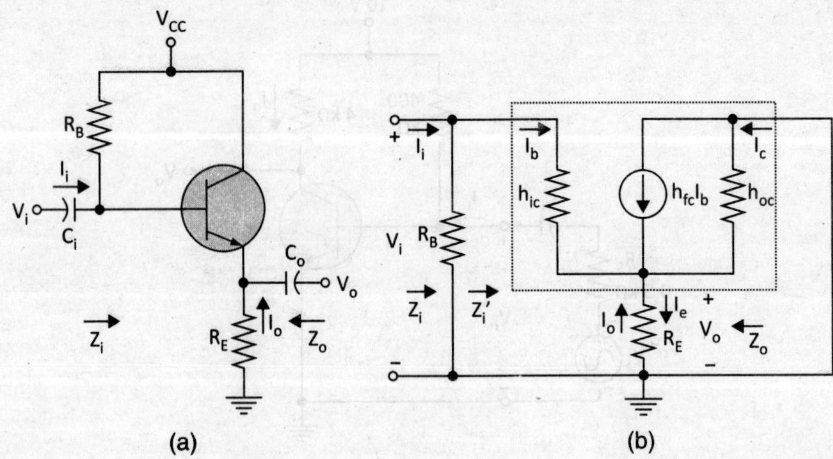

Fig. 4.25: (a) Circuit diagram of emitter-follower configuration (b) simplified h-parameter equivalent model

The output impedance Z_o can be determined as follows.

The base current I_b is given by:

$$I_b = \frac{V_i}{Z_i'} \tag{4.80}$$

The emitter current I_e is then given by:

$$I_e = -h_{fc}I_b = (h_{fe}+1)I_b = (h_{fe}+1)\times\frac{V_i}{Z_i'} \tag{4.81}$$

Substituting the value of Z_i' in the above equation we get,

$$I_e = (h_{fe}+1)\times\frac{V_i}{h_{ie}+(h_{fe}+1)R_E} = \frac{V_i}{h_{ie}/(h_{fe}+1)+R_E} \tag{4.82}$$

Figure-4.26 shows the network defined by eqn. (4.82).

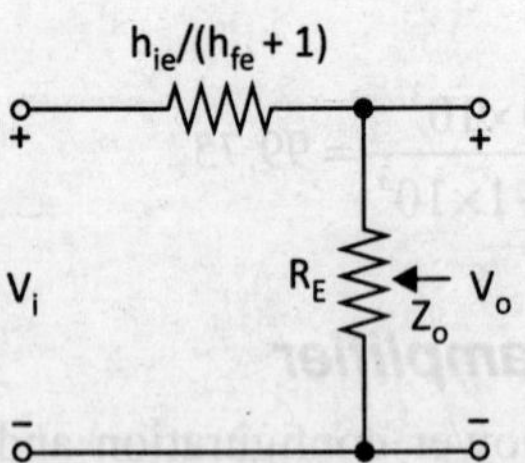

Fig. 4.26: Equivalent network

The output impedance Z_o is defined by setting the input voltage V_i equal to zero. The output impedance Z_o is a parallel combination of resistor R_E and impedance defined by $h_{ie}/(h_{fe}+1)$.

$$Z_o = R_E \,\|\, [h_{ie}/(h_{fe}+1)] \tag{4.83}$$

From Figure-4.26, the output voltage V_o is expressed in terms of the input voltage V_i as:

$$h_{21} = \frac{I_2}{I_1} = -1 \tag{4.84}$$

The voltage gain A_v is then given by:

$$A_v = \frac{V_o}{V_i} = \frac{R_E}{R_E + h_{ie}/(h_{fe}+1)} \tag{4.85}$$

The current gain A_i is given by:

$$A_i = \frac{I_o}{I_i}$$

The output current I_o is given by:

$$I_o = -I_e = h_{fc} I_b = -(h_{fe}+1)I_b$$

From Figure-4.26, the base current I_b is given by:

$$I_b = \frac{R_B}{R_B + Z_i'} \times I_i \tag{4.86}$$

Therefore, A_i is given by:

$$A_i = \frac{-(h_{fe}+1)I_b}{I_i} = \frac{-(h_{fe}+1)R_B}{R_B + Z_i'} \tag{4.84}$$

Example-4.7: A transistor having the following CE h-parameters is to be used as an emitter follower amplifier. Determine (a) The load resistance required to get an input impedance of 300kΩ (b) The overall current gain, voltage gain and power gain if the amplifier is fed from the output of another amplifier having an output impedance of 100kΩ.

h_{ie} = 1000Ω, h_{fe} = 100, h_{oe} = 50μmhos and h_{re} = 0.001

Justify all assumptions made.

Solution: (a) The corresponding CC h-parameters from the given CE h-parameters are given by:

$$h_{ic} = h_{ie} = 1000\Omega$$

$$h_{rc} = (1 - h_{re}) = (1 - 0.001) \cong 1$$

$$h_{fc} = -(1 + h_{fe}) = -101$$

$$h_{oc} = 50 \times 10^{-6}\, mhos$$

The equivalent circuit in CC configuration is given in Figure-4.27.

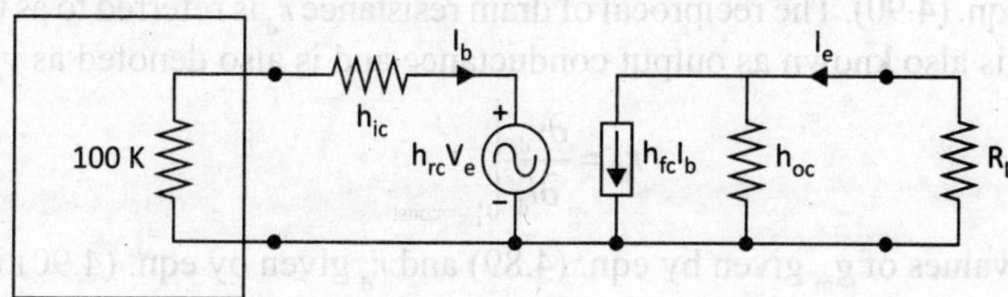

Fig. 4.27: Solution to Example-4.7

The input impedance (R_i) is given by $R_i = h_{ic} + h_{rc} A_i R_L$

Where, the current gain $A_i = -\dfrac{h_{fc}}{1 + h_{oc} R_L}$

Therefore, $R_i = h_{ic} + h_{rc}R_L\left[-\frac{h_{fc}}{1+h_{oc}R_L}\right]$

Substituting the different values, we get the value of load resistance R_L as 3517Ω.

(b) The current gain $A_i = -\frac{h_{fc}}{1+h_{oc}R_L} = -\frac{-101}{1+50\times10^{-6}\times3517} = 86$

The current gain (A_{is}) taking source resistance into account is given by:

$$A_{is} = \frac{A_iR_s}{R_s+R_i} = \frac{86\times100}{100+300} = \frac{86}{4} = 21.5$$

The voltage gain $A_v = \frac{A_iR_L}{R_i} = \frac{86\times3.517}{300} \cong 1$

The voltage gain taking source resistance into account is given by:

$$A_{vs} = \frac{A_vR_i}{R_s+R_i} = \frac{1\times300}{100+300} = 0.75$$

Power gain = Voltage gain × current gain = 0.75 × 21.5 = 16.12

Converting in decibels, we get 12 dB

4.4 SMALL SIGNAL EQUIVALENT CIRCUIT OF FET AMPLIFIERS

The linear small-signal model for FETs can be obtained on similar lines as that for BJTs. The expression for the drain current is given by:

$$I_d = V_{gs}\left.\frac{\partial i_d}{\partial v_{gs}}\right|_{V_{DS}=\text{const.}} + V_{ds}\left.\frac{\partial i_d}{\partial v_{ds}}\right|_{V_{GS}=\text{const.}} \tag{4.88}$$

The parameter g_m is defined as the *transconductance* or the *mutual conductance* and is given by:

$$g_m = \left.\frac{\partial i_d}{\partial v_{gs}}\right|_{V_{DS}=\text{const.}} \tag{4.89}$$

It is also designated as y_{fs} or g_{fs} and is also referred to as forward transadmittance.

The second important parameter used to define the operation of FETs is the *drain resistance* designated as r_d. It is defined by eqn. (4.90). The reciprocal of drain resistance r_d is referred to as the drain conductance (designated as g_d). It is also known as output conductance and is also denoted as y_{os}.

$$r_d = \left.\frac{\partial v_{ds}}{\partial i_d}\right|_{V_{GS}=\text{const.}} \tag{4.90}$$

Substituting the values of g_m given by eqn. (4.89) and r_d given by eqn. (4.90) in eqn. (4.88) we get,

$$I_d = g_mV_{gs} + \frac{1}{r_d}V_{ds} \tag{4.91}$$

The amplification factor *m* of an FET is defined as:

$$\mu = \left.\frac{\partial v_{ds}}{\partial v_{gs}}\right|_{I_D=\text{const.}} \tag{4.92}$$

The parameters g_m, r_d and m are related by the following equation.

$$\mu = r_d g_m \tag{4.93}$$

The low-frequency model of an FET is defined by eqn. (4.91) and is shown in Figure-4.28. As we can see from the figure, it has a Norton's equivalent output circuit with a voltage-dependent current source whose current output is proportional to the gate-source voltage (V_{gs}). Also, the input impedance between the gate and the source terminals is infinite because it is assumed that there is no current flowing through the reverse-biased gate terminal. The above equations and the model in Figure-4.28 are applicable for both JFETs as well as MOSFETs.

When we compare this model of the FET with that of the BJT, we find that there are a few major differences. First, the value of the current generated by the output current source in the case of an FET depends on the input voltage whereas in the case of a BJT it depends upon the input current. Second, in the case of an FET, there is no feedback from the output to the input whereas in the case of a BJT there is feedback between the output and the input circuits through the parameter h_{re}. Lastly, the input impedance of an FET is much larger than that of a BJT. In nutshell, FET iscloser to being an ideal amplifier than a BJT at low frequencies.

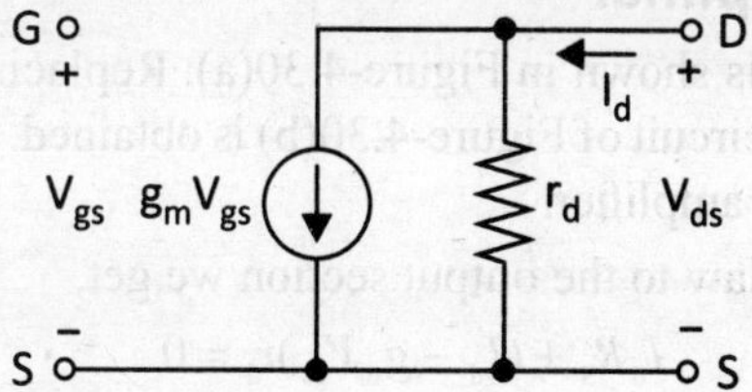

Fig. 4.28: Low-frequency model of an FET

4.4.1 Common Source Amplifier

The common-source FET amplifier is shown in Figure-4.29(a). Replacing the FET by its low-frequency small-signal model, the equivalent circuit of Figure-4.29(b) is obtained.

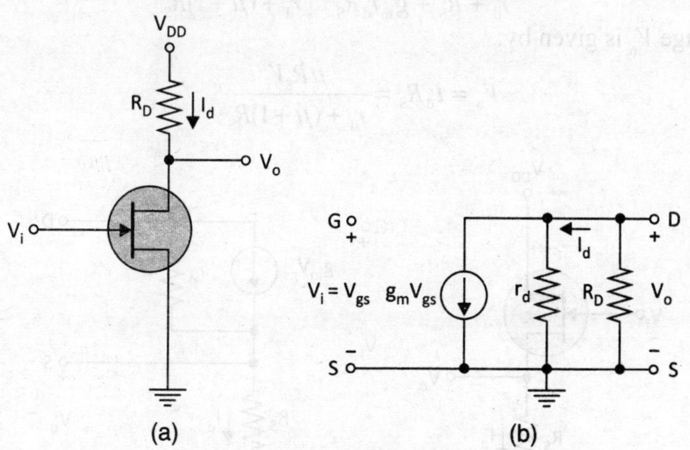

Fig. 4.29: (a) Common-source FET amplifier
(b) low-frequency small-signal equivalent model of the amplifier in (a)

Applying Kirchhoff's voltage law to the output circuit we get

$$I_d R_D + (I_d - g_m V_{gs}) r_d = 0 \tag{4.94}$$

The voltage between the gate and the source terminals (V_{gs}) is equal to the input voltage V_i. Rearranging the terms in equation and substituting $V_{gs} = V_i$, we get,

$$I_d = \frac{g_m r_d V_i}{r_d + R_D} = \frac{\mu V_i}{r_d + R_D} \tag{4.95}$$

The output voltage V_o is given by:

$$V_o = -I_d R_D = -\frac{\mu R_d V_i}{r_d + R_D} \tag{4.96}$$

Therefore, the voltage gain A_v is given by:

$$A_v = \frac{V_o}{V_i} = \frac{\mu R_D}{r_d + R_D} \tag{4.97}$$

For the common-source amplifier with an unbypassed source resistor (R_S), the analysis can be carried out on similar lines and the voltage gain is given by

$$A_v = \frac{\mu R_D}{r_d + R_D + (\mu + 1) R_S} \tag{4.98}$$

4.4.2 Common Drain Amplifier

The common-drain FET amplifier is shown in Figure-4.30(a). Replacing the FET by its low-frequency small-signal model, the equivalent circuit of Figure-4.30(b) is obtained. The analysis is carried on similar lines to that of the common-source amplifier.

Applying Kirchhoff's voltage law to the output section we get,

$$I_d R_S + (I_d - g_m V_{gs}) r_d = 0 \tag{4.99}$$

The gate-source voltage is expressed as:

$$V_{gs} = V_i - I_d R_S \tag{4.100}$$

Combining eqns. (4.99) and (4.100) we get,

$$I_d = \frac{g_m r_d V_i}{r_d + R_S + g_m r_d R_S} = \frac{\mu V_i}{r_d + (\mu + 1) R_S} \tag{4.101}$$

The output voltage V_o is given by:

$$V_o = I_d R_S = \frac{\mu R_S V_i}{r_d + (\mu + 1) R_S} \tag{4.102}$$

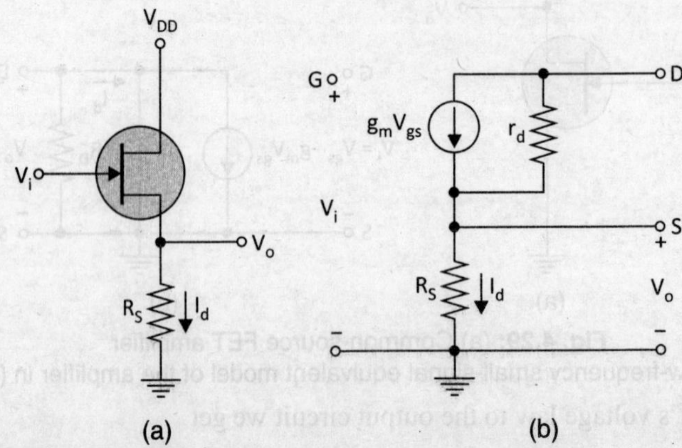

Fig. 4.30: (a) Common-drain amplifier (b) low-frequency small-signal equivalent model

Therefore, the voltage gain A_v is given by:

$$A_v = \frac{V_o}{V_i} = \frac{\mu R_S}{r_d + (\mu+1)R_S} \quad (4.103)$$

For the common-drain amplifier with an unbypassed drain resistor (R_D), the analysis can be carried out on similar lines and the voltage gain is given by:

$$A_v = \frac{\mu R_S}{r_d + R_D + (\mu+1)R_S} \quad (4.104)$$

As the value of μ is very large, therefore the term $(\mu + 1)R_S >> (r_d + R_D)$. Therefore, eqn. (4.104) can by approximated as eqn. 4.105.

$$A_v \cong \frac{\mu R_S}{(\mu+1)R_S} \cong \frac{\mu}{\mu+1} \cong 1 \quad (4.105)$$

Example-4.8: For the self-bias JFET amplifier shown in Figure-4.31, determine the value of (a) Z_i (b) Z_o and (c) A_v. Given that I_{DSS} = 10 mA, V_p = –5 V and r_d = 50 kΩ. The quiescent operating point is V_{GSQ} = –2.5 V and I_{DQ} = 2.5 mA.

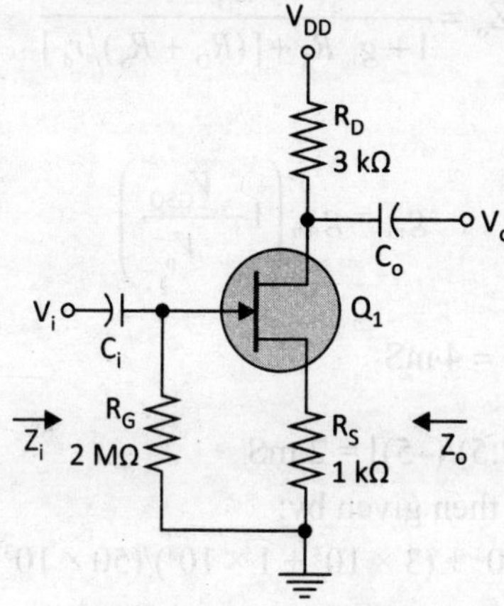

Fig. 4.31: Example-4.8

Solution: The equivalent circuit for the amplifier in Figure-4.31 is given in Figure-4.32.

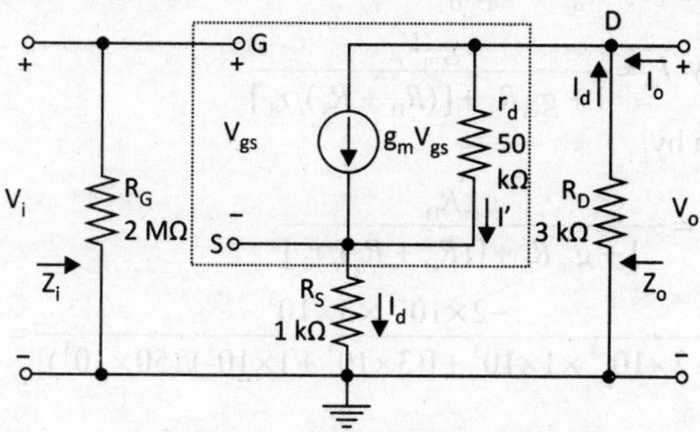

Fig. 4.32: Solution to Example-4.8

The input impedance (Z_i) is given by $Z_i = R_G$. Therefore, Z_i = 2 MΩ.

The output impedance is given by

$$Z_o = \frac{V_o}{I_o}\bigg|_{V_i=0}$$

For $V_i = 0$, the output voltage V_o is defined by $V_o = -I_d R_D$ and the gate-source voltage (V_{gs}) is defined by $V_{gs} = -I_d R_S$.

For $V_i = 0$, the current through resistor r_d is equal to $I' = \frac{V_{rd}}{r_d} = \frac{V_o + V_{gs}}{r_d} = \frac{-I_d(R_D + R_S)}{r_d}$

Applying KCL at the drain node (*D*), $I_d + I_o = I' + g_m V_{gs}$.

Therefore,

$$I_o = -I_d\left(1 + g_m R_S + \frac{R_D + R_S}{r_d}\right)$$

Therefore, Z_o is given by:

$$Z_o = \frac{R_D}{1 + g_m R_S + [(R_D + R_S)/r_d]}$$

The value of g_m is given by:

$$g_m = g_{mo}\left(1 - \frac{V_{GSQ}}{V_P}\right)$$

Now $g_{mo} = \frac{2I_{DSS}}{|V_P|} = \frac{2\times10\times10^{-3}}{5} = 4$ mS

Therefore, $g_m = 4 \times 10^{-3}\,[1 - (-2.5)/(-5)] = 2$ mS

Value of output impedance Z_o is then given by:

$Z_o = 3 \times 10^3/[1 + 2 \times 10^{-3} \times 1 \times 10^3 + (3 \times 10^3 + 1 \times 10^3)/(50 \times 10^3)] = (3 \times 10^3)/(3 + 0.08) = 0.97$ kΩ

Applying KVL to the input section we get $V_{gs} = V_i - I_d R_S$

Applying KCL to the drain node (*D*) we get $I_d = g_m V_{gs} + \frac{V_o - V_{RS}}{r_d}$

Output voltage V_o is given by $V_o = -I_d R_D$.

Therefore, I_d is given by $I_d = \frac{g_m V_i}{1 + g_m R_S + [(R_D + R_S)/r_d]}$

Voltage gain A_v is given by:

$$A_v = \frac{V_o}{V_i} = -\frac{g_m R_D}{1 + g_m R_S + [(R_D + R_S)/r_d]}$$

$$= \frac{-2\times10^{-3}\times3\times10^{3}}{1 + 2\times10^{-3}\times1\times10^{3} + [(3\times10^{3} + 1\times10^{3})/(50\times10^{3})]} = -1.95$$

4.5 FREQUENCY RESPONSE AND EQUIVALENT CIRCUITS OF AMPLIFIERS

As discussed in the earlier part of the chapter, the frequency of the applied input signal has a great effect on the response of the amplifier. The low-frequency response is limited by the coupling and the bypass capacitors as they can no longer be considered as short circuits at these frequencies. The high-frequency response is affected by the stray capacitive elements associated with the active device. Moreover, as the number of amplifier stages increases, the low- and the high-frequency response gets further limited. In the following sections, the low and the high frequency response of the BJT and the FET amplifiers are discussed.

4.5.1 Low Frequency Response and Equivalent Circuits of Amplifiers

In this section, we shall discuss the low-frequency response of the BJT and FET amplifiers.

4.5.1.1 BJT Amplifiers

In the low-frequency region of operation, a BJT or an FET amplifier's response is affected by the R–C combinations formed by the capacitors including the coupling capacitors and bypass capacitors and the resistive elements. The effect of these capacitors on the low frequency response of the BJT amplifier configuration with voltage divider bias is discussed here . The results can be generalized to any BJT amplifier configuration. Figure-4.33 shows the voltage-divider BJT amplifier configuration. C_i is the input-coupling capacitor and is connected between the applied input source and the active device. C_o is the output-coupling capacitor and is connected between the output of the active device and the load.

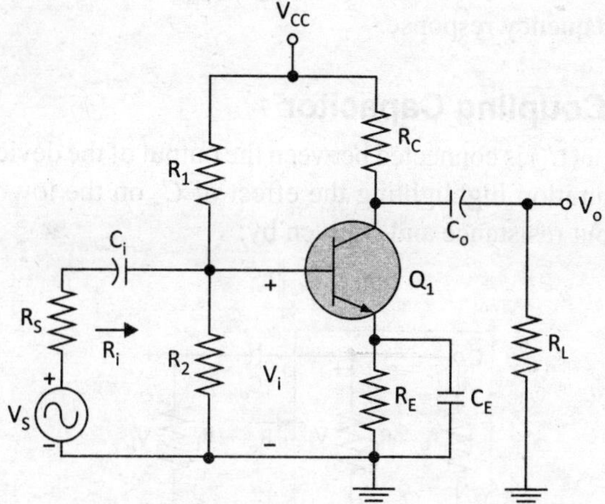

Fig. 4.33: Voltage-divider BJT amplifier configuration

Effect of Input Coupling Capacitor

The capacitor C_i forms an RC network with R_i as shown in Figure-4.34. R_i is the input resistance of the amplifier as seen by the source and is given by parallel combination of R_1, R_2 and h_{ie}:

$$R_i = R_1 \| R_2 \| h_{ie} \quad (4.106)$$

The voltage V_i applied to the input of the active device is calculated by using the voltage-divider rule. Therefore, voltage V_i is given by:

$$V_i = \frac{R_i}{R_s + R_i - jX_{C_i}} \times V_s \quad (4.107)$$

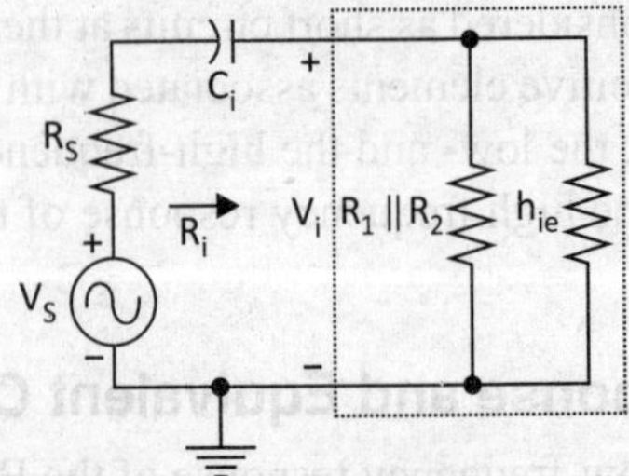

Fig. 4.34: Determining the effect of input-coupling capacitor on the low-frequency response

At mid- and high frequencies, the reactance of capacitors C_i and C_o will be sufficiently small to permit a short-circuit approximation. Therefore, the input voltage at mid-band frequencies ($V_{i\text{-mid}}$) is given by:

$$V_{i\text{-mid}} = \frac{R_i}{R_s + R_i} \times V_s \tag{4.108}$$

The cut-off frequency established by the capacitor C_i is given by:

$$f_{LC_i} = \frac{1}{2\pi(R_i + R_s)C_i} \tag{4.109}$$

At f_{LCi} the voltage V_i will be 0.707 times the voltage $V_{i\text{-mid}}$ assuming that C_i is the only capacitive element effecting the low-frequency response.

Effect of the Output-Coupling Capacitor

The output-coupling capacitor (C_o) is connected between the output of the device and the load. Figure-4.35 shows the simplified configuration highlighting the effect of C_o on the low-frequency response of the amplifier. R_o is the total output resistance and is given by:

$$R_o = R_C \| r_o \tag{4.110}$$

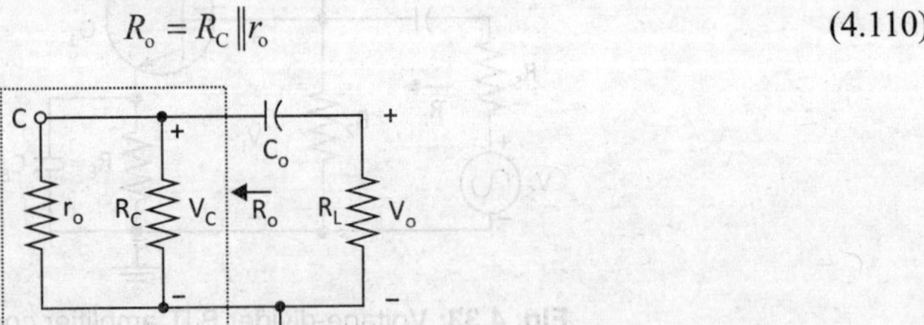

Fig. 4.35: Determining the effect of output-coupling capacitor on the low-frequency response

The cut-off frequency as established by C_o is given by:

$$f_{LC_o} = \frac{1}{2\pi(R_o + R_L)C_o} \cong \frac{1}{2\pi(R_C + R_L)C_o} \tag{4.111}$$

The output voltage V_o will be 70.7% of its mid-band value at the frequency f_{LCo} assuming that C_o is the only capacitive element controlling the low-frequency response.

Effect of Bypass Capacitor

Figure-4.36 shows the network as seen by the bypass capacitor C_E. The value of the equivalent resistance R_e is given by:

$$R_e = R_E \| [(R_s' + h_{ie})/h_{fe}] \tag{4.112}$$

where $R_s' = R_s \| R_1 \| R_2$.

The cut-off frequency as established by resistance R_e and capacitor C_E is given by

$$f_{LC_E} = \frac{1}{2\pi R_e C_E} \tag{4.113}$$

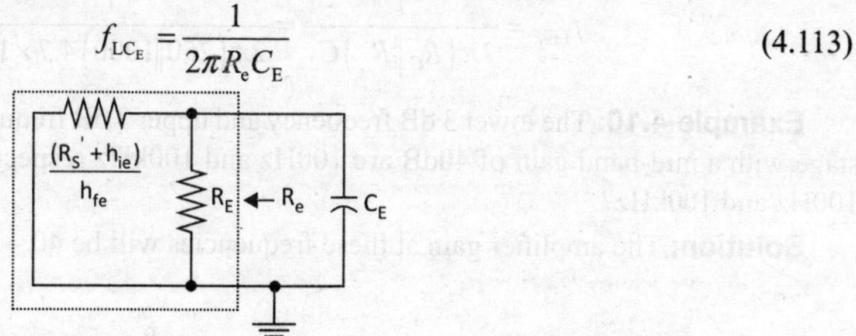

Fig. 4.36: Determining the effect of bypass capacitor on the low-frequency response

The effect of bypass capacitor C_E can be explained qualitatively by considering that at low frequencies the capacitor C_E acts like an open circuit and whole of the resistor R_E appears in the gain equation, resulting in minimum value of gain. As the frequency increases, the reactance of the capacitor C_E decreases resulting in decrease in the value of parallel impedance of resistor R_E and capacitor C_E. The gain is maximum when the impedance of the capacitor C_E reduces so much that it can be considered as a short circuit.

It may be mentioned here that the input- and the output-coupling capacitors and the bypass capacitors affect only the low-frequency response. At the mid-band frequency range, they are considered as short-circuit equivalent and do not affect the gain at these frequencies. If the cut-off frequencies resulting from effect of these capacitors when considered one at a time are far apart, then the highest cut-off frequency due to the three capacitors essentially determines the cut-off frequency of the entire system. If the cut-off frequencies are closer to each other, the effect will be to raise the lower cut-off frequency of the entire system. That is, there is an interaction between the capacitive elements resulting in increased lower cut-off frequency for the entire system.

Example-4.9: Refer to the CE amplifier shown in the Figure-4.37. Given that $\beta = 100$, $g_m = 0.3861$ A/V, $R_S = 1\text{k}\Omega$, $R_B = 93\text{k}\Omega$, $R_C = 250\Omega$, $R_L = 1\text{k}\Omega$, $C_1 = \infty$ and $C_2 = 4.7\mu\text{F}$. Determine the lower cut-off frequencies due to capacitors C_1 and C_2?

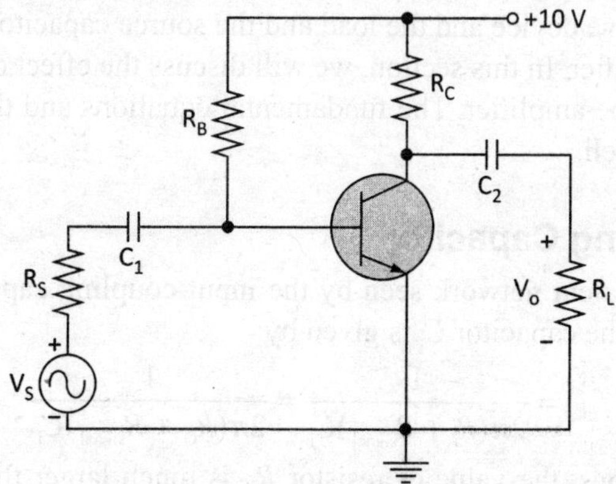

Fig. 4.37: Example-4.9

Solution: As the value of capacitor $C_i = \infty$, therefore the value of lower cut-off frequency due to $C_1 = 0$.

The lower cut-off frequency due to C_2 is given by:

$$f_{LC_2} = \frac{1}{2\pi\left(R_C \| R_L\right)C_2} = \frac{1}{2\pi\left(250\|1000\right)4.7\times10^{-6}} = 27.1Hz$$

Example-4.10: The lower 3 dB frequency and upper 3 dB frequency of a common-emitter amplifier stage with a mid-band gain of 40dB are 100Hz and 100kHz respectively. What is the amplifier gain at 100Hz and 100kHz?

Solution: The amplifier gain at these frequencies will be 40 – 3 = 37dB

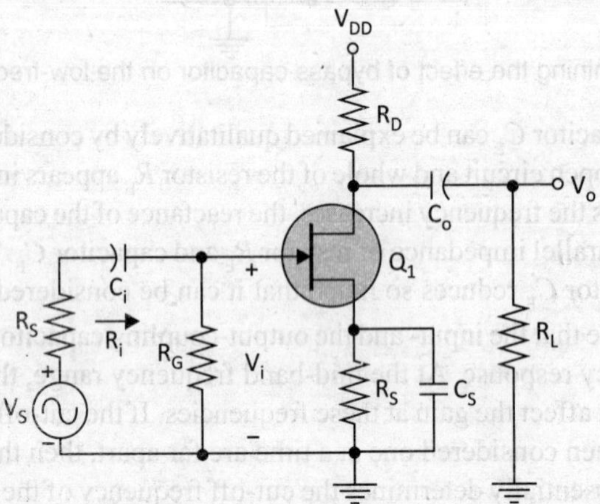

Fig. 4.38: JFET-based amplifier

4.5.1.2 FET Amplifiers

The low-frequency response of FET amplifiers is quite similar to that of BJT amplifiers discussed in the preceding section. In the case of FET amplifiers also, there are three capacitors that affect the low-frequency response, namely, the coupling capacitor C_i between the source and the FET, the coupling capacitor C_o between the active device and the load and the source capacitor C_S. Figure-4.38 shows the circuit of a JFET-based amplifier. In this section, we will discuss the effect of all the three capacitors on the frequency response for the amplifier. The fundamental equations and the procedure apply to other amplifier configurations as well.

Effect of Input-Coupling Capacitor

Figure-4.39 shows the equivalent network seen by the input-coupling capacitor C_i. The lower cut-off frequency as determined by the capacitor C_i is given by:

$$f_{LC_i} = \frac{1}{2\pi(R_i + R_{signal})C_i} = \frac{1}{2\pi(R_G + R_{signal})C_i} \tag{4.114}$$

In most of the applications, the value of resistor R_G is much larger than the value of the resistor R_{signal}. Therefore, the lower cut-off frequency (f_{LCi}) is primarily determined by the values of resistor R_G and capacitor C_i.

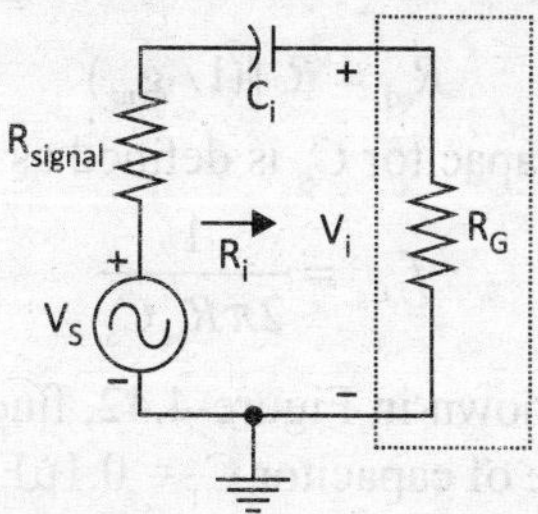

Fig. 4.39: Effect of input-coupling capacitor on the low-frequency response

Effect of Output-Coupling Capacitor

Figure-4.40 shows the network as seen by the output-coupling capacitor. The output resistance (R_o) is determined by:

$$R_o = R_D \| r_d \tag{4.115}$$

The resulting cut-off frequency f_{LCo} is given by:

$$f_{LC_o} = \frac{1}{2\pi(R_o + R_L)C_o} = \frac{1}{2\pi(R_D \| r_d + R_L)C_o} \tag{4.116}$$

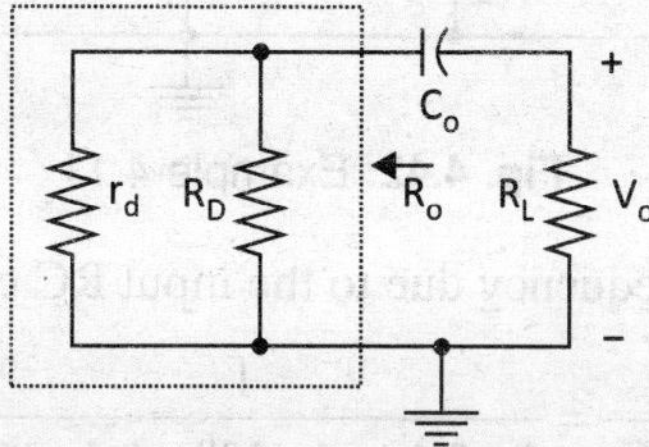

Fig. 4.40: Effect of output-coupling capacitor on the low-frequency response

Effect of Source Capacitor

The equivalent network seen by the source capacitor C_S is shown in Figure-4.41.

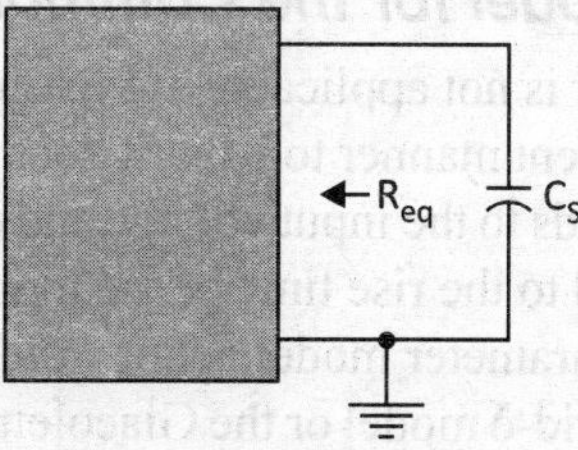

Fig. 4.41: Effect of source capacitor on response the low-frequency

The equivalent resistance as seen by the capacitor C_S is given by:

$$R_{eq} = \frac{R_S(r_d + R_D \| R_L)}{R_S(1 + g_m r_d) + r_d + R_D \| R_L} \tag{4.117}$$

As the value of resistance r_d is very large, assuming $r_d = \infty$ we get,

$$R_{eq} = R_S \| (1/g_m) \tag{4.118}$$

The cut-off frequency due to the capacitor C_S is defined as eqn. 4.119.

$$f_{LC_S} = \frac{1}{2\pi R_{eq} C_S} \tag{4.119}$$

Example-4.11: For the circuit shown in Figure-4.42, find the lower cut-off frequency due to the input RC circuit? (Given that the value of capacitor $C_1 = 0.1\mu F$)

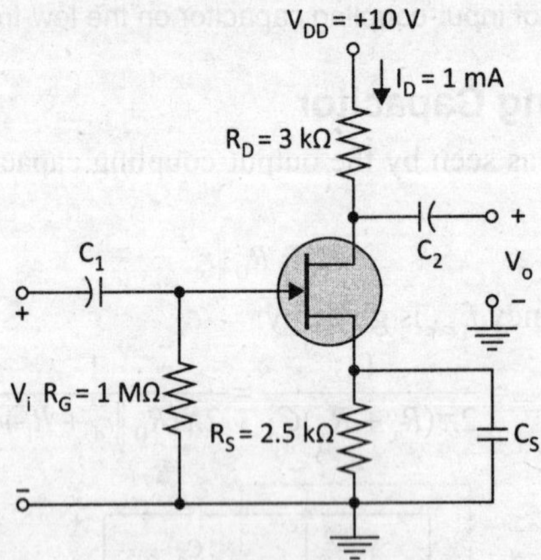

Fig. 4.42: Example-4.11

Solution: The lower cut-off frequency due to the input RC circuit is given by:

$$f_c = \frac{1}{2\pi R_G C_1} = \frac{1}{2\times 3.14\times 1\times 10^6 \times 0.1\times 10^{-6}} = 1.59Hz$$

4.5.2 High Frequency Response and Equivalent Circuits of Amplifiers

In this section are discussed the high frequency response of BJT and MOSFET based amplifier circuits.

4.5.2.1 High-Frequency Model for the Common-Emitter Amplifier

The h-parameter model of a transistor is not applicable at high frequencies because at high frequencies, the transistor behaves in a quite different manner to what it does at low frequencies. At low frequencies, it is assumed that the transistor responds to the input voltage and current instantly as the diffusion time of the carriers is very small as compared to the rise time of the input signal. However, at high frequencies, this is not the case and hence the h-parameter model is not valid at high frequencies. A commonly used method at high frequencies is the hybrid-ð model or the Giacoletto model. This model gives a fairly good approximation of the transistor's behavior at high frequencies.

Figures-4.43(a) and (b) show the circuit of a common-emitter NPN transistor and its hybrid-ð model, respectively. The node B' is an internal node and is not physically accessible. All the components, both capacitive as well as resistive, are assumed to be independent of frequency. They are dependent on the quiescent operating conditions, but under a given bias condition, they do not vary much for small input signal variations.

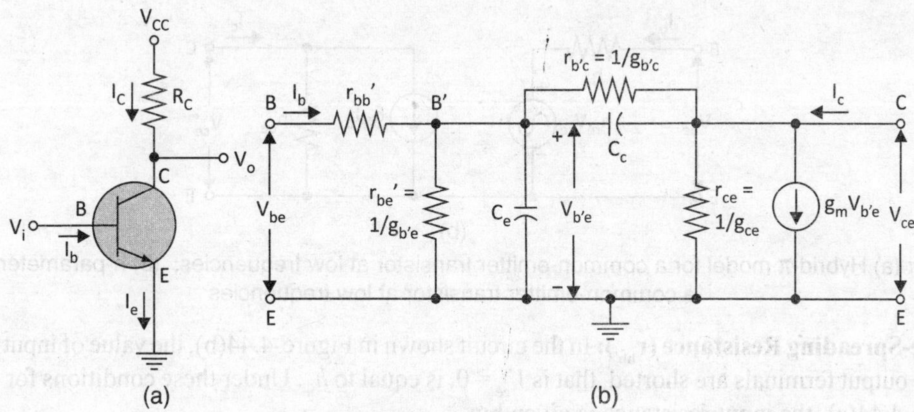

Fig. 4.43: (a) Common-emitter NPN transistor (b) hybrid-π model

Various circuit components are the base-spreading resistance ($r_{bb'}$), conductance between terminals B′ and E ($g_{b'e}$), conductance between terminals C and E (g_{ce}), conductance between terminals B′ and C ($g_{b'c}$), current source between terminals C and E ($g_m V_{b'e}$), collector-junction barrier capacitance (C_c) and diffusion capacitance between terminals B′ and C (C_e). The ohmic base-spreading resistance ($r_{bb'}$) is represented as a lump parameter between the external base terminal (B) and the node B′. The conductance ($g_{b'e}$) considers the increase in the recombination base current due to the increase in the minority carriers in the base region. g_{ce} is the conductance between the collector and the emitter terminals. The conductance ($g_{b'c}$) considers the feedback effect between the output and the input due to Early effect. Early effect results in modulation of the width of the base region due to varying collector-emitter voltage, which in turn causes a change in the emitter and the collector currents as the slope of the minority-carrier distribution in the base region changes.

Small changes in the value of voltage $V_{b'e}$ cause excess minority carriers, proportional to the voltage $V_{b'e}$, to be injected in to the base region. This results in small-signal collector current. Hence, the magnitude of the collector current for shorted collector and emitter terminals is proportional to the voltage $V_{b'e}$. The current generator $g_m V_{b'e}$ considers this effect. Note that g_m is the transconductance of the transistor and C_c is the collector-junction barrier capacitance. Sometimes, this capacitance is split into two parts, namely, the capacitance between C and B′ terminals and the capacitance between C and B terminals. The capacitance between C and B terminals is also referred to as the overlap-diode capacitance. The expressions for different components of the hybrid- π model are derived in terms of h-parameters in the following paragraphs.

Hybrid-π Conductances

Figure-4.44(a) shows the hybrid-π model for a common-emitter transistor amplifier applicable at low frequencies and Figure-4.44(b) shows the h-parameter model for the same. As the hybrid-π model is drawn for low frequencies, the capacitive elements are considered as open circuit.

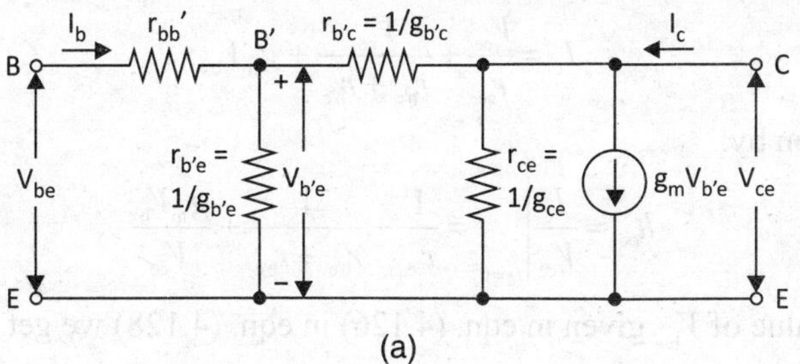

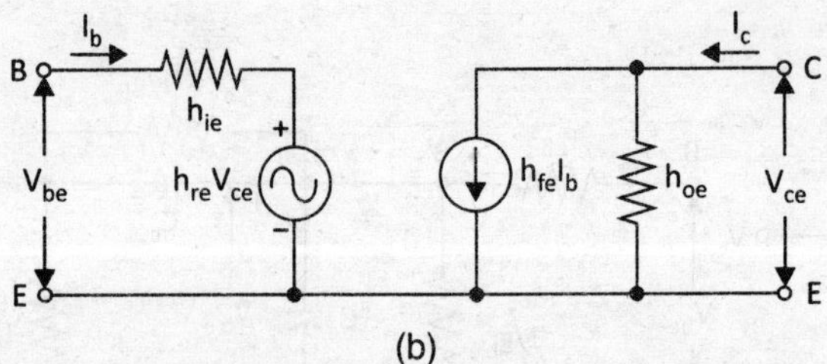

Fig. 4.44: (a) Hybrid-π model for a common-emitter transistor at low frequencies; (b) h-parameter model for a common-emitter transistor at low frequencies

Base-Spreading Resistance ($r_{bb'}$): In the circuit shown in Figure-4.44(b), the value of input resistance when the output terminals are shorted, that is $V_{ce} = 0$, is equal to h_{ie}. Under these conditions for the circuit in Figure-4.44(a), the input resistance is given by:

$$Z_i\Big|_{V_{ce}=0} = r_{bb'} + r_{b'e} \| r_{b'c} \tag{4.120}$$

Therefore

$$h_{ie} = r_{bb'} + r_{b'e} \| r_{b'c} \tag{4.121}$$

As $r_{bc} >> r_{b'e}$, therefore eqn. (4.121) can be approximated as:

$$h_{ie} = r_{bb'} + r_{b'e} \tag{4.122}$$

Conductance between Terminals B′ and C or the Feedback Conductance ($g_{b'c}$): For the circuit in Figure-4.44(b), if the input terminals are open-circuited, then h_{re} is the reverse voltage gain. In terms of the circuit in Figure-4.44(a), the value of h_{re} is given by:

$$h_{re} = \frac{V_{b'e}}{V_{ce}} = \frac{r_{b'e}}{r_{b'e} + r_{b'c}} \tag{4.123}$$

Arranging the terms in eqn. (4.123), we get,

$$r_{b'e}(1 - h_{re}) = h_{re} r_{b'c} \tag{4.124}$$

As the value of h_{re} is in the range of 10^{-4}, that is, $h_{re} << 1$, therefore eqn. (4.124) can be approximated by:

$$r_{b'e} = h_{re} r_{b'c} \quad \text{or} \quad g_{b'c} = h_{re} g_{b'e} \tag{4.125}$$

The equation also verifies that the value of resistance $r_{b'c}$ is much larger than resistance ($r_{b'e}$), that is, $r_{b'c} >> r_{b'e}$.

Conductance between Terminals C and E (g_{ce}): For the circuit in Figure-4.44(b), if the input terminals are open circuit, then

$$V_{b'e} = h_{re} V_{ce} \tag{4.126}$$

For the circuit in Figure-4.44(a), with the input terminals open, that is with $I_b = 0$, the collector current I_c is given by:

$$I_c = \frac{V_{ce}}{r_{ce}} + \frac{V_{ce}}{r_{b'e} + r_{b'c}} + g_m V_{b'e} \tag{4.127}$$

Value of h_{oe} is given by:

$$h_{oe} = \frac{I_c}{V_{ce}}\Big|_{I_b=0} = \frac{1}{r_{ce}} + \frac{1}{r_{b'e} + r_{b'c}} + \frac{g_m V_{b'e}}{V_{ce}} \tag{4.128}$$

Substituting the value of $V_{b'e}$ given in eqn. (4.126) in eqn. (4.128) we get,

$$h_{oe} = \frac{1}{r_{ce}} + \frac{1}{r_{b'e} + r_{b'c}} + g_m h_{re} \tag{4.129}$$

Substituting the value of h_{re} as $g_{b'c}/g_{b'e}$, $1/r_{ce}$ as g_{ce}, $1/r_{b'c}$ as $g_{b'c}$ and assuming that $r_{b'c} >> r_{b'e}$, eqn. (4.129) can be rewritten as eqn. 4.130.

$$h_{oe} = g_{ce} + g_{b'c} + g_m \frac{g_{b'c}}{g_{b'e}} \tag{4.130}$$

We will derive latter that the value of g_m is given by:

$$g_m = h_{fe} g_{b'e} \tag{4.131}$$

Substituting the value of g_m given by eqn. (4.131) in eqn. (4.130), we get

$$h_{oe} = g_{ce} + g_{b'c} + g_{b'c} h_{fe} \tag{4.132}$$

Rearranging the terms in the above equation we get

$$g_{ce} = h_{oe} - (1 + h_{fe}) g_{b'c} \tag{4.133}$$

As the value of $h_{fe} >> 1$, eqn. (4.133) can be approximated as

$$g_{ce} \cong h_{oe} - h_{fe} g_{b'c} \cong h_{oe} - g_m h_{re} \tag{4.134}$$

Conductance between Terminals B′ and E or the Input Conductance ($g_{b'e}$): In the circuit shown in Figure-4.44(a) as the value of resistance ($r_{b'c}$) is much greater than resistance ($r_{b'e}$), most of the current I_b flows into $r_{b'e}$ and the value of the voltage ($V_{b'e}$) is given by:

$$V_{b'e} \cong I_b r_{b'e} \tag{4.135}$$

The short-circuit collector current (I_c) is given by

$$I_c = g_m V_{b'e} \cong g_m I_b r_{b'e} \tag{4.136}$$

The short-circuit current gain (h_{fe}) is defined as:

$$h_{fe} = \left.\frac{I_c}{I_b}\right|_{V_{ce}=\text{const.}} = g_m r_{b'e} \tag{4.137}$$

Rearranging the terms in eqn. (4.137), we get

$$r_{b'e} = \frac{h_{fe}}{g_m} \quad \text{or} \quad g_{b'e} = \frac{g_m}{h_{fe}} \tag{4.138}$$

Transistor's Transconductance (g_m): The transconductance of a transistor (g_m) is defined as the ratio of the change in the value of collector current to change in the value of voltage $V_{b'e}$ for constant value of collector–emitter voltage.

For a common-emitter transistor configuration, the expression for collector current is given by:

$$I_c = I_{CO} + \alpha I_e \tag{4.139}$$

The short-circuit collector current is given by $g_m V_{b'e}$; therefore, the value of g_m is given by

$$g_m = \left.\frac{\partial I_c}{\partial V_{b'e}}\right|_{V_{CE}=\text{const.}} = \alpha \frac{\partial I_e}{\partial V_{b'e}} = \alpha \frac{\partial I_e}{\partial V_e} \tag{4.140}$$

The partial derivative of the emitter voltage with respect to the emitter current (i.e., $\partial V_e/\partial I_e$) can be represented as the emitter diode resistance (r_e). As we know, the dynamic resistance of a forward-biased diode (r_d) is given as:

$$r_d = \frac{V_T}{I_D} \tag{4.141}$$

where V_T is the volt equivalent of temperature and I_D is the diode current. Therefore, the value of g_m can be generalized as

$$g_m = \frac{\alpha I_e}{V_T} = \frac{I_c - I_{CO}}{V_T} \tag{4.142}$$

As the value of $I_c >> I_{CO}$, therefore, the value of g_m for an NPN transistor is positive. For a PNP transistor, the analysis can be carried out on similar lines and the value of g_m in the case of a PNP transistor is also positive. Therefore, the expression for g_m can be written as:

$$g_m = \frac{|I_c|}{V_T} \tag{4.143}$$

Hybrid-π Capacitances

In the hybrid-π model shown in Figure-4.44(b), there are two capacitances namely the collector-junction barrier capacitance (C_c) and the emitter-junction diffusion capacitance (C_e).

Collector-Junction Capacitance (C_c): The capacitance C_c is the output capacitance of the common-base transistor configuration with the input open ($I_E = 0$). It is also specified as C_{ob}. As the collector-base junction is reverse-biased, C_c is the transition capacitance and it varies as V_{CB}^{-n}, where n is 1/2 for abrupt junction and 1/3 for a graded junction.

Emitter-Junction Capacitance (C_e): The capacitance C_e is the diffusion capacitance of the forward-biased emitter junction and is proportional to the emitter-bias current (I_E) and is almost independent of temperature.

4.5.2.2 Variation of Hybrid-π Parameters

The variations in the values of hybrid-π parameters with change in collector current (I_C), collector-emitter voltage (V_{CE}) and temperature (T) are highlighted in Table-4.3.

Table-4.3: Variations in the Values of Hybrid-Π Parameters

Parameter	I_C↑	V_{CE}↑	T↑
g_m	Linear	Independent	Inverse
$r_{bb'}$	Decreases	Complex relation	Increases
$r_{b'e}$	Inverse	Increases	Increases
C_e	Linear	Decreases	Complex relation
C_c	Independent	Decreases	Increases

4.6 COMMON-EMITTER AND COMMON BASE SHORT-CIRCUIT CURRENT GAIN

In continuation of our discussion on high frequency response of BJT amplifiers, in this section, we shall discuss short circuit current gain's upper cut-off frequency and the current gain-bandwidth product for common-emitter and common-base amplifier configurations. Let us first consider a single-stage common-emitter amplifier with the value of the collector resistor (R_C) equal to zero. In this case as the collector resistor acts as the load resistor, this means that the load is a short circuit. Figure-4.45(a) shows the circuit connection and Figure-4.45(b) shows the hybrid-π equivalent model for the circuit. The input source is a sinusoidal source and furnishes a sinusoidal input current I_i. The load current produced is I_L. The equivalent model shown in the figure can be simplified to that shown in Figure-4.45(c). The assumptions made in the simplified model are that the conductance $g_{b'c}$ can be neglected as the value of $g_{b'c} << g_{b'e}$. The conductance g_{ce} has also been removed as it is placed across short-circuited terminals. Another approximation is that the current delivered directly to the output through the conductance $g_{b'c}$ and capacitance C_c has been neglected.

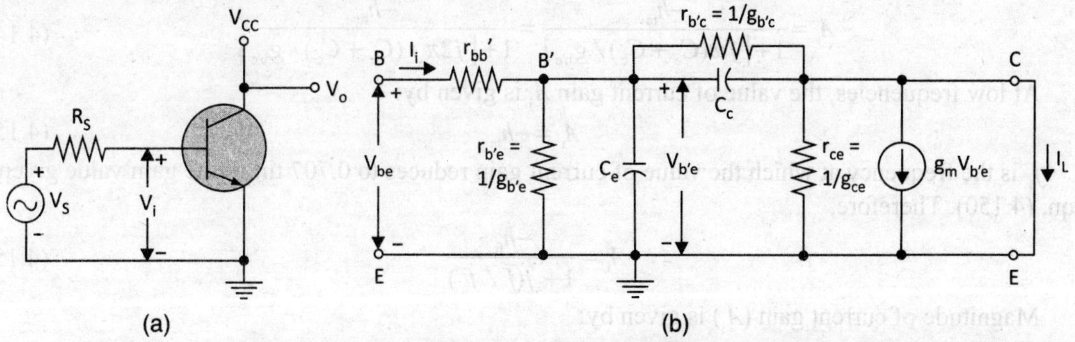

Fig. 4.45: (a) Common-emitter amplifier with short-circuit load (b) hybrid-π equivalent model (c) simplified hybrid-π equivalent model

The parameters of interest are the b-cut-off frequency (f_b) and the short-circuit gain bandwidth product (f_T). f_b is the frequency at which the value of short-circuit common-emitter gain reduces to 0.707 times its mid-band value. In other words, at the b-cut-off frequency, the short-circuit common-emitter current gain is 3 dB below its mid-band value. Thus, f_b represents the maximum attainable current-gain bandwidth for the common-emitter amplifier. The actual maximum bandwidth depends upon the circuit connections. f_T is the frequency at which the short-circuit common-emitter current gain value is unity or 0 dB. The parameter in common-base configuration corresponding to f_b in common-emitter configuration is the a-cut-off frequency f_a. These parameters are briefly described in the following paragraphs.

4.6.1 β-CUT-OFF FREQUENCY

For the circuit shown in Figure-4.45(c), the value of load current (I_L) is given by:

$$I_L = -g_m V_{b'e} \tag{4.144}$$

The value of $V_{b'e}$ is given by:

$$V_{b'e} = \frac{I_i}{g_{b'e} + j\omega(C_e + C_c)} \tag{4.145}$$

The value of current gain (A_i) under short-circuit condition is:

$$A_i = \frac{I_L}{I_i} \tag{4.146}$$

Substituting the values of I_L and I_i given by eqns. (4.144) and (4.145), respectively, in eqn. (4.146) we get,

$$A_i = \frac{-g_m}{g_{b'e} + j\omega(C_e + C_c)} \tag{4.147}$$

Rearranging the terms in eqn. (4.147) we get,

$$A_i = \frac{-g_m / g_{b'e}}{1 + [j\omega(C_e + C_c)/g_{b'e}]} \tag{4.148}$$

From eqn. (4.138) we know that

$$g_{b'e} = \frac{g_m}{h_{fe}}$$

Therefore, the value of current gain A_i is given by

$$A_i = \frac{-h_{fe}}{1+[j\omega(C_e + C_c)/g_{b'e}]} = \frac{-h_{fe}}{1+[j2\pi f(C_e + C_c)/g_{b'e}]} \tag{4.149}$$

At low frequencies, the value of current gain A_i is given by:

$$A_i = -h_{fe} \tag{4.150}$$

f_b is the frequency at which the value of current gain reduces to 0.707 times the gain value given in eqn. (4.150). Therefore,

$$A_i = \frac{-h_{fe}}{1+j(f/f_{\hat{a}})} \tag{4.151}$$

Magnitude of current gain (A_i) is given by:

$$|A_i| = \frac{h_{fe}}{\sqrt{1+(f/f_{\hat{a}})^2}}$$

The value of f_b is given by:

$$f_{\hat{a}} = \frac{g_{b'e}}{2\pi(C_e+C_c)} \tag{4.152}$$

As we can see from eqn. (4.150), the value of A_i is equal to $-h_{fe}$ at zero and low frequencies. Remember that h_{fe} is the low-frequency short-circuit current gain of the common-emitter configuration.

4.6.2 Gain-Bandwidth Product

The frequency f_T is the frequency at which the magnitude of the short-circuit current gain in the common-emitter amplifier becomes unity. As the value of $h_{fe} >> 1$, the magnitude of the current gain A_i becomes unity at the frequency given by the product of h_{fe} and f_b. Therefore, f_T is given by:

$$f_T \cong h_{fe} f \cong \frac{h_{fe} g_{b'e}}{2\pi(C_e+C_c)} \cong \frac{g_m}{2\pi(C_e + C_c)} \tag{4.153}$$

The parameter f_T is a strong function of the collector current of the transistor. The variation of f_T with collector current (I_c) is highlighted in Figure-4.46.

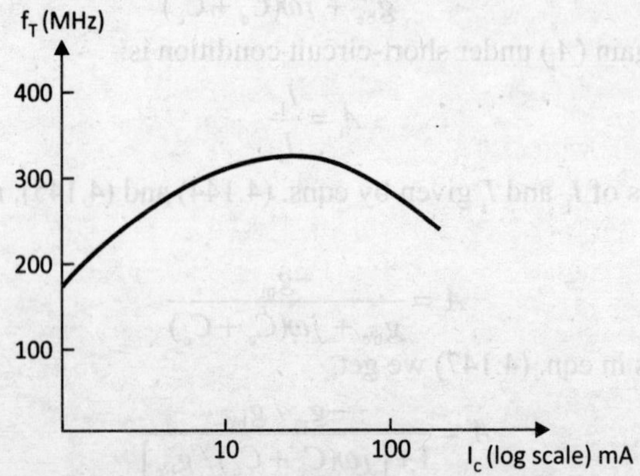

Fig. 4.46: Variation of the frequency f_T with collector current

The expression for current gain A_i can be written as:

$$A_i \cong \frac{-h_{fe}}{1 + jh_{fe}(f / f_T)} \tag{4.154}$$

Figure-4.47 shows the variation of the current gain of a short-circuit common-emitter configuration with frequency. The bold dotted lines indicate the asymptotic curves while the regular bold line shows the actual curve. The two asymptotes intersect each other at $f = f_b$ and the gain thereafter decreases at a rate of 20 dB/decade. The actual gain at $f = f_b$ is 3 dB down (or 0.707 times) the value of mid-band gain.

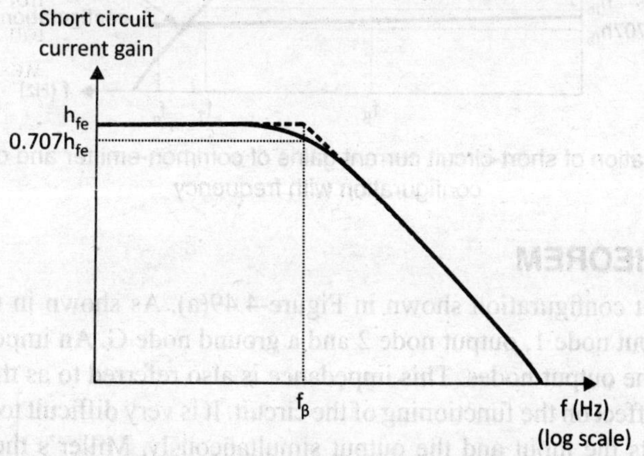

Fig. 4.47: Variation of short-circuit common-emitter current gain with frequency

4.6.3 α-Cut-Off Frequency

The α-cut-off frequency is the frequency at which the short-circuit current gain value in the common-base configuration drops by 3-dB from its value at low frequencies. It is represented as f_{α}. It may be mentioned here that the transistor used in common-base configuration has a much higher value of 3- dB frequency as compared to the transistor used in common-emitter configuration. In other words, the value of f_{α} is much larger than the value of f_{β}.

The expression for the current gain in a common-base configuration is given by eqn. 4.155.

$$A_i = \frac{-h_{fb}}{1 + j(f / f_{\alpha})} \tag{4.155}$$

where f_{α} is the α-cut-off frequency. The expression for the α-cut-off frequency is given by eqn. 4.156.

$$f_{\alpha} = \frac{1}{2\pi r_{b'e}(1 + h_{fb})C_e} \tag{4.156}$$

As the value of $h_{fe} \cong 1/(1 + h_{fb})$, eqn. (4.156) can be rewritten as:

$$f_{\alpha} \cong \frac{h_{fe}}{2\pi r_{b'e} C_e} \tag{4.157}$$

Multiplying and dividing eqn. (4.157) by $(C_e + C_c)$ and substituting the value of f_{β} in the equation, we get,

$$f_{\alpha} \cong \frac{h_{fe} f_{\beta} (C_e + C_c)}{C_e} \tag{4.158}$$

The bandwidth offered by the common-base amplifier is much higher than that offered by a common-emitter amplifier, although the latter has much higher value of gain. Figure- 4.48 shows how the gain of common-emitter and common-base configurations varies with frequency.

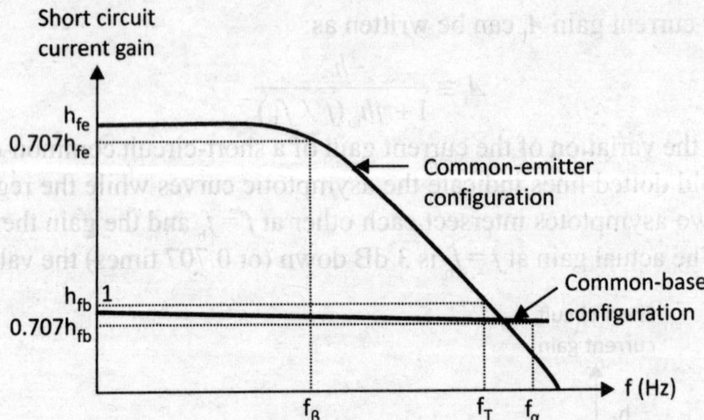

Fig. 4.48: Variation of short-circuit current gains of common-emitter and common-base configuration with frequency

4.7 MILLER'S THEOREM

Let us consider a circuit configuration shown in Figure-4.49(a). As shown in the figure, it comprises three nodes, namely, input node 1, output node 2 and a ground node G. An impedance (Z) is connected between the input and the output nodes. This impedance is also referred to as the feedback impedance. This impedance has an effect on the functioning of the circuit. It is very difficult to analyze such a network as the impedance affects the input and the output simultaneously. Miller's theorem helps to analyze such circuit configurations. According to Miller's theorem, the circuit with feedback impedance can be replaced by an equivalent circuit such that the feedback impedance is split into two impedances: one between the input terminal and the ground (Z_{in}) and the other between the output terminal and the ground (Z_{out}). Figure-4.49(b) shows the Miller's equivalent circuit of the network shown in Figure-4.49(a). In the subsequent paragraphs, we derive the expressions for Z_{in} and Z_{out}.

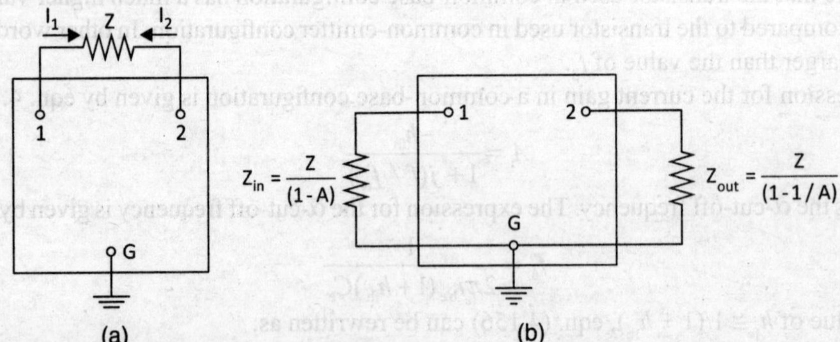

Fig. 4.49: (a) Circuit configuration with feedback impedance (b) Miller's equivalent circuit

Let the voltages at nodes 1 and 2 be V_1 and V_2, respectively. Let the ratio of V_2/V_1 be represented as A. Using Miller's theorem, the impedance connected between nodes 1 and 2 can be replaced by two impedances: one between node 1 and ground node G (Z_{in}) and the other between node 2 and ground node G (Z_{out}).

The value of current I_1 is given by:

$$I_1 = \frac{V_1 - V_2}{Z} \tag{4.159}$$

The value of V_2 is given by $V_2 = AV_1$

Therefore, current I_1 is given by:

$$I_1 = \frac{V_1 - AV_1}{Z} = \frac{V_1(1-A)}{Z} \tag{4.160}$$

From eqn. (4.160), the ratio of V_1/I_1 is given by:

$$\frac{V_1}{I_1} = \frac{Z}{1-A} \tag{4.161}$$

V_1/I_1 is the equivalent impedance of Z as seen from the input side of the circuit. Therefore, Z_{in} is equal to the ratio V_1/I_1 and is given by

$$Z_{in} = \frac{Z}{1-A} \tag{4.162}$$

The impedance Z_{in} appears in parallel with the input terminals of the network.

The expression for output impedance Z_{out} can be derived as follows. The value of current I_2 is given by

$$I_2 = \frac{V_2 - V_1}{Z} \tag{4.163}$$

Voltage V_1 is expressed in terms of voltage V_2 as:

$$V_1 = \frac{V_2}{A}$$

Substituting this value of V_1 in eqn. (4.163) we get,

$$I_2 = \frac{V_2 - (V_2/A)}{Z} = \frac{V_2[1-(1/A)]}{Z} \tag{4.164}$$

The ratio V_2/I_2 is given by:

$$\frac{V_2}{I_2} = \frac{Z}{[1-(1/A)]} \tag{4.165}$$

The ratio V_2/I_2 is the equivalent impedance of Z as seen from the output terminals. It is therefore equal to Z_{out}. The expression for Z_{out} is given by:

$$Z_{out} = \frac{Z}{1-(1/A)} \tag{4.166}$$

Example 4.12: For the circuit shown in Figure-4.50, determine the values of following parameters: (a) R_i (b) $R_{i'}$ (c) amplifier voltage gain (A_v) (d) system voltage gain (A_{vs}) (e) amplifier current gain (A_i) and (f) system current gain ($A_{i'}$). The value of transistor's h-parameters are $h_{ie} = 1$ kΩ, $h_{re} = 1 \times 10^{-4}$, $h_{fe} = 100$ and $h_{oe} = 25 \times 10^{-6}\Omega^{-1}$.

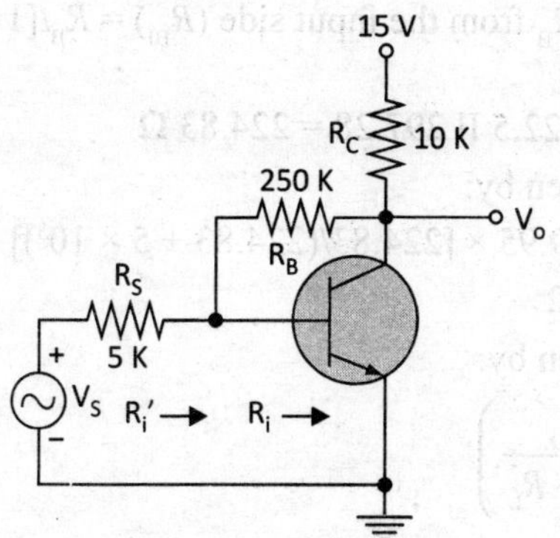

Fig. 4.50: Example-4.12

Solution: The resistor R_B can be replaced by the Miller's equivalent components as shown in Figure-4.51 as itis the feedback resistor between the input and the output terminals.

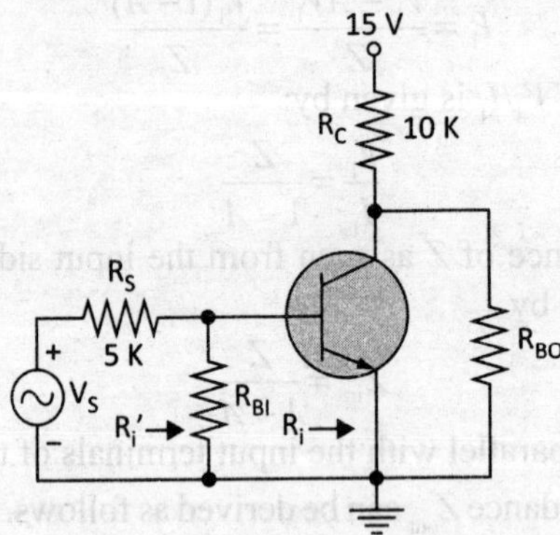

Fig. 4.51: Solution to Example-4.12

The equivalent impedance of R_B as seen from the output terminals (R_{BO}) is given by $R_B/[1-(1/A_v)]$. A_v is the voltage gain from base to collector. As the value of voltage gain is much larger than 1, therefore, value of $R_{BO} \cong R_B$ @ 250 kΩ.

The effective load resistance $(R_L') = R_C$ II R_{BO} = 10 × 10³ II 250 × 10³ = 9.61 × 10³ Ω = 9.61 kΩ.

Current gain A_i is given by:

$$A_i = -\frac{h_{fe}}{1+h_{oe}R_L'} = \frac{-100}{1+25\times10^{-6}\times9.61\times10^3} = \frac{-100}{1.24} = -80.63$$

Input resistance R_i is given by:

$$R_i = h_{ie} - \frac{h_{re}h_{fe}R_L'}{1+h_{oe}R_L'}$$

$$= 1\times10^3 - \frac{1\times10^{-4}\times100\times9.61\times10^3}{1+25\times10^{-6}\times9.61\times10^3} = 1000 - \frac{96.1}{1.24} = 1000 - 77.5 = 922.5\ \Omega$$

Voltage gain A_V is given by:

$$A_v = \frac{A_i R_L'}{R_i} = \frac{-80.63\times9.61\times10^3}{922.5} = -839.95$$

Effective value resistance of R_B from the input side $(R_{BI}) = R_B/[1-A_v]$ = 250 × 10³/ [1 – (-839.95)] = (250 × 10³)/840.95 = 297.28 Ω

The value of $R_i' = R_i$ II R_{BI} = 922.5 II 297.28 = 224.83 Ω

System voltage gain A_{vs} is given by:

$A_{vs} = A_v \times [R_i'/(R_i' + R_s)]$ = -839.95 × [224.83/(224.83 + 5 × 10³)]

= -839.95 × 0.043 = -36.12

System current gain A_i' is given by:

$$A_i' = A_i \times \left(\frac{R_{RI}}{R_i + R_{BI}}\right) \times \left(\frac{R_{BO}}{R_{BO} + R_L}\right)$$

$$= -80.63 \times \frac{297.28}{922.5 + 297.28} \times \frac{250 \times 10^3}{250 \times 10^3 + 10 \times 10^3} = -80.63 \times \frac{297.28}{1219.78} \times \frac{250}{260}$$

$$= -80.63 \times 0.244 \times 0.96 = -18.89$$

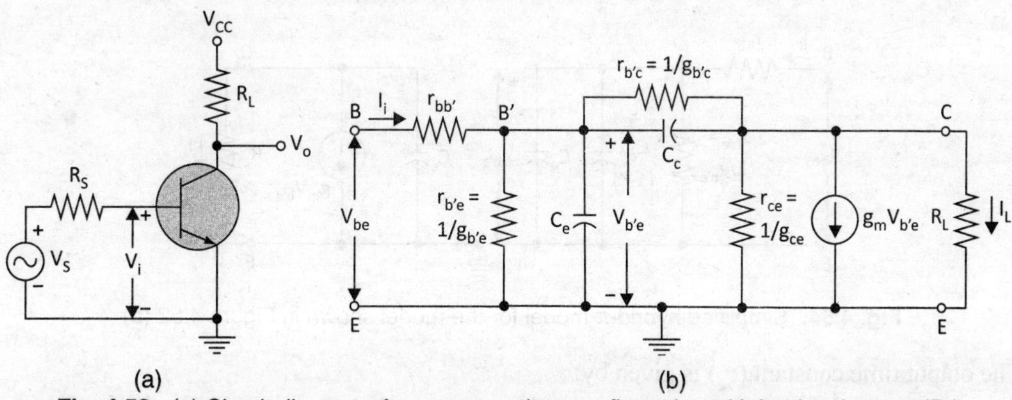

Fig. 4.52: (a) Circuit diagram of common-emitter configuration with load resistance (R_L)
(b) hybrid-π equivalent model

4.8 COMMON-EMITTER CURRENT GAIN WITH RESISTIVE LOAD

Figure-4.52(a) shows the circuit diagram of the common-emitter configuration with load resistor (R_L) and Figure-4.52(b) shows its hybrid-π equivalent model. The conductance $g_{b'c}$ can be replaced by its Miller's equivalent components. The conductance component due to $g_{b'c}$ on the input side is given by $g_{b'c}$ (1 – K), where K = $V_{ce}/V_{b'e}$. The value of K is equal to $-g_m R_L$. The conductance component due to $g_{b'c}$ on the output side is given by $g_{b'c}$ [(K – 1)/K]. The Miller's component of the capacitance C_c on the input side is given by C_c (1 – K) and on the output side is given by C_c [(K – 1)/K]. Figure-4.53 shows the equivalent circuit with components $g_{b'c}$ and C_c being replaced by their Miller's equivalent components.

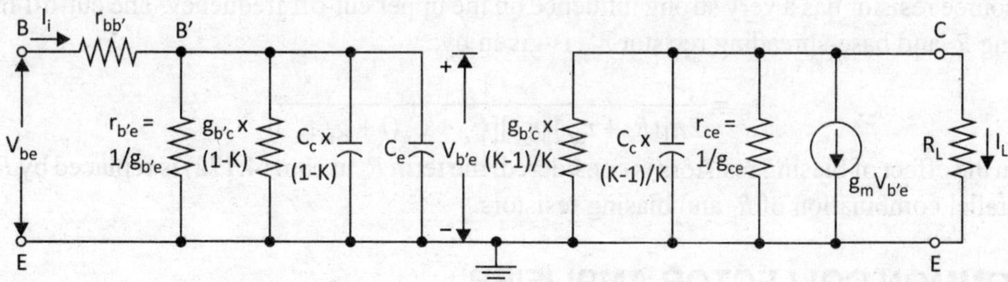

Fig. 4.53: Hybrid-π model making use of Miller's theorem for the model shown in Figure-4.52(b)

The circuit has two time constants, one associated with the input section and the other associated with the output section. As the value of $K >> 1$, therefore the value of $[(K-1)/K] \cong 1$. Therefore, $g_{b'c}$ $[(K-1)/K] \cong g_{b'c}$ and $C_c\ [(K-1)/K] \cong C_c$. The total load resistance R_L' is given by

$$R_L' = R_L \| (1/g_{b'c}) \| (1/g_{ce}) \tag{4.167}$$

In most cases, the value of $g_{b'c} << g_{ce}$ ($r_{b'c}$ » 4–5 MΩ and $r_{ce} \approx$ 80–100 kW), therefore $g_{b'c}$ can be ignored from the output section. The value of load resistor R_L is in the range of 2–5 kΩ. Therefore, the conductance g_{ce} can be neglected as compared to $1/R_L$. Therefore, resistor $R_L' \cong R_L$.

The input conductance (g_i) is given by:

$$g_i = g_{b'e} + g_{b'c}(1-K) \tag{4.168}$$

In most of the cases, the magnitude of the capacitance $g_{b\not{c}c}(1 - K)$ is very small as compared to the value of $g_{b'e}$. Therefore, $g_i \cong g_{b'e}$. Figure-4.54 shows the further simplified hybrid-π equivalent model.

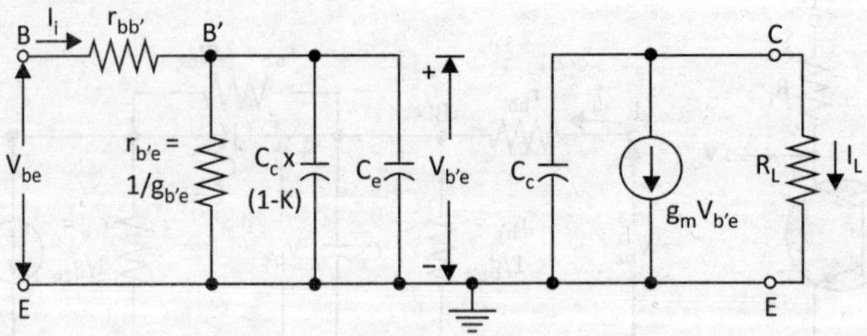

Fig. 4.54: Simplified hybrid-π model for the model shown in Figure-4.52 (b)

The output time constant (t_{oc}) is given by:

$$t_{oc} = R_L' C_c \approx R_L C_c \tag{4.169}$$

The input time constant (t_{ic}) is given by:

$$t_{ic} = (1/g_i) \times [C_e + C_c(1 + g_m R_L)] \approx (1/g_{b'e}) \times [C_e + C_c(1 + g_m R_L)] \tag{4.170}$$

In practical situations, the output time constant is negligible as compared to the input time constant and hence can be ignored. It may be mentioned here that if the transistor works into a highly capacitive load, then the output time constant will also be predominant and cannot be ignored.

The upper 3 dB frequency in this case is given by:

$$f_H = \frac{1}{2\pi r_{b'e}[C_e + C_c(1 + g_m R_L)]} \tag{4.171}$$

The above equation has been derived by neglecting the effect of the source resistance (R_s). The value of source resistor has a very strong influence on the upper cut-off frequency. The cut-off frequency considering R_s and base-spreading resistor $r_{bb'}$ is given by:

$$f_H = \frac{1}{2\pi[(R_s + r_{bb'}) \| r_{b'e}][C_e + C_c(1 + g_m R_L)]} \tag{4.172}$$

When the effect of biasing resistors is considered, the term R_s in eqn. (4.172) is replaced by $R_{s'}$, where $R_{s'}$ is a parallel combination of R_s and biasing resistors.

4.9 COMMON COLLECTOR AMPLIFIER

In this section, we discuss the high-frequency response of a common-collector transistor amplifier. Figure-4.55(a) shows the common-collector transistor amplifier. Capacitance C_L is included in parallel with the load resistor R_L as the common-collector transistor due to its low output resistance is often used to drive capacitive loads. Figure-4.55(b) shows the hybrid-ð equivalent model for the common-collector amplifier shown in Figure-4.55(a).

Applying Miller's theorem to the hybrid-π equivalent circuit of Figure-4.55(b), we get the equivalent circuit as shown in Figure-4.55(c). The parameter K is given by the ratio of voltages V_{ec} and $V_{b'c}$ (i.e., $K = V_{ec}/V_{b'c}$). The input time constant t_{ic} is given by:

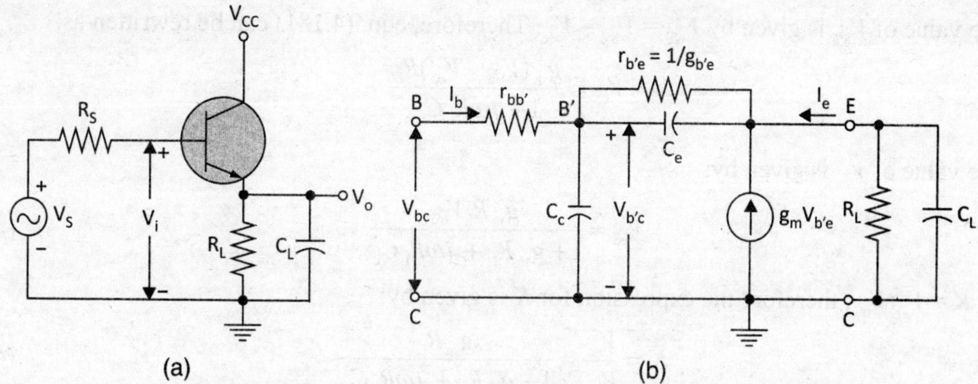

Fig. 4.55: (a) Common-collector amplifier (b) hybrid-π equivalent model of the common-collector amplifier (c) simplified hybrid-π equivalent model of the common-collector amplifier

$$t_{ic} = \left[(R_s + r_{bb'}) \left\| \left\{ \frac{1}{g_{b'e}(1-K)} \right\} \right. \right] [C_c + C_e(1-K)] \tag{4.173}$$

As the low-frequency gain of the emitter–follower configuration is approximately equal to unity, therefore $(1 - K) \cong 0$. Therefore, the expression for t_{ic} can be approximated by:

$$t_{ic} \cong (R_s + r_{bb'})C_c \tag{4.174}$$

The output time constant (t_{oc}) is given by:

$$t_{oc} = \left[R_L \left\| \left\{ \frac{1}{g_{b'e}(K-1)/K} \right\} \right. \right] [C_L + C_e(K-1)/K] \tag{4.175}$$

As the value of $(K - 1) \cong 0$, the above equation can be simplified as:

$$t_{oc} \cong R_L C_L \tag{4.176}$$

As we have assumed that the output load is highly capacitive, therefore the value of $C_L >> C_c$. Hence,

$$R_L C_L >> (R_s + r_{bb'})C_c \tag{4.177}$$

This implies that the value of output time constant (t_{oc}) is much larger than the input time constant (t_{ic}). Hence the upper 3 dB frequency is determined mostly by the output circuit alone.

The impedance of the output circuit (Z_o) is given by:

$$Z_o = R_L \left\| \frac{1}{g_{b'e}(K-1)/K} \right\| \frac{1}{j\omega\{C_L + C_e(K-1)/K\}} \tag{4.178}$$

Substituting $(K - 1) \cong 0$, we get,

$$Z_o \cong R_L \left\| \frac{1}{j\omega C_L} \right. \tag{4.179}$$

The value of voltage V_{ec} is given by:

$$V_{ec} = g_m V_{b'e} Z_o \cong g_m V_{b'e} \left(R_L \left\| \frac{1}{j\omega C_L} \right. \right) \tag{4.180}$$

Rearranging the terms, we get,

$$V_{ec} = \frac{g_m V_{b'e}}{(1/R_L) + j\omega C_L} = \frac{g_m V_{b'e} R_L}{1 + j\omega R_L C_L} \tag{4.181}$$

The value of $V_{b'e}$ is given by $V_{b'e} = V_{b'c} - V_{ec}$. Therefore, eqn. (4.181) can be rewritten as:

$$V_{ec} = \frac{g_m (V_{b'c} - V_{ec}) R_L}{1 + j\omega R_L C_L}$$

The value of V_{ec} is given by:

$$V_{ec} = \frac{g_m R_L V_{b'c}}{1 + g_m R_L + j\omega R_L C_L} \tag{4.182}$$

As $K = V_{ec}/V_{b'c}$, therefore the expression for K is given by:

$$K = \frac{V_{ec}}{V_{b'c}} = \frac{g_m R_L}{1 + g_m R_L + j\omega R_L C_L} \tag{4.183}$$

Multiplying and dividing eqn. (4.183) by $(1 + g_m R_L)$ we get

$$A = \left(\frac{g_m R_L}{1 + g_m R_L}\right) \frac{1}{1 + [j\omega R_L C_L / (1 + g_m R_L)]} \tag{4.184}$$

Eqn. (4.184) can be rewritten as eqn. (4.185).

$$A = \left(\frac{g_m R_L}{1 + g_m R_L}\right)\left(\frac{1}{1 + (jf / f_H)}\right) \tag{4.185}$$

where $f_H = (1 + g_m R_L)/2\pi C_L R_L$

The value of f_H can be expressed as:

$$f_H = \frac{1 + g_m R_L}{2\pi R_L C_L} \cong \frac{g_m}{2\pi C_L} \tag{4.186}$$

The value of unity gain bandwidth (f_T) is given by:

$$f_T = \frac{g_m}{2\pi (C_e + C_c)} \tag{4.187}$$

As the value of C_e for a transistor is much larger than C_c, therefore f_T can be approximated by:

$$f_T \cong \frac{g_m}{2\pi C_e} \tag{4.188}$$

Substituting this value of f_T in eqn. (4.186) we get,

$$f_H \cong \frac{f_T C_e}{C_L} \tag{4.189}$$

Since the input impedance between terminals B′ and C is much large as compared to $(R_s + r_{bb'})$, therefore K is approximately the overall voltage gain (A_{VS}), that is,

$$K \cong A_{VS} = \frac{V_{ec}}{V_s} \tag{4.190}$$

4.10 HIGH-FREQUENCY RESPONSE OF AN FET AMPLIFIER

The high-frequency response of an FET amplifier is similar to that of a BJT amplifier. Figure-4.56 shows the high-frequency model for an FET, which is also valid for a MOSFET. The high-frequency model is similar to the low-frequency model with the addition of junction capacitances.

The capacitance C_{gs} represents the barrier capacitance between the gate and the source terminals. C_{gd} is the barrier capacitance between the gate and the drain terminals. C_{ds} is the drain-to-source capacitance of the channel. These capacitors offer high impedance at lower frequencies and can be considered as open circuit. However, at high frequencies, due to these capacitances feedback exists between the input and output circuits and voltage amplification drops rapidly as the frequency increases.

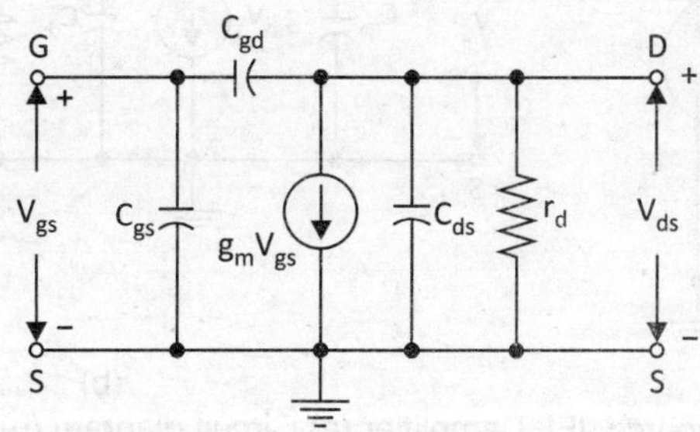

Fig. 4.56: High-frequency model of an FET

In this section, we shall discuss the high-frequency response of the common-source and common-drain FET amplifiers. The derivations are done for a JFET. The expressions derived here apply equally well to MOSFET-based amplifiers.

4.10.1 Common Source amplifier

Figure-4.57(a) shows the circuit diagram for the common-source JFET amplifier and Figure-4.57(b) shows its high-frequency equivalent model. The output voltage V_o is given by the product of short-circuit current (I) and the impedance seen among the output terminals (Z). Therefore,

$$V_o = ZI \tag{4.191}$$

Z is determined by shorting the input terminals, that is, $V_s = 0$. Hence, there is no current flowing through the current generator g_mV_s. Therefore, the value of Z is given by the parallel combination of R_L, C_{ds}, r_d and C_{gd} and is given by:

$$Y = \frac{1}{Z} = G_L + Y_{ds} + g_d + Y_{gd} \tag{4.192}$$

where $G_L = 1/R_L$ is the conductance corresponding to load R_L. If the load is represented by an impedance Z_L, then G_L will be replaced by Y_L (Y_L is the admittance corresponding to impedance Z_L). Also, $Y_{ds} = jwC_{ds}$ is the admittance corresponding to C_{ds}; $g_d = 1/r_d$ is the conductance corresponding to r_d; $Y_{gd} = jwC_{gd}$ is the admittance corresponding to C_{gd}.

The current I flowing from the drain to the source terminal with output terminals shorted is given by:

$$I = -g_mV_s + V_sY_{gd} \tag{4.193}$$

Therefore, the output voltage V_o is given by:

$$V_o = \frac{(-g_m + Y_{gd})V_s}{G_L + Y_{ds} + g_d + Y_{gd}} \tag{4.194}$$

The value of voltage gain (A_v) is therefore given by:

$$A_v = \frac{V_o}{V_s} = \frac{-g_m + Y_{gd}}{G_L + Y_{ds} + g_d + Y_{gd}} \tag{4.195}$$

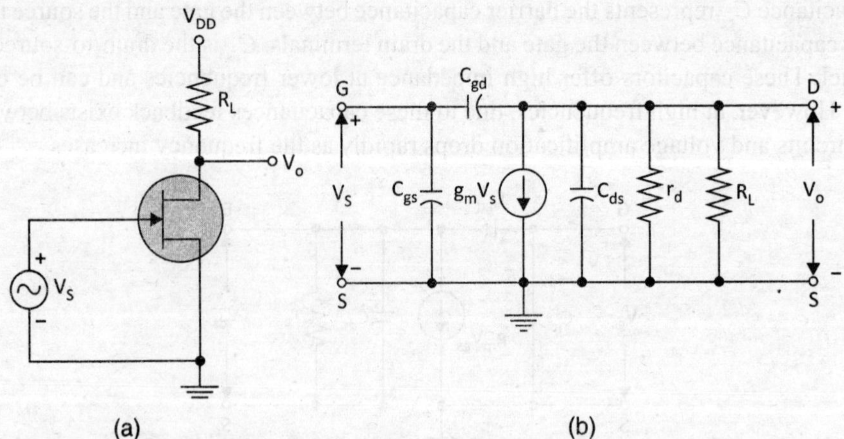

Fig. 4.57: Common-source JFET amplifier (a) Circuit diagram (b) high-frequency model

At low frequencies, the FET capacitances can be neglected and hence $Y_{ds} = Y_{gd} = 0$. Therefore, the value of gain at low frequencies is given by:

$$A_v = \frac{-g_m}{G_L + g_d} = \frac{-g_m R_L r_d}{R_L + r_d} = -g_m R_L' \tag{4.196}$$

where $R_L' = R_L \| r_d$.

The input admittance and the input capacitance can be calculated as follows. As it is evident from Figure-4.57(b) that there is a coupling between the gate and the drain terminals through capacitance C_{gd}. The admittance offered by the capacitance (Y_{gd}) can be replaced by $Y_{gd}(1 - A_V)$ between the gate and the source terminals and by $Y_{gd}[1 - (1/A_V)]$ between the drain and the source terminals. The input admittance (Y_i) is therefore given by:

$$Y_i = Y_{gs} + (1 - A_V)Y_{gd} = Y_{gs} + (1 + g_m R_L')C_{gd} \tag{4.197}$$

The input capacitance (C_i) is given by:

$$C_i = C_{gs} + (1 - A_V)C_{gd} = C_{gs} + (1 + g_m R_L')C_{gd} \tag{4.198}$$

This input capacitance is important in the case of cascaded amplifiers where the input impedance of a stage acts in parallel with the output impedance of the preceding stage. As the reactance of a capacitance decreases with frequency, the input impedance decreases and hence the gain of the cascaded amplifier also decreases with increase in frequency.

The output is obtained by the impedance looking into the drain and the source terminals, with the input voltage (V_i) set equal to zero. With $V_i = 0$, the resistance r_d and capacitances C_{ds} and C_{gd} are in parallel. Therefore, the output admittance (Y_o) is given by:

$$Y_o = g_d + Y_{ds} + Y_{gd} \tag{4.199}$$

4.10.2 Common Drain amplifier

Figure-4.58(a) shows the circuit of a common-drain or a source-follower amplifier. Figure-4.58(b) shows its small-signal high-frequency equivalent circuit.

The output voltage V_o is given by the product of the short-circuit current and the impedance between the source and the ground terminals. By carrying out analysis in a manner similar to that for the common-source amplifier, the expression for the voltage gain (A_v) for a common-drain amplifier is given by:

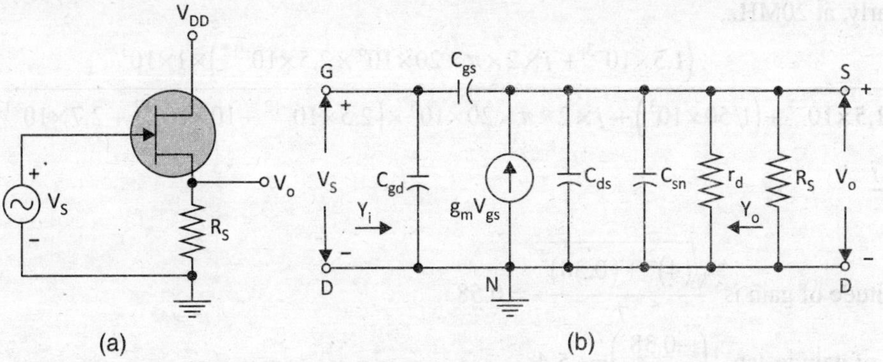

Fig. 4.58: Common-drain amplifier (a) circuit diagram (b) small-signal equivalent

$$A_v = \frac{(g_m + j\omega C_{gs})R_s}{1+[g_m + g_d + j\omega(C_{gs} + C_{ds} + C_{sn})]R_s} \tag{4.200}$$

At low frequencies, the value of reactance offered by the capacitances C_{gs}, C_{ds} and C_{sn} is infinity. Therefore, at low frequencies, the value of voltage gain (A_v) is given by:

$$A_v = \frac{g_m R_s}{1+(g_m + g_d)R_s} \tag{4.201}$$

As we can see from the above equation, the value of A_v is slightly less than unity as generally $g_m R_s >> 1$.

Input admittance (Y_i) is obtained by using the Miller's theorem in a manner similar to that done for the common-source FET amplifier. The expression for (Y_i) is given by:

$$Y_i = j\omega C_{gd} + j\omega C_{gs}(1 - A_v) \cong j\omega C_{gd} \tag{4.202}$$

One of the major advantages of the common-drain amplifier over the common-source amplifier is that it offers lower input capacitance as compared to the common-source amplifier.

The output admittance (Y_o) can also be determined in a manner similar to that for the common-drain FET amplifier. It is given by:

$$Y_o = g_m + g_d + j\omega C_T \tag{4.203}$$

Example-4.13: A common drain MOSFET amplifier has a source resistance R_S of 1kΩ. The MOSFET parameters are g_m = 1.5mA/V, r_d = 50kΩ, C_{gs} = 2.5pF, C_{ds} = 1pF, C_{gd} = 2.8pF and C_{is} = 2.7pF. Calculate the voltage gain at operating frequency of (a) 20 kHz (b) 20 MHz.

Solution: Voltage gain of a common drain amplifier is $A_V = \dfrac{\left(g_m + j\omega C_{gs}\right)R_S}{1+\left[g_m + g_d + j\omega\left(C_{gs} + C_{ds} + C_{is}\right)\right]R_S}$

At 20 kHz, substituting different values we get

$$A_V = \frac{\left(1.5\times10^{-3} + j\times2\times\pi\times20\times10^3\times2.5\times10^{-12}\right)\times1\times10^3}{1+\left[1.5\times10^{-3} + \left(1/50\times10^3\right) + j\times2\times\pi\times20\times10^3\times\left(2.5\times10^{-12} + 10\times10^{-12} + 2.7\times10^{-12}\right)\right]\times1\times10^3}$$

$$= \frac{1.5 + 314.2\times10^{-6}j}{2.52 + 779.15\times10^{-6}j}$$

As the imaginary parts are negligible compared to the real parts, therefore the magnitude of gain is given by 1.5/2.52 = 0.595 and the angle of gain is given by 0°.

Similarly, at 20MHz,

$$A_V = \frac{\left(1.5\times10^{-3} + j\times2\times\pi\times20\times10^{6}\times2.5\times10^{-12}\right)\times1\times10^{3}}{1+\left[1.5\times10^{-3}+\left(1/50\times10^{3}\right)+j\times2\times\pi\times20\times10^{6}\times\left(2.5\times10^{-12}+10\times10^{-12}+2.7\times10^{-12}\right)\right]\times1\times10^{3}}$$

$$= \frac{4-0.38j}{7}$$

Magnitude of gain is $\frac{\sqrt{(4)^2+(0.38)^2}}{7} = 0.58$

Phase of gain is $\tan^{-1}\left(\frac{-0.38}{4}\right) = -5.4°$

GLOSSARY

α-Cut-Off frequency (f_α): The a-cut-off frequency is the frequency at which the short-circuit current gain value in the common-base configuration is 0.707 times its mid band value or drops by 3 dB from its mid band value.

Amplification factor (m): It is the ratio of the change in the instantaneous value of drain voltage to change in instantaneous value of gate-source voltage for a constant value of drain current.

Current gain (A_i): Current gain is defined as the ratio of the current through the load resistance (I_L) to the input current (I_i).

f_β : f_β is the frequency at which the value of short circuit current gain of common emitter configuration reduces to 0.707 times the mid band gain value or 3 dB below the mid band gain value.

Gain-bandwidth product (f_T): Itis the frequency at which the magnitude of the short-circuit current gain in the common-emitter amplifier becomes unity.

Hybrid parameter model (h-parameter model): In the case of h-parameter model, input current (I_i) and output voltage (V_o) are taken as independent variables. The other two variables, namely, the input voltage (V_i) and the output current (I_o) are expressed in terms of these two independent variables. Transistors are generally modelled using the hybrid parameter model or the h-parameter model.

Input impedance (Z_i): The input impedance Z_i is defined as the impedance seen looking into the input terminals of the amplifier.

Miller's theorem: According to Miller's theorem, the circuit with feedback impedance can be replaced by an equivalent circuit such that the feedback impedance is split into two impedances: one between the input terminal and the ground (Z_{in}) and the other between the output terminal and the ground (Z_{out}).

Open-circuit output admittance parameter (h_{22} or h_o): It is the ratio of the change in the instantaneous value of output current to the change in the instantaneous value of the output voltage for constant value of input current. It is measured in Siemens.

Open-circuit reverse transfer voltage ratio parameter (h_{12} or h_r): It is the ratio of the instantaneous change in the input voltage to the instantaneous change in the output voltage for constant value of input current. It is a dimensionless quantity.

Output admittance (Y_o): The output admittance (Y_o) is defined as the reciprocal of the output impedance (Z_o)by setting the voltage source (V_S) to zero.

Short-circuit forward transfer current ratio parameter (h_{21} or h_f): It is the ratio of the change in the instantaneous value of output current to the change in the instantaneous value of the input current for constant value of output voltage. It is a dimensionless parameter.

Short-circuit input impedance parameter (h_{11} or h_i): It is the ratio of the instantaneous change in the input voltage to the instantaneous change in the input current for constant value of output voltage. It has the units of impedance, that is, ohms.

Transconductance or the mutual conductance (g_m): The transconductance of a transistor is defined as the ratio of the change in the value of collector current to change in the value of voltage $V_{b'e}$ for constant value of collector-emitter voltage. The transconductance of a FET is defined as the ratio of the change in the value of drain current to change in the value of voltage V_{gs} for constant value of drain-source voltage.

Voltage gain (A_v): The voltage gain A_v is given by the ratio of the output voltage (V_o) to the input voltage (V_i).

SUMMARY OF IMPORTANT FORMULAE

1. Hybrid parameters (h-parameters)

$$V_i = h_{11}I_i + h_{12}V_o$$

$$I_o = h_{21}I_i + h_{22}V_o$$

$$h_{11} = \left.\frac{V_i}{I_i}\right|_{V_o=0} \qquad h_{12} = \left.\frac{V_i}{V_o}\right|_{I_i=0} \qquad h_{21} = \left.\frac{I_o}{I_i}\right|_{V_o=0} \qquad h_{22} = \left.\frac{I_o}{V_o}\right|_{I_i=0}$$

2. Complete h-parameter model of a transistor amplifier

Current gain A_i is $A_i = -\dfrac{h_f}{1+h_oR_L}$

Input impedance Z_i is $Z_i = h_i - \dfrac{h_rh_fR_L}{1+h_oR_L}$

Voltage gain A_v is $A_{vs} = \dfrac{A_vZ_i}{Z_i+R_S}$

Output admittance (Y_o) is $Y_o = h_o - \dfrac{h_fh_r}{h_i+R_s}$

3. Analysis of Transistor Configurations using Simplified h-Parameter Model

Common Emitter Amplifier - Fixed-Bias Configuration

$$Z_i = R_B \| h_{ie}$$

$$Z_o = R_C \| (1/h_{oe})$$

$$A_v = \frac{-h_{fe} \times [R_C \| (1/h_{oe})]}{h_{ie}}$$

$$A_i = \frac{h_{fe} \times R_B}{R_B + h_{ie}}$$

Common Emitter Amplifier - Voltage-Divider Configuration

$$Z_i = (R_{B1} \| R_{B2}) \| h_{ie}$$

$$Z_o = R_C \| (1/h_{oe})$$

$$A_v = \frac{-h_{fe} \times [R_C \| (1/h_{oe})]}{h_{ie}}$$

$$A_i = \frac{h_{fe} \times (R_{B1} \| R_{B2})}{(R_{B1} \| R_{B2}) + h_{ie}}$$

Common Emitter Amplifier - Emitter-Bias Configuration with Unbypassed Emitter Resistor

$$Z_i' = \frac{V_i}{I_b} = h_{ie} + (h_{fe} + 1)R_E$$

$$Z_i = R_B \| Z_i'$$

$$A_v = -\frac{h_{fe} R_C}{h_{ie} + (h_{fe} + 1)R_E}$$

$$A_i = \frac{h_{fe} R_B}{R_B + h_{ie} + (h_{fe} + 1)R_E}$$

Common Base Amplifier

$$Z_i = R_E \| [h_{ie} / (h_{fe} + 1)]$$

$$Z_o = R_C \| (1/h_{oe}) \cong R_C$$

$$A_v = \frac{h_{fe} R_C}{h_{ie}}$$

$$A_i = \frac{h_{fb} R_E}{R_E + h_{ie}/(1 + h_{fe})} \cong h_{fb}$$

$$Z_i' = h_{ie} + (h_{fe} + 1)R_E$$

$$Z_i = R_B \| Z_i'$$

$$Z_o = R_E \| [h_{ie}/(h_{fe} + 1)]$$

$$A_v = \frac{V_o}{V_i} = \frac{R_E}{R_E + h_{ie} / (h_{fe} + 1)}$$

$$A_i = \frac{-(h_{fe} + 1)R_B}{R_B + Z_i'}$$

4. **FET amplifiers**

Transconductance or the mutual conductance, $g_m = \left. \frac{\partial i_d}{\partial v_{gs}} \right|_{V_{DS} = \text{const.}}$

Drain conductance or output conductance, $r_d = \left. \frac{\partial v_{ds}}{\partial i_d} \right|_{V_{GS} = \text{const.}}$

Amplification factor, $\mu = \left.\frac{\partial v_{ds}}{\partial v_{gs}}\right|_{I_D = \text{const.}}$

$\mu = r_d g_m$

Common Source amplifier $A_v = -\frac{\mu R_D}{r_d + R_D + (\mu+1)R_S}$

Common Drain amplifier $A_v = \frac{\mu R_S}{r_d + R_D + (\mu+1)R_S} \cong \frac{\mu R_S}{(\mu+1)R_S} \cong \frac{\mu}{\mu+1} \cong 1$

5. Low Frequency response

Effect of Input Coupling Capacitor

The cut-off frequency established by the capacitor C_i is given by:

$$f_{LC_i} = \frac{1}{2\pi(R_i + R_s)C_i}$$

Effect of the Output-Coupling Capacitor

The cut-off frequency established by the capacitor C_o is given by:

$$f_{LC_o} = \frac{1}{2\pi(R_o + R_L)C_o} \cong \frac{1}{2\pi(R_C + R_L)C_o}$$

Effect of Bypass Capacitor

$$R_e = R_E \| [(R_s' + h_{ie})/h_{fe}]$$

$$f_{LC_E} = \frac{1}{2\pi R_e C_E}$$

Effect of Input-Coupling Capacitor

$$f_{LC_i} = \frac{1}{2\pi(R_G + R_{signal})C_i}$$

Effect of Output-Coupling Capacitor

$$f_{LC_o} = \frac{1}{2\pi(R_D \| r_d + R_L)C_o}$$

Effect of Source Capacitor

The equivalent resistance as seen by the capacitor C_S is given by:

$$R_{eq} = \frac{R_S(r_d + R_D \| R_L)}{R_S(1 + g_m r_d) + r_d + R_D \| R_L}$$

The cut-off frequency due to the capacitor C_S is defined as:

$$f_{LC_S} = \frac{1}{2\pi R_{eq} C_S}$$

6. High-Frequency Model for the Common-Emitter Transistor Amplifier

$h_{ie} = r_{bb'} + r_{b'e}$

$r_{b'e} = h_{re} r_{b'c}$ or $g_{b'c} = h_{re} g_{b'e}$

$$h_{\mathrm{oe}} = \frac{1}{r_{\mathrm{ce}}} + \frac{1}{r_{\mathrm{b'e}} + r_{\mathrm{b'c}}} + g_{\mathrm{m}} h_{\mathrm{re}}$$

$$g_{\mathrm{ce}} \cong h_{\mathrm{oe}} - h_{\mathrm{fe}} g_{\mathrm{b'c}} \cong h_{\mathrm{oe}} - g_{\mathrm{m}} h_{\mathrm{re}}$$

$$r_{\mathrm{b'e}} = \frac{h_{\mathrm{fe}}}{g_{\mathrm{m}}} \quad \text{or} \quad g_{\mathrm{b'e}} = \frac{g_{\mathrm{m}}}{h_{\mathrm{fe}}}$$

$$g_{\mathrm{m}} = \left.\frac{\partial I_{\mathrm{c}}}{\partial V_{\mathrm{b'e}}}\right|_{V_{\mathrm{CE}} = \mathrm{const.}} = \alpha \frac{\partial I_{\mathrm{e}}}{\partial V_{\mathrm{b'e}}} = \alpha \frac{\partial I_{\mathrm{e}}}{\partial V_{\mathrm{e}}}$$

$$r_{\mathrm{d}} = \frac{V_{\mathrm{T}}}{I_{\mathrm{D}}} \qquad g_{\mathrm{m}} = \frac{|I_{\mathrm{c}}|}{V_{\mathrm{T}}}$$

$$A_{\mathrm{i}} = \frac{-h_{\mathrm{fe}}}{1 + j(f / f_{\hat{a}})}$$

$$|A_{\mathrm{i}}| = \frac{h_{\mathrm{fe}}}{\sqrt{1 + (f / f_{\hat{a}})^2}}$$

$$f_{\hat{a}} = \frac{g_{\mathrm{b'e}}}{2\pi(C_{\mathrm{e}} + C_{\mathrm{c}})}$$

$$f_{\mathrm{T}} \cong h_{\mathrm{fe}} f \cong \frac{h_{\mathrm{fe}} g_{\mathrm{b'e}}}{2\pi(C_{\mathrm{e}} + C_{\mathrm{c}})} \cong \frac{g_{\mathrm{m}}}{2\pi(C_{\mathrm{e}} + C_{\mathrm{c}})}$$

The expression for current gain A_{i} can be written as:

$$A_{\mathrm{i}} \cong \frac{-h_{\mathrm{fe}}}{1 + jh_{\mathrm{fe}}(f / f_{\mathrm{T}})}$$

The expression for the current gain in a common-base configuration is given by:

$$A_{\mathrm{i}} = \frac{-h_{\mathrm{fb}}}{1 + j(f / f_{\alpha})}$$

$$f_{\acute{a}} = \frac{1}{2\pi r_{\mathrm{b'e}}(1 + h_{\mathrm{fb}}) C_{\mathrm{e}}}$$

$$f_{\acute{a}} \cong \frac{h_{\mathrm{fe}}}{2\pi r_{\mathrm{b'e}} C_{\mathrm{e}}}$$

$$f_{\acute{a}} \cong \frac{h_{\mathrm{fe}} f (C_{\mathrm{e}} + C_{\mathrm{c}})}{C_{\mathrm{e}}}$$

7. Miller's theorem

$$Z_{\mathrm{in}} = \frac{Z}{1 - A}$$

$$Z_{\mathrm{out}} = \frac{Z}{1 - (1/A)}$$

REVIEW QUESTIONS

1. Why is the h-parameter model of a transistor suitable only for small signal, low frequency analysis of transistor amplifiers?
2. With the help of hybrid equivalent circuit of a transistor, briefly describe the different h-parameters?
3. Describe the two types of capacitances that you observe in hybrid-π model?
4. Draw the simplified hybrid-π model for the circuit shown in Figure-4.59. What is the β cut-off frequency and the gain bandwidth product for the given circuit.

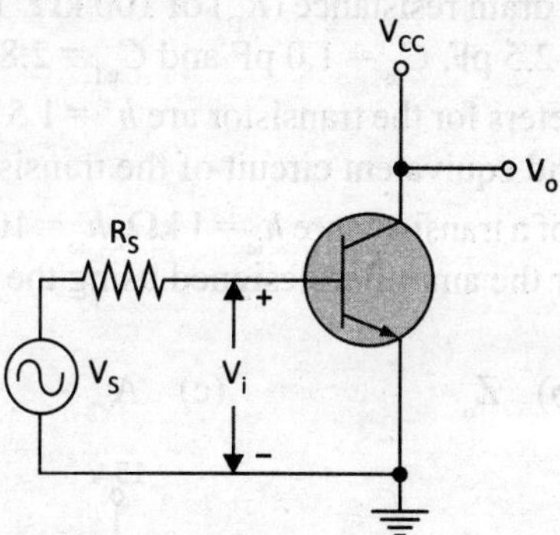

Fig. 4.59: Review question-4

5. What is Miller's theorem and where it can be useful? Derive the expressions for input and output impedances using the theorem?
6. Draw the frequency response of an RC-coupled amplifier and a DC-coupled amplifier. Also explain the main difference between the frequency responses of the two amplifiers.
7. Draw the comprehensive h-parameter model of a transistor. Also draw the approximate h-parameter model, highlighting the assumptions made in drawing it.
8. Derive the expressions for the voltage and current gains, input and output impedances of a collector-to-base feedback common-emitter configuration using simplified h-parameter equivalent model.
9. Draw the equivalent circuit model for a FET amplifier and explain its different parameters.
10. Draw the small-signal equivalent circuit for a common-source FET amplifier and briefly describe its different components.
11. Differentiate between:
    (a) The α-cut-off frequency and the b-cut-off frequency.
    (b) The high-frequency response of a common-base amplifier and a common-emitter amplifier.
    (c) Hybrid parameters for low-frequency analysis and hybrid-π parameters for high-frequency analysis.
12. Explain why the 3-dB frequency for the current gain is not the same as the 3-dB frequency for the voltage gain.

PROBLEMS

1. For the amplifier shown in Figure-4.60, determine the values of V_i, Z_i, V_o/V_i and V_o/V_s.

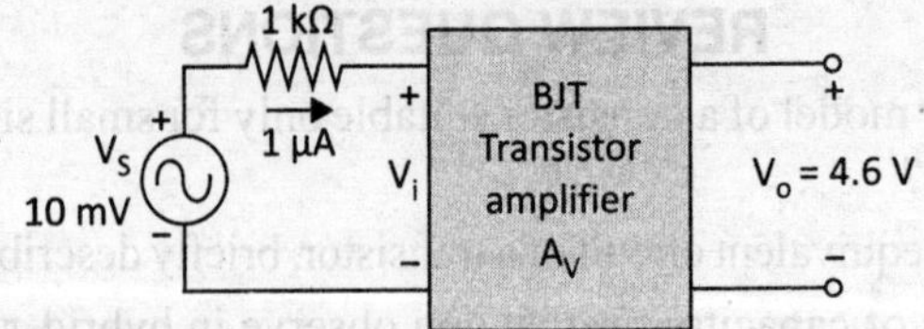

Fig. 4.60: Problem-1

2. Calculate the voltage gain of the common-source MOSFET amplifier at operating frequencies of 20 kHz and 20 MHz with drain resistance (R_D) of 100 kΩ. The MOSFET parameters are g_m = 1.5 mA/V, r_d = 50 kΩ, C_{gs} = 2.5 pF, C_{ds} = 1.0 pF and C_{gd} = 2.8 pF.
3. Given that the hybrid parameters for the transistor are h_{ie} = 1.5 kΩ, h_{fe} = 150, h_{re} = 1 × 10^{-4} and h_{oe} = 20 mmhos. Draw the hybrid equivalent circuit of the transistor in all the three configurations.
4. Given that the h-parameters of a transistor are h_{ie} = 1 kΩ, h_{fe} = 100, h_{oe} = 40 × 10^{-6} mhos. Determine the following parameters for the amplifier designed using the above transistor shown in Figure-4.61.

   (a) Z_i (b) Z_o (c) A_v (d) A_i

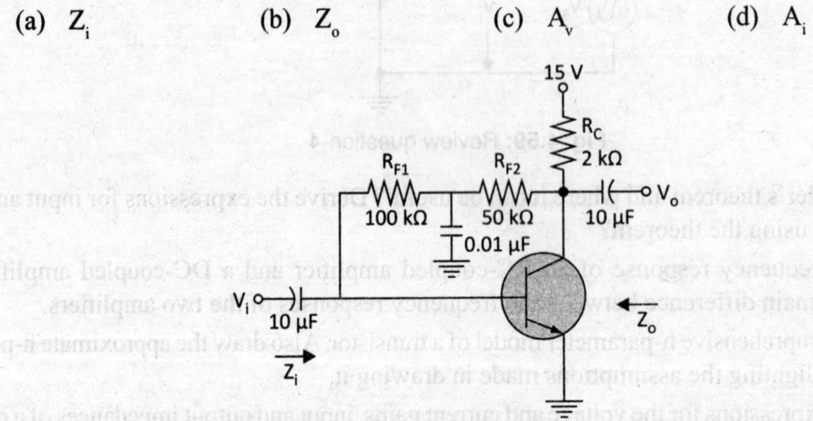

Fig. 4.61: Problem-4

5. Figure-4.62 shows the input and output signal waveforms for a CE amplifier while square wave testing. What is the 3 dB frequency of the amplifier?

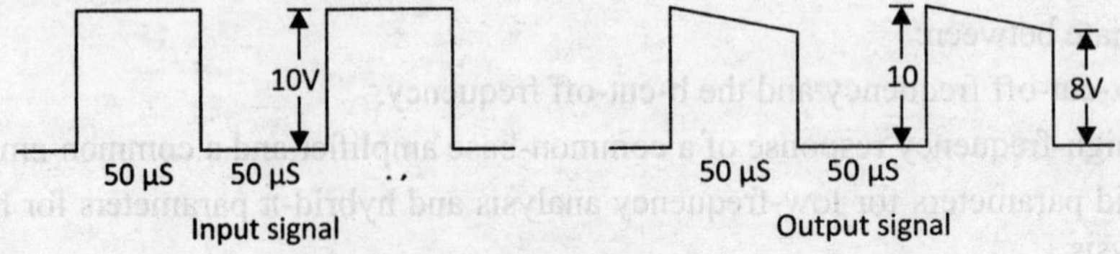

Fig. 4.62: Problem-5

6. Determine the lower cut-off frequency of the BJT amplifier shown in Figure-4.63. Sketch the frequency response using Bode plot. Given that the h-parameters of the transistor are h_{ie} = 1.5 kΩ and h_{fe} = 100.

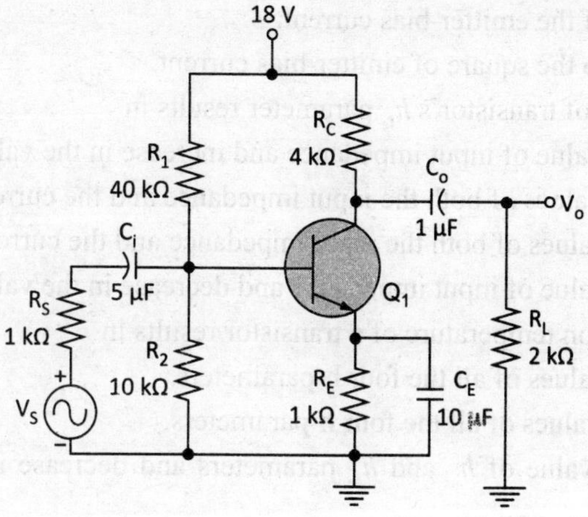

Fig. 4.63: Problem-6

7. Refer to the circuit shown in Figure-4.64. Given that the transconductance of the MOSFET is 1mA/V, find the lower cut-off frequency of the circuit?

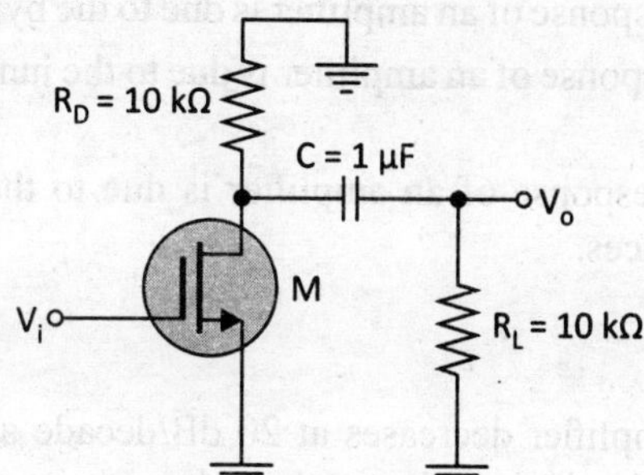

Fig. 4.64: Problem-7

8. A given BJT has the following parameters: g_m = 38 milli-mhos, $r_{b'e}$ = 5.9 kΩ, h_{ie} = 6 kΩ, $r_{bb'}$ = 100 Ω, $C_{b'c}$ = 12 pF, $C_{b'e}$ = 63 pF, f_T = 80 MHz and h_{fe} = 224 at 1 kHz. Determine the a- and b-cut-off frequencies for the given transistor and the value of common-emitter short-circuit current gain at these frequencies.

MULTIPLE CHOICE QUESTIONS

1. The parameter h_{oe} can be determined by:
   (a) taking the slope of the output characteristic curve at the operating point.
   (b) taking the slope of the input characteristic curve at the operating point.
   (c) cannot be determined using the input and output characteristic curves.
   (d) by taking the collector current increment for a fixed value of collector-emitter voltage.
2. The emitter diffusion capacitance for a transistor
   (a) is proportional to the emitter-bias current.
   (b) is inversely proportional to the emitter-bias current.

(c) is independent of the emitter-bias current.

(d) is proportional to the square of emitter-bias current.

3. Increase in the value of transistor's h_{fe} parameter results in

(a) decrease in the value of input impedance and increase in the value of current gain.

(b) decrease in the values of both the input impedance and the current gain.

(c) increase in the values of both the input impedance and the current gain.

(d) increase in the value of input impedance and decrease in the value of current gain.

4. Increase in the junction temperature of a transistor results in

(a) increase in the values of all the four h-parameters.

(b) decrease in the values of all the four h-parameters.

(c) increase in the value of h_{ie} and h_{fe} parameters and decrease in the values of h_{re} and h_{oe} parameters.

(d) decrease in the value of h_{ie} and h_{fe} parameters and increase in the values of h_{re} and h_{oe} parameters.

5. Which of the following statement(s) is/are true?

(a) The low-frequency response of an amplifier is due to the bypass and the coupling capacitors.

(b) The high-frequency response of an amplifier is due to the bypass and the coupling capacitors.

(c) The low-frequency response of an amplifier is due to the junction capacitances and the stray-wiring capacitances.

(d) The high-frequency response of an amplifier is due to the junction capacitances and the stray-wiring capacitances.

(e) Both (a) and (d).

(f) Both (b) and (c).

6. The voltage gain of an amplifier decreases at 20 dB/decade above 100 kHz. If the mid-band frequency gain is 80 dB, what is the value of the voltage gain at 2 MHz?

(a) 60 dB (b) 52 dB (c) 54 dB (d) 64 dB

7. In the h-parameter model the input and the output sections are modelled as

(a) voltage sources.

(b) current sources.

(c) input section as voltage source and output section as current source.

(d) input section as current source and output section as voltage source.

8. The Ohmic base spreading resistance is represented as

(a) the increase in the recombination base current due to the increase in the minority carriers in the base region.

(b) the conductance between the collector and the emitter terminals.

(c) a lump parameter between the external base terminal and the node B′.

(d) the feedback effect between the output and the input due to the Early effect.

9. Larger the spacing between the curves of the output characteristics of a transistor

(a) smaller is the value of h_{fe}

(b) larger is the value of h_{fe}

(c) h_{fe} is independent of the spacing

(d) h_{fe} can increase or decrease depending upon the circuit configuration

10. The value of α-cut-off frequency is

(a) smaller than the β-cut-off frequency.

(b) greater than the β-cut-off frequency.

(c) can be more or less than the β-cut-off frequency.

(d) equal to the β-cut-off frequency.

SOLUTIONS TO MULTIPLE CHOICE QUESTIONS

1. (a)	2. (a)	3. (a)	4. (c)	5. (e)	6. (d)
7. (c)	8. (c)	9. (b)	10. (b)		

SOLUTION TO PROBLEMS

1. $V_i = V_s - 1\times10^{-6}\times1\times10^{3} = 10\times10^{-3} - 1\times10^{-3} = 9mV$

$$Z_i = \frac{V_i}{I_i} = \frac{9\times10^{-3}}{1\times10^{-6}} = 9k\Omega$$

$$\frac{V_o}{V_i} = \frac{4.6}{9\times10^{-3}} = 511.11$$

$$\frac{V_o}{V_s} = \frac{4.6}{10\times10^{-3}} = 460$$

2. **For operating frequency of 20 kHz**

$Y_{gs} = jwC_{gs} = j\times2\times p\times20\times10^{3}\times2.5\times10^{-12} = j3.14\times10^{-7}\Omega^{-1}$

$Y_{ds} = jwC_{ds} = j\times2\times p\times20\times10^{3}\times1.0\times10^{-12} = j1.26\times10^{-7}\Omega^{-1}$

$Y_{gd} = jwC_{gd} = j\times2\times p\times20\times10^{3}\times2.8\times10^{-12} = j3.52\times10^{-7}\Omega^{-1}$

$g_d = 1/r_d = 1/(50\times10^{3}) = 2\times10^{-5}\Omega^{-1}$

$G_D = 1/R_D = 1/(100\times10^{3}) = 1\times10^{-5}\Omega^{-1}$

Voltage gain (A_v) is given by:

$$A_v = \frac{-g_m + Y_{gd}}{G_D + Y_{ds} + g_d + Y_{gd}}$$

$$= \frac{-1.5\times10^{-3} + j3.52\times10^{-7}}{1\times10^{-5} + j1.26\times10^{-7} + 2\times10^{-5} + j3.52\times10^{-7}} = \frac{-1.5\times10^{-3} + j3.52\times10^{-7}}{3\times10^{-5} + j4.78\times10^{-7}}$$

The imaginary terms are negligible in comparison with the real terms. Therefore, the value of voltage gain $A_v = (-1.5\times10^{-3})/(3\times10^{-5}) = -50$

For operating frequency of 20 MHz

$Y_{gs} = jwC_{gs} = j\times2\times p\times20\times10^{6}\times2.5\times10^{-12} = j3.14\times10^{-4}\Omega^{-1}$

$Y_{ds} = jwC_{ds} = j \times 2 \times p \times 20 \times 10^6 \times 1.0 \times 10^{-12} = j1.26 \times 10^{-4}\Omega^{-1}$
$Y_{gd} = jwC_{gd} = j \times 2 \times p \times 20 \times 10^6 \times 2.8 \times 10^{-12} = j3.52 \times 10^{-4}\Omega^{-1}$
$g_d = 1/r_d = 1/(50 \times 10^3) = 2 \times 10^{-5}\Omega^{-1}$
$G_D = 1/R_D = 1/(100 \times 10^3) = 1 \times 10^{-5}\Omega^{-1}$
Voltage gain (A_v) is given by:

$$A_v = \frac{-g_m + Y_{gd}}{G_D + Y_{ds} + g_d + Y_{gd}}$$

$$= \frac{-1.5\times10^{-3} + j3.52\times10^{-4}}{1\times10^{-5} + j1.26\times10^{-4} + 2\times10^{-5} + j3.52\times10^{-4}} = \frac{-1.5\times10^{-3} + j3.52\times10^{-4}}{3\times10^{-5} + j4.78\times10^{-4}}$$

Multiplying and dividing by ($3 \times 10^{-5} - j4.78 \times 10^{-4}$), we get

$$A_v = \frac{(-1.5\times10^{-3} + j3.52\times10^{-4})\times(3\times10^{-5} - j4.78\times10^{-4})}{(3\times10^{-5} + j4.78\times10^{-4})\times(3\times10^{-5} - j4.78\times10^{-4})}$$

$$= \frac{-4.5\times10^{-8} + j7.17\times10^{-7} + j10.56\times10^{-9} + 16.83\times10^{-8}}{9\times10^{-10} + 22.85\times10^{-8}}$$

$$= \frac{-12.33\times10^{-8} + j7.28\times10^{-7}}{22.94\times10^{-8}}$$

$|A_v| = \sqrt{[(12.33 \times 10^{-8})^2 + (7.28 \times 10^{-7})^2]}/(22.94 \times 10^{-8}) = 3.22$
$\angle A_v = \tan^{-1} [(-7.28 \times 10^{-7})/(12.33 \times 10^{-8})] = \tan^{-1}(-5.9) = -80.38°$

3. Figure-4.65(a) shows the hybrid equivalent circuit for the transistor in the common-emitter configuration.

   The values of hybrid parameters in the common-collector configuration are $h_{ic} = h_{ie}$, $h_{rc} = 1$, $h_{fc} = -(1 + h_{fe})$ and $h_{oc} = h_{oe}$.

   Therefore, $h_{ic} = 1.5$ kΩ, $h_{rc} = 1$, $h_{fc} = -151$ and $h_{oc} = 20$ mmhos.

   Figure-4.65(b) shows the hybrid equivalent circuit of the transistor in the common-collector configuration.

   The values of hybrid parameters in the common-base configuration are

$$h_{ib} = \frac{h_{ie}}{1 + h_{fe}} = (1.5\times10^3)/151 = 9.93\ \Omega$$

$$h_{rb} = \frac{h_{ie}h_{oe}}{1 + h_{fe}} - h_{re} = (1.5\times10^3 \times 20\times10^{-6})/(151 - 1\times10^{-4}) = 0.99\times10^{-4}$$

$$h_{fb} = -\frac{h_{fe}}{1 + h_{fe}} = -150/151 = -0.99$$

$$h_{ob} = \frac{h_{oe}}{1 + h_{fe}} = (20\times10^6)/151 = 0.13\times10^{-6}$$

   Figure-4.65(c) shows the hybrid equivalent of the transistor in the common-base configuration.

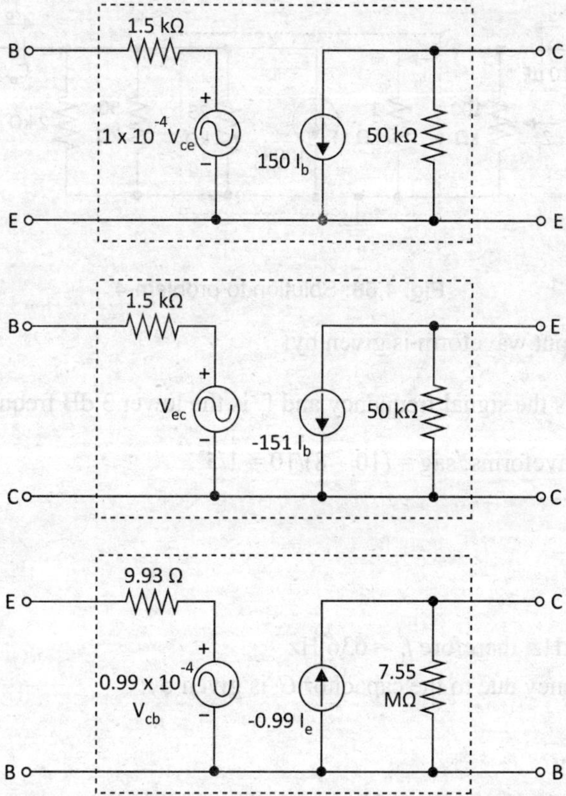

Fig. 4.65: Solution to problem-3

4. The AC equivalent circuit for the amplifier in Figure-4.61 is shown in Figure-4.66.

Input impedance $Z_i = R_{F1} \| h_{ie} = 300 \times 10^3 \| 1 \times 10^3 = 0.99\ \text{k}\Omega$

Output impedance (Z_o) is given by

$$Z_o = R_{F2} \| R_C \| (1/h_{oe}) = 50 \times 10^3 \| 2 \times 10^3 \| 25 \times 10^3 = 1.79 \times 10^3 = 1.79\ \text{k}\Omega$$

Voltage gain A_v is given by

$$A_v = \frac{-h_{fe} \times [R_{F2} \| R_C \| (1/h_{oe})]}{h_{ie}} = \frac{-100 \times 1.79 \times 10^3}{1 \times 10^3} = -1.79$$

The current gain A_i is given by

$$A_i = \frac{h_{fe} R_{F1} \left[R_{F2} \| R_C \| (1/h_{oe}) \right]}{(R_{F1} + h_{ie}) \left[R_{F2} \| R_C \| (1/h_{oe}) + R_C \right]}$$

$$= \frac{100 \times 100 \times 10^3 \times (50 \times 10^3 \| 2 \times 10^3 \| 25 \times 10^3)}{(100 \times 10^3 + 1 \times 10^3) \times (50 \times 10^3 \| 2 \times 10^3 \| 25 \times 10^3 + 2 \times 10^3)} = \frac{10^7 \times 1.79 \times 10^3}{101 \times 10^3 \times 3.79 \times 10^3} = 46.76$$

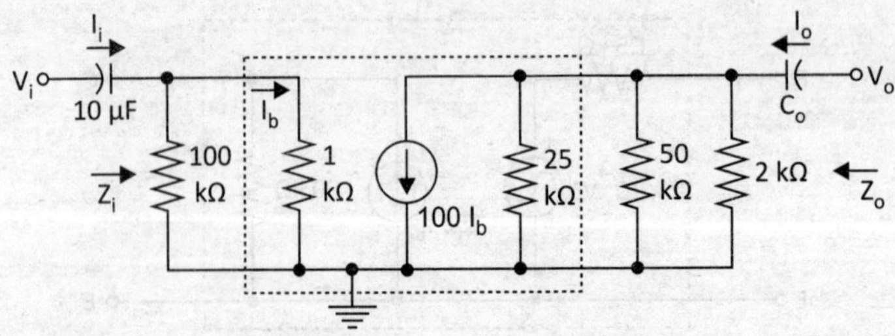

Fig. 4.66: Solution to problem-4

5. The sag in the output waveform is given by:

$\left(\frac{\pi f_L}{f}\right)$, where f is the signal frequency and f_L is the lower 3 dB frequency.

From the given waveforms, sag = (10 – 8)/10 = 1/5

Therefore,

$$\left(\frac{\pi f_L}{f}\right) = 0.2$$

Given that f = 10kHz, therefore f_L = 636 Hz

6. The cut-off frequency due to the capacitor C_i is given by:

$$f_{LC_i} = \frac{1}{2\pi(R_i + R_s)C_i}$$

The value of R_i is given by:

$$R_i = R_1 \| R_2 \| h_{ie} = 40\times10^3 \| 10\times10^3 \| 1.5\times10^3 = 1.26\times10^3 = 1.26\ \text{k}\Omega$$

Therefore f_{LCi} = 1/2 × π × (1.26 × 10^3 + 1 × 10^3) × 5 × 10^{-6} = 14.08 Hz

The cut-off frequency due to capacitor C_E is given by:

$$f_{LC_E} = \frac{1}{2\pi R_e C_E}$$

The value of resistance R_e is

$$R_e = R_E \| [(R_s \| R_1 \| R_2 + h_{ie})/h_{fe}] = 1\times10^3 \| [(1\times10^3 \| 40\times10^3 \| 10\times10^3 + 1.5\times10^3)/100] = 23.33\ \Omega$$

Therefore f_{LCE} = 1/2 × π × (23.33) × 10 × 10^{-6} = 682 Hz

The cut-off frequency due to capacitor C_o is given by

$$f_{LC_o} = \frac{1}{2\pi(R_C + R_L)C_o} = \frac{1}{2\pi(4\times10^3 + 2\times10^3)\times1\times10^{-6}} = 26.53\ \text{Hz}$$

As we can see f_{LCE} is significantly higher than f_{LCo} and f_{LCi}, hence f_{LCE} is the predominant factor in determining the low-frequency response for the complete system.

Hence the cut-off frequency for the overall system is approximately equal to 682 Hz.

Figure- 4.67 shows the asymptotic curves using the Bode plot.

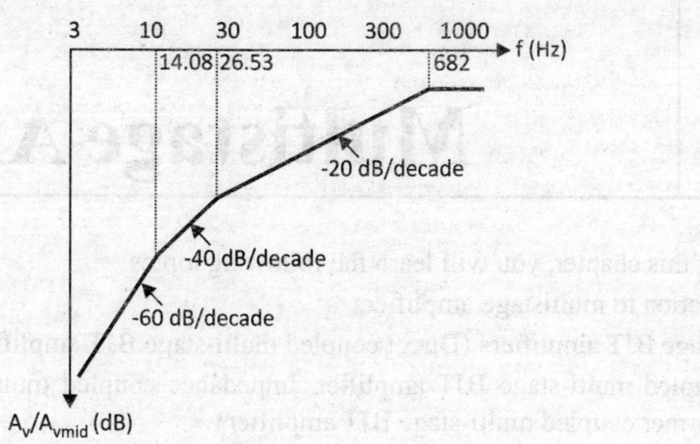

Fig. 4.67: Solution to problem-6

7. The lower cut-off frequency is given by:

$$f_L = \frac{1}{2\pi(R_L + R_D)C} = \frac{1}{2\times3.14\times\left(10\times10^3 + 10\times10^3\right)\times1\times10^{-6}} = 8Hz$$

8. The a-cut-off frequency is given by $f_{\hat{a}} = \dfrac{h_{fe}}{2\pi r_{b'e} C_e} = \dfrac{224}{2\times\pi\times5.9\times10^3\times63\times10^{-12}} = 95.91$ MHz

The b-cut-off frequency is given by $f_{\hat{a}} = \dfrac{g_{b'e}}{2\pi(C_e + C_c)}$

Now, $g_{b'e} = 1/r_{b'e} = 1/(5.9 \times 10^3) = 1.69 \times 10^{-4}$

Therefore, $f_b = 1.69 \times 10^{-4}/[2 \times \pi \times (63 \times 10^{-12} + 12 \times 10^{-12})] = 358.63$ kHz

Common-emitter short-circuit current gain is given by:

$$A_i = \frac{-h_{fe}}{1 + j(f / f_{\hat{a}})}$$

For $f = f_a$, $A_i = -224/[1 + j\{(95.91 \times 10^6)/(358.63 \times 10^3)\}] = -224/(1 + 267.43j)$

$|A_i| = 224/\sqrt{(1^2 + 267.43^2)} = 0.838$, $\angle A_i = 90° - \tan^{-1}(267.43) = 90° - 89.786° = 0.21°$

For $f = f_b$, $A_i = -224/[1 + j\{(358.63 \times 10^3)/(358.63 \times 10^3)\}] = -224/(1 + j)$

$|A_i| = 224/\sqrt{2} = 158.39$, $\angle A_i = 90° - \tan^{-1}1 = 90° - 45° = 45°$

5 Multistage Amplifiers

After completing this chapter, you will learn the following topics.

— Introduction to multistage amplifiers

— Multistage BJT amplifiers (Direct coupled multi-stage BJT amplifier,

— RC coupled multi-stage BJT amplifier, Impedance coupled multi-stage BJT amplifier and Transformer coupled multi-stage BJT amplifier)

— Multistage FET amplifiers

— Darlington amplifiers

— Cascode amplifiers

— Frequency response of cascaded amplifier stages

Introduction

This chapter is dedicated to different types of and the frequency response of multistage amplifiers. The chapter begins with a general introduction to multistage amplifiers. This is followed by discussion on multistage BJT amplifiers including direct-coupled multi-stage amplifiers, R-C coupled multi-stage amplifiers, impedance-coupled multi-stage amplifiers and transformer-coupled multi-stage BJT amplifiers. Following this are covered the multistage FET amplifiers. This is further followed up by a discussion on Darlington and cascade amplifiers. At the end of the chapter, Frequency Response of cascaded amplifier stages is discussed towards the end of the chapter. Different topics discussed in the chapter are amply illustrated with solved examples. In addition, there are a number of problems given towards the end of the chapter along with brief solutions. A self-evaluation exercise containing multiple-choice questions along with answers concludes the chapter.

5.1 MULTISTAGE AMPLIFIERS

Many a time, the gain of a single-amplifier stage is not sufficient for the intended application or the input or the output impedance of the amplifier is not of the correct magnitude for the given application. In such cases, two or more amplifier stages are cascaded, that is, the output of a given stage is connected to the input of the next amplifier stage. A cascade connection of amplifiers is a series connection where the output of one stage is applied to the input of the next stage. A cascaded arrangement of common-emitter amplifier stages is used to provide power gain. A common-collector amplifier stage may be used as the last stage in the cascade arrangement to drive low resistance loads due to its low output resistance. It may also be used as the first-stage due to its high input impedance.

Figure 5.1 shows a generalized cascaded amplifier connection. The total gain is the product of the gains of the individual amplifiers under loaded conditions. The overall gain (A_v) is therefore given by

$$A_v = A_{v1} \times A_{v2} \times A_{v3} \times \cdots \times A_{vn} \tag{5.1}$$

where A_v is the overall voltage gain; A_{v1} is the voltage gain of stage 1 with the input impedance of stage 2 acting on it; A_{v2} is the voltage gain of stage 2 with the input impedance of stage 3 acting on it and its source impedance is the output impedance of stage 1; A_{v3} is the voltage gain of stage 3 with the input impedance of stage 4 acting on it and its source impedance is the output impedance of stage 2; A_{vn} is the voltage gain of stage *n* with the load impedance acting on it and its source impedance is the output impedance of stage $(n - 1)$.

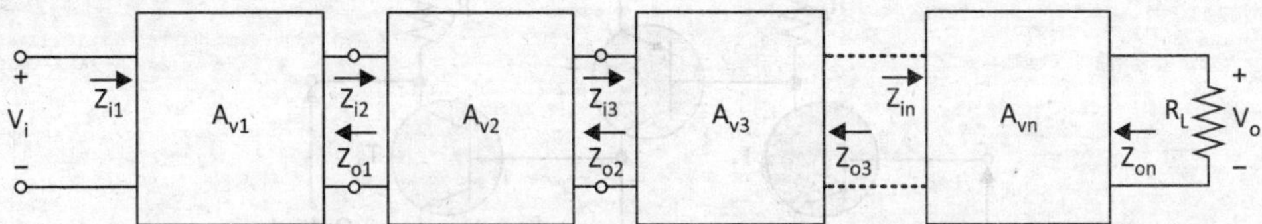

Fig. 5.1: Generalized cascaded amplifier connection

The overall current gain is given by:

$$A_i = -A_v \times \left(\frac{Z_{i1}}{R_L}\right) \tag{5.2}$$

where A_i is the overall current gain; A_v is the overall voltage gain; Z_{i1} is the input impedance of the stage 1; R_L is the load resistance.It may be mentioned here that the DC bias conditions for the cascaded amplifier stages can be determined on similar lines as that for single stage amplifiers.

Example 5.1: A three stage amplifier has a first stage with a voltage gain of 400, second stage with voltage gain of 200 and third stage with voltage gain of 100. Find the overall gain of the cascaded amplifier in dB.

Solution: First stage voltage gain in dB = 20 $\log_{10}$ 400 = 52 dB

Second stage voltage gain in dB = 20 $\log_{10}$ 200 = 46 dB

Third stage voltage gain in dB = 20 $\log_{10}$ 100 = 400 dB

Overall voltage gain = 52 + 46 + 40 = 138 dB

Example 5.2: Three amplifier stages are working in cascade with 0.02V peak-peak input signal providing 20V peak-peak output signal. Given that the voltage gain of the first stage is 20 and the input to the third stage is 2V peak-peak. Determine (a) Overall voltage gain (b) Voltage gain of 3rd stage (c) Voltage gain of 2nd stage (d) Input voltage of 2nd stage.

Solution:

(a) Overall voltage gain $A_V = \dfrac{20}{0.02} = 1000$

(b) Voltage gain of the third stage $A_{V3} = \dfrac{20}{2} = 10$

(c) Voltage gain of the second stage $A_{V2} = \dfrac{A_V}{A_{V1}A_{V3}} = \dfrac{1000}{20 \times 10} = 5$

(d) Input voltage of second stage = Output voltage of first stage = 0.02 × 20 = 0.4V peak-peak

5.2 MULTISTAGE BIPOLAR TRANSISTOR AMPLIFIERS

Different types of multi-stage bipolar transistor amplifiers, which includes direct-coupled, R-C coupled, impedance-coupled and transformer-coupled configurations, are briefly described in the following paragraphs. The amplifier configurations.

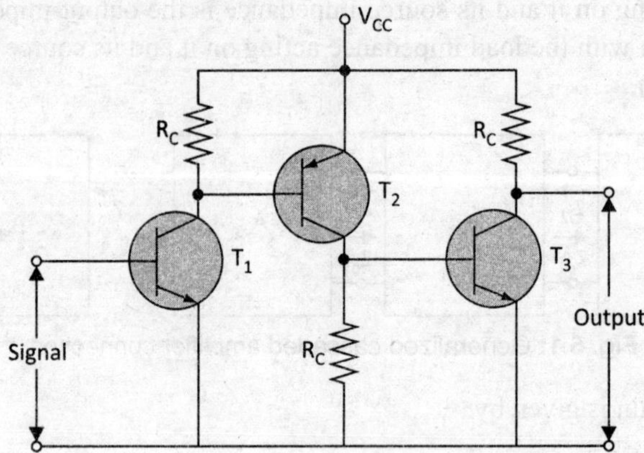

Fig. 5.2: 3-stage direct-coupled BJT amplifier

5.2.1 Direct-coupled Multi-stage Amplifier

In the case of a direct-coupled multi-stage amplifier, each amplifier stage is directly connected to the succeeding amplifier stage without the use of any coupling components such as coupling capacitors and coupling transformers. Figure 5.2 shows a three-stage direct coupled amplifier circuit.The input signal applied to the base of bipolar transistor Q_1 is amplified by this common-emitter stage and the amplified signal appearing at the collector terminal of Q_1 is then directly coupled to the base of bipolar transistor Q_2. The simplified signal is further amplified by the common-emitter stage configured around transistor Q_2. The third amplifying stage further amplifies the signal in the common-emitter stage configured around transistor Q_3. The network of resistors used for providing biasing voltages for different stages is not shown in the circuit diagram for the sake of simplicity.

Direct-coupled amplifiers are simple due to absence of large number of resistors and are low cost due to absence of bulky and expensive coupling components.Direct-coupled amplifiers offer excellent frequency response and are capable of amplifying signals down to zero frequency or DC. It may be mentioned here that coupling components become very bulky if these were to offer an acceptable low frequency cut-off frequency. The frequency response of a direct-coupled amplifier is only affected by the amplifying component itself. The main disadvantage of direct coupling is the shift in operating point due to temperature variations. Small changes in the DC bias voltages, due to temperature and power supply variations, are amplified by successive stages, which can result in some significant drift in the DC levels throughout the circuit. An operational amplifier is a very good example of a direct-coupled amplifier in which direct coupling is used to interconnect different stages. This permits the opamp to amplify signals right down to DC.

Example 5.3: For the DC coupled 2-stage amplifier shown in Figure 5.3, determine the voltage gains of transistors Q_1 and Q_2 and the overall voltage gain of the amplifier. Given that $r_e = 25/I_E$ (I_E is in mA), $\beta_1 = \beta_2 = 100$. Assume $V_{BE} = 0$.

Solution: Calculating the voltage gains of individual stages,

The voltage across resistor R_2 is $V_{TH} = V_{CC}\left(\frac{R_2}{R_1+R_2}\right) = 12\left(\frac{20\times10^3}{100\times10^3+20\times10^3}\right) = 2V$

The emitter current of transistor Q_1 is given by $I_{E1} = \frac{V_{TH}}{R_4} = \frac{2}{2000} = 1mA$

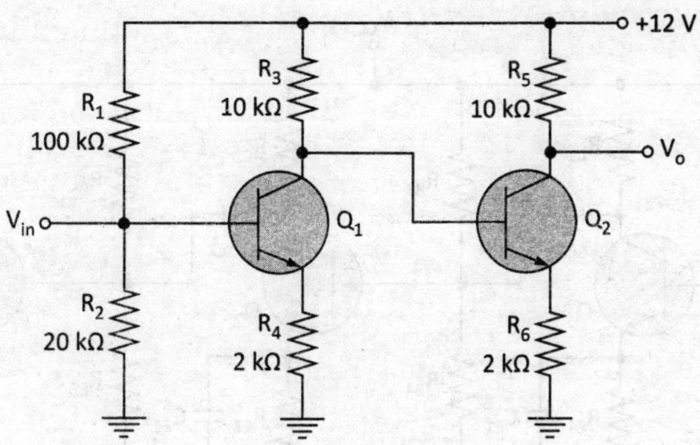

Fig. 5.3: Example 5.3

$$r_{e1} = \frac{25mV}{1mA} = 25\Omega$$

$$V_{R6} = V_{E2} = V_{B2} = V_{C1} = V_{CC} - I_{E1}R_3 = 12 - 1\times10^{-3}\times10\times10^3 = 2V$$

$$I_{E2} = \frac{V_{R6}}{R_6} = \frac{2}{2000} = 1mA$$

$$r_{e2} = \frac{25mV}{1mA} = 25\Omega$$

$$R_{r2} = \beta_2\left(r_{e2} + R_6\right) = 100\left(25 + 2000\right) = 202500\Omega$$

$$\mathrm{R_{e1}} = R_3 \| R_{r2} = 10000 \| 202500 \cong 10000\Omega$$

$$\mathrm{R_{e2}} = R_5 = 10000\Omega$$

$$A_{V1} = \frac{\mathrm{R_{e1}}}{r_{e1} + R_4} = \frac{10000}{25 + 2000} = 4.9$$

$$A_{V2} = \frac{\mathrm{R_{e2}}}{r_{e2} + R_6} = \frac{10000}{25 + 2000} = 4.9$$

Overall voltage gain $A_V = A_{V1}A_{V2} = 4.9\times4.9 = 24$

5.2.2 R-C Coupled Multi-stage Amplifier

In the case of an R-C coupled multi-stage amplifier, the individual stages of the amplifier are connected together using a resistor-capacitor combination due to which it gets its name as *R-C coupled amplifier*.R-C coupling is the most widely used method of coupling in multistage amplifiers, particularly in the design of small signal amplifiers. Since R-C coupling is the most commonly employed mode of coupling in discrete multi-stage amplifiers; we shall describe the operation of R-C coupled multi-stage amplifier in a little more detail by considering a three-stage amplifier configuration shown in Figure 5.4. Let the h-parameters of the transistor Q_1 be h_{ie1}, h_{fe1}, h_{re1} and h_{oe1}; of transistor Q_2 be h_{ie2}, h_{fe2}, h_{re2} and h_{oe2} and that of transistor Q_3 be h_{ie3}, h_{fe3}, h_{re3} and h_{oe3}.

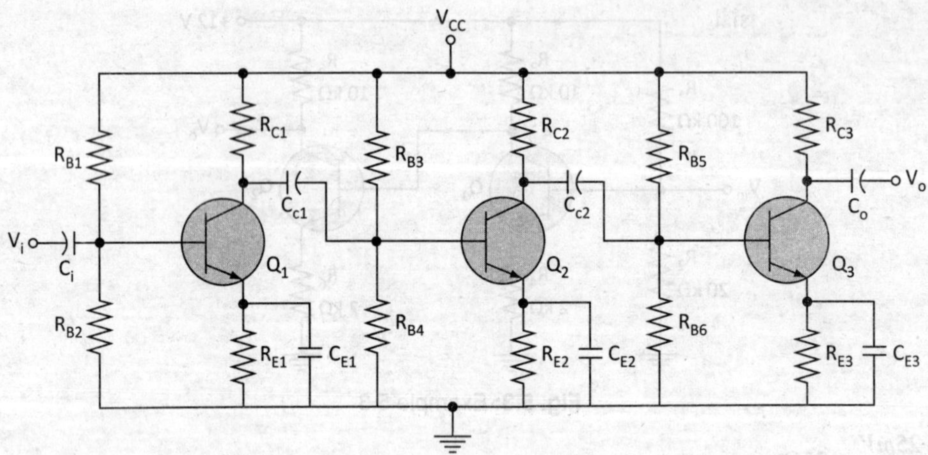

Fig. 5.4: Cascaded three-stage RC-coupled BJT amplifier

The voltage gain of the third stage is given by:

$$A_{v3} = \frac{-h_{fe3} \times [R_{C3} \| (1/h_{oe3})]}{h_{ie3}} \quad (5.3)$$

Assuming $1/h_{oe} >> R_{C3}$, the equation can be simplified as:

$$A_{v3} = \frac{-h_{fe3} \times R_{C3}}{h_{ie3}} \quad (5.4)$$

Similarly, the gain for the second stage A_{v2}, assuming $1/h_{oe2} >> R_{B5} \| R_{B6} \| R_{C2} \| h_{ie3}$ is given by:

$$A_{v2} = \frac{-h_{fe2} \times (R_{B5} \| R_{B6} \| R_{C2} \| h_{ie3})}{h_{ie2}} \quad (5.5)$$

The gain for the first stage A_{v1}, assuming $1/h_{oe1} >> R_{B3} \| R_{B4} \| R_{C1} \| h_{ie2}$ is given by:

$$A_{v1} = \frac{-h_{fe1} \times (R_{B3} \| R_{B4} \| R_{C1} \| h_{ie2})}{h_{ie1}} \quad (5.6)$$

The overall voltage gain A_v is given by the product of the voltage gains of the three stages.

$$A_v = A_{v1} \times A_{v2} \times A_{v3} \quad (5.7)$$

The overall input impedance of the amplifier is the same as the input impedance of stage 1 and is given by:

$$Z_i = R_{B1} \| R_{B2} \| h_{ie1} \quad (5.8)$$

The output impedance of the amplifier is equal to the output impedance of the last stage and is given by:

$$Z_o = R_{C3} \| (1/h_{oe3}) \quad (5.9)$$

Frequency response of an R-C coupled amplifier can be qualitatively described as follows. At *low frequencies* of the order of few 10's of Hertz, the reactance of coupling capacitors, C_{C1} and C_{C2} in Figure 5.4, is quite high and hence very small part of the signal will pass from one stage to the next stage. Again, emitter bypass capacitors, C_{E1}, C_{E2} and C_{E3} in Figure 5.4, cannot respectively shunt the emitter resistors R_{E1}, R_{E2} and R_{E3} effectively because of their large reactance at low frequencies. These two factors cause the dropping of voltage gain at low frequencies. In the *mid frequency region* between low frequency cut-off and high frequency cut-off frequencies, the voltage gain of the amplifier is constant. The effect of coupling capacitor in this frequency range is such that the voltage gain remains uniform. As the frequency increases in this range, reactance of coupling capacitors decreases, which in turn increases the voltage gain. At the same time, lower reactance of coupling capacitors means a higher loading effect of a given amplifier stage on the preceding amplifier stage feeding it. This leads to a decrease in gain. These two factors result in a uniform gain in the mid frequency region. At *high frequencies* above few 10's of kHz, the reactance of various coupling capacitors is quite small with the result that they behave like a short circuit. This increases the loading effect of next stage and results in decreased voltage gain. Again, at high frequencies, capacitive reactance of base-emitter junction is low which in result increases the base current. This causes decrease in current amplification factor β. These two factors cause the dropping of voltage gain at high frequencies.

RC coupling, however, does have a few disadvantages. The resistors use DC power, which leads to loss of efficiency. The capacitor tends to limit the low-frequency response of the amplifier and the amplifying device itself limits the high-frequency response. Multi-stage R-C coupled amplifiers have low voltage and power gains due to the loading effect of different stages in the cascade arrangement on the immediately preceding stages feeding them. Impedance matching is an issue in R-C coupled amplifiers.

Example 5.4: Figure 5.5 shows a two-stage CE amplifier. Determine (a) Voltage gain for each stage and (b) Overall voltage gain. Also, draw the output waveform

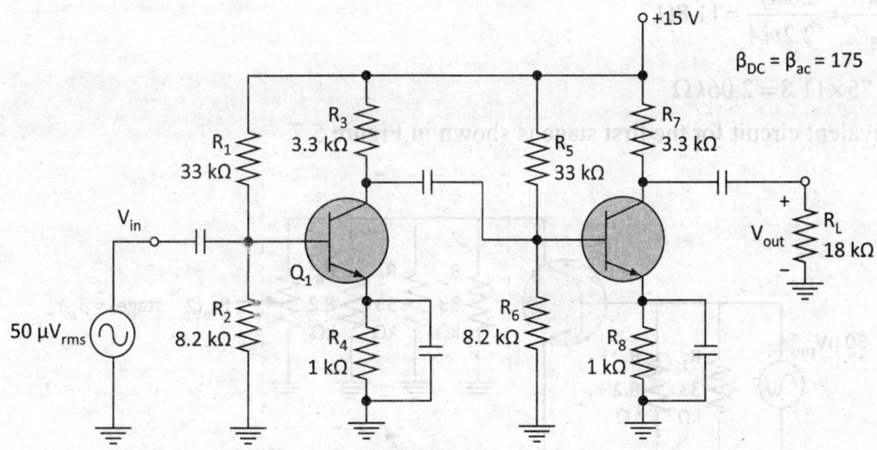

Fig. 5.5: Example 5.4

Solution: Let us do the DC analysis of first transistor. Figure 5.6 shows the DC equivalent circuit of the first transistor.

$$V_{TH} = \left(\frac{R_2}{R_1 + R_2}\right)V_{CC} = \left(\frac{8.2\times10^3}{33\times10^3 + 8.2\times10^3}\right)\times15 = 2.98V$$

$$R_{TH} = R_1 \| R_2 = 33\times10^3 \| 8.2\times10^3 = 6.57k\Omega$$

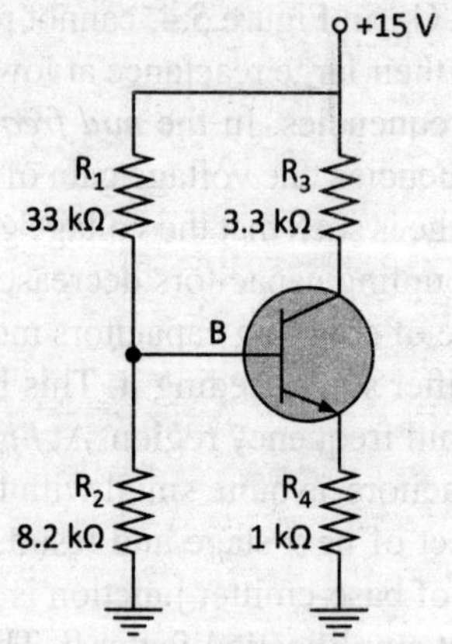

Fig. 5.6: Solution of example 5.4

$$I_B = \frac{V_{TH} - V_{BE}}{R_{TH} + (\beta_{DC}+1)R_4} = \frac{2.98 - 0.7}{6.57\times10^3 + (175+1)1\times10^3} = 12.5\mu A$$

$$I_E = (\beta_{DC}+1)I_B = (175+1)12.5\times10^{-6} = 2.2mA$$

As $R_1 = R_5$, $R_2 = R_6$, $R_3 = R_7$ and $R_4 = R_8$, therefore the DC voltages for Q_1 and Q_2 are the same.

Let us now do the AC analysis

$$r_e = \frac{26mV}{I_E} = \frac{26mV}{2.2mA} = 11.8\Omega$$

$$\beta_{ac} r_e = 175\times11.8 = 2.06k\Omega$$

The equivalent circuit for the first stage is shown in Figure 5.7.

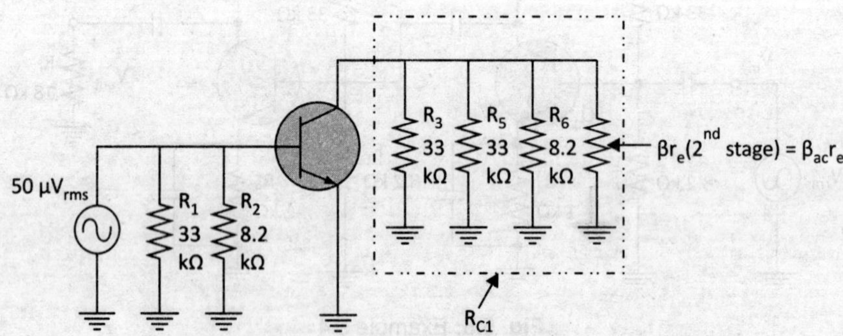

Fig. 5.7: Equivalent circuit for stage 1 (Example 5.4)

$$R_{e1} = R_3 \| R_5 \| R_6 \| \beta r_e \text{ (2nd stage)} = 3.3\times10^3 \| 33\times10^3 \| 8.2\times10^3 \| 2.06\times10^3 = 1.06k\Omega$$

Therefore, gain of the first stage

$$A_{V1} = -\frac{R_{e1}}{r_e} = -\frac{1.06\times10^3}{11.8} = -90.15$$

The equivalent circuit for stage 2 is shown in Figure 5.8.

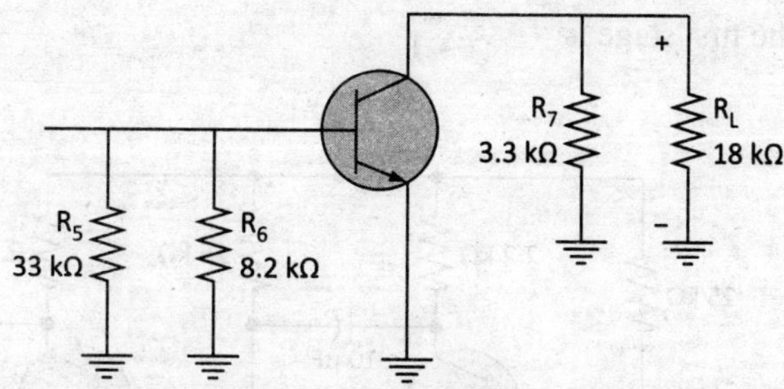

Fig. 5.8: Equivalent circuit for stage 2

$$R_{e2} = R_7 \| R_L = 3.3\times10^3 \| 18\times10^3 = 2.8k\Omega$$

Therefore, gain of the second stage $A_{V2} = -\dfrac{R_{e2}}{r_e} = -\dfrac{2.8\times10^3}{11.8} = -236.3$

Overall voltage gain $A_V = A_{V1}A_{V2} = (-90.15)\times(-236.3) = 21305$

Voltage gain $A_V = \dfrac{V_{out}}{V_{in}}$

Therefore,

$$V_{out} = A_V \times V_{in} = 21305\times50\times10^{-6}\,V_{rms} = 1.06V_{rms} = 1.06\times\sqrt{2}\text{V(peak)}\text{=1.506V(peak)}$$

Figure 5.9 shows the output and the input waveforms.

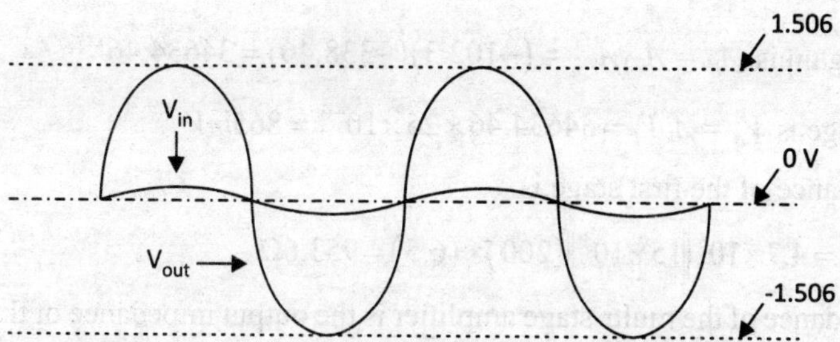

Fig. 5.9: Input and output waveforms for Example 5.4

Example 5.5: For the multi-stage amplifier shown in Figure 5.10, determine the following

(a) Overall voltage gain

(b) Output voltage of transistors Q_1 and Q_2

(c) Input impedance of first stage

(d) Output impedance of second stage

Solution:

(a) The dc bias analysis is done first

$V_B = 4.7V$, $V_E = 4.0V$, $V_C = 11V$, $I_E = 4mA$

$$r_e = \frac{26mV}{I_E} = \frac{26mV}{4mA} = 6.5\Omega$$

The voltage gain of the first stage is

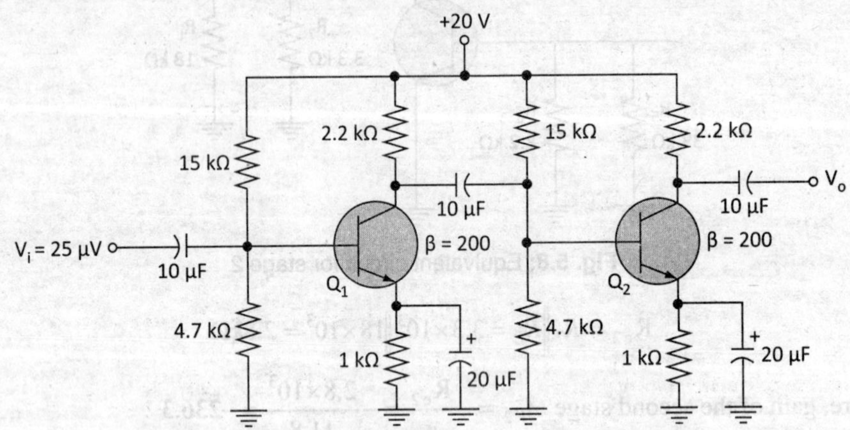

Fig. 5.10: Example 5.5

$$A_{V1} = -\frac{R_4 \| (R_5 \| R_6 \| \beta r_e)}{r_e} = -\frac{(2.2\times10^3) \| \left[15\times10^3 \| 4.7\times10^3 \| (200\times6.5)\right]}{6.5} = -\frac{665}{6.5} = -102.3$$

The voltage gain of the second stage is

$$A_{V2} = -\frac{R_7}{r_e} = -\frac{2.2\times10^3}{6.5} = -338.46$$

Overall voltage gain is $A_V = A_{V1}A_{V2} = (-102.3)(-338.46) = 34634.46$

The output voltage is $V_o = A_V V_i = 34634.46\times25\times10^{-6} = 865mV$

The input impedance of the first stage is

$$Z_{i1} = R_1 \| R_2 \| \beta r_e = 4.7\times10^3 \| 15\times10^3 \| (200)\times(6.5) = 953.6\Omega$$

The output impedance of the multi-stage amplifier is the output impedance of the second stage which in turn is equal to R_7. Therefore, output impedance is equal to 2.2kΩ.

5.2.3 Impedance-coupled Multi-stage Amplifier

Impedance coupling is very similar to R-C coupling. The difference lies in the use of an impedance device such as a coil to replace the load resistor in the first stage. Figure 5.11 shows the circuit diagram of a two-stage impedance-coupled amplifier. In this case, coil L_1 is the load for transistor Q_1 and it handles the output signal of the first stage as shown in Figure 5.11. Since the DC resistance of the coil is low, the efficiency of the amplifier stage is increased. The amplitude of the signal provided by the output of the first stage depends on the inductive reactance of L_1. Load inductors are most effective at high frequencies because the inductance of the coil increases with frequency. This explains why impedance coupling is not used for audio amplifiers. The other components in the network continue working in a manner similar to their counterparts in the R-Ccoupling network. C_1 couples the signal between stages while blocking the DC and the input signal to the second stage is taken across R_5.

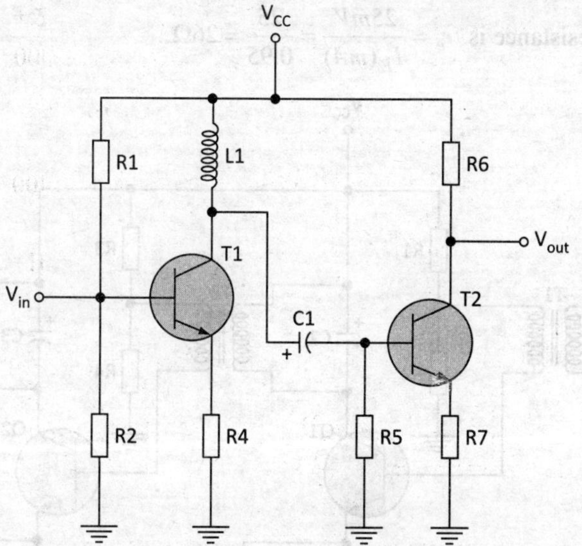

Fig. 5.11: Impedance coupling between two BJT transistors

5.2.4 Transformer-coupled Multi-stage Amplifier

In a *transformer-coupled amplifier*, the previous stage is connected to the next stage using a coupling transformer. This type of coupling is very popular for amplifiers handling radio frequencies (RF). Figure 5.12 shows a transformer coupled two-stage BJT amplifier. Selecting the turns ratio in the transformer appropriately allows either the voltage or the current to be increased. Transformer T_1 is used to couple the input signal to be amplified to the input of first stage. The transformer action of T_2 couples the signal from the first stage to the second stage. The primary of T_2 acts as the load on the first stage configured around Q_1 and the secondary of T_2 acts as the impedance for the second stage configured around Q_2. The transformer action couples the signal between the primary and the secondary of T_2. Transformer T_3 couples the amplified output signal to the load.

The transformer-coupled amplifiers offer a relatively narrow frequency response. At lower frequencies, the reactance of primary winding of the coupling transformer begins to fall, resulting in a decreased gain. At higher frequencies, the capacitance between adjacent turns of windings acts as a bypass capacitor to reduce the output voltage and hence gain.

Some of the advantages of this coupling scheme are that no signal power is lost in the collector or base resistors, because of the low winding resistance of the transformer. It provides a higher voltage gain than R-C coupled amplifier and it provides an excellent resistance matching between the stages.

Major disadvantages include that the coupling transformer is expensive and bulky, particularly when operated at audio frequencies and it tends to produce 'hum' in the circuit.

Example 5.6: Figure 5.13 shows a two stage transformer-coupled transistor amplifier. Determine the voltage gains of the individual stages and the overall voltage gain. Assume that $V_{BE} = 0$.

Solution:

The emitter current is $I_E = \dfrac{V_{CC}}{R_E + \dfrac{R_B}{\beta}} = \dfrac{10}{(1\times10^3)+\left(\dfrac{470\times10^3}{50}\right)} A = 0.96 mA$

AC emitter diode resistance is $r_e = \dfrac{25mV}{I_E(mA)} = \dfrac{25}{0.95} = 26\Omega$

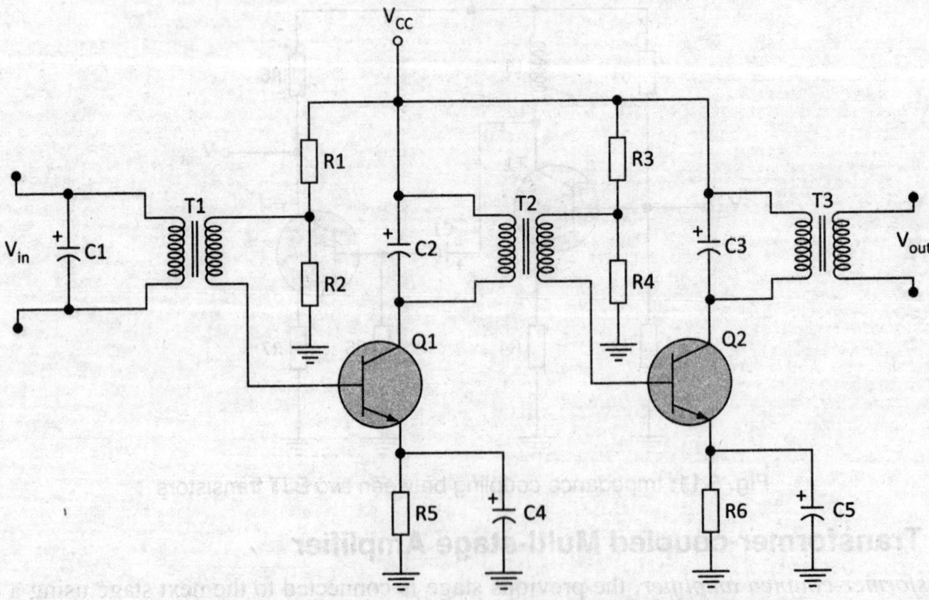

Fig. 5.12: Transformer coupled two-stage BJT amplifier

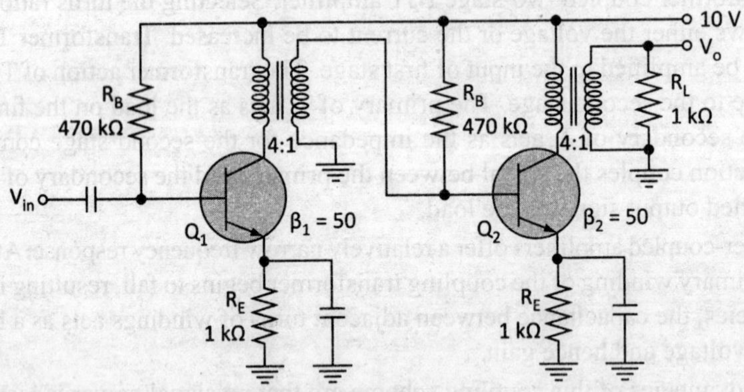

Fig. 5.13: Example 5.6

Input resistance of the first stage is $R_{i1} = R_B \| (\beta r_{e1}) = (470 \times 10^3) \| (50 \times 26)\Omega = 1296\Omega$

Input resistance of the second stage is $R_{i2} = R_B \| (\beta r_{e2}) = (470 \times 10^3) \| (50 \times 26)\Omega = 1296\Omega$

The input resistance of the second stage, transformed to the primary side is given by:

$R_{i2}' = a^2 R_{i2} = (4)^2 \times 1296 = 20736\Omega$

Output resistance of the first stage = Input resistance of the second stage = 20736Ω

Output resistance of the second stage, transformed to the primary side is given by:

$$R_{o2} = a^2 R_L = (4)^2 \times 1000 = 16000\Omega$$

Voltage gain of the first stage $A_{V1} = \frac{R_{o1}}{r_{e1}} = \frac{20736}{26} = 797.5$

Voltage gain of the second stage $A_{V2} = \frac{R_{o2}}{r_{e2}} = \frac{16000}{26} = 615.4$

Overall voltage gain $A_V = A_{V1}A_{V2} = 797.5 \times 615.4 = 490782$

5.3 MULTISTAGE FET AMPLIFIERS

The principles of BJT multistage amplifiers apply equally well to multi-stage FET amplifiers. R-C coupled multi-stage FET amplifiers, which is the most common of all types, is briefly discussed in the following paragraphs.

Figure 5.14 shows a cascaded three-stage RC-coupled JFET amplifier. The gains of the first, second and third stages are given respectively by eqns. (5.10), (5.11) and (5.12).

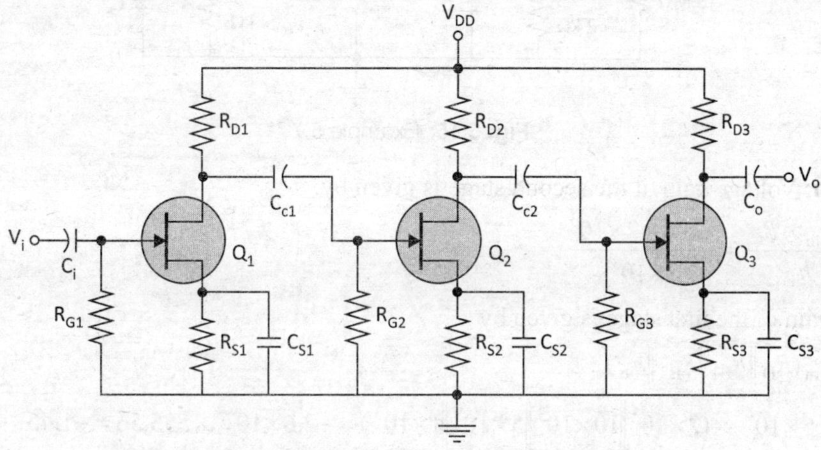

Fig. 5.14: Cascaded three-stage RC-coupled JFET amplifier

$$A_{v1} = -g_{m1}R_{D1} \tag{5.10}$$

$$A_{v2} = -g_{m2}R_{D2} \tag{5.11}$$

$$A_{v3} = -g_{m3}R_{D3} \tag{5.12}$$

where R_{D1}, R_{D2} and R_{D3} are the drain resistors for stage-1, stage-2 and stage-3 amplifiers respectively; g_{m1}, g_{m2} and g_{m3} are the transconductance values for the stage-1, stage-2 and stage-3 amplifiers, respectively. The overall gain A_v is given by:

$$A_v = A_{v1} \times A_{v2} \times A_{v3} \tag{5.13}$$

The input impedance Z_i of the cascaded amplifier is the same as the input impedance of the stage 1.

$$Z_i = R_{G1} \tag{5.14}$$

The output impedance Z_o is given by the output impedance of the last stage.

$$Z_o = R_{D3} \tag{5.15}$$

A combination of FET and BJT stages can also be used to provide both high value of voltage gain as well as high value of input impedance.

Example 5.7: Figure 5.15 shows a two-stage cascaded amplifier with a common-source JFET amplifier as the first stage feeding a common-emitter BJT amplifier. Calculate the voltage gain, input and output impedances of the amplifier. Given that h_{ie} and h_{fe} parameters of the transistor are 1 kΩ and 100, respectively. Assume that the effect of h_{oe} is negligible. The transconductance g_m of the JFET is 2.6 mS.

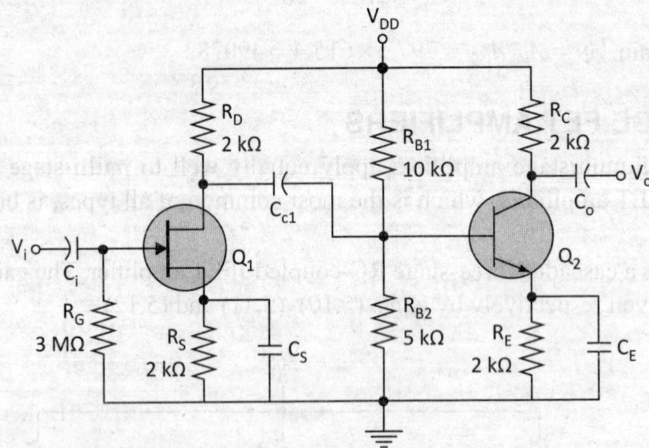

Fig. 5.15: Example 5.7

Solution: Voltage gain of the second stage is given by:

$$A_{v2} = \frac{-h_{fe} \times R_C}{h_{ie}} = \frac{-100 \times 2 \times 10^3}{1 \times 10^3}$$

Voltage gain of the first stage is given by

$$A_{v1} = -g_m (R_D \| R_{B1} \| R_{B2} \| h_{ie})$$

$$= -2.6 \times 10^{-3} \times (2 \times 10^3 \| 10 \times 10^3 \| 5 \times 10^3 \| 1 \times 10^3) = -2.6 \times 10^{-3} \times 555.56 = -1.45$$

Overall voltage gain is given by $A_v = A_{v1} \times A_{v2} = -200 \times -1.45 = 290$.

The input impedance of the amplifier Z_i is given by $Z_i = R_G$. Therefore, $Z_i = 3$ MΩ.

The output impedance of the amplifier is given by $Z_o = R_C \| (1/h_{oe})$. As the effect of h_{oe} is negligible, therefore $Z_o = R_c = 2$ kΩ.

Example 5.8: Figure 5.16 shows a two stage amplifier. Determine the values of (a) voltage gain of the amplifier (b) input impedance of the amplifier and (c) output impedance of the amplifier. It is given that h_{ie} =1200Ω, h_{fe} = 120, effect of h_{oe} is negligible and g_m = 3mS.

Solution:

(a) Voltage gain of the first stage is given by $A_{V1} = \dfrac{h_{fe} \times (R_C \| R_G)}{h_{ie}} = \dfrac{120 \times (2 \times 10^3 \| 2 \times 10^6)}{1200} = -200$

Voltage gain of the second stage $A_{V2} = -g_m R_D = -3 \times 10^{-3} \times 2 \times 10^3 = -6$

Overall voltage gain, $A_V = A_{V1} A_{V2} = -200 \times -6 = 1200$

(b) Input resistance of the amplifier, $R_i = R_{B1} \| R_{B2} \| h_{ie} = 10\times10^3 \| 5\times10^3 \| 1.2\times10^3 = 882.12\Omega$

(c) The output impedance of the amplifier is $Z_o = R_D = 2k\Omega$

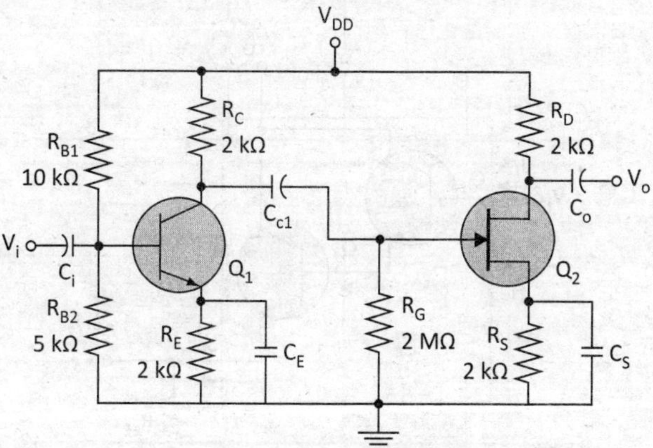

Fig. 5.16: Example 5.8

5.4 DARLINGTON AMPLIFIERS

Darlington amplifiers refer to the connection of two bipolar transistors wherein their collector terminals are tied together and the emitter terminal of one of the transistors is connected to the base terminal of the other transistor. In other words, the Darlington connection can be considered as two cascaded emitter followers, with the first stage having an infinite emitter resistance. The composite transistor acts as a single unit as shown in Figure 5.17, with a current gain approximately equal to the product of the current gains of the individual transistors. If the individual transistors have current gains of β_1 and β_2, then the Darlington connection provides an approximate current gain of β_D given by:

$$\beta_D = \beta_1 \times \beta_2 \tag{5.16}$$

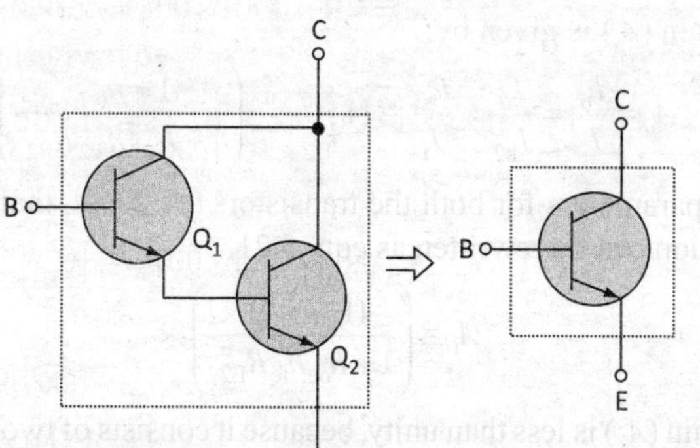

Fig. 5.17: Darlington transistor

It offers other advantages like significantly increased input impedance and reduced output impedance. The values of these parameters are derived in the subsequent paragraphs. Figure 5.18 shows a circuit configuration employing a Darlington pair. The biasing network for Q_1 has not been included for simplicity of analysis.

The current gain for the second transistor Q_2 is given by:

$$A_{i2} = \frac{I_o}{I_{b2}} = \frac{1 + h_{fe2}}{1 + h_{oe2} R_{E2}} \cong 1 + h_{fe2} \tag{5.17}$$

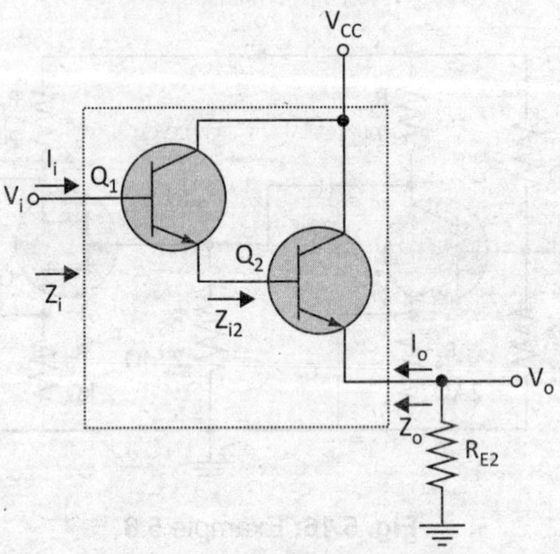

Fig. 5.18: Circuit using a Darlington transistor

The input resistance of the second stage is given by:

$$Z_{i2} = h_{ie2} + (1 + h_{fe2}) R_{E2} \cong (1 + h_{fe2}) R_{E2} \tag{5.18}$$

Z_{i2} is the effective load resistance for the first-stage Q_1 and the current gain for the first stage (A_{i1}) is given by:

$$A_{i1} = \frac{I_{e1}}{I_i} = \frac{I_{b2}}{I_i} = \frac{1 + h_{fe1}}{1 + h_{oe1} Z_{i2}}$$
$$\cong \frac{1 + h_{fe1}}{1 + h_{oe1}(1 + h_{fe2}) R_{E2}} \cong \frac{1 + h_{fe1}}{1 + h_{oe1} h_{fe2} R_{E2}} \tag{5.19}$$

The overall current gain (A_i) is given by:

$$A_i = \frac{I_o}{I_i} = \frac{I_o}{I_{b2}} \times \frac{I_{b2}}{I_i} \cong (1 + h_{fe2}) \left(\frac{1 + h_{fe1}}{1 + h_{oe1} h_{fe2} R_{E2}} \right) \tag{5.20}$$

Assuming that the h-parameters for both the transistors are equal, that is, $h_{fe1} = h_{fe2} = h_{fe}$ and $h_{oe1} = h_{oe2} = h_{oe}$, the above equation can be rewritten as eqn. 5.21.

$$A_i \cong \left(\frac{(1 + h_{fe})^2}{1 + h_{oe} h_{fe} R_{E2}} \right) \tag{5.21}$$

The overall voltage gain (A_v) is less than unity, because it consists of two emitter followers in cascade, each offering a voltage gain of slightly less than unity.

$$A_v = \frac{V_o}{V_i} \cong \left(1 - \frac{h_{ie}}{Z_{i2}} \right) \tag{5.22}$$

Assuming that $A_v \cong 1$, the overall input impedance (Z_i) is given by:

$$Z_i = \frac{A_i R_{E2}}{A_v} \cong A_i R_{E2} \cong \frac{(1 + h_{fe})^2 R_{E2}}{1 + h_{oe} h_{fe} R_{E2}} \tag{5.23}$$

The output impedance (Z_o) is given by:

$$Z_o \cong \frac{R_S + h_{ie}}{(1+h_{fe})^2} + \frac{h_{ie}}{1+h_{fe}} \tag{5.24}$$

where R_S is the value of the source resistance.

In deriving the above equations, we have omitted the biasing network for transistor Q_1 to simplify the analysis. The biasing network mainly affects the input impedance of the network. Figure 5.19(a) shows the biasing arrangement. Let us now consider the effect of the biasing network of transistor Q_1 on the input impedance of the network.

The overall input impedance (Z_i') is given by:

$$Z_i' = Z_i \| R \tag{5.25}$$

where $R = R_{B1} \| R_{B2}$.

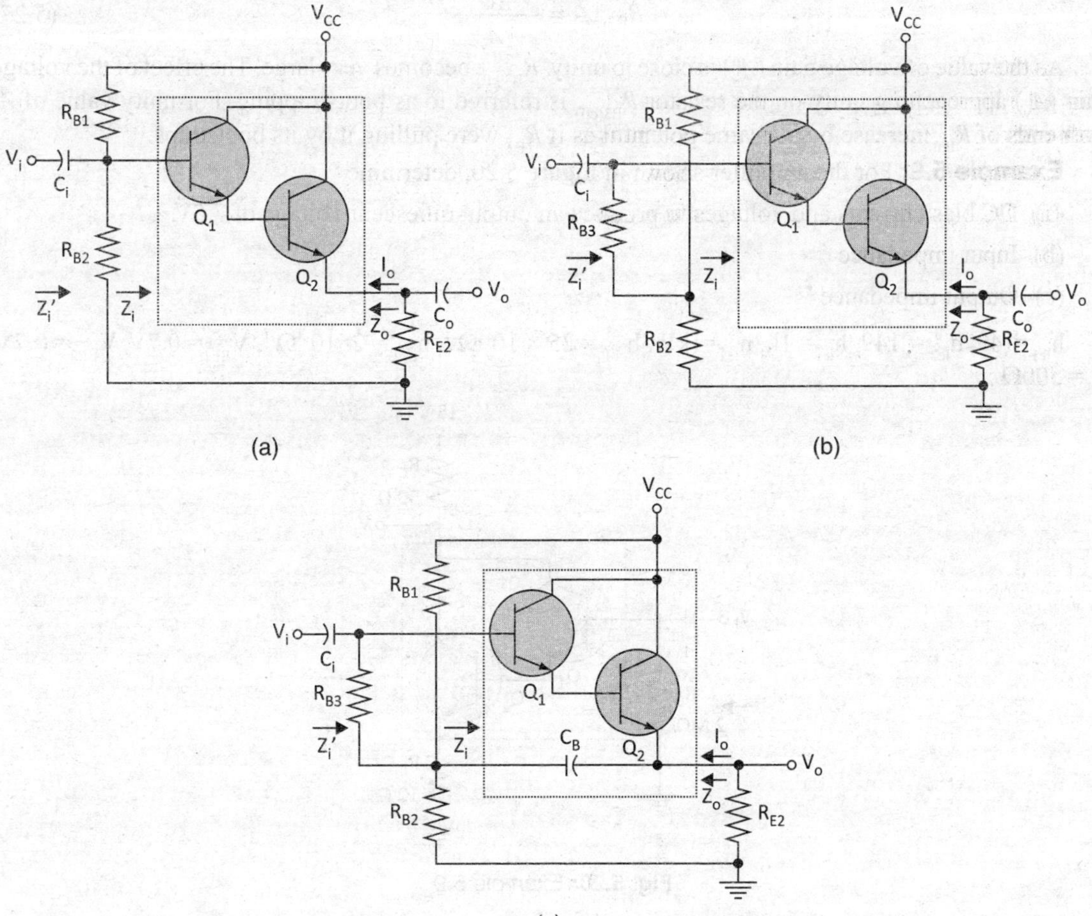

Fig. 5.19: (a) Darlington amplifier with input bias circuit (b) Darlington amplifier with modified input bias circuit (c) bootstrapping in Darlington amplifier

The value of R (i.e., parallel combination of R_{B1} and R_{B2}) is much less than the value of Z_i. Therefore, the overall input impedance (Z_i') is appreciably smaller than Z_i. This nullifies one of the major advantages of high input impedance offered by a Darlington amplifier.

This can be partially overcome by adding a resistor R_{B3} as shown in Figure 5.19(b). The new value of R is now given by:

$$R = R_{B1} \| R_{B2} + R_{B3} \tag{5.26}$$

The value of R is still less than Z_i. The value of R can be substantially improved if we add a capacitor C_B in addition to resistor R_B [Figure 5.19(c)]. The reactance of the capacitor is negligible at the low frequencies at which the amplifier is to be used. Hence, the capacitor (C_B) directly couples the output voltage V_o to the lower side of resistor R_{B3}. The other end of the resistor R_{B3} is connected to the input voltage V_i, which is approximately equal to the output voltage V_o. Therefore, there is very small AC voltage drop across the resistor R_{B3}. Hence, it draws a very small AC current from the input voltage V_i. Therefore, the effective value of R_{B3} has increased manifold. The effective value of R_{B3} can be calculated by making use of Miller's effect and is given by eqn. 5.27.

$$R_{B3(eff)} = \frac{R_{B3}}{1 - A_v} \tag{5.27}$$

As the value of voltage gain (A_v) is close to unity, $R_{B3(eff)}$ becomes very large. The effect of the voltage gain (A_v) approaching unity on the resistor $R_{B3(eff)}$ is referred to as bootstrapping. For unity value of A_v both ends of R_{B3} increase by the same potential as if R_{B3} were pulling it by its bootstraps.

Example 5.9: For the amplifier shown in Figure 5.20, determine

(a) DC bias currents and voltages to produce an output quiescent voltage of 7.5V.

(b) Input impedance

(c) Output impedance

h_{fe1}=149, h_{fe2} = 149, h_{ie1}= 1k, h_{ie2}=1kW, h_{oe1} = 25 × $10^{-4}\Omega^{-1}$, h_{oe2} = $2510^{-4}\Omega^{-1}$, V_{BE1}= 0.7V, V_{BE2}= 0.7V, R_S= 500Ω

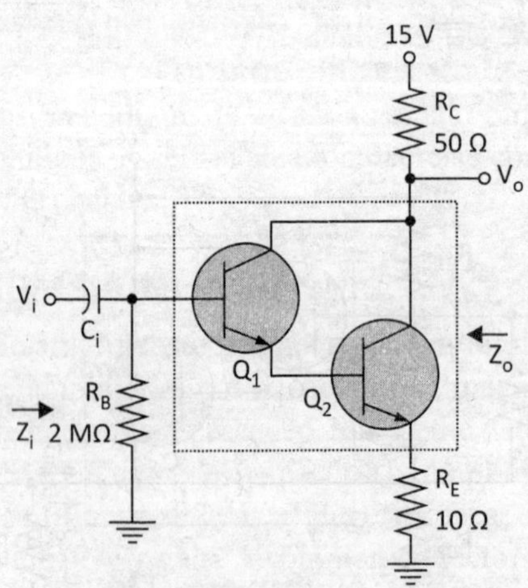

Fig. 5.20: Example 5.9

Solution: The collector current of Q_2 for a quiescent output voltage of 7.5V is $I_{C2} = \frac{15 - 7.5}{50} = 150mA$

Therefore, the emitter current of $Q_2 \cong$ 150mA

The emitter current of Q_1 $I_{E1} = \frac{I_{E2}}{1 + h_{fe}} = \frac{150 \times 10^{-3}}{150} A = 1mA$

Base current of transistor $Q_1 = \frac{I_{E1}}{(1+h_{fe})} = \frac{1\times10^{-3}}{150} = 6.67\mu A$

Collector voltages of both the transistors = 7.5V

Emitter voltage of transistor Q_2 = 10 × 150 × 10^{-3} = 1.5V

Value of emitter voltage of transistor Q_1 = Value of base voltage of transistor Q_2 = 2.2V

$$Z_i' = \frac{(1+h_{fe})^2 R_E}{1+h_{oe}h_{fe}R_E} = \frac{(150)^2 \times 10}{1+25\times10^{-4}\times149\times10} = 47.62k\Omega$$

$$Z_i = Z_i' \| R_B = 46.5k\Omega$$

$$Z_o = \frac{R_s + h_{ie}}{(1+h_{fe})^2} + \frac{h_{ie}}{(1+h_{fe})} = \frac{500+1000}{(150)^2} + \frac{1000}{(150)} = 6.73\Omega$$

5.5 CASCODE AMPLIFIERS

Cascode amplifiers are two-stage amplifiers comprising a transconductance amplifier followed by a current buffer. They offer advantages like high input–output isolation, high input impedance and high output impedance. In a BJT Cascode amplifier configuration, the common-emitter transistor is followed by a common-base connection. Figure 5.21(a) shows the circuit diagram of a Cascode amplifier wherein the transistor Q_1 is configured as common-emitter amplifier and transistor Q_2 is configured as common-base amplifier. The common-base amplifier configured around transistor Q_2 offers large bandwidth, but its input impedance is low. Because of the low input impedance of Q_2, the voltage gain of Q_1 is low. Therefore, the Miller component of capacitance of transistor Q_1 is small and the bandwidth of the cascode amplifier is wider than for the common-emitter stage. Hence, it is used for high-frequency operation.

In the case of an FET-based cascode amplifier, common-source amplifier is followed by common-gate amplifier as shown in Figure 5.21(b).

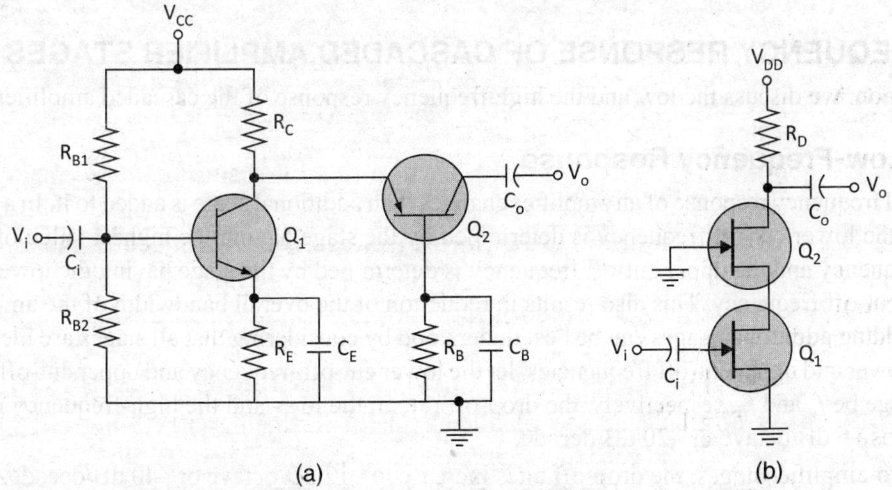

Fig. 5.21: (a) BJT cascode amplifier (b) FET cascode amplifier

Example 5.10: Refer to the Cascode amplifier circuit shown in Figure 5.22. Determine the values of resistors R_E, R_1 and R_2 such that the operating point is I_{CQ} = 10 mA and V_{CEQ} = 10 V. Given that the value of β = 100 and V_{BE} of each transistor is 0.7 V.

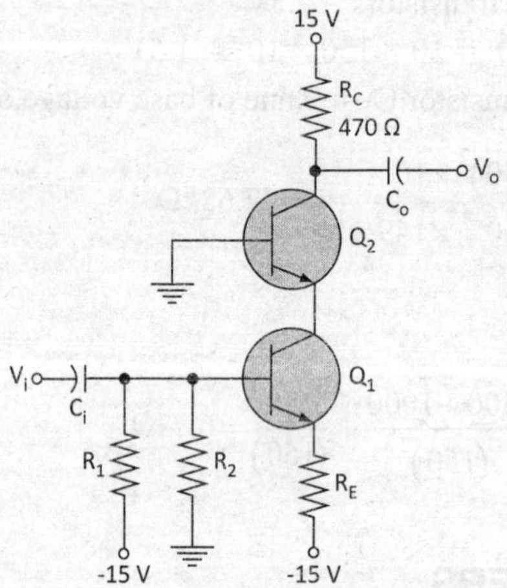

Fig. 5.22: Example 5.10

Solution: DC voltage drop across the resistor R_C is given by 470 × 10 × 10^{-3} = 4.7 V

Therefore, the voltage drop across the resistor R_E is 15 – 4.7 – 10 – 10 – (– 15) = 30 – 24.7 = 5.3 V

Value of resistor R_E is approximately equal to 5.3/10 × 10^{-3} = 5.3 × 10^3 = 5.3 kΩ

Voltage at the base of transistor Q_1 is given by –15 + 5.3 + 0.7 = –9 V

For good bias stability, current through resistor R_2>>I_{BQ1}. Value of R_2 should not be so large such that this condition is not met and also it should not be too small to have an undue load on the power supply.

Assume R_2 = 10 kΩ. Current through R_2 is 9/(10 × 10^3) = 0.9 mA

Current through resistor R_1 = 0.9 × 10^{-3} – 10 × 10^{-3}/100 = 9 × 10^{-3} – 10 × 10^{-5} = 0.89 × 10^{-3} = 0.89 mA

Voltage drop across R_1 is 15 – 9 = 6 V

Therefore, value of resistor R_1 = 6/(0.89 × 10^{-3}) = 6.74 kΩ

5.6 FREQUENCY RESPONSE OF CASCADED AMPLIFIER STAGES

In this section, we discuss the low and the high frequency response of the cascaded amplifier stages.

5.6.1 Low-Frequency Response

The overall frequency response of an amplifier changes if an additional stage is added to it. In a multistage amplifier, the lower cut-off frequency is determined by the stage having the highest value of the lower cut-off frequency and the upper cut-off frequency is determined by the stage having the lowest value of the upper cut-off frequency. This also results in reduction of the overall bandwidth of the amplifier. The effect of adding additional stages can be best understood by considering that all stages are identical with the same lower and upper cut-off frequencies. let the lower cut-off frequency and upper cut-off frequency of each stage be f_L and f_H, respectively. the drop-off rate in the low- and the high-frequency regions for each stage is –6 dB/octave or –20 dB/decade.

For two-amplifier stages, the drop-off rates increase to –12 dB/octave or –40 dB/decade. The lower cut-off frequency (f_L') where the amplitude falls by 3 dB is given by:

$$f_L' = \frac{f_L}{\sqrt{2^{1/2}-1}} = \frac{f_L}{0.64} = 1.56 f_L \tag{5.28}$$

The upper cut-off frequency f_H' for a two-stage amplifier is given by:

$$f_H' = f_H\sqrt{2^{1/2}-1} = 0.64 f_H \tag{5.29}$$

Figure 5.23 shows the response of the two-stage amplifier. The asymptotic response is shown in Figure 5.23(a) whereas the actual response is shown in Figure 5.23(b). Also the response of single-stage amplifiers is shown to highlight the effect of cascading the two stages.

The above discussion can be generalized for n stages. let the gain of each individual stage in the mid frequency region be A_{vmid} and the gain in the low-frequency region be A_{vlow}. Let the overall mid-frequency gain be $A_{vmid\text{-}overall}$ and the overall low-frequency gain be $A_{vlow\text{-}overall}$. Also, the lower and the upper cut-off frequencies for the individual stages are f_L and f_H, respectively, and the lower and the upper cut-off frequencies for the overall amplifier are f_{Ln} and f_{Hn}, respectively.

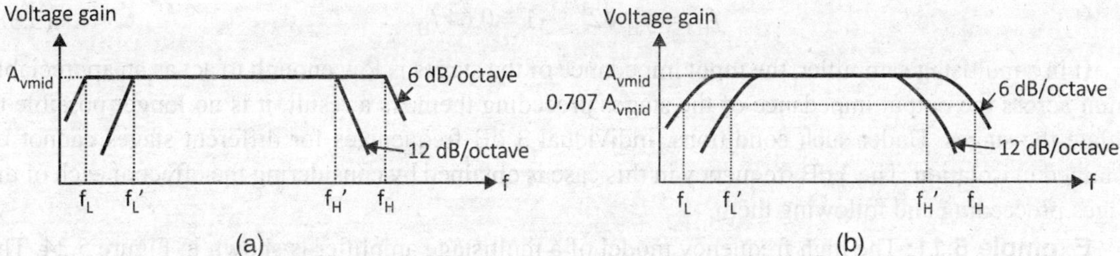

Fig. 5.23: Frequency response (a) Asymptotic response (b) actual response

Therefore,

$$A_{vmid\text{-}overall} = (A_{vmid})^n \tag{5.30}$$

$$A_{vlow\text{-}overall} = (A_{vlow})^n \tag{5.31}$$

Taking the ratio of eqns. (5.30) and (5.31) we get,

$$\frac{A_{vlow\text{-}overall}}{A_{vmid\text{-}overall}} = \left(\frac{A_{vlow}}{A_{vmid}}\right)^n \tag{5.32}$$

$$\frac{A_{vlow\text{-}overall}}{A_{vmid\text{-}overall}} = \left(\frac{1}{(1 - jf_L/f)}\right)^n \tag{5.33}$$

Let the frequency at which the magnitude of the expression given by Eqn. (5.33) become $1/\sqrt{2}$ (–3 dB) be f_{Ln}. Therefore,

$$\frac{1}{\sqrt{[1+(f_L/f_{Ln})^2]^n}} = \frac{1}{\sqrt{2}} \tag{5.34}$$

On solving Eqn. (5.34), we get,

$$f_{Ln} = \frac{f_L}{\sqrt{2^{1/n}-1}} \tag{5.35}$$

Similarly, the overall upper cut-off frequency (f_{Hn}) is given by:

$$f_{Hn} = f_H\sqrt{2^{1/n}-1} \tag{5.36}$$

It may be mentioned here that increase in the number of stages is not always associated with decrease in the bandwidth. If the value of mid-band gain is kept fixed then the bandwidth may increase with increase in the number of stages.

5.6.2 High-frequency Response

The overall frequency response of an amplifier changes if an additional stage isadded to it. In a multistage amplifier, the upper cut-off frequency is determined by the stage having the smallest value of the upper cut-off frequency.

The upper cut-off frequency (f_{Hn}) for "n" identical non-interactive stage amplifiers is given by:

$$f_{Hn} = f_H\sqrt{2^{1/n} - 1} \tag{5.37}$$

where f_H is the upper cut-off frequency of each individual stage. The upper cut-off frequency of a two-stage amplifier (f_{H2}) is therefore given by:

$$f_{H2} = f_H\sqrt{2^{1/2} - 1} = 0.64 f_H \tag{5.38}$$

If in a multistage amplifier, the input impedance of the stages is low enough to act as an appreciable shunt across the output impedance of the stages preceding them.As a result, it is no longer possible to isolate the stages. Under such conditions, individual 3 dB frequencies for different stages cannot be obtained in isolation. The 3 dB frequency in this case is obtained by considering the effect of each of the stages proceeding and following them.

Example 5.11: The high frequency model of a multistage amplifier is shown in Figure 5.24. The values of the gains are $A_1 = 10$, $A_2 = -100$, $A_3 = -10$ and $A_4 = 1$. The values of resistances $R_{o1} = 100\Omega$, $R_{o2} = 10\Omega$, $R_{o3} = 1k\Omega$ and $R_{o4} = 100\Omega$. The values of capacitors $C_2 = 10nF$, $C_3 = 10nF$ and $C_4 = 1pF$.

Calculate the following (A) ignoring the effect of capacitor C_C and (B) with $C_C = 1nF$.

(a) Midband gain, the break frequencies and voltage gain as a function of frequency

(b) Magnitude bode plot of the voltage gain

(c) Phase of the overall gain as a function of frequency

(d) If the above amplifier is to be used in a feedback circuit, for what values of β, the feedback amplifier is stable.

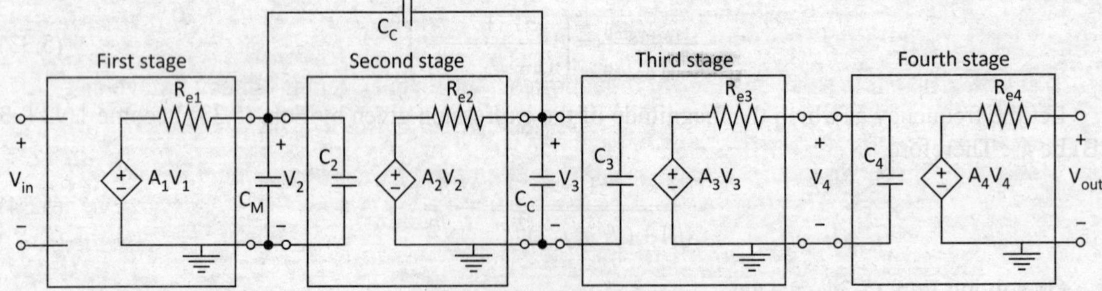

Fig. 5.24: Example 5.11

Solution: A. Without considering the effect of C_C

(a) Voltage gain is

$$A_V(j\omega)=\frac{A_1A_2A_3A_4}{\left(1+j\frac{\omega}{\omega_1}\right)\left(1+j\frac{\omega}{\omega_2}\right)\left(1+j\frac{\omega}{\omega_3}\right)}$$

$A_{mid} = A_1A_2A_3A_4 = 10^4$

Therefore, $(A_{mid})dB = 80dB$

$$\omega_1=\frac{1}{R_{o1}C_2}=\frac{1}{(100)(10\times10^{-9})}=10^6\ rad/s$$

$$\omega_2=\frac{1}{R_{o2}C_3}=\frac{1}{(10)(10\times10^{-9})}=10^7\ rad/s$$

$$\omega_3=\frac{1}{R_{o3}C_4}=\frac{1}{(1000)(10^{-12})}=10^9\ rad/s$$

(b) The magnitude bode plot is shown as the graph with bold lines in Figure 5.25.

(c) The phase plot is shown as the graph with bold lines in Figure 5.26.

(d) Critical frequency is $\omega_c \cong 10^8$ rad/sec where $|A(j\omega_c)|_{dB} = 20dB$

Therefore, $A(j\omega_c)=10$

$$\beta A(j\omega_c)\le -1 \text{ or } 10\beta \le 1$$

Therefore, $\beta \le 0.1$

B. When Considering C_C

(a) With C_C, C_2 and C_3 are modified

$$C_M = C_C(1+A_2)=\left(10^{-9}\right)101\cong 100\times10^{-9}F$$

$$C_2^{'} = C_2 + C_M = 110\times10^{-9}F$$

Therefore, $\omega_1^{'}=\dfrac{1}{R_{o1}C_2^{'}}\cong 10^4\ rad/sec$

$$C_3^{'} = C_3 + C_C = 11\times10^{-9}F$$

Therefore, $\omega_2^{'}=\dfrac{1}{R_{o2}C_3^{'}}\cong 10^7\ rad/sec$

$$\omega_3 = 10^9\ rad/sec$$

(b) The magnitude bode plot is shown as the graph with dotted lines in Figure 5.25.

(c) The phase plot is shown as the graph with dotted lines in Figure 5.26.

(d) Critical frequency is $\omega_c^{'} \cong 10^8$ rad/sec.

$$|A(j\omega_c)|_{dB} = -20dB$$

Then with C_C, feedback amplifier is stable for any $\beta \le 1$, since $|A(j\omega_c)|_{dB} < 0$

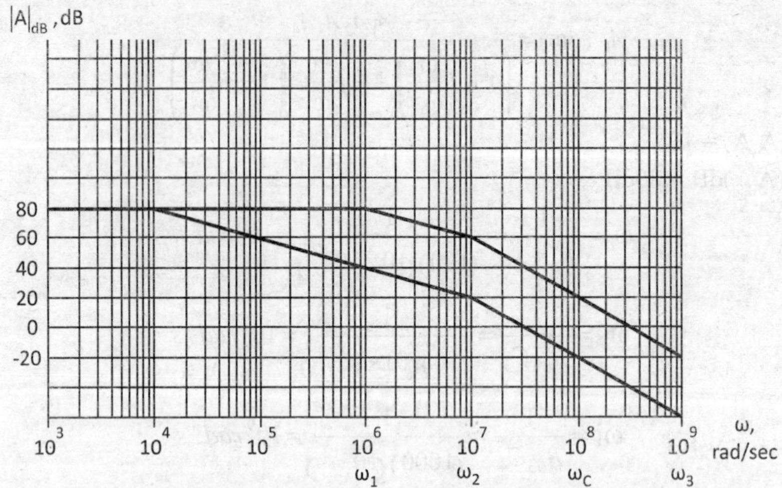

Fig. 5.25: Magnitude bode plot of example 5.11

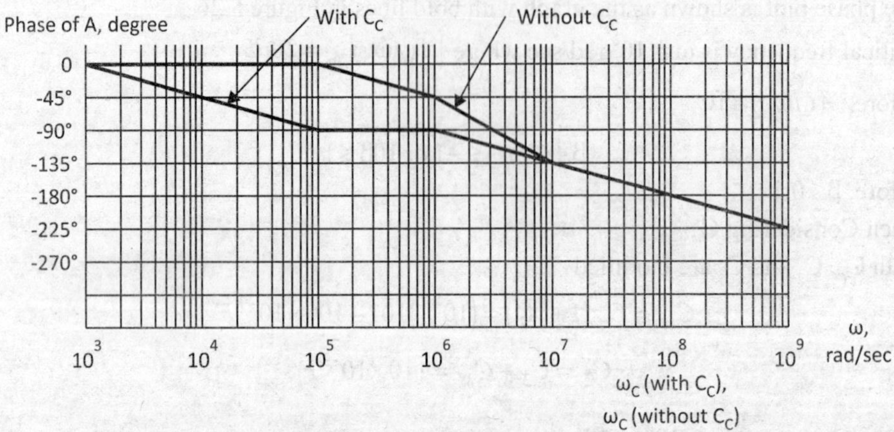

Fig. 5.26: Phase plot of example 5.11

Example 5.12: For the cascaded amplifier shown in Figure 5.27, determine the overall upper cut-off frequency of the amplifier given that h_{ie} for each transistor is 1000 Ω, $r_{b¢e}$ is 800 Ω, $r_{bb¢}$ is 200 Ω, C_c is 5 pF, C_e is 40 pF and $g_m = 60 \times 10^{-3}$ mhos.

Solution: The overall upper cut-off frequency can be determined by determining the upper cut-off frequency for each stage.

The upper cut-off frequency for the third stage amplifier (f_{H3}) is given by:

$$f_{H3} = \frac{1}{2\pi R_{3'}[C_e + C_c(1 + g_m R_{C3})]}$$

$$R_{3'} = \frac{(R_{C2} \| R_{B5} \| R_{B6} + r_{bb'3}) \times r_{b'e3}}{(R_{C2} \| R_{B5} \| R_{B6} + h_{ie3})}$$

$$= \frac{(1000 \| 2000 \| 200 + 200) \times 800}{(1000 \| 2000 \| 200 + 1000)} = 245.34\Omega$$

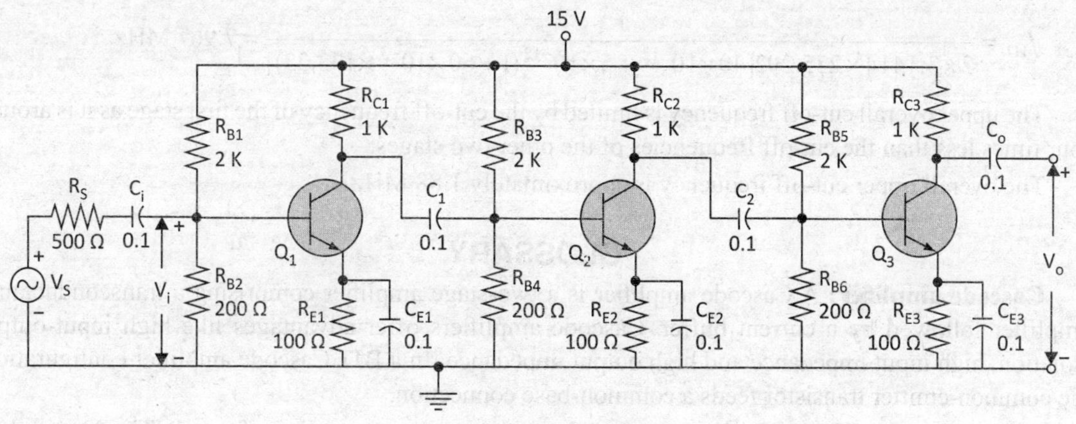

Fig. 5.27: Example 5.12

$$f_{H3} = \frac{1}{2\times 3.1414\times 245.34[40\times 10^{-12} + 5\times 10^{-12}(1+60\times 10^{-3}\times 1\times 10^{3})]} = 1.88 \text{ MHz}$$

The upper cut-off frequency for the second stage (f_{H2}) is given by:

$$f_{H2} = \frac{1}{2\pi R_{2'}[C_e + C_c(1+g_m R_{L2'})]}$$

The effective value of load resistance for the second stage ($R_{L2'}$) is given by:

$$R_{L2'} = R_{C2}\|R_{B5}\|R_{B6}\|h_{ie3} = 1000\|2000\|200\|1000 = 133.33\Omega$$

The value of $R_{2'}$ is given by:

$$R_{2'} = \frac{(R_{C1}\|R_{B3}\|R_{B4} + r_{bb'2})\times r_{b'e2}}{(R_{C1}\|R_{B3}\|R_{B4} + h_{ie2})} = \frac{(1000\|2000\|200+200)\times 800}{(1000\|2000\|200+1000)} = 245.34\Omega$$

$$f_{H2} = \frac{1}{2\times 3.1414\times 245.34[40\times 10^{-12} + 5\times 10^{-12}(1+60\times 10^{-3}\times 133.33)]}$$

$$= 7.632 \text{ MHz}$$

The upper cut-off frequency for the first stage (f_{H1}) is given by:

$$f_{H1} = \frac{1}{2\pi R_{1'}[C_e + C_c(1+g_m R_{L1'})]}$$

The effective load resistance for the first stage ($R_{L1\acute{}}$) is given by:

$$R_{L1'} = R_{C1}\|R_{B3}\|R_{B4}\|h_{ie2} = 1000\|2000\|200\|1000 = 133.33\Omega$$

The value of $R_{1'}$ is given by:

$$R_{1'} = \frac{(R_s\|R_{B1}\|R_{B2} + r_{bb'1})\times r_{b'e1}}{(R_s\|R_{B1}\|R_{B2} + h_{ie1})}$$

$$= \frac{(500\|2000\|200+200)\times 800}{(500\|2000\|200+1000)} = \frac{(133.33+200)\times 800}{133.33+1000} = 235.292\Omega$$

$$f_{H1} = \frac{1}{2\times 3.1414\times 235.292[40\times 10^{-12}+5\times 10^{-12}(1+60\times 10^{-3}\times 133.33)]} = 7.967\text{ MHz}$$

The upper overall cut-off frequency is limited by the cut-off frequency of the first stage as it is around four times less than the cut-off frequencies of the other two stages.

The overall upper cut-off frequency is approximately 1.88 MHz.

GLOSSARY

Cascode amplifier: A Cascode amplifier is a two-stage amplifier comprising a transconductance amplifier followed by a current buffer. Cascode amplifiers offer advantages like high input-output isolation, high input impedance and high output impedance. In a BJT Cascode amplifier configuration, the common-emitter transistor feeds a common-base connection.

Darlington amplifier: ADarlington amplifier refers to the connection of two BJTs wherein their collector terminals are tied together and the emitter terminal of one of the transistors is connected to the base terminal of the other transistor. In other words, the Darlington connection can be considered as two cascaded emitter-follower stages, with the first stage having an infinite emitter resistance.

Direct-coupled multi-stage amplifier: In a direct-coupled multi-stage amplifier, output of one stage directly feeds the input of the following stage without the use of any coupling element such as coupling capacitor. Different amplifying stages inside an opamp are, for instance, direct-coupled. Direct coupling is also used for interconnecting common-emitter amplifier stages with emitter-follower stages.

Impedance-coupled multi-stage BJT amplifier: This type of coupling is very similar to RC coupling. The load resistor of the first stage is replaced by a coil, which also handles the output signal of the first stage. Since the DC resistance of the coil is low, the efficiency of the amplifier stage is increased.

Multistage Amplifiers: Multistage amplifier is a cascade connection of amplifiers. It is a series connection where the output of one stage feeds the input of the following stage.

R-C coupled multi-stage BJT amplifier: In an R-C coupled amplifier, a resistor and a capacitor are used for coupling from one stage to another.

Transformer-coupled multi-stage BJT amplifier: This type of coupling is very popular for amplifiers handling radio frequencies (RF). The transformer action couples the signal from one stage to another.

SUMMARY OF IMPORTANT FORMULAE

Multi-stage Amplifiers

1. A multistage amplifier the overall gain (A_v) is therefore given by:

$$A_v = A_{v1}\times A_{v2}\times A_{v3}\times\cdots\times A_{vn}$$

2. For a multistage amplifier the overall current gain is given by:

$$A_i = -A_v\times\left(\frac{Z_{i1}}{R_L}\right)$$

R-C coupled multi-stage BJT amplifier (Refer to Figure 5.4)

3. The voltage gain of the third stage is given by:

$$A_{v3} = \frac{-h_{fe3} \times [R_{C3} \| (1/h_{oe3})]}{h_{ie3}}$$

4. Similarly, the gain for the second stage A_{v2}, assuming $1/h_{oe2} >> R_{B5} \| R_{B6} \| R_{C2} \| h_{ie3}$ is given by:

$$A_{v2} = \frac{-h_{fe2} \times (R_{B5} \| R_{B6} \| R_{C2} \| h_{ie3})}{h_{ie2}}$$

5. The gain for the first stage A_{v1}, assuming $1/h_{oe1} >> R_{B3} \| R_{B4} \| R_{C1} \| h_{ie2}$ is given by:

$$A_{v1} = \frac{-h_{fe1} \times (R_{B3} \| R_{B4} \| R_{C1} \| h_{ie2})}{h_{ie1}}$$

6. The overall gain A_v is given by

$$A_v = A_{v1} \times A_{v2} \times A_{v3}$$

7. The overall input impedance of the amplifier is the same as the input impedance of stage 1

$$Z_i = R_{B1} \| R_{B2} \| h_{ie1}$$

8. The output impedance of the amplifier is equal to the output impedance of the last stage

$$Z_o = R_{C3} \| (1/h_{oe3})$$

n-stage RC-coupled JFET amplifier (Refer to Figure 5.14)

9. Overall gain A_v is given by:

$$A_v = A_{v1} \times A_{v2} \times A_{v3}$$

where $A_{v1} = -g_{m1} R_{D1}$, $A_{v2} = -g_{m2} R_{D2}$ and $A_{v3} = -g_{m3} R_{D3}$

10. The input impedance Z_i of the cascaded amplifier is the same as the input impedance of the stage 1

$$Z_i = R_{G1}$$

11. The output impedance Z_o is given by the output impedance of the last stage

$$Z_o = R_{D3}$$

Darlington Amplifier (Refer to Figure 5.18)

12. Current gain $\beta_D = \beta_1 \times \beta_2$

13. The overall current gain (A_i) is given by:

$$A_i \cong \left(\frac{(1 + h_{fe})^2}{1 + h_{oe} h_{fe} R_{E2}} \right)$$

14. The overall input impedance (Z_i) is given by:

$$Z_i = \frac{A_i R_{E2}}{A_v} \cong A_i R_{E2} \cong \frac{(1 + h_{fe})^2 R_{E2}}{1 + h_{oe} h_{fe} R_{E2}}$$

15. The output impedance (Z_o) is given by:

$$Z_o \cong \frac{R_S + h_{ie}}{(1 + h_{fe})^2} + \frac{h_{ie}}{1 + h_{fe}}$$

16. For two amplifier stages, the drop-off rates increase to –12 dB/octave or –40 dB/decade. The lower cut-off frequency (f_L') where the amplitude falls by 3 dB is given by:

$$f_L' = \frac{f_L}{\sqrt{2^{1/2}-1}} = \frac{f_L}{0.64} = 1.56 f_L$$

17. For two amplifier stages, the upper cut-off frequency f_H' is given by:

$$f_H' = f_H\sqrt{2^{1/2}-1} = 0.64 f_H$$

For a n-stage amplifier

18. $A_{vmid\text{-}overall} = (A_{vmid})^n$

19. The overall lower cut-off frequency (f_{Ln}) is given by:

$$f_{Ln} = \frac{f_L}{\sqrt{2^{1/n}-1}}$$

20. Similarly, the overall upper cut-off frequency (f_{Hn}) is given by:

$$f_{Hn} = f_H\sqrt{2^{1/n}-1}$$

REVIEW QUESTIONS

1. Draw the frequency response of an RC-coupled amplifier and a DC-coupled amplifier. Also explain the primary difference between the frequency response of the two amplifiers.
2. Why are Darlington transistors also referred to as super-beta transistors? Explain the concept using the internal schematic of Darlington transistors.
3. Explain the effect of cascading amplifier stages on the overall frequency response of the amplifier.
4. What are cascode amplifiers? What are the advantages offered by Cascode amplifiers?
5. What are multistage amplifiers? Write the expressions for overall voltage gain in terms of voltage gains of individual stages in dB.

PROBLEMS

1. Figure 5.28 shows a two-stage CC-CB amplifier. The values of input and output impedances and the voltage gains for each stage are shown in the figure. All the values are for no-load conditions. However, the input impedance and the output impedance of the first stage are under loaded conditions. Determine (a) loaded voltage gain for each stage(b) overall voltage gain of the amplifier and (c) total system voltage and current gain.

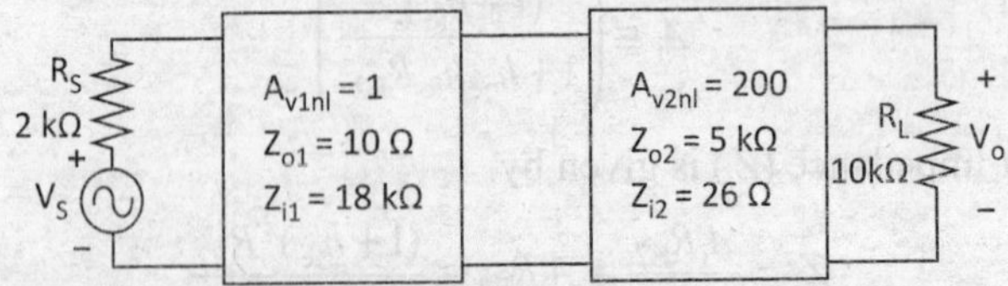

Fig. 5.28 : Problem 1

2. Figure 5.29 shows a two-stage BJT cascaded amplifier. Calculate the voltage gain, input and output impedance of the amplifier, given that h_{ie} and h_{fe} parameters of both the transistors are 1 kΩ and 100, respectively. Assume that the effect of h_{oe} is negligible.

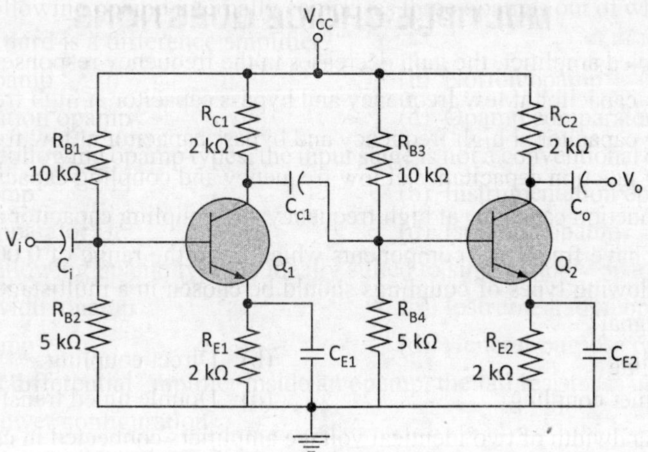

Fig. 5.29: Problem 2

3. For the circuit shown in Figure 5.30, determine the values of input resistances, output resistances, current gain and voltage gain for both the stages.

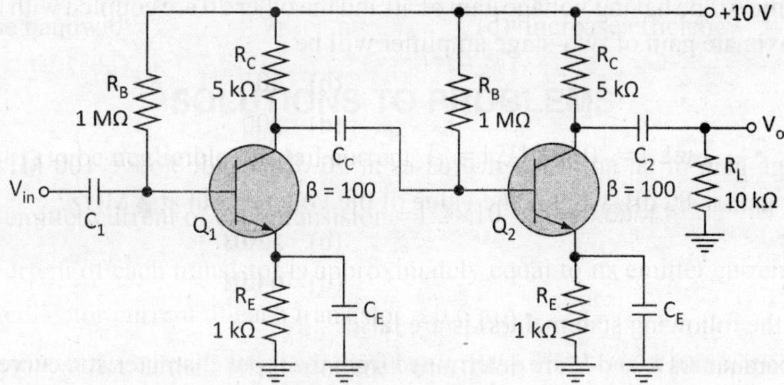

Fig. 5.30: Problem 3

4. Figure 5.31 shows a Darlington amplifier. The two transistors Q_1 and Q_2 are identical and the h-parameters for both the transistors are h_{ie} = 1 kΩ, h_{fe} = 100 and h_{oe} = 40 × 10^{-6} mhos. The values of the voltages V_{CC} = 15 V, V_{BE1} = 0.7 V and V_{BE2} = 0.7 V. Determine the following.
   (a) DC voltage and currents
   (b) Input impedance
   (c) Output impedance
   (d) Voltage gain
   (e) Current gain

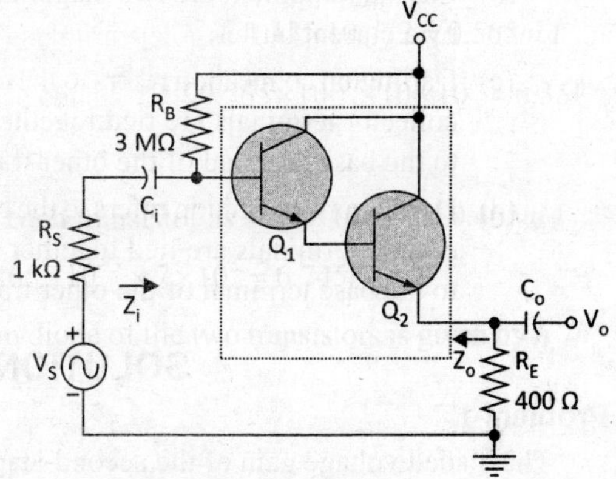

Fig. 5.31: Problem 4

MULTIPLE-CHOICE QUESTIONS

1. In an RC coupled amplifier, the gain decreases in the frequency response due to the
   (a) Coupling capacitor at low frequency and bypass capacitor at high frequency.
   (b) Coupling capacitor at high frequency and bypass capacitor at low frequency
   (c) Coupling junction capacitance at low frequency and coupling capacitor at high frequency.
   (d) Device junction capacitor at high frequency and coupling capacitor at low frequency.
2. A signal may have frequency components which lie in the range of 0.001Hz to 10 Hz. Which one of the following types of couplings should be chosen in a multistage amplifier designed to amplify the signal?
   (a) RC coupling (b) Direct coupling
   (c) Transformer coupling (d) Double tuned transformer coupling.
3. The overall bandwidth of two identical voltage amplifiers connected in cascade will
   (a) Remain the same as that of a single stage
   (b) Be better than that of a single stage
   (c) Be worse than that of a single stage
   (d) Be better if stage gain in low and worse if stage gain is high
4. Two amplifiers, one having voltage gain of 40 and the other 20 are coupled with negligible loading. The approximate gain of two-stage amplifier will be
   (a) 20 (b) 40
   (c) 60 (d) 800
5. The voltage gain of an amplifier decreases at 20 dB/decade above 100 kHz. If the mid-band frequency gain is 80 dB, what is the value of the voltage gain at 2 MHz?
   (a) 60dB (b) 52dB
   (c) 54dB (d) 64dB
6. Which of the following statement(s) is/are false?
   (a) The parameters h_i and h_r are determined from the input characteristic curves of the transistors whereas the parameters h_f and h_o are determined from the output or the collector characteristics.
   (b) Cascode amplifiers are two-stage amplifiers comprising a transconductance amplifier followed by a current buffer.
   (c) Darlington connection refers to the connection of two bipolar junction transistors wherein their collector terminals are tied together and the emitter terminal of one transistor is connected to the base terminal of the other transistor.
   (d) Darlington connection refers to the connection of two bipolar junction transistors wherein their emitter terminals are tied together and the collector terminal of one transistor is connected to the base terminal of the other transistor.

SOLUTIONS TO PROBLEMS

Problem-1:

The loaded voltage gain of the second-stage, that is, the CB amplifier is given by

$$A_{v2} = A_{v2nl} \times [R_L / (R_L + Z_{o2})]$$

$$= 200 \times [(10 \times 10^3) / (10 \times 10^3 + 5 \times 10^3)] = 133.33$$

The loaded voltage gain of the first stage, that is, the CC amplifier is given by

$$A_{v1} = A_{v1nl} \times [Z_{i2} / (Z_{i2} + Z_{o1})] = 1 \times [26/(26+10)] = 26/36 = 0.722$$

The overall voltage gain of the amplifier = $A_{v1} \times A_{v2}$ = 0.722 × 133.33 = 96.26

The total system gain

$A_{vs} = A_v \times [Z_{i1}/(Z_{i1} + R_s)] = 96.26 \times [(18 \times 10^3)/(18 \times 10^3 + 2 \times 10^3)] = 86.63$

The value of the total system current gain is given by:

$$\mathbf{A_{is} = -(A_{vs} \times Z_{i1})/R_L = (86.63 \times 18 \times 10^3)/(10 \times 10^3) = -155.93}$$

Problem-2:

Voltage gain of the second stage is given by:

$$A_{v2} = \frac{-h_{fe2} \times R_{C2}}{h_{ie2}} = \frac{-100 \times 2 \times 10^3}{1 \times 10^3} = -200$$

Voltage gain of the first stage is given by

$$A_{v1} = \frac{-h_{fe1} \times (R_{B3} \| R_{B4} \| R_{C1} \| h_{ie2})}{h_{ie1}}$$

$$= \frac{-100 \times (10 \times 10^3 \| 5 \times 10^3 \| 2 \times 10^3 \| 1 \times 10^3)}{1 \times 10^3} = \frac{-100 \times 555.56}{1 \times 10^3} = -55.556$$

Overall voltage gain is given by $A_v = A_{v1} \times A_{v2}$ = –200 × –55.556 = 11111.2

The input impedance of the amplifier Z_i is given by

$$Z_i = R_{B1} \| R_{B2} \| h_{ie1} = 10 \times 10^3 \| 5 \times 10^3 \| 1 \times 10^3 = 769.05 \text{ ©}$$

The output impedance of the amplifier is given by $Z_o = R_{C2} \| (1/h_{oe2})$. As the effect of h_{oe} is negligible, therefore $Z_o = R_{c2}$ = 2 kΩ.

Problem-3:

The input resistance for the first and the second stages

$$I_E = \frac{V_{CC}}{R_E + \frac{R_B}{\beta}} = \frac{10}{1 \times 10^3 + \frac{1 \times 10^4}{100}} = 0.91mA$$

$$r_e = \frac{25mV}{I_E} = \frac{25mV}{0.91mA} = 27.5\Omega$$

The input resistance of the first stage is $R_{i1} = \beta r_e = 100 \times 27.5 = 2750\Omega$

The input resistance of the second stage is $R_{i2} = \beta r_e = 100 \times 27.5 = 2750\Omega$

The output resistance for the first stage is $R_{o1} = R_C \| R_{i2} = 5000 \| 2750 = 1774\Omega$

The output resistance for the second stage is $R_{o2} = R_C \| R_L = 5000 \| 10000 = 3333\Omega$

Voltage gain of the first stage $A_{V1} = \dfrac{R_{o1}}{r_e} = \dfrac{1774}{27.5} = 64.5$

Voltage gain of the second stage $A_{V2} = \dfrac{R_{o1}}{r_e} = \dfrac{3333}{27.5} = 121.2$

Overall voltage gain $V = A_{V1}A_{V2} = 64.5 \times 121.2 = 7817.$

Problem-4:

The base bias current of the Darlington amplifier I_{B1} is given by:

$$I_{B1} = \frac{V_{CC} - V_{BE1} - V_{BE2}}{R_B + (1+h_{fe})^2 R_E} = \frac{15 - 0.7 - 0.7}{3\times 10^6 + (101)^2 \times 400} = 1.92\mu A$$

Emitter current of the Darlington amplifier is given by:

$I_{E2} = (1 + h_{fe})^2 I_{B1} = (101)^2 \times 1.92 \times 10^{-6}\mu A = 19.6$ mA

The collector current $I_C \cong I_E = 19.6$ mA

The collector emitter voltage $V_{CE} = V_C - V_E = 15 - 19.6 \times 10^{-3} \times 400 = 7.16$ V

Input impedance is

$$Z_i = R_B \| \frac{(1+h_{fe})^2 R_{E2}}{1 + h_{oe}h_{fe}R_{E2}}$$

$$= 3\times 10^6 \left\| \frac{(101)^2 \times 400}{1 + 40\times 10^{-6} \times 100 \times 400} = 3\times 10^6 \right\| 1.57\times 10^6 = 1.03\ M\Omega$$

Output impedance is given by:

$$Z_o \cong \frac{R_s + h_{ie}}{(1+h_{fe})^2} + \frac{h_{ie}}{1+h_{fe}} = \frac{1\times 10^3 + 1\times 10^3}{(101)^2} + \frac{1\times 10^3}{101} = 0.196 + 9.9 = 10.1\Omega$$

Voltage gain A_v is given by:

$$A_v = 1 - \frac{h_{ie}}{(1+h_{fe})R_{E2}} = 1 - \frac{1\times 10^3}{101\times 400} = 1 - 0.025 = 0.975$$

Current gain A_i is given by:

$$A_i = \frac{R_B}{Z_i + R_B} \times \left(\frac{(1+h_{fe})^2}{1 + h_{oe}h_{fe}R_{E2}} \right) = \frac{3\times 10^6}{3\times 10^6 + 1.03\times 10^6} \times \frac{(101)^2}{1 + 40\times 10^{-6} \times 100 \times 400}$$

$$= 0.74 \times 3923.46 = 2903.36$$

ANSWERS TO MULTIPLE-CHOICE QUESTIONS

1. (d) 2. (b) 3. (c) 4. (d)
5. (d) 6. (d)

6 Large Signal Amplifiers

After completing this chapter, you will learn the following topics.

- Classes of amplifiers
- Class-A amplifiers (Direct-coupled class-A amplifiers, Transformer-coupled class-A amplifiers and Push-pull class A amplifiers)
- Class-B amplifiers (Transformer-coupled push–pull configuration, Complementary-symmetry push–pull configuration and Quasi-complementary push–pull configuration)
- Class-AB amplifiers
- Class-C and Class-D amplifiers

Introduction

Large signal amplifiers also called power amplifiers provide power amplification and are used in applications to provide sufficient power to the load or a power device. The output power delivered by these amplifiers is of the order of few watts to few tens of watts. In this chapter we shall discuss different classes of power amplifiers, their characteristic parameters and different circuit configurations. Different classes of amplifiers covered in this chapter include class-A amplifiers (Directly-coupled Class-A amplifier, Transformer-coupled class-A amplifier and push-pull class-A amplifier), class-B amplifiers (Transformer-coupled push-pull class-B amplifier, Complementary-symmetry push-pull class-B amplifier and Quasi-complementary push-pull class-B amplifier), class-AB amplifiers, class-C amplifiers and class-D amplifiers. Different topics discussed in the chapter are amply illustrated with solved examples. In addition, there are a number of problems given towards the end of the chapter along with brief solutions. A self-evaluation exercise containing multiple-choice questions along with answers concludes the chapter.

6.1 CLASSES OF AMPLIFIERS

On the basis of the circuit configuration and principle of operation, amplifiers are classified into different classes. Different classes of large signal amplification include class-A, class-B, class-AB, class-C, class-D, class-E and class-F. Each of these amplifiers has both merits and shortcomings, which will be evident as we go through the details in subsequent sections. In this section, a brief introduction togeneral characteristic parameters and specification and different classes of amplification is presented. Class-E and -F amplifiers are very rarely used. Hence, only class-A, class-B, class-AB, class-C and class-D amplifiers are described in detail.

6.2 CLASS-A AMPLIFIERS

The active device in a class-A amplifier operates during the whole of the input cycle and the output signal is an amplified replica of the input signal with no clipping. In other words, in class-A amplifiers, the amplifying element is so biased that it operates over the linear region of its output characteristics during the full period of the input cycle and is always conducting to some extent. Class-A amplifiers offer very poor efficiency and a theoretical maximum of 50% efficiency is possible in these amplifiers. In a practical scenario, with capacitive coupling and inductive loads such as loud speakers, the efficiency can be as low as 25%. They are generally used for implementing small-signal amplifiers. Figure-6.1 shows the input and output waveforms of class-A amplifiers.

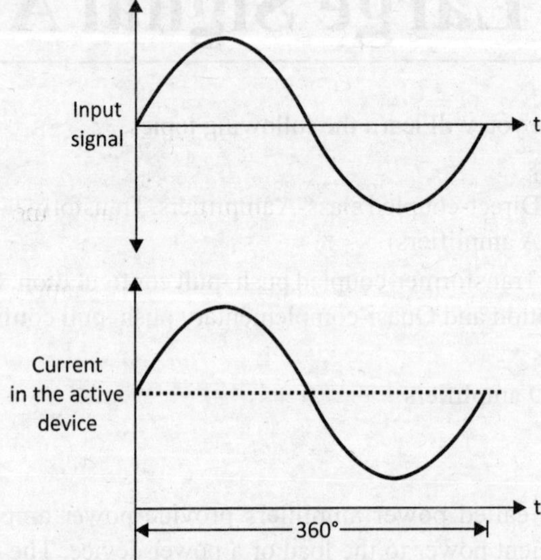

Fig. 6.1: Waveforms of class A amplifiers

Class-A amplifiers can be further classified into three types

(a) Direct-coupled resistive load class-A amplifiers
(b) Transformer coupled class-A amplifiers
(c) Push-pull class-A amplifier

6.2.1 Direct-coupled Resistive Load Class-A Amplifiers

These amplifiers are very rarely used as power amplifiers because of the several disadvantages offered by them, including low efficiency (maximum of 25%), large output impedance of the transistor and very low load impedances. However, they offer few advantages including simple design and low cost. They are used in audio signal amplifiers. These amplifiers are discussed here for completion of the topic.

Figure-6.2 shows a direct-coupled resistive load class A amplifier or a series-fed class A amplifier. The resistor R_C is the load resistor. The signal levels here are of the order of volts and the transistor used here is a power transistor which is capable of operating in the range of several watts to few tens of watts.

The value of the quiescent base current is given by

$$I_{BQ} = \frac{V_{TH} - V_{BE}}{R_{TH} + (\beta + 1)R_E}$$

Where,

$$R_{TH} = R_{B1} \| R_{B2} = \frac{R_{B1}R_{B2}}{R_{B1} + R_{B2}}$$

$$V_{TH} = \frac{R_{B2}V_{CC}}{R_{B1} + R_{B2}}$$

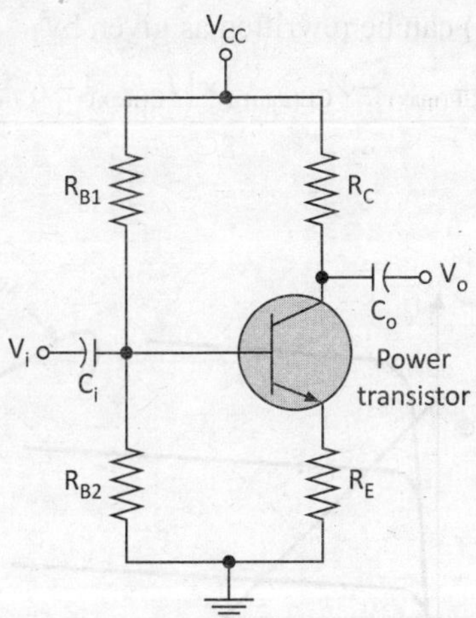

Fig. 6.2: Class A amplifier with direct-coupled resistive load

The value of quiescent collector current (ICQ) and the quiescent collector–emitter voltage (V_{CEQ}) are given by eqns. 6.1(a) and 6.1(b) respectively.

$$I_{CQ} = \beta I_{BQ} \quad (6.1(a))$$

$$V_{CEQ} = V_{CC} - I_{CQ}(R_C + R_E) \quad (6.1(b))$$

The DC bias determines the quiescent point, which in turn determines the maximum possible collector current swing and the collector–emitter voltage swing when the AC signal is applied at the input. Figure-6.3(a) shows the output characteristics and the current and voltage waveforms for the amplifier for a small input signal and Figure-6.3(b) shows the output characteristics and the current and voltage waveforms for the amplifier for a large input signal. The input signal applied to the base is a sinusoidal waveform and assuming the output characteristics to be equidistant, the output current and voltage waveforms are also sinusoidal. When an AC signal is applied to the base of the amplifier, the base current will vary above and below the DC bias point, which in turn will cause the collector current and the collector–emitter voltage to vary around its DC bias point. The output current and voltage varying around the bias point provide AC power to the load.

6.2.1.1 Output Power

The AC output power delivered to the load is given by

$$P_o = V_{ce(RMS)} I_{c(RMS)} = I_{c(RMS)}{}^2 R_L \quad (6.2)$$

Where, $V_{ce(RMS)}$ is the RMS value of the collector–emitter voltage; $I_{c(RMS)}$ the RMS value of the collector current; R_C the load resistance.

Therefore, the RMS value of collector–emitter voltage ($V_{ce(RMS)}$) is expressed in terms of the maximum collector voltage ($V_{CE(max)}$) and minimum collector voltage ($V_{CE(min)}$) as

$$V_{ce(RMS)} = \frac{V_{CE(max)} - V_{CE(min)}}{2\sqrt{2}}$$

The RMS value of collector voltage ($I_{c(RMS)}$) is expressed in terms of the maximum collector current ($I_{C(max)}$) and minimum collector current ($I_{C(min)}$) as given by the following eqn.

$$I_{c(RMS)} = \frac{I_{C(max)} - I_{C(min)}}{2\sqrt{2}}$$

Therefore, output AC power (P_o) can be rewritten as given by

$$P_o = \frac{\left(V_{CE(max)} - V_{CE(min)}\right) \times \left(I_{C(max)} - I_{C(min)}\right)}{8} \tag{6.3}$$

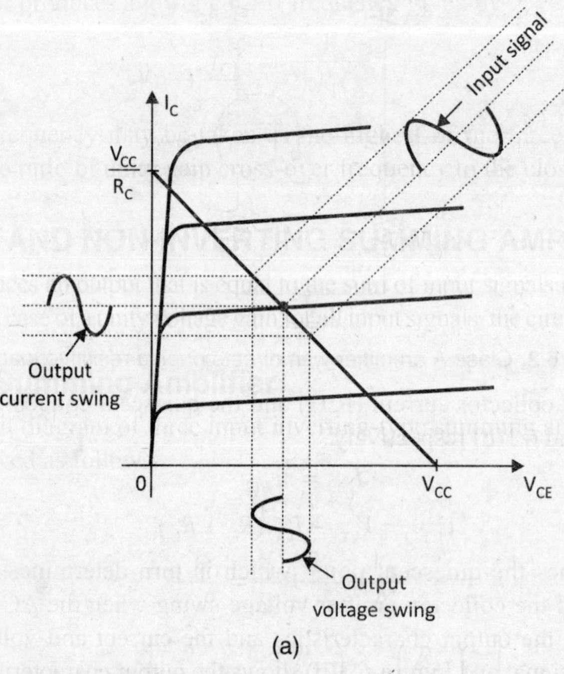

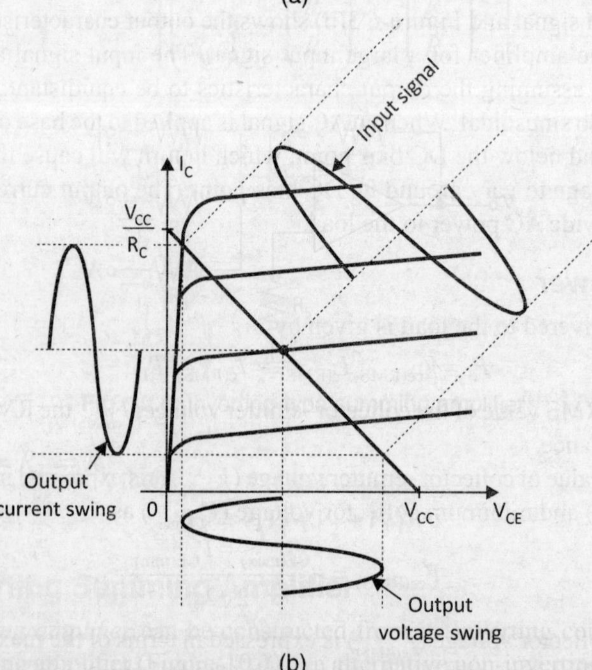

Figure-6.3: (a) Input and output waveforms for the series fed class A amplifier – small input signal; (b) input and output waveforms for the series fed class A amplifier – large input signal

6.2.1.2 Maximum Efficiency

The maximum value of efficiency can be calculated by making ideal assumptions like the characteristics curves of the active device are equally spaced in the region of operation, the input signal has zero minimum value, maximum value of collector–emitter voltage ($V_{CE(max)}$) is equal to V_{CC} and the maximum value of collector current ($I_{C(max)}$) is equal to V_{CC}/R_C.

The maximum value of power output ($P_{o(max)}$) is given by

$$P_{o(max)} = \frac{(V_{CC}) \times (V_{CC} / R_C)}{8} = \frac{V_{CC}^2}{8R_C} \tag{6.4}$$

The value of the input power (P_i) is equal to the product of the supply voltage (V_{CC}) and the quiescent value of the collector current (I_{CQ}). Assuming that the operating point is in the center of the output characteristics, the value of quiescent collector current (I_{CQ}) is equal to $V_{CC}/2R_C$. The value of input power (P_i) is therefore given by

$$P_i = V_{CC} \times I_{CQ} = V_{CC} \times \frac{V_{CC}}{2R_C} = \frac{V_{CC}^2}{2R_C} \tag{6.5}$$

The maximum efficiency is given by the ratio of the maximum AC output power given in eqn. (6.4) to the input power given in eqn. (6.5). The maximum value of efficiency is equal to 25%. In other words, the upper limit of the conversion efficiency in case of a series-fed class A amplifier is 25%. It may be mentioned here that in most of the practical class A series-fed amplifiers, the efficiency is much less than 25%.

Example-6.1: A direct coupled class A power amplifier is shown in Figure-6.4. When a sinusoidal signal is applied to it, it generates a peak base current of 9mA. Given that b = 50 and V_{BE} = 0.7V, determine the efficiency of the amplifier.

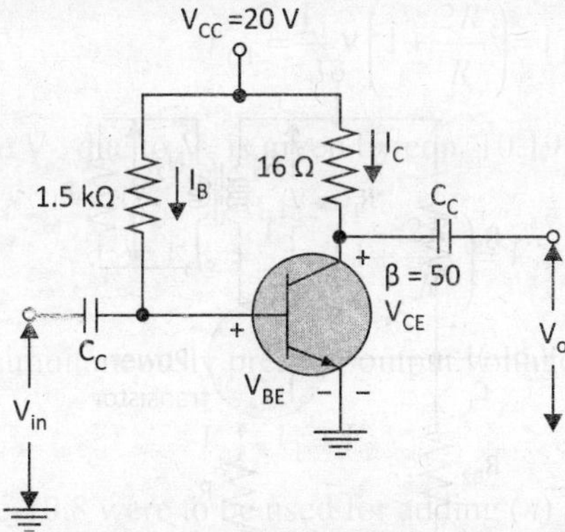

Fig. 6.4: Example 6.1

The quiescent base current is given by

$$I_{BQ} = \frac{V_{CC} - V_{BE}}{R_B} = \frac{(20-0.7)}{1.5 \times 10^3} A = 12.87mA$$

The quiescent collector current is given by

$$I_{CQ} = \beta I_{BQ} = 50 \times 12.87 \times 10^3 = 643.5mA$$

The collector emitter voltage is the quiescent collector-emitter voltage and is also represented as V_{CE}.

$$V_{CE} = V_{CC} - I_{CQ}R_C = 20 - 643.5\times10^{-3}\times16 = 9.7V$$

Therefore, the DC input power

$$P_{dc} = V_{CE}I_{CQ} = 9.7\times643.5\times10^{-3} = 6.24W$$

Given that the peak value of base current is 8mA. Therefore, the peak value of collector current is 400mA. Therefore, the rms value of collector current is $\dfrac{400mA}{\sqrt{2}} = 282.88mA$

$$P_{ac} = \frac{I_m{}^2 R_C}{2} = \frac{\left(282.88\times10^{-3}\right)^2\times16}{2} = 0.64W$$

$$\eta = \frac{P_{ac}}{P_{dc}}\times100\% = \frac{0.64}{6.24}\times100\% = 10.26\%$$

6.2.2 Transformer-coupled class-A amplifier

Class A amplifier with transformer-coupled load employs a transformer-coupled output stage as shown in Figure-6.5. This configuration offers better efficiency as compared to a class A amplifier with a resistive load. This is so because in the case of direct coupling, the transistor quiescent current passes through the load resistance which results in wastage of power as it does not contribute to the AC component of the output power. In the case of a transformer-coupled load, the primary of the transformer has negligible DC resistance; therefore there is negligible power loss. In fact, the efficiency can be increased by a factor of 2 by using transformer coupling. However, in this case it is important to use an output-matching transformer in order to transfer a significant power to the load.

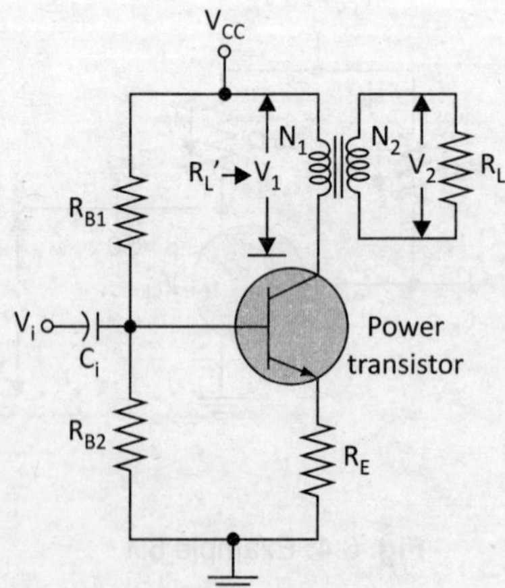

Fig. 6.5: Transformer-coupled class A amplifier

The relationship between the transformer's primary and secondary voltages and currents and its turns ratio are given by eqns. 6.6 and 6.7, respectively:

$$\frac{V_1}{V_2} = \frac{N_1}{N_2} \tag{6.6}$$

where V_1 is the primary voltage; V_2 the secondary voltage; N_1 the number of primary turns; N_2 the number of secondary turns.

$$\frac{I_1}{I_2} = \frac{N_2}{N_1} \tag{6.7}$$

where I_1 is the primary current; I_2 the secondary current; N_1 the number of primary turns; N_2 the number of secondary turns.

From eqns. 6.6 and 6.7 we get

$$\frac{V_1}{I_1} = n^2 \times \frac{V_2}{I_2} \tag{6.8}$$

where V_1/I_1 represents reflected load resistance R_L', V_2/I_2 is equal to the output resistance load resistance R_L, n is equal to the ratio of the primary turns to secondary turns (N_1/N_2).

Eqn. 6.8 can be rewritten as

$$R_L' = n^2 \times R_L \tag{6.9}$$

Figure-6.6 shows the transistor collector characteristics along with the DC and the AC load lines for the transformer-coupled class A amplifier. The output current and voltage waveforms are also shown alongwith.

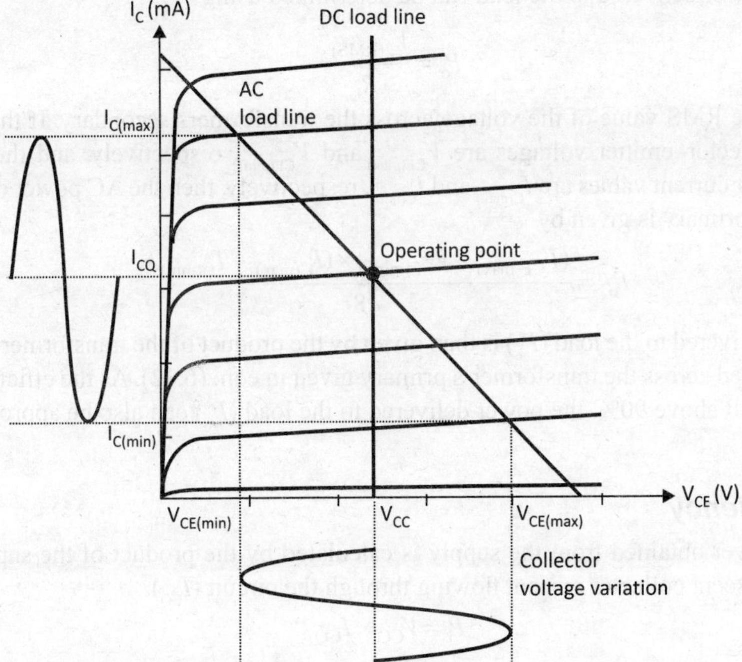

Fig. 6.6: Transistor collector characteristics along with the DC and the AC load lines for the transformer-coupled class A amplifier

For the transformer-coupled amplifier, the DC load line is drawn vertically from $V_{CE} = V_{CC}$. This is so as the resistance of the transformer's primary is negligible. The AC load line is drawn with a slope proportional to $-1/R_L'$.

The main design objective is to design a circuit that will deliver maximum output power to the load for a small allowable distortion. To deliver maximum output power, the AC load line is drawn tangent to the hyperbola curve of maximum power dissipation. The point of tangency is where the DC load line intersects the hyperbola. The load line must be drawn so as not to violate the maximum collector–emitter voltage of transistor. This is usually done by making $V_{CC} \le V_{CE(max)}/2$

In the case of transformer-coupled class A amplifier, the maximum power dissipated ($P_{D(max)}$) is twice the AC output power (P_o'). Here P_o' is the power developed across the transformer's primary. The Q-point is located at

$$I_{CQ} = \frac{2P_o'}{V_{CC}}, \quad V_{CEQ} = V_{CC}$$

If the Q-point is located at the mid-point of the load line then

$$R_L' = \frac{V_{CC}^2}{2P_o'} \tag{6.10}$$

R_L' is the reflected load resistance seen by the primary. The transformer chosen should be such that the actual load R_L on the secondary looks like R_L in the primary.

6.2.2.1 Output Power

The output AC power delivered to the load can be determined using

$$P_o = \frac{V_{2(RMS)}^2}{R_L} \tag{6.11}$$

where $V_{2(RMS)}$ is the RMS value of the voltage across the transformers secondary. If the maximum and the minimum collector–emitter voltages are $V_{CE(max)}$ and $V_{CE(min)}$, respectively, and the maximum and minimum collector current values are $I_{C(max)}$ and $I_{C(min)}$, respectively, then the AC power developed across the transformer's primary is given by

$$P_o' = \frac{(V_{CE(max)} - V_{CE(min)}) \times (I_{C(max)} - I_{C(min)})}{8} \tag{6.12}$$

The power delivered to the load (P_o) is then given by the product of the transformer's efficiency and the power developed across the transformer's primary given in eqn. (6.12). As the efficiency of efficient transformers is well above 90%, the power delivered to the load (P_o) can also be approximated by eqn. (6.12).

6.2.2.2 Efficiency

The input DC power obtained from the supply is calculated by the product of the supply DC voltage (V_{CC}) and the quiescent collector current flowing through the circuit (I_{CQ}).

$$P_i = V_{CC} \times I_{CQ} \tag{6.13}$$

The efficiency of the amplifier is given by

$$\eta = \frac{P_o}{P_i} \times 100\% \tag{6.14}$$

The main source of power loss is that dissipated by the transistor in the form of heat and is approximately equal to the difference between the power that is drawn from the DC power supply and the

AC power delivered to the load. When the input signal is small, little AC power is delivered to the load and maximum power is dissipated by the transistor. When the input signal is large, large amount of power is delivered to the load and less power is dissipated by the transistor. In other words, in a transformer-coupled class A amplifier the power loss is minimum when the load is drawing maximum power from the circuit and is maximum when the load is disconnected from the amplifier.

The maximum value of efficiency can be calculated by making certain assumptions like the characteristic curves of the active device are equally spaced in the region of operation, the input signal has zero minimum value and the operating point is in the center of the output characteristics.

Under the already mentioned ideal conditions,

$$I_{CQ} = \frac{I_{c(max)} - I_{c(min)}}{2} \text{ and } V_{CC} = \frac{V_{CE(max)} + V_{CE(min)}}{2}$$

Therefore,

$$P_i = \frac{(V_{CE(max)} + V_{CE(min)})}{2} \times \frac{(I_{C(max)} - I_{C(min)})}{2} \tag{6.15}$$

Substituting the values of P_o given by eqn. (6.12) and P_i given by eqn. (6.15) in eqn. (6.14) we get

$$\eta = 50\left(\frac{V_{CE(max)} - V_{CE(min)}}{V_{CE(max)} + V_{CE(min)}}\right)\% \tag{6.16}$$

Therefore, the upper limit for theoretical efficiency for a transformer-coupled class A power amplifier is 50% which is twice that of a series-fed class A circuit.

6.2.2.3 Variation of Output Power with Load

Figure-6.7 shows the variation of output power and total harmonic distortion with the load resistance. As we can see from the curve, the load that provides minimum value of total distortion is different from the load that yields maximum output power. However, the output power curve is largely flat in the region of maximum power, so a well-designed amplifier would work properly for a load that gives slightly less than maximum output power as it will give significantly lower value of total distortion.

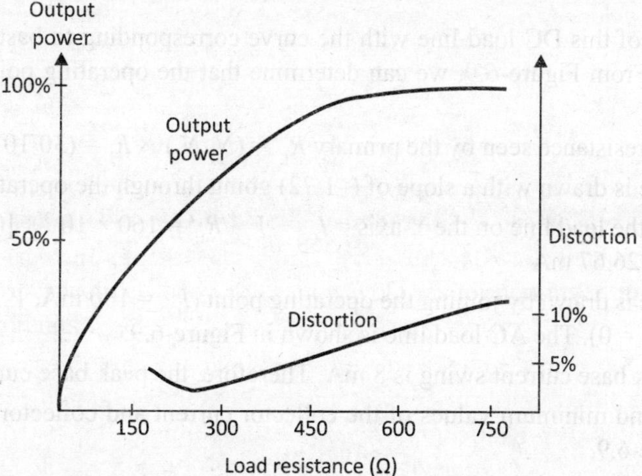

Fig. 6.7: Variation of output power and total distortion with load resistance

6.2.2.4 Disadvantages of Transformer-Coupled Class A Amplifier

The value of total harmonic distortion is quite large in the case of these amplifiers. Moreover, the maximum output power is generated at a load resistance value that is different from the value that offers minimum harmonic distortion. Also, the output transformer is subject to saturation problems as a relatively large DC collector current flows under zero signal conditions.

Example-6.2: Determine the AC power delivered to the speaker in the circuit shown in Figure-6.8(a). The value of the quiescent base current is 8 mA and the input signal results in a peak-to-peak base current swing of 8 mA. The output characteristics of the transistor are shown in Figure-6.8(b).

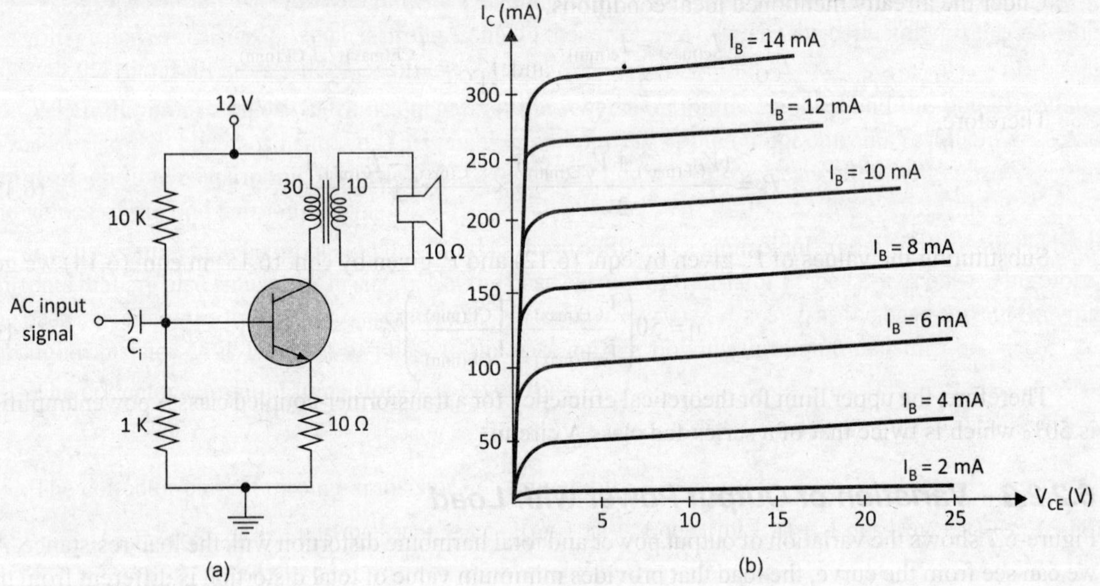

Fig. 6.8: Example 6.2

Solution: The DC load line is obtained by drawing a vertical line from the point (0, V_{CC}), that is, from (0, 12 V).

The intersection of this DC load line with the curve corresponding to base current of 8 mA gives the operating point. From Figure-6.9, we can determine that the operating point is I_{CQ} = 160 mA and V_{CEQ} = 12 V.

The effective ac resistance seen by the primary $R_L' = (N_1/N_2)^2 \times R_L = (30/10)^2 \times R_L = 9 \times 8\ \Omega = 72\ \Omega$

The AC load line is drawn with a slope of (–1/72) going through the operating point.

The intercept of the load line on the Y-axis = $I_{CQ} + V_{CC}/R_L' = 160 \times 10^{-3} + [(12)/(72 \times 10^3)]$ A = 160 mA + 166.67 mA = 326.67 mA

The AC load line is drawn by joining the operating point (I_{CQ} = 160 mA, V_{CEQ} = 12 V) and the point (I_C = 326.67 mA, V_{CE} = 0). The AC load line is shown in Figure-6.9.

The peak-to-peak base current swing is 8 mA. Therefore, the peak base current swing is 4 mA.

The maximum and minimum values of the collector current and collector–emitter voltage can be obtained from Figure-6.9.

$V_{CE(min)}$ = 4.5 V, $V_{CE(max)}$ = 20 V, $I_{C(min)}$ = 60 mA and $I_{C(max)}$ = 260 mA

The AC power delivered to the load is equal to

$$P_o = \frac{(V_{CE(max)} - V_{CE(min)}) \times (I_{C(max)} - I_{C(min)})}{8}$$

$$P_o = [(20 - 4.5) \times (260 \times 10^{-3} - 60 \times 10^{-3})] / 8 \text{ W}$$

$$= (15.5 \times 200)/8 \text{ mW} = 387.5 \text{ mW} = 0.3875 \text{ W}$$

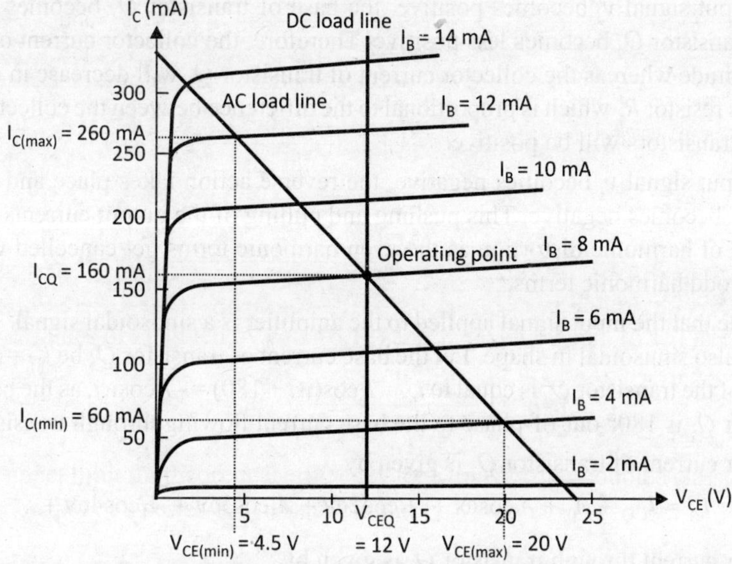

Fig. 6.9: Solution to Example 6.2

6.2.3 Push-pull class-A amplifier

Push–pull amplifiers employ two active devices which are fed with input signals that are 180° out-of-phase with each other. These amplifiers usually have a center-tapped output transformer. Push–pull configuration offers advantages such as cancellation of second harmonic distortion term and reduction in the power supply ripple voltage.

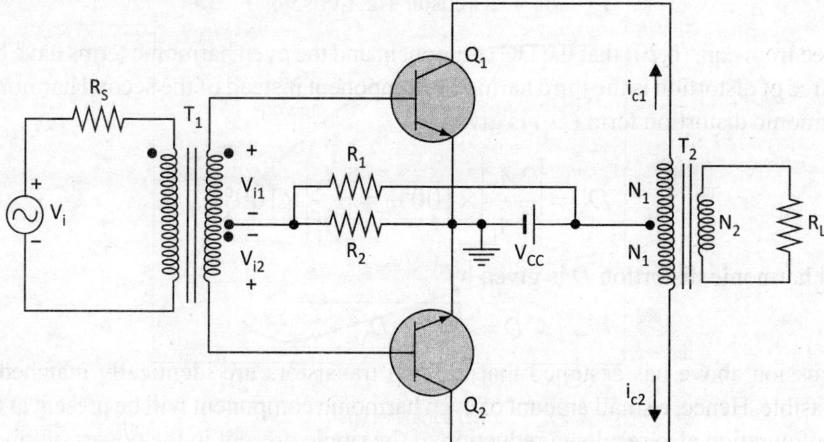

Fig. 6.10: Class A push–pull amplifier

Figure-6.10 shows the circuit configuration of a class A push–pull amplifier. The transformer at the input end (T_1) provides a phase-splitting and the two voltages to the base of the transistors Q_1 and Q_2 that are 180° out-of-phase w. r. t. each other. Resistors R_1 and R_2 are so chosen that both the transistors conduct for the whole input signal cycle. The collector currents of both the transistors pass through the windings of the output transformer (T_2) in opposite directions. Therefore, their magnetizing effects cancel with the result that there is no magnetic saturation problems in the output transformer.

When the input signal v_s becomes positive, the base of transistor Q_1 becomes more positive and the base of the transistor Q_2 becomes less positive. Therefore, the collector current of transistor Q_1 will increase in magnitude whereas the collector current of transistor Q_2 will decrease in magnitude. Hence, the voltage across resistor R_L which is proportional to the difference between the collector currents flowing through the two transistors will be positive.

When the input signal v_s becomes negative, the reverse action takes place and the output voltage across resistor R_L becomes negative. This pushing and pulling of the output currents results in decrease in the magnitude of harmonic distortion as the even harmonic terms get cancelled without increase in the values of the odd harmonic terms.

Let us assume that the input signal applied to the amplifier is a sinusoidal signal. This results in base currents that are also sinusoidal in shape. Let the base current of transistor Q_1 be $i_{b1} = I_b \cos wt$. Therefore, the base current of the transistor Q_2 is equal to $i_{b2} = I_b \cos(wt + 180) = -I_b \cos wt$, as the base current flowing through transistor Q_2 is 180° out-of-phase to the base current flowing through transistor Q_1.

The collector current of transistor Q_1 is given by

$$i_{c1} = I_{CQ} + A_0 + A_1\cos\omega t + A_2\cos 2\omega t + A_3\cos 3\omega t + A_4\cos 4\omega t + \ldots \tag{6.17}$$

The collector current through transistor Q_2 is given by

$$i_{c2} = I_{CQ} + A_0 + A_1\cos(\omega t + \pi) + A_2\cos 2(\omega t + \pi) + A_3\cos 3(\omega t + \pi) + A_4\cos 4(\omega t + \pi) + \ldots \tag{6.18}$$

On simplifying eqn. (6.18) we get

$$i_{c2} = I_{CQ} + A_0 - A_1\cos\omega t + A_2\cos 2\omega t - A_3\cos 3\omega t + A_4\cos 4\omega t + \ldots \tag{6.19}$$

The output voltage is directly proportional to the difference of the collector currents flowing through transistors Q_1 and Q_2.

$$i_{c1} - i_{c2} = 2A_1\cos\omega t + 2A_3\cos 3\omega t + \ldots \tag{6.20}$$

We can see from eqn. (6.20) that the DC component and the even harmonic terms have been cancelled. The main source of distortion is the third harmonic component instead of the second harmonic component. The third harmonic distortion term (D_3) is given by

$$D_3 = \left|\frac{2A_3}{2A_1}\right| \times 100\% = \left|\frac{A_3}{A_1}\right| \times 100\% \tag{6.21}$$

The total harmonic distortion D is given by

$$D = \sqrt{D_3^2 + D_5^2 + \ldots} \tag{6.22}$$

The discussion above has assumed that the two transistors are identically matched, which is not practically feasible. Hence, a small amount of even harmonic component will be present at the output. The push–pull configuration also results in reduction of the ripple present in the power supply voltage (V_{CC}).

6.3 CLASS B AMPLIFIERS

Class B amplifiers operate only during the half of the input cycle as shown in Figure-6.11. However they also create a large amount of distortion. A single class B amplifier is rarely used in practical systems. Two class B amplifiers are used either as a complementary pair or in a push–pull arrangement.

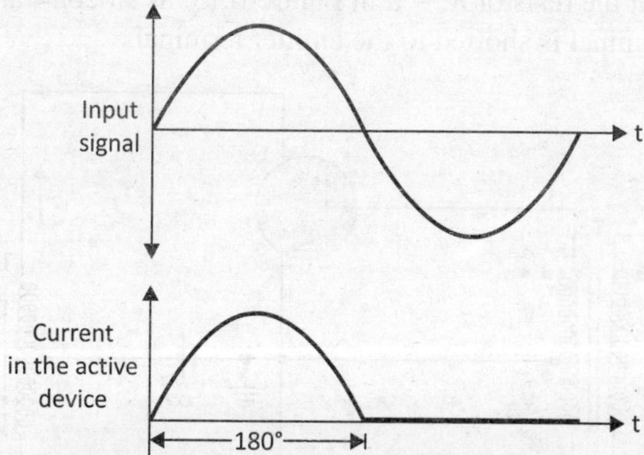

Fig. 6.11: Waveforms of class B amplifiers

In a class B amplifier, the active device is biased at zero DC level. Therefore, it provides an output signal varying over one-half of the input signal cycle as the active device conducts for only one-half of the input signal cycle. To obtain output for full input cycle, push–pull configuration or complementary pair arrangement is used, that is, two active devices are used wherein each conducts for opposite half-cycles and the combined operation provides full cycle of the output signal. Figure-6.12 shows the block schematic of a push–pull configuration.

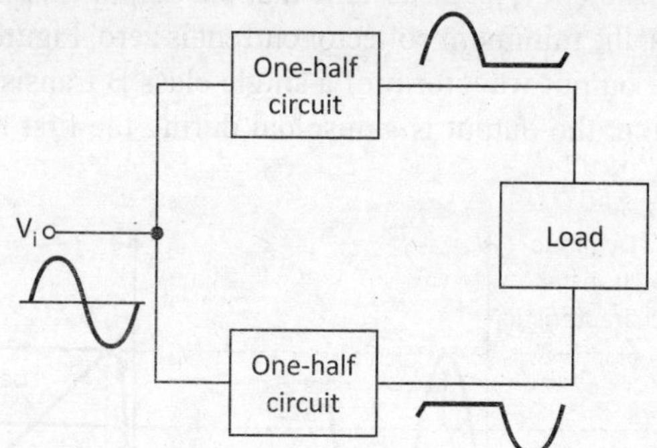

Fig. 6.12: Block schematic of push–pull configuration

Class B amplifier offers higher power output, higher efficiency (theoretical maximum of 78.5%) and there is negligible power loss under quiescent conditions, that is, when no input signal is applied. However, they have higher harmonic distortion, self-bias configuration cannot be used here and power supply voltages must have good regulation.

A number of circuit arrangements are possible for obtaining class B operation. These include

(a) Transformer-coupled push–pull configuration

(b) Complementary-symmetry push–pull configuration

(c) Quasi-complementary push- pull configuration

Each of these circuit configurations is explained in the following sections.

6.3.1 Transformer-coupled push-pull class-B amplifier

Figure-6.13 shows the circuit for a transformer-coupled push–pull class B amplifier. It is essentially the same as a push–pull class A amplifier except that the active devices in this case are biased in the cut-off region. If we compare the circuit of Figure-6.13 with the circuit of class A push–pull amplifier in Figure-6.10, we can see that the resistor $R_2 = 0$ in Figure-6.13, as silicon transistor, is essentially in the cut-off region if its base terminal is shorted to the emitter terminal.

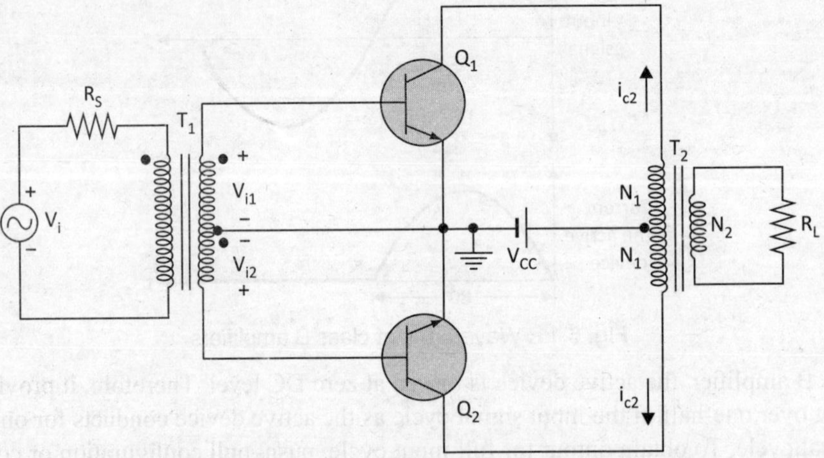

Fig. 6.13: Transformer-coupled push–pull class B amplifier

6.3.1.1 Conversion Efficiency

To determine the conversion efficiency, let us assume that the output characteristics of the active device are equally spaced and also that the minimum collector current is zero. Figure-6.14(a) shows the graphical schematic for determining the output waveform of a single class B transistor stage. As we can see that for a sinusoidal input excitation, the output is sinusoidal during the first half of the input cycle and is zero during the second half cycle.

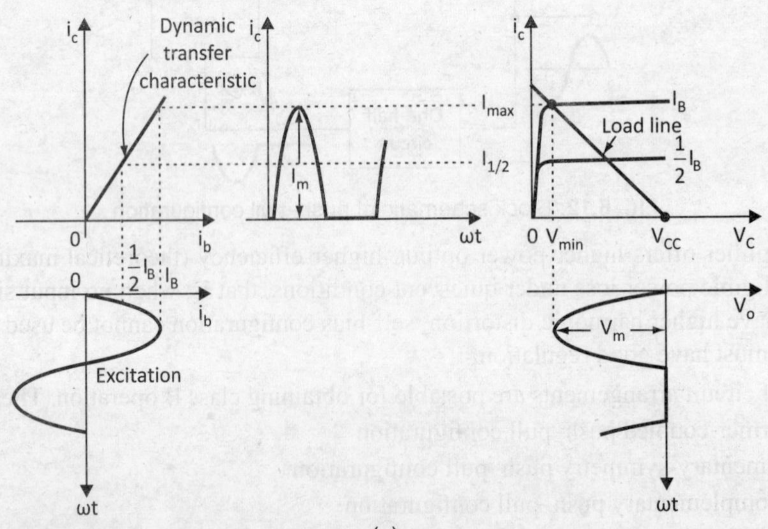

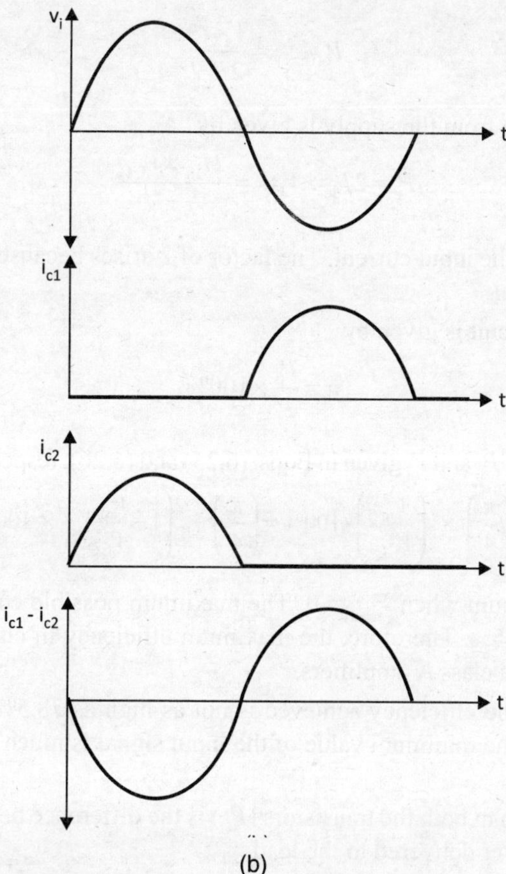

(b)

Fig. 6.14: (a) Output waveform of a single class B transistor stage (b) output waveforms for class B push–pull amplifiers

The effective value of load resistance (R_L') is given by

$$R_L' = \left(\frac{N_1}{N_2}\right)^2 \times R_L \tag{6.23}$$

where N_1 is the number of primary turns to the center tap and N_2 the number of secondary turns.

Figure-6.14(b) shows the collector current waveforms of transistors Q_1 and Q_2. As is clear from the figure, the output waveform of transistor Q_2 is 180° out-of-phase to that of transistor Q_1. The load current is proportional to the difference between the collector currents flowing through the transistors Q_1 and Q_2. It is therefore a perfect sine wave for ideal conditions. The output power (P_o) is given by

$$P_o = \frac{I_m V_m}{2} = \frac{I_m}{2} \times (V_{CC} - V_{min}) \tag{6.24}$$

The maximum power ($P_{o(max)}$) that can be delivered to the load occurs for the conditions $V_m = V_{CC}$, $V_{min} = 0$ and the operating point is at the center of the output characteristics of the transistor. The value of $P_{o(max)}$ is given by

$$P_{o(max)} = \frac{V_{CC}^2}{2R_L}, \tag{6.25}$$

The DC input power (P_i) from the supply is given by

$$P_i = 2I_{dc} \times V_{CC} = \frac{2I_m \times V_{CC}}{\pi} \tag{6.26}$$

where I_{dc} is the DC value of the input current. The factor of 2 arises because the two transistors are used in push–pull configuration.

The efficiency of the circuit is given by

$$\eta = \frac{P_o}{P_i} \times 100\% \tag{6.27}$$

Substituting the values of P_o and P_i given in Eqns. (6.25) and (6.26), respectively, in Eqn. (6.27), we get

$$\eta = \left(\frac{\pi}{4}\right) \times \left(\frac{V_m}{V_{CC}}\right) \times 100\% = \left(\frac{\pi}{4}\right) \times \left(1 - \frac{V_{min}}{V_{CC}}\right) \times 100\% \tag{6.28}$$

The efficiency is maximum when $V_{min} = 0$. The maximum possible conversion efficiency is equal to 25ð which is equal to 78.5%. Therefore, the maximum efficiency in class B amplifiers is 78.5% as compared to that of 50% in a class A amplifiers.

For practical systems, the efficiency achieved is not as high as 78.5% but the value of efficiency is higher in systems where the minimum value of the input signal is much less than the supply voltage (i.e., $V_{min} << V_{CC}$).

The collector dissipation in both the transistors (P_C) is the difference between the input power to the collector circuit and the power delivered to the load

$$P_C = P_i - P_o = \frac{2V_{CC} \times V_m}{\pi R_L}, \frac{V_m^2}{2R_L} \tag{6.29}$$

When $V_m = 0$, $P_C = 0$. As V_m increases, the value of the power dissipated in the transistors (P_C) increases and it is maximum for $V_m = 2V_{CC}/\pi$. The peak value of power dissipation in both the transistors ($P_{C(max)}$) is given by

$$P_{C(max)} = \frac{2V_{CC}^2}{\pi^2 R_L}, \tag{6.30}$$

Therefore,

$$P_{C(max)} = \frac{4}{\pi^2} \times P_{o(max)} \approx 0.4 P_{o(max)} \tag{6.31}$$

Hence, we can obtain a power output of five times the specified power dissipation of a single transistor. As an example, to deliver 10 W from a class B push–pull amplifier, the transistors should have a collector dissipation of 2 W each.

6.3.1.2 Harmonic Distortion

The output of a push–pull system has a mirror symmetry. Therefore, $I_Q = 0$, $I_{max} = -I_{min}$ and $I_{+1/2} = -I_{-1/2}$. The values of different harmonic distortion components are given by

$$A_0 = A_2 = A_4 = 0 \tag{6.32}$$

$$A_1 = \frac{2}{3} \times (I_{max} + I_{+1/2}) \tag{6.33}$$

$$A_3 = \frac{1}{3} \times (I_{max} - 2I_{+1/2}) \tag{6.34}$$

Therefore, there is no even-harmonic distortion. The principal contributor to the harmonic distortion is the third harmonic distortion component (D_3) given by

$$D_3 = \left|\frac{A_3}{A_1}\right| \times 100\% \tag{6.35}$$

The total output power (P_o), taking harmonic distortion into account, is given by

$$P_o = (1 + D_3^{\,2}) \times \frac{A_1^{\,2} R_L{'}}{2} \tag{6.36}$$

6.3.1.3 Crossover Distortion

Crossover distortion refers to the non-linearity in the output signal when the output signal crosses from positive to negative or from negative to positive. In other words, crossover distortion refers to the distortion resulting at low values of the input signal in the vicinity of the zero region. The output of the transistor collector current is not a perfect half-sine-wave and it results in crossover distortion. This arises as the value of the transistor's *b* is quite low near the cut-off region for small values of collector current compared to the rest of the input signal. Figure-6.15 shows the output waveform with crossover distortion.

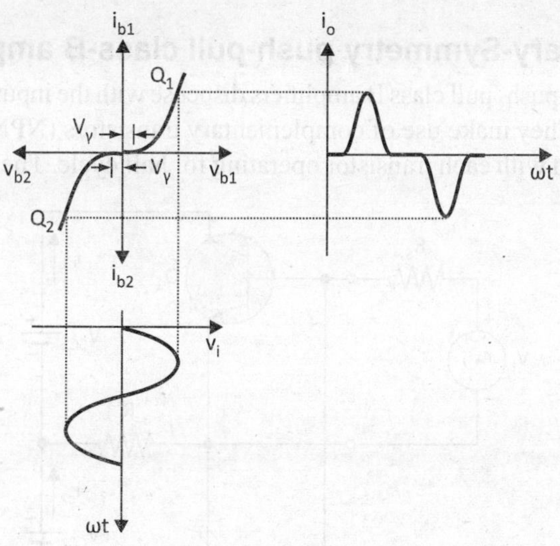

Fig. 6.15: Crossover distortion

Example-6.3: Determine the efficiency of a class B amplifier for a supply voltage of 25V with the output load peak voltage of 5V and 10V?

Solution: Efficiency of a class B amplifier is given by $\eta = 78.5\frac{V_L(p)}{V_{CC}}\%$

Where, $V_L(p)$ is the load peak voltage and V_{CC} is the supply voltage

For a load peak voltage of 5V, the efficiency is $\eta = 78.5\frac{V_L(p)}{V_{CC}}\% = 78.5\times\frac{5}{25}\% = 15.7\%$

For a load peak voltage of 10V, the efficiency is $\eta = 78.5\frac{V_L(p)}{V_{CC}}\% = 78.5\times\frac{10}{25}\% = 31.4\%$

Example-6.4: Given a class B amplifier with the following parameters

- Load 16 ohms
- Output peak signal 20V
- Power supply voltage 30V

Determine the DC input power, AC output power and the efficiency

Solution: $V_P = 20V$, $R_L = 16W$

$$\text{DC input power } P_{DC} = \frac{2V_{CC}V_P}{\pi R_L} = \frac{2\times30\times20}{\pi\times16} = 23.87W$$

$$\text{AC output power } P_{AC} = \frac{V_P^{\ 2}}{2R_L} = 12.5W$$

$$\eta = \frac{P_{AC}}{P_{DC}}\times100\% = 52.37\%$$

6.3.2 Complementary-Symmetry push-pull class-B amplifier

Complementary-symmetry push–pull class B amplifiers dispense with the input and the output transformers as shown in Figure-6.16. They make use of complementary transistors (NPN and PNP) to obtain a full-cycle output across the load with each transistor operating for half cycle. The same input is applied to the

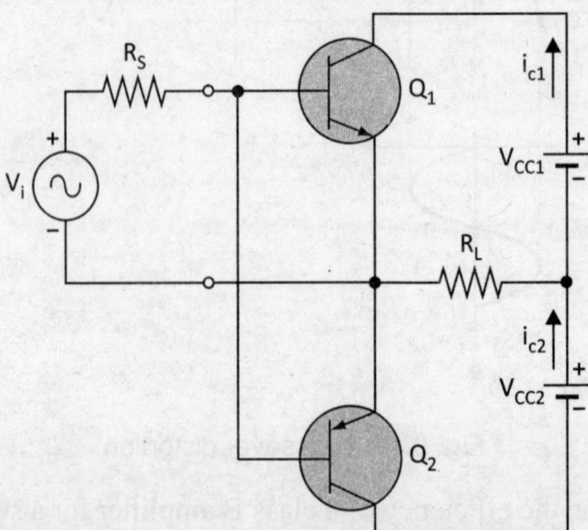

Fig. 6.16: Complementary-symmetry push–pull class B amplifier

base terminals of both the transistors. The NPN transistor is so biased that it conducts during the positive half of the input signal whereas the PNP transistor conducts during the negative half of the input signal. The output appears across the load for the full cycle of the input signal.

However, there are two main drawbacks of this configuration. First, it requires two different voltage supplies. Second, the output signal suffers from crossover distortion. This is so because the transistors conduct partially near the zero-voltage condition.

A more practical version of a complementary-symmetry push–pull class B amplifier is the one employing Darlington-connected transistors as shown in Figure-6.17. The circuit offers higher output current capability and lower output resistance.

6.3.3 Quasi-Complementary push-pull class-B amplifier

Another variation of the complementary-symmetry amplifier is the quasi-complementary class B amplifier shown in Figure-6.18. The push–pull operation is achieved by using a pair of complementary transistors. Transistors Q_1 and Q_3 form a Darlington connection that provides output from a low-impedance emitter follower. Transistors Q_2 and Q_4 form a feedback pair and they provide a low-impedance drive to the load. The crossover distortion can be minimized by adjusting the value of the resistor R_2.

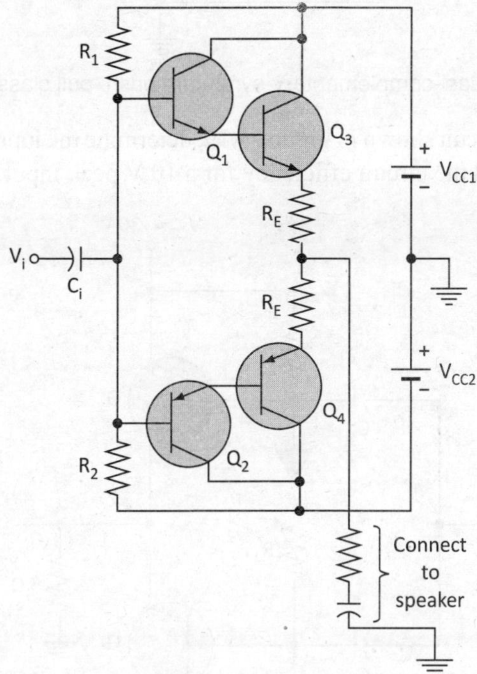

Fig. 6.17: Complementary-symmetry push–pull class B amplifier with Darlington transistors

One of the main advantages of using the quasi-complementary configuration is that it employs matched NPN transistors as high current devices and does not require a high-power PNP transistor as required in case of complementary-symmetry amplifiers. It may be mentioned here that quasi-complementary push–pull amplifier is the most popular form of power amplifiers.

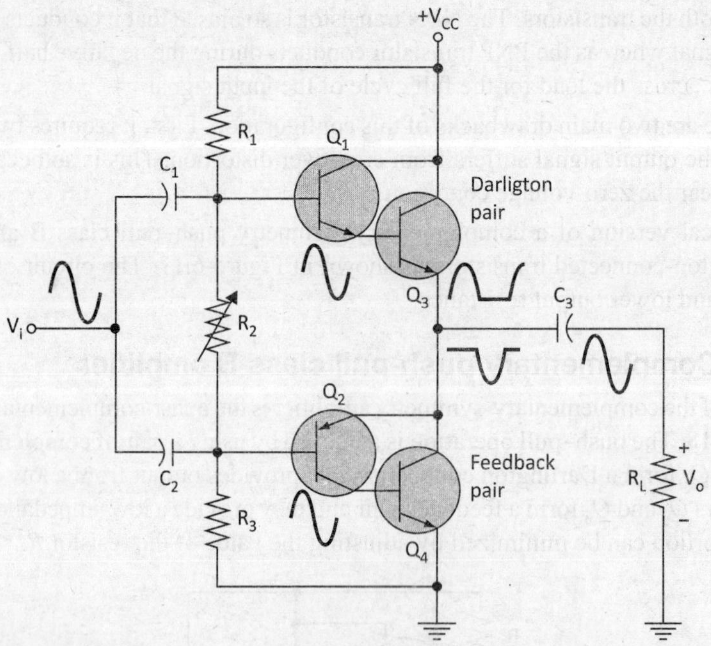

Fig. 6.18: Quasi-complementary-symmetry push–pull class B amplifier

Example-6.5: For the circuit shown in Figure-6.19, determine the input power, output power, power handled by each transistor and the circuit efficiency for a 10 V peak input signal.

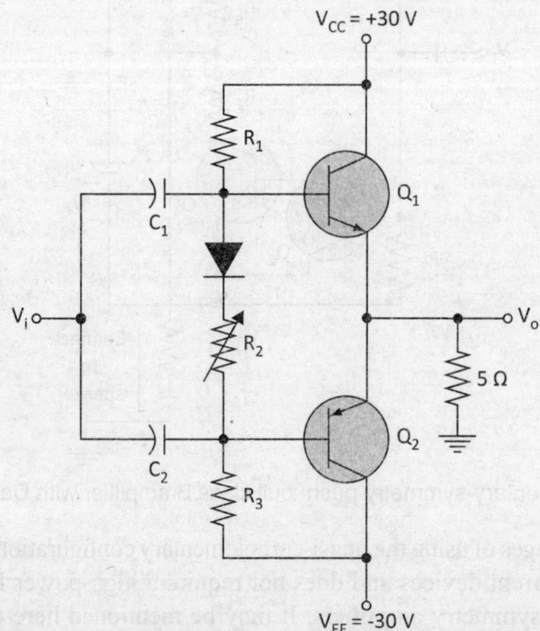

Fig. 6.19: Example 6.5

Solution: The ideal voltage gain of the amplifier is unity. Therefore, the resulting voltage across the load resistance is ideally the same as the input signal. That is, $V_L(p) = 10$ V.

The output power across the load resistor (R_L) is given by $P_o = [V_L(p)]^2/(2 \times R_L) = (10)^2/(2 \times 5) = 100/10 = 10$ W

Peak load current $I_L(p) = V_L(p)/R_L = 10/5 = 2$ A

The DC current drawn from the power supply $I_{dc} = (2/\pi) \times I_L(p) = (2/\pi) \times 2 = 1.27$ A

Input power $P_i = V_{CC} \times I_{dc} = 30 \times 1.27 = 38.2$ W

Total power dissipated $P_D = P_i - P_o = 38.2 - 10 = 28.2$ W

Power dissipated in each transistor = $P_D/2 = 28.2/2 = 14.1$ W

The efficiency at the given input signal is $h = (P_o/P_i) \times 100\% = (10/38.2) \times 100\% = 26.18\%$

6.4 CLASS AB AMPLIFIERS

In a class AB amplifier, the amplifying device conducts for a little more than half of the input waveform. They sacrifice some efficiency over class B amplifiers but they offer better linearity than class B amplifiers. However, they offer much more efficiency than class A amplifiers. Figure-6.20 shows the waveforms of class AB amplifiers.

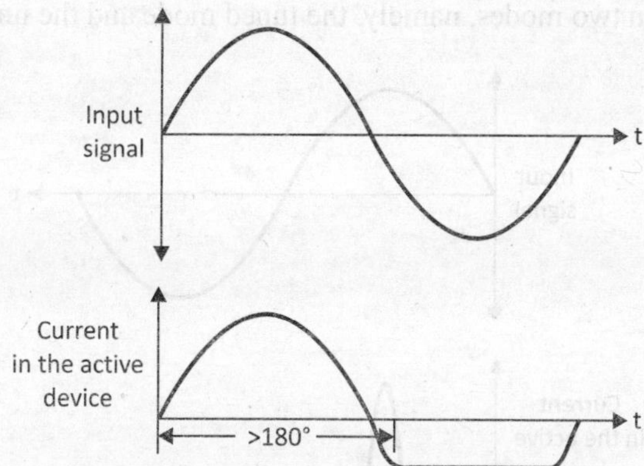

Fig. 6.20: Input and output waveforms of class AB amplifiers

Class AB amplifiers do not suffer from the problem of crossover distortion as in these amplifiers, a small current flows even at zero input signal level. Figure-6.21 shows the configuration of a class AB push–pull amplifier. The circuit is essentially the same as that for class A amplifier. The voltage drop across resistor R_2 is approximately equal to the cut-in voltage of the transistor. When an AC signal is applied to the base, the collector current starts flowing immediately. This biases the transistor away from class B slightly towards class A. Resistors R_e are referred to as the emitter-stabilizing resistors and reduce the amount of distortion produced. However they cause a decrease in the output power due to the negative feedback effect.

6.5 CLASS C AMPLIFIERS

The amplifiers discussed so far, that is, class A, class B and class AB amplifiers, are linear amplifiers where the amplitude and phase of the output signal is directly related to the amplitude and phase of the input signal. In applications where linearity is not the main issue and efficiency is of primary concern, class C, class D, class E and class F amplifiers are used.

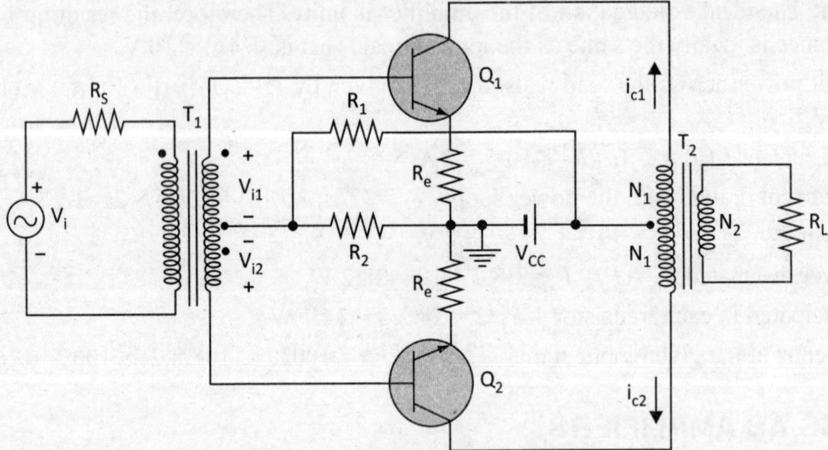

Fig. 6.21: Class AB amplifier

Class C amplifiers conduct for less than 50% of the input signal (Figure-6.22) resulting in a very high efficiency upto 90%. However, they are associated with a very high level of distortion at the output. Class C amplifiers operate in two modes, namely, the tuned mode and the untuned modes.

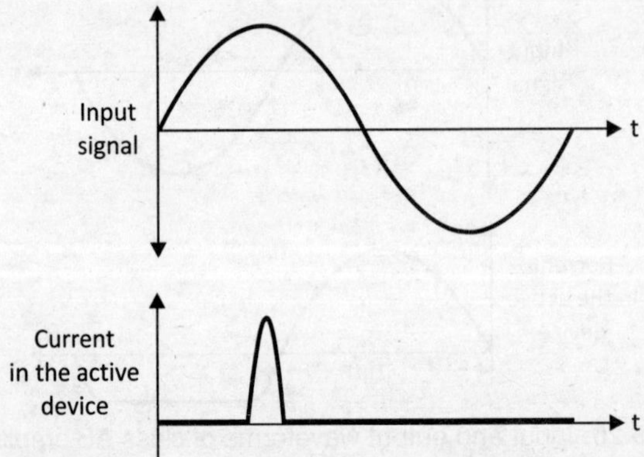

Fig. 6.22: Input and output waveforms of class C amplifiers

The active device in case of class C amplifiers is so biased that it conducts for less than one half of the input cycle, that is, it operates for less than 180° of the input cycle. Only a small portion of the input cycle is passed through the amplifier. This distorts the input signal and hence class C amplifiers are not used for audio applications. They are widely used as RF and IF amplifiers. They offer very high efficiencies of the order of 90%.

Class C amplifiers operate in two modes, namely, the untuned mode and the tuned mode. However, mostly they are operated in the tuned mode. Figure-6.23 shows a tuned class C amplifier configuration. The tuned circuit provides a full cycle of the output signal at the fundamental or the resonant frequency of the tuned circuit. Hence, the unwanted frequencies are drastically suppressed. Other residual harmonics can be removed by using a filter. Class C amplifiers are generally used in RF transmitters and are primarily not intended for use as large signal or power amplifiers.

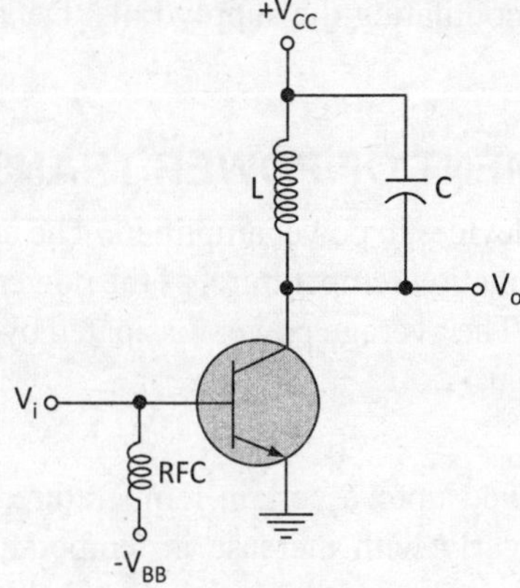

Fig. 6.23: Tuned class C amplifier

6.6 CLASS D AMPLIFIERS

Class D amplifiers use the active device in switching mode to regulate the output power. Hence, these amplifiers offer high efficiency and do not require heat sinks and transformers. These amplifiers use pulse width modulation (PWM), pulse density modulation or sigma delta modulation to convert the input signal into a string of pulses. Figure-6.24 shows how a sinusoidal input waveform is converted into a string of digital pulses using PWM technique. As we can see from the figure, the pulse width of the PWM output waveform at any time instant is directly proportional to the amplitude of the input signal.

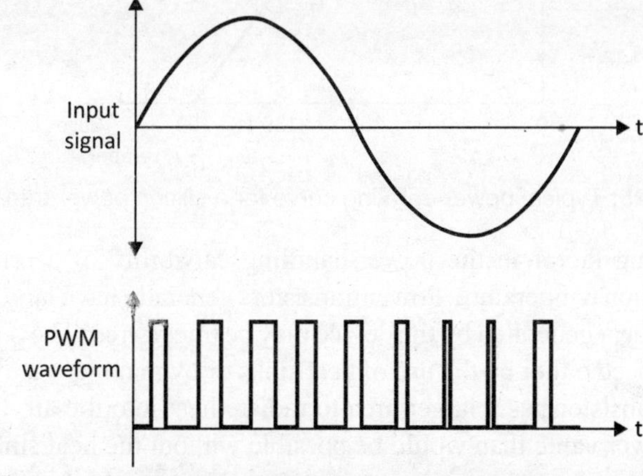

Fig. 6.24: Class D amplifier waveforms

6.7 OTHER CLASSES OF POWER AMPLIFIERS

Class E and class F amplifiers are switching power amplifiers offering very high efficiency levels. They are used at very high frequencies where the switching time is comparable to the duty time. Class G amplifiers are efficient versions of class AB amplifiers. They employ rail switching to decrease power consumption and increase efficiency. The amplifier has several power rails at different voltages and it switches between the rails as the output signal approaches each rail value. Class H amplifiers create infinite number of supply rails by modulating the supply rails. Detailed description of these classes is beyond the scope of the book.

6.8 THERMAL MANAGEMENT OF POWER TRANSISTORS

Power transistors are used as active devices in power amplifiers. The maximum power that can be handled by an active device is related to its junction temperature, as the power dissipated by the device causes an increase in its junction temperature. The average power dissipated by the transistor can be approximated by the following equation:

$$P_D = V_{CE} I_C \tag{6.37}$$

This power dissipation is allowed upto a certain temperature, above which the value of power dissipation capability decreases linearly with increase in temperature such that it reduces to zero at the maximum device case temperature. Larger the power handled by the transistor, higher is the case temperature. It may be mentioned here that the silicon transistors offer larger maximum temperature ratings than germanium transistors. Figure-6.25 shows the typical power derating curve for a silicon power transistor.

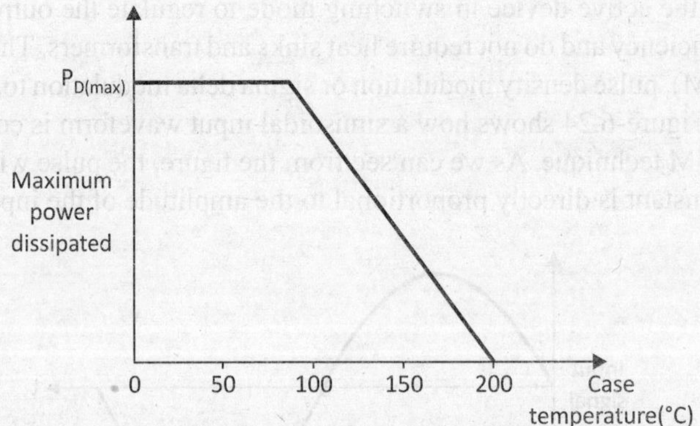

Fig. 6.25: Typical power derating curve for a silicon power transistor

Therefore, the limiting factor in the power-handling capability of a transistor is its maximum permissible collector junction temperature. Power transistors generally have large metal cases to provide a large area from which the heat generated by the device may be transferred. The power-handling capability of the device can be enhanced either by the use of heat sinks or by making use of thermoelectric coolers. With the heat sink, the transistor has a larger area to radiate heat into the air, thereby holding the case temperature to a much lower value than would be possible without the heat sink.

Thermoelectric coolers are solid-state heat pumps and are used in applications which require cooling below the ambient temperature, or where temperature cycling or precise temperature stabilization is required. Thermoelectric coolers are based on the Peltier effect, according to which the DC current applied across two dissimilar materials results in a temperature differential. These coolers transfer heat from one side of the active device to the other side against the temperature gradient. The cooling effect depends upon the amount of DC current and how well the heat from the hot side can be removed. Detailed description of thermoelectric cooling principle and application is beyond the scope of the present text.

GLOSSARY

Class A amplifiers: The active device in a class A amplifier operates during the whole of the input cycle and the output signal is an amplified replica of the input signal with no clipping. In other words, in class A amplifiers, the amplifying element is so biased that it operates over the linear region of its output characteristics during the full period of the input cycle and is always conducting to some extent.

Class AB amplifier: In a class AB amplifier, the amplifying device conducts for a little more than half of the input waveform. They sacrifice some efficiency over class B amplifiers but they offer better linearity than class B amplifiers. However, they offer much more efficiency than class A amplifiers.

Class B Amplifiers: Class B amplifiers operate only during the half of the input cycle. However they also create a large amount of distortion. A single class B amplifier is rarely used in practical systems. Two class B amplifiers are used either as a complementary pair or in a push–pull arrangement.

Class C amplifiers: Class C amplifiers conduct for less than 50% of the input signal resulting in a very high efficiency upto 90%. However, they are associated with a very high level of distortion at the output. Class C amplifiers operate in two modes, namely, the tuned mode and the untuned mode.

Class D amplifiers: Class D amplifiers use the active device in switching mode to regulate the output power. Hence, these amplifiers offer high efficiency and do not require heat sinks and transformers. These amplifiers use pulse width modulation (PWM), pulse density modulation or sigma delta modulation to convert the input signal into a string of pulses.

Class E and class F amplifiers: Class E and class F amplifiers are switching power amplifiers offering very high efficiency levels. They are used at very high frequencies where the switching time is comparable to the duty time.

Class G amplifiers: Class G amplifiers are efficient versions of class AB amplifiers. They employ rail switching to decrease power consumption and increase efficiency. The amplifier has several power rails at different voltages and it switches between the rails as the output signal approaches each rail value.

Class H amplifiers: Class H amplifiers create infinite number of supply rails by modulating the supply rails.

Complementary-symmetry push-pull class B amplifiers: Complementary-symmetry push–pull class B amplifiers dispense with the input and the output transformers. They make use of complementary transistors (NPN and PNP) to obtain a full-cycle output across the load with each transistor operating for half cycle. The same input is applied to the base terminals of both the transistors.

Crossover distortion: Crossover distortion refers to the non-linearity in the output signal when the output signal crosses from positive to negative or from negative to positive. In other words, crossover distortion refers to the distortion resulting at low values of the input signal in the vicinity of the zero region.

Directly Coupled Class A Amplifier: A simple emitter-coupled transistor amplifier with power transistor is a direct-coupled or a series-fed class A amplifier

Peltier effect: According to Peltier effect, the DC current applied across two dissimilar materials results in a temperature differential. These coolers transfer heat from one side of the active device to the other side against the temperature gradient. The cooling effect depends upon the amount of DC current and how well the heat from the hot side can be removed.

Push-pull class-A amplifier: Push–pull amplifiers employ two active devices which are fed with input signals that are 180° out-of-phase with each other. These amplifiers usually have a center-tapped output transformer.

Quasi-complementary class B amplifier: It is another variation of the complementary-symmetry amplifier where the push–pull operation is achieved by using a pair of complementary transistors.

Thermoelectric coolers: Thermoelectric coolers are solid-state heat pumps and are used in applications which require cooling below the ambient temperature, or where temperature cycling or precise temperature stabilization is required. Thermoelectric coolers are based on the Peltier effect.

Transformer-coupled class-A amplifier: Class A amplifier with transformer-coupled load employs a transformer-coupled output stage. This configuration offers better efficiency as compared to a directly coupled class A amplifier.

Transformer-coupled push-pull class-B amplifier: A transformer-coupled push–pull class B amplifier is the same as a push–pull class A amplifier except that the active devices in this case are biased in the cut-off region.

SUMMARY OF IMPORTANT FORMULAE

1. The efficiency of a directly coupled class A amplifier is

$$\eta = \frac{\text{Output Power}}{\text{Input Power}} = \frac{P_{ac}}{P_{dc}} = \frac{(V_{\max} - V_{\min})(I_{max} - I_{min})}{8V_{CC}I_{CQ}}$$

2. The efficiency of a transformer-coupled class-A amplifier is

$$\eta = 50\left(\frac{V_{CE(max)} - V_{CE(min)}}{V_{CE(max)} + V_{CE(min)}}\right)\%$$

3. The efficiency of a transformer-coupled push-pull class-B amplifier is

$$\eta = \left(\frac{\pi}{4}\right)\times\left(\frac{V_m}{V_{CC}}\right)\times 100\% = \left(\frac{\pi}{4}\right)\times\left(1 - \frac{V_{min}}{V_{CC}}\right)\times 100\%$$

4. The average power dissipated by the transistor can be approximated by

$$P_D = V_{CE}I_C$$

REVIEW QUESTIONS

1. Figure-6.26 shows the Q-points of different power amplifiers. Label the graph by highlighting which Q-point belongs to which type of power amplifier?

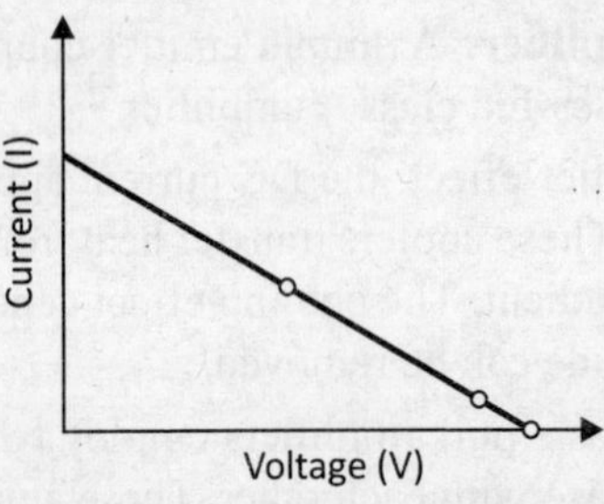

Fig. 6.26: Review Question 1

2. What is the difference between Class A, AB, B operation of amplifiers and class C operation of amplifiers?
3. Explain how the active device in a class A amplifier dissipates less power when a signal is applied to it as compared to when there is no input signal.
4. Explain the operation of the class-B push pull power amplifier with neat diagram and list its advantages
5. Explain the difference between a voltage amplifier and a power amplifier
6. What is crossover distortion? What are the main factors that lead to crossover distortion and how can they be removed?
7. Sketch the circuit diagram of a complementary-symmetry class B push–pull amplifier. Also draw the relevant current and voltage input and output waveforms.
8. Draw the circuit diagram of class A push–pull amplifier and explain its principle of operation.
9. Explain in detail how the use of heat sinks results in enhancement in the power dissipation capability of the transistor.
10. What is the difference between harmonic distortion and crossover distortion?

PROBLEMS

1. A class B amplifier operating on a supply voltage of 20V, provides a 15V peak output signal to a 10W load. What is the efficiency of the amplifier?
2. Calculate the harmonic distortion components for an output signal having fundamental amplitude of 6V, second harmonic of 0.5V, third harmonic of 0.1V and fourth harmonic of 0.04V. What is the value of total harmonic distortion?
3. Calculate the efficiency of the amplifier circuit shown in Figure-6.27. The input voltage applied is such that it produces a base-current of 10 mA peak. The base-emitter voltage of the transistor is equal to 0.7 V.

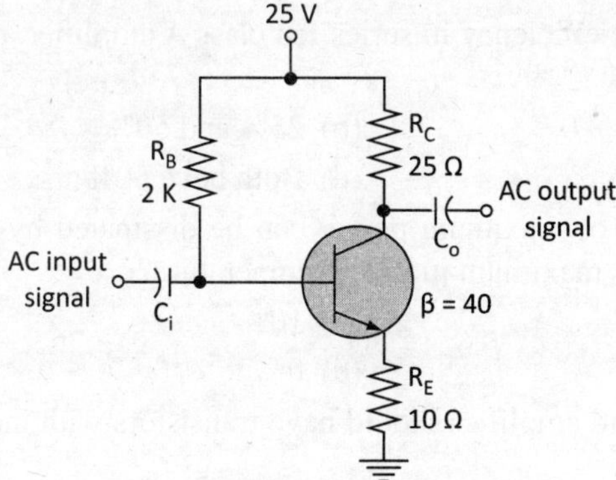

Fig. 6.27: Problem-3

4. A class B amplifier provides a 20 V peak output signal to 15 Ω load. The system operates on a power supply of 25 V. Determine the efficiency of the amplifier.

MULTIPLE CHOICE QUESTIONS

1. Which of the following statements are TRUE
   (a) Class B systems offer higher efficiency as no current flows in a class B amplifier when there is no input signal excitation whereas there is a quiescent current flowing through the active device in a class A amplifier in the absence of input signal
   (b) The dissipation in class B amplifiers is zero in the absence of input signal and it increases with excitation
   (c) In the case of a class A amplifier, dissipation is maximum at zero input and decreases as the signal increases
   (d) All the above
2. Which of the following amplifier class suffers mainly from the problem of crossover distortion?
   (a) Class A (b) Class B
   (c) Class AB (d) Class C
3. Which of the following best describes a class A amplifier?
   (a) High efficiency and high distortion (b) Low efficiency and high distortion
   (c) Low efficiency and low distortion (d) High efficiency and low distortion
4. Heat sinks are used in power transistors to
   (a) reduce the transistor power (b) reduce the junction temperature
   (c) increase the ambient temperature (d) increase the collector current
5. In which class of amplifiers it is theoretically possible to achieve 100% efficiency?
   (a) Class D (b) Class A
   (c) Class AB (d) Class C
6. In which of the following amplifier classes, the active device operates for the whole of the input signal cycle?
   (a) Class A (b) Class AB
   (c) Class B (d) Class C
7. The maximum possible efficiency in series fed class A amplifier and transformer coupled class A amplifiers are
   (a) 50% and 25% (b) 25% and 50%
   (c) Both have 25% (d) Both have 50%
8. How much percentage of maximum power can be dissipated by a transistor for an operating temperature equal to its maximum junction temperature?
   (a) 100% (b) 10%
   (c) 50% (d) 0%
9. A 5 W class B push–pull amplifier should have transistors with individual collector dissipation of
   (a) 2W (b) 1W
   (c) 5W (d) 10W
10. Class A amplifiers are generally used as
    (a) power amplifiers (b) RF amplifiers
    (c) audio amplifiers (d) none of these

SOLUTIONS TO PROBLEMS

Problem-1:

Peak load current $I_{L(P)} = \frac{15}{10} = 1.5A$

The DC value of the current drawn from the power supply is $I_{DC} = \frac{2}{\pi} \times I_{L(P)} = \frac{2}{\pi} \times 1.5A = 0.955A$

Input power delivered by the supply voltage $P_i = V_{CC} \times I_{DC} = 20 \times 0.955W = 19.11W$

Output power delivered to the load $P_o = \frac{V_{L(P)}^2}{2R_L} = \frac{(15)^2}{2 \times 10} W = 11.25W$

Efficiency $\eta = \frac{P_o}{P_i} \times 100\% = \frac{11.25}{19.11} \times 100\% = 58.87\%$

Problem-2:

Second harmonic distortion component is $D_2 = \left|\frac{A_2}{A_1}\right| \times 100\% = \left|\frac{0.5}{6}\right| \times 100\% = 8.33\%$

Third harmonic distortion component is $D_3 = \left|\frac{A_3}{A_1}\right| \times 100\% = \left|\frac{0.1}{6}\right| \times 100\% = 1.67\%$

Fourth harmonic distortion component is $D_4 = \left|\frac{A_4}{A_1}\right| \times 100\% = \left|\frac{0.04}{6}\right| \times 100\% = 0.67\%$

Total harmonic distortion (D) is

$$D = \sqrt{D_2^2 + D_3^2 + D_4^2 + ...} = \sqrt{(8.33)^2 + (1.67)^2 + (0.67)^2} = 8.52\%$$

Problem-3:

The value of the base current at the Q-point is given by $I_{BQ} = (V_{CC} - 0.7)/[R_B + (b + 1)R_E] = (25 - 0.7)/(2 \times 10^3 + 41 \times 10) = 24.3/2410 = 10.08 \times 10^{-3}$ A = 10.08 mA

The value of the collector current I_{CQ} is given by $b'I_{BQ} = 40 \times 10.08 \times 10^{-3}$ A = 403.3 mA

$V_{CEQ} = V_{CC} - I_C R_C - I_E R_E = 25 - 403.3 \times 10^{-3} \times 25 - 403.3 \times 10^{-3} \times 10 = 14.09$ V

The input power $P_i = V_{CC} \times I_{CQ} = 25 \times 403.3 \times 10^{-3} = 10.08$ W

The output power $P_o = [I_{C(p)}^2 \times R_C]/2$

$I_{C(p)} = b \times I_{B(p)} = 40 \times 10 \times 10^{-3} = 400 \times 10^{-3} = 400$ mA

$P_o = [(400 \times 10^{-3})^2 \times 25]/2 = 2$ W

Efficiency $h = (P_o/P_i) \times 100\% = (2/10.08) \times 100\% = 19.84\%$

Problem-4:

The peak load current $I_L(p) = 20/15 = 1.33$ A

The DC value of current drawn from the supply $I_{dc} = (2/\pi) \times I_L(p) = 0.847$ A

Input power delivered by the supply voltage $P_i = V_{CC} \times I_{dc} = 25 \times 0.847 = 21.175$ W

Output power delivered to the load $P_o = V_L(p)^2/2R_L = 20^2/(2 \times 15) = 400/30 = 13.33$ W

Efficiency $h = (P_o/P_i) \times 100\% = (13.33/21.175) \times 100\% = 62.95\%$

ANSWERS TO MULTIPLE CHOICE QUESTIONS

1. (d)	2. (b)	3. (c)	4. (b)
5. (a)	6. (a)	7. (b)	8. (d)
9. (b)	10. (c)		

7 Feedback Amplifiers

After completing this chapter, you will learn the following topics.

— Classification of amplifiers (Voltage amplifiers, Trans-resistance amplifiers, Trans-conductance amplifiers and Current amplifiers)

— Effect of negative feedback in amplifiers (effect on gain factor, de-sensitivity or stability of gain, bandwidth, noise, non-linear distortion, input impedance and output impedance)

— Feedback topologies (Voltage-series or the series–shunt feedback topology, Voltage-shunt or the shunt–shunt feedback topology, Current-series or the series–series feedback topology and the Current-shunt or the shunt–series feedback topology)

Introduction

This chapter is dedicated to description of concept of negative feedback in amplifiers and the effect of negative feedback on important performance parameters of amplifiers such as gain, gain stability, bandwidth, noise and distortion levels, input and output impedances. Different feedback topologies used in amplifiers are also discussed in detail. The chapter begins with a discussion on classification of amplifiers including the voltage amplifiers, trans-resistance amplifiers, trans-conductance amplifiers and current amplifiers. This is followed by discussion on the effect of negative feedback on gain factor, de-sensitivity or stability of gain, bandwidth, noise, non-linear distortion, input impedance and output impedance. Further to this, are discussed in detail different feedback topologies including voltage-series or the series–shunt feedback topology, voltage-shunt or the shunt–shunt feedback topology, current-series or the series–series feedback topology and the current-shunt or the shunt–series feedback topology. Different topics discussed in the chapter are amply illustrated with solved examples. In addition, there are a number of problems given towards the end of the chapter along with brief solutions. A self-evaluation exercise containing multiple-choice questions along with answers concludes the chapter.

7.1 CLASSIFICATION OF AMPLIFIERS

On the basis of the input and output parameters of interest, amplifiers are classified as voltage amplifiers, current amplifiers, trans-resistance amplifiers and trans-conductance amplifiers.

7.1.1 Voltage Amplifier

In the case of a *voltage amplifier*, a small change in the input voltage produces a large change in the output voltage. Voltage gain, which is the ratio of the change in the output voltage to change in the input voltage, is the gain parameter. The input and output circuits of a voltage amplifier are represented by Thevenin's equivalent circuits as shown in Figure 7.1. The circuit of Figure 7.1 will act like a true voltage amplifier when the input resistance of the amplifier represented by R_i and output resistance of the amplifier represented by R_o in Figure 7.1 respectively are infinite and zero. This would allow the whole of applied input voltage to appear across the amplifier input irrespective of the value of source resistance R_s and also whole of amplified input voltage to appear across the load resistance R_L irrespective of the value of R_L. In a practical voltage amplifier circuit, R_i is much larger than R_s and R_o is much smaller than R_L.

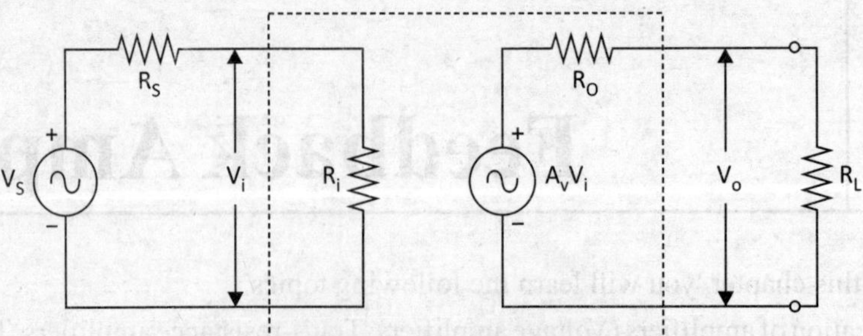

Fig. 7.1: Equivalent circuit of voltage amplifier

7.1.2 Trans-resistance Amplifier

In the case of a *trans-resistance amplifier*, a small change in the input current produces a large change in the output voltage. Ratio of the change in the output voltage to the change in the input current is the gain parameter, which has the units of resistance. The input and output circuits of a trans-resistance amplifier are, respectively, represented by Norton's and Thevenin's equivalent circuits as shown in Figure 7.2. For a true trans-resistance amplifier, the input resistance of the amplifier, represented by R_i in Figure 7.2, should ideally be zero so that the whole of applied input current flows through the amplifier input irrespective of the value of source resistance R_s. In a practical trans-resistance amplifier circuit, R_i is much smaller than R_s. Also, the output resistance R_o should ideally be zero so that the output voltage appears across the load resistance R_L irrespective of the value of R_L. In a practical circuit, R_o is much smaller than R_L. To summarize, trans-resistance amplifiers have very low input and output resistances, which in ideal case should be zero. Trans-resistance amplifiers make excellent current-to-voltage converters.

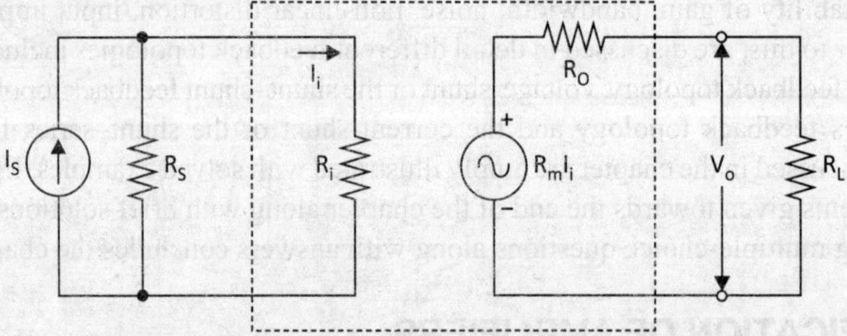

Fig. 7.2: Equivalent circuit of trans-resistance amplifier

7.1.3 Trans-conductance Amplifier

In a*trans-conductance amplifier*, a small change in the input voltage produces a large change in the output current. Ratio of the change in the output current to the change in the input voltage is the gain parameter, which has the units of conductance. The input and output circuits of a trans-conductance amplifier are, respectively, represented by Thevenin's and Norton's equivalent circuits as shown in Figure 7.3. For a true trans-conductance amplifier, the input resistance of the amplifier represented by R_i in Figure 7.3 should ideally be infinite so that the whole of applied input voltage appears across the amplifier input irrespective of the value of source resistance R_s. In a practical trans-conductance amplifier circuit, value of resistance R_i is much larger than R_s. Also, the output resistance R_o should ideally be infinite so that the output current flows through the load resistance R_L irrespective of the value of R_L. In a practical circuit, R_o is much larger than R_L.

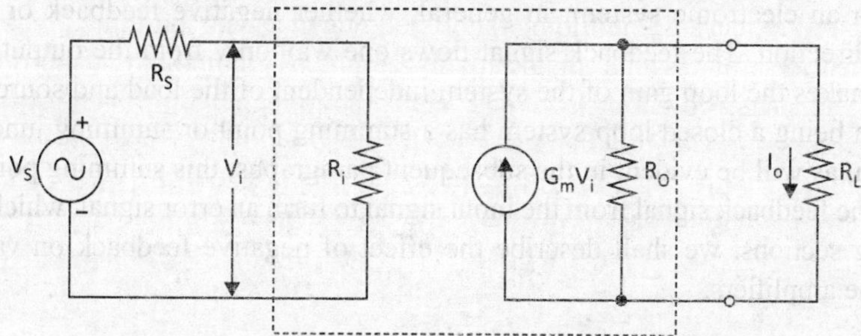

Fig. 7.3: Equivalent circuit of trans-conductance amplifier

7.1.4 Current Amplifier

For a *current amplifier*, a small change in the input current produces a large change in the output current. Current gain, which is the ratio of the change in the output current to the change in the input current, is the gain parameter. The input and output circuits of a current amplifier are represented by Norton's equivalent circuits as shown in Figure 7.4. For a true current amplifier, the input resistance of the amplifier represented by R_i in Figure 7.4 should ideally be zero so that the whole of applied input current flows through the amplifier input irrespective of the value of source resistance R_s. In a practical current amplifier circuit, R_i is much smaller than R_s. Also, the output resistance R_o should ideally be infinite so that whole of amplified input current flows through the load resistance R_L irrespective of the value of R_L. In a practical current amplifier circuit, R_o is much larger than R_L.

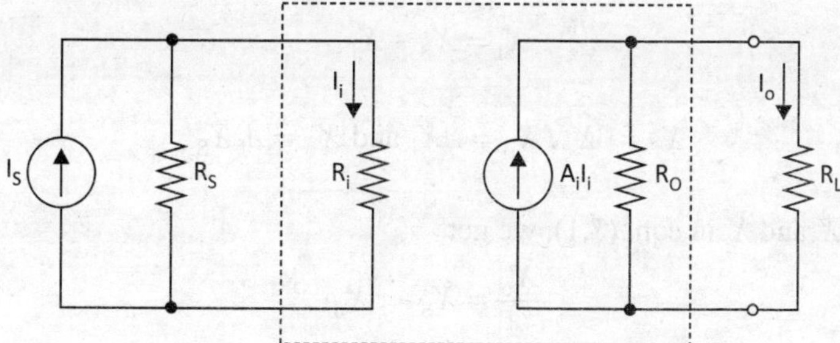

Fig. 7.4: Equivalent circuit of current amplifier

7.2 NEGATIVE FEEDBACK IN AMPLIFIERS

With reference to electronic amplifiers, negative feedback is a mechanism by which a fraction of the output signal, either a voltage or a current, is fed back to the input with the result that the actual input to the amplifier is the resultant of the applied input signal and the feedback signal. The feedback signal in this case is opposite in polarity or is in phase opposition to the input signal. On the other hand, in the case of positive feedback, the feedback signal is of the same polarity as the input signal or is in phase with the input signal. Positive feedback is not desirable in amplifiers. It is used in case of oscillators discussed in the following chapter. Negative feedback has the effect of reducing the overall gain of the amplifier with the degree of reduction being related to the gain of the amplifier in the absence of negative feedback; in the process minimizing the sensitivity of the gain parameter to external factors. Negative feedback also has effects of reducing distortion and noise, improving bandwidth, input and output impedances.

Feedback in an electronic system, in general, whether negative feedback or positive feedback, is unilateral in direction. The feedback signal flows one way only from the output to the input of the system, which makes the loop gain of the system independent of the load and source impedances. The feedback system being a closed loop system has a summing point or summing junction. In a negative feedback system, as will be evident in the subsequent paragraphs, this summing point or junction at its input subtracts the feedback signal from the input signal to form an error signal, which drives the system. In the following sections, we shall describe the effect of negative feedback on various performance parameters of the amplifiers.

7.2.1 Effect on Gain Factor

Let us consider a negative-feedback amplifier as shown in Figure 7.5. The actual signal applied to the amplifier input X_i is the difference of externally applied input signal X_s and the feedback signal X_f. It is given by eqn. 7.1.

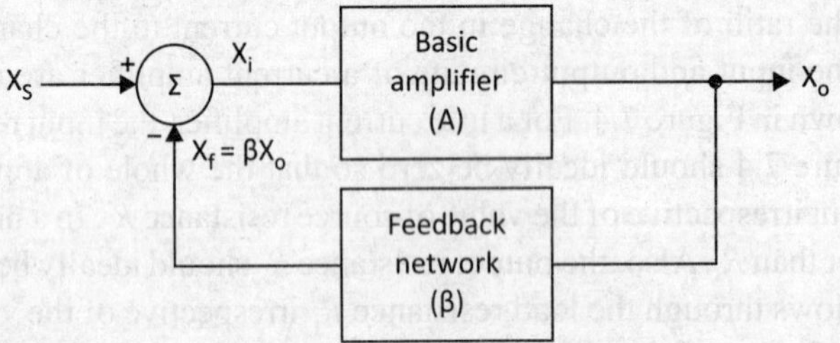

Fig. 7.5: Block schematic of amplifier with negative feedback

$$X_i = X_S - X_f \tag{7.1}$$

Also,
$$X_f = \beta X_o, X_o = AX_i \text{ and } X_o = A_f X_S, \tag{7.2}$$

Substituting for X_i and X_f in eqn. (7.1), we get,

$$\frac{X_o}{A} = X_S - \beta X_o \tag{7.3}$$

Simplifying eqn. (7.3), we get the expression for A_f as follows:

$$A_f = \frac{X_o}{X_S} = \frac{A}{1+\beta A} \tag{7.4}$$

An important parameter relevant to negative-feedback amplifiers is the loop gain. It is given by (-βA) with minus sign indicating negative feedback. Another relevant term is the quantum of feedback expressed in decibels. It is given by:

$$\text{dB of feedback} = 20\log\left|\frac{A_f}{A}\right| = 20\log\left|\frac{1}{1+\beta A}\right| \tag{7.5}$$

It may be mentioned here that for eqn. (7.4) and equations for input and output impedances derived in the case of amplifiers with negative feedback in the latter part of the chapter to be valid, three fundamental assumptions should be satisfied for the feedback network. These include the following.

1. Forward transmission through feedback network is zero. In other words, the input signal is transmitted to the output through the amplifier only and not through the feedback network. This further implies that if the gain of the amplifier were reduced to zero, the output must drop to zero.
2. Reverse transmission through amplifier is zero, that is the feedback signal is transmitted from output to input through feedback network only.
3. The feedback factor is independent of load and source resistances.

Example 7.1: A negative feedback amplifier has a closed loop gain of 100 and an open loop gain of 10000. Determine the feedback factor. If for the same feedback factor, the open loop gain reduces to 1000, what is the percentage change in closed loop gain corresponding to this factor of reduction of 10 in the open loop gain of the amplifier?

Solution: Closed loop gain is

$$A_f = \frac{A}{1+A\beta} = 100$$

A is given as 10000. Solving the above equation, we get

$$A\beta = \frac{10^4}{100} - 1 = 99 \text{ or } \beta = \frac{99}{10^4} = 9.9\times10^{-3}$$

When A is changed to 1000, then,

$$A_f = \frac{A}{1+A\beta} = \frac{1000}{1+1000\times9.9\times10^{-3}} = 91.74$$

Percentage change in closed loop gain with respect to open loop gain is given by:

$$\frac{\Delta A_f}{A_f}\times100\% = \left(\frac{91.74-100}{100}\right)\times100\% = -8.26\%$$

Example 7.2: Refer to the non-inverting amplifier circuit of Figure 7.6. The closed-loop gain of this amplifier is usually considered as being equal to [(1 + (R_2/R_1)]. Given that the open-loop gain of the op-amp is 100 000, values of R_1 and R_2 are 10 KW and 100 KW, respectively, and the value of the applied input voltage V_i is 2 V, determine the percentage error incurred in computing the output voltage by using this expression.

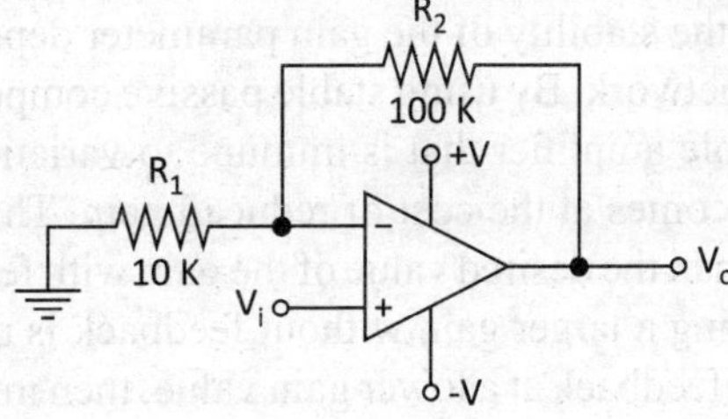

Fig. 7.6: Example 7.2

Solution: Closed-loop gain ignoring the effect of finite value of open loop gain = 1 + (R_2/R_1).
Substituting for R_1 and R_2,
Closed loop gain = 11

Output voltage = 11 × 2 = 22 V

The true value of closed-loop gain is given by $[A/(1 + bA)]$.

Where A = Open-loop gain = 100 000 and

β = Feedback factor = $[R_1/(R_1 + R_2)] = 1/11$

The true value of the closed-loop gain is, therefore, given by:

$[100000/\{(1 + 100000)/11\}] = 10.998$

True value of output voltage = 2 × 10.998 = 21.99758 V.

Percentage error = [(22- 21.99758)/22] × 100 = 0.011%

7.2.2 De-sensitivity (or Stability) of Gain

Introduction of negative feedback makes the amplifier insensitive to variations in the values of the components and parameters of the active devices used in building the amplifier.

Differentiating eqn. 7.4 with respect to A, we get,

$$\frac{dA_f}{dA} = \frac{d}{dA}\left[\frac{A}{1+\beta A}\right] = \frac{(1+\beta A)-\beta A}{(1+\beta A)^2} = \frac{1}{(1+\beta A)^2} \tag{7.6}$$

$$dA_f = \frac{dA}{(1+\beta A)^2} = \left(\frac{dA}{A}\right)\times\left[\frac{A}{(1+\beta A)^2}\right] = \left(\frac{dA}{A}\right)\times\left[\frac{A_f}{1+\beta A}\right]$$

$$\frac{dA_f}{A_f} = \left[\frac{1}{1+\beta A}\right]\times\left(\frac{dA}{A}\right)$$

$$\left|\frac{dA_f}{A_f}\right| = \left|\frac{1}{1+\beta A}\right|\times\left|\frac{dA}{A}\right| \tag{7.7}$$

$|(1 + \beta A)|$ is called the de-sensitivity parameter D. Thus, percentage variation in gain with feedback is equal to the percentage variation in gain without feedback divided by the de-sensitivity parameter D. As a special case, when $\beta A >> 1$, A_f equals $1/\beta$ and therefore becomes independent of the open-loop gain of the amplifier. In that case, the stability of the gain parameter depends only on the stability of the components used in the feedback network. By using stable passive components in the feedback network, it is indeed possible to have a stable amplifier that is immune to variations in parametric values of the amplifier. Remember that all this comes at the cost of reduced gain. This implies that the gain without feedback needs to be much larger than the desired value of the gain with feedback. If increase in instability in the amplifier on account of having a larger gain without feedback is not significantly higher than the instability of the amplifier without feedback at a lower gain value, then introduction of negative feedback certainly improves the stability by a significant margin.

7.2.3 Effect on Bandwidth

Bandwidth increases with introduction of negative feedback. Increase in bandwidth results from the fact that amplifiers exhibit a constant gain-bandwidth product. Reduction in gain is, therefore, accompanied by increase in bandwidth. Bandwidth increases by the same de-sensitivity factor $D = (1 + \beta A)$ by which the gain reduces. Bandwidth of amplifier with feedback is given by

$$(BW)_{\mathrm{f}} = BW \times (1 + \beta A) \tag{7.8}$$

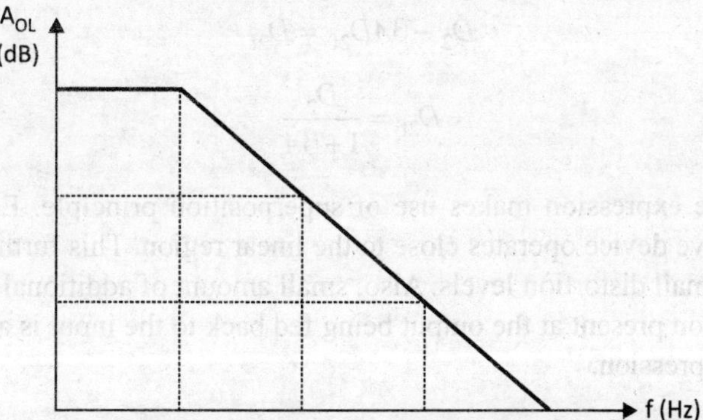

Fig. 7.7: Effect of negative feedback on bandwidth

Figure 7.7 shows the gain-bandwidth curve of a typical operational amplifier. The gain-bandwidth product is given by the unity gain crossover frequency. We can see how bandwidth can be traded for closed-loop gain. Increase in bandwidth with introduction of negative feedback can also be explained as follows. As the gain rolls off with increase in frequency, reduced output signal amplitude means reduced feedback. Reduced negative feedback means increase in the magnitude of effective input signal which increases the output. In other words, output remains at its mid-band-value up to a higher frequency.

7.2.4 Effect on Noise

Introduction of negative feedback acts on the noise generated in the amplifier in the same manner as it does on the non-linear distortion. Reduction in noise is governed by:

$$N_{\mathrm{f}} = \frac{N}{1 + \beta A} \tag{7.9}$$

N_{f} and N are, respectively, the noise levels with and without negative feedback. However, if reduction in gain resulting from introduction of negative feedback is compensated by adding an amplifier stage, the overall system may turn out to be noisier than before. In order to benefit from the positive effect of negative feedback on noise, it is important that the reduced gain is compensated by readjustment of amplifier parameters for a higher gain without feedback so that the amplifier with feedback gives the desired gain.

7.2.5 Effect on Non-linear Distortion

Non-linear distortion arises from the existence of non-linear transfer characteristics of the active device and the input and output signal swings that are large enough to drive the active device to operate in the non-linear region of the characteristics. Non-linear distortion can be assumed to be predominantly second harmonic distortion. Introduction of negative feedback reduces distortion provided that reduction in gain caused by negative feedback is compensated by increased gain in the preamplifier stages rather than introducing an additional gain stage. Remember that the non-linear distortion mainly occurs in the last stage of amplification and increasing the gain of previous stages does not add significantly to the overall distortion level.

Non-linear distortion decreases by the de-sensitivity factor $D = (1 + \beta A)$. Let us assume that the distortion levels without and with negative feedback are D_2 and D_{2f}, respectively. Suffix "2" implies second harmonic distortion. D_2 is the distortion contributed by the active device. In the presence of feedback, D_{2f} appears as $-\beta AD_{2f}$ at the input of the amplifier. The expression for D_{2f} is therefore given by eqn. (7.10).

$$D_2 - \beta AD_{2f} = D_{2f} \tag{7.10}$$

Which gives,

$$D_{2f} = \frac{D_2}{1+\beta A} \tag{7.11}$$

Derivation of above expression makes use of superposition principle. Eqn. (7.11) is, therefore, valid only when the active device operates close to the linear region. This further means that the above expression is valid for small distortion levels. Also, small amount of additional distortion arising out of small fraction of distortion present at the output being fed back to the input is assumed to be negligible in deriving the above expression.

7.2.6 Effect on Input Resistance

Input resistance in an amplifier with negative feedback is affected depending upon how the feedback signal (voltage or current) is connected to the source of external input signal. The input resistance increases if the feedback signal is connected in series with the source of input signal and decreases if the feedback signal is connected across it in shunt. Increase or decrease, as the case may be, is by de-sensitivity factor $D = (1 + \beta A)$. Thus, in the case of voltage-series and current-series feedback, input resistance with feedback R_{if} is given by eqn. (7.12).

$$R_{if} = R_i \times (1+\beta A) \tag{7.12}$$

Where, R_i is the input resistance without feedback. Input resistance in the case of voltage-shunt and current-shunt feedback is given by eqn. (7.13).

$$R_{if} = \frac{R_i}{1+\beta A} \tag{7.13}$$

7.2.7 Effect on Output Resistance

Negative feedback affects the output resistance of the amplifier depending upon the nature of the output signal fed back to the input. In case output voltage is sampled; output resistance decreases. In case output current or a voltage proportional to the output current is sampled; output resistance increases. Output resistance with feedback R_{of} in the case of current-series and current-shunt feedback is given by eqn. (7.14).

$$R_{of} = R_o \times (1+\beta A) \tag{7.14}$$

Where, R_o is the output resistance without feedback.

Output resistance in the case of voltage-series and voltage-shunt feedback is given by eqn. 7.15.

$$R_{of} = \frac{R_o}{1+\beta A} \tag{7.15}$$

Example 7.3: An amplifier without feedback has a voltage gain of 1000. The designer decides to use 10% negative feedback. Determine the gain of the amplifier in the presence of feedback. If the desired value of gain with feedback is 50, what should in that case be the feedback factor?

Solution: Gain with feedback = $A/(1 + \beta A)$

Where A = Gain without feedback and

β = Feedback factor

Gain with feedback = $1000/(1 + 0.1 \times 1000) = 1000/101 = 9.9$

If the gain with feedback needs to be equal to 50,

Then $50 = 1000/(1 + \beta \times 1000)$

Solving for β, we get,

$1000b + 1 = 20$

That is, $\beta = 0.019$ or 1.9%.

Example 7.4: The total harmonic distortion of an amplifier reduces from 10% to 1% on introduction of 10% negative feedback. Determine the open-loop and closed-loop gain values.

Solution: Distortion (with feedback) = Distortion (without feedback)/$(1 + \beta A)$, where A is the open-loop gain.

$0.01 = 0.1/(1 + 0.1A)$

Which gives $1 + 0.1A = 10$ or $A = 90$.

Therefore, open-loop gain = 90.

Closed-loop gain = $90/(1 + 0.1 \times 90) = 9$

Example 7.5: A negative-feedback amplifier has -40 dB of feedback. Determine the loop gain.

Solution: Negative feedback in dB = 20 log (Gain with feedback/Gain without feedback) = -40.

Log (Gain with feedback/Gain without feedback) = -2.

Gain with feedback/Gain without feedback = 0.01= $1/(1 + \beta A)$.

This gives $(1 + \beta A) = 100$, or $\beta A = 99$

Loop gain $= -\beta A = -99$

Example 7.6: The overall gain of a multistage amplifier is 140. When negative voltage feedback is applied, the gain is reduced to 17.5. Find the fraction of the output that is feedback to the input.

Solution: Gain with feedback A_f is related to gain without feedback A by

$$A_f = \frac{A}{1+\beta A}$$

Given $A_f = 17.5$, A = 140. Substituting these values in the above equation, we get

$\beta = 0.05$

Example 7.7: When negative voltage feedback is applied to an amplifier of gain 100, the overall gain falls to 50.

(a) Calculate the fraction of the output voltage feedback

(b) If this fraction is maintained, calculate the value of the amplifier gain required if the overall gain is to be 75.

Solution: (a) Gain without feedback A = 100

Gain with feedback $A_f = 50$

Gain with feedback A_f is related to gain without feedback A by the following equation.

$$A_f = \frac{A}{1+\beta A}$$

Solving the above equation, we get b = 0.01

(b) New value of overall gain (A_f') = 75

Given value of $\beta = 0.01$

Substituting the values in the equation $A_f = \dfrac{A}{1+\beta A}$

We get the value of A is 300.

Example 7.8: If the open loop gain of an opamp is 100 and the feedback factor in the amplifier configuration in which it is used is 0.1; determine the percentage change in the gain of the amplifier configuration if the open loop gain falls by 6dB due to aging.

Solution: Gain with feedback A_f is related to gain without feedback A by:

$$A_f = \frac{A}{1+\beta A}$$

For A = 100 and $\beta = 0.1$, gain with feedback is given by:

$$A_f = \frac{100}{1+100\times 0.1} = 9.09$$

Fall in open loop gain = 6dB

Let the new value of gain be A'.

Therefore, the new value of open loop gain is given by:

$$20\log\frac{A}{A'} = 6$$

Solving the above equation, we get A' = 50

New value of gain with feedback is given by:

$$A_f' = \frac{50}{1+50\times 0.1} = 8.33$$

Percentage change in the system gain is given by:

$$\left(\frac{9.09-8.33}{9.09}\right)\times 100\% = 8.36\%$$

7.3 FEEDBACK TOPOLOGIES

There are four feedback topologies classified on the basis of the nature of sampled signal and the mode in which it is fed back to the input,. These include the following.

1. Voltage-series or the series–shunt feedback topology
2. Voltage-shunt or the shunt–shunt feedback topology
3. Current-series or the series–series feedback topology
4. Current-shunt or the shunt–series feedback topology

Each one of these feedback topologies is described in the following sections.

7.3.1 Voltage Series or Series-Shunt Feedback Topology

In the case of voltage-series or the series-shunt feedback, output voltage is sampled and mixed in series with the externally applied input signal. Figure 7.8 shows the block schematic arrangement of a generalized feedback amplifier with voltage-series feedback and Figure 7.9 shows its equivalent circuit.

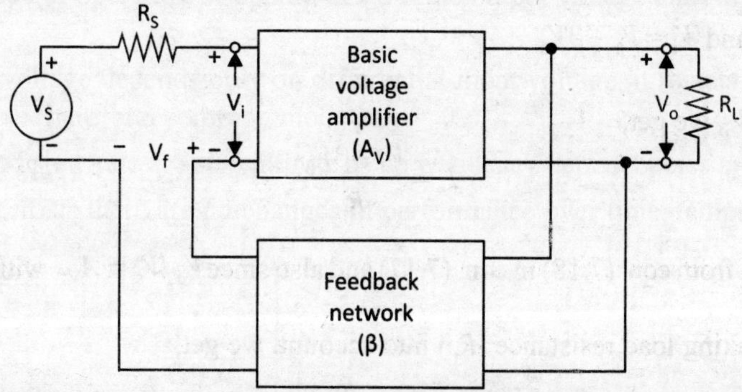

Fig. 7.8: Schematic arrangement of voltage-series (series–shunt) feedback

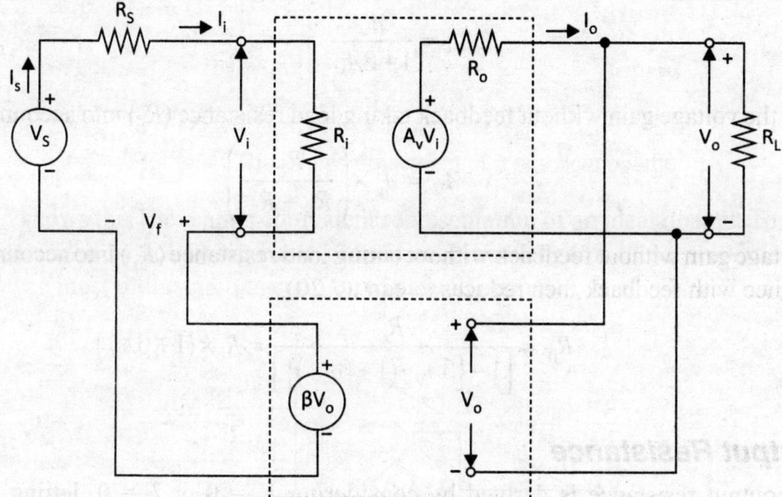

Fig. 7.9: Equivalent circuit for schematic arrangement of Figure 7.8

7.3.1.1 *Gain*

The gain parameter in this case is the voltage gain. Eqn. 7.16 gives the expression for voltage gain with feedback in terms of gain without feedback and the feedback factor.

$$A_{Vf} = \frac{A_V}{1+\beta A_V} \tag{7.16}$$

where A_V and A_{Vf} are the voltage gains without and with feedback considering the load resistance R_L.

7.3.1.2 Input Resistance

Expression for input resistance is derived as follows.

$$R_{\text{if}} = \frac{V_s}{I_s} = \frac{V_s}{I_i} \tag{7.17}$$

Now $I_i = V_i/R_i$ and $V_i = V_s - \beta V_o$

Substituting for V_i, we get,

$$I_i = \frac{V_s - \beta V_o}{R_i} \tag{7.18}$$

Substituting for I_i from eqn. (7.18) in eqn. (7.17) and also since $V_o/V_s = A_{\text{Vf}}$ with A_{Vf} being the voltage gain with feedback taking load resistance (R_L) into account, we get,

$$R_{\text{if}} = \frac{R_i}{1 - \beta A_{\text{Vf}}} \tag{7.19}$$

Now,

$$A_{\text{Vf}} = \frac{A_V}{1 + \beta A_V}$$

where A_V is the voltage gain without feedback taking load resistance (R_L) into account. It is given by:

$$A_V = A_v \times \left(\frac{R_L}{R_o + R_L} \right)$$

A_v is the voltage gain without feedback without taking load resistance (R_L) into account. The equation for input resistance with feedback then reduces to eqn. (7.20).

$$R_{\text{if}} = \frac{R_i}{\left[1 - \{\beta A_V/(1 + \beta A_V)\}\right]} = R_i \times (1 + \beta A_V) \tag{7.20}$$

7.3.1.3 Output Resistance

Expression for output resistance is derived by considering $V_s = 0$ or $I_s = 0$, letting load resistance $R_L = \infty$ and applying a voltage V across the output. Ratio of applied voltage V to the resulting current I gives the output resistance.

$$I = \frac{V - A_v V_i}{R_o}$$

For

$$V_s = 0,\ V_i = -V_f = -\beta V$$

Therefore,

$$I = \frac{V + \beta A_v V}{R_o}$$

$$R_{\text{of}} = \frac{V}{I} = \frac{R_o}{1 + \beta A_v} \tag{7.21}$$

It may be mentioned here that R_{of} is the output resistance with feedback with $R_L = \beta$. From eqn. (7.21), we see that it is equal to R_o divided by the factor $(1 + \beta A_v)$, which contains the voltage gain A_v and not A_V. Considering the effect of load resistance R_L, the output resistance with feedback R_{of}' is given by parallel combination of R_{of} and R_L. R_{of}' can also be expressed by:

$$R_{of}' = \frac{R_o'}{1+\beta A_V} \text{ where } R_o' = \frac{R_o \times R_L}{R_o + R_L} \quad (7.22)$$

Remember, A_V is the voltage gain without feedback taking load resistance (R_L) into account.

7.3.1.4 Practical Circuits

Common-drain amplifier or the source-follower circuit as shown in Figure 7.10 is an example of voltage-series feedback as the output voltage appearing across the source resistor R_S is fed back in series with the externally applied input signal. The bipolar transistor counterpart of source follower is the emitter-follower, which is another example of voltage-series feedback. Source-follower and emitter-follower are examples of 100% feedback with the result that the closed-loop gain is approximately unity.

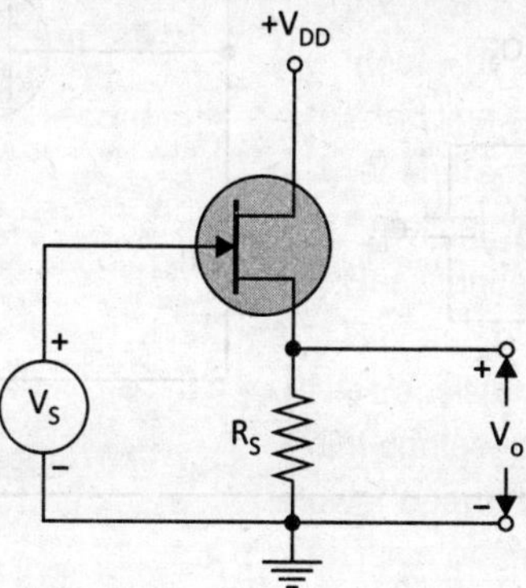

Fig. 7.10: Source follower amplifier circuit

A non-inverting amplifier circuit configured around an op-amp as shown in Figure 7.11 is yet another example of voltage-series feedback. In this case, the feedback voltage appears across R_1.

In this case, the feedback voltage $= V_o \times R_1/(R_1 + R_2)$

The feedback voltage V_f is in series with externally applied input voltage V_i. Also, it is in phase opposition with the external input as V_i and V_f are, respectively, applied to non-inverting and inverting inputs of the op-amp.

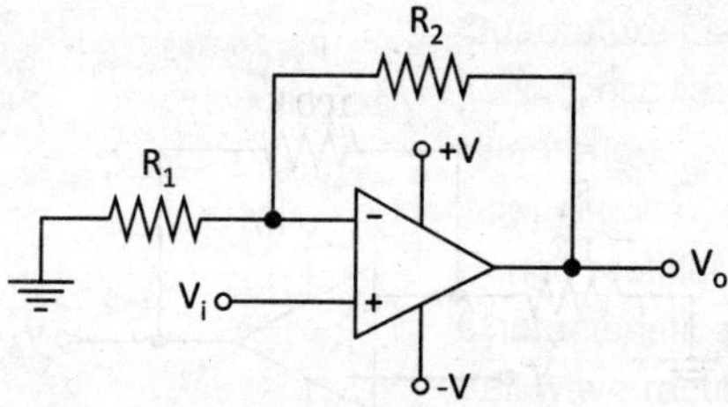

Fig. 7.11: Voltage-series feedback in non-inverting amplifier

Another non-inverting amplifier configuration with voltage-series negative feedback is shown in Figure 7.12. The circuit shown is a cascade arrangement of two common-emitter amplifier stages. Since each common-emitter stage introduces a phase shift of 180°; the total phase shift introduced by cascade arrangement is 360° or 0°. The emitter resistor of the first stage is split into two series-connected resistors. Relatively much smaller of the two resistance values is un-bypassed and forms a part of the potential divider arrangement with another resistor connected from the output. The feedback voltage, which is the voltage across R_1, opposes the applied input voltage. The feedback factor is given by $R_1/(R_1 + R_2)$.

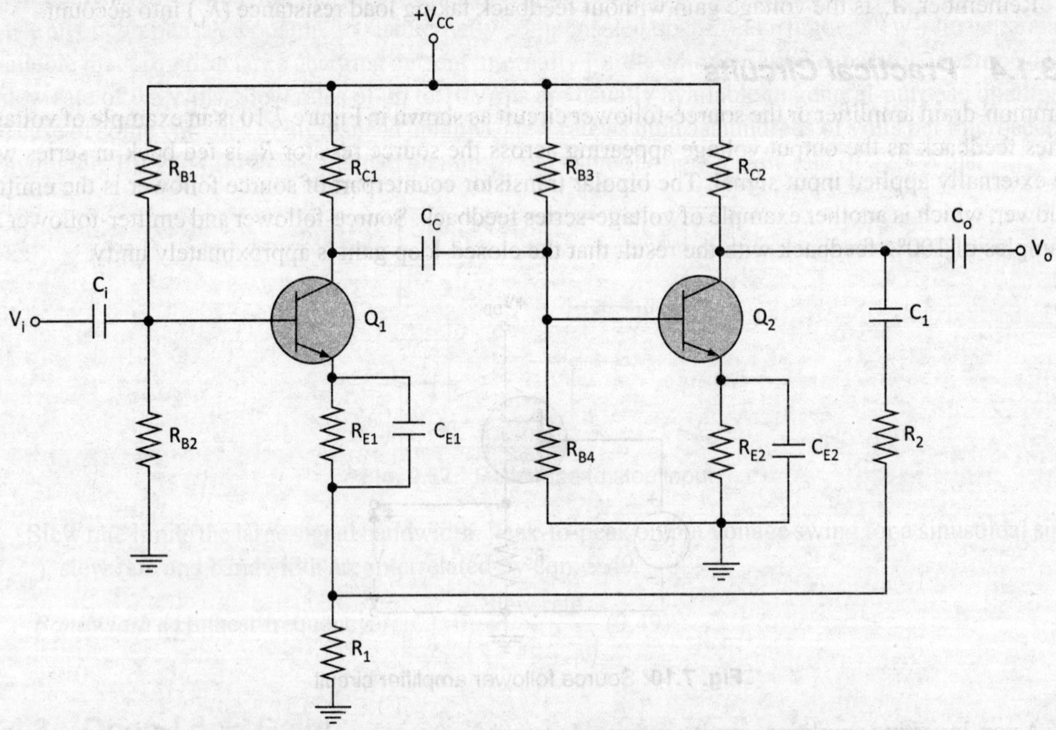

Fig. 7.12: Two-stage common emitter amplifier with voltage-series feedback

Example 7.9: For the amplifier shown in Figure 7.13, determine the voltage gain and the input impedance. Given that open-loop gain, and the input impedance of the op-amp are 80 dB and 1 MW, respectively.

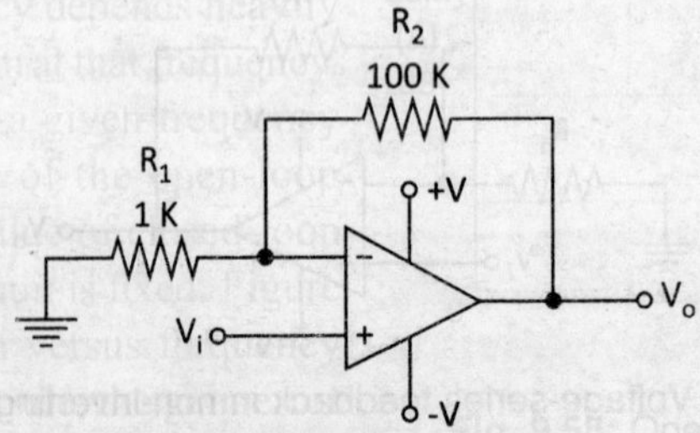

Fig. 7.13: Example 7.9

Solution: Open-loop gain, $A = 80$ dB

Therefore, A = 10000

Feedback factor, $\beta = R_1/(R_1 + R_2) = 1 \times 10^3/(1 \times 10^3 + 100 \times 10^3) = 1/101 = 0.0099$

Therefore, de-sensitivity factor, $D = 1 + \beta A = 1 + 10000/101 = 100.0099$

Gain with feedback = 10000/100.0099 = 99.99

Input impedance of the op-amp = 1 MΩ.

Since it is a case of series feedback, input impedance would increase by the de-sensitivity factor

That is, input impedance with feedback = $1 \times 10^6 \times 100.0099 = 100$ MΩ

Example 7.10: Refer to circuit of Figure 7.14. Identify the type of feedback. Also, determine the voltage gain, input resistance and output resistance in the presence of voltage-series feedback.

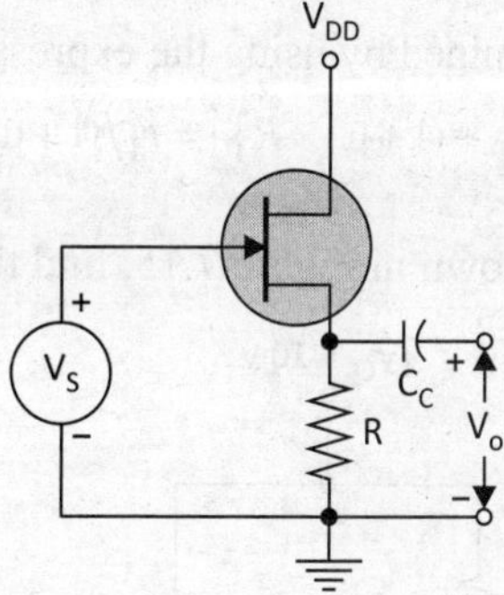

Fig. 7.14: Example 7.10

Solution: The feedback voltage here is the voltage developed across resistance R with the polarities as shown. As is evident from the circuit diagram, the feedback voltage is in series with and in phase opposition to applied input signal.. Therefore, it is a voltage-series negative feedback.

In the absence of negative feedback, voltage gain A_V would be expressed by:

$$A_V = V_o/V_s = \{g_m \times (r_d \| R) \times V_s\}/V_s = (g_m \times r_d \times R \times V_s)/\{(r_d + R) \times V_s\}$$

Therefore, $A_V = (g_m \times r_d \times R)/(r_d + R)$

Also $g_m \times r_d = \mu$. This gives $A_V = (\mu \times R)/(r_d + R)$.

De-sensitivity factor, $D = 1 + \beta A_V = 1 + [(\mu \times R)/(r_d + R)] = [\{r_d + (1+\mu) \times R\}/(r_d + R)]$ as $\beta = 1$

Therefore, $A_{Vf} = A_V/D = [(\mu \times R)/\{r_d + (1+\mu)R\}]$

The input impedance of an FET for all practical purposes is infinite. Therefore, input resistance with feedback, $R_{if} = R_i \times D$ is also infinite.

Output resistance with feedback $R_{of} = R_o/(1 + \beta A_v)$.

Here $R_o = r_d$ considering the load resistance R to be an open circuit.

Also, $A_v = m$.

Therefore, $R_{of} = r_d/(1+\mu)$.

If R_{of}' is the output resistance with feedback taking load resistance into account, then

$$R_{of}' = R_o'/D, \text{ where } R_o' = (r_d \times R)/(r_d + R) \text{ and } D = \{r_d + (1+\infty) \times R\}/(r_d + R)$$

This gives $R_{of}' = \left[(r_d \times R)/\{r_d + (1+\mu)\times R\}\right]$

The value of R_{of} can also be determined by using the expression

$$R_{of} = \lim_{R\to\infty} R_{of}' = \lim_{R\to\infty}\left[(r_d \times R)/\{r_d + (1+\mu)\times R\}\right] = r_d/(1+\mu)$$

Example 7.11: For the circuit shown in Figure 7.15, find the input impedance.

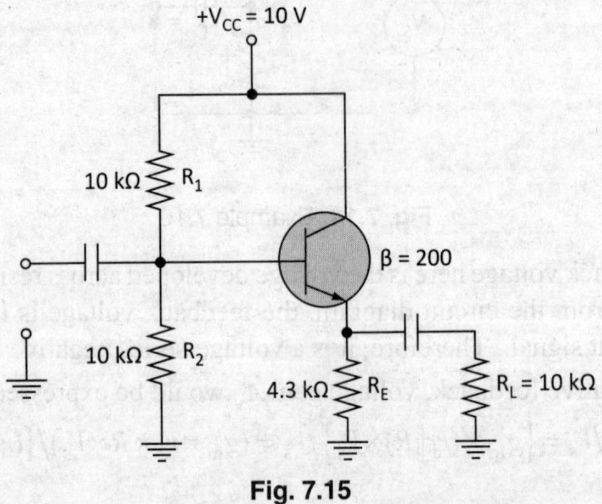

Fig. 7.15

Solution:

Voltage across resistor R_2 is $V_2 = \left(\dfrac{V_{CC}}{R_1 + R_2}\right) \times R_2 = \left(\dfrac{10}{10\times10^3 + 10\times10^3}\right) \times 10\times10^3 = 5V$

Voltage across resistor R_E is $V_E = V_2 - V_{BE} = 5 - 0.7 = 4.3V$

Emitter current $I_E = \dfrac{V_E}{R_E} = \dfrac{4.3}{4.3\times10^3} = 1mA$

Emitter resistance $r_e = \dfrac{25mV}{I_E(mA)} = \dfrac{25mV}{1mA} = 25\Omega$

Effective external emitter resistance is $R_E' = R_E \| R_L = 4.3\times10^3 \| 10\times10^3 = 3k\Omega$

The input impedance looking into the base terminal of the transistor

$$R_{in} = \beta\left(r_e + R_E^{'}\right) = 200(25 + 3000) = 605k\Omega$$

The input impedance of the emitter follower configuration is

$$R_{in}^{'} = R_1 \| R_2 \| R_{in} = 10\times10^3 \| 10\times10^3 \| 605\times10^3 = 4.96k\Omega$$

Example 7.12: Consider the opamp circuit shown in Figure 7.16. Given that the opamp has infinite value of input impedance, zero output impedance and finite value of open-loop gain A.

(a) Find the value of feedback factor b

(b) If R_1 = 10kW, find the value of R_2 that results in A_f = 10V/V for the following three cases

(i) A = 1000V/V (ii) A = 100V/V (iii) A = 12V/V

(c) For each of the three cases in (b), find the percentage change in A_f that results when A decreases by 20%. Comment on the results.

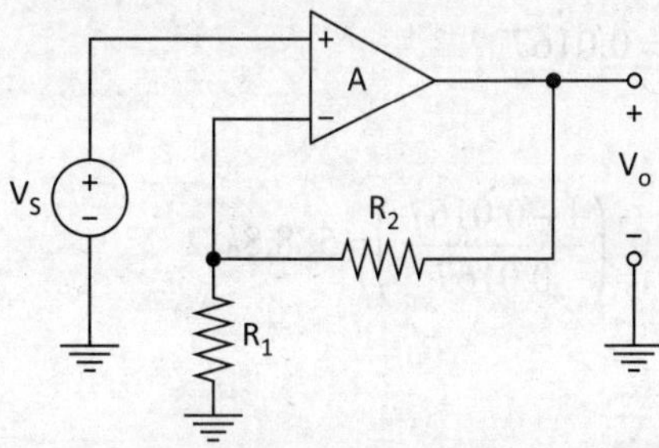

Fig. 7.16: Example 7.12

Solution:

(a) The equivalent circuit of the opamp circuit is shown in Figure 7.17.

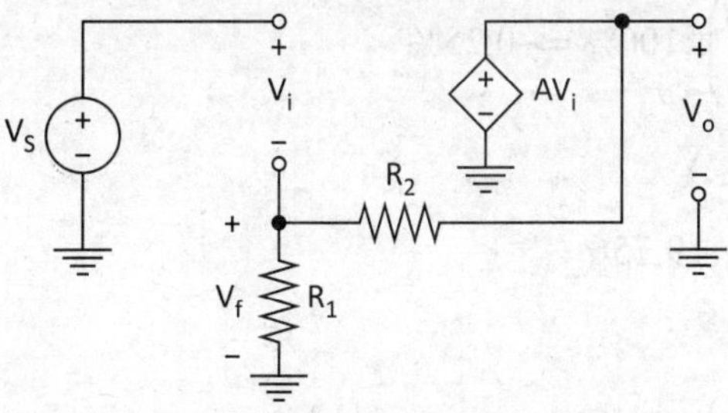

Fig. 7.17: Example 7.12

Solution to Example 7.12

$$V_f = \left(\frac{R_1}{R_1 + R_2}\right)V_o = \beta V_o$$

Therefore, $\beta = \left(\dfrac{R_1}{R_1 + R_2}\right)$

(b)

(i) $A_f = \dfrac{A}{1+\beta A} \Rightarrow \beta = \dfrac{1}{A_f} - \dfrac{1}{A} = \dfrac{1}{10} - \dfrac{1}{10^3} = 0.099$

$$\beta = \left(\frac{R_1}{R_1 + R_2}\right) \Rightarrow R_2 = R_1\left(\frac{1-\beta}{\beta}\right) = 10\times 10^3\left(\frac{1-0.099}{0.099}\right) = 91.01k\Omega$$

(ii) $\beta = \dfrac{1}{A_f} - \dfrac{1}{A} = \dfrac{1}{10} - \dfrac{1}{100} = 0.09$

$$R_2 = R_1\left(\frac{1-\beta}{\beta}\right) = 10\times 10^3\left(\frac{1-0.09}{0.09}\right) = 101.11k\Omega$$

(iii) $\beta = \dfrac{1}{A_f} - \dfrac{1}{A} = \dfrac{1}{10} - \dfrac{1}{12} = 0.0167$

$$R_2 = R_1\left(\frac{1-\beta}{\beta}\right) = 10\times 10^3\left(\frac{1-0.0167}{0.0167}\right) = 588.8k\Omega$$

(c) If A decreases by 20%

(i) A = 0.8 ′ 1000 = 800V/V

$$A_f = \frac{800}{1+(0.099)(800)} = 9.975$$

$$\frac{\Delta A_f}{A} = \left(\frac{9.975-10}{10}\right)\times 100\% = -0.25\%$$

(ii) A = 0.8 ′ 100 = 80V/V

$$A_f = \frac{80}{1+(0.09)(80)} = 9.756$$

$$\frac{\Delta A_f}{A} = \left(\frac{9.756-10}{10}\right)\times 100\% = -2.44\%$$

(iii) A = 0.8 ′ 12 = 9.6V/V

$$A_f = \frac{9.6}{1+(0.0167)(9.6)} = 8.27$$

$$\frac{\Delta A_f}{A} = \left(\frac{8.27-10}{10}\right)\times 100\% = -17.26\%$$

7.3.2 Voltage shunt or Shunt-Shunt feedback

In the case of voltage-shunt or shunt–shunt feedback, output voltage is sampled and mixed in shunt with the externally applied input signal. Figure 7.18 shows the block schematic arrangement of a generalized feedback amplifier with voltage-shunt feedback and Figure 7.19 shows its equivalent circuit.

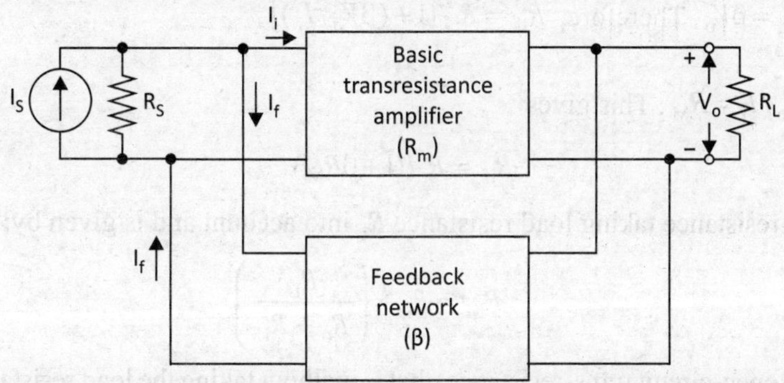

Fig. 7.18: Schematic arrangement of voltage-shunt (shunt–shunt) feedback

7.3.2.1 Gain

The gain parameter in this case is the trans-resistance. Equation 7.23 gives the expression for trans-resistance with feedback R_{Mf} in terms of trans-resistance without feedback R_M and the feedback factor *b*.

$$R_{Mf} = \frac{R_M}{1+\beta R_M} \tag{7.23}$$

7.3.2.2 Input Resistance

Expression for input resistance is derived as follows.

$$R_{if} = \frac{V_i}{I_s} = \frac{R_i \times I_i}{I_s} \tag{7.24}$$

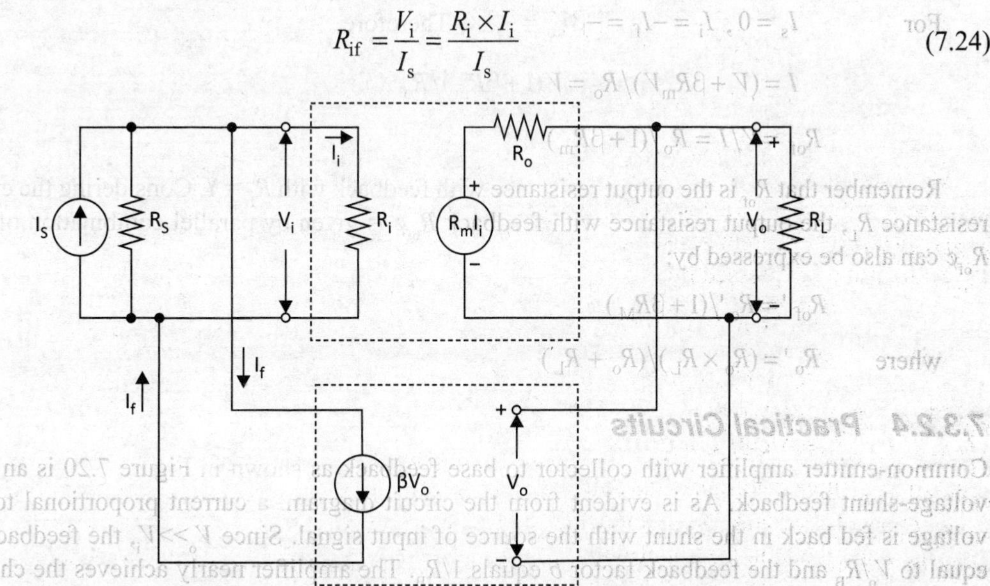

Fig. 7.19: Equivalent circuit for schematic arrangement of Figure 7.18

Substituting $I_s = I_i + I_f$ in eqn. (7.24), we get,

$$R_{if} = \frac{R_i \times I_i}{I_i + I_f} = \frac{R_i}{(I_i + I_f)/I_i} = \frac{R_i}{1+(I_f/I_i)}$$

Now, $\quad I_f = \beta V_o$. Therefore, $R_{if} = R_i/[1+(\beta V_o/I_i)]$

Also, $\quad V_o/I_i = R_M$. This gives

$$R_{if} = R_i/(1+\beta R_M) \tag{7.25}$$

R_M is the trans-resistance taking load resistance R_L into account and is given by:

$$R_M = R_m \times \left(\frac{R_L}{R_o + R_L}\right)$$

where R_m is the open-circuit trans-resistance, that is, without taking the load resistance R_L into account and can be expressed as:

$$R_m = \lim_{R_L \to \infty} R_M$$

7.3.2.3 Output Resistance

Expression for output resistance is derived by considering $I_s = 0$, letting load resistance R_L = ¥ and applying a voltage V across the output. Ratio of applied voltage V to the resulting current I gives the output resistance.

$$I = (V - R_m I_i)/R_o$$

For $\quad I_s = 0,\ I_i = -I_f = -\beta V_o = -\beta V$. Therefore,

$$I = (V + \beta R_m V)/R_o = V(1+\beta R_m)/R_o$$

$$R_{of} = V/I = R_o/(1+\beta R_m) \tag{7.26}$$

Remember that R_{of} is the output resistance with feedback with R_L = ¥. Considering the effect of load resistance R_L, the output resistance with feedback R_{of}¢ is given by parallel combination of R_{of} and R_L. R_{of}¢ can also be expressed by:

$$R_{of}' = R_o'/(1+\beta R_M)$$

where $\quad R_o' = (R_o \times R_L)/(R_o + R_L) \quad (7.27)$

7.3.2.4 Practical Circuits

Common-emitter amplifier with collector to base feedback as shown in Figure 7.20 is an example of voltage-shunt feedback. As is evident from the circuit diagram, a current proportional to the output voltage is fed back in the shunt with the source of input signal. Since $V_o >> V_i$, the feedback current is equal to V_o/R_B and the feedback factor b equals $1/R_B$. The amplifier nearly achieves the characteristics of a trans-resistance amplifier.

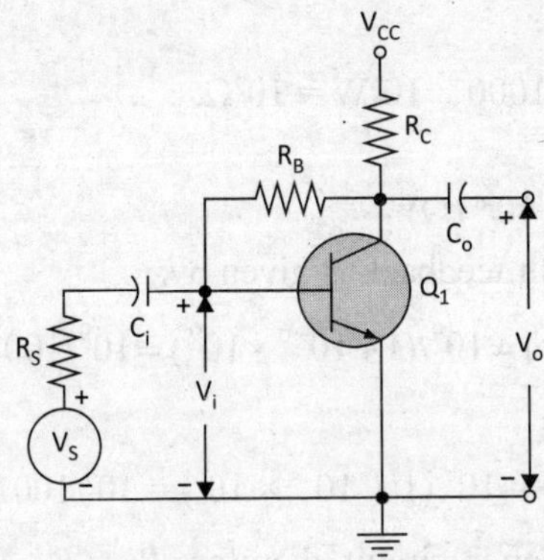

Fig. 7.20: Common-emitter amplifier circuit with voltage-shunt feedback.

Figure 7.21 shows the op-amp version of voltage-shunt feedback topology. The circuit shown is that of an inverting amplifier. The input current given by V_S/R_S flows through the feedback resistance R_f to produce an output voltage equal to $-I_S R_f$. The gain parameter is the trans-resistance R_f.

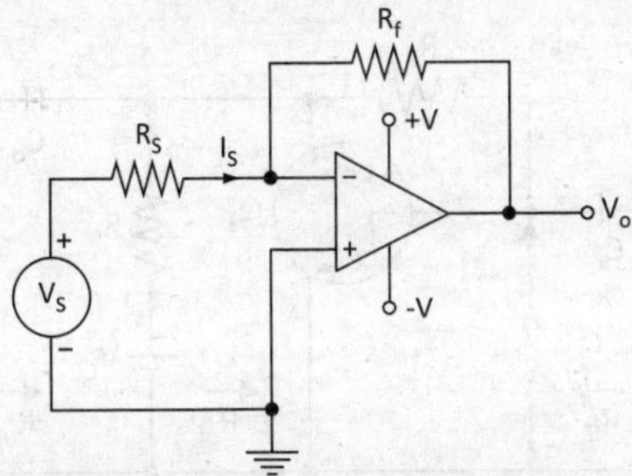

Fig. 7.21: Inverting amplifier with voltage-shunt feedback

Example 7.13: Refer to Figure 7.22. Identify the type of negative feedback. Determine the trans-impedance gain, the input impedance and output impedance of the amplifier, given that trans-impedance, input impedance and output impedance parameters of the op-amp without feedback are 1000 MΩ, 10 MΩ and 100 Ω, respectively.

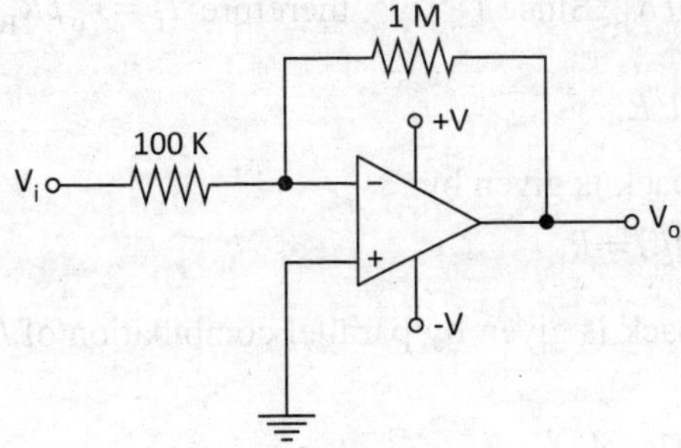

Fig. 7.22: Example 7.13

Solution: The feedback in this case is given by ratio of current flowing through 1M resistance to the output voltage V_o. The feedback signal here is in shunt across the input voltage. Therefore, the feedback of the given op-amp circuit is of voltage-shunt type.

Trans-impedance is given by:

$$R_M = 1000\ \text{M}\Omega = 1000 \times 10^6\text{W} = 10^9\Omega.$$

Feedback factor is given by:

$$\beta = 1/10^6\ (\Omega)^{-1} = 10^{-6}\ (\Omega)^{-1}$$

Therefore, trans-impedance with feedback is given by:

$$R_{\text{Mf}} = R_{\text{M}}/(1+\beta R_{\text{M}}) = 10^9/(1+10^{-6}\times 10^9) = 10^9/1001 = 0.999\times 10^6\Omega = 999\ \text{k}\Omega$$

Input impedance is given by:

$$R_{\text{if}} = R_{\text{i}}/(1+\beta R_{\text{M}}) = 10^7/(1 + 10^{-6} \times 10^9) = 10^7/1001 = 9.99\ \text{K}\Omega.$$

As the output is seen across an open-circuit, therefore $R_m = R_M$.

Output impedance is given by:

$$R_{\text{of}} = R_{\text{o}}/(1+\beta R_{\text{m}}) = 100/(1 + 10^{-6} \times 10^9) = 100/1001 = 0.099\ \Omega.$$

Example 7.14: Refer to the circuit of Figure 7.23. Derive expressions for feedback factor, trans-resistance, input resistance and output resistance with feedback.

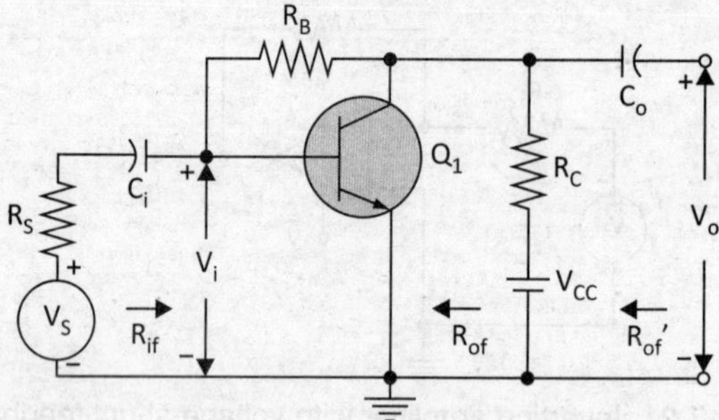

Fig. 7.23: Example 7.14

Solution: The given circuit employs voltage-shunt feedback.

The feedback factor *b*is given by $I_{\text{f}}/V_{\text{o}}$.

Now, $I_{\text{f}} = (V_{\text{o}} - V_{\text{i}})/R_{\text{B}}$ .Since $V_o >> V_i$, therefore $I_{\text{f}} = V_{\text{o}}/R_{\text{B}}$

That is, $\beta = I_{\text{f}}/V_{\text{o}} = 1/R_{\text{B}}$

Trans-resistance with feedback is given by:

$$R_{\text{Mf}} = V_{\text{o}}/I_{\text{s}} \cong 1/\beta = R_{\text{B}}$$

Input resistance with feedback is given by parallel combination of h_{ie} and Miller component of R_B appearing across input.

That is, $R_{if} = h_{\text{ie}} \| R_B/(1 - A_{\text{V}})$

Where A_V is the voltage gain

Voltage gain $A_{\text{V}} = -h_{\text{fe}} R_{\text{c}}'/h_{\text{ie}}$, where $R_C' = R_C \|$(Miller component of R_B appearing across output).

Now, Miller component of R_B appearing across output $= R_{\text{B}} \times [A_{\text{V}}/(A_{\text{V}} - 1)] \cong R_{\text{B}}$

Therefore, $R_C' = R_C \| R_B$

Input resistance with feedback, R_{if} therefore can be determined by substituting the value of A_V in the expression for R_{if} and simplifying the resultant expression.

Output resistance with feedback R_{of} is given by parallel combination of Miller component of R_B appearing across output and R_C.

$R_{of} \cong R_C$

R_B, which is further equal to $(R_C \times R_B)/(R_C + R_B)$

7.3.3 Current series or Series-Series feedback

In the case of current-series or series–series feedback, output current (usually a voltage proportional to the output current) is sampled and mixed in series with the externally applied input signal. Figure 7.24 shows the block schematic arrangement of a generalized feedback amplifier with current-series feedback and Figure 7.25 shows its equivalent circuit.

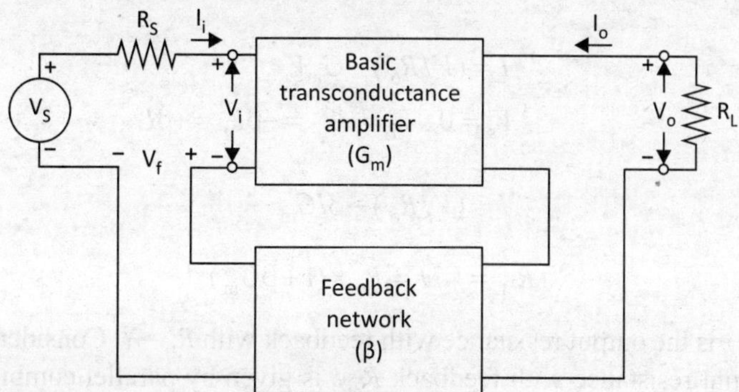

Fig. 7.24: Schematic arrangement of current-series (series–series) feedback

Equivalent circuit for schematic arrangement of Figure 7.24

7.3.3.1 Gain

The gain parameter in this case is the trans-conductance. Equation (7.28) gives the expression for trans-conductance with feedback G_{Mf} in terms of trans-conductance without feedback G_M and the feedback factor *b*.

$$G_{Mf} = \frac{G_M}{1 + \beta G_M} \tag{7.28}$$

7.3.3.2 Input Resistance

Expression for input resistance is derived as follows:

$$R_{if} = V_s / I_s = V_s / I_i = (V_i + V_f)/I_i \tag{7.29}$$

Now, $I_i = V_i / R_i$. Substituting the value of I_i in eqn. (7.29), we get,

$$R_{if} = (V_i + V_f) \times (R_i / V_i) = R_i \times [1 + (V_f / V_i)]$$

Also, $V_f = \beta I_o$. Therefore,

$$R_{if} = R_i \times [1 + (\beta I_o / V_i)] = R_i \times (1 + \beta G_M) \tag{7.30}$$

G_M is the trans-conductance taking load resistance R_L into account. It is expressed as:

$$G_M = G_m \times \left(\frac{R_o}{R_o + R_L} \right)$$

where G_m is the short-circuit trans-conductance, that is, without taking the load resistance R_L into account. It is also expressed as:

$$G_m = \lim_{R_L \to 0} G_M$$

7.3.3.3 Output Resistance

Expression for output resistance is derived by considering $V_s = 0$, letting load resistance R_L = ¥ and applying a voltage V across the output. Ratio of applied voltage V to the resulting current I gives the output resistance:

$$I = (V/R_o) - G_m V_i$$

For

$$V_s = 0\ ,\ V_i = -V_f = -\beta I_o = +\beta I.$$

Therefore,

$$I = (V/R_o) - \beta I G_m$$

$$R_{of} = V/I = R_o \times (1 + \beta G_m) \tag{7.31}$$

Remember that R_{of} is the output resistance with feedback with R_L = ¥. Considering the effect of load resistance R_L, the output resistance with feedback R_{of}¢ is given by parallel combination of R_{of} and R_L. R_{of}¢ can also be expressed by:

$$R_{of}' = R_o' \times [(1 + \beta G_m)/(1 + \beta G_M)]$$

where $R_o' = R_o \| R_L$ (7.32)

7.3.3.4 Practical Circuits

Common-emitter amplifier with un-bypassed emitter resistor as shown in Figure 7.26 is an example of current-series feedback. As is evident from the circuit diagram, a voltage proportional to the output current is fed back in series with the source of input signal. This is true if the base current were considered as negligible. The feedback factor *b* in this case equals $-R_E$. The amplifier nearly achieves the characteristics of a trans-conductance amplifier. Although the output current is proportional to the output voltage, this configuration should not be misunderstood as a case of voltage-series feedback. If it were considered one, then the feedback factor would equal $-R_E/R_C$. This violates one of the fundamental assumptions of negative-feedback amplifiers according to which the feedback factor should be independent of load and source resistances.

Similarly, common source amplifier with un-bypassed source resistor is also a case of current-series feedback. Also, an op-amp wired as a non-inverting amplifier where the output taken is the current I_o across the feedback resistor R_2 is an example of current-series feedback. As shown in Figure 7.27, it is the voltage developed across R_1 ($= -I_o \times R_1$) that is fed back in series with the input.

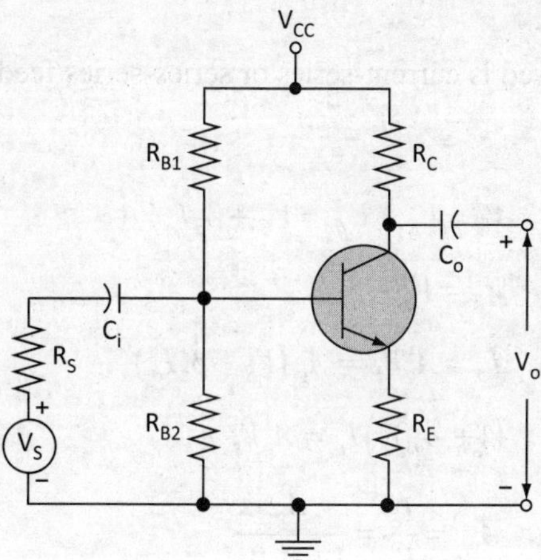

Fig. 7.26: Common-emitter amplifier with current-series feedback

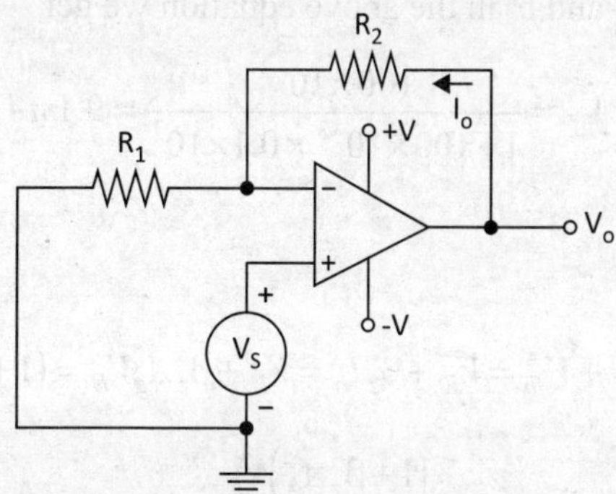

Fig. 7.27: Op-amp based amplifier circuit with current-series feedback

Example 7.15: For the circuit shown in Figure 7.28, given that A_g = 100mA/V, R_i = 10kΩ, R_o = 10kΩ and β_z = 100W. Determine the following

(a) The type of feedback used
(b) Derive the expression for the closed loop voltage gain and determine its value
(c) Derive the expression for closed loop input resistance and determine its value
(d) Derive the expression for closed loop output resistance and determine its value

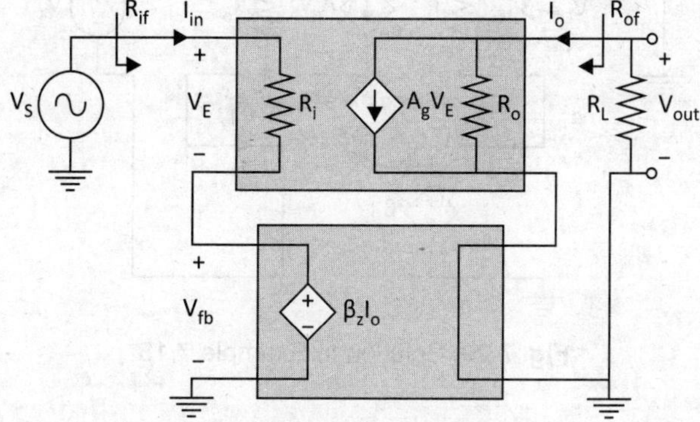

Fig. 7.28: Example 7.15

Solution:

(a) The type of feedback used is current-series or series-series feedback

(b) $I_o = A_g V_E$

$$V_s = V_E + V_{fb} = V_E + \beta_z I_o$$

Therefore, $$V_E = V_S - \beta_z I_o$$

Hence, $$I_o = A_g V_E = A_g\left(V_S - \beta_z I_o\right)$$

Or $$\left(1 + A_g \beta_z\right) I_o = A_g V_s$$

Closed loop gain $$A_{gf} = \frac{I_o}{V_s} = \frac{A_g}{1 + A_g \beta_z}$$

Substituting the values of A_g and b_z in the above equation we get

$$A_{gf} = \frac{100 \times 10^{-3}}{1 + 100 \times 10^{-3} \times 0.1 \times 10^{3}} = 9.1 mA/V$$

(c) $R_{if} = \dfrac{V_s}{i_{in}}$

$$V_s = V_E + V_{fb} = V_E + \beta_z I_o = V_E + \beta_z A_g V_E = \left(1 + \beta_z A_g\right) V_E$$

$$R_{if} = \frac{V_s}{i_{in}} = \frac{\left(1 + \beta_z A_g\right) V_E}{i_{in}} = \left(1 + \beta_z A_g\right) R_{in}$$

Therefore, $R_{if} = \left[1 + \left(100 \times 10^{-3}\right)\left(0.1 \times 10^{3}\right)\right]\left(10 \times 10^{3}\right) = 110 k\Omega$

(d)To determine R_{of}, make $V_s = 0$ and connect a source V_x at the output side as shown in Figure 7.29.

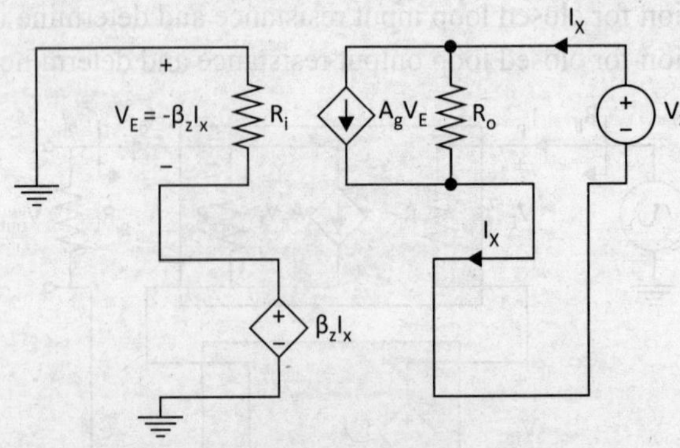

Fig. 7.29: Solution to Example 7.15

Then $R_{of} = \dfrac{V_x}{I_x}$

Current I_x is given by $I_x = \dfrac{V_x}{R_o} + A_g V_E = \dfrac{V_x}{R_o} + \left(-\beta_z A_g\right) I_x$

Therefore, $\left(1+\beta_z A_g\right) I_x = \dfrac{V_x}{R_o}$

Therefore, $R_{of} = \dfrac{V_x}{I_x} = \left(1+\beta_z A_g\right) R_o$

Substituting different values, we get $R_{of} = \left[1+\left(100\times10^{-3}\right)\left(0.1\times10^{3}\right)\right]\left(10\times10^{3}\right) = 110k\Omega$

Example 7.16: Refer to the opamp circuit shown in Figure 7.30.

(a) Assume that the opamp has infinite input resistance and zero output resistance. What is the expression for the feedback factor?

(b) What is the condition under which the closed loop gain is almost determined by the feedback network?

Solution:

(a) The feedback factor is given by $\beta = \dfrac{R_1}{R_1 + R_2}$

(b) The gain with feedback is given by $A_f = \dfrac{A}{1+A\beta}$

If Ab>>1, then $A_f \cong \dfrac{A}{A\beta} \cong \dfrac{1}{\beta}$

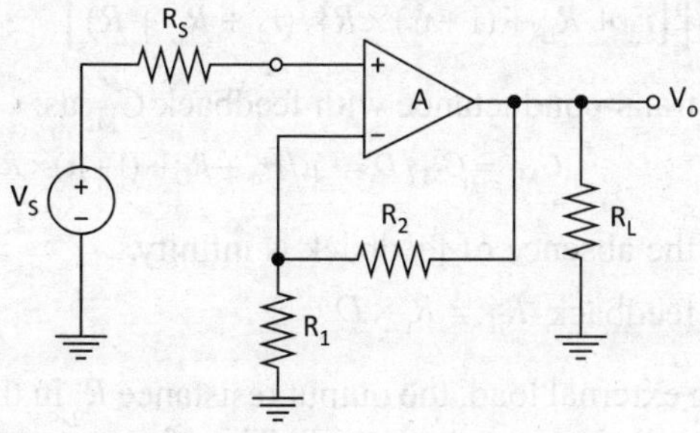

Fig. 7.30: Example 7.16

Example 7.17: Refer to the common-source FET amplifier circuit with un-bypassed source resistor as shown in Figure 7.31. Derive expressions for trans-conductance, input resistance and output resistance with and without feedback.

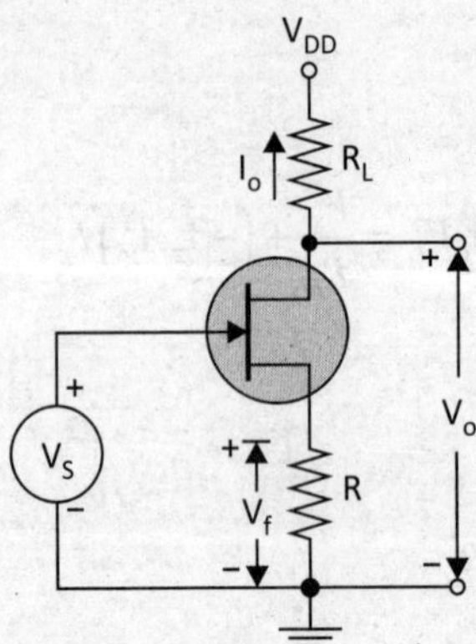

Fig. 7.31: Example 7.17

Solution: The feedback voltage appears across source resistor R. Therefore, $V_f = -I_o \times R$

This gives feedback factor, $\beta = V_f / I_o = -R$

In the absence of any negative feedback, the signal V_{gs} appearing across the input of the amplifier is the same as the externally applied input signal V_s. Therefore, trans-conductance without feedback G_M is given by:

$$G_M = I_o / V_{gs} = I_o / V_s$$

I_o is given by $\quad I_o = -(g_m \times V_{gs} \times r_d)/(r_d + R_L + R)$

This gives $\quad G_M = -(g_m \times r_d)/(r_d + R_L + R)$

Now, $\quad g_m \times r_d = \mu$

Therefore, $\quad G_M = -\mu/(r_d + R_L + R)$

De-sensitivity factor, D is given by:

$$D = 1 + \beta G_M = 1 + [(\mu \times R)/(r_d + R_L + R)]$$

$$= [\{r_d + R_L + (1+\mu) \times R\}/(r_d + R_L + R)]$$

This gives expression for trans-conductance with feedback G_{Mf} as:

$$G_{Mf} = G_M / D = -\mu / [r_d + R_L + (1+\mu) \times R]$$

The input resistance R_i in the absence of feedback is infinity.

The input resistance with feedback $R_{if} = R_i \times D = \infty$.

If R_L is considered to be an external load, the output resistance R_o in the absence of feedback without considering the load resistance R_L is given by $r_d + R$. Therefore, output resistance with feedback R_{of} without considering R_L is given by:

$$R_{of} = R_{of} = R_o \times (1 + \beta G_m).$$

Where G_m is the short-circuited value of G_M. That is, $G_m = \lim_{R_L \to 0} G_M$

Now, $G_m = -\mu/(r_d + R)$. This gives,

$$R_{of} = R_o \times (1 + \beta G_m) = (r_d + R) \times \left[\{r_d + (1+\mu) \times R\}/(r_d + R)\right]$$
$$= r_d + (1+\mu) \times R$$

Output resistance with feedback R_{of}' considering the effect of R_L is given by parallel combination of R_{of} and R_L.

An alternative expression for R_{of}' is given by:

$R_{of}' = R_o' \times [(1 + \beta G_m)/(1 + \beta G_M)]$

7.3.4 Current shunt or Shunt-Series feedback

In the case of current-shunt (shunt–series) feedback, output current is sampled and mixed in shunt with the externally applied input signal. Figure 7.32 shows the block schematic arrangement of a generalized feedback amplifier with current-shunt feedback and Figure 7.33 shows its equivalent circuit.

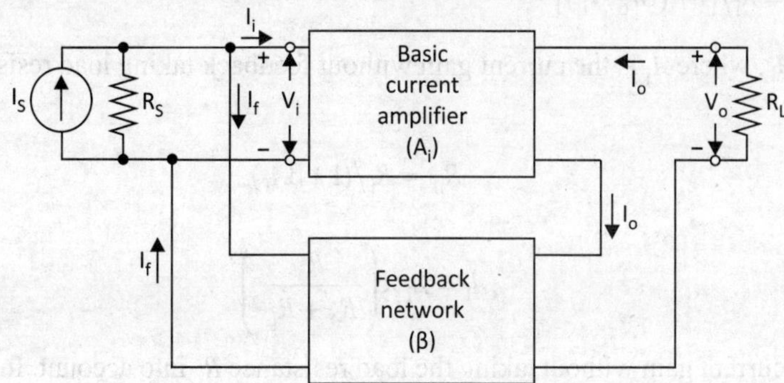

Fig. 7.32: Schematic arrangement of current-shunt (shunt–series) feedback.

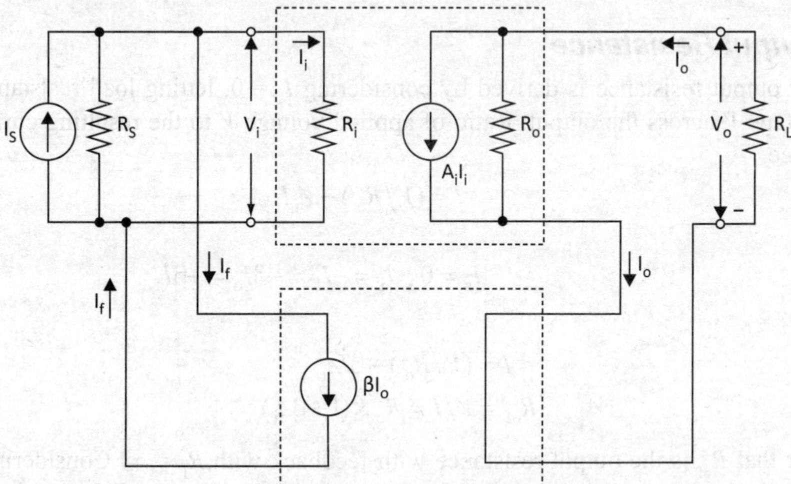

Fig. 7.33: Equivalent circuit for schematic arrangement of Figure 7.32

7.3.4.1 Gain

The gain parameter in this case is the current gain. Equation (7.33) gives the expression for current gain with feedback A_{If} in terms of current gain without feedback A_I and the feedback factor *b*.

$$A_{If} = \frac{A_I}{1+\beta A_I} \tag{7.33}$$

7.3.4.2 Input Resistance

The expression for input resistance is derived as follows.

$$R_{if} = V_i/I_s = (R_i \times I_i)/I_s \tag{7.34}$$

Substituting $I_s = I_i + I_f$ in eqn. (7.34), we get

$$R_{if} = R_i \times [I_i/(I_i + I_f)] = R_i/[(I_i + I_f)/I_i] = R_i/[1 + (I_f/I_i)]$$

Now, $I_f = \beta I_o$.

Therefore, $R_{if} = R_i/[1 + (\beta I_o/I_i)]$

Also, $I_o/I_i = A_I$, where A_I is the current gain without feedback taking load resistance into account.

This gives,

$$R_{if} = R_i/(1 + \beta A_I) \tag{7.35}$$

A_I is given by:

$$A_I = A_i \times \left(\frac{R_o}{R_o + R_L}\right)$$

where A_i is the current gain without taking the load resistance R_L into account. In fact, it is the short-circuited current gain. It can also be expressed as $A_i = \lim_{R_L \to 0} A_I$

7.3.4.3 Output Resistance

Expression for output resistance is derived by considering $I_s = 0$, letting load resistance $R_L = \infty$ and applying a voltage V across the output. Ratio of applied voltage V to the resulting current I gives the output resistance.

$$I = (V/R_o) - A_i I_i$$

For $$I_s = 0,\ I_i = -I_f = -\beta I_o = +\beta I.$$

Therefore,

$$I = (V/R_o) - \beta I A_i$$
$$R_{of} = V/I = R_o \times (1 + \beta A_i) \tag{7.36}$$

Remember that R_{of} is the output resistance with feedback with $R_L = \infty$. Considering the effect of load resistance R_L, the output resistance with feedback R_{of}' is given by parallel combination of R_{of} and R_L. R_{of}' can also be expressed by:

$$R_{of}' = R_o' \times [(1+\beta A_i)/(1+\beta A_I)] \tag{7.37}$$

where $R_o' = R_o \| R_L$

Also, for $R_L = \infty$, $R_o' = R_o$ and $A_I = 0$, Eqn. (7.37) reduces to

$$R_{of}' = R_o \times (1+\beta A_i) \tag{7.38}$$

7.3.4.4 Practical Circuits

A cascade arrangement of two common-emitter amplifier stages with feedback from emitter of the second stage to the base of the first stage as shown in Figure 7.34 is an example of current-shunt feedback. The voltage across emitter resistor of the second stage is out of phase with the base voltage of the first stage, which confirms this to be a case of negative feedback. Also, it can be proved that the feedback current, that is the current flowing through resistor R, is proportional to the output current and the proportionality factor b is equal to $[R_e/(R_e + R)]$. Current-shunt feedback leads to very high output impedance and very low input impedance. These are the desirable traits of a good current amplifier. That is how the negative feedback in the circuit of Figure 7.34 stabilizes the current gain parameter.

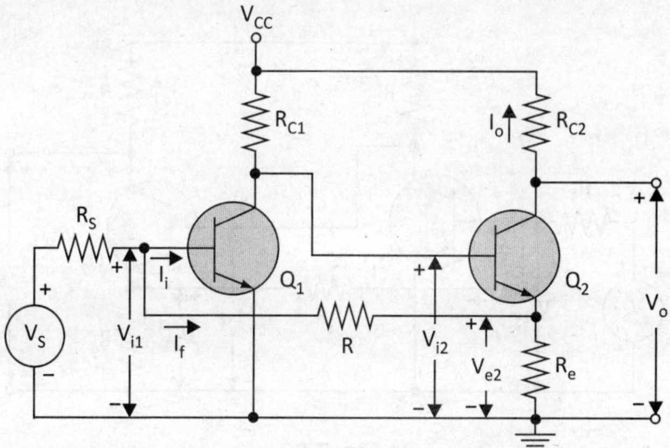

Fig. 7.34: Cascade arrangement of common emitter amplifier stages with current-shunt feedback

Figure 7.35 shows op-amp-based inverting current amplifier. This circuit too has current-shunt feedback. One can see the similarities between this circuit and the transistorized circuit shown in Figure 7.34. The feedback factor in this case is given by $[R_1/(R_1 + R_2)]$.

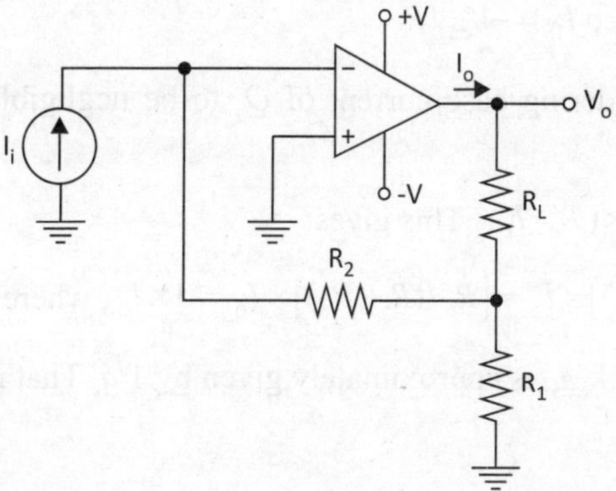

Fig. 7.35: Op-amp-based current amplifier with current-shunt feedback

Example 7.18: An amplifier without feedback has a voltage gain of 50, input and output resistances of 1000W and 2500W respectively. A feedback amplifier is built using this amplifier with a feedback factor of 0.2 using current-shunt topology. Determine the input impedance of this amplifier?

Solution: In the current-shunt amplifier, $R_{if} = \dfrac{R_i}{1+\beta A_i}$

Where $A_i = \left(\dfrac{R_i}{R_o}\right)A_v = \left(\dfrac{1000}{2500}\right)50 = 20$

Therefore, $R_{if} = \dfrac{1000}{1+0.2\times 20} = 200\Omega$

Example 7.19: Refer to the cascade arrangement of two CE amplifier stages as shown in Figure 7.36. Prove that the circuit has current-shunt feedback. Derive an expression for the feedback factor β. What is the current gain with feedback?

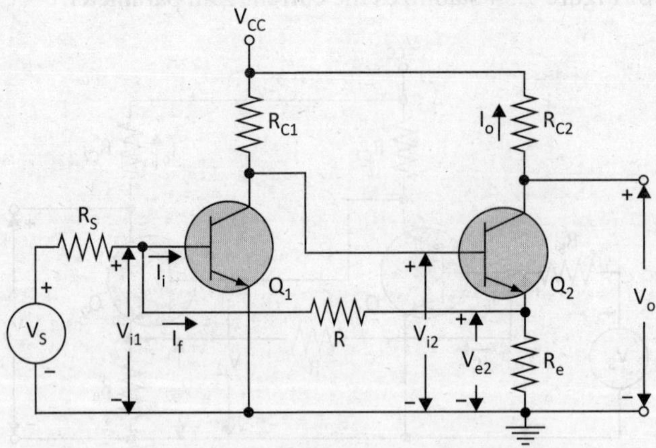

Fig. 7.36

Solution: As we can see from Figure 7.36, the output current is sampled and fed back in shunt with the input current I_i. Therefore, the circuit employs current-shunt feedback.

The feedback current I_f is given by $I_f = (V_{i1} - V_{e2})/R$

Assuming $V_{e2} >> V_{i1}$, we get $I_f = -V_{e2}/R$

$V_{e2} = (I_f - I_o)\times R_e$ considering base current of Q_2 to be negligible as compared to its collector current.

Therefore, $I_f = (I_o - I_f)\times(R_e/R)$. This gives:

$I_f = (R_e/R)\times[R/(R+R_e)]\times I_o = [R_e/(R+R_e)]\times I_o = \beta\times I_o$, where $\beta = R_e/(R+R_e)$

Current gain with feedback A_{If} is approximately given by $1/\hat{a}$. That is $A_{If} \cong (R+R_e)/R_e$

7.4 CONCEPT OF STABILITY, GAIN MARGIN AND PHASE MARGIN

7.4.1 Stability

A system is considered stable, if it remains at rest for all time unless it is excited by an external source of input. Such a system would return to its state of rest, when the excitation is removed. The stability is defined in several ways. One way to express system stability is to determine the impulse response of the system. If the system's impulse response approaches zero as the time approaches infinity, the system is considered stable. Another definition says that the system is stable, if every bounded input (an input whose magnitude is less than some finite value for all values of time t) produces a bounded output. It is important to note here that if a system produces a bounded output for a certain specific bounded input, it does not guarantee stability.

7.4.2 Relative Stability

Relative stability is a measure of how close or far a stable system is from becoming unstable. A given system may be highly stable or only marginally stable. Relative stability of a system is expressed in terms of parameters like gain margin and phase margin.

7.4.2.1 Gain Margin

Gain margin is defined as the reciprocal of the magnitude of the open loop transfer function at the phase crossover frequency. The phase crossover frequency is the one at which the phase of the open loop transfer function is 180°.

The gain margin is calculated by eqn.7.39.

$$\text{Gain Margin}=\frac{1}{\left|GH\left(j\omega_{\pi}\right)\right|} \tag{7.39}$$

Where, w_p is the phase crossover frequency.

7.4.2.2 Phase Margin

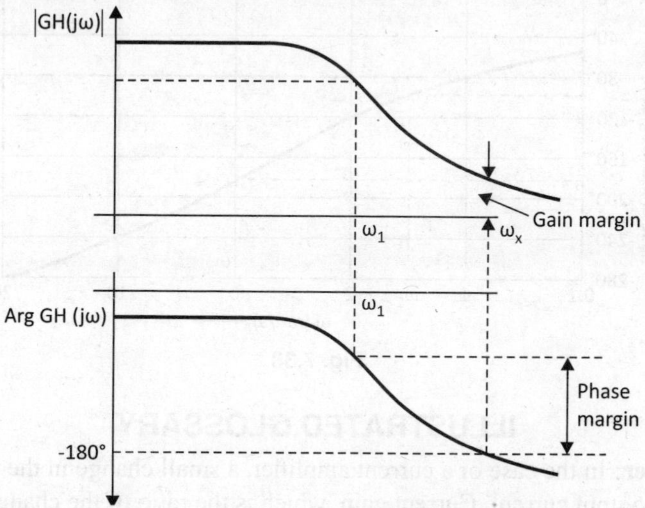

Fig. 7.37: Gain margin and phase margin

Phase margin is defined as 180° plus a phase angle (f_1). f_1 is the phase angle of the open loop transfer function evaluated at a frequency ω_1, where ω_1 is the gain crossover frequency at which $|GH(j\omega)|=1$.

$$\text{Phase Margin}=180° + Arg\,(j\omega_1) \tag{7.40}$$

Figure 7.37 shows the magnitude and phase of the gain curve to calculate the gain margin and the phase margin respectively.

Example 7.20: Figures 7.38(a) and (b) show the Bode plots for a certain amplifier. Determine the gain and phase margins for the amplifier. Also determine how much we can afford to increase the gain factor without making the system unstable, if a phase margin of 60° or better were acceptable.

Solution: From Figure 7.38(b), phase crossover frequency w_p = 5rad/s

From Figure 7.38(a), gain margin = 15dB

Also, from Figure 7.38(b), phase angle at gain crossover frequency = -100°

Therefore, phase margin = 180° – 100° = 80°

If a phase margin of 60° is acceptable, the corresponding phase angle is -120°

From Figure 7.38(b), the new gain crossover frequency is 2 rad/s

Now at w = 2rad/s, from Figure 7.38(a), the new gain margin = 5dB

That is, the gain factor could now be increased by a factor of 1.78

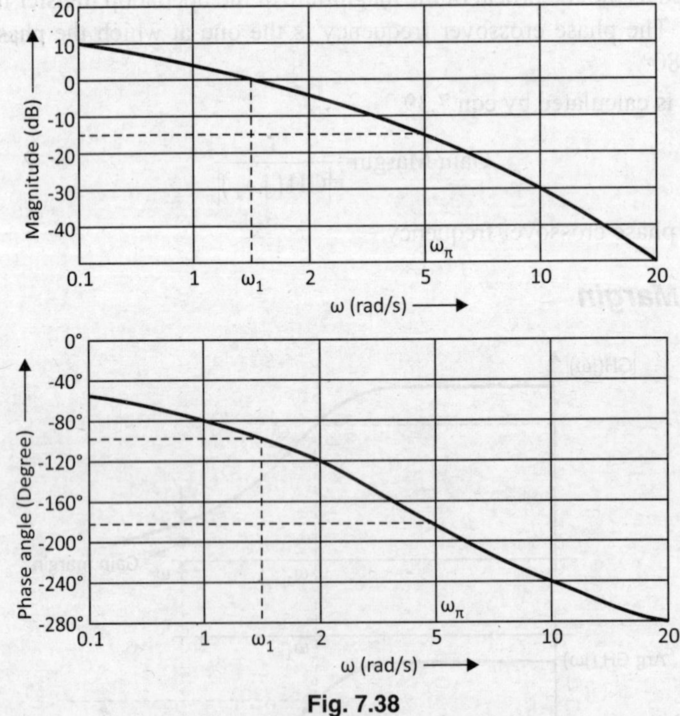

Fig. 7.38

ILLUSTRATED GLOSSARY

Current amplifier: In the case of a current amplifier, a small change in the input current produces a large change in the output current. Current gain, which is the ratio of the change in the output current to the change in the input current, is the gain parameter.

Current-Series or Series-Series feedback: In the case of current-series (series–series) feedback, output current (usually a voltage proportional to the output current) is sampled and mixed in series with the externally applied input signal.

Current-Shunt or Shunt-Series feedback: In the case of current-shunt (shunt–series) feedback, output current is sampled and mixed in shunt with the externally applied input signal.

De-sensitivity parameter:ï$(1 + bA)$ï is called the de-sensitivity parameter D. Percentage variation in gain with feedback is equal to the percentage variation in gain without feedback divided by the de-sensitivity parameter D.

Trans-conductance amplifier: In the case of a trans-conductance amplifier, a small change in the input voltage produces a large change in the output current. Ratio of the change in the output current to the change in the input voltage is the gain parameter. The gain parameter has the units of conductance.

Trans-resistance amplifier: In the case of a trans-resistance amplifier, a small change in the input current produces a large change in the output voltage. Ratio of the change in the output voltage to the change in the input current is the gain parameter. The gain parameter has the units of resistance.

Voltage amplifier: In the case of a voltage amplifier, a small change in the input voltage produces a large change in the output voltage. Voltage gain, which is the ratio of the change in the output voltage to change in the input voltage, is the gain parameter.

Voltage-Series or the Series-Shunt feedback: In the case of voltage-series (series–shunt) feedback, output voltage is sampled and mixed in series with the externally applied input signal.

Voltage shunt or Shunt-Shunt feedback: In the case of voltage-shunt or shunt–shunt feedback, output voltage is sampled and mixed in shunt with the externally applied input signal.

SUMMARY OF IMPORTANT FORMULAE

General formulae valid for all feedback topologies

1. Gain with feedback is related to gain without feedback by:

   $$A_f = \frac{A}{1+\beta A}$$

   Where the terms have their usual meaning
2. Feedback factor in decibels in given by:

   $$\text{dB of feedback} = 20\log\left|\frac{A_f}{A}\right| = 20\log\left|\frac{1}{1+\beta A}\right|$$

3. Bandwidth with feedback is related to bandwidth without feedback by:

   $$(BW)_f = BW \times (1+\beta A)$$

4. Noise with feedback is related to noise without feedback by:

   $$N_f = \frac{N}{1+\beta A}$$

5. Second harmonic distortion in the presence of feedback is related to its value in the absence of feedback by:

$$D_{2f} = \frac{D_2}{1+\beta A}$$

Voltage-series or the series-shunt feedback topology

6. Voltage gain with feedback is related to voltage gain without feedback by:

$$A_{Vf} = \frac{A_V}{1+\beta A_V}$$

7. Input resistance with feedback is related to input resistance without feedback by:

$$R_{if} = R_i \times (1+\beta A_V)$$

8. Output resistance with feedback is related to output resistance without feedback without taking load resistance into account by:

$$R_{of} = \frac{R_o}{1+\beta A_v}$$

9. Output resistance with feedback is related to output resistance without feedback taking load resistance into account by:

$$R_{of}' = \frac{R_o'}{1+\beta A_V} \quad R_{of}' = \frac{R_o'}{1+\beta A_V}$$

where $R_o' = \dfrac{R_o \times R_L}{R_o + R_L}$

Different terms in expressions 6 to 9 have their usual meaning.

Voltage-shunt or shunt-shunt feedback

10. The gain parameter in this case is trans-resistance. Trans-resistance with feedback is related to trans-resistance without feedback by:

$$R_{Mf} = \frac{R_M}{1+\beta R_M}$$

11. Input resistance with feedback is related to input resistance without feedback by: $R_{if} = R_i/(1+\beta R_M)$

$$R_M = R_m \times \left(\frac{R_L}{R_o + R_L}\right)$$

$$R_m = \lim_{R_L \to \infty} R_M$$

12. Output resistance with feedback is related to output resistance without feedback ignoring the effect of load resistance by:

$$R_{of} = R_o/(1+\beta R_m)$$

13. Output resistance with feedback is related to output resistance without feedback considering the effect of load resistance by:

$$R_{of}' = R_o'/(1+\beta R_M)$$

$$R_o' = (R_o \times R_L)/(R_o + R_L)$$

Different terms used in expressions 10 to 13 have their usual meaning.

Current-series or series-series feedback

14. The gain parameter in this case is the trans-conductance. Trans-conductance with feedback is related to trans-conductance without feedback by:

$$G_{Mf} = \frac{G_M}{1+\beta G_M}$$

15. Input resistance with feedback is related to input resistance without feedback by:

$$R_{if} = R_i \times (1+\beta G_M)$$

$$G_M = G_m \times \left(\frac{R_o}{R_o + R_L}\right)$$

$$G_m = \lim_{R_L \to 0} G_M$$

16. Output resistance with feedback is related to output resistance without feedback ignoring the effect of load resistance by:

$$R_{of} = R_o \times (1+\beta G_m)$$

17. Output resistance with feedback is related to output resistance without feedback considering the effect of load resistance by:

$$R_{of}' = R_o' \times [(1+\beta G_m)/(1+\beta G_M)] \; R_{of}' = R_o' \times [(1+\beta G_m)/(1+\beta G_M)]$$

$$R_o' = R_o \| R_L$$

Different terms used in expressions 14 to 17 have their usual meaning.

Current-shunt or shunt-series feedback

18. The gain parameter in this case is the current gain. Current gain with feedback is related to current gain without feedback by:

$$A_{If} = \frac{A_I}{1+\beta A_I}$$

19. Input resistance with feedback is related to input resistance without feedback by:

$$R_{if} = R_i/(1+\beta A_I)$$

$$A_I = A_i \times \left(\frac{R_o}{R_o + R_L}\right)$$

20. Output resistance with feedback is related to output resistance without feedback ignoring the effect of load resistance by:

$R_{of} = R_o \times (1 + \beta A_i)$

21. Output resistance with feedback is related to output resistance without feedback considering the effect of load resistance by:

$R_{of}' = R_o' \times [(1 + \beta A_i)/(1 + \beta A_I)]$

$R_o' = R_o \| R_L$

Different terms used in expressions 18 to 21 have their usual meaning.

REVIEW QUESTIONS

1. Classify amplifiers based on the nature of input and output signals?
2. What is the difference between positive and negative feedback? What type of feedback is used in amplifiers and why?
3. Are there any demerits of introduction of negative feedback in amplifiers? Please mention if any.
4. What type of negative feedback should be introduced in an amplifier to make it work like a true (a) current-to-voltage converter and (b) voltage-to-current converter? Give reasons for your answer.
5. How will the input impedance of an amplifier be affected by introduction of (a) voltage-series feedback and (b) voltage-shunt feedback?
6. How will the output impedance of an amplifier be affected by introduction of (a) current-series feedback and (b) current-shunt feedback?
7. Give two examples of practical amplifier circuits representative of the following types of negative feedback.

   a. Shunt–series feedback

   b. Series–shunt feedback
8. "A common-emitter amplifier with un-bypassed emitter resistor is representative of current-series feedback and not voltage-series feedback." Is the above statement true. If yes, why?
9. " The gain parameter in a negative-feedback amplifier depends exclusively on the components of feedback network when the open-loop gain becomes very large. " Is the above statement true. If yes, why?
10. What is the difference between trans-impedance and trans-conductance amplifiers? Give one example each of the two types of amplifiers.

PROBLEMS

1. An amplifier with an open circuit voltage of 1000 has an output resistance of 100 ohms and it feeds a resistive load of 900 ohms. Negative voltage feedback is provided by connecting a resistive voltage divider across the output and one-fiftieth of the output voltage is feedback in series with the input signal. Determine the voltage gain with negative feedback.
2. Figure 7.39 shows the basic common-emitter amplifier circuit with un-bypassed emitter resistor. Derive expressions for trans-conductance, input resistance and output resistance with and without feedback. Also prove that the trans-conductance parameter in this circuit is stabilized due to presence of current-series feedback.

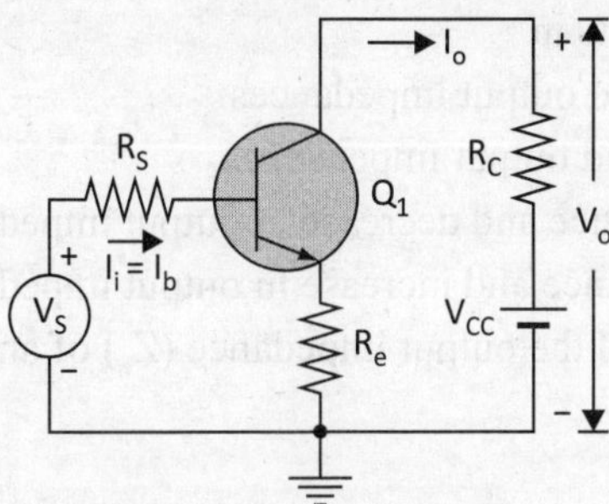

Fig. 7.39: Problem-2

3. An amplifier has an open loop gain of 100,000. A negative feedback of 10dB is applied. Find the value of voltage gain with feedback and the feedback fraction.
4. A voltage amplifier is characterized by voltage gain of 1000, input resistance of 100 KΩ and output resistance of 1 KΩ in the absence of any feedback. Find the modified values of these parameters if 5% of output voltage were feedback in series and phase opposition with the input.
5. A voltage amplifier is a cascade arrangement of three identical amplifier stages each having an open loop gain of A_1. The output from the final stage is fed back in series and phase opposition with the input of the first stage to get an overall closed loop gain of A_f. Derive an expression for overall open loop gain A in terms of open loop gain stability $|dA_1/A_1|$ of individual stages and overall closed loop gain stability $|dA_f/A_f|$.
6. Determine the percentage reduction in gain of an amplifier due to 40 dB of negative feedback.
7. Figure 7.40 shows an amplifier with feedback. Given that g_m = 2000 mS and r_d = 1 kΩ. Find out the voltage gain with feedback.

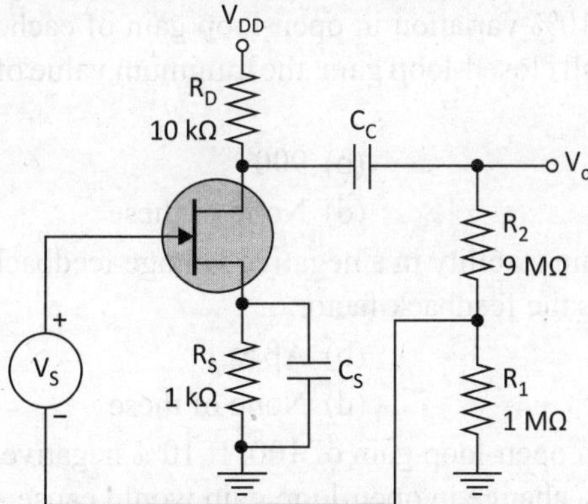

Fig. 7.40: Problem-7

MULTIPLE-CHOICE QUESTIONS

1. Voltage-series feedback results in
   (a) increase in both input and output impedances
   (b) decrease in both input and output impedances
   (c) increase in input impedance and decrease in output impedance
   (d) decrease in input impedance and increase in output impedance

2. Current-shunt feedback results in
   (a) increase in both input and output impedances
   (b) decrease in both input and output impedances
   (c) increase in input impedance and decrease in output impedance
   (d) decrease in input impedance and increase in output impedance
3. The input impedance (Z_i) and the output impedance (Z_o) of an ideal transconductance amplifier are
   (a) $Z_i = 0, Z_o = 0$
   (b) $Z_i = 0, Z_o = \infty$
   (c) $Z_i = \infty, Z_o = 0$
   (d) $Z_i = \infty, Z_o = \infty$
4. If the voltage gain of an amplifier without feedback is 20 and with negative voltage feedback is 12, then the feedback fraction is
   (a) 1.66 (b) 0.6
   (c) 0.2 (d) 0.033
5. For the expression of gain with feedback $A_f = A/(1 + \beta A)$ in the case of negative-feedback amplifier to be valid,
   (a) feedback factor β should be independent of load and source resistances
   (b) forward transmission through the feedback network should be zero
   (c) reverse transmission through amplifier should be zero
   (d) all the above should be true
6. A voltage amplifier consists of cascade arrangement of two identical stages. Negative feedback is introduced from output of second stage to input of first stage to get a stable overall closed-loop gain of 45. In order that 10% variation in open-loop gain of each stage does not produce more than 1% variation in overall closed-loop gain, the minimum value of open-loop gain of each stage should be
   (a) 30 (b) 900
   (c) 45 (d) None of these
7. In order to obtain good gain stability in a negative voltage feedback amplifier with A as the gain without feedback and b as the feedback factor
   (a) $A\beta = 1$ (b) $A\beta >> 1$
   (c) $A\beta < 1$ (d) None of these
8. A voltage amplifier has an open-loop gain of 100. If 10% negative feedback were introduced in the amplifier, then an 11% change in open-loop gain would cause
   (a) 1% change in closed-loop gain (b) 11% change in closed-loop gain
   (c) 1.1% change in closed-loop gain (d) 0.1% change in closed-loop gain
9. In the case of a negative-feedback amplifier, which of the following is true?
   (a) Closed-loop gain can be less than or more than the open-loop gain depending upon the type and amount of feedback.
   (b) Closed-loop gain is always less than the open-loop gain.
   (c) Closed-loop gain is always more than the open-loop gain.
   (d) Closed-loop gain and bandwidth are always less than the corresponding open-loop values.

10. Feedback circuit is
    (a) independent of frequency (b) strongly dependent on frequency
    (c) moderately dependent on frequency (d) none of the above

SOLUTIONS TO PROBLEMS

1. Figure 7.41 shows the equivalent circuit of the amplifier along with the feedback circuit.

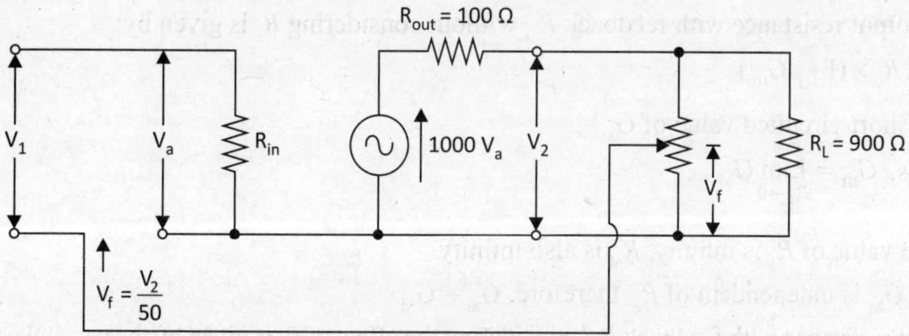

Figure 7.41: Solution to Problem-1

Voltage gain of the amplifier without feedback is given by:

$$A_v = \frac{A_o R_L}{R_{out} + R_L} = \frac{1000 \times 900}{100 + 900} = 900$$

Voltage gain with feedback is

$$A_{vf} = \frac{A_v}{1 + \beta A_v} = \frac{900}{1 + 900 \times (1/50)} = 47.4$$

2. The feedback voltage appears across emitter resistor R_e. Therefore, $V_f = -I_o \times R_e$

This gives feedback factor, $\beta = V_f / I_o = -R_e$

In absence of any negative feedback, signal V_i appearing across the input of amplifier is same as the externally applied input signal V_s.

Therefore, trans-conductance without feedback G_M is given by $I_o/V_i = I_o/V_s = -(h_{fe} \times I_b)/V_s$

Now, $V_s/I_b = R_s + h_{ie} + R_e$

Therefore, $G_M = -h_{fe}/(R_s + h_{ie} + R_e)$

De-sensitivity factor, $D = (1 + \beta G_M) = 1 + [(h_{fe} \times R_e)/(R_s + h_{ie} + R_e)]$

Therefore, $D = \left[\{R_s + h_{ie} + (1 + h_{fe}) \times R_e\}/(R_s + h_{ie} + R_e)\right]$

This gives expression for trans-conductance with feedback G_{Mf} as:

$G_{Mf} = G_M / D = -h_{fe} / [R_s + h_{ie} + (1 + h_{fe}) \times R_e]$

Since $(1 + h_{fe}) \times R_e >> (R_s + h_{ie})$ and also $h_{fe} >> 1$, expression for G_{Mf} simplifies to $G_{Mf} \cong -1/R_e$

This proves that G_{Mf} is independent of transistor parameters and is only dependent on R_e.

The input resistance in the absence of feedback is given by $R_i = R_s + h_{ie} + R_e$

The input resistance with feedback is given by:

$R_{if} = R_i \times D = R_s + h_{ie} + (1 + h_{fe}) \times R_e$

Output resistance in the absence of feedback R_o without considering the collector load resistance R_c is infinity.

The output resistance with feedback R_{of} without considering R_c is given by:

$R_{of} = R_o \times (1 + \beta G_m)$

G_m is short-circuited value of G_M

That is, $G_m = \lim\limits_{R_c \to 0} G_M$

As the value of R_o is infinity, R_{of} is also infinity.

Since G_M is independent of R_c, therefore, $G_m = G_M$

Output resistance with feedback R_{of}' considering the effect of R_c is given by the parallel combination of R_{of} and R_c. As the value of R_o is infinity, R_{of}' equals R_c

An alternative expression for R_{of}' is given by $R_{of}' = R_o \times [(1 + \beta G_m)/(1 + \beta G_M)]$

3. dB voltage gain without feedback = 20log100,000 = 100dB

   Voltage gain with feedback = 100 – 10 = 90 dB

   Now, 20log(A_f) = 90

   Therefore, A_f = 31622

   Now, $A_f = \dfrac{A}{1 + A\beta}$

   Substituting the values of Af and A we get,

   $31622 = \dfrac{100000}{1 + 100000\beta}$ $31622 = \dfrac{100000}{1 + 100000\beta}$

   Therefore, b = 2.17′10^{-5}

4. Open-loop gain A = 1000 and feedback factor b = 0.05

   Closed-loop gain = 1000/(1 + 0.05×1000) = 1000/51 = 19.6

   Since the feedback signal is in series with input, modified input resistance is given by:

   100 × 10^3 ×(1 + 0.05 × 1000) = 5100 KW

   Since it is fraction of the output voltage that is fed back to the input, modified output resistance is given by:

   1 × 10^3 × /(1 + 0.05 × 1000) = 1000/51W = 19.6W

5. Open-loop gain, $A = A_1^{\;3}$. Therefore, $dA = 3A_1^{\;2} dA_1$

   This gives $dA/A = 3A_1^{\;2} \times (dA_1 / A_1^{\;3}) = 3dA_1/A_1$

Now, $dA_f / A_f = 1/|1+\beta A| \times (dA/A)$

$|dA_f / A_f| = 1/|1+\beta A| \times 3 \times |dA_1 / A_1|$

Also, $1/|1+\beta A| = A_f / A$

Therefore, $A = 3A_f \times |dA_1 / A_1| / |dA_f / A_f|$

6. dB of feedback $= 20\log\left|\frac{A_f}{A}\right|$

Therefore, $-40 = 20\log\left|\frac{A_f}{A}\right|$ or $A_f = 0.01A$

$$\text{Percentage reduction in gain} = \left(\frac{A - A_f}{A}\right) \times 100\% = \left(\frac{A - 0.01A}{A}\right) \times 100\% = 99\%$$

7. Voltage gain without feedback $= -\dfrac{g_m (r_d \times R_D)}{(r_d + R_D + R_S)}$

Therefore, $A = -\dfrac{2000 \times 10^{-6}\left(1 \times 10^3 \times 10 \times 10^3\right)}{\left(1 \times 10^3 + 10 \times 10^3 + 1 \times 10^3\right)} = -1.67$

Feedback factor $\beta = \dfrac{-1 \times 10^6}{1 \times 10^6 + 9 \times 10^6} = -\dfrac{1}{10}$

Gain with feedback $= \dfrac{-1.67}{1 + (-1.67)\left(-\dfrac{1}{10}\right)} = -1.43$

ANSWERS TO MULTIPLE-CHOICE QUESTIONS

1. (c) 2. (d) 3. (d) 4. (d) 5. (d) 6. (a) 7. (b) 8. (a) 9. (b) 10. (a)

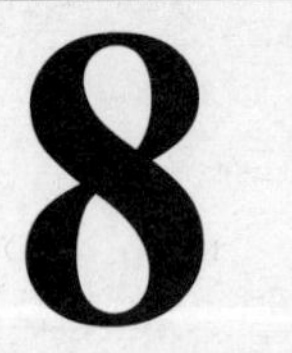

Oscillators - Sinusoidal and Non-sinusoidal

After completing this chapter, you will learn the following topics.

- Review of the basic concept - Barkhausen criterion
- Sinusoidal oscillators - RC oscillators, LC oscillators and crystal oscillators
- RC oscillators - Phase shift, Buffered RC phase shift, Wien-bridge, Bubba, Quadrature and Twin-T oscillators
- LC oscillators - Hartley, Colpitt, Clapp and Armstrong oscillators
- Crystal oscillators
- Frequency stability of oscillators
- Voltage controlled oscillator
- Non-sinusoidal oscillators - astable multivibrators and blocking oscillators

Introduction

The topics covered in this chapter include the Barkhausen condition i.e. the condition of oscillations, sinusoidal oscillators, non-sinusoidal oscillators, voltage controlled oscillators and frequency stability of oscillators. The sinusoidal oscillators covered include the RC oscillators, LC oscillators and crystal oscillators. Different types of RC oscillators covered include Phase shift, Buffered RC Phase shift, Wien-bridge, Bubba, Quadrature and Twin-T oscillators. Hartley, Colpitt, Clapp and Armstrong oscillators are covered under LC oscillators. Important formulae and keywords are listed at the end of the chapter. Different topics discussed in the chapter are amply illustrated with solved examples. In addition, there are a number of problems given towards the end of the chapter along with brief solutions. A self-evaluation exercise containing multiple-choice questions along with answers concludes the chapter.

8.1 BARKHAUSEN CRITERION: CONDITIONS FOR OSCILLATIONS

An oscillator circuit is essentially an amplifier circuit with a frequency-selective feedback network. The feedback network feeds a fraction of the amplifier output back to its input in such a way as to satisfy the two fundamental requirements of occurrence of sustained oscillations. These requirements are commonly known by the name of *Barkhausen criterion*.

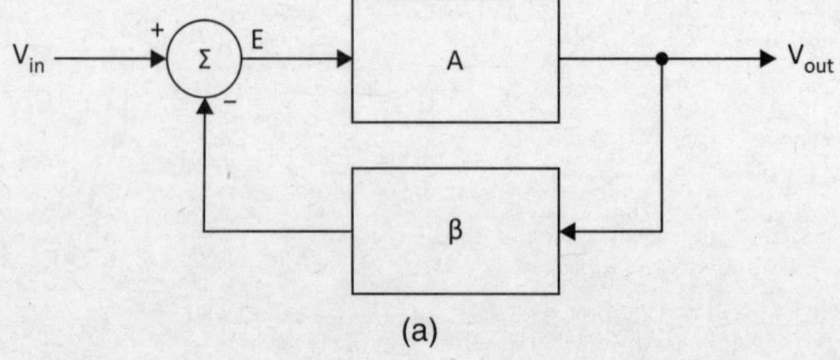

(a)

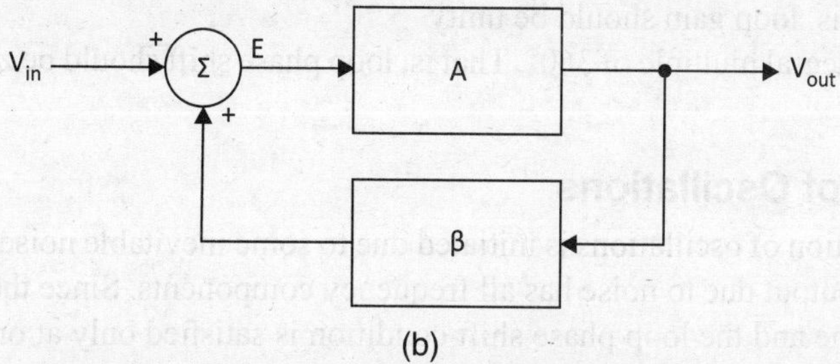

Fig. 8.1: Canonical form of feedback systems (a) Negative feedback system (b) Positive feedback system

Consider the canonical form of negative and positive feedback systems as shown in Figures 8.1(a) and (b), respectively. Canonical form is the simplest form of representation of any class of systems without any loss of generality. The transfer function in the case of negative feedback system of Figure 8.1(a) can be derived as follows. Remember that in the case of a negative feedback system, the summing point is a subtractor. That is, the error signal is the sum of input signal and the phase-inverted feedback signal:

$$E = V_{IN} - \beta \times V_{OUT} \tag{8.1}$$

Now $E = V_{OUT}/A$, substituting the same in Eqn. 8.1, we get

$$\frac{V_{OUT}}{A} = V_{IN} - \beta \times V_{OUT} \tag{8.2}$$

This simplifies to

$$\frac{V_{OUT}}{V_{IN}} = \frac{A}{(1+\beta A)} \tag{8.3}$$

In the case of a positive feedback system in which the summing point is an adder, the transfer function is given by

$$\frac{V_{OUT}}{V_{IN}} = \frac{A}{(1-\beta A)} \tag{8.4}$$

If $\beta A = -1 = 1\angle -180°$ in the case of negative feedback system and $\beta A = 1 = 1\angle 0°$ in the case of positive feedback system, the system works like an oscillator. In the case of the former, the conditions specify magnitude of loop gain as unity and loop phase shift as 180. In the case of latter, the conditions specify magnitude of loop gain as unity and loop phase shift as 0 or 360 . The condition for the magnitude of the loop gain is the same in the two cases. If we carefully examine the two cases, we will find that the loop phase shift condition is also the same as phase inversion implied by the negative sign at the summing point. This restores the overall phase shift at the point of amplifier input. Essentially the two conditions mean the following:

1. The magnitude of loop gain is unity, which ensures that the feedback signal has the same magnitude as that of the input signal.
2. The magnitude of loop phase shift is such that the feedback signal is in-phase with the input signal when it reaches the input of the amplifier.

These two conditions define what is known as Barkhausen criterion of oscillations. Satisfying Barkhausen criterion ensures that oscillator circuits do not need an external applied input signal. Instead they use fraction of the output signal as the input signal.

In practical oscillator circuits, the summing point is an adder and therefore the Barkhausen criterion of oscillations is written as follows:

1. $|\beta A| = 1$. That is, loop gain should be unity.
2. $\angle \beta A = 0°$ or integral multiple of 360°. That is, loop phase shift should be zero or integral multiple of 360°.

8.1.1 Initiation of Oscillations

The process of generation of oscillations is initiated due to some inevitable noise present at the amplifier input. The amplified output due to noise has all frequency components. Since the feedback network is a frequency selective one and the loop phase shift condition is satisfied only at one frequency, the signal fed back to the input has a single frequency component at which the loop phase shift condition of the Barkhausen criterion is satisfied. This leads to the oscillator circuit producing a sinusoidal output.

The essential condition for the magnitude of loop gain for the oscillations to occur is that loop gain is precisely unity. There is every possibility that with change in parameters of the transistor or other active devices used in the amplifier part of the oscillator due to ageing or replacement, one lands up with loop gain less than unity. In that case there will be no oscillations. So, in practice, loop gain is kept slightly greater than unity to ensure that oscillator works even if there is a slight change in the circuit parameters. Moreover, there is no harm in keeping loop gain slightly greater than unity as the output cannot increase infinitely as it appears because the output amplitude will be limited due to onset of non-linearity of active device used. However, if A is much larger than unity, the oscillator output will have lot of distortion.

Example 8.1: Determine the gain or phase shift as the case may be for the following oscillator circuits.

Case 1: If the feedback network of an oscillator provides 0.1% positive feedback, what should be the minimum gain for the amplifier section of the oscillator for sustained oscillations?

Case 2: The amplifier gain in an oscillator is 500. What should be the percentage feedback for sustained oscillations?

Solution:

Case 1: A feedback of 0.1% means $\beta = 0.001$.

Therefore, amplifier's minimum gain is $1/\beta = 1000$.

Case 2: Amplifier gain = 500

Therefore, feedback factor $\beta = 1/500 = 0.002$, Percentage feedback = 0.2%

Example 8.2: What is the value of C required for the circuit shown in Figure 8.2 to function as a sinusoidal oscillator of frequency 1kHz?

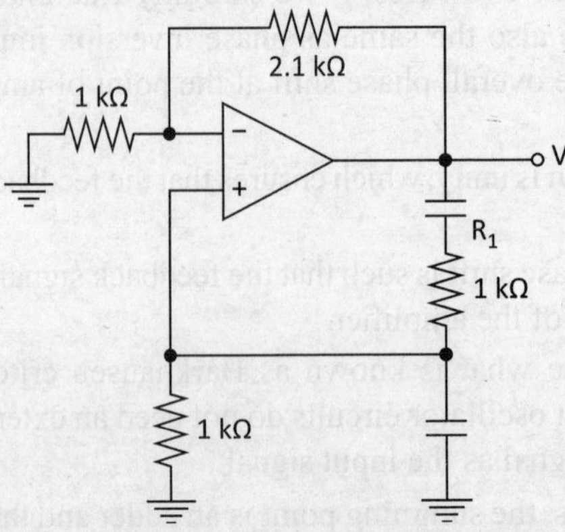

Fig. 8.2: Example 8.2

Solution: Let the voltage at the non-inverting input of the opamp be Vi. Let the capacitor be denoted as C and both the 1k? resistors as R. Applying KCL at the non-inverting input of the op-amp we get

$$\frac{V_i}{R}+\frac{V_i}{1/j\omega C}+\frac{V_i-V_o}{R+(1/j\omega C)}=0$$

Solving the above equation, we get

$$\frac{V_o}{V_i}=\frac{j\omega C}{R}\left(-\frac{1}{\omega^2 C^2}+R^2\right)+3$$

For oscillations to occur, imaginary part should be zero. Therefore,

$$\frac{\omega C}{R}\left(-\frac{1}{\omega^2 C^2}+R^2\right)=0 \quad \text{or}$$

$$C=\frac{1}{\omega R}=\frac{1}{2\pi\times 10^3\times 10^3}F=\frac{1}{2\pi}\mu F$$

8.2 SINUSOIDAL OSCILLATORS

Sinusoidal oscillators are oscillators that produce sine or cosine waveforms at the output. They are classified on the basis of the type of frequency-selective network used in the feedback loop. Different types include the following.

1. RC oscillators 2. LC oscillators 3. crystal oscillators

All the three types of oscillators are discussed in this section.

8.2.1 RC oscillators

In the case of RC oscillators, multiple RC sections are used to provide the required phase shift. Remember that a single section RC or RL network provides up to a maximum of 90° of phase shift due to existence of a single pole in its transfer function. A minimum of two sections would therefore be required to provide the required 180° of phase shift. Cascade arrangement of three RC sections is used in practical RC phase shift oscillators with each section providing 60° of phase shift. This provides a larger value of rate of change of phase with frequency around the operational frequency (dϕ/dω), which gives improved performance in terms of frequency stability. Frequency stability issues are discussed in detail in the latter part of the chapter. Figure 8.3 shows the plot of phase as a function of frequency in the case of multiple RC arrangements.

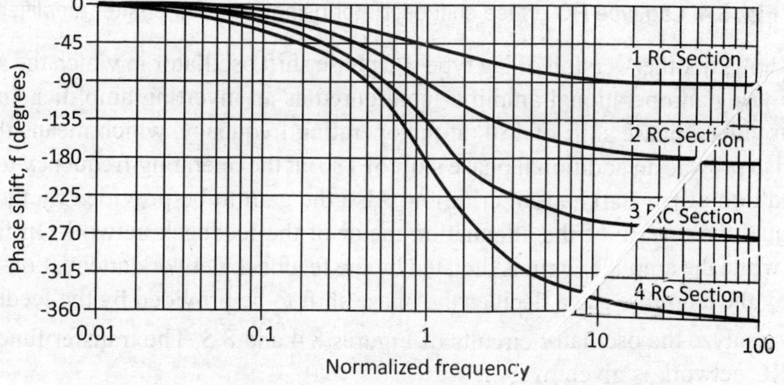

Fig. 8.3: Phase versus frequency plot of RC sections

Prominent candidates in the category of RC oscillators include the RC phase shift oscillator, twin-T oscillator, Wein bridge oscillator, Bubba oscillator and Quadrature oscillator. Each of these oscillator types are covered in the following paragraphs.

8.2.1.1 RC phase shift oscillator

The basic RC phase shift oscillator comprises a single-stage amplifier whose output is fed back to its input through a feedback network. The amplifier portion is usually implemented by employing either a bipolar transistor-based common-emitter amplifier stage, junction-FET based common-source amplifier or an operational amplifier wired as an inverting amplifier. The feedback network comprises a cascade arrangement of three identical sections of either lag- or lead-type RC network. Figure 8.4 shows the circuit schematic of an RC phase shift oscillator using a common-emitter amplifier stage and a lag-type RC feedback network.

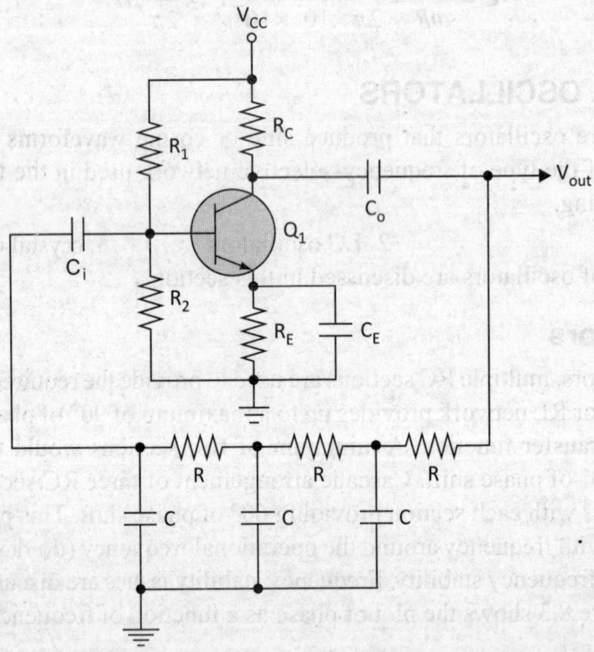

Fig. 8.4: Lag type RC phase shift oscillator using common-emitter amplifier

Figure 8.5 shows another version of lag type RC phase shift oscillator in which the amplifier portion is implemented using an operational amplifier configured as an inverting amplifier. In both the cases, the amplifier provides a phase shift of 180 at the operating frequency, which means that the feedback network must also provide an additional phase shift of 180 at the operating frequency to satisfy the loop phase shift condition of the Barkhausen criterion. Also the gain to be provided by the amplifier stage must at least equal the inverse of the attenuation factor of the feedback network. In fact, in the phase shift oscillator, while the amplifier gain is dictated by the feedback network attenuation factor; the phase shift provided by the amplifier stage decides the phase shift to be provided by the feedback network.

Let us now analyze the oscillator circuits of Figures 8.4 and 8.5. The transfer function of a single-stage lag-type RC network is given by:

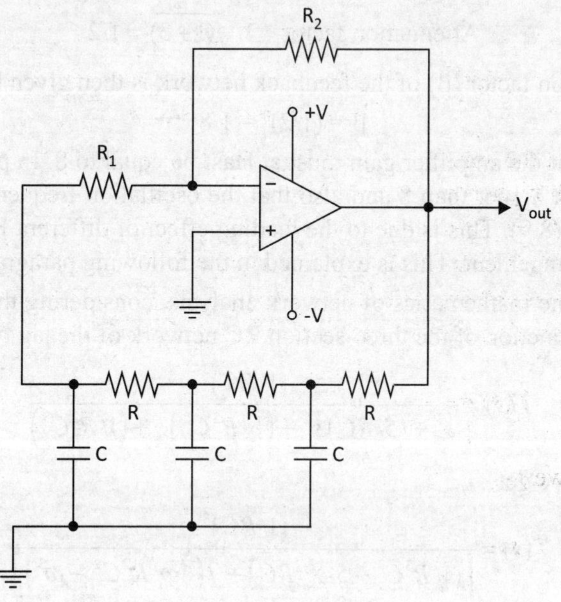

Fig. 8.5: Lag type RC phase shift oscillator using operational amplifier

$$T(s) = \frac{1}{(1+RCs)} \tag{8.5}$$

where $s = j\omega$

Assuming that the RC sections in the cascade arrangement are independent of each other, that is, individual RC sections do not load each other, then the transfer function of the cascade arrangement of three sections is given by

$$T(s) = \left[\frac{1}{(1+RCs)}\right]^3 \tag{8.6}$$

Now, the single-section RC network provides a phase shift (θ) given by

$$\theta = \tan^{-1}(\omega RC)$$
$$\tan\theta = \omega RC \tag{8.7}$$

$$\omega = \frac{\tan\theta}{RC} \tag{8.8}$$

If this single RC section were to provide the desired phase shift of 60 so as to produce a total phase shift of 180 from the feedback network, then the operational frequency of the oscillator would be given by:

$$\omega = \frac{\tan 60^{\circ}}{RC} = \frac{\sqrt{3}}{RC}, \text{ which gives } f = \frac{\sqrt{3}}{2\pi RC} \tag{8.9}$$

Attenuation factor provided by single-section RC network is given by

$$\text{Attenuation factor (single-section RC network)} = \frac{1}{\sqrt{1+\omega^2 R^2 C^2}} \tag{8.10}$$

Substituting the value of (ω) from Eqn. (8.9), we get

$$\text{Attenuation factor} = 1/\sqrt{(1+3)} = 1/2$$

The overall attenuation factor (β) of the feedback network is then given by:

$$\beta = (1/2)^3 = 1/8 \tag{8.11}$$

Eqn. 8.11 implies that the amplifier gain must at least be equal to 8. In practice, it is observed that the required gain is much higher than 8 and also that the oscillation frequency is also higher than the computed by using Eqn. (8.9). This is due to the loading effect of different RC sections when they are connected in cascade arrangement. This is explained in the following paragraphs.

Without going into the mathematics of network analysis, considering the loading effect, it can be proved that the transfer function of the three-section RC network of the lag type is given by

$$T(s) = \frac{(1/RC)^3}{s^3 + (5/RC)s^2 + (6/R^2C^2)s + (1/R^3C^3)} \tag{8.12}$$

Substituting $s = j\omega$, we get

$$T(s) = \frac{(1/RC)^3}{\left[(1/R^3C^3 - 5\omega^2/RC) + j(6\omega/R^2C^2 - \omega^3)\right]}$$

Multiplying both numerator and denominator by R^3C^3, we get

$$T(s) = \frac{1}{\left[(1 - 5\omega^2R^2C^2) + j(6\omega RC - \omega^3R^3C^3)\right]} \tag{8.13}$$

If the feedback network were to provide an overall phase shift of 180 , then the imaginary part should be equal to zero. That is, $6\omega\ RC - \omega^3\ R^3C^3 = 0$, which gives

$$\omega = \sqrt{6}/RC \tag{8.14}$$

Substituting the value of from Eqn. (8.14)in Eqn. (8.13), we get the expression for the feedback factor as

$$\text{Feedback factor, } \beta = 1/(1\text{–}30) \tag{8.15}$$

This gives,

$$|\beta| = 1/29 \tag{8.16}$$

Eqns (8.14) and (8.16) specify the required conditions for loop phase shift and loop gain respectively. The oscillation frequency is given by Eqn. (8.14) and Eqn. (8.16) tells that the amplifier gain must at least be equal to 29.

A similar analysis can be done in the case of lead-type RC phase shift network too. The expressions for the transfer function and the phase shift provided by single-section lead network are given by Eqns. (8.17) and (8.18), respectively.

$$T(s) = \frac{RCs}{(1+RCs)} \tag{8.17}$$

$$\theta = \tan^{-1}(1/\omega RC), \text{ which gives } \omega = 1/(\sqrt{3}RC) \text{ for } \theta = 60 \tag{8.18}$$

Considering the loading effect, the transfer function for the cascade arrangement of three-section lead-type RC network is given by Eqn. (8.19). This equation is similar to Eqn. (8.13) written for the cascade arrangement of lag network.

$$T(s) = \frac{1}{\{1-5/(\omega^2 R^2 C^2)\} - j\{6/(\omega RC) - 1/(R^3 C^3 \omega^3)\}} \quad (8.19)$$

Again, if the feedback network were to provide an overall phase shift of 180, then the imaginary part should be equal to zero. That is,

$$6/\omega RC - 1/R^3 C^3 \omega^3 = 0\text{, which gives } \omega = 1/(\sqrt{6}RC) \quad (8.20)$$

Substituting the value of from Eqn. (8.20) in Eqn. (8.19), we get expression for the feedback factor as given by Eqn. (8.22).

$$\text{Feedback factor, } \beta = 1/(1-30) \quad (8.10)$$

$$\text{This gives, } |\beta| = 1/29 \quad (8.22)$$

Eqns. (8.20) and (8.22) respectively specify the required conditions for loop phase shift and loop gain for RC phase shift oscillators employing lead-type RC phase shift network. The oscillation frequency is given by Eqn. (8.20) and Eqn. (8.22) tells that the amplifier gain must at least be equal to 29. Figure 8.6 shows circuit schematic of RC phase shift oscillator using lead-type phase shift network. The circuit uses op-amp-based amplifier stage. The oscillator circuit using transistorized amplifier stage would be similar to the one shown in Figure 8.4 except for the feedback network.

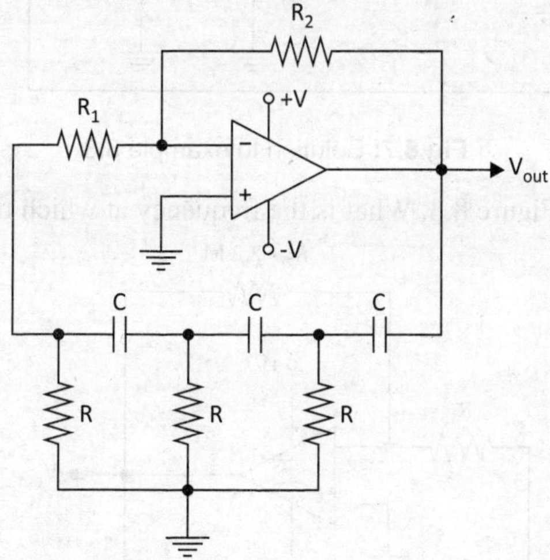

Fig. 8.6: Lead type op-amp-based RC phase shift oscillator

To summarize, in the case of an RC phase shift oscillator, the frequency of oscillation is given by $f = [\sqrt{6}/(2\pi RC)]$ if the feedback network employed lag-type RC sections and $f = [1/(2\pi\sqrt{6}RC)]$ if the feedback circuit used lead-type RC sections. Minimum amplifier gain in both cases is 29.

RC phase shift oscillator has limitations when it comes to designing a variable frequency oscillator as it is impractical to simultaneously vary three capacitance values equally. Also, adjustment of resistance values is not recommended because variation of resistance values will alter the loop gain of the oscillator circuit and there is likelihood of it not satisfying Barkhausen criterion for sustained oscillations. However, higher $d\phi/d\omega$ resulting from steep phase versus frequency slope provided by the three-section RC network gives a reasonably high frequency stability.

Example 8.3: Design a lead type phase-shift oscillator for a frequency of 800Hz. The capacitors are to be of 10nF.

Solution: The value of resistors needed in the feedback circuit is given by

$$R = \frac{1}{2\pi\sqrt{6}fC} = \frac{1}{2\pi\sqrt{6}\left(800\times10\times10^{-9}\right)} \cong 8.2k\Omega$$

The value of the feedback resistor is given by

$$R_f = 29R = 29\times8.2\times10^3\,\Omega = 238k\Omega$$

Figure 8.7 shows the circuit.

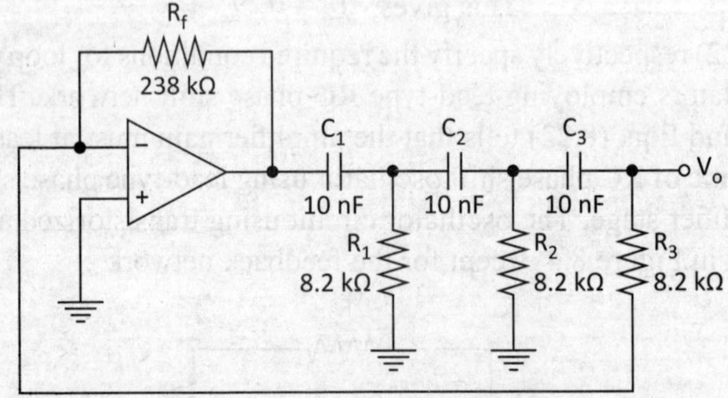

Fig.8.7: Solution to example 8.3

Example 8.4: Refer to Figure 8.8. What is the frequency at which this circuit would oscillate?

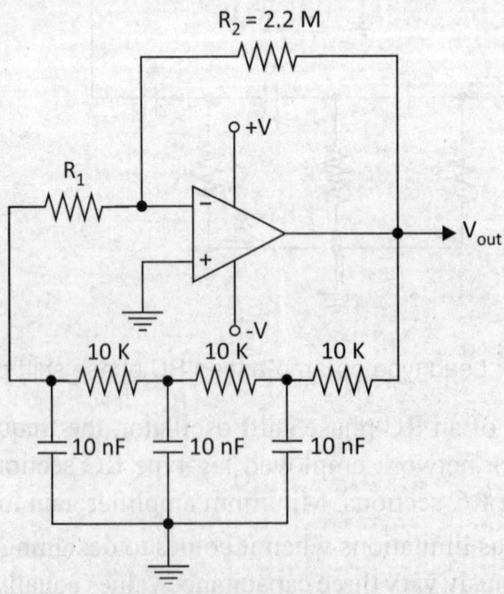

Fig. 8.8: Example 8.4

Solution: The oscillation frequency (f) is given by $f = \sqrt{6}/2\pi RC$

Therefore, $f = \sqrt{6}/(6.283 \times 10 \times 10^3 \times 10 \times 10^{-9}) = 3.9$ kHz

Example 8.5: In the oscillator shown in Figure 8.8, determine the maximum value of resistance (R_1) for sustained oscillations. How would the oscillation frequency change if the positions of R and C in the feedback network were interchanged?

Solution: Minimum gain to be provided by the amplifier = 29

|Gain| = R_2/R_1 = 29

This gives $R_1 = 2.2 \times 10^6/29 = 75.86$ kΩ

R_1 should therefore be less than 75.86 kΩ

When the positions of *R* and *C* are interchanged, the oscillation frequency is given by $f = 1/2\pi\sqrt{6}RC$

Substituting the values of R and C, we get f = 650 Hz

8.2.1.2 Buffered RC Phase shift oscillator

There are buffered versions of both lead type and lag type RC phase shift oscillators. They overcome the loading effect of different RC sections in the conventional phase shift oscillator. The oscillator performs very nearly at the computed values of frequency and amplifier gain. The lag type buffered RC phase shift oscillator is shown in Figure 8.9.The oscillation frequency in this case is given by Eqn. (8.23) and the minimum value of the amplifier gain for sustained oscillations is 8.

$$f = \sqrt{3}/(2\pi RC) \tag{8.23}$$

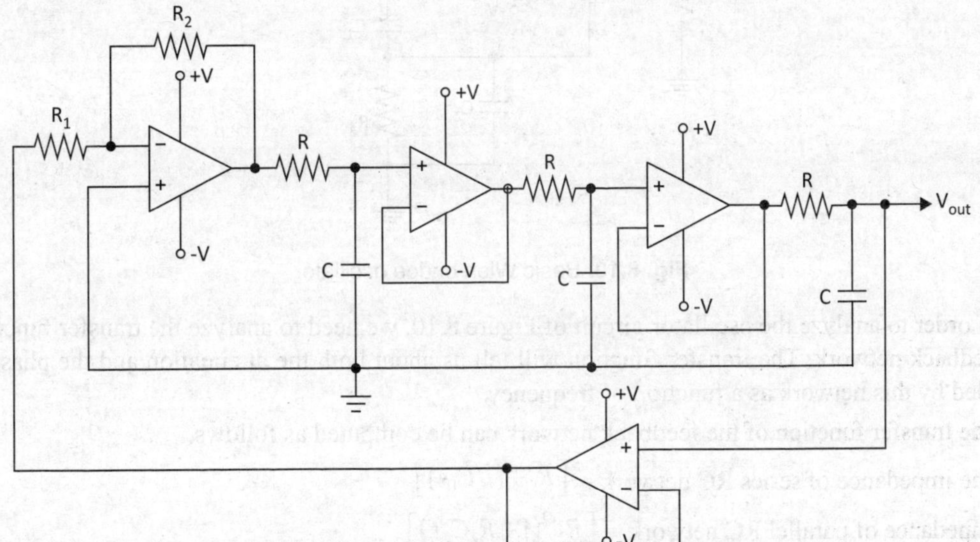

Fig. 8.9: Lag type Buffered RC phase shift oscillator

In the case of lead-type buffered RC phase shift oscillator, the oscillation frequency would be given by

$$f = 1/(2\pi\sqrt{3}RC) \tag{8.24}$$

Example 8.6: If the oscillator in the example 8.4 is a buffered RC oscillator, what would be the frequency of oscillations?

Solution: The oscillation frequency (f) is given by $f = \sqrt{3}/2\pi RC$

Therefore, $f = 3/(6.283 \times 10 \times 10^3 \times 10 \times 10^{-9}) = 2.76$ kHz

8.2.1.3 Wien-bridge oscillator

The Wien bridge oscillator is the most widely used RC oscillator configuration for low-frequency applications due to simplicity of the circuit, very good frequency stability and its amenability to variable frequency operation. The only major disadvantage is that these oscillators suffer from relatively higher amplitude distortionsat the output unless special measures are taken to minimize them. Modified Wien bridge oscillator designs that minimize distortion are also discussed in the subsequent paragraphs in this section. The basic Wien bridge oscillator circuit comprises a single-stage amplifier whose output is fed back to its input through a feedback network. The amplifier portion is usually implemented by an operational amplifier wired as a non-inverting amplifier. The feedback network comprises a cascade arrangement of a series RC network and a parallel RC network. Figure 8.10 shows the circuit schematic of the basic Wien bridge oscillator configured around an operational amplifier.

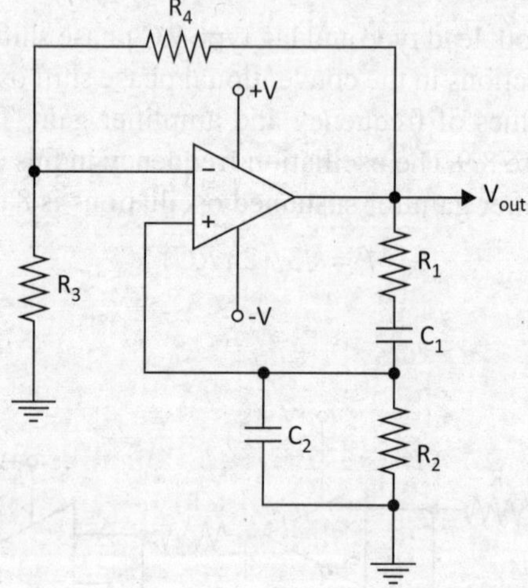

Fig. 8.10: Basic Wien bridge oscillator

In order to analyze the oscillator circuit of Figure 8.10, we need to analyze the transfer function of the feedback network. The transfer function will tell us about both the attenuation and the phase shift provided by this network as a function of frequency.

The transfer function of the feedback network can be computed as follows.

The impedance of series RC network = $\left[R_1 + (1/C_1 s)\right]$

Impedance of parallel RC network = $\left[R_2/(1+R_2C_2 s)\right]$

The transfer function of the feedback network can therefore be written as

$$T(s) = \beta = \frac{\left[R_2/(1+R_2C_2s)\right]}{\left[(R_1+1/C_1s)+R_2/(1+R_2C_2s)\right]} \tag{8.25}$$

Eqn (8.25) can be simplified to

$$\beta = \frac{R_2C_1s}{\left[R_1C_1R_2C_2s^2+(R_1C_1+R_2C_2+R_2C_1)s+1\right]} \tag{8.26}$$

Substituting $s = j\omega$ in Eqn. (8.26), we get

$$\beta = \frac{j\omega R_2 C_1}{\left[\left(1-\omega^2 R_1 C_1 R_2 C_2\right) + j\omega\left(R_1 C_1 + R_2 C_2 + R_2 C_1\right)\right]} \quad (8.27)$$

The magnitude and phase responses of β are

$$\text{Magnitude of } \beta,\ |\beta| = \frac{\omega R_2 C_1}{\sqrt{\left[\left(1-\omega^2 R_1 C_1 R_2 C_2\right)^2 + \omega^2\left(R_1 C_1 + R_2 C_2 + R_2 C_1\right)^2\right]}} \quad (8.28)$$

$$\text{Phase angle, } \theta = 90° - \tan^{-1}\left[\left\{\omega\left(R_1 C_1 + R_2 C_2 + R_2 C_1\right)\right\} / \left(1-\omega^2 R_1 C_1 R_2 C_2\right)\right] \quad (8.29)$$

In order that the loop phase shift is zero, the feedback network must provide a phase shift of zero. For this to happen, following condition should be satisfied in Eqn.8.29.

$$1-\omega^2 R_1 C_1 R_2 C_2 = 0$$

which gives the frequency of oscillation as

$$\omega = \frac{1}{\sqrt{R_1 C_1 R_2 C_2}} \quad (8.30)$$

Substituting the value of from Eqn.(8.30) in Eqn. (8.28) and simplifying, we get

$$|\beta| = \frac{R_2 C_1}{\left(R_1 C_1 + R_2 C_2 + R_2 C_1\right)} \quad (8.31)$$

In the Wien bridge oscillator, $R_1 = R_2 = R$ and $C_1 = C_2 = C$. In that case,

$$|\beta| = 1/3 \quad (8.32)$$

This implies that the amplifier gain should at least be equal to 3. Also

$$\omega = \frac{1}{RC} \quad (8.33)$$

If we carefully examine the feedback network, we will notice that it is a combination of a lag network formed by R_1 and C_2 and a lead network formed by R_2 and C_1. The operating frequency is the geometric mean of the two cut-off frequencies given by $(1/R_1C_2)$ and $(1/R_2C_1)$.

Distortions in Wien Bridge Oscillator: As outlined earlier, Wien bridge oscillator is associated with relatively higher output distortion unless design measures are taken to minimize it. High output distortion results from the fact that the output amplitude is at power supply rails. This saturates the output transistors inside the op-amp and causes clipping of the output signal at both the supply rails, thus producing several odd and even harmonics.

Distortion can be minimized by applying non-linear feedback. Figure 8.11 shows one such circuit. Initially, diodes D_1 and D_2 are non-conducting. The feedback resistance in that case is sum of R_2 and R_3. For larger signals, voltage across R_3 is large enough to make D_1 and D_2 conduct, respectively, during positive and negative half cycles. Conducting diodes (D_1 or D_2) decrease effective R_3, thus reducing the gain.

In another configuration, a non-linear component such as an incandescent lamp or a thermistor with positive temperature coefficient of resistance replaces the gain determining resistance connected from inverting input of the op-amp to ground. Figure 8.12 shows the modified circuit schematic using a non-linear resistor. The nominal value of resistance of the non-linear resistor is chosen to be equal to half of the feedback resistance at the current established by the two resistors. In the absence of any oscillations, the non-linear resistance value will be lower, causing the gain to be greater than 3. This initiates oscillations. As the oscillations build up, the current through the non-linear resistance heats it up and causes its resistance to increase thus lowering the gain and stabilizing the output. The non-linear relationship between the current and the resistance ensures that a small change in output voltage causes a large change in the resistance value. This keeps the op-amp output away from saturation. In this way, the distortion is minimized. It is observed that the distortion in the circuit of the type shown in Figure 8.12 is more than an order of magnitude better than that observed in the case of oscillator circuit of Figure 8.10.

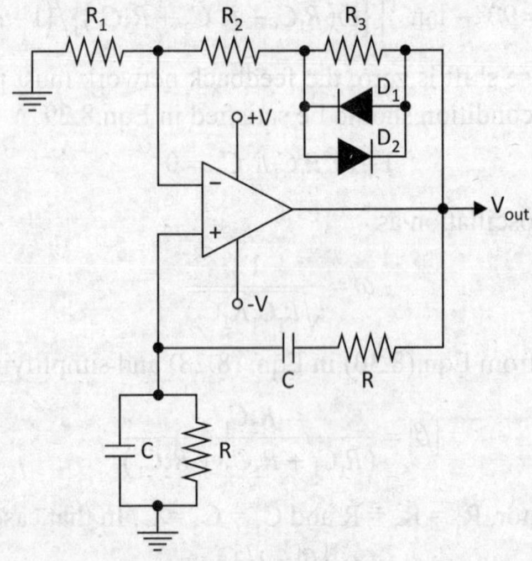

Fig. 8.11: Wien bridge oscillator with non-linear feedback

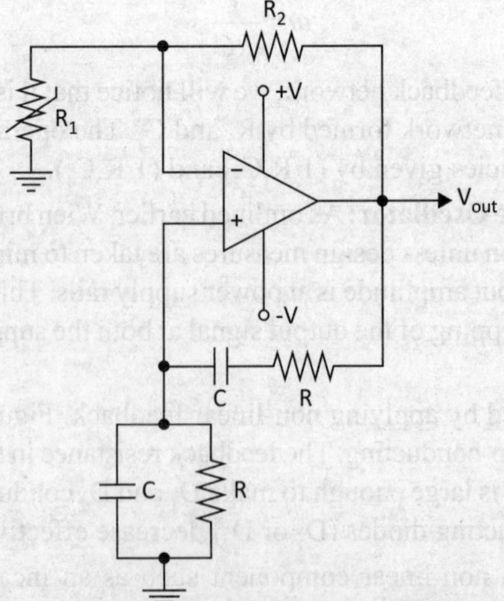

Fig. 8.12: Wien bridge oscillator with a non-linear resistor

Another possible circuit configuration that achieves low level of output distortion is shown in Figure 8.13. The circuit employs an n-channel JFET whose drain-to-source ON-resistance RDS(ON) is controlled by a negative gate voltage. This negative gate voltage is in turn proportional to the peak amplitude of the output signal. The drain-to-source resistance of the JFET is a part of the gain-determining network as is evident from the circuit. Any increase in output amplitude causes increased negative voltage at the JFET gate terminal. Increased negative voltage causes drain-to-source resistance to increase and therefore the gain to decrease. The circuit arrangement therefore provides automatic gain control. Various resistance values are so chosen as to have an initial gain of greater than 3 to start oscillations. Thereafter, the gain is automatically controlled.

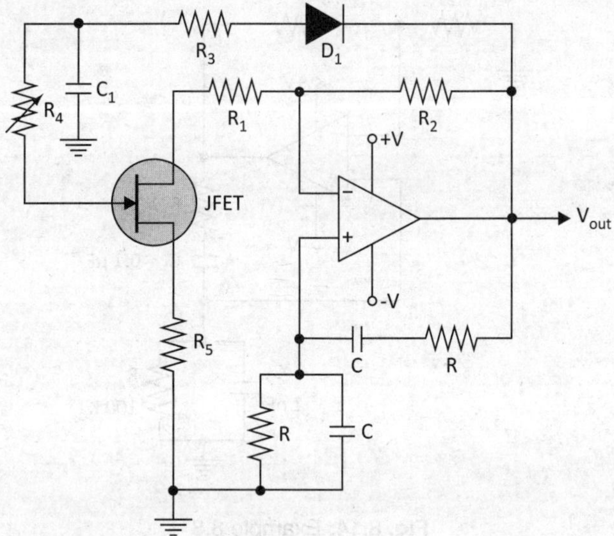

Fig. 8.13: Wien bridge oscillator with automatic gain control

Example 8.7: Calculate the values of R and C for a 100Hz output Wien Bridge oscillator and explain why is it necessary to have an amplifier with a very high input impedance?

Solution: Oscillation frequency of a Wien Bridge oscillator is given by $f = \dfrac{1}{2\pi RC}$

Assume C = 0.001 μF, therefore $R = \dfrac{1}{2\pi fC} = \dfrac{1}{2\times\pi\times100\times0.001\times10^{-6}}\Omega = 1.6M\Omega$

If the amplifier input impedance is not very high as compared to the calculated value of R (1.6MΩ in this case), it will load the resistance R and hence change the frequency of oscillations. That is why, an opamp or a FET amplifier stage is normally used instead of a transistor amplifier stage.

Example 8.8: Refer to the RC oscillator circuit of Figure 8.14. Identify the type of oscillator. Also, determine the operating frequency and preferred value of R_3.

Solution: The oscillator shown in Figure 8.14 is a Wien bridge oscillator.

Operating frequency is given by $\omega = 1/(R_1R_2C_1C_2)$. Therefore, $\omega = 1/\sqrt{(1 \times 10^3 \times 100 \times 10^3 \times 0.1 \times 10^{-6} \times 1 \times 10^{-9})} = 10^4$ rad/s

$f = \omega/2\pi = 104/6.283$ Hz = 1.592 kHz

Attenuation provided by feedback network is given by

$|\beta| = R_2C_1/(R_1C_1 + R_2C_2 + R_2C_1)$

Therefore, $|\beta| = (100 \times 10^3 \times 0.1 \times 10^{-6})/(1 \times 10^3 \times 0.1 \times 10^{-6} + 100 \times 10^3 \times 1 \times 10^{-9} + 100 \times 10^3 \times 0.1 \times 10^{-6}) = 10^{-2}/(10^{-4} + 10^{-4} + 10^{-2}) = 1/1.02$

Therefore, minimum value of required gain = 1.02. That is, $1 + (R_4/R_3) = 1.02$, $R_4/R_3 = 0.02$

$R_3 = 2.2 \times 10^3/0.02 = 110\ \text{k}\Omega$

Since the required gain has to be slightly greater than 1.02, preferred value of R_3 therefore should be slightly less than 110 kΩ.

R_3 may be chosen to be 100 kΩ.

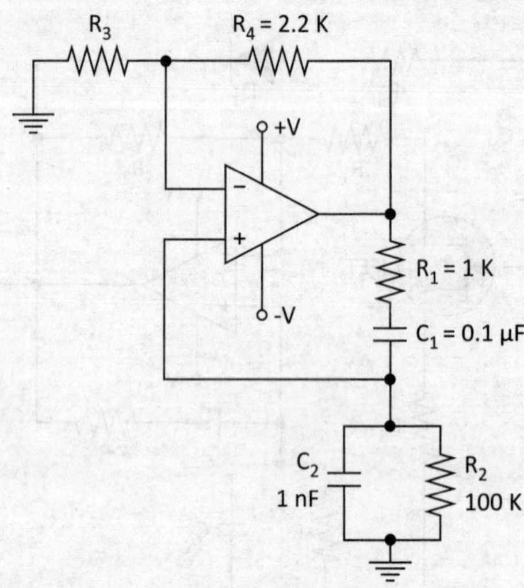

Fig. 8.14: Example 8.8

8.2.1.4 Bubba oscillator

Bubba oscillator is a slight variation of the buffered RC phase shift oscillator. Figure 8.15 shows the circuit schematic of the Bubba oscillator. The difference between the two is that the Bubba oscillator uses four RC sections in the feedback network with each RC section contributing a phase difference of 45°. This offers two distinctive advantages. One, taking outputs from alternate sections yields low impedance quadrature outputs. Two, use of four RC sections provides higher $d\phi/d\omega$, which in turn leads to relatively higher frequency stability. The expression for the transfer function of the feedback network is given by Eqn. (8.34). Remember that different sections in the feedback network are buffered and therefore there is no loading effect.

$$\beta = \left[\frac{1}{1+RCs}\right]^4 \tag{8.34}$$

Single-section RC section provides a phase shift of 45° for = 1/RC. Substituting this value of ω in Eqn. (8.34) we get

$$|\beta| = \left|\frac{1}{(1+j)^4}\right| = \frac{1}{4} \tag{8.35}$$

Eqn. (8.35) tells that the gain of the amplifier must at least be 4 for oscillations to occur. As explained earlier, the gain is chosen to be 10-15% higher than this value.

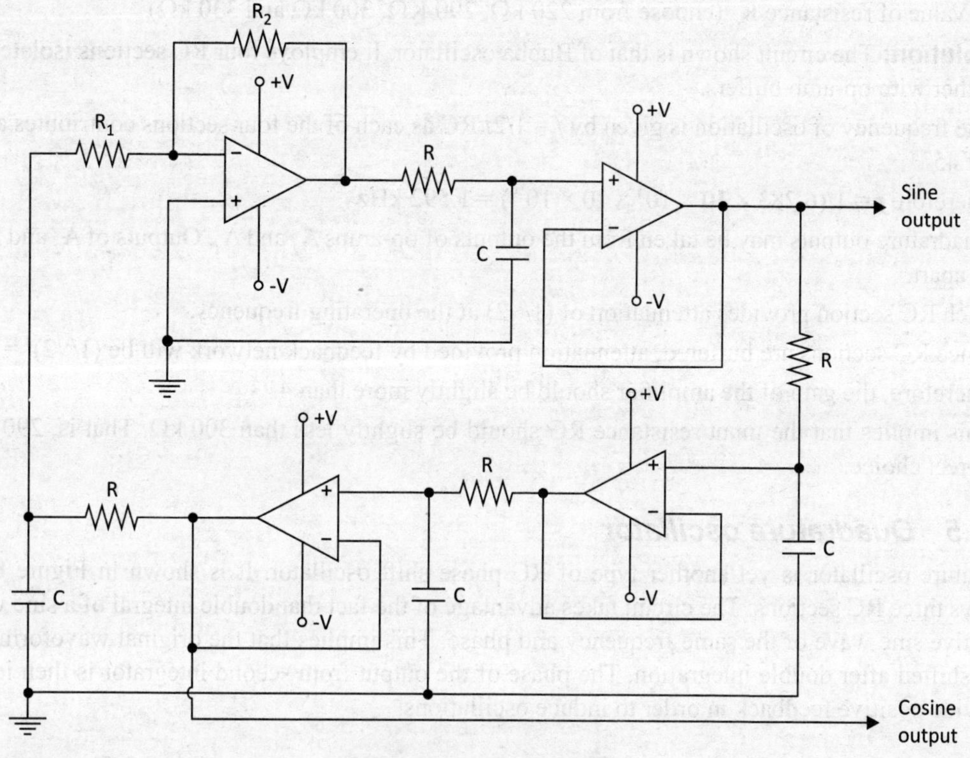

Fig. 8.15: Bubba oscillator

Example 8.9:

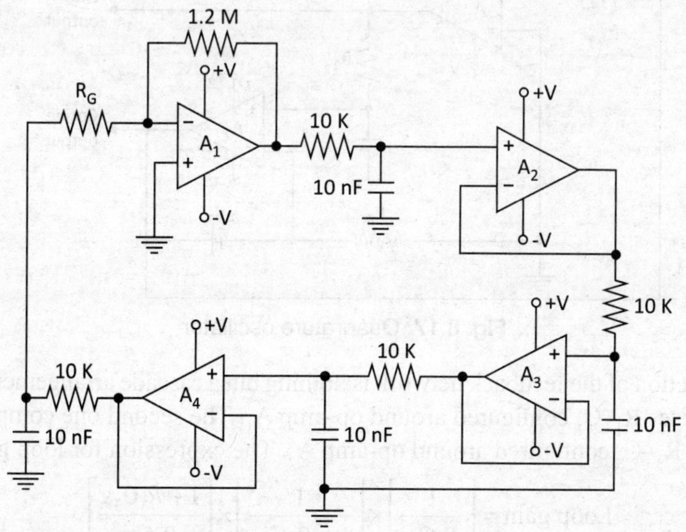

Fig. 8.16: shows an oscillator circuit. Determine the following.

a. Frequency of oscillation

b. Possible points in the circuit for quadrature outputs

c. Value of resistance R_G (choose from 220 kΩ, 290 KΩ, 300 kΩ and 330 kΩ)

Solution: The circuit shown is that of Bubba oscillator. It employs four RC sections isolated from each other with op-amp buffers.

The frequency of oscillation is given by $f = 1/2\pi RC$ as each of the four sections contributes a phase shift of 45°.

Therefore $f = 1/(6.283 \times 10 \times 10^3 \times 10 \times 10^{-9}) = 1.592$ kHz

Quadrature outputs may be taken from the outputs of op-amps A_2 and A_4. Outputs of A_2 and A_4 will be 90° apart.

Each RC section provides attenuation of $(1/\sqrt{2})$ at the operating frequency.

Since RC sections are buffered, attenuation provided by feedback network will be $(1/\sqrt{2})^4 = 1/4$.

Therefore, the gain of the amplifier should be slightly more than 4.

This implies that the input resistance RG should be slightly less than 300 kΩ. That is, 290 kΩ is the correct choice.

8.2.1.5 Quadrature oscillator

Quadrature oscillator is yet another type of RC phase shift oscillator. It is shown in Figure 8.17. It employs three RC sections. The circuit takes advantage of the fact that double integral of a sine wave is a negative sine wave of the same frequency and phase. This implies that the original waveform is 180 phase-shifted after double integration. The phase of the output from second integrator is then inverted to provide positive feedback in order to induce oscillations.

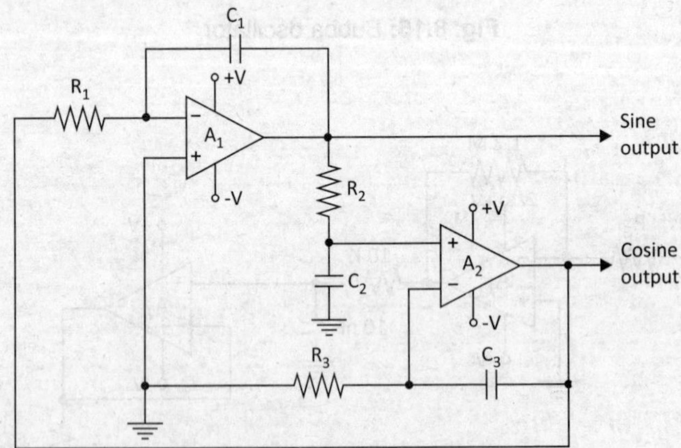

Fig. 8.17: Quadrature oscillator

The transfer function of the feedback network is nothing but a cascade arrangement of three networks. The first one comprises R_1–C_1 configured around op-amp A_1. The second one comprises R_2–C_2 and the third one comprises R_3–C_3 configured around op-amp A_2. The expression for loop gain is given by

$$\text{Loop gain} = \left[\frac{1}{R_1C_1s}\right] \times \left[\frac{1}{1+R_2C_2s}\right] \times \left[\frac{1+R_3C_3s}{R_3C_3s}\right] \tag{8.36}$$

If $R_1C_1 = R_2C_2 = R_3C_3 = RC$ and we substitute $\omega = 1/RC$, the first network provides a phase shift of 90°, the second and third networks provide phase shift of 45° each so as to provide a total phase shift of 180°. Op-amp A_1 too provides a phase shift of 180°, which leads to loop phase shift of 0°. Also, Eqn. (8.36) reduces to the following equation:

$$\text{Loop gain} = \frac{1}{(RCs)^2} = 1\angle -180° \qquad (8.37)$$

The circuit provides sine and cosine outputs (quadrature outputs) because of 90° phase difference between the two signals present at the outputs of the two op-amps.

Example 8.10: Figure 8.18 shows the circuit diagram of a quadrature oscillator. Determine the operating frequency. Also determine the phase difference between the signals appearing at the outputs of op-amps A_1 and A_2. If the peak amplitude of the signal appearing at the output of A_1 is 2 V, determine the peak amplitude of the signal at the junction of R_2 and C_2 and also at the output of A_2.

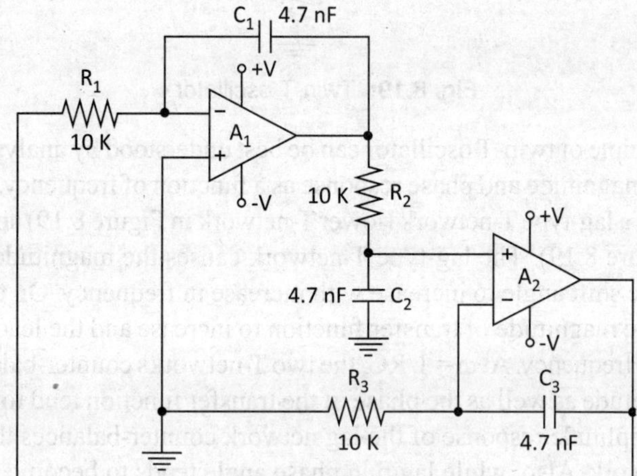

Fig. 8.18: Example 8.10

Solution: The frequency of oscillation is given by $f = 1/2\pi RC$.

Substituting the values of R and C, we get $f = 1/(6.283 \times 10 \times 10^3 \times 4.7 \times 10^{-9}) = 3.386$ kHz

The transfer function from output of A_1 to junction of $R_2 - C_2$ is given by $1/(1 + R_2C_2s)$. At $\omega = 1/R_2C_2$, it produces a phase shift of 45°.

The transfer function from junction of $R_2 - C_2$ to the output of A_2 is given by $(1 + R_3C_3s)/R_3C_3s$. At $= 1/R_3C_3$, it produces a phase shift of –45°. Since $R_2C_2 = R_3C_3$, the phase shift from output of A_1 to the output of A_2 will be 90°.

It is clear from the transfer functions mentioned above that the two networks respectively provide attenuation and gain of $1/\sqrt{2}$ and $\sqrt{2}$.

Therefore, peak amplitude of signal at junction of R_2–C_2 is $2/\sqrt{2} = \sqrt{2}$V and that at the output of A_2 is $\sqrt{2} \times \sqrt{2} = 2$V.

8.2.1.6 Twin-T oscillator

The twin-T oscillator employs a twin-T-type of notch filter network as the frequency selective component in the feedback network. Figure 8.19 shows the basic circuit schematic of a twin-T oscillator. The circuit employs both positive as well as negative feedback. The positive feedback necessary to produce oscillations is provided by a voltage divider network of R_1 and R_2. The negative feedback is through the frequency selective twin-T network.

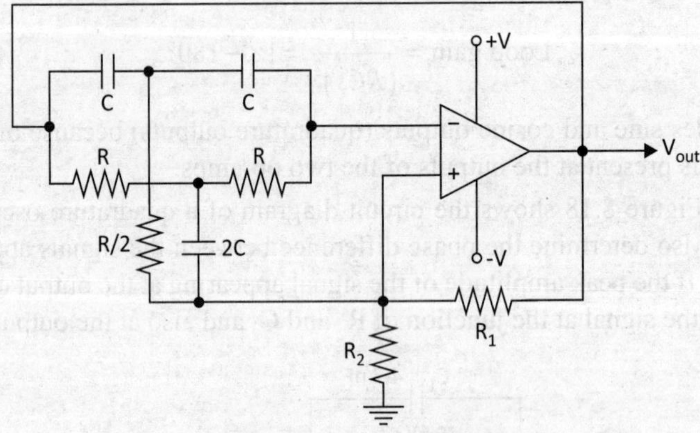

Fig. 8.19: Twin-T oscillator

The operational principle of twin-T oscillator can be best understood by analyzing its transfer function and thereby studying its magnitude and phase response as a function of frequency. In fact, twin-T network is a parallel connection of a lag-type T-network (lower T-network in Figure 8.19) and a lead-type T-network (upper T-network in Figure 8.19). The lag-type T-network causes the magnitude of transfer function to fall and the lagging phase shift angle to increase with increase in frequency. On the other hand, the lead-type T-network causes the magnitude of transfer function to increase and the leading phase shift angle to decrease with increase in frequency. At ω = 1/RC, the two T-networks counter-balance each other with the result that both the magnitude as well as the phase of the transfer function tend to become zero. In fact, at ω = 1/RC, decreasing amplitude response of the lag network counter-balances the increasing amplitude response of the lead network. Also, while lagging phase angle tends to become –90°, the leading phase angle tends to become +90 . Figure 8.20 shows the amplitude and phase response of the twin-T network as a function of normalized frequency. The value of frequency f_c equals [1/(2πRC)].

The same can be explained with the help of expression for transfer function of the twin-T network. Without going into mathematical details, the transfer function of the twin-T network can be expressed as

$$T(s) = \frac{1-\omega^2 R^2 C^2}{1-\omega^2 R^2 C^2 + j4\omega CR} \tag{8.38}$$

The magnitude of T(s) is

$$|T(s)| = \frac{1-\omega^2 R^2 C^2}{\sqrt{\left(1-\omega^2 R^2 C^2\right)^2 + (4\omega CR)^2}} \tag{8.39}$$

The phase angle of T(s) is

$$\theta = \tan^{-1}[4\omega CR/(1-\omega^2 C^2 R^2)] \tag{8.40}$$

Substituting ω = 1/RC in eqns. (8.39) and (8.40), we get the magnitude of transfer function as zero and the phase angle as either –90 or +90°. This small computation thus vindicates what was said in the preceding paragraph.

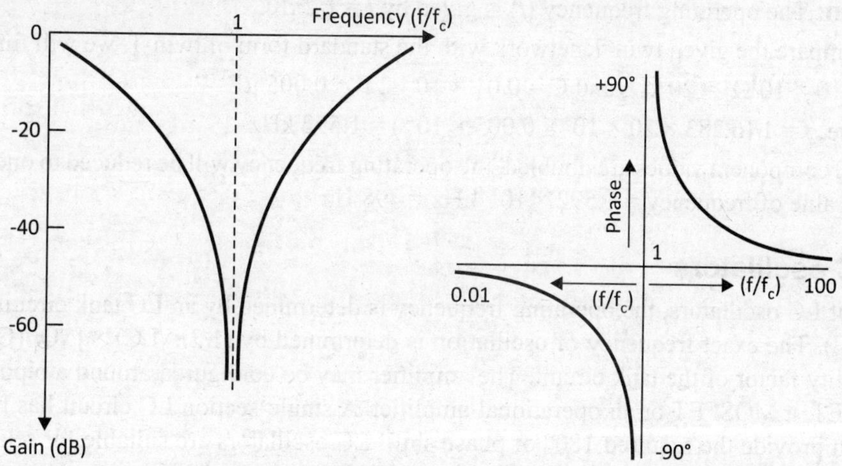

Fig. 8.20: (a) Magnitude response of twin-T network (b) phase response of twin-T network

A zero amplitude for the transfer function implies zero negative feedback at $\omega = 1/RC$. At all other frequencies, there will be very high negative feedback thus allowing the circuit to oscillate only very close to the notch frequency. Resistance R_2 is a thermistor with a positive temperature coefficient. An incandescent lamp may also be used in place of thermistor. The positive temperature coefficient of resistance of tungsten filament used in incandescent lamp is used for the purpose. A low value of R2 initially produces a large amount of positive feedback to initiate oscillations. Once the oscillations build up, the current flowing through R_2 heats it and thus raises its temperature. Increase in temperature increases the value of R_2 thus reducing the positive feedback to stabilize the magnitude of oscillations.

Twin-T oscillator produces a low distortion sinusoidal output. This is primarily because of two reasons. First, harmonics are subjected to a very high level of negative feedback, thus severely attenuating them. Second, the operating point of the oscillator is very delicately balanced between positive and negative feedback. This necessitates a very small amount of non-linearity to stabilize the amplitude.

Example 8.11: Refer to the twin-T oscillator of Figure 8.21. Determine the frequency of the output signal. How would the frequency change if all component values in the twin-T network are doubled?

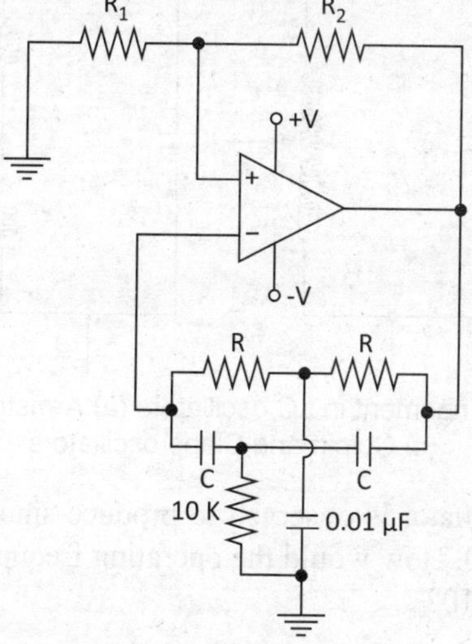

Fig. 8.21: Example 8.11

Solution: The operating frequency (f) is given by $f = 1/2\pi RC$

If we compare the given twin-T network with the standard form of twin-T, we will find that

$R = 2 \times 10 \times 10^3 \Omega = 20\ k\Omega$ and $C = 0.01 \times 10^{-6}/2\ F = 0.005\ \mu F$

Therefore, $f = 1/(6.283 \times 20 \times 10^3 \times 0.005 \times 10^{-6}) = 1.592$ kHz

When all component values are doubled, the operating frequency will be reduced to one-fourth. That is, changed value of frequency $= 1.592 \times 10^3/4$ Hz $= 398$ Hz

8.2.2 LC oscillators

In the case of LC oscillators, the operating frequency is determined by an LC tank circuit and is given by $(1/2\pi\sqrt{LC})$. The exact frequency of oscillation is determined by $(1/2\pi\sqrt{LC}) \times [\sqrt{Q^2/(Q^2 + 1)}]$. Here Q is the quality factor of the tank circuit. The amplifier may be configured around a bipolar transistor, a junction FET, a MOSFET or an operational amplifier. A single-section LC circuit has two poles and therefore can provide the required 180° of phase shift. LC oscillators are suitable for relatively higher operational frequencies due to the fact that inductors operating at low frequencies are expensive, bulky and highly non-ideal. RC oscillators are preferred at lower frequencies.

LC oscillators are usually classified by the name of its inventor. The common ones are Armstrong oscillator, Hartley oscillator, Colpitt oscillator and Clapp oscillator. They are also classified as series-fed or shunt-fed oscillators depending upon the manner in which DC power is applied to the active device. In the case of series-fed LC oscillators, DC power is applied to the active device through the tank circuit or a part of the tank circuit. In shunt-fed LC oscillators, DC power is applied through a separate path that is parallel to the tank circuit. Each of the LC oscillators mentioned above can be constructed either way.

Also, LC oscillators (Armstrong, Hartley, Colpitt and Clapp) are identifiable by the manner in which feedback signal is coupled to the input. In the case of Armstrong oscillator, the feedback signal is magnetically coupled [Figure 8.22(a)]. In the case of Hartley oscillator, a tapped or a split coil is used for the purpose [Figure 8.22(b)]. Split capacitor arrangement is used in the case of Colpitt and Clapp oscillators [Figure 8.22(c)]. Each of these oscillators is described in the following sections.

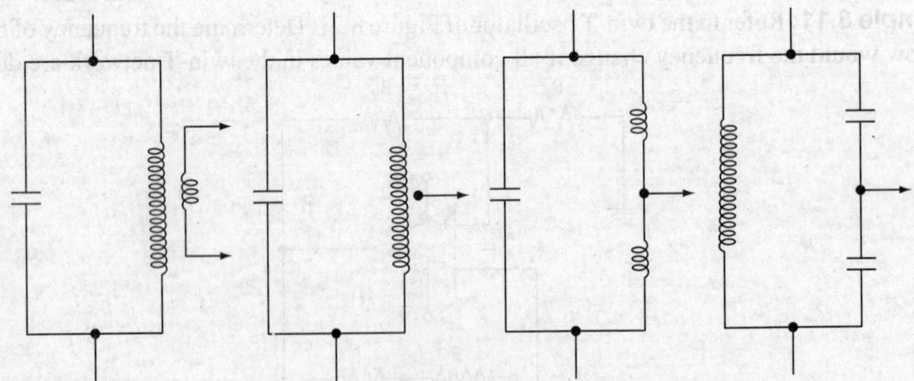

Fig. 8.22: Feedback coupling arrangement in LC oscillators (a) Armstrong oscillator (b) Hartley oscillator (c) Colpitt and Clapp oscillators

Example 8.12: An LC oscillator is observed to produce sine wave output at 10MHz when the Q-factor of the LC circuit was 100. How would the operating frequency change, if at all it would, with the value of Q-factor dropping to 10?

Solution: The oscillation frequency for a LC oscillator is given by $f = \dfrac{1}{2\pi\sqrt{LC}}\sqrt{\dfrac{Q^2}{(Q^2+1)}}$

For Q = 100, $f = \dfrac{1}{2\pi\sqrt{LC}}\sqrt{\dfrac{10000}{10001}} \cong \dfrac{1}{2\pi\sqrt{LC}} = 10MHz$

For Q = 10, $f = \dfrac{1}{2\pi\sqrt{LC}}\sqrt{\dfrac{100}{101}} \cong 10\times10^6 \times \sqrt{\dfrac{100}{101}} = 9.95MHz$

8.2.2.1 Hartley oscillator

Hartley oscillator uses a tapped or split coil for the purpose of generating feedback signal. This is where a Hartley oscillator differs from an Armstrong oscillator, which uses a separate coil called tickler coil. In the case of Hartley oscillator, current flow through one section of the tapped coil induces a voltage in the other section to provide the feedback. The feedback signal is 180° out-of-phase with the one that produces it.

Figure 8.23 shows the circuit schematic of Hartley oscillator configured around a bipolar transistor. Incidentally, the circuit shown is that of a series-fed oscillator. Figure 8.24 shows the Hartley oscillator configured around an op-amp.

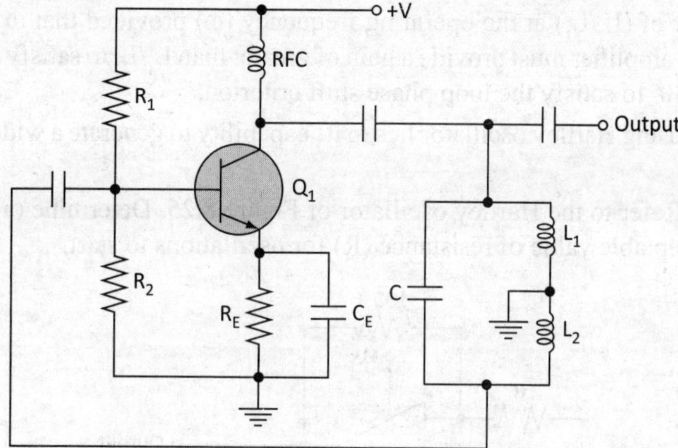

Fig. 8.23: Hartley oscillator configured around bipolar transistor

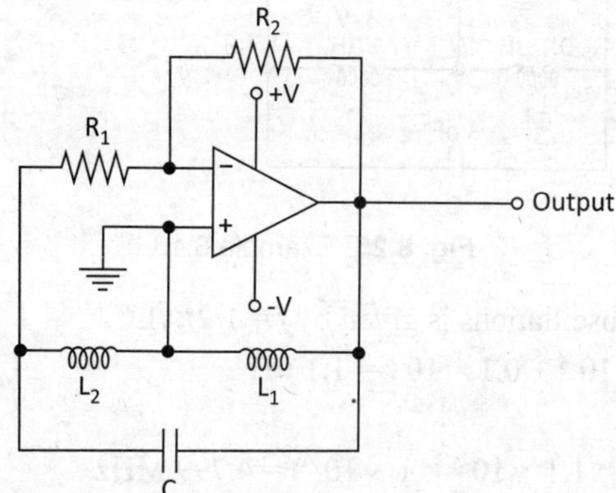

Fig. 8.24: Hartley oscillator configured around op-amp

The attenuation factor and the phase shift provided by the feedback network can be determined from the transfer function of the feedback network. The feedback network in the present case is a pi-network with capacitive series element and inductive shunt element. The transfer function is given by

$$T(s) = \beta = \frac{-\omega^2 L_2 C}{(1-\omega^2 L_2 C)} = \frac{-(1-\omega^2 L_1 C)}{\omega^2 L_1 C} \tag{8.41}$$

Negative sign implies phase shift of 180°.

Also,

$$|\beta|^2 = \left[\frac{\omega^2 L_2 C}{(1-\omega^2 L_2 C)}\right] \times \left[\frac{(1-\omega^2 L_1 C)}{\omega^2 L_1 C}\right] = \left(\frac{L_2}{L_1}\right) \times \left[\frac{(1-\omega^2 L_1 C)}{(1-\omega^2 L_2 C)}\right]$$

Substituting $\omega = 1/\sqrt{(L_1 + L_2)C}$ in the above equation, we get

$$|\beta|^2 = \left(\frac{L_2}{L_1}\right)^2$$

$$|\beta| = \left(\frac{L_2}{L_1}\right) \tag{8.42}$$

Eqns (8.41) and (8.42) imply that the feedback network introduces a phase shift of 180° and signal attenuation by a factor of (L_2/L_1) at the operating frequency (ω) provided that $\omega = 1/(L_1 + L_2)C$. This further implies that the amplifier must provide a gain of greater than L_1/L_2 to satisfy the loop gain criterion and a phase shift of 180° to satisfy the loop phase shift criterion.

The advantage of using Hartley oscillator lies in its capability to generate a wide range of frequencies and its easy tunability.

Example 8.13: Refer to the Hartley oscillator of Figure 8.25. Determine (a) operating frequency and (b) maximum acceptable value of resistance (R) for oscillations to start.

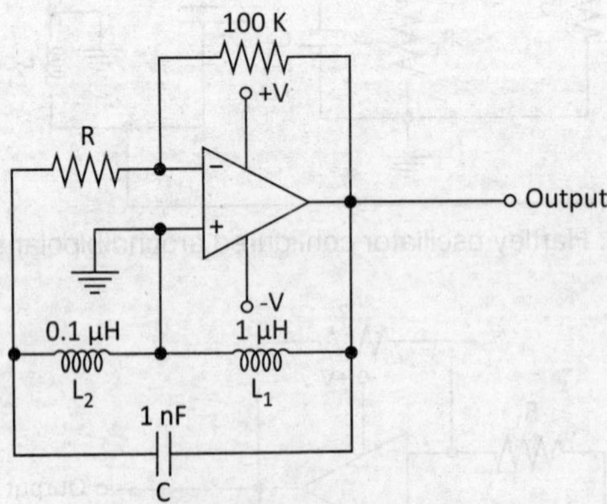

Fig. 8.25: Example 8.13

Solution: Frequency of oscillations is given by $f = 1/2\pi\sqrt{LC}$.

Now, $L = L_1 + L_2 = 1.0 \times 10^{-6} + 0.1 \times 10^{-6} = 1.1\ \mu H$

and C = 1 nF

Therefore, $f = 1/(6.283 \times \sqrt{1.1 \times 10^{-6} \times 1 \times 10^{-9}}) = 4.799$ MHz

Feedback factor = $(0.1 \times 10^{-6})/(1.0 \times 10^{-6}) = 0.1$

Therefore, minimum required gain = 10.

Value of gain = $100 \times 10^3/R$.

Therefore, maximum value of R = $10^5/10 = 10^4\Omega = 10\ k\Omega$

Example 8.14: Refer to the circuit in Figure 8.26. Which oscillator does it represent? Determine the oscillation frequency and the value of resistor R_1 for sustained oscillations?

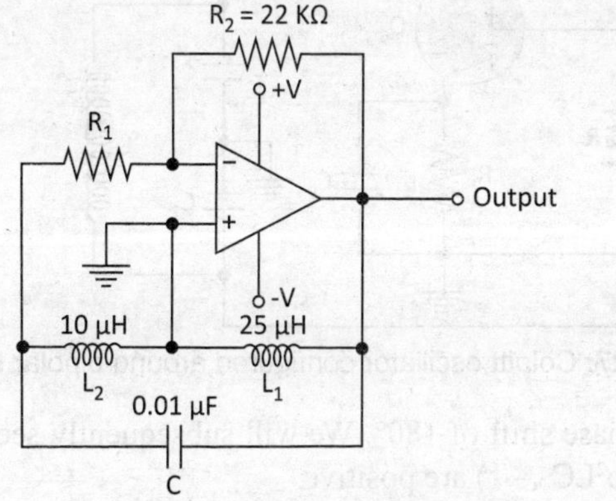

Fig. 8.26: Example 8.14

Solution: The circuit shown is Hartley oscillator

The frequency of oscillations is given by $f = \dfrac{1}{2\pi\sqrt{(L_1 + L_2)C}}$

Given that, $L_1 = 25\mu H$, $L_2 = 10\mu H$, $C = 0.01\mu F$

Therefore, $f = \dfrac{1}{2\pi\sqrt{(25\times10^{-6} + 10\times10^{-6})\times0.01\times10^{-6}}} = 269\times10^3\ Hz = 269kHz$

The minimum gain provided by the amplifier should be $\left(\dfrac{L_1}{L_2}\right) = \dfrac{25\times10^{-6}}{10\times10^{-6}} = 2.5$

Therefore, $\left(\dfrac{R_2}{R_1}\right) = 2.5$ Hence, $R_1 = \dfrac{R_2}{2.5} = \dfrac{22\times10^3}{2.5} = 8.8k\Omega$

8.2.2.2 Colpitt oscillator

Colpitt oscillator uses a pair of capacitors and an inductor in the tank circuit to produce the regenerative-feedback signal. In fact, the feedback network in this case is an electrical dual of the feedback network of Hartley oscillator. Figures 8.27 and 8.28 show the Colpitt oscillator circuits configured around bipolar transistor and op-amp, respectively. An FET could also be used as the active device instead. As is obvious from the two circuit schematics, the output signal is developed across capacitor C_1 and the feedback signal is generated across capacitor C_2.

The attenuation factor and the phase shift provided by the feedback network can be determined from the transfer function of the feedback network. The feedback network in the present case is a pi-network with inductive series element and capacitive shunt elements. The transfer function is given by

$$T(s) = \beta = -(\omega^2 LC_1 - 1) = \frac{-1}{(\omega^2 LC_2 - 1)} \quad (8.43)$$

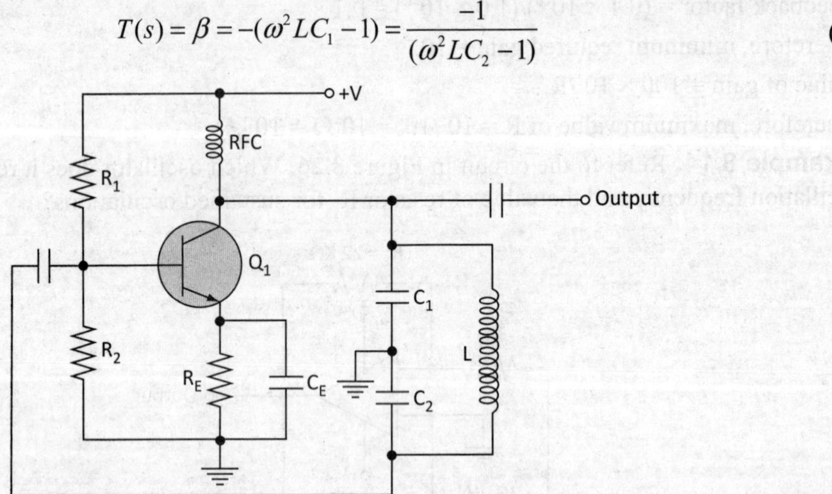

Fig. 8.27: Colpitt oscillator configured around bipolar transistor

Negative sign implies phase shift of 180°. We will subsequently see that for $\omega = 1/\sqrt{[LC_1C_2/(C_1 + C_2)]}$, both $(\omega^2 LC_1 - 1)$ and $(\omega^2 LC_2 - 1)$ are positive.

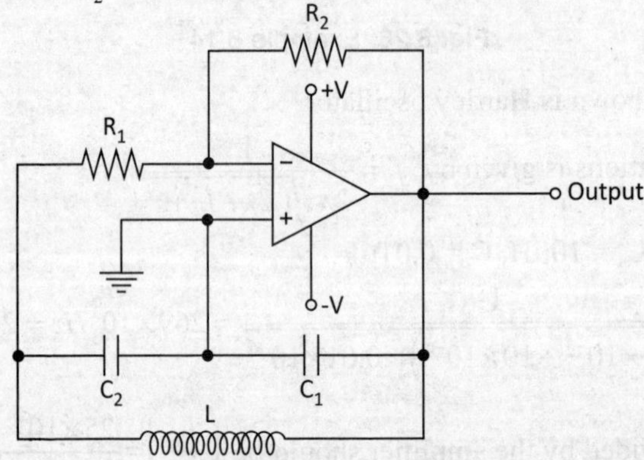

Fig. 8.28: Colpitt oscillator configured around op-amp

Also,

$$|\beta|^2 = \frac{(\omega^2 LC_1 - 1)}{(\omega^2 LC_2 - 1)}$$

For $\omega = 1/\sqrt{[LC_1C_2/(C_1 + C_2)]}$, the magnitude of ? is given by

$$|\beta| = \left(\frac{C_1}{C_2}\right) \quad (8.44)$$

Eqns. (8.43) and (8.44) imply that the feedback network introduces a phase shift of 180° and signal attenuation by a factor of C_1/C_2 at the operating frequency (ω) provided that $\omega = 1/\sqrt{[LC_1C_2/(C_1 + C_2)]}$. This further implies that the amplifier must provide a gain of greater than C_2/C_1 to satisfy the loop gain criterion and a phase shift of 180 to satisfy the loop phase shift criterion.

In practice, the operating frequency is affected by the junction capacitance whose Miller components appear across C_1 and C_2. This problem is overcome in Clapp oscillator configuration, which is discussed next.

Example 8.15: Refer to the oscillator of Figure 8.29. Does the given oscillator circuit resemble any standard oscillator configuration? If yes, identify the oscillator configuration. Also, determine its frequency of oscillations and the required minimum value of amplifier gain.

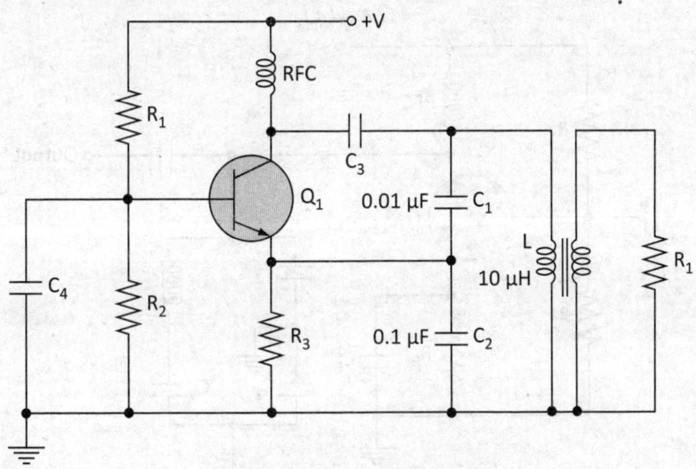

Fig. 8.29: Example 8.15

Solution: If we carefully examine the given circuit, we find that it is Colpitt oscillator configuration.

The feedback circuit in this case is a tank circuit comprising a pair of series connected capacitors C_1 and C_2 and an inductor L.

Also, the amplifier has been wired in common-base configuration. Note that the base terminal is effectively grounded for AC signal through capacitor C_4.

The output in this case appears across series combination of capacitors C_1 and C_2. (The output appeared across C_1 only in the case of Colpitt oscillator configured around common-emitter amplifier). The feedback signal appears across C_2 in both cases.

The feedback factor in this case is therefore given by $[C_1 \times C_2/(C_1 + C_2)]/C_2$, which simplifies to $C_1/(C_1 + C_2)$.

The required minimum value of amplifier gain is therefore $(C_1 + C_2)/C_1$.

Frequency of oscillations can be computed from $f = 1/2\pi\sqrt{LC}$, where $C = C_1 \times C_2/(C_1 + C_2)$.

Now $C = 0.01 \times 10^{-6} \times 0.1 \times 10^{-6}/(0.01 \times 10^{-6} + 0.1 \times 10^{-6}) = 0.009\ \mu F$

Therefore, $f = 1/2\pi\sqrt{(10 \times 10^{-6} \times 0.009 \times 10^{-6})} = 530.5$ kHz

Feedback factor $= 0.01 \times 10^{-6}/(0.01 \times 10^{-6} + 0.1 \times 10^{-6}) = 1/11$

Also, required minimum value of amplifier gain = 11

8.2.2.3 Clapp oscillator

Clapp oscillator circuit is a slight modification of the Colpitt oscillator circuit configuration. The feedback circuit in the case of Clapp oscillator uses an extra capacitor (C_3 in Figure 8.30) in series with the coil. The function of C_3 is to minimize the effect of junction capacitance on the operating frequency.

The operating frequency (f) is given by

$$f = \frac{1}{2\pi} \times \sqrt{\left[\frac{1}{L} \times \left\{\left(\frac{1}{C_1}\right) + \left(\frac{1}{C_2}\right) + \left(\frac{1}{C_3}\right)\right\}\right]} \tag{8.45}$$

If C_3 is chosen to be much smaller than either C_1 or C_2, then expression for frequency (f) simplifies to

$$f = \frac{1}{2\pi\sqrt{LC_3}} \tag{8.46}$$

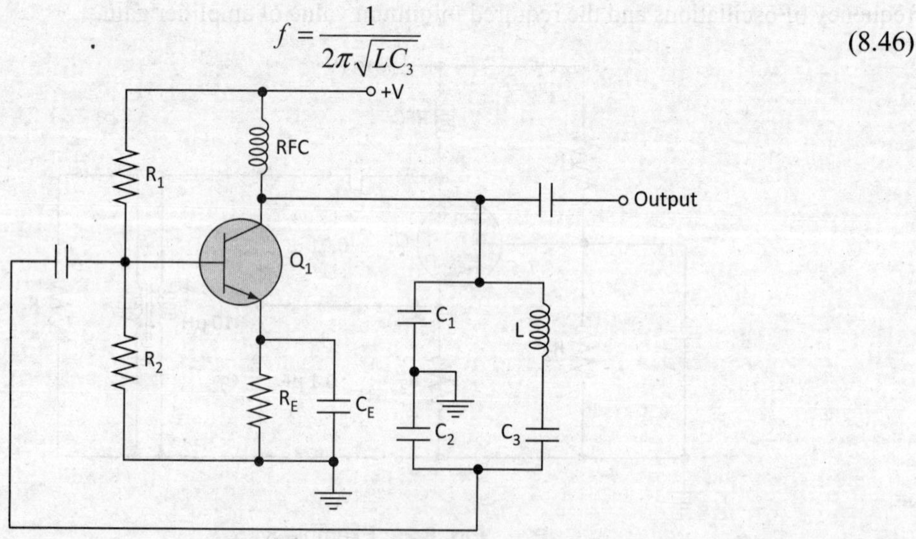

Fig. 8.30: Clapp oscillator

Remember that we still need C_1 and C_2 to provide the required phase shift for the regenerative feedback. Clapp oscillator is preferred over Colpitt oscillator for designing variable frequency oscillators. The adjustment of tuning element (C_3 in Clapp oscillator) does not alter the attenuation factor in Clapp oscillator. The attenuation factor is decided by C_1 and C_2. In the case of Colpitt oscillator, any attempt to vary the frequency by varying either C_1 or C_2 might cause cessation of oscillations over a portion of desired frequency range.

Example 8.16: Refer to Figure 8.31. What is the circuit functioning as?

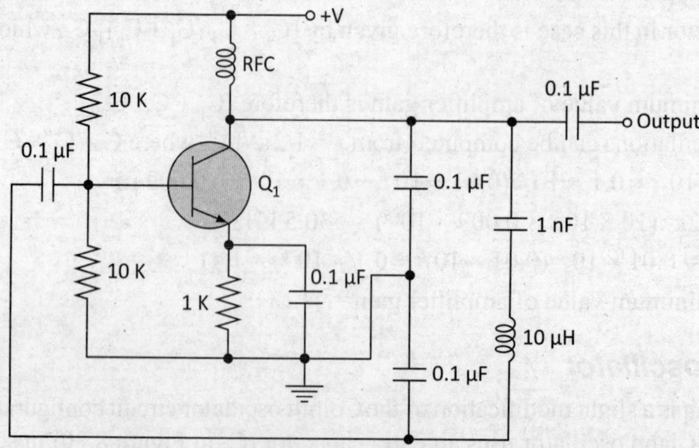

Fig. 8.31: Example 8.16

Solution: As is evident from the circuit of Figure 8.31, it is an oscillator circuit comprising an amplifier and a feedback network that provides a positive feedback. The feedback network employs a split capacitor and a series L-C arrangement across it. The circuit is therefore the Clapp oscillator configuration.

Example 8.17: Determine frequency of oscillations for the oscillator circuit in Figure 8.31?

Solution: The frequency of oscillations is given by $f = 1/2$ LC.

In the present case, C, is given by $1/C = (1/C_1) + (1/C_2) + (1/C_3)$.

Substituting for C_1, C_2 and C_3, we get $1/C = 1/(0.01 \times 10^{-6}) + 1/(0.1 \times 10^{-6}) + 1/(1 \times 10^{-9})$.

This gives C = 0.0009 μF

Therefore, $f = 1/(6.283 \times \sqrt{10 \times 10^{-6} \times 0.0009 \times 10^{-6}}) = 1.677$ MHz

8.2.2.4 Armstrong oscillator

Armstrong oscillator, also known as Meissner oscillator, uses magnetic coupling as means of feeding part of output signal back to input to provide oscillations. It is also called a Tickler oscillator due to use of magnetic coupling between the tickler coil and the coupling coil. In case of a vacuum tube based Armstrong oscillator, tickler coil is the name given to a small coil connected in series with the plate circuit of a vacuum tube and coupled inductively to the grid circuit to provide feedback. In the case of a bipolar junction transistor or an FET, the tickler coil is placed in series with collector or drain circuit and is inductively coupled to the base or gate circuit. A capacitor is placed across either the tickler coil or the coupling coil to form a tank circuit that decides the operating frequency. Figures 8.32(a) and (b) show the basic circuit arrangements in the two cases with n-channel junction FET used as the active device. Biasing components are omitted for the sake of simplicity.

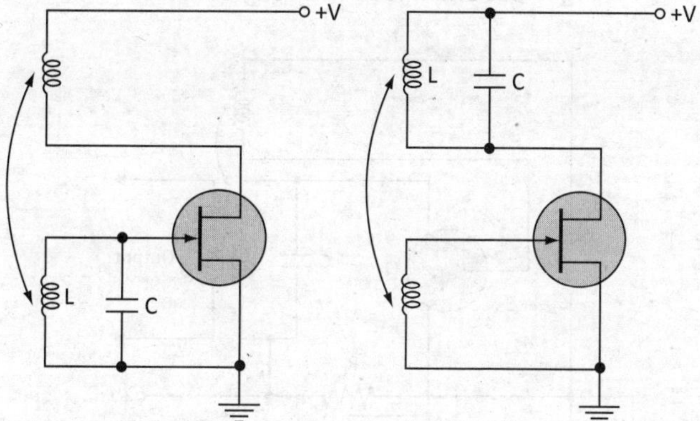

Fig. 8.32: Basic Armstrong oscillator configurations

The frequency of oscillation is primarily determined by the tank circuit and is given by

$$f = \frac{1}{2\pi\sqrt{LC}} \quad (8.47)$$

Here L is the inductance of the coupling coil in the case of circuit shown in Figure 8.32(a) and that of the tickler coil in the case of circuit shown in Figure 8.32(b). In practice, the frequency of oscillations is slightly different from the one computed by using Eqn. (8.47) because of stray capacitances, loading of tank circuit, etc. The feedback factor in this case is given by ratio of mutual inductance between the two coils to the inductance in the tank circuit. Minimum gain required to start oscillations is reciprocal of the feedback factor.

Figure 8.33 shows the circuit schematic of Armstrong oscillator configured around a bipolar transistor. The transistor is wired in common-emitter configuration and thus provides a phase shift of 180°. Another 180° phase shift is provided by magnetic coupling as indicated by placement of dots. Operating frequency is decided by tank circuit comprising capacitor C and inductance of transformer primary coil. Note that Armstrong oscillator of Figure 8.33 is a shunt-fed oscillator. The circuit schematic of a series-fed Armstrong oscillator would look like the one shown in Figure 8.34.

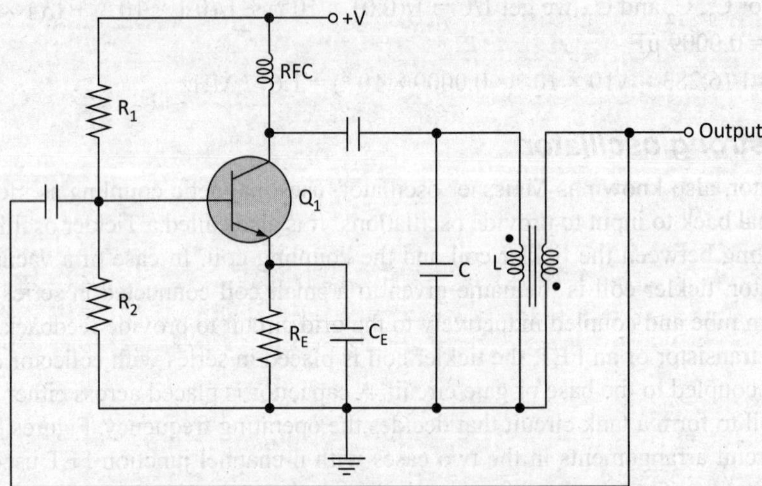

Fig. 8.33: Shunt-fed Armstrong oscillator

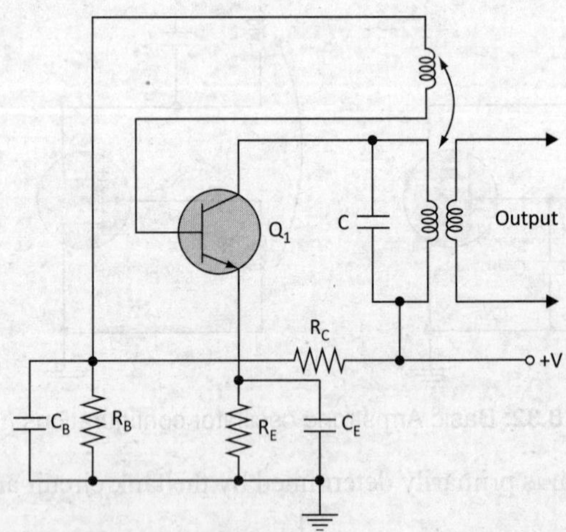

Fig. 8.34: Series-fed Armstrong oscillator

Example 8.18: Refer to Figure 8.35. Determine the frequency of oscillations and the minimum amplifier gain required to start oscillations if the value of Q is very high. How would the oscillation frequency change if the loaded Q-factor of the tank circuit were given to be 10?

Solution: When Q is high, frequency of oscillations,

$f = 1/2\pi\sqrt{LC} = 1/(6.283\sqrt{3.6 \times 10^{-6} \times 0.1 \times 10^{-6}} = 265.3$ kHz

Feedback factor = $0.1 \times 10^{-6}/3.6 \times 10^{-6} = 1/36$

Therefore, minimum value of amplifier gain required to start oscillations = 36

Q-factor of the tank circuit = 5

Frequency of oscillation will reduce by a factor equal to $[\sqrt{Q^2/(Q^2 + 1)}]$.

Therefore, new frequency of oscillations will be $265.3 \times 10^3 \times [\sqrt{10^2/(10^2 + 1)}] = 263.98$ kHz

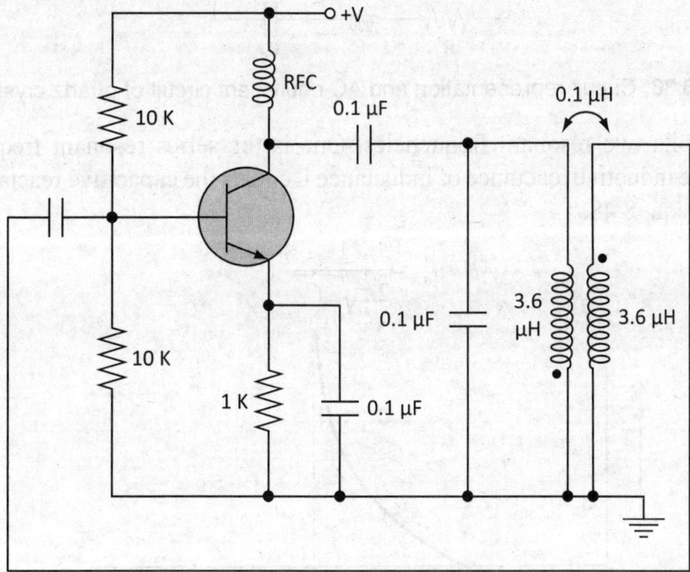

Fig. 8.35: Example 8.18

8.2.3 Crystal oscillator

In crystal oscillators, crystal resonator provides the electrical equivalent of frequency-selective network. Crystal oscillators are the most stable of the three types due to their extremely high rate of change of phase with frequency at the operating frequency ($d\phi/d\omega$). Crystal oscillators are not practical at lower operating frequencies due to their size, weight and cost restrictions.

In the case of a crystal oscillator, a quartz crystal with the desired value of resonant frequency forms part of the frequency-selective feedback network. Crystal oscillator is the natural choice when the accuracy and stability of oscillation frequency is of paramount importance. In order to understand the operation of crystal oscillators, it is important that we first study and analyze the AC equivalent circuit of the crystal as a component.

8.2.3.1 AC Equivalent Circuit

Figure 8.36 shows the circuit representation and AC equivalent circuit of the quartz crystal. R, L and C_S, respectively, represent the resistance, inductance and capacitance of the piezoelectric crystal element. C_M represents the mounting capacitance. It is in fact the capacitance due to the parallel-plate capacitor formed by the connecting electrodes and the piezoelectric element constituting the dielectric. Typically, R is in the range of few hundreds of ohms to a few kilo-ohms; L is of the order of few tens of milli-henries to few Henries, CS is a very small fraction of a pico-farad and C_M is few pico-farads. The Q-factor of the crystal is given by $Q = \omega L/R = 1/\omega C_S R$.

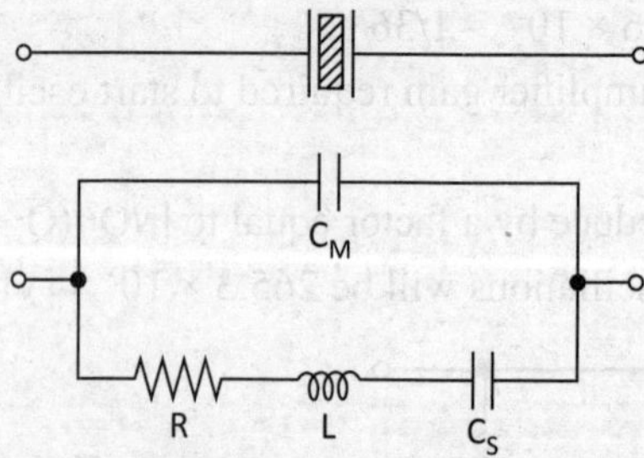

Fig. 8.36: Circuit representation and AC equivalent circuit of quartz crystal

The crystal exhibits two resonant frequencies. One is the series resonant frequency f_S. It is the frequency at which the inductive reactance of inductance L equals the capacitive reactance of capacitance C_S. It is expressed as eqn. 8.48.

$$f_s = \frac{1}{2\pi\sqrt{LC_s}} \tag{8.48}$$

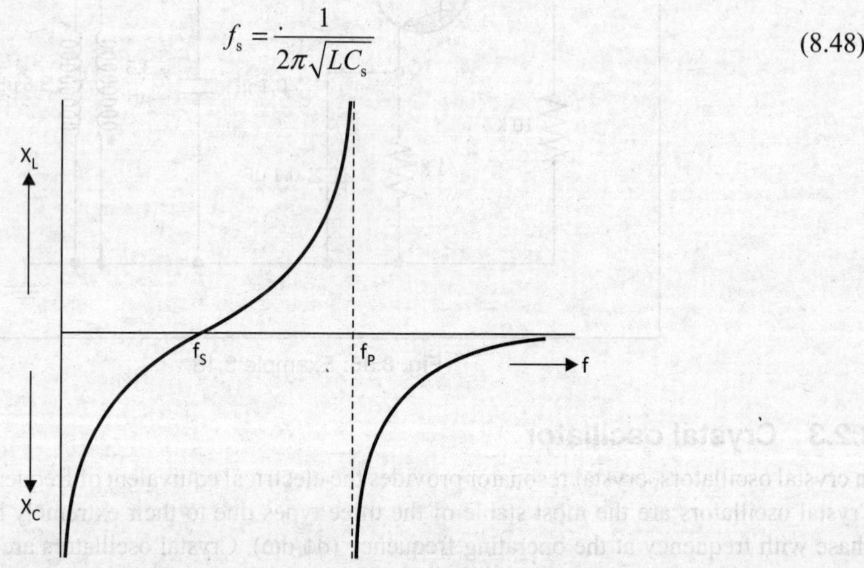

Fig. 8.37: Reactance versus frequency plot

Figure 8.37 shows the plot of reactance versus frequency for the equivalent circuit of Figure 8.36. Quite understandably, the impedance is a capacitive reactance below the series resonant frequency and an inductive reactance above it. The second resonant frequency called the parallel resonant frequency (f_P) occurs at a value where the inductive reactance equals the capacitive reactance due to equivalent capacitance of the tank circuit. Parallel resonance occurs at a frequency where the circulating loop current is at its maximum. Since circulating loop current flows through series combination of C_S and C_M, therefore the equivalent capacitance of the parallel tuned circuit is given by eqn. 8.49.

$$C_P = \frac{C_M \times C_S}{(C_M + C_S)} \tag{8.49}$$

Parallel resonant frequency is given by eqn. 8.50.

$$f_p = \frac{1}{2\pi\sqrt{LC_p}} \tag{8.50}$$

Since C_S is much smaller than C_M, C_P is only marginally less than C_S with the result that f_S and f_P are very close to each other. The apparent difference between f_S and f_P as shown in Figure 8.38 is an exaggerated one to explain the operation of the crystal.

The two resonant frequencies described in the previous paragraph are the fundamental resonant frequencies. Remember that the specified crystal frequency is between f_S and f_P. This area of frequencies between f_S and f_P is known as the area of usual parallel resonance or simply parallel resonance. A crystal can also resonate at harmonics of the fundamental frequency called overtones. The fundamental resonant frequency of the crystal is usually limited to less than 30 MHz due to the smallest physical dimension the crystal can be cut to. Operation in the overtone mode allows stable output at much higher frequencies.

8.2.3.2 Extremely High Frequency Stability

The extremely high frequency stability of a crystal oscillator comes from its extremely stable values of inductance and capacitance and a very high value of its Q-factor. Remember that the oscillation frequency of an LC oscillator in addition to the values of L and C also depends upon the Q-factor of the LC circuit. The generalized expression is given by

$$f = \left[1/(2\pi\sqrt{LC})\right] \times \sqrt{Q^2/(Q^2+1)} \tag{8.51}$$

A very high value of Q-factor in the case of quartz crystal ensures that the oscillation frequency exclusively depends upon the operational stability of crystal elements. As a component, it is extremely stable.

A high value of Q-factor also produces a high value of rate of change of phase with respect to frequency ($d\theta/d\omega$), where θ represents phase. It implies that even infinitesimally small change in ω will produce a sufficient change in θ to restore the frequency to the original value. Quartz crystal has a Q-factor approaching tens of thousands and as a component, it is extremely stable.

8.2.3.3 Crystal Oscillator Circuits

As is evident from the impedance versus frequency characteristics of the crystal, depending upon the circuit characteristics, it can act like a capacitor, an inductor, a series-tuned circuit or a parallel-tuned circuit. There are a large number of crystal oscillator circuit configurations depending upon the mode in which the crystal is used. In one of the categories of crystal oscillator circuits, crystal is connected in series with the LC tank circuit in the feedback path. Each of the LC oscillator circuits (Armstrong, Hartley, Colpitt and Clapp) can be configured as a crystal-controlled oscillator by connecting a crystal in series with the tank circuit.

Figure 8.38 shows one such oscillator circuit. It is the modified Colpitt oscillator circuit. The circuit operates as follows. The LC tank circuit is tuned to the series resonant frequency of the crystal. The crystal offers minimum impedance at the series resonant frequency and thus allows the feedback signal to reach the input with practically no additional attenuation. A slight variation in frequency increases the impedance of the crystal to a very large value. The feedback signal is attenuated to an extent that loop gain criterion is not met and the oscillations stop. Thus the oscillator can oscillate only at the resonant frequency of the crystal, thus significantly improving the frequency stability of the oscillator. Armstrong, Hartley and Clapp oscillator circuits can similarly be modified by introducing a quartz crystal in series with the respective tank circuits.

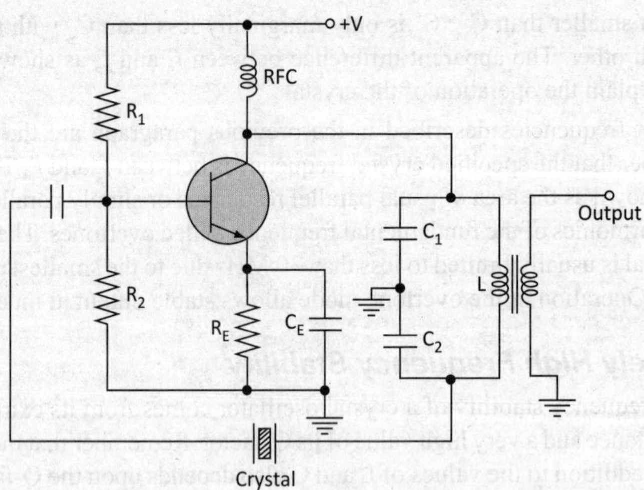

Fig. 8.38: Crystal controlled Colpitt oscillator

Figure 8.39 shows another variation of crystal-controlled Colpitt oscillator circuit. Here crystal forms a part of the tank circuit. The crystal acts like an inductor that resonates with capacitors C_1 and C_2. The resonant frequency is somewhere between the series and parallel resonant frequencies of the quartz crystal. Figure 8.40 shows a slightly modified Colpitt oscillator circuit that uses common-base amplifier configuration instead of common-emitter configuration used in the oscillator circuit of Figure 8.39. Common-base amplifier configuration allows operation at relatively higher oscillation frequencies.

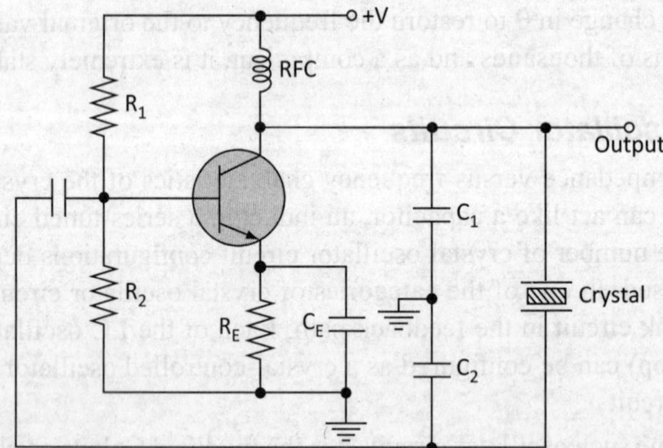

Fig. 8.39: Crystal-based Colpitt oscillator with common-emitter amplifier

Yet another application of Colpitt oscillator configuration is found in what is popularly known as *Pierce oscillator*. Figure 8.41 shows the basic circuit implementation of a Pierce oscillator. An FET (JFET or MOSFET) is used as the active device and the crystal along with the inter-electrode capacitances C_{gs} and C_{ds} constitute the feedback network. Pierce oscillator of Figure 8.41 is redrawn in Figure 8.42 to demonstrate its resemblance to Colpitt oscillator configuration. The oscillation frequency is the parallel resonant frequency of the crystal and the inter-electrode capacitances do not play any role in determining oscillation frequency. The feedback factor and therefore the required amplifier gain are determined by C_{gs} and C_{ds}. In fact, it is observed that the oscillator stops oscillating as the oscillation frequency is reduced to below about 2 MHz due to insufficient feedback. In a situation like this, it becomes imperative to have external capacitors between gate-source and drain-source terminals. Pierce oscillator works very well in VHF and UHFfrequency ranges. Purpose of putting radio-frequency choke (RFC) is to prevent the high-frequency output from getting grounded through drain power supply.

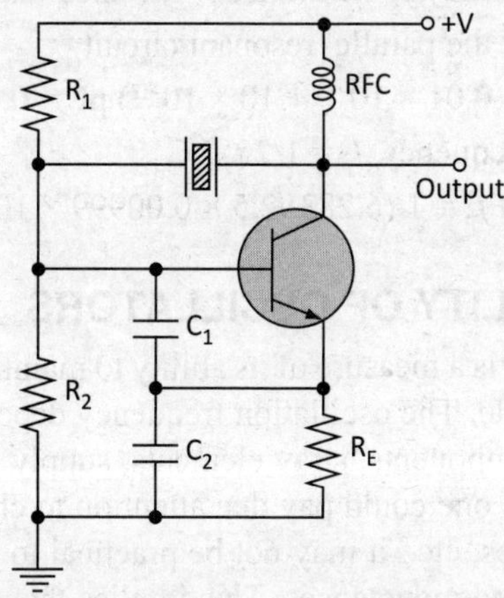

Fig. 8.40: Crystal-based Colpitt oscillator with common-base amplifier

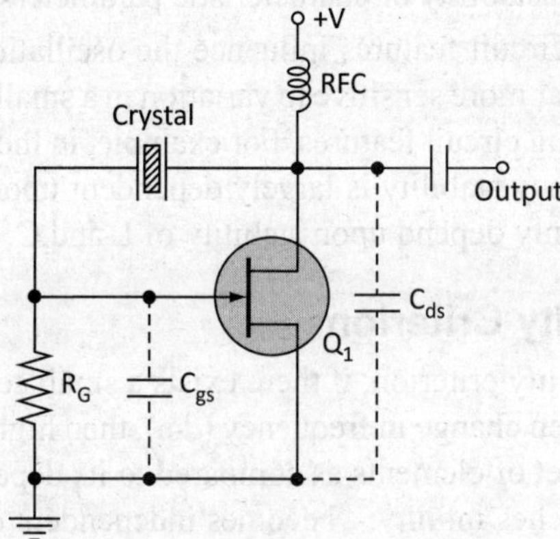

Fig. 8.41: Basic Pierce oscillator

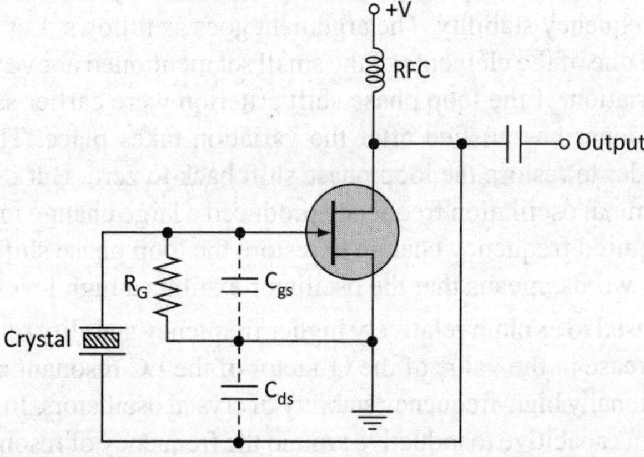

Fig. 8.42: Pierce oscillator with inter-electrode capacitances

Example 8.19: A quartz crystal is characterized by L = 2.5 H, R = 1 kΩ, C_S = 0.01 pF and C_P = 10 pF. Determine the series and parallel resonant frequencies of the crystal.

Solution: Series resonant frequency, $f_S = 1/2\pi\sqrt{LC_S} = 1/(6.283\sqrt{2.5 \times 0.01 \times 10^{-12}})$ Hz = 1.006614 MHz

Equivalent capacitance CP for the parallel resonant circuit

$C_P = 0.01 \times 10^{-12} \times 10 \times 10^{-12}/(0.01 \times 10^{-12} + 10 \times 10^{-12})$ pF = 0.00999 pF

Therefore, parallel resonant frequency, $f_P = 1/2\pi\sqrt{LC_P}$.

Substituting the values, we get $f_P = 1/(6.283\sqrt{2.5 \times 0.00999 \times 10^{-12}})$ Hz = 1.007117 MHz

8.3 FREQUENCY STABILITY OF OSCILLATORS

Frequency stability of an oscillator is a measure of its ability to maintain a constant oscillation frequency for as long a time period as possible. The oscillation frequency depends upon a large number of circuit features, which include circuit components, stray elements, supply voltages, characteristic parameters of active devices and so on. While one could pay due attention to choice of circuit components, use of clean and regulated supply voltages, etc., it may not be practical to identify location and estimation of magnitude of stray capacitances and inductances. This implies that it would be extremely hard to take remedial measures to counter the frequency drift caused by these elements. Equally impractical would be neutralizing the ill effects of instability of characteristic parameters of active devices.

Fortunately though, not all circuit features influence the oscillation frequency to the same extent. Oscillation frequency is usually far more sensitive to variation in a small number of circuit features than it is to the large number of remaining circuit features. For example, in the case of RC phase shift and Wien bridge oscillator circuits, frequency stability is largely dependent upon stability of R and C. Similarly, in an LC oscillator, it would mainly depend upon stability of L and C.

8.3.1 Frequency Stability Criterion

According to the frequency stability criterion, if there exists a small set of elements which introduces a large phase change ($d\theta$) for a given change in frequency ($d\omega$), then higher the value of $d\omega/d\omega$, more will be the dependence of ω on this set of elements as compared to its dependence on other circuit features. In the limit when $d\theta/d\omega$ approaches infinity; becomes independent of all other features and depends only on this small set of elements.

It can also be argued that $d\theta/d\omega$ is a measure of frequency stability of the oscillator and a higher value of $d\theta/d\omega$ means higher frequency stability. The argument goes as follows. Let us assume that one of the circuit features other than one of the elements of the small set mentioned above undergoes a variation. As a consequence of this variation, if the loop phase shift criterion were earlier satisfied at the operational frequency, it would no longer be satisfied after the variation takes place. The operational frequency must therefore shift in order to restore the loop phase shift back to zero. But if there were a small set of elements which at the nominal osciilation frequency produced a large change in phase for a given change in frequency, then the required frequency change to restore the loop phase shift condition would also be very small. This, in other words, means that the oscillator exhibits a high level of frequency stability.

This concept can be used to explain relatively higher frequency stability of LC oscillators in general, which improves with increase in the value of the Q-factor of the LC resonant circuit. It can similarly be used to explain the exceptionally high-frequency stability of crystal oscillators. In the case of LC oscillators, the reactance changes from capacitive to inductive around the frequency of resonance. Higher the Q-factor of the LC circuit, more abrupt is this change of phase. This further implies that higher Q-factor leads to a higher dθ/dω and consequently higher frequency stability. The frequency stability can be quantified by computing the magnitude of dθ/dω at the nominal oscillation frequency by differentiating the expression for the phase angle for the transfer function of the feedback network with respect to ω.

Example 8.20: Derive the relevant expression to prove that the Wien bridge oscillator exhibits better frequency stability at relatively lower operating frequencies and that the frequency stability deteriorates with increase in frequency.

Solution: The expression for phase angle (θ) as a function of frequency (ω) in the case of Wien bridge oscillator can be written as $\theta = 90° - \tan^{-1}[3\omega RC/(1 - \omega^2R^2C^2)]$. This equation is obtained by substituting $R_1 = R_2 = R$ and $C_1 = C_2 = C$ in eqn. (8.29).

Phase angle, $\theta = 90° - \tan^{-1}\left[\{\omega(R_1C_1 + R_2C_2 + R_2C_1)\}/\left(1 - \omega^2 R_1C_1R_2C_2\right)\right]$

The above equation can also be written as $\theta = \tan^{-1}[(1 - \omega^2R^2C^2)/3\omega RC]$.

In general $(d/dx)(\tan^{-1}u) = [1/(1 + u^2)] \times du/dx$

Using this formula, dθ/dω = KRC, where K is a constant.

The above expression implies that product RC needs to have a higher value in order to have higher dθ/dω and therefore higher stability.

Higher RC means lower oscillation frequency as the oscillation frequency of a Wien Bridge oscillator is given by $f = 1/(2\pi RC)$.

This proves that the Wien bridge oscillator exhibits better frequency stability at lower oscillation frequency and that the frequency stability deteriorates as the frequency of oscillations increases.

8.4 VOLTAGE CONTROLLED OSCILLATOR

A voltage controlled oscillator (VCO) is an oscillator circuit in which the frequency of oscillations can be varied by an applied DC control voltage. This is achieved by having a voltage-dependent capacitor commonly known as varicap or a varactor diode as a part of the frequency-determining tank circuit.

Hartley and Clapp oscillator configurations are particularly suited to building VCOs as in both cases, the frequency-determining LC circuit has a single capacitor and tuning can be easily done by replacing this capacitor by a varactor diode. Figure 8.43 shows the basic voltage-controlled Hartley oscillator configured around a junction FET. A similar circuit could be configured around a bipolar transistor also. In the circuit shown in Figure 8.43, the amplifier is configured as common-drain amplifier with voltage gain slightly less than unity. In this case, the feedback factor is greater than 1 as the output signal appears across portion of the coil between source terminal and ground and the feedback signal appears across the whole of the coil winding.

Use of a single varactor diode is usually discouraged. This is because of the reason that for small values of DC control voltages, the varactor diode may start conducting at either of the peaks of the RF signal depending upon how it is connected in the circuit. Conducting diode reduces the Q-factor of the tank circuit and deteriorates the phase noise performance. Back-to-back connection of two varactor diodes overcomes this problem.

Another application of VCO is in fine tuning of crystal oscillators. The oscillator frequency may be varied by few tens of parts per million as the high value of Q-factor in the case of crystals allows pulling only over a small range. Fine tuning of crystal oscillator frequency may be needed to adjust output frequency to either match or be an exact multiple of some external reference. Voltage-controlled fine tuning of crystal oscillators may also be employed in temperature-compensated VCOs (TCVCXO) to correct the temperature dependence of oscillator frequency.

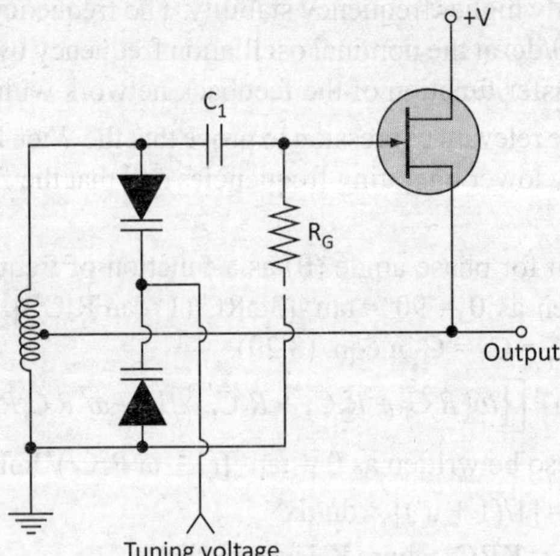

Fig. 8.43: Voltage-controlled Hartley oscillator

8.5 NON-SINUSOIDAL OSCILLATORS

Non-sinusoidal oscillators are oscillators which generate waveforms other than sinusoidal waveform. They produce waveforms such as square, rectangular, sawtooth or triangle wave.Astable multivibrators produce square or rectangular waveforms. Output of a square wave or rectangular wave oscillators when connected to integrators produce triangular waveforms or sawtooth waveforms (under special conditions). Multivibrators are described in this section with particular emphasis on astable multivibrators. The triangular and sawtooth wave generators have been covered in the chapters on op-amps.

8.5.1 Multivibrators

A multivibrator like the familiar sinusoidal oscillator is a circuit with regenerative feedback with the difference that it produces a pulsed output. There are three basic types of multivibrator circuits. These include Bistable multivibrator, monostable multivibrator and astable multivibrator.

8.5.1.1 Bistable multivibrator

A Bistable multivibrator circuit is the one in which both LOW and HIGH output states are stable. Irrespective of the logic status of the output, LOW or HIGH, it stays in that state unless a change is induced by applying an appropriate trigger pulse. As we will see subsequently, the operation of a Bistable multivibrator is identical to that of a flip-flop. Figure 8.44(a) shows the basic Bistable multivibrator circuit. This is the fixed-bias type of Bistable multivibrator. Other configurations are self-bias type and the emitter-coupled type. However, operational principle of all types is the same.

In the circuit arrangement of Figure 8.44(a), it can be proved that both the transistors (Q_1 and Q_2) cannot be simultaneously ON or OFF. If Q_1 is ON, the regenerative feedback ensures that Q_2 is OFF and when Q_1 is OFF, the feedback drives transistor Q2to the ON state. In order to vindicate this statement, let us assume that both Q_1 and Q_2 are conducting simultaneously. Owing to slight circuit imbalance, which is always there, collector current in one transistor will always be greater than that in the other. Let us assume that $I_{c2} > I_{c1}$. Lesser I_{c1} means a higher V_{c1}. Since V_{c1} is coupled to Q_2-base, rise in V_{c1} leads to increase in Q_2-basevoltage. Increase in Q_2-basevoltage results in increase in I_{c2} and associated reduction in V_{c2}. Reduction in V_{c2} leads to reduction of Q_1-base voltage and an associated fall in I_{c1} with the result that V_{c1}

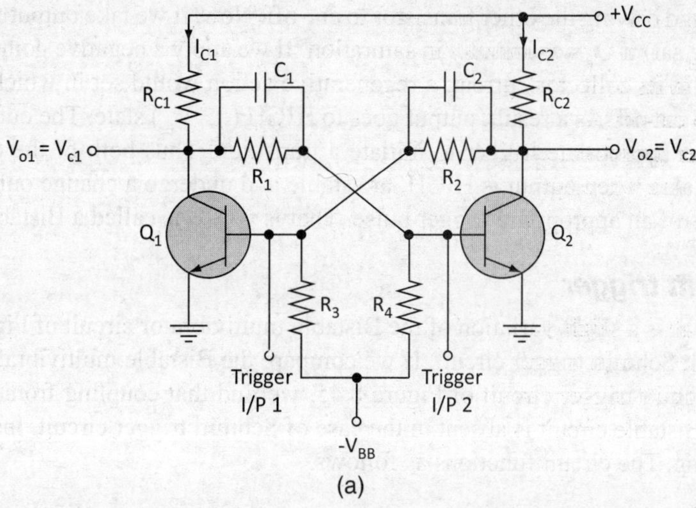

(a)

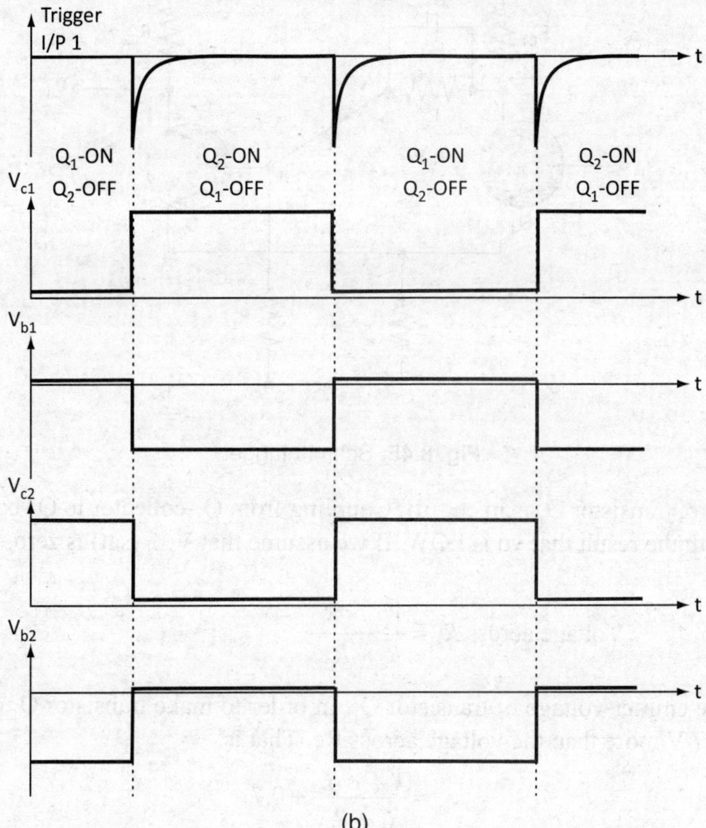

(b)

Fig. 8.44: (a) Bistable multivibrator (b) timing waveforms for the Bistable multivibrator of Figure 8.44(a)

increases further. Thus a slight circuit imbalance has initiated a regenerative action which culminates in transistor Q_1 going to cut-off and transistor Q_2 getting driven to saturation. To sum up, whenever there is a tendency of one of the transistors to conduct more than the other, it will end up with that transistor going to saturation and driving the other transistor to cut-off. Now, if we take output from Q_1 collector, it will be LOW (= V_{CE1} sat) if Q_1 was initially in saturation. If we apply a negative going trigger to Q_1-base to cause a decrease in its collector current, a regenerative action would set in which would drive Q_2 to saturation and Q_1 to cut-off. As a result, output goes to HIGH (= $+V_{cc}$) state. The output will stay HIGH till we apply another appropriate trigger to initiate a transition. Thus both of the output states, when output is LOW and also when output is HIGH, are stable and undergo a change only when a transition is induced by means of an appropriate trigger pulse. That is why it is called a Bistable multivibrator.

8.5.1.2 Schmitt trigger

Schmitt trigger circuit is a slight variation of the Bistable multivibrator circuit of Figure 8.44(a). Figure 8.45 shows the basic Schmitt trigger circuit. If we compare the Bistable multivibrator circuit of Figure 8.44(a) with the Schmitt trigger circuit of Figure 8.45, we find that coupling from Q_2-collector to Q_1-base in the case of Bistable circuit is absent in the case of Schmitt trigger circuit. Instead, resistance Re provides the coupling. The circuit functions as follows.

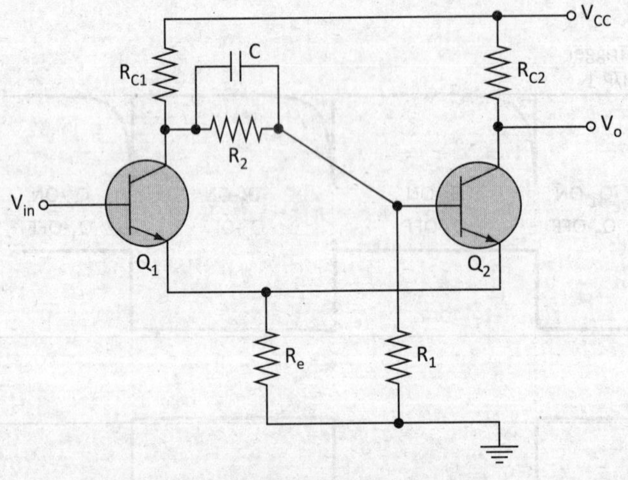

Fig. 8.45: Schmitt trigger

When vinis zero, transistor Q_1 is in cut-off. Coupling from Q_1-collector to Q_2-base drives transistor Q_2 to saturation with the result that vo is LOW. If we assume that V_{CE2} (sat) is zero, then voltage across Re is given by

$$\text{Voltage across } R_e = \frac{V_{CC} \times R_e}{R_e + R_{C2}} \tag{8.52}$$

This is also the emitter voltage of transistor Q_1. In order to make transistor Q_1 conduct, v_{in} must at least be equal to 0.7 V more than the voltage across Re. That is,

$$v_{in} = \frac{V_{CC} \times R_e}{R_e + R_{C2}} + 0.7 \tag{8.53}$$

When vinexceeds this voltage, Q_1 starts conducting. The regenerative action again drives Q_2 to the cut-off. The output goes to the HIGH state. Voltage across Rechanges to a new value given by

$$\text{Voltage across } R_e = \frac{V_{CC} \times R_e}{R_e + R_{C1}} \tag{8.54}$$

Q_1 will continue to conduct as long as vin is equal to or greater than the value given by

$$v_{in} = \frac{V_{CC} \times R_e}{R_e + R_{C1}} + 0.7 \tag{8.55}$$

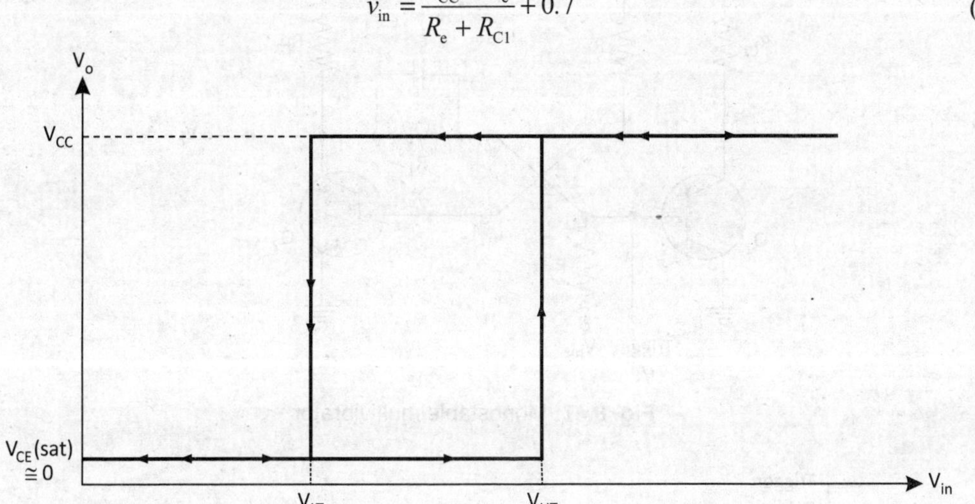

Fig. 8.46: Transfer characteristics of the Schmitt trigger circuit

If v_{in} falls below this value, Q_1 tends to come out of saturation and conduct less heavily. The regenerative action does the rest with the process culminating in Q1going to cut-off and Q_2 to saturation. Thus the state of output (HIGH or LOW) depends upon input voltage level. The HIGH and LOW states of the output correspond to two distinct input levels given by eqns. (8.53) and (8.55) and therefore the values of R_{C1}, R_{C2}, Reand V_{CC}. Schmitt trigger circuit of Figure 8.45 therefore exhibits hysteresis. Figure 8.46 shows the transfer characteristics of the Schmitt trigger circuit. The lower trip point (V_{LT})and upper trip point (V_{UT})of these characteristics are, respectively, given by eqns. (8.56) and (8.57):

$$V_{LT} = \frac{V_{CC} \times R_e}{R_e + R_{C1}} + 0.7 \tag{8.56}$$

$$V_{UT} = \frac{V_{CC} \times R_e}{R_e + R_{C2}} + 0.7 \tag{8.57}$$

8.5.1.3 Monostable multivibrator

A monostable multivibrator, also known as monoshot, is the one in which one of the states is stable and the other is quasi-stable. The circuit is initially in the stable state. It goes to the quasi-stable state when appropriately triggered. It stays in the quasi-stable state for a certain time period, after which it comes back to the stable state. Figure 8.47 shows the basic monostable multivibrator circuit. The circuit functions as follows. Initially, transistor Q_2 is in saturation as it gets its base bias from $+V_{CC}$ through R. Coupling from Q_2-collector to Q_1-base ensures that Q_1 is in cut-off. When a positive trigger pulse of short duration and sufficient magnitude is applied to the base of transistor Q_1, Q_1 starts conducting. As the voltage across the capacitor C cannot change instantly, negative voltage is applied to the base of transistor Q_2 and it turns OFF. Therefore, the output goes to the HIGH state. Since there is no direct coupling from Q_1-collector to Q_2-base, which is necessary for a regenerative process to set in, Q_1 is not necessarily in saturation. However, it conducts some current. The Q_1-collector voltage falls by $I_{c1}R_{c1}$and Q_2-base voltage falls by the same amount as voltage across a capacitor (C in this case) cannot change instantaneously.

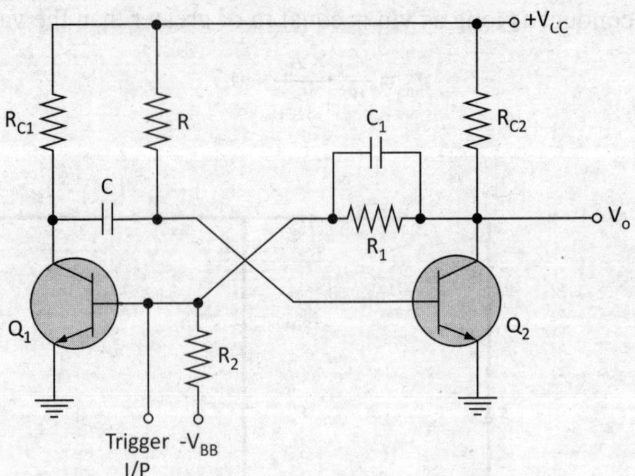

Fig. 8.47: Monostable multivibrator

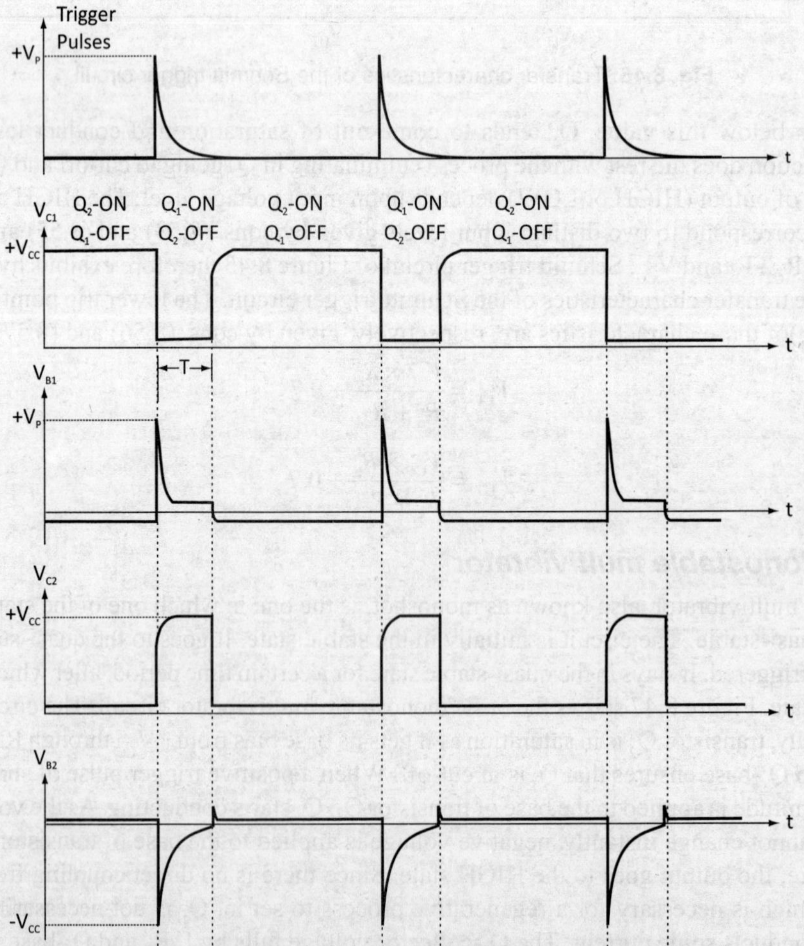

Fig. 8.48: Timing waveforms of monostable multivibrator

To sum up, the moment we applied the trigger, Q_2 went to cut-off and Q_1 started conducting. But now there is a path for capacitor C to charge from V_{CC} through R and the conducting transistor. The polarity of voltage across C is such that Q_2-base potential rises. The moment Q_2-base voltage exceeds the cut-in voltage, it turns Q_2ON, which due to coupling through R_1 turns Q_1 OFF. And we are back to the original state, the stable state. Figure 8.48 shows the relevant timing diagrams. Whenever, we trigger the circuit into the other state, it does not stay there permanently and returns back after a time period that depends upon R and C. Larger the time constant (RC), larger is the time for which it stays in the other state called quasi-stable state. The width of the quasi-stable state is given by

$$T = 0.693 \times R \times C \tag{8.58}$$

8.5.1.4 Astable multivibrator

In the case of an astable multivibrator, neither of the two states is stable. Both output states are quasi-stable. The output switches from one state to the other and the circuit functions like a free-running square wave oscillator. Figure 8.49 shows the basic astable multivibrator circuit.

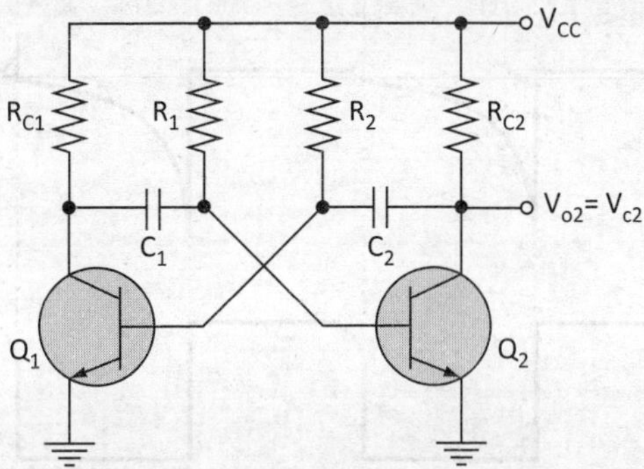

Fig. 8.49: Astable multivibrator

Value of resistors R_1 and R_2 are typically 10 times the value of R_{C1} and R_{C2}, respectively. It can be proved that in this type of circuit, neither of the output states is stable. Both states, LOW as well as HIGH, are quasi-stable. The time periods for which the output remains LOW and HIGH depends upon R_2C_2 and R_1C_1 time constants, respectively. For $R_1C_1=R_2C_2$, the output is a symmetrical square waveform. The circuit functions as follows. When power is applied, one transistor will conduct more than the other because of some circuit imbalances. Let us assume that transistor Q_1 conducts more than transistor Q_2. The regenerative action will force transistor Q_1 to saturation and transistor Q_2 to cut-off. Capacitor C_2 will charge rapidly to V_{CC} through resistor R_{C2} and the base-emitter junction of transistor Q_1. This results in momentary increase in the base voltage of transistor Q_1. Capacitor C_1 had previously charged through resistor R_{C1} upto V_{CC} when transistor Q_2 was conducting. Now when Q_1 is conducting, C_1 discharges through R_1 and Q_1. The initial pulse of discharge current from C_1through R_1 results in a negative pulse at the base of transistor Q_2 as shown in Figure 8.50. This turns transistor Q_2 OFF and the output goes to HIGH state. Transistor Q_1 keeps conducting from V_{CC} through resistor R_2. The OFF-time of transistor Q_2 depends upon the time constant R_1C_1. When the base voltage of the transistor reaches the base-switching voltage, transistor Q_2 is no longer in cut-off and starts to conduct allowing capacitor C_1 to be recharged rapidly through resistor R_{C1}. This results in momentary increase in positive voltage at the base of the transistor Q_2 leading to its fast turning ON. Therefore, the output goes to the LOW state. Now capacitor C_2 discharges through transistor Q_2 and resistor R_2. The initial pulse of discharge current from C_2 through R_2 makes the base of transistor Q_1 very negative. This turns OFF Q_1. Q_1 is held in the OFF state depending upon the time constant R_2C_2 after which Q_1 begins to conduct. This process continues and due to both the couplings (Q_1-collector to Q_2-base and Q_2-collectorto Q_1-base) being capacitive, neither of the states is stable. The rounding off in the rising edge of $V_{C1}$is because of the voltage drop across resistor R_{C1} while capacitor C_1 is recharging. Similarly the rounding off in the rising edge of V_{C2} is because of the voltage drop across resistor R_{C2} while capacitor C_2 is recharging. Figure 8.50 shows the relevant timing diagrams.

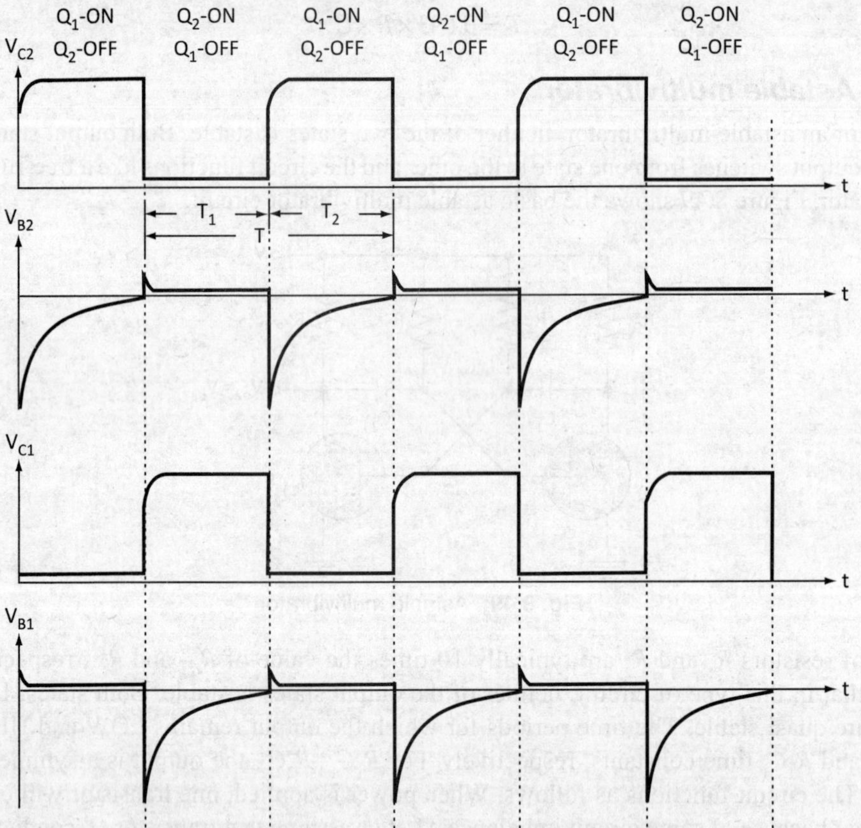

Fig. 8.50: Timing waveforms of astable multivibrator

The base voltage of transistor Q_2 during discharge of capacitor C_1 is given by:

$$v_{B2} = V_{CC} - i_{C1}R_1 \tag{8.59}$$

Since, the capacitor charges to approximately V_{CC}, the initial value of current (i_{C1}) is

$$i_{C1} = \frac{V_{CC} + V_{CC}}{R_1} = \frac{2V_{CC}}{R_1}$$

The current decays exponentially with a time constant of R_1C_1. Therefore, the voltage v_{B2} is given by

$$v_{B2} = V_{CC} - 2V_{CC}e^{-t/R_1C_1} \tag{8.60}$$

The base-switching voltage for silicon transistors is 0.5 V and that for germanium transistors is 0.2 V, which is very small as compared to the VCC voltage. Therefore, it can be assumed that the transistor will switch when $v_{B2} = 0$ V. The time required to switch ON transistor Q_2, that is, the OFF time of the transistor Q_2 (T_2) is given by

$$0 = V_{CC} - 2V_{CC}e^{-T_2/R_1C_1}$$

Therefore,

$$T_2 = R_1C_1 \ln 2 = 0.694R_1C_1 \tag{8.61}$$

T_2 is also the ON time of transistor Q_1. Similarly, the ON time (T_1) of transistor Q_2 which is equal to the OFF time of transistor Q_1 is given by

$$T_1 = R_2C_2 \ln 2 = 0.694R_2C_2 \tag{8.62}$$

The total time period of the wave is T which is given by

$$T = T_1 + T_2 = 0.694(R_1C_1 + R_2C_2) \tag{8.63}$$

For $R_1 = R_2 = R$ and $C_1 = C = C$, the time period is equal to and the frequency (*f*) is given by

$$f = \frac{1}{1.388RC}$$

8.5.2 Blocking oscillator

A blocking oscillator is basically a transformer coupled pulse generator which could work both in the monostable as well as in the astable mode. Figure 8.51 shows the basic blocking oscillator that works in the astable mode. Transistor Q gets its base bias through resistor R. The transistor which is connected in the CE configuration provides thephase inversion and if the transformer polarities are so chosen as to provide another phase inversion, there are conditions for positive feedback. When the transistor conducts, there are oscillations at the resonant frequency of the primary winding. If the amount of positive feedback is very high, the oscillations will build up very rapidly. There is a burst of current in the base, which charges the capacitor in a direction to drive the transistor to cut-off. The capacitor starts discharging through R. After it has discharged to an extent that it cannot keep the transistor in cut-off, the transistor conducts again followed by burst of base current, which discharges the capacitor again to drive the transistor to cut-off and the process continues. The natural frequency of such an oscillator also called the relaxation oscillator is (n+1/RC).

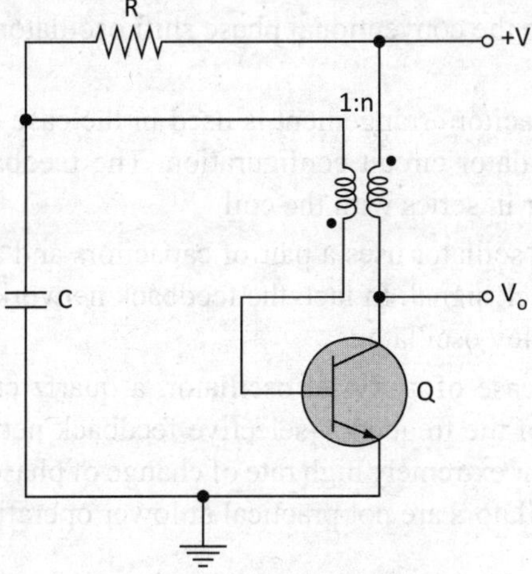

Fig. 8.51: Blocking Oscillator

In synchronised blocking oscillators, conduction of the transistor is synchronised with the synchronising pulses. If in the blocking configuration, the natural frequency is kept slightly lower than the frequency of the synchronising pulses, the blocking oscillator output will be synchronised with the applied sync pulse input. Synchronised blocking oscillators are of considerable practical importance and are invariably used in the horizontal and vertical scanning sections of the television receivers. The horizontal deflection oscillator is synchronised with the horizontal sync and vertical deflection oscillator is synchronised with the vertical sync pulses.

GLOSSARY

Armstrong oscillator: Armstrong oscillator, also known as Meissner oscillator, uses magnetic coupling as means of feeding part of output signal back to input to provide oscillations. It is also called a Tickler oscillator due to use of magnetic coupling between the tickler coil and the coupling coil.

Astable multivibrator: In the case of an astable multivibrator, neither of the two states is stable. Both output states are quasi-stable. The output switches from one state to the other and the circuit functions like a free-running square wave oscillator.

Barkhausen criterion of oscillations: The following two conditions for Barkhausen criterion need to be satisfied for sustained oscillations.

1. The magnitude of loop gain is unity, which ensures that the feedback signal has the same magnitude as that of the input signal.
2. The magnitude of loop phase shift is such that the feedback signal is in-phase with the input signal when it reaches the input of the amplifier.

Bistable multivibrator: A Bistable multivibrator circuit is the one in which both LOW and HIGH output states are stable. Irrespective of the logic status of the output, LOW or HIGH, it stays in that state unless a change is induced by applying an appropriate trigger pulse.

Blocking oscillator: A blocking oscillator is basically a transformer coupled pulse generator which could work both in the monostable as well as in the astable mode.

Bubba oscillator: Bubba oscillator is a slight variation of the buffered RC phase shift oscillator. It uses four RC sections in the feedback network with each RC section contributing a phase difference of 45 .

Buffered RC Phase shift oscillator: The buffered RC phase shift oscillator overcomes the loading effect of different RC sections in the conventional phase shift oscillator by employing a buffer between different RC stages.

Clapp oscillator: Split capacitor arrangement is used in the case of Clapp oscillator. It is a slight modification of the Colpitt oscillator circuit configuration. The feedback circuit in the case of Clapp oscillator uses an extra capacitor in series with the coil.

Colpitt oscillator: Colpitt oscillator uses a pair of capacitors and an inductor in the tank circuit to produce the regenerative-feedback signal. In fact, the feedback network in this case is an electrical dual of the feedback network of Hartley oscillator.

Crystal oscillator: In the case of a crystal oscillator, a quartz crystal with the desired value of resonant frequency forms part of the frequency-selective feedback network. Crystal oscillators are the most stable oscillators due to their extremely high rate of change of phase with frequency at the operating frequency ($d\theta/d\omega$). Crystal oscillators are not practical at lower operating frequencies due to their size, weight and cost restrictions.

Hartley oscillator: In the case of Hartley oscillator, a tapped or a split coil is used. Here, the current that flows through one section of the tapped coil induces a voltage in the other section to provide the feedback. The feedback signal is 180° out-of-phase with the one that produces it.

LC oscillators: In the case of LC oscillators, the operating frequency is determined by an LC tank circuit and is given by ($1/2\pi\sqrt{LC}$). The exact frequency of oscillation is determined by ($1/2\pi\sqrt{LC}$) × [Q2/(Q2 + 1)], where Q is the quality factor of the oscillator.

Monostable multivibrator: A monostable multivibrator, also known as monoshot, is the one in which one of the states is stable and the other is quasi-stable. The circuit is initially in the stable state. It goes to the quasi-stable state when appropriately triggered. It stays in the quasi-stable state for a certain time period, after which it comes back to the stable state.

Multivibrator: A multivibrator like the sinusoidal oscillator is a circuit with regenerative feedback with the difference that it produces a pulsed output. There are three basic types of multivibrator circuits. These include Bistable multivibrator, monostable multivibrator and astable multivibrator.

Non-sinusoidal oscillators: Non-sinusoidal oscillators are oscillators which generate waveforms other than sinusoidal waveform. They produce waveforms such as square, rectangular, sawtooth or triangle wave.

Pierce oscillator: It is a variation of Colpitt oscillator. An FET (JFET or MOSFET) is used as the active device and the crystal along with the inter-electrode capacitances constitute the feedback network.

Quadrature oscillator: Quadrature oscillator is a type of RC phase shift oscillator which employs three RC sections.

RC oscillators: In the case of RC oscillators, multiple RC sections are used to provide the required phase shift.

RC phase shift oscillator: The basic RC phase shift oscillator comprises a single-stage amplifier whose output is fed back to its input through a feedback network. The amplifier portion is usually implemented by either a bipolar transistor-based common-emitter amplifier stage or an operational amplifier wired as an inverting amplifier. The feedback network comprises a cascade arrangement of three identical sections of either lag- or lead-type RC network.

Series-fed LC oscillators: In the case of series-fed LC oscillators, DC power is applied to the active device through the tank circuit or a part of the tank circuit.

Shunt-fed LC oscillators: In shunt-fed LC oscillators, DC power is applied through a separate path that is parallel to the tank circuit.

Sinusoidal oscillators: Sinusoidal oscillators are oscillators that produce sine or cosine waveforms at the output.

Twin-T oscillator: The twin-T oscillator employs a twin-T-type of notch filter network as the frequency selective component in the feedback network.

Voltage controlled oscillator: A voltage-controlled oscillator (VCO) is an oscillator circuit in which the frequency of oscillations can be varied by an applied DC control voltage. This is achieved by having a voltage-dependent capacitor commonly known as varicap or a varactor diode as a part of the frequency-determining tank circuit.

Wien-bridge oscillator: The Wien bridge oscillator is the most widely used RC oscillator configuration for low-frequency applications. It comprises a single-stage amplifier whose output is fed back to its input through a feedback network. The amplifier portion is usually implemented by an operational amplifier wired as a non-inverting amplifier. The feedback network comprises a cascade arrangement of a series RC and a parallel RC network.

SUMMARY OF IMPORTANT FORMULAE

1. Barkhausen criterion of oscillations

(a) $|\beta A| = 1$. That is, loop gain should be unity.

(b) $\sqrt{\beta A} = 0°$ or integral multiple of 360°

2. Lag-type RC phase shift oscillator

(a) Frequency of oscillation $f = [\sqrt{6}/(2\pi RC)]$

(b) Feedback factor $|\beta| = 1/29$

(c) Minimum value of oscillator gain = 29

3. Lead-type RC phase-shift oscillator

(a) Frequency of oscillation $f = [1/(2\pi\sqrt{6}RC)]$

(b) Feedback factor $|\beta| = 1/29$

(c) Minimum value of oscillator gain = 29

4. Buffered Lag-type RC Phase shift oscillator

(a) Frequency of oscillation $f = \sqrt{3}/(2\pi RC)$

(b) Feedback factor $|\beta| = 1/8$

(c) Minimum value of oscillator gain = 8

5. Buffered Lead-type RC Phase shift oscillator

(a) Frequency of oscillation $f = 1/(2\pi\sqrt{3}RC)$

(b) Feedback factor $|\beta| = 1/8$

(c) Minimum value of oscillator gain = 8

6. Wein Bridge oscillator

(a) Frequency of oscillation $f = 1/(2\pi RC)$

(b) Feedback factor $|\beta| = 1/3$

(c) Minimum value of oscillator gain = 3

7. Bubba oscillator

(a) Frequency of oscillation $f = 1/(2\pi RC)$

(b) Feedback factor $|\beta| = 1/4$

(c) Minimum value of oscillator gain = 4

8. Quadrature oscillator

(a) Frequency of oscillation $f = 1/(2\pi RC)$

(b) Feedback factor $|\beta| = 1/\sqrt{2}$

(c) Minimum value of oscillator gain = $\sqrt{2}$

9. Twin-T oscillator

Frequency of oscillation $f = 1/(2\pi RC)$

10. LC Oscillator

Generalized expression for frequency of oscillation is given by:

$$f = \left[1/(2\pi\sqrt{LC})\right] \times \sqrt{Q^2/(Q^2+1)}$$

11. Hartley oscillator

(a) Frequency of oscillation $f = \frac{1}{2\pi\sqrt{(L_1 + L_2)C}}$

(b) Feedback factor $|\beta| = \left(\frac{L_2}{L_1}\right)$

(c) Minimum value of oscillator gain $\left(\frac{L_1}{L_2}\right)$

12. Colpitt oscillator

(a) Frequency of oscillation $f = \frac{LC_1C_2}{2\pi\sqrt{(C_1 + C_2)L}}$

(b) Feedback factor $|\beta| = \left(\frac{C_1}{C_2}\right)$

(c) Minimum value of oscillator gain $\left(\frac{C_2}{C_1}\right)$

13. Clapp oscillator

Frequency of oscillation $f = \frac{1}{2\pi} \times \sqrt{\frac{1}{L} \times \left\{\left(\frac{1}{C_1}\right) + \left(\frac{1}{C_2}\right) + \left(\frac{1}{C_3}\right)\right\}}$

14. Armstrong oscillator

Frequency of oscillation $f = \frac{1}{2\pi\sqrt{LC}}$

15. Crystal oscillator

(a) Series resonant frequency $f_s = \frac{1}{2\pi\sqrt{LC_s}}$

(b) Parallel resonant frequency $f_p = \frac{1}{2\pi\sqrt{LC_p}}$

16. Monostable multivibrator

Width of the quasi-stable state $T = 0.693 \times R \times C$

17. Astable multivibrator

(a) Total time period of the wave $T = T_1 + T_2 = 0.694(R_1C_1 + R_2C_2)$

For $R_1 = R_2 = R$ and $C_1 = C_2 = C$, $T = 1.388RC$ and $f = \frac{1}{1.388RC}$

REVIEW QUESTIONS

1. List three differences between an oscillator circuit and an amplifier circuit? With the help of a suitable block diagram, explain the different constituents of an oscillator circuit.
2. Briefly describe the necessary conditions for sustained oscillations?

3. With the help of relevant circuit diagram, briefly describe the operation of an RC phase shift oscillator configured around an op-amp and a lag-type feedback network. What should be the minimum value of amplifier gain for sustained oscillations? What is the phase shift introduced by each of the three RC sections in the feedback network at the operating frequency?
4. "Wien bridge oscillators exhibit better frequency stability at relatively lower operating frequencies" Comment on the statement in detail.
5. What are buffered RC phase shift oscillators? How does the operating frequency in the case of a buffered oscillator differ from that of conventional non-buffered counterpart?
6. Briefly describe the operation of quadrature oscillator with particular reference to its ability to produce sine and cosine outputs.
7. Why are LC oscillators not suitable for relatively lower frequencies? How does the frequency stability of an LC oscillator depend upon the Q-factor of the LC circuit?
8. What are crystal oscillators? What makes crystal oscillator exhibit exceptionally high frequency stability?
9. With the help of basic circuit diagram, briefly describe the operation of a Pierce oscillator. How does it differ from a Colpitt oscillator?
10. What is a voltage controlled oscillator? Why is it important to use back-to-back connected varactor diodes instead of a single diode?
11. Explain in detail on which parametersdoes frequency stability of an oscillator depend onand why?
12. How does an astable multivibrator function as an oscillator?
13. How is a blocking oscillator different from a sinusoidal oscillator?

PROBLEMS

1. If in an oscillator, the amplifier portion is a two-stage CE configuration, what should be the phase shift to be introduced by the feedback network at the oscillation frequency for sustained oscillations?
2. Figure 8.52 shows an RC phase shift oscillator using an op-amp as the active device. The oscillator is oscillating at the correct frequency but the output is distorted severely near the signal peaks. What could be the possible causes?

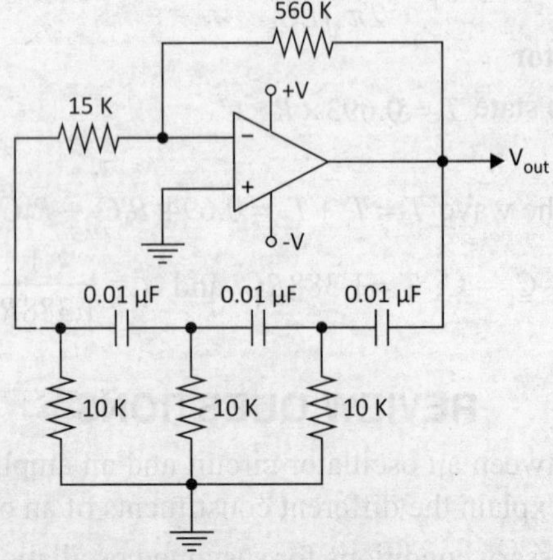

Fig. 8.52: Problem 2

3. Refer to the Wien bridge oscillator circuit of Figure 8.53. Determine the oscillator frequency and the preferred value of R_1.

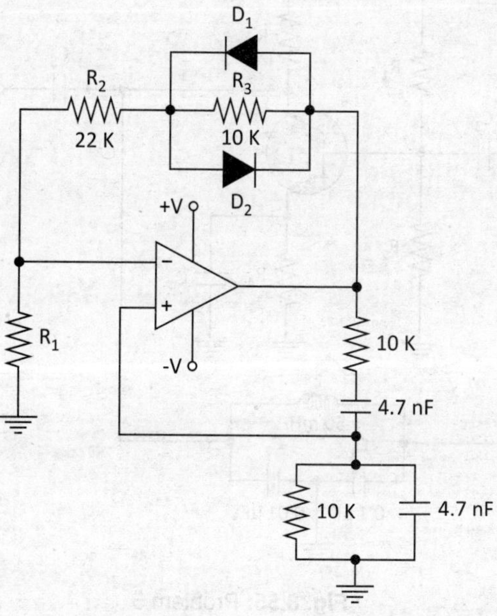

Fig. 8.53: Problem 3

4. Refer to the Colpitt oscillator of Figure 8.54. Determine (a) frequency of oscillations and (b) minimum gain required to start oscillations.

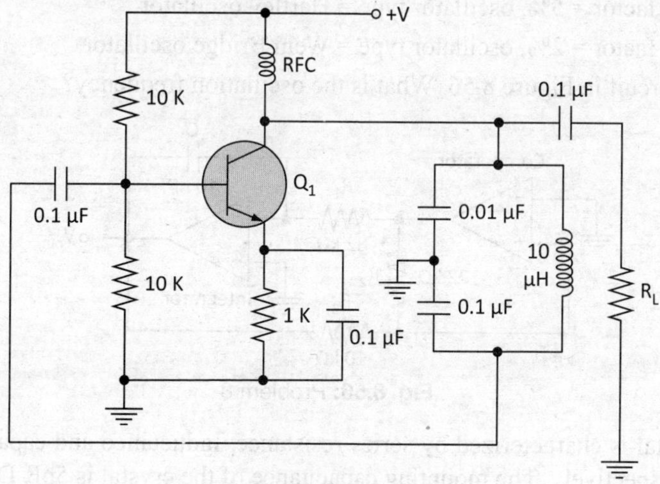

Fig. 8.54: Problem 4

5. Determine the frequency for the oscillator circuit shown in Figure 8.55, assuming that the quality factor is very large and there is negligible loading on the feedback circuit?

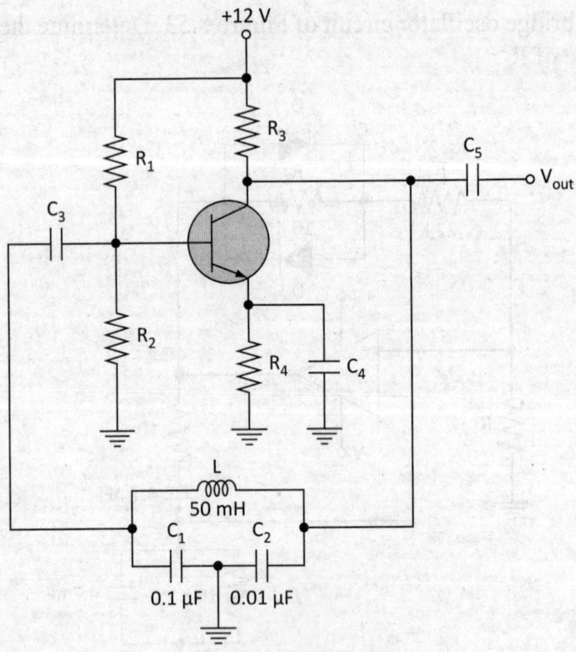

Fig. 8.55: Problem 5

6. For the oscillator circuit of problem-5, determine the oscillation frequency if the quality factor were to drop to 10?
7. Determine the minimum amplifier gain and phase shift required to be introduced by the amplifier for the following cases
   (a) Feedback factor = 5%, oscillator type = Hartley oscillator
   (b) Feedback factor = 2%, oscillator type = Wein Bridge oscillator
8. Refer to the circuit in Figure 8.56. What is the oscillation frequency?

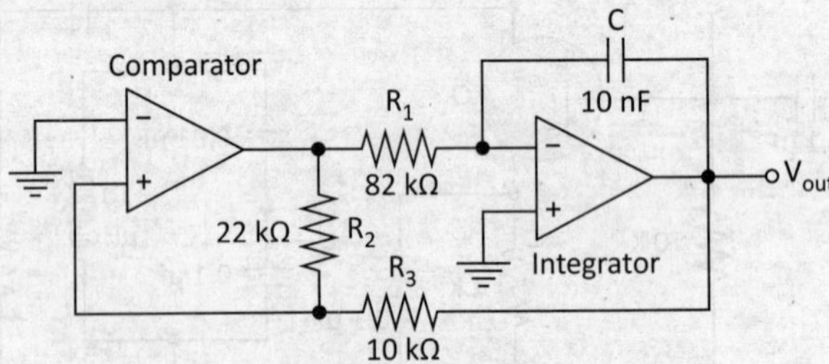

Fig. 8.56: Problem 8

9. A quartz crystal is characterized by series resistance, inductance and capacitance of 500Ω, 2H and 0.01pF respectively. The mounting capacitance of the crystal is 5pF. Determine the
   (a) Series resonant frequency of the crystal
   (b) Parallel resonant frequency of the crystal
10. If the crystal given in question 9 is employed in a pierce oscillator, determine its oscillation frequency?

MULTIPLE-CHOICE QUESTIONS

1. The output waveform for the circuit in Figure 8.57 is

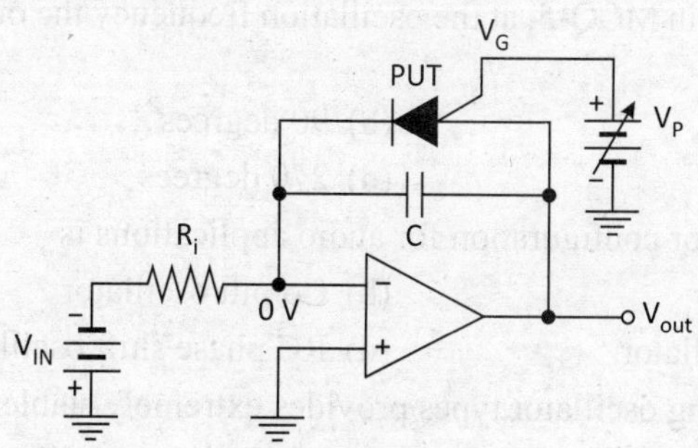

Fig. 8.57: MCQ-1

(a) sawtooth wave (b) triangle wave
(c) square wave (d) sine wave

2. The condition that decides the oscillator's output frequency is
(a) loop gain should at least be unity
(b) loop phase shift should be zero or integral multiple of 2 radians
(c) loop gain should be precisely unity
(d) loop phase shift should be precisely zero radian

3. In a crystal oscillator, the crystal acts like a
(a) Band-pass filter (b) Resonant circuit
(c) Notch filter (d) Power source

4. In a conventional transistor RC phase shift oscillator using lead-type feedback network, frequency of oscillations is given by

(a) $f = \dfrac{1}{2\pi RC}$ (b) $f = \dfrac{1}{2\pi\sqrt{RC}}$

(c) $f = \dfrac{1}{2\pi\sqrt{6}RC}$ (d) $f = \dfrac{1}{2\pi\sqrt{3}RC}$

5. Refer to the circuit shown in Figure 8.58. It is a

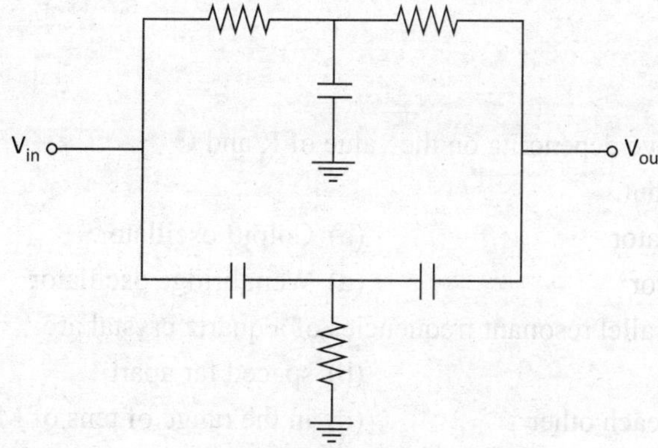

Fig. 8.58: MCQ-5

(a) Wein Bridge oscillator network (b) Twin-t oscillator network

(c) Quadrature oscillator network (d) None of the above

6. For the circuit shown in MCQ-5, at the oscillation frequency the output of this network is phase-shifted by

(a) 0 degrees (b) 90 degrees

(c) 180 degrees (d) 270 degrees

7. Most popular oscillator configuration for audio applications is

(a) Hartley oscillator (b) Colpitt oscillator

(c) Wein bridge oscillator (d) RC phase shift oscillator

8. Which of the following oscillator types provides extremely stable output frequency?

(a) Hartley oscillator (b) Wein bridge oscillator

(c) Crystal oscillator (d) Clapp oscillator

9. The oscillator circuit shown in Figure 8.59 has an ideal inverting amplifier. The oscillation frequency is given by

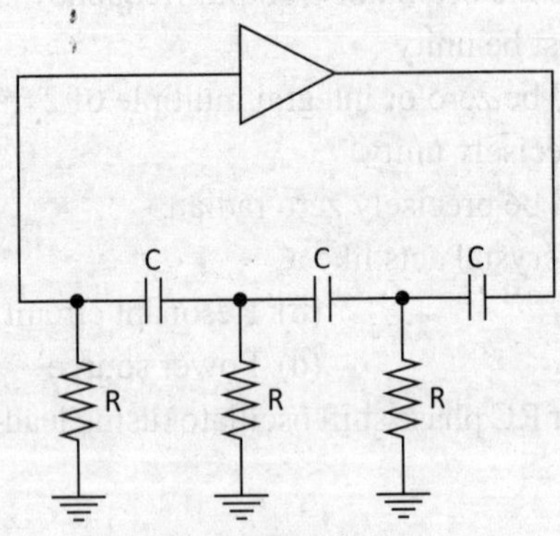

Fig. 8.59: MCQ-9

(a) $\dfrac{1}{2\pi\sqrt{6}RC}$

(b) $\dfrac{1}{2\pi RC}$

(c) $\dfrac{1}{\pi\sqrt{6}RC}$

(d) All of the above depending on the value of R and C

10. Pick the odd-one out.

(a) Hartley oscillator (b) Colpitt oscillator.

(c) Clapp oscillator (d) Wein bridge oscillator

11. The series and parallel resonant frequencies of a quartz crystal are

(a) the same (b) spaced far apart

(c) very close to each other (d) in the range of tens of MHz

12. A Schmitt trigger circuit is a type of
    (a) Bistable multivibrator circuit (b) Monostable multivibrator circuit
    (c) Astable multivibrator circuit (d) none of these
13. In the case of a buffered RC phase shift RC oscillator, the required minimum value of amplifier gain is
    (a) 29 (b) 8
    (c) 3 (d) 16
14. According to the frequency stability criterion,
    (a) higher |dθ/dω| means higher frequency stability
    (b) higher |dθ/dω| means lower frequency stability
    (c) frequency stability is independent of |dθ/dω|
    (d) higher value of Q-factor means lower frequency stability
15. For the circuit shown in Figure 8.60, in the stable state the voltages at the collector terminals of transistors Q1 and Q2 respectively are

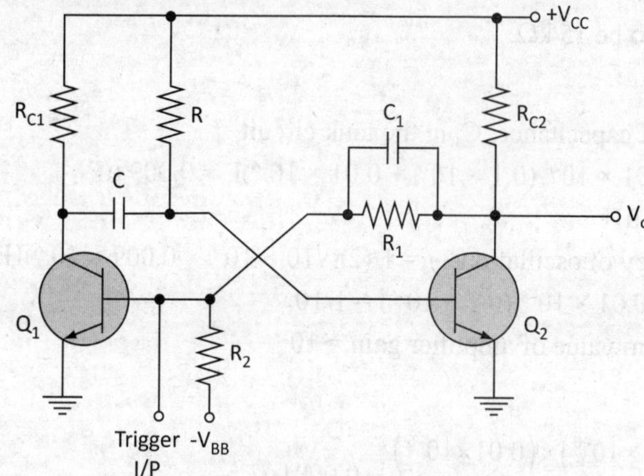

Fig. 8.60: MCQ-15

(a) 0 and V_{CC} (b) V_{CC} and 0
(c) V_{CC} and V_{CC} (d) 0 and 0

SOLUTIONS TO PROBLEMS

Problem-1:

A two-stage CE amplifier provides a phase shift of 2 radians.

Therefore, the feedback network must not introduce any more phase shift or introduce phase shift equal to multiples of 2 radians in order to satisfy Barkhausen criterion for sustained oscillations.

Poblem-2:

The minimum amplifier gain requirement is 29.

In order to ensure that we get sustained oscillations and the device replacement and ageing have no effects, the amplifier gain is chosen to be slightly more than what is demanded by the Barkhausen criterion.

It may exceed the minimum required gain value by 10-15%. Too large a gain can cause signal clipping near the peaks.

The gain magnitude in the present case is given by $560 \times 10^3/15 \times 103 \cong 37.3$, which exceeds the required minimum by approximately 30%. This explains the distortion observed in the output.

Problem-3:

Oscillator frequency is given by $f = 1/2$ RC where R = 10 kΩ and C = 4.7 nF

Therefore, $f = 1/(6.283 \times 10 \times 10^3 \times 4.7 \times 10\ 9)$Hz = 3.386 kHz

Required minimum value of amplifier gain = 3

Amplifier gain = $1 + [(R_2 + R_3)/R_1]$

This gives $(R_2 + R_3)/R_1 = 2$, $R_1 = (22 \times 10^3 + 10 \times 10^3)/2 = 16 \times 10^3\Omega = 16$ kΩ

Since the required gain has to be slightly greater than 3, preferred value of R1 therefore should be slightly less than 16 kΩ.

R_1 may be chosen to be 15 kΩ.

Problem-4:

Equivalent value of capacitance, C, in the tank circuit

$C = 0.1 \times 10^{-6} \times 0.01 \times 10^{-6}/(0.1 \times 10^{-6} + 0.01 \times 10^{-6})F = 0.009\ \mu F$

Inductance, L = 10 μH

Therefore, frequency of oscillations, $f = 1/(2\pi\sqrt{10 \times 10^{-6} \times 0.009 \times 10^{-6}})$Hz = 530.5 kHz

Feedback factor = $0.01 \times 10^{-6}/(0.1 \times 10^{-6}) = 1/10$

Therefore, minimum value of amplifier gain = 10

Problem-5:

$$C = \frac{C_1C_2}{C_1 + C_2} = \frac{(0.1\times10^{-6})\times(0.01\times10^{-6})}{(0.1\times10^{-6} + 0.01\times10^{-6})} = 0.0091\mu F$$

The oscillation frequency with high value of quality factor (Q) is given by:

$$f = \frac{1}{2\pi\sqrt{LC}} = \frac{1}{2\pi\sqrt{50\times10^{-3}\times0.0091\times10^{-6}}} Hz = 7.46kHz$$

Problem-6:

When value of Q = 10,

$$f = \frac{1}{2\pi\sqrt{LC}}\sqrt{\frac{Q^2}{Q^2+1}} = 7.46\times10^3 \times \sqrt{\frac{100}{101}} Hz = 7.4kHz$$

Problem-7:

(a) Feedback factor = 5% = 5/100 = 0.05

Minimum value of amplifier gain = 1/0.05 = 20

For a Hartley oscillator, the feedback network provides a phase shift of 180º.

Hence, the minimum phase shift the amplifier should introduce is 180º.

(b) Feedback factor = 2% = 2/100 = 0.02

Minimum value of amplifier gain = 1/0.02 = 50

For a Wein bridge oscillator, the feedback network provides a phase shift of 0 . Hence, the minimum phase shift the amplifier should introduce is 0º.

Problem-8:

The oscillation frequency is given by:

$$f = \frac{1}{4R_1C}\left(\frac{R_2}{R_3}\right) = \frac{1}{4\times 82\times 10^3\times 10\times 10^{-9}}\times\left(\frac{22\times 10^3}{10\times 10^3}\right)Hz = 671Hz$$

Problem-9:

(a) Given that L = 2H, C_s = 0.01pF

Series resonant frequency of the crystal is given by

$$f_s = \frac{1}{2\pi\sqrt{LC_s}} = \frac{1}{2\times 3.1416\times\sqrt{2\times 0.01\times 10^{-12}}}Hz = 1.125MHz$$

(b) Given that L = 2H, C_s = 0.01pF and C_M = 5pF

Parallel resonant frequency of the crystal is given by

$$f_p = \frac{1}{2\pi\sqrt{L\left(\frac{C_sC_M}{Cs+C_M}\right)}} = \frac{1}{2\times 3.1416\times\sqrt{2\times\left(\frac{0.01\times 10^{-12}\times 5\times 10^{-12}}{0.01\times 10^{-12}+5\times 10^{-12}}\right)}}Hz = 1.126MHz$$

Problem-10:

The oscillation frequency of a pierce oscillator is the same as the parallel resonant frequency. Therefore, the oscillation frequency = 1.126MHz.

SOLUTION TO MULTIPLE-CHOICE QUESTIONS

1 (a)	2 (b)	3 (b)	4 (c)
5 (b)	6 (c)	7 (c)	8 (c)
9 (a)	10 (d)	11 (c)	12 (a)
13 (b)	14 (a)	15 (b)	

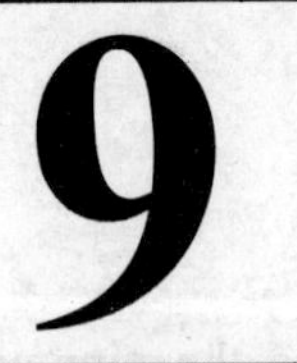

Introduction to Operational Amplifiers

After completing this chapter, you will learn the following topics.

— Internal architecture of an operational amplifier and description of different stages constituting an operational amplifier
— Current mirror basics and different current mirror configurations
— Introduction to operational amplifiers
— Types of operational amplifiers
— Operational amplifier parameters

Introduction

This chapter introduces operational amplifier. The chapter begins with brief description of an important building block called current mirror of the internal architecture of an operational amplifier. This is done to make it easier for the readers to understand the other building blocks comprising the internal architecture. Difference between ideal and practical opamps, opamp parameters defining opamp performance, types of opamps and their preferred application areas are the other topics discussed in this chapter. Important formulae and keywords are listed at the end of the chapter. Different topics discussed in the chapter are amply illustrated with solved examples. In addition, there are a number of problems given towards the end of the chapter along with brief solutions. A self-evaluation exercise containing multiple-choice questions along with solutions concludes the chapter.

9.1 CURRENT MIRROR

A *current mirror* is a circuit block that produces a copy of the current flowing into or out of an input terminal by replicating the current in an output terminal. A current mirror circuit is characterized by a high output impedance and a low input impedance. A high output resistance helps to keep the output current constant regardless of load conditions and a low input resistance helps to keep the input current constant regardless of drive conditions. The current being 'copied' can be, and often is, a varying signal current. The current mirror is often used to provide bias currents and active loads in amplifier stages.As an example, the collector and emitter resistors in the differential amplifier constituting the input stage of an operational amplifier invariably use current mirror circuit. There are various current mirror circuits exploited for designing constant current sources. In the following sections, are briefly described the basic current mirror circuits and the variations to the basic current mirror including Widlar and Wilson current sources.

9.1.1 Basic Current Mirror

The basic concept of an ideal current mirror can be explained with the help of block schematic representation of Figure 9.1. Figures 9.1 (a) and (b) respectively demonstrate use of current mirror circuit block as current sink and a current source. In the case of current mirror used a current sink as shown in Figure 9.1 (a), the input is a current source.The input section of the current mirror looks like a virtual short circuit and reflects this current to produce a current sink by swapping the direction of flow of current. In the case of current mirror used as current source, the current sink is the input and the current mirror reflects this current to control current source. A current mirror therefore consists of a low impedance input stage connected to a high impedance output current stage. We can also say that conceptually, an ideal current mirror is simply an ideal inverting current amplifier with a gain of unity.

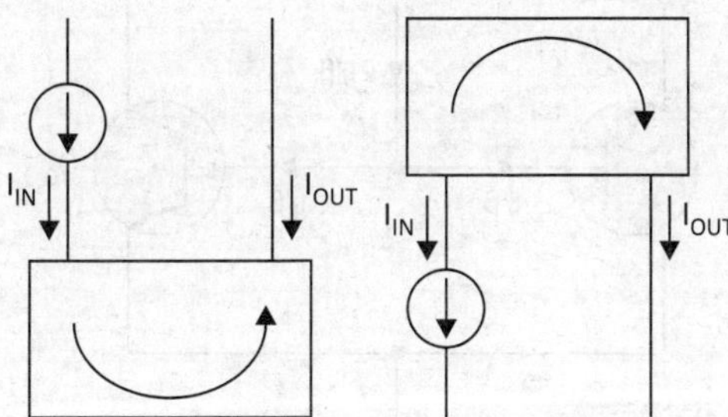

Fig. 9.1: Current mirror concept (a) as current sink (b) as current source

9.1.1.1 BJT-based Current Mirror

Figure 9.2 shows the basic current mirror circuit using bipolar junction transistors (BJT). The simple two transistor implementation of the current mirror using either bipolar junction transistors as shown in the circuit of Figure 9.2 or field effect transistors is based on the fundamental relationship that two equal size transistors at the same temperature with the same V_{GS} for a MOSFET or V_{BE} for a BJT have the same drain or collector current. Again, referring to Figure 9.2, if the two transistors were perfectly matched, they could be assumed to have same values of base-emitter voltage drops and DC current gains. This is possible to achieve when the two transistors are fabricated on the same integrated circuit (IC) chip at the same time. Transistor (Q_1) with its collector terminal shorted to its base-terminal is wired like a diode. A semiconductor diode has not been used instead as that would have made the matching of characteristics of the diode and the base-emitter junction diode of the transistor (Q_2) difficult to achieve. If we analyze this current mirror circuit of Figure 9.2; we find that it comprises an input section that converts current (I_{IN}= I) to a voltage (V_{BE}) and an output section that converts voltage (V_{BE} in this case) into a current (I_2= I). With the help of simple mathematics, it can be proved that current (I) flowing through (Q_2) equals the current (I_{IN}) flowing through (R_1).

Since the two transistors have identical values of DC current gain (b) and base current (I_B), they would have identical collector and emitter currents as shown in Figure 9.1.

Thus, the current (I_{IN}) set by (V_{CC}) and (R_1) is mirrored as the collector current of (Q_2). It may be mentioned here that more than one matched transistor can be connected to the base of (Q_1). The current through the collector of each of the transistors equals the current flowing through the collector of left-half transistor. Higher the value of (b), closer the mirrored current approximates the set value as is obvious from eqn. 9.1. Figure 9.3 shows another current mirror circuit in which JFET current regulating diode sets the constant current. The set value of current in this case equals (I_{DSS}), which makes $I = I_{DSS}$. It may be mentioned here that in the circuit arrangement of Figure 9.2, current through (R_1) would vary with variation in the supply voltage with the result that the current (I) though a mirror image of current (I_{IN}) will not be constant. The current mirror configuration of Figure 9.2, where transistor (Q_1) is driven by a constant current source, overcomes this problem.

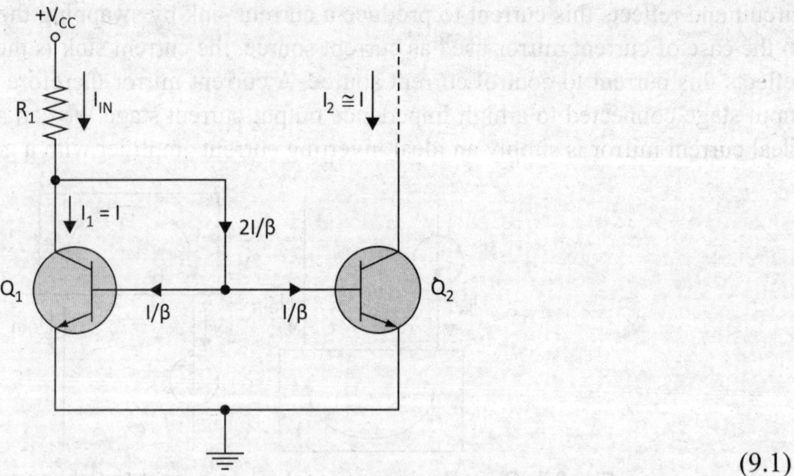

Fig. 9.2: Current mirror implemented with bipolar transistor

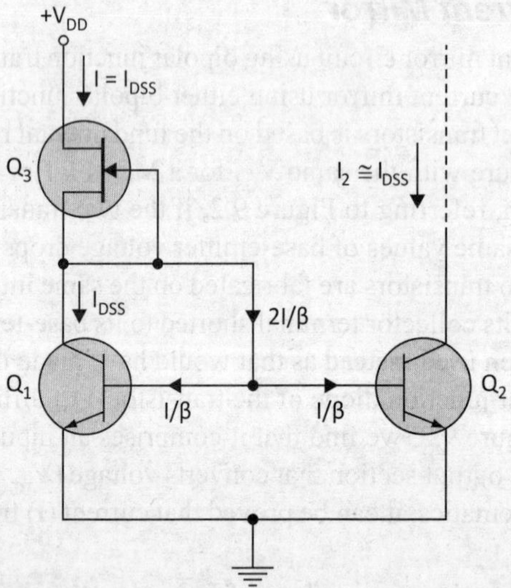

Fig. 9.3: Current mirror with JFET providing constant current

9.1.1.2 MOSFET-based Current Mirror

Figure 9.4 shows the circuit diagram of basic current mirror implemented with enhancement MOSFETs. It comprises an input section configured around MOSFET M_1 (functioning as current to voltage converter) and an output section configured around MOSFET M_2 (functioning as voltage to current converter). The drain current $I_D (= I_{IN})$ of a MOSFET is a function of both the gate to source voltage V_{GS} and the drain to gate voltage V_{DG} of the MOSFET. Input current I_{IN} is a known current and can be provided by a resistor as shown in the figure, or by a threshold-referenced or self-biased current source to ensure that it is constant, independent of voltage supply variations. For $V_{DG} = 0$, I_{IN} sets the value of V_{GS}. The V_{GS} set by I_{IN} is then applied to MOSFET M_2. If M_2 also were biased with zero V_{DG} and if MOSFETs M_1 and M_2 had matched characteristics, $I_{OUT} = I_{IN}$.

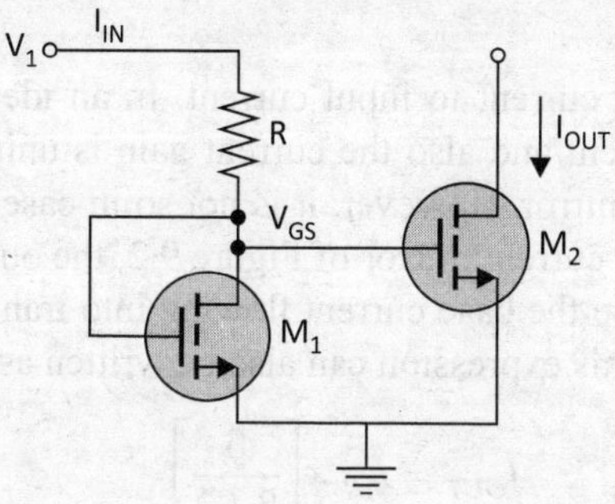

Fig. 9.4: MOSFET-based current mirror

The generalized expressions for I_{IN} and I_{OUT} are given by eqns. 9.2 and 9.3.

$$I_{IN} = \frac{1}{2} \times K_n \times \left(\frac{W}{L}\right)_{M1} \times (V_{GS} - V_{TH})^2 \times (1 + \lambda V_{DS}) \tag{9.2}$$

$$I_{OUT} = \frac{1}{2} \times K_n \times \left(\frac{W}{L}\right)_{M2} \times (V_{GS} - V_{TH})^2 \times (1 + \lambda V_{DS}) \tag{9.3}$$

Where K_n = Technology related constant

λ = Channel length modulation constant

W and L are respectively the channel width and channel length of the MOSFETs.

Ignoring the effect of channel length modulation due to drain-source voltage bias, we get

$$I_{IN} = \frac{1}{2} \times K_n' \times (V_{GS} - V_{TH})^2 \tag{9.4}$$

$$I_{OUT} = \frac{1}{2} \times K_n' \times (V_{GS} - V_{TH})^2 \tag{9.5}$$

Where $$K_n' = K_n \times \left(\frac{W}{L}\right)$$

If the two MOSFETs are identical and their characteristics are perfectly matched, we get,

$$I_{IN} = I_{OUT} \tag{9.6}$$

9.1.2 Characteristics of Current Mirror

A current mirror as described earlier is a current amplifier with a gain of unity. A current amplifier is characterized by following parameters.

1. Current gain, A_I also called Mirror Gain or Current Transfer Ratio
2. Input resistance, R_i
3. Output resistance, R_o
4. Minimum input voltage, V_{IN} (MIN)
5. Minimum output voltage, V_{OUT} (MIN) also called Compliance Voltage

An ideal current mirror is characterized by a current gain of unity, input resistance of zero and output resistance of infinity. A practical current mirror however has a current gain that is slightly less than unity, very low input resistance and very high output resistance.

9.1.2.1 Current Gain

Current gain is the ratio of output current to input current. In an ideal current mirror, output current is linearly related to the input current and also the current gain is unity. Figure 9.5 shows the transfer characteristics of an ideal current mirror. However, it is not so in case of a practical current mirror. As an example, in the basic BJT-based current mirror of Figure 9.2, the output current is less than the input current by an amount equal to twice the base current flowing into transistors Q_1 and Q_2. That is, $I_{OUT} = I_{IN} - 2I_B$. I_B in this case equals I/b. This expression can also be written as eqn. 9.7.

$$I_{OUT} = I_{IN} \times \left[\frac{\beta}{\beta+2}\right] \tag{9.7}$$

A significant advantage of the MOS current mirror is the absence of base current induced error that BJT current mirrors suffer from. Different variants of current mirror that offer improvement over the basic current mirror address this issue.

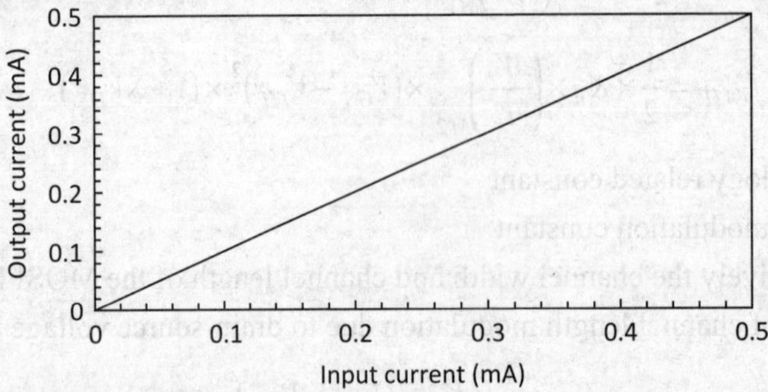

Fig. 9.5: Current transfer characteristics of ideal current mirror

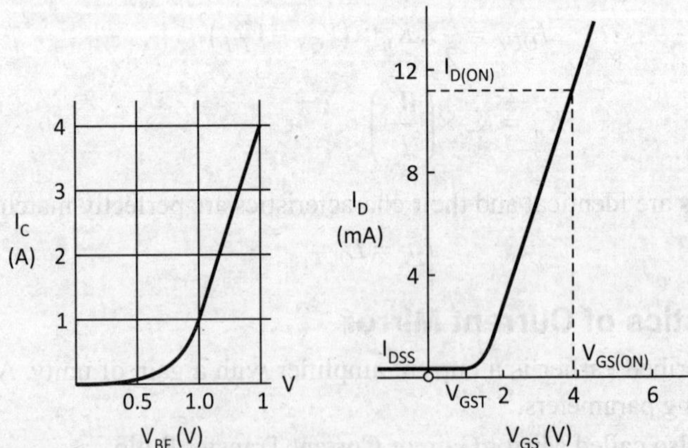

Fig. 9.6: Input resistance of current mirror (a) BJT current mirror (b) MOSFET current mirror

Current mirror gain of other than unity can be obtained by connecting more than one transistors in parallel on the input side or output side or both input and output sides. If N identical devices in are paralleled on the input side and M identical devices are connected in parallel on the output side; the mirror gain will be M/N as all transistors share the same V_{BE} voltage. While input current gets divided equally among the parallel-connected input transistors; the identical mirrored currents on the output side add up. Figure 9.7 shows one such arrangement. The mirror gain in this case is 1.5. The current mirror configuration of the type shown in Figure 9.7 can also be used to generate multiple constant currents from a single reference current.

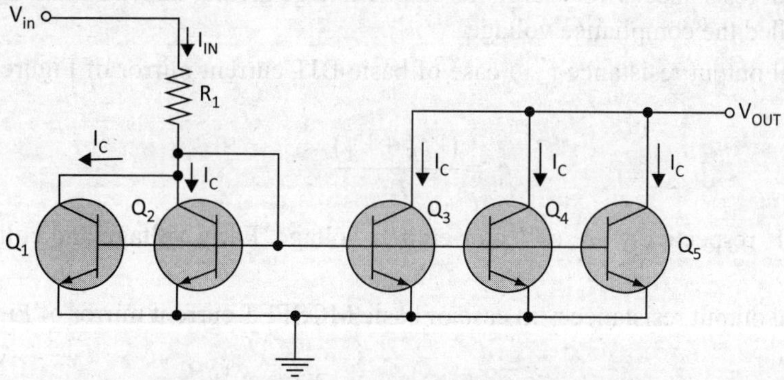

Fig. 9.7: Current mirror with non-unary mirror gain

Figure 9.8 shows a MOSFET-based current mirror that can be used to generate multiple currents from a single reference current. The mirrored currents will be equal to reference current if all MOSFETs were identical. In the case of MOSFET current mirror, it is possible to have mirrored currents with amplitudes different from the reference current. This is achieved by having channel W/L ratio different from that of input MOSFET. It may be mentioned that it is easy to fabricate MOSFETs with different channel dimensions on a common integrated circuit chip.

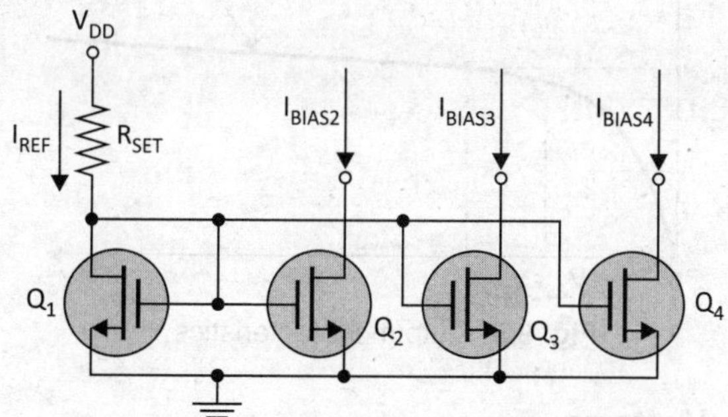

Fig. 9.8: MOSFET current mirror with non-unary mirror gain

9.1.2.2 Input Resistance

In case of an ideal current mirror, *input resistance* should be zero. In practical current mirrors, it is very small and in the range of few hundreds of ohms to few kilo-ohms. A minimum input voltage parameter called V_{IN} (MIN) is defined as the range of input voltage over which the input resistance is not very small. In the case of a BJT current mirror of Figure 9.2, collector current I versus base-emitter voltage V_{BE} of the input transistor Q_1 defines the input resistance (Figure 9.6a). In the case of MOSFET current mirror of Figure 9.4, it would be drain current I versus V_{GS} of the input MOSFET M_1 (Figure 9.6b).

9.1.2.3 Output Resistance

Incremental output resistance in an ideal current mirror should be infinite. In case of practical current mirror circuits, it is very large in the range of hundreds of kilo-ohms to few Giga-ohms. The incremental output resistance also called AC output resistance determines how much the output current varies with the voltage seen at the mirror output. Incremental output resistance is defined by output characteristics, that is, output current versus output voltage characteristics as shown in Figure 9.9. As is evident from Figure 9.7, the output resistance is very large for output voltage greater than a certain minimum voltage V_{OUT} (MIN) also called the compliance voltage.

The incremental output resistance r_o in case of basic BJT current mirror of Figure 9.2 is given by eqn. 9.8.

$$r_o = \frac{(V_{CE} + V_A)}{I_C} \tag{9.8}$$

where V_{CE}, V_A and I_C respectively are collector-emitter voltage, Early voltage and collector current of output transistor Q_2.

The incremental output resistance r_o in case of basic MOSFET current mirror of Figure 9.4 is given by eqn. 9.9.

$$r_o = \frac{\left[(1/\lambda) + V_{DS}\right]}{I_D} \tag{9.9}$$

where l, V_{DS} and I_D respectively are channel length modulation constant, drain-source voltage and drain current of output MOSFET M_2.

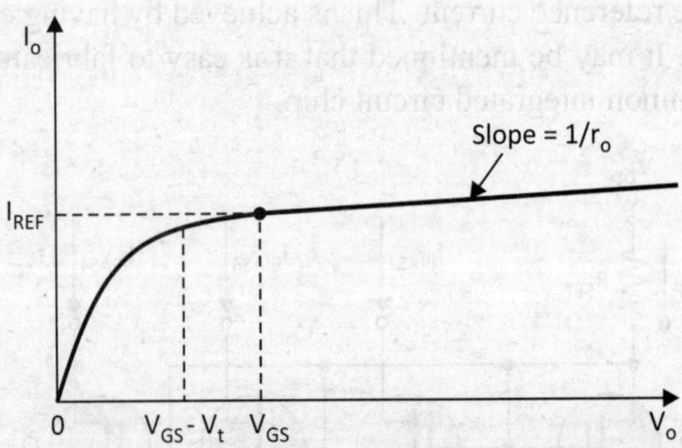

Fig. 9.9: Output characteristics

9.1.2.4 Compliance Voltage

Compliance voltage is the minimum voltage drop required across the output leg of the current mirror necessary to maintain the desired output current. This minimum voltage, called compliance voltage, is determined by the need to keep the output transistor of the BJT current mirror in the active region (Figure 9.10a) or MOSFET current mirror in saturation region (Figure 9.10b).

In the case of basic BJT current mirror, the compliance voltage $V_{CV} = V_{BE}$ under bias conditions with the output transistor at the output current level I_C and with $V_{CB} = 0$ V. It can also be expressed by eqn. 9.10.

$$V_{CV} = V_T \times \ln\left(\frac{I_C}{I_S}\right) \tag{9.10}$$

Where V_T is the thermal voltage; I_C and I_S are respectively collector current and reverse saturation current.

The compliance voltage V_{CV} in case of MOSFET current mirror of Figure 9.4 is given by eqn. 9.11.

$$V_{CV} = V_{GS} \ \ (\text{for } I_D \text{ at } V_{GS} = 0) \qquad (9.11)$$

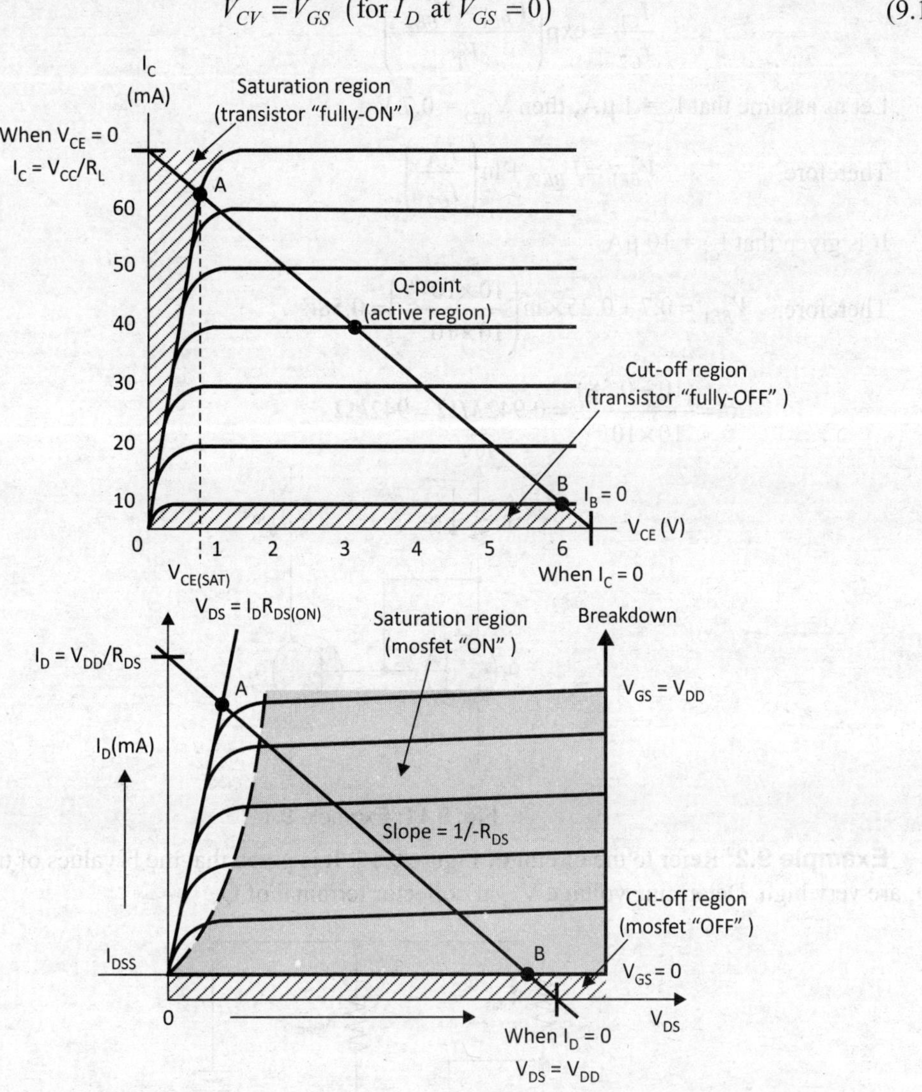

Fig. 9.10: Output characteristics (a) BJT current mirror (b) MOSFET current mirror

Example 9.1: Refer to the BJT current mirror circuit of Figure 9.11. Determine R_1 for I_O= 10μA. Q_1, Q_2 have V_{BE}=0.7V for I_C=1μA.

Solution:

We know that $$V_{BE} = V_T \times \ln\left(\frac{I_C}{I_S}\right)$$

This leads to $$I_C = I_S \times \exp\left(\frac{V_{BE}}{V_T}\right)$$

If I_{C1} and I_{C2} were the collector currents of Q_1 and Q_2, then we can write the following expression.

$$\frac{I_{C1}}{I_{C2}} = \exp\left(\frac{V_{BE1} - V_{BE2}}{V_T}\right)$$

Let us assume that I_{C2} = 1 μA, then V_{BE2} = 0.7 V

Therefore, $$V_{BE1} = V_{BE2} + \ln\left(\frac{I_{C1}}{I_{C2}}\right)$$

It is given that I_{C1} = 10 μA

Therefore, $$V_{BE1} = 0.7 + 0.25 \times \ln\left(\frac{10 \times 10^{-6}}{10 \times 10^{-3}}\right) = 0.58V$$

$$R_1 = \frac{(10 - 0.58)}{10 \times 10^{-6}} = 0.942M\Omega = 942k\Omega$$

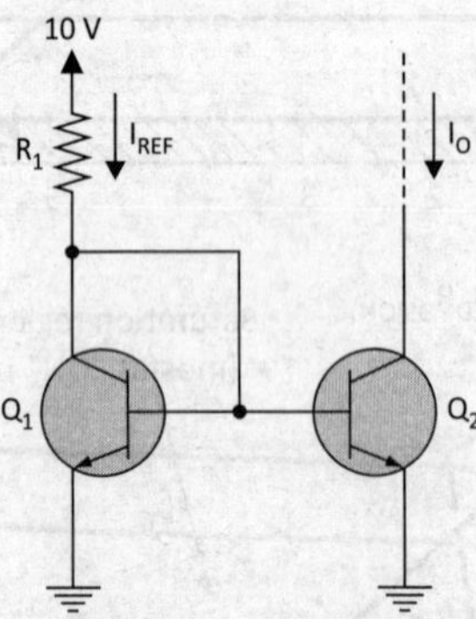

Fig. 9.11: Example 9.1

Example 9.2: Refer to the circuit of Figure 9.12. It is given that the b-values of transistors Q_1 and Q_2 are very high. Determine voltage V_{C2} at collector terminal of Q_2.

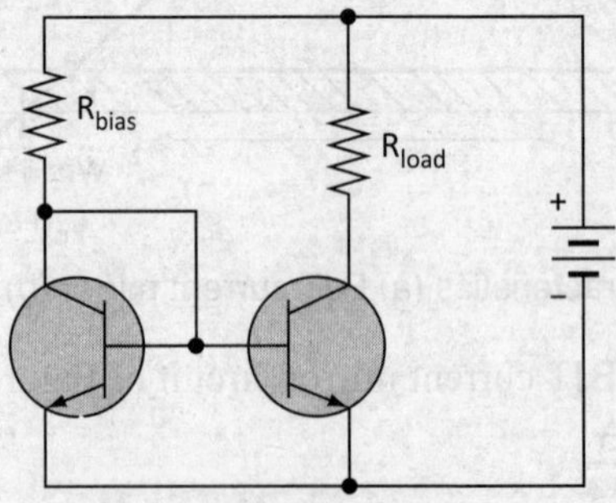

Fig. 9.12: Example 9.12

Solution: The circuit shown in Figure 9.12 is that of basic BJT-based current mirror.

The input current = 5 mA

Since the b values for the transistors are very high, $I_O = I_{REF}$

Therefore, mirrored current flowing through 1 kΩ resistor is also 5 mA.

Voltage, $V_{C2} = 12 - 1 \times 10^3 \times 5 \times 10^{-3} = 7V$

Example 9.3: Design a MOSFET current mirror shown in Figure 9.13 for an output current of 100 μA given that V = 5V, V_{TH} = 2V and $K_n¢$ = 100 mA/V². Assume the two MOSFETs to be identical and ignore channel length modulation effect.

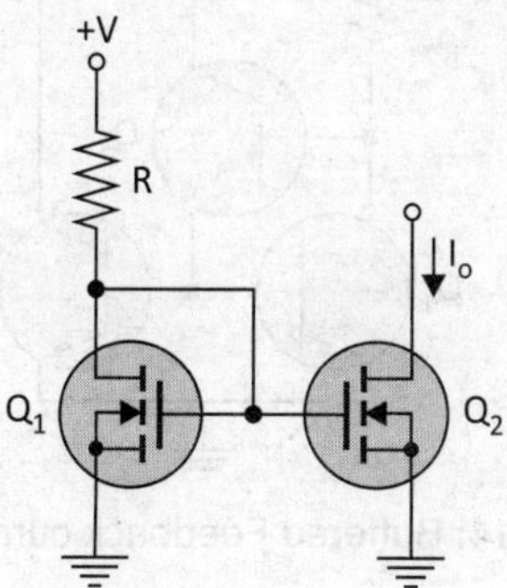

Fig. 9.13: Example 9.3

Solution: The design essentially reduces to determining resistance value of R.

$$I_O = 100\times10^{-6} = \frac{1}{2}\times K_n'\times(V_{GS}-V_{TH})^2$$

$$10^{-4} = \frac{1}{2}\times100\times10^{-3}\times(V_{GS}-2)^2$$

Or $\quad (V_{GS}-2)^2 = 2\times10^{-3}$

Solving the above equation for V_{GS}, we get

$$V_{GS}^2 - 4V_{GS} + 3.998 = 0$$

Or $\quad V_{GS}$ = 2.045V, 1.956V

Since $\quad V_{GS}$ has to be greater than equal to V_{TH}

Therefore, $\quad V_{GS}$ = 2.045V

Since $\quad I_O = I_{IN}$

R = (5 - 2.045)/100 MW = 0.03 MW = 30 kΩ

9.1.3 Different Variants of Current Mirror

Different variants of the basic current mirror circuit have been proposed to overcome the shortcomings and improve upon the performance of the basic current mirror circuits discussed in the preceding paragraphs. Three common variants include the *buffered feedback current mirror*, *Widlar current source* and the *Wilson current source*. These are briefly discussed in the following paragraphs.

9.1.3.1 Buffered Feedback Current Mirror

In *buffered feedback current mirror*, also known as *base current compensation current mirror*, the collector terminal of input transistor is wired to base terminals of input and output transistors (Q_1 and Q_2) through an emitter follower buffer as shown in the circuit diagram of Figure 9.14. High current gain of the buffer stage greatly reduces the gain error caused by finite values of base currents of Q_1 and Q_2 in case of basic current mirror.

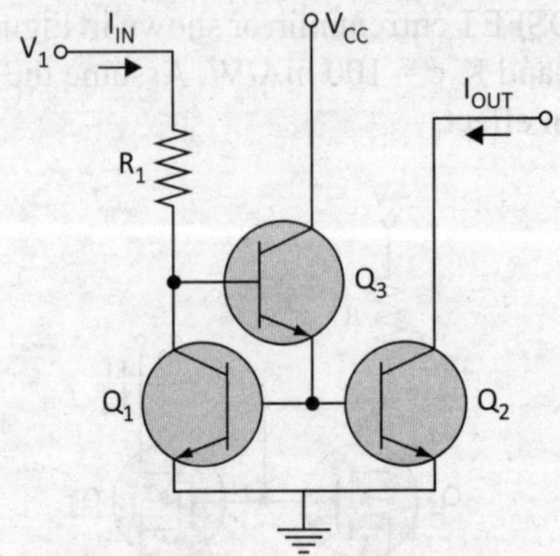

Fig. 9.14: Buffered Feedback current mirror

In order to ensure that the output current closely matches the input current; the collector-emitter voltage of Q_1 and Q_2 should be the same, that is, $2 \times V_{BE}$. Also, I_{IN} in case of buffered feedback current mirror is given by eqn. 9.12.

$$I_{IN} = \frac{(V_1 - V_{BE1} - V_{BE3})}{R_1} \tag{9.12}$$

The relationship between I_{IN} and I_{OUT} can be derived as follows.

$$I_{IN} = I_{C1} + I_{B3} \tag{9.13}$$

Where I_{C1} and I_{B3} respectively are Q_1 collector current and Q_3 base current. Eqn. 9.13 can be re-written as eqn. 9.14.

$$I_{C2} + \frac{(I_{B1} + I_{B2})}{(\beta + 1)} \tag{9.14}$$

Where I_{C2}, I_{B1}, I_{B2} and b respectively are Q_2 collector current, Q_1 base current, Q_2 base current and DC current gain of Q_1, Q_2 and Q_3.

Now $\quad I_{B1} + I_{B2} = 2I_B = \dfrac{2I_{OUT}}{\beta}$

Therefore, eqn. 9.14 can be further written as eqn. 9.15.

$$I_{IN} = I_{OUT} + \frac{(2I_{OUT}/\beta)}{(\beta+1)} = I_{OUT} \times \left[1 + \left\{\frac{2}{\beta(\beta+1)}\right\}\right]$$

Since $\beta >> 1$, then

$$I_{IN} = I_{OUT} \times \left[1 + \left(\frac{2}{\beta^2}\right)\right] \tag{9.15}$$

The incremental output resistance R_o of this current mirror configuration is same as the incremental output resistance r_o of the transistor Q_2. This can be derived from the equivalent circuit as shown in Figure 9.15 drawn by replacing transistors by their small signal equivalent hybrid-pmodels. It is assumed that different transistors are identical.

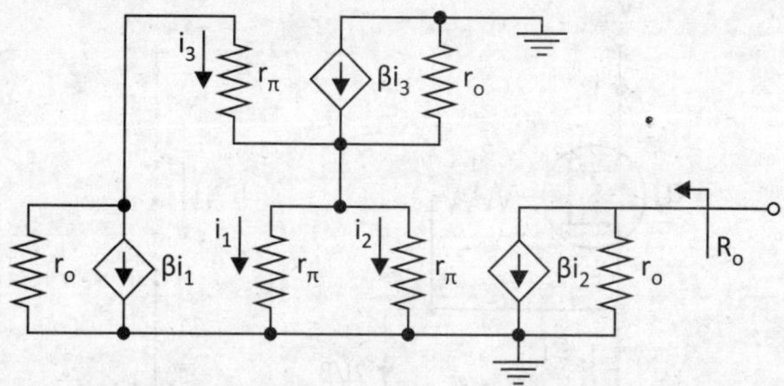

Fig. 9.15: Small signal equivalent circuit of buffered feedback current mirror

Let us take $i_{B1} = \dfrac{v}{r_\pi} = i_{B2}$

Replacing the output Norton circuit of small signal equivalent of Q_1 by its Thevenin's counterpart, we get the circuit of Figure 9.16. If we examine the left hand side loop, we notice the following.

1. There is no independent source
2. There is no controlled source controlled by a parameter external to this loop

Therefore, all currents are zero and so is voltage v. It is therefore concluded that $R_o = r_o$.

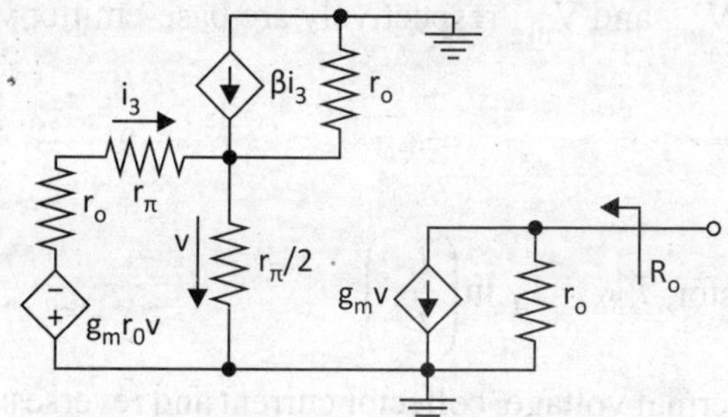

Fig. 9.16: Re-arranged circuit of Figure 9.15

In buffered feedback current mirror, if there were to be a significant capacitance between the base connection common to Q_1 and Q_2 and ground, it could lead to an undesirable response to fast changes in I_{IN} due to vastly unequal currents available for charging and discharging of this capacitance. While the available current to charge this capacitance is potentially equal to b (Q_3) times I_{IN}; the current available to discharge this capacitance is merely $2I_B$. The charging current is much larger than the discharge current.

9.1.3.2 Widlar Current Source circuit

A constant current source should ideally have infinite incremental output impedance. Widlar current source as shown in Figure 9.17 is an improvement over the basic current mirror circuits of Figures 9.2 and 9.3 and offers much higher incremental output impedance. This is achieved by connecting a resistor (R_2 in this case) in series with the emitter terminal of (Q_2). This resistor introduces a current feedback around (Q_2), thus increasing its incremental output resistance. Again, in order to have a constant load current, the circuit must be driven by a constant current rather than (R_1). The expressions for output current and incremental output resistance are derived as follows.

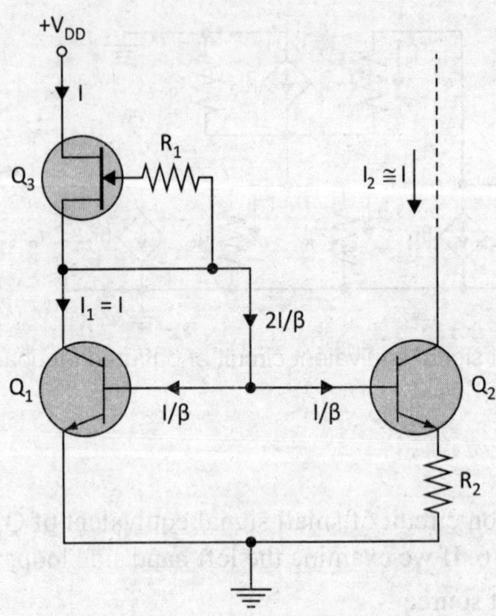

Fig. 9.17: Widlar current source

Refer to Figure 9.17. Applying KVL around base-emitter loop of Q_1 and Q_2 we get,

$V_{BE1} - V_{BE2} - I_o R_2 = 0$; V_{BE1} and V_{BE2} respectively are base-emitter voltages of Q_1 and Q_2.

Or $V_{BE1} = V_{BE2} + I_o R_2$

$$V_{BE1} - V_{BE2} = I_o R_2 \tag{9.16}$$

Now, for a bipolar transistor, $V_{BE} = V_T \ln\left(\dfrac{I_C}{I_S}\right)$

Where V_T, I_C and I_S are thermal voltage, collector current and reverse saturation current respectively. Therefore,

$$V_{BE1} - V_{BE2} = V_T \ln\left(\frac{I_{C1}}{I_{C2}}\right) = V_T \ln\left(\frac{I_{IN}}{I_O}\right) \tag{9.17}$$

This leads to expression for I_2 as eqn. 9.18.

$$I_O R_2 = V_T \ln\left(\frac{I_{IN}}{I_O}\right) \tag{9.18}$$

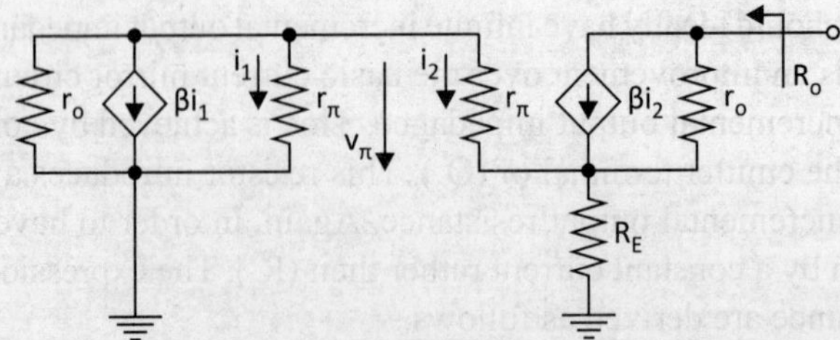

Fig. 9.18: Small signal equivalent circuit of Widlar current mirror

The expression for incremental output resistance R_O of Widlar current mirror can also be derived by replacing the current mirror circuit by its small signal equivalent circuit. The equivalent circuit is shown in Figure 9.18. Note that the equivalent circuit of Figure 9.18 ignores the FET-based constant source feeding the input current I_1.

If we consider $i_{B1} = \frac{v}{r_\pi}$; then current source βi_{B1} can be replaced with an equivalent voltage source $g_m v$, which in turn can be replaced by a $(1/g_m)$ resistor in accordance with voltage source absorption theorem. According to the voltage source absorption theorem, if in one branch of the circuit with current i, there is a voltage source controlled by i, the source can be replaced by a simple impedance with value equal to the source controlling factor. Figure 9.19 shows further simplification of the equivalent circuit of Figure 9.18. In the right hand side loop, the Norton circuit has been replaced by its Thevenin's equivalent.

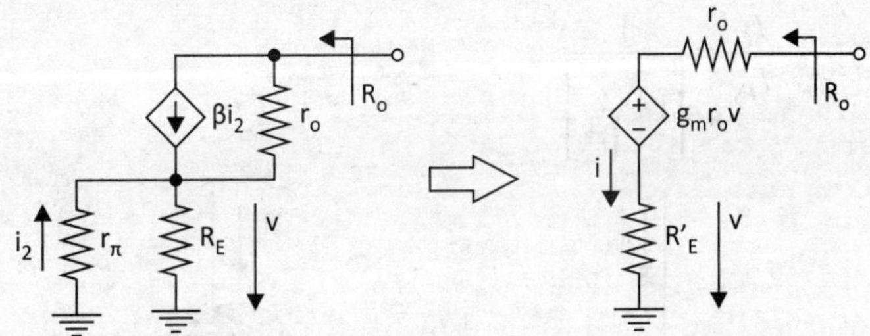

Fig. 9.19: Simplification of equivalent circuit shown in Figure 9.18

The voltage source $g_m r_O v$ can be transformed to $g_m r_O R_E' i$, which can be replaced by a resistance equal to $g_m r_O R_E'$. Therefore, expression for incremental output resistance R_O can be written as eqn. 9.19.

$$R_o = r_o + R_E' + g_m r_o R_E'$$

Since, $\quad R_E' = r_\pi$

$$R_o = r_o + r_\pi + g_m r_o R_E'$$

Since r_p is very small, it may be ignored.

$$R_o = r_o\left(1 + g_m R_E'\right) + r_\pi \cong r_o\left(1 + g_m R_E'\right)$$

9.1.3.3 Wilson Current Source

Wilson current source as shown in Figure 9.20 has the advantage of virtually eliminating the base current mismatch of the conventional current mirror configuration. The other advantage is its higher incremental output resistance. The expressions for output current and incremental output resistance are derived as follows.

$$I_{IN} = I_{C1} + I_{B3} = I_{C2} + \frac{I_O}{\beta} \tag{9.19}$$

$$I_{C2} = I_{E3} - I_{B1} - I_{B2} = I_{E3} - \frac{2I_{C2}}{\beta}$$

Or

$$I_{C2} = \left[\frac{\beta}{(\beta + 2)}\right] I_{E3} \tag{9.20}$$

Now, $I_{E3} = \left[\frac{(\beta + 1)}{\beta}\right] I_O$

Substituting for I_{E3} in eqn. 9.20, we get eqn. 9.21.

$$I_{C2} = \left[\frac{(\beta+1)}{(\beta+2)}\right] I_O \tag{9.21}$$

Substituting for I_{C2} in eqn. 9.19, we get eqn. 9.22.

$$I_{IN} = I_{C2} + \frac{I_O}{\beta} = \left[\frac{(\beta+1)}{(\beta+2)}\right] I_O + \frac{I_O}{\beta} \tag{9.22}$$

$$= \left[\frac{(\beta^2+2\beta+2)}{(\beta^2+2\beta)}\right] I_O = \left[1+\frac{2}{\beta(\beta+2)}\right] I_O \cong \left[1+\frac{2}{\beta^2}\right] I_O$$

$$\frac{I_{IN}}{I_O} = \left[1+\frac{2}{\beta^2}\right] I_{IN}/I_O \text{ or } \frac{I_O}{I_{IN}} = \frac{1}{\left[1+\frac{2}{\beta^2}\right]} \tag{9.23}$$

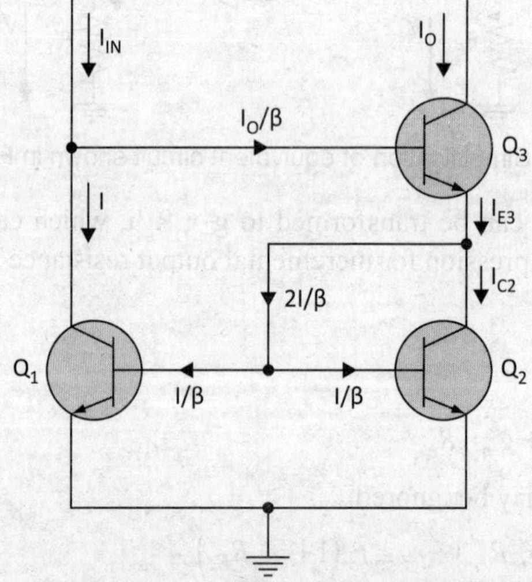

Fig. 9.20: Wilson current source

The incremental output resistance R_O can be determined again by drawing the small signal equivalent circuit of the Wilson current mirror circuit of Figure 9.20 as shown in Figure 9.21.

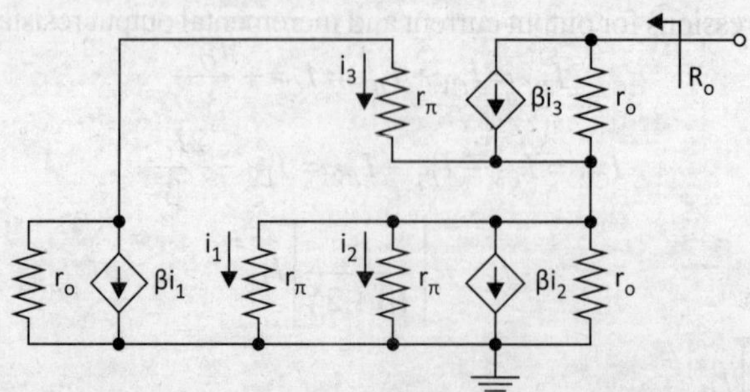

Fig. 9.21: Small signal equivalent circuit of Wilson current mirror circuit of Figure 9.20

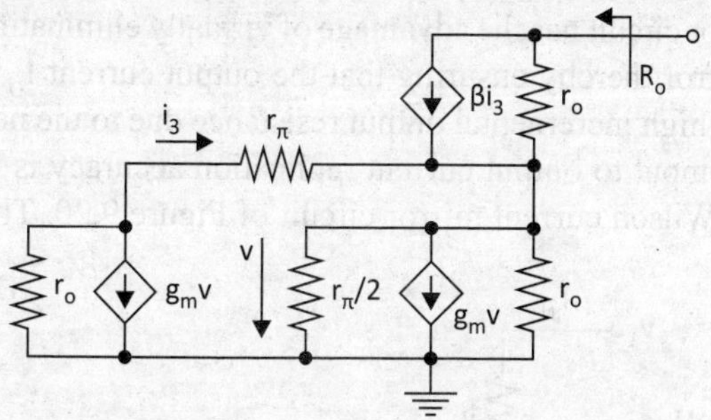

Fig. 9.22: Simplification of circuit of Figure 9.21

Assuming $i_{B1} = i_{B2} = v/r_\pi$, the equivalent circuit of Figure 9.21 modifies to circuit of Figure 9.22. The gmv current source on the right hand side may be replaced by a resistance (= $1/g_m$), which will be much smaller than the parallel combination of r_o and $r_\pi/2$. Also, we replace the g_{mv} Norton source on the left hand side by its Thevenin's equivalent; we get the circuit of Figure 9.23.

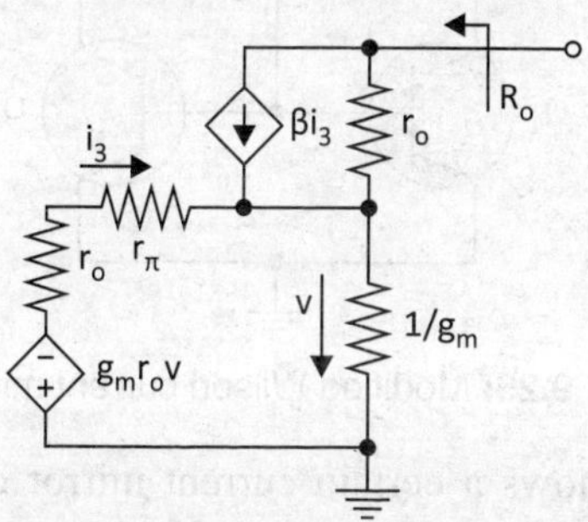

Fig. 9.23: Further simplification of circuit of Figure 9.22

In the circuit of Figure 9.23, $r_o >> r_\pi$. Therefore rp can be ignored. Reverting the Thevenin's source back to Norton's source and replacing the Norton's source by an equivalent resistor (= $1/g_m$), we get the equivalent circuit of Figure 9.24 (a). The circuit of Figure 9.24 (a) is successively transformed, as shown in Figures 9.24 (b) and (c), bearing in mind that $i_{B3} = g_m v$, that $v = i/2g_m$ and that the source $\beta r_o i/2$ may be replaced by a resistor with value $br_o/2$.

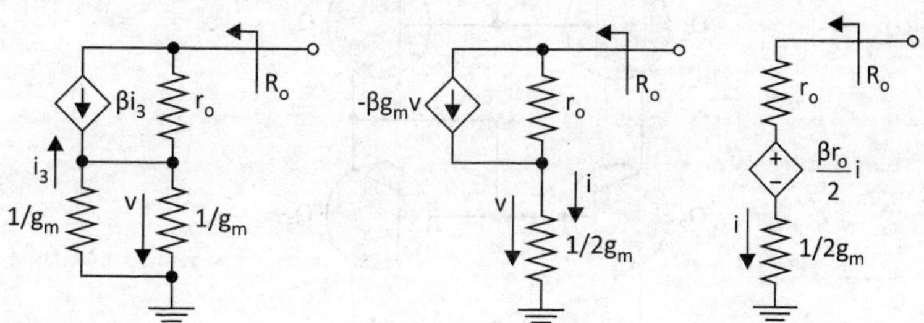

Fig. 9.24: Transformation of equivalent circuit of Figure 9.23

The output resistance R_O is therefore given by:

$$R_O = r_O + \frac{\beta r_O}{2} + \frac{1}{2g_m} \cong r_O + \frac{\beta r_O}{2} \cong r_O\left(1 + \frac{\beta}{2}\right) \cong \frac{\beta r_O}{2} \quad (9.24)$$

The Wilson current mirror circuit has the advantage of virtually eliminating the base current mismatch of the basic BJT current mirror thereby ensuring that the output current I_O is almost equal to the input current I_{IN}. It also has a very high incremental output resistance due to the negative feedback through Q_1 back to the base of Q_3. The input to output current replication accuracy is further improved by adding a fourth transistor Q_4 to the Wilson current mirror circuit of Figure 9.20. The modified circuit is shown in Figure 9.25.

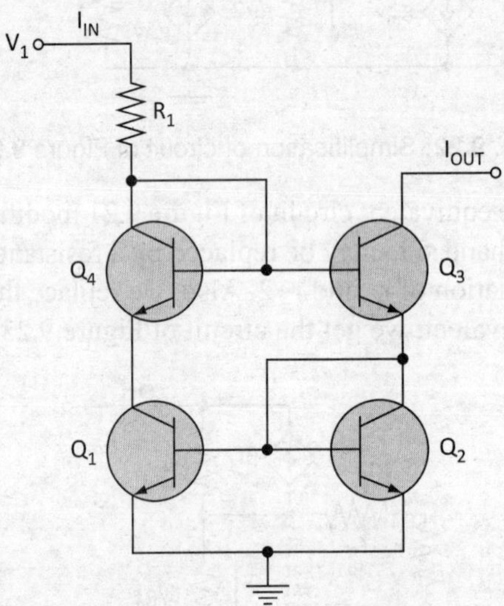

Fig. 9.25: Modified Wilson current mirror

Example 9.4: Figure 9.26 shows a certain current mirror circuit. Identify the current mirror configuration. If all bipolar transistors were identical and had a very high value of β; determine V_{DC}.

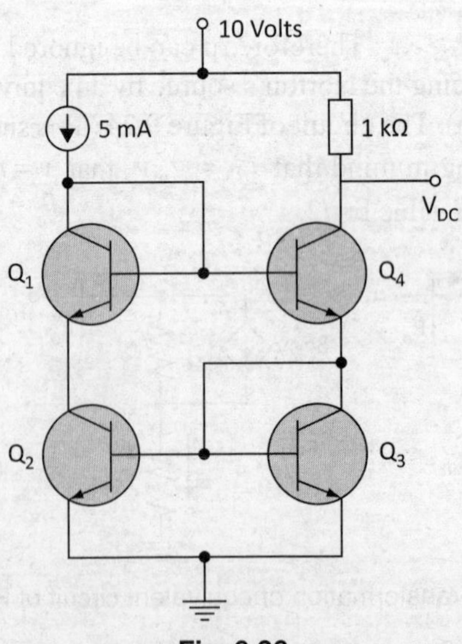

Fig. 9.26

Solution: The current mirror circuit of Figure 9.26 is that of modified Wilson current mirror. The output current that would flow through 1 kΩ resistor is given by:

$$I_O = \frac{I_{IN}}{\left[1+\frac{2}{\beta^2}\right]}$$ $I_O = I_{IN} \times (1 + 2/\beta^2)$....check

Since b is given to be very large,

$I_O \cong I_{IN}$

$I_{IN} = 5$ mA, which gives $I_o = 5$ mA

Therefore, $V_{DC} = 10 - 5 \times 1 = 5V$

Example 9.5: Design a Widlar current source as shown in Figure 9.27 to provide a constant current source of 10 μA with $V_{CC} = 12V$, $R_1 = 33$ kΩ, â =100 and $V_{BE} = 0.7V$.

Solution:

$$I_{OUT} \times R_2 = V_T \times \ln\left(\frac{I_{C1}}{I_O}\right) = V_T \times \ln\left(\frac{I_{IN}}{I_O}\right)$$

$$I_{OUT} = 10\times10^{-6}\ A$$

$$V_T = \frac{T}{11600} = 0.026 \text{ (for } T = 300K)$$

$$I_{IN} = \frac{(12-0.7)}{33\times10^3} = 0.342mA$$

Substituting the values of V_T, I_{OUT} and I_{IN}, we get

$$10\times10^{-6}\times R_2 = 0.026\times\ln\left(\frac{0.342\times10^{-3}}{10\times10^{-6}}\right) = 0.026\times\ln(34.2) = 0.026\times3.532 = 0.092$$

$$\text{Therefore, } R_2 = \frac{0.092}{10\times10^{-6}} = 9.2k\Omega$$

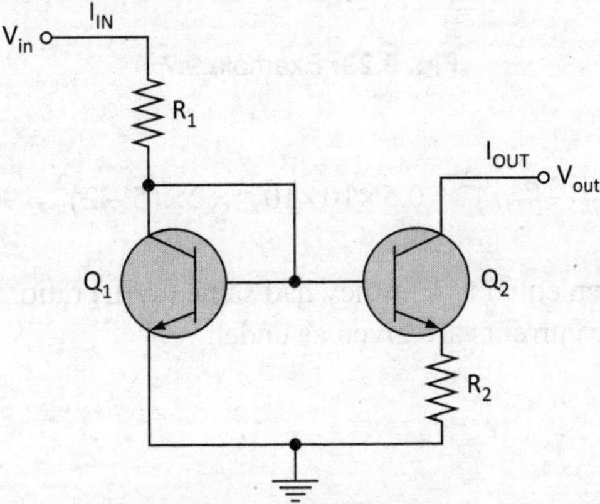

Fig. 9.27: Example 9.5

Example 9.6: Refer to the current mirror circuit of Figure 9.28. Given that all seven transistors are identical; determine I_{OUT} for $I_{IN} = 100$ mA.

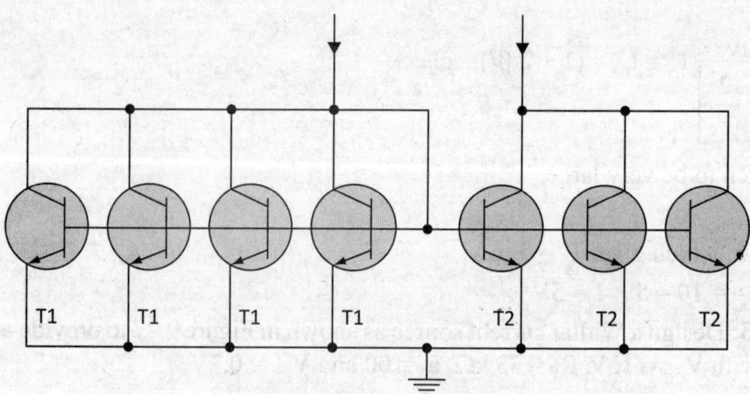

Fig. 9.28: Example 9.6

Solution: There are four parallel-connected transistors on the input side and three parallel-connected transistors on the output side.

Therefore, mirror gain ratio = ¾

I_{IN} = 100 mA; therefore, I_{OUT} = 100 × ¾ = 75 mA.

Example 9.7: Refer to the MOSFET current mirror circuit of Figure 9.29. All MOSFETs are identical except for (W/L) ratio, which is governed by $(W/L)_4 = 2(W/L)_3 = 4(W/L)_2 = 8(W/L)_1$. $(W/L)_1 = 2$, $K_n = 10\ mA/V^2$, $V_{GS} = 5V$ and $V_{TH} = 2V$. Assuming that channel length modulation effects are negligible; determine I_1, I_2, I_3 and I_4.

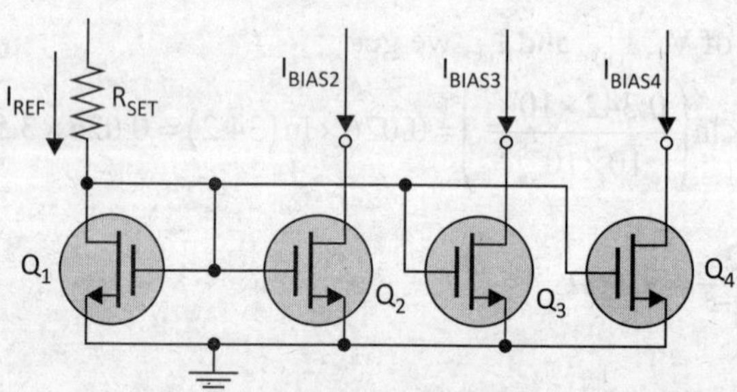

Fig. 9.29: Example 9.7

Solution:

$$I_1 = 0.5 \times K_n \times \left(\frac{W}{L}\right)_1 \times (V_{GS} - V_{TH})^2 = 0.5 \times 10 \times 10^{-3} \times 2 \times (5-2)^2 = 90mA$$

I_2, I_3 and I_4 would have been equal to I_1 if they had same (W/L) ratio. Since they have (W/L) ratios different from that of M_1, these currents are given as under.

I_2 = 2 × 90 = 180 mA

I_3 = 4 × 90 = 360 mA

I_4 = 8 × 90 = 720 mA

Example 9.8: Figure 9.30 shows the circuit diagram for BJT-based Wilson current mirror. Given that V_{CC} = 12V, V_{BE} = 0.7V, R = 47 kΩ, R_L = 33 kΩ and β = 100; determine the load current I_{LOAD}. What would have been the load current if β were 10?

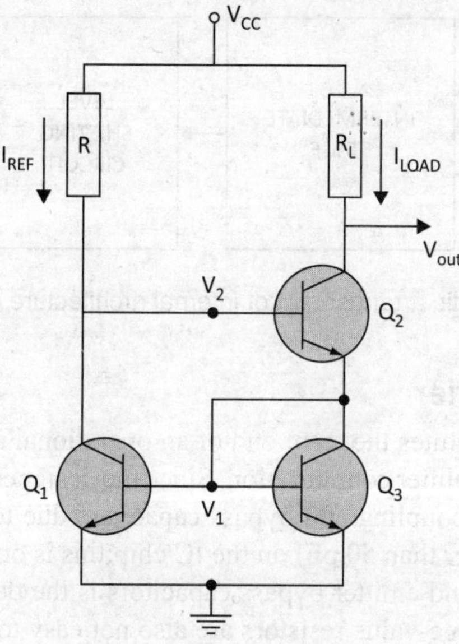

Fig. 9.30: Example 9.8

Solution:

$V_1 = V_{BE} = 0.7V$

$V_2 = 2V_{BE} = 1.4V$

$$I_{REF} = \frac{(12-1.4)}{47\times10^3}A = \frac{10.6}{47}mA = 0.226mA \qquad \frac{I_{LOAD}}{I_{REF}} = \frac{1}{\left(1+\frac{2}{\beta^2}\right)}$$

$$\text{Therefore, } I_{LOAD} = 0.226 \times \left(1+\frac{2}{10000}\right)mA = 0.226 \times 1.0002mA = 0.226mA$$

If transistor b were 10, then

$$I_{LOAD} = 0.226 \times \left(1+\frac{2}{100}\right)mA = 0.226 \times 1.02mA = 0.231mA$$

9.2 INTERNAL ARCHITECTURE OF OPERATIONAL AMPLIFIER

The internal architecture of a typical operational amplifier consists of a differential amplifier input stage that is followed by one or more differential amplifier gain stages and an output stage. Generally, the input differential amplifier provides a differential output and the gain stages provide a single-ended output. The number of gain stages may be different for different opamps. The output of the final gain stage feeds the input of an output stage through an emitter emitter-follower buffer stage. The output stage is a class-B push-pull amplifier that acts like a level translator and output driver. Figure 9.31 shows the block schematic arrangement of the internal circuit of a typical operational amplifier with a differential input and a single- ended output. The output voltage equals product of input voltage and open loop voltage gain, i.e. voltage gain in the absence of any negative feedback. In the following sections, we shall look at the basic circuits used to implement each of the building blocks of the operational amplifier.

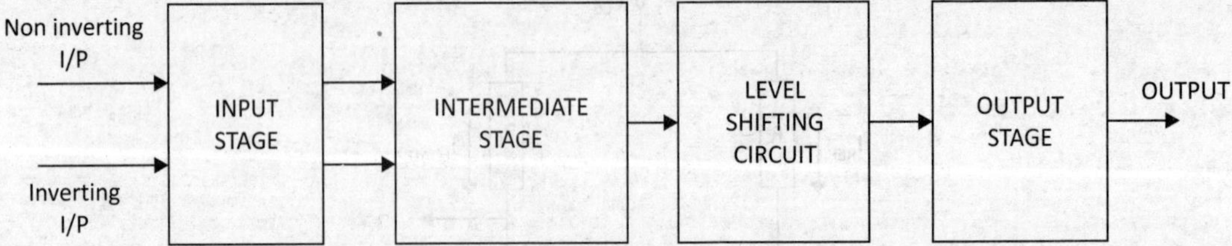

Fig. 9.31: Block schematic arrangement of internal architecture of operational amplifier

9.2.1 Differential Amplifier

Differential amplifier stage constitutes the front end of an operational amplifier. Figure 9.32 shows the basic single-stage differential amplifier configuration. Since the designers of integrated circuit amplifiers do not have the luxury of using coupling and bypass capacitors due to non-practicality of fabricating large large-value capacitors (larger than 50 pF) on the IC chip;this is one of the reasons that differential amplifier requiring no coupling and emitter bypass capacitors is the designers' preferred choice as the opamp front-end circuit. Even large-value resistors are also not easy to fabricate in the IC form. These too are simulated by suitable transistor configurations.

The differential amplifier configuration is also sometimes called a long tail pair as the two transistors share a common emitter resistor. The current through this resistor is called the tail current. Figure 9.32 shows the basic configuration of a differential amplifier with differential input and differential output. In the circuit of Figure 9.32, if the output is single ended and is taken from the collector of transistor Q_2, then the base terminal of Q_1 is the non-inverting input and base terminal of transistor Q_2 is the inverting input. The output is inphase with the signal applied at non-inverting input and out-of-phase with the signal applied at inverting input. This further implies that if two different input signals are applied to inverting and non-inverting inputs, the output is given by eqn. 9.25.

$$V_O = A_d \times (V_1 - V_2) \tag{9.25}$$

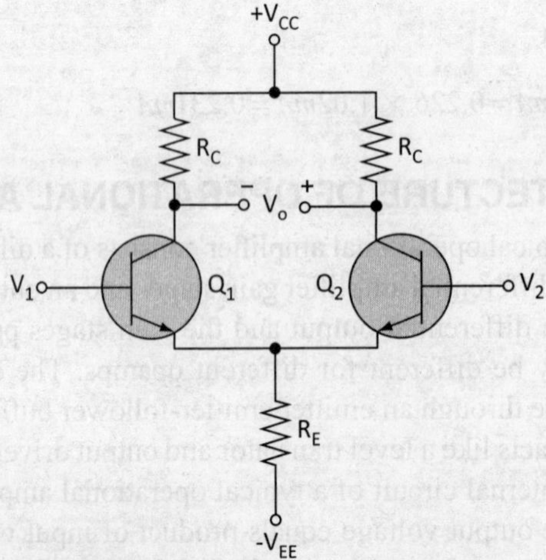

Fig. 9.32: Basic differential amplifier

9.2.1.1 Basic Concept

For DC analysis, if we ignore the voltage drop across base-emitter junctions of the two transistors, the common common-emitter point for all practical purposes is at ground potential. That is, the tail current is given by V_{EE}/R_E, which is constant. The tail current is divided into two separate paths, one through Q_1 and the other through Q_2. As the two halves are symmetrical, total current sharing depends upon the voltages applied to the two inputs. Figure 9.33 shows the circuit diagram and signal wave shapes at relevant points when the signal is applied to inverting and non-inverting inputs separately.

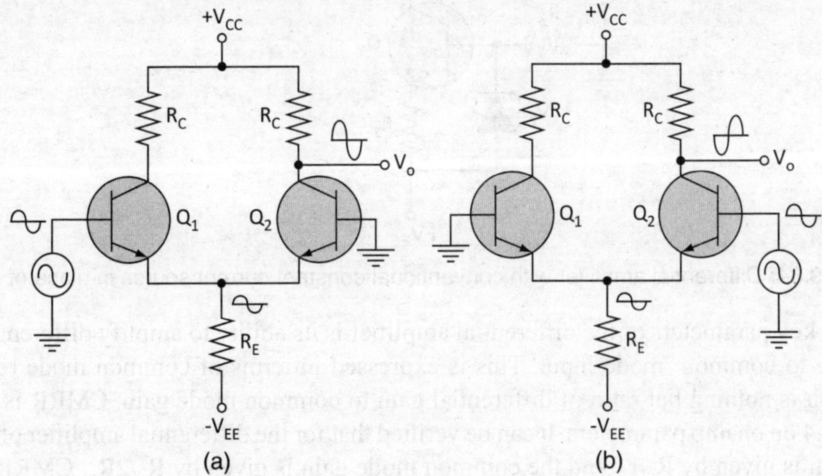

Fig. 9.33: Differential amplifier with signal applied to (a) non-inverting input; (b) inverting input

Let us consider the operation of circuit shown in Figure 9.33 (a). The base of Q_2 (inverting input) is grounded and a sinusoidal signal is applied to the base of Q_1 (Non-inverting input). Initially, same current flows through the two transistors as the two halves are symmetrical. The sum of the two currents equals the constant current flowing through R_E (= V_{EE}/R_E). When the signal applied to the non-inverting input goes through positive half cycle; collector current of Q_1 increases proportionally. Since the sum of two collector currents has to be constant; Q_2-collector current decreases by same proportion. As a result of this, voltage drop across R_C of Q_2 decreases thereby increasing the output voltage V_O. Therefore, during the positive half cycle of input signal, the output also goes through a positive half cycle. Similarly, during the negative half cycle of input signal, the output also goes through negative half cycle. That is, output signal is in phase with input signal. Thus, our contention that Q_1-base is the non-inverting input of the differential amplifier stage is proven to be correct. The amplitude however depends upon gain of the differential amplifier stage, which is discussed in a subsequent paragraph.

Let us now consider the operation of circuit shown in Figure 9.33 (b). The base of Q_1 (Non-inverting input) is grounded and a sinusoidal signal is applied to the base of Q_2 (Inverting input). When the signal applied to the inverting input goes through positive half cycle; collector current of Q_2 increases proportionally. Since the sum of two collector currents has to be constant; Q_1-collector current decreases by same proportion. As a result of this, voltage drop across R_C of Q_2 increases thereby decreasing the output voltage V_O. Therefore, during the positive half cycle of input signal, the output also goes through a negative half cycle. Similarly, during the negative half cycle of input signal, the output also goes through positive half cycle. That is, output signal is out of phase with input signal. Thus, our contention that Q_2-base is the inverting input of the differential amplifier stage is proven to be correct. The amplitude however depends upon gain of the differential amplifier stage, as mentioned in the previous paragraph.

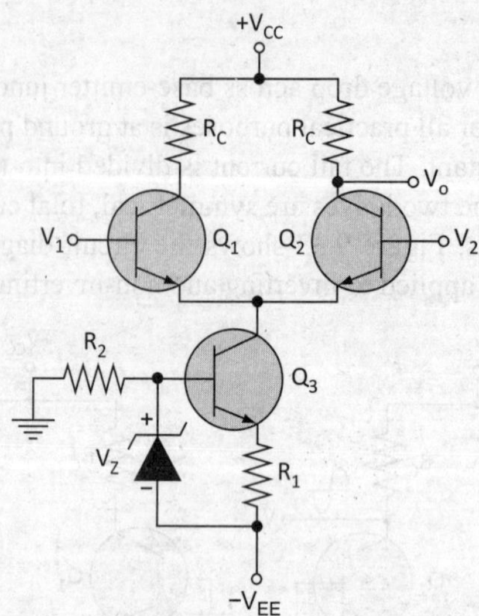

Fig. 9.34: Differential amplifier with conventional constant current source in place of R_E

One of the key parameters of the differential amplifier is its ability to amplify differential input and its insensitivity to common mode input. This is expressed in terms of common mode rejection ratio (CMRR), which is nothing but ratio of differential gain to common mode gain. CMRR is described in detail section 9.4 on opamp parameters. It can be verified that for the differential amplifier of Figure 9.32, differential gain is given by R_C/r_e' and the common mode gain is given by $R_C/2R_E$. CMRR therefore is given by $2R_E/r_e'$, where. r_e' is the dynamic resistance of the base-emitter junctions of the two transistors. Expressions for differential gain, common mode gain and common mode rejection ratio are derived in the latter section.

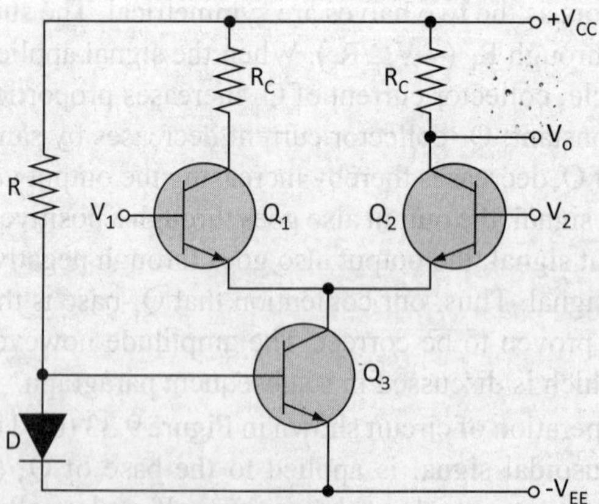

Fig. 9.35: Differential amplifier with current mirror constant current source in place of R_E

It is evident from the expression for CMRR that the value of R_E should be as high as possible. That is why in practical opamp circuits, R_E is replaced by a constant current source. A current mirror configuration is also used to implement a constant current source. Figures 9.34 shows differential amplifier circuits with a conventional constant current source. The constant current in this case is the current flowing through R_1, which is further equal to $(V_Z - V_{BE})/R_1$.

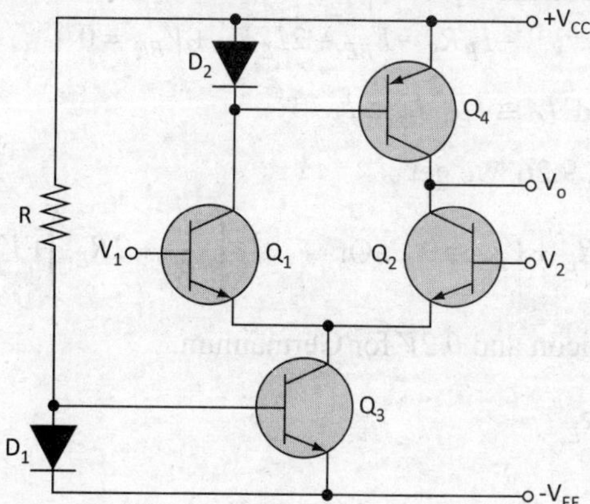

Fig. 9.36: Differential amplifier with current mirrors used in place of emitter and collector resistors

The current mirror comprising resistor R, diode D and transistor Q_3 works as follows. If the diode connected across the base-emitter junction and the base-emitter junction diode of the transistor had matched current-voltage characteristics, the collector current of the transistor equals the current through resistor R. In other words, the collector current is a mirror image of the resistor current. In the basic current mirror circuit discussed in the earlier part of the chapter employs a transistor with its collector shorted to the base to simulate a diode function. Different current mirror circuits were discussed in section 9.1. As it is very easy to match the current-voltage characteristics of a diode and base-emitter junction diode of a transistor in ICs because of both being on same chip, current mirror configuration is commonly used as current source and active load in IC opamps. Figure 9.36 shows a differential amplifier stage with current mirrors being used instead of emitter resistor R_E and collector resistor R_C.

9.2.1.2 Design of BJT-based Differential Amplifier

Design of differential amplifier involves DC analysis to determine the operating point values I_{CQ} and V_{CEQ} of the two bipolar transistors used in the circuit. The DC equivalent circuit of the differential amplifier is obtained by reducing all AC signals to zero as shown in Figure 9.37.

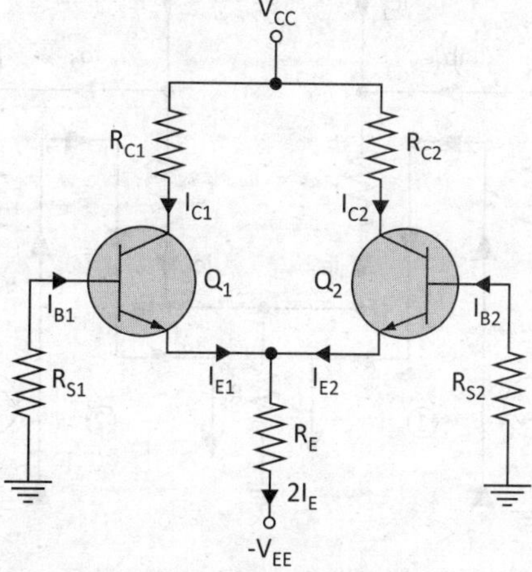

Fig. 9.37: DC equivalent circuit of differential amplifier

Applying KVL to base-emitter loop of Q_1,

$$-I_B R_S - V_{BE} - 2I_E R_E + V_{EE} = 0 \tag{9.26}$$

Since $\quad I_C = \beta I_B$ and $I_C \cong I_E$, $I_B \cong I_E/\beta$

Substituting for I_B in eqn. 9.26, we get

$$\frac{-I_E}{\beta} R_S - V_{BE} - 2I_E R_E + V_{EE} = 0 \quad \text{Or} \quad -I_E\left(\frac{R_S}{\beta} + 2R_E\right) + V_{EE} - V_{BE} = 0$$

Where $V_{BE} = 0.7V$ for Silicon and $0.2V$ for Germanium.

Also, $\quad \left(\frac{R_S}{\beta}\right) << 2R_E$

Therefore,
$$I_E = \frac{(V_{EE} - V_{BE})}{2R_E} \tag{9.27}$$

Eqn. 9.27 establishes two things, one that I_E is independent of R_C and two that R_E determines the emitter current of Q_1 and Q_2.

Also, $V_E = -V_{BE}$ as the voltage drop across R_S being negligible can be ignored.

$$V_{CE} = V_C - V_E = V_{CC} - I_C R_C - V_E = V_{CC} - I_C R_C - (-V_{BE}) = V_{CC} + V_{BE} - I_C R_C \tag{9.28}$$

Since Q_1 and Q_2 are identical; eqns. 9.27 and 9.28 can be used to establish the operating point values for both.

That is, $I_C \cong I_E = \dfrac{(V_{EE} - V_{BE})}{2R_E}$ and $V_{CE} = V_{CC} + V_{BE} - I_C R_C$

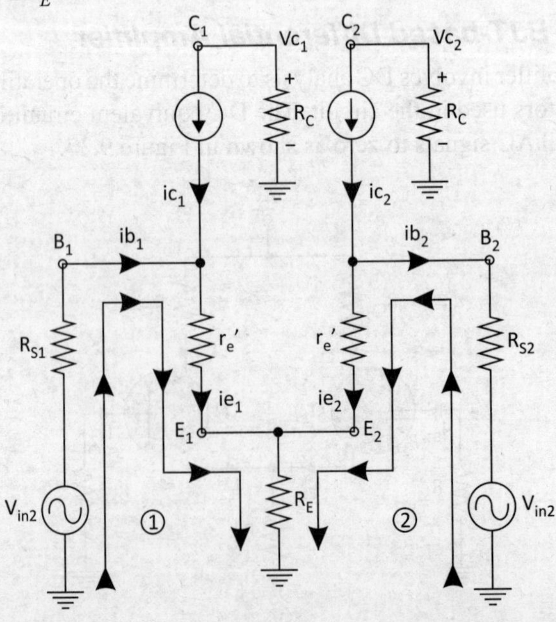

Fig. 9.38: AC equivalent circuit of differential amplifier

Differential gain, differential input resistance, output resistance and common mode rejection ratio (CMRR) can be determined by doing AC analysis of the differential amplifier circuit. Figure 9.38 shows the ac equivalent circuit of the differential amplifier. This is obtained by replacing all DC voltage sources by short circuits and the two bipolar transistors by their equivalent models.

Differential Voltage Gain

Since both DC emitter currents are equal, $r_{e1}^{'} = r_{e2}^{'} = r_e^{'}$

Applying KVL in loop 1 and 2, we get eqns. 9.29 and 9.30.

$$V_{in1} = R_{S1} i_{b1} + i_{e1} r_e^{'} + (i_{e1} + i_{e2}) R_E \tag{9.29}$$

$$V_{in2} = R_{S2} i_{b2} + i_{e2} r_e^{'} + (i_{e1} + i_{e2}) R_E \tag{9.30}$$

Now, $i_{b1} = \frac{i_{c1}}{\beta} \cong \frac{i_{e1}}{\beta}$ and $i_{b2} = \frac{i_{c2}}{\beta} \cong \frac{i_{e2}}{\beta}$

Substituting for I_{b1} and I_{b2} in eqns. 9.29 and 9.30, we get eqns. 9.31 and 9.32.

$$V_{in1} = \left(\frac{R_{S1}}{\beta}\right) i_{e1} + i_{e1} r_e^{'} + (i_{e1} + i_{e2}) R_E \tag{9.31}$$

$$V_{in2} = \left(\frac{R_{S2}}{\beta}\right) i_{e2} + i_{e2} r_e^{'} + (i_{e1} + i_{e2}) R_E \tag{9.32}$$

Since R_{s1} and R_{s2} are very small value resistances, R_{S1}/β and R_{S2}/β will be negligible as compared to R_E and r_e'. Eqns. 9.31 and 9.32 reduce to eqns. 9.33 and 9.34 respectively.

$$V_{in1} = i_{e1}\left(r_e^{'} + R_E\right) + i_{e2} R_E \tag{9.33}$$

$$V_{in2} = i_{e2}\left(r_e^{'} + R_E\right) + i_{e1} R_E \tag{9.34}$$

We can determine expressions for i_{e1} and i_{e2} by solving eqns. 9.33 and 9.34.

$$i_{e1} = \frac{\left[V_{in1}\left(r_e^{'} + R_E\right) - V_{in2} R_E\right]}{\left(r_e^{'} + R_E\right)^2 - R_E^{\,2}} \tag{9.35}$$

$$i_{e2} = \frac{\left[V_{in2}\left(r_e^{'} + R_E\right) - V_{in1} R_E\right]}{\left(r_e^{'} + R_E\right)^2 - R_E^{\,2}} \tag{9.36}$$

Differential output voltage,

$$V_o = V_{C2} - V_{C1} = -R_C i_{C2} - (-R_C i_{C1}) = R_C \times (i_{C1} - i_{C2}) \cong R_C \times (i_{e1} - i_{e2}) \tag{9.37}$$

Substituting for i_{e1} and i_{e2} in eqn. 9.37, we get expression for V_o as:

$$V_o = \frac{\left[R_C \times (V_{in1} - V_{in2})\left(r_e^{'} + 2R_E\right)\right]}{\left[r_e^{'}\left(r_e^{'} + 2R_E\right)\right]}$$

Or $V_o = \left(\frac{R_C}{r_e'}\right)(V_{in1} - V_{in2})$

Therefore, differential gain, $A_d = \frac{V_o}{(V_{in1} - V_{in2})} = \left(\frac{R_C}{r_e'}\right)$ (9.38)

Common Mode Gain

Common mode gain of a differential amplifier can be determined by using the half circuit concept where the differential amplifier circuit is divided into two identical halves as shown in Figure 9.39. The emitter current I_E in this case is equally divided as $I_E/2$ into the two half circuits. Also, R_E becomes $2R_E$ in the two halves. The half circuit concept is valid as long as the resistance seen looking into each emitter is the same.

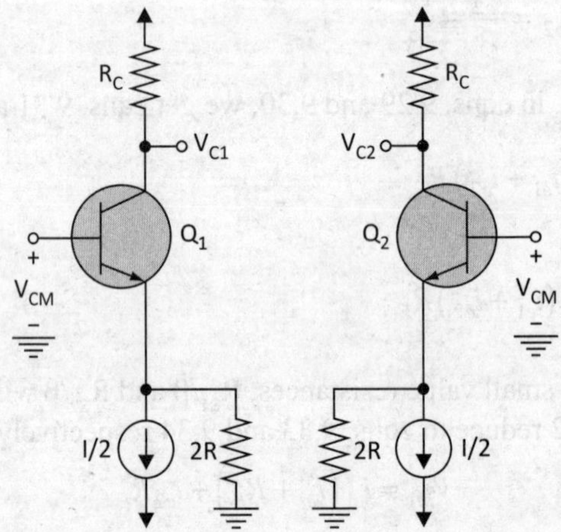

Fig. 9.39: Common mode analysis of differential amplifier

The magnitude of common mode gain, $A_{CM} = \frac{V_o}{V_{CM}} = \left(\frac{\beta R_C}{r_\pi + 2(\beta+1)R_E}\right)$

Since $\beta >> 1$ and $2\beta R_E >> r_\pi$

$$A_{CM} \cong \frac{R_C}{2R_E} \tag{9.39}$$

Differential Input Resistance

Differential Input Resistance is the equivalent resistance measured across either of input terminals and ground. Thus, R_{i1} and R_{i2} can be determined by respectively grounding V_{in2} and V_{in1}.

$$R_{i1} = \frac{V_{in1}}{I_{b1}} \text{ (for } V_{in2}=0) = \frac{\beta V_{in1}}{I_{e1}}$$

Substituting for i_{e1} from eqn. 9.35,

$$R_{i1} = \beta V_{in1} \Bigg/ \left\{\frac{\left[V_{in1}\left(r_e' + R_E\right) - V_{in2}R_E\right]}{\left(r_e' + R_E\right)^2 - R_E^2}\right\}$$

$$R_{i1} = \beta \Big/ \left\{ \frac{\left(r_e' + R_E\right)}{\left(r_e'^2 + 2r_e' R_E\right)} \right\} = \left\{ \beta r_e' \left(r_e' + 2R_E\right) \right\} \Big/ \left(r_e' + R_E\right) \quad (9.40)$$

Since $R_E >> r_e'$

Therefore, $\left(r_e' + 2R_E\right) \cong 2R_E$ and $\left(r_e' + R_E\right) \cong R_E$

Eqn. 9.41 reduces to eqn. 9.42.

$$R_{i1} \cong 2\beta r_e' \quad (9.41)$$

Similarly, $R_{i2} \cong 2\beta r_e'$ (9.42)

Output Resistance

Here, we are referring to the single-ended output resistance. It is the resistance between the collector terminal of the one of the transistors and ground.

$$R_{o1} = R_{o2} = R_C \quad (9.43)$$

Common Mode Rejection Ratio

Common mode rejection ratio (CMRR) is the ratio of differential gain to common mode gain. It is the ability of the differential amplifier to amplify only the differential input signal and reject common mode signals. The effectiveness of rejection of common mode input signal depends on the matching of the two common-emitter stages used in the differential amplifier. CMRR is generally expressed in decibels.

$$CMRR = \frac{A_d}{A_{cm}}$$

$$A_d = \frac{R_C}{r_e'} \text{ and } A_{cm} = \frac{R_C}{2R_E}$$

Therefore, $CMRR = \left(\frac{R_C}{r_e'}\right) \Big/ \left(\frac{R_C}{2R_E}\right) = \frac{2R_E}{r_e'}$ (9.44)

In the ideal case, common mode gain is zero. Therefore, CMRR is ideally infinite. CMRR is generally expressed in decibels and is given by:

$$CMRR\ (in\ decibels) = 20 \log \left| \frac{A_d}{A_{cm}} \right| \quad (9.45)$$

9.2.1.3 Design of MOSFET-based Differential Amplifier

Figure 9.40 shows the basic MOSFET-based differential amplifier. In the following paragraphs, we shall derive expressions for differential gain, common mode gain and common mode rejection ratio. The overall gain offered by the differential amplifier has contributions from differential gain and common mode gain. Differential gain A_d is the gain offered by differential amplifier to differential input i.e. $(V_{in1} - V_{in2})$. Common mode gain A_c is the gain offered by the differential amplifier to common mode input i.e. $(V_{in1} + V_{in2})/2$.

Mathematically, $V_o = A_d \times \left(V_{in1} - V_{in2}\right) + A_c \times \left[\frac{\left(V_{in1} + V_{in2}\right)}{2}\right]$ (9.46)

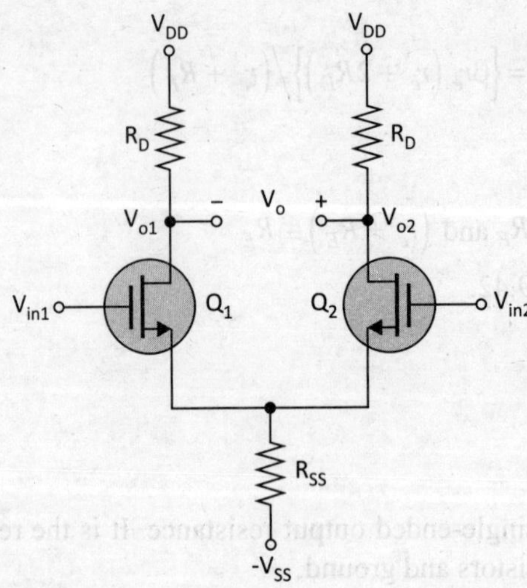

Fig. 9.40: Basic MOSFET-based differential amplifier

Common Mode Gain

Common mode gain can be computed by applying the same common mode input to both inverting and non-inverting inputs as shown in Figure 9.41 (a). A simple approach to computing the common mode gain is to break the circuit into two identical half circuits as shown in Figure 9.41 (b). The two half circuits are nothing but two identical common source amplifier circuits with source resistor.

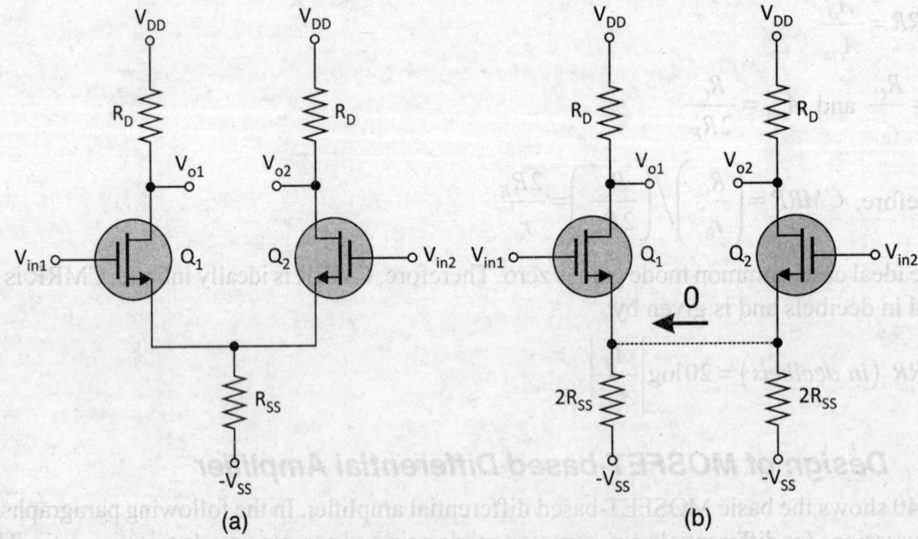

Fig. 9.41: computation of common mode gain

Therefore, common mode gain $A_c = \frac{V_{o1}}{V_c} = \frac{V_{o2}}{V_c} = -\frac{g_m R_D}{\left(1 + 2g_m R_{SS} + \frac{R_D}{r_o}\right)}$ (9.47)

$$g_m = \text{Transconductance of MOSFET} = \sqrt{2K_n\left(\frac{W}{L}\right)I_d} = \frac{2I_d}{(V_{GS} - V_{TH})}$$

In the expression for A_c, the term $2g_mR_{SS}$ in the denominator is much larger than the remaining term $(1 + R_D/r_o)$. Therefore, the expression reduces to eqn. 9.48.

$$A_{cm} = \frac{R_C}{2R_{SS}} \tag{9.48}$$

Input Common Mode Range

Input common mode range (ICMR) is the range of common mode input voltages for which the differential amplifier maintains linear relationship between the output and differential input. That is, throughout the input common mode range, the amplifier works with the same differential gain. For operation to be linear, neither of the two MOSFETs should come out of saturation. The input common mode range is approximately 50% of $V_{DD} - V_{SS}$.

Differential Gain

For computation of differential gain also, the differential amplifier circuits can be broken into two identical half circuits as shown in Figure 9.42.

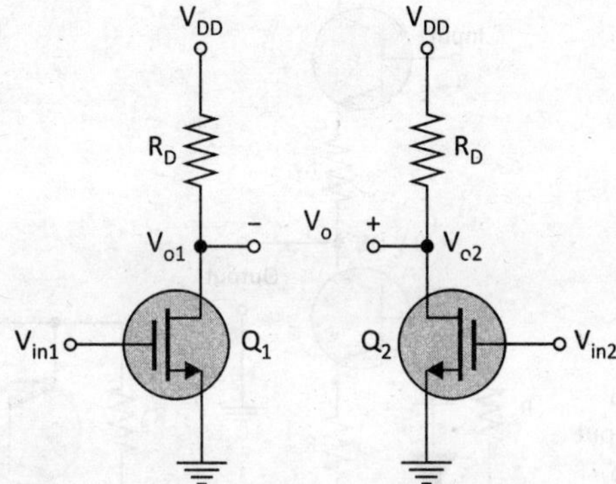

Fig. 9.42: Computation of differential gain

$$\text{Differential gain, } A_d = \frac{\text{Differential output}}{\text{Differential input}} = \frac{(V_{o2} - V_{o1})}{(V_{in2} - V_{in1})} = -g_m \times (r_o \| R_D)$$

For $R_D >> r_o$, $A_d = -g_m \times R_D$

9.2.2 Intermediate Gain Stage

Referring to block schematic arrangement of the internal architecture of an operational amplifier as shown in Figure 9.31 earlier; the input stage is a dual input balanced output differential amplifier which provides most of the voltage gain of amplifier and also establishes the input resistance of operational amplifier. The *intermediate stage* of operational amplifier is another differential amplifier stage that also contributes to the overall voltage gain. It is driven by the differential output of the first stage. The intermediate differential amplifier stage is usually a differential (balanced) input and single-ended (unbalanced) output stage as shown in Figure 9.43.

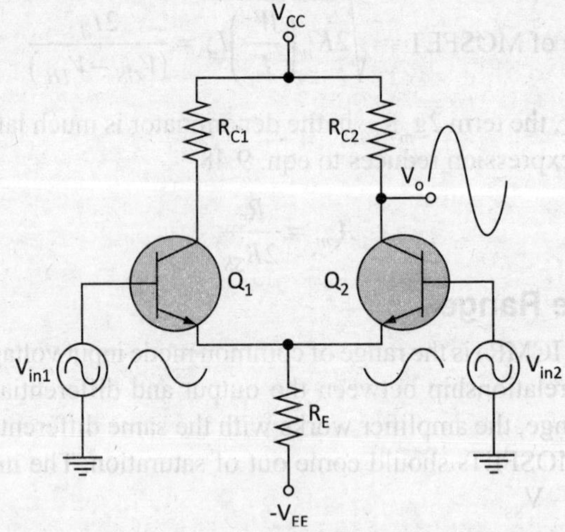

Fig. 9.43: Balanced-input, unbalanced output differential amplifier

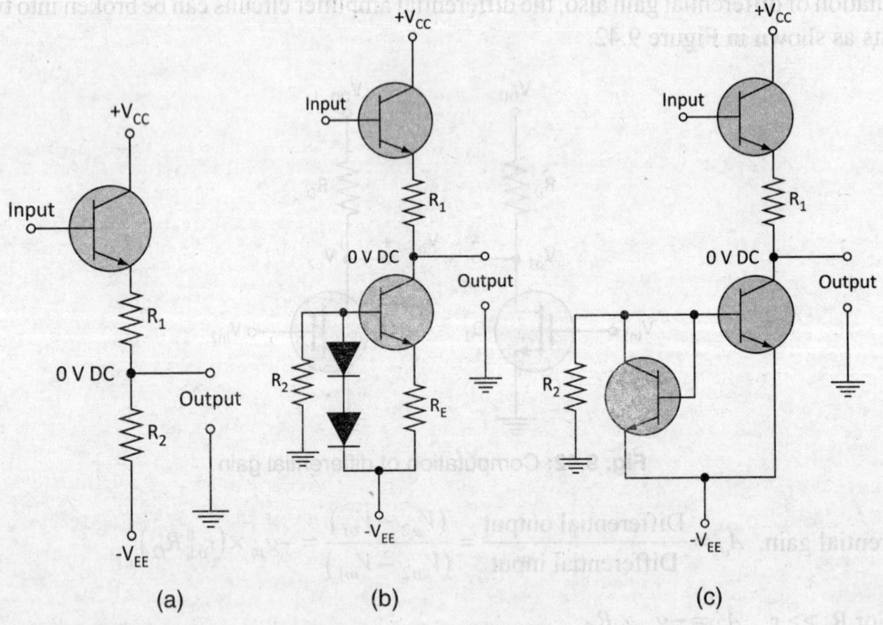

Fig. 9.44: Level shifting stage

9.2.3 Level Shifting Stage

Operational amplifiers are direct coupled (DC) amplifiers. The input stage as described earlier is a differential amplifier, which is then followed by one or more intermediate differential amplifier gain stages. We often assume perfect symmetry and ideally matched devices for differential amplifiers so that the differential common mode output is zero. In practice, while each amplifier stage produces AC amplification of the signal but at the same time a small DC voltage present at the input due to offsets also gets amplified in successive stages due to direct coupling. The problem becomes severe due to high gain of multi-stage differential amplifier stages in an operational amplifier. This can limit the voltage swing and even cause distortions at the output. To address this problem, a *level shifter* or *translator stage* is used following intermediate differential amplifier stage. The level shifter or translator circuit shifts DC level to zero. Level translator is an emitter follower stage. Different circuit configurations are in use. We can use voltage divider emitter follower circuit as shown in Figure 9.44 (a) for the purpose. Here, DC voltage is determined by the ratio of R_1 and R_2. A current mirror bias (Figure 9.44b) or a diode current bias (Figure 9.44c) may be used for better results.

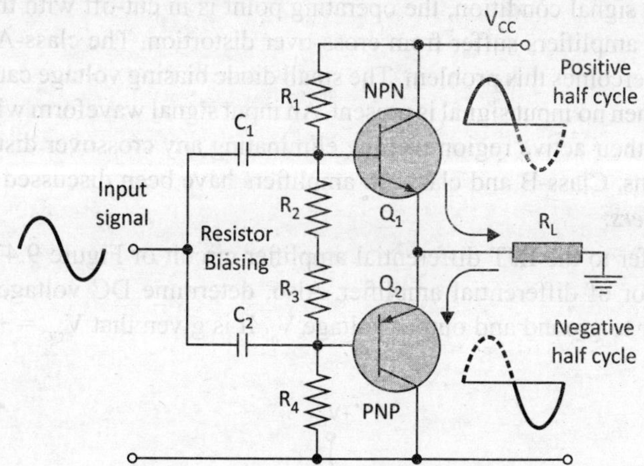

Fig. 9.45: Class-B complementary symmetry push-pull amplifier

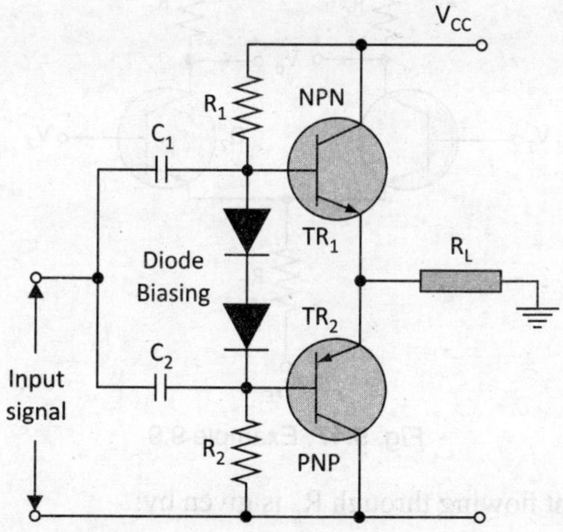

Fig. 9.46: Class-AB complementary symmetry push-pull amplifier

9.2.4 Output Stage

Key functions of *output stage of an operational amplifier include efficient delivery of power to load implying increased output voltage swing and current delivery capability; providing low output resistance and handling large signals with low total harmonic distortion (THD). Various circuit configurations are available for the purpose. These include class-A, class-B and class-AB amplifiers. The output stage in an operational amplifier* is usually a complementary symmetry class-B or class-AB push-pull amplifier. Basic

Class-B and class-AB push-pull amplifier configurations are shown in Figures 9.45 and 9.46 respectively. Class-B amplifiers use two or more transistors that are biased in such a way that each transistor conducts only during one half cycle of the input waveform. The term complementary symmetry has its origin in the fact that one of the transistors is NPN type and the other is PNP type and also that they are made with the same material and technology and are of same maximum ratings. The resistors R_1 and R_2 provide the voltage divider bias to forward bias the emitter-base Junction of transistor Q_1. Similarly, resistors R_3 and R_4 provide the voltage divider bias for emitter-base junction of transistor Q_2. The resistor values are so selected that under zero signal condition, the operating point is in cut-off with the result that collector current is zero. Class-B amplifiers suffer from cross-over distortion. The class-AB amplifier circuit as shown in Figure 9.46 overcomes this problem. The small diode biasing voltage causes both transistors to slightly conduct even when no input signal is present. An input signal waveform will cause the transistors to operate as normal in their active region thereby eliminating any crossover distortion present in pure Class B amplifier designs. Class-B and class-Ab amplifiers have been discussed at length in chapter-5 on *Large Signal Amplifiers*.

Example 9.9: Refer to the BJT differential amplifier circuit of Figure 9.47. Estimate dc emitter current in each transistor of differential amplifier. Also, determine DC voltage from Q_1-collector to ground and Q_2-collector to ground and output voltage V_o. It is given that V_{CC} = + 12V, V_{EE} = –12V, R_C = 15K and R_E = 30K.

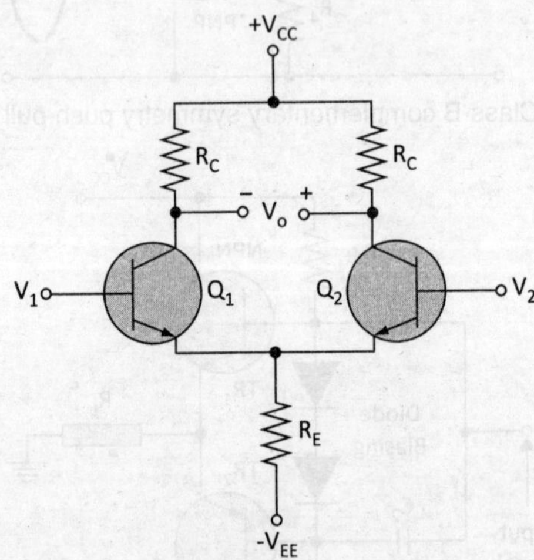

Fig. 9.47: Example 9.9

Solution: The tail current flowing through R_E is given by:

$$I_E = \frac{(V_{EE} - V_{BE})}{R_E} \cong \frac{V_{EE}}{R_E} = \frac{12}{30 \times 10^3} = 0.4mA$$

This current gets equally divided among the two transistors.

Since $I_C = I_E$; collector current in each of the two transistors = 0.2 mA

$$V_{CE1} = V_{CC} - I_{C1} \times R_C = 12 - 0.4 \times 15 = 6V$$

Similarly, V_{CE2} = 6V

$$V_o = V_{CE2} - V_{CE1} = 6 - 6 = 0V$$

Example 9.10: Refer to the differential amplifier circuit of Figure 9.48. If this differential amplifier were to provide a differential gain (A_d) of 50 V/V; determine tail current (I), collector resistance (R_c) and differential input resistance (R_{id}). The differential amplifier operates from ± 5V supplies and the design should be such that the quiescent power dissipation does not exceed 2 mW. Assume transistor b = 100.

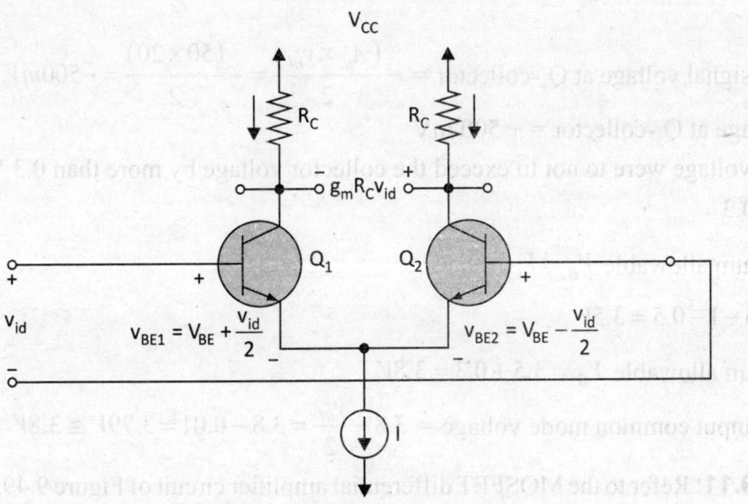

Fig. 9.48: Example 9.10

Solution: Differential gain $A_d = g_m \times R_C$

Now, $g_m = \dfrac{I_C}{V_T}$

where V_T = Thermal voltage taken as equal to 25 mV

I_c = Collector current

Therefore, $A_d = \dfrac{(I_C \times R_C)}{V_T}$

Hence, $I_C \times R_C = 40 \times 25 = 1000mV = 1V$

Quiescent power dissipation = $I \times [5-(-5)] = 10I \leq 2mW$

Therefore, I ≤ 0.2 mA

For I = 0.2 mA, I_c = I/2 = 0.1 mA

Substituting the value of I_c in the equation for $(I_C \times R_C)$ derived earlier, we get

$$R_C = \frac{1}{0.1 \times 10^{-3}} = 10k\Omega$$

Differential input resistance, $R_{id} = 2r_\pi = 2\beta r_e' = \dfrac{2\beta}{g_m}$

$$g_m = \frac{I_C}{V_T} = \frac{0.1}{26} = 0.004A/V$$

Therefore, $R_{id} = \dfrac{2 \times 100}{0.004} = 50k\Omega$

Example 9.11: For the differential amplifier circuit of Figure 9.48, if $v_{id} = 20$ mV; determine the signal voltage at each collector terminal. Also, if V_B were not to exceed V_c by more than 0.3 V to keep the transistors away from saturation; determine the maximum allowable common mode input voltage.

Solution: Differential input voltage v_{id} is equally divided among two transistors in a differential amplifier.

Therefore, signal voltage at Q_1-collector $= -\frac{(A_d \times v_{id})}{2} = -\frac{(50\times 20)}{2} = -500mV$

Signal voltage at Q_2-collector = + 500 mV

If the base voltage were to not to exceed the collector voltage by more than 0.3 V; then

$V_B \le V_C + 0.3$

Or maximum allowable $V_B = V_C + 0.3$

$$V_{C1} = 5 - 1 - 0.5 = 3.5V$$

$\Rightarrow$ Maximum allowable $V_B = 3.5 + 0.3 = 3.8V$

Maximum input common mode voltage $= 3.8 - \frac{v_{id}}{2} = 3.8 - 0.01 = 3.79V \cong 3.8V$

Example 9.11: Refer to the MOSFET differential amplifier circuit of Figure 9.49. MOSFETs Q_1 and Q_2 are identical. $R_D = 500$ ohms, $V_{TH} = 0.5$ V, $I_{D3} = 2$ mA, $V_{OV3} = 0.5$ V and $K_n¢ = 8$ mA/V². Compute V_S, V_D, V_{DS}' and V_{GS} for $V_G = 0$ V. Assume l= 0. Also, V_{OV} for any MOSFET = (V_{GS}- V_{TH}) for that MOSFET.

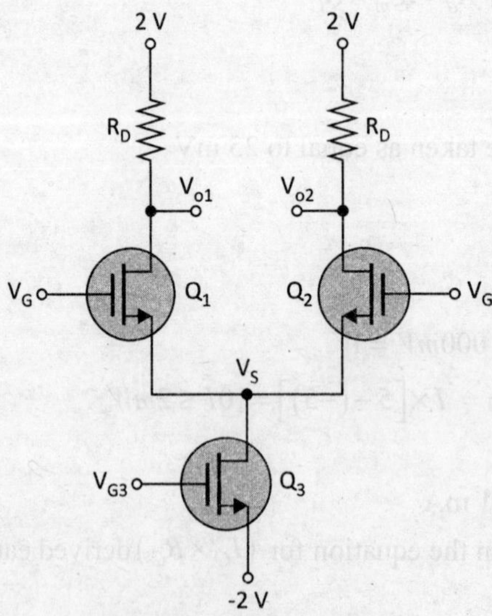

Fig. 9.49: Example 9.11

Solution:

I_{D3} gets equally divided among I_{D1} and I_{D2}.

Therefore, $I_{D1} = I_{D2} = 2/2 = 1$ mA

$$V_{D1} = V_{D2} = V_D - 1\times 10^{-3} \times 500 = 1.5V$$

Assuming Q_1 to be in saturation,

$$I_{D1} = 0.5K_n'V_{OV1}^2 \times (1+\lambda V_{DS1}) \cong 0.5K_n'V_{OV1}^2 \text{ (for l = 0)}$$

$$I_{D1} = 0.5 \times 8 \times V_{OV1}^2 = 1 \times 10^{-3}$$

This gives $V_{OV1} = 0.5$ V

Also, $V_{OV1} = V_{GS1} - V_{TH}$

Or $V_{GS1} = V_{OV1} + V_{TH} = 0.5 + 0.5 = 1V$

Now,

$$V_{DS1} = V_{D1} - V_S = V_{D1} + (V_{GS1} - V_{G1}) = V_{D1} + (V_{OV1} + V_{TH}) - V_{G1} = V_{OV1} + (V_{D1} + V_{TH} - V_{G1})$$

Substituting different values,

$$V_{DS1} = V_{OV1} + (1.5 + 0.5 - V_{G1}) = V_{OV1} + (2 - V_{G1})$$

For $V_{G1} = 0$,

$$V_{DS1} = V_{OV1} + 2 = 0.5 + 2 = 2.5V$$

Now, $V_S = V_{G1} - V_{GS1} = 0 - 1 = -1V$

To summarize results,

V_S = -1 V, V_D = 1.5 V, V_{DS} = 2.5 V and V_{GS} = 1 V

Example 9.12: Find the differential gain and (W/L) of all transistors in the differential amplifier circuit of Figure 9.50. Q_3 and Q_4 are matched and so are Q_1 and Q_2. All transistors have V_{OV} = 0.2 V, $i_n C_{ox}$ = 400 ìA/V², $i_p C_{ox}$ = 100 ìA/V², and $|V_A|$= 3.6 V for both n-channel and p-channel MOSFETs. Ignore channel-length modulation in biasing calculations.

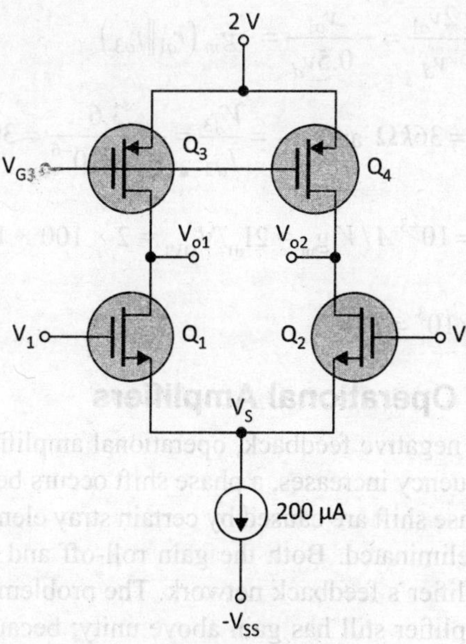

Figure 9.50: Example 9.12

Solution: Since Q_1 and Q_2 are matched; $I_{d1} = I_{d2} = 200/2 = 100\ \mu A$

Also, $I_{d1} = I_{d3}$ and $I_{d2} = I_{d4}$

Since Q_3 and Q_4 are also matched,

Therefore, $I_{d1} = I_{d2} = I_{d3} = I_{d4} = 100\mu A$

$$I_{d1} = 100\times10^{-6} = 0.5\times\alpha_n\times C_{ox}\times\left(\frac{W}{L}\right)_1\times V_{OV1}{}^2$$

$$= 0.5\times400\times10^{-6}\times\left(\frac{W}{L}\right)_1\times(0.2)^2 = 8\times10^{-6}\times\left(\frac{W}{L}\right)_1$$

Therefore, $\left(\frac{W}{L}\right)_1 = \frac{100\times10^{-6}}{8\times10^{-6}} = 12.5 = \left(\frac{W}{L}\right)_2$

Also, $I_{d3} = 100\times10^{-6} = 0.5\times\alpha_n\times C_{ox}\times\left(\frac{W}{L}\right)_3\times V_{OV3}{}^2$

$$= 0.5\times100\times10^{-6}\times\left(\frac{W}{L}\right)_3\times(0.2)^2 = 2\times10^{-6}\times\left(\frac{W}{L}\right)_3$$

Therefore, $\left(\frac{W}{L}\right)_3 = \frac{100\times10^{-6}}{2\times10^{-6}} = 50 = \left(\frac{W}{L}\right)_4$

Differential gain, $A_d = \frac{(v_{o2} - v_{o1})}{v_d}$

Since $v_{o2} = -v_{o1}$

Therefore, $A_d = -\frac{2v_{o1}}{v_d} = -\frac{v_{o1}}{0.5v_d} = -g_m\left(r_{o1}\|r_{o3}\right)$

Now, $r_{o1} = \frac{V_{A1}}{I_{d1}} = \frac{3.6}{100\times10^{-6}} = 36k\Omega$ and $r_{o3} = \frac{V_{A3}}{I_{d3}} = \frac{3.6}{100\times10^{-6}} = 36k\Omega$

$g_m = \frac{2I_{d1}}{V_{OV1}} = \frac{2\times100\times10^{-6}}{0.2} = 10^{-3}\ A/V$ $g_m = 2I_{d1}/V_{OV1} = 2\times100\times10^{-6}/0.2 = 10^{-3}$ A/V

Therefore, $A_d = -10^{-3}\times18\times10^3 = -18$

9.2.5 Compensation in Operational Amplifiers

Gain of a typical amplifier with negative feedback, operational amplifier being no exception, falls off with frequency. Also, as the frequency increases, a phase shift occurs between the input and the output. Both the gain roll-off and the phase shift are caused by certain stray elements such as stray capacitances etc. that cannot be completely eliminated. Both the gain roll-off and input-to-output phase shift are generally dominated by the amplifier's feedback network. The problem actually arises when the phase shift reaches 180° while the amplifier still has gain above unity; because then, the negative feedback turns into positive feedback and the amplifier goes into oscillations thereby becoming unstable. Figures

9.51 (a) and (b) show typical gain and phase plots of unstable and stable amplifiers. The problem can be more severe or more likely in an operational amplifier because of it being a multi-stage amplifier and each amplifier stage adding phase shift. Gain margin and phase margin are often used to quantify the stability of a generalized control system with negative feedback. Gain margin is the factor by which gain needs to be increased or decreased to make the loop gain equal to unity at the frequency where the phase angle is –180°. In other words, the gain margin is (1/G) if (G) is the gain at the –180° phase frequency. Phase margin is the difference between the input-to-output phase shift at unity gain and 180°.

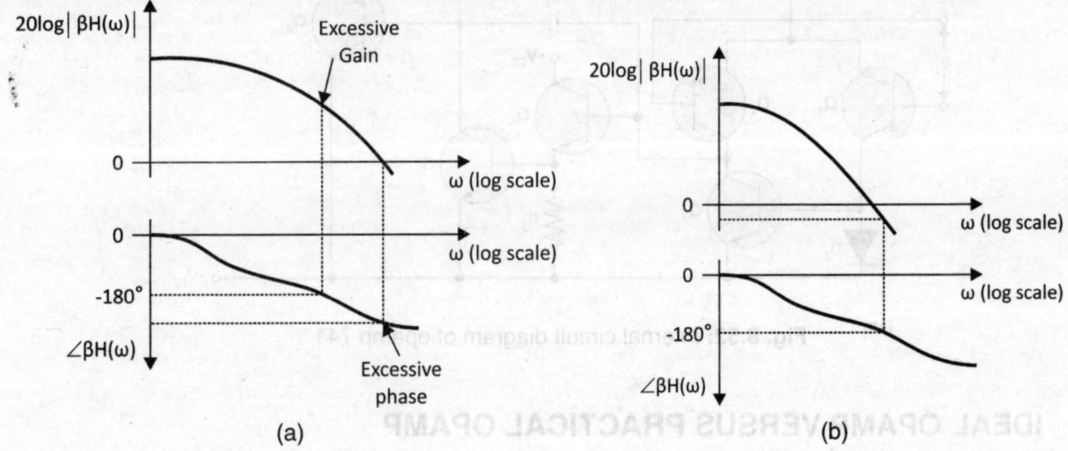

Fig. 9.51: Gain and phase plots for unstable and stable amplifiers

Compensation or frequency compensation, to be more precise, is used to ensure that the amplifier remains stable and does not go to oscillations throughout its usable frequency range. Compensation ensures that the amplifier gain would have fallen below unity or 0 dB if the input-to-output phase shift reached 180° in the frequency range of interest. Compensation is the process of adding an extra feedback component, usually a capacitor, to roll off the gain at a particular rate regardless of the feedback circuit. In this way the gain can be guaranteed to be unity or zero dB by the time the phase shift reaches 180 degrees. Frequency compensation can be internal to the chip(by the manufacturer) or external (by the user) or both. It consists of adding one low pass RC stage in series to reduce the bandwidth so that higher frequencies are not amplified or appear as noise. The resistance value is generally built inside the chip and the user has to connect a low value external capacitor across the designated terminals to provide compensation. Most present day operational amplifiers are internally compensated; which makes them stable right up to gain of unity.

It is pertinent to mention here that Internally compensated opamps are not unconditionally stable. They are stable when used in accordance with the applications. Internal compensation is accomplished in several ways, but the most common method is to connect a capacitor across the collector-base junction of a transistor in a gain stage, usually the intermediate gain stage. If the intermediate gain stage transistor were fed from a buffer stage; the compensation capacitor may be connected from collector of gain providing transistor to base of buffer transistor as shown in Figure 9.52. The circuit diagram shown in Figure 9.52 is incidentally internal circuit diagram of industry standard opamp 741. Here, C_1 is the compensation capacitor. The Miller effect multiplies the capacitor value by an amount approximately equal to the stage gain. Miller effect allows use of small value capacitors for compensation.

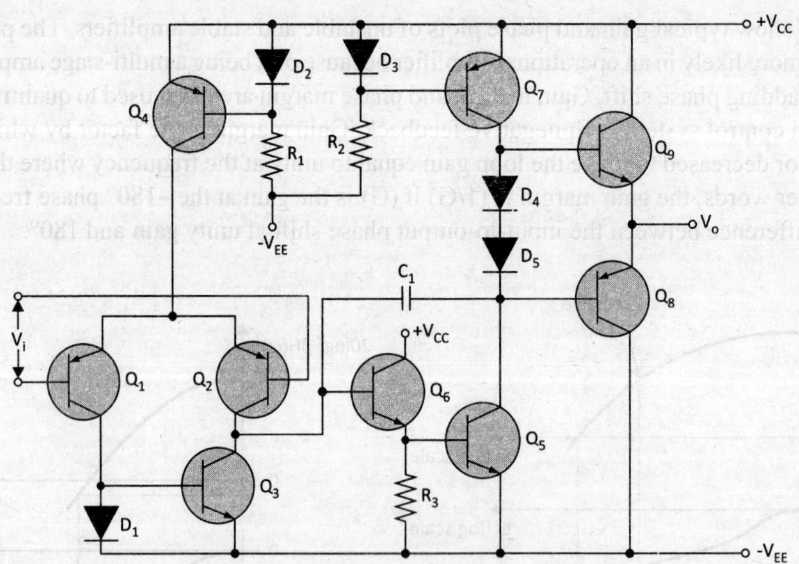

Fig. 9.52: Internal circuit diagram of opamp 741

9.3 IDEAL OPAMP VERSUS PRACTICAL OPAMP

An opamp is a direct-coupled high gain, high bandwidth differential amplifier with very high value of input impedance and very low value of output impedance. Figure 9.53 shows the Thevenin's equivalent circuit model of a generalized amplifier fed at the input from a source having a source resistance R_S and the amplified output feeding a load resistance R_L. Due to finite values of R_i and R_o, the effective value of the gain is less than what it would have been had Ri and Ro been infinite and zero, respectively.

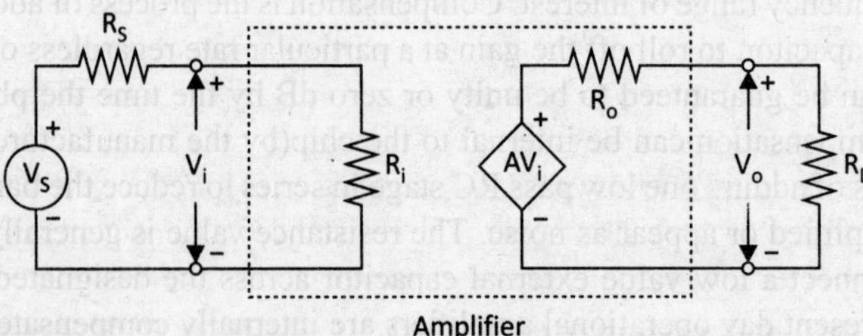

Fig. 9.53: Thevenin's equivalent circuit model of a generalized amplifier

Figure 9.54 shows the Thevenin's equivalent of the opamp. V_I and V_{NI} are, respectively, inverting and non-inverting inputs and A_d is the open- loop differential voltage gain. This is the equivalent circuit model of a practical opamp. There are loading effects at the input and output ports due to finite values of input and output resistances. The ideal opamp model was derived to simplify circuit calculations. The ideal opamp model makes the following three assumptions.

1. Input resistance, Ri = ∞
2. Output resistance, Ro = 0
3. Open- loop gain, Ad = ∞

From the three above-mentioned primary assumptions, other assumptions can be derived. These include the following.

1. Since $R_i = \infty$, $I_I = I_{NI} = 0$.
2. Since $R_o = 0$, $V_o = A_d \times V_d$
3. For linear mode of operation of opamp and a finite output voltage and infinite differential gain, $V_d = 0$.
4. Since output voltage depends only on differential input voltage, it rejects any voltage common to both inputs. Therefore, common mode gain = 0.
5. Bandwidth and slew rate are also infinite as no frequency dependencies are assumed.
6. Drift is also zero as there are no changes in performance over time, temperature, power supply variations and so on.

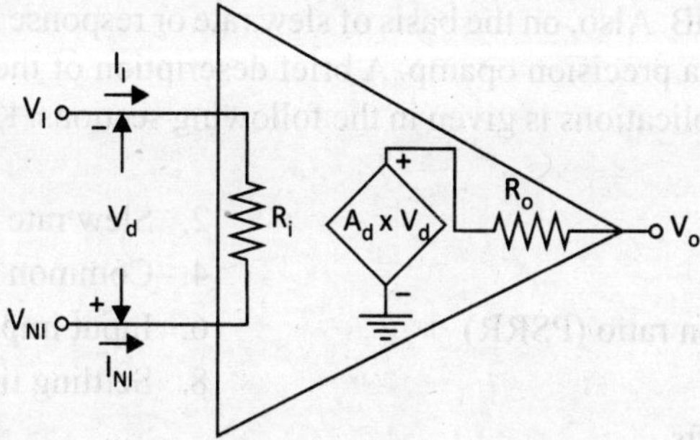

Fig. 9.54: Thevenin's equivalent of a practical opamp

Figure 9.55 shows the Thevenin's equivalent representation of an ideal opamp. To sum up, an ideal opamp is characterized by following basic properties. Knowledge of these properties is sufficient to design and analyze most of the circuits configured around opamps.

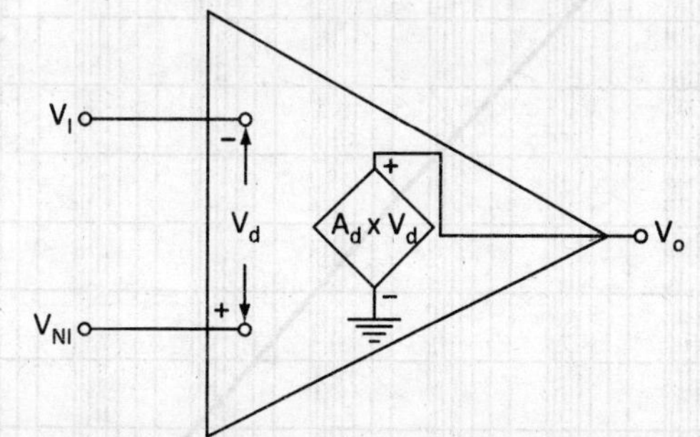

Fig. 9.55: Thevenin's equivalent of an ideal opamp

1. Infinite open-loop differential voltage gain
2. Infinite input impedance
3. Zero output impedance
4. Infinite bandwidth
5. Zero DC input and output offset voltages
6. Zero input differential voltage

Open-loop gain is the differential voltage gain in the absence of any positive or negative feedback. Practical opamps have open-loop gain in the range of 10,000 to 100,000. Input impedance of an ideal opamp is infinite. In the case of real devices, it could vary from hundreds of kilo-ohms for some low-grade opamps to tera-ohms for high-grade opamps. An ideal opamp acts like a perfect voltage source with zero internal impedance. For real devices, output impedance may be in the range of 10 to 100 ohms. The ideal opamp amplifies all signals from DC to highest AC frequencies. In the case of real devices, bandwidth is rather limited and is specified by gain-bandwidth product. An ideal opamp produces a zero output when both the inputs are grounded. In the case of real devices, there may be some finite DC output, referred to as output offset voltage, even when both the inputs are grounded. Output offset may vary from few nano-volts for ultra- low offset opamps to few milli-volts for general-purpose opamps. In the case of ideal opamps, voltage appearing at one input also appears at the other input for linear mode of operation.

9.4 PERFORMANCE PARAMETERS OF OPAMPS

Key performance parameters of an opamp to decide its suitability for a particular application. For instance, an opamp with a CMRR of 120 dB is much better suited for building a differential amplifier than another opamp having CMRR of 80 dB. Also, on the basis of slew rate or response time specifications, we cannot evaluate the performance of a precision opamp. A brief description of the key parameters of an opamp along with their practical implications is given in the following sections. Key opamp parameters include the following.

1. Bandwidth
2. Slew rate
3. Open-loop gain
4. Common mode rejection ratio (CMRR)
5. Power supply rejection ratio (PSRR)
6. Input impedance
7. Output impedance
8. Settling time
9. Offsets and offset drifts

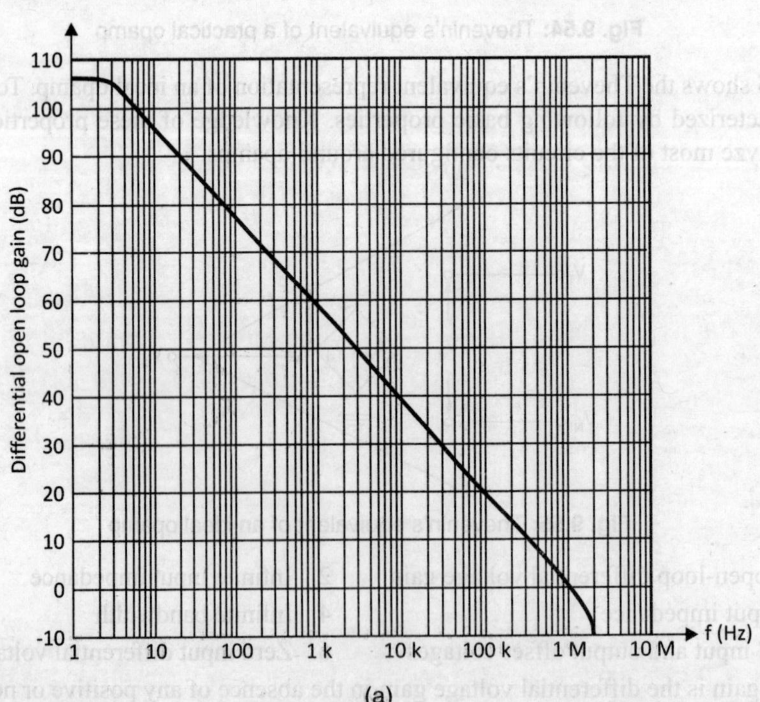

(a)

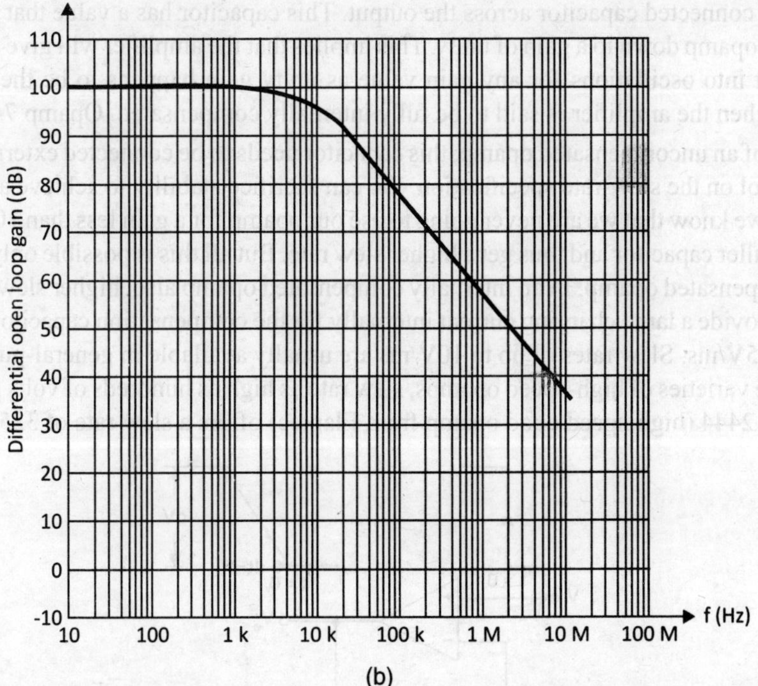

Fig. 9.56: Small signal bandwidth (a) of opamp 741 (b) high-speed opamp AD829

9.4.1 Bandwidth

Bandwidth of an opamp tells us about the range of frequencies it can amplify for a given amplifier gain. The frequency response curve of a typical opamp looks like the graph of Figure 9.56 (a). It is nothing but the frequency response of the general-purpose opamp 741 and the graph has been reproduced from the data sheet of the said opamp. The high-frequency roll-off is attributed to capacitive effects appearing in shunt. Beyond cut-off, the frequency falls at a rate of 6 dB per octave or 20 dB per decade. When the opamp is used in the closed-loop mode, the bandwidth increases at the cost of the gain. The bandwidth is usually expressed in terms of the *unity gain crossover frequency* (also called gain-bandwidth product). It is 1 MHz in the case of opamp 741 as is evident from the graph. It could be as high as 1500 MHz in the case of high bandwidth opamps. Figure 9.56 (b) shows the frequency response of high-speed opamp AD829. It may be mentioned here that the plots shown in Figure 9.56 represent the small signal bandwidth of the opamp. That is, the output signal amplitude and the signal frequency are such that the rate of change of output is less than the slewing rate of the opamp. If it is not so, the signal is termed as large signal and the large signal bandwidth is slew-rate limited. Slew rate and the large signal bandwidth are discussed in the following section.

9.4.2 Slew Rate

Slew rate is one of the most important parameters of an opamp. It gives us an idea as to how well the opamp output follows a rapidly changing waveform at the input. It is defined as the rate of change of output voltage with time. It is determined by applying a step input and monitoring the output as shown in Figure 9.57. The step input simulates the large signal conditions. The incapability of the opamp to follow rapidly rising and falling input is, respectively, due to the minimum charge and discharge times required by an internally connected capacitor across the output. This capacitor has a value that guarantees stable operation of the opamp down to a gain of unity. This implies that the amplifier will give a stable operation and will not get into oscillations for any gain value as unity gain happens to be the worst condition. Now if it is so, then the amplifier is said to be fully internally compensated. Opamp 741 is an example.

In the case of an uncompensated opamp, this capacitor needs to be connected externally. In that case, we have a control on the slew-rate specification. We can sacrifice stability to achieve a higher slew rate. For instance, if we know that we are never going to use our opamp for a gain less than 10; we could afford to connect a smaller capacitor and thus get a higher slew rate. But all this is possible only when we decide to use an uncompensated opamp. In an internally compensated opamp also, higher slew-rate versions are available that provide a large charging current internally for the compensation capacitor. Opamp 741 has a slew rate of 0.5V/ms. Slew rates of up to 10V/ms are usually available in general-purpose opamps. In the case of some varieties of high-speed opamps, slew rate as high as hundreds of volts per microseconds is available. EL 2444 (high-speed quad opamp from Elantec) offers a slew rate of 325 V/ms.

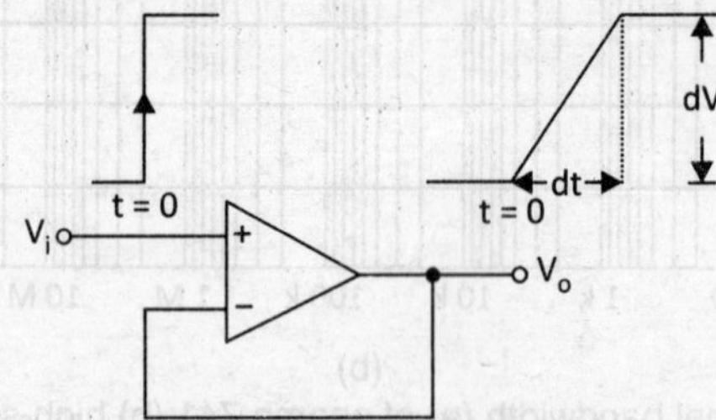

Fig. 9.57: Response to step input

Slew rate limits the large signal bandwidth. Peak-to-peak output voltage swing for a sinusoidal signal ($V_{p\text{-}t\text{-}p}$), slew rate and bandwidth are interrelated by eqn. 9.49.

$$\textit{Bandwidth}\ (\text{Highest frequency}, f_{\max}) = \frac{\text{Slew rate}}{(\pi \times V_{p-t-p})} \quad (9.49)$$

9.4.3 Open-Loop Gain

Open-loop gain is the ratio of single-ended output to the differential input. This parameter has a great bearing on the gain accuracy specification of the opamp wired as an amplifier. The ratio of the open-loop gain to the closed-loop gain (which depends upon the application circuit) is called the loop gain. Accuracy at any given frequency depends heavily on the magnitude of the loop gain at that frequency. The magnitude of loop gain at a given frequency depends directly on the value of the open-loop gain at that frequency as the value of closed-loop gain for a given application circuit is fixed. Figure 9.58 shows the open-loop gain versus frequency curve of an opamp. As a thumb rule, the gain error at any given frequency is given by the ratio of the

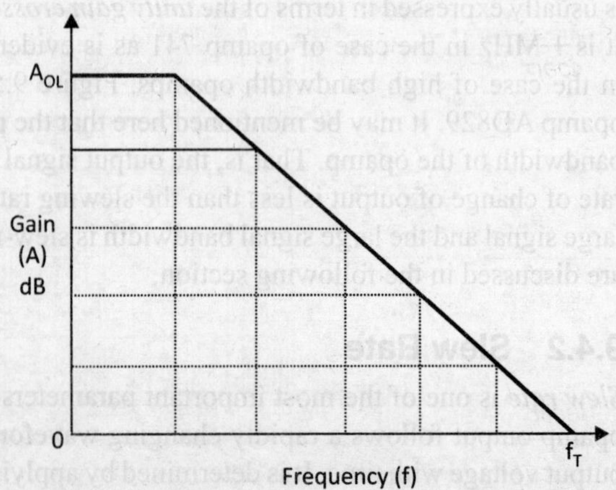

Fig. 9.58: Open-loop gain versus frequency

closed-loop gain to the open-loop gain. Thus, a higher open-loop gain gives a smaller error for a given closed-loop gain.

9.4.4 Common Mode Rejection Ratio

Common mode rejection ratio(*CMRR*) is a measure of the ability of the opamp to suppress common mode signals. It is the ratio of the desired differential gain (A_d) to the undesired common mode gain (A_c). The ratio CMRR is usually expressed as CMR given by 20 log (A_d/A_c) dB. A lower CMRR or CMR reflects in terms of smaller variation in the output of a differential amplifier due to variation in the common mode input when the differential input stays put. The common mode input is the average value of the two inputs. The common mode input affects the bias point of the input differential pair. Owing to lack of perfect symmetry in the two halves of the input differential pair, change in bias point changes the offset voltage. This in turn changes the output voltage. CMRR is also defined as the ratio of the change in the common mode input to the corresponding change in the output offset voltage.

CMRR is always specified for a given input voltage range. Exceeding the input voltage range would degrade the CMRR specification. In some opamps, the input voltage range is specified separately, which implies that the given value of CMRR is guaranteed over the listed input voltage range. CMRR as published in data sheet is a DC parameter. CMRR when graphed versus frequency falls with increase in frequency as shown in Figure 9.59. The graph shown in the Figure 9.59 is taken from data sheet of opamp 741.

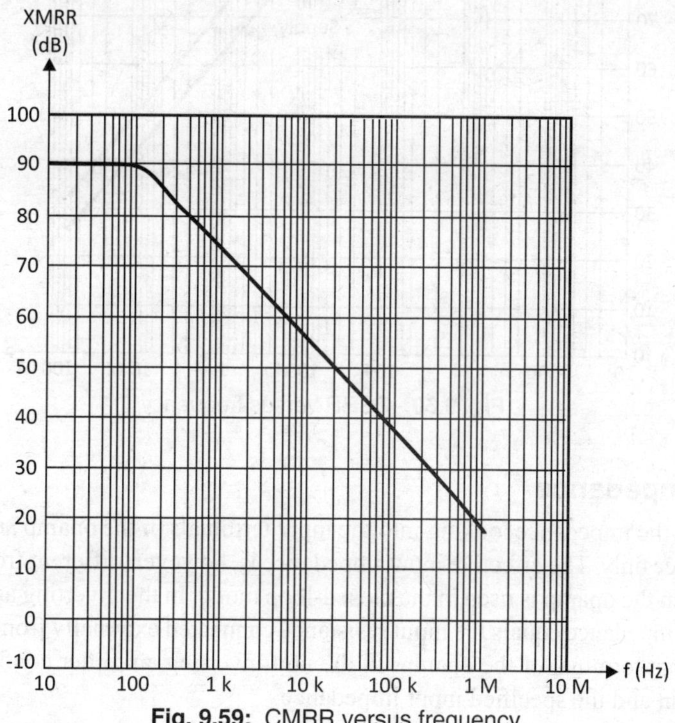

Fig. 9.59: CMRR versus frequency

9.4.5 Power Supply Rejection Ratio

Power supply rejection ratio(*PSRR*) is defined as the ratio of change in the power supply voltage to corresponding change in the output voltage. The mechanism that produces PSRR is the same as that responsible for CMRR. The power supply affects the bias point of the input differential amplifier stage of the opamp. Owing to inherent mismatch in the input circuitry, changes in bias point changes the offset voltage, which in turn changes the output voltage. PSRR is also defined as the ratio of the change in the input offset voltage to the change in one of the power supply voltages, with the other power supply voltage held constant.

PSRR like CMRR too is a DC parameter and its value falls with increase in frequency. The parameter is particularly significant as switched mode power supplies can have noise in the frequency range of 20 kHz to 200 kHz and even higher. PSRR is almost zero at these frequencies with the result that power supply noise appears as noise at the output of the opamp. Figure 9.60 shows PSRR versus frequency graph of opamp type AD 829.

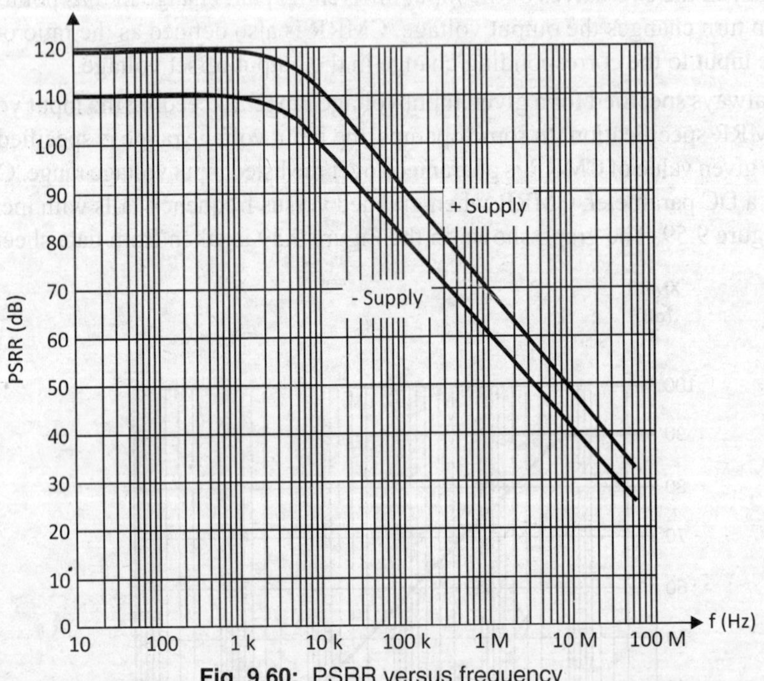

Fig. 9.60: PSRR versus frequency

9.4.6 Input Impedance

Input impedance is the impedance looking into the input terminals of the opamp and is mostly expressed in terms of resistance only. The effective input impedance is, however, different from what is specified in the data sheets when the opamp is used in the closed-loop mode. In the inverting amplifier configuration, the effective input impedance equals the input resistance connected externally from source of input signal to the inverting input terminal of the opamp. In the non-inverting amplifier configuration, it equals the product of loop gain and the specified input impedance.

9.4.7 Output Impedance

Output impedance is defined as the impedance between the output terminal of the opamp and ground. Common-emitter (bipolar) and common-source (CMOS) output stages used in rail-to-rail output opamps have higher output impedance than emitter-follower output stages. Output impedance becomes a critical parameter when using rail-to-rail output opamps to drive heavy loads. If the load were mainly resistive, it would decide how close the output can be to the rails. If the load were capacitive, the additional phase shift caused will erode the phase margin. Figure 9.61 shows the effect of output impedance on the output signal assuming that the output impedance is resistive in the case of a predominantly resistive load R_L [Figure 9.61 (a)] and a capacitive load C_L [Figure 9.61 (b)]. In the case of resistive load, eqn.9.50 describes the output. Eqn.9.51 gives the expression for the output in the case of capacitive load.

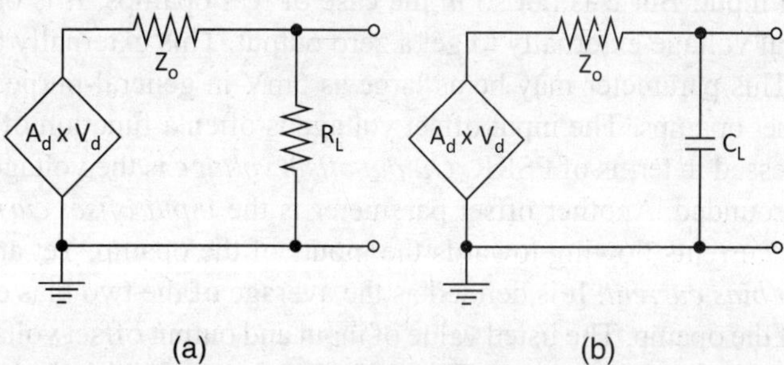

Fig. 9.61: (a) Effect of resistive load R_L on output signal; (b) effect of capacitive load C_L on output signal

$$V_o = A_d \times V_d \times \left[\frac{R_L}{R_L + Z_o}\right] \tag{9.50}$$

$$V_o = A_d \times V_d \times \left[\frac{1}{j(f/f_o)+1}\right] \tag{9.51}$$

where $f_o = \dfrac{1}{2\pi Z_o C_L}$

9.4.8 Settling Time

Settling time is a parameter specified in the case of high-speed opamps or opamps with a high value of gain-bandwidth product. It gives the response of the opamp to larger step inputs. It is expressed as the time taken by the opamp output to settle within a specified percentage of the final value, usually 0.1% or 0.01% of the final expected value, in response to a step at its input (Figure 9.62). The settling time is usually specified for opamp wired as a unity gain amplifier and it worsens for a closed-loop gain greater than 1.

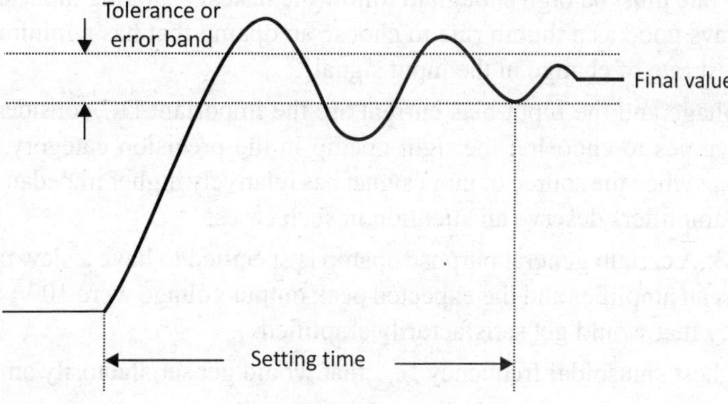

Fig. 9.62 : Settling time

Settling time is a design issue in data acquisition circuits when signals are changing rapidly. This parameter is very important when the opamp is being used as a sample and hold circuit at the input of an analog-to-digital converter or at the output of a high-speed digital-to-analog converter.

9.4.9 Offsets and Offset Drifts

Offset is a commonly used term with reference to opamps. An ideal opamp should produce a zero output for a zero differential input. But it is not so in the case of real opamps. It is observed that we need to apply a DC differential voltage externally to get a zero output. This externally applied input is then the *input offset voltage*. This parameter may be as large as 5mV in general-purpose opamps and as small as 200mV in low offset opamps. The input offset voltage is often a function of power supply voltages. This variation is expressed in terms of PSRR. *Output offset voltage* is the voltage at the output with both the input terminals grounded. Another offset parameter is the *input offset current*. It is the difference between the two bias currents flowing towards the inputs of the opamp. Yet another important opamp parameter is the *input bias current*. It is defined as the average of the two bias currents flowing into the two input terminals of the opamp. The listed value of input and output offset voltages and input offset and bias currents tend to drift with temperature. This drift is also specified in the datasheets. Some general-purpose opamps (741 for instance) have a provision for externally nullifying the input offset voltage by usually connecting the fixed terminals of a potentiometer of a given resistance value across the designated terminals and connecting the center terminal to the negative supply voltage.

9.5 SELECTING THE RIGHT OPAMP

Having briefly described the key parameters in respect of different categories of opamps, the opamp selection should be no problem. Based on the circuit objectives, the first thing to be decided is the opamp category that would do the required job economically. Having made up our mind on the broad class of opamps, that is, we need a general-purpose opamp or a high-speed opamp or for that matter an instrumentation opamp, we can go through the specifications of the devices available in the chosen category to choose a device that suits our needs the best. We should give due attention to both AC as well as DC considerations. One of the major AC considerations, for instance, is the desired loop gain. As an example, if we wanted the opamp to yield an accuracy of 0.1% while amplifying an AC signal of 10 kHz by a gain of 10, then the opamp must have an open-loop gain of 10,000 at the operating frequency of 10kHz. Opamp 741 will certainly not serve the purpose here. The open-loop gain for a given frequency can be verified from the gain versus frequency plot.

Similarly, slew rate must be high enough to follow the fastest changing input signal without causing distortion. It is always good as a thumb rule to choose an opamp that has a minimum slew rate of 25% larger than the fastest rate of change in the input signal.

Input offset voltage and the input bias current are the important DC considerations besides open-loop gain when it comes to choosing the right opamp in the precision category. Input bias current is particularly important when the source of input signal has relatively higher impedance. FET-input opamps or instrumentation amplifiers deserve an attention in such cases.

Example 9.13: A certain general purpose opamp is specified to have a slew rate of 0.5 V/ms. If the opamp were used as an amplifier and the expected peak output voltage were 10 V; determine the highest sinusoidal frequency that would get satisfactorily amplified.

Solution: Highest sinusoidal frequency f_{MAX} that would get satisfactorily amplified is given by:

$$f_{MAX} = \frac{\text{Slew rate}}{(2\pi \times V_p)}$$

where V_p is the expected peak output voltage

In the present case, slew rate = 0.5 V/ms and V_p = 10 V

$$\text{Therefore,} \quad f_{MAX} = \frac{(0.5 \times 10^6)}{(2\pi \times 10)} = 7.96 kHz$$

Example 9.14: The differential voltage gain and CMRR of an opamp when expressed in decibels are 110 dB and 100 dB, respectively. Determine the common mode gain expressed as a ratio.

Solution:

$$CMRR \text{ (in dB)} = 20 \log \left(\frac{A_d}{A_{CM}} \right)$$

where A_d and A_{CM} are, respectively, the differential and common mode gain values

$$CMRR \text{ (in dB)} = 20 \log A_d - 20 \log A_{CM}$$

$$\text{That is,} \quad 20 \log A_{CM} = 20 \log A_d - CMRR \text{ (in dB)} = 110 - 100 = 10 dB$$

$$\text{This gives} \quad \log A_{CM} = \frac{10}{20} = 0.5$$

$$\text{Therefore,} \quad A_{CM} = \text{antilog}(0.5) = 3.16$$

Example 9.15: In the case of a certain opamp, 1V change in common mode input causes a DC output offset change of 1mV. Determine CMRR in dB.

Solution:

1. $CMRR = \frac{\Delta V_{CM}}{\Delta V_{OS}} = \frac{1}{1 \times 10^{-6}} = 10^6$, 2. $CMRR$ in dB $= 20 \log 10^6 = 120 dB$

9.6 TYPES OF OPAMPS

Opamps can be categorized on the basis of the performance specifications and consequently their application area and also on the basis of their internal structure as general-purpose opamps, high-speed and high-bandwidth opamps, precision opamps, power opamps, instrumentation opamps, Norton opamps (also known as current differencing opamps), opamp comparators and isolation opamps.

9.6.1 General-Purpose Opamps

The term *general-purpose opamp* is generally used with reference to that category of opamps which has moderate or say reasonably good values for all the key parameters. In the case of general-purpose opamps, none of the major specifications as outlined earlier can be said to be exceptionally good or state-of-the-art and also none of the specifications is extremely poor. Within the broad category of general-purpose opamps, some type numbers may have slightly better overall performance specifications and thus called as high-performance general-purpose opamps. A general-purpose opamp of the type 741 may have an open-loop gain of typically 10^4–10^5, input impedance of 0.5–1 MW, output impedance of 50–100W, CMRR of the order of 70–100dB, output offset voltage of the order of a few milli-volts and an open-loop bandwidth in the range of 1 MHz. Those general-purpose opamps that have a JFET-based input differential amplifier stage have relatively much larger input impedance (typically 10^{12}W) and much better noise specifications. So, general-purpose opamps due to overall good performance specifications are used in a wide range of applications in low cost designs.

JEFT-input opamps (opamps with the input differential amplifier stage constructed with JEFTs) are preferred in applications where high-input impedance and low noise are the main considerations.

9.6.2 High-Speed Opamps

High-speed opamps have high slew rate and bandwidth specifications. Today opamps with slew rate in hundreds of volts per microsecond and bandwidth in hundreds of MHz are commercially available. As an illustration, opamp type AD 829 from Analog Devices has a slew and unity gain small signal bandwidth specifications of 230 V/ms and 600MHz, respectively. EL 2444 from Elantec is yet another high-speed opamp. It is a quad opamp with slew rate and unity gain small signal bandwidth specifications of 325V/ms and 60MHz, respectively.

9.6.3 Precision Opamps

Precision opamps have extremely low offsets and a very high value of open-loop differential gain. The output offset voltage in such opamps may be of the order of several tens of microvolts. The open-loop gain approaches 120dB.

9.6.4 Power Opamps

The power supply voltages and consequently the output voltage swing are no longer limited to ±18 V or so. Opamps with supply voltage rating of the order of several hundred volts and current delivering capability of the order of several amperes are also available. These are called *power opamps*. However, these devices are very expensive and are manufactured by a few select manufacturers internationally.

9.6.5 Opamps Comparators

Theseare opamps specially designed for use in comparator applications. These have much faster response time (typically from a few nanoseconds to several tens of nanoseconds) than that of a conventional general purpose opamp (typically of the order of 1 μs). Comparator, in which one of the inputs is normally a reference voltage, switches between two states at the output depending upon whether the other input is higher or lower than the reference. In the case of general-purpose opamps being used as comparators, the output switches between two levels that are fixed and depends upon the supply voltages. These levels may not be compatible with the load requirement which in most of the applications is a logic circuit. There might therefore be a need for the comparator output to be compatible to a certain logic family like TTL or CMOS. The response time and the output compatibility happen to be the two most important specifications in the case of opamp comparators. A comparator forms the basic building block in circuits like zero crossing detectors, level detectors, Schmitt triggers, square and triangle waveform generators.

9.6.6 Norton Opamps

A *Norton opamp* also known as the current differencing opamp differs from a conventional opamp in its internal circuit design. While in a conventional opamp, the input stage is a differential amplifier to achieve inverting and non-inverting input functions, in the case of a Norton opamp, the non-inverting input function is derived from the inverting input function by using a current mirror configuration. The non-inverting input current is derived from the one entering at the inverting input. While we talk about differential input voltage in the case of a conventional opamp, it is differential input current in the case of a Norton opamp. Single supply operation and the fact that most of the general-purpose opamp applications can be realized without significantly sacrificing performance characteristics coupled with low cost per opamp make Norton opamp a very attractive choice. A Norton opamp has a definite edge over a general-purpose opamp (of 741 types) in single supply operation. When a general-purpose opamp is used on a single supply, the minimum input voltage that can be applied while ensuring that the opamp responds to a differential input is limited by the minimum common mode input range (typically ±2V in general-purpose opamps). This is rather large. In addition, general-purpose opamps when used on single supply have poorer output voltage swing. Norton opamps have no such limitations. A Norton opamp is represented in a circuit by the circuit symbol of Figure 9.63 (b). The conventional opamp is represented by the circuit symbol of Figure 9.63 (a).

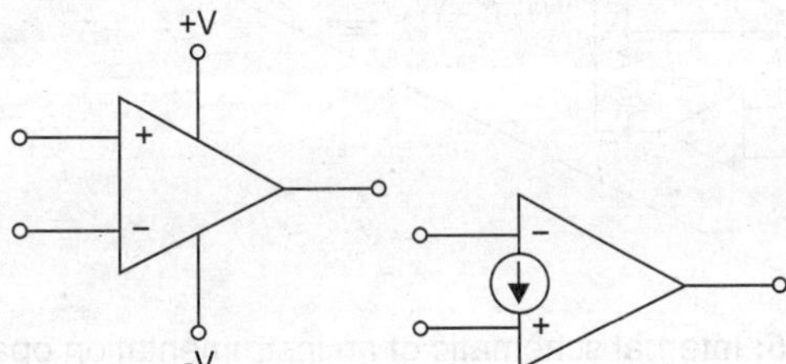

Fig. 9.63: Circuit representation: (a) Conventional opamp; (b) Norton opamp

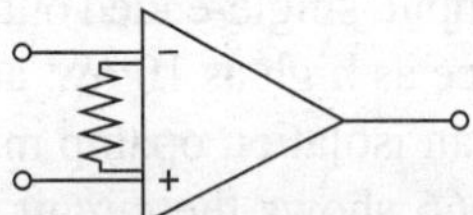

Fig. 9.64: Circuit representation of an instrumentation opamp

9.6.7 Instrumentation Opamp

An *instrumentation opamp* is a differential amplifier with a very high value of input impedance, very large CMRR and extremely low values of offsets and offset drifts. Like an opamp of the type described in the earlier paragraphs, it is differential input single-ended output gain block. Gain in an instrumentation opamp, if we so call it, is usually set with a single resistor whereas in a conventional opamp, the same in achieved with the help of two resistors. Instrumentation opamps are available in single IC packages. Figure 9.64 shows the circuit representation of an instrumentation opamp. Typical internal schematic of such a device is shown in Figure 9.65. As is clear from the schematic arrangement of Figure 9.65, it is a combination of three opamps. The output opamp has been wired as a differential amplifier with its non-inverting and inverting inputs fed from the outputs of the other two opamps wired as non-inverting amplifiers. The gain setting resistor (R_{gain}) is connected external to the device. Thus, the two major problems in a conventional opamp, namely, the low effective input impedance loading on to the signal source with comparatively high value of output impedance and the gain setting requiring simultaneous adjustment of two resistors leading to inaccuracies are overcome.

The essential characteristics of instrumentation opamps as outlined above make them very useful in amplifying low-level differential signals with high value of common mode content. Transducers such as thermocouples, biological probes, strain gauge bridges and current shunts produce small differential signals superimposed on common mode bias voltages. Instrumentation opamp is an excellent choice in such cases for meaningful acquisition and analysis of data in addition to its use in general-purpose applications requiring a precision high quality differential amplifier. Some of these applications are discussed in chapter-9 on opamp application circuits.

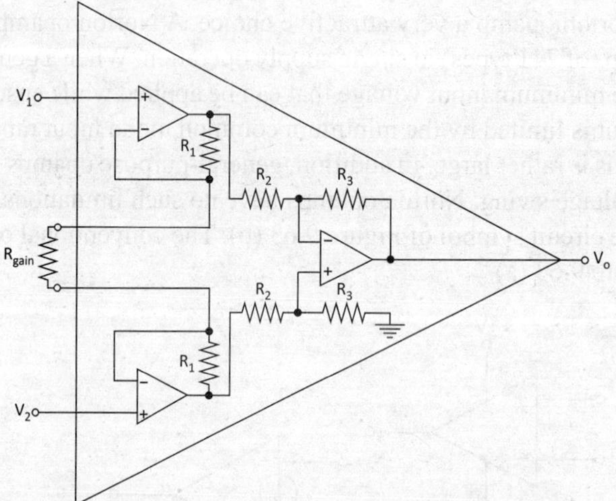

Fig. 9.65: Internal schematic of an instrumentation opamp

9.6.8 Isolation Opamp

An *isolation opamp* is again a differential input, single-ended output amplifier with its output electrically isolated from the input. Isolation impedance as high as 10^{12}&! and an isolation voltage of about 1000V are common. The differential amplifier in an isolation opamp may be an ordinary differential amplifier or an instrumentation amplifier. Figure 9.66 shows the circuit symbol of isolation opamp. There are transformer-coupled isolation opamps [Figure 9.67 (a)] mainly used in applications where linearity, gain accuracy, etc. are important and there optically coupled isolation opamps [Figure 9.67 (b)] used in applications where speed and bandwidth are important.

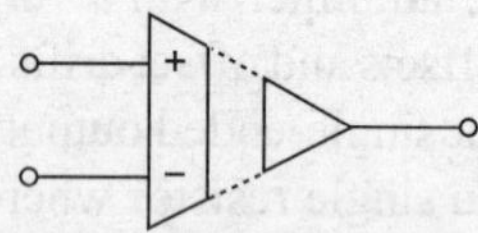

Fig. 9.66: Circuit symbol of an isolation opamp

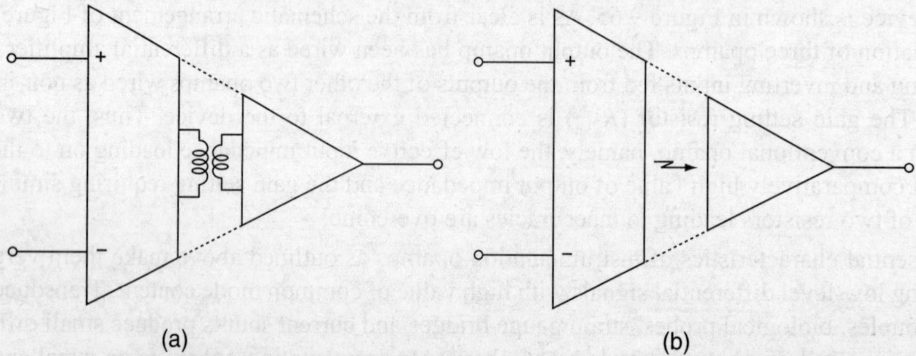

Fig. 9.67: (a) Transformer coupled isolation opamp; (b) optically coupled isolation opamp

Isolation opamps are used for those applications where electrical isolation between the source and the output is desirable. For instance, in medical instrumentation where the transducer or sensor is in physical contact with the patient, isolation opamp is an excellent interface between the transducer and the equipment (Figure 9.68). The isolation opamp provides a floating input for the signal source output and need for source ground connections is completely eliminated.

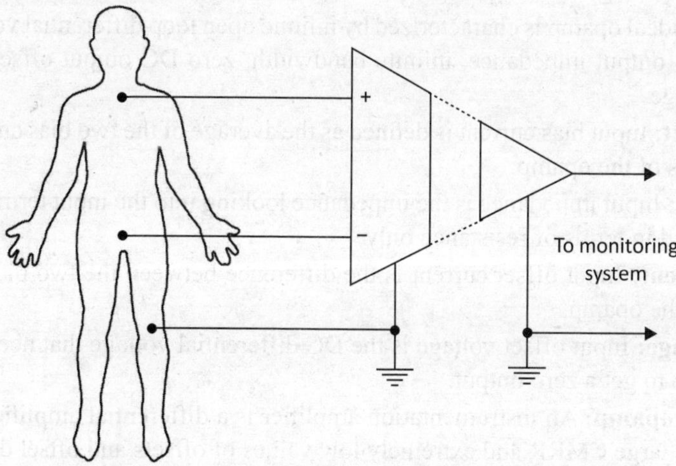

Fig. 9.68: Isolation opamp used in medical instrumentation

GLOSSARY

Bandwidth: Bandwidth of an opamp tells us about the range of frequencies it can amplify for a given amplifier gain.

Base current compensation mirror: See *Buffered feedback current mirror*

Buffered feedback current mirror: Inbuffered feedback current mirror, also known as *base current compensation current mirror*, the collector terminal of input transistor is wired to base terminals of input and output transistors (Q_1 and Q_2) through an emitter follower buffer. High current gain of the buffer stage greatly reduces the gain error caused by finite values of base currents of Q_1 and Q_2 in case of basic current mirror.

Common mode rejection ratio: Common mode rejection ratio (CMRR) is a measure of the ability of the opamp to suppress common mode signals. It is the ratio of the desired differential gain to the undesired common mode gain. It is usually expressed in decibels (dB) and is given by CMRR = 20 log (A_d/A_c).

Compliance voltage (Current mirror): Compliance voltage is the minimum voltage drop required across the output leg of the current mirror necessary to maintain the desired output current. This minimum voltage, called compliance voltage, is determined by the need to keep the output transistor of the BJT current mirror in the active region (Figure 9.10a) or MOSFET current mirror in saturation region (Figure 9.10b)

Current gain (Current mirror): Current gain is the ratio of output current to input current. In an ideal current mirror, output current is linearly related to the input current and also the current gain is unity.

Current mirror: A current mirror is a circuit block that produces a copy of the current flowing into or out of an input terminal by replicating the current in an output terminal. A current mirror circuit is characterized by a high output impedance and a low input impedance.

Fully internally compensated opamp: Fully internally compensated opamps have an internally connected capacitor that guarantees stable operation of the opamp down to a gain of unity.

General- purpose opamp: The term general purpose opamp is generally used with reference to that category of opamps which has moderate or say reasonably good values for all the key parameters.

High-speed opamp: High speed opamps have high slew rate and bandwidth specifications.

Ideal opamp: An ideal opamp is characterized by infinite open loop differential voltage gain, infinite input impedance, zero output impedance, infinite bandwidth, zero DC output offset voltage and zero input differential voltage.

Input bias current: Input bias current is defined as the average of the two bias currents flowing into the two input terminals of the opamp.

Input impedance: Input impedance is the impedance looking into the input terminals of the opamp and is mostly expressed in terms of resistance only.

Input offset current: Input offset current is the difference between the two bias currents flowing towards the inputs of the opamp.

Input offset voltage: Input offset voltage is the DC differential voltage that needs to be applied to the input of the opamp to get a zero output.

Instrumentation opamp: An instrumentation amplifier is a differential amplifier with a very high input impedance, very large CMRR and extremely low values of offsets and offset drifts.

Isolation opamp: An isolation amplifier is a differential input single ended output amplifier with its output electrically isolated from the input. Isolation impedance as high as 10^{12} ohms and an isolation voltage of about 1000 volts are common.

Loop gain: Ratio of the open loop gain to the closed loop gain (which depends upon the application circuit) is called the loop gain.

Miller capacitance: If there is some capacitance between the input and output of an inverting voltage amplifier such as between base and collector in a bipolar transistor amplifier or between gate and drain in a FET-based amplifier,it will appear to be multiplied by the gain of the amplifier. This extra capacitance is due to the *Miller effect,* and so is known as Miller capacitance.

Norton opamp: A Norton opamp also known as the current differencing opamp has the non-inverting input function derived from the inverting input function by using a current mirror configuration. The non-inverting input current is derived from the one entering at the inverting input.

Opamp: An opamp is basically a high gain differential amplifier capable of amplifying signals right down to DC.

Opamp comparator: These are opamps specially designed for use in comparator applications. These have much faster response time (typically from a few nanoseconds to several tens of nanoseconds) than that of a conventional general purpose opamp (typically of the order of 1 microsecond). The response time and output compatibility happen to be the two most important specifications in case of opamp comparators.

Open-loop gain: Open loop gain is the ratio of single ended output to the differential input. This parameter has a great bearing on the gain accuracy specification of the opamp wired as an amplifier.

Output impedance: Output impedance is defined as the impedance between the output terminal and ground.

Output offset voltage: It is the voltage at the output with both the input terminals grounded.

Power opamp: Power opamps are those with supply voltage rating of the order of several hundred volts and current delivering capability of the order of several amperes.

Precision opamp: Precision opamps have extremely low offsets and a very high value of open loop differential gain.

Power supply rejection ratio: Power supply rejection ratio (PSRR) is defined as the ratio of change in power supply voltage to corresponding change in output voltage.

Settling time: Settling time is expressed as the time taken by the opamp output to settle within a specified percentage of the final value, usually 0.1 percent or 0.01 percent of the final expected value, in response to a step at its input

Slew rate: Slew rate of an opamp is defined as rate of change of output voltage with time.

Uncompensated opamp: In the case of an uncompensated opamp, there is no capacitor connected internally across the output as is the case with compensated opamps.

Widlar current source: It is a variant of basic current mirror configuration that is an improvement on the basic configuration achieved by connecting a resistor in series with the emitter terminal of output transistor.

Wilson current source: Wilson current source is a variant of basic current mirror that has the advantage of virtually eliminating the base current mismatch of the conventional current mirror configuration. The other advantage is its higher incremental output resistance.

SUMMARY OF IMPORTANT FORMULAE

1. In a conventional two-transistor current mirror configuration, input and output currents are related by:

$$I_{IN} = I_{OUT} \times \left[\frac{(\beta+2)}{\beta}\right]$$

2. In a conventional two-MOSFET current mirror configuration, input and output currents are given by following expressions.

$$I_{IN} = \frac{1}{2} \times K_n \times \left(\frac{W}{L}\right)_{M1} \times (V_{GS} - V_{TH})^2 \times (1+\lambda V_{DS})$$

$$I_{OUT} = \frac{1}{2} \times K_n \times \left(\frac{W}{L}\right)_{M2} \times (V_{GS} - V_{TH})^2 \times (1+\lambda V_{DS})$$

Where K_n = Technology related constant l = Channel length modulation constant

W and L are respectively the channel width and channel length of the MOSFETs

3. Mirror gain in conventional BJT current mirror is given by:

$$\text{Mirror gain} = \left[\frac{\beta}{\beta+2}\right]$$

4. Mirror gain in conventional MOSFET current mirror is given by:

$$\text{Mirror gain} = \left[\left(\frac{W}{L}\right)_{M2} \bigg/ \left(\frac{W}{L}\right)_{M1}\right]$$

M1 and M2 are respectively input and output MOSFETs

(W) and (L) are respectively channel width and length of MOSFETs

5. If in a conventional current mirror circuit, N identical devices in are paralleled on the input side and M identical devices are connected in parallel on the output side; then mirror gain is given by:

   $$\text{Mirror gain} = \left[\frac{M}{N}\right]$$

6. In basic two-transistor differential amplifier circuit with collector resistance R_C, emitter resistance R_E, the differential gain, common mode gain and CMRR are given by following expressions.

   Differential gain, $A_d = \frac{R_C}{r_e}$, Common mode gain, $A_{cm} = \frac{R_C}{2R_E}$

   $$CMRR = \frac{2R_E}{r_e}$$

7. In basic two-MOSFET differential amplifier circuit with drain resistance R_D, source resistance R_{SS}, the differential gain, common mode gain and CMRR are given by following expressions.

   Differential gain, $A_d = -g_m \times R_D$

   Common mode gain, $A_c = \frac{R_D}{2R_{SS}}$

   $$CMRR = -2g_m R_{SS}$$

   Where g_m = transconductance of MOSFET = $\sqrt{2K_n\left(\frac{W}{L}\right)I_d} = \frac{2I_d}{(V_{GS} - V_{TH})}$

8. Generalized expression for Common Mode Rejection Ratio (CMRR) is given by:

   $$CMRR = \frac{A_d}{A_{cm}} \text{ and } CMRR \text{ (in dB)} = 20\log\left(\frac{A_d}{A_{cm}}\right)$$

9. Slew rate limited bandwidth of an opamp is given by:

REVIEW QUESTIONS

1. What is a current mirror circuit? What is the importance of current mirror circuit with reference to operational amplifiers?
2. With the help of a suitable circuit diagram, briefly describe operation of basic two-transistor current mirror. Derive expression for mirror gain.
3. With the help of suitable circuit diagram, briefly describe operation of basic MOSFET-based current mirror and derive expression for mirror gain. What are the advantages of MOSFET-based current mirror over BJT-based current mirror?
4. How do Widlar and Wilson current mirror configurations improve upon the performance of basic current mirror? Explain with the help of relevant circuit diagrams.
5. With the help of a suitable diagram, explain how multiple transistors can be used in a current mirror circuit to achieve a mirror gain of other than unity. Derive generalized expression for mirror gain.
6. What is an operational amplifier? How does it differ from common-emitter amplifier constructed using discrete components?

7. How would you characterize an ideal opamp? How does a practical opamp differ from an ideal opamp? Use Thevenin's equivalent circuit model to compare an ideal opamp with a practical opamp.
8. With the help of a suitable block diagram, briefly describe internal architecture of a typical operational amplifier. Explain the functions of different building blocks constituting the operational amplifier.
9. What is primarily responsible for giving an opamp the following characteristics?
   (a) High input impedance
   (b) Low output impedance
   (c) High open-loop gain
   (d) High common mode rejection ratio
   (e) Frequency response down to DC
10. Briefly describe the reasons for the following:
    (a) Why it is not possible to have an infinite CMRR?
    (b) Why internally compensated opamps have relatively lower slew rate?
11. Briefly describe the following opamp parameters with particular reference to their criticality for a given application circuit.
    (a) Slew rate
    (b) Open-loop gain
    (c) Settling time
    (d) Common mode rejection ratio
12. Briefly describe the following types of opamps with reference to major performance parameters.
    (a) High-speed opamps
    (b) Instrumentation opamps
    (c) Opamp comparators
    (d) General-purpose opamps

PROBLEMS

1. Refer to the differential amplifier circuit of Figure 9.69. Determine the quiescent DC voltage at the collector terminal of each transistor assuming V_{BE} of the two transistors to be negligible. What will be the quiescent DC values if V_{BE} is taken as 0.7 V?

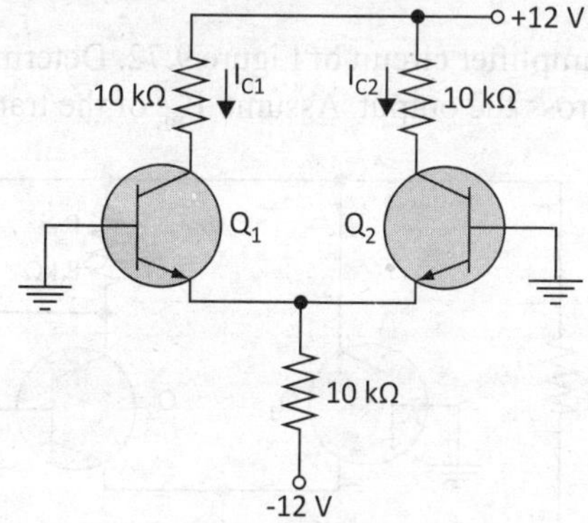

Fig. 9.69: Problem-1

2. Refer to the differential amplifier circuit of Figure 9.70. Determine the quiescent DC voltage at the collector terminal of each transistor assuming V_{BE} of the two transistors to be equal to 0.7 V?
3. If the transistors used in the differential amplifier circuit of Figure 9.70 have h_{ie} = 1 kΩ and h_{fe} = 50, determine the differential voltage gain.

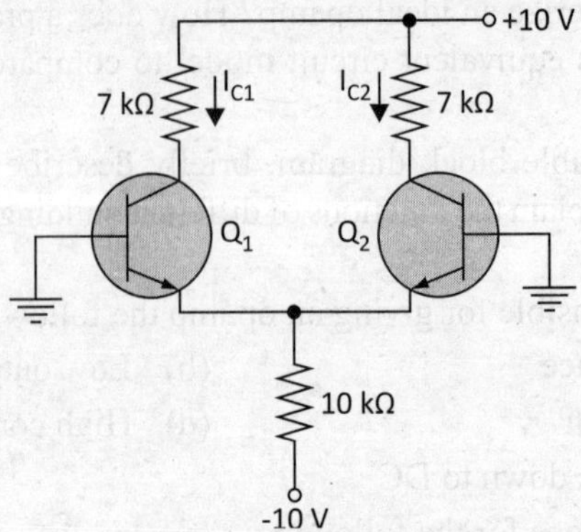

Fig. 9.70: Problem-2

4. Refer to the differential amplifier circuit diagram of Figure 9.71. Determine the differential voltage given that the transistors used in the circuit have h_{ie} = 1 kW and h_{fe} = 40

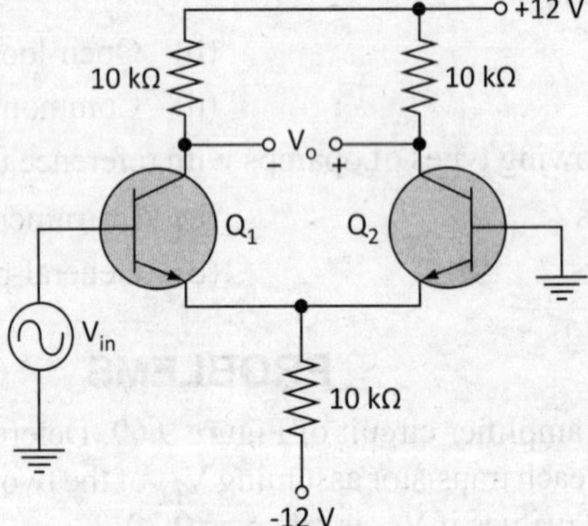

Fig. 9.71: Problem-4

5. Refer to the differential amplifier circuit of Figure 9.72. Determine the tail current I_T and also the quiescent DC voltage across the output. Assume V_{BE} of the transistors to be 0.7 V.

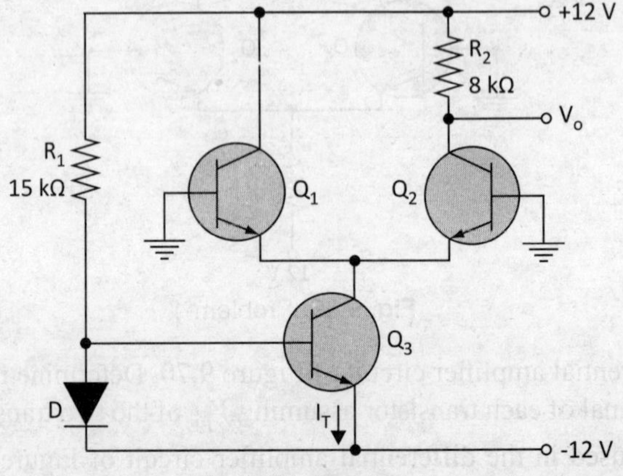

Fig. 9.72: Problem-5

6. Opamp LF 356 is specified to have a slew rate of 5.0 V/ms. If the opamp were used as an amplifier and the expected peak output voltage were 12 V, determine the large signal bandwidth.
7. Design a differential amplifier of the type shown in Figure 9.48 so as to provide a differential input resistance of at least 10 KΩ and differential voltage gain of 100V/V. Assume V_{CC} = 5V and b (for Q_1 and Q_2) = 100.
8. Refer to the MOSFET-based current mirror of Figure 9.13. Determine (R) for an output current of 200 μA given that V = 5V, V_{TH} = 1V, W/L (for Q_1 and Q_2) = 10 and K_n = 10 mA/V². Assume the two MOSFETs to be identical and ignore channel length modulation effect.
9. The differential voltage gain and CMRR of an opamp when expressed in decibels are 120 dB and 100 dB, respectively. Determine the common mode gain expressed as a ratio.
10. In the case of a certain opamp, 2.0 V change in common mode input causes a DC output offset change of 5.0 mV. Determine CMRR in dB.
11. The frequency response of an opamp shows the cut-off frequency to be equal to 10 Hz. If the mid-band voltage gain is 120 dB, determine the frequency at which the closed-loop gain will be unity.
12. A conventional BJT current mirror employs two parallel-connected transistors on the input side and five parallel-connected transistors on the output side. If the output current were 5 mA; determine input current. Assume all transistors to be identical.

MULTIPLE CHOICE QUESTIONS

1. In a basic two-MOSFET current mirror, if W_1 and W_2 are the channel widths of input and output MOSFETs respectively; L_1 and L_2 are channel lengths of input and output MOSFETs respectively; then mirror gain I_O/I_I is given by: (Ignore channel length modulation effect)
   (a) W_2L_1/W_1L_2 (b) W_1L_2/W_2L_1
   (c) W_2L_2/W_1L_1 (d) W_1L_1/W_2L_2
2. One of the following current mirror configurations takes care of the imbalance in the input and output currents caused by Early effect.
   (a) Buffered feedback current mirror (b) Widlar current mirror
   (c) Wilson current mirror (d) None of these
3. The key advantage of using current mirror configuration as the active load in place of resistor in the input differential amplifier stage of an opamp is
   (a) it provides higher efficiency
   (b) it provides better matching between the two active devices
   (c) it largely eliminates biasing problems caused by large value load resistors
   (d) None of these
4. An opamp can amplify
   (a) DC signals only (b) AC signals only
   (c) both AC as well as DC signals (d) neither DC nor AC signals
5. A conventional BJT current mirror used three parallel connected bipolar transistors on the input side and five parallel connected transistors on the output side. If all eight transistors were identical and input current were 12 mA; the output current would be

(a) 20 mA (b) 7.2 mA
(c) 10 mA (d) None of these

6. Which of the following statements describes an opamp the best?
(a) It is a differential amplifier
(b) It is a large bandwidth amplifier
(c) It is direct-coupled amplifier
(d) It is a direct-coupled high-gain differential amplifier

7. If collector current in each of the two bipolar transistors in the long tail differential pair were 10 mA under zero signal input conditions; then the tail current would be
(a) 10 mA (b) 20 mA
(c) 5 mA (d) It cannot be computed from given data

8. The input stage of an opamp in most of the cases is a
(a) high-gain common-emitter amplifier (b) differential amplifier
(c) emitter-follower buffer (d) none of these

9. The common mode rejection ratio is
(a) same as the common mode gain
(b) ratio of common mode gain to differential gain
(c) ratio of differential gain to common mode gain
(d) ratio of output DC offset voltage to change in common mode input

10. The input offset current is
(a) zero (b) less than input bias current
(c) more than input bias current (d) none of these

11. One of the following opamp parameters limits the large signal bandwidth.
(a) Slew rate (b) CMRR
(c) Settling time (d) Unity gain bandwidth

12. The frequency response of an opamp shows the cut-off frequency to be equal to 100 Hz. If the mid-band voltage gain is 100 dB, then the unity gain cross-over frequency will be
(a) 1.0 MHz (b) 100 MHz
(c) 10 MHz (d) indeterminate from given data

13. An opamp has open-loop gain and unity gain bandwidth specifications of 120 dB and 10 MHz, respectively. The open-loop cut-off frequency will be
(a) 10 Hz (b) 100 Hz
(c) 1000 Hz (d) 1 Hz

14. The compensating capacitor connected externally in the case of uncompensated opamps is to
(a) increase large signal bandwidth (b) prevent oscillations
(c) improve slew rate (d) increase CMRR

15. Identify the opamp type in which the output stage is designed to be compatible with some logic family.
(a) Opamp comparator (b) High speed opamp
(c) Isolation opamp (d) Instrumentation opamp

16. Which of the following opamp internally comprises three opamps out of which two are wired as buffers and the third is a difference amplifier?
(a) Isolation opamp (b) Norton opamp
(c) Instrumentation opamp (d) Opamp comparator
17. In which of the following opamp types, the input stage is not a conventional differential amplifier.
(a) Norton opamp (b) Instrumentation opamp
(c) Opamp comparator (d) Isolation opamp
18. Which of the following opamp types is ideally suited to single supply operation?
(a) High bandwidth opamp (b) Instrumentation opamp
(c) Norton opamp (d) General-purpose opamp
19. In the front-end differential amplifier inside an opamp, the tail resistor is usually replaced by
(a) emitter-follower configuration
(b) current mirror configuration
(c) common-emitter amplifier configuration
(d) a junction diode
20. In the internal circuit of an opamp, collector resistors are usually replaced by active loads to
(a) increase differential gain (b) decrease common mode gain
(c) increase bandwidth (d) increase efficiency

SOLUTIONS TO PROBLEMS

1. Assuming V_{BE} to be negligible, the tail current $I_T = 12/10\times10^3 = 1.2mA$

Therefore, emitter current of each transistor $= 1.2\times10^{-3}/2 = 0.6mA$

Collector current of each transistor is approximately equal to its emitter current

Therefore, collector current of each transistor = 0.6 mA

Quiescent DC voltage at the collector of each transistor $= 12 - 0.6\times10^{-3}\times10\times10^3 = 6V$

If $V_{BE} = 0.7$V, tail current $= (12-0.7)/10\times10^3 = 1.13mA$

This gives emitter and hence collector current of each transistor as $1.13\times10^{-3}/2 = 0.565mA$

Quiescent DC voltage at each collector in that case equals $12 - 0.565\times10^{-3}\times10\times10^3 = 6.35V$

2. $V_{BE} = 0.7$V, tail current $= (10-0.7)/10\times10^3 = 0.93mA$

This gives emitter and hence collector current of each transistor as $0.93\times10^{-3}/2 = 0.465mA$

Quiescent DC voltage at each collector $= 10 - 0.465\times10^{-3}\times7\times10^3 = 6.745V$

3. Dynamic resistance r_e' of the base-emitter junction diode of the two transistors is given by h_{ie}/h_{fe}.

Therefore, $r_e' = \dfrac{1000}{40} = 25\Omega$

Differential voltage gain $A_d = \dfrac{R_C}{r_e'}$

Therefore, $A_d = \frac{10000}{25} = 400$

4. Dynamic resistance r_e' of the base-emitter junction diode of the two transistors is given by h_{ie}/h_{fe}

   Therefore, $r_e' = \frac{1000}{50} = 20\Omega$

   Differential voltage gain is given by

   Therefore,

5. Current I_R flowing through resistor R_1 is given by $I_R = (12+12-0.7)/(15\times10^3) = 1.553mA$

   1.553 mA

   The tail current $I_T = I_R = 1.553$ mA

   Current flowing through each transistor is equal to half of the total tail current

   Therefore, current through each transistor = 1.553 ′ $10^{-3}/2$ = 0.7765 mA

   Quiescent DC voltage across output $= 12 - 0.7765\times10^{-3}\times8\times10^3 = 5.788V$

6. Highest sinusoidal frequency f_{MAX} that would get satisfactorily amplified is given by:

   $f_{MAX} = \frac{\text{Slew rate}}{2\pi V_P}$, where V_P is the expected peak output voltage

   In the present case, slew rate = 5 V/ms and V_P = 12V.

   $$f_{MAX} = \frac{5\times10^6}{2\pi\times12} = 66.348kHz$$

   Therefore, large signal bandwidth = 66.348 kHz

7. Differential gain $A_d = g_m \times R_C$

   Differential input resistance, $R_{id} = 2r_\pi = 2\beta r_e = \frac{2\beta}{g_m}$

   $$g_m = \frac{2\beta}{R_{id}} = \frac{200}{10\times10^3} = 20\times10^{-3}\,A/V$$

   Therefore, $A_d = 100 = 20\times10^{-3}\times R_C$

   Or $R_C = 100/20\times10^{-3} = 5k\Omega$

   Also, $g_m = \frac{I_C}{V_T}$

   Or $I_C = g_m \times V_T = 20\times10^{-3}\times26\times10^{-3} = 0.52mA$

   Therefore, tail current, $I = 2\times0.52\times10^{-3}\,A = 1.04mA$

8. $I_O = 200\times10^{-6} = 0.5\times K_n \times\left(\frac{W}{L}\right)\times(V_{GS}-V_{TH})^2$

   $$2\times10^{-4} = 0.5\times10\times10^{-3}\times10\times(V_{GS}-1)^2$$

Or $(V_{GS}-1)^2 = 4\times10^{-3}$

Solving the above equation for V_{GS}, we get

$V_{GS}{}^2 - 2V_{GS} + 0.996 = 0$

Or $V_{GS} = 1.063, 0.937$

Since V_{GS} has to be greater than equal to V_{TH}

Therefore, $V_{GS} = 1.063V$

Since $I_O = I_{IN}$

$$R = \frac{(5-1.063)}{200} M\Omega = 20k\Omega$$

9. $CMRR\ (\text{in dB}) = 20\log\left(\frac{A_d}{A_{cm}}\right)$

where A_d and A_{CM} are, respectively, the differential and common mode gain values

$CMRR\ (\text{in dB}) = 20\log A_d - 20\log A_{cm}$

That is, $20\log A_{cm} = 20\log A_d - CMRR\ (\text{in dB}) = 120 - 100 = 20$ dB

This gives $\log A_{CM} = 20/20 = 1$

Therefore, A_{CM} = Antilog 1 = 10

10. $CMRR = \frac{\Delta V_{CM}}{\Delta V_{OS}} = \frac{2}{5\times10^{-6}} = 4\times10^5$

$CMRR$ in dB $= 20\log\left(4\times10^5\right) = 20\times5.6 = 112dB$

11. Mid-band gain = 120 dB = 10^6

If (f) is the frequency at which gain is unity,

Then, f × 1 = 10 × 10^6

Or f = 10 MHz

12. $I_{OUT} = I_{IN}\times(5/2)$

Therefore, $I_{IN} = I_{OUT}\times(2/5) = \left(5\times10^{-3}\right)\times(2/5) = 2mA$

SOLUTIONS TO MULTIPLE CHOICE QUESTIONS

1. (a)	2. (b)	3. (c)	4. (c)
5. (a)	6. (d)	7. (b)	8. (b)
9. (c)	10. (b)	11. (a)	12. (c)
13. (a)	14. (b)	15. (a)	16. (c)
17. (a)	18. (c)	19. (b)	20. (a)

10 Opamp Circuits

After completing this chapter, you will learn the following application circuits using opamps.

- Voltage follower
- Inverting and non-inverting amplifiers
- Inverting summing and non-inverting summing amplifiers
- Subtractor
- Inverting comparator
- Non-inverting comparator
- Window comparator
- Nonlinear amplifiers
- Peak detector
- Half wave and full wave rectifiers
- Integrators and differentiators
- Phase shifters
- Active filters – low pass, high pass and band pass
- Relaxation oscillator
- Instrumentation amplifier
- Clipping and clamping circuits
- Current-to-voltage and voltage-to-current converters
- Averager circuit
- Absolute value circuit

Introduction

This chapter discusses the simple opamp circuits including the inverting and non-inverting amplifiers, voltage follower, summing and difference amplifiers, averager, integrators and differentiators, rectifiers, clippers and clampers, peak detector circuit, absolute value circuit, comparators, phase-shifters, instrumentation amplifiers, non-linear amplifiers, relaxation oscillators, current-to-voltage and voltage-to-current converters. Opamp based oscillators are discussed in chapter 8 on oscillators. Important formulae and keywords are listed at the end of the chapter. Different topics discussed in the chapter are amply illustrated with solved examples. In addition, there are a number of problems given towards the end of the chapter along with brief solutions. A self-evaluation exercise containing multiple-choice questions along with solutions concludes the chapter.

10.1 VOLTAGE FOLLOWER

Voltage follower is nothing but a non-inverting amplifier circuit with unity gain. Figure-10.1 shows the basic voltage-follower circuit. The name has its origin in the fact that the output follows the input. In an ideal opamp with negative feedback, the voltage at inverting terminal is equal to the voltage at non-inverting terminal. Since the inverting terminal is connected to the output; the output voltage is equal to the input voltage. In case, input signal is an Ac signal; suitable capacitors are connected in series with input and output terminals.

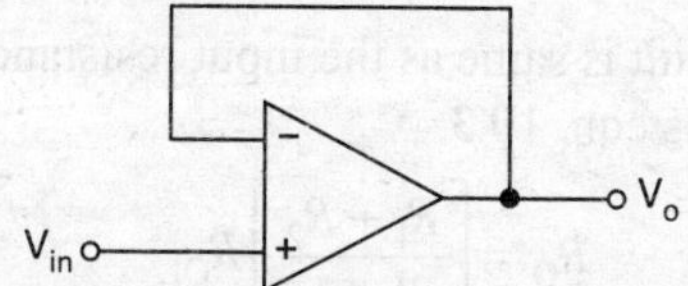

Fig. 10.1: DC voltage-follower circuit

Voltage-follower circuit has many advantages. Owing to its extremely high input impedance, extremely low output impedance and unity gain; it acts as an ideal interface between a high impedance source and a low impedance load. Also, unity closed-loop gain leads to a very high closed-loop bandwidth equal to the unity gain cross-over frequency of the opamp. The output offset error is also very low because due to unity closed-loop gain, input errors are not amplified.

10.2 INVERTING AMPLIFIER

An *inverting amplifier* changes both amplitude and polarity of the signal in the case of DC input and changes the amplitude and reverses the phase of the input signal in the case of AC input. Figure-10.2 shows the basic circuit diagram of an inverting amplifier configured around an opamp.

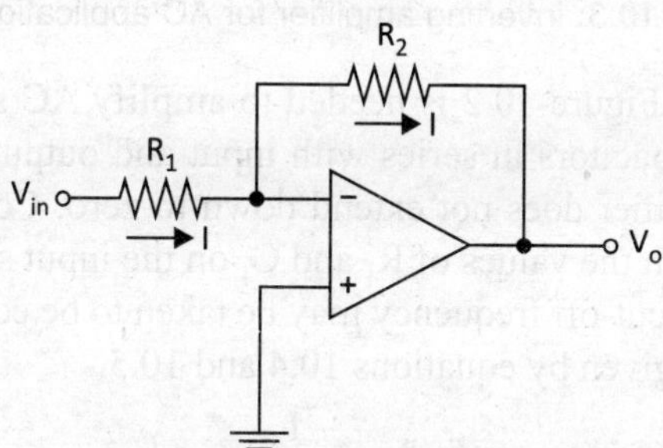

Fig. 10.2: Inverting amplifier

The expression for the closed-loop gain A_{CL} for the inverting amplifier circuit of Figure-10.1 is given by eqn. 10.1.

$$A_{CL} = -\frac{A_{OL} R_2}{R_1 + R_2 + A_{OL} R_1} \cong -\frac{R_2}{\left[R_1 + \left(R_2/A_{OL}\right)\right]} \tag{10.1}$$

Where,

A_{OL} is the open-loop gain of the opamp.

When ratio R_2/A_{OL} is much smaller than R_1, the gain expression reduces to the gain expression of eqn. 10.2.

$$A_{CL} = -\left(\frac{R_2}{R_1}\right) \tag{10.2}$$

The above equation can be easily derived by assuming that no current flows into the inverting input of the opamp. That is, the current flowing through resistor R_1 is same as that flowing through R_2. Since, inverting input behaves as virtual earth; voltage drop across R_1 is equal to voltage drop across R_2, which leads to eqn. 10.2.

The input impedance of this circuit is same as the input resistance value, R_1. The output impedance of this circuit (R_O) is approximated as eqn. 10.3.

$$R_O = \left[\frac{R_1 + R_2}{R_1 A_{OL}}\right] R_{OL} \tag{10.3}$$

Where,

R_{OL} is the open-loop output impedance of the opamp.

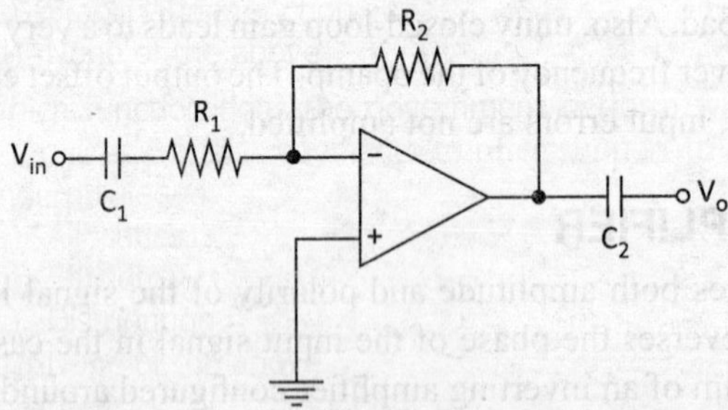

Fig. 10.3: Inverting amplifier for AC applications

If the inverting amplifier of Figure-10.2 is needed to amplify AC signals only, the circuit may be modified to include coupling capacitors in series with input and output as shown in Figure-10.3. The frequency response of this amplifier does not extend down to zero. Coupling capacitors give a lower cut-off frequency depending upon the values of R_1 and C_1 on the input side and R_L (load resistance) and C_2 on the output side. The lower cut-off frequency may be taken to be equal to higher of the two values. The two cut-off frequencies are given by equations 10.4 and 10.5.

$$f_{CL1} = \frac{1}{2\pi R_1 C_1} \tag{10.4}$$

$$f_{CL2} = \frac{1}{2\pi R_L C_2} \tag{10.5}$$

Closed-loop bandwidth or upper cut-off frequency (f_{CH}) is given by eqn. 10.6

$$f_{CH} = \frac{\text{Unity gain cross-over frequency}}{A_{CL}} \tag{10.6}$$

10.3 NON-INVERTING AMPLIFIER

Figure-10.4 shows a non-inverting amplifier for DC applications.

The ideal closed-loop voltage gain (A_{CL}) is given by eqn. 10.7.

$$A_{CL} = 1 + \frac{R_2}{R_1} \tag{10.7}$$

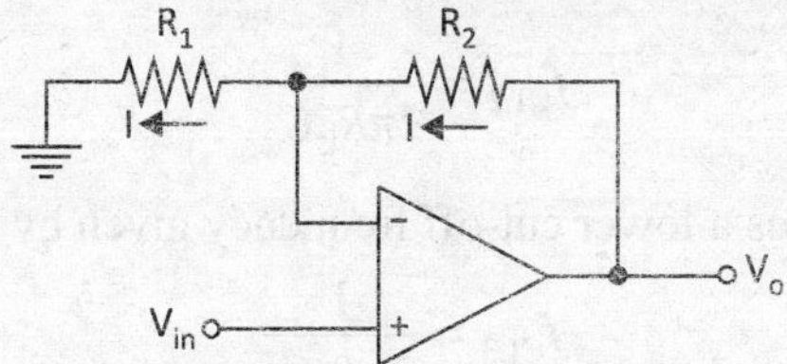

Fig. 10.4: Non-inverting amplifier

The actual gain expression in the case of a non-inverting amplifier is given by eqn. 10.8.

$$A_{CL} = \frac{A_{OL}(R_1 + R_2)}{R_1 + R_2 + A_{OL} R_1} \quad (10.8)$$

The input impedance (R_i) of this configuration is given by eqn. 10.9.

$$R_i = R_{IL} A_{OL} \left(\frac{R_1}{R_1 + R_2} \right) \quad (10.9)$$
$$= R_{IL} \times \text{Loop gain}$$

Where,

R_{IL} is the open-loop input impedance

loop gain is the open-loop gain/closed-loop gain.

The output impedance (R_o) can be computed from the following equation

$$R_O = \frac{R_{OL}}{\text{Loop gain}} \quad (10.10)$$

Where,

R_{OL} is the open-loop output impedance of the opamp

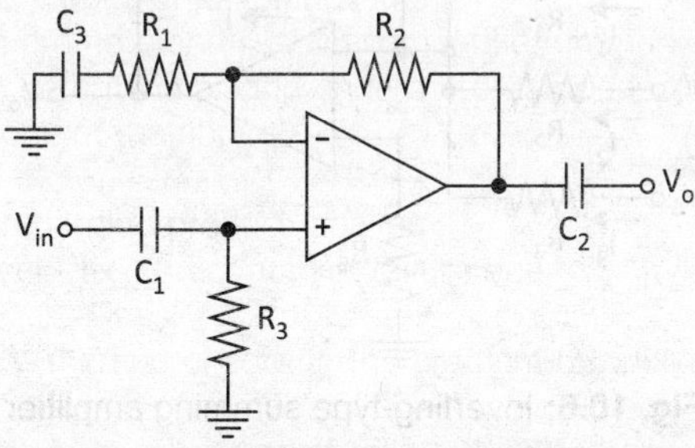

Fig. 10.5: Non-inverting amplifier for AC signal

In case the non-inverting amplifier of Figure-10.3 is needed to amplify AC signals only, the circuit may be modified to include coupling capacitors C_1 and C_2 in series with input and output, respectively, and a bypass capacitor C_3 as shown in Figure-10.4. Coupling capacitors give a lower cut-off frequency depending upon the values of R_3 and C_1 on the input side and R_L (load resistance) and C_2 on the output side. The two cut-off frequencies are given by the following equations

$$f_{CL1} = \frac{1}{2\pi R_3 C_1} \quad (10.11)$$

$$f_{CL2} = \frac{1}{2\pi R_L C_2} \tag{10.12}$$

The bypass capacitor produces a lower cut-off frequency given by

$$f_{CL3} = \frac{1}{2\pi R_1 C_3} \tag{10.13}$$

The lower cut-off frequency may be taken as the highest of the three values. The upper cut-off frequency is given by the ratio of unity gain cross-over frequency to the closed-loop gain.

10.4 INVERTING AND NON-INVERTING SUMMING AMPLIFIERS

Summing amplifier produces an output that is equal to the sum of input signals multiplied by corresponding voltage gain values. In the case of a unity voltage gain for all input signals, the circuit becomes an adder circuit.

10.4.1 Inverting Summing Amplifier

Figure 10.6 shows circuit diagram of three input inverting-type summing amplifier. Expression for the output voltage V_o is derived as follows.

$$I = I_1 + I_2 + I_3 \tag{10.14}$$

$$-\frac{V_O}{R} = \frac{V_1}{R_1} + \frac{V_2}{R_2} + \frac{V_3}{R_3} \tag{10.15}$$

$$V_o = -\left[\left(\frac{R_4}{R_1}\right)V_1 + \left(\frac{R_4}{R_2}\right)V_2 + \left(\frac{R_4}{R_3}\right)V_3\right] \tag{10.16}$$

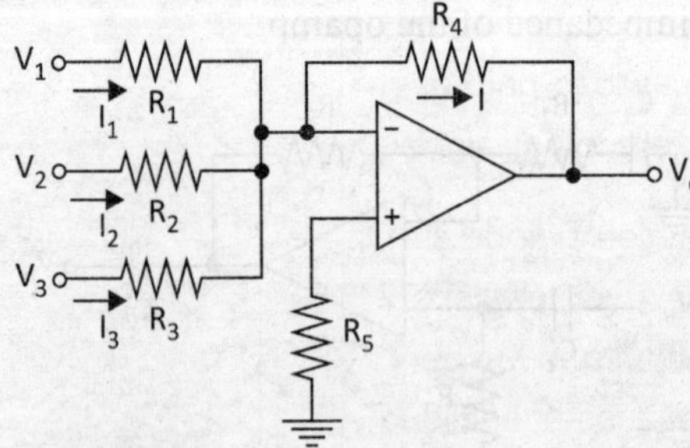

Fig. 10.6: Inverting-type summing amplifier

If $R_1 = R_2 = R_3 = R_4 = R$, then

$$V_o = -(V_1 + V_2 + V_3) \tag{10.17}$$

10.4.2 Non-inverting Summing Amplifier

A *non-inverting summing amplifier* can be constructed from its inverting counterpart by cascading it with a unity gain inverting amplifier (Figure-10.7). An alternative non-inverting adder circuit, where the summing has been done at the non-inverting input, is shown in Figure-10.8. The given circuit behaves like a non-inverting amplifier with a gain of unity to both the inputs. This can be verified as follows. .

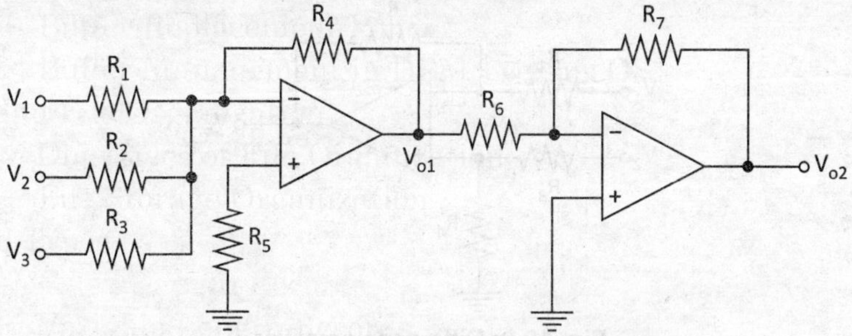

Fig. 10.7: Non-inverting summing amplifier

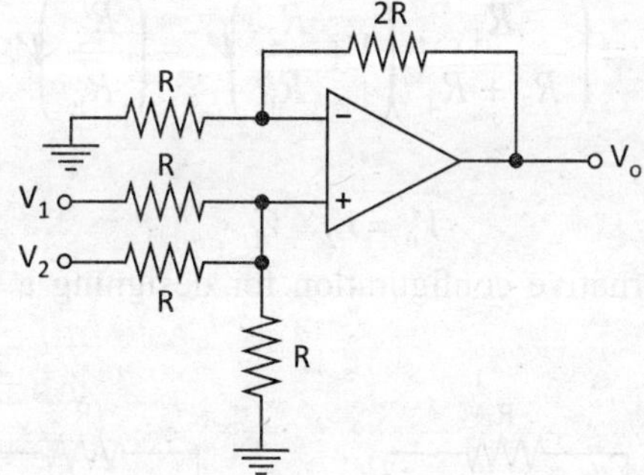

Fig. 10.8: Non-inverting adder with single opamp

Taking one input at a time, the output voltage V_{o1} due to V_1 is given by eqn. 10.18.

$$V_{O1} = \frac{V_1}{3} \times \left(1 + \frac{2R}{R}\right) = V_1 \tag{10.18}$$

Similarly, the output voltage V_{o2} due to V_2 is given by eqn. 10.19

$$V_{O2} = \frac{V_2}{3} \times \left(1 + \frac{2R}{R}\right) = V_2 \tag{10.19}$$

In case both V_1 and V_2 are simultaneously present, output voltage V_o is given by eqn. 10.20.

$$V_o = V_1 + V_2 \tag{10.20}$$

If the adder circuit of Figure-10.8 were to be used for adding (n) inputs, the feedback resistor value would be equal to nR.

10.5 DIFFERENCE AMPLIFIER AND SUBTRACTOR

A *difference amplifier* produces an output that is equal to the difference of the two input signals multiplied by corresponding voltage gain values. In the case of voltage gain being unity for the two input signals, the circuit becomes a *subtractor* circuit. Figure-10.9 shows the generalized form of a difference amplifier.

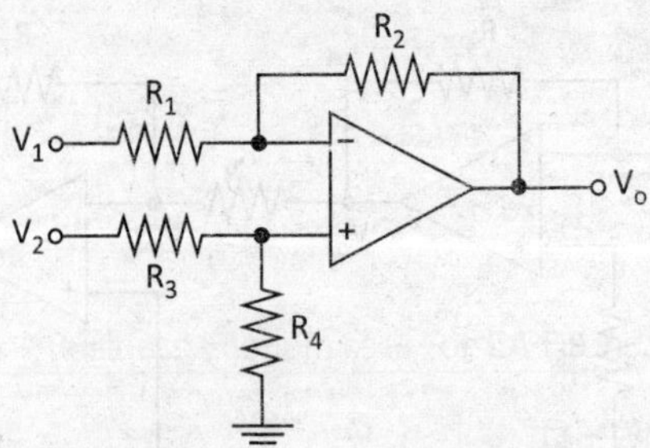

Fig. 10.9: Difference amplifier

The output voltage V_o is given by eqn. 10.21.

$$V_o = \left(\frac{R_4}{R_3 + R_4}\right)\left(1 + \frac{R_2}{R_1}\right)V_2 - \left(\frac{R_2}{R_1}\right)V_1 \tag{10.21}$$

For $R_1 = R_2 = R_3 = R_4$

$$V_o = V_2 - V_1 \tag{10.22}$$

Figure-10.10 shows an alternative configuration for designing a subtractor circuit, with output voltage V_o equal to V_1-V_2.

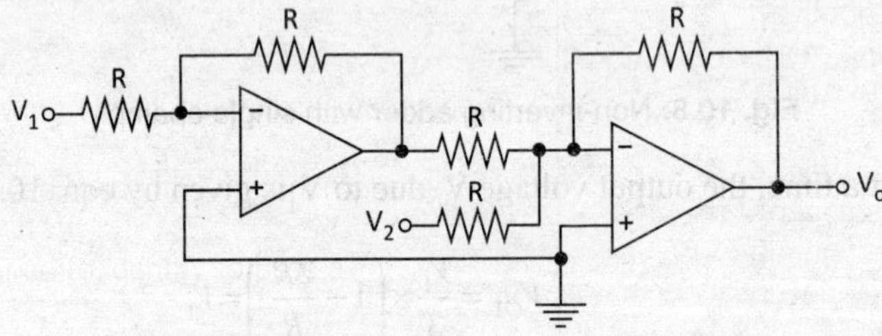

Fig. 10.10: Alternative form of subtractor circuit

Example-10.1: Figure-10.11 shows an inverting amplifier using an opamp. Given that R_1 = 10 kW and R_2 = 100 kW and the slew rate of the opamp is 0.5 V/ms. For an input signal with peak amplitude varying from 100 to 300 mV, what is the maximum possible input signal frequency that would be faithfully amplified?

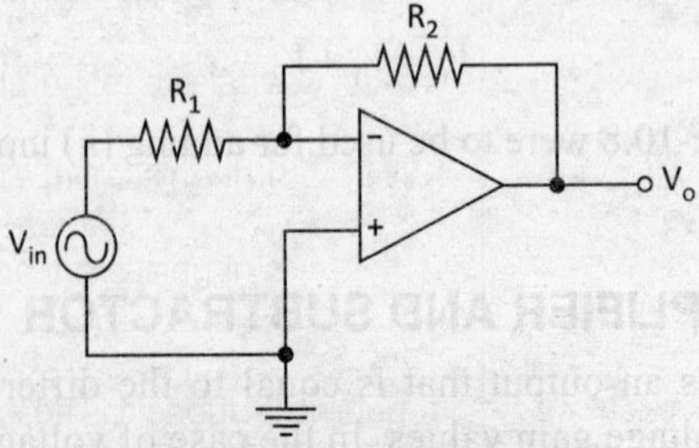

Fig. 10.11: Example-1

Solution: The largest input signal amplitude = 300 mV.

Corresponding output signal = $300 \times 10^{-3} \times \left(100 \times 10^3 / 10 \times 10^3\right) = 3000mV = 3V$.

Highest sinewave frequency that would be faithfully amplified is given by:

$$f_{MAX} = \left[\frac{\text{Slew rate}}{2\pi V_O(\text{max})}\right] = \left[\frac{0.5\times10^6}{2\pi\times3}\right] Hz = 26.5kHz$$

Example-10.2: For the amplifier circuit of Figure-10.12, determine output voltage V_o.

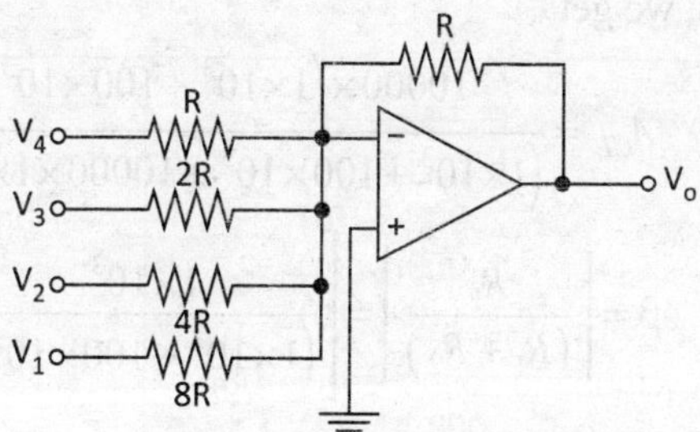

Fig. 10.12: Example-2

Solution: Let us assume that V_{o1}, V_{o2}, V_{o3} and V_{o4} are respectively the outputs for only V_1, V_2, V_3 and V_4 present one at a time with other inputs grounded.

Then, $$V_{o4} = -V_4 \times \left(\frac{R}{R}\right) = -V_4$$

$$V_{o3} = -V_3 \times \left(\frac{R}{2R}\right) = -\frac{V_3}{2}$$

$$V_{o2} = -V_2 \times \left(\frac{R}{4R}\right) = -\frac{V_2}{4} \text{ and}$$

$$V_{o1} = -V_1 \times \left(\frac{R}{8R}\right) = -\frac{V_1}{8}$$

With all inputs are present simultaneously, $V_o = -\left[V_4 + \frac{V_3}{2} + \frac{V_2}{4} + \frac{V_1}{8}\right]$

Example-10.3: For the op-amp based amplifier shown in Figure-10.13, what is the value of voltage gain and the input impedance? Given that open loop gain and the input impedance of the opamp are 80 dB and 1MW respectively.

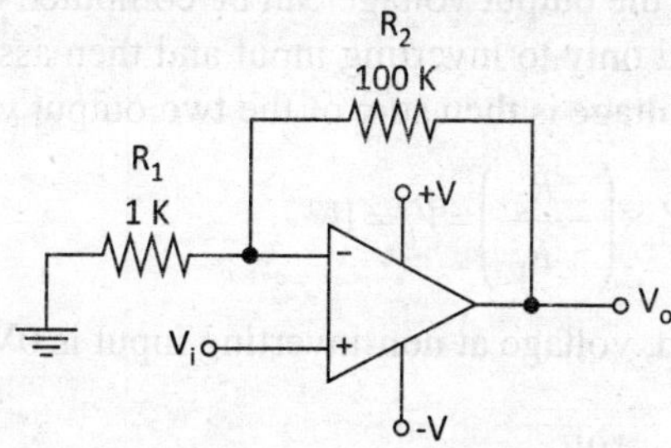

Fig. 10.13: Example 3

Solution: The closed loop gain can be computed from:

$$A_{CL} = \frac{A_{OL}(R_1 + R_2)}{R_1 + R_2 + A_{OL}R_1} \quad A_{CL} = \frac{A_{OL}(R_1 + R_2)}{R_1 + R_2 + A_{OL}R_1}$$

Now, open loop gain, $A_{OL} = 80$ dB = 10000

Substituting different values, we get,

$$A_{CL} = \frac{10000 \times (1\times10^3 + 100\times10^3)}{(1\times10^3 + 100\times10^3 + 10000\times1\times10^3)} = 99.99$$

Now, Feedback factor, $\beta = \left[\frac{R_1}{(R_1 + R_2)}\right] = \left[\frac{1\times10^3}{(1\times10^3 + 100\times10^3)}\right] = \frac{1}{101}$

Therefore, de-sensitivity factor, $D = (1 + \beta A) = 1 + \frac{10000}{101} = 100.0099$

De-sensitivity factor is also the loop gain. Loop gain is ratio of open loop gain to closed loop gain.

Therefore, Input impedance = Input impedance of opamp × (1 + βA) =1×100.0099MΩ = 100MΩ

Closed loop gain can also be computed by dividing the open loop gain by de-sensitivity factor.

That is, Closed loop gain= $\frac{10000}{100.0099} = 99.99$

Example-4: Figure-10.14 shows an op-amp based circuit. Determine the value of output voltage (in volts) when the switch S is (a) open (b) closed.

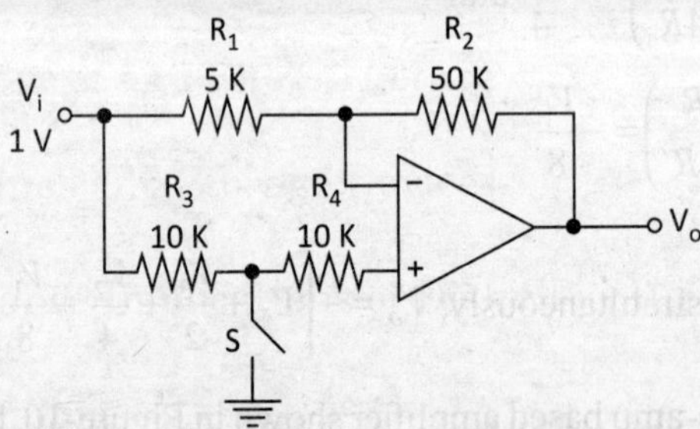

Fig. 10.14: Example-4

Solution:

(a) When the switch is open, the output voltage can be computed by using superposition principle by first assuming that V_i is applied only to inverting input and then assuming that V_i is applied only to non-inverting input. The output voltage is then sum of the two output voltages.

That is, $V_o = V_i \times \left(1 + \frac{R_2}{R_1}\right) + V_i \times \left(-\frac{R_2}{R_1}\right) = V_i = 1V$

(b) When the switch is closed, voltage at non-inverting input is 0V.

Therefore, $V_o = V_i \times \left(-\frac{R_2}{R_1}\right) = -10V$

10.6 COMPARATORS

A *comparator* circuit is a two-input, one-output building block that produces a high or low output depending upon the relative magnitudes of the two inputs. An opamp can be very conveniently used as a comparator when used without negative feedback. Because of very large value of open-loop voltage gain, it produces either positively saturated or negatively saturated output voltage depending upon whether the amplitude of the voltage applied at the non-inverting input terminal is more or less positive than the voltage applied at the inverting input terminal.

One of the inputs of the comparator is generally applied a reference voltage and the other input is fed with the input voltage that needs to be compared with the reference voltage. In a special case where the reference voltage is zero, the circuit is referred to as *zero-crossing detector*. Figure-10.15 shows the basic circuit arrangement of a non-inverting type of zero-crossing detector along with its transfer characteristics. It is called a non-inverting zero-crossing detector because an input more positive than zero leads to a positively saturated output voltage. Diodes D_1 and D_2 connected at the input are to protect the sensitive input circuits inside the opamp from excessively large input voltages. Some opamps are specially designed and optimized for use as comparators. These devices have in-built protection diodes and therefore do not require external diode clamps. R is the current-limiting resistor.

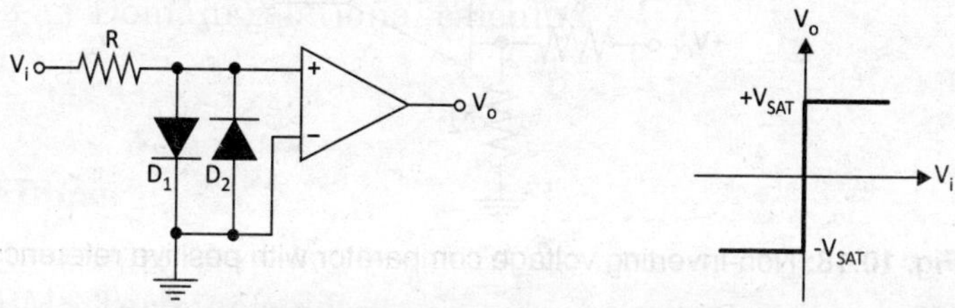

Fig. 10.15: Non-inverting zero-crossing detector

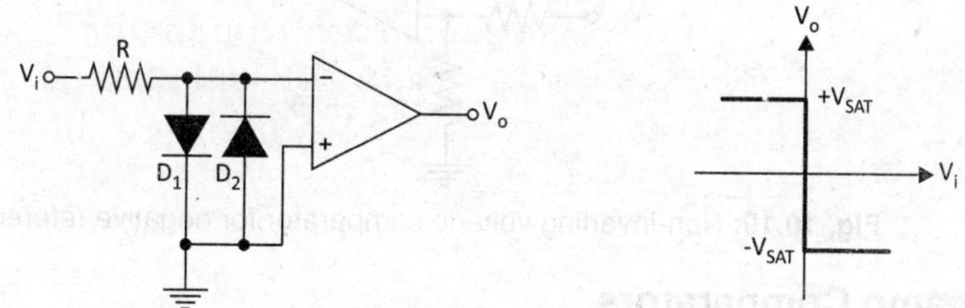

Fig. 10.16: Inverting zero-crossing detector

Figure-10.16 shows the inverting type of zero-crossing detector along with its transfer characteristics. In this case, input voltage slightly more positive than zero produces a negatively saturated output voltage. One common application of zero-crossing detector is to convert sine wave signal to a square wave signal. Figures-10.17(a) and (b) respectively show relevant waveforms for non-inverting and inverting type of zero-crossing detector circuits.

In the generalized case, reference voltage may be a positive or a negative voltage. Figure-10.18 shows the circuit diagram of non-inverting comparator for a positive reference voltage. V_{REF} in this case is given by $+V_{CC} \times [R_2/(R_1 + R_2)]$. Figure-10.19 shows the circuit diagram of non-inverting comparator for a negative reference voltage. Reference voltage V_{REF} is given by $-V_{CC} \times [R_2/(R_1 + R_2)]$.

Inverting-type voltage comparators can similarly be built for positive and negative reference voltages.

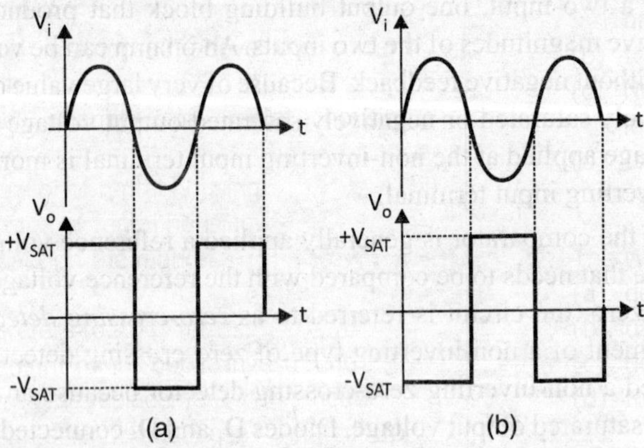

Fig. 10.17: Waveforms of zero-crossing detector

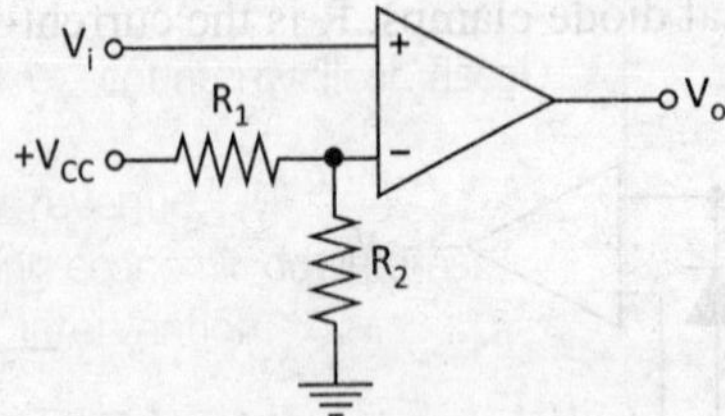

Fig. 10.18: Non-inverting voltage comparator with positive reference

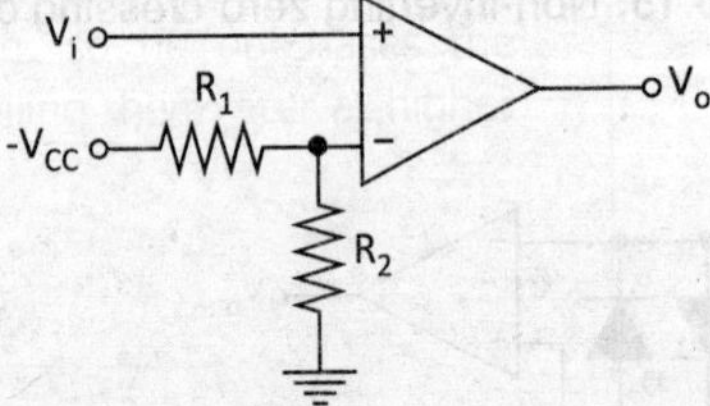

Fig. 10.19: Non-inverting voltage comparator for negative reference

10.6.1 Opamp Comparators

In the preceding paragraphs, we have discussed use of general-purpose opamps as voltage comparators. As outlined earlier, there are opamps that are particularly designed and optimized for use as comparators. General-purpose opamp when used as a comparator suffers from slew rate limitation. Relatively lower slew rate forces the transition time from one state to the other to be prohibitively large. Though this problem can be overcome by using a high-speed opamp with a higher slew rate specification; a better design approach to overcoming this limitation is by eliminating the compensation capacitor. It may be mentioned here that comparator works as a non-linear circuit and therefore elimination of compensation capacitor has no derogatory effect on the performance. With compensation capacitor removed, the only capacitance remaining is the stray capacitance across the output. Thus, slew rates can be very high.

Another important parameter of a comparator is its ability to operate from a single supply and interface conveniently with popular logic families. Input circuit of opamp comparator is tailored to meet these two requirements. Figure-10.20 shows the simplified schematic diagram of opamp comparator. As shown in the figure, the output has an open-collector output stage. For the output stage to work properly, the output terminal needs to be connected to the positive supply voltage through an external resistor called pull-up resistor. It is called pull-up resistor as it pulls the output voltage to the supply voltage when the output transistor Q_5 (in Figure-10.20) is in cut-off state. Not all comparators have an open-collector output stage. In fact, pull-up resistor slows down the response time of the comparator. There are opamp comparators with active pull-up output stage. These opamp comparators are capable of producing relatively much faster switching times. These comparators need dual power supplies.

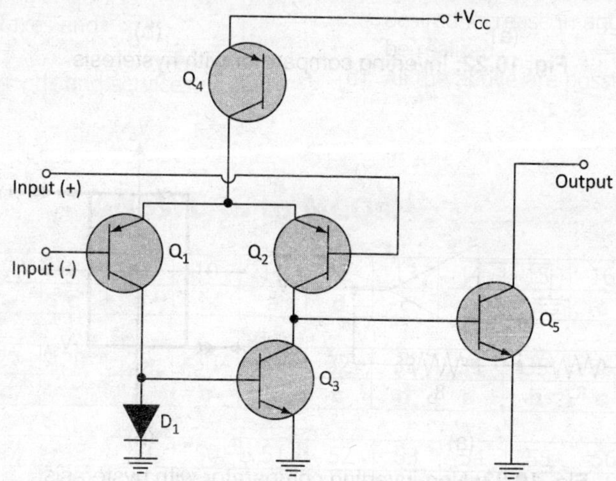

Fig. 10.20: Basic circuit schematic arrangement of opamp comparator

10.6.2 Comparator with Hysteresis

When the input signal to comparator contains noise; transitions at the output around the trip point tend to become highly erratic. Instead of being smooth from one state to the other, transition around the trip point is a cluster of pulses with randomly varying pulse width. The problem becomes particularly severe if the input signal were changing slowly. This phenomenon is demonstrated in Figure-10.21.

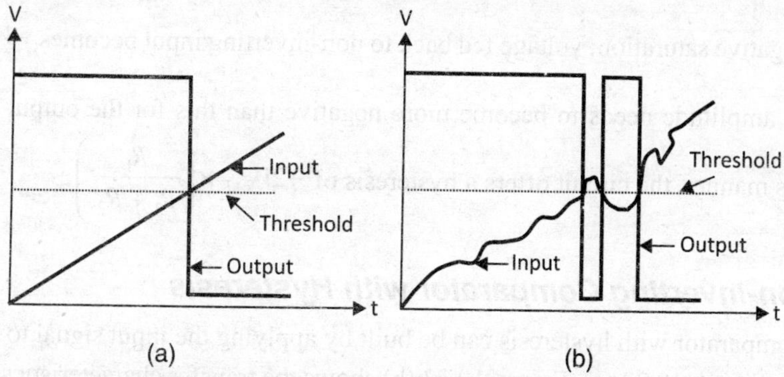

Fig. 10.21: Erratic transitions caused by noisy input signal:
(a) Ideal input signal; (b) noisy input signal

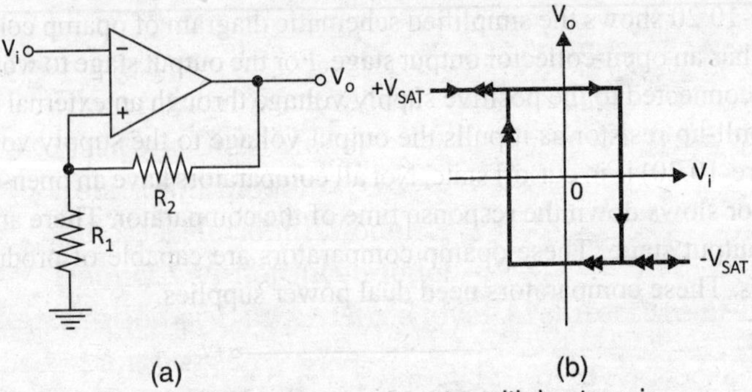

Fig. 10.22: Inverting comparator with hysteresis

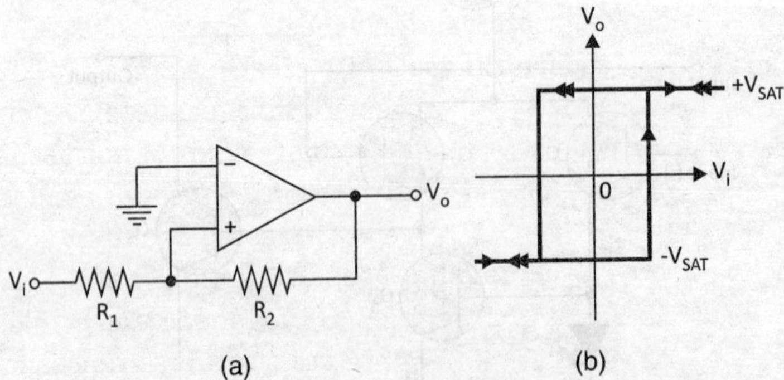

Fig. 10.23: Non-inverting comparator with hysteresis

10.6.2.1 Inverting Comparator with Hysteresis

Figure-10.22(a) shows the circuit schematic of an inverting comparator with hysteresis. Figure-10.22 (b) shows its transfer characteristics. The circuit functions as follows. Let us assume that the output is in positive saturation. Voltage at non-inverting input in this case is $+V_{SAT} \times \left(\frac{R_1}{R_1 + R_2}\right)$. Now, the input signal needs to be more positive than this voltage for the output to go to negative saturation. Once the output goes to negative saturation; voltage fed back to non-inverting input becomes $-V_{SAT} \times \left(\frac{R_1}{R_1 + R_2}\right)$. The input signal amplitude needs to become more negative than this for the output to go to positive saturation. In this manner, the circuit offers a hysteresis of $+2V_{SAT} \times \left(\frac{R_1}{R_1 + R_2}\right)$.

10.6.2.2 Non-inverting Comparator with Hysteresis

Non-inverting comparator with hysteresis can be built by applying the input signal to the non-inverting input as shown in Figure-10.23 (a). Figure-10.23 (b) shows the transfer characteristics. Operation of the circuit can be explained on lines similar to that of its inverting counterpart. Upper and lower trip points are, respectively, given by $+V_{SAT} \times \left(\frac{R_1}{R_2}\right)$ and $-V_{SAT} \times \left(\frac{R_1}{R_2}\right)$. Hysteresis in this case is equal to $+2V_{SAT} \times \left(\frac{R_1}{R_2}\right)$.

10.6.3 Window Comparator

In the case of a conventional comparator, the output changes state when the input voltage goes above or below the preset reference voltage. In a window comparator, there are two reference voltages called the lower and the upper trip points. Output is in one state when the input is inside the window created by the lower and upper trip points and in the other state when it is outside the window. Figure-10.24 shows the basic circuit diagram of one such window comparator. The circuit functions as follows. When the input voltage is less than the voltage reference corresponding to the lower trip point (LTP), output of opamp A_1 is at $+V_{SAT}$ and that of opamp A_2 is at $-V_{SAT}$. Diodes D_1 and D_2 are respectively forward- and reverse-biased. Consequently, output across R_L is at $+V_{SAT}$. When the input voltage is greater than the reference voltage corresponding to the upper trip point (UTP), the output of opampA_1 is at $-V_{SAT}$ and that of opamp A_2 is at $+V_{SAT}$. Diodes D_1 and D_2 are respectively reverse- and forward-biased with the result that the output across R_L is again at $+V_{SAT}$. When the input voltage is greater than LTP voltage and lower than UTP voltage, the outputs of both opamps are at negative saturation with the result that diodes D_1 and D_2 are reverse-biased and the output across R_L is zero.

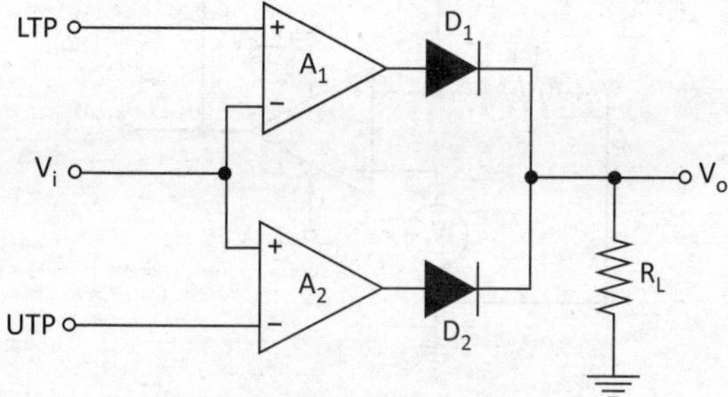

Fig. 10.24: Window comparator

Figure-10.25 (a) shows the transfer characteristics of the window comparator whose circuit is shown in Figure-10.24. The transfer characteristics shown in Figure-10.25 (b) can be obtained if we interchange the positions of LTPs and UTPs and the two opamp comparators used have open collector outputs. In this case a pull-up resistor will be connected from the output pin of the comparator to the supply terminal.

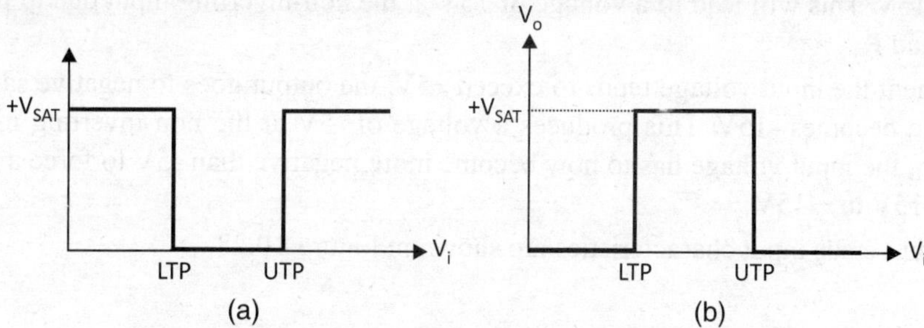

Fig. 10.25: Transfer characteristics of window comparator

Example-5: Refer to the opamp-based non-inverting zero crossing detector circuit of Figure-10.26. The opamp is characterized by saturation voltages of ±10 V and a slew rate specification of 10V/μs.

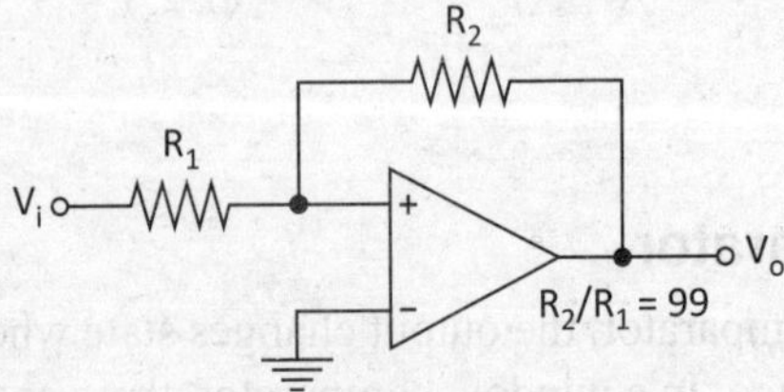

Fig. 10.26: Example-5

Solution: Saturation voltage = 10 V

Therefore, hysteresis voltage $= 10\times\dfrac{R_1}{(R_1+R_2)} = \dfrac{10}{(1+R_2/R_1)}$

Now, $R_2/R_1 = 99$

Therefore, hysteresis $= 10/(1+99) = 0.1V = 100mV$

Example-10.6: Refer to the opamp circuit of Figure-10.27. Identify the circuit and draw output versus input characteristics indicating magnitudes of relevant voltages.

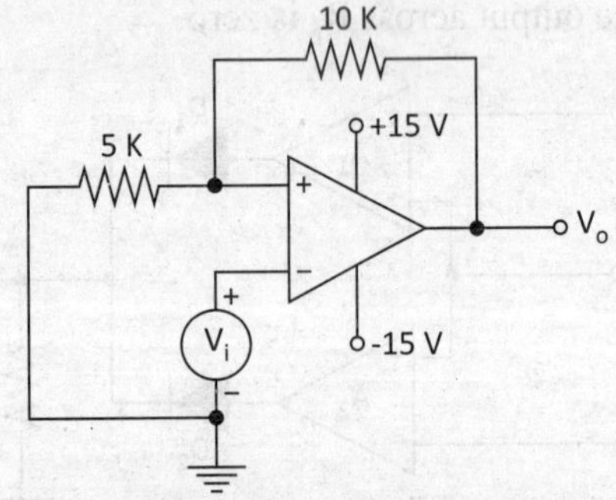

Fig. 10.27: Example 10.6

Solution: The circuit shown in Figure-10.27 does not have a negative feedback. Instead, it has a positive feedback. Also, input is applied to inverting input terminal of opamp. Therefore, it is an inverting comparator with hysteresis.

Let us assume that the output is initially in positive saturation. The output voltage in that case would be equal to +15V. This will lead to a voltage of +5V at the non-inverting input due to potential divider action of R_1 and R_2.

The moment the input voltage tends to exceed +5V; the output goes to negative saturation and the output voltage becomes -15V. This produces a voltage of -5V at the non-inverting input terminal of opamp. Again, the input voltage has to now become more negative than -5V to force a transition at the output from -15V to + 15V.

The output versus input characteristics are shown in Figure-10.28.

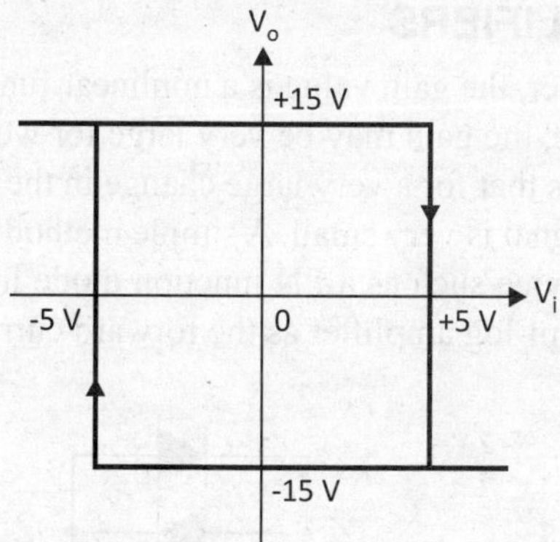

Fig. 10.28: Solution to Example-10.6

Example-10.7: Figure-10.29 shows a window comparator configured around opamp comparators having open collector outputs. Draw the transfer characteristics and determine the two trip points.

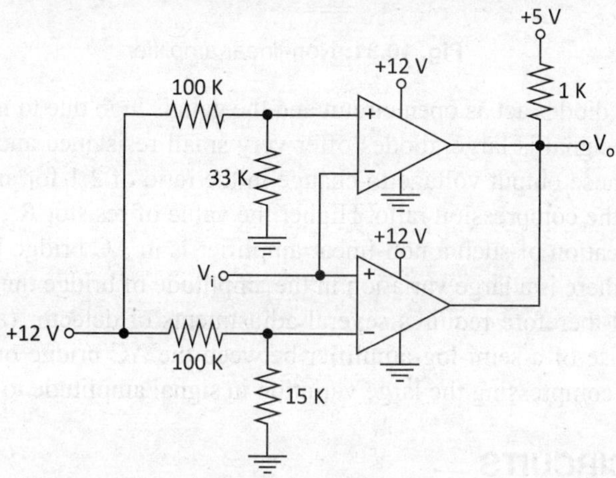

Fig. 10.29: Example-10.7

Solution: The upper trip point (LTP) = 12 × 33/133 = 2.977V

The lower trip point (UTP) = 12 × 15/115 = 1.565V

When the input voltage is either less than the LTP or greater than the UTP; the output is pulled down to zero. When the input is greater than the LTP and less than the UTP; the output is pulled up to +5V. Fig. 10.30: shows transfer characteristics.

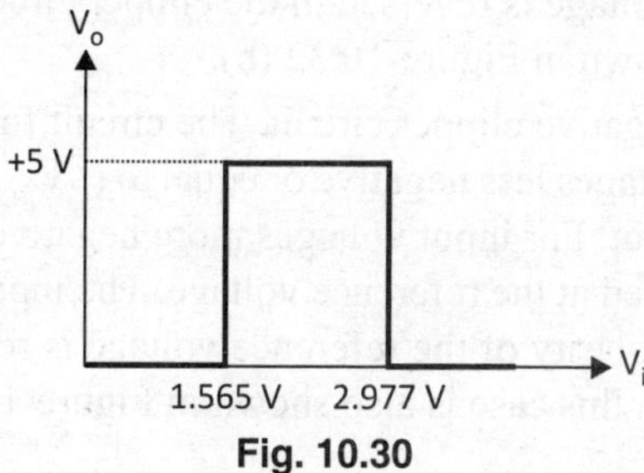

Fig. 10.30

10.7 NONLINEAR AMPLIFIERS

In the case of a nonlinear amplifier, the gain value is a nonlinear function of the amplitude of the signal applied at the input. For example, the gain may be very large for weak input signals and very small for large input signals, which implies that for a very large change in the amplitude of input signal, resultant change in amplitude of output signal is very small. A simple method to achieve non-linear amplification is by connecting a non-linear device such as a PN junction diode in the feedback path (Figure-10.31). The amplifier thus becomes a semi-log amplifier as the forward current through silicon diodes varies as log of applied voltage.

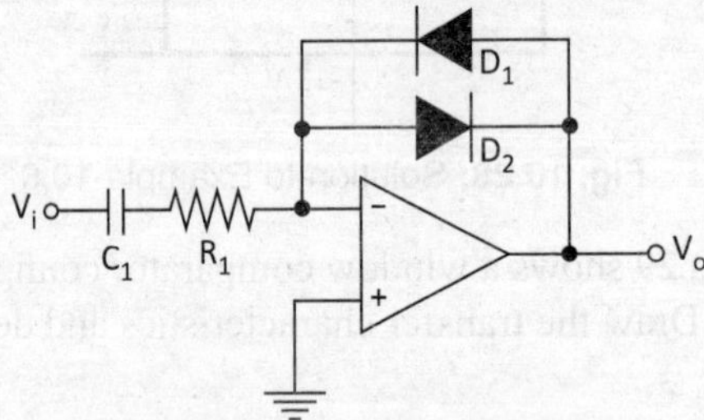

Fig. 10.31: Non-linear amplifier

With zero voltage, diodes act as open circuit and the gain is high due to minimum feedback. When the amplitude of input signal is large, diodes offer very small resistance and thus gain is low. Such a circuit may typically cause output voltage to change in the ratio of 2:1 for an input change of 1000:1. Resistance R_1 decides the compression ratio. Higher the value of resistor R_1, lesser is the compression ratio. A common application of such a non-linear amplifier is in AC bridge balance detectors. In case of AC bridge balance, there is a large variation in the amplitude of bridge output signal around the null point. Obtaining a null therefore requires several adjustments of detector (an AC milli-voltmeter for example) sensitivity. Use of a semi-log amplifier between the AC bridge output and the meter input addresses this issue by compressing the large variation in signal amplitude to a small variation.

10.8 CLIPPER CIRCUITS

Figure-10.32 (a) shows a positive clipper circuit, a clipper circuit that clips positive half cycles above a certain positive reference voltage. The circuit functions as follows. During positive half cycles, for input voltages less than or equal to reference voltage (V_{REF}), the opamp output goes to positive saturation and diode (D_1) is reverse-biased with the result that the input appears as such at the output. The situation is same during negative half cycles. When the input voltage exceeds the reference voltage, the opamp output goes to negative saturation and the diode gets forward-biased. The output gets shorted to inverting input and the output is clamped to V_{REF}. The input and output waveforms are shown in Figure-10.32 (b). If the polarity of the reference voltage is reversed in the clipper circuit of Figure-10.32 (a), the clipping occurs below zero voltage as shown in Figure-10.32 (b).

Figure-10.33 (a) shows a negative clipper circuit. The circuit functions as follows. During positive half cycles and also for input voltages less negative or equal to ($-V_{REF}$), diode (D_1) is reverse-biased. The input appears as such at the output. For input voltages more negative than $-V_{REF}$, diode (D_1) is forward-biased and the output gets clamped at the reference voltage. The input and output waveforms are shown in Figure-10.33 (b). When the polarity of the reference voltage is reversed, clipping occurs above zero voltage. The output waveform in this case is also shown in Figure-10.33 (b).

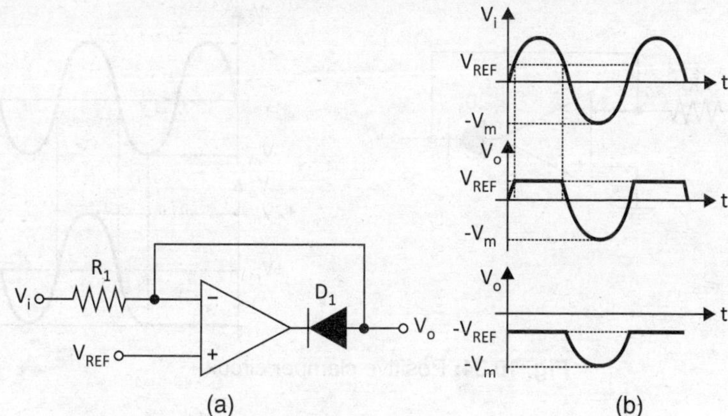

Fig. 10.32: Positive clipper circuit and relevant waveforms

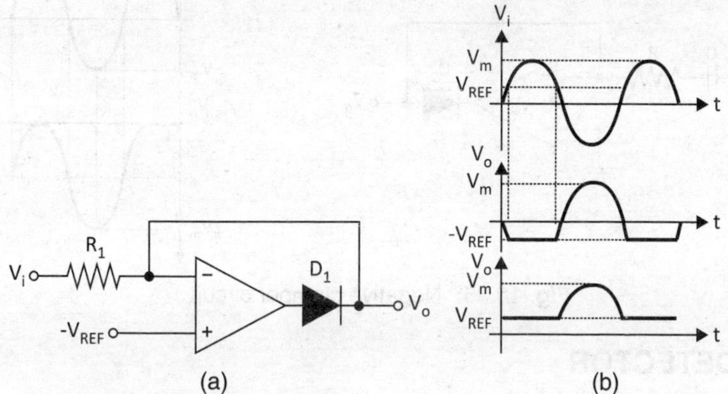

Fig. 10.33: Negative clipper circuit and relevant waveforms

10.9 CLAMPER CIRCUITS

Figure-10.34 shows the positive clamper circuit that clamps the negative peaks to zero. The circuit operates as follows. During the first negative half cycle, diode D_1 gets forward-biased and capacitor C charges through resistance R and the forward-biased diode to the peak of the negative half cycle voltage. During the positive cycle, the diode gets reverse-biased. There is no rapid discharge path for the capacitor and in this case, the output equals the input voltage plus the voltage across the capacitor. The negative peaks are thus clamped to zero voltage. If the non-inverting input is applied a reference voltage (V_{REF}), positive or negative, the negative peaks are clamped at V_{REF} instead of zero. Figure-10.35 shows the negative clamper circuit that clamps positive peaks to zero. Again, if the non-inverting input is applied a reference voltage V_{REF}, positive or negative, the positive peaks are clamped at V_{REF} instead of zero.

The conventional clamper circuit cannot function as a clamper if the peak input signal is less than 0.7 V. The opamp-based clamper circuit has no such limitation. It functions as if the diode is ideal. This implies that the circuit can be used to clamp even milli-volt signals.

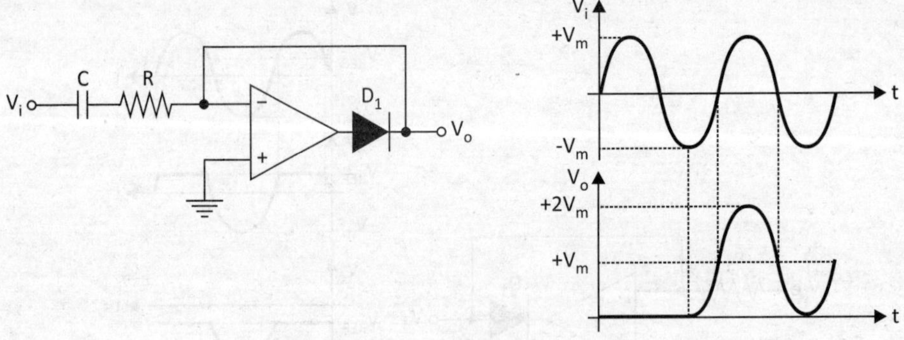

Fig. 10.34: Positive clamper circuit

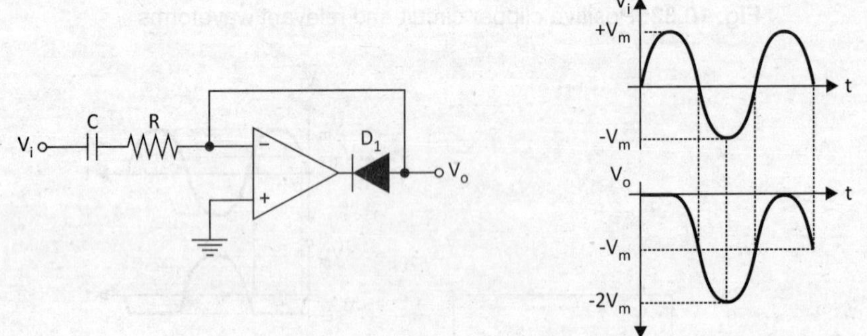

Fig. 10.35: Negative clamper circuit

10.10 PEAK DETECTOR

Peak detector circuit produces a voltage at the output equal to peak amplitude (positive or negative) of the input signal. Figure-10.36 shows a positive peak detector circuit. As we can see, it is essentially a clipper circuit with a parallel resistor-capacitor connected at its output. The clipper here reproduces the positive half cycles. During this period, the diode is forward-biased. The capacitor rapidly charges to the positive peak from the output of the opamp through the ON resistance of the forward-biased diode. As the input starts decreasing beyond the peak; the diode gets reverse-biased, thus isolating the capacitor (C) from the output of the opamp. The capacitor can now discharge only through the resistor (R) connected across it. The value of the resistor (R) is much larger than the forward-biased diode's ON resistance. The purpose of this resistor is to allow a discharge path so that the output can respond to changing amplitudes of the signal peaks, decreasing amplitudes of the signal peaks to be more precise. The buffer circuit connected ahead of the capacitor prevents any discharge of the capacitor due to loading effects of the following circuit. The circuit can be made to respond to the negative peaks by reversing the polarity of the diode. Rest of the circuit is the same.

The parallel R-C circuit time constant is typically 100 times the time period corresponding to the minimum frequency of operation. The R-C time constant also controls the response time. The response time is nothing, but the time needed to respond to a decreasing amplitude. Surely, a large time constant would make the response more sluggish. An attempt to reduce the time constant to improve the response time increases the output ripple. The chosen time constant is a compromise of the two conflicting requirements. Slew rate is the primary specification that needs to be looked into while choosing the right opamp for the clipper portion. The desired slew rate is such that the slew rate limited frequency, which is a function of peak-to-peak output swing and the slew rate, is at least equal to the highest frequency of operation. The peak-to-peak voltage swing at the output of the opamp is equal to $V_{pk} - (-V_{SAT}) = (V_{pk} + V_{SAT})$. Here V_{pk} is the maximum peak amplitude of the input signal and $-V_{SAT}$ is the maximum negative output voltage of the opamp.

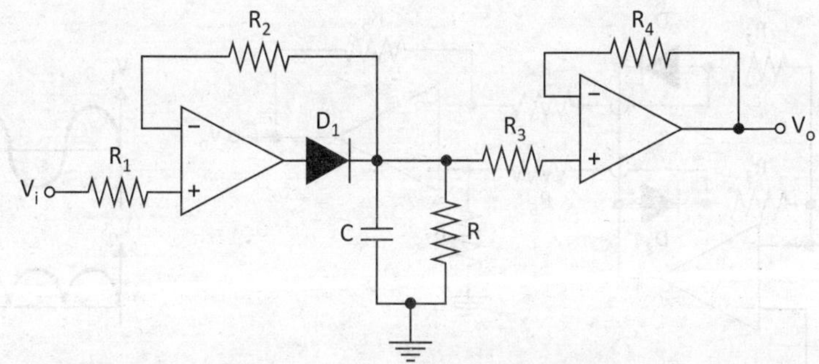

Fig. 10.36: Peak detector circuit

10.11 RECTIFIER CIRCUITS

Conventional rectifier circuits do not produce an ideal rectified waveform at the output due to forward-biased voltage drop across the diode, which is 0.7 V in the case of silicon diodes. This problem is overcome in opamp-based rectifier circuits. Figure 10.37 shows the generalized half-wave rectifier circuit built around an opamp. The circuit functions as follows. Owing to non-inverting input of the opamp being at ground potential, during positive half cycles, diode (D_1) is forward-biased and the diode (D_2) is reverse-biased. The positive half cycles appear as negative half cycles due to phase inversion. Similarly, during negative half cycles, diode (D_1) is reverse-biased and diode (D_2) is forward-biased with the result that negative half cycles appear as positive half cycles again due to phase inversion. Remember that the moment input increases by a few milli-volts either in positive or in negative direction, the output tends to go to negative or positive saturation, respectively. It is therefore not necessary for the input to exceed the diode drop to produce the output. However, maximum values of peak positive output and peak negative output are $(V_{SAT} - 0.7)$ and $(-V_{SAT} + 0.7)$, respectively.

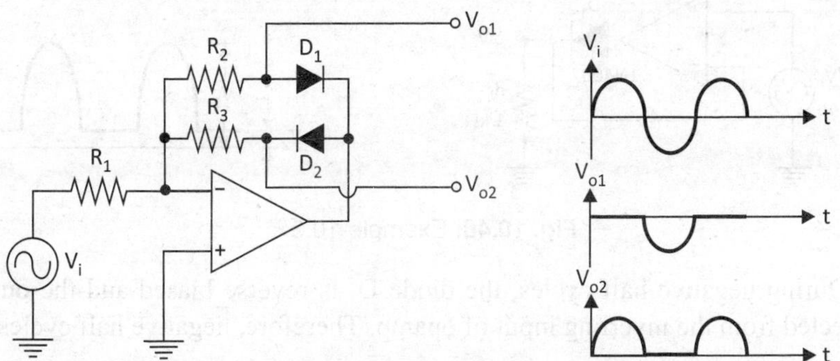

Fig. 10.37: Half-wave rectifier

The two half-wave rectified outputs can be summed up in another opamp stage to get a full-wave rectified output as shown in Figure-10.38.

Figure-10.39 shows an alternative circuit arrangement for building a full-wave rectifier. During positive half cycle of the input signal, the diode is reverse-biased and therefore the feedback resistor is disconnected from the output of the opamp. The positive half cycles appear as such at the output. During negative half cycles, the diode is forward-biased. The negative half cycles get inverted and again appear as positive half cycles. Thus, the output is a full-wave rectified signal.

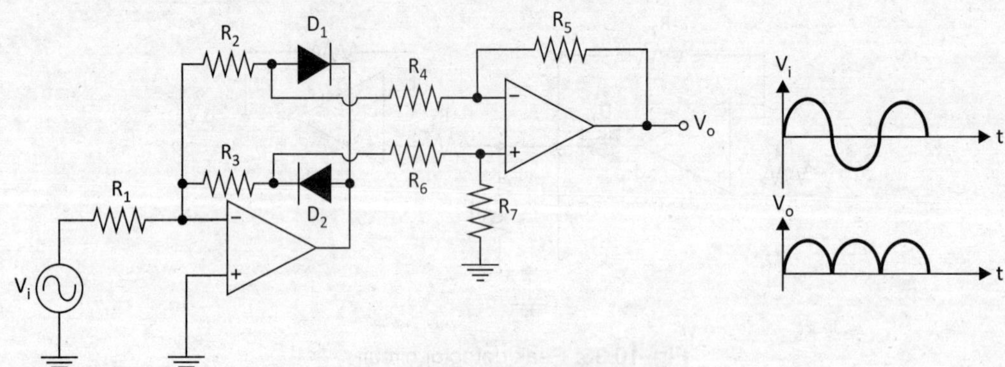

Fig. 10.38: Full-wave rectifier

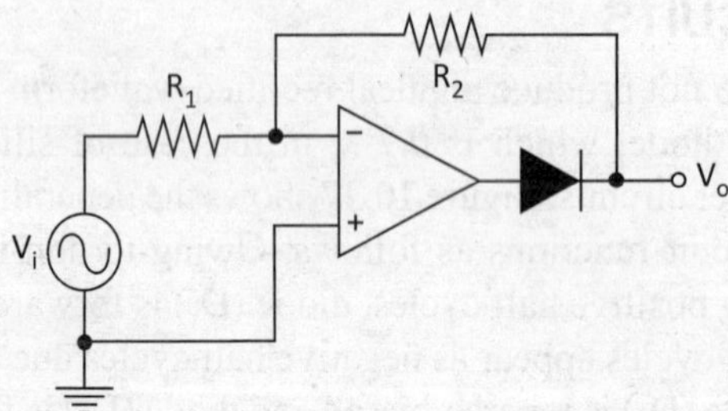

Fig. 10.39: Full-wave rectifier – alternative arrangement

Example-10.8: Figure-10.40 shows an opamp-based half-wave rectifier circuit and the associated rectified output waveform. What is the value of V_1 and V_2 given that opamp has an open-loop gain of 100 dB and diode D_1 has a cut-in voltage of 0.7 V?

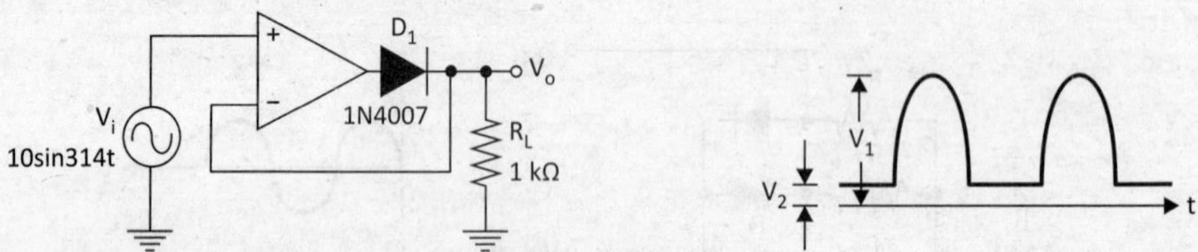

Fig. 10.40: Example-10.8

Solution: During negative half cycles, the diode D_1 is reverse biased and the output of opamp remains disconnected from the inverting input of opamp. Therefore, negative half cycles do not appear at the output.

During positive half cycles, diode D_1 will get forward biased only when the output voltage exceeds 0.7V. This happens when the amplitude of input sinusoidal signal exceeds $0.7/A_{OL}$ where A_{OL} is the open loop gain of the opamp. After that, the input signal appears at the output.

V_1 = positive peak amplitude of input signal = 10 V.

$V_2 = 0.7/A_{OL}$, where A_{OL} is the open-loop gain of opamp.

A_{OL} = 100 dB = 100,000. Therefore, V_2 = 0.7/100,000 = 7 mV

Example-10.9: Figure-10.41 shows a precision rectifier circuit configured around an ideal opamp. Assuming that diodes D_1 and D_2 are practical diodes, determine the transfer characteristics of the circuit.

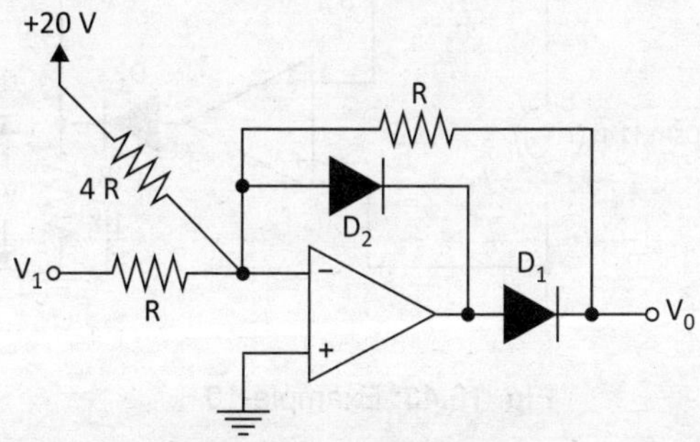

Figure-10.41: Example-9

Solution: DC input of +20V appears as -5V at the output. Also, input voltage v_1 appears as $-v_1$ at the output. Therefore, as long as input voltage v_1 remains equal to or greater than -5V; the net output voltage remains equal or greater than zero. This keeps both diodes as forward biased with the result that the output voltage remains zero.

The moment input voltage becomes more negative than -5V; the diodes become reverse biased and the net output voltage equals $(-v_1 - 5)$ volts. That is, when input voltage varies from -5V to -10V; the output voltage varies from 0 to +5V. Figure-10.42 shows the transfer characteristics. We can also find the solution by applying Kirchhoff's current law (KCL) at the inverting input terminal of opamp.

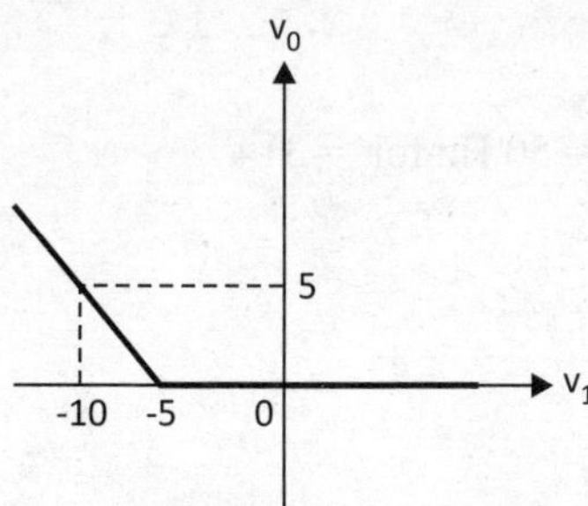

Fig. 10.42: Solution to Example-10.9

At $V_1 = -10$ V, applying KCL at the inverting terminal of the opamp, we get

$$\frac{(0-20)}{4R} + \frac{[0-(-10)]}{R} + \frac{(0-V_o)}{R} = 0$$

Therefore, $V_o = +5$V

At $V_1 = -5$V, applying KCL at the inverting terminal of the opamp, we get

$$\frac{(0-20)}{4R} + \frac{[0-(-5)]}{R} + \frac{(0-V_o)}{R} = 0$$

Therefore, $V_o = 0V$

For $V_1 > -5V$, both diodes are conducting. Therefore, $V_o = 0$ V

Example-10.10: Refer to the clamping circuit of Figure-10.43. What is the peak value of the clamped waveform at the output? Also, determine minimum value of capacitor C1 for the circuit to function properly. Assume the diode to be ideal.

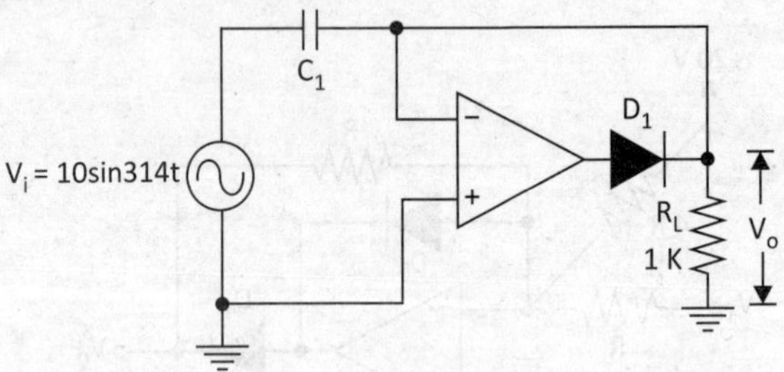

Fig. 10.43: Example-10

Solution: The circuit shown in Figure-10.43 is that of a positive clamper. During the first positive half cycle, diode D1 is reverse biased and therefore, the output remains at ground potential. During the first negative half cycle, diode D_1 gets forward-biased and capacitor C charges through the forward-biased diode to the peak of the negative half cycle voltage. The output side of capacitor goes from zero to +10V. During the positive cycle, the diode gets reverse-biased. Since, there is no rapid discharge path for the capacitor; the output equals the input voltage plus the voltage across the capacitor. That is, the peak value of output voltage goes to +20V at the time instant of peak value of second positive half cycle.

Therefore, peak value of clamped output waveform = +20V.

If T is the time period of input signal; the recommended value of $R_L C_1$ time constant is given by 10T.

That is, $C_1 = \dfrac{(10\times T)}{R_1}$

Now, frequency of input signal, f = 50 Hz for = 314

Therefore, T = 1/f = 20ms

$$C_1 = \frac{\left(10\times 20\times 10^{-3}\right)}{1000} = 200\infty F$$

10.12 AVERAGER CIRCUIT

An averager circuit produces an output that is equal to average of the amplitudes of the applied input signals. Figure-10.44 shows the generalized form of an averager circuit for n inputs. The circuit configuration is similar to that of an inverting-type summing amplifier. The expression for output voltage can be derived by considering one input voltage at a time and then applying superposition principle. Considering only V_1 and assuming all other inputs to be zero; we get,

$$V_o = -\frac{V_1}{n} \quad (10.23)$$

Considering only V_2 and assuming all other inputs to be zero, we get,

$$V_o = -\frac{V_2}{n} \quad (10.24)$$

We can write similar expressions for other inputs, when taken one at a time, as follows.

$$V_o = -\frac{V_3}{n} \tag{10.25}$$

$$V_o = -\frac{V_4}{n} \tag{10.26}$$

$$V_o = -\frac{V_n}{n} \tag{10.27}$$

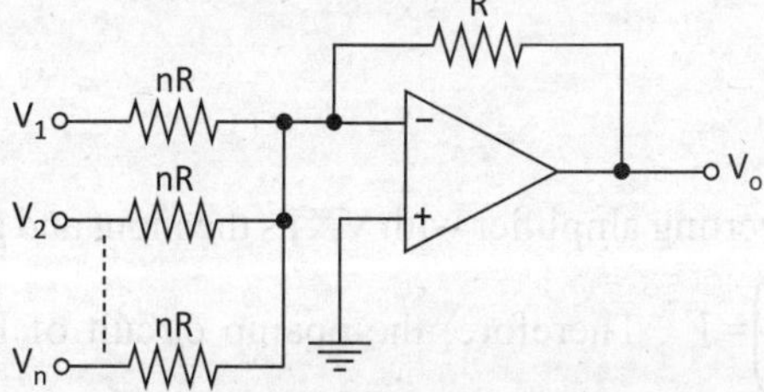

Fig. 10.44: Averager circuit

Considering all input voltages to be present simultaneously, the output voltage V_o is given by eqn. 10.28.

$$V_o = -\left(\frac{V_1 + V_2 + V_3 + \cdots + V_n}{n}\right) \tag{10.28}$$

A non-inverting averager may be built by connecting a unity gain inverting amplifier at the output of the circuit shown in Figure-10.44.

10.13 ABSOLUTE VALUE CIRCUIT

The absolute value circuit reproduces the input voltage at the output irrespective of its polarity. That is, both +V and -V at the input will produce +V at the output. Figure-10.45 shows one possible opamp configuration that produces at its output a voltage equal to the absolute value of the input voltage. The circuit shown is a dual half-wave rectifier circuit discussed earlier followed by a difference amplifier.

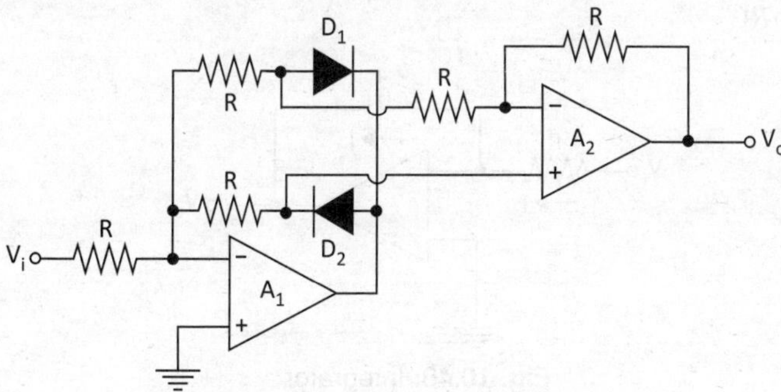

Fig. 10.45: Absolute value circuit

When the applied input is of positive polarity (say +V), diode D_1 is forward-biased and diode D_2 is reverse-biased. In this case, opamps A_1 and A_2 function as unity gain inverting amplifiers and the output is equal to +V.

When the applied input is of negative polarity (say –V), diode D_1 is reverse-biased and diode D_2 is forward-biased. In this case, voltage appearing at non-inverting terminal of opamp A_2 can be determined by applying Kirchhoff's current law (KCL) at the inverting terminal of the opamp A_1 as follows. Assume voltage at non-inverting input terminal of opamp A_2 to be V_X. Applying KCL at the inverting input of opamp A_1, we get,

$$-\frac{V}{R}+\frac{V_x}{R}+\frac{V_x}{2R}=0 \tag{10.29}$$

Or $$\frac{3V_x}{2R}=\frac{V}{R}$$

Or $$V_x=\frac{2V}{3}$$

A_2 here functions as a non-inverting amplifier with VX as the input and gain equal to (1 + R/2R) = 3/2.

Therefore, $V_o=\left(\frac{2V}{3}\right)\times\left(\frac{3}{2}\right)=V$. Therefore, the opamp circuit of Figure-10.45 functions as an absolute value circuit.

10.14 INTEGRATOR

An integrator circuit is the one that produces an output proportional to the integral of the input. Figure-10.46 shows the circuit diagram. Since non-inverting input terminal has been grounded, virtual earth appears at R-C junction. Thus, the voltage V_o effectively is the voltage across the capacitor C. Theexpression for output voltage V_o is derived as follows.

$$\frac{V_i}{R}=-C\frac{dV_o}{dt}$$

Or $$dV_o=-\left(\frac{V_i}{RC}\right)dt$$

Or $$V_o=-\frac{1}{RC}\int V_i dt=K\int V_i dt \tag{10.30}$$

Where, $K=-1/RC$

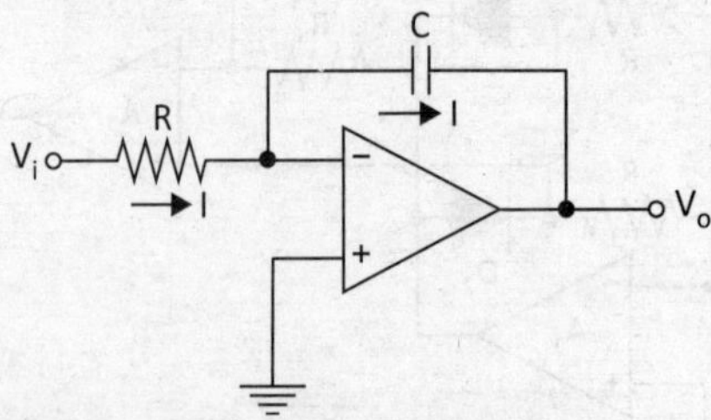

Fig. 10.46: Integrator

The basic integrator circuit suffers from DC instability problems. The circuit offers a very high gain to DC which means that even in the absence of any input, small input offset voltage might cause the output to go to positive or negative saturation. This problem can be overcome by connecting a relatively large value resistor across C. This resistor limits the DC gain to a lower value and it may be chosen to be 10 times the input resistor. Non-inverting integrator may be built by connecting a unity gain inverting amplifier at the output of inverting integrator circuit of Figure-10.46.

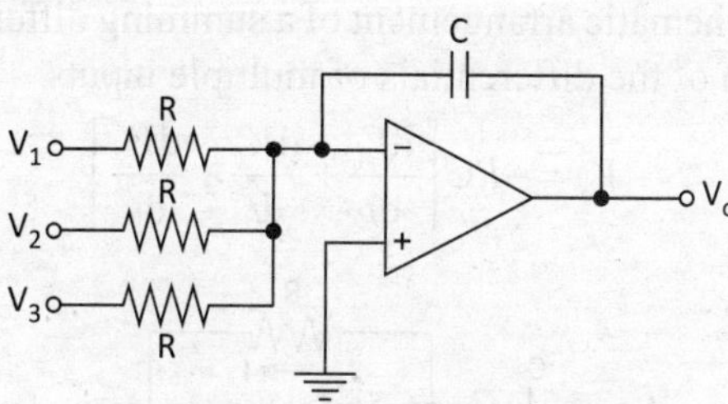

Fig. 10.47: Summing integrator

Figure-10.47 shows another variation of integrator circuit. It is a summing integrator that produces an output proportional to sum of integrals of multiple inputs. That is,

$$V_o = K\left(\int V_1 dt + \int V_2 dt + \int V_3 dt\right) \tag{10.31}$$

Where, $K = -1/RC$

Again, a non-inverting summing integrator may be built by connecting a unity gain inverting amplifier at the output of inverting integrator circuit of Figure-10.47.

10.15 DIFFERENTIATOR

A differentiator circuit is the one that produces an output proportional to the differential of the input. Figure-10.48 shows the circuit diagram. Since non-inverting input terminal has been grounded, virtual earth appears at R-C junction. Thus, the voltage V_o effectively is the voltage across resistor R.

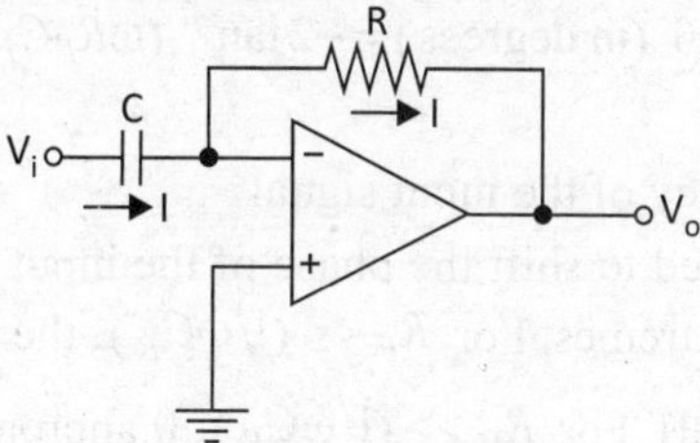

Fig. 10.48: Differentiator

The expression for output voltage V_o is derived as follows.

$$C\frac{dV_i}{dt} = -\frac{V_o}{R}$$

$$V_o = -RC\frac{dV_i}{dt} = K\frac{dV_i}{dt} \tag{10.32}$$

Where, $K = -RC$

Basic differentiator circuit tends to go into oscillations at relatively higher frequencies. The problem can be overcome by connecting a resistor in series with the input capacitor. The resistor limits the gain at higher frequencies. The value of this resistor may be chosen to be in the range of one-tenth to one-hundredth of the feedback resistor. Non-inverting differentiator circuit may be built by connecting a unity gain inverting amplifier at the output of inverting differentiator circuit of Figure-10.48.

Figure-10.49 shows the schematic arrangement of a summing differentiator. The circuit produces an output proportional to the sum of the differentials of multiple inputs.

$$V_o = -RC\left[\frac{dV_1}{dt} + \frac{dV_2}{dt} + \frac{dV_3}{dt}\right] \tag{10.33}$$

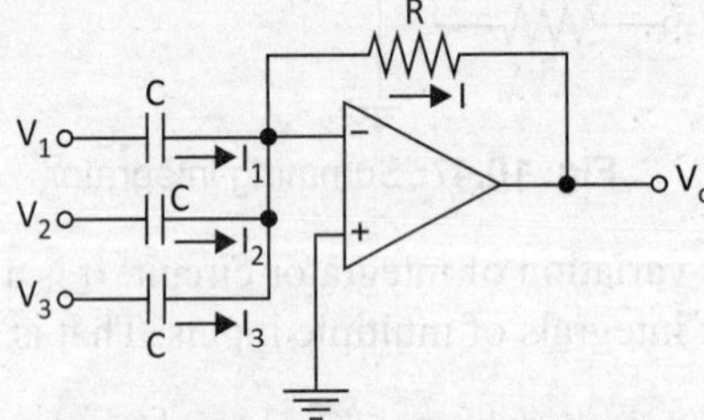

Fig. 10.49: Summing differentiator

10.16 PHASE SHIFTERS

In this section, we shall describe phase shifter circuits, both lagging and leading type, configured around one or more opamps.

10.16.1 Lag-Type Phase Shifter

Figure-10.50 shows the circuit diagram of single opamp-based lagging-type phase shifter circuit. The output lags the input by an angle (θ) given by eqn. 10.34.

$$\theta \text{ (in degrees)} = -2\tan^{-1}(\omega R_P C_P) \tag{10.34}$$

Where,

$\omega = 2\pi f$, f being the frequency of the input signal

This simple circuit can be used to shift the phase of the input signal over a wide range by varying R_p with 0° and –180° being the extremes. For $R_P << (1/\omega C_P)$, the phase shift is near zero. (It will be 0° when $R_p = 0$ which is not practical). For $R_P >> (1/\omega C_P)$, θ approaches –180° (θ = –180° only for R_p = infinity which is again not feasible.) For $R_P = (1/\omega C_P)$, $\theta = -90°$. Two such sections can be used in cascade to vary the phase shift over full 360°. Figure-10.51 shows the circuit diagram.

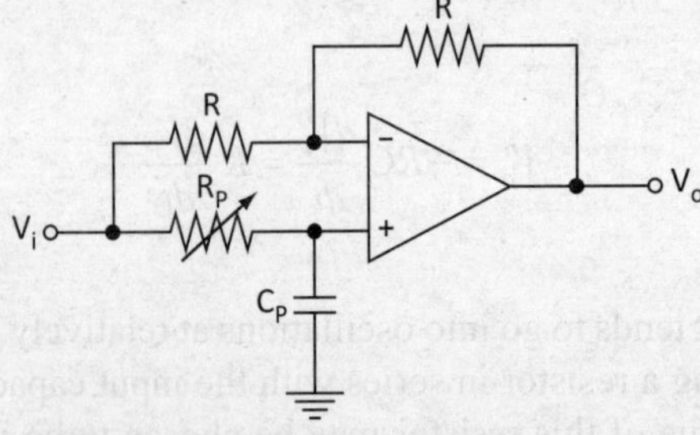

Fig. 10.50: Lagging-type phase shifter

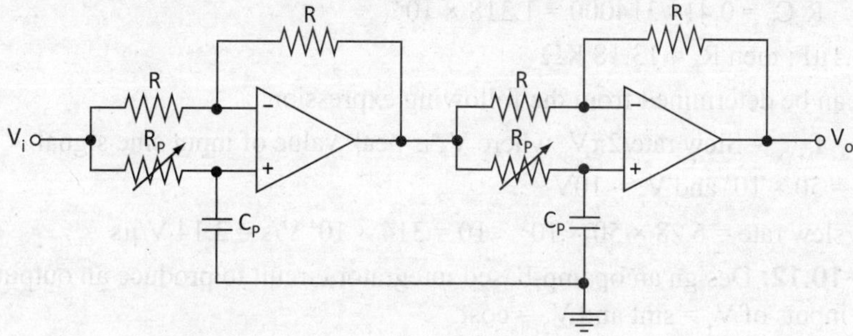

Fig. 10.51: Two-stage lagging-type phase shifter

10.16.2 Lead-Type Phase Shifter

Figure-10.52 shows the circuit diagram of lead-type phase shifter. The circuit shown here is just the redrawn version of lagging-type phase shifter of Figure-10.50 with positions of R_p and C_p interchanged. The phase difference (è) is given by eqn. 10.35.

$$\theta \text{ (in degrees)} = 2\tan^{-1}(\omega R_P C_P) \tag{10.35}$$

For this circuit, when $R_p = (1/\omega C_p)$, $\theta = 90°$, when $R_p >> (1/\omega C_p)$, $\theta = 180°$, and when $R_p << (1/\omega C_p)$, $\theta = 0°$.

Cascade arrangement of two lead-type filter stages can be used for varying phase shift over full 360°.

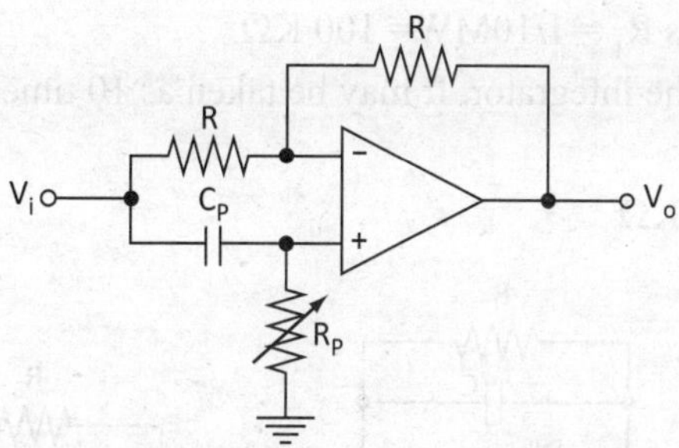

Fig. 10.52: Lead-type phase shifter

Example-10.11: Refer to the lag-type phase shifter of Figure-10.50. Determine the values of resistor R_p and capacitor C_p if a sine wave signal applied at the input has to undergo a phase shift of -45°. Also, if the peak value of the applied sine wave signal is 10V and the highest input signal frequency is 50 kHz; what should be the slew rate of the opamp?

Solution: Phase shift is given by:

$$\theta \text{ (in degrees)} = -2\tan^{-1}(\omega R_P C_P)$$

Or $$\tan^{-1}(\omega R_P C_P) = \frac{\theta}{2} = 22.5°$$

Or $$(\omega R_P C_P) = \tan 22.5° = 0.414$$

Now, $\omega = 2\pi f = 6.28 \times 50 \times 10^3 = 314000$

Therefore, $R_PC_P = 0.414/314000 = 1.318 \times 10^{-6}$

Let $C_P = 0.1\mu F$; then $R_P = 13.18\ K\Omega$

Slew rate can be determined from the following expression.

f_{MAX} = Slew rate/$2\pi V_P$ where V_P is peak value of input sine signal

Now, $f_{MAX} = 50 \times 10^3$ and $V_P = 10V$

Therefore, slew rate = $6.28 \times 50 \times 10^3 \times 10 = 314 \times 10^4$ V/s = 3.14 V/µs

Example-10.12: Design an opamp-based integrator circuit to produce an output V_o = (sint - cost) from available inputs of V_1 = sint and V_2 = cost.

Solution: Figure-10.53 shows the circuit. The first opamp stage is the inverting summing integrator with V_1 and V_2 as its two inputs. Product R_1C here equals 1.0 second. The output of this stage is given by:

$$-\left(\int V_1 + \int V_2\right)$$

The second stage is a unity gain inverting amplifier.

Therefore, $V_o = \left(\int V_1 + \int V_2\right)$

Now, V_1 = sint and V_2 = cost

This gives $V_o = \left(\int \sin t dt + \int \cos t dt\right) = -\cos t + \sin t = \sin t - \cos t$

Values of R_1 and C can be computed from:

$R_1C = 1$

Let C = 10µF, which gives R_1 = 1/10MW= 100 KΩ

R_2 limits the DC gain of the integrator. It may be taken as 10 times R_1.

Therefore, $R_2 = 1M\Omega$

R_3 may be taken to be 10 KΩ

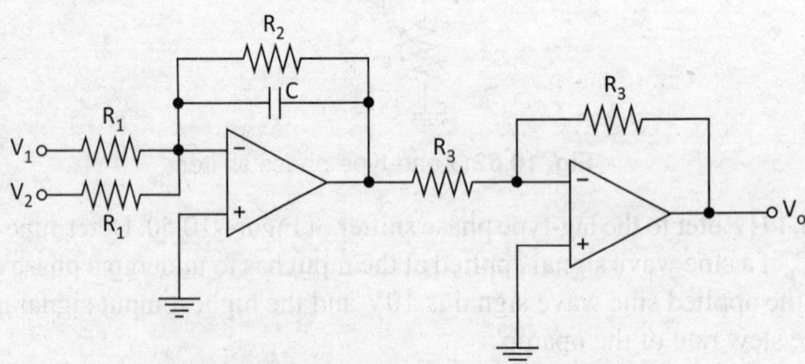

Fig. 10.53: Solution to Example-10.12

Example-10.13: Design an opamp based differentiator circuit to produce the same outputas in Example-10.11 from the same available inputs.

Solution: Figure-10.54 shows the circuit. The opamp stage is the inverting summing differentiator with V_1 and V_2 as its two inputs. Product R_1C here equals 1.0 second. The output of this stage is given by:

$$-\left[\frac{d}{dt}(V_1) + \frac{d}{dt}(V_2)\right]$$

Therefore, $V_o = -\left[\frac{d}{dt}(V_1) + \frac{d}{dt}(V_2)\right]$

Now, V_1 = sint and V_2 = cost

This gives $V_o = -\left[\frac{d}{dt}(\sin t) + \frac{d}{dt}(\cos t)\right] = -\cos t + \sin t = \sin t - \cos t$

Values of R_1 and C can be computed from:

$R_1C = 1$

Let C = 10μF, which gives R_1 = 1/10 MW = 100 KW

R_2 here may be taken as 0.01 times R_1

Therefore, R_2 = 1KW

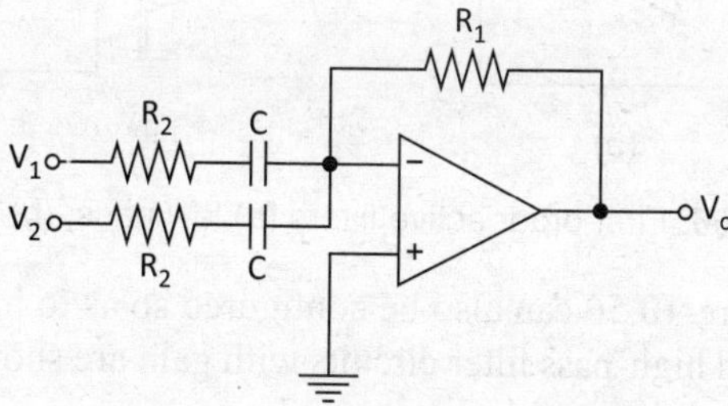

Fig. 10.54: Solution to Example-10.13

Example-10.14: Identify the opamp circuit of Figure-10.55. Also, determine the output voltage.

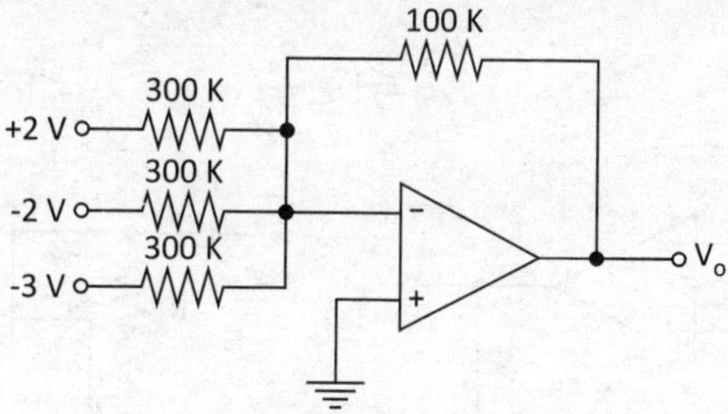

Fig. 10.55: Example-10.14

Solution: The resistance value of each of the three input resistors is three times the resistance of feedback resistor. This makes it an inverting averager circuit.

Therefore, V_o = -(2 - 2 - 3)/3 = 1V

10.17 ACTIVE FILTERS

Active filters configured around opamps are discussed in this section. Types of filters covered include first and second order low-pass, high-pass, band-pass and band-reject active filters. Order of an active filter is determined by number of *R-C* sections (or poles) used in the filter, which for a few exceptions equals the number of capacitors.

10.17.1 First-Order Filters

The simplest low-pass and high-pass active filters are constructed by connecting lag and lead type of *R-C* sections, respectively, to the non-inverting input of the opamp wired as a voltage follower. Figures-10.56 (a) and (b) respectively show such first-order low-pass and high-pass filter circuits. The cut-off frequency in both cases is given by eqn.10.36. The gain rolls off at a rate of 6 dB per octave or 20 dB per decade beyond the cut-off point. The output is 0.707 times the input when the signal frequency is such as to make capacitive reactance equal to the resistance value. This is called the cut-off frequency. Roll-off rate beyond the cut-off point in the case of *n*-order filter is 6*n* dB per octave or 20*n* dB per decade. Operation of the high-pass circuit can also be explained on similar lines.

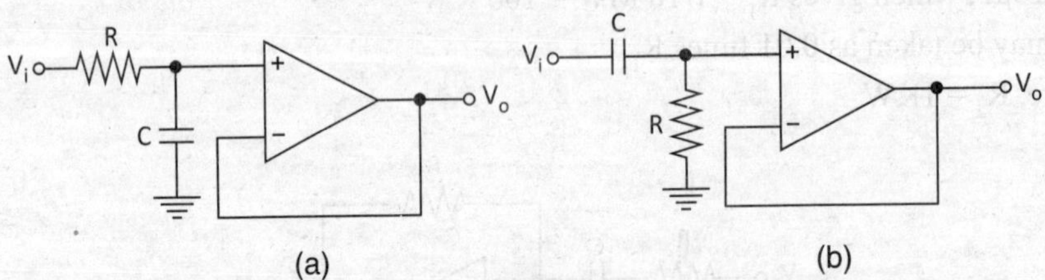

Fig. 10.56: First-order active filters (a) low pass; (b) high pass

The filters shown in Figure-10.56 can also be configured so as to have the desired amplification of the input signal. Low-pass and high-pass filter circuits with gain are shown in Figures-10.57 (a) and (b), respectively. The voltage gain A_v is given by eqn. 10.37.

$$f_c = \frac{1}{2\pi RC} \tag{10.36}$$

$$A_v = 1 + \frac{R_3}{R_2} \tag{10.37}$$

Fig. 10.57: First-order filters with gain: (a) low pass; (b) high pass

Single-order filters shown in Figures-10.56 and 10.57 employ non-inverting type of amplifier configuration. These filters could also be implemented using inverting amplifier configuration. Relevant circuits are shown in Figures-10.58. Cut-off frequency and mid-band gain values in the case of low-pass filter are, respectively, given by eqns. 10.38 and 10.39.

$$f_c = \frac{1}{2\pi R_2 C_1} \tag{10.38}$$

$$A_v = -\frac{R_2}{R_1} \tag{10.39}$$

The same in the case of high-pass filter are given by eqns.10.40 and 10.41.

$$f_c = \frac{1}{2\pi R_1 C_1} \tag{10.40}$$

$$A_v = -\frac{R_2}{R_1} \tag{10.41}$$

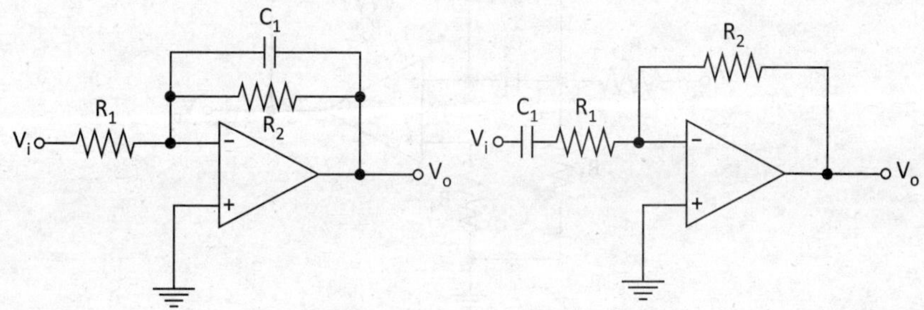

Fig. 10.58: First-order filters using inverting configuration: (a) low pass; (b) high pass

10.17.2 Second-Order Filters

Figure-10.59 shows the generalized form of a second-order Butterworth active filter. Butterworth filter, also called *maximally flat filter*, offers a relatively flat pass and stop band response but has the disadvantage of relatively sluggish roll-off. Other commonly used filters are the Chebychev and Cauer filters. Chebychev filters offer much faster roll-off but their pass band has ripple. Cauer filters have rippled pass and stop bands. There are other types of filters such as Bessel filters with their unique properties. Discussion on all these types is beyond the scope of the present text.

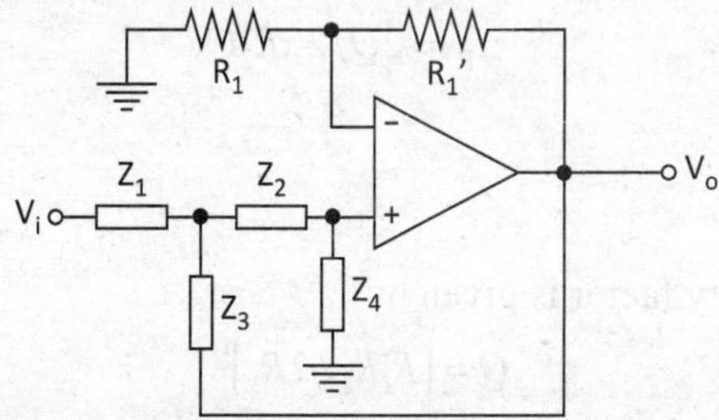

Fig. 10.59: Generalized form of second-order Butterworth filter

In the case of generalized form of second-order Butterworth filter, shown in Figure-10.60, we have the following:

1. If $Z_1 = Z_2 = R$ and $Z_3 = Z_4 = C$, we get a second-order low-pass filter.
2. If $Z_1 = Z_2 = C$ and $Z_3 = Z_4 = R$, we get a second-order high-pass filter.

The cut-off frequency is given by eqn. 10.42.

$$f_C = \frac{1}{2\pi RC} \tag{10.42}$$

The value of pass band gain (A_F) can be computed from eqn. 10.43.

$$A_F = 1 + \frac{R_1'}{R_1} \tag{10.43}$$

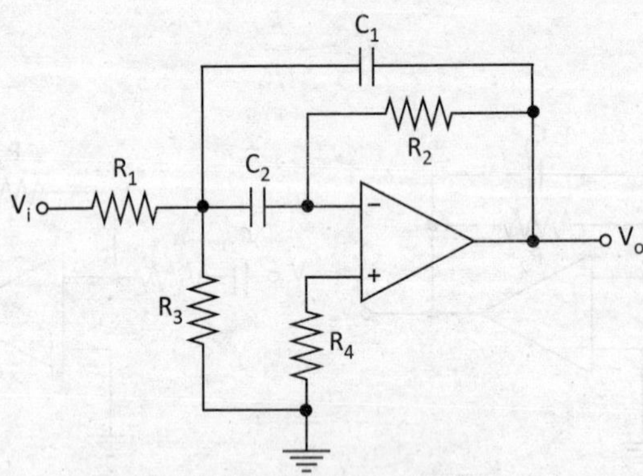

Fig. 10.60: Narrow band-pass filter

Band-pass filters can be formed by cascading the high-pass and the low-pass filter sections. These filters are simple to design and offer large bandwidth. To construct a narrow band-pass filter, one needs to employ multiple feedback as shown in Figure-10.60. At very low frequencies, C_1 and C_2 offer very high reactance. As a result, the input signal is prevented from reaching the output. At very high frequencies, the output is shorted to the inverting input, which converts the circuit to an inverting amplifier with zero gain. Again, there is no output. Thus, at both very low and very high frequencies, the output is zero. At some intermediate band of frequencies, the gain provided by the circuit offsets the loss due to the potential divider R_1 - R_3. Mathematical expressions governing the design of the filter circuit are given in eqns.10.44, 10.45 and 10.46.

Resonant frequency,
$$f_R = 2Q/2\pi R_2 C \tag{10.44}$$

where

Q is the quality factor.

For $C_1 = C_2 = C$, the quality factor is given by

$$Q = [R_1 R_2 / 2R_3]^{1/2} \tag{10.45}$$

The voltage gain is

$$A_v = Q/2\pi R_1 f_R C \tag{10.46}$$

Figure-10.61 shows the circuit diagram of second-order band reject filter. It uses a twin-T network that is connected in series with the non-inverting input of the opamp. A twin-T network offers very high reactance at the resonance frequency and very low reactance at frequencies off-resonance. This phenomenon explains the behaviour of the circuit. Another way of explaining the behaviour of the circuit is as follows. Very low frequency signals find their way to the output via the low-pass filter formed by R_1–

R_2–C_3. Very high frequency signals reach the output through the high-pass filter constituted by C_1–C_2–R_3. In an intermediate band of frequencies, both filters pass the signal to some extent, but the negative phase shift introduced by low-pass filter is cancelled out by an identical positive phase shift by high-pass filter with the result that at any instant, the net signal reaching the non-inverting input and hence the output is zero. Component values of the twin-T network are chosen according to the following eqns.10.47 to 10.50.

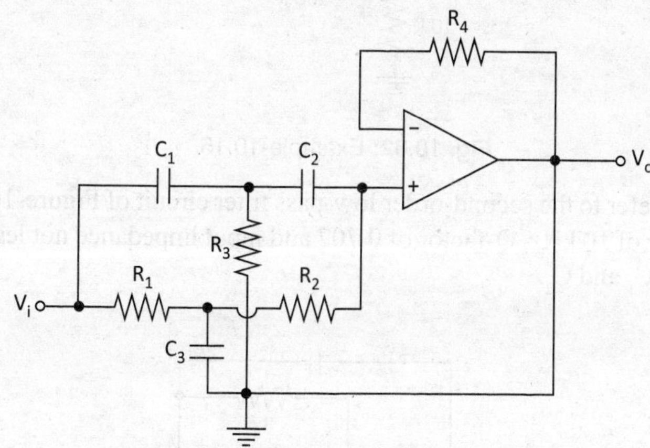

Fig. 10.61: Second-order band reject filter

$$R_1 = R_2 = R, R_3 = R/2 \tag{10.47}$$

$$C_1 = C_2 = C, C_3 = 2C \tag{10.48}$$

$$0 \le R_4 \le (R_1 + R_2) \tag{10.49}$$

$$f_R = \frac{1}{2\pi RC} \tag{10.50}$$

Example-10.15: Refer to the low pass active filter circuit of Figure-10.62. Determine cut-off frequency, mid band gain and gain at 100 kHz.

Solution: Cut-off frequency $= 1/\left(2\pi \times 10 \times 10^3 \times 1000 \times 10^{-12}\right) = 15.92 kHz$

Mid band gain = 1 + 100/10 = 11

Now, generalized expression for gain can be written as follows.

$$Gain = \frac{V_o}{V_i} = 11 \times \left[\frac{1}{(1 + j\omega RC)}\right]$$ where R = 10kW and C = 1000pF

$$\text{Magnitude of gain} = \frac{11}{\sqrt{\left(1+\omega^2 R^2 C^2\right)}}$$

For f = 100 kHz, w = 2pf = 6.28 × 100 × 10^3= 6.28 × 10^5

$$\text{Magnitude of gain} = \frac{11}{\sqrt{\left(1+\left(6.28\times10^5\right)^2 \times \left(10\times10^3\right)^2 \times \left(10^{-9}\right)^2\right)}} = 1.73 = 4.76 dB$$

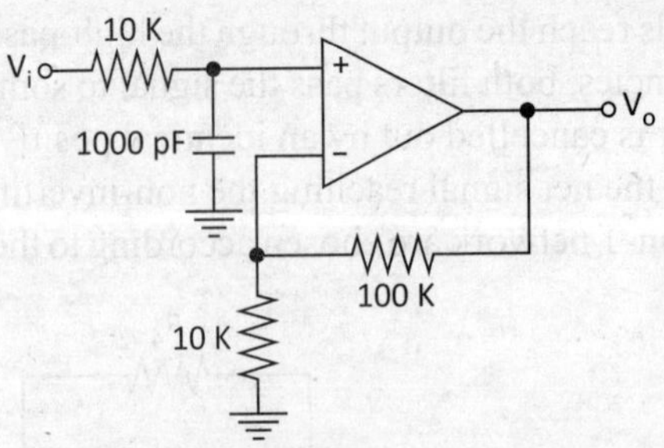

Fig. 10.62: Example-10.15

Example-10.16: Refer to the second-order low-pass filter circuit of Figure-10.63. If the filter were to have cut-off frequency of 10 kHz, Q-factor of 0.707 and input impedance not less than 10 k; calculate the values of R_1, R_2, R_3, C_1 and C_2.

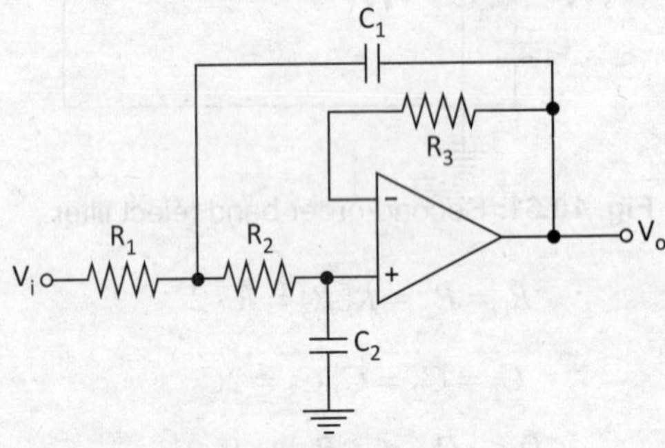

Fig. 10.63: Example-10.16

Solution:

The quality factor, Q is given by: $Q = (1/2)\times\sqrt{C_1/C_2}$

For Q = 0.707, $C_1 = 2C_2$

$R_1 = R_2 = R$ and $R_3 = R_1 + R_2$

Cut-off frequency is given by:

$f_c = 1/2\pi R\sqrt{C_1C_2}$

For a minimum input impedance of 10 kΩ, $R_1 = 10\text{ k}\Omega = R_2$ and $R_3 = 20\text{ k}\Omega$

Substituting the values of R and f_C, we get,

$$10\times10^3 = 1/\left(2\pi\times10\times10^3\sqrt{C_1C_2}\right)$$

$$\text{Or } C_1C_2 = 1/\left(2\pi\times10\times10^3\times10\times10^3\right)^2$$

$$\text{Or } C_2^{\,2} = 1/2\times\left(2\pi\times10\times10^3\times10\times10^3\right)^2$$

$$C_2 = 1.126nF = 0.0011\mu F$$

And $C_1 = 2C_2 = 0.0022\ \mu\text{F}$

Example-10.17: Design a twin-T network based band reject filter around an opamp. The desired notch frequency is 1 MHz.

Solution: Figure-10.64 shows the circuit diagram of a twin-T network based notch filter using an opamp. For this circuit to behave as a notch filter, the design equations are as follows.

1. $R_1 = R_2 = R$ and $R_3 = R/2$
2. $C_1 = C_2 = C$ and $C_3 = 2C$
3. Notch frequency, $f_o = \dfrac{1}{2\pi RC}$

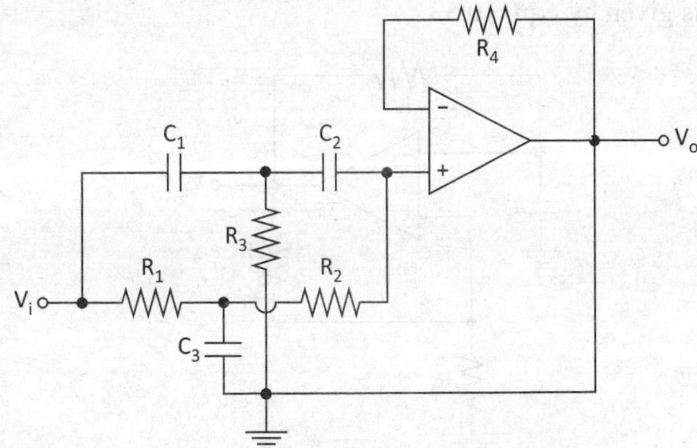

Fig. 10.64: Solution to Examle-10.17

Let $C_1 = 10\text{pF} = C_2$; then, $C_3 = 20\text{pF}$

$$f_o = \frac{1}{2\pi RC} = 10^6$$

Or
$$R = \frac{1}{2\pi \times 10^6 \times 10 \times 10^{-12}} = 15.9k\Omega$$

Therefore, $R_1 = R_2 = 15.9$ kW and $R_3 = 7.95$ kΩ

10.18 RELAXATION OSCILLATOR

A *relaxation oscillator* is a circuit that produces a repetitive non-sinusoidal output having a time period that depends on the charge and discharge of a capacitor. The capacitor voltage may change exponentially when charged or discharged through a resistor from a constant voltage, or linearly when charged or discharged through a constant current source. Opamps adapt very well to construction of relaxation oscillator circuits that produce a rectangular output. Figure-10.65 shows the basic opamp-based relaxation oscillator circuit. Operation of relaxation oscillator of Figure-10.65 can be explained as follows. Let us assume that the output is initially in positive saturation. As a result, voltage at non-inverting input of opamp is given by eqn. 10.51.

$$V_o = +V_{SAT} \times \left(\frac{R_1}{R_1 + R_2} \right) \tag{10.51}$$

Since capacitor C is initially in fully discharged state, voltage at inverting input is zero, which forces the output in positive saturation. Capacitor C starts charging towards $+V_{SAT}$ through R. The moment the capacitor voltage exceeds the voltage appearing at the non-inverting input, the output switches to -V_{SAT}. The voltage appearing at non-inverting input is now given by eqn. 10.52.

$$V_o = -V_{SAT} \times \left(\frac{R_1}{R_1 + R_2} \right) \tag{10.52}$$

The capacitor starts discharging and after reaching zero, it begins to charge towards -V_{SAT}. Again, as soon as it becomes more negative than the negative threshold appearing at non-inverting input of the opamp, the output switches back to +V_{SAT}. The cycle repeats thereafter. The output is a rectangular wave. The expression for time period of output waveform can be derived from the exponential charging and discharging process and is given by eqn. 10.53.

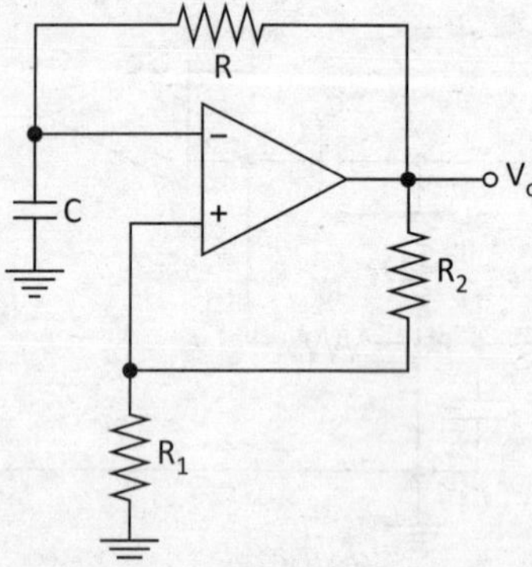

Fig. 10.65: Relaxation oscillator

$$T = 2RC \ln\left(\frac{1+B}{1-B} \right) \tag{10.53}$$

Where, $B = \left(\frac{R_1}{R_1 + R_2} \right)$

Figure-10.66 shows the relevant waveforms. The time period of output may be conveniently varied by varying the resistance value of R.

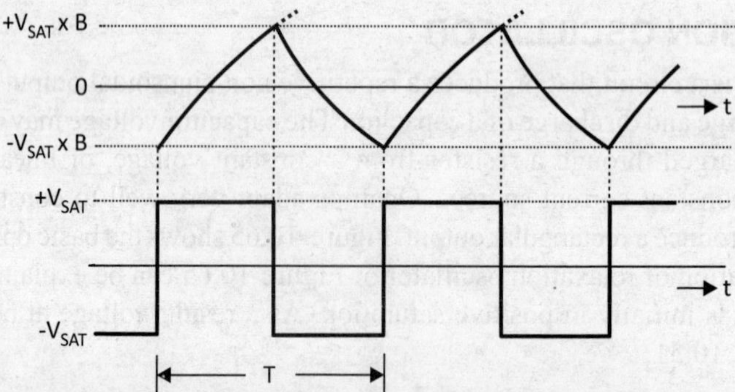

Fig. 10.66: Relevant waveforms of relaxation oscillator

Relaxation oscillator forms the basis of waveform-generation circuits configured around opamps. If the output of relaxation oscillator circuit is cascaded with an opamp based integrator circuit; the output of integrator circuit would be a triangular waveform. Figure-10.67 shows the circuit.

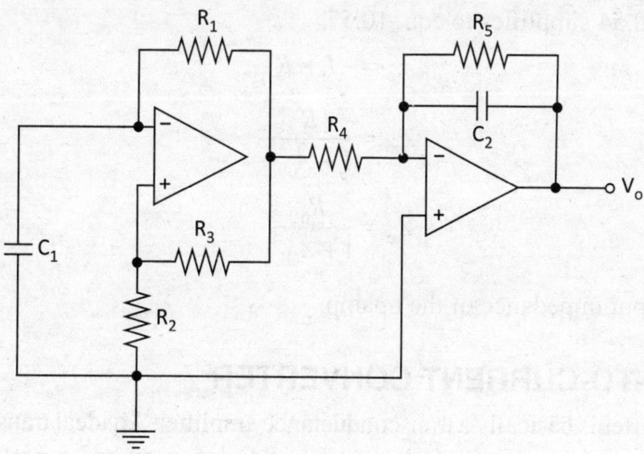

Fig. 10.67: Triangular waveform generator

10.19 CURRENT-TO-VOLTAGE CONVERTER

Current-to-voltage converter is basically a transimpedance amplifier. An ideal transimpedance amplifier with its zero input and output impedances makes a perfect current-to-voltage converter. Figure-10.68 shows an opamp circuit wired as transimpedance amplifier. The circuit is characterized by voltage shunt feedback, which implies that the circuit offers near zero input and output impedances. The circuit very closely approaches a perfect current-to-voltage converter. The expressions for output voltage, closed-loop input and output impedances are given as eqns. 10.54, 10.57, 10.58 and 10.59.

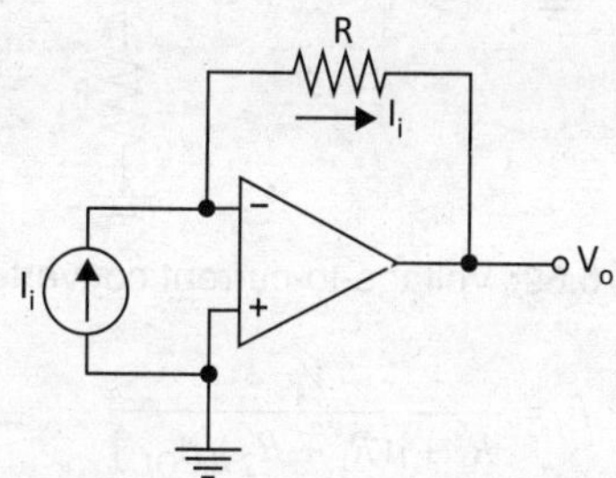

Fig. 10.68: Current-to-voltage converter

$$V_o = -I_i \times R \times \left(\frac{A_{OL}}{1 + A_{OL}}\right) \tag{10.54}$$

Eqn. 10.54 represents expression for output voltage in case of a practical opamp. Eqn. 10.54 can be derived by determining the magnitude of actual current that would flow through R. It is given by eqn. 10.55.

$$\text{Current flowing through } R = \frac{I_i \times R}{[R + R/A_{OL}]} \tag{10.55}$$

Eqn. 10.55 simplifies to eqn. 10.56.

$$\text{Current flowing through } R = I_i \times \left[\frac{A_{OL}}{1 + A_{OL}}\right] \tag{10.56}$$

For A_{OL}>> 1, eqn. 10.54 simplifies to eqn. 10.57.

$$V_o = -I_i \times R \tag{10.57}$$

$$Z_{in} = \frac{R}{1 + A_{OL}} \tag{10.58}$$

$$Z_o = \frac{R_o}{1 + A_{OL}} \tag{10.59}$$

Where, R_o is the output impedance of the opamp.

10.20 VOLTAGE-TO-CURRENT CONVERTER

Voltage-to-current converter is basically a transconductance amplifier. An ideal transconductance amplifier with its infinite input impedance and infinite output impedance makes a perfect voltage-to-current converter. An opamp based transconductance amplifier very closely approaches a perfect voltage-to-current converter. Figure-10.69 shows the basic circuit arrangement. The circuit is characterized by current-series feedback. Expressions for output voltage, closed-loop input and output impedances are given in eqns. 10.60 to 10.63.

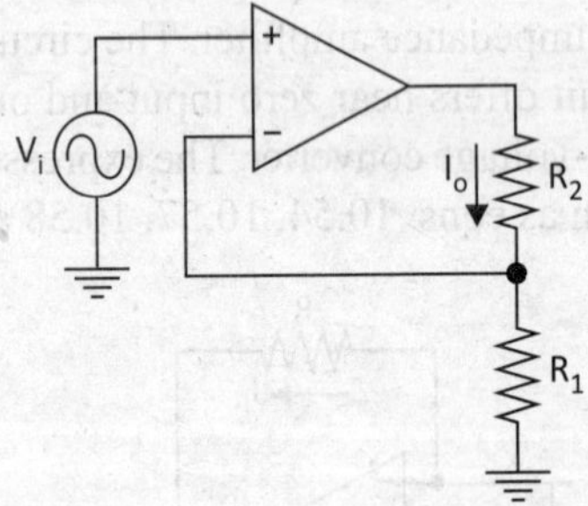

Fig. 10.69: Voltage-to-current converter

$$I_o = \frac{V_i}{R_1 + [(R_1 + R_2)/A_{OL}]} \tag{10.60}$$

Eqn. 10.60 can be derived by applying KVL across input loop consisting of input voltage, differential input voltage across opamp inputs and voltage across R_1. The three voltages respectively are V_i, $I_o(R_1 + R_2)/A_{OL}$ and I_oR_1.

For A_{OL}>> 1, eqn. 10.60 simplifies to the eqn. 10.61.

$$I_o = \frac{V_i}{R_1} \tag{10.61}$$

Applying principle of voltage shunt feedback, closed-loop input impedance is given by eqn. 10.62.

$$Z_{in} = R_i \times \left(1 + A_{OL} \times \frac{R_1}{R_1 + R_2}\right) \tag{10.62}$$

Where, R_i is the input impedance of the opamp.

Applying principle of voltage shunt feedback, closed-loop output impedance is given by eqn. 10.63.

$$Z_o = R_1 \times \left(1 + A_{OL} \times \frac{R_1}{R_1 + R_2}\right) \tag{10.63}$$

Voltage-to-current converter of Figure-10.69 operates with a floating load, which is not always convenient. Monolithic opamps specially designed as transconductance amplifiers to feed single-ended load resistances are commercially available.

10.21 INSTRUMENTATION AMPLIFIER

Instrumentation amplifier is nothing but a differential amplifier that has been optimized to nearly approach the DC performance of an ideal opamp. An instrumentation amplifier is characterized by a high differential gain, high common mode rejection ratio (CMRR), high input impedance and low input offsets and low temperature drifts. Figure-10.70 shows the classical internal schematic arrangement of an instrumentation amplifier. The two input opamps A_1 and A_2 are wired as non-inverting amplifiers,called pre-amplifiers, to provide gain and very high input impedance and the output opamp A_3 is wired as difference amplifier with unity gain. The resistors used in the output stage are ultra-high precision, low temperature drift resistors.

The instrumentation amplifier of Figure-10.70 is analyzed here for its common-mode and differential-input performance. Let us assume that the common-mode input is V_{IN}(CM). Owing to same positive voltage applied to both the non-inverting inputs, voltages appearing at the output of opamps A_1 and A_2 and also at R_1–R_2 and R_3–R_4 junctions are equal with the result that point A is floating. This further implies that A_1 and A_2 act like voltage followers. In other words, common-mode gain A_{CM} of the preamplifier stage is unity. Tolerance specification of R_1 and R_2 has no effect on the common-mode gain of the pre-amplifier stage.

On the other hand, when a differential signal is applied to the input, signals appearing at R_1–R_2 and R_3–R_4 junctions are equal and opposite creating a virtual ground at point A. The differential gain of this stage is therefore $(1 + R_2/R_1)$.

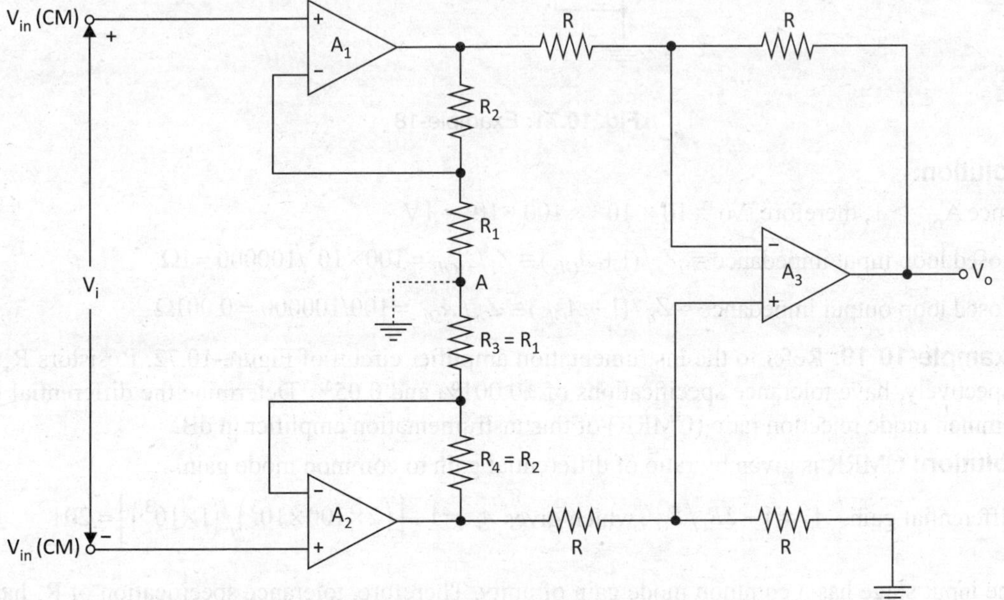

Fig. 10.70: Instrumentation amplifier

The difference amplifier stage has a common-mode gain equal to ±2DR/R, where DR represents how closely the resistors are matched. Differential gain of this stage is unity. If we combine the results, we can say that the overall common-mode gain is equal to the common-mode gain of the difference amplifier stage and overall differential is equal to the differential gain of the pre-amplifier stage. That is, the differential gain is given by eqn. 10.64.

$$A_V = 1 + \frac{R_2}{R_1} \tag{10.64}$$

Since point A is a virtual ground and not a mechanical ground, we can use a single resistor instead of two separate resistors. If this single resistor were R_G, then $R_1 = R_3 = R_G/2$.

Therefore,

$$A_V = 1 + \frac{2R_2}{R_G} \tag{10.65}$$

The overall common-mode gain is given by eqn. 10.66.

$$A_{CM} = \pm 2\Delta R/R \tag{10.66}$$

In the integrated circuit instrumentation opamps, all the components except R_G are integrated on the chip. R_G is connected externally and is used to control the voltage gain.

Example-10.18: For current-to-voltage converter circuit of Figure-10.71, determine output voltage, closed loop input impedance and output impedances, given that the opamp has open-loop trans-impedance gain of 100,000, input impedance of 100 kW and output impedance of 100 W.

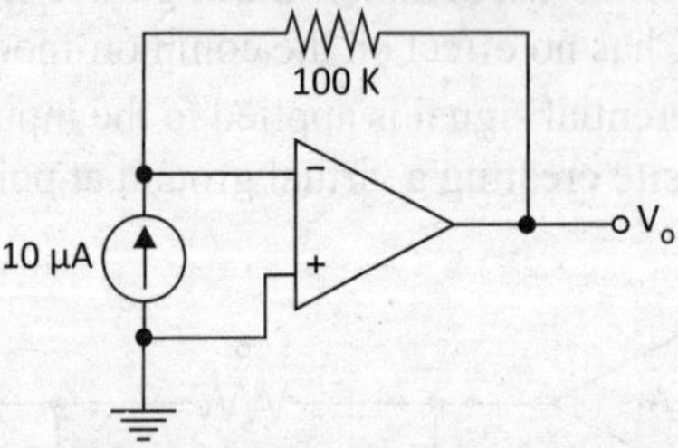

Fig. 10.71: Example-18

Solution:

Since $A_{OL} >> 1$, therefore, $Vo = 10 \times 10^{-6} \times 100 \times 10^3 = 1V$

Closed loop input impedance $= Z_i/(1 + A_{OL}) \cong Z_i/A_{OL} = 100 \times 10^3/100000 = 1\Omega$

Closed loop output impedance $= Z_o/(1 + A_{OL}) \cong Z_o/A_{OL} = 100/100000 = 0.001\Omega$

Example-10.19: Refer to the instrumentation amplifier circuit of Figure-10.72. Resistors R_1 and R_2, respectively, have tolerance specifications of ±0.001% and 0.05%. Determine the differential gain and common mode rejection ratio (CMRR) of this instrumentation amplifier in dB.

Solution: CMRR is given by ratio of differential gain to common mode gain.

Differential gain, $A_V = 1 + 2R_1/R_G$, which gives $A_V = 1 + \left[\left(2 \times 100 \times 10^3\right)/\left(1 \times 10^3\right)\right] = 201$

The input stage has a common mode gain of unity. Therefore, tolerance specification of R_1 has no bearing on common mode gain of instrumentation amplifier.

Common mode gain of difference amplifier = $\pm 2\Delta R_2/R_2 = \pm 2\times$Tolerance of R_2

Therefore common-mode gain = $2\times 0.0005 = 0.001$

Or CMRR = 201/0.001 = 201000

CMRR (in dB) = 20 log 201000 H ≈ 106 dB

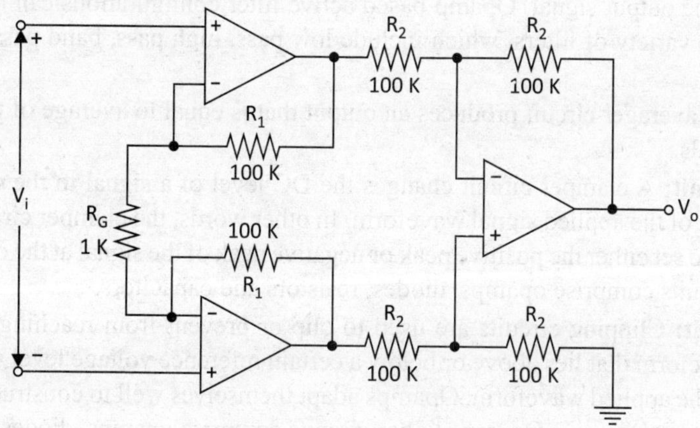

Fig. 10.72: Example-10.19

Example-10.20: The relaxation oscillator circuit of Figure-10.73 operates on a power supply voltage of ±15V. Given that the opamp has positive and negative saturation output voltages of +13V and -13V respectively; determine the peak-to-peak amplitude and frequency of the output V_o.

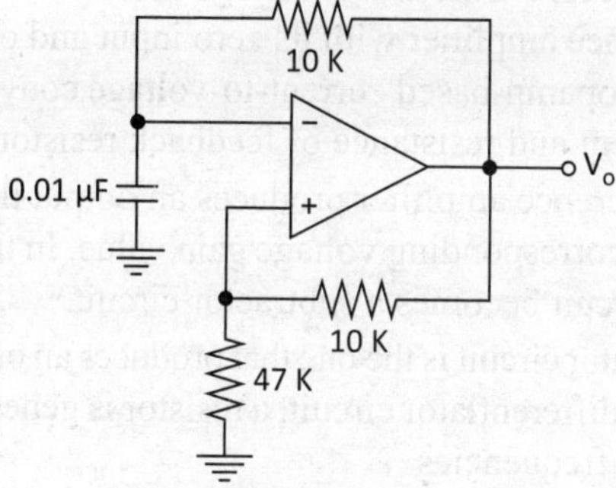

Fig. 10.73: Example-20

Solution: The output of relaxation oscillator switches between +VSAT and -VSAT. The time period of output waveform is given by:

$$T = 2RC\ln\left(\frac{1+B}{1-B}\right)$$

Now, $B = 47\times10^3 / \left(47\times10^3 + 10\times10^3\right) = 0.825$

Therefore, $T = 2\times10\times10^3\times0.01\times10^{-6}\ \ln\left(\frac{1+0.825}{1-0.825}\right) = 0.4688ms$

Frequency, $f = \frac{1}{T} = \frac{1}{0.4688\times10^{-3}}\ Hz = 2.133kHz$

GLOSSARY

Active filter: Active filter is an analog circuit that implements electronic filters using active and passive components. These filters use active components such as operational amplifiers, transistors or FET's within their circuit design. They draw their power from an external power source and use it to boost or amplify the output signal. Opamp based active filter configurations can be conveniently used to implement large variety of filters, which include low pass, high pass, band pass, band reject and all pass filters.

Averager: An averager circuit produces an output that is equal to average of the amplitudes of the applied input signals.

Clamper circuit: A clamper circuit changes the DC level of a signal to the desired level without changing the shape of the applied signal waveform. In other words, the clamper circuit moves the whole signal up or down to set either the positive peak or negative peak of the signal at the desired level. Opamp-based clamper circuits comprise opamps, diodes, resistors and capacitors.

Clipper circuit: Clipping circuits are used to clip or prevent from reaching the output a part of applied signal waveform that lies above or below a certain reference voltage level without distorting the remaining part of the applied waveform. Opamps adapt themselves well to constructing both positive as well as negative clipper circuits. Opamp clipper circuits comprise opamps, diodes and resistors.

Comparator: A comparator circuit is a two-input, one-output building block that produces a high or low output depending upon the relative magnitudes of the two inputs. The opamp comparator compares one analog voltage level with another analog voltage level, or some preset reference voltage, V_{REF} and produces an output signal based on this voltage comparison.

Current-to-voltage converter: Current-to-voltage converter is nothing but a transimpedance amplifier. An ideal transimpedance amplifier with its zero input and output impedances makes a perfect current-to-voltage converter. In opamp-based current-to-voltage converter using an ideal opamp, output voltage is product of input current and resistance of feedback resistor.

Difference amplifier: Difference amplifier produces an output that is equal to the difference of the two input signals multiplied by corresponding voltage gain value. In the case of voltage gain being unity for the two input signals, the circuit becomes a subtractor circuit.

Differentiator: A differentiator circuit is the one that produces an output proportional to the differential of the input. In an opamp-based differentiator circuit, a resistor is generally connected in series with input capacitor to limit gain at higher frequencies.

Instrumentation amplifier: Instrumentation amplifier is nothing but a differential amplifier that has been optimised for DC performance to nearly approach the DC performance of an ideal opamp. As a result, instrumentation amplifier is characterized by a high differential gain, high CMRR, high input impedance and low input offsets and low temperature drifts. An instrumentation amplifier comprises three opamps with two opamps on the input side wired as buffers and the third opamp on the output wired as differential amplifier.

Integrator: An integrator circuit is the one that produces an output proportional to the integral of the input. In an opamp-based integrator circuit, a resistor is generally connected across the feedback resistor to limit DC gain.

Inverting amplifier: An inverting amplifier is the one, which in addition to changing the amplitude of the signal, changes the polarity of the input signal in the case of DC input and reverses the phase of the input signal in the case of AC input.

Logarithmic amplifier: A logarithmic amplifier produces an output signal that is directly proportional to natural log of input signal.

Non-inverting amplifier: A non-inverting amplifier is the one in which the amplified output signal is in phase with the input. Opamp based non-inverting amplifier is characterized by extremely high input impedance. In the special case of gain being unity, it becomes a voltage follower.

Non-linear amplifier: In the case of non-linear amplifier, the gain value is non-linear function of the amplitude of the input signal. That is, a change in input signal does not produce a proportional change in output. A logarithmic amplifier is a type of nonlinear amplifier.

Peak detector circuit: Peak detector circuit produces a voltage at the output equal to peak amplitude (positive or negative) of the input signal.

Phase shifter: It is used to introduce phase shift, lagging or leading, in the input signal.

Relaxation oscillator: Relaxation oscillator is an oscillator circuit that produces a non-sinusoidal output whose time period is dependent on the charging time of a capacitor connected as a part of the oscillator circuit.

Summing amplifier: Summing amplifier produces an output that is equal to sum of input signals multiplied by corresponding voltage gain values. In the case of voltage gain being unity for all input signals, the circuit becomes an adder circuit.

Voltage follower: Voltage follower is nothing but a non-inverting amplifier circuit with a unity gain. It can be used as an ideal buffer between a high impedance source and a low impedance load.

Voltage-to-current converter: Voltage to current converter is a case of a transconductance amplifier. An ideal transconductance amplifier makes a perfect voltage controlled current source or a voltage-to-current converter.

Window comparator: In a window comparator, there are two reference voltages called the lower and upper trip points. Output is in one state when the input is inside the window created by lower and upper trip points and in the other state when it is outside the window.

SUMMARY OF IMPORTANT FORMULAE

1. Voltage gain of an opamp-based inverting amplifier, $A_{CL} = -\frac{A_{OL} R_2}{R_1 + R_2 + A_{OL} R_1} \cong -\frac{R_2}{\left[R_1 + (R_2/A_{OL})\right]}$

   Where R_1 is the input resistor, R_2 is the feedback resistor and A_{OL} is the open loop gain of opamp.

2. Voltage gain of an ideal opamp-based inverting amplifier, $A_{CL} = -\left(\frac{R_2}{R_1}\right)$

3. Voltage gain of an opamp-based non-inverting amplifier, $A_{CL} = \frac{A_{OL}(R_1 + R_2)}{R_1 + R_2 + A_{OL} R_1}$ Where R_1 is the resistor connected from non-inverting input to ground, R_2 is the feedback resistor and A_{OL} is open loop voltage gain. For A_{OL} = Infinity, closed loop gain is given by: $A_{CL} = 1 + \frac{R_2}{R_1}$

4. Voltage gain of an ideal opamp-based non-inverting amplifier,

5. For an averager circuit, $V_o = -\left(\dfrac{V_1 + V_2 + V_3 + \cdots + V_n}{n}\right)$

6. The output in case of opamp-based difference amplifier is given by:

$$V_o = \left(\frac{R_4}{R_3 + R_4}\right)\left(1 + \frac{R_2}{R_1}\right)V_2 - \left(\frac{R_2}{R_1}\right)V_1$$

Where R_1 is connected between first input V_1 and inverting input of opamp; R_2 is connected between inverting input and output; R_3 is connected between second input V_2 and non-inverting input and R_4 is connected from non-inverting input and ground.

For an integrator circuit, $V_o = -\dfrac{1}{RC}\int V_i dt = K\int V_i dt$

Where R is the input resistor and C is the feedback capacitor.

7. For a differentiator circuit, $V_o = -RC\dfrac{dV_i}{dt} = K\dfrac{dV_i}{dt}$

Where C is the input capacitor and R is the feedback resistor.

8. In an opamp-based current-to-voltage converter with R as the feedback resistor, the output voltage is given by:

$$V_o = -I_i \times R \times \left(\frac{A_{OL}}{1 + A_{OL}}\right)$$

A_{OL} is the open loop gain of opamp.

9. In an opamp-based voltage-to-current converter, the output current I_o is given by:

$$I_o = \frac{V_i}{R_1 + [(R_1 + R_2)/A_{OL}]}$$

where R_1 is the resistance connected from inverting input to ground and R_2 is the resistance connected between output and inverting input terminals. A_{OL} is open loop gain of opamp.

10. In an opamp-based relaxation oscillator circuit, the time period T of the output waveform is given by:

$$T = 2RC\ln\left(\frac{1+B}{1-B}\right) \text{ where } B = R_1/(R_1 + R_2)$$

R is the charging resistor connected from output terminal to inverting input terminal, C is the charging capacitor connected from inverting input to ground, R_1 is the resistor connected from non-inverting input to ground and R_2 is the resistor connected between output and non-inverting input terminals.

11. The phase shift introduced by a single stage opamp-based lag-type phase shifter is given by:

$$\theta \text{ (in degrees)} = -2\tan^{-1}(\omega R_P C_P)$$

where $\omega = 2\pi f$ being the frequency of the input signal; R_P is resistor connected in series with non-inverting input and C_P is capacitor connected between non-inverting input and ground.

12. The phase shift introduced by a single stage opamp-based lead-type phase shifter is given by:

$$\theta \text{ (in degrees)} = 2\tan^{-1}(\omega R_P C_P)$$

where w = 2ðf, *f* being the frequency of the input signal; R_P is resistor connected between non-inverting input and ground and C_P is capacitor connected in series with non-inverting input.

13. For a Twin-T notch filter, the resonant frequency f_R is given by:

$$f_R = \frac{1}{2\pi RC}$$

where $R_1 = R_2 = R$, $R_3 = R/2$ and $C_1 = C_2 = C$, $C_3 = 2C$

REVIEW QUESTIONS

1. With the help of circuit diagrams, briefly describe the operation of opamp-based inverting and non-inverting amplifiers. Derive expressions for voltage gain, input impedance and output impedance in the two cases assuming practical opamp.
2. What opamp parameters decide the maximum operating frequency of inverting and non-inverting amplifier configurations in case of sinusoidal input signal for a given value of voltage gain?
3. With the help of circuit diagram, explain the operation of a subtractor that can be used to subtract two DC voltages V_1 and V_2 to produce V_1-V_2.
4. Draw the basic circuit schematic of a classical three-opamp instrumentation amplifier. Briefly describe its operational principle with particular reference to the role of the two opamps constituting the input stage and the output opamp wired as differential amplifier.
5. What is the key advantage of an opamp-based rectifier over conventional rectifier? With the help of relevant circuit diagrams, explain the functional principle of a half- wave rectifier that clips (a) positive half cycles and (b) negative half cycles.
6. With the help of a circuit diagram, describe the operation of an opmp-based circuit that can produce an output equal to average of three unequal inputs.
7. Draw the circuit diagram of (a) phase shifter circuit that can introduce a phase shift in the range of 0° to +120 and (b) phase shifter circuit that can introduce a phase shift of 0° to -120° in a sine wave input signal.
8. Draw the circuit diagram of opamp-based current-to-voltage converter. Derive generalized expression for output voltage. What decides the maximum value of feedback resistance to be used in the circuit?
9. What is a window comparator? Draw the circuit diagrams of window comparators that produce (a) high output for input signal inside the window and a low output for input outside the window and (b) high output for input signal inside the window and a low output for input outside the window.
10. What is an absolute value circuit? Draw the circuit schematic of one such circuit configured around opamp and briefly describe its functional principle.
11. With the help of transfer characteristics, briefly describe why a comparator with hysteresis is preferred over a conventional comparator.
12. With the help of relevant circuit schematic of an inverting comparator with hysteresis, briefly describe its operation and draw its transfer characteristics.

13. What is a relaxation oscillator? Draw the circuit diagram of opamp-based relaxation oscillator circuit and derive expression for the frequency of output voltage waveform. What is the magnitude of peak-to-peak output voltage waveform?
14. Draw circuit diagrams of opamp-based first order low pass and high pass active filters with gain and briefly describe their operation.
15. With the help of circuit diagram, describe the operation of an opamp-based adder circuit that produces an output equal to algebraic sum of multiple input DC voltages.

PROBLEMS

1. For the amplifier circuit of Figure-10.74, derive an expression for output voltage.

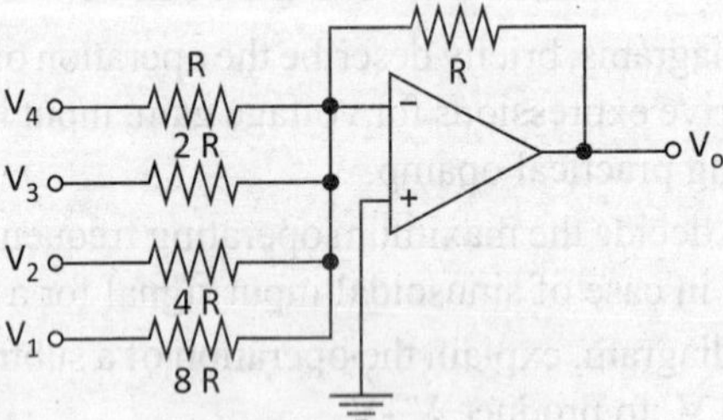

Fig. 10.74: Problem-1

2. For the opamp circuit of Figure-10.75, derive expression for current I_F. What would be the input impedance of this circuit for $R_1 = 10K$, $R_F = 100K$, open loop input impedance of opamp equal to 1M and open loop gain, $A_{OL} = 100000$. What would be the output voltage equal to if the non-inverting input of opamp were grounded and the opamp had specified input offset voltage $V_{io} = 2mV$.

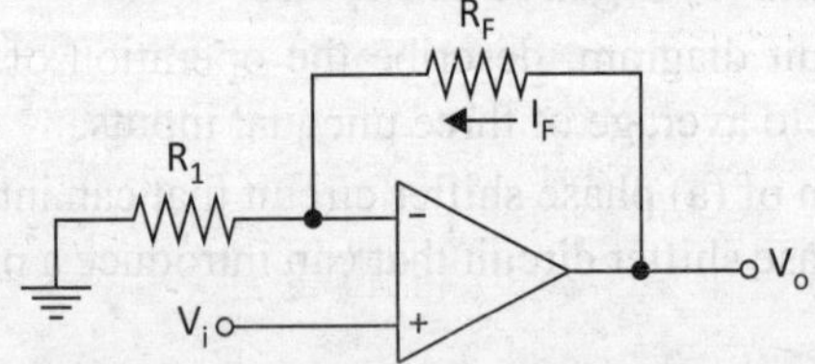

Fig. 10.75: Problem-2

3. For the opamp circuit of 10.76, derive expression for the output voltage.

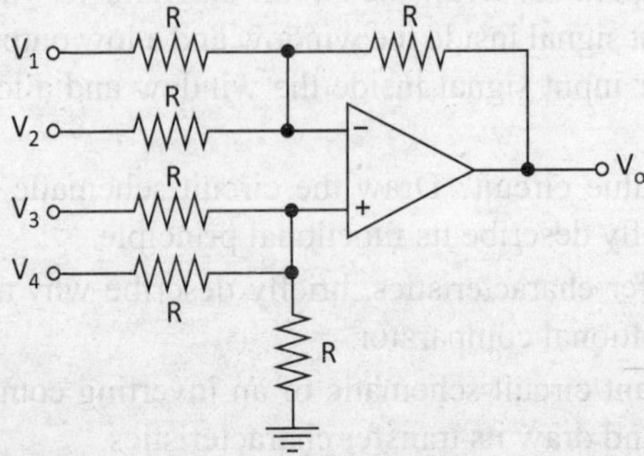

Fig. 10.76: Problem-3

4. For the opmp-based laser diode driver circuit of Figure-10.77 and the given waveform for the input V_{IN}, draw the waveform for the output current flowing through the laser diode.

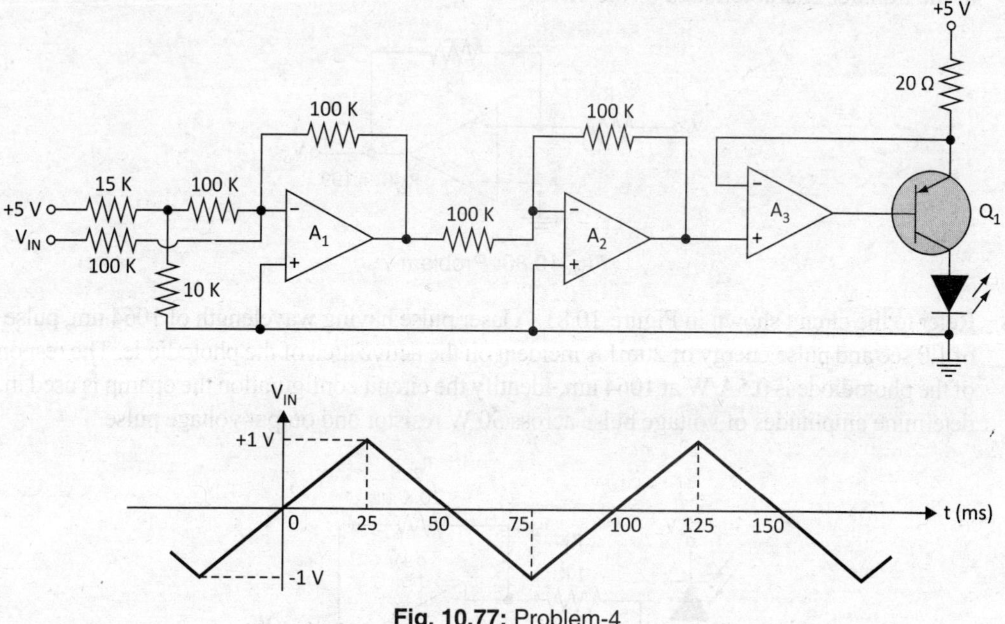

Fig. 10.77: Problem-4

5. Refer to the opamp-based amplifier circuit of Figure-10.78. Determine voltage gain of the amplifier when the variable terminal of the potentiometer is at (a) point A and (b) point B.

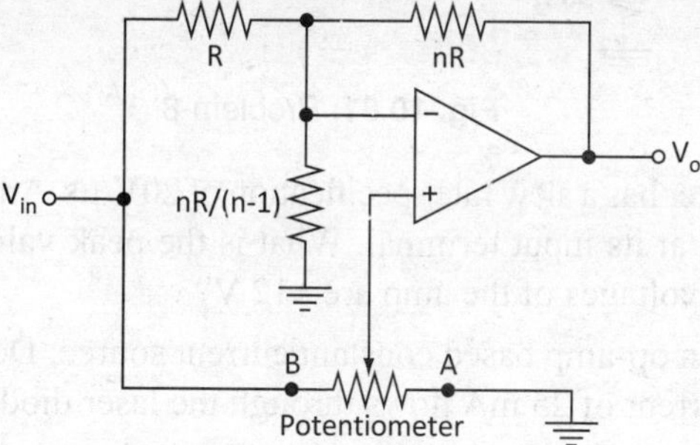

Fig. 10.78: Problem-5

6. Figure-10.79 shows opamp-based voltage follower circuit. If the unity gain cross-over frequency of opamp were 1 MHz and the peak-to-peak voltage observed across the load of 10 W were 98 mV; determine the no load output voltage.

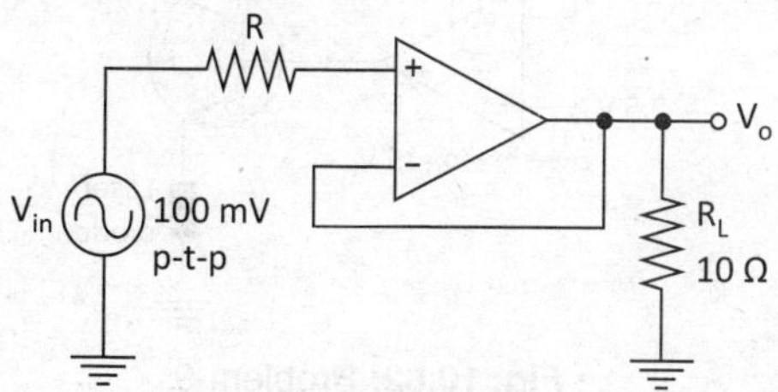

Fig. 10.79: Problem-6

7. Refer to the non-inverting zero crossing detector circuit of Figure-10.80. Given that output saturation voltages are +12V and -12V and the slew rate is 10V/µs; determine hysteresis present in the transfer characteristics of the circuit.

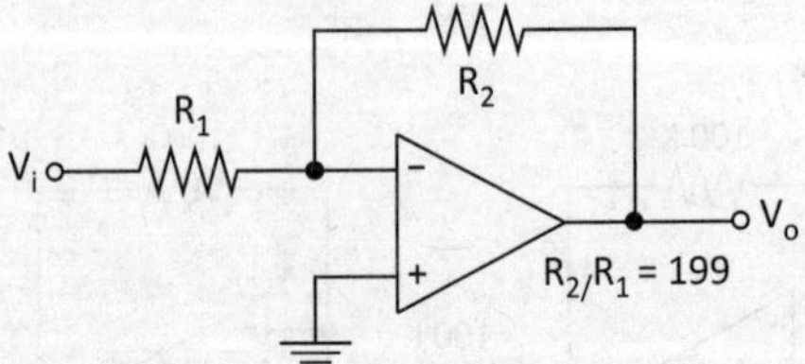

Fig. 10.80: Problem-7

8. Refer to the circuit shown in Figure-10.81. A laser pulse having wavelength of 1064 nm, pulse width of 1.0 sec and pulse energy of 20mJ is incident on the active area of the photodiode. The responsivity of the photodiode is 0.5A/W at 1064 nm. Identify the circuit configuration the opamp is used in. Also, determine amplitudes of voltage pulse across 50 W resistor and output voltage pulse.

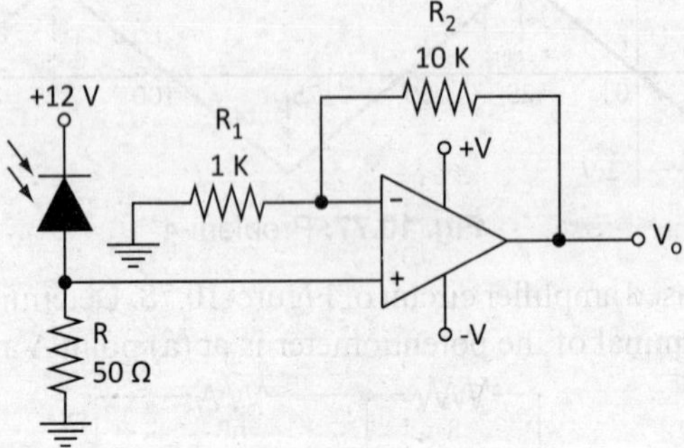

Fig. 10.81: Problem-8

9. An operational amplifier has a slew rate specification of 20V/µs. An input signal having a frequency of 10 MHz is applied at its input terminal. What is the peak value of the output signal in volts given that the supply voltages of the amp are ±12 V?

10. Figure-10.82 shows an op-amp based constant current source. Determine the value of resistor *R* in ohms), so that a current of 25 mA flows through the laser diode?

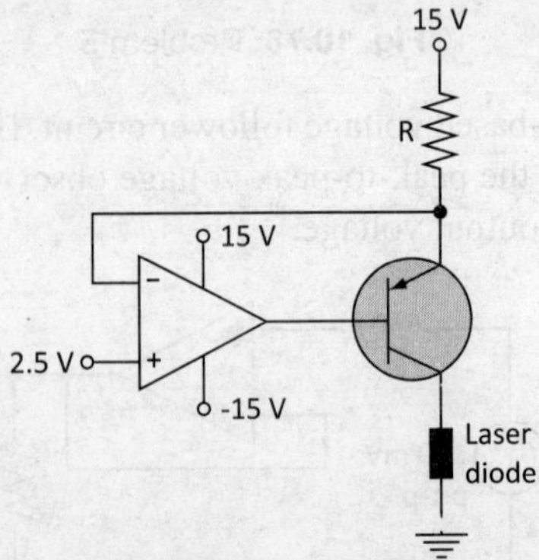

Fig. 10.82: Problem-9

11. For the inverting amplifier circuit of Figure-10.83, the JFET has R_{DS} = 200 W and V_{GS}(OFF) = - 6V. Determine the voltage gain of the circuit when the voltage applied to the gate of junction FET is (a) 0 V and (b) 6V

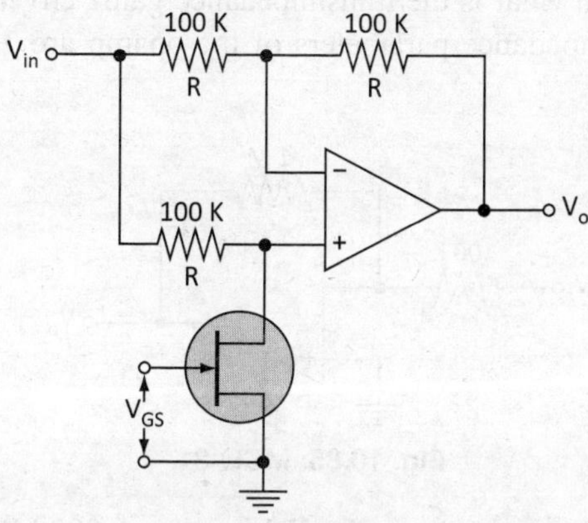

Fig. 10.83: Problem-10

12. Consider the Schmidt trigger circuit of Figure-10.84. A triangular wave which goes from -12V to +12V is applied to the inverting input of the opamp. Given that the output of the opamp swings from +15V to – 15V; determine the voltage extremes the voltage at non-inverting input switches between.

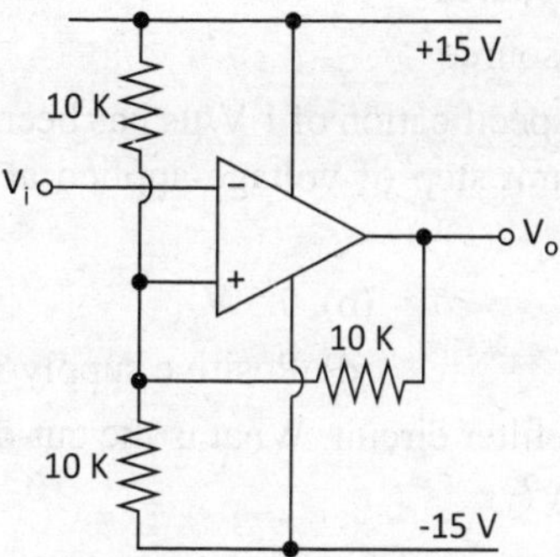

Fig. 10.84: Problem-11

MULTIPLE CHOICE QUESTIONS

1. In an opamp circuit, '*N*' DC inputs are connected to the inverting input through individual resistances, which are of the same value. The feedback resistance connected from output to inverting input is of resistance value that is $(1/N)^{th}$ of the input resistance value. Non-inverting input is grounded. The output in this case is

   (a) indeterminate from given data (b) average of all inputs
   (c) sum of all inputs (d) none of these

2. In an inverting summer circuit using opamp, DC voltages of +1 V, –2 V and +2 V are, respectively, applied to the input through 10 kW, 20 kWand 50 kW resistors. If the feedback resistance were 50 kW, the output voltage would then be

(a) +2 V (b) –2 V

(c) –3 V (d) +3 V

3. Refer to the opamp based inverting amplifier circuit of Figure-10.85. Which type of negative feedback is employed and what is the transimpedance gain? Given that transimpedance, input impedance and output impedance parameters of the opamp are 1 M&!, 10 M&! and 100 W respectively.

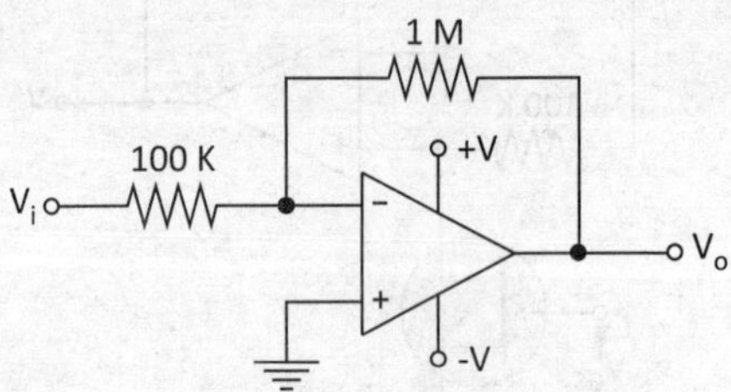

Fig. 10.85: MCQ-3

(a) Voltage shunt, 91 kW (b) Voltage shunt, 900 kW

(c) Current series, 990 kW (d) Current series, 900 kW

4. An operational amplifier is an example of
   (a) Current controlled control source
   (b) Voltage controlled voltage source
   (c) Current controlled voltage source
   (d) Voltage controlled current source

5. An op-amp having a slew-rate specification of 1 V/μs has been connected in the voltage follower configuration. The input is a unit step of voltage applied at instant t = 0. What is the output magnitude at t = 500 ns?

(a) 1 V (b) 0.5 V

(c) 0 V (d) Positive supply voltage

6. Figure-10.86 shows a low pass filter circuit. What is the cut-off frequency and the gain value at four times the cut-off frequency?

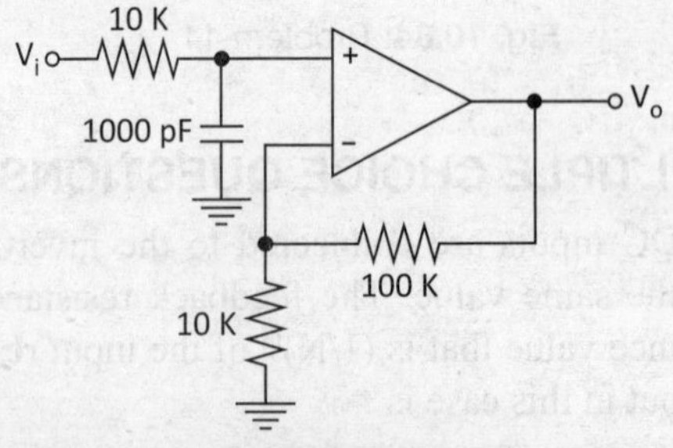

Fig. 10.86: MCQ-6

(a) 15.7 kHz, 8.8 dB (b) 15.9 kHz, 8.8 dB

(c) 15.1 kHz, 8.8 dB (d) 15.9 kHz, 8.9 dB

7. For the comparator circuit of Figure-10.87, diodes D_1 and D_2 have forward-biased voltage drop equal to 0.7 V each. What is the state of LED-1 and LED-2 (whether ON or OFF) when the switch SW-1 is in position-A?

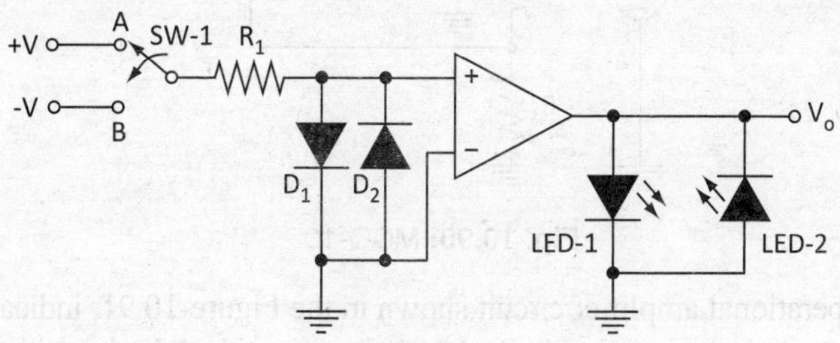

Fig. 10.87: MCQ-7

(a) LED-1 ON, LED-2 OFF (b) LED-1 ON, LED-2 ON

(c) LED-1 OFF, LED-2 ON (d) LED-1 OFF, LED-2 OFF

8. Figure-10.88 shows an op-amp circuit. Given that the op-amp is ideal and $R_2/R_1 = 5$.

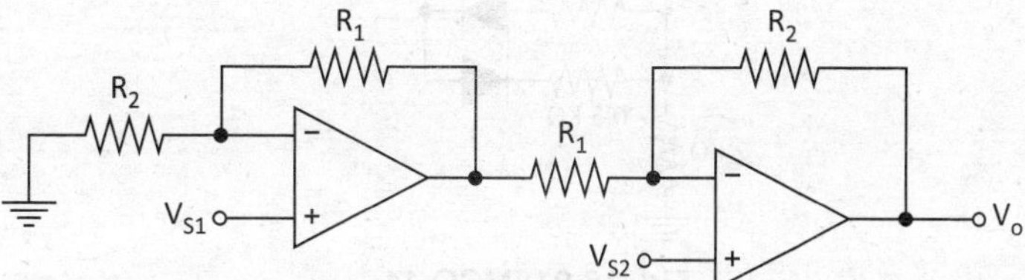

Fig. 10.88: MCQ-8

The mathematical operation performed by the amplifier circuit is

(a) Subtractor (b) Multiplier (c) Adder (d) Divider

9. Figure-10.89 shows a filter circuit. Identify the circuit.

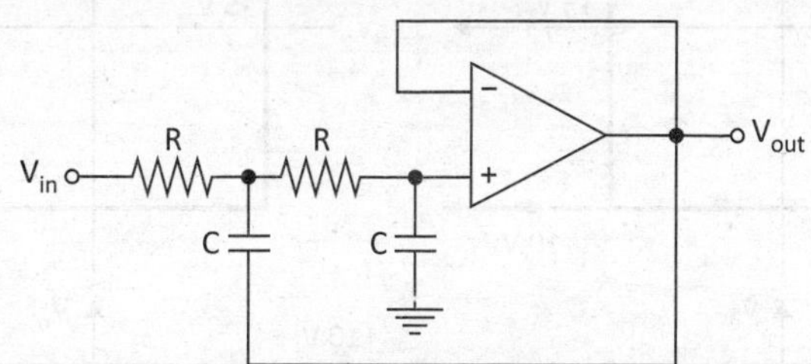

Fig. 10.89: MCQ-9

(a) First order low pass filter (b) Second order low pass filter

(c) First order high pass filter (d) Second order high pass filter

10. Assuming the opamp to be ideal, the voltage gain of the amplifier shown in Figure-10.90 is

(a) $-\dfrac{R_2}{R_1}$ (b) $-\dfrac{R_3}{R_1}$

(c) $-\left(\dfrac{R_2 \| R_3}{R_1}\right)$ (d) $-\left(\dfrac{R_2 + R_3}{R_1}\right)$

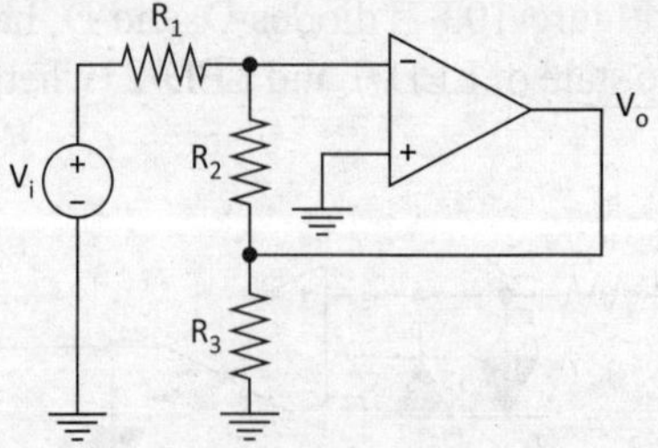

Fig. 10.90: MCQ-10

11. Given the ideal operational amplifier circuit shown in the Figure-10.91, indicate the correct transfer characteristics from choices given in Figure-10.92 assuming ideal diodes with zero cut-in voltage.

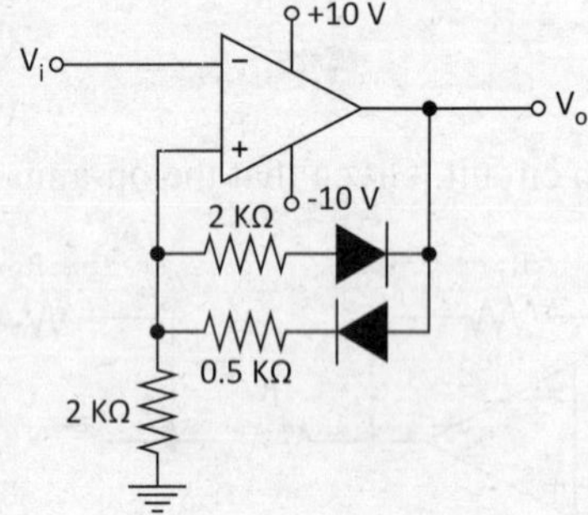

Fig. 10.91: MCQ-11

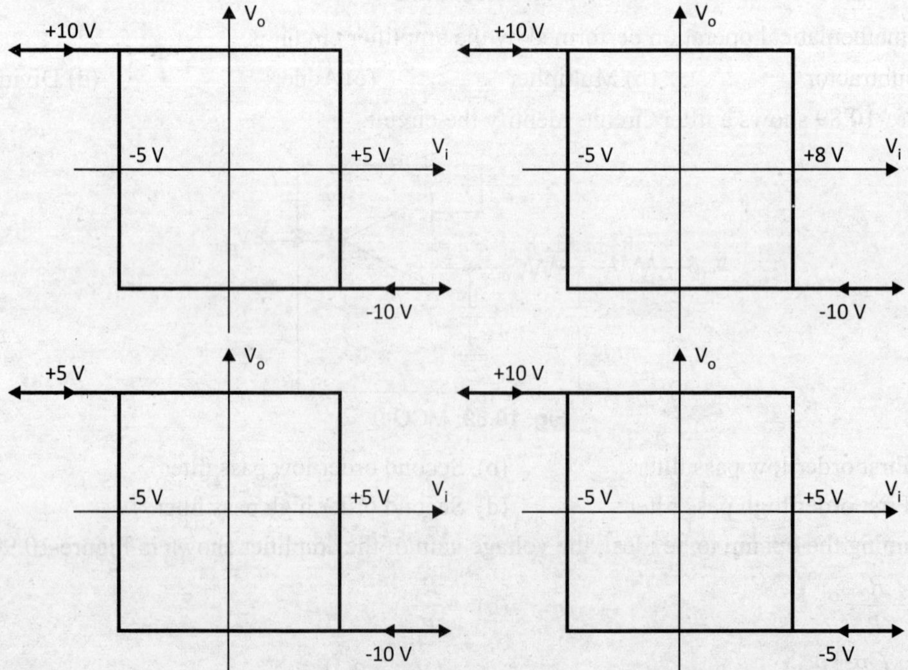

Fig. 10.92: MCQ-12

12. In the circuit shown in Figure-10.93, the op-amps are ideal. V_{OUT} in volts is
    (a) 4 V (b) 6 V
    (c) 8 V (d) 10 V

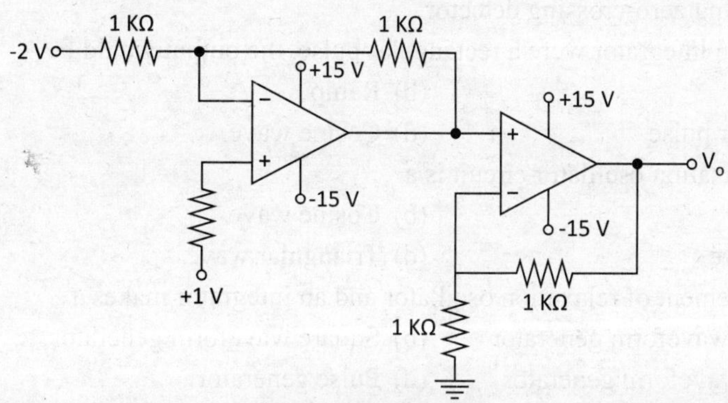

Fig. 10.93: MCQ-13

13. Figure-10.94 shows transfer characteristics of some opamp circuit. It could possibly be
    (a) an inverting comparator
    (b) a non-inverting comparator
    (c) an inverting amplifier with hysteresis
    (d) a non-inverting amplifier with hysteresis

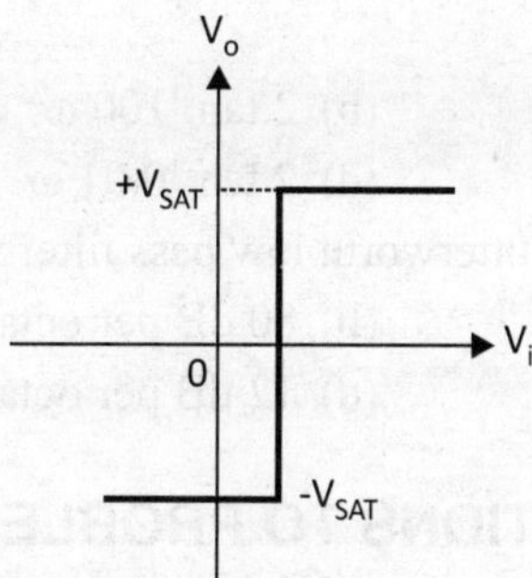

Fig. 10.94: MCQ-14

14. Refer to the transfer characteristics shown in Figure-10.95. Identify the circuit.

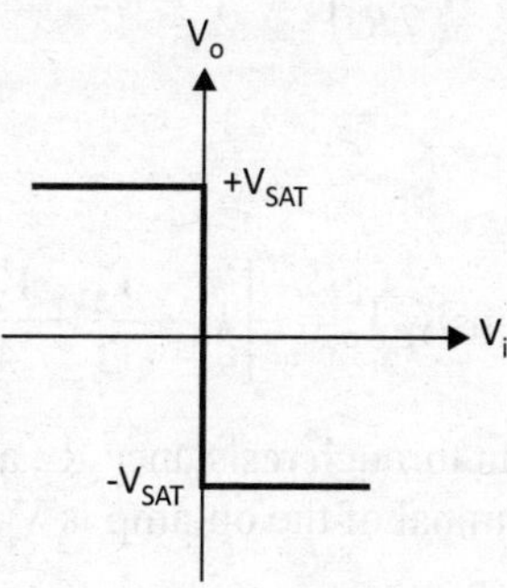

Fig. 10.95

(a) Inverting comparator
(b) Non-inverting comparator
(c) Inverting zero-crossing detector
(d) Non-inverting zero-crossing detector

15. If the input to an integrator were a rectangular pulse, the output would be
(a) Sine wave (b) Ramp
(c) Rectangular pulse (d) Cosine wave

16. Output of a relaxation oscillator circuit is a
(a) Sine wave (b) Cosine wave
(c) Square wave (d) Triangular wave

17. Cascade arrangement of relaxation oscillator and an integrator makes a
(a) Triangular waveform generator (b) Square waveform generator
(c) Sawtooth waveform generator (d) Pulse generator

18. Introduction of hysteresis in a comparator makes it
(a) Prone to false triggering caused by noisy input signal
(b) Immune to false triggering caused by noisy input signal.
(c) A square waveform generator.
(d) None of these

19. The phase shift introduced by a single stage lagging type phase shifter comprising 100kW resistance and 0.1μF capacitor as the phase determining components at an operating frequency of ω rad/s is
(a) $-2\tan^{-1}0.01\omega$ (b) $2\tan^{-1}100\,\omega$
(c) $-2\tan^{-1}(1/0.01\,\omega)$ (d) $2\tan^{-1}0.01\,\omega$

20. The roll-off rate in fourth order Butterworth low pass filter will be
(a) 80 dB per decade (b) 80 dB per octave
(c) 24 dB per decade (d) 12 dB per octave

SOLUTIONS TO PROBLEMS

1. Let us assume that V_{o1}, V_{o2}, V_{o3} and V_{o4} are the outputs, respectively, for only V_1, V_2, V_3 and V_4 present one at a time with other inputs grounded.

$$V_{o4} = -V_4 \times \left(\frac{R}{R}\right) = -V_4,\ V_{o3} = -V_3 \times \left(\frac{R}{2R}\right) = -\frac{V_3}{2},\ V_{o2} = -V_2 \times \left(\frac{R}{4R}\right) = -\frac{V_2}{4} \text{ and}$$

$$V_{o1} = -V_1 \times \left(\frac{R}{8R}\right) = -\frac{V_1}{8}$$

With all inputs present simultaneously, $V_o = -\left[V_4 + \frac{V_3}{2} + \frac{V_2}{4} + \frac{V_1}{8}\right]$

2. Current I_F is the same as the current through resistance R_1, as the input impedance of the op-amp is infinite. Voltage at inverting terminal of the op-amp is V_i.

Therefore, current $I_F = V_i/R_1$

Input impedance R_i is given by:

$$R_i = \text{Open loop input impedance} \times A_{OL} \times \left[\frac{R_1}{(R_1+R_2)}\right]$$

$$R = 1 \times 100000 \times \left[\frac{10\times10^3}{\left(10\times10^3+100\times10^3\right)}\right] = 9090.9M\Omega$$

When the non-inverting input is grounded; the output is only due to input offset voltage. It is equal to input offset voltage multiplied by closed loop gain.

Therefore, output voltage $= \pm\left(\frac{2\times10^{-3}\times110}{10}\right) = \pm22mV$ (Offset may be positive or negative)

3. Let us assume that V_{o1}, V_{o2}, V_{o3} and V_{o4} are the outputs, respectively, for V_1, V_2, V_3 and V_4 present one at a time with other inputs grounded.
With only V_1 present and all other inputs grounded, output $V_{o1} = -V_1$.
With only V_2 present and all other inputs grounded, output $V_{o2} = -V_2$.
With only V_3 present and all other inputs grounded, voltage appearing at non-inverting input is given by $(V_3 \times R/2)/[R+(R/2)] = V_3/3$. This gives output $V_{o3} = V_3$.
Similarly, with only V_4 present and all other inputs grounded, output $V_{o4} = V_4$.

   When all inputs are present simultaneously, output V_o equals algebraic sum of V_{o1}, V_{o2}, V_{o3} and V_{o4}.
That is, $V_o = V_3 + V_4 - V_2 - V_1$

4. Assuming that the base current of Q_1 is negligible as compared to emitter current; laser diode current is same as the current flowing through 20 ohm resistor.
Therefore, laser diode current = $(5 - V_E)/20$ A, where V_E = Voltage at Q_1-emitter
Now V_E is equal to voltage at inverting input of amplifier A_3. A_1 is a unity gain inverting summer; A_2 is a unity gain inverting amplifier. Voltage at non-inverting input of A_3 is therefore sum of V_{IN} and voltage appearing across 10 kW resistor at the input of A_1.

   Voltage across 10 kW resistor $= [(5\times10)/25]V = 2V$

   Therefore, at positive peak of V_{IN}, $V_E = 2+1 = 3V$ and at negative peak of V_{IN}, $V_E = 2-1 = 1V$ and for $V_{IN} = 0$ V, $V_E = 2$ V

   Therefore, at the positive peak of V_{IN}, laser diode current $= [(5-3)/20]A = 100mA$

   At the negative peak of V_{IN}, laser diode current $= [(5-1)/20]A = 200mA$.

   Also, at $V_{IN} = 0$, laser diode current $= [(5-2)/20]A = 150mA$

   Therefore, the waveform for current flowing through light emitting diode is as shown in Figure-10.96.

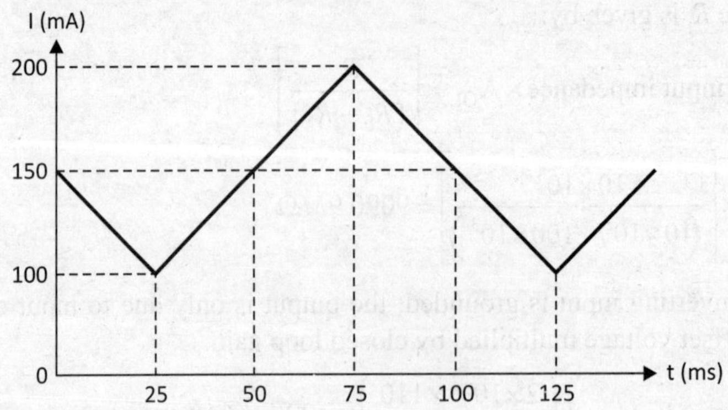

Fig. 10.96: Solution to Problem-4

5. (a) When the variable terminal of the potentiometer is at A, the non-inverting terminal is grounded. The amplifier is a simple inverting amplifier with a voltage gain of -(nR/R) = -n.

   (b) When the variable terminal of the potentiometer is at B, the non-inverting terminal has input V_{in} applied to it. Voltage gain in this condition is equal to an inverting gain and a non-inverting voltage gain.

   Inverting voltage gain is given by $(-nR/R) = -n$.

   In case of non-inverting gain, the resistance connected between inverting input and ground is parallel combination of R and nR/(n-1), which is equal to $nR/(2n-1)$.

   Therefore, non-inverting voltage gain is given by:

$$1 + \frac{nR}{nR/(2n-1)} = 1 + 2n - 1 = 2n$$

   Net voltage gain due to both inverting and non-inverting gains = $2n - n = n$.

6. The circuit shown in Figure-10.79 is that of a voltage follower. Therefore, no load peak-to-peak output voltage is 100 mV.

7. $R_2/R_1 = 199$

   Hysteresis = $\pm 12 \times R_1/(R_1 + R_2) = \pm 12/[(R_1 + R_2)/R_1]$

   $= \pm 12/(1 + R_2/R_1) = \pm 12/200 = \pm 60$ mV = 120 mV.

8. The opamp here is used as non-inverting amplifier. The gain value is 1 + 10/1 = 11.

   The incident light pulse has an energy of 20 mJ and a pulse width of 1 second.

   Therefore, the input peak power = $20 \times 10^{-3}/1$ = 20 mW.

   Output current from the photodiode = $0.5 \times 20 \times 10^{-3}$ = 10 mA.

   Voltage across the resistance R = $50 \times 10 \times 10^{-3}$ = 0.5 V.

   Amplitude of output pulse = 0.5×11 = 5.5V.

9. Frequency and slew rate are related by:

   f_{MAX} = Slew rate/(p × $V_{p\text{-}t\text{-}p}$)

   Slew rate = 20V/μs = 20×10^6 V/s

   Therefore, Vp-t-p = Slew rate/(π × f_{MAX}) = $20 \times 10^6/(\pi \times 10 \times 10^6) = 2/\pi$ = 0.6366V

Or peak value of output = 0.6366/2 = 0.3183V.

10. Current flowing through laser diode is same as that flowing through resistance R assuming that the base current is the transistor is negligible.
    Also, Voltage at the inverting terminal of the op-amp and therefore emitter terminal of transistor is the same as the voltage at the non-inverting terminal.
    Voltage across resistor R is therefore = 15 – 2.5 = 12.5 V.
    Therefore, 12.5/R = 25 × 10^{-3}. Therefore, R = 12.5/25 × 10^{-3} = 500Ω.
11. (a) When V_{GS}(OFF) = 0, JFET is conducting and its R_{DS} = 200 W. Since the externally connected drain resistance of 100K is much larger than R_{DS}; the non-inverting terminal is grounded for all practical purposes.
    Therefore, voltage gain = (-100 × 10^3)/(100 × 10^3) = –1.
    (b) When V_{GS}(OFF) = -6 V, JFET is in cut-off state. The circuit in this case acts both like a non-inverting amplifier and an inverting amplifier simultaneously.
    Non-inverting voltage gain is given by:
    1 + (100 ×10^3/(100 ×10^3) = 2.
    Inverting voltage gain is given by:
    (–100 × 10^3)/(100 × 10^3) = –1.
    Therefore, overall voltage gain = 2 – 1 = 1
12. Let the voltage at the non-inverting input be V_{ni}.
    Applying KCL at the non-inverting node of the amplifier, we get
    $$\left[(V_{ni}-15)/10\times10^3\right]+\left[(V_{ni}-(-15))/10\times10^3\right]+\left[(V_{ni}-V_o)/10\times10^3\right]=0$$
    Solving this equation, we get, $V_{ni}=V_o/3$
    Since the output voltage swings from –15V to +15V, therefore the input voltage at the non-inverting input of the opamp swings from – 5V to +5V.

SOLUTIONS TO MULTIPLE CHOICE QUESTIONS

1. (b): Each of the 'N' inputs when taken alone with other inputs grounded appears at the output divided by 'N'. When all inputs are present simultaneously; the output is equal to sum of all inputs divided by 'N' or in other words the average of all inputs.
2. (b): The three inputs respectively experience gain values of 5, 2.5 and 1. Outputs due to three inputs respectively are -5V, +5V and -2V. Therefore, output voltage, which is equal to algebraic sum of three outputs, is -2V.
3. (a): The feedback signal is a voltage and it is in shunt with the input signal. Therefore, the feedback is of voltage shunt type.
   Transimpedance, R_M = 1MΩ= 10^6Ω.
   Feedback factor, β = 1/$10^6$$\Omega^{-1}$ = $10^{-6}$$\Omega^{-1}$
   Transimpedance with feedback,
   $R_{Mf}=R_M/(1+\beta R_M)=10^6/(1+10\times10^{-6}\times10^6)=90.9k\Omega=91k\Omega$.
4. (b)

5. (b): The output voltage changes by 1V in 1 μs. Therefore, it would change by 0.5V in 0.5 μs or 500 ns.
6. (b): Cut-off frequency = $1/2\pi RC = 1/\left(2\pi\times10\times10^3\times1000\times10^{-12}\right) = 15.9kHz$

   Gain 1 + 10 = 11

   Gain (in dB) = 20 log 11 = 20.8 dB

   The roll-off is 6 dB per octave.

   Therefore, at four times the cut-off frequency, gain would reduce by 12 dB.

   Or Gain = 20.8 - 12 = 8.8 dB.
7. (a): When the switch SW-1 is in position-A, voltage appearing at non-inverting input is +0.7 V (equal to forward-biased voltage drop across D_1). That is, voltage at non-inverting input is more positive with respect to voltage at inverting input. Therefore, opamp output goes to positive saturation with the result that LED-1 is ON and LED-2 is OFF.
8. (a): $V_o = V_{s1}\left(1+\frac{R_1}{R_2}\right)\left(-\frac{R_2}{R_1}\right)+V_{s2}\left(1+\frac{R_2}{R_1}\right) = V_{s1}\left(1+\frac{1}{5}\right)(-5)+V_{s2}(1+5) = 6(V_{s2}-V_{s1})$

   Therefore, the circuit is a subtractor.
9. (b)
10. (a): The circuit given is that of an inverting amplifier with a load resistor (R_3) connected at the output.

    Therefore, gain of the amplifier is - (R_2/R_1).
11. (b): Let us assume that the output voltage is positive i.e. + 10V.

    The lower diode conducts in this situation and the voltage at the non-inverting terminal of the opamp is $\left[\left(2\times10^3\right)/\left(2\times10^3+0.5\times10^3\right)\right]\times10V = 8V$.

    When the input voltage V_i at the inverting terminal exceeds + 8V the output goes from positive saturation voltage (+10V) to negative saturation voltage (–10V).

    The upper diode conducts in this situation and the voltage at the non-inverting terminal of the opamp is $\left[\left(2\times10^3\right)/\left(2\times10^3+2\times10^3\right)\right]\times(-10V) = -5V$

    When the input voltage V_i at the inverting terminal goes below – 5V, the output goes from negative saturation voltage (–10V) to positive saturation voltage (+10V).

    Therefore, transfer characteristics shown in option (b) are correct.
12. (c): Output voltage of the first opamp is $1\times\left[1+\left(1\times10^3/1\times10^3\right)\right]-2\left[-1\times10^3/1\times10^3\right] = 4V$

    Output voltage of the second opamp is $4\times\left[1+\left(1\times10^3/1\times10^3\right)\right] = 8V$
13. (b): The output voltage transits from negative saturation voltage to positive saturation voltage when the input voltage exceeds a certain positive voltage.
14. (c): The output transits from positive saturation voltage to negative saturation voltage at zero cross-over point.

15. (b) 16. (c) 17. (a) 18. (b) 19. (a) 20. (a)

11 Digital-to-Analog and Analog-to-Digital Converters

After completing this chapter, you will learn the following topics.

— Operational basics of D/A converters
— Performance specifications of D/A converters
— Different modes of operation of D/A converters
— Different types of D/A converters
— Performance specifications of A/D converters
— Different types of A/D converters

Introduction

Digital-to-Analog (D/A) and Analog-to-Digital (A/D) converters are important building blocks of any digital system including both communication and non-communication systems besides having other applications. D/A converter is important not only because it is needed at the output of most of the digital systems where it converts a digital signal into an analog voltage or current; it is also important because it forms an indispensable part of majority of the A/D converter types. An A/D converter forms an essential interface when it comes to transmitting analog data with a digital communication system. It is invariably used in all digital readout test and measuring equipment. In this chapter, we shall discuss the operational fundamentals, major performance specifications, different types of digital-to-analog and analog-to-digital converters. Different concepts are illustrated with the help of a large number of problems. A glossary of important words concludes the chapter.

11.1 DIGITAL-TO-ANALOG CONVERTERS

A D/A converter takes digital data at its input and converts it into an analog voltage or current that is proportional to weighted sum of digital inputs. In the following paragraphs is briefly explained how different bits in the digital input data contribute a different quantum to the overall output analog voltage or current and also that the LSB has the least and the MSB the highest weight.

11.1.1 Resistive Network for D/A Conversion

Simple resistive networks can be used to convert a digital input into an equivalent analog output. Figure-11.1 shows one such resistive network that can convert a 3-bit digital input into an analog output. This network, however, can be extended further to enable it to perform digital to analog conversion of digital data with larger number of bits. In the network of Figure-11.1, if R_L is much larger than R, it can be proved with the help of simple network theorems that the output analog voltage is given by eqn. 11.1.

$$V_A = \frac{[(V_1/R)+\{V_2/(R/2)\}+\{V_3/(R/4)\}]}{[(1/R)+\{1/(R/2)\}+\{1/(R/4)\}]} = \frac{V_1+2V_2+4V_3}{7} \qquad (11.1)$$

Eqn. 11.1 can be further expressed as eqn. 11.2.

$$V_A = \frac{V_1 \times 2^0 + V_2 \times 2^1 + V_3 \times 2^2}{2^3 - 1} \quad V_A = \frac{V_1 \times 2^0 + V_2 \times 2^1 + V_3 \times 2^2}{2^3 - 1} \tag{11.2}$$

Eqn. 11.2 can be extended further to an n-bit D/A converter to get a generalized expression given in eqn. 11.3.

$$V_A = \frac{V_1 \times 2^0 + V_2 \times 2^1 + V_3 \times 2^2 + \cdots + V_n \times 2^{n-1}}{2^n - 1} \tag{11.3}$$

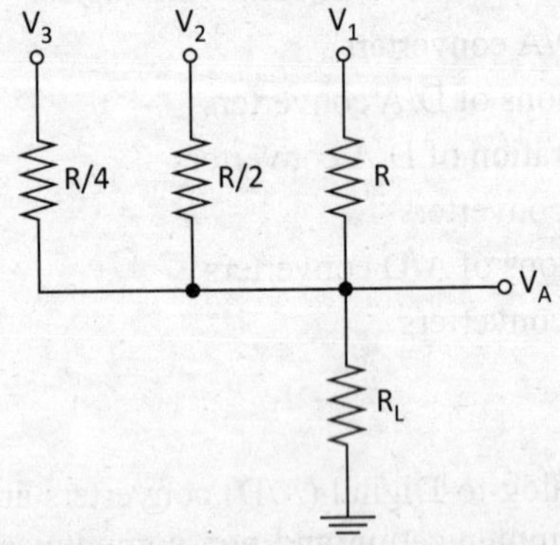

Fig. 11.1: Simple resistive network for D/A conversion

Substituting $V_1 = V_2 = \ldots = V_n = V$ in eqn. 11.3, then a logic '1' at the LSB position would contribute $V/(2^n - 1)$ to the analog output, a logic '1' in the next adjacent higher bit position would contribute $2V/(2^n - 1)$ to the output. The contributions of successive higher bit positions in case of a logic '1' would then be:

$$\frac{4V}{2^n - 1}, \frac{8V}{2^n - 1}, \frac{16V}{2^n - 1} \ldots$$

That is, contribution of any given bit position due to the presence of a logic '1'is twice the contribution of the adjacent lower bit position and half of the adjacent higher bit position. When all input bit positions have logic '1', the analog output is given by eqn. 11.4.

$$V_A = \frac{V(2^0 + 2^1 + 2^2 + \cdots + 2^{n-1})}{2^n - 1} = V \tag{11.4}$$

In the case of all inputs being in logic '0' state, $V_A = 0$. Therefore, analog output varies from 0 to V volts as the digital input varies from an all 0's to an all 1's input. Principally, this how a resistive divider network type D/A conversion process works.

11.1.2 Binary Ladder Network for D/A Conversion

The simple resistive divider network of Figure-11.1 has two serious drawbacks namely:

1. Each resistor in the network is of a different value. Since these networks use precision resistors, the added expense becomes unattractive.

2. The resistor used for the most significant bit (MSB) is required to handle a much larger current than the LSB resistor. For example, in an 8-bit network, current through MSB resistor will be about 125 times the current through LSB resistor.

To overcome these drawbacks, a second type of resistive network called *binary ladder*(or *R*/2*R* ladder) is used in practical D/A converters. The binary ladder too is a resistive network which produces an analog output that equals weighted sum of digital inputs. Figure-11.2 shows the binary ladder network for a four-bit D/A converter. As is clear from the figure, the ladder is made up of only two different values of resistor. This overcomes one of the drawbacks of the resistive divider network. It can be proved with the help of simple mathematics that the analog output voltage (V_A) in the case of binary ladder network is given by eqn. 11.5.

$$V_A = \frac{V_1 \times 2^0 + V_2 \times 2^1 + V_3 \times 2^2 + V_4 \times 2^3}{2^4} \quad (11.5)$$

In general, for an *n*-bit D/A converter using binary ladder network, V_A is given by eqn. 11.3. Using eqn. 11.3, for $V_1 = V_2 = V_3 = ... = V_n = V$, we get eqn. 11.6.

$$V_A = \left(\frac{2^n - 1}{2^n}\right) \times V \; V_A = \left(\frac{2^n - 1}{2^n}\right) \times V \quad (11.6)$$

and for $V_1 = V_2 = V_3 = ... = V_n = 0$, we get $V_A = 0$.

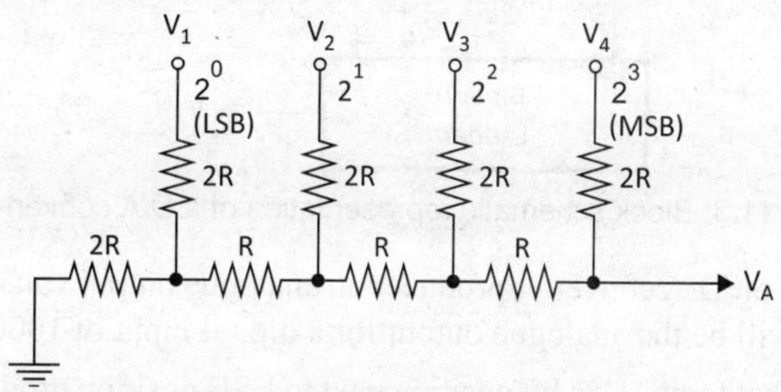

Fig. 11.2: Binary ladder network for D/A conversion

In the case of D/A conversion using binary ladder network; for all 0's input, $V_A = 0$

and for 1's input, $V_A = \left(\frac{2^n - 1}{2^n}\right) \times V$

Also, in case of resistive divider network, the LSB contribution to the analog output is equal to:

$$\left(\frac{1}{2^n - 1}\right) \times V$$

This is also the minimum possible incremental change in the analog output voltage. The same in the case of binary ladder network would be:

$$\left(\frac{1}{2^n}\right) \times V$$

Binary ladder network is the most widely used network for digital-to-analog conversion for obvious reasons. Though actual D/A conversion takes place in this network, a practical D/A converter device has additional circuitry such as a register for temporary storage of input digital data and level amplifiers to ensure that the digital signals presented to the resistive network are all of the same level. Figure-11.3 shows block schematic representation of a complete n-bit D/A converter. D/A converters of different sizes (8-bit, 12-bit, 16-bit etc.) are available in the form of integrated circuits.

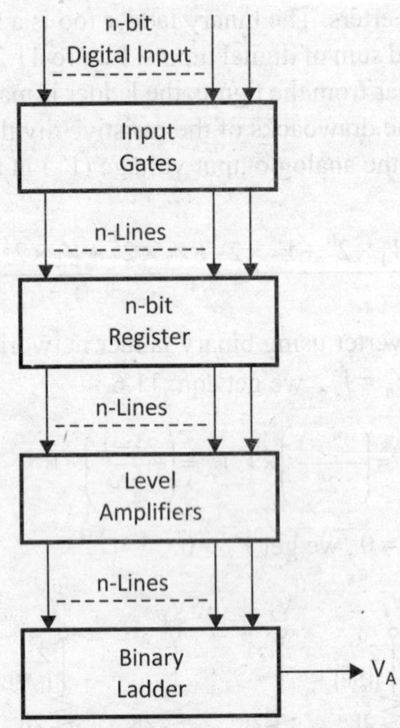

Fig. 11.3: Block schematic representation of a D/A converter

Example-11.1: An 8-bit D/A converter produces an analogue output voltage of 50 mV for a digital input of 00000010. What will be the analogue output for a digital input of 10000000?

Solution: It is given that logic '1' in bit position next to LSB position produces an output of 50 mV. This implies that logic '1' in the LSB position, second, third, fourth, fifth, sixth, seventh and eighth bit positions shall produce outputs of 25 mV, 100 mV, 200 mV, 400 mV, 800 mV, 1.6 V and 3.2 V respectively.

The analogue output for a digital input of 10000000 will be 3.2 V.

Example-11.2: In an 8-bit D/A converter, logic '1' is represented by a DC voltage of 5 Volts. Determine the following.

(a) Analog output voltage for an all 1's input sequence if the converter used a simple resistive divider network.

(b) Analog output voltage for an all 1's input sequence if the converter used binary ladder network.

Solution:

(a) Analog output voltage = $V = 5\ V$

(b) Analog output voltage = $V_A = \left(\dfrac{2^n - 1}{2^n}\right) \times V = \left(\dfrac{2^8 - 1}{2^8}\right) \times V = \left(\dfrac{255}{256}\right) \times 5V = 4.98\,\text{V}$

Example-11.3: In an 8-bit D/A converter using a binary ladder network, the analog output is 460 millivolts for a digital input of 00010111. Determine the analog output for a digital input of 00011000.

Solution: In a binary ladder network based D/A converter, minimum incremental analog voltage

$= \text{Voltage corresponding to 1 LSB change} = \left(\frac{1}{2^n}\right) \times V = \frac{V}{256}$

Therefore, $460 = (V/256) + (V/128) + (V/64) + (V/16) = (23/256) \times V$

Or $V = (256 \times 460)/23 = 5.12V$.

Analog output corresponding to digital input sequence of 00011000 is given by:

$(V/32) + (V/16) = (3/32) \times 5.12 = 480mV$

11.2 SPECIFICATIONS – D/A CONVERTERS

Major performance specifications of a D/A converter include the following.

1. Resolution
2. Accuracy
3. Conversion speed
4. Dynamic Range
5. Non-linearity (NL) and differential non-linearity (DNL)
6. Monotonicity

11.2.1 Resolution

Resolution

Resolution of a D/A converter is the number of states (2^n) that the full scale range is divided or resolved into. Here (n) is the number of bits in the input digital word. Higher the number of bits, better is the resolution. An 8-bit D/A converter has 255 resolvable levels. It is said to have a percentage resolution of $(1/255) \times 100 = 0.39\%$ or simply 8-bit resolution. Similarly, 10-bit and 12-bit D/A converters would have percentage resolution figures of 0.098% [= (1/1023))×100] and 0.0244% (= [(1/4095)×100] respectively. In general, for an n-bit D/A converter, percentage resolution is given by $(1/2^n\text{-}1) \times 100$. Resolution in millivolts for the three cases for a full scale output of 5 volts is approximately 20 mV (for 8-bit converter), 4.9 mV (for 10-bit converter) and 1.2 mV (for 12-bit converter).

11.2.2 Accuracy

Accuracy

Accuracy of a D/A converter is the difference between the actual analog output and the ideal expected output for a given applied digital input. Sources of error include the *Gain Error* (or full scale error), *Offset Error* (or zero scale error), *Nonlinearity Errors* and a drift of all these factors. Gain error is the difference between the actual and ideal output voltage expressed as a percentage of full scale output. It is also expressed in terms of LSB. As an example, accuracy of ± 0.1% implies that the analog output voltage may be off by as much as ±10 mV for a full scale output of 10 volts throughout the analog output voltage range. The offset error is the error at analog zero. Figures 11.4 (a) and (b) illustrate gain and offset errors respectively.

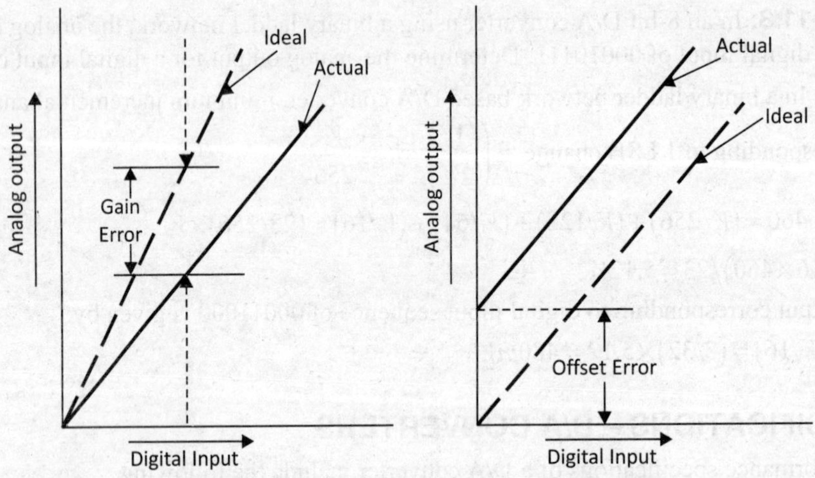

Fig. 11.4: (a) Gain error and (b) Offset error

11.2.3 Conversion Speed or Settling Time

Conversion Speed

Conversion Speed of a D/A converter is expressed in terms of its settling time. *Settling Time* is the time period that has elapsed for the analog output to reach its final value within a specified error band after a digital input code change has been affected. General purpose D/A converters have a settling time of several microseconds while some of the high speed D/A converters have a settling time of a few nanoseconds. Settling time specification for D/A converter type number AD 9768 from Analog Devices U.S.A., for instance, is 5 ns.

11.2.4 Dynamic Range

It is the ratio of the largest output to the smallest output excluding zero expressed in dB. For linear D/A converters, it is $\left(20\times\log 2^n\right)$,which is approximately equal to (*6n*). For Companding type D/A converters to be discussed in section-11.3, it is typically 66 dB or 72 dB.

11.2.5 Non-linearity and Differential Non-linearity

Non-linearity (NL) is the maximum deviation of analogue output voltage from a straight line drawn between the end points expressed as a percentage of the full scale range or in terms of LSBs. *Differential Non-linearity* (DNL) is the worst case deviation of any adjacent analogue outputs from the ideal 1 LSB step size.

11.2.6 Monotonicity

A D/A converter is considered as monotonic if its analog output either increases or remains same but does not decrease as the digital input code advances in 1 LSB steps. In an ideal D/A converter, the analog output should increase by an identical step size for every 1 LSB increment in the digital input word. When the input of such a converter is fed from the output of a counter, the converter output would be a perfect staircase waveform as shown in Figure-11.5. In such cases, the converter is said to be exhibiting perfect *Monotonocity*. If the Differential Nonlinearity (DNL) error of the converter is less than or equal to twice its worst case Nonlinearity error, it guarantees Monotonocity.

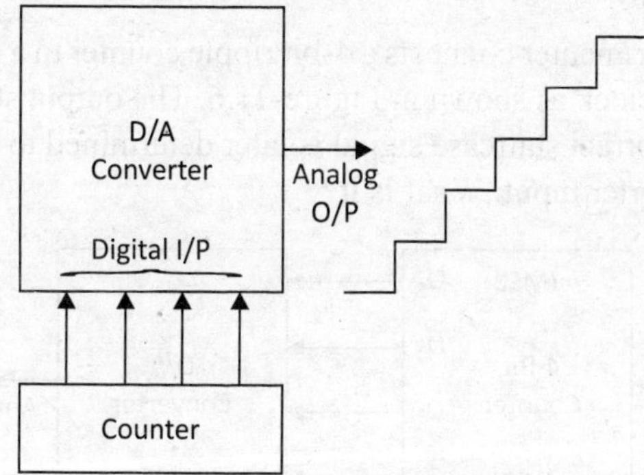

Fig. 11.5: Monotonocity in a D/A converter

Example-11.4: An 8-bit D/A converter has a step size of 20 mV. Determine the full scale output and percentage resolution.

Solution: Step size is same as the resolution.

Therefore, $\left(1/2^8\right)\times V = 20\times10^{-3}$

where V is voltage corresponding to a logic '1'

This gives, $V = 20\times10^{-3}\times2^8 = 5.12V$

Full scale output $= \left[\left(2^n-1\right)/2^n\right]\times V = \left[\left(2^8-1\right)/2^8\right]\times5.12 = 5.1V$

Percentage resolution $= \left[1/\left(2^n-1\right)\right]\times100\% = (100/255)\% = 0.392\%$

Percentage resolution can also be determined from:

Percentage resolution $= [\text{step size}/\text{full scale output}]\times100\% = \left(20\times10^{-3}/5.1\right)\times100\% = 0.392\%$

Example-11.5: A computer is used to control the speed of a motor. The computer output is interfaced to the motor input through an n-bit D/A converter. If the motor speed is to be controlled from 0 to 1000 RPM and if the motor speed is to be within 1.5 RPM of the desired speed, determine the size in number of bits of D/A converter.

Solution: For a n-bit D/A converter number of steps are $\left(2^n-1\right)$

This gives $\left(2^n-1\right)\geq(1000/1.5)\geq666.67$ or $2^n\geq667.67$

or $n\geq\left(\log 667.67/\log 2\right) = 9.382$

Since (n) is an integer, (n) must at least be 10.

Therefore, D/A converter should be a 10-bit D/A converter

Example-11.6: Determine the step size and percentage resolution of a D/A converter with 12-bit binary input. The full scale output is 9.99 V.

Solution: Step size$=\dfrac{\text{Full scale output}}{\text{Number of steps}}$

In case of binary input, step size $= \left[9.99/\left(2^{12}-1\right)\right] = [9.99/4095] = 2.44mV$

Percentage Resolution $= [1/4095] \times 100\% = 0.0244\%$

Example-11.7: An experimenter connects a 4-bit ripple counter to a 4-bit D/A converter to perform a staircase test using a 1 kHz clock as shown in Figure-11.6. The output staircase waveform is shown in Figure-11.7. The cause of incorrect staircase signal is later determined to be wrong connection between counter output and D/A converter input. What is it?

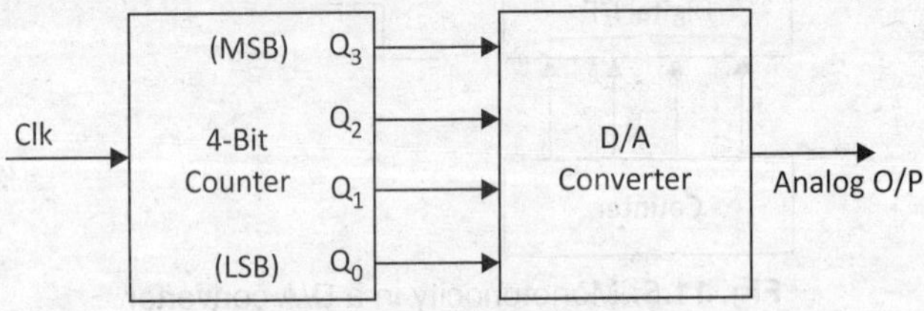

Fig. 11.6: Example 11.7

Solution: The correct staircase waveform would be generated at the output of D/A converter if the counter outputs Q0 (LSB), Q1, Q2 and Q3 (MSB) are connected to the corresponding inputs of the D/A converter in the same order. If we carefully examine the given staircase waveform and recall the sequence in which counter shall advance, it can be visualized that the given staircase waveform would result if the interconnections of LSB and the next adjacent higher bit of the counter output and the corresponding inputs of D/A converter are interchanged. While in one complete cycle, the counter counts as 0000, 0001, 0010, 0011, 0100, 0101, 0110, 0111, 1000, 1001, 1010, 1011, 1100, 1101, 1110 and 1111; the D/A converter, due to interchanged connections, gets inputs as 0000, 0010, 0001, 0011, 0100, 0110, 0101, 0111, 1000, 1010, 1001, 1011, 1100, 1110, 1101 and 1111. Corresponding analogue outputs are 0, 2, 1, 3, 4, 6, 5, 7, 8, 10, 9, 11, 12, 14, 13 and 15 volts as shown in staircase waveform of Figure-11.7.

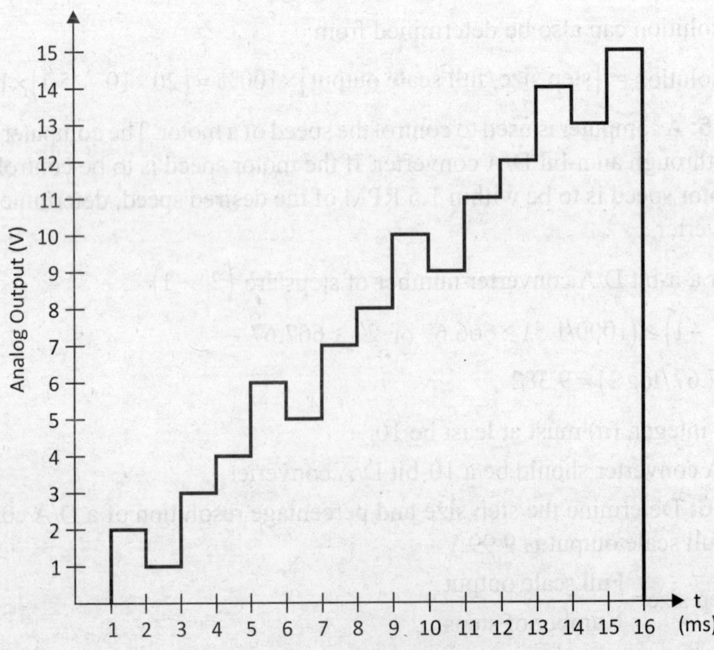

Fig. 11.7: Solution to Example 11.7

11.3 TYPES OF D/A CONVERTERS

The D/A converters discussed in this section include the following.

1. Multiplying Type D/A Converters
2. Bipolar Output D/A Converters
3. Companding D/A Converters

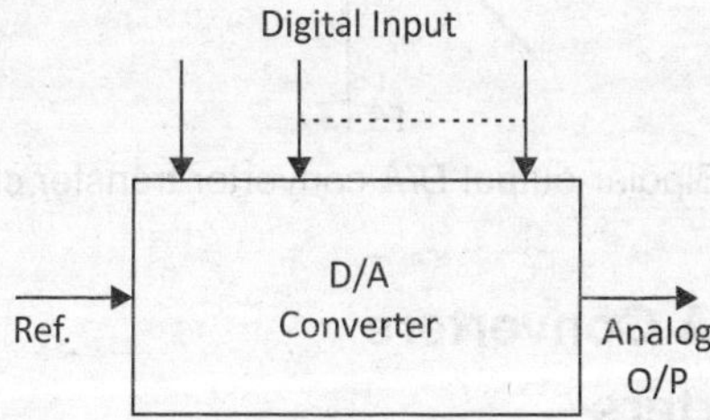

Fig. 11.8: Multiplying-type D/A converter

11.3.1 Multiplying D/A Converters

Multiplying D/A Converters

In a *Multiplying Type D/A Converter*, the converter multiplies an analog reference by the digital input. Figure-11.8 shows the circuit representation. Some D/A converters can multiply only positive digital words by a positive reference. This is known as single quadrant (QUAD-I) operation. Two quadrant operation (QUAD-I and QUAD-III) can be achieved in a D/A converter by configuring the output for bipolar operation. This is accomplished by off-setting the output by a negative MSB (equal to analogue output of 1/2 of full scale range) so that MSB becomes the sign bit. Some D/A converters provide even 4-quadrant operation by allowing the use of both positive as well as negative reference. Multiplying D/A converters are extensively used in digitally programmable analog signal attenuators. Figure-11.9 shows a typical circuit where a D/A converter has been used to produce a digitally programmable analog output.

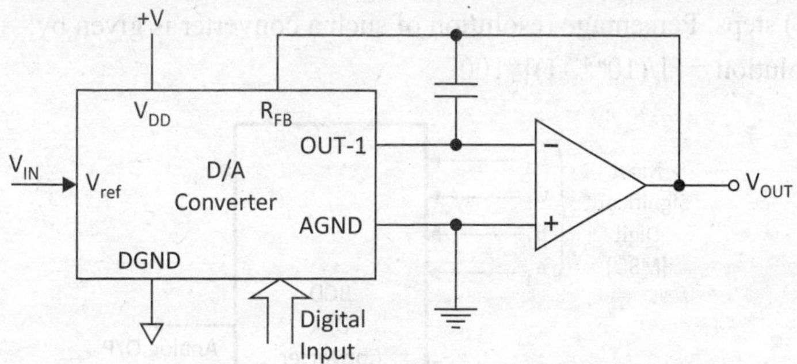

Fig. 11.9: Digitally programmable analog signal attenuator

11.3.2 Bipolar Output D/A Converters

Biplor Output D/A Converters

In *Bipolar Output D/A Converters*, the analog output signal range includes both positive and negative values. The transfer characteristics of an ideal 2-Quadrant bipolar output D/A converter are shown in Figure-11.10.

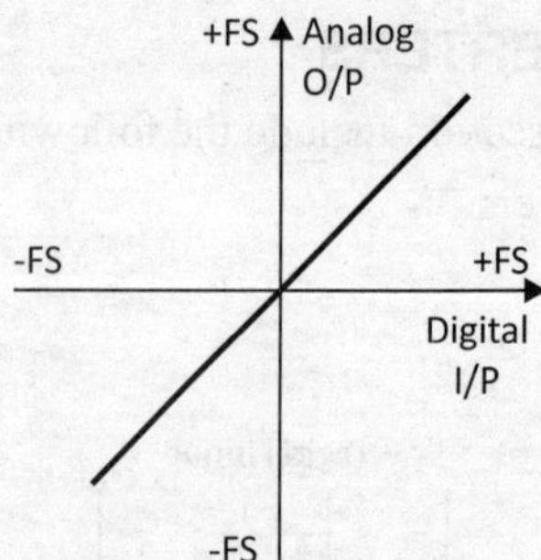

Fig. 11.10: Bipolar-output D/A converter transfer characteristics

11.3.3. Companding D/A Converters

Companding D/A Converters

Companding Type D/A Converters are so constructed that the more significant bits of the digital input have a larger than binary relationship to the less significant bits. This decreases the resolution of more significant bits, which in turn increases the analog signal range. The effect of this is to compress more data into more significant bits.

11.4 BCD-INPUT D/A CONVERTERS

A BCD input D/A converter accepts BCD equivalent of decimal digits at its input. A 2-digit BCD D/A converter for instance is an 8-bit D/A converter. Figure-11.11 shows circuit representation of an 8-bit BCD type D/A converter. Such a converter has 99 steps and accepts decimal digits 00 to 99 at its input. A 12-bit converter will have 999 steps. The weight of different bits in the least significant digit (LSD) will be 1 (for A_0), 2 (for B_0), 4 (for C_0) and 8 (for D_0). The weights of the corresponding bits in the next higher digit will be 10 times the weights of corresponding bits in the lower adjacent digit. For the D/A converter shown in Figure-11.11, the weight of different bits in the most significant digit (MSD) will be 10 (for A_1), 20 (for B_1), 40 (for C_1) and 80 (for D_1). In general, an n-bit D/A converter of BCD input type will have $(10n/4 - 1)$ steps. Percentage resolution of such a converter is given by:

Percentage resolution = $[1/(10^{n/4} - 1)] \times 100$

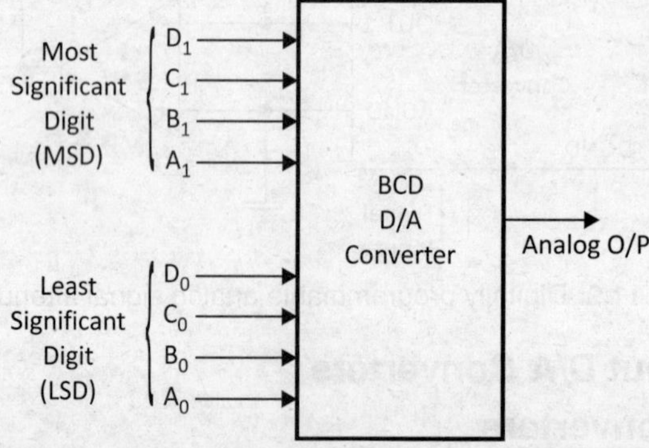

Fig. 11.11: 2-digit (8-bit) BCD-input D/A converter

Example-11.8: Refer to Figure-11.12. This BCD D/A converter has a step size of 6.25 mV. Determine the full scale output.

Solution: Step size of 6.25 mV implies that A_0 has a weight of 6.25 mV. Weights of B_0, C_0 and D_0 would respectively be 12.5 mV, 25 mV and 50 mV. Now weight of A_1 will be ten times the weight of A_0 *i.e.* weight of A_1 will be 62.5 mV. Weights of B_1, C_1 and D_1 will accordingly be 125 mV, 250 mV and 500 mV respectively. On similar lines weights of A_2, B_2, C_2 and D_2 will respectively be 625 mV, 1.25 V, 2.5 V and 5 V.

For full scale output, input will be decimal 999. Each of the three 4-bit groups will be 1001.

Therefore, full scale analog output $= (6.25 + 50) + (62.5 + 500) + (625 + 5000)$ mV

$= (56.25 + 562.5 + 5625)$ mV

$= 6.24375$ V

Full scale analog output can also be determined from the product of step size and number of steps. That is, full scale output = 6.25 × 999 = 6.24375V

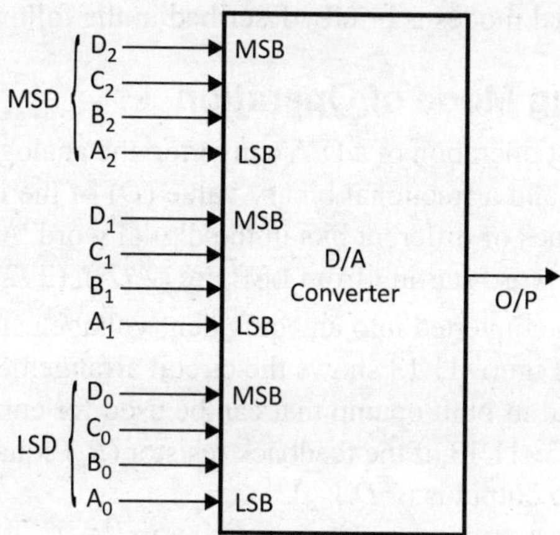

Fig. 11.12: Example 11.8

Example-11.9: Compare the step size and percentage resolution of a D/A converter with 8-bit binary input with a D/A converter having an8-bit BCD input. Both have a full scale output of 5 V.

Solution: Step size = Full scale output/Number of steps

In case of binary input, step size = $5/\left(2^8 - 1\right) = 5/255V = 20mV$

Percentage Resolution = $(1/255)\times 100\% = 0.392\%$

In case of BCD input, step size = 5/99 = 51 mV

Percentage Resolution = $(1/99)\times 100\% = 1.01\%$

Example-11.10: A 12-bit binary input and a 12-bit BCD input D/A converter have the same full-scale output voltage. What would be the resolution of 12-bit binary D/A converter in mV if the resolution of BCD input converter were 10 mV?

Solution: Full-scale output in case of BCD input D/A converter = 10 × 999 = 9.99 V

Therefore, the step size in case of binary input D/A converter is

$$\frac{9.99}{2^n - 1} = \frac{9.99}{4095} = 2.44 \text{ mV}$$

Example-11.11: An eight-bit BCD-input D/A converter produces an analog output voltage of 50 mV for a digital input of 00000010. Determine analog output for a digital input of 10100000.

Solution: It is given that logic '1' in bit position next to LSB position produces an output of 50 mV. This implies that logic '1' in the LSB position, second, third, and MSB position of the least significant digit shall produce outputs of 25 mV, 50 mV, 100 mV and 200 mV respectively. This also further implies that the LSB and the next three higher bits of the most significant digit of the digital input shall produce analog outputs of 250 mV, 500 mV, 1 V and 2 V respectively. Therefore, the analog output for a digital input of 10000000 is given by 2 + 0.5 = 2.5 V.

11.5 MODES OF OPERATION OF D/A CONVERTERS

D/A converters are usually operated in either of the following two modes of operation.

1. Current steering mode
2. Voltage switching mode

Either of the two operational modes is briefly described in the following paragraphs.

11.5.1 Current Steering Mode of Operation

In the *Current Steering Mode* of operation of a D/A converter, the analog output is a current equal to the product of a reference voltage and a fractional binary value (*D*) of the input digital word. (*D*) is equal to sum of fractional binary values of different bits in the digital word. Also, fractional binary values of different bits in an *n*-bit digital word starting from LSB are $(2^0/2^n)$, $(2^1/2^n)$, $(2^2/2^n)$,... $(2^{n-1}/2^n)$.

The output current is often converted into an equivalent voltage using an external opamp wired as a current to voltage converter. Figure-11.13 shows the circuit arrangement. Majority of D/A converters in integrated circuit form has an in-built opamp that can be used for current to voltage conversion. For the circuit arrangement of Figure-11.13, if the feedback resistor (R_F) equals the ladder resistance (*R*), the analog output voltage at opamp output is $(-D.V_{ref})$.

The arrangement of a 4-bit D/A converter of Figure-11.13 can be conveniently used to explain the operation of a D/A converter in the current steering mode. The R-2R ladder network divides the input current (*I*) due to a reference voltage (V_{ref}) applied at the reference voltage input of the D/A converter into binary weighted currents as shown. These currents are then steered to either the output designated Out-1 or Out-2 by the current steering switches. The positions of these current steering switches are controlled by digital input word. A logic '1' steers the corresponding current to Out-1 whereas a logic '0' steers it to Out-2. For instance, a logic '1' in MSB position will steer the current (*I*/2) to Out-1. A logic '0' steers it to Out-2, which is the ground terminal. In the 4-bit converter of Figure-11.13, the analog output current (or voltage) will be maximum for a digital input of (1111). The analog output current in this case will be (*I*/2 + *I*/4+ *I*/8+ *I*/16) = (15/16) *I*. The analog output voltage will be $(-15/16)\, IR_F = (-15/16)\, IR$. Also, $I = (V_{ref}/R)$ as the equivalent resistance of the ladder network across (V_{ref}) is also (*R*). The analog output voltage is then given by:

$$\left[\left(\frac{-15}{16}\right)\times\left(\frac{V_{ref}}{R}\right)\right]\times R = \left[\left(\frac{-15}{16}\right)\times V_{ref}\right]$$

(15/16) here is nothing but the fractional binary value of digital input (1111). In general, maximum analog output voltage is given by $\left[-\left(1-2^{-n}\right)\right]\times V_{ref}$ where (*n*) is number of bits in the input digital word.

11.5.2 Voltage Switching Mode of Operation

In the *Voltage Switching Mode* of operation of *R –2R* ladder type D/A converter, the reference voltage is applied to Out-1 terminal and the output is taken from reference voltage terminal. Out-2 is joined to analog ground. Figure-11.14 shows the 4-bit D/A converter of *R–2R* ladder type in voltage switching mode of operation. The output voltage is product of fractional binary value of the digital input word and the reference voltage applied at Out-1 terminal i.e. ($D.V_{ref}$). As the positive reference voltage produces a positive analog output voltage; the voltage switching mode of operation is possible with a single supply. As the circuit produces analog output voltage; it obviates the need for an opamp and the feedback resistor. However, the reference voltage applied to Out-1 terminal in this case will see different input impedances for different digital inputs. For this reason, the source of input is buffered as is also shown in the circuit of Figure-11.14.

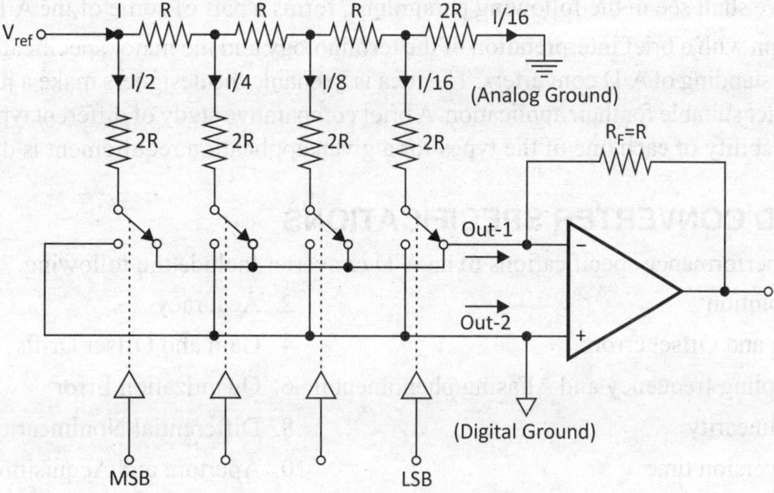

Fig. 11.13: Current steering mode of operation of D/A converter

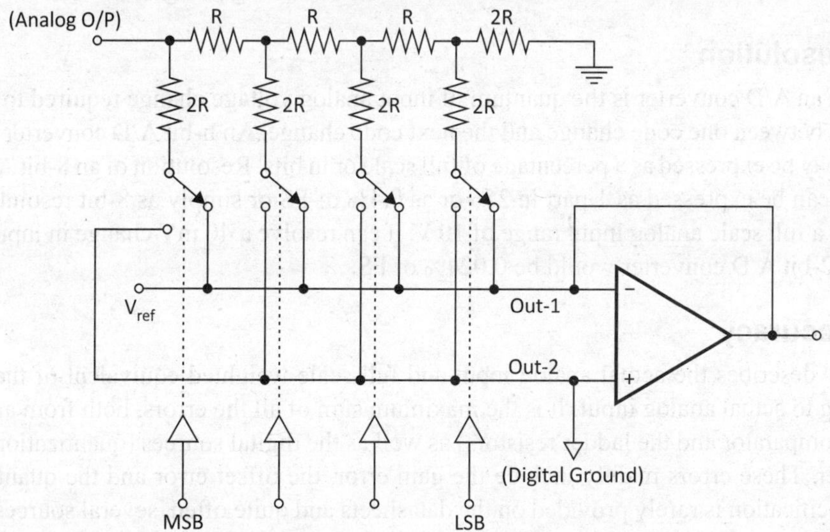

Fig. 11.14: Voltage switching mode of operation of D/A converter

11.6 ANALOG-TO-DIGITAL CONVERTERS

Analog-to-digital (A/D) converters are discussed in this and following sections. An A/D converter forms an essential interface when it comes to analyzing analog data with a digital computer. It is an indispensable part of any digital communication system where the analog signal to be transmitted is digitized at the sending end with the help of an A/D converter. It is invariably used in all digital readout test and measuring equipment. Be it a digital voltmeter or a laser power meter or for that matter even a pH-meter, an A/D converter is at the core of all of them.

A/D converter takes at its input an analog voltage and after a certain amount of time, produces a digital output code representing the analog input. A/D conversion process is generally more complex than the D/A conversion process There are various techniques developed for the purpose of A/D conversion and these techniques have different advantages and disadvantages with respect to one another. A D/A converter circuit, as we shall see in the following paragraphs, forms a part of some of the A/D converter types.

We begin with a brief interpretation of the terminology and the major specifications that are relevant to the understanding of A/D converters. The idea is to enable the designers make a judicious choice of an A/D converter suitable for their application. A brief comparative study of different types of A/D converters and the suitability of each one of the types for a given application requirement is discussed thereafter.

11.7 A/D CONVERTER SPECIFICATIONS

The major performance specifications of an A/D converter include the following.

1. Resolution
2. Accuracy
3. Gain and Offset errors
4. Gain and Offset Drifts
5. Sampling frequency and Aliasing phenomenon
6. Quantization Error
7. Nonlinearity
8. Differential Nonlinearity
9. Conversion time
10. Aperture and Acquisition times
11. Code width

Each of these specifications is briefly described in the following paragraphs.

11.7.1 Resolution

Resolution of an A/D converter is the quantum of input analog voltage change required to increment its digital output between one code change and the next code change. An n-bit A/D converter can resolve 1 part in 2^n. It may be expressed as a percentage of full scale or in bits. Resolution of an 8-bit A/D converter, for example, can be expressed as 1 part in 256 or as 0.4% of FS or simply as 8-bit resolution. If such a converter has a full scale analog input range of 10 V; it can resolve a 40 mV change in input. Resolution figure for a 12-bit A/D converter would be 0.024% of FS.

11.7.2 Accuracy

The *accuracy* describes the actual analog input and full-scale weighted equivalent of the output code corresponding to actual analog input. It is the maximum sum of all the errors, both from analog sources (mainly the comparator and the ladder resistors) as well as the digital sources (quantization error) of the A/D converter. These errors mainly include the gain error, the offset error and the quantization error. Accuracy specification is rarely provided on the datasheets and quite often, several sources of errors are listed separately.

11.7.3 Gain and Offset Errors

Gain error is the difference between the actual full-scale transition voltage and the ideal full-scale transition voltage. It is expressed either as percentage of full-scale range (% of FSR) or in LSBs. *Offset error* is the error at analog zero for an A/D converter operating in the bipolar mode. It is measured in % of FSR or in LSBs.

11.7.4 Gain and Offset Drifts

Gain Drift is the change in the full-scale transition voltage measured over the entire operating temperature range. It is expressed in FS per degree Celsius or PPM of FS per degree Celsius or LSBs. *Offset Drift* is the change with temperature of the analogue zero for an A/D converter operating in the bipolar mode. It is generally expressed in PPM of FS per degree Celsius or LSBs.

11.7.5 Sampling Frequency and Aliasing Phenomenon

If the rate at which the analog signal to be digitized is sampled is at least twice the highest frequency in the analog signal, which is what is embodied in the Shannon-Nyquist sampling theorem, then the analog signal can be faithfully reproduced from its quantized values by using a suitable interpolation algorithm. The accuracy of the reproduced signal is however limited by quantization error. In case the sampling rate is inadequate, i.e. it is less than the Nyquist rate; then the reproduced signal is not a faithful reproduction of original signal and these spurious signals called aliases are produced. The frequency of aliased signal is difference between the signal frequency and the sampling frequency. For example, a 2 kHz sine wave if sampled at 1.5 kHz rate would be reconstructed as a 500 Hz sine wave. This problem is called aliasing and in order to avoid aliasing, the analog input signal is low pass filtered to remove all frequency components above half of the sampling rate. This filter, called anti-aliasing filter, is used in all practical A/D converters.

11.7.6 Quantization Error

Quantization error is inherent to digitizing process. For a given analog input voltage range, it can be reduced by increasing the number of digitized levels. An A/D converter having an n-bit output can only identify (2^n) output codes while there exist an infinite number of analog input values adjacent to the LSB of the A/D converter which are assigned the same output code. For instance, if we are digitizing an analog signal with a peak value of 7 V using 3 bits; then in that case all analog voltages equal to or more than 5.5 V and less than or equal to 6.5 V will be represented by same output code i.e. 110 (if the output coding is in straight binary form). The error is ± 0.5V or ± 1/2 LSB as 1 LSB change in the output corresponds to an analogue change of 1 V in this case. The ± 1/2 LSB limit to resolution is known as the fundamental *quantization error*. Expressed in percentage, the quantization error in an 8-bit converter is 1 part in 256 or 0.4%.

11.7.7 Nonlinearity

Nonlinearity specification (also referred to as the *Integral nonlinearity*, INL by some manufacturers) of an A/D converter describes its departure from a linear transfer curve. Nonlinearity error does not include gain, offset and quantization errors. It is expressed as a % of FS or in LSBs.

11.7.8 Differential Nonlinearity

Differential nonlinearity indicates the worst case difference between the actual analog voltage change and the ideal 1 LSB voltage change. DNL specification is as important as the INL specification as an A/D converter having a good INL specification may have a poor quality transfer curve if DNL specification is poor. DNL is also expressed in % of FS or in LSBs. DNL in fact explains the smoothness of the transfer characteristics and is thus of great importance to the user. Figure-11.15(a) shows the transfer curve for 3-bit A/D converter with 7 V full-scale range, (1/4) LSB INL and 1LSB DNL. Figure-11.15 (b) shows the same for 7 V FS range, 1LSB NL and 1/4 LSB DNL. Although the former has much better INL specification; the latter with better DNL specification has a much better and smoother curve and may thus be preferred. Too high a value of DNL may even grossly degrade the converter resolution. In a 4-bit converter with ± 2LSB DNL, the 16-step transfer curve may be reduced to a 6-step curve. DNL specification should in no case be ignored unless the INL specification is tight enough to guarantee the desirable DNL.

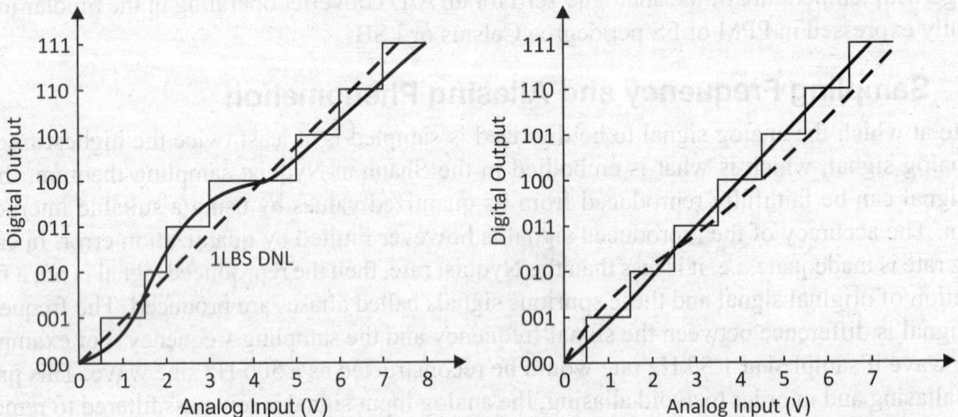

Fig. 11.15: Transfer characteristics of a three-bit A/D converter (a) INL = 1/4LSB, DNL = 1LSB (b) INL = 1 LSB, DNL = 1/4LSB

11.7.9 Conversion Time

It is the time that elapses from the time instant of the start of conversion signal until the conversion complete signal occurs. It ranges from a few nanoseconds for flash type A/D converters to a few microseconds for successive approximation type A/D converters and may be as large as tens of milliseconds for dual slope integrating A/D converters.

11.7.10 Aperture and Acquisition Times

When a rapidly changing signal is digitized; the input signal amplitude would have changed even before the conversion is complete with the result that output of the A/D converter does not represent the signal amplitude at the start. A sample and hold circuit with a buffer amplifier is used at the input of the A/D converter to overcome this problem. Aperture and acquisition times are the parameters of the sample and hold circuit. The signal to be digitized is sampled with an electronic switch that can be rapidly turned on and off. The sampled amplitude is then stored on the hold capacitor. The A/D converter digitizes the stored voltage and after the conversion is complete, a new sample is taken and held for the next conversion. *Acquisition time* is the time required by the electronic switch to close and the hold capacitor to charge while *Aperture time* is the time needed by the switch to completely open after the occurrence of hold signal. Ideally, both the times should be zero. The maximum sampling frequency is thus determined by the aperture and acquisition times in addition to the conversion time.

11.7.11 Code Width

The quantum of input voltage change that occurs between the output code transitions expressed in LSBs of full-scale is the *Code width*. *Code width uncertainty* is the dynamic variation or Jitter in the code width due to noise.

11.8 A/D CONVERTER TERMINOLOGY

Some of the more commonly used terms while interpreting the specifications and salient features of A/D converters are briefly described in the following paragraphs.

11.8.1 Unipolar Mode Operation

Unipolar Mode Operation

In Unipolar mode of operation, the analogue input to the A/D converter varies from 0 to full-scale voltage of one polarity only.

11.8.2 Bipolar Mode Operation

Bipolar Mode Operation

A/D converter configured to convert both positive as well as negative analogue input voltages is said to be operating in bipolar mode.

11.8.3 Coding

Coding

Coding defines the nature of A/D converter output data format. Commonly used formats include straight binary, offset binary, complementary binary, 2's complement, low byte and high byte.

11.8.4 Low Byte And High Byte

Low Byte And High Byte

In A/D converters with resolution greater than 8-bits, some products are offered in high byte or low byte format to simplify their interface with 8-bit microprocessor systems. The low byte output contains the least significant bit and some or all of the lower 8 bits of the A/D converter output. In the high byte, output contains the MSB and some or all of the upper 8 bits.

11.8.5 Right Justified Data, Left Justified Data

Right Justified Data, Left Justified Data

In the byte oriented data output format, data bit sets shorter than 8 bits are placed starting with the right side of the data output transfer register. This could apply to upper or lower byte. For example, a 12-bit ADC will have 4 extra bits which could be right justified. In the left justified data, data bit sets shorter than 8-bits are placed starting with the left side of data output transfer register. This could apply to the lower or the upper byte. For example, a 12-bit ADC will have 4 extra bits which could be left justified.

11.8.6 Command Register, Status Register

Command register is an internal register of the ADC that can be programmed by the user to select various modes of operation such as unipolar or bipolar mode selection, range selection, data output format selection etc. Status register indicates the current status of the analogue to digital conversion with a 'Busy' or 'Conversion Complete' signal.

11.8.7 Control Lines

Control Lines

Digital input/output pins that activate/monitor and control ADC operation are called control lines. Some of the examples are Chip Select, Write, Start Convert, Conversion Complete, etc.

Example-11.12: Determine the resolution of a 12-bit A/D converter having a full scale analog input voltage of 5 volts.

Solution: A 12-bit A/D converter resolves analog input voltage into $\left(2^{12}-1\right)$ levels. Resolution is nothing but the step size.

Resolution $= 5/\left(2^{12}-1\right)V = 1.22mV$

Example-11.13: The data sheet of a certain 8-bit A/D converter lists the following specifications:

Resolution: 8-bits

Full scale error: 0.02% of Full scale

Full scale analog input: + 5 volts

Determine (a) Quantization error in volts (b) Total possible error in volts

Solution: (*a*) 8-bit A/D converter has $\left(2^{8}-1\right) = 255 steps$

Therefore, Quantization error $= (5/255)V = 19.607mV$

(*b*) Full scale error $= 0.02\%$ of FS$= ((0.02\times 5000)/100) = 1mV$

Total possible error = Quantization error + Full scale error $= 19.607 + 1 = 20.607\ mV$

11.9 TYPES OF A/D CONVERTERS

Analog to Digital converters are often classified according to the conversion process or the conversion technique used to digitize the signal. Based on various conversion methodologies, common types of A/D converters include the following.

1. Flash or simultaneous or direct conversion A/D Converter
2. Half flash A/D converter
3. Counter type A/D converter
4. Tracking A/D Converter
5. Successive approximation type A/D converter
6. Single slope, dual slope and multi-slope A/D converters
7. Sigma-Delta A/D converter

Each of the above mentioned types of A/D converters is described in the following paragraphs.

11.9.1 Simultaneous or Flash A/D Converters

The simultaneous method of A/D conversion is based on using a number of comparators. The number of comparators needed for n-bit A/D conversion is $(2^n - 1)$. One such system capable of converting an analog input signal into a 2-bit digital output is shown in Figure-11.16. The analog signal to be digitized serves as one of the inputs to each of the three comparators. The second input for each of the comparators is a reference input, different for each comparator. The reference voltages to be used for comparators are in general $(V/2^n)$, $(2V/2^n)$, $(3V/2^n)$, $(4V/2^n)$ and so on. (V) is the maximum amplitude of the analog signal that the A/D converter can digitize and (n) is the number of bits in the digitized output. In the present case of 2-bit A/D converter, the reference voltages for the three comparators will be (V/4), (V/2) and (3V/4). If we wanted a 3-bit output, the reference voltages would have been (V/8), (V/4), (3V/8), (V/2), (5V/8), (3V/4) and (7V/8). Referring to Figure-11.16, the output status of various comparators depends upon the input analog signal (V_A). For instance, when the input (V_A) lies between (V/4) and (V/2), output (C_1) is HIGH whereas both (C_2) and (C_3) outputs are LOW. The results are summarized in Table-11.1. The three comparator outputs can then be fed to a coding network (comprising of logic gates etc.) to provide two bits, which are digital equivalent of input analog voltage. The bits at the output of the coding network can then be entered into a flip-flop register for storage. Figure-11.17 shows the arrangement of a 3-bit simultaneous type A/D converter.*Simultaneous A/D converters* are also known as *Flash A/D converters*.

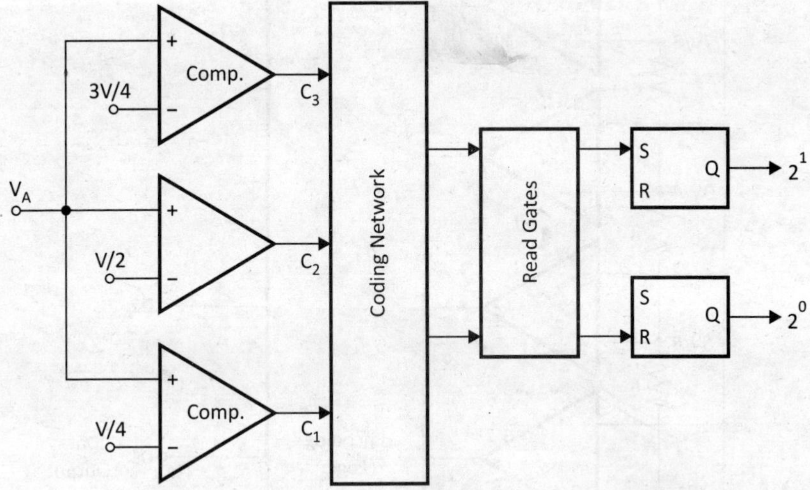

Fig. 11.16: Two-bit simultaneous A/D converter

Table-11.1: Simultaneous or Flash A/D converter

Input analogue voltage (v_a)	C_1	C_2	C_3	2^1	2^2
0 to $\frac{v}{4}$	Low	Low	Low	0	0
$\frac{v}{4}$ to $\frac{v}{2}$	High	Low	Low	0	1
$\frac{v}{2}$ to $\frac{3v}{4}$	High	High	Low	1	
$\frac{3v}{4}$ to V	High	High	High		

The construction of a simultaneous A/D converter is quite straightforward and relatively easy to understand. However, as the number of bits in the desired digital signal increases, the number of comparators required to perform A/D conversion increases very rapidly and it may not be feasible to use this approach once the number of bits exceeds 6 or so. The greatest advantage of this technique lies in its capability to execute extremely fast analog to digital conversion.

11.9.2 Half Flash A/D Converter

Half flash A/D converter, also known as *Pipeline A/D converter*, is a variant of flash type converter that overcomes to a large extent the primary disadvantage of requirement of a prohibitively large number

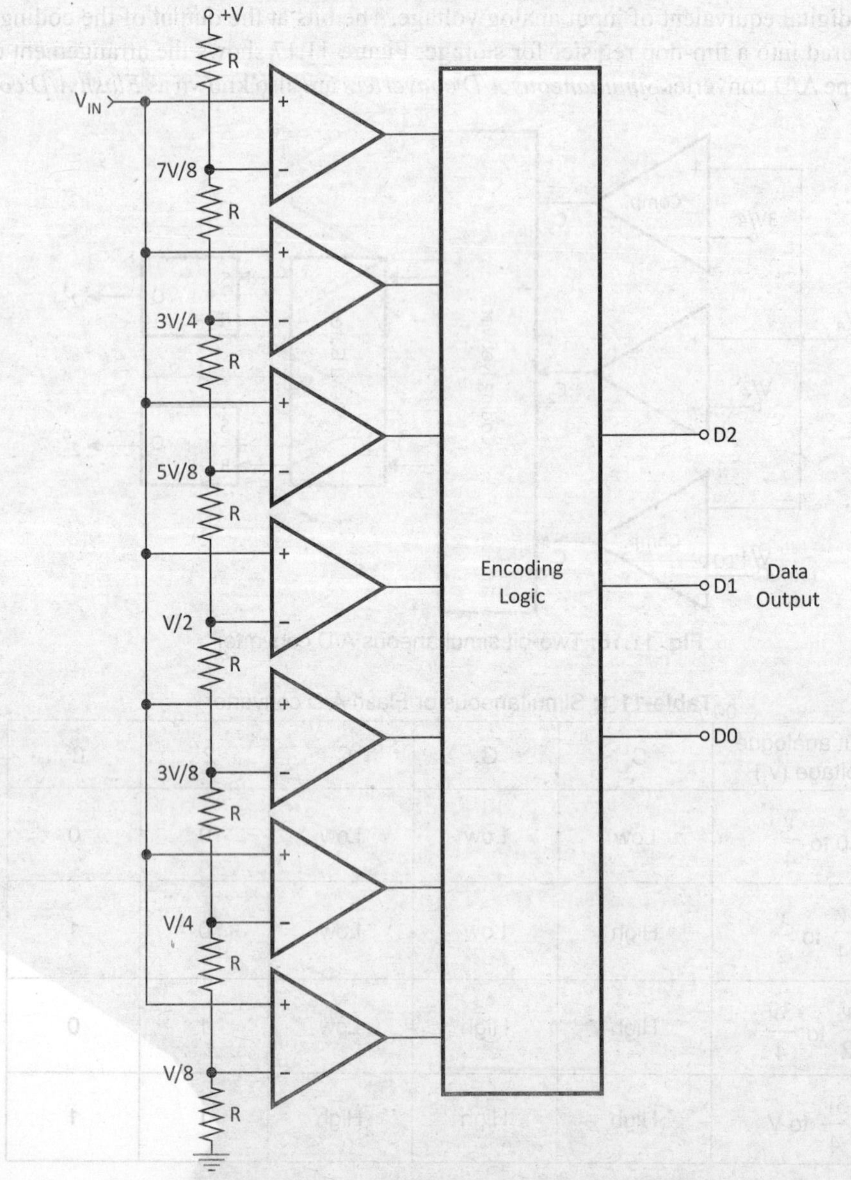

Fig. 11.17: Three-bit simultaneous A/D converter

of comparators in high resolution full-flash converters without significantly degrading its high speed conversion performance. When compared to a full flash converter of certain resolution, while the number of comparators and associated resistors reduce drastically in a half-flash converter; conversion time increases approximately by a factor of 2. For an n-bit flash converter, number of comparators required is 2^n [(2^n-1) for encoding of amplitude and one comparator for polarity], the same for an equivalent half-flash converter would be $2\times(2^{n/2})$. In case of an 8-bit converter, the number is 32 (for half-flash) against 256 (for full-flash). It is further explained in the following paragraphs considering the example of an 8-bit half-flash converter.

A half-flash converter uses two full-flash converters with each full-flash converter having a resolution equal to half the number of bits of the half-flash converter. That is, an 8-bit half-flash converter uses two 4-bit full-flash converters. In addition, it uses a 4-bit D/A converter and an 8-bit latch. Figure-11.18 shows the basic architecture of such a converter. The timing and control circuitry is omitted for the sake of simplicity. The circuit functions as follows.

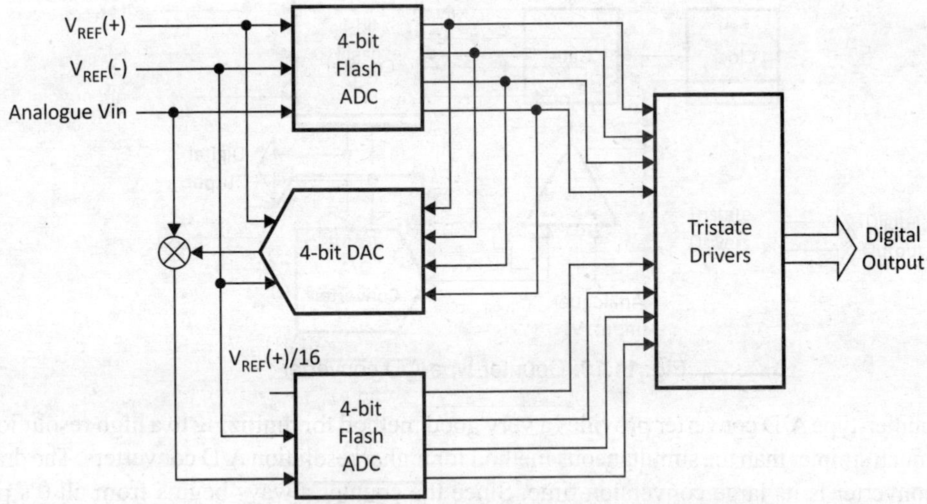

Fig. 11.18: Eight-bit half-flash A/D converter

The most significant 4-bit A/D converter converts the input analog signal into a corresponding 4-bit digital code; which is stored in the most significant 4 bits of the output latch. This 4-bit digital code however represents the low resolution sample of the input. Simultaneously, it is converted back into an equivalent analog signal with a 4-bit D/A converter. The approximate value of the analog signal so produced is then subtracted from the sampled value and the difference is converted into digital code using least significant 4-bit A/D converter. Least significant A/D converter is referenced to $1/16^{th}$ ($= 1/2^4$) of the reference voltage used by most significant A/D converter. The new 4-bit digital output is stored in least significant 4 bits of the output latch. The latch now contains the 8-bit digital equivalent of the analog input. The digitized output is the same as would be produced by an 8-bit full-flash converter. The only difference is that the conversion process takes a little longer. It may also be mentioned here that 8-bit half-flash converter can be either used as a 4-bit full-flash converter or 8-bit half-flash converter. Some half-flash converters use a single full-flash converter and reuse it for both conversions. This is achieved by using additional sample and hold circuitry.

11.9.3 Counter Type A/D Converter

It is possible to construct higher resolution A/D converters with a single comparator by using a variable reference voltage. One such A/D converter is the *counter type A/D converter* represented by the block schematic of Figure-11.19. The circuit functions as follows. To begin with, the counter is reset to all 0's. When a convert signal appears on the start-line, the input gate is enabled, and the clock pulses are allowed to the counter's clock-input. The counter advances through its normal binary count sequence. Counter output feeds a D/A converter and the staircase waveform generated at the output of D/A converter forms one of the inputs of the comparator. The other input to the comparator is the analog input signal. Whenever the D/A converter output exceeds the analog input voltage, the comparator changes state. The gate is disabled and the counter stops. The counter output at that instant of time is then the required digital output corresponding to analog input signal.

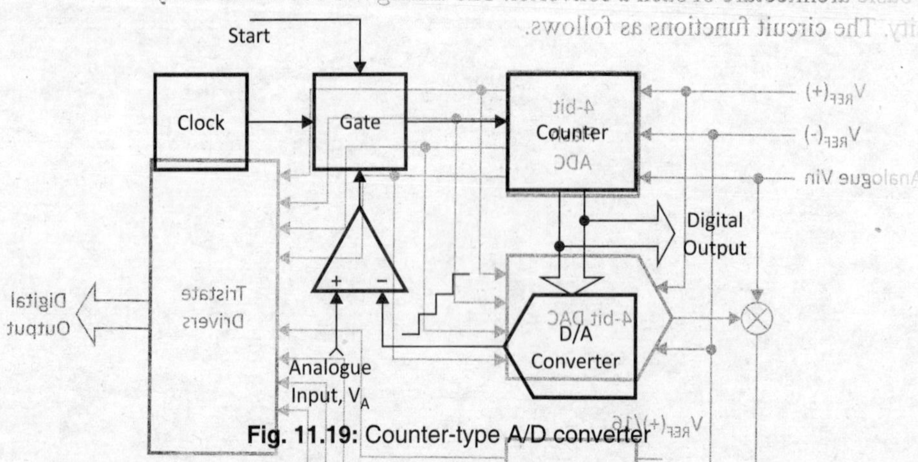

Fig. 11.19: Counter-type A/D converter

The counter-type A/D converter provides a very good method for digitizing to a high resolution. This method is much simpler than the simultaneous method for higher resolution A/D converters. The drawback with this converter is its large conversion time. Since the counter always begins from all 0's position and counts through its normal binary sequence; it may require as many as 2^n counts before conversion is complete. The average conversion time can be taken to be $2^n/2 = 2^{n-1}$ counts. One clock cycle gives one count. As an illustration, if we have a 4-bit converter and a 1 MHz clock, the average conversion time would be 8 µs. It would be as large as 0.5 ms for a 10-bit converter of this type at 1 MHz clock-rate. In fact, the conversion time doubles for each bit added to the converter. Thus, resolution can be improved only at the cost of a longer conversion time. This makes counter type of A/D converter unsuitable for digitizing rapidly changing analog signals.

11.9.4 Tracking Type A/D Converter

Tracking type A/D converter, also called *Delta encoded A/D converter*, is a modified form of counter type converter that overcomes to some extent the shortcoming of a longer conversion time of the latter. In the modified arrangement, the counter, which is primarily an UP-counter in case of counter type A/D converter, is replaced by an UP/DOWN counter. It counts in upward sequence whenever D/A converter output analog voltage is less than the analog input voltage to be digitized and it counts in the downward sequence whenever D/A converter output analog voltage is greater than analog input voltage. In this type of converter, whenever a new conversion is to begin, the counter is not reset to zero; in fact, it begins counting either up or down from its last value depending upon the comparator output. The D/A converter output staircase waveform contains both positive going and negative going staircase signals that track the input analogue signal.

11.9.5 Successive Approximation Type A/D Converter

Successive approximation type A/D converter aims at approximating the analog signal to be digitized by trying only one bit at a time. The process of A/D conversion by this technique can be illustrated with the help of an example. Let us take a 4-bit successive approximation type A/D converter. Initially, the counter is reset to all 0's. The conversion process begins with MSB being set by the start pulse. That is, the flip-flop representing the MSB is set. The counter output is converted into an equivalent analog signal and then compared with the analog signal to be digitized. A decision is then taken whether the MSB is to be left-in (i.e. flip-flop representing MSB remains set) or it is to be taken out (i.e. flip flop is reset) when the first clock pulse sets the second MSB. Once the second MSB is set, again a comparison is made, and a decision taken whether the second MSB is to remain set or not when the subsequent clock pulse sets the third MSB. The process continues till we go down to LSB. We will notice that every time we make a comparison; we tend to narrow down the difference between the analog signal to be digitized and the analog signal representing the counter count. The operational diagram of Figure-11.20 illustrates the concept. It is clear from the diagram that to reach any count from 0000 to 1111, the converter requires 4 clock cycles. In general, the number of clock cycles required for each conversion will be (n) for n-bit A/D converter of this type.

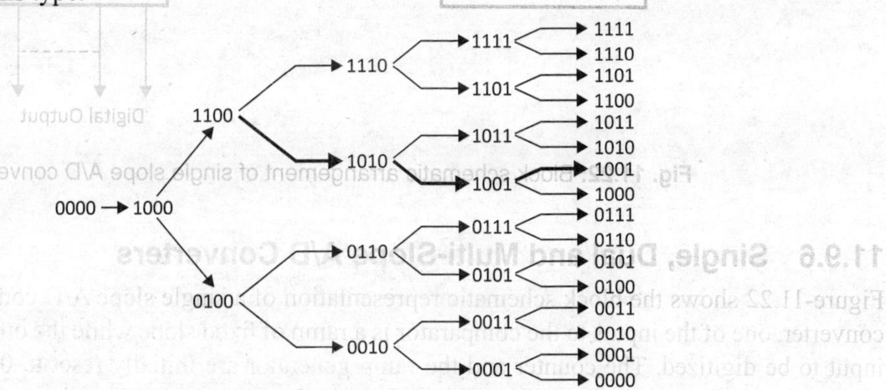

Fig. 11.20: Conversion process in a successive approximation A/D converter

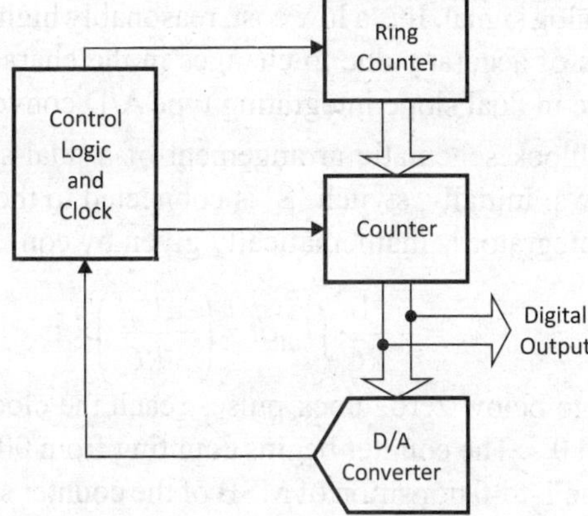

Fig. 11.21: Block schematic arrangement of successive approximation A/D converter

Figure-11.21 shows the block-schematic representation of a successive approximation type of A/D converter. Since only one flip flop (in the counter) is operated upon at one time, a ring counter which is nothing but a circulating register (serial shift register with outputs Q and Q' of the last flip flop connected to J and K inputs respectively of the first flip flop) is used to do the job. Referring to Figure-11.20, the dark lines show the sequence in which the counter arrives at the desired count, assuming that 1001 is the desired count. This type of A/D converter is much faster than the counter-type A/D converter previously discussed. In an n-bit converter, the counter-type A/D converter on an average would require (2^{n-1}) clock cycles for each conversion whereas successive approximation type converter requires only (n) clock cycles. That is, an 8-bit A/D converter of this type operating on 1 MHz clock has a conversion time of 8 μs.

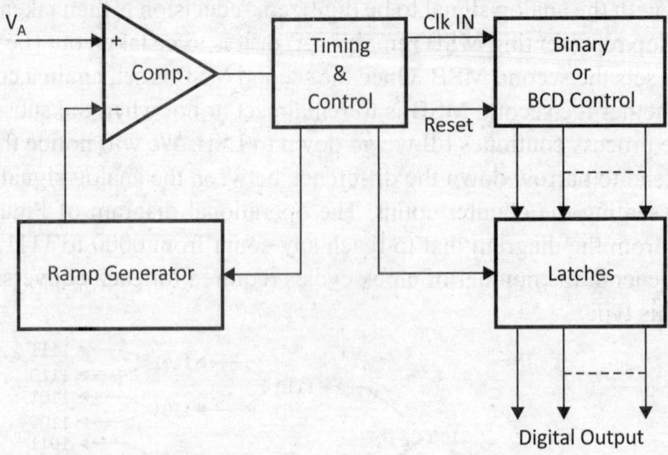

Fig. 11.22: Block schematic arrangement of single slope A/D converter

11.9.6 Single, Dual and Multi-Slope A/D Converters

Figure-11.22 shows the block schematic representation of a single slope A/D converter. In this type of converter, one of the inputs to the comparator is a ramp of fixed slope while the other input is the analog input to be digitized. The counter and the ramp generator are initially reset to 0's. The counter starts counting with the first clock cycle input. The ramp is also synchronized to start with the first clock input. The counter stops when the ramp amplitude equals the analog input. In this case, the counter count is directly proportional to the analog signal. It is a low cost, reasonably high accuracy converter but it suffers from the disadvantage of loss of accuracy due to changes in the characteristics of the ramp generator. This shortcoming is overcome in dual slope integrating type A/D converter.

Figure-11.23 shows the block schematic arrangement of a dual-slope integrating A/D converter. The converter works as follows. Initially, switch 'S' is connected to the analog input voltage (V_A) to be digitized. The output of the integrator is mathematically given by eqn. 11.7.

$$v_o = -\frac{1}{RC}\int V_A dt = \left(-\frac{V_A}{RC}\right) \times t \tag{11.7}$$

The moment v_o tends to go below zero, clock pulses reach the clock input terminal of the counter, which is initially cleared to all 0's. The counter begins counting from 0000 ...0. At the (2^n)th clock pulse, the counter is again cleared, the 1-to-0 transition of MSB of the counter sets a flip-flop, which controls the state of switch 'S', which now connects the integrator input to a reference voltage of polarity opposite to that of analog input. The integrator output moves in the positive direction; the counter has again started counting after it got reset (at say $t = T_1$). The moment, the integrator output tends to exceed zero; the counter stops as the clock pulses no longer reach the counter's clock input. The counter output at this stage (say at $t = T_2$) is proportional to the analog input. Mathematically, it can be proved that $n = (V_A/V_R).2^n$ where (n) here is the count recorded in the counter at $t = T_2$. Figure-11.24 illustrates the concept further with the help of relevant waveforms. This type of A/D converter is very popular in digital voltmeters due to its good conversion accuracy and low cost. Also, accuracy is independent of both the integrator capacitance and the clock frequency as they affect the negative and positive slope in the same manner. Yet another advantage of the dual slope integrator A/D converter is that the fixed analog input integration period results in rejection of noise frequencies present in the analog input and having time periods that are equal to or sub-multiple of the integration time. Proper choice of integration time can therefore achieve excellent rejection of 50/60 Hz line ripple.

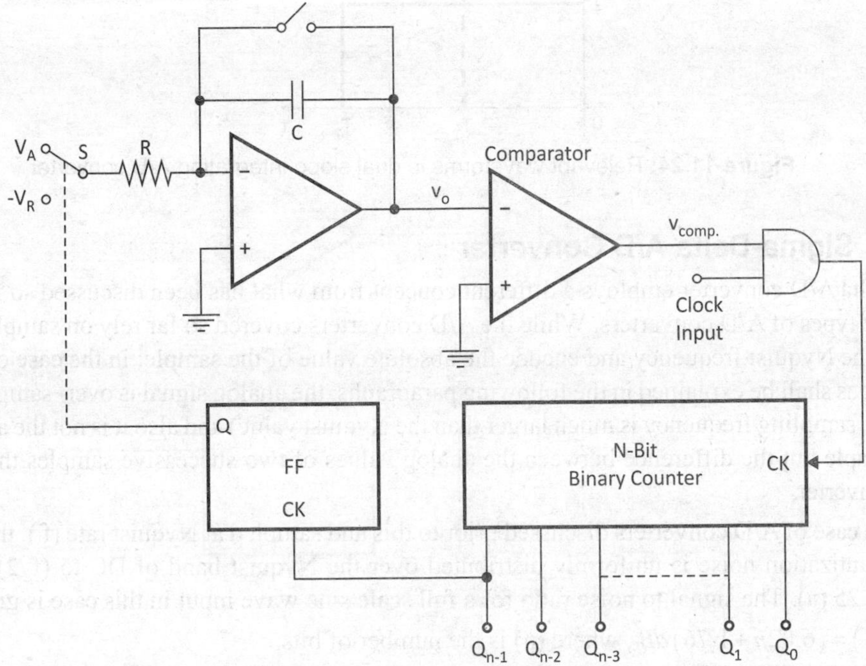

Fig. 11.23: Block schematic arrangement of dual-slope integrating A/D converter

There are multi-slope converter architectures too aimed at further enhancing the performance of integrating A/D converters. For example, the triple-slope architecture is used to increase the conversion speed at the cost of added complexity. Increase in conversion speed is accomplished by carrying out integration from reference voltage at two distinct rates, a high speed rate and a low speed rate. The counter is also divided into two sections, one for MSB bits and the other for LSB bits. A properly designed triple-slope converter achieves increased conversion speed without compromising the inherent linearity, differential linearity and stability characteristics of dual slope converter.

Bias currents offset voltages and gain errors associated with operational amplifiers used as integrator and comparator do introduce some errors. These can be cancelled by using additional charge/discharge cycles and then using the results to correct the initial measurement. One such A/D converter is quad-slope converter that uses two charge/discharge cycles as compared to one charge/discharge cycle in case of dual-slope converter. Quad-slope A/D converters have a much higher accuracy than dual slope counterparts.

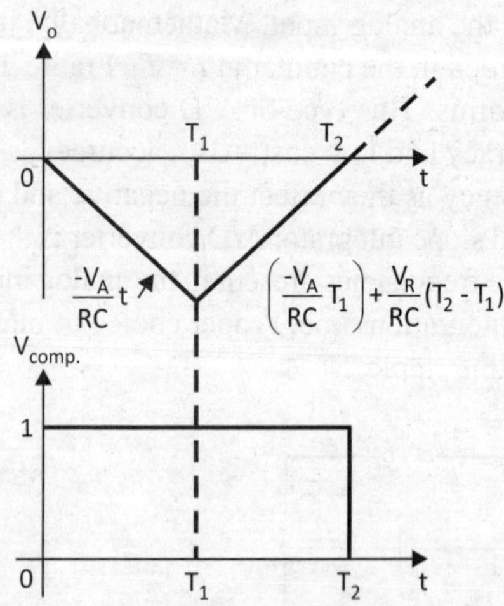

Figure-11.24: Relevant waveforms in dual slope integrating A/D converter

11.9.7 Sigma-Delta A/D Converter

Sigma-delta A/D converter employs a different concept from what has been discussed so far in the case of various types of A/D converters. While the A/D converters covered so far rely on sampling of analog signal at the Nyquist frequency and encode the absolute value of the sample; in the case of sigma-delta converter, as shall be explained in the following paragraphs, the analog signal is over- sampled by a large factor (i.e. sampling frequency is much larger than the Nyquist value) and also it is not the absolute value of the sample but the difference between the analog values of two successive samples that is encoded by the converter.

In the case of A/D converters discussed prior to this and sampled at Nyquist rate (f_s), the RMS value of the quantization noise is uniformly distributed over the Nyquist band of DC to ($f_s/2$) as shown in Figure-11.25 (a). The signal to noise ratio for a full scale sine wave input in this case is given by:

$(S/N) = (6.02n + 1.76)\,dB$, where (n) is the number of bits.

The only way to increase the signal to noise ratio is by increasing number of bits. On the other hand, a sigma-delta converter attempts to enhance signal to noise ratio by over sampling the analog signal, which has the effect of spreading the noise spectrum over a much larger bandwidth, and then filtering out the desired band. If the analog signal were sampled at a rate of (Kf_s), the quantization noise gets spread over DC to ($Kf_s/2$) as shown in Figure-11.25 (b). (K) is a constant referred to as oversampling ratio. Enhanced S/N ratio means higher resolution, which is achieved by other types of A/D converters by way of increasing number of bits.

It may be mentioned here that if we simply use oversampling to improve resolution, it would be required to oversample by a factor of (2^{2N}) to achieve an N-bit increase in resolution. Sigma-delta converter does not require to be oversampled by such a large factor because it not only limits the signal pass band but also shapes the quantization noise in such a way that most of it falls outside this pass band as shown in Figure-11.25 (c). In the following paragraphs is explained the operational principle of sigma-delta A/D converter.

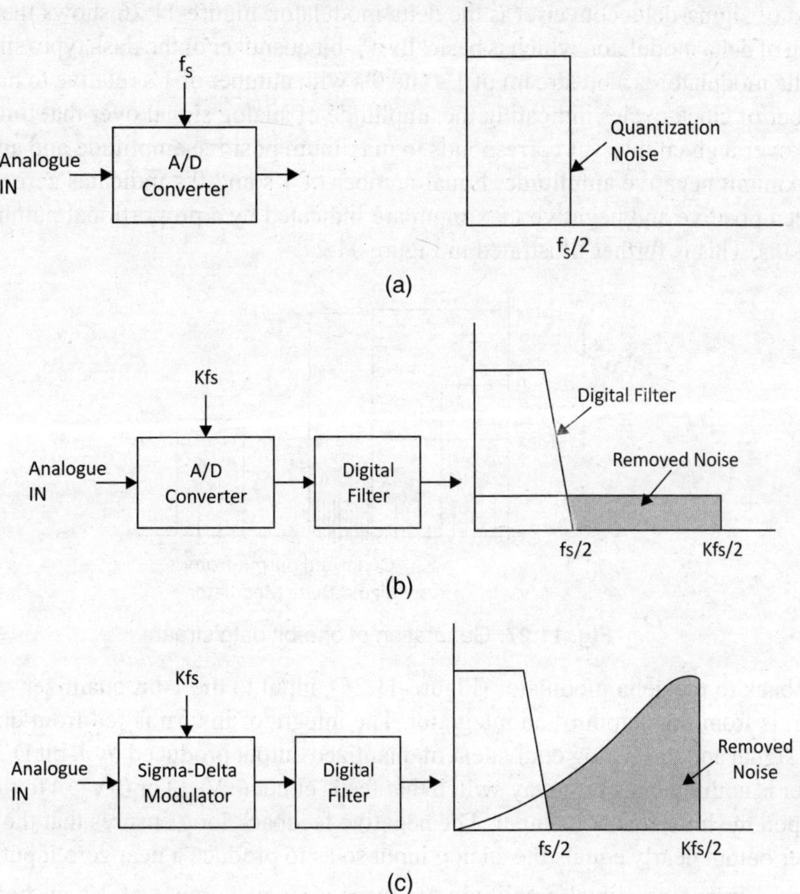

Fig. 11.25: Quantization noise spectrum (a) with sampling at Nyquist rate (b) with oversampling (c) with oversampling in a sigma-delta converter

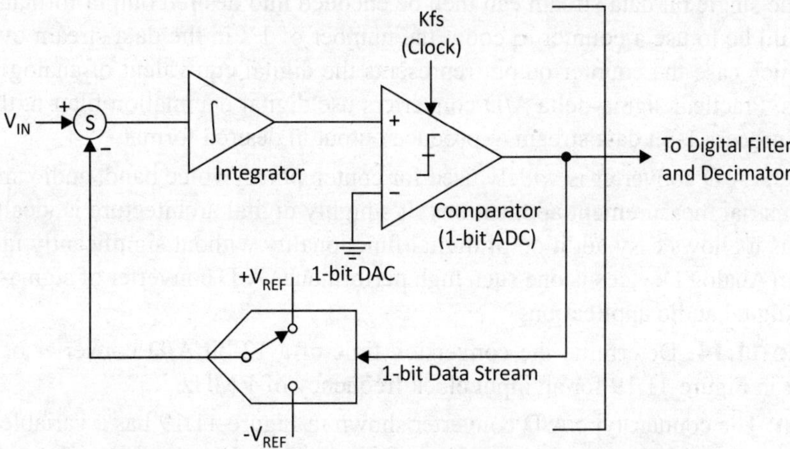

Fig. 11.26: Block schematic representation of delta modulator

The heart of sigma-delta converter is the delta modulator. Figure-11.26 shows the block schematic representation of delta modulator, which is basically a 1-bit quantizer of the flash type (single comparator). Output of delta modulator is a bit stream of 1's and 0's with number of 1's relative to number of 0's over a given number of clock cycles indicating the amplitude of analog signal over that time interval. An all 1's sequence over a given interval corresponds to maximum positive amplitude and an all 0's sequence indicates maximum negative amplitude. Equal number of 1's and 0's indicates zero amplitude. Other values between positive and negative maximum are indicated by a proportional number of 1's relative to number of 0's. This is further illustrated in Figure-11.27.

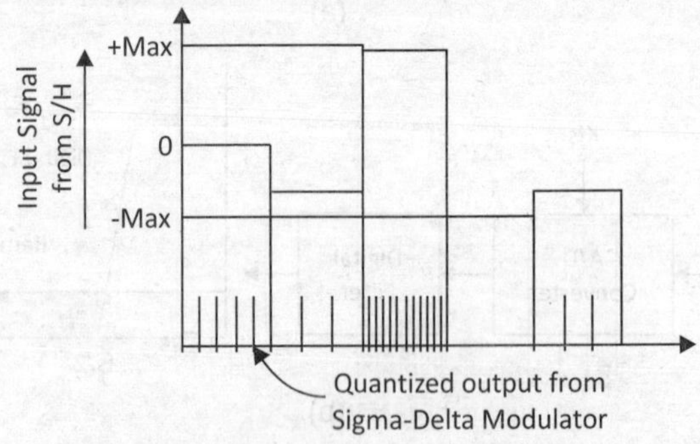

Fig. 11.27: Generation of one-bit data stream

Coming back to the delta modulator (Figure-11.26), input to the 1-bit quantizer, which is basically a comparator, is from the output of an integrator. The integrator in turn is fed from difference between analog input signal and the analog equivalent of quantized output produced by 1-bit D/A converter. 1-bit D/A converter is nothing but a two-way switch that feeds either ($+V_{REF}$) or ($-V_{REF}$) to the summing point depending upon the bit status at its input. The negative feedback loop ensures that the average value of D/A converter output nearly equals the analog input so as to produce a near zero input to the integrator.

An increase in analog signal amplitude produces a larger number of 1's at the quantizer output and consequently a higher average value of the analog signal at D/A converter output. This means that number of 1's in the quantizer output bit stream over a given time interval represents the analog signal amplitude. The single bit data stream can then be encoded into desired output format. One simple way to do this could be to use a counter to count the number of 1's in the data stream over fixed intervals of time in which case the counter output represents the digital equivalent of analog signal over those time intervals. Practical sigma-delta A/D converters use digital decimation filter at the output of delta modulator to process 1-bit data stream to produce output in desired format.

Sigma-delta A/D converter is widely used for contemporary voice band, audio and high resolution precision industrial measurement applications. It's highly digital architecture is ideally suited for such applications as it allows easy addition of digital functionality without significantly increasing the cost. AD 1871 from Analog Devices is one such high performance A/D converter of sigma-delta architecture intended for digital audio applications.

Example-11.14: Determine the conversion time of a 12-bit A/D converter of the counter type shown earlier in Figure-11.19 for an input clock frequency of 1 MHz.

Solution: The counter type A/D converter shown in Figure-11.19 has a variable conversion time, which is the maximum when the input analog voltage is just below the full scale analog input voltage. An average conversion time equal to half of the maximum conversion time is usually defined in case of such converters.

Maximum conversion time = Time taken by $\left(2^{12}-1\right)=4095$ cycles of clock input.

Clock time period = $\left[1/\left(1\times10^{6}\right)\right]=1\mu s$

Therefore, maximum conversion time = 4095 × 1 = 4095 μs = 4.095 ms

Average conversion time = (4.095/2) = 2.047 ms

Example-11.15: The A/D converter of Example-11.14 has a full scale analog input of 10 volts. Determine the digital output produced by this converter for an analog input of 3.56 volts.

Solution: Full scale analog input = 10 volts

Size of each step (or resolution) = 10/4095 = 2.442mV

Therefore, number of steps required for an analog input of 3.56 V is given by:

$3.56/\left(2.442\times10^{-3}\right)=1457.8=1458$ steps

The digital output will therefore be equal to binary equivalent of 1458.

Digital Output = 010110110010

Example-11.16: The D/A converter of a counter type A/D converter (Refer to Fig. 11.19) produces a staircase output having a step size of 10 mV. The A/D converter has a 10-bit resolution and is specified to have a quantization error of ± 1/2 LSB. Determine the digital output for an analog input of 4.012 volts. Assume that the comparator has a comparison threshold of 1 mV.

Solution: The comparator has a comparison threshold of 1 mV. With reference to Figure-11.19, it implies that for the comparator to change state, the voltage at the relevant input should be 1 mV more than the voltage at the other input. Now, one of the inputs to the comparator is the analog input voltage (= 4.012 V in the present case). The other input to the comparator is a voltage that is equal to sum of D/A converter output voltage and a fixed voltage corresponding ½ LSB. This is the case when the quantization error of A/D converter is specified to be ± ½ LSB. In case the quantization error is 1 LSB, the D/A converter directly feeds the other input of comparator.

In the present case, 1 LSB corresponds to 10 mV

Therefore, ½ LSB corresponds to 5 mV.

For an analog input of 4.012 V, the voltage at the other input needs to be 4.013 V (due to comparator threshold of 1 mV). This implies that D/A converter output needs to be 4.008 V.

Therefore, number of steps = $4.008/\left(10\times10^{-3}\right)=400.8=401mV$

Digital output is binary equivalent of (401)10, which equals 0110010001.

Example-11.17: A 10-bit A/D converter of the successive approximation type has a resolution (or quantization error) of 10 mV, Determine the digital output for an analog input of 4.365 Volts.

Solution: In case of a successive approximation type of A/D converter, the final analog output of its D/A converter portion always settles at a value below the analog input voltage to be digitized within the resolution of the converter.

Analog input voltage = 4.365 V

Resolution = 10 mV

Number of steps = $4.365/\left(10\times10^{-3}\right)=436.5$

Step number 436 will produce a D/A converter output of 436 × 10 = 4360 mV = 4.36 V and step number 437 will produce a D/A converter of 4.37 V. The A/D converter will settle at step 436. The digital output will be the binary equivalent of (436)10 , which is 0110110100.

Note: When this converter actually performs the conversion, in the tenth clock cycle, the LSB will be set to '1' initially. This would produce a D/A converter output of 4.37 V which exceeds the analog input voltage of 4.365 V. The comparator changes state, which in turn resets the LSB to '0' bringing the D/A converter output to 4.36 V. This is how a converter of this type settles. The D/A converter output settles at a value that is one step below the value that makes it exceed the analogue input to be digitized.

Example-11.18: Compare the average conversion time of an 8-bit counter type A/D converter with that of an 8-bit successive approximation type A/D converter if both are working at 10 MHz clock frequency.

Solution: Clock time period = 0.1 μs

Average conversion time in case of counter type A/D converter is given by:

$$\left[\frac{(2^8 - 1)}{2}\right] \times 0.1 = 12.75 \mu s$$

Conversion time in case of successive approximation type A/D converter is given by 8 × 0.1 = 0.8 μs.

Example-11.19: The data sheet of a certain eight-bit A/D converter lists the following specifications: Resolution: Eight bits; Full-scale error: 0.02% of full-scale; Full-scale analog input: +5 V. Determine the total possible error (in millivolts).

Solution: An eight-bit A/D converter has the following number of steps = $2^8 - 1$ = 255 steps

Therefore, the quantization error is therefore given by:

$$\frac{5}{255} V = \frac{5000}{255} mV = 19.607 \text{ mV}$$

The full-scale error, which is 0.02% of full scale, is given by:

$$\frac{0.02 \times 5000}{100} = 1 \text{ mV}$$

Therefore, the total possible error = 19.607 + 1 = 20.607 mV

Example-11.20: What will be conversion time in ms of an 8-bit successive approximation type A/D converter for an analog input of 2.0 volts and operating at 1.0 MHz? What will be the conversion time if the analog input were 4.0 volts?

Solution: Conversion time in case of successive approximation A/D converter is equal to (n) clock periods irrespective of the magnitude of the input analog voltage to be digitized. Therefore, whether the input analog voltage is 2.0 volts or 4.0 volts; the conversion time will be the same. The conversion time therefore for both cases is given by eight clock periods.

Clock period = 1 μs (for f = 1 MHz)
Conversion time = 8 μs

GLOSSARY

Accuracy (A/D converter): Accuracy describes the actual analog input and full-scale weighted equivalent of the output code corresponding to actual analog input.

Accuracy (D/A converter): Accuracy of a D/A converter is the difference between the actual analog output and the ideal expected output for a given applied digital input. Sources of error include the *Gain Error* (or full scale error), *Offset Error* (or zero scale error), *Nonlinearity Errors* and a drift of all these factors.

Acquisition time (A/D converter): Acquisition time is the time required by the electronic switch to close and the hold capacitor to charge while

A/D converter: A/D converter takes at its input an analog voltage and after a certain amount of time, produces a digital output code representing the analog input.

Aperture time (A/D converter): Aperture time is the time needed by the switch to completely open after the occurrence of hold signal.

BCD-input D/A converter: A BCD input D/A converter accepts BCD equivalent of decimal digits at its input. A 2-digit BCD D/A converter for instance is an 8-bit D/A converter.

Binary Ladder Network (D/A conversion): It is a resistive network that uses two different values of resistors. The binary ladder too produces an analog output that equals weighted sum of digital inputs.

Bipolar mode of operation(A/D converter): A/D converter configured to convert both positive as well as negative analogue input voltages is said to be operating in bipolar mode.

Bipolar output D/A converter: In bipolar output D/A converters, the analog output signal range includes both positive and negative values.

Code width (A/D converter): The quantum of input voltage change that occurs between the output code transitions expressed in LSBs of full-scale is the code width.

Companding type D/A converter: Companding type D/A converters are so constructed that the more significant bits of the digital input have a larger than binary relationship to the less significant bits. This decreases the resolution of more significant bits, which in turn increases the analog signal range.

Conversion time (A/D converter): It is the time that elapses from the time instant of the start of conversion signal until the conversion complete signal occurs.

Conversion speed (D/A converter): Conversion speed of a D/A converter is expressed in terms of its settling time. *Settling time* is the time period that has elapsed for the analog output to reach its final value within a specified error band after a digital input code change has been affected.

Counter type A/D converter: In counter type A/D converter, the counter is initially reset to all 0's. When a convert signal appears on the start-line, the input gate is enabled, and the clock pulses are allowed to the counter's clock-input. The counter, which is an UP-counter, advances through its normal binary count sequence. Counter output feeds a D/A converter and the staircase waveform generated at the output of D/A converter forms one of the inputs of the comparator, whose other input is the analog input signal. Whenever the D/A converter output exceeds the analog input voltage, the comparator changes state and the counter stops. The counter output at that instant of time is the required digital output. Counter type A/D converter has the disadvantage of a longer conversion time. Average conversion time is (2^{n-1}) clock periods.

Current Steering Mode (D/A conversion): In the current steering mode of operation of a D/A converter, the analog output is a current equal to the product of a reference voltage and a fractional binary value (D) of the input digital word. (D) is equal to sum of fractional binary values of different bits in the digital word.

D/A converter: A D/A converter takes digital data at its input and converts it into an analog voltage or current that is proportional to weighted sum of digital inputs.

Differential nonlinearity (A/D converter): Differential nonlinearity indicates the worst case difference between the actual analog voltage change and the ideal 1 LSB voltage change.

Differential nonlinearity (D/A converter): Differential Non-linearity (DNL) is the worst case deviation of any adjacent analog outputs from the ideal 1 LSB step size.

Dual-slope integrating type A/D converter: Dual-slope integrating A/D converter uses a counter, a comparator and an integrator. In dual slope type A/D converter, the integrator generates two different ramps, one with the known analog input voltage V_A generating a negative ramp and another with a known reference voltage $-V_{REF}$ generating a positive ramp. It offers better accuracy than the single-slope converter and accuracy is independent of both the integrator capacitance and the clock frequency as they affect the negative and positive slope in the same manner.

Dynamic range (D/A converter): It is the ratio of the largest output to the smallest output excluding zero expressed in dB. For linear D/A converters, it is $20\times\log2n$,which is approximately equal to $(6n)$.

Flash A/D converter: See *simultaneous A/D converter*

Gain drift (A/D converter): Gain drift is the change in the full-scale transition voltage measured over the entire operating temperature range. It is expressed in FS per degree Celsius or PPM of FS per degree Celsius or LSBs.

Gain error (A/D convertor): Gain error is the difference between the actual full-scale transition voltage and the ideal full-scale transition voltage. It is expressed either as percentage of full-scale range (% of FSR) or in LSBs.

Half-flash A/D converter: Half-flash A/D converter, also known as *Pipeline A/D converter*, is a variant of flash type converter that overcomes to a large extent the primary disadvantage of requirement of a prohibitively large number of comparators in high resolution full-flash converters without significantly degrading its high speed conversion performance. For an n-bit flash converter, number of comparators required is 2^n [$(2^n$-1) for encoding of amplitude and one comparator for polarity], the same for an equivalent half-flash converter would be $2\times(2^{n/2})$.

Monotonocity (D/A converter): A D/A converter is considered as monotonic if its analogue output either increases or remains same but does not decrease as the digital input code advances in 1 LSB steps.

Offset drift (A/D converter): Offset drift is the change with temperature of the analog zero for an A/D converter operating in the bipolar mode. It is generally expressed in PPM of FS per degree Celsius or LSBs.

Offset error (A/D converter): Offset error is the error at analog zero for an A/D converter operating in the bipolar mode. It is measured in % of FSR or in LSBs.

Multiplying type D/A converter: In a multiplying type D/A converter, the converter multiplies an analog reference by the digital input.

Nonlinearity (A/D converter): Nonlinearity specification (also referred to as the Integral nonlinearity, INL by some manufacturers) of an A/D converter describes its departure from a linear transfer curve. Nonlinearity error does not include gain, offset and quantization errors. It is expressed as a % of FS or in LSBs.

Nonlinearity (D/A converter): Non-linearity (NL) is the maximum deviation of analogue output voltage from a straight line drawn between the end points expressed as a percentage of the full scale range or in terms of LSBs.

Quantization error (A/D converter): It is the maximum deviation that can occur in the magnitude of analog voltage corresponding to digitized output from the actual magnitude of the analog signal being digitized due to process of analog signal sampling. It is equal to ± ½ LSB. It decreases with increase in number of bits for a given full scale range.

Resolution (A/D converter): Resolution of an A/D converter is the quantum of input analog voltage change required to increment its digital output between one code change and the next code change. An n-bit A/D converter can resolve 1 part in 2^n. It may be expressed as a percentage of full scale or in bits.

Resolution (D/A converter): Resolution of a D/A converter is the number of states (2^n) that the full scale range is divided or resolved into. Here (n)is the number of bits in the input digital word. An 8-bit D/A converter has 255 resolvable levels. It is said to have a percentage resolution of (1/255) × 100 = 0.39% or simply 8-bit resolution.

Sigma-delta A/D converter: Sigma-delta converter, unlike other types of A/D converters that sample analog signal at Nyquist rate, over-sample the analog signal by a large factor (i.e. sampling frequency is much larger than the Nyquist value) and also it is not the absolute value of the sample but the difference between the analog values of two successive samples that is encoded by the converter. Sigma-delta A/D converter is widely used for contemporary voice band, audio and high resolution precision industrial measurement applications. It's highly digital architecture is ideally suited for such applications as it allows easy addition of digital functionality without significantly increasing the cost.

Simultaneous A/D converter: The simultaneous method of A/D conversion is based on using a number of comparators. The number of comparators needed for n-bit A/D conversion is (2^n-1). Simultaneous A/D converters are also known as *Flash A/D converters*. The greatest advantage of this technique lies in its capability to execute extremely fast analog to digital conversion. The disadvantage is that as the number of bits in the desired digital signal increases, the number of comparators required to perform A/D conversion increases very rapidly.

Single-slope integrating type A/D converter: Single-slope integrating type A/D converter uses a counter, a comparator and an integrator. In this type of converter, one of the inputs to the comparator is a ramp of fixed slope while the other input is the analog input to be digitized. The counter and the ramp generator are initially reset to 0's. The counter starts counting with the first clock cycle input. The ramp is also synchronized to start with the first clock input. The counter stops when the ramp amplitude equals the analog input. In this case, the counter count is directly proportional to the analog signal. Single-slope A/D converter has the disadvantage of loss of accuracy due to changes in the characteristics of the ramp generator.

Successive approximation type A/D converter: Successive approximation type A/D converter aims at approximating the analog signal to be digitized by trying only one bit at a time. Conversion time for n-bit A/D converter of this type is (n) clock periods irrespective of magnitude of analog signal to be digitized.

Tracking type A/D converter: Tracking type A/D converter, also called Delta encoded A/D converter, is a modified form of counter type converter that overcomes to some extent the shortcoming of a longer conversion time of the latter. In the modified arrangement, the counter, which is primarily an UP-counter in case of counter type A/D converter, is replaced by an UP/DOWN counter. In this type of converter, whenever a new conversion is to begin, the counter is not reset to zero; in fact, it begins counting either up or down from its last value depending upon the comparator output.

Unipolar mode of operation (A/D converter): In Unipolar mode of operation, the analogue input to the A/D converter varies from 0 to full-scale voltage of one polarity only.

SUMMARY OF IMPORTANT FORMULAE

1. In a resistive divider type n-bit D/A converter, the analog output voltage is given by:

$$V_A = \frac{V_1 \times 2^0 + V_2 \times 2^1 + V_3 \times 2^2 + \cdots + V_n \times 2^{n-1}}{2^n - 1}$$

2. In a binary ladder type n-bit D/A converter, the analog output voltage is given by:

$$V_A = \frac{V_1 \times 2^0 + V_2 \times 2^1 + V_3 \times 2^2 + \cdots + V_n \times 2^{n-1}}{2^n}$$

3. Percentage resolution in an n-bit D/A Converter is given by:

$$\text{Percentage resolution} = \frac{1}{2^n - 1} \times 100$$

4. Percentage resolution in an n-bit BCD-input D/A converter is given by:

$$\text{Percentage resolution} = \left(\frac{1}{10^{n/4} - 1}\right) \times 100$$

5. The analog voltage at opamp output for current steering mode of operation for $R_F = R$ is given by:

$$-D.V_{REF}$$

Where D is the fractional binary value of input digital word and V_{REF} is the reference voltage.

6. Number of comparators required to construct an n-bit simultaneous or flash A/D converter is given by:

$2^n - 1$ (2^n including one for polarity)

7. The number of comparators required to construct n-bit half-flash A/D converter is given by:

$2 \times (2^{n/2})$

8. The average conversion time in an n-bit counter-type A/D converter is 2^{n-1} clock cycles.
9. The conversion time in an n-bit successive approximation type A/D converter equals n clock periods irrespective of amplitude of analog signal to be digitized.

REVIEW QUESTIONS

1. Briefly describe the process of digital to analog conversion in a binary ladder network. How does it overcome the shortcomings of the simple resistive network used for the same purpose? Write expression for output analog voltage for an n-bit binary ladder network.
2. Briefly describe *Resolution*, *Accuracy*, *Conversion* time and *Monotonocity* specifications of a D/A converter.
3. Briefly describe the following with reference to D/A converters.
   (a) Multiplying type D/A converter
   (b) Companding type D/A converter
   (c) Current steering mode of operation
   (d) Voltage switching mode of operation
4. With reference to A/D converters, differentiate between:
   (a) Resolution and Accuracy
   (b) Non-linearity (NL) and Differential nonlinearity (DNL)
   (c) Aperture and Acquisition times
   (d) Gain error and quantization error
5. Briefly describe the principle of operation of a Simultaneous or Flash type A/D converter. What are the merits and demerits of this type of converter? How does the architecture of flash converter differ from that of a half-flash converter?

6. Describe with the help of a schematic diagram the operation of a tracking type A/D converter. Explain how it overcomes the inherent disadvantage of a longer conversion time of the conventional counter type A/D converter.
7. Describe with the help of a schematic diagram the principle of operation of a successive approximation type A/D converter. Explain the sequence of operation of conversion of an analog signal to its digital equivalent when the expected digital output is 1011.
8. Explain the following :
   (a) Why a tracking type A/D converter is particularly suitable for fast changing analog signals?
   (b) How a sigma-delta A/D converter methodology differ from those of other types of A/D converters?
   (c) Why dual slope integrating type A/D converter has higher accuracy than a single slope integrating type A/D converter?
   (d) What does oversampling of analog signal achieve in a sigma-delta A/D converter and how does it do so?

PROBLEMS

1. An eight-bit D/A converter has a step size of 10 mV. Determine percentage resolution and full-scale output voltage.
2. Determine percentage resolution in case of a D/A converter having a step size of 10 mV and full-scale output of 5 V.
3. A 12-bit D/A converter has a resolution of 2.44 mV. Determine its analog output for a digital input of 111111111111.
4. A 12-bit binary input and a 12-bit BCD input D/A converter have the same full-scale output voltage. What would be the resolution of 12-bit binary D/A converter in mV if the resolution of BCD input converter were 10 mV?
5. Determine the resolution of a 12-bit A/D converter having a full-scale analog input voltage of 5 volts.
6. Determine average conversion time of an eight-bit counter-type A/D converter run by a 10 MHz clock. Also, determine the conversion time if it were a successive approximation type A/D converter.
7. The D/A converter of a counter type A/D converter shown earlier in Figure-11.19 produces a staircase output having a step size of 6 mV. The A/D converter has 10-bit resolution and is specified to have a quantization error of ± 1/2 LSB. Determine the digital output for an analog input of 3.65 volts. Assume that the comparator has a comparison threshold of 1 mV.
8. A 12-bit A/D converter of the successive approximation type has a resolution (or quantization error) of 6 mV, Determine the digital output for an analog input of 3.65 Volts.
9. Determine conversion time of a successive approximation type eight-bit A/D converter operating at a clock frequency of 2 MHz for analog input voltages of 2V, 3V and 4V given that full scale output voltage of 5V.
10. The data sheet of a certain 12-bit A/D converter lists the following specifications: Resolution: 12 bits; Full-scale error: 0.03% of full-scale; Full-scale analog input:+5 V. Determine the total possible error (in millivolts).

MULTIPLE CHOICE QUESTIONS

1. The resolution of an eight-bit BCD-input D/A converter with a full-scale output of 9.9 V will be
   (a) 9.9 mV (b) 99 mV
   (c) 100 mV (d) None of these
2. The conversion time in the case of an n-bit successive approximation-type A/D converter is 0.8 μs when run by a 10 MHz clock. The number of bits n is
   (a) 8 (b) 10
   (c) 12 (d) Indeterminate from given data
3. The percentage resolution of an n-bit D/A converter can be computed from
   (a) $\frac{100}{2^n}$ (b) $\frac{n}{100}$
   (c) $\frac{2^{n-1}}{100}$ (d) $\left(\frac{1}{2^n-1}\right)\times 100$
4. An analog output from a certain six-bit D/A converter for a digital input of 000100 is 400 mV. Determine the analog output for a digital input of 010101.
   (a) Indeterminate from given data (b) 2.1V
   (c) 2.65 V (d) 10.6 V
5. Among the following types of A/D converters, name the one in which the analog signal is sampled at a frequency much higher than the Nyquist rate.
   (a) Tracking-type A/D converter (b) Dual-slope integrating-type A/D converter
   (c) Half-flash A/D converter (d) Sigma–delta A/D converter
6. Architecture of a 16-bit half-flash converter comprises of
   (a) Two eight-bit-flash converters
   (b) Four four-bit-flash converter
   (c) Modified form of 16-bit-flash converter
   (d) None of these
7. A 10-bit successive approximation type A/D converter has quantization error of 10 mV. The digital output corresponding to analog input of 4.365 V would be
   (a) 0110110110 (b) 0100100100
   (c) 0110110100 (d) 1101101100
8. A successive approximation type A/D converter when run by 1 MHz clock offered a conversion time of 8 μs. What would be the conversion time if the same converter were run by a clock of 5 MHz?
   (a) 40 μs (b) 1.6 μs
   (c) 8 μs (d) None of these
9. Arrange the following A/D converter types in the ascending order of conversion speed (i.e. A/D converter with highest conversion time or lowest speed to come first and all have the same number of bits): Simultaneous A/D converter; Counter-type A/D converter; Successive approximation

A/D converter; Half-flash A/D converter

(a) Counter-type A/D converter; Successive approximation A/D converter; Half-flash A/D converter; Simultaneous A/D converter

(b) Simultaneous A/D converter; Half-flash A/D converter; Counter-type A/D converter; Successive approximation A/D converter

(c) Successive approximation A/D converter; Counter-type A/D converter; Half-flash A/D converter; Simultaneous A/D converter

(d) Counter-type A/D converter; Successive approximation A/D converter; Simultaneous A/D converter; Half-flash A/D converter

10. A 0001 input to a four-bit D/A converter produces a 1 V output. The analog output corresponding to 1000 input would be

(a) 4 V
(b) 8 V
(c) 15 V
(d) Indeterminate from given data

11. An 8 bit successive approximation A/D converter has full-scale reading of 2.55 V and its conversion time for an analog input of 1 V is 20μ. The conversion time for a 2 V input will be:

(a) 10 μs
(b) 20 μs
(c) 40 μs
(d) 50 μs

12. The number of comparators in a four-bit-flash ADC is:

(a) 4
(b) 5
(c) 15
(d) 16

13. A digital system is required to amplify a binary-encoded audio signal. The user should be able to control the gain of the amplifier from a minimum to a maximum in 100 increments. The minimum number of bits required to encode, in straight binary, is:

(a) 8
(b) 6
(c) 5
(d) 7

14. A 12-bit D/A converter has a resolution of 2.44 mV. Determine its analog output for a digital input of 111111111111.

(a) Indeterminate from given data
(b) 10 V
(c) 5 V
(d) 2.44 V

15. The number of comparators required to build an eight-bit half-flash A/D converter is

(a) 256
(b) 255
(c) 64
(d) 32

SOLUTIONS TO PROBLEMS

1. Percentage resolution can be computed as follows.

$$\left(\frac{1}{2^n-1}\right)\times 100 = \frac{100}{255} = 0.392\%$$

The step size is same as the resolution

Therefore, $\left(\frac{1}{2^8}\right)\times V = 10\times10^{-3}$

Where V is voltage corresponding to a logic '1'. This gives

$V = 10 \times 10^{-3} \times 256 = 2.56$ V

Therefore, the full-scale output is

$$\left(\frac{2^n-1}{2^n}\right)\times V = \left(\frac{2^8-1}{2^8}\right)\times 2.56 = \frac{255}{256}\times 2.56 = 2.55 \text{ V}$$

2. Percentage resolution $= \left(\frac{\text{Step size}}{\text{Full-scale output}}\right)\times 100$

$$= \left(\frac{10\times10^{-3}}{5}\right)\times 100$$

$$= 0.2\%$$

3. The resolution can be expressed by:

$$\frac{\text{Full-scale output voltage}}{2^n-1}$$

Therefore, the full-scale output voltage is given by:

$$2.44\times\left(2^n-1\right) = 2.44\times4095 = 10000mV = 10V$$

4. Full-scale output in case of BCD input D/A converter = 10 × 999 = 9.99 V

Therefore, the step size in case of binary input D/A converter is given by:

$$\frac{9.99}{2^n-1} = \frac{9.99}{4095} = 2.44 \text{ mV}$$

5. A 12-bit A/D converter resolves analog input voltage into $2^{12} - 1$ levels. The resolution is nothing but the step size. Therefore, the resolution is given by:

$$\frac{5}{2^{12}-1} = \frac{5000}{4096-1} = \frac{5000}{4095} = 1.22 \text{ mV}$$

6. The average conversion time of an n-bit counter-type A/D converter is given by 2^{n-1}clock cycles.

Therefore, the average conversion time is given by:

$2^7 = 128$ clock cycles = 128 × 0.1 µs = 12.8 µs

Conversion time in case of n-bit successive approximation A/D converter = n clock periods

Clock period = 0.1 µs

Therefore, conversion time = 8 × 0.1 = 0.8 µs

7. The comparator has a comparison threshold of 1 mV. With reference to Figure-11.19, it implies that for the comparator to change state, the voltage at the relevant input should be 1 mV more than the voltage at the other input.

Now, one of the inputs to the comparator is the analog input voltage (= 3.65 V in the present case). The other input to the comparator is a voltage that is equal to sum of D/A converter output voltage and a fixed voltage corresponding ½ LSB. This is the case when the quantization error of A/D converter is specified to be ± ½ LSB. In case the quantization error is 1 LSB, the D/A converter directly feeds the other input of comparator.

In the present case, 1 LSB corresponds to 6 mV

Therefore, ½ LSB corresponds to 3 mV.

For an analog input of 3.65 V, the voltage at the other input needs to be 3.651 V (due to comparator threshold of 1 mV). This implies that D/A converter output needs to be 3.648 V.

Therefore, number of steps $= 3.648/\left(10\times10^{-3}\right) = 364.8$

Digital output is binary equivalent of $(365)_{10}$, which equals 0101101101

8. In case of a successive approximation type of A/D converter, the final analog output of its D/A converter portion always settles at a value below the analog input voltage to be digitized within the resolution of the converter.

   Analog input voltage = 3.65 V

   Resolution = 6mV

   Number of steps $= 3.65/\left(6\times10^{-3}\right) = 608.33$

   Step number 608 will produce a D/A converter output of 608 × 6 = 3.648 V and step number 609 will produce a D/A converter of 3.654 V. The A/D converter will settle at step 608. The digital output will be the binary equivalent of (608)10 , which is 001001100000.

9. In a successive approximation A/D converter, conversion time depends only on number of bits and the clock speed. It is independent of analog input voltage to be digitized and other parameters.

   Clock frequency= 2 MHz

   Clock period = 1/2 μs = 0.5 μs

   Therefore, conversion time for all three cases = 8 × 0.5 = 4 μs

10. Number of steps in a 12-bit A/D converter is given by:

    $\left(2^{12}-1\right) = 4095$ steps

    $1600+400+100 = 2100\text{ mV} = 2.1\text{ V}$ $1600+400+100 = 2100\text{ mV} = 2.1\text{ V}$

    Therefore, the quantization error is given by:

    $$\frac{5}{4095} = \frac{5000}{4095} = 1.221\text{ mV}$$

    The full-scale error, which is 0.03% of full scale, is

    $$\frac{0.03\times5000}{100} = 1.5\text{ mV}$$

    Therefore, the total possible error is given by:

    1.221 + 1.5 = 2.721 mV

SOLUTIONS TO MULTIPLE CHOICE QUESTIONS

1. (c)

   The resolution of the given converter is given by:

   $\frac{9.9}{99} = 0.1\text{ V} = 100\text{ mV}$

2. (a)

   Conversion time in this case equals n clock cycles. For 10 MHz clock, each cycle is for 0.1ms. Since the conversion time is given to be 0.8 ms; the A/D converter has 8 bits.

3. (d)

   This is the standard formula for calculating percentage resolution of an n-bit D/A converter.

4. (b)

   The LSB here corresponds to 100 mV. Therefore, the output is obtained as follows:

   $1600 + 400 + 100 = 2100\text{ mV} = 2.1\text{ V}$

5. (d)

   Sigma-delta A/D converters are sampled at a frequency much higher than Nyquist rate to increase S/N ratio. It does so by spreading the noise over a much larger bandwidth.

6. (a)

   It is inherent to internal architecture of a half flash A/D converter.

7. (c)

   The analog input voltage is 4.365 V; the resolution is 10 mV. Therefore, the number of steps is given by:

   $$\frac{4.365}{10\times10^{-3}} = 436.5$$

   The step number 436 will produce the D/A converter output of $436 \times 10 = 4360\text{ mV} = 4.36\text{ V}$. Also, the step number 437 will produce a D/A converter of 4.37 V. The A/D converter will settle at step 436. The digital output will be the binary equivalent of $(436)_{10}$, that is, 0110110100.

8. (b)

   Conversion time is equal to n clock cycles where n is number of bits. It is an 8-bit converter as the clock period is 1.0 ms and conversion time is given to be 8.0 ms. Multiplying the clock frequency by 5 will reduce clock period by a factor of 5, which reduces the conversion time by a factor of 5.

9. (a)

   Of the types mentioned, counter type A/D converter is the slowest (average conversion time for n-bit converter = 2^{n-1} clock cycles) and simultaneous type A/D converter (conversion time depending upon only the propagation delay) is the fastest.

10. (b)

    LSB corresponds to 1 V. The other higher order bits therefore correspond to 2 V, 4 V and 8 V. Thus, the analog output corresponding to 1000 input would be 8 V.

11. (b)

    The conversion time in case of successive approximation A/D converter is independent of analog voltage to be digitized.

12. (c)

    Number of comparators = 2^n-1 (Excluding the comparator needed for polarity)

13. (d)

    From the given data, we have $2^n \geq 100$, which gives n =7.

14. (b)

    The resolution is given by:

    Therefore, the full-scale output voltage is therefore given by:

15. (d)

    The number of comparators required to construct n-bit half-flash A/D converter is equal to $2\times(2^{n/2})$ where (n) is the number of bits.

    Here, n = 8

    Therefore, required number of comparators = $2 \times 2^4 = 32$

12 Switched Capacitor Circuits

After completing this chapter, you will learn the following topics.

— Basic concepts related to switched capacitor circuits
— Switched capacitor resistors
— Switched capacitor amplifiers
— Switched capacitor integrators
— Switched capacitor filters
— Switched capacitor circuit applications in D/A converters
— Switched capacitor applications in A/D converters

Introduction

This chapter covers switched capacitor circuits. Beginning with an introduction to switched capacitor as an electronic circuit element, other important topics covered in the chapter include basic building blocks used in switched capacitor circuits and applications of switched capacitors along with opamps in a variety of electronic circuits such as amplifiers, integrators, active filters, digital-to-analog and analog-to-digital circuits. Different topics are amply illustrated with solved examples. In addition, there are a number of problems given towards the end of the chapter along with brief solutions. A self-evaluation exercise containing multiple-choice questions along with answers concludes the chapter.

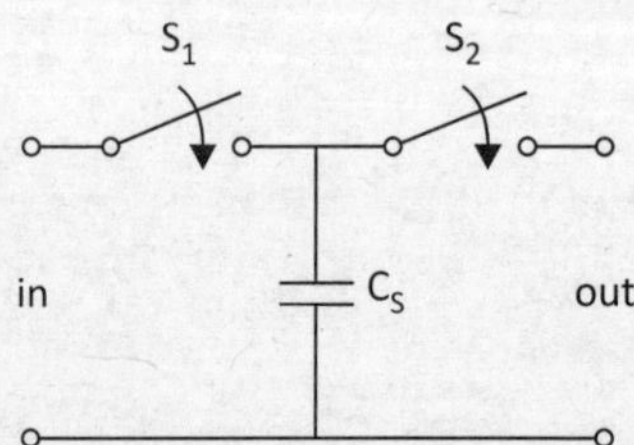

Fig. 12.1: Switched capacitor resistor

12.1 SWITCHED CAPACITORS

A *switched capacitor* is an electronic circuit element comprising MOS-based capacitors and analog switches. These are used in discrete time signal processing of analog signals. A switched capacitor works by transferring charge into and out of a capacitor when switches are rapidly opened and closed usually employing non-overlapping control signals. All switched capacitor circuits including amplifiers, integrators and filters employ only capacitors, analog switches and opamps. Resistor function in these circuits is also simulated with switched capacitors. One MOS capacitor and two MOS switches can be used to approximate a resistor (Figure 12.1). Switches S_1 and S_2 are driven by non-overlapping control signals derived from a clock signal. Switched capacitor resistors and other application circuits configured around switched capacitors are discussed in detail in the latter part of the chapter.

Switched-capacitor techniques were developed primarily to allow for the integration of both analog and digital functions on a single chip. We know that very large scale integrated (VLSI) circuits rely on MOS transistors and pico-farad range MOS capacitors for implementing different circuit functions, which implies that realization of analog circuit functions on a chip will also have to use these elements. Referring to conventional analog circuits, ratio of resistances set the transfer functions of amplifiers; magnitudes of resistances determine the operation of current-to-voltage and voltage-to-current converters and finally, the values of RC products are used in active filters and signal generators determine their frequency responses. But when these analog circuit functions are to be implemented on a silicon chip;the objective is to use MOS technology to achieve the same functionality in a much reduced area. Since switches, small-value capacitors, and decent op-amps are easily realizable in MOS technology and the fact that resistors can be replaced by MOS switches that are rapidly turned on and off, and MOS capacitors; switched-capacitor became an important building block for implementing a variety of analog and digital circuit functions in integrated circuits. Also, the time constants associated with these simulated resistances and the MOS capacitors are given in the form of capacitance ratios that are tunable through change of driving clock frequency. These time constants also have the advantage of the superior matching of capacitances fabricated on silicon, as well as their ability to track each other with temperature.

Although the initial motivation behind development of switched-capacitors was to be able to integrate analog active filters along with digital functions on a single silicon chip;besides filters, they are used to implement a large variety of analog circuit functions, which include instrumentation amplifiers, voltage-to-frequency converters, data converters, programmable capacitor arrays, balanced modulators, peak detectors, and oscillators. The advantages of using switched capacitor circuits will be further evident when we discuss different types of circuits in subsequent sections.

12.2 BUILDING BLOCKS OF SWITCHED CAPACITOR CIRCUITS

Basic building blocks of switched capacitor circuits include capacitors, switches, non-overlapping clock generating circuit and opamps or operational transconductance amplifiers (OTAs). *Double poly capacitors* that make use of capacitance between two poly-silicon layers are often used in switched capacitor circuits. Though double poly-silicon capacitors have a substantial parasitic capacitance associated with them; they offer a highly linear capacitance between the two poly-silicon layers. Figure 12.2 shows the construction of a double poly capacitor (Figure 12.2a) and its equivalent circuit (Figure 12.2b).

MOS switches are invariably used in switched capacitor circuits. The OFF-resistance of MOS switches at room temperature is of the order of Giga-ohms, which is a desirable feature. Also, the ON-resistance should be as small as possible. MOSFET switches with their small ON-resistance of the order of few tens of ohms that can be further reduced by increasing the width of the transistor during fabrication makes

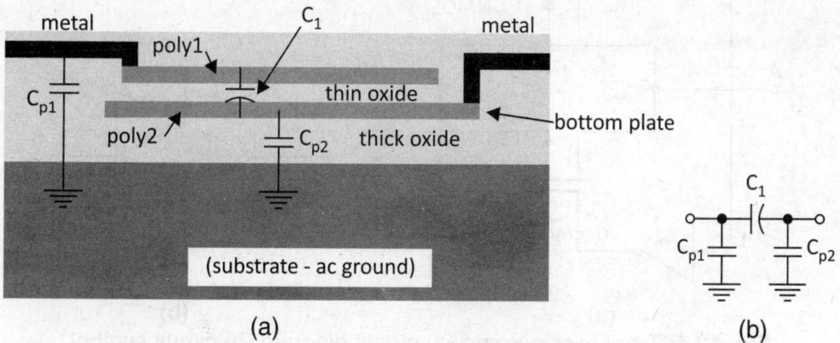

Fig. 12.2: Double poly capacitor (a) construction (b) equivalent circuit

them highly suitable for use in switched capacitor circuits. Increase in width however is associated with a consequent increase in parasitic capacitance and leakage current. Also, unlike bipolar transistors, MOS switches are free from offsets. Another advantage of MOS transistor when used as a switch is that it can be in ON-state while carrying zero current. Also, its source and drain voltages are not pinned to the gate voltage, which means that if the gate voltage varies, the source or drain voltage need not follow that variation. On the contrary, bipolar transistors lack both of these features, typically necessitating complex circuits to perform sampling.

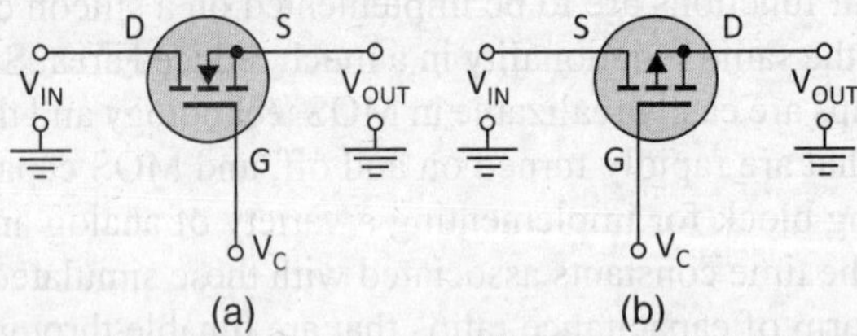

Fig. 12.3: MOS transistor switch (a) NMOS switch (b) PMOS switch

Figures 12.3 (a) and (b) respectively show use of N-channel and P-channel MOSFETs as analog switches. The N-channel MOSFETs,as shown in Figure 12.3 (a),can be used for transmission of analog signals. Assuming that the drain and source terminals are identical, the input is connected to the drain terminal and the control signal to the gate terminal. When the gate control voltage, V_C is HIGH,the NMOS transistor is turned on and it passes the input voltage to the output. If the control voltage V_C is LOW; the NMOS transistor is turned off; and the output terminal is disconnected from the input. The control voltage at the gate terminal therefore determines whether the N-channel MOSFET switch is open or closed. For proper operation of N-channel MOSFET switch, it is important that the control voltage is significantly greater than the channel threshold voltage. Operation of a P-channel MOSFET as a switch is similar to that of N-channel MOSFET with current in this case flowing in the opposite directionfrom source to drain. In the case of a P-channel MOSFET switch, the input is connected to the source terminal and the control signal to the gate terminal as shown in Figure 12.3 (b). When the gate control voltage, V_C is LOW (or negative), the P-channel MOSFET is turned on and the input voltage is passed onto the output. If it is HIGH, the MOSFET is turned off and the output terminal is disconnected from the input. Thus, the control voltage applied to the gate determines whether the transistor switch is in open or closed state. For proper operation of the P-channel MOSFET switch, V_{GS} must be significantly less than the channel threshold voltage.

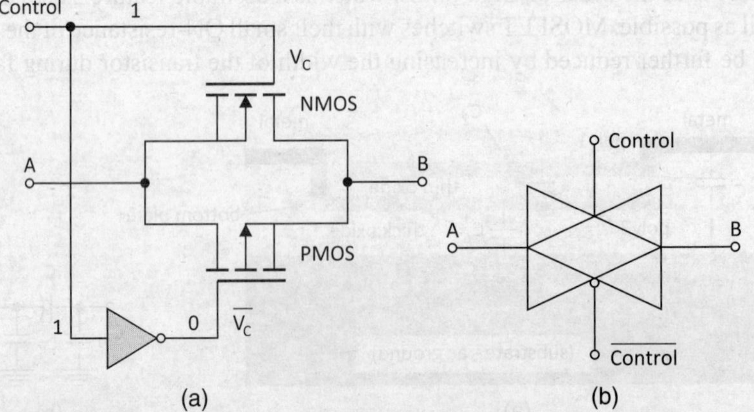

Fig. 12.4: Transmission gate (a) circuit diagram (b) circuit symbol

As described in the previous paragraph, a positive gate-to-source voltage causes current to flow in one direction from drain-to-source, while for the PMOS device, a negative gate-to-source voltage will result in current flowing in the reverse direction from source-to-drain. Thus, by combining the characteristics of the N-channel and P-channel MOSFET devices, it is possible to transmit a signal value in either direction without any degradation. This then forms the basis of a *Transmission Gate* described in the following paragraph.

Transmission gate is a bilateral switch i.e. input and output terminals are interchangeable. A transmission gate is constructed by connecting N-channel and P-channel MOSFETs in parallel. This bilateral operation is shown in the transmission gate symbol of Figure 12.4 (b), which shows two superimposed triangles pointing in opposite directions to indicate the two signal directions. An inverter connected between the gate terminals of the N-channel and P-channel MOSFETs to provide the two complementary control voltages. When the input control signal, V_C is LOW, both the MOSFETs are in the cut-off region and the switch is open. When V_C is HIGH, both devices are biased into conduction and the switch is closed. The bubble in the transmission gate symbol of Figure 12.4 (b) is indicative of gate terminal of the P-channel MOSFET. The Boolean expression defining the operation of a transmission gate is B = A.CONTROL i.e. B equals A AND CONTROL.

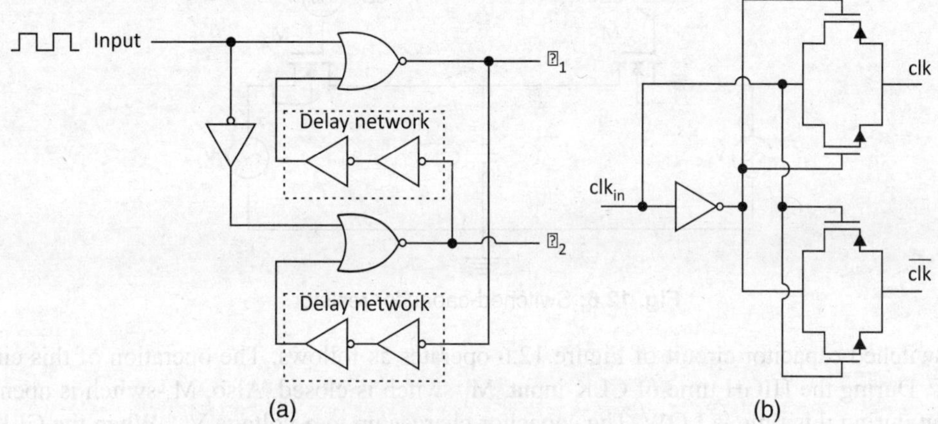

Fig. 12.5: Complementary clock generating circuit

The next important building block of a switched capacitor circuit is the *non-overlapping or complementary clock generating circuit*. As shown earlier in Figure 12.1, the basic switched capacitor circuit element i.e. a switched capacitor resistor comprises a capacitor and two MOS switches. These MOS switches are driven by complementary clock signals to function as a resistor. Various circuit configurations are possible to implement the complementary clock generating circuit. Two such circuits are shown in Figures 12.5 (a) and (b). The two circuits are self-explanatory.

Opamps or *Operational Transconductance amplifiers* (OTAs) are integral part of most switched capacitor circuits. While an opamp is a voltage controlled voltage source; OTA is a voltage controlled current source. OTA is simpler than a conventional opamp. Opamps can drive resistive loads while OTAs cannot do so. Also, OTAs have a relatively higher output impedance. While opamps are better suited to RC filters; OTAs are preferred for switched capacitor filters. As regards different characteristic parameters, DC gain sets the accuracy of charge transfer and hence transfer function accuracy; unity gain cross-over frequency, slew rate and phase margin decide the maximum clock frequency. Unity gain crossover frequency should at least be five times the clock frequency. Also, DC offsets should be as small as possible. High DC offsets lead to high output DC offsets. There are techniques available that significantly reduce the offset and also reduce (1/f) noise.

12.3 SWITCHED-CAPACITOR RESISTOR

Switched-capacitor resistor is the basic building block of switched-capacitor circuits used to implement different analog circuit functions. Figure-12.6 shows the basic circuit diagram of a switched-capacitor resistor. As is seen from the circuit diagram, it comprises a MOS capacitor and two N-channel MOSFETs. The two MOSFETs designated M_1 and M_2 are used as switches. These are driven by complementary clock pulse trains designated CLK and CLK'. The MOSFETs are turned ON when the clock pulse or the gate voltage is HIGH and turned OFF when the clock pulse or the gate voltage is LOW. The ON and OFF conditions of the MOSFETs represent the closed and open positions of the switch. Since the two MOSFETs are driven by complementary clock pulse trains; the two MOSFETs are not simultaneously ON or OFF. When M_1 is ON; M_2 is OFF and vice versa.

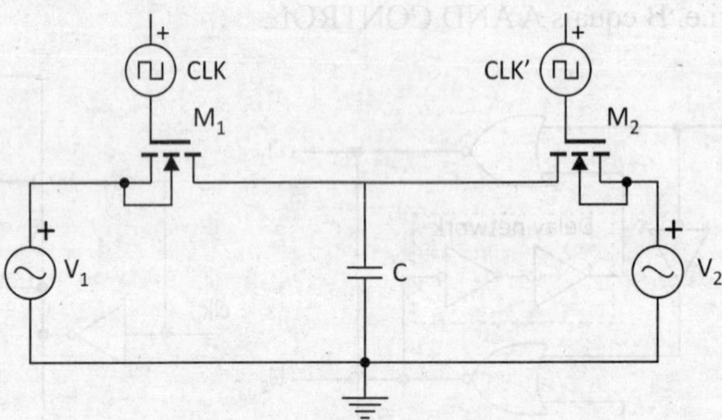

Fig. 12.6: Switched-capacitor resistor

The switched-capacitor circuit of Figure 12.6 operates as follows. The operation of this circuit is as follows. During the HIGH time of CLK input, M_1-switch is closed. Also, M_2-switch is open as the CLK' input during this time is LOW. The capacitor charges up to a voltage V_1 . When the CLK input goes to LOW state; M_1-switch becomes open while M_2-switch closes. The capacitor discharges down to/charges up to a voltage V_2 depending upon whether V_2 is smaller or greater than V_1. As a result of consecutive switching operations, there is a net charge transfer, which assuming V_1 to be greater than V_2 is given by eqn. 12.1.

$$\Delta Q = C \times \Delta V = C \times (V_1 - V_2) \tag{12.1}$$

For a clock frequency of f_{CLK}, the net charge transferred to capacitor is given by eqn. 12.2.

$$\text{Charge transferred per unit time} = \Delta Q \times f_{CLK} = C \times \Delta V = C \times f_{CLK} \times (V_1 - V_2) \tag{12.2}$$

Charge transferred per unit time is the average current, I_{av} given by eqn. 12.3.

$$I_{av} = C \times f_{CLK} \times (V_1 - V_2) \tag{12.3}$$

If the clock frequency were much higher than the frequency of the applied V_1 and V_2 signals; the switching process can be considered to be continuous and the switched capacitor can be modelled as an equivalent resistance as shown in Figure 12.7. The magnitude of this equivalent resistance is given by eqn. 12.3.

$$R_{eq} = \frac{(V_1 - V_2)}{I_{av}} = \frac{1}{(C \times f_{CLK})} = \frac{T}{C} \tag{12.4}$$

Where T is the time period of the clock signal.

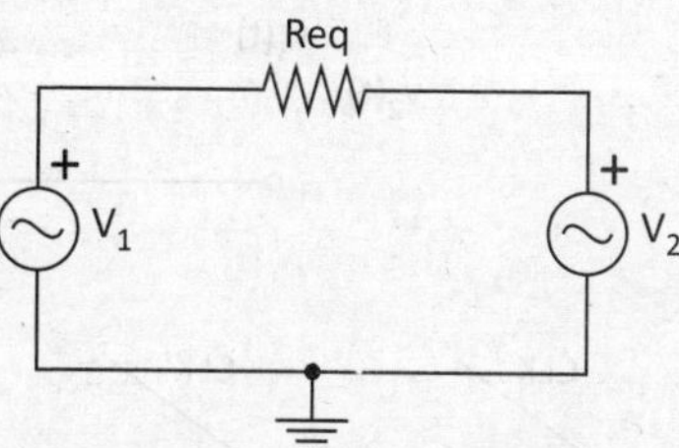

Fig. 12.7: Switched-capacitor as an equivalent resistance

Switched-capacitor resistors bring a number of advantages when it comes to integrating analog circuit functions on a chip. The important ones include the following.

1. It allows implementation of large value resistors in a very small area on the chip. As an example, a 10 MW resistor may be realized with a 10 pF capacitor switched at a clock frequency of 10 kHz.
2. Switched-capacitor topology allows realization of time constants with high accuracy. The time constant is the product of resistance value of switched-capacitor resistor and the capacitance. Since equivalent resistance is proportional to $(1/(C \times f_{CLK})$; the time constant therefore is proportional to ratio of two capacitances and inversely proportional to the clock frequency. Capacitor ratios, particularly in monolithic form, are very robust against temperature changes and clock frequencies can also be strictly controlled. This makes it possible to realize accurate time constants using switched-capacitor circuits.

Switched-capacitor topology comes with certain constraints, the principle one being the need for the clock frequency to be much higher than the critical frequency dictated by the RC products in the circuit. Another major constraint is the need to have zero impedance nodes on either side of MOSFET switches. Some of the other design constraints include the following. In switched-capacitor circuits using opamps, there is a need for the feedback path around the opamp to be closed continuously to ensure stability. A switched-capacitor resistor with its sampled data construction cannot be used in the feedback path all by itself. Secondly, all circuit nodes must have a resistive path to ground so as to prohibit charge build-up on the capacitor plates. Thirdly, the bottom plates of MOS capacitors must be connected to AC ground or a voltage source so that the parasitic capacitance associated with the bottom plate does not affect the overall response of switched-capacitor filter. And finally, the non-inverting terminal of the opamp should be kept at a constant voltage and should not be connected to the signal in any way. This would ensure that the inverting input is always at virtual ground thereby eliminating an undesirable change in filter response due to MOS capacitor's parasitic capacitance.

There are switched capacitor circuit arrangements other than the one shown in Figure 12.6 and discussed in the preceding paragraphs that can be used to emulate a resistor. While the switched -capacitor circuit shown in Figure 12.6 is known as the parallel configuration; other circuit configurations are called *series*, *series-parallel* and *bilinear*. Series, series-parallel and bilinear configurations are respectively shown in Figures 12.8 (a), (b) and (c).

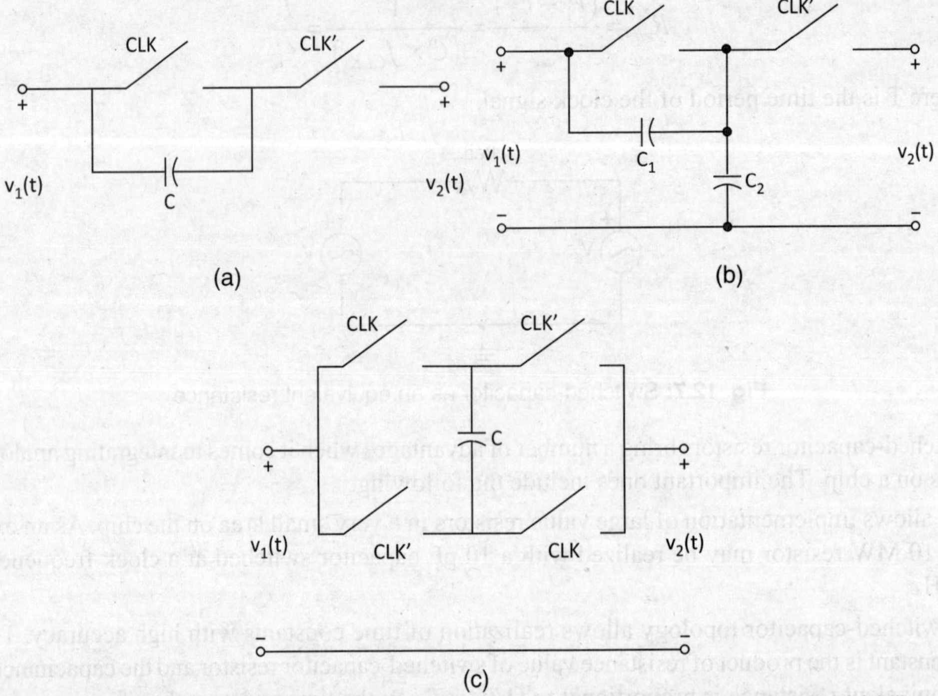

Fig. 12.8: Oher forms of switched-capacitor resistors (a) series (b) series-parallel (c) bilinear

In the case of series configuration, equivalent resistance value is given by eqn. 12.5.

$$R_{eq}(series) = \frac{1}{(C \times f_{CLK})} = \frac{T}{C} \tag{12.5}$$

In the case of series-parallel configuration, equivalent resistance value is given by eqn. 12.6.

$$R_{eq}(series-parallel) = \frac{1}{((C_1 + C_2) \times f_{CLK})} = \frac{T}{(C_1 + C_2)} \tag{12.6}$$

In the case of bilinear configuration, equivalent resistance value is given by eqn. 12.7.

$$R_{eq}(bi-linear) = \frac{1}{(4C \times f_{CLK})} = \frac{T}{4C} \tag{12.7}$$

Example-12.1: Refer to the switched capacitor resistor circuit of Figure 12.9. Determine the capacitance C to emulate a resistance of 1 MW assuming that the frequency of clock signal and is 100kHz.

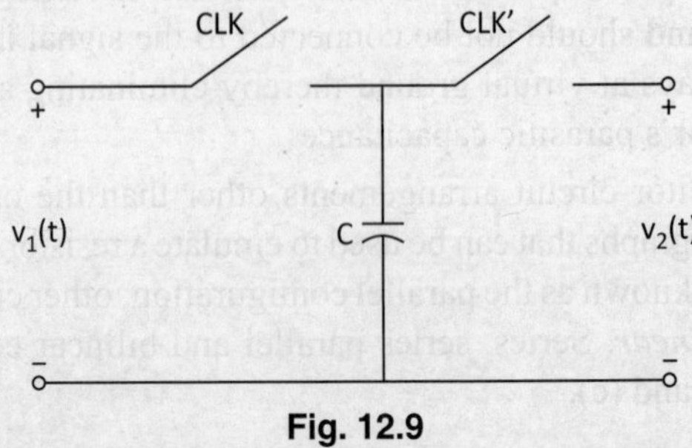

Fig. 12.9

Solution: Equivalent resistance value for the switched capacitor resistor shown in Figure 12.9 is given by:

$$R_{eq} = \frac{1}{(C \times f_{CLK})}$$

Therefore, $C = \dfrac{1}{(R_{eq} \times f_{CLK})} = \dfrac{1}{(1 \times 10^6 \times 100 \times 10^3)} = 10\,pF$

Example-12.2: At what clock frequency should a series-parallel switched-capacitor resistor circuit of Figure 12.10 be clocked to emulate a resistance value of 1 MΩ if $C_1 = C_2 = 10$ pF. f_1 and f_2 here represent complementary clock signals.

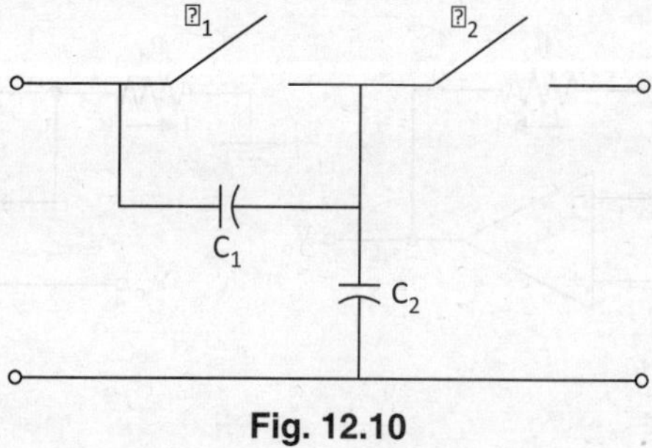

Fig. 12.10

Solution:

$$R_{eq}(series - parallel) = \frac{1}{[(C_1 + C_2) \times f_{CLK}]} = \frac{T}{(C_1 + C_2)}$$

For $C_1 = C_2 = C$

$R_{eq}(series - parallel) = \dfrac{T}{2C}$, where T = Clock signal time period

Which gives, $T = 2CR_{eq}$

It is given that C = 10 pF and R_{eq} = 1 MΩ

Therefore, $T = 2 \times 10 \times 10^{-12} \times 1 \times 10^6 = 2 \times 10^{-5}\ s$

This gives $f = \dfrac{1}{2 \times 10^{-5}} Hz = 50 kHz$

12.4 SWITCHED CAPACITOR AMPLIFIERS

As discussed earlier in section 12.1, VLSI circuits rely heavily on MOS technology and the fact that Pico-Farad capacitors, MOS switches and opamps with decent specifications can be conveniently implemented using MOS technology; switched capacitor circuits are commonly used to implement a variety of analog circuit functions. When used to build amplifiers, they overcome some of the important shortcomings associated with bipolar amplifiers. It may be mentioned here that the gain accuracy largely depends upon the magnitude of open loop gain, which is evident from the generalized expressions for closed loop voltage gain in the case of inverting and non-inverting amplifier configurations. The two configurations are shown in Figures 12.11 (a) and (b). The corresponding expressions for voltage gain are given in eqns. 12.8 (inverting amplifier) and 12.9 (non-inverting amplifier). As isevident from these expressions; assuming that open loop gain A_{OL} is infinite, the expressions for closed loop voltage gain reduce to eqns. 12.10 (inverting amplifier) and 12.11 (non-inverting amplifier). Any value of AOL less than infinity affects the gain accuracy. Lower the open loop gain, higher is the inaccuracy. Opamp circuits are discussed in detail in chapter-10.

$$A_{CL} = \frac{A_{OL}(R_1 + R_2)}{R_1 + R_2 + A_{OL} R_1} \tag{12.9}$$

$$A_{CL} = -\left(\frac{R_2}{R_1}\right) \tag{12.10}$$

$$A_{CL} = 1 + \frac{R_2}{R_1} \tag{12.11}$$

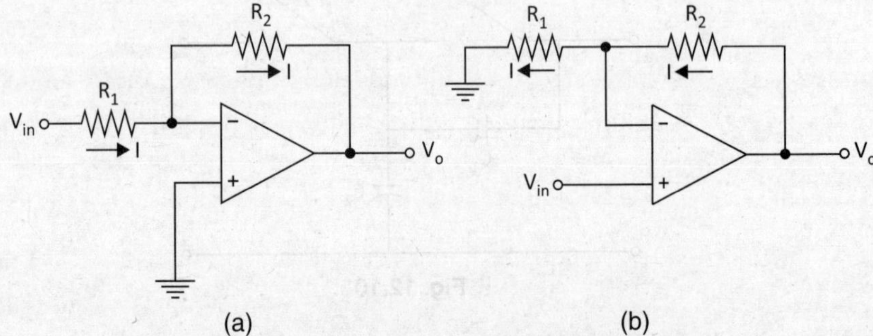

Fig. 12.11: Amplifiers (a) inverting (b) non-inverting

In CMOS opamps, open loop output resistance of the opamp is maximized to increase the magnitude of open loop gain to achieve an acceptable gain accuracy. R_2 tends to reduce the output resistance and hence the gain accuracy. One possible remedy is to use capacitors in place of resistors as shown in the inverting amplifier configuration of Figure 12.12 (a). The voltage gain provided by this circuit is given by eqn. 12.12.

$$A_{CL} = -\left(\frac{C_1}{C_2}\right) \tag{12.12}$$

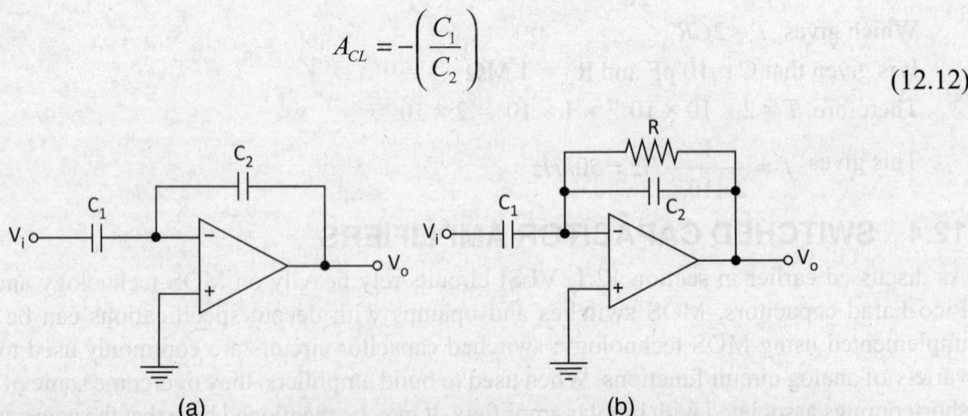

Fig. 12.12: Continuous time amplifiers using capacitors (a) without feedback resistor (b) with feedback resistor

A disadvantage with this circuit is the issue of setting of bias at the junction of C_1 and C_2. This may be overcome by connecting a large value resistance across C_2 as shown in Figure 12.12 (b). The associated disadvantage is that the RC_2 product makes it a high pass amplifier and therefore renders it unsuitable for amplifying wideband signals. Also, the closed loop gain A_{CL} for the circuit of Figure 12.12 (b) is given by eqn. 12.13.For w>> $(1/RC_2)$, the product (RC_2s) becomes much greater than 1 with the result that eqn. 12.13 reduces to eqn. 12.14. Satisfying this condition often leads to prohibitively large values of R and C_2.

$$\frac{V_o(s)}{V_i(s)} = -\frac{RC_1s}{(RC_2s+1)} \tag{12.13}$$

$$\frac{V_o(s)}{V_i(s)} = -\frac{C_1}{C_2} \tag{12.14}$$

Therefore, there is need to identify other techniques for establishing the bias while using capacitive feedback networks. It is where switched capacitor technology comes in. Switched capacitor amplifier fundamentals and different amplifier configurations are discussed in the following sections.

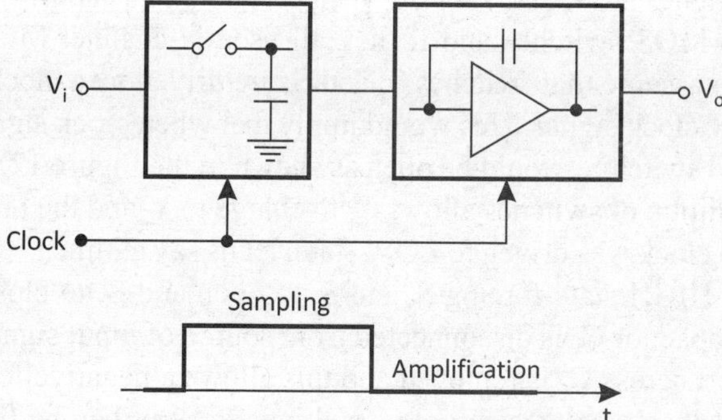

Fig. 12.13: Basic building blocks of switched capacitor amplifier

12.4.1 Basic Switched Capacitor Amplifier

Figure 12.13 shows the arrangement of the basic building blocks of a switched capacitor amplifier. A switched capacitor amplifier operates in two phases namely the *sampling phase* and the *amplification phase*. The two phases are controlled by a clock signal, which is usually a set of two complementary clock signals. During the sampling phase, the input capacitor is charged to V_i. The output voltage V_o during this phase is zero as the feedback path is kept shorted. During the amplification phase, the charged input capacitor becomes disconnected from the source of input signal; the short across the feedback path is removed and the stored charge is transferred to the feedback capacitor thereby producing an amplified output signal. The processes of sampling and amplification can be best explained with the help of a typical switched capacitor amplifier circuit as shown in Figure 12.14.

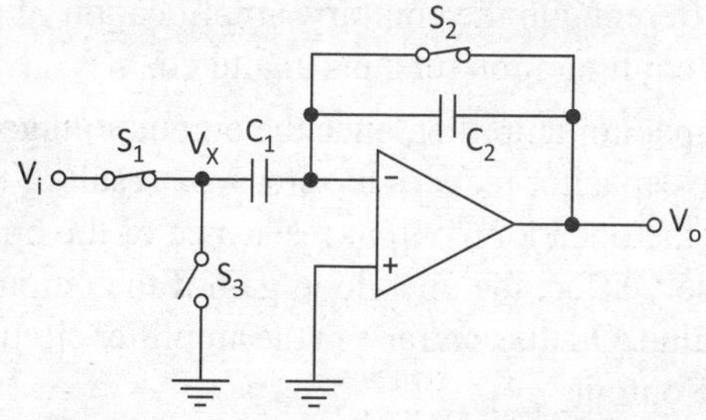

Fig. 12.14: A typical switched capacitor amplifier

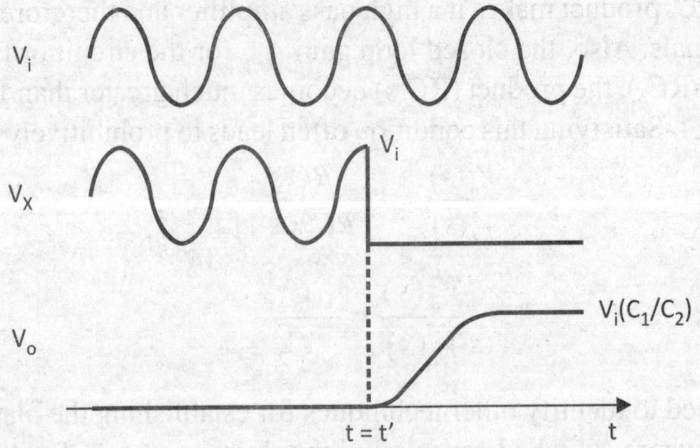

Fig. 12.15: Relevant waveforms for the circuit of Figure-12.14

Let us assume that switches S_1, S_2 and S_3 close when clock signal is HIGH and open when the clock signal is LOW. These are MOS switches and if they all used N-channel MOSFETs, the assumption would be valid. Let us also assume that switches S_1 and S_2 are driven by a clock signal and switch S_3 is driven by a complementary clock signal. This would imply that when clock signal is HIGH, switches S_1 and S_2 would be closed and switch S_3 would be open as shown in the Figure 12.14. This is the set-up for sampling phase as the condition of switches allows C_1 to charge to V_i and the output voltage V_o is forced to remain zero. Now, if the clock was driven to LOW state, let us say at time t = t'; complementary clock signal would be driven to HIGH state forcing S_1 and S_2 to open and S_3 to close. This is the set-up for the amplification phase. Capacitor C_1 is disconnected from source of input signal and its positive side is grounded through S3. Short across C_2 is removed and this allows a negative feedback through C_2. Due to presence of negative feedback, voltage across C_1 is driven to zero thereby forcing transfer of charge from C_1 to C_2. That is, $C_1.V_i = C_2.V_o$. The output voltage Vo is therefore amplified V_i. Waveforms shown in Figure 12.15 further illustrate this point.

Therefore,
$$\frac{V_o}{V_i} = \frac{C_1}{C_2} \tag{12.15}$$

There are certain distinct features of a switched capacitor amplifier of Figure 12.14, which distinguish it from a continuous time implementation shown in circuit diagrams of Figure 12.11. These include the following.

1. The switched capacitor amplifier, as briefly described in the previous paragraphs, has two distinct phases. When the input signal is being sampled; the output is set to zero and there is no amplification. In the second phase, there is no sampling of input signal and the input signal sampled during preceding phase is amplified. Also, the two circuit configurations in the two phases is considerably different. On the contrary, amplification of input signal is on continuous time basis and the circuit configuration remains unaltered.

2. In the case of switched capacitor amplifier, once the output voltage settles to the amplified input value; current through the capacitor reduces to zero. As a result of this, there is no loading effect of feedback capacitor on the open loop output resistance of the opamp. The feedback capacitor therefore does not adversely affect the open loop gain if the output voltage were given enough time to settle to its final value. On the contrary, in the amplifier circuits of Figure 12.11, resistance R_2 continuously loads the output.

3. Switched capacitor amplifiers are highly amenable to implementation with CMOS technology as compared to their implementation in bipolar and other technologies. This is because the two most desirable requirements of discrete time operations are the switches and high input impedance, and both are conveniently available in CMOS technology.

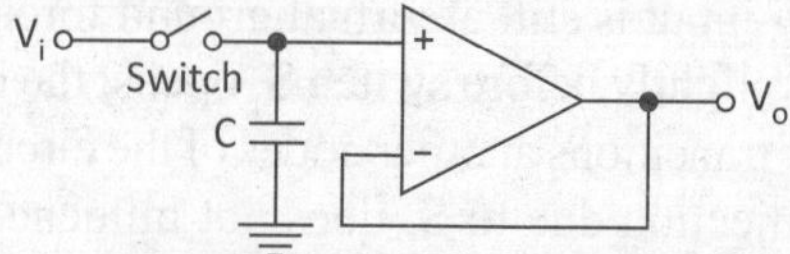

Fig. 12.16: Unity gain buffer

12.4.2 Switched Capacitor Unity Gain Buffer

Switched capacitor unity gain buffer essentially comprises a sampling circuit followed by a unity gain opamp buffer. Figure 12.16 shows one such circuit configuration. This circuit however suffers from certain shortcomings. Switched capacitor circuits use MOS switches. For a MOSFET to be ON, there has to be a channel of charge carriers at the oxide-silicon interface. The channel charge is input voltage dependent. When the MOSFET is turned OFF, a fraction of the channel charge is injected onto the capacitor leading to inaccuracy in stored charge, which depending upon capacitance of the sampling capacitor causes inaccuracy in the magnitude of sampled voltage. The channel charge of MOS switch is equal to the product of channel capacitance and threshold voltage. Channel capacitance in turn is given by product of C_{ox}, W and L where C_{ox}, W and L respectively are oxide capacitance per unit area, channel width and channel length. Inaccuracy or gain error and offset error is input voltage dependent. Another source of inaccuracy is the clock feed through gate-drain or gate-source capacitance. Thermal noise voltage introduced by the ON-resistance of MOS switch also contributes to charge stored on the capacitor and is yet another source of error. Thermal noise voltage is approximately equal to $\sqrt{KT/C}$. Also, non-linear dependence of MOSFET's threshold voltage V_{TH} on V_i causes nonlinearity. These shortcomings to a large extent are overcome in the unity gain buffer circuit of Figure 12.17.

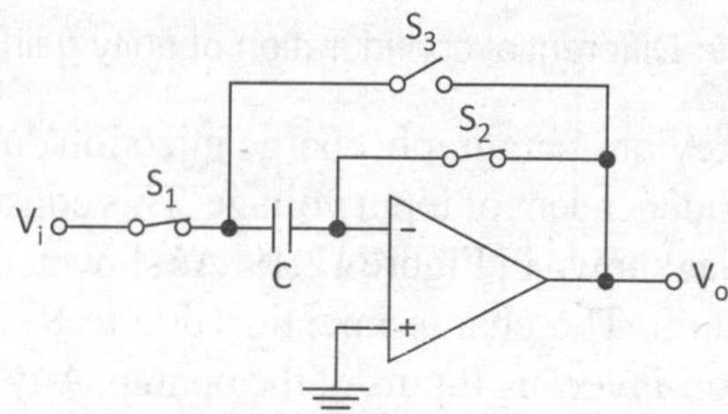

Fig. 12.17: Improved unity gain buffer (a) sampling (b) amplification

During the sampling phase, switches S_1 and S_2 are closed and switch S_3 is open as shown in Figure 12.17. The clock signal applied to S_3 is complement of the clock signal applied to S_1 and S_2. At the time of S_1 and S_2 switching to open state and S_3 switching to closed state, the capacitor C would have charged to a certain voltage V. After the switches S_1, S_2 and S_3 change state, the circuit diagram effectively reduces to the one shown in Figure 12.18. The charge stored in the capacitor at the time of switches changing state is conserved and the output voltage is equal to V. This is how the circuit functions as a unity gain buffer.

Let us now study the effect of charge injection due to switches S_1, S_2 and S_3. It is observed that with proper clock signal timing to ensure that switch S_2 opens slightly before switch S_1 rather than the two switches opening simultaneously, channel charge injection due to S_1 causes only an offset error that is independent of input voltage and has no adverse effect on gain error. Also, it does not contribute to input-output circuit non-linearity. Also, channel charge injection due to S_1 and S_3 is unimportant and has no adverse effect on either gain error or offset error. It may be mentioned here that at the time of opening of switch S_2, inverting input is at virtual ground and charge stored in the capacitor is frozen at CV. After the feedback path is restored, inverting input is still at virtual ground forcing capacitor C to carry the same charge. Also, when switch S_2 opens slightly before switch S_1 opens; the inverting input floats maintaining a constant total charge regardless of transitions at other nodes of the circuit. As a result, when the feedback configuration is restored, charge injection due to S_1 does not influence the output voltage. The charge on capacitor C is also unaffected by closing of switch S_3. The channel charge required to turn S_3 on is supplied entirely by the opamp.

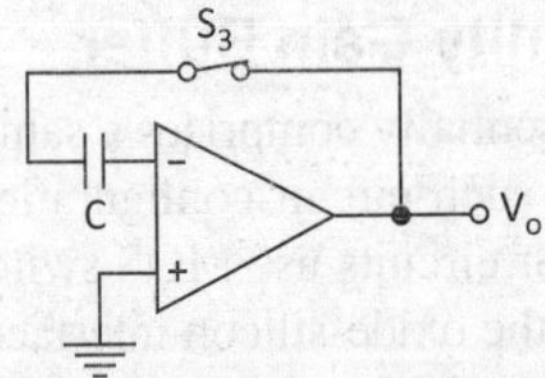

Fig. 12.18: Unity gain buffer in amplification mode

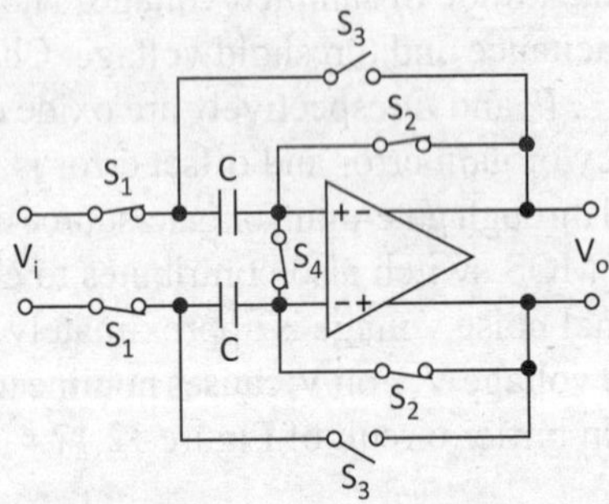

Fig. 12.19: Differential configuration of unity gain buffer

As already mentioned in the previous paragraph, charge injection due to opening of switch S_2 causes an offset error that is constant and independent of input voltage. This constant offset error can be cancelled by using differential configuration as shown in Figure 12.19. As shown, the circuit employs a differential opamp with two sampling capacitors. The charge injection due to S_2 and S_2' appear as common ode disturbances at the inverting and non-inverting inputs of the opamp. Any mismatch in the charge injected by turning off of S_2 and S_2' is further equalized by using another switch S_4 between inverting and non-inverting input nodes of the opamp and making this switch turn off slightly after S_2 and S_2' and before S_1 and S_1'. This helps in equalizing charges at inverting and non-inverting input nodes of the opamp.

The output voltage and gain error of the unity gain buffer circuit described in this section are respectively given by eqns. 12.16 and 12.17.

Output voltage,
$$V_o = \frac{V}{\left[1 + \dfrac{1}{A_V\left\{\dfrac{C_{in}}{C} + 1\right\}}\right]} \tag{12.16}$$

Gain error,
$$\frac{\Delta V_o}{\Delta V} = -\frac{1}{A_V\left\{\frac{C_{in}}{C}+1\right\}} \tag{12.17}$$

Where C_{in} is the input capacitance of the opamp.

For $C_{in}/C << 1$ and $A_v \rightarrow$ infinity, $V_o = V$

Equations 12.16 and 12.17 underline the importance of an opamp with a very high open loop gain and a small input capacitance. Though a lower value of C_{in} is important from the viewpoint of achieving higher speed; it should be minimized even if speed is not the consideration.

12.4.3 Non-inverting Amplifier

Non-inverting amplifier switched capacitor amplifier was discussed earlier in earlier part of section 12.3. The non-inverting amplifier circuit was shown earlier in Figure 12.14. Again, with proper timing, the output voltage can be made free from the effects of charge injection due to S_1 and charge absorption due to S_3. Also, constant offset error due to charge injection from S_2 can be taken care of by employing differential configuration. Figure 12.20 shows differential circuit realization of a switched capacitor non-inverting amplifier.

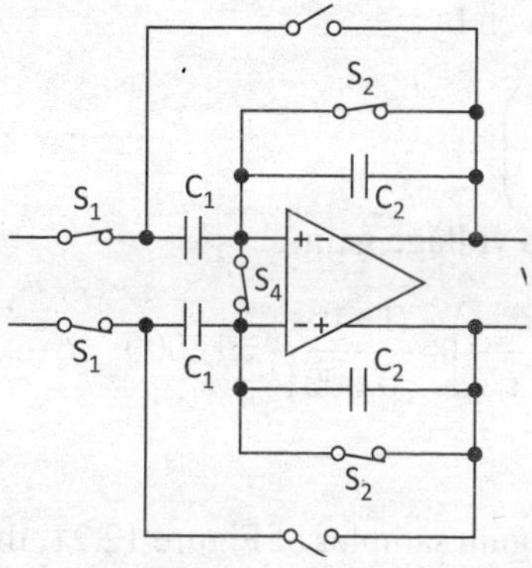

Fig. 12.20: Differential configuration of non-inverting amplifier

The voltage gain and gain error of the non-inverting amplifier described in this section are respectively given by eqns. 12.18 and 12.19.

Voltage gain,
$$\frac{V_o}{V_i} = \frac{C_1}{\left[C_2 + (C_1 + C_2 + C_{in})/A_V\right]} \tag{12.18}$$

Gain error,
$$\frac{\Delta V_o}{\Delta V} = \frac{(C_1 + C_2 + C_{in})}{A_V C_2} \tag{12.19}$$

Where, C_{in} is the input capacitance of the opamp.

For $A_v \rightarrow$ infinity, $\frac{V_o}{V_i} = \frac{C_1}{C_2}$

A non-inverting amplifier with a relatively high closed loop gain suffers from precision and speed degradation. Inferior precision and speed of response in the case of non-inverting amplifier with a larger closed loop gain as compared to a unity gain buffer is due to lower feedback factor in the case of former.

Equations 12.16 and 12.17 also underline the importance of an opamp with a very high open loop gain and a small input capacitance. Though a lower value of C_{in} is important from the viewpoint of achieving higher speed; it should be minimized even if speed is not the consideration. Also, the gain error in case of non-inverting amplifier is greater than in case of a unity gain buffer. The gain error depends upon the value of gain. if C_{in} is considered negligible, we shall find that the gain error in non-inverting amplifier configuration having unity gain is twice that in the case of unity gain buffer configuration.

Example-12.3: Figure 12.21 shows a unity gain buffer both in sampling and amplification modes. If the input capacitance of the opamp is 1 pF; then determine the minimum acceptable value of open loop gain to ensure that the gain accuracy of not poorer than 0.01%.

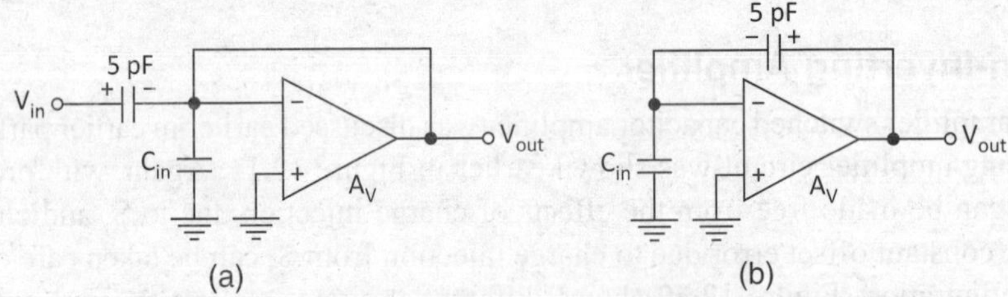

Fig. 12.21: Example-12.3 (a) sampling mode (b) amplification mode

Solution: Gain accuracy is given by:

$$\text{Gain error} = \left(\frac{1}{A_V}\right)\times\left(1+\frac{C_{in}}{C}\right)$$

Therefore, Minimum open loop voltage gain,

$$A_v(\min) = \left(\frac{1}{\text{Gain error}}\right)\times\left(1+\frac{C_{in}}{C}\right) = \frac{(1+0.2)}{0.0001} = 12000$$

Therefore A_v (min) = 12000

Example 12.4: If in the unity gain sampler of Figure 12.21, the opamp used had an open loop gain of 50000 and the input capacitance were 0.5 pF; what would be the percentage gain error?

Solution: $\text{Gain error} = \left(\frac{1}{A_V}\right)\times\left(1+\frac{C_{in}}{C}\right)$

Now, A_v = 50000, C_{in} = 0.5 pF

$$\text{Therefore, Gain error} = \left(\frac{1}{50000}\right)\times(1+0.1) = \frac{1.1}{50000} = 0.000022 = 0.0022\%$$

The result underlines the importance of reduced input capacitance and increased open loop gain.

Example 12.5: Refer to the differential amplifier realization of a switched capacitor non-inverting amplifier as shown in Figure 12.22. Given that C_1 = 2 pF, C_2 = 1 pF, channel capacitance WLC_{ox} = 50 fF and V_{TH} = 0.5V; determine DC offset voltage appearing at the output assuming a threshold voltage mismatch of 10 mV between S_2 and S_2' and also that all of the channel charge of S_2 and S_2' is respectively injected into non-inverting and inverting inputs of the opamp.

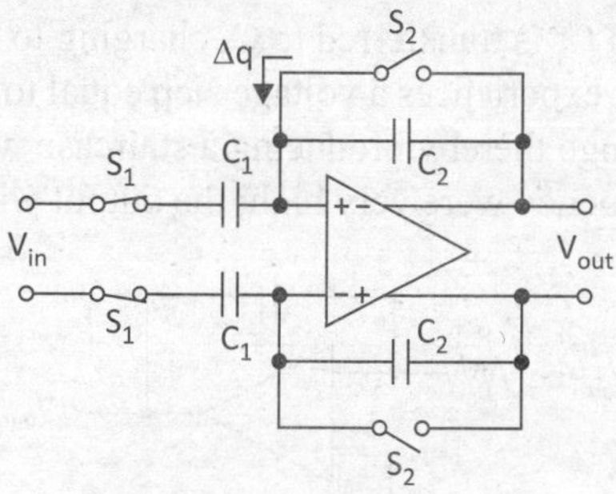

Fig. 12.22: Example 12.5

Solution: Injected charge = Channel capacitance × Threshold voltage mismatch

$$= 50\times10^{-15}\times10\times10^{-3} = 5\times10^{-16}\,Coulomb$$

With non-inverting input being at virtual ground, there is a negligible change in voltage across C_1. The injected charge resides primarily on C_2.

Therefore, DC offset voltage at output $= \dfrac{5\times10^{-16}}{10^{-12}}V = 0.5mV$

Example-12.6: In the non-inverting amplifier circuit of Figure 12.14, $C_1 = 5$ pF, $C_2 = 1$ pF and $C_{in} = 0.5$ pF. If the gain error were not to exceed 0.1%; determine the minimum value of open loop gain of opamp. What would be the gain error if open loop gain of the chosen opamp had infinite open loop gain.

Solution: Gain error in a non-inverting amplifier as given by eqn. 12.19 $= \dfrac{(C_1 + C_2 + C_{in})}{A_V C_2}$

Substituting for maximum allowed gain error, C_1, C_2 and C_{in}, we get:

$$0.001 = \frac{(5+1+0.5)}{A_V \times 1} = \frac{6.5}{A_V(\min)}$$

Therefore, $A_V(\min) = \dfrac{6.5}{0.001} = 6500$

For $A_V \to \infty$, gain error $= \dfrac{6.5}{\infty} = 0$

12.5 SWITCHED CAPACITOR INTEGRATOR

An integrator is an important building block of a number of analog circuit functions including a variety of filters, analog to digital converters etc. Figure 12.23 the basic continuous time opamp-based RC integrator circuit. Assuming a very large open loop gain of the opamp, the output voltage V_{out} is given by eqn. 12.20.

$$V_{out} = -\frac{1}{RC}\int V_{in}\,dt \tag{12.20}$$

If we replace resistance *R*is replaced by its switched capacitor counterpart, we get the discrete circuit equivalent of the continuous time integrator of Figure 12.23. Figure 12.24 (a) shows the discrete circuit integrator. It is an inverting integrator. When fed with a constant input voltage at the input, the circuit functions as follows.

MOS switches S_1 and S_2 are driven by complementary clock signals, which means when S_1 is closed or on, switch S_2 is open or off and vice versa. When S_1 is closed, capacitor C_1 charges to V_i. When S_1 opens and S_2 closes; the charge stored in C_1 is transferred to C_2 charging to a voltage equal to $(C_1/C_2)V_i$. Thus, during one clock cycle, the output experiences a voltage step equal to $(C_1/C_2)V_i$. Every subsequent clock cycle produces a similar step change thereby producing a staircase waveform at the output as shown in Figure 12.24 (b). If the clock frequency were very high; the output will tend towards a continuous ramp.

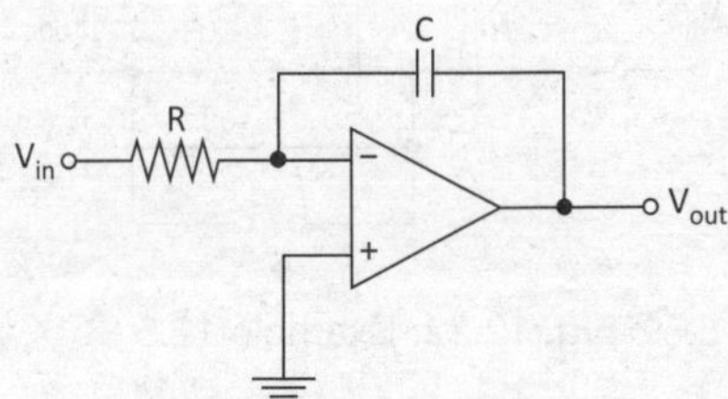

Fig. 12.23: Continuous time RC integrator

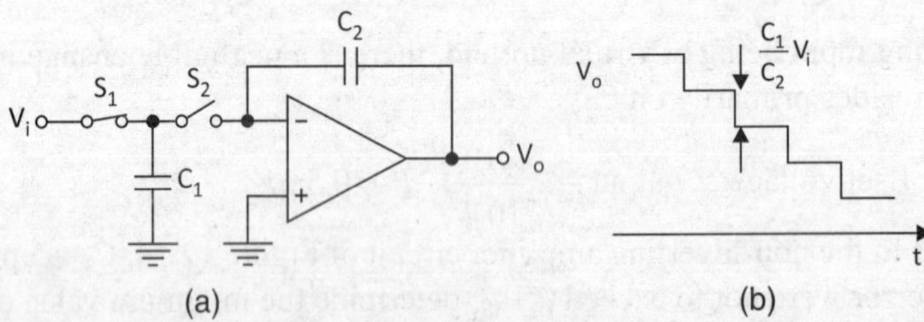

Fig. 12.24: Switched capacitor inverting integrator (a) circuit diagram (b) output waveform

If the input to the integrator were an AC signal of frequency (f) and if the clock frequency were much higher than (f); then the transfer function of the switched capacitor integrator of Figure 12.24 (a) are given by eqn. 12.21.

(12.21)

Now, $R_{eq} = \dfrac{1}{C_1 f_{CLK}}$, which gives $\dfrac{V_o}{V_i} = \dfrac{(1/C_2 s)}{R_{eq}}$

$$\frac{V_o}{V_i} = -\left(\frac{C_1}{C_2 s}\right) \times f_{CLK} = -\left(\frac{C_1}{j2\pi f C_2}\right) \times f_{CLK} = -\frac{1}{j(f/f_o)} \qquad (12.22)$$

Where $f_o = \dfrac{1}{2\pi}\left(\dfrac{C_1}{C_2}\right) f_{CLK}$

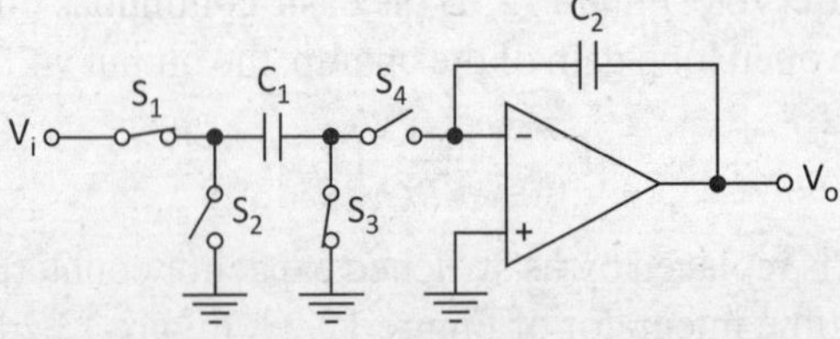

Fig. 12.25: Stray-insensitive switched capacitor non-inverting integrator

The switched capacitor integrator of Fig. 12.24(a) has some drawbacks. First, the input dependent charge injection of MOS switch S_1 introduces nonlinearity in the charge stored on C_1 thereby affecting the output voltage. Second, when capacitor C_1 is switched to inverting input of the opamp; the nonlinear capacitance due to the source-to-drain junctions of MOS switches S_1 and S_2 also results in a nonlinear charge-to-voltage conversion. It is because of these reasons that the integrator circuit of Figure 12.24 (a) is also referred to as stray-sensitive integrator. Figure 12.25 shows modified integrator circuit that is stray-insensitive; that is, it overcomes both these shortcomings. Figure 12.26 shows an alternative representation of the integrator circuit of Figure 12.25. In Figure 12.26, an SPDT switch S_1 replaces two SPST switches S_1 and S_2 and an SPDT switch S_2 replaces two SPST switches S_3 and S_4. Figure 12.27 shows stray-insensitive inverting integrator. During charging process, C_1 and C_2 are in series. Both will acquire same charge $Q = V_i \times [C_1C_2/(C_1 + C_2)]$. As a result, voltage across C_1 and C_2 will respectively be Q/C_1 and Q/C_2. The polarities of the voltages will be as shown in Figure 12.27. When the switches switch over to the other position (as indicated in Figure 12.27), C_1 gets shorted and discharged to zero voltage.

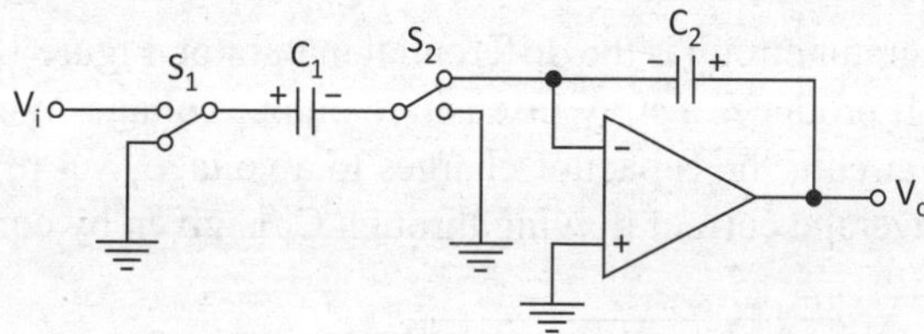

Fig. 12.26: Stray-insensitive non-inverting integrator-Alternative representation

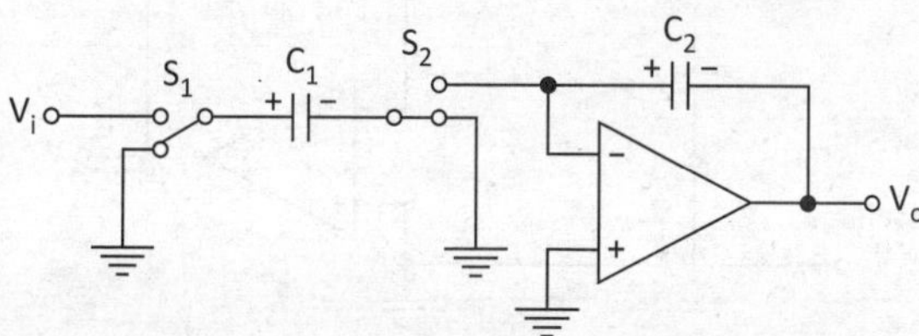

Fig. 12.27: Stray-insensitive inverting integrator-Alternative representation

In the case of stray-insensitive integrator of Figure 12.25, when a transition is being made to the integration mode, S_3 is turned off first followed by turning off of S_1. Since S_3 turns off first, it introduces only a constant offset voltage on C_1, which can be suppressed by differential operation. The charge injection or absorption of S_1 and S_2 contributes no error. Also, since inverting input node of opamp is a virtual ground; the charge injected or absorbed by S_4 is constant and independent of V_i. Another point worth mentioning here is that the voltage across nonlinear junction capacitances of S_3 and S_4 goes from near zero in the sampling mode to virtual ground in the integration mode. As a consequence of very small change in voltage across these stray capacitances, the resulting nonlinearity is also negligible.

Another common integrator circuit is the summing integrator used for producing an output equal to sum of integrals of multiple inputs. Figure 12.28 shows the circuit diagram of a summing integrator with two inputs. The output voltage V_o in this case is given by eqn. 12.23.

$$V_o = -\frac{1}{(jf/f_1)} \times V_1 - \frac{1}{(jf/f_2)} \times V_2 \tag{12.23}$$

Where $f_1 = \frac{1}{2\pi}\left(\frac{C_1}{C_3}\right) f_{CLK}$ and $f_2 = \frac{1}{2\pi}\left(\frac{C_1}{C_2}\right) f_{CLK}$

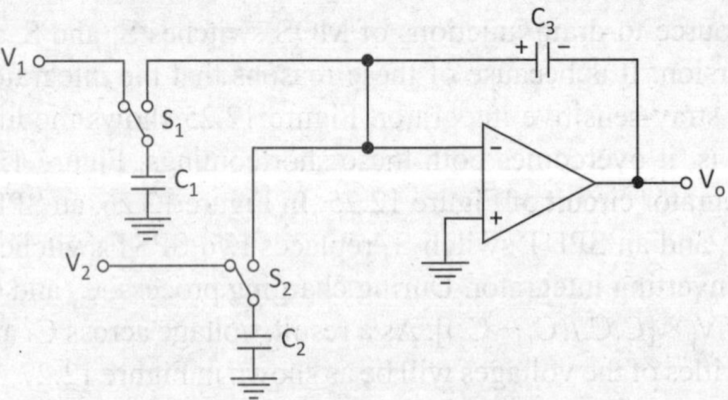

Fig. 12.28: Inverting summing integrator

Another important integrator circuit is the differential integrator. Figure 12.29 shows circuit diagram of a differential integrator. It produces a stray insensitive output voltage. When C_1 is connected to both V_1 and V_2 as shown in the circuit; the capacitor charges to a voltage (V_1-V_2). If the clock frequency is sufficiently high, then the average current flowing through C_1 is given by eqn. 12.24.

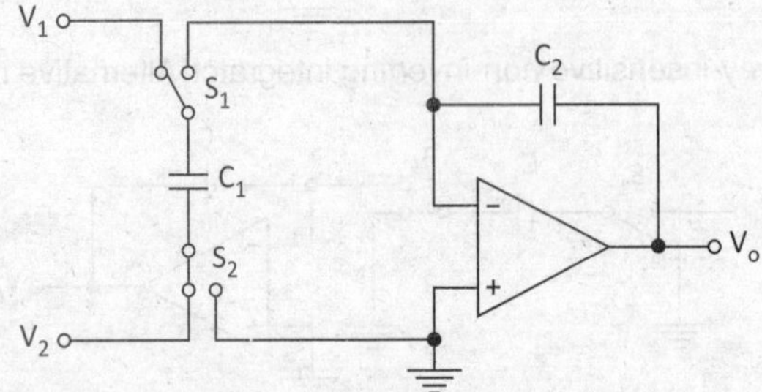

Fig. 12.29: Differential integrator

$$I_{av} = f_{CLK} \times C_1 \times (V_1 - V_2) \tag{12.24}$$

Therefore, $$V_o = -\left(\frac{1}{j\omega C_2}\right) \times f_{CLK} \times C_1 \times (V_1 - V_2) \tag{12.25}$$

Equation 12.25 can also be written as eqn. 12.26.

Where $$V_o = \left(\frac{1}{j(f/f_o)}\right) \times (V_2 - V_1) \tag{12.26}$$

Example-12.7: The switches S_1 and S_2 in the switched capacitor integrator of Figure 12.24 (a) are driven by non-overlapping clock signal of 100 kHz frequency. What should be the value of capacitance C_1 to simulate a resistance of 1M? If the input were 1VDC and C_2 = 100 pF; determine the amplitude of the resulting staircase waveform at the output at t = 100 µs.

Solution: Time period of clock signal, $T = \dfrac{1}{100 \times 10^3} = 10\mu s$

Therefore, $R = \dfrac{T}{C_1} = \dfrac{10 \times 10^{-6}}{C_1}$

Therefore, $C_1 = \dfrac{10\times10^{-6}}{10^6} = 10\,pF$

The step change in output voltage for every clock cycle $= 1\times\left(\dfrac{10}{100}\right)\times V = 0.1V$

At the end of 100 μs, there will be a total number of 10 voltage steps.

Therefore, the output will rise to $0.1\times10V = 1V$

Example-12.8: In the differential integrator circuit of Figure 12.29, switches S_1 and S_2 are connected respectively to V_1 and V_2 at t = 0. Both switches are driven by a symmetrical clock signal of 50 kHz. If V_1 = 1V, V_2 = 2V, C_1 = 1 pF and C_2 = 10 pF; then what would be the output voltage at t = 100 μs?

Solution: At t = 0, C_1 is simultaneously connected to V_1 and V_2.

For every clock cycle, V_1 contributes a step voltage change of $V_1\times\left(\dfrac{C_1}{C_2}\right) = 0.1V$ at the output and V_2 contributes a step voltage change of $V_2\times\left(\dfrac{C_1}{C_2}\right) = 0.2V$ at the output.

Thus, every clock cycle contributes 0.3V to the output.

Since clock period is 20 ms (for f_{CLK} = 50 kHz); at t = 100 μs, 5 clock cycles would have been completed.

Therefore, output voltage V_o at the end of 100 μs = (0.3 × 5)V = 1.5V

The output voltage in this case will be staircase waveform of the type shown earlier in Figure 12.24 (b).

12.6 SWITCHED CAPACITOR FILTERS

In this section, we shall describe some common filter circuits implemented using switched capacitor circuits. Switched capacitor filters can be hardware implemented by replacing resistors in the R-C continuous time filter circuits with switched capacitor equivalents. We shall illustrate the operation of switched capacitor filters by first considering first order low pass and high pass filter configurations obtained from the corresponding continuous time filter circuits. This is then followed up with a detailed description of biquad filter configuration and simultaneous implementation of low pass, high pass, band pass and band reject filters using this configuration. Again, discussion begins with a detailed analysis of continuous time biquad filter configuration by deriving transfer functions for different filters. Corresponding switched capacitor filter circuits can then be simply obtained by replacing resistors by their switched capacitor equivalents.

12.6.1 First Order Filters

Figure 12.30 shows generalized form of a first order active filter. It can be used to implement low pass, high pass and all pass filters. The s-domain transfer function of this filter circuit can be written as eqn. 12.27.

$$H(s) = \frac{V_o(s)}{V_i(s)} = \frac{(a_1 s \pm a_0)}{(s + b_0)} \qquad (12.27)$$

For $a_1 = 0$, we get a low pass filter

For $a_0 = 0$, we get a high pass filter

For $a_1 \neq 0$ and $a_0 \neq 0$, we get an all pass filter

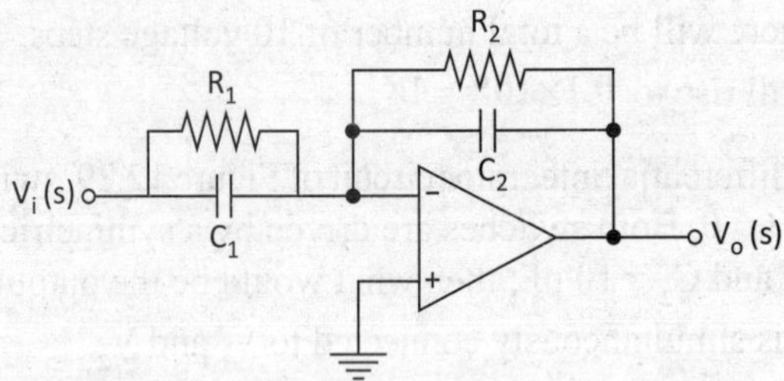

Fig. 12.30: Generalized form of first order continuous time filter

Transfer function of the filter circuit shown in Figure 12.30 is given by eqn. 12.28.

$$\frac{V_o(s)}{V_i(s)} = -\left(\frac{R_2}{R_1}\right)\frac{(sR_1C_1+1)}{(sR_2C_2+1)} \tag{12.28}$$

In the following paragraphs, we shall briefly describe first order low pass, high pass and all-pass filters derived from the generalized first order filter configuration shown in Figure 12.30.

First Order Low Pass Filter

As mentioned above, for a low pass circuit, $a_1 = 0$, which implies that $C_1 = 0$

The transfer function of the low pass filter circuit is given by eqn. 12.29.

$$\frac{V_o(s)}{V_i(s)} = -\left(\frac{R_2}{R_1}\right)\left(\frac{1}{sR_2C_2+1}\right) \tag{12.29}$$

The switched capacitor equivalent of the first order low pass filter can be drawn by replacing R_1 and R_2 by their parasitic-insensitive switched capacitor equivalents. It may be mentioned here that the switched capacitor equivalent of resistance R_1 given here is a two-port network that offers a negative trans-resistance and switched capacitor equivalent of R_2 given here offers a positive trans-resistance. You can notice the difference in phases of clock signal in the two cases. Before we do that; let us assume $a_1 = a_0 T$ and $a_2 = b_0 T$ where (T) is the time period of the clock signal used to control the MOS switches in switched capacitor equivalent of the first order low pass filter of Figure 12.30 and shown in Figure 12.31. The transfer function given by the expression of eqn. 12.29 can be rewritten as eqn. 12.30. Note that capacitor C_2 in the feedback path in Figure 12.30 is C_1 in the equivalent switched capacitor circuit of Figure 12.31. Also, a_1C_1 and a_2C_1 are respectively the capacitors that along with MOS switches construct resistors R_1 and R_2.

$$\frac{V_o(s)}{V_i(s)} \cong -\left(\frac{\alpha_1}{\alpha_2}\right)\left(\frac{1}{(sT/\alpha_2)+1}\right) = -\left(\frac{\alpha_1}{sT+\alpha_2}\right) = -(\alpha_1/T)\times\left(\frac{1}{s+(\alpha_2/T)}\right) \tag{12.30}$$

Here, $T = 1/f_{CLK}$; f_{CLK} is the clock frequency.

If we examine the transfer function expression of eqn. 12.30, we shall notice that it has the generalized form of a first order low pass filter as expressed by eqn. 12.27 earlier and reproduced in eqn. 12.31.

$$\frac{V_o(s)}{V_i(s)} = \left(\frac{a_0}{s+b_0}\right) \tag{12.31}$$

where $a_0 = (\alpha_1/T)$ and $b_0 = (\alpha_2/T)$

Figure 12.31 shows the switched capacitor equivalent of the continuous time first order low pass filter of Figure 12.30. The s-domain transfer function as expressed by eqn. 12.30 can also be expressed in z-domain, which is the discrete time equivalent of s-domain. z-domain and s-domain are interrelated by $z = e^{sT}$ where (T) is the sampling time interval, which with reference to switched capacitor circuits is the clock signal time period.

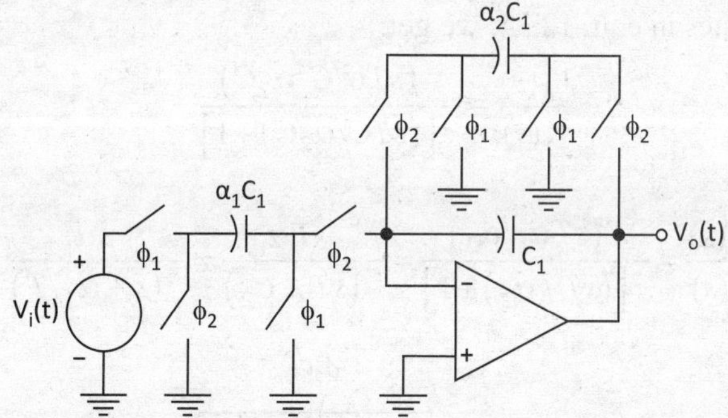

Fig. 12.31: Non-inverting first order low pass switched capacitor filter

Figure 12.32 shows the inverting first order low pass filter circuit. The transfer function of this filter is given by eqn. 12.32.

$$\frac{V_o(s)}{V_i(s)} = (\alpha_1/T)\times\left(\frac{1}{s+(\alpha_2/T)}\right) \tag{12.32}$$

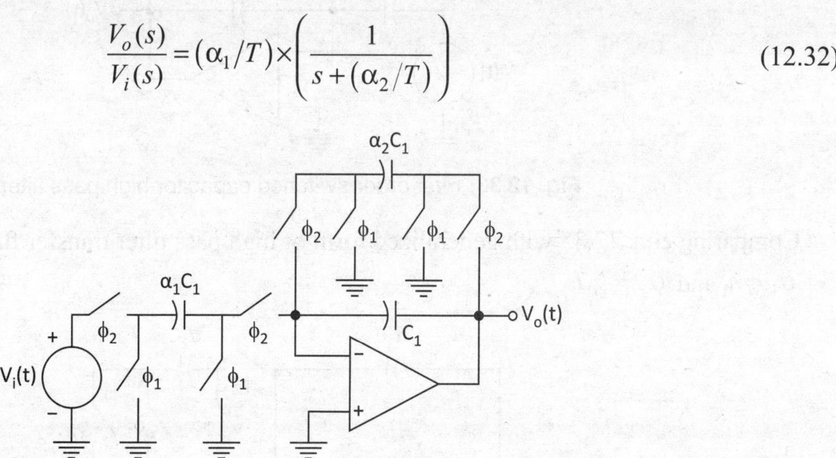

Fig. 12.32: Inverting first order low pass switched capacitor filter

First Order High Pass Filter

First order high pass filter can also be derived from the generalized circuit of Figure 12.30. The transfer function for the circuit of Figure 12.30 as given by eqn. 12.27 is reproduced as eqn. 12.33.

$$\frac{V_o(s)}{V_i(s)} = -\left(\frac{R_2}{R_1}\right)\frac{(sR_1C_1+1)}{(sR_2C_2+1)} \tag{12.33}$$

Figure 12.33 shows the first order high pass circuit. The transfer function is obtained from eqn. 12.33 by considering R_1 as open circuit i.e. substituting R_1 = ¥. Equation 12.34 gives the transfer function.

$$\frac{V_o(s)}{V_i(s)} = -\left(\frac{sR_2C_1}{sR_2C_2+1}\right) \tag{12.34}$$

Referring to Figure 12.33, $R_2 = T/\alpha_2 C$, $C_1 = \alpha_1 C$ and $C_2 = C$

Substituting these values in eqn. 12.34, we get:

$$\frac{V_o(s)}{V_i(s)} \cong -\frac{(sT\alpha_1 C/\alpha_2 C)}{[(sTC/\alpha_2 C)+1]}$$

$$\frac{V_o(s)}{V_i(s)} = -\frac{(sT\alpha_1/\alpha_2)}{[(sT/\alpha_2)+1]} = -\frac{sT\alpha_1}{(sT+\alpha_2)} = -\frac{s\alpha_1}{(s+\alpha_2/T)} \tag{12.35}$$

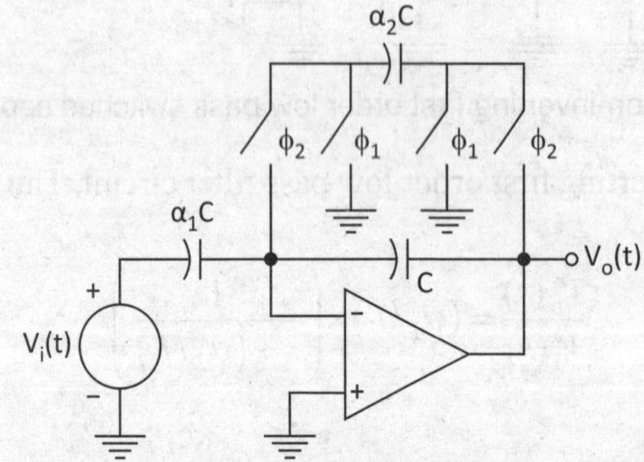

Fig. 12.33: First order switched capacitor high pass filter

Comparing eqn. 12.35 with generalized form of high pass filter transfer function, we get:
$\alpha_1 = a_1$ and $\alpha_2 = b_0 T$

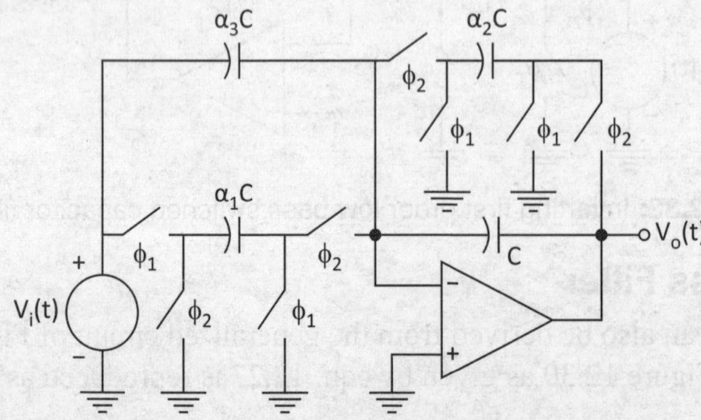

Fig. 12.34: First order switched capacitor all pass filter

First Order All Pass Filter

A low pass filter was earlier obtained by removing C_1 from the generalized circuit diagram of Figure 12.30 and replacing R_2 by its switched capacitor equivalent. A high pass filter was obtained by removing R_1 and replacing R_2 by its switched capacitor equivalent. An all-pass filter passes all frequency components of the input signal with equal gain but provides predictable phase shifts for different frequencies of the input signal. They are also called phase equalizers or delay equalizers. Figure 12.30 shown earlier represents generalized form of first order all-pass filter circuit. The switched capacitor all pass filter can be obtained by replacing R_1 and R_2 by their switched capacitor equivalents. Figure 12.34 shows the circuit diagram.

The transfer function of the generalized filter configuration of Figure 12.30 given earlier by eqn. 12.28 is reproduced in eqn. 12.36.

$$\frac{V_o(s)}{V_i(s)} = -\left(\frac{R_2}{R_1}\right)\frac{(sR_1C_1+1)}{(sR_2C_2+1)} \tag{12.36}$$

Comparing the generalized filter circuits of Figure 12.30 and 12.34, we get:

$R_1 = \alpha_3 C$ and $R_2 = C$

Also, $R_1 = (T/\alpha_1 C)$ and $R_2 = (T/\alpha_2 C)$

Substituting these values in eqn. 12.36, we get:

$$\frac{V_o(s)}{V_i(s)} = -\left(\frac{\alpha_1}{\alpha_2}\right)\times\left[\frac{\{(sT\alpha_3/\alpha_1)+1\}}{\{(sT/\alpha_2)+1\}}\right] = -\frac{\{\alpha_3 s + (\alpha_1/T)\}}{\{s+(\alpha_2/T)\}} \tag{12.37}$$

Comparing the expression for transfer function with the generalized form, we get:

$\alpha_3 = a_1$, $\alpha_1/T = a_0$ and $a_2/T = b_0$

12.6.2 Biquad Filters

A biquad filter is a second order IIR (Infinite Impulse Response) filter. An IIR filter is one of the two primary types of digital filters used in digital signal processing applications. The other type is the FIR (Finite Impulse Response) filter. The advantage of IIR filters vis-à-vis FIR filters is that they can achieve given filtering characteristics using relatively less memory and calculations than a similar FIR filter. Also, most electronic and digital filters are examples of time invariant systems and infinite impulse response is a property that applies to many time-invariant systems. A biquad filter is one of the most commonly used forms of IIR filters. A biquad is a second order IIR filter implementing a quadratic function in (s) in both numerator and denominator. A biquad can simultaneously implement second order low pass, high pass, band pass and band reject (or Notch) filters.

A biquad transfer function can be realized with a pair of integrators configured around opamps and connected in series. Each integrator introduces a factor (1/s). Figure 12.35 shows the biquad filter circuit. Opamp A_1 is configured as an inverting summer used to combine low pass filter output and the input signal. The opamp A_1 also acts as a non-inverting amplifier for the third input, which is also the band pass filter output or the output of first integrator. Resistor (R) and capacitor (C) determine the natural frequency and the potential divider R2-R3 provides positive feedback to determine damping ratio. Opamps A_2 and A_3 are configured as integrators. The inverting summer configured around opamp A_4 is used to implement band reject filter and may be omitted if band reject function is not required. All filter outputs have identical second order denominator in (s) and the appropriate numerator terms will exist for each particular filter. In the following paragraphs, we shall analyze transfer function of each of the four filter types that can be implemented with a biquad. Low pass, high pass, band pass and band reject filter functions are respectively available at the outputs of A_3, A_1, A_2 and A_4.

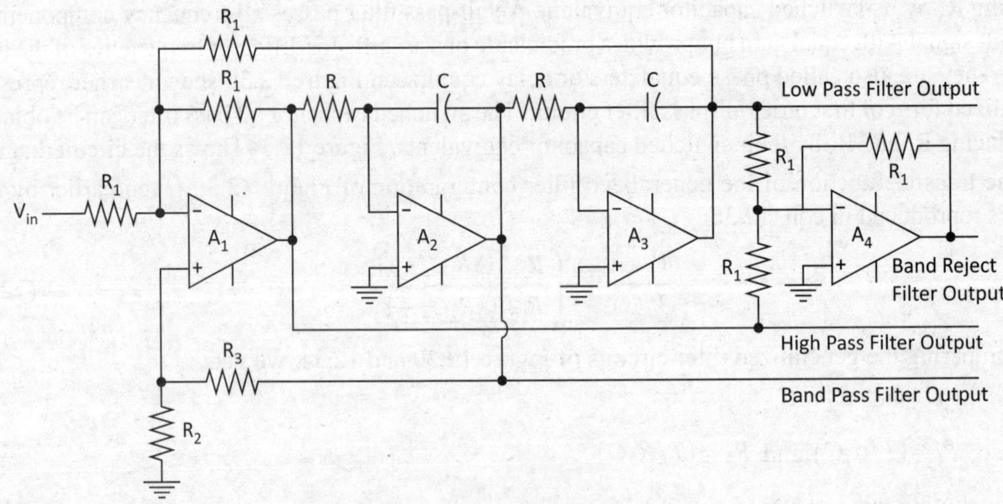

Fig. 12.35: Biquad filter

Low Pass Filter

Refer to Figure 12.35.

Low pass filter output (output of A_3), $V_{LP} = -\dfrac{V_{BP}}{RCs}$ (12.37)

Where V_{BP} = Band pass filter output

Also, $V_{BP} = -\dfrac{V_{HP}}{RCs}$ (12.38)

Where V_{HP} = High pass filter output

Therefore, $$V_{LP} = \frac{V_{HP}}{R^2C^2s^2} \quad (12.39)$$

Now, $$V_{HP} = -V_{LP} - V_{in} + 3 \times V_{BP} \times \left[\frac{R_2}{(R_2+R_3)}\right] \quad (12.40)$$

Substituting for V_{HP} and V_{BP} in eqn. 12.40, we get:

$$V_{HP} = -V_{in} - \frac{V_{HP}}{R^2C^2s^2} - 3 \times \left(\frac{V_{HP}}{RCs}\right) \times \left[\frac{R_2}{(R_2+R_3)}\right] \quad (12.41)$$

Rearranging different terms in eqn. 12.41, we get expression for high pass filter output.

$$V_{HP} = -\frac{V_{in}s^2}{s^2 + \dfrac{3}{RC}\left(\dfrac{R_2}{R_2+R_3}\right)s + \dfrac{1}{R^2C^2}} \quad (12.42)$$

Substituting for VHP in eqn. 12.39, we get expression for V_{LP} as given in eqn. 12.43.

$$V_{LP} = -\frac{\left(V_{in}/R^2C^2\right)}{s^2 + \frac{3}{RC}\left(\frac{R_2}{R_2+R_3}\right)s + \frac{1}{R^2C^2}} \tag{12.43}$$

High Pass Filter

High pass filter response is already derived and is given by eqn. 12.42.

Band Pass Filter

Band pass filter response is given by eqn. 12.38. Substituting for VHP in eqn. 12.38, we get response for VBP as given by eqn. 12.44.

$$V_{BP} = \frac{\left(V_{in}s/RC\right)}{s^2 + \frac{3}{RC}\left(\frac{R_2}{R_2+R_3}\right)s + \frac{1}{R^2C^2}} \tag{12.44}$$

Band Reject Filter

Band reject filter response is obtained by adding low pass filter and high pass filter responses.

That is, Band reject filter response, $V_{BR} = -V_{LP} - V_{HP}$

Substituting for V_{LP} and V_{HP}, we get expression for V_{BR}.

$$V_{BR} = -\frac{V_{in}\left[\left(-s^2\right)-\left(1/R^2C^2\right)\right]}{\left[s^2 + \frac{3}{RC}\left(\frac{R_2}{R_2+R_3}\right)s + \frac{1}{R^2C^2}\right]} = \frac{V_{in}\left[\left(s^2\right)+\left(1/R^2C^2\right)\right]}{\left[s^2 + \frac{3}{RC}\left(\frac{R_2}{R_2+R_3}\right)s + \frac{1}{R^2C^2}\right]}$$

Having discussed responses of low pass, high pass, band pass and band reject filters, we shall now look at some important design equations. If we examine the responses of different filters asgiven by eqns. 12.43 (low pass filter), 12.42 (high pass filters), 12.44 (band pass filter) and 12.45 (band reject filter); we find that all responses have the same denominator. We can compare the denominator with the standard form of second order denominator to determine the natural frequency and damping ratio. The standard form of second order denominator is given by:

$$s^2 + 2\zeta\omega_n s + \omega_n{}^2$$

Comparing the denominator of the filter response with the standard form we get:

$$\omega_n = \frac{1}{RC} \tag{12.46}$$

$$2\zeta\omega_n = \frac{3}{RC}\left(\frac{R_2}{R_2+R_3}\right) \tag{12.47}$$

Substituting for w_n from eqn. 12.46 in eqn. 12.47, we get:

$$\zeta = \frac{\frac{3}{RC}\left(\frac{R_2}{R_2+R_3}\right)}{2\omega_n} = \frac{\frac{3}{RC}\left(\frac{R_2}{R_2+R_3}\right)}{(2/RC)} = \frac{3}{2}\left(\frac{R_2}{R_2+R_3}\right) = \frac{3}{2}\left(\frac{1}{1+(R_3/R_2)}\right) \quad (12.48)$$

Quality factor (Q-factor) of the filter is related to damping factor by eqn. 12.49.

$$Q = \frac{1}{2\zeta} = \left(\frac{1+(R_3/R_2)}{3}\right) \quad (12.49)$$

$$\left(\frac{R_3}{R_2}\right) = 3Q - 1 \quad (12.50)$$

C may be computed from the empirical relationship expressed by eqn. 12.51.

$$C(\text{in Farad}) = \frac{4\times10^{-7}}{\sqrt{F_n}}$$

Where F_n is the natural frequency in Hz.

R can be computed from eqn. 12.52.

$$R = \frac{1}{2\pi F_n C} \quad (12.52)$$

Where F_n = Natural frequency in Hz

Also,
$$Q = \frac{F_n}{\text{Bandwidth}} \quad (12.53)$$

Having discussed at length the functioning of a generalized biquad filter configuration, it may be mentioned here that there can be several possible biquad filter circuit configurations derived from the biquad filter configuration of Figure 12.35 depending upon nature of desired filter function. The circuit for switched capacitor biquad filter can be obtained from its continuous time counterpart by replacing different resistors by their parasitic-insensitive switched capacitor equivalents.

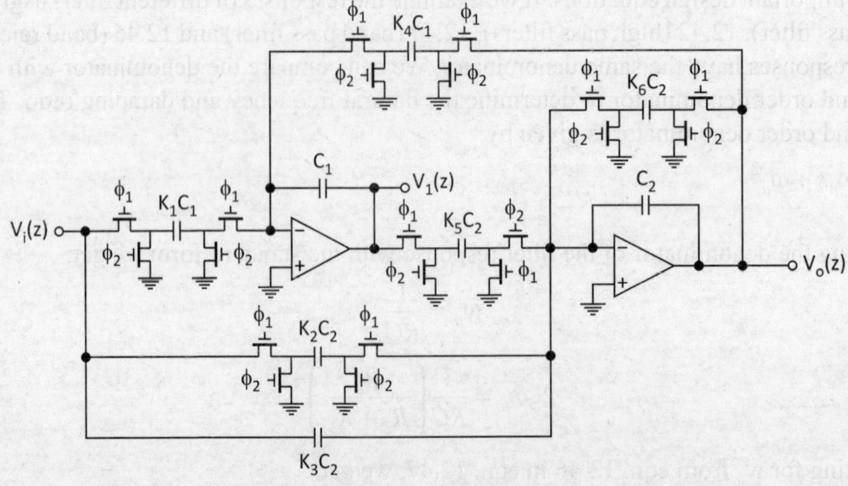

Fig. 12.36: Low-Q switched capacitor biquad filter

Figure 12.36 shows one such switched capacitor biquad filter circuit. The biquad of Figure 12.36 is best suited to design of low-Q filters. The transfer function of this filter circuit is given by eqn. 12.54.

$$\frac{V_o(z)}{V_i(z)} = -\frac{(K_2+K_3)z^2+(K_1K_5-K_2-2K_3)z+K_3}{(1+K_6)z^2+(K_4K_5-K_6-2)z+1} \tag{12.54}$$

Figure 12.37 shows circuit diagram of high-Q switched capacitor biquad filter. The transfer function of this filter circuit is given by eqn. 12.55.

$$\frac{V_o(z)}{V_i(z)} = -\frac{K_3z^2+(K_1K_5+K_2K_5-2K_3)z+K_3-K_2K_5}{z^2+(K_4K_5+K_5K_6-2)z+(1-K_5K_6)} \tag{12.55}$$

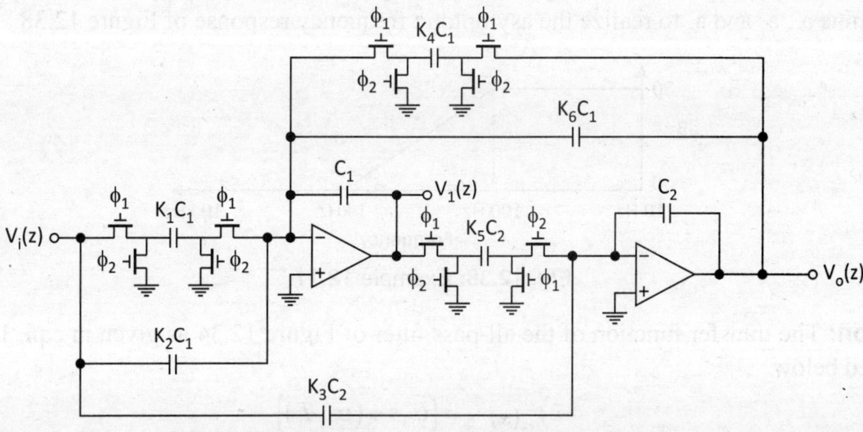

Fig. 12.37: High-Q switched capacitor biquad filter

Example-12.9: Determine the values of a_1 and a_2 for the first-order low pass filter of the type shown earlier in Figure 12.31 for a low frequency cut-off frequency of 5 kHz and low frequency gain of +10. Assume clock frequency to be equal to 200 kHz.

Solution: Referring to Figure 12.31, low frequency gain $= \left(\frac{\alpha_1 C_1}{\alpha_2 C_1}\right) = \left(\frac{\alpha_1}{\alpha_2}\right) = 10$

Also, from eqn. 12.32, transfer function, $\frac{V_o(s)}{V_i(s)} = (\alpha_1/T)\times\left(\frac{1}{s+(\alpha_2/T)}\right)$

This gives cut-off frequency in radians/sec $= \frac{\alpha_2}{T} = \alpha_2 f_{CLK}$, where f_{CLK} is the clock frequency in Hz.

Therefore, $\alpha_2 f_{CLK} = 5000$

Which gives $\alpha_2 = (5000/200000) = (1/40) = 0.025$

Since $(\alpha_1/\alpha_2) = 10$; $\alpha_1 = 0.25$

$\alpha_1 = 0.25$ and $\alpha_2 = 0.025$

Example-12.10: In the first order high pass filter circuit of Figure 12.33, and . Determine high frequency gain and the clock frequency at which the filter circuit would need to be driven to achieve a 3 dB cut-off frequency of 10 kHz.

Solution: Referring to Figure 12.33, high frequency gain$=\frac{\alpha_1}{\alpha_2}=\frac{0.8}{0.04}=20$

Also, 3-dB frequency in radians/s=6.28×10^4=62800 radians/s=(α_2/T)

Where (T) is the time period of clock signal.

This gives, $T=(\alpha_2/62800)=(0.04/62800)s=0.637\mu s$

Therefore, clock frequency = 1/0.637 MHz = 1.57 MHz

Example-12.11: The first order all pass filter of Figure 12.34 is driven by a clock frequency of 100 kHz. Determine a_1, a_2 and a_3 to realize the asymptotic frequency response of Figure 12.38.

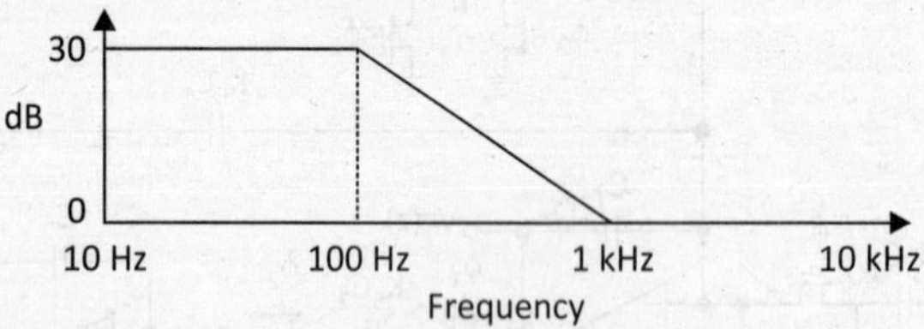

Fig, 12.38: Example 12.11

Solution: The transfer function of the all-pass filter of Figure 12.34 as given in eqn. 12.37 earlier is reproduced below.

$$\frac{V_o(s)}{V_i(s)}=-\frac{\{\alpha_3 s+(\alpha_1/T)\}}{\{s+(\alpha_2/T)\}}$$

Desired value of DC gain = 30 dB

That is, gain ratio = Antilog 1.5 = 31.622

Also, DC gain$=\frac{\alpha_1}{\alpha_2}=31.622$

From the frequency response of Figure 12.38, we can see that there is zero at 1000 Hz and a pole at 100 Hz.

Therefore, $\frac{\alpha_1}{T\alpha_3}=2\pi\times1000=6280$ and $\frac{\alpha_2}{T}=2\pi\times100=628$

Solving these two equations, we get, $\frac{\alpha_1}{\alpha_2\alpha_3}=\frac{6280}{628}=10$

Substituting for (α_1/α_2), we get $\alpha_3=(10/31.622)=0.316$

Now clock frequency = 100 kHz

Therefore, T = (1/100) ms = 10 μs

Substituting for (T), we get $\alpha_2=628\times10\times10^{-6}=0.00628$ and $\alpha_1=0.00628\times31.622=0.2$

12.7 SWITCHED CAPACITOR D/A CONVERTERS

Digital-to-analog (D/A) converters were discussed at length in the previous chapter. The heart of a D/A converter is an R-2R binary ladder. The digital input is applied to the binary ladder network through a switch matrix. Both current and voltage steering modes of operation of D/A converter were discussed in the previous chapter. In both modes of operation, magnitude of analog output voltage is equal to product of reference voltage and fractional binary value of the digital input word. The architecture of a 4-bit D/A converter operated in current steering mode is reproduced in Figure 12.39. The analog output voltage here varies from 0 to $-(15/16)\times V_{REF}$ for digital input varying from 0000 to 1111. In general, for an N-bit converter, the analog output varies from 0 to $-\left(2^{N-1}/2^{N}\right)\times V_{REF}$.

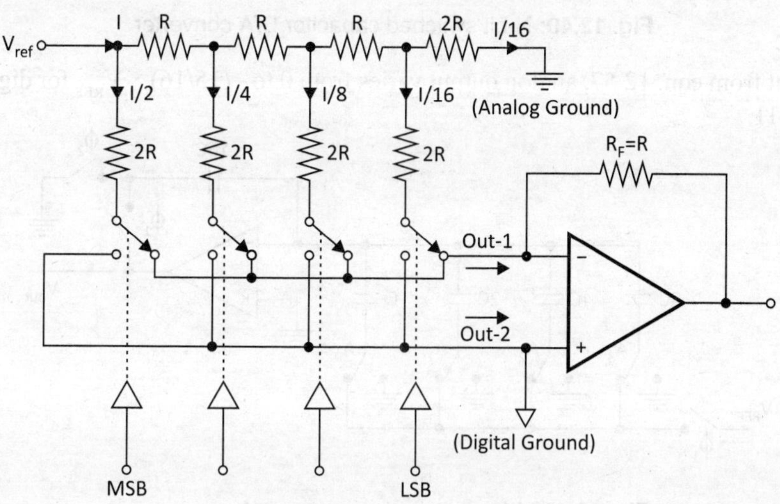

Fig. 12.39: 4-bit D/A converter

A switched capacitor D/A converter uses a switched capacitor network instead of a switched resistor network. Figure 12.40 shows the circuit diagram of an N-bit switched capacitor D/A converter. The switch matrix comprising MOS switches controls application of digital input. As shown in the figure, different switches are used to connect the corresponding inputs of the capacitor network to either ground or V_{REF}. Also, capacitance values of different capacitors are binary weighted and are 2^0C (for LSB), 2^1, 2^2, …………., 2^{N-2}C and 2^{N-1}C (for MSB). The feedback capacitance is 2^NC. The analog output voltage in this case is given by eqn. 12.56.

$$V_o = -\left(\frac{Q}{2^N C}\right) \tag{12.56}$$

Where $Q = V_{REF}\times\left(A_0 2^0 C + A_1 2^1 C + A_2 2^2 C + \ldots\ldots\ldots\ldots + A_{N-1}2^{N-1}C\right)$

Four a 4-bit converter, eqn. 12.56 reduces to eqn. 12.57.

$$V_o = -\left(\frac{V_{REF}}{16C}\right)\times\left(A_0 C + A_1 2C + A_2 4C + A_3 8C\right) \tag{12.57}$$

Figure 12.41 shows the circuit diagram of a 4-bit converter.

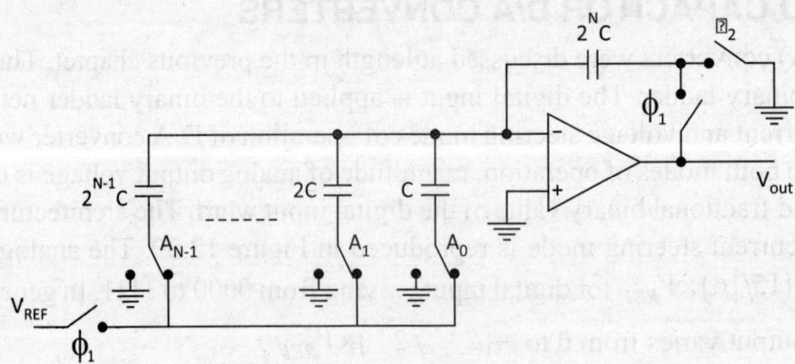

Fig. 12.40: N-bit switched capacitor D/A converter

As is evident from eqn. 12.57, analog output varies from 0 to - (15/16) × V_{REF} for digital input going from 0000 to 1111.

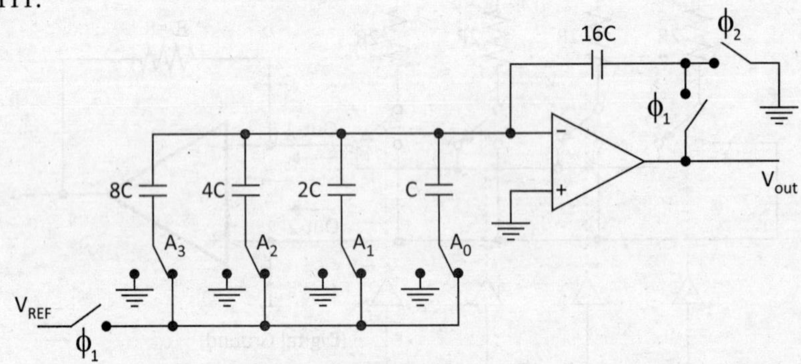

Fig. 12.41: 4-bit switched capacitor D/A converter

The D/A converter of Figure 12.40 is prone to analog output voltage fluctuations during clock changes. The modified circuit of Figure 12.42 helps in maintaining the output voltage during clock changes. C1 here is used to hold the output voltage of the previous cycle during the time digital input word is changing states.

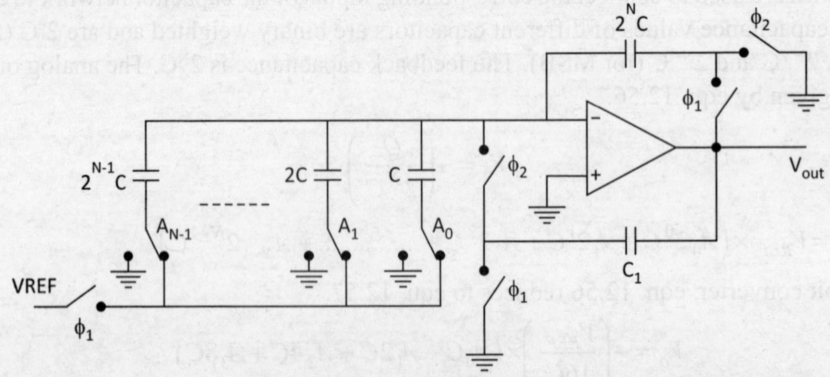

Fig. 12.42: Modified 4-bit switched capacitor D/A converter

An alternative D/A converter architecture that uses same value capacitors in the switched capacitor of network is shown in Figure 12.43. The D/A converter functions as follows. The input digital word to be converted into equivalent analog voltage is expressed in unary code, also sometimes called thermometer code. In unary code for non-negative natural numbers, bitsx_1, x_2, ..., $x_M$are such that if the integer value of the input word is m, the bits x_1, x_2, ..., x_m equal 1 and the remaining bits are 0. Since the input digital word to be fed to the converter is written in unary code; though not shown in the figure, a binary to unary decoder is required at the input. All capacitors in the switched capacitor network are of equal capacitance value (=C) and the feedback capacitance is (MC). As an example, for a 4-bit converter, there will be 15 capacitors (C_1 to C_{15}) of capacitance C each and the feedback capacitance (C_f) will be 16C. During the reset phase (f_1=1), the feedback capacitor (C_f) is discharged and all input capacitors are charged to the reference voltage V_{REF}. Next, during the conversion phase(f_2=1), only the first (m) input capacitors are discharged into (C_f) The analog output voltage V_o is given by eqn. 12.58.

$$V_o = \left(\frac{mC}{C_f}\right) \times V_{REF} = \left(\frac{m}{M}\right) \times V_{REF} \tag{12.58}$$

For a 4-bit D/A converter, M = 16. As an illustration, for a digital input of 0011, corresponding integer value is 3. Therefore, $V_o = \left(\frac{3}{16}\right) \times V_{REF}$

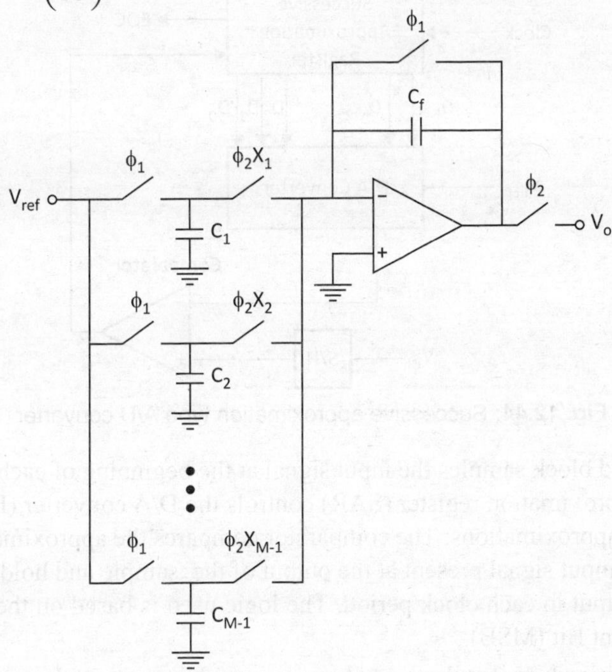

Fig. 12.43: An alternative switched capacitor D/A converter topology

Since during the reset phase. All capacitors are charged to V_{REF} and only (m) of the (M -1) input capacitors are discharged during conversion phase; capacitors C_{m+1} to C_{M-1} may be discharged during the conversion phase to eliminate signal dependent loading of V_{REF}. Another issue with this circuit topology is that nominally equal valued capacitors are more likely to be mismatched. The problem becomes more severe for smaller value of capacitors, which is the case if the converter were to operate at faster clock rates. This introduces nonlinearity making it difficult to achieve even a 10-bit resolution. However, techniques are available for analog correction of matching errors. Discussion on the techniques for correction of matching errors is beyond the scope of the resent text.

12.8 SWITCHED CAPACITOR A/D CONVERTERS

An examination of architectures of different types of analog-to-digital (A/D) converters discussed at length in the previous chapter clearly reveals that all with the exception of perhaps one or two have D/A converter as a dominant building block. From counter type A/D converter to successive approximation type A/D converter and further on to sigma-delta converter; all of these use D/A converter as an important building block. Switched capacitor D/A converters have been discussed in the previous section. Switched capacitor A/D converters would primarily mean replacement of the D/A converter block by its switched capacitor equivalent. This concept has been put to use in successive approximation type A/D converters. For the purpose of continuity of discussion, block schematic representation of a successive approximation type A/D converter is reproduced here in Figure 12.44. Integrating type A/D converters invariably use an integrator block, which could be replaced by their switched capacitor equivalent in order to add switched capacitor component in those converters.

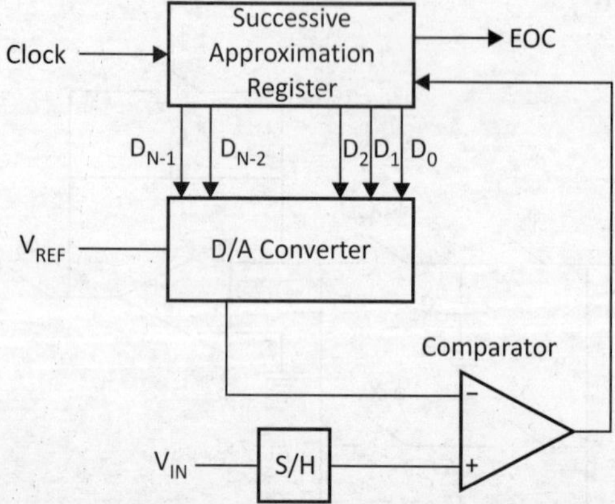

Fig. 12.44: Successive approximation type A/D converter

The sample and hold block samples the input signal at the beginning of each conversion cycle. The output of successive approximation register (SAR) controls the D/A converter (DAC), which generates the proper sequence of approximations. The comparator compares the approximations generated by the D/A converter with the input signal present at the output of the sample and hold circuit and determines one bit of the digital output in each clock period. The logic used is based on the binary search starting from the Most Significant Bit (MSB).

It is pertinent to mention here that the overall accuracy and linearity of the successive approximation A/D converter is determined primarily by the internal D/A converter block. Until recently, most precision A/D converters of this type used laser-trimmed thin-film D/A converters to achieve the desired accuracy and linearity. The thin-film resistor trimming process adds cost. Also, the thin-film resistor values may be affected when subjected to the mechanical stresses of packaging. Use of switched capacitor D/A converter block inside successive approximation A/D converters has addressed this issue. The use of switched capacitor D/A converter in an A/D converter is that it eliminates the need for either an external sample and hold circuit or allocation of chip area for a separate integral sample and hold circuit. The D/A converter itself behaves as a sample-and-hold circuit. Figure 12.45 shows architecture of AD 7641 A/D converter.

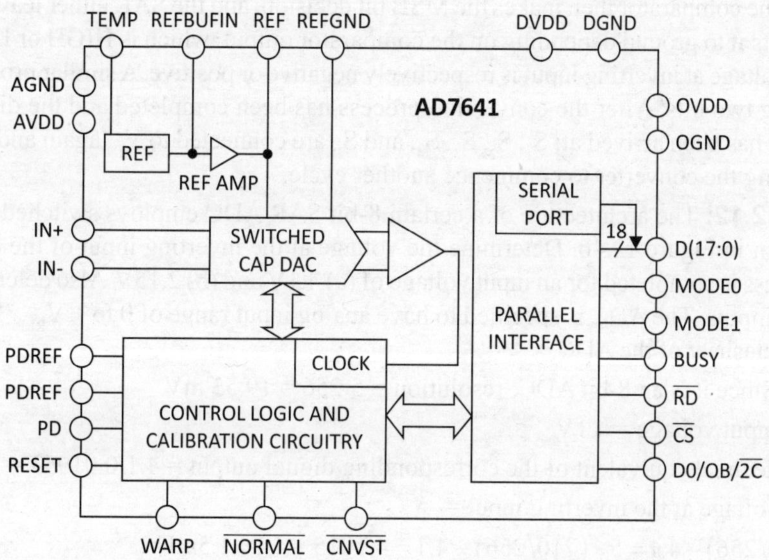

Fig. 12.45: Internal architecture of AD 7641 from Analog Devices

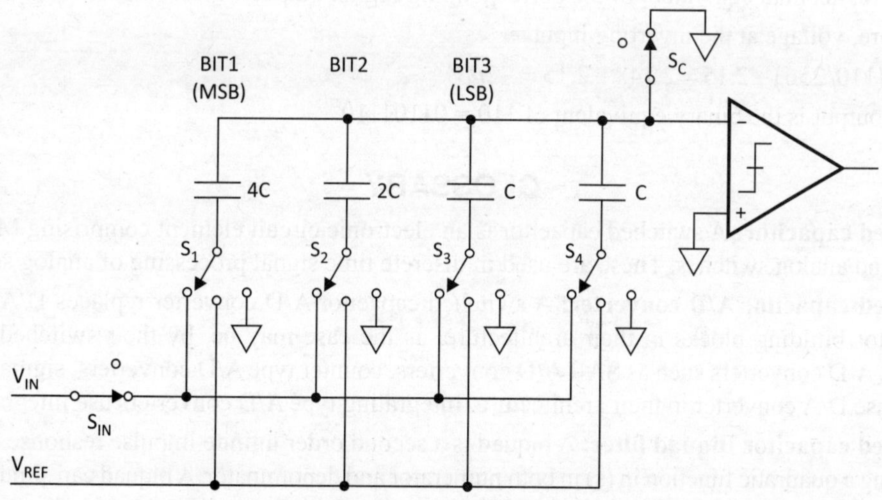

Fig. 12.46: 3-bit switched capacitor D/A converter

Figure 12.46 shows a representative architecture of the switched capacitor D/A converters found inside most switched capacitor successive approximation type A/D converters. The figure shows architecture of a 3-bit converter only to depict the topology. The position of switches as shown in the figure represents *sample mode* where the analog input voltage, V_{IN} is being sampled by charging parallel combination of all the capacitors. Following sampling mode, switch S_{IN} is opened to initiate he *hold mode* leaving the sampled analog input voltage on the capacitor array. Switch S_C is then opened allowing the voltage at inverting input to move as the bit switches are manipulated. If S_1, S_2, S_3, and S_4 are all connected to ground, a voltage equal to $-V_{IN}$ appears at inverting input. Connecting S_1 to V_{REF} adds a voltage equal to $V_{REF}/2$ to $-V_{IN}$. The comparator then makes the MSB bit decision, and the SAR either leaves S_1 connected to V_{REF} or connects it to ground depending on the comparator output, which is HIGH or LOW depending on whether the voltage at inverting input is respectively negative or positive. A similar process is followed for the remaining two bits. After the conversion process has been completed and the digital equivalent of sampled input has been arrived at; S_1, S_2, S_3, S_4, and S_{IN} are connected to V_{IN} again and S_C is connected to ground enabling the converter to commence another cycle.

Example-12.12: The architecture of a certain 8-bit SAR ADC employs switched capacitor DAC of the type shown in Figure 12.46. Determine the voltage at the inverting input of the opamp after the conversion process is completed for an input voltage of (a) 4.1V and (b) 2.15V. Also determine the digital output for these inputs. The ADC is specified to have analog input range of 0 to + V_{REF}. V_{REF} is specified as + 5V in the datasheet of the ADC.

Solution: Since it is an 8-bit ADC; resolution = 5/256 = 19.53 mV

(a) Analog input voltage = 4.1V

Therefore, decimal equivalent of the corresponding digital output = 4.1/0.01953 = 209.93 = 210

Therefore, voltage at the inverting input =

$$V_{REF} \times (210/256) - 4.1 = 5 \times (210/256) - 4.1 = 4.1015 - 4.1 = 1.5mV$$

Digital output is the binary equivalent of 210 = 11010010

(b) Analog input voltage = 2.15V

Therefore, decimal equivalent of the corresponding digital output = 2.15/0.01953 = 110.08 = 110

Therefore, voltage at the inverting input =

$$V_{REF} \times (110/256) - 2.15 = 2.148 - 2.15 = -2mV$$

Digital output is the binary equivalent of 110 = 01101110

GLOSSARY

Switched capacitor: A switched capacitor is an electronic circuit element comprising MOS-based capacitors and analog switches. These are used in discrete time signal processing of analog signals.

Switched capacitor A/D converter: A switched capacitor A/D converter replaces D/A converter and integrator building blocks in their architecture, as the case may be, by their switched capacitor equivalents. A/D converters such as SAR A/D converters, counter type A/D converters, sigma delta A/D converters use D/A converter in their architecture. Integrating type A/D converters use integrator block.

Switched capacitor Biquad filter: A biquad is a second order infinite impulse response (IIR) filter implementing a quadratic function in (s) in both numerator and denominator. A biquad can simultaneously implement second order low pass, high pass, band pass and band reject (or Notch) filters. Switched capacitor biquad filter replaces all resistors in the continuous time biquad filters by their switched capacitor equivalents.

Switched capacitor amplifier: A switched capacitor amplifier uses MOS switches, capacitors and opamps rather than resistors and opamps. The voltage gain in this case depends upon ratio of capacitance values. It operates in two phases namely the sampling phase and the amplification phase. During the sampling phase, energy is stored in the input capacitor and the output is kept zero. During the amplification phase, the stored charge is transferred to the output capacitor thereby producing an amplified output signal.

Switched capacitor D/A converter: A switched capacitor D/A converter uses a switched capacitor network instead of a switched resistor network.

Switched capacitor filter: Switched capacitor filter uses switched capacitor equivalents of resistors used in the corresponding R-C continuous time filter circuits.

Switched capacitor integrator: Switched capacitor integrator uses a switched capacitor resistor in place of a conventional resistor. Used in continuous time integrator.

Switched capacitor unity gain buffer: Switched capacitor unity gain buffer essentially comprises a sampling circuit followed by a unity gain opamp buffer.

SUMMARY OF IMPORTANT FORMULAE

1. Equivalent resistance of a parallel switched capacitor resistor topology is given by:

$$R_{eq}(\text{parallel}) = \frac{1}{(C \times f_{CLK})} = \frac{T}{C}$$

2. Equivalent resistance of a series switched capacitor resistor topology is given by:

$$R_{eq}(series) = \frac{1}{(C \times f_{CLK})} = \frac{T}{C}$$

3. Equivalent resistance of a series-parallel switched capacitor resistor topology is given by:

$$R_{eq}(series - parallel) = \frac{1}{((C_1 + C_2) \times f_{CLK})} = \frac{T}{(C_1 + C_2)}$$

4. Equivalent resistance of a bi-linear switched capacitor resistor topology is given by:

$$R_{eq}(bi - linear) = \frac{1}{(4C \times f_{CLK})} = \frac{T}{4C}$$

5. Closed loop voltage gain of inverting switched capacitor amplifier is given by:

$A_{CL}(inverting) = -\left(\frac{C_1}{C_2}\right)$; C_1 and C_2 are respectively the input and feedback capacitors.

6. Closed loop voltage gain of a non-inverting switched capacitor amplifier is given by:

$A_{CL}(\text{non-inverting}) = \left(\frac{C_1}{C_2}\right)$; C_1 and C_2 are respectively the input and feedback capacitors.

7. Gain error in a unity gain switched capacitor buffer is given by:

$$\text{Gain error} = -\left(\frac{1}{A_V}\right) \times \left(1 + \frac{C_{in}}{C}\right)$$

C is feedback capacitance and C_{in} is the parasitic capacitance appearing from inverting input to ground

8. Gain error in a switched capacitor amplifier is given by:

$$\text{Gain error} = -\left(\frac{1}{A_V C_2}\right) \times (C_1 + C_2 + C_{in})$$

Where C_1 and C_2 are respectively input and feedback capacitances and C_{in} is the input capacitance of the opamp.

9. Transfer function of an inverting integrator is given by:

$$\frac{V_o(s)}{V_i(s)} = -\left(\frac{C_1}{C_2 s}\right) \times f_{CLK}$$

Where C_1 and C_2 are respectively input and feedback capacitors.

10. Transfer function of a switched capacitor first order low pass filter is given by:

$$\frac{V_o(s)}{V_i(s)} = \frac{\alpha_1/T}{\left[1/(s+\alpha_2/T)\right]}$$

a_1/a_2 is the input to feedback capacitor ratio.

11. Transfer function of a switched capacitor first order high pass filter is given by:

$$\frac{V_o(s)}{V_i(s)} = -\frac{s\alpha_1}{(s+\alpha_2/T)}$$

a_1/a_2 is the input to feedback capacitor ratio.

12. Transfer function of a switched capacitor first order all pass filter is given by:

$$\frac{V_o(s)}{V_i(s)} = -\frac{\{\alpha_3 s+(\alpha_1/T)\}}{\{s+(\alpha_2/T)\}}$$

13. Analog output voltage in an N-bit switched capacitor D/A converter is given by:

$$V_o = -\left(\frac{V_{REF}}{2^N C}\right) \times \left(A_0 C + A_1 2C + A_2 4C + \ldots\ldots\ldots + A_{N-1} 2^{N-1} C\right)$$

$A_0, A_1, A_2, \ldots\ldots\ldots\ldots\ldots\ldots, A_{N-1}$ represent logic status (0 or 1) of N input bits.

REVIEW QUESTIONS

1. What are the advantages of using switched capacitor circuits in implementing analog circuit functions such as amplifiers, integrators and filters?
2. What are the basic components of the basic switched capacitor circuit element? Briefly describe the function of each component.
3. With the help of circuit diagram, briefly describe the operation of a switched capacitor resistor. Derive an expression for the magnitude of resistance.
4. Give the circuit diagrams of two-port switched capacitor network with positive and negative trans-resistances as their transfer functions. Derive expressions for trans-resistance.
5. Draw the circuit diagram of an inverting switched capacitor amplifier and briefly explain its operation. Derive an expression for the voltage gain. What are the key advantages of such an amplifier over the one that uses resistors.
6. Draw the circuit diagram of an inverting switched capacitor integrator and briefly explain its operation. Derive an expression for the transfer function. What are the key advantages of such an amplifier over the one that uses discrete resistors.

7. Draw the circuit diagram of a 4-bit switched capacitor D/A converter. Briefly describe the process of digital to analog conversion for one complete cycle. What key advantages a switched capacitor D/A converter brings when used in A/D converters?
8. What do you understand by the problem of charge injection in switched capacitor circuits? Which parameters does it affect and how is that problem overcome?
9. What are the main advantages of switched capacitor filters over continuous time filters? With the help of a suitable circuit diagram, briefly describe operation of a first order low pass switched capacitor filter.
10. What is a biquad filter? What is common to low pass, high pass, band pass and notch biquad filter transfer functions? What is the key advantage of using a biquad filter configuration with reference to tuning and damping requirements?

PROBLEMS

1. Refer to the basic switched capacitor resistor circuit of Figure 12.1. Determine the clock frequency at which the two switches should be driven for the circuit to emulate a resistance value of 100 K given that C = 5 pF.
2. Figure 12.47 shows a switched capacitor unity gain buffer in the sampling mode. If the input capacitance of the opamp is 2 pF and the open loop gain is 10000; determine the percentage gain error.

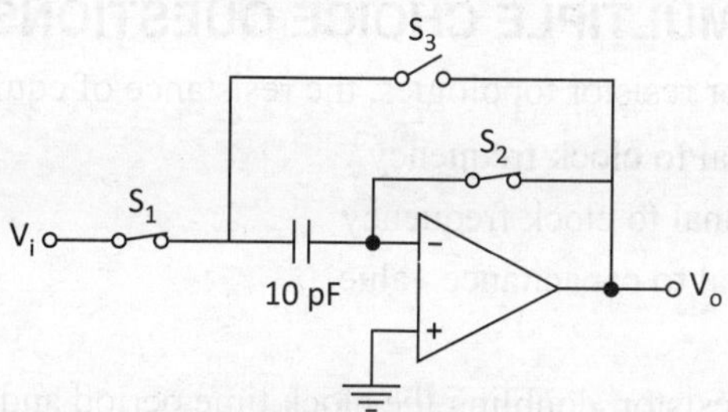

Fig. 12.47: Problem-2

3. In the non-inverting amplifier circuit of Figure 12.48, C_1 = 10 pF, C_2 = 2 pF and C_{in} = 0.5 pF. If the gain error were not to exceed 0.1%; determine the minimum value of open loop gain of opamp.

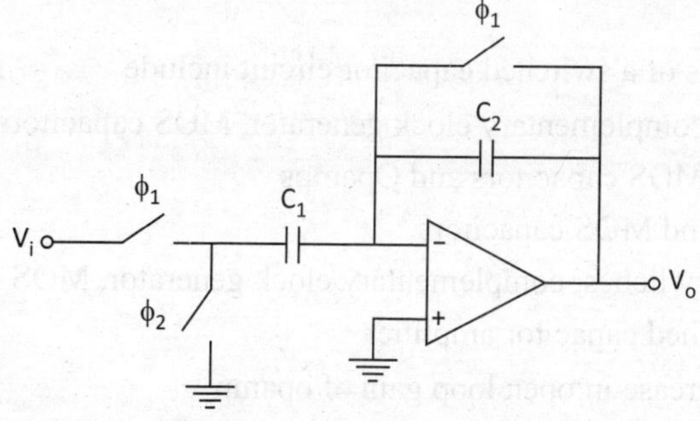

Fig. 12.48: Problem-3

4. The first order all pass filter of Figure 12.34 is driven by a clock frequency of 250 kHz. Determine a_1, a_2 and a_3 to realize the asymptotic frequency response of Figure 12.49.

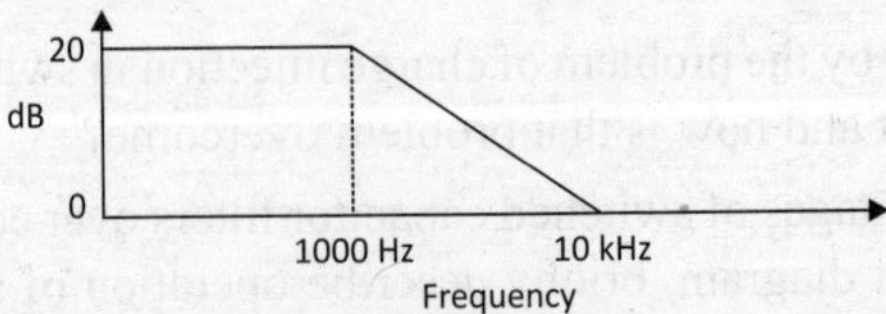

Fig. 12.49: Problem-4

5. The series-parallel switched capacitor circuit of Figure 12.50 emulates a resistor. When the clock frequency is doubled and value of C_1 and C_2 halved; the resistance value becomes 100 K. Determine the resistance value before these changes are implemented.

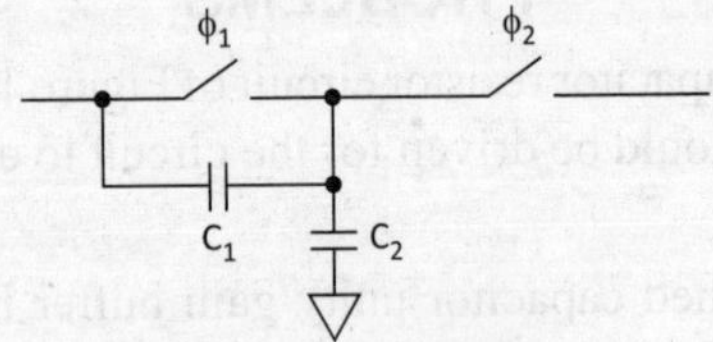

Fig. 12.50: Problem-5

MULTIPLE CHOICE QUESTIONS

1. In all switched capacitor resistor topologies, the resistance of equivalent resistor is
   (a) directly proportional to clock frequency
   (b) inversely proportional to clock frequency
   (c) directly proportional to capacitance value
   (d) None of these
2. In switched capacitor resistor, doubling the clock time period and capacitance value
   (a) keeps the value of equivalent resistance unchanged
   (b) doubles the equivalent resistance value
   (c) halves the equivalent resistance value
   (d) None of these
3. Basic building blocks of a switched capacitor circuit include
   (a) MOS switches, complementary clock generator, MOS capacitors and opamps
   (b) MOS switches, MOS capacitors and Opamps
   (c) MOS switches and MOS capacitors
   (d) resistors, MOS switches, complementary clock generator, MOS capacitors and opamps
4. Gain error in a switched capacitor amplifier
   (a) reduces with increase in open loop gain of opamp
   (b) increases with decrease in capacitance value of feedback capacitor
   (c) reduces with decrease in parasitic input capacitance appearing from inverting input to ground
   (d) All of the above

5. Magnitude of closed loop gain of a switched capacitor inverting amplifier is given by:
   (a) Output capacitance/Input capacitance
   (b) Input capacitance/Output capacitance
   (c) 1 + (Output capacitance/Input capacitance)
   (d) 1 + (Input capacitance/Output capacitance)
6. Magnitude of closed loop gain of a switched capacitor non-inverting amplifier is given by:
   (a) Output capacitance/Input capacitance
   (b) Input capacitance/Output capacitance
   (c) 1 + (Output capacitance/Input capacitance)
   (d) 1+ (Input capacitance/ Output capacitance)
7. Magnitude of transfer function of a switched capacitor inverting first order low pass filter is expressed by:
   (a) $H(s)=\frac{\alpha_1\left[1/(s+\alpha_2/T)\right]}{T}$ (b) $H(s)=\frac{\alpha_1}{(s+\alpha_2/T)}$
   (c) $H(s)=\frac{\alpha_1 s}{(sT+\alpha_2)}$ (d) None of these
8. Magnitude of transfer function of a switched capacitor first order high pass filter is expressed by:
   (a) $H(s)=\frac{s\alpha_1}{(s+\alpha_2/T)}$ (b) $H(s)=\frac{\alpha_1}{(s+\alpha_2/T)}$
   (c) $H(s)=\frac{s\alpha_1}{s(s+\alpha_2/T)}$ (d) None of these
9. In a switched capacitor 4-bit D/A converter, analog output voltage is expressed by:
   (a) $V_o=-\left(\frac{V_{REF}}{16C}\right)\times(A_0C+A_12C+A_24C+A_38C)$
   (b) $V_o=-V_{REF}\times(A_0C+A_12C+A_24C+A_38C)$
   (c) $V_o=-V_{REF}/(A_0C+A_12C+A_24C+A_38C)$
   (d) None of these
10. In a biquad filter,
    (a) band pass filter response is integral of low pass filter response
    (b) high pass filter response is integral of band pass filter response
    (c) band pass filter response is integral of high pass filter response
    (d) None of these
11. In a biquad filter,
    (a) low pass filter response is integral of band pass filter response
    (b) high pass filter response is integral of band pass filter response
    (c) band pass filter response is integral of low pass filter response
    (d) None of these

12. One of the following statements is true with reference to a biquad filter.
   (a) It is a fourth order active filter with a cut-off slope of 24 dB/octave.
   (b) It is a second order filter with finite impulse response.
   (c) It is a second order infinite impulse response (IIR) filter with cut-off slope of 12 dB/octave
   (d) The architecture primarily comprises an integrator and a differentiator block in series.
13. In a biquad filter, in order to achieve a cut-off slope of 80 dB/decade,
   (a) four bi-quads are cascaded.
   (b) two bi-quads are cascaded.
   (c) three bi-quads are cascaded
   (d) cut-off slope of 80 dB/decade is not possible with any cascaded arrangement of bi-quad Filters
14. In a switched capacitor amplifier,
   (a) clock frequency is equal to signal frequency
   (b) clock frequency is much lower than signal frequency
   (c) clock frequency is much larger than signal frequency
   (d) clock frequency is independent of signal frequency
15. One of the following statements is best applied to switched capacitor filters.
   (a) The cut-off frequency can be changed by changing capacitance ratio and clock frequency.
   (b) They are prone to frequency aliasing problem
   (c) They occupy a large chip area when implemented in integrated circuit form.
   (d) Both (a) and (b) are true
16. The basic 8-bit switched capacitor D/A converter would have (N) capacitors.
   (a) N = 9 (b) N = 8
   (c) N = 256 (d) N = 257
17. Refer to the two-port switched capacitor trans-resistance network of Figure 12.51. Assume that clock frequency is much larger than signal frequency. f_1 and f_2 represent MOS switches driven by complementary clock signals. The transfer function of this network is given by:
   (a) T/C (b) C/T
   (c) –T/C (d) –1/TC

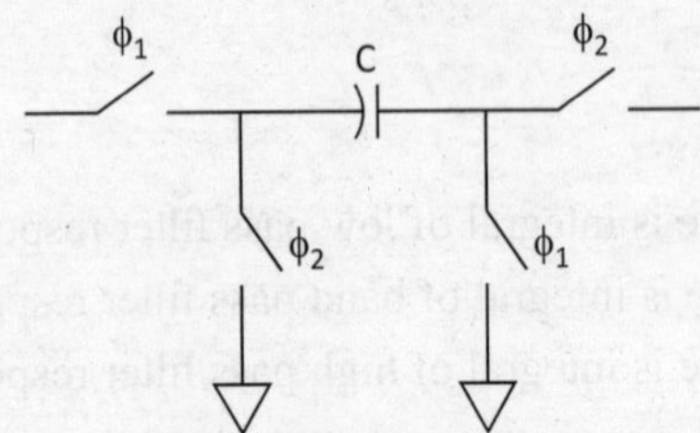

Fig. 12.51: MCQ-17

18. Refer to the two-port switched capacitor trans-resistance network of Figure 12.52. Assume that clock frequency is much larger than signal frequency. f_1 and f_2 represent MOS switches driven by complementary clock signals. The transfer function of this network is given by:
   (a) –T/C (b) T/C
   (c) 1/TC (d) None of these

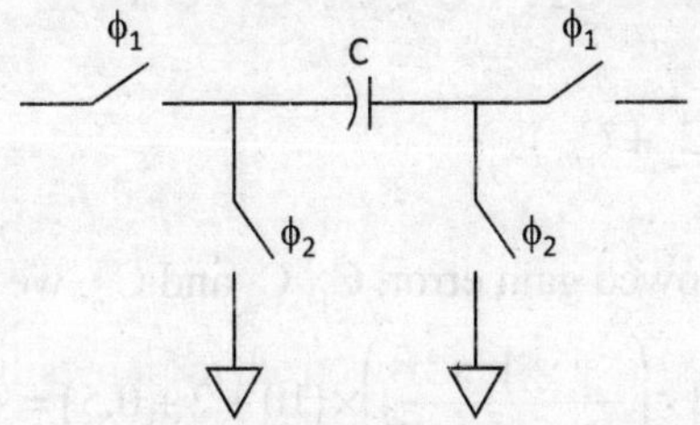

Fig. 12.52 : MCQ-18

19. In a switched capacitor equivalent of an SAR ADC, which building blocks of the internal architecture are replaced by switched capacitor technology?
    (a) D/A converter
    (b) Successive approximation register (SAR)
    (c) D/A converter and SAR
    (d) Control circuit
20. Identify the switched capacitor circuit of Figure 12.53.
    (a) First order low pass filter
    (b) First order high pass filter
    (c) Unity gain buffer
    (d) Stray-sensitive integrator

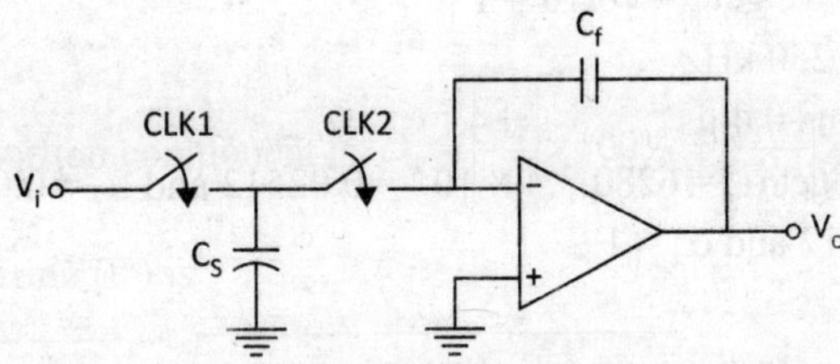

Figure 12.53 : MCQ-20

SOLUTIONS TO PROBLEMS

Problem-1

$$R_q = \frac{1}{(C \times f_{CLK})}$$

Therefore, $f_{CLK} = \frac{1}{\left(R_{eq} \times C\right)} = \frac{1}{\left(1 \times 10^5 \times 5 \times 10^{-12}\right)} = 2\,MHz$

Problem-2

$$\text{Gain error} = \left(\frac{1}{A_V}\right) \times \left(1 + \frac{C_{in}}{C}\right) = \left(\frac{1}{10000}\right) \times \left[1 + \left(\frac{2}{10}\right)\right] = \frac{1.2}{10000} = 0.000012$$

Therefore, percentage gain error = 0.0012%

Problem-3

$$\text{Gain error} = \left(\frac{1}{A_V C_2}\right) \times (C_1 + C_2 + C_{in})$$

Substituting for maximum allowed gain error, C_1, C_2 and C_{in}, we get:

$$0.001 = \left(\frac{1}{A_V(\min) \times 1}\right) \times (10 + 2 + 0.5) = \frac{12.5}{A_V(\min)}$$

Therefore, A_v (min) = 12.5/0.001 = 12500

Problem-4

$$\frac{V_o(s)}{V_i(s)} = -\frac{\{\alpha_3 s + (\alpha_1/T)\}}{\{s + (\alpha_2/T)\}}$$

DC gain = 20 dB

Therefore, gain ratio = 10

Also, DC gain = $\alpha_1/\alpha_2 = 10$

From the frequency response of Figure 12.49, we can see that there is zero at 10000 Hz and a pole at 1000 Hz.

Therefore, $\alpha_1/T\alpha_3 = 2\pi \times 10000 = 62800$ and $\alpha_2/T = = 2\pi \times 1000 = 6280$

Solving these two equations, we get, $\alpha_1/\alpha_2\alpha_3 = 62800/6280 = 10$

Substituting for (α_1/α_2), we get $_3$ = 10/10 = 1

Now clock frequency = 250 kHz

Therefore, T = (1/250) ms = 4 μs

Substituting for (T), we get $\alpha_2 = 6280 \times 4 \times 10^{-6} = 0.02512$ and $\alpha_1 = 0.02512 \times 10 = 0.2512$

$\alpha_1 = 0.2512$, $\alpha_2 = 0.02512$ and $\alpha_3 = 1$

Problem-5

$R = T/(C_1 + C_2)$ where T = Clock time period = $1/f_{CLK}$

Changed value of T = 0.5T

Changed value of $C_1 = 0.5C_1$ and changed value of $C_2 = 0.5C_2$

Therefore, changed value of $R = 0.5T/[0.5 \times (C_1 + C_2)] = T/(C_1 + C_2) = 100k\Omega$ = original value of R

Therefore, R remains unchanged

SOLUTIONS TO MULTIPLE CHOICE QUESTIONS

1. (b)	2. (a)	3. (a)	4. (d)
5. (b)	6. (b)	7. (a)	8. (a)
9. (a)	10. (c)	11. (a)	12. (c)
13. (b)	14. (c)	15. (d)	16. (a)
17. (c)	18. (b)	19. (a)	20. (d)

INDEX

S

T

U

V

W

Z